Religion, Culture and Society

Religion, Culture and Society

A READER IN THE SOCIOLOGY OF RELIGION

Edited by

Louis Schneider

Professor of Sociology, University of Illinois

John Wiley & Sons, Inc., New York · London · Sydney

Foreword

The term sociology of religion is in present-day usage evidently a quite comprehensive one. Max Weber's studies of major religions go under the title of sociology of religion. No one hesitates to label Durkheim's work on the elementary forms of the religious life, with its focus on aboriginal Australian religion, sociology of religion. Gabriel Le Bras' preoccupations with such matters as rural parishes in France or the geography of religious practice in that country or, generally, with adherence to or deviation from standards of practice set by the Catholic Church get published under the title *Études de Sociologie Religieuse*. While there is some tendency in relevant literature to distinguish "sociologie religieuse" (with a practical orientation to needs of the ministry) and "sociologie des religions" (with a greater sweep and without practical goals in immediate view), these terms are often used interchangeably and it is certainly not grossly misleading to translate Le Bras' title as *Studies in the Sociology of Religion*. Sociology of religion also appears to do service as a term covering a considerable body of studies of parishes and sects; analyses of church attendance or non-attendance, for instance in cities and rural areas, in different social strata, on the part of men and on that of women; investigations of social solidarity and of conflict religiously generated or significantly influenced by religion; formulations such as that of Gustav Mensching (suggested in Part Four of this Volume) on the self-destroying quality of universal religions impelled to conquer all men but bound to sacrifice their high religious standards in the very effort of conquest.

There is much more that could be put into an illustrative listing and, indeed, much more will be found in this volume. A simple listing does not in itself afford the best evidence of fundamental diversity. Obviously, there could be important elements of unity in what appeared superficially to be quite heterogeneous. And in truth there are significant elements of unity in a good deal, at least, that goes under the name of sociology of religion. A "field" without elements of unity would scarcely deserve the name. And this volume has of course been put together on the presumption that the sociology of religion is an authentic field. The elements of unity are, then, surely worthy of stress. But the impression of diversity also persists, and the diversity is in plain fact also a reality.

No effort has been made in the selection of the following materials or in the commentaries thereon to legislate this diversity out of existence. The field is very young and the danger of being foolish or arbitrary about what should go into it and what not very real. To be sure, an enterprise such as this is unlikely to please everyone, partly just for the reason that some will be convinced that there are unfortunate omissions (and inept inclusions). But, in any case, there has been no intention to compile this volume in any unconscionably restrictive spirit or in favor of some deeply cherished but intolerably idiosyncratic view of the compass of the sociology of religion. Rather, the reader may allow that a certain catholicity has attended the making of the selections.

But if a certain catholicity is indeed granted and if this has worked out, as it would evidently have to, in a wide range of selections, it may be asked on what more special bases the selections have been made and organized. Much of the answer to this can be obtained simply from the reading of what follows, with close scrutiny of the introductions to the subparts, which are indispensable for understanding of the various choices made. It may nevertheless be useful to afford at this early point an explicit statement of the motivation of organization and content. Four matters should be given main stress in this connection. They have to do with what may be called essential structure, particular theoretical notions, perspectives, and "interestingness."

It will be evident that the bulk of the content of this volume is to be found in Parts Three, Four, and Five. The remaining Parts (One, Two and Six) are not by any means unimportant, in my view, and I shall recur to them briefly, but Three, Four, and Five not only carry a very heavy share of the content but exhibit the essential structure of the book. These central Parts concentrate on matters relating to *function, culture,* and *social interaction* or *society*—three categories here employed to effect a rough, general classification of the basic materials of the sociology of religion. The categories can be taken as suggesting main concerns of the field of sociology itself. Functional (or structural-functional) analysis has clearly been one of the guiding orientations in the general field. Preoccupation with culture has also been important from the inception of modern sociology and has of course at times been intensified by the example of specialists in other fields, such as anthropology. Concern with social interaction and the formation of "society" out of interaction has very plainly been central in the field at large. This is as good a place as any to say initially (the matter is alluded to again in the Introduction to Part Five) something that is notably unoriginal but (perhaps partly for that very reason) appreciably important, namely, that the sociology of religion is . . . sociology, precisely, and is the more likely to prosper as it maintains contact with, is influenced by, and in turn influences the field at large. If the employment of the categories of function, culture, and social interaction helps to make it plain that the sociology of religion is sociology and can be reasonably and comprehensively presented under rubrics that make a kind of general sociological "sense," there is considerable usefulness in this already.

The categories are useful, also, in another way, just because they have been allowed to have a certain roughness or looseness. Thus, for reasons of convenience as well as for reasons of a kind of "natural" hang-together of certain materials, it seemed well to combine in Part Four "religion as culture" with "structural differentiation" and with "nonreligious activities." Structural differentiation as understood in Part Four is not strictly a cultural phenomenon, although it undoubtedly has significant connections with cultural phenomena. The inclusion in Part Four of "religion and nonreligious activities," again if Part Four be conceived as primarily designed to deal with religion as culture, has a clear justification, particularly when meanings, values, and symbols (taken as the content of culture) are to the fore *both* on the "religious" and the "nonreligious" side. But the justification might not hold particularly well in a number of cases as the "nonreligious" phenomena involved became less strictly or unqualifiedly "cultural." This is freely acknowledged. The general rubric of culture has been serviceable—and, very usefully, roughly serviceable. Without this quality of roughness of the heading of culture, I might have been constrained to try refinements of classification of the material that I suspect would not have been especially helpful and that could well have interfered with other motives of classification to which I have been able to give scope.

Part Five, on Religion and Society, here described as concentrating on social interaction, also features a somewhat rough heading, although, again, I would submit, a most useful one, and certainly no more rough a one than is found in Part Four. Interactions of course build into social structures, and in this sense— that structures such as sects and churches, solidified out of interaction, are prominent in Part Five—Part Five obviously goes beyond sheer interaction. The Part ends with a piece on institutionalization, which alone might suggest the closeness of some of its materials to "culture." But this kind of closeness is of course inevitable. Interactions are unavoidably shot through with "content," and to have sought to represent them without it would have been to try for an impossible end—and an undesirable one; and this can be affirmed with particular confidence for a field like religion, where cultural content looms very large. The description of Part Three as concentrating on functions affords perhaps the least rough heading afforded by any of the several categories. But the matter is hardly worth arguing in detail. Again the category involved has proved usefully absorptive. It has taken up a good deal of significant material and it still exhibits, I believe, a quite adequate unity for the objects of an anthology in the field that must control its materials while allowing them range and variety.

The particular sequence observed— from function to culture to social interaction or society—might be vindicated in a number of ways. My own bias is that the functional outlook (whatever its limitations) sets out some orientations without which the sociology of religion

can hardly "get off the ground." It is therefore evidently well to start with this. To get then to religion as culture and some related matters is to get to a number of things that should most certainly not be excluded from the sociology of religion (such as the things discussed in the items by Sorokin and Mensching) and that an overenthusiastic empiricism might too hastily press to exclude. For the rest, there are matters included in Part Four, surely, which everyone would readily acknowledge a place for. Both these and the other matters in which there is perhaps a greater danger of exclusion may serve as items on which the reader can try out and develop a theoretical sense that, it may be hoped, will have been nourished by Part Three. By the time the reader is well launched into Part Five he should have a rich sense of the whole field and be prepared for an assault on a number of its most central problems. The positions of Parts Four and Five might possibly have been reversed, although Part Five might be regarded as penetrating to the very core of the field and therefore as properly placed after Parts Three and Four to emphasize its "climactic" character. If the reader wishes to regard this as a somewhat perfunctory vindication of the particular sequence adopted, I shall have no great objection. The utility of the three main categories and the reasonableness of the sequence adopted both appear plain enough to me, and I trust they will to others.

The use of these categories should not obscure the circumstance that the phenomena they point to and organize can be involved in constant interaction. Thus, cultural phenomena and social phenomena can surely have their "functions." What other phenomena than cultural and social ones, indeed, would in their "functioning" interest a sociologist primarily? It has already been suggested that interactions are inevitably shot through with "content." Thereby "social interactions" or "society" and "culture" evidently come into intimate contact. This line of argument could well be elaborated, and it would have been desirable to have more interplay than has been made evident in the relations of Parts Three, Four, and Five. I have to plead that I could only select readings and could otherwise exercise very little control over their content. Hopefully, too, something may be left to the imagination and talents of the reader.

The choice of the three categories of function, culture, and social interaction and the order in which they have been put have hardly been uninfluenced by theoretical considerations, but other theoretical notions have also affected the structure, the ordering, and the contents of the present volume. These (additional or more particular) theoretical notions may be said to have shaped the volume within the framework established by the three major rubrics. Under the general heading of function, the problems emergent for both social agents and social theorists through the becoming manifest of latent functions of religion have seemed to me to be most significant, and the reader will note both from the Introduction to Part Three and from some of the content of the Part itself that certain selections have been made with an eye to these problems. Also, the selections are placed where they are in the context of Part Three because latent-functions-become-manifest-and-subsequently-treated-as-goals reveal a very striking kind of change. All this will be much more understandable once the reader turns to Part Three. Again as a matter of theoretical interest that has influenced both selection and organization, reference may be made to the intellectual tension that arises from the constraints, on the one hand, to stress ritual and practice in religions and, on the other, their dogmatic or idea components. This states the fact of the tension too briefly and crudely, but it will be found somewhat

more fully stated in the Introductions to Parts Three and Four. For another illustration of the influence of particular theoretical notions, the selection and organization of materials in Part Five have been influenced by the desire to stress contrasting (but quite possibly mutually richly involved) functions of sects—those that have been called compensatory and maintenance functions versus those that have been called escalator functions.

Other theoretical notions will be found which have had a plain effect on content and its ordering. The above is only an illustrative listing. But there has been no intention to develop the notions referred to in great detail. I have thought that a reader in this field should, and indeed must, give a fair amount of guidance and thereby go beyond the exceedingly brief kind of statement that may be allowable in readers in some other areas, in which an editor relies very heavily on the notion that well-selected and well-ordered materials will effectively tell their own tale. At the same time, a reader does not strike me as the most appropriate medium for a full-scale exposition of one's own views. I am well aware that there is much in my introductory statements that I might have elaborated and refined. The matter of dogma, ritual, and feeling and their interrelations, for one, is susceptible of considerably more elaboration than I have given it. I might have said considerably more than I have about religion as "communal" and as "associational" (see the selection from Lenski in Part Four, Section B), although I have not left the whole matter untreated. I have tended to take rather for granted the general notion of culture in Part Four and that of social interaction or society in Part Five. I resisted the temptation to write a lengthy introduction to Part Six to afford a more detailed justification of choices therein. I hope that what I have provided in the way of expository and synthetic efforts in the matter prefacing each Part will indeed prove helpful and that at least the strategy I have adopted in the introductions will not alienate both those who prefer exceedingly clipped editorial statements in readers and those who want a detailed exposition of an editor's own relevant views, while it quite fails to charm still others who might in principle be attracted by some compromise in such matters.

Aside from essential structure and various particular theoretical notions, a desire to allow scope to certain "perspectives" has been indulged in this volume and has influenced the process of selection, at least. It has seemed important to have comparative and historical perspective represented here. The range of the materials over the world is fairly wide, and, while it may be argued that it would have been desirable to have more historical matter than has been included, the reader may at any rate get the minimum notion that the history of religion and the sociology of religion are not necessarily areas implacably alien to one another. For the rest, the idea of perspective may be understood as a kind of analogue to the idea of theoretical notion but at the same time as something "weaker," more inchoate, perhaps less suggestive of possibilities of systematic thought than a theoretical notion. Perspectives in this sense—and they can in their own fashion be quite valuable— that are pertinent in the field of sociology of religion are of course often provided by persons who are not professed sociologists. Thus, Frank Russell Earp provides a most helpful perspective in the brief statement on Greek religion reproduced in Section B of Part Three. Both the desirability of comparative and historical perspective and of perspective in the broad sense of direction-giving and provocative notions (that yet may be said to fall short of being "theoretical") have made it the case that this volume contains contributions not only by professed sociologists but also by persons whose most evident affiliation is—wholly expectably—with comparative religion and history, and also with areas such as anthropology, philosophy, psychology, and theology.

A fourth and final matter of stress is that an effort has been made to find readings that are interesting. Again, the most obvious influence of this occurred in the process of selection. I mention this criterion without hesitation and in full realization that others may not invariably agree with me about what is most interesting. If I had the choice of two items, each equally well illustrative of a point, while one seemed dull and another stimulating, I was of course inclined toward the latter. Some of the points particular readings are designed to bring out are quite simple and might perhaps have been made more briefly than they have, but a relatively large amount of space for a point readily made has occasionally been allowed because the point has been made in such fashion as to challenge attention to significant matters transcending the point itself. Ostensibly "incidental" matter in the social sciences (as indeed elsewhere) has often proved most instructive, and it does no harm to recognize this circumstance nor even to allow one's self to be guided by it in some degree.

A word may here be added about Parts One, Two, and Six. While Parts Three, Four, and Five are admittedly central, One, Two, and Six have not been included by way of casual adornment. The matter of obstacles to understanding and need for knowledge treated in Part One is hardly a trivial one, and if some of the definitional issues posed in Part Two are neither easy to resolve nor, in all probability, most advantageously attacked at this still relatively early point in a more or less determinedly scientific approach to religious phenomena, they should surely be presented to the reader nevertheless. As regards Part Six, while it is perforce brief it will be noted from the Introduction to the Part and from its contents that an attempt has been made to include within it, too, a considerable range of materials. Theoretical concerns, perspectives, and intrinsic interest of materials presented have also affected choices made for Parts One, Two, and Six. While Parts One through Five may appeal to the reader as setting out a content and following a sequence that are at least sensible, Part Six may look like a somewhat arbitrary addendum. Certainly, an appreciable part of the motivation to include it has been to meet the interests of an American audience in particular. If there is an element of the arbitrary or adventitious in this, it should still be clear that the contents of Part Six—the subject-matter and the treatments thereof —are such as to ally the Part easily with the rest of the volume.

The elements influencing structure, ordering and selection that have been discussed above explain much of the character of this volume, but not quite all. Also influencing selection, for example, and working in intimate connection with the desire to afford comparative material, was the notion that it was additionally desirable to afford some sense of the character of the sociology of religion outside the United States. A limited amount of new translation of relevant materials has been provided, but there is more material it would have been helpful to have, and it would have been made available were it not for the scarcity of the resources that have to be devoted to translation. The materials it proved feasible to present even influenced organization. Had it not been possible to provide Mensching's exceptionally lucid statement on folk and universal religion (in Part Four, Section B), for example, it is likely that Part Four would have been differently organized and not designed to give so much stress as it does to structural differentiation.

Again as regards selection, the length of a number of otherwise valuable items

that were examined was too great, while editing them into appropriate brevity was either not feasible or would have taken an inordinate amount of time. Accessibility of items was not allowed to influence choices much. This was a very secondary matter indeed. High inaccessibility can be a concomitant of high irrelevance. Some of the items reprinted here have been reprinted elsewhere, but to the best of my knowledge, these are really quite few in number. Hans Meyerhoff says, neatly, in the preface to his collection of papers on the *Philosophy of History in our Time* (Garden City, New York: Doubleday, 1959): "I decided to exclude any writings that had already found their way into some other anthology. To anthologize anthologies seemed supererogatory." The decision for this reader in the sociology of religion has been different. It seemed to me most important that the volume should stand on its own and that the question of what had happened to be included elsewhere or not was a quite incidental one, as long as my anthologizing of anthologies was evidently so strictly limited.

The whole matter of omissions and inclusions could obviously be discussed at far too great length. I have tried here to give the field of the sociology of religion a certain kind of structure, at least in an incipient fashion. There was no way to do so except by being selective, and it is perfectly evident that some sort of selection would in any case have had to be operative as long as confines narrower than those of the whole literature of the field were to be set. I regret certain omissions and I am sure my choices have not always been the wisest possible. (Even a fairly sizable reader must omit much that it is hard to omit and I would have been glad to include in Section D of Part Four, in particular, as many as a dozen more selections—among them a few I wanted very much and resisted excluding until the last possible moment —than the seven it was feasible to have.)

But these are unavoidable hazards. At the same time, there are some kinds of omissions or insufficiencies of stress that are more disturbing than others. Too little has been forthcoming recently from sociologists on some important aspects of religion which have accordingly not received the emphasis they might have. I refer to such phenomena as have been described as constituting "the dark side of religion"—if one will, its nastier aspects, featured, for example, in a variety of bloody activities. The conflict of religious organizations with one another or of nonreligious organizations (such as the state in Soviet Russia) with religion also now appear to be rather too much slighted by sociologists.

These "dark" sides and conflicts are hardly unimportant and there is perhaps some danger that sociologists may become oversophisticated about them in an effort to be profound and to repudiate concern with "what anybody can see," leaving it to others to develop what they should seek to develop themselves. There is nothing necessarily wrong, of course, with an effort to be profound, and it would be utter foolishness to throw away the gains that contemporary sociological outlooks on religion have made. Some rather naively rationalistic and positivistic views of religion have been very advantageously left by the way. Moreover, it is not easy to accommodate "everything" in the most tentative and delicate frameworks of analysis that sociologists have been likely to have at their disposal at any particular time. There is still such a thing as looking away too much from certain realities, after all valid excuses have been made, and to indulge it is not

likely to enhance the vitality of a discipline. But, at the risk of seeming excessively cautious and almost to retract what has just been said, I must also say that the extent to which sociologists overlook or understress phenomena of the kind now referred to can be exaggerated. And, for better or for worse, I am one of those firmly persuaded that a determined hostility to functional analysis will prove of very slight help in these matters.

In the end, I am not greatly inclined to make apology for the character of this volume. That it has limitations is evident. I hope and believe that it also has virtues. I would expect it to have the defects of such virtues as it may in fact possess. It sets out points of view. If it did not, it would be worthless. Although these points of view are not developed in ideal fullness, for reasons already suggested, I trust they are set out fully enough to be clear—and challengeable, if they need to be challenged.

A last word on the content of selections. Some writers I have drawn from make explicit theological statements or show certain religious inclinations. I could not have eliminated all trace of these, had I desired to do so, without badly marring texts. There may even be advantages in allowing a few such statements to appear and a few such inclinations to be quite plainly revealed in a volume such as this. But it is of course to be understood that sociology of religion, whatever its breadth, is not to be confused with theology or any particular religious disposition. Such confusion obviously could produce nothing but harm.

Urbana, Illinois, 1964   LOUIS SCHNEIDER

Acknowledgments

It is a pleasure to acknowledge assistance received in the making of this volume. Joseph Gusfield, Harry Johnson, and Bernard Lazerwitz gave me much sagacious comment, from which I would undoubtedly have profited more had my own sagacity been greater. I could not do justice to the aid given by my wife in a sentence much larger than this, but at least I can acknowledge it with a brevity which I trust is becoming where greater length would be pointless.

L. S.

CONTENTS

Part One

OBSTACLES TO UNDERSTANDING AND RESEARCH AND THE NEED FOR KNOWLEDGE

PARTS One and Two of this volume take up preliminary issues, and, in a sense, we do not reach the heart of our subject until Part Three, on the functional analysis of religion. But Parts One and Two set out problems that confront a serious student of religion early in his endeavors and that do not by any means always resolve themselves neatly even after prolonged study and research. Moreover, the discussions by Ernst Benz, and H. Paul Douglass and Edmund de S. Brunner at points suggest issues that are important beyond the matters with which we are concerned here. For example, Benz writes of "the common preference we attribute to theology, the doctrinal part of religion," and notes that "this preference is a specific sign of Christianity, especially Western Christianity of the Protestant variety." He states that the preference has led some Westerners to put undue stress on the teachings and philosophy of non-Christian religions, and that he was "extremely surprised" to find

that "in contemporary Buddhism a much more central role is played by liturgical and cultic elements." These are most important observations, and they point forward to some of the matters to be taken up in Part Three, in which will be found, among other things, a plain statement by Frank R. Earp of the significance of *practice* and the relative unimportance of dogma in the religion of classical Greece.

These observations by Benz make up an indispensable part of his main discussion while, at the same time, they are a kind of additional bonus that comes from the discussion. But the observations are included for the primary reason that they touch upon common misunderstandings, obstacles to our comprehension of the non-Christian religions of the Orient. It is a truism for a sociology of religion that aspires to scope and significance that if it does not make a determined effort to comprehend non-Christian religions its aspirations are quite vain. A comparative perspective is, bluntly, indispensable for

1

anything but a hopelessly provincial and cripplingly limited "science of religion." It is well to begin with a reading that takes for granted the need for a comparative perspective.

The second selection in Part One, Douglass and Brunner's "The Church as a Social Institution," deals with some hindrances to the acquisition of knowledge that operate on a more restricted scene—the scene of an American endeavor to obtain sociological understanding of religion that was launched by the Institute of Social and Religious Research more than a generation ago. Some notion of the scope of the work of the Institute, on which Douglass and Brunner drew, in the volume from which the selection here presented has been taken is given by this statement in their preface to that volume:[1]

> Beginning with the *Church and Community Survey of Salem County, New Jersey,* published in 1922, and following with some twenty volumes, large and small, which conserved and completed surveys undertaken by the Interchurch World Movement, the Institute of Social and Religious Research up to the present writing (July, 1934) has carried out forty-eight research projects published in seventy-eight volumes.

It is a fair presumption that the account given in the chapter of Douglass and Brunner here reproduced is based on rather considerable experience. The chapter is somewhat complex but certainly intelligible enough. It is presented here as it was originally published, and there should be no difficulty in discerning amid its components that large element that stresses hindrances to the development of a sociology of religion.

The final selection in this Part, Benson Y. Landis' "Confessions of a Church Statistician," brief though it be, will convey some sense of difficulties that have been experienced in obtaining reliable numerical data, even of a rather rudimentary sort, on matters having to do with religious activity. It is a tremendous handicap to analysis that basic statistical data bearing on religious affiliation and a variety of other religiosocial circumstances are often lacking or have often been so loosely compiled that little confidence can be placed in them and their very meaningfulness can be questioned. Much has been achieved in the study of religion with rather little in the way of reliable numerical data. But undoubtedly much more could be achieved if such data were abundant. The need for knowledge here is indeed great. There is at least good ground for the suspicion that religion is no adventitious or fleeting feature of human life. On a phenomenon that may even in some sense be a permanent and omnipresent feature of life in human societies it would appear reasonable to desire, and to strive for, very detailed and very accurate knowledge. Fortunately, we are not entirely without resources in the way of pertinent statistical data that have a measure of reliability, but until those resources can be improved and extended—ideally, in such fashion that excellent and full data shall be available on a worldwide scale—it is salutary to have the kind of reminder that Landis' comments supply.[2]

[1] H. Paul Douglass and Edmund de S. Brunner, *The Protestant Church as a Social Institution,* New York: Harper and Brothers, 1935, Preface, p. V.

[2] It will be noted that Landis begins with a reference to federal census work on religion. A more recent contribution than his to the subject of religious statistics (William Petersen, "Religious Statistics in the United States," in *Journal for the Scientific Study of Religion,* vol. 1, 1962, pp. 165–178) enters an interesting plea for further census concern with such statistics.

1 · On Understanding Non-Christian Religions

ERNEST BENZ

As I came to understand the essence of one non-Christian religion, it became at once increasingly clear to me to what extent and to what degree of depth our Western attitude, our intellectual, emotional, and volitional reaction to other religions, is modified by the European Christian heritage. It is one of the basic rules of the phenomenological study of religions to avoid judgment of other religions by criteria of one's own. However, I was repeatedly surprised by how difficult it is in practice to observe this rule. Our scientific-critical thinking, our total experience of life, our emotional and volitional ways of reaction, are strongly shaped by our specific Christian presuppositions and Western ways of thought and life. This is true even as regards the pseudoforms, and secularized forms of thought and life, which are antithetical to the claims of Christianity. Indeed, we are frequently, in most cases even totally, unconscious of these presuppositions. Permit me to mention three points in this connection.

1. Our Western Christian thinking is qualified in its deepest philosophical and methodological ideas by a personalistic idea of God. This concept makes it particularly difficult to understand the fundamental disposition of Buddhism, which knows of no personalistic idea of God. The traditional Western reaction, in Christian theology as well as in Western philosophy, is to characterize Buddhist

SOURCE. Reprinted from *The History of Religions: Essays in Methodology*, Mircea Eliade and Joseph M. Kitagawa, eds., The University of Chicago Press, Chicago, 1959, pp. 120–130, by permission of The University of Chicago Press.

theology as "atheistic." It is difficult for a Westerner to comprehend the specifically Buddhist form of the approach to the transcendent. As for me, I had theoretical knowledge from my acquaintance with Buddhist literature, of the nontheistic tenets of Buddhism. But it became clear to me only when attending Buddhist "worship services," or in conversation with Buddhist priests and lay people. It is difficult for us to understand the nontheistic notion of Buddhism because the personalistic idea of God plays such a fundamental part in our Western logic. It took constant effort and new trials on my part to realize that the basic difference between the two is not one of abstract theological concepts. It goes deeper than that, because this particular form of expression is attained by a certain training in meditation. It is here that the experience of the transcendent is cultivated and secured for the total life of Buddhism.

From Christian lecterns and pulpits we hear proclaimed in noisy and confident terms detailed information concerning the essence of God, the exact course of his providential activity and the inner life of the three Divine Persons in the unity of the divisive substance. But the reverent silence of the Buddhists before the "emptiness" of the transcendent, beyond all dialectic of human concepts, is pregnant with its own beneficence.

Buddhist art was the most important help to me in overcoming this intellectual "scared-rabbit" attitude toward the theological "atheism" of Buddhism. I was especially impressed by the representations of Buddha himself in the various positions of meditation. Our traditional theological ideas and concepts of God are a serious obstacle in understanding the Buddhist forms of transcendental experience. At best, Meister Eckhart's idea of the divine Nothingness, or Jacob Boehme's notion of the Non-ground (*Ungrund*) in God may serve as bridges of understanding from a Christian experience of the transcendent to a Buddhist one.

2. Hindu and Shinto polytheism confronted me with still another problem. I simply felt incapable of understanding why a believer preferred just one god or goddess among the vast pantheon. What attracts the wealthy can manufacturer of Kyoto to the shrine of the rice god Inari and causes him to donate whole pyramids of his cans and his pickles? I saw such offerings literally piled up beside other pyramids of rice wine casks and cognac bottles which other dealers had donated to the god of this shrine. In the Shinto pantheon of 800,000 gods this singling out of one of them was a real enigma to me. What moves the devout Hindu to pass by the Kali temple and the Vishnu temple on one day, and hurry to the sanctuary of Krishna to offer him his sacrifice of flowers and his prayers and to participate the next day in the Kali festival? In the mind of the devotee what role does the individual god play beside the other gods? Our understanding of all these problems is blocked by many factors. Consider for example the vigorous denouncements by the Old Testament prophets of idols and idolatry among the ancients. Consciously or unconsciously, the modern Christian is influenced by such traditional attitudes. Nor can he fully appraise the strength of these attitudes if he reduces them to theological arguments. The battle waged against polytheistic practices by the Mosaic and Christian religions must be seen as a total emotional response which penetrates our attitudes more deeply than any intellectual affirmations.

Even the various European renais-sances of classical antiquity have not appreciably changed this. We are still accustomed to seeing the ancient abode of the gods in the light of the poetic transfigurations of Humanism and Classicism. This whole world of gods' defamed by Christianity, flares up once again in a kind of aesthetic romanticism. But these gods are for us at best only allegories. We are no longer able to imagine the religious significance that they had as gods for the faithful who prayed and sacrificed to them.

In Asian lands, however, polytheism is encountered not as literary mythology, but as genuine religious belief and as living cultic practice. It appears in an overwhelming diversity and at the most varied levels of religious consciousness. As in the Hellenistic religions of late antiquity there occurred also in India a development toward monotheism. The Hindu deities Krishna, Vishnu, Kali, and others were worshiped as manifestations of Brahma, the one transcendental God, the Hindu God, much more reverently, however, than was the God of Plotinus, because the Hindu religion presupposes a plurality of worlds as over against the geocentric narrowing of the world picture of classical antiquity.

This development is the result of a profound change in the religious consciousness of India. In Shintoism, however, this change has not yet occurred. Its 800,000 gods have hardly been put into hierarchical order, each god being a particular manifestation of the Numinous by itself. While visiting Shinto shrine festivals, I often asked myself what moved the Shinto faithful to prefer this or that particular god, to sacrifice to him and worship him in a special way. (The shrines require rather substantial sacrifices after all state support has been withdrawn.) To seek the answer to this question in custom or convention in the relationship of certain occupational groups to certain deities is only to put off the question.

Rather it seems to be the case that one worships the divine in such form as it has emerged impressively and effectively in one's own life, whether it be as helper, as bringer of luck, as protector and savior, or as a power spreading horror and awakening fear. It is the experience of the *numen praesens* which is primary and decisive for cultic devotion. Manilal Parekh, in his book on Zoroaster, puts this thought into an excellent phrase when he writes of the devotees of the Rig-Veda epoch: "They invoke a god because they need something from him, and for the time being he fills all their horizon. Thus it happens that there is no god who is supreme in this pantheon."

I asked my Shinto friends repeatedly: What is the essence of Shintoism in the veneration of the numerous gods at the various great and small shrines? One of them, a priest at a Shinto shrine, answered that it is the devotion to the creative forces in the universe in the bodily, the cosmic, the ethical, the intellectual, and the aesthetic realms. This answer doubtless meets the most important point. Decisive for this stage of the religious consciousness is the encounter with the self-realization of the transcendent in its individual form and expression of power. This encounter is the crucial factor, whether it occurs on a holy mountain or at a holy tree or fountain or in the meeting with an ethical hero. Correspondingly, the world of the gods is never finished; only the dead polytheism of our classic literary antiquity is "perfect," its Olympus complete, and philologically conceptualized. Living polytheism constantly creates new gods. One of the most important Shinto shrines is dedicated to the veneration of General Nogis, who in 1921 committed a demonstrative hara-kiri which was consummated in all the liturgical forms of religious self-sacrifice. By his act the dangers of Westernization were called to the attention of Japanese youth who habitually sense, recognize,

and worship the transcendent in constantly new forms of appearances. It is precisely from Shintoism that in recent times there have emerged not only new gods, but also new religions. Living polytheism, therefore, is extraordinarily flexible and is open to systematization and a hierarchical organization. It is also capable of being accommodated to the various high-religions, as was the case in the monotheism of the Vedas, and also in Buddhism. Only Judaism understood the idea of the unity of God in the exclusive sense that all other gods beside Yahweh are "nothing." In the tradition of Jewish monotheism the Christian Church has used the exclusive interpretation of the unity of God to denounce the non-Christian gods of its neighbors as demons and to abolish their cults. Christian theology itself has screened the Christian doctrine of the Trinity, sometimes interpreted in a polytheistic sense, in such a way that the understanding of genuine polytheism was no longer possible.

3. The third point is that Hinduism, like Buddhism and Shintoism, lacks one other distinction so fundamental for our Christian thinking: the belief in the basic essential difference between creation and Creator. For our Western Christian thought this absolute discontinuity between Creator and creation is normative, but it does not exist in Buddhism and Shintoism. The same central importance that the idea of the absolute otherness of Creator and creation has for us, the idea of the unity of being has within Buddhist and Shinto thought. This idea of unity is connected not only with the particular method of direct religious experience, meditation and vision but also has a bearing on logic and conceptualization even where they are wholly unrelated to religious experiences as such.

Many other points might be mentioned in this connection, such as the relationship of man to nature, to the universe, and especially the idea of deification. It is baffling to the visitor from the West to note again and again how in the Eastern religions outstanding personalities are swiftly elevated to the rank of god, or recognized and worshiped as incarnations of certain divine attributes. This, however, only surprises one who holds the basic Western presupposition of the absolute discontinuity of divine and human existence. Viewed from the idea of the unity of existence, this step is self-explanatory just as the impassable gulf between Creator and creation is self-evident to us.

Another basic assumption which we hold as part of our Western Christian thinking is the common preference we attribute to theology, the doctrinal part of religion, when it comes to the interpretation of the forms of religious expression. But this preference is a specific sign of Christianity, especially Western Christianity of the Protestant variety. Whenever this viewpoint has been applied to the critical examination of Asiatic religions, an emphasis on their didactic and doctrinal elements has resulted. Thus, in interpreting Buddhism and Hinduism, some Western authors have placed undue stress on their teachings and philosophy.

I myself was extremely surprised to find that in contemporary Buddhism, a much more central role is played by its liturgical and cultic elements. One element of religious life, which has almost completely vanished from religious practice in Western Christianity, the exercise of meditation as a spiritual and ascetic discipline, is accorded a tremendous importance in Buddhism. This became clear to me only as I had the opportunity of seeing it first hand.

Meditation in Buddhism is not the privilege of a few specialists, but a practice directly shared by the majority of Buddhist lay people. To this day it is assumed in Buddhist countries that before taking over an important position in government, administration, science, or

elsewhere in the social and military life, men must have undergone some training in meditation. Today it is still customary among many educated Buddhists to spend their vacations as temporary novices in a monastery and to give themselves to meditation. In Hinduism, too, meditation is still very much alive and is practiced in an astounding variety of forms and methods, because most of the great Gurus and founders of ashrams have developed their own form of meditation and Yoga and transmitted it to their disciples.

The importance of Eastern meditation has gradually been recognized in the modern Western literature on the science of religion and elucidated in various technical studies. However, the whole vast area of the symbolic language of Eastern religions as well as of their liturgy and cults has hardly been noticed. I was surprised over and over by the power of the symbol in Buddhist worship services. Symbolic details were often explained to me by obliging priests. Especially in Buddhism does this symbolic language appear highly inaccessible. Above all, the symbolism of the movements of hands, arms, and fingers is very strongly developed. This hand and finger symbolism has in Eastern religions been brought to high perfection in two fields. It plays a role in the liturgical dances of India, where to this day a large number of symbolic hand and finger movements (*mudras*) have been preserved. It also figures in the practice of meditation and in the cult of two Buddhist schools, the Tendai and Shingon schools. Within the esoteric tradition of these schools, hand and finger symbolism was cultivated to an incredibly skilful and complicated system of expression which makes it possible to express through finger and hand symbols the whole content of the school's secret doctrine in one worship service. Just as significant are the symbolic positions of one's body, hands, and fingers during meditation. This is so because the person meditating puts himself into the position corresponding to the position of Buddha or some Bodhisattva on his way toward attaining full enlightenment.

It is often said that the religious life of Christianity is not confined to its teachings and its theology. This is certainly even more true for Buddhism, which, in essence, is practiced religion, practical meditation, symbolic representation, and cultic liturgical expression.

The Western Christian also must beware of transferring to the Eastern religions his own ideas concerning the organization of religion. We always assume more or less consciously the ecclesiastical model of Christianity when analyzing other religions. This approach suits neither Hinduism nor Buddhism nor Shintoism. The Japanese Buddhists do not form a Buddhist "church." Buddhism is, in fact, represented by a diversity of schools with their own temples and monasteries, and their own educational institutions and universities. These are not co-ordinated in any organizational fashion. Moreover, within the individual schools there is only a minimal organizational connection between the temples and monasteries. They are basically autonomous and economically independent units. A Buddhist federation was only very recently formed in Japan. This, incidentally, was inspired by the formation of the "Buddhist World Fellowship" in connection with the Sixth Buddhist Congress in Rangoon in 1954–56. But its concern is merely the representation of common interests among the different Japanese and Buddhist groups. It has nothing to do with ecclesiastical organization.

It would be equally misleading to apply to Eastern religions the idea that a person can be a member of only one religious community. This is a notion which stems specifically from confessional Christianity. It does not apply to Japan,

nor to China, where, in the life of the individual Taoism, Confucianism, and Buddhism mix and interpenetrate, as Shintoism and Buddhism do in Japan. The Japanese is a Shintoist when he marries since the wedding ceremony is conducted by the priest at the Shinto shrine; and he is a Buddhist when he dies, since the funeral rites are conducted by Buddhist priests, the cemeteries are connected with Buddhist temples, and the rituals for the souls of the dead are held in Buddhist temples. Between the wedding and funeral, the Japanese celebrates, according to private taste, preference, and family tradition, the Shinto shrine festivals and the Buddhist temple festivals. After the occupation, when the Americans took a religious census in connection with the religious legislation carried out by them, it was found, to their great surprise, that Japan, with only 89,000,000 inhabitants, registered 135,-000,000 as the number of the faithful of all religious groups. In point of fact, there was no fraud involved. The curious surplus of religious adherents had resulted from individuals registering as members of both Shinto and Buddhist temple communities. For this reason they appeared twice in the religious census. The "Pure Buddhism" mentioned in our textbooks of the history of religions does not exist at all. For even in the various Buddhist centers of meditation and teaching, Buddhism is amalgamated with various levels of religious consciousness expressed in local mythologies.

I had occasion to attend the celebration of the consecration of a Buddhist priest. According to the ritual, the newly consecrated priest first offers his obeisance to the Sun-Goddess Amaterasu and afterwards to the person of the Emperor. This type of connection between Buddhism and Shintoism occurred in Japan as early as the eighth century. It followed from the teachings of Kobo-Daishi, who in his sermons taught the people that the

Shinto gods are identical with the Bod-hisattvas of the Buddhist doctrines. This identification occurred not only on the intellectual theological level, but on all levels of the liturgy, the cult, the religious symbolic language, and the mythology. It led to practical forms of conduct which cannot be judged by criteria of dogmatic thought and the division of religions on a doctrinal basis.

Another aspect of Eastern religions which was difficult for me to understand was that of magic and sorcery. I came into contact not only with exorcism and sorcery, but also with forms of magic in cultic dance, words, writings, and pictures. Here the Western Christian finds access to a wide dimension of religion otherwise completely barred to him by his own tradition. Christianity denounced the whole aspect of magic as "demonic" and banned it from the realm of Christian faith. This is just another of those surprising examples of how in Hinduism and Buddhism all levels of religious consciousness and all varieties of religion continue to exist side by side and to intermingle with each other. The European observer always feels himself pressed to create divisions and differentiations. Hindu friends of mine have observed that many European visitors interested in Hinduism ask the same question. Observing the devotion of Hindus in their temples, they ask: How is it possible for such variant and mutually exclusive opposites to exist side by side in Hinduism? Together with the highest spiritual and ethical form of monotheism and the most elevated form of asceticism and of meditation, they are amazed to find such primitive sorcery and magic as might be seen in African fetishism. The Hindu's answer to this question will always be that such things are not at all mutually exclusive opposites, but represent stages in the development of religious consciousness.

There is a similar situation in Bud-dhism. Many of the cult rituals that I was permitted to attend were based on completely magical notions. I was particularly impressed, for example, by the new year's service in a Zen monastery. On three consecutive days the festival of the so-called Daihanya, the physical turning-over of books, was celebrated. The basic idea of this festival is to set into motion the total content of the teachings of Buddha. But since this doctrine fills about 600 volumes, it is quite impossible for a small monastic community to recite it in its entirety in one service of worship. Such a recitation of the canon could only take place at an occasion such as the Sixth Council of Buddhism, where thousands of monks were occupied for a long period of time reciting the sutras consecutively.

Instead, at the Zen monastery, the spiritual moving of the content of the 600 volumes is magically accomplished by moving them physically. Piled on a low table in front of each monk are some ten to fifteen volumes of the canon. During the worship service each one of the volumes, written on a continuous folded strip, is unfolded like an accordion and folded again with a fluent ritual movement. The monk swings it briskly over his head while he calls out its title and first and last line. The idea is that through this physical motion the spiritual content of the books is actually set into motion. This liturgy counts as particularly meritorious, both for the liturgists themselves and for other Buddhists too.

For our Western thinking it appears absurd to set into motion the spiritual content of a book by liturgically leafing through it. We no longer have a sense for the meaning of magic, any more than for the difference between black and white magic. The peculiar basic assumptions on the relationship of spirit and matter underlying this idea are foreign to our thought and difficult for us to comprehend. These assumptions operate on a still more primitive level in the system of Buddhist-Lamaist prayer mills. This system consists of producing the spiritual content of a prayer through physical movements of the parchment on which the prayer is written.

It was equally difficult for me to understand the practice of sacrificing and its meaning. The ultimate emotional and spiritual motives for a sacrifice, the estimated value of a sacrifice, the enormous variety of sacrifices (sacrifices of flowers, incense, drink, animals, all with manifold liturgical and ritual variations) are extremely hard to fathom. This whole world is one which is largely closed to Europeans, especially to those of Protestant persuasion. It is a world to which we lost access centuries ago. The abyss separating us from the ancient idea of sacrifice cannot be bridged simply by an intellectual jump. There are, however, a few European philosophers of religion whose work is significant here. In studying the various types of sacrifice in the history of religions, Franz von Baader, for example, has been able to understand something about the mystery of sacrifice.

One other danger of misunderstanding lies in evaluating the mission of non-Christian religions. Here, too, Western observers are easily inclined to presuppose the Christian form of mission and propaganda, and its methods and practices among the non-Christian high-religions. Such assumptions can only lead to misunderstanding. It is true that a certain analogy exists between the expansion of Hinduism and Buddhism on the one hand, and the mission of Byzantium and of the Nestorian Church of the fifth to the tenth centuries on the other hand. The basis of mission here is not, however, a missionary organization, but the free and partly improvised activity of charismatic personalities who, as itinerant monks, counselors, and teachers, collected a group of disciples around them. As a rule, this type of activity is related to the formation of monastic centers. In Hinduism we note the appearance of individual leaders who founded ashrams, and from these ashrams began missionary expansion or reform activity. In the same way the history of the expansion of Buddhism is most strongly connected with the appearance of such charismatic personalities. As itinerant preachers and founders of monastic communities, these men contributed their own particular forms of teaching and meditation. It has been only in very recent times that Buddhism adopted an organized mission activity. In this case, it is significant to note that the model for its methods of propaganda, as well as for its organization, is furnished by the organization and method of the Christian world mission.

2 · The Church as a Social Institution

H. PAUL DOUGLASS AND EDMUND DE S. BRUNNER

The historic significance of the church and, no less, its essential present mean-

SOURCE. H. Paul Douglass and Edmund de S. Brunner, *The Protestant Church as a Social Institution,* Ch. 1 (pp. 3–18), copyright 1935. Harper and Row, Publishers, Incorporated. From cloth bound editions.

ings, hinge upon belief in a cosmic situation consisting of mundane and supramundane aspects in intercommunication. The validation of any concept of this sort is essentially religious. It is based upon the reliability of subjective insights. It holds for religious people. It asserts realities of a spiritual order. In religious language, it must be "apprehended by faith."

The specific characteristics of the church originate in its relation to the spiritual order and bear the marks of their source. But a vast institutional fabric and an extensive system of secondary mores have built themselves about these central ideas and convictions and have accumulated bulk, prestige and variety throughout the ages.

The Church a Phase of Human Society

Whatever, then, the church may be specifically, generally it is a social institution and bears the marks of the class of phenomena to which it belongs. The studies of the Institute of Social and Religious Research have primarily addressed themselves to the institutionalized aspects of religion. They have treated the church as an aspect and phase of human society. They have dealt effectively with whatever habitual behaviors, practices, attitudes, and experiences they have found grouped under the term religious as traits of human groups. These they have observed and sometimes measured, but without raising any question of the validity of the conceptions and beliefs underlying them.

The reasons for this limitation have been two: first, the belief that the Institute had a distinctive contribution to make to the understanding of the church; and that this involved the maintenance of a distinctive point of view. Everyone else was regarding the church religiously. It was time for someone to regard it scientifically. Here was a novel enterprise in the field of institutional religion. It adopted the rules of the scientific game. It confined itself to the objective viewpoint to see what would happen. What happened was at least this: some new

ability to direct the church toward its own higher goals.

In the second place, however, no other basis than the scientific one would have been possible in the nearly fifty studies relating to the church. The more or less representative persons who sponsored, directed and carried out the studies could never have agreed on any set of postulates with respect to the church as a phase of a supra-mundane society. Acceptable generalizations could be made and tentative conclusions reached about the church and its external aspects. But the research students were in no position to choose between the competing religious interpretations offering conflicting accounts of the specific inner aspects of the phenomena in question. However limited the objective vision of the church might appear to the eye of faith, it at least made research possible for whatever it might be worth. The unity and comparability of the studies grow out of their confinement to the objective viewpoint and to scientific methods of investigation.

Object of Study versus Object of Faith

Now at the end of fourteen years' experience in making objective studies of the church as a social institution the Institute has to testify that its effort has been under continuous suspicion and has frequently aroused resistance and opposition. The religious point of view has been habitually jealous for the specific character which a church gets from its supra-mundane realm, and has resented examination and comparison with other societies.

This assertion is not contradicted by the fact that most of the Institute's projects were undertaken upon definite request of ecclesiastical leaders or agencies and that their results have been often used and greatly valued, especially by those in charge of the affairs of the church as an institution. Moreover, this has been true even when the facts disclosed have constituted a criticism of the church's management.

Opposition to objective studies merely carries the issue a step farther back. The more aggressively religious mood within the church is at outs with the viewpoints of practical administration quite as truly as it is at outs with the scientific attitude. The ecclesiastical leaders are themselves suspected of being more concerned with externals of the church as an institution than with the great realities behind it.

This acute and continuing conflict between the view that the church as an object of faith is not amenable to objective study and the effort to make objective studies has, in a very real sense, conditioned the success of the effort. To be sure, the studies have gone right on. They have been backed by extensive private resources which have given them freedom from any and all ecclesiastical agencies for support or control. They have had no other interference. But in spite of these extraordinary advantages they have all along had to struggle against undercurrents of resistance. Virtually all the Institute's studies were first-hand studies. As such, they have had to depend upon the willingness of the object of study to stand examination. Would the church do this? Would it open its books and permit observance of its processes? Generally, though often with some pressure, it would! The religious viewpoint has, nevertheless, presented many real obstacles with reference both to the comprehension of what was intended and the readiness to give serious coöperation. It has shut many doors and opened others but narrowly.

Opposition has naturally been more definite with respect to some projects than to others. In general, little objec-tion has been raised to territorial or community studies directly concerned with local church units, especially when their results pointed out remedies for already acknowledged evils. When it came, however, to studies touching the organization or functioning of the church in general or of its ministry, objections began to be more vocal.

Moreover, in the last analysis, attention to the published studies and the willingness to follow their conclusions were even more conditioned by suspicion of or dissent from the objective viewpoint with respect to the churches. The studies indeed might be made, but would the religious viewpoint prevent many from reading the reports or taking them seriously?

All told, then, resistance to the scientific study of the church from church sources has been thrown into relief as a major phenomenon by fourteen years of experience. This is itself data of first significance as to the frequent conflict of the scientific attitude and the religious spirit.

The actual objections which objective church studies have had to meet did not all draw the issue in such single theoretical terms as has been done in the preceding pages. Each objection had its own tone and expressed itself in its own version. The further functions of the present introductory chapter are therefore two: (1) to examine the grounds of the resistances encountered in their variety as well as in their common insistence upon a special viewpoint; and (2) to confess and make explicit the ways in which the Institute, in its own mind, had met them.

Sources of Resistance

Ignoring private individualists whose criticisms were simply the indulgence of their temperaments, and also ignoring the occasional person who was palpably affronted by the discovery of unwelcome facts about his particular institution, we find that two continuously significant sources of resistance to objective studies of the church based on the religious viewpoint have made themselves manifest.

Shocked and Grieving Piety. The first consists of a rather large number of simple-minded and sincerely religious folks who have been now shocked and now grieved by the attempt to take a scientific attitude with respect to something as holy to them as the church is. They have never heard of the like before and they suspect the scientific approach of failure to sense the inner values which they apprehend. The church, to them, remains a society projected into the supra-mundane sphere —something whose dominant aspect is out of sight or, perhaps better, something too dazzling for sight to bear— something incandescent and glorious. Nevertheless, familiarly known in its human aspect, it possesses dear and revered qualities. The devout believer is sure that the power to stir his emotions is something resident in the phenomena themselves, not merely something imported by his own mind. The scientific viewpoint is consequently charged, first, with ignoring the invisible part and aspect of the church and, secondly, with illicitly treating the visible part as though it were mere cold phenomenon; whereas the religious person has inside knowledge that the phenomenon is not cold, but warm and palpitating. Piety, therefore, inclines to conclude that no true account of the realities of a religious institution can be given by one who thinks of its merely as an objective entity.

The scientific viewpoint as such has obviously no applicable answer to difficulties which arise in subjective feeling and sentiment. It can only point out that science has been most successful when its mood has been most completely divorced from the private concerns of individual human beings. A giant lens is to be poured from molten glass. If successful, it will bring the planets twice as near as they have ever been before. Success means profits to investors, credit and fame to technicians and craftsmen and the satisfaction of insatiable curiosity to pure scientists. These motivations of the hearts of men may rage passionately behind the event. But the more forgotten they are for the moment, the steadier the hand that pours the flood of glass into the mold.

Science may challenge piety to recognize a sort of twin in single-handed and complete dedication to truth, as well as a genuine morality in the stern discipline of concentration upon an honest accounting with observable facts. Investigators in the objective realm acknowledge compelling loyalties in behalf of which they know labor and anguish. This is the best, perhaps the only hopeful ground of appeal for understanding as between the scientific spirit and naïve piety.

Rationalized Objections. When it comes to answering resistances coming from the second source, namely, a varied group of criticisms alleging rational objections, the scientific attitude is on more accustomed ground.

These criticisms arise out of: (1) special versions of the nature of the church in its religious and universal aspect; (2) special evaluations of the actual present church; and (3) general attitudes toward the whole tendency to institutionalize religion. Objective studies of the church have been criticized, for example, for not taking sides in controversies as to its nature; for being diverted by an interest in institutional phenomena when they ought to spend the time calling upon an unfaithful church to repent; and for not repudiating institutionalism, root and branch, instead of possibly bolstering it up with facts, the knowledge of which may lead to greater institutional efficiency.

Now, in view of the rationalized objections and resistances which it has all along met, the long series of Institute studies represent more than mere persistence in a scientific undertaking. Implicitly they constitute an answer to criticism. Repeated objection has forced repeated reappraisal of the theory of objective studies as related to the church, in connection with which a definite attitude toward the church as an institution has matured. The church has been observed and considered objectively for fourteen years. For the observer, after all this time, to have experienced no change of attitude and reached no fresh generalization would be less than scientific. A well-developed attitude derived from steady attention to objective considerations might rightfully be anticipated. The Institute, in some measure, has acquired such an attitude. In order to exhibit it concretely, it is appropriate to note how it meets the main points of rationalized objection. In this way the grounds upon which its persistence in objective studies finally justifies itself may be made clear.

The Nature of the Church. Among sources of rationalized challenge to the validity of the objective studies of the church, one has first to consider conflicting versions of the nature of the church.

The divisions of American religious opinion among the historic doctrines of the church were intensively explored in the series of Institute studies on church coöperation and unity. The results showed the persistence and currency of deep-rooted differences between Protestant and Catholic viewpoints.[1]

[1] See chapter xv, p. 332 of *The Protestant Church as a Social Institution.*

To the radical Protestant, religion consists of direct and unique personal relations between God and the individual. The sum total of the persons who have realized these relationships constitutes the church, which is to be described as an essentially spiritual entity, and only very secondarily as a social institution.

In the characteristic Catholic viewpoint, on the contrary, the essence of religion is found in God's corporate relations to men effectualized through the church as an ordained channel of life. The church is definitely a divinely constituted social institution. Its sacraments convey grace, its priesthood is essential to the valid performance of the church's saving functions. Both of these views are easily turned into grounds of objection to scientific studies of the church.

High-Church Resistance. The consequences drawn from the high-church version of the church ought logically to be favorable to objective studies. The divine authority ascribed to the external institutions should permit free examination of it, since its authority is beyond challenge from any conclusions which investigation may reach. The really robust Catholic mind has never hesitated to put a Pope or two in hell, because the private character of popes makes no difference to the sanctity of the church. The scientist surely can do it no greater damage.

Nevertheless the priestly consciousness does not easily consent to any curious and unabashed inquiry into its functions, especially one which might throw light upon its inner psychology. The prestige of religious professionals suffers from any exhibition of shortcoming in their institutions. Ministers of religion, consequently, have often shown extreme sensitiveness with respect to objective studies. Curiously, however, this sensitiveness does not follow denominational lines. The objection of ministers to keeping time schedules or to having their work examined in its aspects as a job, their resentment against a consideration of employer-employé relations as involving themselves or of equity as between the superior and the subordinate members of a staff, are quite as prevalent among the common or garden type as they are among convinced high-churchmen. The former, with no claim to be priests, have appropriated a personal high-church attitude.

Protestant Resistance. Historic Protestanism in its most characteristic version intended no absolute break with Catholic tradition and took middle ground in defining the church as both spiritual and corporate. It is the total body of those who are inwardly in vital relations with God; outwardly it is the set of institutions which both symbolize and realize this fact.

In consulting the opinion of the American religious public, the actual crux of the difference between this and the Catholic position was located in the varying consequences drawn from the assertion that the church is both spiritual and corporate. If it is corporate, one should be able to list its invariable marks as an institution. But to this proposal an overwhelming majority of opinion replied that "the church can be identified by spiritual marks only." In tests on this point nine-tenths of 624 church leaders responding affirmed the proposition in this form. The proportion of agreement reached more than eight-tenths with all denominations except the Protestant Episcopal, which historically reflects a somewhat diluted Catholic tradition.[2]

Studies of church unity have further established the fact that the religious masses of the United States habitually contrast the external and organic aspects

of the church with the spiritual aspects. They deliberately stress the subordination of the church to the gospel. They fear institutional mechanics as an obstacle to the Holy Spirit. They are unimpressed by objective measurements of church phenomena because they wish to devote all their stress to the imponderables. These tendencies reflect a deeply-rooted folk-attitude. The majority of American Christians fear too close an identification of the church with the visible institution bearing that name. This fear reflects a burnt-finger attitude toward the church as an institution, based on experience of the evils of institutionalism in the past. Its concrete index is found in traditional opposition to the Roman Catholic church.

Minds holding this point of view are naturally hard to interest in objective investigations of the church as a social institution. It is not so much that such investigations wrong the church as that they touch no important point or aspect of the church as religiously understood and defined.

It turns out, then, that both the superiority complex of professionals and the burnt-finger attitude of the Protestant masses are in instinctive rebellion against objective studies of the church and are inclined to give them grudging coöperation, if any.

Evaluation of the Present Church. A second source of rationalized challenge to objective studies of the church is found in a considerable body of Protestant opinion, which has reached a highly unfavorable estimate of the religious values of the present church. At this point the low theoretical estimate accorded the visible church by the Protestant masses is reinforced by a very poor opinion of its current quality. Not content with depreciating the church in theory in order to exalt the gospel, opinion is widespread in many circles that the

[2] Douglass, *Church Unity Movements in the United States,* p. 260.

church has very largely failed the gospel, either in proclaiming or in living it. This opinion is echoed from many sides and by spiritually-minded and socially-minded people alike. Both are grieved by the discrepancy between the dream and the reality; both regard the visible church with a certain irritation as an institution that has somehow contrived to let religion down. In particular, stress upon church organization is regarded as a hindrance to the appreciation of its need of recovering inner values. Such views come naturally to persons of the fundamentalist frame of mind, as contrasted with institutionalists, according to Professor Kirsopp Lake's apt distinction. And they are especially numerous among people belonging to that party in the church which labels itself Fundamentalist.

All told, the prevalence in many Protestant circles of a scolding mood with respect to the church constitutes a rather curious and portentous phenomenon. It contrasts sharply with the invariable pity awakened in Catholics in behalf of the church "sore oppressed." The church as an institution is a sort of Protestant whipping-boy. It is beaten as disappointed heathens beat their idols. In extreme cases this position carries over into an almost Manichean mood, as though the embodiment of religion in an institution were a sort of pollution. Such a viewpoint inclines to envisage the unholy church throughout the world, in eternal conflict with the inner and unorganized virtues of the spirit. To teach tricks of institutional survival and efficiency to such an apostate or defiled church is to do a disservice to true religion. Such attitudes are in implicit resistance, if not in vocal opposition, to objective "engineering" studies of the church; and, from this viewpoint, such studies as the Institute's have often been berated as a waste of money and mistaken expenditure of effort.

Critical Anti-Institutionalism. In addition, however, to popular, professional, and doctrinaire resistance to scientific methods of studying the church, others are to be distinguished which may be denominated critically anti-institutionalist. These positions have no quarrel with the scientific method as such; indeed, some of those holding this view believe themselves to have something of a monopoly on that method as applied to religion. These include doctrinal and ethical radicals, people perhaps with confessed humanistic leanings; also unconventional mystics who keep their religion in one mental compartment in order that they may be strictly scientific in another. Neither of these groups can be thought of as motivated by traditional religious qualms. From both, nevertheless, objections to scientific studies of the church as an institution have been heard; because, it is alleged, these studies assume or at least do not preclude the perpetuation of the church in its present institutional forms.

Radical anti-institutionalism, from the standpoint of advanced doctrinal and social thinking, is well expressed, for example, in a pamphlet, issued by the Community Church of New York, entitled "Religion Without a Church." Religion, it is conceded, cannot exist without social expression. Indeed it is inherently social. But a fatal choice was made when it was attempted to embody religion primarily in an ecclesiastical institution and to put it in custody of organized agencies. The same error, it is held, applies to medicine, law, teaching, and economic enterprises. All have developed separate, segregated, and rival institutions without power to generate the ideals necessary to control themselves or the society to which they belong. Religion confined within a specialized institution is equally powerless. Religion, it is held, must be released from the church and diffused through all the agencies of the community. The church naturally resists such a recall and redistribution of its prerogatives. But this is what must happen if religion is to rule society. The present churches can only be regarded as vestigial growths surviving beyond their time and possibly as centers of infection rather than of helpful life.[3]

The attitude of such a viewpoint toward objective studies is in effect this:

> In not taking sides against the present churches, your studies are in fact helping them to succeed. We want them to fail. The more you show them how to survive, the more damage they are in position to do to truth and progress.

Such a statement is an almost literal transcription of explanations actually given of unwillingness to coöperate in studies of the church as an institution.

From a different and essentially mystical standpoint a highly attractive alternative to the present church has appeared in the vision of a church without ecclesiasticism. This makes especially persuasive appeal in what may be called its cosmopolitan-liberal form. Such a viewpoint controlled certain passages of *Rethinking Missions,* the recent Laymen's Foreign Missions Inquiry report. Convinced of the impertinence of much of the baggage of western ecclesiasticism as imposed upon Oriental Christians by missionaries; and impressed by widespread revolt of nationalism against "cultural imperialism" as it is expressed in the western church, many of the finest minds of the present generation take very kindly to the notion of a free fellowship in religion, in which historic forms shall be completely subordinated to personal relationships of spiritually kindred

spirits. Within such a fellowship, it is hoped, the essential genius of religion would find untrammeled expression. The following quotations from the Laymen's report eloquently express such moods.

> . . . Many times during the history of western Christianity men's hearts have turned from the rigidity of the ecclesiastical institution in which the spirit of Christ's religion seemed to them to be smothered, from the stiff and hardened phrases in which the living faith of the Founder seemed to them to be stifled, and they have longed for what a medieval prophet called the Eternal Gospel, expressed in free ways through a universal Church, vital, spiritual, and growing and expanding with the life of men.
> . . . The approach might thus have been the charm and attractive power of a great personal life rather than metaphysical statements about his essential nature.
> . . . Experiments in number have been tried to effect a return to the simplicity of the Gospel, and to inaugurate a movement free enough and spiritual enough to grow into a universal Church. Every such experiment in the West, however, finds itself in rivalry with the churches of the ecclesiastical type already holding the field.
> . . . The freer type of church might well have brought over into itself the most important leaders of life and thought in all three (Oriental) lands and have marked the beginning of a new era in the life of Christianity.[4]

Such viewpoints find very little to im-

---

[3] McAfee, *Community Religion; Religion Without a Church* (New York, The Community Church of New York, 1928), No. 2.

[4] *Rethinking Missions: Report of the Commission of Appraisal of the Laymen's Foreign Missions Inquiry* (New York: Harper and Brothers, 1932), Chapter V, pp. 3, 4, 5.

press them in objective studies of the church as an institution; since the very institutionalization of religion is viewed as something artificial and unhealthy.

All types of anti-institutionalist argument sooner or later appeal to the long story of struggle between the ecclesiastical and prophetic elements in religion. Institutionalism has always stoned the prophets. It is easy to bring forward plenty of terribly convincing evidence on this point.

All these varied evidences of the sensitiveness of the church to the objective approach to its phenomena, and of its habitual and quick resort to defense mechanisms, confirm what was earlier insisted upon, namely, that the widespread and reiterated fact of resistance to objective studies is one of the most important data which these studies reveal.

Piecemeal Reply to Objections. Now the projects of the Institute, each in its own particular order and detail, have had to overcome more or less resistance from one or another or, sometimes, from all the sources catalogued above. Each project has turned criticism aside and has gone ahead on the plea of having limited objectives. Each has said in effect: We are not dealing with the church in general; we only want to discover something about this narrow group of facts and to appraise them on their own merits. Your religious qualms are not properly involved; since we have no bias against you and do not pretend to penetrate into the realms in which your qualms originate.

Explanations of this sort have never fully satisfied objections to particular projects, and they cannot well satisfy as an explanation of the persistence of the Institute in the total body of its objective research.

Now that this total product is being reviewed and summarized, it seems permissible to dramatize the situation as implying a sort of convergence, at one time, of all the objections which have been made separately to the several projects. Imagine, then, all the objectors uniting in the demand to know what, after so many years of research, is the underlying implication with respect to the church of the continued use of scientific method. The Institute studies have repeatedly exposed unacknowledged assumptions on the part of the subjects of their investigations. Is it not fair for the Institute to take its own medicine at least to the extent of trying to explain what, now at length and at the end of the process, it has arrived at by way of basic conclusions with respect to the church as an institution, and with respect to the institutionalization of religion which turned out to be the crucial point of nearly all of the objections.

Reappraisal of Institutionalized Religion

In response to an actually persistent demand thus dramatized, no literal consultation of the entire group of those who have made the Institute's researches has been or could have been held. It thus remains for the writers to make as representative a generalization as they can in behalf of the entire series of studies.

With respect to the institutionalization of religion, that generalization may be expressed in a word, as follows: institutionalization is inevitable, dangerous, yet manageable. Institutionalized religion may conceivably be made to serve the interests of modern society, and no less the ends apprehended and professed by religious insight.

Inevitability of Institutionalization. To state the grounds of this conclusion carries one back into some of the fairly familiar commonplaces of social psychology and sociology. Institutions are simply the more important and deeply rooted of the social habits of men, and are as inherent and inescapable as are any set of habits. Psychology reveals that even the most casual meetings of groups resolve themselves into milder or less mild struggles between personalities for ascendancy, as measured by attention or admiration. But these struggles from their most primitive beginnings have always been controlled by convention which defines behavior: as for example between the older and the younger, the male and the female; and which varies according to the particular kinds of occasions within which the casual grouping takes place. These examples show the all but universal formalization of social conduct which is the root of institutionalization.

Sociology goes on to show that virtually all religious types exhibit highly developed stages and degrees of formalization. Those most critical of what they consider the institutionalism of the church themselves exhibit it. Sects, for example, like the Primitive Baptist, representing extreme anti-ecclesiastical attitudes, maintaining the utmost simplicity and freedom in worship and an unpaid ministry, are genuinely shocked by the excesses of the Holy Rollers as the latter appear in mountain communities. Yet the truth is that the mountain preacher who most loudly proclaims that he receives his sermon by direct inspiration of God is asserting a highly-developed religious convention. Even in the most informal intercourse of his group he is subject to the dead hand of social ritualism. In the mountain community the father-character is so formalized that the intimate life of the family, generation after generation, is terribly robbed of spontaneity. The intercourse of loafers seated on the village lumber pile has a special ritual of greeting and for the conduct of conversation. Peculiar religious diction and intonation are universally employed in primitive religious services to signify the inter-communion between the human and the divine members of a common society. One who has witnessed the "speaking with tongues" of the wilder religions is sure to have been impressed by the imitative manner of vocalization. Institutionalization, then, has no exclusive connection with prayerbooks or a sacerdotal order of clergy.

Moreover, in religious groups whose ecclesiasticism is least developed, formalized group judgments defining and evaluating the person are more frequent and burdensome than in the ritualistic churches. As marks of the individual, the fulfillment of religious obligations like churchgoing and Bible reading completely outrank intelligence and interestingness. The conventicle type of religious organization, which lodges authority in the local congregation and denies the necessity of any universal church, is heavier handed and more capricious in the discipline and control of its members than an ecclesiastical inquisition ever was. In short, the doctrine which denies the corporate reality of the church in the interest of its spiritual nature becomes locally corporate with a vengeance. "Presbyter" is simply "Priest writ large."

Even if religion originates in a person-to-person relation between God and the individual, it is logically and historically inevitable that a duplication of that relation between God and many men will involve person-to-group relations. This takes place as soon as the social implications of individual religious ties develop. New Testament history accurately points out the crucial character of the moment when believers begin to multiply in number. As has often been observed, religions newly originating with a lone prophet and his disciples cannot outlast a single generation in pure and original form; since every successful attempt of a religion to perpetuate itself involves means of propaganda, education and discipline, and these are impossible without institutionalization.

All American sects have continuously become more churchly in doctrine, ethics and administration, particularly as social isolation has broken down. Even in the freest churches prayer becomes stereotyped. Testimony repeats old patterns. The religious originality of the first generation slips down into the institutionalized custom of succeeding ones. The ecclesiasticism of the sect is a different sort from that of the established church, but it is not a whit less institutionalized.

The attempt, then, to conceive of a non-institutionalized religion for modern man is sociologically infantile. It is an attack on rationality and ethical stability themselves. Religion cannot have currency without developing some generalized form, and generalized form implies habits resistant to change which are the essence of institutionalization.

Danger of Institutionalism. On the other hand, no extensive and objective study of the church as an institution can have failed to impress the minds of those making the study with the dangers of institutionalism.

Probably no body of data ever assembled constitutes so staggering an indictment of the actual evils and futilities of current religious institutionalism as the Institute's studies of the American church. The utter incoherence and colossal wastefulness of the church and its impotence to lift itself out of its pitiable traditional entanglements have never been so dispassionately set forth nor in so impressive factual terms.

The church, in other words, is often like a spider trapped in its own web. Moreover, the difficulty of the situation is that it is paradoxical. Thus Professor George A. Coe defines institutionalism as the "defect of a virtue." Its virtue is to give permanence and power to the creative religious insights of prophetic spirits.

Its defect is to give these insights a holdover authority after they have ceased to have pertinence and timeliness.

". . . Institutions," Dr. Coe goes on to say, "*qua* institutions, have an inherent gravitation away from creativity toward self-imitation.

"The church is a permanent necessity; if what we call churches should disappear, some institution that bears a different name would assume their functions. . . . But churches, in common with all other institutions, acquire a momentum that is repetitious and mechanical rather than personal and creatively variant. Religion comes to mean being loyal and obedient to the partial insight and the institutional creation of yesterday. Precedents, the product of a particular time, place, and state of mind, become controlling assumptions, as though they were the eternal truth, the will of God, or a finished creation." [5]

There is nothing novel about this conclusion, but the Institute's studies, in their total import, would seem to justify it.

Manageability of Institutionalism. Nevertheless, it is also a fair conclusion from these studies that, in the large, the desirable possibilities of institutionalism outweigh its evils; and that, inevitable as it is, it is subject to control.

Objective studies of the church have contributed much to the understanding of the possibility and technique of change. The scientific method, in turn, has been a discipline in fair-mindedness, helping one to see the frequent need of change. Its consequent mood brings anything but joy to the standpatter; and its results almost inevitably constitute an apologetic for institutional plasticity.

[5] *What Is Christian Education?* (New York: Charles Scribner's Sons, 1929), pp. 240, 241.

The scientific viewpoint has also increasingly made possible a temperate account of specialization in religion; and of the necessity of dividing, concentrating and relating undifferentiated religious functions under some relatively stable scheme of organization; yet without delivering religion over to monopolistic implications at the hands of a specialized clergy nor to hard and fast forms in doctrine, rites and ethical practices. In brief, institutionalization with plasticity gives the maximum power to religious values.

As to the implementation of such a conclusion the further verdict of Professor Coe appears sound and significant:

> . . . Nothing, in fact, could be more religious, than finding and putting into operation a method for the continuous self-criticism (which means self-testing and judging) of religion and of religious institutions.[6]

In no defense, then, of the existing churches beyond the strength of facts objectively discovered, and on express condition that radical self-criticism shall continuously be exercised, the result of long experience in objective studies may easily be that one comes to a renewed belief in the church; that is to say, in the institutionalized aspect of religion, a church whose naturalness and inevitability are accepted, whose dangers and paradoxes are recognized, and whose processes and results are critically evaluated and controlled.

Practical Value of Studies of Institutionalized Religion

Having thus dealt faithfully with both emotional and rational objections on the theoretical basis of objective studies of the church, and having offered a positive

[6] Ibid., pp. 241, 242.

apologetic for such studies, the way should be open to emphasize their secondary but very real practical values. Besides the fact that they are on the side of institutional plasticity and self-criticism, one quickly thinks of several obvious contributions of objective studies to the value of the church as an aspect of modern civilization.

(1) The period of the world's history during which these studies have been in process has served to emphasize the central importance as a social force of the phenomena with which they have been concerned. Russia, Italy, China, Germany in turn have found in organized religion the strongest challenge to their respective versions of a totalitarian state. The national and international implications of the organized church for politics were never more pronounced nor acute: all the more reason then for attempting to understand it.

(2) The church has obviously been a badly-conducted institution in many respects. Its duplicatory congregations and plants and much of the cost of its propagation have been socially wasteful. These factors, coupled with the sectarian division of community life by the churches, have often rendered it positively demoralizing. Nothing can be more shocking than such a situation as chapter vi reveals in which Christian ministers in the United States are compelled to serve superfluous churches on salaries that are below any decent standards of living and even below the present meager economic levels of the working classes. Anything that adds reason and expertness to the conduct of so chaotic an enterprise must be reckoned as of the highest social utility.

(3) The wobbly character and the failure of the church at so many points is a burden not merely to the purse but also to the faith of multitudes of poor and pious people. Unnecessary failure, the failure of unwise and futile organization

saddled upon them by religious tradition or by the deliberate drive of denominational zeal, has proved in the long run a terribly undermining influence in religious morale. As chapter x shows, the cost per individual of churches of inferior quality is frequently actually greater than that of the best churches. This religious overcharge, at the expense of those least able to bear it, never can be brought to light so long as the church is allowed to shelter itself behind the skirts of ecclesiastical sanctity. Objective studies immediately reveal it for what it is, an atrocious scandal.

(4) One of the most useful services of objective studies of the church has been to reveal the vital possibilities of coöperation and unity among the sadly divided religious fragments politely generalized under the term, the American church. A tracing of progress made in this line and a demonstration of the possibilities of rapid further progress stand among the most valuable discoveries of studies using the scientific approach to religion.

(5) Objective studies of the church show the infinite importance of good institutional techniques in the agency which after all creates the best oppor-

tunity that the inner values of religion have to take hold of the individual. The school can only expose the pupil to education; its high percentage of failure is proverbial; yet in no other way can he be so well and thoroughly exposed. Similarly the church can only expose the individual to religion; but it can do this; and objective studies of its institutionalized methods help to show how this may be done in the most effective way.

Finally, the scientific viewpoint on the whole strengthens the conviction that the inner and outer aspects of religion are but two sides of a single whole. Institutionalized religion really symbolizes and in a sense measures the energy of the inner meanings for which the religious viewpoint contends. Something beyond a consistently fair-minded attitude toward religion may thus easily eventuate from long attention to objective studies. At most they do not contradict a warmly sympathetic attitude toward religion. At best they may serve to confirm faith in the treasure of the spirit which lies within the earthen vessels of institutionalism and in those imponderable values which multitudes testify to, as more real to them than all objective facts.

3 · Confessions of a Church Statistician

BENSON Y. LANDIS[1]

The most valuable book on church statistics ever published in the United States, in my opinion, was the report of the federal Census of Religious Bodies for 1926. Published by the U.S. Bureau of

SOURCE. National Council Outlook, Vol. 7, February, 1957, p. 3.
[1] Dr. Benson Y. Landis is associate executive director of the Council's department of research and survey and editor of the Yearbook of American Churches.

the Census, it contained information on church membership, religious education, and church finance, gathered from local churches by uniform methods from one office as of a particular date, and distributed the information by states, counties, and major cities. We have had nothing of the same scope since, although fortunately a special foundation grant has made possible a church distribution study which contains data by states, counties, etc., for over 100 denominations with almost three-fourths of the church members.[2]

For almost 40 years I have compiled and studied church statistics on an inter-denominational basis. During that time I have been interested in noting the various responses to the publication of my elementary summaries and compilations. They may be grouped under these heads:

1. Most people who have published comments have, in my opinion, over-estimated the value or significance of these products of simple arithmetic and an ordinary adding machine.

2. Some will have nothing to do with them because they are church statistics. In this group are eminent social scientists.

3. Others, possibly a small group, have sought to make careful use of church statistics, have tried to understand the nature of the sources, and have engaged in inquiry concerning their meaning.

Because of a wish to enlarge and extend the third category, this article is being written.

Since the federal Census of Religious Bodies, 1926, there have been no compilations for U.S.A. by uniform methods, gathered at one time, with the relatively full cooperation of the local churches. The federal census of 1936 was marred because of the non-cooperation of about 20 per cent of the local churches. That of 1946 was begun and never completed. In 1956 the Executive Branch of a government with leaders vocal on religion did not bother to request an appropriation from Congress, and, so far as the record of hearings goes, no member of Congress, Republican or Democrat, even made a simple inquiry about the matter.

[2] Information about the church distribution study may be obtained from the National Council's Publication and Distribution Department.

For creation of this situation the non-cooperation of local churches and the indifference of government officials both are responsible.

Many religious bodies make annual reports of the figures that they obtain from their local churches. But it is not even known how many of the 268 religious bodies gather such information annually. Perhaps half of them do.

Thus much of the quality of the reporting is dependent on what the local churches have by way of records and on the willingness of pastors or lay people to make careful accountings. It has often been said that pastors, priests, and rabbis are not distinguished for their work with figures. At present many of the published figures come from local church records that are apparently not carefully kept, either by clergymen or lay people.

What about those that do not make annual collections of reports from local churches? Some gather figures at irregular intervals, and others simply make crude estimates of their constituencies.

Just as local churches vary in the care of their reporting, so the various religious bodies vary in their conceptions of membership and of the formality with which people are related to their churches. There has never been a compilation of definitions of church membership. In some Protestant denominations it is only by custom, and not by formal action, that many persons are taken into full membership at age 13.

Also, a number of Protestant bodies do count all baptized children, including infants; it is not correct to say that Protestants, of course, only count persons aged 13 years and over. In 1945, I estimated carefully and found 5,000,000 Protestant church members officially reported under age 13.

Roman Catholics include all baptized persons. Jewish congregations include all Jews in communities having congregations. The Eastern Orthodox include all persons in the cultural or nationality or racial group served.

It is perhaps no secret that the relation of many Negro families to their churches is a very informal one, and that it is difficult for these churches to keep records. Yet an informal relationship can be a most vital one. In Montgomery, Alabama, the Negro churches certainly appear to have had the loyalty of their people; and the pastors of these churches have been close to, and have understood, the aspirations of their people.

In a suburb I know there is a well-organized church with 900 members. For 200 of these persons there is not a post-office address available. They do not live in the community where their names are on the church roll. It is possible that a proportion of these are also on other church rolls. The great migrations have brought problems for the churches, one of which may be a higher proportion of non-resident and inactive members than in former years.

We may also be getting to a place where duplication of membership is more than negligible. We may, as in the Orient, be getting a number of people who belong to two denominations. But in the Orient they seem to be deliberate about it and always aware of it. In the U.S.A. it comes about because people are not aware of it.

There are careful observers who think that it is in the suburbs that much of the current church activity, including building, is taking place. There are many "inner cities" and rural communities whose churches do not seem to be gaining membership, and are thus not participating in the over-all gains whereby officially reported church membership has been increasing more rapidly than population.

And what, finally, do these things imply?

There is no substitute for careful records and careful reporting in the local churches. All other reporting is dependent upon that.

Beyond the local church there are also large responsibilities. One is that we try to move out of the stage of being in the beginning of the beginning on church statistics, to make careful and regular reports, and to produce reports that can be directly compared with previous reports. If every denomination printing a yearbook were to print the name of the county in which a church is located, that would help. (The Disciples of Christ, the Roman Catholics, and others do.)

There should come a day when church statistics generally are presented to consumers more carefully than other statistics. At present that day is far from dawning. In simple justice to consumers, there should be intensive cooperation toward that end.

Part Two

PROBLEMS IN DEFINITION

IT is easy to exaggerate the importance of definitions of religion. The famous German sociologist, Max Weber, began that portion of his major work which is devoted to the sociology of religion by stating:

> To define "religion," to say what it *is*, is not possible at the start of a presentation such as this. Definition can be attempted, if at all, only at the conclusion of the study.[1]

A definition may function as a kind of resolution or agreement to study under the rubric of "religion" a prematurely delimited set of phenomena—prematurely because it may soon appear that for a variety of substantial reasons the delimitation is an unfortunate one. But delimitations can change and may be looked upon as only tentatively useful devices. The impulse to define, here as elsewhere, hardly requires repression for the reason that it is likely to result in something that will not last forever. Students of religion can, however—and in fact they often do this—rely on a degree of implicit or explicit agreement that certain phenomena, whatever detailed examination may reveal about them, are

in any case "religious." Then, later, when more is known about the phenomena, fairly rigorous definition of the category of the religious may be sought. Some such view of this matter was probably entertained by Weber. Also, there may exist a certain confidence that close analysis of definitions that are in some sense "representative" would reveal more agreement among those affording definitions than appears on the surface. Yet, even if we retain a degree of skepticism, in the present state of relevant knowledge, about very intense and determined efforts to define religion (especially where they seem to be based on the notion that a rigorous definition of a field is indispensable before the field can be usefully approached), a moderate amount of attention to the entire matter of definition can be instructive.

The four readings in Part Two have been chosen partly on ordinarily inevitable grounds (such as availability of material and feasibility of reproducing it) and partly for the variety of sources from which the definitions presented in them come. The first reading is from the main contribution to the sociology of religion made by the eminent French sociologist, Emile Durkheim. It presents more than a brief definition, of course, and is rather a kind of definitional ex-

[1] Max Weber, *The Sociology of Religion*, Boston: Beacon Press, 1962, p. 1.

plication. The second reading, from Gustav Mensching (whose work will be encountered again in this volume), presents a succinct definition whose crucial term is "the holy," and Mensching follows this with a very condensed statement of Rudolph Otto's conception of the holy, on which he relies heavily. Mensching is a student of comparative religion (he holds a chair in this field at the University of Bonn), whose publications include a volume on the sociology of religion published in 1947. Mensching's short statement is followed by Morris R. Cohen's piece on baseball as a national religion. Cohen was a noted American philosopher who did not hold to a supernaturalistic view, who wrote an essay on "the dark side of religion" which is contained in the same volume from which the item on baseball has been taken, but who also had a certain sympathy with some conventional expressions of religion and, as his autobiography[2] particularly shows, was partial to "piety" in the sense of loyalty to the sources of one's being. Joachim Wach, represented by "Universals in Religion," was a broad-gauged student of religion whose writings covered numerous aspects of that total phenomenon. Those writings include a sizable volume on the sociology of religion. Perhaps Wach, like Mensching, is best described, in view of the entirety of his work, as a student of comparative religion. In these four several pieces, then, by Durkheim, Mensching, Cohen, and Wach, variety of provenience (within unavoidable limits, to be sure) is achieved. Durkheim was a sociologist, Cohen a philosopher, Wach a comparative religionist; and Mensching is also a comparative religionist (although the last two have shown marked sociological interests).

Obviously, religion can be approached

[2] *A Dreamer's Journey*, Glencoe: The Free Press, 1949.

from a number of points of view, and legitimate abstractions can be made from the whole phenomenon by students with different concerns, by psychologists, comparative religionists, philosophers and others, certainly including sociologists. But, aside from particular modes of abstraction, elements of unity can often be seen to run through a variety of definitions. A few words about such elements seem called for. Durkheim's essay in definition displays a tendency that the definitional endeavors of others also display repeatedly: the tendency to affirm the importance to religion of a special realm, variously called the sacred, the holy, the transcendent, the ultimate. "A religion is a unified system of beliefs and practices relative to sacred things," writes Durkheim. These sacred things are "set apart and forbidden." Point-for-point correspondence between Durkheim's conceptions and those of others is hardly to be expected but, to adduce only a single relevant instance, it is quite clear that the "holy," in the sense of Otto and Mensching, has a strong affinity with Durkheim's "sacred"; the language of the "set apart and forbidden" is not at all alien to the language of "the distant, unapproachable and deeply mysterious God." Wach, for his part, writes of a response of the total being to "what is apprehended as ultimate reality." And Cohen refers to a "mystic unity with a larger life," and his conception of this, half whimsically developed, clearly does not take him far from Durkheim, Mensching, or Wach. If we rely on these sources, religion would appear to involve a transcendent sphere, at the least transcending the individual human being, at the most transcending human life altogether and signifying a "beyond" with which human life may come into contact (sometimes fearfully hesitant contact) but which it cannot encompass or contain.

When it is said, as just above, that

religion would appear to "involve" a transcendent realm, what is meant is that man as religious actor, or as actor in the realm of religion, conceives and responds to a conceived transcendent realm. This suggests many problems which cannot be considered here (and it is not even denied that more careful attention may be needed for the words transcendent, ultimate, and so on, that are here taken as loosely synonymous), but it should certainly be noted that considerable theological differences may exist side by side with, say, an agreement that the conception or sentiment of the existence of a transcendent realm on the part of human agents is a crucial feature of religion. Thus, Durkheim's "theology" is in a very clear sense nontheistic. What human agents (and Australian primitives in particular) conceive of as transcendent or sacred is, for Durkheim himself, merely the reality of society expressed in symbolic form. On the other hand, it is possible to hold to the view that the transcendent or sacred or ultimate or holy or the like has an authentic, irreducible existence and that it thereby refers to an objective reality variously apprehended and approached by men in different societies but existent no matter how it happens to be apprehended. The point is plain enough, but it is stressed in order that it be entirely evident that to note an agreement among different students that religion involves the presumption of the existence of "another realm" (a presumption entertained by humans who are religious) is *not* to mark an agreement on the theological or ontological question of the objective existence or nature of the transcendent realm itself.

Indeed, in so far as there is agreement that men who are religious distinctively presume that there is a transcendent realm, it is agreement on a point that it is quite fair to label "sociological." If an entity such as a nation is what is taken

to be transcendent and is worshipfully regarded, a theologian may be inclined to speak of "idolatry" and to decry such worship. But this rests on a theological judgment. It is possible that there are significant sociological differences where there are certain theological differences —as in the case of one group for which a nation constitutes a transcendent entity, by contrast with another for which a "nonidolatrous" entity alone is transcendent. It is possible that faith falters more easily where transcendent entities are "idolatrous," since men have some reserve feeling that idolatrous entities are not authentically transcendent. These and other matters undoubtedly suggest problems of some importance. But if we modify Mensching's definition so that it asserts that religion is experiential encounter with what human beings sense or conceive as the holy (transcendent, sacred, ultimate) and the responsive action of those beings influenced by what they conceive as the holy, one vein of exploration of possibly greater implicit agreement on definitions among a variety of persons doing the defining than appears superficially is at least opened up. Sociological "constants" in religious activity may emerge from this line of exploration which, clearly, does not involve theological commitment and, indeed, deliberately avoids it.

Even more unequivocally sociological is the stress that there is covenanting, as Wach puts it, *about* the transcendent realm or entity—associating, assembling, organizing of men. Religion may be said to involve a transcendent realm, in the sense of the above, and it is a realm about which men engage in association. The response to the holy, in Mensching's language, is at least in part a response made in assemblies, associations, or organizations. Of course, simple as this point is, it is crucial for the sociology of religion. And here it is even easier to reconcile a variety of views of religion.

Durkheim and Cohen (whose piece may indeed be said to have a rather Durkheimian flavor) and Wach and Menger can agree on the elementary fact of association about what is conceived as the transcendent. Undoubtedly, many others who have no special sociological concern and have not stressed the fact of association about the transcendent would nevertheless concede it. Whether the fact of association in religious context would be crucial to a definition of religion as such or not, it might well be made an indispensable part of the definition of the sociology of religion, so that for the latter it might be said that religion, minimally, constitutes experential encounter with what is humanly sensed or conceived as the holy and human response to what is thus sensed or conceived, particularly as that response involves association.

But we need not attempt to go on from here. It should be entirely plain by now that there is merit in Weber's view, quoted at the beginning of this section, which implies that a genuinely valuable definition of religion (and, no doubt, also of the sociology of religion) must rest on considerable knowledge of the phenomenon itself. It is not enough, in the end, to juggle different definitions and to preoccupy one's self with their points of agreement or disagreement. This can all too easily degenerate into verbal play.

The suggestions above made on elements of unity in definitions should be taken precisely as undeveloped suggestions. If they, or other suggestions, should not now be susceptible of fruitful development, there is still room at least for considerable "denotative" agreement (as has indeed already also been suggested), that kind of agreement whereby it is clear that when one student "points" to some particular phenomenon and proposes to call it religious a goodly number of others are willing to "go along." Failing all else, such agreement is by no means useless.

In the selections that follow, Durkheim affords us a kind of extended definition and Mensching a briefer one. Cohen discusses baseball as a national religion, but his piece is included because it quite definitely suggests a certain view of religion, which in fact rests on the notion that such phenomena as baseball teams and cities can constitute transcendent entities with which men may feel a kind of "mystic unity" and that thereby such phenomena can have religious significance. Wach's paper presents more than a definition, and it is included because it is thought that a search for universal components in religion may afford a path toward more rigorous specification of the religious reality itself.

1 · Search for a Positive Definition

EMILE DURKHEIM

Religious phenomena are naturally arranged in two fundamental categories:

SOURCE. Emile Durkheim, "Search for a Positive Definition," from Emile Durkheim, *The Elementary Forms of the Religious Life*, tr. J. W. Swain, New York: Macmillan, 1926, pp. 36–47. Reprinted with permission of The Free Press of Glencoe. First published in 1954.

beliefs and rites. The first are states of opinion, and consist in representations; the second are determined modes of action. Between these two classes of facts there is all the difference which separates thought from action.

The rites can be defined and distinguished from other human practices, moral practices, for example, only by the special nature of their object. A moral rule prescribes certain manners of acting to us, just as a rite does, but which are addressed to a different class of objects. So it is the object of the rite which must be characterized, if we are to characterize the rite itself. Now it is in the beliefs that the special nature of this object is expressed. It is possible to define the rite only after we have defined the belief.

All known religious beliefs, whether simple or complex, present one common characteristic: they presuppose a classification of all the things, real and ideal, of which men think, into two classes or opposed groups, generally designated by two distinct terms which are translated well enough by the words *profane* and *sacred* (*profane, sacré*). This division of the world into two domains, the one containing all that is sacred, the other all that is profane, is the distinctive trait of religious thought; the beliefs, myths, dogmas and legends are either representations or systems of representations which express the nature of sacred things, the virtues and powers which are attributed to them, or their relations with each other and with profane things. But by sacred things one must not understand simply those personal beings which are called gods or spirits; a rock, a tree, a spring, a pebble, a piece of wood, a house, in a word, anything can be sacred. A rite can have this character; in fact, the rite does not exist which does not have it to a certain degree. There are words, expressions and formulæ which can be pronounced only by the mouths of consecrated persons; there are gestures and movements which everybody cannot perform. If the Vedic sacrifice has had such an efficacy that, according to mythology, it was the creator of the gods, and not merely a means of winning their favour, it is because it possessed a virtue comparable to that of the most sacred beings. The circle of sacred objects cannot be determined, then, once for all. Its extent varies infinitely, according to the differ

ent religions. That is how Buddhism is a religion: in default of gods, it admits the existence of sacred things, namely, the four noble truths and the practices derived from them.[1]

Up to the present we have confined ourselves to enumerating a certain number of sacred things as examples: we must now show by what general characteristics they are to be distinguished from profane things.

One might be tempted, first of all, to define them by the place they are generally assigned in the hierarchy of things. They are naturally considered superior in dignity and power to profane things, and particularly to man, when he is only a man and has nothing sacred about him. One thinks of himself as occupying an inferior and dependent position in relation to them; and surely this conception is not without some truth. Only there is nothing in it which is really characteristic of the sacred. It is not enough that one thing be subordinated to another for the second to be sacred in regard to the first. Slaves are inferior to their masters, subjects to their king, soldiers to their leaders, the miser to his gold, the man ambitious for power to the hands which keep it from him; but if it is sometimes said of a man that he makes a religion of those beings or things whose eminent value and superiority to himself he thus recognizes, it is clear that in any case the word is taken in a metaphorical sense, and that there is nothing in these relations which is really religious.[2]

On the other hand, it must not be lost to view that there are sacred things of every degree, and that there are some in relation to which a man feels himself relatively at his ease. An amulet has a sacred character, yet the respect which

[1] Not to mention the sage and the saint who practise these truths and who for that reason are sacred.

[2] This is not saying that these relations cannot take a religious character. But they do not do so necessarily.

it inspires is nothing exceptional. Even before his gods, a man is not always in such a marked state of inferiority; for it very frequently happens that he exercises a veritable physical constraint upon them to obtain what he desires. He beats the fetich with which he is not contented, but only to reconcile himself with it again, if in the end it shows itself more docile to the wishes of its adorer.[3] To have rain, he throws stones into the spring or sacred lake where the god of rain is thought to reside; he believes that by this means he forces him to come out and show himself.[4] Moreover, if it is true that man depends upon his gods, this dependence is reciprocal. The gods also have need of man; without offerings and sacrifices they would die. We shall even have occasion to show that this dependence of the gods upon their worshippers is maintained even in the most idealistic religions.

But if a purely hierarchic distinction is a criterium at once too general and too imprecise, there is nothing left with which to characterize the sacred in its relation to the profane except their heterogeneity. However, this heterogeneity is sufficient to characterize this classification of things and to distinguish it from all others, because it is very particular: *it is absolute*. In all the history of human thought there exists no other example of two categories of things so profoundly differentiated or so radically opposed to one another. The traditional opposition of good and bad is nothing beside this; for the good and the bad are only two opposed species of the same class, namely morals, just as sickness and health are two different aspects of the same order of facts, life, while the sacred and the profane have always and everywhere been conceived by the human mind as two distinct classes, as two

worlds between which there is nothing in common. The forces which play in one are not simply those which are met with in the other, but a little stronger; they are of a different sort. In different religions, this opposition has been conceived in different ways. Here, to separate these two sorts of things, it has seemed sufficient to localize them in different parts of the physical universe; there, the first have been put into an ideal and transcendental world, while the material world is left in full possession of the others. But howsoever much the forms of the contrast may vary,[5] the fact of the contrast is universal.

This is not equivalent to saying that a being can never pass from one of these worlds into the other: but the manner in which this passage is effected, when it does take place, puts into relief the essential duality of the two kingdoms. In fact, it implies a veritable metamorphosis. This is notably demonstrated by the initiation rites, such as they are practised by a multitude of peoples. This initiation is a long series of ceremonies with the object of introducing the young man into the religious life: for the first time, he leaves the purely profane world where he passed his first infancy, and enters into the world of sacred things. Now this change of state is thought of, not as a simple and regular development of pre-existent germs, but as a transformation *totius substantiae*—of the whole being. It is said that at this moment the young man dies, that the person that he was ceases to exist, and that another is instantly substituted for it. He is re-born under a new form. Ap-

[3] Schultze, *Fetichismus*, p. 129.
[4] Examples of these usages will be found in Frazer, *Golden Bough*, 2 edit., I, pp. 81 ff.

[5] The conception according to which the profane is opposed to the sacred, just as the irrational is to the rational, or the intelligible is to the mysterious, is only one of the forms under which this opposition is expressed. Science being once constituted, it has taken a profane character, especially in the eyes of the Christian religions; from that it appears as though it could not be applied to sacred things.

propriate ceremonies are felt to bring about this death and re-birth, which are not understood in a merely symbolic sense, but are taken literally.[6] Does this not prove that between the profane being which he was and the religious being which he becomes, there is a break of continuity?

This heterogeneity is even so complete that it frequently degenerates into a veritable antagonism. The two worlds are not only conceived of as separate, but as even hostile and jealous rivals of each other. Since men cannot fully belong to one except on condition of leaving the other completely, they are exhorted to withdraw themselves completely from the profane world, in order to lead an exclusively religious life. Hence comes the monasticism which is artificially organized outside of and apart from the natural environment in which the ordinary man leads the life of this world, in a different one, closed to the first, and nearly its contrary. Hence comes the mystic asceticism whose object is to root out from man all the attachment for the profane world that remains in him. From that come all the forms of religious suicide, the logical working-out of this asceticism; for the only manner of fully escaping the profane life is, after all, to forsake all life.

The opposition of these two classes manifests itself outwardly with a visible sign by which we can easily recognize this very special classification, wherever it exists. Since the idea of the sacred is always and everywhere separated from the idea of the profane in the thought of men, and since we picture a sort of logical chasm between the two, the mind irresistibly refuses to allow the two corresponding things to be confounded, or even to be merely put in contact with each other; for such a promiscuity, or even too direct a contiguity, would contradict too violently the dissociation of these ideas in the mind. The sacred thing is *par excellence* that which the profane should not touch, and cannot touch with impunity. To be sure, this interdiction cannot go so far as to make all communication between the two worlds impossible; for if the profane could in no way enter into relations with the sacred, this latter could be good for nothing. But, in addition to the fact that this establishment of relations is always a delicate operation in itself, demanding great precautions and a more or less complicated initiation,[7] it is quite impossible, unless the profane is to lose its specific characteristics and become sacred after a fashion and to a certain degree itself. The two classes cannot even approach each other and keep their own nature at the same time.

Thus we arrive at the first criterium of religious beliefs. Undoubtedly there are secondary species within these two fundamental classes which, in their turn, are more or less incompatible with each other.[8] But the real characteristic of religious phenomena is that they always suppose a bipartite division of the whole universe, known and knowable, into two classes which embrace all that exists, but which radically exclude each other. Sacred things are those which the interdictions protect and isolate; profane things, those to which these interdictions are ap-

[6] See Frazer, "On Some Ceremonies of the Central Australian Tribes" in *Australian Association for the Advancement of Science,* 1901, pp. 313 ff. This conception is also of an extreme generality. In India, the simple participation in the sacrificial act has the same effects; the sacrificer, by the mere act of entering within the circle of sacred things, changes his personality. (See, Hubert and Mauss, *Essai sur le Sacrifice* in the *Année Sociologique,* II, p. 101.)

[7] See what was said of the initiation above, p. 29.

[8] We shall point out how, for example, certain species of sacred things exist, between which there is an incompatibility as all-exclusive as that between the sacred and the profane (*El. Forms,* Bk. III, ch. v, § 4).

plied and which must remain at a distance from the first. Religious beliefs are the representations which express the nature of sacred things and the relations which they sustain, either with each other or with profane things. Finally, rites are the rules of conduct which prescribe how a man should comport himself in the presence of these sacred objects.

When a certain number of sacred things sustain relations of co-ordination or subordination with each other in such a way as to form a system having a certain unity, but which is not comprised within any other system of the same sort, the totality of these beliefs and their corresponding rites constitutes a religion. From this definition it is seen that a religion is not necessarily contained within one sole and single idea, and does not proceed from one unique principle which, though varying according to the circumstances under which it is applied, is nevertheless at bottom always the same: it is rather a whole made up of distinct and relatively individualized parts. Each homogeneous group of sacred things, or even each sacred thing of some importance, constitutes a centre of organization about which gravitate a group of beliefs and rites, or a particular cult; there is no religion, howsoever unified it may be, which does not recognize a plurality of sacred things. Even Christianity, at least in its Catholic form, admits, in addition to the divine personality which, incidentally, is triple as well as one, the Virgin, angels, saints, souls of the dead, etc. Thus a religion cannot be reduced to one single cult generally, but rather consists in a system of cults, each endowed with a certain autonomy. Also, this autonomy is variable. Sometimes they are arranged in a hierarchy, and subordinated to some predominating cult, into which they are finally absorbed; but sometimes, also, they are merely rearranged and united. The religion which we are going to study will furnish us with an example of just this latter sort of organization.

At the same time we find the explanation of how there can be groups of religious phenomena which do not belong to any special religion; it is because they have not been, or are no longer, a part of any religious system. If, for some special reason, one of the cults of which we just spoke happens to be maintained while the group of which it was a part disappears, it survives only in a disintegrated condition. That is what has happened to many agrarian cults which have survived themselves as folk-lore. In certain cases, it is not even a cult, but a simple ceremony or particular rite which persists in this way.[9]

Although this definition is only preliminary, it permits us to see in what terms the problem which necessarily dominates the science of religions should be stated. When we believed that sacred beings could be distinguished from others merely by the greater intensity of the powers attributed to them, the question of how men came to imagine them was sufficiently simple: it was enough to demand which forces had, because of their exceptional energy, been able to strike the human imagination forcefully enough to inspire religious sentiments. But if, as we have sought to establish, sacred things differ in nature from profane things, if they have a wholly different essence, then the problem is more complex. For we must first of all ask what has been able to lead men to see in the world two heterogeneous and incompatible worlds, though nothing in sensible experience seems able to suggest the idea of so radical a duality to them.

However, this definition is not yet complete, for it is equally applicable to two sorts of facts which, while being related to each other, must be distinguished nevertheless: these are magic and religion.

[9] This is the case with certain marriage and funeral rites, for example.

Magic, too, is made up of beliefs and rites. Like religion, it has its myths and its dogmas; only they are more elementary, undoubtedly because, seeking technical and utilitarian ends, it does not waste its time in pure speculation. It has its ceremonies, sacrifices, lustrations, prayers, chants and dances as well. The beings which the magician invokes and the forces which he throws in play are not merely of the same nature as the forces and beings to which religion addresses itself; very frequently, they are identically the same. Thus, even with the most inferior societies, the souls of the dead are essentially sacred things, and the object of religious rites. But at the same time, they play a considerable rôle in magic. In Australia[10] as well as in Melanesia,[11] in Greece as well as among the Christian peoples,[12] the souls of the dead, their bones and their hair, are among the intermediaries used the most frequently by the magician. Demons are also a common instrument for magic action. Now these demons are also beings surrounded with interdictions; they too are separated and live in a world apart, so that it is frequently difficult to distinguish them from the gods properly so-called.[13] Moreover, in Christianity itself, is not the devil a fallen god, or even leaving aside all question of his origin, does he not have a religious character from the mere fact that the hell of which he has charge is something indispensable to the Christian religion? There are even some regular and official deities who are

invoked by the magician. Sometimes these are the gods of a foreign people; for example, Greek magicians called upon Egyptian, Assyrian or Jewish gods. Sometimes, they are even national gods: Hecate and Diana were the object of a magic cult; the Virgin, Christ and the saints have been utilized in the same way by Christian magicians.[14]

Then will it be necessary to say that magic is hardly distinguishable from religion; that magic is full of religion just as religion is full of magic, and consequently that it is impossible to separate them and to define the one without the other? It is difficult to sustain this thesis, because of the marked repugnance of religion for magic, and in return, the hostility of the second towards the first. Magic takes a sort of professional pleasure in profaning holy things;[15] in its rites, it performs the contrary of the religious ceremony.[16] On its side, religion, when it has not condemned and prohibited magic rites, has always looked upon them with disfavour. As Hubert and Mauss have remarked, there is something thoroughly anti-religious in the doings of the magician.[17] Whatever relations there may be between these two sorts of institutions, it is difficult to imagine their not being opposed somewhere; and it is still more necessary for us to find where they are differentiated, as we plan to limit our researches to religion, and to stop at the point where magic commences.

Here is how a line of demarcation can be traced between these two domains.

The really religious beliefs are always common to a determined group, which

[10] See Spencer and Gillen, *Native Tribes of Central Australia,* pp. 534 ff.; *Northern Tribes of Central Australia,* p. 463; Howitt, *Native Tribes of S.E. Australia,* pp. 359–361.
[11] See Codrington, *The Melanesians,* ch. xii.
[12] See Hubert, art. *Magia* in *Dictionnaire des Antiquités.*
[13] For example, in Melanesia, the *tindalo* is a spirit, now religious, now magic (Codrington, pp. 125 ff., 194 ff.).

[14] See Hubert and Mauss, *Théorie Générale de la Magie,* in *Année Sociologique,* vol. VII, pp. 83–84.
[15] For example, the host is profaned in the black mass.
[16] One turns his back to the altar, or goes around the altar commencing by the left instead of by the right.
[17] *Loc. cit.,* p. 19.

makes profession of adhering to them and of practising the rites connected with them. They are not merely received individually by all the members of this group; they are something belonging to the group, and they make its unity. The individuals which compose it feel themselves united to each other by the simple fact that they have a common faith. A society whose members are united by the fact that they think in the same way in regard to the sacred world and its relations with the profane world, and by the fact that they translate these common ideas into common practices, is what is called a Church. In all history, we do not find a single religion without a Church. Sometimes the Church is strictly national, sometimes it passes the frontiers; sometimes it embraces an entire people (Rome, Athens, the Hebrews), sometimes it embraces only a part of them (the Christian societies since the advent of Protestantism); sometimes it is directed by a corps of priests, sometimes it is almost completely devoid of any official directing body.[18] But wherever we observe the religious life, we find that it has a definite group as its foundation. Even the so-called private cults, such as the domestic cult or the cult of a corporation, satisfy this condition; for they are always celebrated by a group, the family or the corporation. Moreover, even these particular religions are ordinarily only special forms of a more general religion which embraces all;[19] these

restricted Churches are in reality only chapels of a vaster Church which, by reason of this very extent, merits this name still more.[20]

It is quite another matter with magic. To be sure, the belief in magic is always more or less general; it is very frequently diffused in large masses of the population, and there are even peoples where it has as many adherents as the real religion. But it does not result in binding together those who adhere to it, nor in uniting them into a group leading a common life. *There is no Church of magic.* Between the magician and the individuals who consult him, as between these individuals themselves, there are no lasting bonds which make them members of the same moral community, comparable to that formed by the believers in the same god or the observers of the same cult. The magician has a clientele and not a Church, and it is very possible that his clients have no other relations between each other, or even do not know each other; even the relations which they have with him are generally accidental and transient; they are just like those of a sick man with his physician. The official and public character with which he is sometimes invested changes nothing in this situation; the fact that he works openly does not unite him more regularly or more durably to those who have recourse to his services.

It is true that in certain cases, magicians form societies among themselves: it happens that they assemble more or less periodically to celebrate certain rites in common; it is well known what a place these assemblies of witches hold in European folk-lore. But it is to be remarked

[18] Undoubtedly it is rare that a ceremony does not have some director at the moment when it is celebrated; even in the most crudely organized societies, there are generally certain men whom the importance of their social position points out to exercise a directing influence over the religious life (for example, the chiefs of the local groups of certain Australian societies). But this attribution of functions is still very uncertain.
[19] At Athens, the gods to whom the domestic cult was addressed were only specialized

forms of the gods of the city (Ζεὺς κτήσιος, Ζεὺς ἑρκεῖος). In the same way, in the Middle Ages, the patrons of the guilds were saints of the calendar.
[20] For the name Church is ordinarily applied only to a group whose common beliefs refer to a circle of more special affairs.

that these associations are in no way indispensable to the working of the magic; they are even rare and rather exceptional. The magician has no need of uniting himself to his fellows to practise his art. More frequently, he is a recluse; in general, far from seeking society, he flees it. "Even in regard to his colleagues, he always keeps his personal independence." [21] Religion, on the other hand, is inseparable from the idea of a Church. From this point of view, there is an essential difference between magic and religion. But what is especially important is that when these societies of magic are formed, they do not include all the adherents to magic, but only the magicians; the laymen, if they may be so called, that is to say, those for whose profit the rites are celebrated, in fine, those who represent the worshippers in the regular cults, are excluded. Now the magician is for magic what the priest is for religion, but a college of priests is not a Church, any more than a religious congregation which should devote itself to some particular saint in the shadow of a cloister, would be a particular cult. A Church is not a fraternity of priests; it is a moral community formed by all the believers in a single faith, laymen as well as priests. But magic lacks any such community.[22]

But if the idea of a Church is made to enter into the definition of religion, does that not exclude the private religions which the individual establishes for himself and celebrates by himself? There is scarcely a society where these are not found. Every Ojibway, as we shall see below, has his own personal *manitou*, which he chooses himself and to which he renders special religious services; the Melanesian of the Banks Islands has his *tamaniu;*[23] the Roman, his *genius;*[24] the Christian, his patron saint and guardian angel, etc. By definition all these cults seem to be independent of all ideas of the group. Not only are these individual religions very frequent in history, but nowadays many are asking if they are not destined to be the pre-eminent form of the religious life, and if the day will not come when there will be no other cult than that which each man will freely perform within himself.[25]

But if we leave these speculations in regard to the future aside for the moment, and confine ourselves to religions such as they are at present or have been in the past, it becomes clearly evident that these individual cults are not distinct and autonomous religious systems, but merely aspects of the common religion of the whole Church, of which the individuals are members. The patron saint of the Christian is chosen from the official list of saints recognized by the Catholic Church; there are even canonical rules prescribing how each Catholic should perform this private cult. In the same way, the idea that each man necessarily has a protecting genius is found, under different forms, at the basis of a great number of American religions, as well as of the Roman religion (to cite only these two examples); for, as will be seen later, it is very closely connected with the idea of the soul, and this idea of the soul is not one of those which can be left entirely to individual choice. In a

[21] Hubert and Mauss, *loc. cit.*, p. 18.
[22] Robertson Smith has already pointed out that magic is opposed to religion, as the individual to the social (*The Religion of the Semites*, 2 edit., pp. 264–265). Also, in thus distinguishing magic from religion, we do not mean to establish a break of continuity between them. The frontiers between the two domains are frequently uncertain.

[23] Codrington, *Trans. and Proc. Roy. Soc. of Victoria*, XVI, p. 136.
[24] Negrioli. *Dei Genii presso i Romani.*
[25] This is the conclusion reached by Spencer in his *Ecclesiastical Institutions* (ch. xvi), and by Sabatier in his *Outlines of a Philosophy of Religion, based on Psychology and History* (tr. by Seed), and by all the school to which he belongs.

word, it is the Church of which he is a member which teaches the individual what these personal gods are, what their function is, how he should enter into relations with them and how he should honour them. When a methodical analysis is made of the doctrines of any Church whatsoever, sooner or later we come upon those concerning private cults. So these are not two religions of different types, and turned in opposite directions; both are made up of the same ideas and the same principles, here applied to circumstances which are of interest to the group as a whole, there to the life of the individual. This solidarity is even so close that among certain peoples,[26] the ceremonies by which the faithful first enter into communication with their protecting geniuses are mixed with rites whose public character is incontestable, namely the rites of initiation.[27]

There still remain those contemporary aspirations towards a religion which would consist entirely in internal and subjective states, and which would be constructed freely by each of us. But howsoever real these aspirations may be, they cannot affect our definition, for this is to be applied only to facts already realized, and not to uncertain possibilities. One can define religions such as they are, or such as they have been, but not such as they more or less vaguely tend to become. It is possible that this religious individualism is destined to be realized in facts; but before we can say just how far this may be the case, we must first know what religion is, of what elements it is made up, from what causes it results, and what function it fulfils—all questions whose solution cannot be foreseen before the threshold of our study has been passed. It is only at the close of this study that we can attempt to anticipate the future.

Thus we arrive at the following definition: *A religion is a unified system of beliefs and practices relative to sacred things, that is to say, things set apart and forbidden—beliefs and practices which unite into one single moral community called a Church, all those who adhere to them.* The second element which thus finds a place in our definition is no less essential than the first; for by showing that the idea of religion is inseparable from that of the Church, it makes it clear that religion should be an eminently collective thing.[28]

[26] Notably among numerous Indian tribes of North America.

[27] This statement of fact does not touch the question whether exterior and public religion is not merely the development of an interior and personal religion which was the primitive fact, or whether, on the contrary, the second is not the projection of the first into individual consciences. The problem will be directly attacked (*El. Forms,* Bk. II, ch. v, § 2, cf. the same book, ch. vi and vii, § 1). For the moment, we confine ourselves to remarking that the individual cult is presented to the observer as an element of, and something dependent upon, the collective cult.

[28] It is by this that our present definition is connected to the one we have already proposed in the *Année Sociologique.* In this other work, we defined religious beliefs exclusively by their obligatory character; but, as we shall show, this obligation evidently comes from the fact that these beliefs are the possession of a group which imposes them upon its members. The two definitions are thus in a large part the same. If we have thought it best to propose a new one, it is because the first was too formal, and neglected the contents of the religious representations too much. It will be seen, in the discussions which follow, how important it is to put this characteristic into evidence at once. Moreover, if their imperative character is really a distinctive trait of religious beliefs, it allows of an infinite number of degrees; consequently there are even cases where it is not easily perceptible. Hence come difficulties and embarrassments which are avoided by substituting for this criterium the one we now employ.

2 · Religion and the Holy

GUSTAV MENSCHING

Religion is experiential encounter with the holy and the responsive action of the human being influenced by the holy.

R. Otto marked off the direct and rationally inaccessible essence of the holy through the basic experiences that may be encountered in all religion. He made use of three concepts in this connection, concepts that have since been taken up in the science of religion: the holy is, we may say, first of all the "mysterium tremendum," the mystery that evokes trembling; for the holy acts on the person who encounters it so that it elevates yet at the same time oppresses him, as it arouses in him dreadful awe and the feeling of the alien. The distant, unapproachable and

SOURCE. From Gustav Mensching, *Die Religion*, Stuttgart: C. E. Schwab, 1959. pp. 18–19 and 130. Translated by the editor.

deeply mysterious God is meant here. This powerful and majestic divinity makes man tremble in his nothingness and creatureliness, as in the sense of the words, "I have taken upon me to speak with thee, although I am dust and ashes." (*Genesis* 18:27) Additionally, we encounter, in a curious harmony of contrast, the experience of the holy as an experience of the attractive, the gladsome, the desirable. Otto named this factor in the reality of the holy the "fascinans." As a third factor, we may add the "august," by which term we may designate the experience of the holy as lofty value. In the light of this, man perceives his unworthiness as a profane creature, i.e., one not belonging to the world of the holy. Isaiah expresses this experience of the holy (*Isaiah* 6) in these words: "I am a man of unclean lips and I dwell in the midst of a people of unclean lips."

3 · Baseball as a National Religion

MORRIS R. COHEN

In the world's history baseball is a new game: hence new to song and story and uncelebrated in the fine arts of painting, sculpture, and music. Now, as Ruskin has pointed out, people generally do not see beauty or majesty except when it has been first revealed to them in pictures or other works of art. This is peculiarly true

SOURCE. Morris R. Cohen, *The Faith of a Liberal*, Henry Holt, New York, 1946, pp. 334–336; published in *The Dial*, Vol. 67, p. 57 (July 26, 1919).

of the people who call themselves educated. No one who prides himself on being familiar with Greek and Roman architecture and the classic masters of painting would for a moment admit that there could be any beauty in a modern skyscraper. Yet when two thousand years hence some Antarctic scholar comes to describe our civilization, he will mention as our distinctive contribution to art our beautiful office buildings, and perhaps offer in support of his thesis colored plates of some of the ruins of those temples of commerce. And when he comes to speak of America's contribution to religion, will he not mention baseball? Do not be shocked, gentle or learned reader! I know full well that baseball is a boy's game, and a professional sport, and that a properly cultured, serious person always feels like apologizing for attending a baseball game instead of a Strauss concert or a lecture on the customs of the Fiji Islanders. But I still maintain that, by all the canons of our modern books on comparative religion, baseball is a religion, and the only one that is not sectarian but national.

The essence of religious experience, so we are told, is the "redemption from the limitations of our petty individual lives and the mystic unity with a larger life of which we are a part." And is not this precisely what the baseball devotee or fanatic, if you please, experiences when he watches the team representing his city battling with another? Is there any other experience in modern life in which multitudes of men so completely and intensely lose their individual selves in the larger life which they call their city? Careful students of Greek civilization do not hesitate to speak of the religious value of the Greek drama. When the auditor identifies himself with the action on the stage—Aristotle tells us—his feelings of fear and pity undergo a kind of purification (catharsis). But in baseball the identification has even more of the religious quality, since we are absorbed not only in the action of the visible actors but more deeply in the fate of the mystic unities which we call the contending cities. To be sure, there may be people who go to a baseball game to see some particular star, just as there are people who go to church to hear a particular minister preach; but these are phenomena in the circumference of the religious life. There are also blasé persons who do not care who wins so long as they can see what they call a good game—just as

there are people who go to mass because they admire the vestments or intoning of the priest—but this only illustrates the pathology of the religious life. The truly religious devotee has his soul directed to the final outcome; and every one of the extraordinarily rich multiplicity of movements of the baseball game acquires its significance because of its bearing on that outcome. Instead of purifying only fear and pity, baseball exercises and purifies all of our emotions, cultivating hope and courage when we are behind, resignation when we are beaten, fairness for the other team when we are ahead, charity for the umpire, and above all the zest for combat and conquest.

When my revered friend and teacher William James wrote an essay on "A Moral Equivalent for War," I suggested to him that baseball already embodied all the moral value of war, so far as war had any moral value. He listened sympathetically and was amused, but he did not take me seriously enough. All great men have their limitations, and William James's were due to the fact that he lived in Cambridge, a city which, in spite of the fact that it has a population of 100,000 souls (including the professors), is not represented in any baseball league that can be detected without a microscope.

Imagine what will happen to the martial spirit in Germany if baseball is introduced there—if any Social Democrat can ask any Herr von Somebody, "What's the score?" Suppose that in an exciting ninth-inning rally, when the home team ties the score, Captain Schmidt punches Captain Miller or breaks his helmet. Will the latter challenge him to a duel? He will not. Rather will he hug him frenziedly or pummel him joyfully at the next moment when the winning run comes across the home plate. And after the game, what need of further strife? When Jones of Philadelphia meets Brown of New York there may be a slight touch of condescension on one side, or a hidden strain of envy on the other side, but they take each other's arm in fraternal fashion, for they have settled their differences in an open, regulated combat on a fair field. And if one of us has some sore regrets over an unfortunate error which lost the game, there is always the consolation that we have had our inning, and though we have lost there is another game or season coming. And what more can a reasonable man expect in this imperfect world than an open chance to do his best in a free and fair fight?

Every religion has its martyrs; and the greatest of all martyrdoms is to make oneself ridiculous and to be laughed at by the heathen. But whatever the danger,

I am ready to urge the claims of international baseball as capable of arousing far more national religious fervor than the more monotonous game of armaments and war. Those who fear "the deadly monotony of a universal reign of peace" can convince themselves of the thrilling and exciting character of baseball by watching the behavior of crowds not only at the games but also at the baseball score-boards miles away. National rivalries and aspirations could find their intensest expression in a close international pennant race, and yet such rivalry would not be incompatible with the establishment of the true Church Universal in which all men would feel their brotherhood in the Infinite Game.

4 · Universals in Religion

JOACHIM WACH

I

The careful research of many a generation of scholars, the travel reports, not only of adventurers, missionaries and explorers, but of many a person you and I count among our personal acquaintances, have brought home to well-nigh all of us a realization of the variety of religious ideas and practices that exist in the world. The result of this realization has been bewilderment and confusion in many hearts and minds. Roughly three different types of reaction to the situation can be discerned: (i) scepticism, that is, the refusal to see in all these religious ideas and usages more than the expression of igno-

SOURCE. Joachim Wach, *Types of Religious Experience: Christian and Non-Christian,* Chicago: The University of Chicago Press, 1951, Ch. 2 (pp. 30–47 and 237–241). Reprinted by permission of The University of Chicago Press.

rance and folly, in other words a cultural and/or religious "lag"; (ii) relativism, that is, a disposition to dispense with the problem of truth in favour of a noncommittal registration of all there is and has been, an attitude which has found much favour in the latter-day circles of scholars and intellectuals; and finally (iii) the desire to investigate the variety of what goes under the names of religion and religions in order to determine by comparison and phenomenological analysis if anything like a structure can be discovered in all these forms of expression, to what kind of experiences this variegated expression can be traced, and finally, what kind of reality or realities may correspond to the experiences in question. It is the last of the three types of reaction to the predicament characterized above which seems to us the only promising and fruitful one, and we propose to follow it in what we have to say here.

The first difficulty we encounter in trying to bring some order into the bewildering mass of material that geography, anthropology, sociology, archaeology, philology, history, and the history of religions have placed at our disposal, is the need for criteria which would enable us to distinguish between what is religious and what is not. Now you will not expect me to discuss the well-nigh endless series of definitions of religion which have been proposed by the great and the not-so-great during recent decades. We shall also find it impossible to use as our yardstick one of the classical historical formulations evolved in one of the great religious communities itself, say in the Christian. For we should soon discover that it is not possible to identify religion with what we have come to know as Christian or Jewish or Hindu, even if we forget for the moment that it would be far from easy to agree on which of the available formulations we want to use. Some of us might feel, at first thought, that it is after all not so difficult to determine what may be called religious and what is not religious; they would point to the neat divisions which we are accustomed to find in our text-books, dealing with the lives of individuals, societies and cultures, past and present, in which separate chapters deal with man's political views and activities, his economic situation, his interest in the arts, and his religious orientation, or with the social organization, the economics, the legal institutions, the arts and sciences, the moral life, and the religion of a given tribe, people or nation. But, on second thoughts, the unsatisfactory character of such parcelling becomes evident; and that not only in the repetitions and omissions which this procedure entails. No wonder then that some investigators—and we find among them distinguished anthropologists, philosophers, and theologians—have come to the conclusion that religion is not anything distinct and *sui generis*, but is a name given

to the sum of man's aspirations, to the whole of the civilization of a people. If we reject this view, it is not because we want to separate sharply between religion on the one hand and on the other all that makes up an individual's or a society's other experiences and activities. But we are of the opinion that, in order to be able to assess the interrelation and interpenetration of the various interests, attitudes, and activities of man, we have to examine very carefully the nature of his propensities, drives, impulses, actions, and reactions. William James has rightly said:

> The essence of religious experiences, the thing by which we must finally judge them, must be that element or quality in them which we can meet nowhere else. (1)

We disagree with those who are prone to identify religion with just one segment of man's inner existence: feeling, willing, or cogitating. In order to lay down our criteria, we cannot be satisfied to examine only the conceptually articulated perceptions or only the emotions and affections and the respective expressions in which they have become manifest. We propose rather the following *four formal criteria* for a definition of what might be called religious experience:

1. Religious experience is a response to what is experienced as ultimate reality; that is, in religious experiences we react not to any single or finite phenomenon, material or otherwise, but to what we realize as undergirding and conditioning all that constitutes our world of experiences. We agree with Paul Tillich when he says that "the presence of the demand of 'ultimacy' in the structure of our existence is the basis of religious experience" (2). Before him William James said in his book on the *Varieties of Religious Experience* (3)—a passage quoted in Paul Johnson's *Psychology of Religion* (4).

It is as if there were in the human consciousness a sense of reality, a feeling of objective presence, a perception of what we may call "something there," more deep and more general than any of the special and particular "senses" by which the current psychology supposes existent realities to be originally revealed (5).

Or as the author of a recent text-book on Psychology of Religion formulates it (6):

Religious experience is response to stimuli that represent an active reality viewed as divine, or as creative of values.

This response has the tendency to persist, once communion with the source of life and values is established, and man is restless to reassure himself of its continuance.

2. Religious experience is a total response of the total being to what is apprehended as ultimate reality. That is, we are involved not exclusively with our mind, our affections, or our will, but as integral persons (7).

3. Religious experience is the most intense experience of which man is capable. That is not to say that all expression of religious experience testifies to this intensity but that, potentially, genuine religious experience is of this nature, as is instanced in conflicts between different basic drives or motivations. Religious loyalty, if it is religious loyalty, wins over all other loyalties. The modern term "existential" designates the profound concern and the utter seriousness of this experience.

4. Religious experience is practical, that is to say it involves an imperative, a commitment which impels man to act. This activistic note distinguishes it from aesthetic experience, of which it shares the intensity, and joins it with moral experience. Moral judgment, however, does

not necessarily represent a reaction to ultimate reality.

It should be borne in mind that one, two, or three of these criteria would not suffice to reassure us that we are dealing with genuine religious experience. All four would have to be present. If they are, we should have no difficulty in distinguishing between religious and non-religious experiences. However, there are *pseudo-religious* and *semi-religious* experiences. The former are non-religious and known to be such to the person or persons who pretend to them by using forms of expression peculiar to religion. The latter may show the presence of the second, third and fourth characteristics, but refer not to ultimate but to some aspect of "finite" reality. The intense and possibly sacrificial devotion with which somebody may "worship" a loved person, his race, his social group, or his state are instances of semi-religious loyalties. Because they are directed toward finite values, they are idolatrous rather than religious.

Now it is our contention, and this is the first proposition in regard to our topic, that religious experience, as we have just attempted to define it by means of these four criteria, is *universal*. The empirical proof of this statement can be found in the testimonies of explorers and investigators. "There are no peoples, however primitive, without religion and magic," is the opening sentence of one of Malinowski's well-known essays (8). In practically all cases where a rash negative conclusion has been reached, more careful research has corrected the initial error.

A *second* proposition is this: religious experience tends towards *expression*. This tendency is universal. Only in and through its expression does any of our experiences exist for others, does any religious experience exist for us, the students of the history of religion. The religious experience of another person can never become the object of direct observation. Some important hermeneutical consequences result from the recognition of this fact.

Now for the *third* step in our search for universals in religion. A comparative study of the *forms* of the expression of religious experience, the world over, shows an amazing similarity in structure. We should like to summarize the result of such comparative studies by the statement: all expression of religious experience falls under the three headings of *theoretical expression, practical expression,* and *sociological expression* (9). Everywhere and at all times man has felt the need to articulate his religious experience in three ways: conceptually; by action, or practically; and in convenanting, or sociologically. There is no religion deserving of the name in which any one of these three elements is totally lacking, though the degree and, of course, the tempo of this development may vary. Notwithstanding numerous attempts at establishing priority for one of these three modes of expression, we feel that it would be futile to argue that myth precedes cult or that both precede fellowship: history teaches us that the dynamics of religious life is made up of the interpenetration of these three aspects.

Before we can discuss in any greater detail the structure of these fields of expression of religious experience and the common elements to be found within an apparently endless variety of forms, we have to consider briefly some general factors which help to determine their development. Man finds himself always situationally conditioned: whatever he experiences, he experiences in *time* and *space*. Even if, in his religious experience, he seems to transcend these limitations —a feeling to which the mystics of all religions have given vivid and often paradoxical articulation [Eckhart: "Time is what keeps the light from reaching us. There is no greater obstacle to God than Time" (10)]—he cannot but give expression to what he has seen, felt, etc., *per analogiam entis,* by means of *analogy* from what is known and familiar to him (11). The way of negation, of analogy and of eminence is used in all religious language. That we have to remember when we review the concepts of sacred time and of sacred space which are the framework within which religious thought and religious acts enfold themselves. Holy times and holy places are universal notions; no myth or doctrine, no cult or religious association is found without them (12). Closely related to these categories within which religious apprehension expresses itself is the notion of a *cosmic* (that is natural, ritual and social) *order* upon which life, individual and collective, depends. The well-known Chinese concept of *Tao,* the Hindu *ṛta,* the Iranian *asha,* the Greek *dike,* designate the order upon which man and society depend for their existence (13). In the religions of the American Indians, the Africans and Oceanians' the directions, the seasons, the celestial bodies, colours, social organization, all follow this orientation, the cosmic law which the physical, mental and spiritual life of all beings has to obey (14). Nature and its rhythm, culture and its activities, and polity and its structure are but aspects of this order. It is the foundation for all "ethics."

Religious experience, we saw, may be characterized as the total response of man's total being to what he experiences as ultimate reality. In it he confronts a *power* greater than any power which he controls by his own wit or strength. I should like to stress *two* points here. This encounter is not a question of intellectual inference or speculative reasoning, of which there are few traces in many of the lower so-called primitive religions

(15). That is to say, religion is emphatically not a kind of under-developed "science" or "philosophy." This misinterpretation, still widely current, is an unfortunate legacy from the rationalistically-minded era of the Enlightenment. The experience which we call religion is rather an awareness of apprehension, not lacking a cognitive aspect but not defined by it, a reaction to something that is sensed or apprehended as powerful. Rudolf Otto has spoken of a *sensus numinis* (sense of awe) (16), and this term seems to me a very apt designation. We must reject all theories of religion which conceive of it as the fulfilment which imaginative or crafty individuals have supplied for a subjective, that is illusory, need. True, many a testimony to religious experience lets the latter appear as the result of a search, a struggle, but more often this experience has come as a bolt from the blue, with a spontaneity which contradicts the theory of need. Hence we prefer to say that there is a propensity, a *nisus* or *sensus numinis* which is activated in the religious experience proper (17). The aspect of power which the comparative study of religion has recently vindicated as a central notion in the religions of widely different peoples and societies, indicates the "point of contact" between the reality which is confronted in religious experience and life in the everyday world: the "immanence of the transcendent." Religions differ in their notions as to the how, where, and when of the manifestations of power in the phenomenal world. But the acknowledgment that this power manifest itself in experienceable form is universal. To the degree that it appears diffused, we speak of *power-centres* such as are known in all primitive, higher and fully developed cults (18). The Swedish historian of religion, Martin Nilsson, has recently (19) stressed the adjective character of terms for power such as *mana, orenda,* etc. Not the phenomenon, object or person in which this power manifests itself, but a power that *transcends* it, is the object of man's awe. It is of great importance to understand that this power is apprehended as an elementary force which transcends moral or aesthetic qualifications. As such it is "mysterious." It was one of the great insights of the author of the *Idea of the Holy,* Rudolf Otto, that he caught the double notion of the *mysterium magnum* in the twin ideas of its terrifying and its alluring aspect. These *two aspects* are known to the theologians of all religions as Divine Wrath and Divine Love or Grace. Though their natural roles and relationships are differently conceived in different faiths, these two aspects of power are universally recognized. But we can still go one step further in our analysis of universal features in religious experience. It is possible to discern a double consequence of man's apprehension of numinous power at all times and everywhere: he either bows to it in submission, or he reaches out in an attempt to manipulate and control the mysterious forces of which he has become aware. The first, the *religious* way, leads up to the highest religious act, that of adoration; the second, the way of *magic,* sets him on the road to conquer and to appropriate as much of the power as will yield to his command. These two developments are not to be thought of in terms of a chronological and evolutionary sequence: on the one hand the magical is always with us, and on the other the presence of genuinely religious response to the numinous even in the primitive cults cannot be denied. Hence both are universal. It is only the *intention* inherent in it which distinguishes the religious from the magical act. The very complicated question of the origins, the nature of the development of "science" (in the broader as well as the narrower sense of the natural sciences), and of its relation to both magic and religion, can be answered when we are more fully conversant with the nature of knowledge (20), with the psychological motivations for wanting to know (21).

Perhaps the sociology of knowledge will help us at some time in the future. On the cognitive factor in the experience which we call religious we shall have a word to say presently.

II

After these brief remarks, which were meant to put in relief some universally valid features of religious *experience*, we will now turn to the examination of universals in the forms of *expression* of this experience (22). We have said that the very fact that this experience tends to expression constitutes in itself a universal. We shall enlarge this statement now by asking: What *motivates* expression? There is first what I should like to call the demonstrative type of expression with which we are familiar from all kinds of experiences other than religious. The shout of joy or pain, witnessing to a profound emotion, is paralleled by the ejaculatory expression of awe or devotion. Then there is the communicative motif: we like to share our experiences with others, and we can do so only by means of sounds, words or acts. Finally the missionary purpose has to be considered. We want to attract others, a purpose not alien to other types of experience, but constitutive of the religious. Finding these motives making for expression universally valid, we may ask further: What of the *modes* in which the expression of religious experience is cast?

Here we face the difficult question of the interrelationship of what we have called the intellectual, the practical and the sociological expressions of religious experience (23). Bevan, Cassirer, Urban, Susanne Langer and others have studied the problem of symbolism and analysed the structure of logical, aesthetic, and religious symbols (24). The *symbol* is the primary means of expressing the content of any experience which we call religious. The use of symbolic expression is universal. By symbols a meaning is conveyed the nature of which may be conceptually explained, which may be acted upon, and which may serve as an integrating factor in creating religious fellowship. An example of a simple symbol is the *churinga* of the Australians (the bullroarer, standing for the presence of totemic ancestors), on a higher level the *shintai* (sword, mirror, stone) of the Japanese, or finally, in the great world religions, the Buddhist wheel and the Christian cross. In each case theoretical explanations, cultural use and sociological effect contribute to unfold and explain the meaning of the symbol (25). Stages in the development of these modes of expression can be traced: the African Bushmen, awed by the presence of the numinous at a given place, utter a numinous sound in which they express the vivid emotion that grips them, while throwing a few grains into a hole in the hallowed ground, an act which at the same time expresses and reinforces the communion which exists between fellow-worshippers. A second example: in the Egypt of the ancient kingdom the worshippers of a deity are gathered in a hut before the crude therio- or anthropomorphic images which stand as a symbol of the numinous presence. The myth in which the nature and the significance of this manifestation of the divine is illustrated imaginatively, is alive in the minds of those present. A third example: the original intuition or basic religious experience of the founder of Islam is enfolded in the systematic doctrine of Islam, acted out in acts of devotion and charity, and is the foundation upon which the *umma* or congregation of the faithful rests. All this goes to show the universal presence of the three modes of expression of religious experience and their intimate interrelationship.

We now have to discuss the *means* by which religious experience is theoretically, practically and sociologically expressed. Here too our expectation is to find elements present everywhere (26). We begin with the *intellectual* expression. Religious experience, as confrontation of ultimate reality, entails a cognitive element. When Mohammed received his initial revelation, when the Buddha awoke to the realization of the impermanence of the phenomenal world, when Laotse became aware of the nature of the unalterable Tao, this original intuition (*"Ur-intuition"*) in each case implied an apprehension of ultimate reality, of the relation of the visible to the invisible, of the nature of the universe and of man's nature and destiny which invited further conceptual articulation. We do not know to which intuitions the primitive cults owe their existence, but we can infer that generations of seers and priests helped to evolve the mythical concepts in which the numinous experiences of these peoples have come to expression. For *myth* is the *first form* of intellectual explanation of religious apprehensions. "It is," says S. Langer (27), "in the great realm of myth that human conceptions of reality become articulated." "These stories," says Malinowski (28), "live not by idle interest, not as fictions or even as true narratives; but are to the natives a statement of a primeval, greater, and more relevant reality by which the present life, fate and activities of man are determined. Here the imaginative element prevails over the abstract" (29). Contrary to the assumption of the Positivist school—Comte's theory of the stages—this form of expression is universal; it is not bound to any one stage of development, as the use of mythical language in all the great religions indicates. Myth asks the perennial question Why? Why are we here? Where do we

come from? Why do we act in the way we do? Why do we die?—questions which the awakened intellectual curiosity of man is apt to ask and to answer in imaginative, that is symbolic, language. The reason for the persistence of this form of expression of religious experience is to be found in the nature of this experience itself (30). It ultimately transcends rationalization, as the religious thinkers of all times and places well know (31). The *second form* of the intellectual explanation of religious apprehension we call *doctrine*. It grows out of the attempt to unify and systematize variant concepts. Doctrine also is a ubiquitous, that is a universal element. We meet with considerable development or systematization of myth in the priestly schools of Polynesia, in Western Africa, in the Maya and Aztec centres of learning, and we find this process continued in ancient Egypt, in Sumeria, in Israel, in Asia Minor, in India, in ancient Greece and Rome, among the Celts and the Teutonic tribes. In all the major world religions a doctrinal development which includes reactions and protests can be traced. More often than not we meet with short confessions of faith, some of which have developed into creeds (32).

From the examination of the formal side of the intellectual expression of religious experience, we turn to an analysis of its *content*. The great recurrent themes, treated in the myths as well as in the doctrines of all faiths, are (a) the nature and character of supreme reality: the deity of God; evil; the origin, nature and destiny of (b) the world and (c) of man (personality; sin; hope). In articulated theological doctrine these topics are treated in the disciplines known as theology, cosmology, and anthropology and eschatology. "The questions," says P. Tillich (33), "implied in human existence, determine the meaning and the theological interpretation of the answers as they appear in the classical religious concepts." In several of the great civilizations in the history of the world, in Greece, in Persia, in India, in China, theological speculation has developed into philosophy of religion and philosophical thought as such, especially metaphysics. Yet not only philosophy but science in practically all its major branches stems from this source. However important the thinking out of the implications of religious apprehension may be, it should never be identified with the total expression of religious experience. We agree here with Wiemann when he says:

> Events rich in value and events transformative of human existence run deeper than ideas and doctrines and are mightier (34).

The history of religious *thought* is only *one* though an essential and ubiquitous part of the history of religions. There are actually other than purely intellectual yet equally universally present means of expression of religious experience. "Man incited by God," says the author of the best book on worship (E. Underhill) (35), "dimly or sharply conscious of the obscure presence of God, responds to him best not by a single movement of the mind, but by a rich and complex action in which his whole nature is concerned, and which has at its full development the character of a work of art." "Ritual like art is," according to S. Langer, "essentially the active termination of a symbolic transformation of experience."

The phenomenology of the religious *act* shows a great variety of ways of acting which we shall, for our purpose, arrange typologically. It has been claimed that all life, as it is lived and acted, could be regarded as expressing that relationship that is experienced in the awareness of the numen. The great anthropologist R. R. Marett put it in this way:

> Being inwardly assured of its primacy as the ultimate source of vital

and psychic energy, spirit has no need to fear the close intimacy with the natural functions that go with life as pursued on the material plane (36).

Acts which in our view are remote from the religious sphere, such as eating, playing, mating (37), are cultual acts in many primitive and higher religions. In distinction from the general, there are specific cultual acts which we shall call *rites*. They have a special dedicatory character. In and through them the presence of the numen is acknowledged (38). The contact with creative sources of life innervates and stimulates man to action. "Ritual," says S. Langer (39), "is a transformation of the experiences that no other medium can adequately express. It is not prescribed for a practical purpose, even not social solidarity." The range of *media* employed in the cultual act is very wide: it runs the whole gamut from simple and spontaneous utterances and sounds, tones, words, gestures, and movements to highly standardized practices such as liturgy, sacrifice, sacred dance, divination, procession, pilgrimage. However, in order to determine if an act is genuinely religious or not, we have to examine the *intention* with which it is performed. A bow may be a token of respect, a conventional way of saluting one's acquaintances, and yet it may be, if it is executed in the presence of the numen, an expression of religious awe. The kiss, another general sign, is a token of affection or just of greeting; yet it may become the shibboleth of a spiritual brotherhood and part of a ritual pattern. Prayer, on the other hand, is an exclusive act of recollection by which man establishes and cultivates his communion with the source of power. It is a universal form of worship, as the rich phenomenology of prayer which Heiler has presented convincingly demonstrates. The Australian and the Bantu Negro, the Plains Indian and the Ainu, the Chinese and the Hindu, the Jew and the

Christian pray. Universal also are the various types of prayer: silent and vocal, private and collective, spontaneous and standardized.

Life in the universe, in the social unit and in the individual, cannot go on, so it is felt by the religious, if it is not nourished, encouraged, and stimulated by rites which keep it attuned to cosmic or divine powers. *Rites of Passage* (van Gennep) are practised universally. They consecrate the crises and marginal situations in individual and collective life. Prenatal preparations, ceremonies surrounding birth, name-giving, initiation at puberty, marriage, sickness, and burial rites are performed the world over to ward off the dangers lurking in the passage from one stage of life to another and to secure the indispensable contact with the divine source of life. "Ceremonial life," says R. R. Marett, "is the outstanding feature of all primitive cultures" (40). It characterizes, with one great exception—namely, modern Western civilization—all cultures. Not only the extraordinary or crucial events in life but also the regular activities of work and play cannot and must not be carried on unless the accompanying rites render them adequate and effective (41). The making of tools, the building of houses, the construction of boats, the tilling of the soil, hunting and fishing, the making of war, in primitive and higher civilization call for incantation, divination, and dedication. Malinowski has discussed Melanesian garden-ceremonies, Herskovits Dahomean co-operative construction rites, Parsons described the agricultural ritual in the Pueblo settlements. Aztecs and Chinese, Greeks and Romans, Sumerians and Hindus observed the requirements of cosmic orientation in planning their settlements as carefully as the African Yoruba or the nomad North American Omaha. A devout Moslem will not start on any important or even trivial enterprise without placing it, through an

"inshallah," in a deeper context. It is the great vision of all *homines religiosi* everywhere that all life is the expression of worship, that every act and deed witnesses to the continuous communion of man with God. The prophets, saints and mystics of the highest religions join in this vision with the humble folks whom we honour with the name of "Primitive" societies. Perhaps it would not be wrong to say that at no time and nowhere has this vision become actuality. Even if we do not quite agree with P. Radin, who suggests in his book on Primitive Religion (42) that the only men who really can be said to "have religion" and to practise it have been what he calls the "religious formulators," yet we realize that the natural frailty of human nature—man's sinful nature as the Christian would say —prevents him as a rule from enjoying the realization of the Divine presence continually and from expressing it, as it were, uninterruptedly by his deeds and acts. Even in the lives of saints and prophets, their great efforts to sustain this highest level of man's calling have not always been successful. Sluggishness, dullness, disobedience, temptation always work together to cause man to lapse. As he emancipates himself from the power that sustains him, his activities become centrifugal; they become, as we call it, "secularized." Yes, the very acts which were designed to witness to the highest communion lose their meaning, become, if they are still performed, empty, fossilized. It is the function of the prophet to revitalize the old forms or to devise new ways by which man can express in acts and deeds his religious experience. Reformation is a universal phenomenon required by the dialectics of religious life (43).

The world over we find that in different religions certain acts are regarded and recommended as especially efficacious in establishing and strengthening the communion between man and the numen which is the goal of all worship. Such are acts of self-discipline or self-denial or the performance of special duties; acts of *devotion* and acts of *charity*. Some may be expected of everyone, and some be defined as *opera supererogationis*. I should be inclined to think that acts of devotion and service to one's fellow-men are universally valid practical expressions of religious experience. It is the exception rather than the rule that in our modern Western civilization worship of one's God and care for one's brother could become separated and one played against the other. If we can be proud at having left behind the cruder practices of an extreme asceticism, there is less reason for rejoicing that so many of us moderns have at the same time, because we see no motivation for it, abandoned all and every act of self-denial.

With the notion that in certain acts of devotion the religious life may culminate or appear epitomized, the concept of the *sacramental* act developed. This has its roots in primitive religion and has come to fruition in the Hellenistic mystery cults, in Zoroastrianism, in Hinduism and Mahāyāna Buddhism, in Gnosticism and Manichaeism, and above all in Christianity. Aptly has E. Underhill defined a sacrament as "the use of visible things and deeds not merely to signify but to convey invisible realities" (44). Originally (45) the sacramental acts were only special instances of the wider notion (46) according to which the effective and transforming grace of the numinous presence flows into souls (47), especially prepared by acts of dedication; but in the history of our own religion these sacramental foci have become isolated (48) and cut out from the context of the life which they are meant to consecrate.

It behooves us finally to mention one more universal feature of the practical expression of religious experience. All human action will be *conditioned* by the physical *material* in which and with

which alone it can work. The word needs no vehicle, the tone may be enforced by the use of instruments, the performance of service hallowed by wearing a special vestment. There are the simple and the complex instruments used for the purpose of creating a numinous atmosphere, the emblems and "images" which stand for the presence of the unseen, be it the Pueblo feather-sticks, the Plains medicine bundle, the Japanese *shintai*, the Hindu *pratika*, the Hebrew ark, the Greek *agalma*, or the Orthodox ikon. Tone, word, colour, stone, wood and metal are universal media by means of which man has tried to give expression to the profoundest experience of which he is capable. He has become a *secondary creator:* The dangers which must accompany this development have given rise to protests of which the Hebrew prophets, the founder of Islam, and the Christian, Hindu and Buddhist reformers are impressive examples. Some of these protests are directed against the perfunctory or mechanical way in which such acts are all too often performed—cf. the Old Testament prophets and Jesus—others, of a more radical nature, reject all outward forms of expression, as do the spiritualists (49) and some, though not all, mystics. They feel that in spirit and in truth alone can true worship exist, whereas the motto of others is St. Augustine's "Per visibilia ad invisibilia." For both extremes—idolatry and evaporation of the *sensus numinis*—the history of religions affords many an example, but, as W. Temple has rightly said (50):

> The goal is to fuse action and worship into the continuous life of worshipful service; in the holy city which came down from God out of heaven the seer beheld no place of worship because the divine presence pervaded all his life (Rev. xxi, 22).

There is finally, besides the intellectual and the practical, a *third* way in which religious experience expresses itself: the sociological. Here too we meet with a universal trait. We discussed previously the various motives which make for the expression of any kind of experience. True, there is in the confrontation of man with ultimate reality something solitary—the "flight of the Alone to the Alone." The solitary visionary is encountered at all stages of religious development from the lonely American Indian in quest of a Guardian Spirit to Søren Kierkegaard and William James (51), but the desire to communicate, to share, is a powerful motif in association and communication between men (52). Here the problem of communication of religious experience poses itself. We moderns are all too prone to look on it as a technical question to which improved techniques of manipulation will supply the answer (53). The history of religion teaches us otherwise. Wherever a true call is felt, a genuine religious experience is had, the means of communicating it miraculously seem to be at hand. Only in a secondary sense did the prophets and teachers feel that the establishment of contact and of fellowship was in their power. Where men were living in a communion with the great reality, they understood each other.

It would be rash to add religious fellowship to other existing forms of association without qualifications. A religious group is not another type of club. If in religious experience man confronts ultimate reality, it is towards this reality that all communion that is to be called religious must be oriented. "No personal impression," says R. Otto in his book, *The Kingdom of God and the Son of Man* (54), "is as strong as the impression of the numinous or so well fitted to bind together a circle of those who receive the impression." The *first* characteristic which distinguishes the cult-group from all other associations is that it is orientated primarily towards that reality which is apprehended in religious experience. *Secondarily*, it is constituted by the relations existing among its members. These two principles (55), which should guide the work of the sociologist of religion, denote two universal features characteristic of the sociological expression of religious experience. We can test their validity by examining any cult group in primitive, higher, or the highest civilization. What determines the attitude of the members of a secret or mystery society in Polynesia, Africa, or of American Indians but the awareness of power and power centres? What makes the fraternal spirit prevailing in mystery societies, of which we find so many examples in the history of ancient Greece, Rome, and the Near East? The numinous experience reflected in the concept of salvation and acted in the sacred drama! If the atmosphere of the Christian brotherhood is *agape*, can this attitude be meaningful unless it be buttressed by apprehension of the love of God as it is revealed in the life and death of Jesus Christ? All religious communities, furthermore, have specific *notae*, marks by which they desire to be identified (56) (certain visionary experiences, faith, beliefs, a certain esoteric knowledge, an attitude or behaviour).

Universally valid also are the *means* by which the religious community is integrated, namely, a common faith, a common cult, and a common order. Symbols, myths, doctrines, professions of faith, rites and practices, constitute and preserve the identity and integrity of the fellowship. Moreover, every cult-group possesses a structure. Though we find great variety with regard to the degree of differentiation, some differences according to the natural criteria of sex and age, of charismata and skills, knowledge, healing power, etc., make for a diversity of functions. Even in the most egalitarian group reverence is paid to age and experience, to the gift of prophecy or teaching.

We agree with W. Temple (57) that the apparent conflict between *experience* and *authority*, of which we hear so much from our contemporaries, is actually a tension of two indispensable, ubiquitous elements. For the *individual*, Temple says rightly, authority (be it in tribal custom or revelation), is first. He grows and develops within a world in which he finds tradition surrounding him on every side; in the *race*, experience is prior to authority, as can be easily proved. The structure of every religious group implies an *order*. Within this order there is room for freedom and spontaneity as well as for discipline. The history of religions is replete with examples of what happened to religious communities in which one of these two notions was sacrificed for the other.

Leadership is universal, though the sources of its authority and its functions are differently conceived in different cult-groups. Max Weber has convincingly shown that it may be exerted on personal or institutional authority (charisma) (58), the prophet and the priest illustrating these two types of religious leadership.

Here, then, are some universals in religion: man relating himself in the experience which we call religious to ultimate reality. This experience, which is had within the limitations of time and space, tends to be expressed theoretically, practically and sociologically. The forms of this expression, though conditioned by the environment within which it originated, show similarities in structure; there are uinversal themes in religious thought, the universal is always embedded in the particular. Though the differences and conflicts arise from particular loyalties, these cannot simply be left out (as the Enlightenment would have

it). They are the arteries through which the life-blood of religious experience flows. But they have constantly to be checked and purified.

That the particular has not come into its own in this lecture is undeniable, but our topic for to-day was universals in religion. True, we have had to concentrate here on the formal elements which characterize religious experience and its articulation, but this might be also a way of contributing to the important problem of general and special revelation which is vividly discussed in contemporary theology (cf. the controversy between Barth and Brunner). Though we have not indicated here how we conceive of the *relation between* the universal and the particular way in which God has made himself known to man, we have, we feel, demonstrated that there is a ground upon which we can stand in believing that God has at no time and nowhere left himself without witness. We believe, with Temple, that "natural religion ends in a hunger for what would transform it into something other than itself: a specific revelation" (59).

Notes

[1] William James, *The Varieties of Religious Experience* (New York and London: Longmans, Green, 1902).

[2] Paul Tillich, "The Problem of Theological Method," *Journal of Religion*, XXVII (1947), 23.

[3] W. James, op. cit., p. 58.

[4] Paul E. Johnson, *Psychology of Religion* (New York: Abingdon-Cokesbury Press), p. 36.

[5] Émile Durkheim agrees with W. James that "religious beliefs rest upon a specific experience whose demonstrative value is, in one sense, not one bit inferior to that of scientific experiments, though different from them." (*The Elementary Forms of the Religious Life*, trans. J. W. Swain (1915), (Glencoe: Free Press, 1947), p. 417.) He adds, and rightly, that it does not follow

from the fact that a "religious experience exists and has a certain foundation, that the reality which is its foundation conforms objectively to the idea which believers have of it."

[6] Johnson, *Psychology*, p. 47, and John M. Moore, *Theories of Religious Experience* (New York: Round Table Press, 1938), who criticizes Rudolf Otto's assumption of the cognitive nature of the numinous feeling (pp. 86 ff., 95 ff.). We distinguish between apprehension and intellectual expression.

[7] This point is well brought out by Canon B. H. Streeter, *The Buddha and the Christ* (London: Macmillan, 1932), pp. 157 ff.

[8] Bronislaw Malinowski, *Magic, Science, and Religion and other Essays* (Glencoe, Ill.: Free Press, 1948), p. 1.

[9] Cf. the methodological prolegomena in J. Wach, *Sociology of Religion* (London: Kegan Paul, 1947); Part I. Cf. there many references and bibliography for statements in the text above.

[10] Cf. Aldous Huxley, *The Perennial Philosophy* (London: Chatto and Windus, 1945), chap. xii: 'Time and Eternity.'

[11] There is the *analogy* of the senses (sight, hearing, smell, touch; what is experienced is described as "light," voices are heard, sweet odours are smelt), then the analogy of physical phenomena (procreating, eating), that of the various activities of man (warfare, peaceful pursuits; agriculture; pastoral life; other professions), travelling (pilgrimage) and of human relationships (kin, social, marital relations). Professor Bevan has especially studied the symbolic use of time and space notions. Urban again has stressed the analogies of the *sun*—"the Sun with its powerful rays, its warmth and light, its life-giving qualities, becomes a natural symbol for the creating and eliciting power" (Urban, *Language*, p. 589)—and *sex*—"sex love, its heights and its depths, its horrible darkness and its blinding light is never wholly alien to the creative love of which Plato, no less than Christian theologians and philosophers, discourse" (Urban, loc. cit., p. 591). M. A. Ewer (*A Survey of Mystical Symbolism* (London: S.P.C.K., 1933)) analysed the analogies of the senses in mystical symbolic language. E. Underhill has concentrated upon the symbolic notions

of pilgrimage (for divine transcendence), of love and of transmutation (*Mysticism* (London: Methuen, 12th ed., 1930), chap. vi).

[12] Gerardus van der Leeuw, *Religion in Essence and Manifestation* (London: Allen & Unwin, 1938), pp. 655–7. Mircea Eliade, *Traité d'histoire des religions* (Paris: Payot, 1949), chaps. x, xi.

[13] Otto Franke, "Der Kosmische Gedanke in der Philosophie und dem Staat der Chinesen," *Vorträge der Bibliothek Warburg* (Leipzig: Teubner, 1928): Wach, *Sociology of Religion*, pp. 49 ff.; T. W. Rhys Davids, "Cosmic Law in Ancient Thought" (*Proceedings of Brit. Academy* (Oxford: University Press, 1917), pp. 18, 279 ff.). Roger Caillois, "L'homme et le sacré" (*Mythes et religions* (Paris: Leroux, 1939), pp. 9 ff.; Eliade, *Traité*, chaps. x, xi.

[14] "The symbolism of the World Quarters, of the Above, and of the Below, is nowhere more elaborately developed among American Indians than with the *Pueblos*. Analogies are drawn not merely with colours, with plants and animals, and with cult objects and religious ideas, but with human society in all the ramifications of its organization, making of mankind not only the theatric centre of the cosmos, but a kind of elaborate image of its form" (Hartley Alexander, "North American Mythology," in *The Mythology of All Races* (Archaeological Institute of America, 1936), Vol. X., 185.

[15] "He [the savage] encounters the divine stimulus here, there and anywhere within the contents of an experience in which percepts play a far more important part than concepts" (Marett, *Faith, Hope, and Charity in Primitive Religion* (Oxford: Clarendon Press, 1932), p. 144). Cf. also Frankfurt, etc., *Intellectual Adventure of Ancient Man* (Chicago, University Press, 1946), 130 ff.

[16] Cf. below, Chap. X.

[17] Thus the criticism which J. M. Moore (*Theories*, pp. 91 ff., 103 ff.) levels rightly at Rudolf Otto's concept of "feeling" does not apply to our theory.

[18] Van der Leeuw, op. cit., Part I; Eliade, op. cit.

[19] Martin P. Nilsson, 'Letter to Professor A. D. Nock' (*Harvard Theological Review*, XLII (1949), 91).

[20] Cf. the excellent chapter "Curiosity" in Marett, *Faith, Hope and Charity in Primi-*

tive Religion (op. cit., note 15 above), chap. viii. Cf. also: V. Gordon Childe, *Magic, Craftsmanship and Science* (Liverpool: University Press, 1950).

[21] Malinowski, "Myth in Primitive Society" (op. cit., pp. 72 ff., 76, 93 f.). Malinowski's solution—the sociological theory of myth, in his own words—does not satisfy because of his preoccupation with the *pragmatic* aspect of both religious and magical activities. He neglects the problems of meaning, structure and motivation. A more promising approach seems to be Ernesto de Martino's *Il Mondo Magico* (Firenze, Giulio Einaudi, 1948)) who is concerned with the nature of the *reality* to which magic thought and acts refer (p. 11).

[22] Cf. for the general framework: Wach, *Sociology of Religion,* Part I, chap. ii.

[23] Clyde Kluckhohn, "Myths and Rituals: A General Theory" (*Harvard Theol. Review,* XXXV, 1 (1942), 45 ff.; cf. also C. H. Ratschow, *Magic und Religion* (Gütersloh, Bertelsmann, 1947).

[24] Edwyn R. Bevan, *Symbolism and Belief* (London: Allen & Unwin, 1938); Ernst Cassirer, *Philosophie der symbolischen Formen* (Berlin: Cassirer, 1923 ff.); Wilbur M. Urban, *Language and Reality* (London: Allen & Unwin, 1939), esp. chap. xii; Susanne Langer, op. cit., note 27 below (cf. p. 10, n. 2); Mircea Eliade, op. cit., chap. xiii; Wach, *Sociology of Religion,* p. 19; Jean Danielou, "The Problems of Symbolism" (*Thought,* XXV, 1950), 423 ff.

[25] "Images are taken from the narrower and more intelligible relations and used as expressions for more universal and ideal relations which, because of this pervasiveness and ideality, cannot be directly expressed" (Urban, *Language,* pp. 580, 586).

[26] Rich inventories of the wealth of expressions of religious experiences are to be found in Gerardus van der Leeuw's *Religion in Essence and Manifestation,* trans. J. E. Turner (London: Allen & Unwin, 1938), of which a revised French translation appeared recently: *La Religion dans son essence et ses manifestations. Phénoménologie de la religion* (Paris: Payot, 1948); and in Mircea Eliade, *Traité d'histoire des religions. Morphologie du Sacré* (Paris: Payot, 1949).

[27] Susanne K. Langer, *Philosophy in a New Key. A Study in the Symbolism of Reason,*

Rite, and Art (New York: Penguin Books (1942), 1948), p. 169; also Urban, op. cit., pp. 586 ff.

[28] Malinowski, op. cit., p. 86.

[29] Urban, op. cit., pp. 571 ff., 576 ff.

[30] Cf. the penetrating analysis in Maurice Leenhardt, *Do Kamo, La personne et le mythe dans le monde melanésien* (Paris: Gallimard, 5th ed., 1947), esp. chap. XII.

[31] Urban, op. cit., pp. 598 ff.

[32] Cf., as an example, the development in early Christianity, suggestively traced by Oscar Cullmann, *The Earliest Christian Confessions,* trans. J. K. S. Reid (London: Lutterworth, 1949).

[33] Paul Tillich, op. cit., p. 25.

[34] Henry N. Wieman, *The Source of Human Good* (Chicago: University of Chicago Press, 1946), p. 217.

[35] Evelyn Underhill, *Worship.*

[36] Marett, *Sacraments of Simple Folk* (Oxford: Clarendon Press, 1933), p. 18; cf. Ratschow, op. cit., pp. 43 ff., 62, 81 f., 148 f.

[37] Marett, op. cit., chaps. ii, iv.

[38] For the divine 'archetypes' of the cult: cf. M. Eliade, *Le mythe de l'eternal rétour* (Paris: Gallimard, 1949), pp. 44 ff.; cf. also W. Norman Pittenger, *Sacraments, Signs and Symbols* (Chicago, Wilcox and Follet, 1949), I.

[39] Langer, op. cit., p. 39; cf. Theodor H. Gaster, *Thespis; Ritual, Myth and Drama in the Ancient Near East* (New York, H. Schumann, 1950).

[40] Marett, *Sacraments,* p. 12.

[41] "The attitude which is the worshipper's response to the insight given by the sacred symbol is an emotional pattern, which governs all individual lives. It cannot be recognized through any clearer medium than that of formalized gesture; yet in this cryptic form it *is* recognized, and yields a strong sense of tribal or congregational unity, of rightness and security. A rite regularly performed is the constant reiteration of sentiments toward 'first and last things'; it is not a free expression of emotions, but a disciplined rehearsal of 'right attitudes'" (S. Langer, op. cit., p. 124).

[42] Paul Radin, *Primitive Religion, Its Nature and Origin* (London: Hamish Hamilton, 1938), chap. ii.

[43] Cf. *Sociology of Religion,* chap. v, sect. 10: "Reaction: Protest"; and Paul Tillich,

The Protestant Era (Chicago: University of Chicago Press, 1948), esp. sect. iv.

[44] Underhill, *Worship* (London: Nisbet, 1936), chap. iii.

[45] Marett, *Sacraments of Simple Folk;* Ratschow, op. cit.

[46] Cf. the chapter on 'The Sacramental Universe' in W. Temple, *Nature, Man, and God,* Lect. XIX.

[47] The need of sacraments, according to Dr. Inge, is "one of the deepest convictions of the religious consciousness. It rests ultimately on the instinctive reluctance to allow any spiritual fact to remain without an external expression."

"A sacrament is a symbolic act, not arbitrarily chosen, but resting, to the mind of the recipient, on Divine authority, which has no ulterior object except to give expression to, and in so doing effectuate, a relation which is too purely spiritual to find utterance in the customary activities of life" (William R. Inge, *Mysticism in Religion* (London: Hutchinson [1947]; Chicago: University of Chicago Press, 1948), pp. 251 ff.).

[48] The sacraments of Baptism and the Lord's Supper are "symbols of the mystical union between the Christian and his ascended Lord. Baptism symbolizes that union in its inception, the Eucharist in its organic life" (loc. cit.).

[49] The spiritualist teachings of Caspar Schwenckfeld are treated in Chap. VII of Wach, *Types of Religious Experience.*

[50] William Temple, *Nature, Man, and God,* p. 494.

[51] William James, *Varieties,* pp. 30 ff.

[52] Durkheim has stressed this point (op. cit., p. 47), that religion is "something eminently social." But he has not always taken care to qualify this statement, as when he says (p. 10), "They [religious representations and rites] are rich in social elements." The opposite one-sidedness we find in the work of a well-known contemporary of Durkheim, in W. James' classic *The Varieties of Religious Experience,* where the emphasis on the individual dominates. We agree with Durkheim, however, when he states: "In so far as he belongs to society, the individual transcends himself, both when he thinks and when he acts" (pp. 16 f.). Cf. Wach, *Sociology of Religion,* pp. 27 ff.

[53] Lyman Bryson, *The Communication of Ideas (Religion and Civilization Series.* Institute for Rel. and Soc. Studies, New York: Harper, 1948).

[54] R. Otto, *The Kingdom of God and the Son of Man,* trans. Floyd V. Filson and B. L. Lee (London: Lutterworth, 1938), p. 164. Cf. below, Chap. X.

[55] *Symposium on Twentieth-century Sociology,* art. "Sociology of Religion" (chap. xiv).

[56] Cf. Wach, *Types of Religious Experience,* p. 191 for Christian "notae."

[57] William Temple, *Nature, Man, and God,* Lect. XIII.

[58] Max Weber, *The Theory of Social and Economic Organization,* trans. A. M. Henderson and T. Parsons (London: W. Hodge, 1947), pp. 358 ff.; R. Otto, *Kingdom,* Book IV; and J. Wach, *Sociology of Religion,* chap. viii.

[59] Op. cit., LXX.

Part Three

ISSUES IN

FUNCTIONAL ANALYSIS

THE analysis of religion in functional terms has constituted one of the significant approaches to the entire subject that has thus far been developed in sociology and anthropology. The functional mode of analysis is here introduced and broadly set out by Radcliffe-Brown's essay on "Religion and Society." Virtually the first thing Radcliffe-Brown does is to refer to "the usual way of looking at religions . . . as bodies of erroneous beliefs and illusory practices." Perhaps this way is no longer quite so usual as it was even in the mid-forties, less than a generation ago, when Radcliffe-Brown wrote, but the reference to erroneous beliefs and illusory practices is important. In the background of functionalism there hovers what has been called an intellectualist view of religion, of which the anthropologist, Edward B. Tylor, is frequently taken as a leading representative. In the intellectualist view as developed by Tylor and others, primitive man achieves by reflection on such phenomena as dreams (which suggest the idea of a detachable double or spirit) an erroneous "religious" world outlook whose founda-

tion is animism or the belief in spiritual beings. This intellectually indefensible outlook leads to and induces practices which are mere foolishness and which will simply not achieve the effects that those who carry them out think or hope they will. To put the matter thus is perhaps to put it somewhat too baldly, but this is nevertheless the plain tendency of those who wrote in the intellectualist tradition of analysis of religion.

In functionalist approaches to religion, there is no such bias that religion must "begin" as (erroneous) thought activity and end in (foolish, pointless, or "illusory") practice. The relations between religious thought and practice are, indeed, complex, and it often seems appropriate, in the light of what actually confronts the student of religion, to approach religion as primarily or most importantly a matter of practice. The issues here involved are difficult, and one surely need not leap to the conclusion that thought and reasoning in the religious context and elaboration of dogmatic views and the like must in some sense always be secondary or epiphenomenal.

53

Nevertheless, functionalism in religion, partly no doubt in sheer negative reaction to the intellectualist stress on religion as elaboration of erroneous thought and as establishment of practice on the foundation of erroneous thought, has often put its own emphasis on religious practice in the first place. Along with this frequent emphasis on practice has certainly gone the view that religious statements, that is, statements by human agents acting in the religious sphere, *can* indeed be of secondary significance, although they *need* not necessarily be so. They can be secondary in the sense that they are clearly secondary for human agents themselves when these agents regard dogma or the like as unimportant and, in effect, hold that to be a religious man is to be a man who *does* certain things. They can be secondary in the sense that they constitute afterthoughts by way of justification or explanation of practices in the way of rites and ceremonies whose origins or foundations are actually unknown. The readings that follow should be suggestive with regard to these matters.

It has been noted that functionalism has tended to stress practice partly in reaction to an intellectualist bias which sees religion as a tissue of errors underlying silly or useless activity. It should also be noted that stress on practice along with refusal to look at that practice as necessarily action that is engaged in by way of deduction, as to what should be done, from mistaken premises has readily led functionalists to concentrate on the consequences of practice for societies. Religion is now approached as action that has certain results in systems of social arrangements and for human beings. Practice does *not* fade into insignificance as a hardly interesting outcome of a mistaken system of thought, something which cannot really be analyzed on its own with serious intent. (And practice may have consequences

or functions never contemplated in the thought of those who do the practicing, but still most important.) There is a sense in which a strong intellectualism does not treat religion as a matter having to do with society at all. But if functionalism does anything, it does treat religion as a matter of society. It *is* concerned intimately and seriously with the consequences of religious practices for social arrangements and for the humans among whom these prevail. This should be very plain from some of the materials that follow.

Practice in religion has been so important and so often in the past naively regarded as unimportant that it has seemed worthwhile to give it very particular stress and even more so because functionalists have emphasized it to the extent that they have. Hence Radcliffe-Brown's general statement is followed by several pieces that exhibit well the stress on practice that has been put by numerous students of religion. The first of these pieces, in Section B, is from Robertson Smith's work on the religion of the Semites. The selection given is partly quoted in the first essay by Radcliffe-Brown, but this slight repetition does no harm. Robertson Smith's work was a very significant antecedent of Durkheim's, and Smith himself may certainly be said to have adopted a functional outlook on religion. The second item in Section B is a small extract from James Bissett Pratt's early work on the religions of India. The character of its stress is quite plain. (It may serve as a useful reminder of some of Ernst Benz's assertions reproduced in Part One.) Further comment on Pratt, whose work is also drawn on in Section E, is reserved for the moment. It is true that stress on what may be called the practice-character of religion does not necessarily go along with a functional outlook on religion, although, to say it once more, functionalists themselves definitely have tended to emphasize practice.

The third selection in Section B, on the religion of the ancient Greeks, by the classicist, Frank Russell Earp, exhibits a stress on practice-character in a student who, as far as I am aware, did not hold to a functional view of religion. It is surely possible that Earp, who was born in 1871 and died in 1955, was actually influenced by the elements of a functional view of religion that he could have found in the work of classicist near-contemporaries like Jane Ellen Harrison (1850–1928) but, however this may be, we may allow that stress on practice-character need not be accompanied by a functional view. This is to say, minimally, that stress on practice-character need not necessarily be developed into definite concern with the results of practice for social circumstances and the humans involved in them. It may run off into philosophical speculation about the nature of religions at large. It may lead into aesthetic preoccupations. But the point that practice has been most significant for functional thought remains.

Not only have functionalists stressed practice-character. They have also tended to stress the eufunctional nature or eufunctional side of practice-character—its "good" by contrast with its "bad" or dysfunctional side. Good and bad may here be understood in a formal sense. One sets up some criterion such as the "maintenance" of a social system or the preservation of the equilibrium of the human agents involved in it and, if certain phenomena function to maintain or preserve, they may be taken as eufunctional; if they work against maintenance or preservation, as dysfunctional. This is a gross simplification that bypasses much current effort to refine functional notions, but it does suggest that the terms, eufunctional and dysfunctional, may be taken in a value-neutral sense *once* a certain criterion is (or certain criteria are) assumed. If, in this introduction, criteria are not made quite explicit at every point, it hardly follows that they do not exist, and making criteria explicit in each case where either of our two terms is employed would have resulted in (presumably unnecessary) awkwardness and wordiness. But it should be plain that the criteria by which a phenomenon is construed as eufunctional or dysfunctional can themselves be brought into question. (This point comes up again in the reference to Merton's selection two paragraphs below.)

There has been dissatisfaction with various functional analyses on the ground that they have been undertaken in too limited a perspective. Thus, an analyst may exhibit an aspect of mourning ceremonies that functions to mitigate feelings of loss and abandonment on the part of the members of a mourning group. But it may also be possible to show, paradoxically, that the ceremonies intensify such feelings. They may both mitigate and intensify. Or it may be possible to show that the ceremonies consume large quantities of time and energy and thereby raise serious economic questions (if not for those who practice them, then in any case for those who analyze them). Functional analysts have without doubt often tended to be overenthusiastic in their stress on eufunction and have restricted unduly their outlook or range of view. Their net, if one prefers, has frequently not been cast wide enough. Malinowski's writings very often give the impression that the Trobriand Islands he knew were a kind of primitive paradise in which everything functioned beneficently and in which any kind of significant change could only have meant damage to a universal excellence of functioning. If it is nevertheless fair to say that Durkheim and Malinowski and Comte, selections from whose writings comprise Section C of this part, were at least generally aware that religion has often involved or encouraged such things as strife and war and cruelty and the like, they still did not hesitate to give much (and, it may well be argued, over-much) stress to its "good" side. Their relevant writings remain enlightening if not always convincing in detail. They exhibit religion as eufunctional—as working on the line of "maintaining" social systems, preserving the equilibrium of human agents, or the like; as working "positively" (although the sense and delimitations of "positive" should always be kept clear). Perhaps one day we will have a master theory of religion that will shrewdly juxtapose and thoroughly illuminate all its theoretically relevant "sides," including those that are "positive" and those that are not. In the interim, we may yet profit from statements that rest on limited observations and on points of view that have not been fully scrutinized for their relations to other relevant points of view.

But one surely need not overlook the difficulties that are posed by a too enthusiastic espousal of eufunctional outlooks on religion. And some of these have been usefully noted by Merton in the selection from his work in Section D. Merton also makes it clear that the very criteria by which something is taken as eufunctional or dysfunctional may come into question, although there may still be agreement on "what actually happens." Thus he notes in effect that when Marxists and non-Marxist functionalists agree as to what religion "does" (in so far as they agree, for example, that it works to enhance solidarity or integration in so-called bourgeois society) they nevertheless disagree on the *evaluation* of such functioning, for the former can look upon the functioning in this fashion as an effecting of illusory class solidarity and the latter as a binding together of the elements of a community. It is also valuable to be reminded that solidarity and integration are formal terms, in that the conditions they refer to can prevail in societies of widely variant types with widely variant norms.

The first selection in Section C, from Durkheim, has been included for more than one reason. Not only does it construe at least the particular religious phenomena it reviews as eufunctional. Perhaps so much has thus far been made of religious practice that it may seem that emotion in the religious context has been neglected. This has not been the intention, and one of the uses Durkheim's treatment of piacular rites may serve is precisely to enforce the notion of the significance of emotion in religious context. But there is a great deal more in Durkheim's piece. It shows especially plainly that it is at times quite important to be willing to regard "dogma" as secondary. Durkheim's argument indicates specifically why he can regard judgments, "verbalizations" about whether the spirit of a dead man is benevolently or malevolently disposed as symbolic renderings or reflections of a certain state of members of a group. Something of the force of his argument is rendered by the statement that "men do not weep for the dead because they fear them; they fear them because they weep for them." Practice and feeling *can* be primary; "reflections," "thoughts" about the evil, to-be-feared disposition of the spirits of the dead *can* be symbols or reflexes, secondary manifestations of a complex state of emotion and action. Note again that Durkheim writes of the rites of mourning determining "certain of the secondary characteristics of the soul" and ventures the view that "rites are perhaps not foreign to the idea" that the soul survives the body. And there is more in this vein. There is indeed much more of Durkheim's entire theory of religion in this chapter than can or need be mentioned here. But, for present purposes, the chapter above all affords a fine example of stress on religion as eufunctional. The short passage from Malinowski that follows this chapter has been chosen both for what may be regarded as a kind of continuation of Durkheim's interest in death and mourning and, in the present context most significantly, for its further exemplification of a eufunctional perspective on religious activity.

The relations between dogma or ideas and practice, rite, and ceremony again obtrude themselves in virtue of the above remarks about Durkheim. These may be adverted to briefly once more. However, another point may first be noted, a point worth noting in its own right and one that will in fact make the more necessary the subsequently resumed reference to ideas and practice. The point alluded to is that dogma or belief can itself be analyzed functionally. In the intellectualist tradition it is ordinarily not so analyzed. Its putatively erroneous elements are rather held up for exhibition precisely as elements in one long sequence of mistakes in thinking. But dogma can be otherwise analyzed. The short treatment of Catholic dogma afforded by Comte gives a concise analysis of dogma in functional—and, indeed, eufunctional—terms and is included as a very interesting example of functional analysis of dogma coming early in the development of modern sociology. Comte's analysis may even be said to be "shamelessly" functional, so forthrightly is he pointed toward the effects or consequences or functions of dogma rather than toward the question of whether that dogma is itself true or false. Comte's short item should be read for its functional approach and for its eufunctional stress, in the present context, not for the correctness of its every detail. A full understanding of Comte's views in the passage selected would require familiarity with his more general views, but the functional character of his interpretation of dogma in the passage is clear enough.

(It will be noted that in the last few sentences of the passage Comte switches from dogma to sacrament, which he also construes in the functional vein.) He writes of "the political efficacy" of Catholic dogmas and means, at a minimum, their efficacy in preventing the Church from being absorbed by or made an appendage to temporal powers; their efficacy in meeting needs of individual Catholics; their efficacy in exalting the status of the church itself, or of its functionaries. Comte had abandoned the Catholicism of his youth and his doubts of the truth of dogma are here evident (although he later modelled a religion of his own in many ways on Catholicism, as is well known, and evidently never lost a certain regard for Catholicism, which he personally clearly preferred to Protestantism). But it is perhaps unnecessary to develop the point that a functional outlook on dogma by no means need be accompanied or followed by cynicism or by the view that dogma is "good for the masses" while "superior" men are too wise to credit it.

This passage from Comte again makes it relevant to point out that certain kinds of interpretations of dogma are not necessarily exclusive of others. If we think of dogma as part of the whole realm of religious ideas, it must once more be noted that while it may be and often is legitimate to see ideas as reflections and symbolic renderings of other phenomena or to analyze their consequences regardless of their truth-value, it is often *also* legitimate to take them as important elements in their own right. No matter what their origins they frequently have a way of taking on independence of those origins and undergoing great elaboration of their own. In developed, elaborated form they may have tremendous influence on human beings, and questions of their truth-value may become extremely important to the latter—and this importance to the latter is something the sociologist would be most unwise to leave out of account. In being wary of an excessive intellectualism against which functionalists have properly reacted with a sound sense of the importance of practice and the frequently secondary significance of belief or ideas, we need not become antirationalist and unreservedly reductionist. Social and cultural phenomena do present certain complexities; contexts of analysis differ; it is quite possible that the role of ideas in religion is much smaller in primitive than in nonprimitive societies; it is possible that Protestant Christianity is especially notable among religions for the relative importance that ideas have had within it. The problems suggested can hardly be attended to here. (The entire matter of the *interaction* of ideas on the one hand and practice and emotion on the other is most important in the sociology of religion, but can be given only a passing word. A state of emotional desolation produced by a death may be "verbalized" or symbolized in an avowal that the dead person's spirit is malevolent, yet the conception of the spirit as malevolent may reinforce the emotional state—a rudimentary illustration of complexities in interaction.) But it should not be surprising if elsewhere in this volume religious ideas seem to be given much stress for their part. Sociologists are far from ready for a thoroughly systematic, well-grounded statement of the relative importance of religious ideas and practices on a world-wide scale. They must be willing to endure some intellectual tensions and uncertainties in consequence. However, it can be strongly reaffirmed that the stress on practice found in the selections in the present part has been a most useful corrective to intellectualist excesses—as it has been a corrective (as Pratt, for one, notes) to a certain provincialism.

Dissatisfaction with functional approaches to religion (and to other social phenomena) has often taken the form of the contention that functionalism does not or cannot deal adequately with social or cultural change. Some aspects of the problems thus suggested are considered in the paper by Clifford Geertz on ritual and social change. The ethnographic material Geertz presents is interesting in itself and has been left intact in the present reproduction to allow him to make his points as clearly as he originally did. No judgment need be given here as to how valuable Geertz's effort to render functionalism less "static" may be. But it can be said that Geertz is being responsive to intellectual tensions in and about functionalism. The only suggestions that I need make or reinforce is that it would be pointless and, in any case, probably futile to seek simply to abandon the functional outlook and with it its insights and the sensitivity of many of its exponents to a variety of problems that are far from trivial; that it is by now evident that religion is not invariably "integrative" or eliminative of dysphoria or otherwise in some sense eufunctional and that no self-respecting functionalist is obligated to deny this; that *some* of the limitations of the work of functional analysts of religion are to be accounted for by their zeal in combatting what *they* saw as the limitations of intellectualism; that no one could reasonably laud and wish to maintain intact a sociological theory that was genuinely incapable of giving some sort of account of change and that there are at least a number of contemporary functionalists inclined to the view that functional theory may be susceptible of that kind of refinement and extension that would indeed enable it to give an adequate account of at least some significant kinds of change; that in any case the difficult but worthwhile task to undertake in these premises is precisely that of constructing a better conceived theory of religion than earlier functionalists could, one open to a larger range of relevant fact and as alert to dysfunction and change as to eufunction and static condition, but not one that confines itself to stating what are by now obvious reservations (which indeed it was once most useful to make) about a variety of functional interpretations—since this could hardly aspire to the title of theory at all.

The penultimate section of the present part is concerned with a particular kind of change that is highly relevant to functional analysis—the kind of change that occurs when latent functions become manifest. Merton, who has particularly accustomed sociologists to the terms manifest and latent, has indicated in his most relevant paper that this is a form of change to which he deliberately does not there address himself. But the form has nevertheless received attention. The first of the selections in the next-to-last portion of Part Three, Section E, reproduces some of the work of James Bissett Pratt, a psychologist of religion and philosopher who died in 1944. Pratt develops a distinction between objective and subjective worship, defining the former as a kind of worship "which aims at making some kind of effect upon the Deity or in some way communicating with him" and the latter as a kind of worship which "seeks to induce some desired mood or belief or attitude in the worshiper." Pratt was keenly aware that it was possible for worshiping humans to note "beneficent effects" of objective worship, eufunctional byproducts of an activity addressed to other ends. If worship is objective, it may nevertheless thus be "beneficial" to the worshiper. If he is unaware of the beneficent effect that actually occurs, to that extent he is unaware of the functions of objective worship. (The word "functions" has just been used in such a way that it might suggest solely

consequences of action for individuals. Sociologists would prefer to retain it for situations in which it is possible to speak also of consequences for social arrangements or a social system. Pratt, as a psychologist, was disposed to think very immediately in terms of effects on particular individuals of their seeking "subjective" benefit from a worship which they might once have engaged in purely *ad majorem Dei gloriam* but which they had discovered might work to advantage them and had accordingly tried to *make* work to their advantage. But Pratt's distinction and his discussion of it have unmistakable sociological implications and applicability.) If the worshiper is aware of beneficent effect, he is to that extent aware of the functions of objective worship, which are then of course manifest to him. But the *becoming* aware of once latent functions is what is of particular interest.

Indeed, the movement from objective to subjective worship is clearly of major interest to Pratt himself. He regards Catholicism as still relatively considerably oriented toward objective worship and Protestantism as relatively more oriented toward subjective worship. And he is concerned with whether subjective worship will bring its distinctive "benefits" if it is unmingled with anything of an objective character in his sense of "objective." It is plain, too, that he is inclined to think that subjective worship cannot stand alone: worship engaged in because of a desire to benefit the worshiper psychologically is unlikely to achieve its end when the worshiper is well aware that he is no longer actually "worshiping" anything but engaging in "worship" solely to gain psychological benefit. Pratt has more to say about objective and subjective worship, and a good deal of what he has to say is highly relevant to what the sociologist describes as the becoming manifest of latent functions with subsequent recasting of the once latent functions as goals or ends to be pursued. It may be urged that the problems pointed to by all this are most significant. Only one pertinent question by way of very simple illustration of the kinds of problems meant may be posed: If mourners achieve by ceremonies of mourning some appreciable catharsis of feelings of loss and abandonment and if this occurs latently, that is, without the mourners' knowledge, what happens in case this function of mourning does become known to them and they then engage in mourning instrumentally, that is, *in order to* be relieved of distressing feelings? The consequences of the instrumentalization of religion, here regarded as a most important form of religious change, are worth close scrutiny.

Pratt had made his distinction between objective and subjective worship previously in his book on *India and its Faiths*[1] (q.v., at pp. 271, 272, 275, and 383), the book from which the very short item on practice in Hindu religion in the present Part Three has also been extracted. He returned to the distinction again in his notable later work on *The Pilgrimage of Buddhism*[2] (at pp. 134, 362, 372–373, 654, 665). It is of interest that evidently as a kind of mature reflection on Buddhism and objective and subjective worship he gave it as his general view that Buddhism "by no means evaporates into what I have called subjective worship, or the mere attempt to produce a desirable state of mind in oneself." (*The Pilgrimage of Buddhism*, p. 665.) And he continued to hold to the view that if subjective worship is to produce what worshipers (and perhaps also nonworshipers) regard as psychologically desirable results it will have to be

blended with a component of objective worship. His concern with this whole set of problems was maintained in a posthumously published volume on *Eternal Values in Religion*,[3] in which the following statement (op. cit., p. 27) occurs.

After many thousands of years of . . . naively objective worship, more reflective worshipers discovered that the cult in its varied forms exerted an influence not only upon the gods but upon their own spirits . . . The leaders of religion were presumably among the first to discover this fact, and the next stage in the development was for them consciously to conduct the cult in such fashion as not only to influence the gods but also to affect their fellow worshipers. The entire history of religion might be written from the point of view of this process, from the naive attempt to influence the deity to the sophisticated and deliberate effort to bring about a psychological effect upon the worshiper. Both elements of worship still survive in our own day and in our own religion.

This is a broad and general statement, certainly, but it focuses attention plainly on the emergence of awareness of previously latent functions on the part of some ("the leaders of religion") and on the effort to bring about as goals of endeavor these newly realized functions; and it suggests the elements of a process of instrumentalization. All this cannot possibly fail to interest the sociologist concerned with the kind of change that takes place when some human agents become aware of previously latent functions, recast them as goals, and seek then to attain them by an effort instrumentally designed to do so and no longer allow the indirect and unconscious achievement of them which occurred when they were still latent functions. Pratt, it may also

[1] James Bissett Pratt, *India and Its Faiths,* Boston: Houghton Mifflin Co., 1915.
[2] James Bissett Pratt, *The Pilgrimage of Buddhism,* New York: Macmillan, 1928.
[3] James Bissett Pratt, *Eternal Values in Religion,* New York: Macmillan, 1950.

be noted, may have been right when he considered that for subjective worship to "work" it would have to be combined with elements of objective worship. If it is difficult to be dedicated to the deity without any reserve concern whatever for one's self, it may be questioned whether exclusive concern for one's self to the accompaniment of lapse of "authentic belief" will "work." The functional outlook on religion can make us most alert to the problems Pratt poses with his distinction and to others easily suggested by it.

The final reading in Section E of Part Three takes up the manifest-to-latent theme in connection with an examination of popular American inspirational religious literature that attains a certain culmination in the works of Norman Vincent Peale.

Of numerous additional matters that might be put under the heading of "issues in functional analysis," several are suggested in Section F of the present Part. Some of the content of Section F might perhaps have been worked in reasonably well with the content of the prior sections. But the separate section may both help to prevent certain confusions and to give a sharper emphasis than might otherwise be afforded to some matters that need a measure of special stress.

Section F is actually designed to bring out three matters. The first is brought out well enough by the selection from Parsons' essay on "Religious Perspectives." It will be remarked that Parsons gives some weight here to what may be called the "meaning-functions" of religion. Parsons takes man as "a culture-bearing animal" who is impelled to seek "meanings." The inclination to find meaning does not necessarily have to be reducible to something else. Man is the sort of creature who seeks to make sense and coherence out of his world, and the religious imagination is made to work in this direction. The meaning-functions are accordingly of genuine importance. This should be quite evident from Parsons' discussion, which may also serve as a link to Part Four. (Culture receives considerable attention in Part Four, and a stress on meaning is accordant with stress on culture, which is indeed taken, as will be seen, as a realm of meanings, values and symbols.) Parsons' discussion incorporates some material that may have become quite familiar, but the small amount of substantial repetition involved is allowed in order to afford him a needed context for his observations on meaning-functions.

The second selection in Section F is included in order to stress a quite different point. This is that religion can perform eminently "nonconservative" functions. The meaning of this will become clearer from reading of the selection itself. Cohn's paper on "Medieval Millenarism" is not directly or immediately inspired by a functional outlook, but it will not take much imagination to see the relevance of its content to such an outlook; and, in particular, the paper does afford what is here very much to the point: a striking instance of religion as nonconservative or revolutionary.

The last two selections in Section F, from writings by H. Richard Niebuhr and S. M. Lipset, are designed to *suggest* the notion of functional alternatives. The word suggest is italicized lest these extremely brief passages be expected to bear a larger burden than they can. The idea of functional alternatives as now intended might also be stated by speaking of alternative structures that could fulfill the same or like (or at least overlapping) functions or have like social consequences. But there is no special interest in developing a technical vocabulary of functional analysis here. When Niebuhr compares "the socialism of 1848 and later years" to Anabaptism and Quakerism and to Lollardy and the

Waldensian revolt and then observes that the nineteenth-century socialist movement, like the religious movements of previous centuries, "cherished the hope of an inevitable social renewal which would cast down the mighty from their seats and exalt them of low degree" and "provided the oppressed with an emotional escape from the weariness and grime of uneventful and profitless labor" and "brought to consciousness the latent sense of social solidarity and endowed the impoverished individual life with the significance of participation in a cosmic event," he is clearly suggesting that socialism took over some functions previously performed by the religious movements. (No over-all *identity* of functions is presumed by him, but at least some *overlap* of functions is presumed.) Alternative structures ("socialistic," "religious") may, then, perform like functions. Or certain functions may be said to have "choices" among structures that are for certain "purposes" (functionally)

indifferent. But Niebuhr was not interested in a close theoretical analysis of structures and functions. It suffices for our purposes that he does in effect suggest the notion of functional alternatives, which needs much exploration in the sociology of religion. We may also be interested in a relevant hint in the selection from Lipset, but again without seeking to tease out from it more than may be warranted. There is, after all, in this particular selection simply an intimation of "connections between the social roots of political and of religious extremism." One might wish, on the basis of this, to begin to explore the very general notion that political and religious extremism may perform some similar functions. But it is enough for our immediate purposes to have set out the notion of functional or structural alternatives in a context of analysis of religion. That it would be, ideally, desirable to do more than this is quite evident.

A · SOME ESSENTIALS IN THE FUNCTIONAL OUTLOOK ON RELIGION

1 · *Religion and Society**

A. R. RADCLIFFE-BROWN

The Royal Anthropological Institute has honoured me with an invitation to deliver the Henry Myers Lecture on the rôle of religion in the development of human society. That is an important and complex subject, about which it is not possible to say very much in a single lecture, but as it is hoped that this may be only the first of a continuing series of lectures, in which different lecturers will each offer some contribution, I think that the most useful thing I can do is to indicate certain lines along which I believe that an enquiry into this problem can be profitably pursued.

The usual way of looking at religions is to regard all of them, or all except one, as bodies of erroneous beliefs and illusory practices. There is no doubt that the history of religions has been in great part a history of error and illusion. In all ages men have hoped that by the proper performance of religious actions or observances they would obtain some specific benefit: health and long life, children to

SOURCE. A. R. Radcliffe-Brown, *Structure and Function in Primitive Society*, Glencoe, Illinois: The Free Press, 1952, pp. 153–177. Reprinted with permission of The Free Press of Glencoe. First published in 1952.
* The Henry Myers Lecture, 1945.

carry on their line, material well-being, success in hunting, rain, the growth of crops and the multiplication of cattle, victory in war, admission of their souls after death to a paradise, or inversely, release by the extinction of personality from the round of reincarnation. We do not believe that the rainmaking rites of savage tribes really produce rain. Nor do we believe that the initiates of the ancient mysteries did actually attain through their initiation an immortality denied to other men.

When we regard the religions of other peoples, or at least those of what are called primitive peoples, as systems of erroneous and illusory beliefs, we are confronted with the problem of how these beliefs came to be formulated and accepted. It is to this problem that anthropologists have given most attention. My personal opinion is that this method of approach, even though it may seem the most direct, is not the one most likely to lead to a real understanding of the nature of religions.

There is another way in which we may approach the study of religions. We may entertain as at least a possibility the theory that any religion is an important or even essential part of the social ma-

63

chinery, as are morality and law, part of the complex system by which human beings are enabled to live together in an orderly arrangement of social relations. From this point of view we deal not with the origins but with the social functions of religions, i.e. the contribution that they make to the formation and maintenance of a social order. There are many persons who would say that it is only *true* religion (i.e. one's own) that can provide the foundation of an orderly social life. The hypothesis we are considering is that the social function of a religion is independent of its truth or falsity, that religions which we think to be erroneous or even absurd and repulsive, such as those of some savage tribes, may be important and effective parts of the social machinery, and that without these "false" religions social evolution and the development of modern civilisation would have been impossible.

The hypothesis, therefore, is that in what we regard as false religions, though the performance of religious rites does not actually produce the effects that are expected or hoped for by those who perform or take part in them, they have other effects, some at least of which may be socially valuable.

How are we to set to work to test this hypothesis? It is of no use thinking in terms of religion in general, in the abstract, and society in the abstract. Nor is it adequate to consider some one religion, particularly if it is the one in which we have been brought up and about which we are likely to be prejudiced one way or another. The only method is the experimental method of social anthropology, and that means that we must study in the light of our hypothesis a sufficient number of diverse particular religions or religious cults in their relation to the particular societies in which they are found. This is a task not for one person but for a number.

Anthropologists and others have dis-

cussed at length the question of the proper definition of religion. I do not intend to deal with that controversial subject on this occasion. But there are some points that must be considered. I shall assume that any religion or any religious cult normally involves certain ideas or beliefs on the one hand, and on the other certain observances. These observances, positive and negative, i.e. actions and abstentions, I shall speak of as rites.

In European countries, and more particularly since the Reformation, religion has come to be considered as primarily a matter of belief. This is itself a phenomenon which needs to be explained, I think, in terms of social development. We are concerned here only with its effects on the thinking of anthropologists. Among many of them there is a tendency to treat belief as primary: rites are considered as the results of beliefs. They therefore concentrate their attention on trying to explain the beliefs by hypotheses as to how they may have been formed and adopted.

To my mind this is the product of false psychology. For example, it is sometimes held that funeral and mourning rites are the result of a belief in a soul surviving death. If we must talk in terms of cause and effect, I would rather hold the view that the belief in a surviving soul is not the cause but the effect of the rites. Actually the cause-effect analysis is misleading. What really happens is that the rites and the justifying or rationalising beliefs develop together as parts of a coherent whole. But in this development it is action or the need of action that controls or determines belief rather than the other way about. The actions themselves are symbolic expressions of sentiments.

My suggestion is that in attempting to understand a religion it is on the rites rather than on the beliefs that we should first concentrate our attention. Much the same view is taken by Loisy, who justifies his selection of sacrificial rites as the subject of his analysis of religion by saying that rites are in all religions the most stable and lasting element, and consequently that in which we can best discover the spirit of ancient cults.[1]

That great pioneer of the science of religion, Robertson Smith, took this view. He wrote as follows:

In connection with every religion, whether ancient or modern, we find on the one hand certain beliefs, and on the other certain institutions, ritual practices and rules of conduct. Our modern habit is to look at religion from the side of belief rather than that of practice; for, down to comparatively recent times, almost the only forms of religion seriously studied in Europe have been those of the various Christian Churches, and all parts of Christendom are agreed that ritual is important only in connection with its interpretation. Thus the study of religion has meant mainly the study of Christian beliefs, and instruction in religion has habitually begun with the creed, religious duties being presented to the learner as flowing from the dogmatic truths he is taught to accept. All this seems to us so much a matter of course that, when we approach some strange or antique religion, we naturally assume that here also our first business is to search for a creed, and find in it the key to ritual and practice. But the antique religions had for the most part no creed; they consisted entirely of institutions and practices. No doubt men will not habitually follow certain practices without attaching a meaning to them; but as a rule

we find that while the practice was rigorously fixed, the meaning attached to it was extremely vague, and the same rite was explained by different people in different ways, without any question of orthodoxy or heterodoxy arising in consequence. In ancient Greece, for example, certain things were done at a temple, and people were agreed that it would be impious not to do them. But if you asked why they were done you would probably have had several mutually contradictory explanations from different persons, and no one would have thought it a matter of the least religious importance which of these you chose to adopt. Indeed, the explanations offered would not have been of a kind to stir any strong feeling; for in most cases they would have been merely different stories as to the circumstances under which the rite first came to be established, by the command or by the direct example of the god. The rite, in short, was connected not with dogma but with a myth.[2]

. . . It is of the first importance to realise clearly from the outset that ritual and practical usage were, strictly speaking, the sum-total of ancient religions. Religion in primitive times was not a system of belief with practical applications; it was a body of fixed traditional practices to which every member of society conformed as a matter of course. Men would not be men if they agreed to do certain things without having a reason for their action; but in ancient religion the reason was not first formulated as a doctrine and then expressed in practice, but conversely, practice preceded doctrinal theory. Men form general rules of conduct before they begin to express general principles in words; political in-

[1] "Les rites étant dans toutes les religions l'élément le plus consistant et le plus durable, celui, par conséquent, où se découvre le mieux l'esprit des cultes anciens." *Essai historique sur le Sacrifice*, Paris, 1920, p. 1.

[2] W. Robertson Smith, *Lectures on the Religion of the Semites*, 1907, pp. 16–17.

stitutions are older than political theories, and in like manner religious institutions are older than religious theories. This analogy is not arbitrarily chosen, for in fact the parallelism in ancient society between religious and political institutions is complete. In each sphere great importance was attached to form and precedent, but the explanation why the precedent was followed consisted merely of a legend as to its first establishment. That the precedent, once established, was authoritative did not appear to require any proof. The rules of society were based on precedent, and the continued existence of the society was sufficient reason why a precedent once set should continue to be followed.[3]

The relative stability of rites and the variability of doctrines can be illustrated from the Christian religions. The two essential rites of all Christian religions are baptism and the eucharist, and we know that the latter solemn sacrament is interpreted differently in the Orthodox Church, the Roman Church and the Anglican Church. The modern emphasis on the exact formulation of beliefs connected with the rites rather than on the rites themselves is demonstrated in the way in which Christians have fought with and killed one another over differences of doctrine.

Thirty-seven years ago (1908), in a fellowship thesis on the Andaman Islanders (which did not appear in print till 1922), I formulated briefly a general theory of the social function of rites and ceremonies. It is the same theory that underlies the remarks I shall offer on this occasion. Stated in the simplest possible terms the theory is that an orderly social life amongst human beings depends upon the presence in the minds of the members of a society of certain sentiments, which

control the behaviour of the individual in his relation to others. Rites can be seen to be the regulated symbolic expressions of certain sentiments. Rites can therefore be shown to have a specific social function when, and to the extent that, they have for their effect to regulate, maintain and transmit from one generation to another sentiments on which the constitution of the society depends. I ventured to suggest as a general formula that religion is everywhere an expression in one form or another of a sense of dependence on a power outside ourselves, a power which we may speak of as a spiritual or moral power.

This theory is by no means new. It is to be found in the writings of the philosophers of ancient China. It is most explicit in the teachings of Hsün Tzǔ who lived in the third century B.C., and in the *Book of Rites* (the *Li Chi*), which was compiled some time later. The Chinese writers do not write about religion. I am doubtful if there is in Chinese any word which will convey just what we understand by the word religion. They write about *li*, and the word is variously translated as ceremonial, customary morality, rites, rules of good manners, propriety. But the character by which this word is written consists of two parts, of which one refers to spirits, sacrifice and prayer, and the other originally meant a vessel used in performing sacrifices. We may therefore appropriately translate *li* as "ritual." In any case what the ancient philosophers are chiefly concerned with are the rites of mourning and sacrificial rites.

There is no doubt that in China, as elsewhere, it was thought that many or all of the religious rites were efficacious in the sense of averting evils and bringing blessings. It was believed that the seasons would not follow one another in due order unless the Emperor, the Son of Heaven, performed the established rites at the appropriate times. Even under the

[3] *Op. cit.,* p. 20.

Republic a reluctant magistrate of a *hsien* may be compelled by public opinion to take the leading part in a ceremony to bring rain. But there developed among the scholars an attitude which might perhaps be called rationalistic and agnostic. For the most part the question of the efficacy of rites was not considered. What was thought important was the social function of the rites, i.e. their effects in producing and maintaining an orderly human society.

In a text that is earlier than Confucius we read that "sacrifice is that through which one can show one's filial piety and give peace to the people, pacify the country and make the people settled. . . . It is through the sacrifices that the unity of the people is strengthened" (*Ch'u Yü* II, 2).

You know that one of the major points of the teaching of Confucius was the importance of the proper performance of rites. But it is said of Confucius that he would not discuss the supernatural.[4] In the Confucian philosophy, music and ritual are considered as means for the establishment and preservation of social order, and regarded as superior to laws and punishments as means to this end. We take a very different view of music, but I may remind you that Plato held somewhat similar ideas, and I suggest that an anthropological study of the relations between music (and dancing) and religious rituals would provide some interesting results. In the *Book of Rites* one section (the *Yüeh Chi*) is concerned with music. The third paragraph reads:

The ancient kings were watchful in regard to the things by which the mind was affected. And so they instituted ceremonies to direct men's aims aright; music to give harmony to their voices;

laws to unify their conduct; and punishments to guard against their tendencies to evil. The end to which ceremonies, music, punishments and laws conduct is one; they are the instruments by which the minds of the people are assimilated, and good order in government is made to appear.[5]

The view of religion that we are here concerned with might be summed up in the following sentence from the *Book of Rites*, "Ceremonies are the bond that holds the multitudes together, and if the bond be removed, those multitudes fall into confusion."

The later Confucian philosophers, beginning with Hsün Tzŭ, paid attention to the ways in which rites, particularly the mourning and sacrificial rites, performed their function of maintaining social order. The chief point of their theory is that the rites serve to "regulate" and "refine" human feelings. Hsün Tzŭ says:

Sacrificial rites are the expressions of man's affectionate longings. They represent the height of altruism, faithfulness, love and reverence. They represent the completion of propriety and refinement.[6]

Of the mourning rites Hsün Tzŭ says:

The rites (*li*) consist in being careful about the treatment of life and death. Life is the beginning of man, Death is the end of man. When the end and beginning are both good, the way of humanity is complete. Hence the Superior Man respects the be-

[4] *Analects*, VII, 20. Waley translates this passage as: "The Master never talked of prodigies, feats of strength, disorders or spirits."

[5] Legge's translation. An alternative translation of the last sentence would be: "Rites, music, punishments, laws have one and the same end, to unite hearts and establish order."
[6] The translations from Hsün Tzŭ are those of Fung Yu Lan and are quoted from his *History of Chinese Philosophy*, Peiping, 1937.

ginning and venerates the end. To make the end and beginning uniform is the practice of the Superior man, and is that in which lies the beauty of *li* and standards of justice (*i*). For to pay over-attention to the living and belittle the dead would be to respect them when they have knowledge and disrespect them when they have not. . . .

The way of death is this: once dead, a person cannot return again. [It is in realising this that] the minister most completely fulfils the honour due to his ruler, and the son the honour of his parents.

Funeral rites are for the living to give beautified ceremonial to the dead; to send off the dead as if they were living; to render the same service to the dead as to the living; to the absent as to the present; and to make the end be the same as the beginning . . .

Articles used in life are prepared so as to be put into the grave, as if [the deceased] were only moving house. Only a few things are taken, not all of them. They are to give the appearance, but are not for practical use. . . . Hence the things [such as were used] in life are adorned, but not completed, and the "spiritual utensils" are for appearance but not use. . . .[7]

Hence the funeral rites are for no other purpose than to make clear the meaning of death and life, to send off the dead with sorrow and reverence, and when the end comes, to prepare for storing the body away. . . . Service to the living is beautifying their beginning; sending off the dead is beautifying their end. When the end and the beginning are both attended to, the service of the filial son is ended and the way of the Sage is completed. Slighting the dead and over-emphasising the living is the way of Mo (Tzŭ).[8] Slighting the living and over-attention to the dead is the way of superstition. Killing the living to send off the dead is murder.[9] The method and manner of *li* and standards of justice (*i*) is to send off the dead as if they were alive, so that in death and life, the end and the beginning, there is nothing that is not appropriate and good. The Confucian does this.

The view taken by this school of ancient philosophers was that religious rites have important social functions which are independent of any beliefs that may be held as to the efficacy of the rites. The rites gave regulated expression to certain human feelings and sentiments and so kept these sentiments alive and active. In turn it was these sentiments which,

---

[7] Fung Yu Lan translates by the term "spiritual utensils" the Chinese *ming ch'i*, which Legge in the following passage from the *Book of Rites* translates as "vessels to the eye of fancy": "Confucius said, 'In dealing with the dead, if we treat them as if they were entirely dead, that would show a want of affection, and should not be done; or, if we treat them as if they were entirely alive, that would show a want of wisdom, and should not be done. On this account the vessels of bamboo [used in connection with the burial of the dead] are not fit for actual use; those of earthenware cannot be used to wash in; those of wood are incapable of being carved; the lutes are strung, but not evenly; the pandean pipes are complete, but not in tune; the bells and musical stones are there, but they have no stands. They are called vessels to the eye of fancy; that is [the dead] are thus treated as if they were spiritual intelligencies,' " Legge, *The Sacred Books of China*, Part III, The Lî Kî, I–X, Oxford, 1885, p. 148.

[8] Mo Tzŭ was a philosopher who criticised the mourning rites as being wasteful.

[9] Referring to the ancient practice of human sacrifice at the burial of important persons.

by their control of or influence on the conduct of individuals, made possible the existence and continuance of an orderly social life.

It is this theory that I propose for your consideration. Applied, not to a single society such as ancient China, but to all human societies, it points to the correlation and co-variation of different characteristics or elements of social systems. Societies differ from one another in their structure and constitution and therefore in the customary rules of behaviour of persons one to another. The system of sentiments on which the social constitution depends must therefore vary in correspondence with the difference of constitution. In so far as religion has the kind of social function that the theory suggests, religion must also vary in correspondence with the manner in which the society is constituted. In a social system constituted on the basis of nations which make war on one another, or stand ready to do so, a well-developed sentiment of patriotism in its members is essential to maintain a strong nation. In such circumstances patriotism or national feeling may be given support by religion. Thus the Children of Israel, when they invaded the land of Canaan under the leadership of Joshua, were inspired by the religion that had been taught to them by Moses and was centred upon the Holy Tabernacle and its rites.

War or the envisaged possibility of war is an essential element in the constitution of great numbers of human societies, though the warlike spirit varies very much from one to another. It is thus in accordance with our theory that one of the social functions of religion is in connection with war. It can give men faith and confidence and devotion when they go out to do battle, whether they are the aggressors or are resisting aggression. In the recent conflict the German people seem to have prayed to God for

victory not less fervently than the people of the allied nations.

It will be evident that to test our theory we must examine many societies to see if there is a demonstrable correspondence of the religion or religions of any one of them and the manner in which that society is constituted. If such a correspondence can be made out, we must then try to discover and as far as possible define the major sentiments that find their expression in the religion and at the same time contribute to the maintenance of stability in the society as constituted.

An important contribution to our study is to be found in a book that is undeservedly neglected by anthropologists, *La Cité antique*, by the historian Fustel de Coulanges. It is true that it was written some time ago (1864) and that in some matters it may need correction in the light of later historical research, but it remains a valuable contribution to the theory of the social function of religion.

The purpose of the book is to show the point-by-point correspondence between religion and the constitution of society in ancient Greece and Rome, and how in the course of history the two changed together. It is true that the author, in conformity with the ideas of the nineteenth century, conceived this correlation between two sets of social features in terms of cause and effect, those of one set being thought of as the cause producing those of the other set. The men of the ancient world, so the argument runs, came to hold certain beliefs about the souls of the dead. As the result of their beliefs they made offerings at their tombs.

Since the dead had need of food and drink it appeared to be a duty of the living to satisfy this need. The care of supplying the dead with sustenance was not left to the caprice or to the variable sentiments of men; it was obligatory. Thus a complete religion of the dead was established, whose dogmas might soon be effaced, but whose rites endured until the triumph of Christianity.[10]

It was a result of this religion that ancient society came to be constituted on the basis of the family, the agnatic lineage and the gens, with its laws of succession, property, authority and marriage.

A comparison of beliefs and laws shows that a primitive religion constituted the Greek and Roman family, established marriage and paternal authority, fixed the order of relationship, and consecrated the right of property and the right of inheritance. This same religion, after having enlarged and extended the family, formed a still larger association, the city, and reigned in that as it had reigned in the family. From it came all the institutions, as well as all the private law, of the ancients. It was from this that the city received all its principles, its rules, its usages and its magistracies. But, in the course of time, this ancient religion became modified or effaced, and private law and political institutions were modified with it. Then came a series of revolutions, and social changes regularly followed the development of knowledge.[11]

In his final paragraph the author writes:

We have written the history of a belief. It was established and human society was constituted. It was modified, and society underwent a series of revolutions. It disappeared and society changed its character.[12]

[10] *The Ancient City* (trans. Willard Small), p. 23.
[11] Op. cit., p. 12.
[12] Op. cit., p. 529.

This idea of the primacy of belief and of a causal relation in which the religion is the cause and the other institutions are the effect is in accordance with a mode of thought that was common in the nineteenth century. We can, as I indeed do, completely reject this theory and yet retain as a valuable and permanent contribution to our subject a great deal of what Fustel de Coulanges wrote. We can say that he has produced evidence that in ancient Greece and Rome the religion on the one side and the many important institutions on the other are closely united as interdependent parts of a coherent and unified system. The religion was an essential part of the constitution of the society. The form of the religion and the form of the social structure correspond one with the other. We cannot, as Fustel de Coulanges says, understand the social, juridical and political institutions of the ancient societies unless we take the religion into account. But it is equally true that we cannot understand the religion except by an examination of its relation to the institutions.

A most important part of the religion of ancient Greece and Rome was the worship of ancestors. We may regard this as one instance of a certain type of religion. A religious cult of the same general kind has existed in China from ancient times to the present day. Cults of the same kind exist to-day and can be studied in many parts of Africa and Asia. It is therefore possible to make a wide comparative study of this type of religion. In my own experience it is in ancestor-worship that we can most easily discover and demonstrate the social function of a religious cult.

The term "ancestor-worship" is sometimes used in a wide, loose sense to refer to any sort of rites referring to dead persons. I propose to use it in a more limited and more precisely defined sense. The cult group in this religion consists solely of persons related to one another by descent in one line from the same ancestor or ancestors. In most instances descent is patrilineal, through males. But in some societies, such as the Bakongo in Africa and the Nayar in India, descent is matrilineal, and the cult group consists of descendants of a single ancestress. The rites in which the members of the group, and only they, participate have reference to their own ancestors, and normally they include the making of offerings or sacrifices to them.

A particular lineage consists of three or more generations. A lineage of four or five generations will normally be included as a part in one of six or seven generations. In a well-developed system related lineages are united into a larger body, such as the Roman gens, or what may be called the clan in China. In parts of China we can find a large body of persons, numbering in some instances as much as a thousand, all having the same name and tracing their descent in the male line from a single ancestor, the founder of the clan. The clan itself is divided into lineages.

A lineage, if it is of more than three or four generations, includes both living persons and dead persons. What is called ancestor-worship consists of rites carried out by members of a larger or smaller lineage (i.e. one consisting of more or fewer generations) with reference to the deceased members of the lineage. Such rites include the making of offerings, usually of food and drink, and such offerings are sometimes interpreted as the sharing of a meal by the dead and the living.

In such a society, what gives stability to the social structure is the solidarity and continuity of the lineage, and of the wider group (the clan) composed of related lineages. For the individual, his primary duties are those to his lineage. These include duties to the members now living, but also to those who have died and to those who are not yet born. In the carrying out of these duties he is con-

trolled and inspired by the complex system of sentiments of which we may say that the object on which they are centred is the lineage itself, past, present and future. It is primarily this system of sentiments that is expressed in the rites of the cult of the ancestors. The social function of the rites is obvious: by giving solemn and collective expression to them the rites reaffirm, renew and strengthen those sentiments on which the social solidarity depends.

We have no means of studying how an ancestor-worshipping society comes into existence, but we can study the decay of this type of system in the past and in the present. Fustel de Coulanges deals with this in ancient Greece and Rome. It can be observed at the present time in various parts of the world. The scanty information I have been able to gather suggests that the lineage and join-family organisation of some parts of India is losing something of its former strength and solidarity and that what we should expect as the inevitable accompaniment of this, a weakening of the cult of ancestors, is also taking place. I can speak with more assurance about some African societies, particularly those of South Africa. The effect of the impact of European culture, including the teaching of the Christian missionaries, is to weaken in some individuals the sentiments that attach them to their lineage. The disintegration of the social structure and the decay of the ancestral cult proceed together.

Thus for one particular type of religion I am ready to affirm that the general theory of the social function of religions can be fully demonstrated.

A most important contribution to our subject is a work of Emile Durkheim published in 1912. The title is *Les Formes élémentaires de la Vie religieuse*, but the sub-title reads: *La Système totémique en Australie*. It is worth while mentioning that Durkheim was a pupil of Fustel de Coulanges at the École Normale Supérieure and that he himself said that the most important influence on the development of his ideas about religion was that of Robertson Smith.

Durkheim's aim was to establish a general theory of the nature of religion. Instead of a wide comparative study of many religions, he preferred to take a simple type of society and carry out an intensive and detailed analysis, and for this purpose he selected the aboriginal tribes of Australia. He held the view that these tribes represent the simplest type of society surviving to our own times, but the value of his analysis is in no way affected if we refuse to accept this view, as I do myself.

The value of Durkheim's book is as an exposition of a general theory of religion which had been developed with the collaboration of Henri Hubert and Marcel Mauss, starting from those foundations provided by Robertson Smith. Durkheim's exposition of this theory has often been very much misunderstood. A clear, though very brief, statement of it is to be found in the Introduction written by Henri Hubert in 1904 for the French translation of the *Manuel d'Histiore des Religions* of Chantepie de la Saussaye. But it is not possible on this occasion to discuss this general theory. I wish only to deal with one part of Durkheim's work, namely his theory that religious ritual is an expression of the unity of society and that its function is to "recreate" the society or the social order by reaffirming and strengthening the sentiments on which the social solidarity and therefore the social order itself depend.[13] This theory he tests by an examination of the totemic ritual of the Australians. For while Frazer regarded the totemic rites of the Australian tribes as being a matter of magic, Durkheim treats them as religious because the rites themselves are

[13] Op. cit., pp. 323, 497 and elsewhere.

sacred and have reference to sacred beings, sacred places and sacred objects.

In 1912 very much less was known about the Australian aborigines than is known at present. Some of the sources used by Durkheim have proved to be unreliable. The one tribe that was well known, through the writings of Spencer and Gillen and Strehlow—the Aranda—is in some respects atypical. The information that Durkheim could use was therefore decidedly imperfect. Moreover, it cannot be said that his handling of this material was all that it might have been. Consequently there are many points in his exposition which I find unacceptable. Nevertheless, I think that Durkheim's major thesis as to the social function of the totemic rites is valid and only requires revision and correction in the light of the more extensive and more exact knowledge we now have.[14]

The beings to which the Australian cult refers are commonly spoken of as "totemic ancestors," and I have myself used the term. But it is somewhat misleading, since they are mythical beings and not ancestors in the same sense as the dead persons commemorated in ancestor-worship. In the cosmology of the Australian natives the cosmos, the ordered universe, including both the order of nature and the social order, came into existence at a time in the past which I propose to speak of as the World-Dawn, for this name corresponds to certain ideas that I have found amongst the aborigines of some tribes. This order (of nature and of society) resulted from the doings and adventures of certain sacred beings. These beings, whom I shall call the Dawn Beings, are the totemic ancestors of ethnological literature. The explanations of topographical features, of natural species and their characteristics, and

[14] For a criticism of some points in Durkheim's work, see "The Sociological Theory of Totemism" in *Structure and Function*.

of social laws, customs and usages are given in the form of myths about the happenings of the World-Dawn.

The cosmos is ruled by law. But whereas we think of the laws of nature as statements of what invariably does happen (except, of course, in miracles), and of moral or social laws as what ought to be observed but are sometimes broken, the Australian does not make this distinction. For him men and women ought to observe the rules of behaviour that were fixed for all time by the events of the World-Dawn, and similarly the rain ought to fall in its proper season, plants should grow and produce fruit or seed, and animals should bear young. But there are irregularities in human society and in nature.

In what I shall venture to call the totemic religion of the Australian aborigines, there are two main types of ritual. One of these consists of rites carried out at certain spots which are commonly referred to as "totem centres." A totem centre is a spot that is specially connected with some species of object, most commonly with a particular species of animal or plant, or with an aspect of nature such as rain or hot weather. Each centre is associated with one (or occasionally more than one) of the Dawn Beings. Frequently the Being is said to have gone into the ground at this spot. For each totem centre there is a myth connecting it with the events of the World-Dawn. The totem centre, the myth connected with it and the rites that are performed there, belong to the local group that owns the territory within which the totem centre lies. Each totem centre is thought of as containing, in a rock or a tree or a pool of water or a heap of stones, what we may perhaps call the life-spirit or life-force of the totem species.

The rites performed at the toem centre by the members of the local group to which it belongs, or under their leadership and direction, are thought to renew the vitality of this life-spirit of the species. In eastern Australia the totem centre is spoken of as the "home" or "dwelling-place" of the species, and the rites are called "stirring up." Thus, the rite at a rain totem centre brings the rain in its due season, that at a kangaroo totem centre ensures the supply of kangaroos, and that at the baby totem centre provides for the birth of children in the tribe.

These rites imply a certain conception, which I think we can call specifically a religious conception, of the place of man in the universe. Man is dependent upon what we call nature: on the regular successions of the seasons, on the rain falling when it should, on the growth of plants and the continuance of animal life. But, as I have already said, while for us the order of nature is one thing and the social order another, for the Australian they are two parts of a single order. Well-being, for the individual or for the society, depends on the continuance of this order free from serious disturbance. The Australians believe that they can ensure this continuance, or at least contribute to it, by their actions, including the regular performance of the totemic rites.

In the rites that have been described, each group takes care (if we may so express it) of only a small part of nature, of those few species for which it owns totem centres. The preservation of the natural order as a whole therefore depends on the actions of many different groups.

The social structure of the Australian natives is based on two things: a system of local groups, and a system of kinship based on the family. Each small local group is a closed patrilineal descent group; that is, a man is born into the group of his father and his sons belong to his group. Each group is independent and autonomous. The stability and continuity of the social structure depends on the strong solidarity of the local group.

Where there existed the totemic cult which I have just described (and it existed over a very large part of Australia), each local group was a cult group. The totemic ritual served to express the unity and solidarity of the group and its individuality and separation from other groups by the special relation of the group to its *sacra:* the totem centre or centres, the Dawn Beings associated with them, the myths and songs referring to those Beings, and the totems or species connected with the centres. This aspect of the social function of totemism was emphasised, and I think somewhat over-emphasised, by Durkheim.

There is, however, another aspect, for while the local totemic groups are separate individual and continuing social entities, they are also part of a wider social structure. This wider structure is provided by the kinship system. For an individual in Australian native society, every person with whom he has any social contact is related to him by some bond of kinship, near or distant, and the regulation of social life consists essentially of rules concerning behaviour towards different kinds of kin. For example, a man stands in very close relation to his mother's local group and, in many tribes, in a very close relation to its *sacra:* its totems, totem centres and totemic rites.

While Australian totemism separates the local groups and gives each an individuality of its own, it also links the groups together. For while each group is specially connected with certain parts of the natural order (e.g. with rain, or with kangaroo) and with certain of the Beings of the World-Dawn, the society as a whole is related through the totemic religion to the whole order of nature and to the World-Dawn as a whole. This is best seen in another kind of totemic cult, part of which consists of sacred dramas in which the performers impersonate var-

ious Dawn Beings. Such dramatic dances are only performed at those religious meetings at which a number of local groups come together, and it is on these occasions that young men are initiated into manhood and into the religious life of the society.

Australian society is not merely a collection of separate local groups; it is also a body of persons linked together in the kinship system. Australian totemism is a cosmological system by which the phenomena of nature are incorporated in the kinship organisation. When I was beginning my work in Australia in 1910, a native said to me, "*Bungurdi* (kangaroo) [is] my *kadja* (elder brother)." This simple sentence of three words gives the clue to an understanding of Australian totemism. The speaker did not mean that individuals of the kangaroo species are his brothers. He meant that to the kangaroo species, conceived as an entity, he stood in a social relation analogous to that in which a man stands to his elder brother in the kinship system. I am sorry that there is not time on this occasion to expound this thesis more fully.

The account I have just given of Australian totemism differs considerably from that given by Durkheim. But far from contradicting, it confirms Durkheim's fundamental general theory as to the social function of the totemic religion of Australia and its rites. The two kinds of totemic cult are the demonstration, in symbolic action, of the structure of Australian society and its foundations in a mythical and sacred past. In maintaining the social cohesion and equilibrium, the religion plays a most important part. The religion is an intrinsic part of the constitution of society.

I have dwelt, if only cursorily, with two types of religion: ancestor-worship and Australian totemism. In both of them it is possible to demonstrate the close correspondence of the form of religion and the form of the social structure. In both it is possible to see how the religious rites reaffirm and strengthen the sentiments on which the social order depends. Here then are results of some significance for our problem. They point to a certain line of investigation. We can and should examine other religions in the light of the results already reached. But to do this we must study religions *in action;* we must try to discover the effects of active participation in a particular cult, first the direct effects on the individual and then the further effects on the society of which these individuals are members. When we have a sufficient number of such studies, it will be possible to establish a general theory of the nature of religions and their rôle in social development.

In elaborating such a general theory it will be necessary to determine by means of comparative studies the relations between religion and morality. There is only time to refer very briefly here to the question of religion and morality. As representing a theory that seems to be widely held, I quote the following passages from Tylor:

> One great element of religion, that moral element which among the higher nations forms its most vital part, is indeed little represented in the religion of the lower races.[15]
> The comparison of savage and civilised religions brings into view, by the side of a deep-lying resemblance in their philosophy, a deep-lying contrast in their practical action on human life. So far as savage religion can stand as representing natural religion, the popular idea that the moral government of the universe is an essential tenet of natural religion simply falls to the ground. Savage animism is almost devoid of that ethical element

which to the educated modern mind is the very mainspring of practical religion. Not, as I have said, that morality is absent from the life of the lower races. Without a code of morals, the very existence of the rudest tribe would be impossible; and indeed the moral standards of even savage races are to no small extent well-defined and praiseworthy. But these ethical laws stand on their own ground of tradition and public opinion, comparatively independent of the animistic beliefs and rites which exist beside them. The lower animism is not immoral, it is unmoral. . . . The general problem of the relation of morality to religion is difficult, intricate, and requiring immense array of evidence.[16]

I agree with Tylor that the problem of the relation of morality to religion is difficult and intricate. But I wish to question the validity of the distinction he makes between the religions of savages and those of civilised peoples, and of his statement that the moral element "is little represented in the religion of the lower races." I suspect that when this view is held it often means only that in the "lower races" the religion is not associated with the kind of morality which exists in contemporary Western societies. But societies differ in their systems of morals as in other aspects of the social system, and what we have to examine in any given society is the relation of the religion or religions of that society to their particular system of morality.

Dr. R. F. Fortune, in his book on Manus religion, has challenged the dictum of Tylor.[17] The religion of Manus is

[15] Tylor, *Primitive Culture*, 3rd ed., 1891, Vol. I, p. 427.

[16] Op. cit., Vol. II, p. 360.

[17] R. F. Fortune, *Manus Religion*, Philadelphia, 1935, pp. 5 and 356. Dr. Fortune's book is a useful contribution to the study of the social function of religion and deals with a religion of a very unusual type.

what may be called a kind of spiritual-ism, but it is not ancestor-worship in the sense in which I have used the term in this lecture. The Manus code of morals rigidly forbids sexual intercourse except between husband and wife, condemns dishonesty and insists on the conscien-tious fulfilment of obligations, including economic obligations, towards one's rela-tives and others. Offences against the moral code bring down on the offender, or on his household, punishment from the spirits, and the remedy is to be found in confession and reparation for wrong.

Let us now reconsider the case of ancestor-worship. In the societies which practise it, the most important part of the moral code is that which concerns the conduct of the individual in relation to his lineage and clan and the individual members thereof. In the more usual form of ancestor-worship, infractions of this code fall under religious or supernatural sanctions, for they are offences against the ancestors, who are believed to send punishment.

Again we may take as an example of the lower races the aborigines of Aus-tralia. Since the fundamental social struc-ture is a complex system of widely ex-tended recognition of relations of kin-ship, the most important part of the moral code consists of the rules of be-haviour towards kin of different cate-gories. One of the most immoral actions of which a man can be guilty is having sexual relations with any woman who does not belong to that category of his kinsfolk into which he may legally marry.

The moral law of the tribe is taught to young men in the very sacred cere-monies known as initiation ceremonies. I will deal only with the Bora ceremo-nies, as they are called, of some of the tribes of New South Wales. These cere-monies were instituted in the time of the World-Dawn by Baiame, who killed his own son Daramulun (sometimes iden-tified with the sacred bull-roarer) and on the third day brought him back to life. As the ceremony is conducted, the initi-ates all 'die' and are brought back to life on the third day.[18]

On the sacred ceremonial ground where these initiations take place there is usually an image of Baiame made of earth, and sometimes one of Baiame's wife. Beside these images sacred rites are shown to the initiates, and sacred myths about Baiame are recounted.

Now Baiame instituted not only the initiation ceremonies, which are, amongst other things, schools of morals for young men, but also the kinship system with its rules about marriage and behaviour to-wards different categories of kin. To the question, "Why do you observe these complex rules about marriage?" the usual answer is, "Because Baiame established them." Thus Baiame is the divine law-giver, or, by an alternative mode of ex-pression, he is the personification of the tribal laws of morality.

I agree with Andrew Lang and Father Schmidt that Baiame thus closely re-sembles one aspect of the God of the Hebrews. But Baiame gives no assistance in war as Jehovah did for the children of Israel, nor is Baiame the ruler or control-ler of nature, of storms and seasons. That position is held by another deity, the Rainbow-Serpent, whose image in earth also appears on the sacred ceremonial ground. The position held by Baiame is that of the Divine Being who established the most important rules of morality and the sacred ceremonies of initiation.

These few examples will perhaps suf-fice to show that the idea that it is only the higher religions that are specially

[18] The suggestion has been made that we have here the influence of Christianity, but that opinion can be dismissed. The idea of ritual death and rebirth is very widespread in religion, and the three-day period is ex-emplified every month in every part of the world by the death and resurrection of the moon.

concerned with morality, and that the moral element is little represented in the religions of the lower races, is decidedly open to question. If there were time I could provide instances from other parts of the world.

What makes these problems complex is the fact that law, morality and religion are three ways of controlling human conduct which in different types of society supplement one another, and are combined, in different ways. For the law there are legal sanctions, for morality there are the sanctions of public opinion and of conscience, for religion there are religious sanctions. A single wrongful deed may fall under two or three sanctions. Blasphemy and sacrilege are sins and so subject to religious sanctions; but they may also sometimes be punished by law as crimes. In our own society murder is immoral; it is also a crime punishable by death; and it is also a sin against God, so that the murderer, after his sudden exit from this life at the hands of the executioner, must face an eternity of torment in the fires of Hell.

Legal sanctions may be brought into action in instances where there is no question of morality or immorality, and the same is true of religious sanctions. It is held by some of the Fathers or doctors of the Christian churches that an upright and virtuous life devoted to good works will not save a man from Hell unless he has attained grace by accepting as true the specific doctrines taught by a church.

There are different kinds of religious sanctions. The penalty for sin may be conceived simply as alienation from God. Or there may be a belief in rewards and punishments in an after-life. But the most widespread form of the religious sanction is the belief that certain actions produce in an individual or in a community a condition of ritual pollution, or uncleanness, from which it is necessary to be purified. Pollution may result from things done unintentionally and unwit-

tingly, as you may see from the fifth chapter of the Book of Leviticus. One who unwittingly has touched any unclean thing, such as the carcase of an unclean beast, is guilty and has sinned and must bear his iniquity. He must make a sacrifice, a trespass offering, by which he may be cleansed from his sin.

Ritual uncleanness does not in itself involve moral condemnation. We read in the twelfth chapter of the same Book of Leviticus that the Lord instructed Moses that a woman who has borne a male child shall be unclean for seven days and her purification must continue for a further three and thirty days, during which she shall touch no hallowed thing, nor come into the sanctuary. If the child she bears is female, the first period of uncleanness is to be two weeks and the period of purification threescore-and-six days. Thus, it is polluting, but no one can suppose that it is immoral, to bear a child, and more polluting if the child is female than if it is male.

The opposite of pollution or sinfulness is holiness. But holiness comes not from leading an honest and upright life, but from religious exercises, prayer and fasting, the performance of penance, meditation and the reading of sacred books. In Hinduism the son of a Brahmin is born holy; the son of a leather-worker is born unclean.

The field covered by morality and that covered by religion are different; but either in primitive or in civilised societies there may be a region in which they overlap.

To return to our main topic, a writer who has dealt with the social function of religions on the basis of a comparative study is Loisy, who devotes to the subject a few pages of the concluding chapter of his valuable *Essai historique sur le Sacrifice*.[19] Although he differs from Durkheim in some matters, his funda-

[19] 1920, pp. 531–540.

mental theory is, if not identical, at any rate very similar to that of the earlier writer. Speaking of what he calls the sacred action (*l'action sacrée*), of which the most characteristic form is the rite of sacrifice, he writes:

> We have seen its rôle in human societies, of which it has maintained and strengthened the social bonds, if indeed it has not contributed in a large measure to creating them. It was, in certain respects, the expression of them; but man is so made that he becomes more firmly fixed in his sentiments by expressing them. The sacred action was the expression of social life, of social aspirations, it has necessarily been a factor of society. . . .
>
> Before we condemn out of hand the mirage of religion and the apparatus of sacrifice as a simple waste of social resources and forces, it is proper to observe that, religion having been the form of social conscience, and sacrifice the expression of this conscience, the loss was compensated by a gain, and that, so far as purely material losses are concerned, there is really no occasion to dwell on them. Moreover the kind of sacred contribution that was required, without real utility as to the effect that was expected from it, was an intrinsic part of the system of renunciations, of contributions which, in every human society, are the condition of its equilibrium and its conservation.[20]

But besides this definition of the social function in terms of social cohesion and continuity, Loisy seeks for what he calls a general formula (*formule générale*) in which to sum up the part that religion has played in human life. Such a formula is useful so long as we remember that it is only a formula. The one that Loisy

offers is that magic and religion have served to give men confidence.

In the most primitive societies it is magic that gives man confidence in face of the difficulties and uncertainties, the real and imaginary dangers with which he is surrounded.

> A la merci des éléments, des saisons, de ce que la terre lui donne ou lui refuse, des bonnes ou des mauvaises chances de sa chasse ou de sa pêche, aussi du hasard de ses combats avec ses semblables, il croit trouver le moyen de régulariser par des simulacres d'action ces chances plus ou moins incertaines. Ce qu'il fait ne sert à rien par rapport au but qu'il se propose, mais il prend confiance en ses entreprises et en lui-même, il ose, et c'est en osant que réellement il obtient plus ou moins ce qu'il veut. Confiance rudimentaire, et pour une humble vie; mais c'est le commencement du courage moral.[21]

This is the same theory that was later developed by Malinowski in reference to the magical practices of the Trobriand Islanders.

At a somewhat higher stage of development, "when the social organism has been perfected, when the tribe has become a people, and this people has its gods, its religion, it is by this religion itself that the strength of the national conscience is measured, and it is in the service of national gods that men find a pledge of security in the present, of prosperity in the future. The gods are as it were the expression of the confidence that the people has in itself; but it is in the cult of the gods that this confidence is nourished."[22]

At a still higher stage of social development, the religions which give men a promise of immortality give him

---

[20] Op. cit., pp. 535–537.

[21] Op. cit., p. 533.

[22] Loc. cit.

thereby an assurance which permits him to bear courageously the burdens of his present life and face the most onerous obligations. "It is a higher and more moral form of confidence in life." [23]

To me this formula seems unsatisfactory in that it lays stress on what is only one side of the religious (or magical) attitude. I offer as an alternative the formula that religion develops in mankind what may be called a sense of dependence. What I mean by this can best be explained by an example. In an ancestor-worshipping tribe of South Africa, a man feels that he is dependent on his ancestors. From them he has received his life and the cattle that are his inheritance. To them he looks to send him children and to multiply his cattle and in other ways to care for his well-being. This is one side of the matter; on his ancestors he *can* depend. The other side is the belief that the ancestors watch over his conduct, and that if he fails in his duties they will not only cease to send him blessings, but will visit him with sickness or some other misfortune. He cannot stand alone and depend only on his own efforts; on his ancestors he *must* depend.

We may say that the beliefs of the African ancestor-worshipper are illusory and his offerings to his gods really useless; that the dead of his lineage do not really send him either blessings or punishments. But the Confucians have shown us that a religion like ancestor-worship can be rationalised and freed from those illusory beliefs that we call superstition. For in the rites of commemoration of the ancestors it is sufficient that the participants should express their reverential gratitude to those from whom they have received their life, and their sense of duty towards those not yet born, to whom they in due course will stand in the position of revered ancestors. There still remains the sense of dependence. The living depend on those of the past; they have duties to those living in the present and to those of the future who will depend on them.

I suggest to you that what makes and keeps a man a social animal is not some herd instinct, but the sense of dependence in the innumerable forms that it takes. The process of socialisation begins on the first day of an infant's life and it has to learn that it both *can* and *must* depend on its parents. From them it has comfort and succour; but it must submit also to their control. What I am calling the sense of dependence always has these two sides. We can face life and its chances and difficulties with confidence when we know that there are powers, forces and events on which we can rely, but we must submit to the control of our conduct by rules which are imposed. The entirely asocial individual would be one who thought that he could be completely independent, relying only on himself, asking for no help and recognising no duties.

I have tried to present to you a theory of the social function of religion. This theory has been developed by the work of such men as Robertson Smith, Fustel de Coulanges, Durkheim, Loisy. It is the theory that has guided my own studies for nearly forty years. I have thought it worth while to indicate that it existed in embryo in the writings of Chinese philosophers more than twenty centuries ago.

Like any other scientific theory it is provisional, subject to revision and modification in the light of future research. It is offered as providing what seems likely to be a profitable method of investigation. What is needed to test and further elaborate the theory is a number of systematic studies of various types of religion in relation to social systems in which they occur.

[23] Op. cit., p. 534.

I will summarise the suggestions I have made:

1. To understand a particular religion we must study its effects. The religion must therefore be studied *in action.*

2. Since human conduct is in large part controlled or directed by what have been called sentiments, conceived as mental dispositions, it is necessary to discover as far as possible what are the sentiments that are developed in the individual as the result of his participation in a particular religious cult.

3. In the study of any religion we must first of all examine the specifically religious actions, the ceremonies and the collective or individual rites.

4. The emphasis on belief in specific doctrines which characterises some modern religions seems to be the result of certain social developments in societies of complex structure.

5. In some societies there is a direct and immediate relation between the religion and the social structure. This has been illustrated by ancestor-worship and Australian totemism. It is also true of what we may call national religions, such as that of the Hebrews or those of the city states of Greece and Rome.[24] But where there comes into existence a separate independent religious structure by the formation of different churches or sects or cult-groups within a people, the relation of religion to the total social structure is in many respects indirect and not always easy to trace.

6. As a general formula (for whatever such a formula may be worth) it is suggested that what is expressed in all religions is what I have called the sense of dependence in its double aspect, and that it is by constantly maintaining this sense of dependence that religions perform their social function.

[24] ". . . among the ancients what formed the bond of every society was a worship. Just as a domestic altar held the members of a family grouped about it, so the city was the collective group of those who had the same protecting deities, and who performed the religious ceremony at the same altar." Fustel de Coulanges, op. cit., p. 193.

B · THE IMPORTANCE OF
RELIGIOUS PRACTICE

1 · The Method of the Inquiry

W. ROBERTSON SMITH

Before entering upon the particulars of our enquiry, I must still detain you with a few words about the method and order of investigation that seem to be prescribed by the nature of the subject. To get a true and well-defined picture of the type of Semitic religion, we must not only study the parts separately, but must have clear views of the place and proportion of each part in its relation to the whole. And here we shall go very far wrong if we take it for granted that what is the most important and prominent side of religion to us was equally important in the ancient society with which we are to deal. In connection with every religion, whether ancient or modern, we find on the one hand certain beliefs, and on the other certain institutions ritual practices and rules of conduct. Our modern habit is to look at religion from the side of belief rather than of practice; for, down to comparatively recent times, almost the only forms of religion seriously studied in Europe have been those of the

SOURCE. W. Robertson Smith, *Lectures on the Religion of the Semites*, New York: Meridian Books, 1956, pp. 15–22. Reprinted with permission of Meridian Books, The World Publishing Company, Cleveland and New York.

various Christian Churches, and all parts of Christendom are agreed that ritual is important only in connection with its interpretation. Thus the study of religion has meant mainly the study of Christian beliefs, and instruction in religion has habitually begun with the creed, religious duties being presented to the learner as flowing from the dogmatic truths he is taught to accept. All this seems to us so much a matter of course that, when we approach some strange or antique religion, we naturally assume that here also our first business is to search for a creed, and find in it the key to ritual and practice. But the antique religions had for the most part no creed; they consisted entirely of institutions and practices. No doubt men will not habitually follow certain practices without attaching a meaning to them; but as a rule we find that while the practice was rigorously fixed, the meaning attached to it was extremely vague, and the same rite was explained by different people in different ways, without any question of orthodoxy or heterodoxy arising in consequence. In ancient Greece, for example, certain things were done at a temple, and people were agreed that it would be impious not to do them. But if you had asked why they were done, you would probably have had several mutually contradictory explanations from different persons, and no one would have thought it a matter of the least religious importance which of these you chose to adopt. Indeed, the explanations offered would not have been of a kind to stir any strong feeling; for in most cases they would have been merely different stories as to the circumstances under which the rite first came to be established, by the command or by the direct example of the god. The rite, in short, was connected not with a dogma but with a myth.

In all the antique religions, mythology takes the place of dogma; that is, the sacred lore of priests and people, so far as it does not consist of mere rules for the performance of religious acts, assumes the form of stories about the gods; and these stories afford the only explanation that is offered of the precepts of religion and the prescribed rules of ritual. But, strictly speaking, this mythology was no essential part of ancient religion, for it had no sacred sanction and no binding force on the worshippers. The myths connected with individual sanctuaries and ceremonies were merely part of the apparatus of the worship; they served to excite the fancy and sustain the interest of the worshipper; but he was often offered a choice of several accounts of the same thing, and, provided that he fulfilled the ritual with accuracy, no one cared what he believed about its origin. Belief in a certain series of myths was neither obligatory as a part of true religion, nor was it supposed that, by believing, a man acquired religious merit and conciliated the favour of the gods. What was obligatory or meritorious was the exact performance of certain sacred acts prescribed by religious tradition. This being so, it follows that mythology ought not to take the prominent place that is too often assigned to it in the scientific study of ancient faiths. So far as myths

consist of explanations of ritual, their value is altogether secondary, and it may be affirmed with confidence that in almost every case the myth was derived from the ritual, and not the ritual from the myth; for the ritual was fixed and the myth was variable, the ritual was obligatory and faith in the myth was at the discretion of the worshipper. Now by far the largest part of the myths of antique religions are connected with the ritual of particular shrines, or with the religious observances of particular tribes and districts. In all such cases it is probable, in most cases it is certain, that the myth is merely the explanation of a religious usage; and ordinarily it is such an explanation as could not have arisen till the original sense of the usage had more or less fallen into oblivion. As a rule the myth is no explanation of the origin of the ritual to any one who does not believe it to be a narrative of real occurrences, and the boldest mythologist will not believe that. But if it be not true, the myth itself requires to be explained, and every principle of philosophy and common sense demands that the explanation be sought, not in arbitrary allegorical theories, but in the actual facts of ritual or religious custom to which the myth attaches. The conclusion is, that in the study of ancient religions we must begin, not with myth, but with ritual and traditional usage.

Nor can it be fairly set against this conclusion, that there are certain myths which are not mere explanations of traditional practices, but exhibit the beginnings of larger religious speculation, or of an attempt to systematise and reduce to order the motley variety of local worships and beliefs. For in this case the secondary character of the myths is still more clearly marked. They are either products of early philosophy, reflecting on the nature of the universe; or they are political in scope, being designed to supply a thread of union between the various worships of groups, originally distinct, which have been united into one social or political organism; or, finally, they are due to the free play of epic imagination. But philosophy, politics and poetry are something more, or something less, than religion pure and simple.

There can be no doubt that, in the later stages of ancient religions, mythology acquired an increased importance. In the struggle of heathenism with scepticism on the one hand and Christianity on the other, the supporters of the old traditional religion were driven to search for ideas of a modern cast, which they could represent as the true inner meaning of the traditional rites. To this end they laid hold of the old myths, and applied to them an allegorical system of interpretation. Myth interpreted by the aid of allegory became the favourite means of infusing a new significance into ancient forms. But the theories thus developed are the falsest of false guides as to the original meaning of the old religions.

On the other hand, the ancient myths taken in their natural sense, without allegorical gloss, are plainly of great importance as testimonies to the views of the nature of the gods that were prevalent when they were formed. For though the mythical details had no dogmatic value and no binding authority over faith, it is to be supposed that nothing was put into a myth which people at that time were not prepared to believe without offence. But so far as the way of thinking expressed in the myth was not already expressed in the ritual itself, it had no properly religious sanction; the myth apart from the ritual affords only a doubtful and slippery kind of evidence. Before we can handle myths with any confidence, we must have some definite hold of the ideas expressed in the ritual tradition, which embodied the only fixed and statutory elements of the religion.

All this, I hope, will become clearer to us as we proceed with our enquiry, and learn by practical example the use to be made of the different lines of evidence open to us. But it is of the first importance to realise clearly from the outset that ritual and practical usage were, strictly speaking, the sum-total of ancient religions. Religion in primitive times was not a system of belief with practical applications; it was a body of fixed traditional practices, to which every member of society conformed as a matter of course. Men would not be men if they agreed to do certain things without having a reason for their action; but in ancient religion the reason was not first formulated as a doctrine and then expressed in practice, but conversely, practice preceded doctrinal theory. Men form general rules of conduct before they begin to express general principles in words; political institutions are older than political theories, and in like manner religious institutions are older than religious theories. This analogy is not arbitrarily chosen, for in fact the parallelism in ancient society between religious and political institutions is complete. In each sphere great importance was attached to form and precedent, but the explanation why the precedent was followed consisted merely of a legend as to its first establishment. That the precedent, once established, was authoritative did not appear to require any proof. The rules of society were based on precedent, and the continued existence of the society was sufficient reason why a precedent once set should continue to be followed.

Strictly speaking, indeed, I understate the case when I say that the oldest religious and political institutions present a close analogy. It would be more correct to say that they were parts of one whole of social custom. Religion was a part of the organised social life into which a man was born, and to which he conformed through life in the same unconscious way in which men fall into any habitual practice of the society in which they live. Men took the gods and their worship for granted, just as they took the other usages of the state for granted, and if they reasoned or speculated about them, they did so on the presupposition that the traditional usages were fixed things, behind which their reasonings must not go, and which no reasoning could be allowed to overturn. To us moderns religion is above all a matter of individual conviction and reasoned belief, but to the ancients it was a part of the citizen's public life, reduced to fixed forms, which he was not bound to understand and was not at liberty to criticise or to neglect. Religious nonconformity was an offence against the state; for if sacred tradition was tampered with the bases of society were undermined, and the favour of the gods was forfeited. But so long as the prescribed forms were duly observed, a man was recognised as truly pious, and no one asked how his religion was rooted in his heart or affected his reason. Like political duty, of which indeed it was a part, religion was entirely comprehended in the observance of certain fixed rules of outward conduct.

The conclusion from all this as to the method of our investigation is obvious. When we study the political structure of an early society, we do not begin by asking what is recorded of the first legislators, or what theory men advanced as to the reason of their institutions; we try to understand what the institutions were, and how they shaped men's lives. In like manner, in the study of Semitic religion, we must not begin by asking what was told about the gods, but what the working religious institutions were, and how they shaped the lives of the worshippers. Our enquiry, therefore, will be directed to the religious institutions which governed the lives of men of Semitic race.

2 · A Word on the Significance of Practice in Hinduism

JAMES BISSETT PRATT

It is to be hoped that the reader will not suppose that by learning the Hindu views of the Gods, Philosophy, and Fate, he has learned "the Hindu religion." To us Christians it has become so natural to identify religion with creed that it is difficult at first to conceive of religion being anything else. To make such an identification, however, is in fact very provincial—both spatially and temporally. The ancients, for instance, did not view matters at all in our way. A Greek

SOURCE. James Bissett Pratt, *India and Its Faiths,* Boston and New York: Houghton Mifflin Company, 1915, p. 116.

thinker, such as Aristotle, could give up all belief in his country's gods, and yet never be regarded as a heretic provided he fulfilled regularly all the external duties which religious custom demanded. So it is with the Hindu. He has always enjoyed very ample liberty of thought, because he and his fellows have never conceived of religion as being in any way identical with creed. The Hindu atheist is in as good and regular standing as the polytheist, the theist, or the pantheist, and provided he lives according to the ancient customs is never regarded as in any way heretical. In fact Hinduism includes within itself every kind of creed, and from this point of view claims to be the only really universal religion extant. . . .

3 · Greek Religion

FRANK RUSSELL EARP

There is a general impression that the Greeks did not take their religion very seriously. The scandals of mythology, the apparent irreverence with which the gods are treated in Comedy, and even in some religious rites, the way in which they are sometimes depicted in art—these, and similar obvious reasons, leave in the minds of most schoolboys and of many University students a feeling that this kind of thing is not religion. "No doubt," they say to themselves, "the Greeks did perform ceremonies and offer sacrifices to these gods, but either they had ceased by historical times to take them seriously, or else they had never done so." If a doubt arises why the Greeks took so much trouble to propitiate these nugatory gods, an easy answer presents itself. These gods, whatever their shortcomings, furnished excellent material for art and literature, and deserved to be encouraged on that account; and the ceremonies in their honour, sacrifices, processions, dramatic performances, games, and so on, were not only excellent material for art, but beautiful in themselves and very agreeable.

This is hardly a travesty of the impression general among those who have some acquaintance at first or second hand with Greek Art and Literature. Scholars who have gone a little further would somewhat modify the picture.

SOURCE. Frank Russell Earp, *The Way of the Greeks,* London: Oxford University Press, 1929, pp. 67–76, 78. Reprinted with permission of the Clarendon Press, Oxford.

They remember many passages in literature, and even some incidents in Greek history, which forbid them to doubt that some Greeks at least at some times took their religion seriously. Some of these can be explained away. Aeschylus, for instance, was a person of unusual views, and his prophetic fervour cannot be taken as typical; and when the Athenians banished Alcibiades after the affair of the Hermae, and when they put Socrates to death, they were using religion as a pretext to cloak a political grudge. But the instances are too numerous for all to be explained away like these, and so the scholar as a rule is a little perplexed. He cannot deny that this very defective religion had some hold on the Greeks, but in such an intelligent nation it is surprising.

In this perplexity scholars resort to various devices, for they cannot all accept the naïve theory that the Greek gods were somehow providentially created to furnish themes for art. Some scholars, the majority I fancy, drawing on their own minds, believe that the more intelligent Greeks were monotheists, and found it useful for various reasons, such as those mentioned by Gibbon in the case of the Romans, to conform to popular beliefs. This is the most plausible, and in one sense the truest explanation. There were monotheists among the Greeks, probably as early as the sixth century B.C., if not before. Monotheism might occur to a thoughtful man in any age and place, and we know there were monotheists in Greece, and there may have been strict monotheists. But the strict monotheist, he who believes that there is One God and no other, is very different from him who believes in a supreme god with other inferior powers subject to him. And that is the form of monotheism, if it can be so called, which we commonly find in Greek writers. That form is compatible with a belief in any number of subordinate powers. And the example of Plato himself shows how natural such a belief was to the Greek.

This being so, it is misleading to assume that the more intelligent Greeks conformed, hypocritically, to beliefs they did not share. They doubtless did not believe in all the absurdities implied by those beliefs, but when they sacrificed, they were not sacrificing to nothing in order to placate the mob. There was some power, indefinable perhaps, but real enough, to which they were doing homage.

It is hardly necessary at this date to discuss another explanation fashionable some generations ago; the explanation that mythology and ceremonial were deliberately devised, whether benevolently or cynically; by cynics to amuse the multitude, or by benevolent philosophers to convey salutary truths in a form apprehensible by the vulgar. Allegory is sometimes found in poets and philosophers, and the later Greeks often explained offensive legends as allegorical, but the popular religion certainly did not originate in any conscious fiction.

These and similar difficulties, with their attendant growth of explanations, spring from the old root, modern prepossessions. And the shortest way to deal with them is, if possible, to cut that root away; and again the shortest way to do that is to recapitulate the chief points of difference between the Greek conception of religion and ours. The facts are quite familiar, but even accomplished scholars find it hard to keep them in view.

To most people now, in Western Europe at least, religion means in the first place a system of doctrines concerning the nature of God and man, and a system of morality based on those doctrines. As an adjunct to these we find prayer and the performance of ritual and ceremonies, and usually a professional priesthood marked off in various ways from other men. We also find in most cases some belief in a union or communion with God, whether by the aid of ritual or other means. The stress laid upon the last three points varies, but most Christian communities and many others, as the Mohammedans, include all five, and none would omit the first two, doctrine and morality.

When we turn to the Greeks we find of all these five points only one, prayer and ceremonial, as definitely established and recognized. The others, it is true, are not quite excluded. The performance of ceremonies implies belief in a being who can be approached by them, and who when approached has the power and will to help; but it implies nothing more about his nature. Morality again is present in so far as certain gods are guardians of certain rules of morality, and punish their breach. But the idea of gods as more than this, as essentially the source of moral law, and therefore its upholders always—this is no part of religion as commonly understood by the Greek, though poets and other moralists may inculcate it often enough. Again the Greeks have priests, but they do not form a separate class, and their functions do not usually go beyond the performance of ceremonial duties. They are not, as a rule, expected to be teachers or examples to their fellows. The last point mentioned, the belief in a mystic union with God, is also alien to the common religion of Greece. It is found in certain cults, such as the Orphic rites, but these were abnormal and suspect. Only prayer and ceremonial are universal and essential.

The modern student when he discovers

this to be the case, can hardly believe it, and most of his difficulties spring from an endeavour to evade the horrid fact that Greek Religion consisted of ceremonial. Most of all he is troubled by the absence of dogma. This, if he has been well brought up, he feels to be essential, and instinctively tries to provide. He therefore, in some cases, invests the statements of Homer and other early writers with something of the authority of the Bible; and he has this much justification that the Greeks themselves treated Homer as a moral teacher. This however leads him into difficulty. For, having invested Homer with this sanctity, and then observing that the Greeks as early as Xenophanes in the sixth century B.C. began to criticize the theology of Homer, he assumes that these attacks were as alarming to the normal Greek as *Essays and Reviews* and later more drastic criticisms were to a public that believed in the verbal inspiration of Holy Scripture. Our student has failed to notice that, though Homer was popularly treated as a moral teacher, his claim to that position had not been ratified by the decision of any Council, and that in fact there was not in Greece any central authority in matters of religion.

This point is vital, for it bears not only on this but on many other common errors. It is obvious, though often forgotten, that where there is no central authority, there can be no orthodox doctrine. Delphi to the beginner may seem the Rome of Greek Religion, but though its influence at some periods was considerable, it was never an authority on matters of doctrine. There was no central authority. The Greeks derived their ideas of the gods from Homer and the later poets, supplemented by local traditions. These had never been either canonized or systematized, and therefore we are in error if we think that criticism of their statements is comparable to criticism of the Holy Scripture in the eyes of early

Victorian Englishmen or American "Fundamentalists." No doubt the ordinary Greek was somewhat disturbed to hear the current beliefs criticized, whether they were expressed by Homer and the poets, or implied by local traditions, but this was only because human nature always resents disturbance of familiar beliefs. Such criticism was not in itself an attack upon religion. This point is vital and calls for fuller treatment.

In the case of religions which have a systematic theology, to attack any one of their cardinal dogmas is to assail the foundations. But a religion like the Greek, which has no coherent or authorized theology, is obviously not imperilled by any criticism which stops short of denying the existence of the gods and their power to help man. It is at once the strength and the weakness of such religions that they are founded not on dogma, but on ritual. This is a source of strength; for such a religion is more like a forest tree than a building of stone. If you destroy in a building any of its main supports, the whole collapses, but you may lop bough after bough from the tree, and it still lives and puts forth others. The religion of Greece is like a very ancient tree. There are fungi and parasites growing upon it, and some of its boughs decay, or are lopped off, but still it lives. It does not die until vitality forsakes even the root.

And if the root, as we maintain, be ritual, it may even be said that in a sense ancient religion never died, for much of the ritual survives with a new meaning in the observances of the Christian Church. It would be perverse to make too much of this, for the new meaning imposed on the ancient rite was often not merely different from the old, but adverse to it; but nevertheless it is not fantastic to say that the old religion did not wholly die. For if the meaning officially attached later to the rite was quite different, the spirit and ideas of the worshipper were not always so radically changed. In the most essential point of all, the feeling that rites and ceremonies in themselves are a sufficient means for procuring divine favour, paganism has not died yet.

The assertion that ritual is the foundation of Greek Religion will no doubt provoke scruples in many. First, if it is hard to understand how the more intelligent Greeks could swallow the thorns of their mythology, it is still harder to believe that they attached value to ritual not reinforced by theology or morality. Secondly Greek literature and history provide frequent instances of a higher conception of religion. Both these difficulties are serious, but not insuperable.

A religion resting chiefly upon ritual is doubtless unsatisfactory, and doubtless many Greeks felt it to be so. But the position was this. Few Greeks doubted that there were in the universe powers greater than themselves upon whom they were dependent, and who had the power and at least sometimes the will to help them. Sacrifice and ritual were the traditional method of approaching these powers and of obtaining their favour. The performance of such rites, even if the gods did not demand them as a price for favours, was at least a mark of respect and gratitude, and a proof that the worshipper acknowledged his dependence upon a higher power. And seeing that the performance of the rite implied no dogmatic statement as to the nature of the power worshipped, it could be performed in all sincerity by any one except an actual atheist. Greek Religion, in fact, from the first was compatible with a mild agnosticism. Questions and doubts in regard to the nature and ways of the gods go back as far as Homer. This being the case, the man who neglected the customary rites and sacrifices either declared himself an atheist or was guilty of ὕβρις. To disregard any duty enforced by tradition and the custom of his fathers,

came, in the eyes of a Greek, very near to ὕβρις; to refuse to the gods the customary worship, and thus defy their power and imply independence of it, was ὕβρις patent and unmistakable. Therefore we need not be surprised if Greeks as enlightened as Socrates and Aristotle showed regard for religious observances.

The second difficulty, as we saw, was the presence of higher ideas than those implied by a religion of outward observance. Such ideas we find, occasionally, in Homer, and more frequently and more definitely in later writers. It may therefore seem unfair to say that the essence of Greek Religion is ritual; but the statement is true, if rightly understood. It does not imply that the Greek had no ideas of his gods higher than could be inferred from his ritual, though that could be interpreted in a nobler way than as a mere traffic in benefits received in return for rites performed. The statement only implies that the outward observance was the one thing definitely fixed and demanded by custom, and the one which came first in the thoughts of the Greek.

When we inquire into a man's religion, we normally ask first what he believes, and then, if we are more exacting and precise, we ask whether he acts in accordance with his beliefs. We do not so naturally inquire whether he fulfils the outward observances of his religion. We rather assume that he does so; but even if we find that he is negligent in this respect, we do not, when the belief is present, deny that he has a religion at all. Though different communities of Christians would regard such negligence differently, some as venial and others as very serious, the strictest of all would hardly say that a man negligent in observance was therefore not a Christian; they would say rather that he was a "bad Christian."

With the Greek, as with most pagans, this order is reversed. When he asks a foreigner about his religion, he wishes to know what forms of worship he follows. The answer will probably include mention of the gods to whom worship is offered, but this mention will usually not go beyond a statement of their names, or of those of the Greek gods whom they most resemble. If the inquirer is persistent and the informant well informed, he may even elicit one or two of the stories told by these βάρβαροι about their gods, but this is more matter of curiosity than of vital importance. That this was so appears very clearly from descriptions of foreign religions in Herodotus and other writers. Herodotus, indeed, curious about all things human and divine, does tell us not a little of the beliefs and legends of foreign races as well as of their modes of worship. But even with him these are secondary. His frame of mind is not that of a modern traveller, or at least of a modern traveller before the days of anthropology. It is not what people believe, but what they do that is his chief concern. Indeed he even outstrips the anthropologist; for the anthropologist, though trained to observe external practices, observes them to discover the underlying idea. It is this which to him makes the practices worth studying, and he devotes more pains to discovering the beliefs, or non-beliefs of the Australian Arunta than Herodotus to the theology of the ancient Egyptians.

This frame of mind, of which Herodotus is typical, is, when we come to consider it, inevitable from the nature of the case. Where there is no recognized or central authority, no court of appeal in matters of doctrine, beliefs are inevitably fluid, and it is useles to inquire into them too precisely. You will not get a definite answer, or if you do, it will not be valid for all. For when beliefs have not been defined by authority, they vary in detail from man to man. And this variation does not imply that one man is less, or more, orthodox than his neigh-

bour. There is no orthodoxy; there is only piety; and piety is shown by a willing and reverent observance of the customary rites and ceremonies. These are definite and can be known and studied, and therefore it is these to which the ancient Greek looks when he is investigating the religion of a nation or an individual.

But rites and ceremonies, an obstinate questioner may say, are after all but "beggarly elements." If we cannot reasonably look for definite theology, surely we may look for morality. Unless these rites have at least some moral meaning they are obviously worthless, and no rational and reflecting man could take them seriously. The answer to this objection is that the rites undoubtedly have a moral meaning, or at least a moral value, but it is not of the kind which the questioner, if he be a normal modern European, expects at first sight. The average modern takes it for granted that a religion, if worthy of the name, must teach and inspire morality in its adherents. It must itself declare, with authority, in the name of God and as proceeding from him, what the laws of morality are; and must in various ways exact from its followers obedience to those laws, and must furnish incentives thereto, and it must make such obedience a condition and a test of sincere belief. Now Greek Religion does none of these things, or at least does not do them explicitly and directly. We have seen that it does not teach theology, and for the same reason it cannot teach morality. There is no authority to decide the laws of morality any more than the principles of theology. And having no recognized doctrine it cannot furnish clear and definite incentives to moral conduct. Moreover the rites which it employs are in many cases derived from a time of barbarism, and contain elements, and imply ideas, which seem to a civilized man immoral.

In spite of all this however, Greek Religion, even if outward observance is its essence, is far from being morally worthless. To begin with, the rules of the temple, or cult, exact of the worshipper at least ceremonial purity. And if this purity is originally only external, the transition from this to deeper things was easy, and comes early. Even in Homer we feel at times a perception that the gods demand not only clean hands but a pure heart (or at least the Greek equivalent for that, for their conception of moral purity was different). The germ of this belief is latent even in such a phrase as ὅς κε θεοῖς ἐπιπείθηται, μάλα τ᾽ ἔκλυον αὐτοῦ, "the gods hear best the prayer of him that obeys them"; and it appears more clearly elsewhere. In Hesiod the idea grows plainer, and it is reiterated in later literature. That the sacrifice of the righteous man is alone acceptable to the gods is a familiar idea, and it does not concern us here that the righteousness meant is itself somewhat external. So far as this, then, ritual is associated with morality, but it remains true that the essential thing is the ritual. For it alone is stable and definite; its connexion with morality is precarious.

It may well seem that we exaggerate in this the difference between the Greeks and the followers of later religions. Many men at all times, and nearly all men at some time, slip into the sin of regarding worship as a machinery for procuring divine favour. If only the nobler Greeks escaped this error, they were not, it may be said, so much unlike ourselves. But the difference is essential. The Christian and the Mohammedan, and the Jew after the time of the prophets, is explicitly and emphatically taught that a right spirit is more pleasing to God than sacrifice, though that is necessary too. If he fails to bring a right spirit to his sacrifice, it is not from ignorance. But to all but the more thoughtful and intelligent of the Greeks performance of the outward act is the essential. The ordinary pious rustic, sacrificing to Hermes or Pan and the Nymphs, would go away with a quiet mind, if he had decently and reverently offered sacrifice according to his power. He would not examine his conscience to discover whether his frame of mind and his conduct were such as to recommend him to the divine favour. This is clearly an important difference.

We have endeavoured to make good the proposition that the essence of Greek Religion was worship, and not belief or morality, and to show that in spite of this it received and deserved serious respect even from the more intelligent Greeks. If this proposition is true, the consequences are important, but can only be briefly indicated here. One consequence we have already noted. Criticisms of mythology, and even criticisms of particular beliefs about the nature of the gods, are not of necessity attacks upon religion or expressions of general disbelief. When they occur in writers like Pindar and Aeschylus, who are essentially reverent and friendly, such criticisms are rather a proof of belief than of unbelief. They desire to clear the gods of unworthy imputations. This does not imply that the friendly critic accepts as true and edifying those parts of mythology and traditional belief that he does not criticize. It means rather that, theology being fluid, and mythology not subject to any canon, every man is free to take or reject, and to interpret, the tradition according to his ideas of right and probability. The traditions concerning the gods are in fact in the position of the Apocrypha as defined by the Thirty-nine Articles. They may be read for edification, but not to establish doctrine.

C · RELIGION AS EUFUNCTIONAL

1 · Piacular Rites and the Ambiguity of the Notion of Sacredness

EMILE DURKHEIM

Howsoever much they may differ from one another in the nature of the gestures they imply, the positive rites which we have been passing under review have one common characteristic: they are all performed in a state of confidence, joy and even enthusiasm. Though the expectation of a future and contingent event is not without a certain uncertainty, still it is normal that the rain fall when the season for it comes, and that the animal and vegetable species reproduce regularly. Oft-repeated experiences have shown that the rites generally do produce the effects which are expected of them and which are the reason for their existence. Men celebrate them with confidence, joyfully anticipating the happy event which they prepare and announce. Whatever movements men perform participate in this same state of mind: of course, they are marked with the gravity which a religious solemnity always supposes, but this gravity excludes neither animation nor joy.

SOURCE. Emile Durkheim, *The Elementary Forms of the Religious Life*, New York: Macmillan, 1926, pp. 389–414. Reprinted with permission of The Free Press of Glencoe. First published in 1954.

These are all joyful feasts. But there are sad celebrations as well, whose object is either to meet a calamity, or else merely to commemorate and deplore it. These rites have a special aspect, which we are going to attempt to characterize and explain. It is the more necessary to study them by themselves since they are going to reveal a new aspect of the religious life to us.

We propose to call the ceremonies of this sort piacular. The term *piaculum* has the advantage that while it suggests the idea of expiation, it also has a much more extended signification. Every misfortune, everything of evil omen, everything that inspires sentiments of sorrow or fear necessitates a *piaculum* and is therefore called piacular.[1] So this word seems to be very well adapted for designating the rites which are celebrated by those in a state of uneasiness or sadness.

[1] *Piacularia auspicia appellabant quæ sacrificantibus tristia portendebant* (Paul ex Fest., p. 244, ed. Müller). The word *piaculum* is even used as a synonym of misfortune. "*Vetonica herba*," says Pliny, "*tantum gloriæ habet ut domus in qua sita sit tuta existimetur a piaculis omnibus*" (XXV, 8, 46).

I

Mourning offers us a first and important example of piacular rites.

However, a distinction is necessary between the different rites which go to make up mourning. Some consist in mere abstentions: it is forbidden to pronounce the name of the dead,[2] or to remain near the place where the death occurred;[3] relatives, especially the female ones, must abstain from all communication with strangers;[4] the ordinary occupations of life are suspended, just as in feast-time,[5] etc. All these practices belong to the negative cult and are explained like the other rites of the same sort, so they do not concern us at present. They are due to the fact that the dead man is a sacred being. Consequently, everything which is or has been connected with him is, by contagion, in a religious state excluding all contact with things from profane life.

But mourning is not made up entirely of interdicts which have to be observed. Positive acts are also demanded, in which the relatives are both the actors and those acted upon.

Very frequently these rites commence as soon as the death appears imminent. Here is a scene which Spencer and Gillen witnessed among the Warramunga. A totemic ceremony had just been celebrated and the company of actors and spectators was leaving the consecrated ground when a piercing cry suddenly came from the camp: a man was dying there. At once, the whole company commenced to run as fast as they could, while most of them commenced to howl.

"Between us and the camp," say these observers, "lay a deep creek, and on the bank of this, some of the men, scattered about here and there, sat down, bending their heads forwards between their knees, while they wept and moaned. Crossing the creek we found that, as usual, the men's camp had been pulled to pieces. Some of the women, who had come from every direction, were lying prostrate on the body, while others were standing or kneeling around, digging the sharp ends of yam-sticks into the crown of their heads, from which the blood streamed down over their faces, while all the time they kept up a loud, continuous wail. Many of the men, rushing up to the spot, threw themselves upon the body, from which the women arose when the men approached, until in a few minutes we could see nothing but a struggling mass of bodies all mixed up together. To one side, three men of the Thapungarti class, who still wore their ceremonial decorations, sat down wailing loudly, with their backs towards the dying man, and in a minute or two another man of the same class rushed on to the ground yelling and brandishing a stone knife. Reaching the camp, he suddenly gashed both thighs deeply, cutting right across the muscles, and, unable to stand, fell down into the middle of the group, from which he was dragged out after a time by three or four female relatives, who immediately applied their mouths to the gaping wounds while he lay exhausted on the ground." The man did not actually die until late in the evening. As soon as he had given up his last breath, the same scene was re-enacted, only this time the wailing was still louder, and men and women, seized by a veritable frenzy, were rushing about cutting themselves with knives and sharp-pointed sticks, the women battering one another's heads with fighting clubs, no one attempting to ward off either cuts or blows. Finally, after about an hour, a torchlight procession started off across

[2] Spencer and Gillen, *Northern Tribes of Central Australia* (hereafter *Nor. Tr.*), p. 526; Eylmann, *Die Eingeborenen der Kolonie Südaustralien*, p. 239. Cf. *El. Forms*, p. 305.
[3] Brough Smyth, *The Aborigines of Victoria*, I, p. 106; Dawson, *Australian Aborigines*, p. 64; Eylmann, p. 239.
[4] Dawson, p. 66; Eylmann, p. 241.
[5] *Native Tribes*, p. 502; Dawson, p. 67.

the plain, to a tree in whose branches the body was left.[6]

Howsoever great the violence of these manifestations may be, they are strictly regulated by etiquette. The individuals who make bloody incisions in themselves are designated by usage: they must have certain relations of kinship with the dead man. Thus, in the case observed by Spencer and Gillen among the Warramunga, those who slashed their thighs were the maternal grandfather of the deceased, his maternal uncle, and the maternal uncle and brother of his wife.[7] Others must cut their whiskers and hair, and then smear their scalps with pipe-clay. Women have particularly severe obligations. They must cut their hair and cover the whole body with pipe-clay; in addition to this, a strict silence is imposed upon them during the whole period of mourning, which may last as long as two years. It is not rare among the Warramunga that, as a result of this interdiction, all the women of a camp are condemned to the most absolute silence. This becomes so habitual to them that even after the expiration of the period of mourning, they voluntarily renounce all spoken language and prefer to communicate with gestures—in which, by the way, they acquire a remarkable ability. Spencer and Gillen knew one old woman who had not spoken for over twenty-four years.[8]

The ceremony which we have described opens a long series of rites which succeed one another for weeks and even for months. During the days which follow, they are renewed in various forms. Groups of men and women sit on the ground, weeping and lamenting, and kissing each other at certain moments. These ritual kissings are repeated frequently during the period of mourning. It seems as though men felt a need of coming close together and communicating most closely; they are to be seen holding to each other and wound together so much as to make one single mass, from which loud groans escape.[9] Meanwhile, the women commence to lacerate their heads again, and, in order to intensify the wounds they make, they even go so far as to burn them with the points of fiery sticks.[10]

Practices of this sort are general in all Australia. The funeral rites, that is, the ritual cares given to the corpse, the way in which it is buried, etc., change with different tribes,[11] and in a single tribe they vary with the age, sex and social importance of the individual.[12] But the real ceremonies of mourning repeat the same theme everywhere; the variations are only in the details. Everywhere we

---

[6] *Nor. Tr.*, pp. 516–517.
[7] *Ibid.*, pp. 520–521. The authors do not say whether these were tribal or blood relatives. The former hypothesis is the more probable one.
[8] *Nor. Tr.*, pp. 525 f. This interdiction against speaking, which is peculiar to women, though it consists in a simple abstention, has all the appearance of a piacular rite: it is a way of incommoding one's self. Therefore we mention it here. Also, fasting may be a piacular rite or an ascetic one, according to the circumstances. Everything depends upon the conditions in which

it takes place and the end pursued (for the difference between these two sorts of rites, see *El. Forms*, p. 396).
[9] A very expressive illustration showing this rite will be found in *Nor. Tr.*, p. 525.
[10] *Ibid.*, p. 522.
[11] For the principal forms of funeral rites, see Howitt, *Native Tribes*, pp. 446–508, for the tribes of the South-East; Spencer and Gillen, *Nor Tr.*, p. 505, and *Native Tribes*, pp. 497 ff., for those of the centre; Roth, *Nor. Queensland Ethnog.*, Bull. 9, in *Records of the Australian Museum*, VI, No. 5, pp. 365 ff. (*Burial Customs and Disposal of the Dead*).
[12] See, for example, Roth, *loc. cit.*, p. 368; Eyre, *Journals of Exped. into Central Aust.*, II, pp. 344 f.

find this same silence interrupted by groans,[13] the same obligation of cutting the hair and beard,[14] or of covering one's head with pipe-clay or cinders, or perhaps even with excrements;[15] everywhere, finally, we find this same frenzy for beating one's self, lacerating one's self and burning one's self. In central Victoria, "when death visits a tribe there is great weeping and lamentation amongst the women, the elder portion of whom lacerate their temples with their nails. The parents of the deceased lacerate themselves fearfully, especially if it be an only son whose loss they deplore. The father beats and cuts his head with a tomahawk until he utters bitter groans, the mother sits by the fire and burns her breasts and abdomen with a small firestick. Sometimes the burns thus inflicted are so severe as to cause death." [16]

According to an account of Brough Smyth, here is what happens in one of the southern tribes of the same state. As the body is lowered into the grave, "the widow begins her sad ceremonies. She cuts off her hair above her forehead, and becoming frantic, seizes fire-sticks, and burns her breasts, arms, legs and thighs. She seems to delight in the self-inflicted torture. It would be rash and vain to interrupt her. When exhausted, and when she can hardly walk, she yet endeavours to kick the embers of the fire, and to throw them about. Sitting down, she takes the ashes into her hands, rubs them into her wounds, and then scratches her face (the only part not touched by the fire-sticks) until the blood mingles with the ashes, which partly hide her

cruel wounds. In this plight, scratching her face continually, she utters howls and lamentations." [17]

The description which Howitt gives of the rites of mourning among the Kurnai is remarkably similar to these others. After the body has been wrapped up in oppossum skins and put in a shroud of bark, a hut is built in which the relatives assemble. "There they lay lamenting their loss, saying, for instance, 'Why did you leave us?' Now and then their grief would be intensified by some one, for instance, the wife, uttering an ear-piercing wail, 'My spouse is dead,' or another would say, 'My child is dead.' All the others would then join in with the proper term of relationship, and they would gash themselves with sharp stones and tomahawks until their heads and bodies streamed with blood. This bitter wailing and weeping continued all night." [18]

Sadness is not the only sentiment expressed during these ceremonies; a sort of anger is generally mixed with it. The relatives feel a need of avenging the death in some way or other. They are to be seen throwing themselves upon one another and trying to wound each other. Sometimes the attack is real; sometimes it is only pretended.[19] There are even cases when these peculiar combats are organized. Among the Kaitish, the hair of the deceased passes by right to his son-in-law. But he, in return, must go, in company with some of his relatives and friends, and provoke a quarrel with one of his tribal brothers, that is, with a man belonging to the same matrimonial class as himself and one who might therefore have married the daughter of the

[13] Spencer and Gillen, *Native Tribes*, p. 500; *Nor. Tr.*, pp. 507, 508; Eylmann, p. 241; Parker, *Euahlayi*, pp. 83 ff.; Brough Smyth, I, p. 118.

[14] Dawson, p. 66; Howitt, *Native Tribes*, p. 466; Eylmann, pp. 239–240.

[15] Brough Smyth, I, p. 113.

[16] W. E. Stanbridge, *Trans. Ethnological Society of London*, N.S., Vol. I, p. 286.

[17] Brough Smyth, I, p. 14.

[18] Howitt, *Native Tribes*, p. 459. Similar scenes will be found in Eyre, *op. cit.*, II, p. 255, n., and p. 347; Roth, *loc. cit.*, pp. 394, 395, for example; Grey, *Journal of Two Expeditions*, II, pp. 320 ff.

[19] Brough Smyth, I, pp. 104, 112; Roth, *loc. cit.*, p. 382.

dead man. This provocation cannot be refused and the two combatants inflict serious wounds upon each other's shoulders and thighs. When the duel is terminated, the challenger passes on to his adversary the hair which he had temporarily inherited. This latter then provokes and fights with another of his tribal brothers, to whom the precious relic is next transmitted, but only provisionally; thus it passes from hand to hand and circulates from group to group.[20] Also, something of these same sentiments enters into that sort of rage with which each relative beats himself, burns himself or slashes himself: a sorrow which reaches such a paroxysm is not without a certain amount of anger. One cannot fail to be struck by the resemblances which these practices present to those of the vendetta. Both proceed from the same principle that death demands the shedding of blood. The only difference is that in one case the victims are the relatives, while in the other they are strangers. We do not have to treat especially of the vendetta, which belongs rather to the study of juridic institutions; but it should be pointed out, nevertheless, how it is connected with the rites of mourning, whose end it announces.[21]

In certain societies, the mourning is terminated by a ceremony whose effervescence reaches or surpasses that produced by the inaugural ceremonies. Among the Arunta, this closing rite is called *Urpmilchima*. Spencer and Gillen assisted at two of these rites. One was celebrated in honour of a man, the other of a woman. Here is the description they give of the latter.[22]

They commence by making some ornaments of a special sort, called *Chimurilia*

by the men and *Aramurilia* by the women. With a kind of resin, they fixed small animal bones, which had previously been gathered and set aside, to locks of hair furnished by the relatives of the dead woman. These are then attached to one of the head-bands which women ordinarily wear and the feathers of black cockatoos and parrots are added to it. When these preparations are completed, the women assemble in their camp. They paint their bodies different colours, according to their degree of kinship with the deceased. After being embraced by one another for some ten minutes, while uttering uninterrupted groans, they set out for the tomb. At a certain distance, they meet a brother by blood of the dead woman, who is accompanied by some of his tribal brothers. Everybody sits down on the ground, and the lamentations recommence. A *pitchi*[23] containing the Chimurilia is then presented to the elder brother, who presses it against his stomach; they say that this is a way of lessening his sorrow. They take out one of the Chimurilia and the dead woman's mother puts it on her head for a little while; then it is put back into the *pitchi*, which each of the other men presses against his breast, in his turn. Finally, the brother puts the Chimurilia on the heads of two elder sisters and they set out again for the tomb. On the way, the mother throws herself on the ground several times, and tries to slash her head with a pointed stick. Every time, the other women pick her up, and seem to take care that she does not hurt herself too much. When they arrive at the tomb, she throws herself on the knoll and endeavours to destroy it with her hands, while the other women literally dance upon her. The tribal mothers and aunts (sisters of the dead woman's father) follow her example; they also throw

[20] *Nor. Tr.*, pp. 511–512.
[21] Dawson, p. 67; Roth, *loc. cit.*, pp. 366–367.
[22] *Native Tribes*, pp. 508–510.

[23] A little wooden vessel, of which we spoke on p. 334 of *El. Forms*.

themselves on the ground, and mutually beat and tear each other; finally their bodies are all streaming with blood. After a while, they are dragged aside. The elder sisters then make a hole in the earth of the tomb, in which they place the Chimurilia, which had previously been torn to pieces. Once again the tribal mothers throw themselves on the ground and slash each other's heads. At this moment, "the weeping and wailing of the women who were standing round seemed to drive them almost frenzied, and the blood, streaming down their bodies over the white pipe-clay, gave them a ghastly appearance. At last only the old mother was left crouching alone, utterly exhausted and moaning weakly on the grave." [24] Then the others raised her up and rubbed off the pipe-clay with which she was covered; this was the end of the ceremony and of the mourning.[24]

Among the Warramunga, the final rite presents some rather particular characteristics. There seems to be no shedding of blood here, but the collective effervescence is translated in another manner.

Among this people, before the body is definitely interred, it is exposed upon a platform placed in the branches of a tree; it is left there to decompose slowly, until nothing remains but the bones. Then these are gathered together and, with the exception of the humerus, they are placed inside an ant-hill. The humerus is wrapped up in a bark box, which is decorated in different manners. The box is then brought to camp, amid the cries and groans of the women. During the following days, they celebrate a series of totemic rites, concerning the totem of the deceased and the mythical history of the ancestors from whom the clan is descended. When all these ceremonies have been terminated, they proceed to the closing rite.

A trench one foot deep and fifteen feet long is dug in the field of the ceremony. A design representing the totem of the deceased and certain spots where the ancestor stopped is made on the ground a little distance from it. Near this design, a little ditch is dug in the ground. Ten decorated men then advance, one behind another, and with their hands crossed behind their heads and their legs wide apart they stand astraddle the trench. At a given signal, the women run from the camp in a profound silence; when they are near, they form in Indian file, the last one holding in her hands the box containing the humerus. Then, after throwing themselves on the ground, they advance on their hands and knees, and pass all along the trench, between the legs of the men. The scene shows a state of great sexual excitement. As soon as the last woman has passed, they take the box from her, and take it to the ditch, near which is an old man; he breaks the bone with a sharp blow, and hurriedly buries it in the debris. During this time, the women have remained at a distance, with their backs turned upon the scene, for they must not see it. But when they hear the blow of the axe, they flee, uttering cries and groans. The rite is accomplished; the mourning is terminated.[25]

II

These rites belong to a very different type from those which we have studied hitherto. We do not mean to say that important resemblances cannot be found between the two, which we shall have to note; but the differences are more apparent. Instead of happy dances, songs

---

[24] *Native Tribes,* pp. 508–510. The other final rite at which Spencer and Gillen assisted is described on pp. 503–508 of the same work. It does not differ essentially from the one we have analysed.

[25] *Nor. Tr.* pp. 531–540.

and dramatic representations which distract and relax the mind, they are tears and groans and, in a word, the most varied manifestations of agonized sorrow and a sort of mutual pity, which occupy the whole scene. Of course the shedding of blood also takes place in the Intichiuma, but this is an oblation made with a movement of pious enthusiasm. Even though the motions may be the same, the sentiments expressed are different and even opposed. Likewise, the ascetic rites certainly imply privations, abstinences and mutilations, but ones which must be borne with an impassive firmness and serenity. Here, on the contrary, dejection, cries and tears are the rule. The ascetic tortures himself in order to prove, in his own eyes and those of his fellows, that he is above suffering. During mourning, men injure themselves to prove that they suffer. By all these signs, the characteristic traits of the piacular rites are to be recognized.

But how are they to be explained?

One initial fact is constant: mourning is not the spontaneous expression of individual emotions.[26] If the relations weep, lament, mutilate themselves, it is not because they feel themselves personally affected by the death of their kinsman. Of course, it may be that in certain particular cases, the chagrin expressed is really felt.[27] But it is more generally the case that there is no connection between the sentiments felt and the gestures made by the actors in the rite.[28] If, at the very moment when the weepers seem the most overcome by their grief, some one speaks to them of some temporal interest, it frequently happens that they change their features and tone at once, take on a laughing air and converse in the gayest fashion imaginable.[29] Mourning is not a natural movement of private feelings wounded by a cruel loss; it is a duty imposed by the group. One weeps, not simply because he is sad, but because he is forced to weep. It is a ritual attitude which he is forced to adopt out of respect for custom, but which is, in a large measure, independent of his affective state. Moreover, this obligation is sanctioned by mythical or social penalties. They believe, for example, that if a relative does not mourn as is fitting, then the soul of the departed follows upon his steps and kills him.[30] In other cases, society does not leave it to the religious forces to punish the negligent; it intervenes itself, and reprimands the ritual faults. If a son-in-law does not render to his father-in-law the funeral attentions which are due him, and if he does not make the prescribed incisions, then his tribal fathers-in-law take his wife away from him and give him another.[31] Therefore, in order to square himself with usage, a man sometimes forces tears to flow by artificial means.[32]

Whence comes this obligation?

Ethnographers and sociologists are generally satisfied with the reply which the natives themselves give to this question. They say that the dead wish to be lamented, that by refusing them the tribute of sorrow which is their right, men offend them, and that the only way of preventing their anger is to conform to their will.[33]

But this mythological interpretation merely modifies the terms of the problem, without resolving it; it is still necessary to explain why the dead imperatively reclaim the mourning. It may be said that

---

[26] Contrarily to what Jevons says, *Introduction to the History of Religion*, pp. 46 ff.
[27] This makes Dawson say that the mourning is sincere (p. 66). But Eylmann assures us that he never knew a single case where there was a wound from sorrow really felt (*op. cit.*, p. 113).
[28] *Native Tribes*, p. 510.

[29] Eylmann, pp. 238–239.
[30] *Nor. Tr.*, p. 507; *Native Tribes*, p. 498.
[31] *Native Tribes*, p. 500; Eylmann, p. 227.
[32] Brough Smyth, I, p. 114.
[33] *Native Tribes*, p. 510.

it is natural for men to wish to be mourned and regretted. But in making this sentiment explain the complex system of rites which make up mourning, we attribute to the Australian affective exigencies of which the civilized man himself does not always give evidence. Let us admit—as is not evident *a priori* —that the idea of not being forgotten too readily is pleasing to a man who thinks of the future. It is still to be established that it has ever had enough importance in the minds of the living for one to attribute to the dead a state of mind proceeding almost entirely from this preoccupation. It seems especially improbable that such a sentiment could obsess and impassion men who are seldom accustomed to thinking beyond the present moment. So far is it from being a fact that the desire to survive in the memory of those who are still alive is to be regarded as the origin of mourning, that we may even ask ourselves whether it was not rather mourning itself which, when once established, aroused the idea of and the taste for posthumous regrets.

The classic interpretation appears still more unsustainable when we know what the primitive mourning consists in. It is not made up merely of pious regrets accorded to him who no longer is, but also of severe abstinences and cruel sacrifices. The rite does not merely demand that one think of the deceased in a melancholy way, but also that he beat himself, bruise himself, lacerate himself and burn himself. We have even seen that persons in mourning sometimes torture themselves to such a degree that they do not survive their wounds. What reason has the dead man for imposing such torments upon them? Such a cruelty on his part denotes something more than a desire not to be forgotten. If he is to find pleasure in seeing his own suffer, it is necessary that he hate them, that he be thirsty for their blood. This ferocity would undoubtedly appear natural to those for whom every spirit is necessarily an evil and redoubted power. But we know that there are spirits of every sort; how does it happen that the soul of the dead man is necessarily an evil spirit? As long as the man is alive, he loves his relatives and exchanges services with them. Is it not strange that as soon as it is freed from his body, his soul should instantly lay aside its former sentiments and become an evil and tormenting genius? It is a general rule that the dead man retains the personality of the living, and that he has the same character, the same hates and the same affections. So this metamorphosis is not easily understandable by itself. It is true that the natives admit it implicitly when they explain the rite by the exigencies of the dead man, but the question now before us is to know whence this conception came. Far from being capable of being regarded as a truism, it is as obscure as the rite itself, and consequently cannot account for it.

Finally, even if we had found the reasons for this surprising transformation, we would still have to explain why it is only temporary. For it does not last beyond the period of mourning; after the rites have once been accomplished, the dead man becomes what he was when alive, an affectionate and devoted relation. He puts the new powers which he receives from his new condition at the service of his friends.[34] Thenceforth, he is regarded as a good genius, always ready to aid those whom he was recently tormenting. Whence come these successive transfers? If the evil sentiments attributed to the soul come solely from the fact that it is no longer in life, they should remain invariable, and if the mourning is due to this, it should be interminable.

[34] Several examples of this belief are to be found in Howitt, *Native Tribes*, p. 435. Cf. Strehlow, I, 15–16; II, p. 7.

These mythical explanations express the idea which the native has of the rite, and not the rite itself. So we may set them aside and face the reality which they translate, though disfiguring it in doing so. If mourning differs from the other forms of the positive cult, there is one feature in which it resembles them: it, too, is made up out of collective ceremonies which produce a state of effervescence among those who take part in them. The sentiments aroused are different; but the arousal is the same. So it is presumable that the explanation of the joyous rites is capable of being applied to the sad rites, on condition that the terms be transposed.

When some one dies, the family group to which he belongs feels itself lessened and, to react against this loss, it assembles. A common misfortune has the same effects as the approach of a happy event: collective sentiments are renewed which then lead men to seek one another and to assemble together. We have even seen this need for concentration affirm itself with a particular energy: they embrace one another, put their arms round one another, and press as close as possible to one another. But the affective state in which the group then happens to be only reflects the circumstances through which it is passing. Not only do the relatives, who are affected the most directly, bring their own personal sorrow to the assembly, but the society exercises a moral pressure over its members, to put their sentiments in harmony with the situation. To allow them to remain indifferent to the blow which has fallen upon it and diminished it, would be equivalent to proclaiming that it does not hold the place in their hearts which is due it; it would be denying itself. A family which allows one of its members to die without being wept for shows by that very fact that it lacks moral unity and cohesion: it abdicates; it renounces its existence. An individual, in his turn, if he is strongly

attached to the society of which he is a member, feels that he is morally held to participating in its sorrows and joys; not to be interested in them would be equivalent to breaking the bonds uniting him to the group; it would be renouncing all desire for it and contradicting himself. When the Christian, during the ceremonies commemorating the Passion, and the Jew, on the anniversary of the fall of Jerusalem, fast and mortify themselves, it is not in giving way to a sadness which they feel spontaneously. Under these circumstances, the internal state of the believer is out of all proportion to the severe abstinences to which they submit themselves. If he is sad, it is primarily because he consents to being sad, and he consents to it in order to affirm his faith. The attitude of the Australian during mourning is to be explained in the same way. If he weeps and groans, it is not merely to express an individual chagrin; it is to fulfil a duty of which the surrounding society does not fail to remind him.

We have seen elsewhere how human sentiments are intensified when affirmed collectively. Sorrow, like joy, becomes exalted and amplified when leaping from mind to mind, and therefore expresses itself outwardly in the form of exuberant and violent movements. But these are no longer expressive of the joyful agitation which we observed before; they are shrieks and cries of pain. Each is carried along by the others; a veritable panic of sorrow results. When pain reaches this degree of intensity, it is mixed with a sort of anger and exasperation. One feels the need of breaking something, of destroying something. He takes this out either upon himself or others. He beats himself, burns himself, wounds himself or else he falls upon others to beat, burn and wound them. Thus it became the custom to give one's self up to the veritable orgies of tortures during mourning. It seems very probable that blood-revenge and head-hunting have their origin in this. If every death is attributed to some magic charm, and for this reason it is believed that the dead man ought to be avenged, it is because men must find a victim at any price, upon whom the collective pain and anger may be discharged. Naturally this victim is sought outside the group; a stranger is a subject *minoris resistentiæ;* as he is not protected by the sentiments of sympathy inspired by a relative or neighbour, there is nothing in him which subdues and neutralizes the evil and destructive sentiments aroused by the death. It is undoubtedly for this same reason that women serve more frequently than men as the passive objects of the cruellest rites of mourning; since they have a smaller social value, they are more obviously designated as scapegoats.

We see that this explanation of mourning completely leaves aside all ideas of souls or spirits. The only forces which are really active are of a wholly impersonal nature: they are the emotions aroused in the group by the death of one of its members. But the primitive does not know the psychical mechanism from which these practices result. So when he tries to account for them, he is obliged to forge a wholly different explanation. All he knows is that he must painfully mortify himself. As every obligation suggests the notion of a will which obliges, he looks about him to see whence this constraint which he feels may come. Now, there is one moral power, of whose reality he is assured and which seems designated for this rôle: this is the soul which the death has liberated. For what could have a greater interest than it in the effects which its own death has on the living? So they imagine that if these latter inflict an unnatural treatment upon themselves, it is to conform to its exigencies. It was thus that the idea of the soul must have intervened at a later date into the mythology of mourning. But

also, since it is thus endowed with inhuman exigencies, it must be supposed that in leaving the body which it animated, the soul lays aside every human sentiment. Hence the metamorphosis which makes a dreaded enemy out of the relative of yesterday. This transformation is not the origin of mourning; it is rather its consequence. It translates a change which has come over the affective state of the group: men do not weep for the dead because they fear them; they fear them because they weep for them.

But this change of the affective state can only be a temporary one, for while the ceremonies of mourning result from it, they also put an end to it. Little by little, they neutralize the very causes which have given rise to them. The foundation of mourning is the impression of a loss which the group feels when it loses one of its members. But this very impression results in bringing individuals together, in putting them into closer relations with one another, in associating them all in the same mental state, and therefore in disengaging a sensation of comfort which compensates the original loss. Since they weep together, they hold to one another and the group is not weakened, in spite of the blow which has fallen upon it. Of course they have only sad emotions in common, but communicating in sorrow is still communicating, and every communion of mind, in whatever form it may be made, raises the social vitality. The exceptional violence of the manifestations by which the common pain is necessarily and obligatorily expressed even testifies to the fact that at this moment, the society is more alive and active than ever. In fact, whenever the social sentiment is painfully wounded, it reacts with greater force than ordinarily: one never holds so closely to his family as when it has just suffered. This surplus energy effaces the more completely the effects of the interruption which was felt at first, and thus dissipates the feeling of coldness which death always brings with it. The group feels its strength gradually returning to it; it begins to hope and to live again. Presently one stops mourning, and he does so owing to the mourning itself. But as the idea formed of the soul reflects the moral state of the society, this idea should change as this state changes. When one is in the period of dejection and agony, he represents the soul with the traits of an evil being, whose sole occupation is to persecute men. But when he feels himself confident and secure once more, he must admit that it has retaken its former nature and its former sentiments of tenderness and solidarity. Thus we explain the very different ways in which it is conceived at different moments of its existence.[35]

Not only do the rites of mourning determine certain of the secondary characteristics attributed to the soul, but perhaps they are not foreign to the idea that it survives the body. If he is to understand the practices to which he submits on the death of a parent, a man is obliged to believe that these are not an indifferent matter for the deceased. The shedding of blood which is practised so freely during mourning is a veritable sacrifice offered to the dead man.[36] So

[35] It may be asked why repeated ceremonies are necessary to produce the relief which follows upon mourning. The funeral ceremonies are frequently very long; they include many operations which take place at intervals during many months. Thus they prolong and support the moral disturbance brought about by the death (cf. Hertz, *La Répresentation collective de la mort*, in *Année Sociol.*, X, pp. 48 ff.). In a general way, a death marks a grave change of condition which has extended and enduring effects upon the group. It takes a long time to neutralize these effects.

[36] In a case reported by Grey from the observations of Bussel, the rite has all the aspects of a sacrifice: the blood is sprinkled over the body itself (Grey, II, p. 330). In

something of the dead man must survive, and as this is not the body, which is manifestly immobile and decomposed, it can only be the soul. Of course it is impossible to say with any exactness what part these considerations have had in the origin of the idea of immortality. But it is probable that here the influence of the cult is the same as it is elsewhere. Rites are more easily explicable when one imagines that they are addressed to personal beings; so men have been induced to extend the influence of the mythical personalities in the religious life. In order to account for mourning, they have prolonged the existence of the soul beyond the tomb. This is one more example of the way in which rites react upon beliefs.

III

But death is not the only event which may disturb a community. Men have many other occasions for being sorry and lamenting, so we might foresee that even the Australians would know and practise other piacular rites besides mourning. However, it is a remarkable fact that only a small number of examples are to be found in the accounts of the observers.

One rite of this sort greatly resembles those which have just been studied. It will be remembered that among the Arunta, each local group attributes exceptionally important virtues to its collection of churinga: this is this collective palladium, upon whose fate the fate of the community itself is believed to depend. So when enemies or white men succeed in stealing one of these religious treasures, this loss is considered a public calamity. This misfortune is the occasion of a rite having all the characteristics of

other cases, there is something like an offering of the beard: men in mourning cut off a part of their beards, which they throw on to the corpse (*ibid.*, p. 335).

mourning: men smear their bodies with white pipe-clay and remain in camp, weeping and lamenting, during a period of two weeks.[37] This is a new proof that mourning is determined, not by the way in which the soul of the dead is conceived, but by impersonal causes, by the moral state of the group. In fact, we have here a rite which, in its structure, is indistinguishable from the real mourning, but which is, nevertheless, independent of every notion of spirits or evil-working demons.[38]

Another circumstance which gives occasion for ceremonies of the same nature is the distress in which the society finds itself after an insufficient harvest. "The natives who live in the vicinity of Lake Eyre," says Eylmann, "also seek to prevent an insufficiency of food by means of secret ceremonies. But many of the ritual practices observed in this region are to be distinguished from those which have been mentioned already: it is not by symbolic dances, by imitative movements nor dazzling decorations that they try to act upon the religious powers or the forces of nature, but by means of the suffering which individuals inflict upon themselves. In the northern territories, it is by means of tortures, such as prolonged fasts, vigils, dances persisted in up to the exhaustion of the dancers, and physical pains of every sort, that they attempt to appease the powers which are ill-disposed towards men." [39] The torments to which the natives submit themselves for this purpose sometimes leave them in such a state of exhaustion

that they are unable to follow the hunt for some days to come.[40]

These practices are employed especially for fighting against drought. This is because a scarcity of water results in a general want. To remedy this evil, they have recourse to violent methods. One which is frequently used is the extraction of a tooth. Among the Kaitish, for example, they pull out an incisor from one man, and hang it on a tree.[41] Among the Dieri, the idea of rain is closely associated with that of bloody incisions made in the skin of the chest and arms.[42] Among this same people, whenever the drought is very great, the great council assembles and summons the whole tribe. It is really a tribal event. Women are sent in every direction to notify men to assemble at a given place and time. After they have assembled, they groan and cry in a piercing voice about the miserable state of the land, and they beg the *Muramura* (the mythical ancestors) to give them the power of making an abundant rain fall.[43] In the cases, which, by the way, are very rare, when there has been an excessive rainfall, an analogous ceremony takes place to stop it. Old men then enter into a veritable frenzy,[44] while the cries uttered by the crowd are really painful to hear.[45]

Spencer and Gillen describe, under the name of Intichiuma, a ceremony which may well have the same object and the same origin as the preceding ones: a physical torture is applied to make an animal species multiply. Among the Urabunna, there is one clan whose totem is a variety of snake called *wadnun-*

[37] *Native Tribes,* pp. 135–136.

[38] Of course each churinga is believed to be connected with an ancestor. But it is not to appease the spirits of the ancestors that they mourn for the lost churinga. We have shown elsewhere (*El. Forms,* p. 123) that the idea of the ancestor only entered into the conception of the churinga secondarily and late.

[39] *Op. cit.,* p. 207; cf. p. 116.

[40] Eylmann, p. 208.

[41] *Ibid.,* p. 211.

[42] Howitt, *The Dieri,* in *J.A.I.,* XX (1891), p. 93.

[43] Howitt, *Native Tribes,* p. 394.

[44] Howitt, *ibid.,* p. 396.

[45] Communication of Gason in *J.A.I.,* XXIV (1895), p. 175.

gadni. This is how the chief of the clan proceeds, to make sure that these snakes may never be lacking. After having been decorated, he kneels down on the ground, holding his arms straight out. An assistant pinches the skin of his right arm between his fingers, and the officiant forces a pointed bone five inches long through the fold thus formed. This self-mutilation is believed to produce the desired result.[46] An analogous rite is used among the Dieri to make the wild-hens lay: the operators pierce their scrotums.[47] In certain of the Lake Eyre tribes, men pierce their ears to make yams reproduce.[48]

But these partial or total famines are not the only plagues which may fall upon a tribe. Other events happen more or less periodically which menace, or seem to menace, the existence of the group. This is the case, for example, with the southern lights. The Kurnai believe that this is a fire lighted in the heavens by the great god Mungan-ngaua; therefore, whenever they see it, they are afraid that it may spread to the earth and devour them, so a great effervescence results in the camp. They shake a withered hand, to which the Kurnai attribute various virtues, and utter such cries as "Send it away; do not let us be burned." At the same time, the old men order an exchange of wives, which always indicates a great excitement.[49] The same sexual licence is mentioned among the Wiimbaio whenever a plague appears imminent, and especially in times of an epidemic.[50]

Under the influence of these ideas, mutilations and the shedding of blood are sometimes considered an efficient means of curing maladies. If an accident happens to a child among the Dieri, his relations beat themselves on the head with clubs or boomerangs until the blood flows down over their faces. They believe that by this process, they relieve the child of the suffering.[51] Elsewhere, they imagine that they can obtain the same end by means of a supplementary totemic ceremony.[52] We may connect with these the example already given of a ceremony celebrated specially to efface the effects of a ritual fault.[53] Of course there are neither wounds nor blows nor physical suffering of any sort in these two latter cases, yet the rite does not differ in nature from the others: the end sought is always the turning aside of an evil or the expiation of a fault by means of an extraordinary ritual prestation.

Outside of mourning, such are the only cases of piacular rites which we have succeeded in finding in Australia. To be sure, it is probable that some have escaped us, while we may presume equally well that others have remained unperceived by the observers. But if those discovered up to the present are few in number, it is probably because they do not hold a large place in the cult. We see how far primitive religions are from being the daughters of agony and fear from the fact that the rites translating these painful emotions are relatively rare. Of course this is because the Australian, while leading a miserable existence as compared with other more civilized peoples, demands so little of life

[46] *Nor. Tr.*, p. 286.
[47] Gason, *The Dieri Tribe*, in Curr, II, p. 68.
[48] Gason, *The Dieri Tribe;* Eylmann, p. 208.
[49] Howitt, *Native Tribes*, pp. 277 and 430.
[50] *Ibid.*, p. 195.

[51] Gason, *The Dieri Tribe*, in Curr, *Australian Race*, II, p. 69. The same process is used to expiate a ridiculous act. Whenever anybody, by his awkwardness or otherwise, has caused the laughter of others, he asks one of them to beat him on the head until blood flows. Then things are all right again, and the one who was laughed at joins in the general gaiety (*ibid.*, p. 70).
[52] Eylmann, pp. 212 and 447.
[53] See above, p. 385.

that he is easily contented. All that he asks is that nature follow its normal course, that the seasons succeed one another regularly, that the rain fall, at the ordinary time, in abundance and without excess. Now great disturbances in the cosmic order are always exceptional; thus it is noticeable that the majority of the regular piacular rites, examples of which we have given above, have been observed in the tribes of the centre, where droughts are frequent and constitute veritable disasters. It is still surprising, it is true, that piacular rites specially destined to expiate sins, seem to be completely lacking. However, the Australian, like every other man, must commit ritual faults, which he has an interest in redeeming; so we may ask if the silence of the texts on this point may not be due to insufficient observation.

But howsoever few the facts which we have been able to gather may be, they are, nevertheless, instructive.

When we study piacular rites in the more advanced religions, where the religious forces are individualized, they appear to be closely bound up with anthropomorphic conceptions. When the believer imposes privations upon himself and submits himself to austerities, it is in order to disarm the malevolence attributed by him to certain of the sacred beings upon whom he thinks that he is dependent. To appease their hatred or anger, he complies with their exigencies; he beats himself in order that he may not be beaten by them. So it seems as though these practices could not arise until after gods and spirits were conceived as moral persons, capable of passions analogous to those of men. For this reason, Robertson Smith thought it possible to assign a relatively late date to expiatory sacrifices, just as to sacrificial oblations. According to him, the shedding of blood which characterizes these rites was at first a simple process of communion: men poured forth their blood

upon the altar in order to strengthen the bonds uniting them to their god. The rite acquired a piacular and penal character only when its original significance was forgotten and when the new idea which was formed of sacred beings allowed men to attribute another function to it.[54]

But as piacular rites are met with even in the Australian societies, it is impossible to assign them so late an origin. Moreover, all that we have observed, with one single exception,[55] are independent of all anthropomorphic conceptions: there is no question of either spirits or gods. Abstinences and effusions of blood stop famines and cure sicknesses directly and by themselves. No spiritual being introduces his action between the rite and the effect it is believed to produce. So mythical personalities intervened only at a late date. After the mechanism of the ritual had once been established, they served to make it more easily representable in the mind, but they are not conditions of its existence. It is for other reasons that it was founded; it is to another cause that it owes its efficacy.

It acts through the collective forces which it puts into play. Does a misfortune which menaces the group appear imminent? Then the group unites, as in the case of mourning, and it is naturally an impression of uneasiness and perplexity which dominates the assembled body. Now, as always, the pooling of these sentiments results in intensifying them. By affirming themselves, they exalt and impassion themselves and attain a degree of violence which is translated by the corresponding violence of the gestures which express them. Just as at the death of a relative, they utter terrible cries, fly into a passion and feel that they must tear and destroy; it is to satisfy

[54] *The Religion of the Semites*, lect. XI.
[55] This is the case in which the Dieri, according to Jason, invoke the Mura-mura of water during a drought.

this need that they beat themselves, wound themselves, and make their blood flow. When emotions have this vivacity, they may well be painful, but they are not depressing; on the contrary, they denote a state of effervescence which implies a mobilization of all our active forces, and even a supply of external energies. It matters little that this exaltation was provoked by a sad event, for it is real, notwithstanding, and does not differ specifically from what is observed in the happy feasts. Sometimes it is even made manifest by movements of the same nature: there is the same frenzy which seizes the worshippers and the same tendency towards sexual debauches, a sure sign of great nervous over-excitement. Robertson Smith had already noticed this curious influence of sad rites in the Semitic cults: "in evil times," he says, "when men's thoughts were habitually sombre, they betook themselves to the physical excitement of religion as men now take refuge in wine. . . . And so in general when an act of Semitic worship began with sorrow and lamentation—as in the mourning for Adonis, or the great atoning ceremonies which became common in later times—a swift revulsion of feeling followed, and the gloomy part of the service was presently succeeded by a burst of hilarious revelry." [56] In a word, even when religious ceremonies have a disquieting or saddening event as their point of departure, they retain their stimulating power over the affective state of the group and individuals. By the mere fact that they are collective, they raise the vital tone. When one feels life within him—whether it be in the form of painful irritation or happy enthusiasm—he does not believe in death; so he becomes reassured and takes courage again, and subjectively, everything goes on as if the rite had really driven off the danger which was dreaded.

[56] Op. cit., p. 262.

This is how curing or preventive virtues come to be attributed to the movements which one makes, to the cries uttered, to the blood shed and to the wounds inflicted upon one's self or others; and as these different tortures necessarily make one suffer, suffering by itself is finally regarded as a means of conjuring evil or curing sickness.[57] Later, when the majority of the religious forces had taken the form of moral personalities, the efficacy of these practices was explained by imagining that their object was to appease an evil-working or irritated god. But these conceptions only reflect the rite and the sentiments it arouses; they are an interpretation of it, not its determining cause.

A negligence of the ritual acts in the same way. It, too, is a menace for the group; it touches it in its moral existence, for it touches it in its beliefs. But if the anger which it causes is affirmed ostensibly and energetically, it compensates the evil which it has caused. For if it is acutely felt by all, it is because the infraction committed is an exception and the common faith remains entire. So the moral unity of the group is not endangered. Now the penalty inflicted as an expiation is only a manifestation of the public anger, the material proof of its unanimity. So it really does have the healing effect attributed to it. At bottom, the sentiment which is at the root of the real expiatory rites does not differ in nature from that which we have found at the basis of the other piacular rites: it is a sort of irritated sorrow which tends to manifest itself by acts of destruction. Sometimes it is assuaged to the detriment of him who feels it; sometimes

[57] It is also possible that the belief in the morally tempering virtues of suffering (see El. Forms, p. 312) has added something here. Since sorrow sanctifies and raises the religious level of the worshipper, it may also raise him up again when he falls lower than usual.

it is at the expense of some foreign third party. But in either case, the psychic mechanism is essentially the same.[58]

IV

One of the greatest services which Robertson Smith has rendered to the science of religions is to have pointed out the ambiguity of the notion of sacredness.

Religious forces are of two sorts. Some are beneficent, guardians of the physical and moral order, dispensers of life and health and all the qualities which men esteem: this is the case with the totemic principle, spread out in the whole species, the mythical ancestor, the animal-protector, the civilizing heroes and the tutelar gods of every kind and degree. It matters little whether they are conceived as distinct personalities or as diffused energies; under either form they fulfil the same function and affect the minds of the believers in the same way: the respect which they inspire is mixed with love and gratitude. The things and the persons which are normally connected with them participate in the same sentiments and the same character: these are holy things and persons. Such are the spots consecrated to the cult, the objects which serve in the regular rites, the priests, the ascetics, etc.—On the other hand, there are evil and impure powers, productive of disorders, causes of death and sickness, instigators of sacrilege. The only sentiments which men have for them are a fear into which horror generally enters. Such are the forces upon which and by which the sorcerer acts, those which arise from corpses or the menstrual blood, those freed by every profanation of sacred things, etc. The

spirits of the dead and malign genii of every sort are their personified forms.

Between these two categories of forces and beings, the contrast is as complete as possible and even goes into the most radical antagonism. The good and salutary powers repel to a distance these others which deny and contradict them. Therefore the former are forbidden to the latter: any contact between them is considered the worst of profanations. This is the typical form of those interdicts between sacred things of different species, the existence of which we have already pointed out.[59] Women during menstruation, and especially at its beginning, are impure; so at this moment they are rigorously sequestered; men may have no relations with them.[60] Bull-roarers and churinga never come near a dead man.[61] A sacrilegious person is excluded from the society of the faithful; access to the cult is forbidden him. Thus the whole religious life gravitates about two contrary poles between which there is the same opposition as between the pure and the impure, the saint and the sacrilegious, the divine and the diabolic.

But while these two aspects of the religious life oppose one another, there is a close kinship between them. In the first place, both have the same relation towards profane beings: these must abstain from all contact with impure things just as from the most holy things. The former are no less forbidden than the latter:

---

[58] Cf. what we have said of expiation in our *Division du travail social³*, pp. 64 ff.

[59] See *El. Forms*, p. 301.

[60] Spencer and Gillen, *Native Tribes*, p. 460; *Nor. Tr., p.* 601; Roth, *North Queensland Ethnography*, Bulletin No. 5, p. 24. It is useless to multiply references for so well-known a fact.

[61] However, Spencer and Gillen cite one case where churinga are placed on the head of the dead man (*Native Tribes*, p. 156). But they admit that the fact is unique and abnormal (*ibid.*, p. 157), while Strehlow energetically denies it (*Die Aranda . . .* II, p. 79).

they are withdrawn from circulation alike. This shows that they too are sacred. Of course the sentiments inspired by the two are not identical: respect is one thing, disgust and horror another. Yet, if the gestures are to be the same in both cases, the sentiments expressed must not differ in nature. And, in fact, there is a horror in religious respect, especially when it is very intense, while the fear inspired by malign powers is generally not without a certain reverential character. The shades by which these two attitudes are differentiated are even so slight sometimes that it is not always easy to say which state of mind the believers actually happen to be in. Among certain Semitic peoples, pork was forbidden, but it was not always known exactly whether this was because it was a pure or an impure thing[62] and the same may be said of a very large number of alimentary interdictions.

But there is more to be said; it very frequently happens that an impure thing or an evil power becomes a holy thing or a guardian power, without changing its nature, through a simple modification of external circumstances. We have seen how the soul of a dead man, which is a dreaded principle at first, is transformed into a protecting genius as soon as the mourning is finished. Likewise, the corpse, which begins by inspiring terror and aversion, is later regarded as a venerated relic: funeral anthropophagy, which is frequently practised in the Australian societies, is a proof of this transformation.[63] The totemic animal is the pre-eminently sacred being; but for him

who eats its flesh unduly, it is a cause of death. In a general way, the sacrilegious person is merely a profane one who has been infected with a benevolent religious force. This changes its nature in changing its habitat; it defiles rather than sanctifies.[64] The blood issuing from the genital organs of a woman, though it is evidently as impure as that of menstruation, is frequently used as a remedy against sickness.[65] The victim immolated in expiatory sacrifices is charged with impurities, for they have concentrated upon it the sins which were to be expiated. Yet, after it has been slaughtered, its flesh and blood are employed for the most pious uses.[66] On the contrary, though the communion is generally a religious operation whose normal function is to consecrate, it sometimes produces the effects of a sacrilege. In certain cases, the persons who have communicated are forced to flee from one another as from men infected with a plague. One would say that they have become a source of dangerous contamination for one another: the sacred bond which unites them also separates them. Examples of this sort of communion are numerous in Australia. One of the most typical has been observed among the Narrinyeri and the neighbouring tribes. When an infant arrives in the world, its parents carefully preserve its umbilical cord, which is believed to conceal a part of its soul. Two persons who exchange the cords thus preserved communicate together by the very act of this exchange, for it is as though they exchanged their souls. But, at the same time, they are

---

[62] Smith, *Rel. of Semites*, p. 153; cf. p. 446, the additional note, *Holiness, Uncleanness and Taboo.*
[63] Howitt, *Native Tribes*, pp. 448–450; Brough Smyth, I, pp. 118, 120; Dawson, p. 67; Eyre, II, p. 251; Roth, *North Queensland Ethn.*, Bull. Mo. 9, in *Rec. of the Austral. Museum*, VI, No. 5, p. 367.

[64] See *El Forms*, p. 320.
[65] *Nor. Tr.*, p. 599; *Native Tribes*, p. 464.
[66] Among the Hebrews, for example, they sprinkled the altar with the blood of the expiatory victim (Lev. iv, 5 ff.); they burned the flesh and used products of this combustion to make water of purification (Numb. xix).

forbidden to touch or speak to or even to see one another. It is just as though they were each an object of horror for the other.[67]

So the pure and the impure are not two separate classes, but two varieties of the same class, which includes all sacred things. There are two sorts of sacredness, the propitious and the unpropitious, and not only is there no break of continuity between these two opposed forms, but also one object may pass from the one to the other without changing its nature. The pure is made out of the impure, and reciprocally. It is in the possibility of these transmutations that the ambiguity of the sacred consists.

But even if Robertson Smith did have an active sentiment of this ambiguity, he never gave it an express explanation. He confined himself to remarking that, as all religious forces are indistinctly intense and contagious, it is wise not to approach them except with respectful precautions, no matter what direction their action may be exercised in. It seemed to him that he could thus account for the air of kinship which they all present, in spite of the contrasts which oppose them otherwise. But the question was only put off; it still remains to be shown how it comes that the powers of evil have the same intensity and contagiousness as the others. In other words, how does it happen that they, too, are of a religious nature? Also, the energy and force of expansion which they have in common do not enable us to understand how, in spite of the conflict which divides them, they may be transformed into one another or substituted for each other in their respec-

tive functions, and how the pure may contaminate while the impure sometimes serves to sanctify.[68]

The explanation of piacular rites which we have proposed enables us to reply to this double question.

We have seen, in fact, that the evil powers are the product of these rites and symbolize them. When a society is going through circumstances which sadden, perplex or irritate it, it exercises a pressure over its members, to make them bear witness, by significant acts, to their sorrow, perplexity or anger. It imposes upon them the duty of weeping, groaning or inflicting wounds upon themselves or others, for these collective manifestations, and the moral communion which they show and strengthen, restore to the group the energy which circumstances threaten to take away from it, and thus they enable it to become settled. This is the experience which men interpret when

---

[67] Taplin, *The Narrinyeri*, pp. 32–34. When two persons who have thus exchanged their umbilical cords belong to different tribes, they are used as inter-tribal messengers. In this case, the exchange of cords took place shortly after birth, through the intermediary of their respective parents.

[68] It is true that Smith did not admit the reality of these substitutions and transformations. According to him, if the expiatory victim served to purify, it was because it had nothing impure in itself. At first, it was a holy thing; it was destined to re-establish, by means of a communion, the bonds of kinship uniting the worshipper to his god, when a ritual fault had strained or broken them. An exceptionally holy animal was chosen for this operation in order that the communion might be as efficacious as possible, and efface the effects of the fault as completely as possible. It was only when they no longer understood the meaning of the rite that the sacrosanct animal was considered impure (*op. cit.*, pp. 347 ff.). But it is inadmissible that beliefs and practices as universal as these, which we find at the foundation of the expiatory sacrifice, should be the product of a mere error of interpretation. In fact, we cannot doubt that the expiatory victim was charged with the impurity of the sin. We have shown, moreover, that these transformations of the pure into the impure, or the contrary, are to be found in the most inferior societies which we know.

they imagine that outside them there are evil beings whose hostility, whether constitutional or temporary, can be appeased only by human suffering. These beings are nothing other than collective states objectified; they are society itself seen under one of its aspects. But we also know that the benevolent powers are constituted in the same way; they, too, result from the collective life and express it; they, too, represent the society, but seen from a very different attitude, to wit, at the moment when it confidently affirms itself and ardently presses on towards the realization of the ends which it pursues. Since these two sorts of forces have a common origin, it is not at all surprising that, though facing in opposite directions, they should have the same nature, that they are equally intense and contagious and consequently forbidden and sacred.

From this we are able to understand how they change into one another. Since they reflect the abjective state in which the group happens to be, it is enough that this state change for their character to change. After the mourning is over, the domestic group is re-calmed by the mourning itself; it regains confidence; the painful pressure which they felt exercised over them is relieved; they feel more at their ease. So it seems to them as though the spirit of the deceased had laid aside its hostile sentiments and become a benevolent protector. The other transmutations, examples of which we have cited, are to be explained in the same way. As we have already shown, the sanctity of a thing is due to the collective sentiment of which it is the object. If, in violation of the interdicts which isolate it, it comes in contact with a profane person, then this same sentiment will spread contagiously to this latter and imprint a special character upon him. But in spreading, it comes into a very different state from the one it was in at first. Offended and irritated by the profanation

implied in this abusive and unnatural extension, it becomes aggressive and inclined to destructive violences: it tends to avenge itself for the offence suffered. Therefore the infected subject seems to be filled with a mighty and harmful force which menaces all that approaches him; it is as though he were marked with a stain or blemish. Yet the cause of this blemish is the same psychic state which, in other circumstances, consecrates and sanctifies. But if the anger thus aroused is satisfied by an expiatory rite, it subsides, alleviated; the offended sentiment is appeased and returns to its original state. So it acts once more as it acted in the beginning; instead of contaminating, it sanctifies. As it continues to infect the object to which it is attached, this could never become profane and religiously indifferent again. But the direction of the religious force with which it seems to be filled is inverted: from being impure, it has become pure and an instrument of purification.

In résumé, the two poles of the religious life correspond to the two opposed states through which all social life passes. Between the propitiously sacred and the unpropitiously sacred there is the same contrast as between the states of collective well-being and ill-being. But since both are equally collective, there is, between the mythological constructions symbolizing them, an intimate kinship of nature. The sentiments held in common vary from extreme dejection to extreme joy, from painful irritation to ecstatic enthusiasm; but, in any case, there is a communion of minds and a mutual comfort resulting from this communion. The fundamental process is always the same; only circumstances colour it differently. So, at bottom, it is the unity and the diversity of social life which make the simultaneous unity and diversity of sacred beings and things.

This ambiguity, moreover, is not peculiar to the idea of sacredness alone;

something of this characteristic has been found in all the rites which we have been studying. Of course it was essential to distinguish them; to confuse them would have been to misunderstand the multiple aspects of the religious life. But, on the other hand, howsoever different they may be, there is no break of continuity between them. Quite on the contrary, they overlap one another and may even replace each other mutually. We have already shown how the rites of oblation and communion, the imitative rites and the commemorative rites frequently fulfil the same function. One might imagine that the negative cult, at least, would be more sharply separated from the positive cult; yet we have seen that the former may produce positive effects, identical with those produced by the latter. The same results are obtained by fasts, abstinences and self-mutilations as by communions, oblations and commemorations. Inversely, offerings and sacrifices imply privations and renunciations of every sort. The continuity between ascetic and piacular rites is even more apparent: both are made up of sufferings, accepted or undergone, to which an analogous efficacy is attributed. Thus the practices, like the beliefs, are not arranged in two separate classes. Howsoever complex the outward manifestations of the religious life may be, at bottom it is one and simple. It responds everywhere to one and the same need, and is everywhere derived from one and the same mental state. In all its forms, its object is to raise man above himself and to make him lead a life superior to that which he would lead, if he followed only his own individual whims: beliefs express this life in representations; rites organize it and regulate its working.

2 · Death and the Reintegration of the Group

BRONISLAW MALINOWSKI

Of all sources of religion, the supreme and final crisis of life—death—is of the greatest importance. Death is the gateway to the other world in more than the literal sense. According to most theories of early religion, a great deal, if not all, of religious inspiration has been derived from it—and in this orthodox views are on the whole correct. Man has to live his life in the shadow of death, and he who clings to life and enjoys its fullness must dread the menace of its end. And he who is faced by death turns to the promise of life. Death and its denial—Immortality—have always formed, as

SOURCE. Bronislaw Malinowski, *Magic, Science and Religion,* Garden City, New York: Doubleday, pp. 47–53. Reprinted with permission of the publisher. Copyright 1948 by The Free Press.

they form today, the most poignant theme of man's forebodings. The extreme complexity of man's emotional reactions to life finds necessarily its counterpart in his attitude to death. Only what in life has been spread over a long space and manifested in a succession of experiences and events is here at its end condensed into one crisis which provokes a violent and complex outburst of religious manifestations.

Even among the most primitive peoples, the attitude towards death is infinitely more complex and, I may add, more akin to our own, than is usually assumed. It is often stated by anthropologists that the dominant feeling of the survivors is that of horror at the corpse and of fear of the ghost. This twin attitude is even made by no less an authority than Wilhelm Wundt the very nucleus of all religious belief and practice. Yet this assertion is only a half-truth, which means no truth at all. The emotions are extremely complex and even contradictory; the dominant elements, love of the dead and loathing of the corpse, passionate attachment to the personality still lingering about the body and a shattering fear of the gruesome thing that has been left over, these two elements seem to mingle and play into each other. This is reflected in the spontaneous behavior and in the ritual proceedings at death. In the tending of the corpse, in the modes of its disposal, in the post-funerary and commemorative ceremonies, the nearest relatives, the mother mourning for her son, the widow for her husband, the child for the parent, always show some horror and fear mingled with pious love, but never do the negative elements appear alone or even dominant.

The mortuary proceedings show a striking similarity throughout the world. As death approaches, the nearest relatives in any case, sometimes the whole community, forgather by the dying man, and dying, the most private act which a man can perform, is transformed into a public, tribal event. As a rule, a certain differentiation takes place at once, some of the relatives watching near the corpse, others making preparations for the pending end and its consequences, others again performing perhaps some religious acts at a sacred spot. Thus in certain parts of Melanesia the real kinsmen must keep at a distance and only relatives by marriage perform the mortuary services, while in some tribes of Australia the reverse order is observed.

As soon as death has occurred, the body is washed, anointed and adorned, sometimes the bodily apertures are filled, the arms and legs tied together. Then it is exposed to the view of all, and the most important phase, the immediate mourning begins. Those who have witnessed death and its sequel among savages and who can compare these events with their counterpart among other uncivilized peoples must be struck by the fundamental similarity of the proceedings. There is always a more or less conventionalized and dramatized outburst of grief and wailing in sorrow, which often passes among savages into bodily lacerations and the tearing of hair. This is always done in a public display and is associated with visible signs of mourning, such as black or white daubs on the body, shaven or disheveled hair, strange or torn garments.

The immediate mourning goes on round the corpse. This, far from being shunned or dreaded, is usually the center of pious attention. Often there are ritual forms of fondling or attestations of reverence. The body is sometimes kept on the knees of seated persons, stroked and embraced. At the same time these acts are usually considered both dangerous and repugnant, duties to be fulfilled at some cost to the performer. After a time the corpse has to be disposed of. Inhumation with an open or closed grave; exposure in caves or on platforms, in hollow trees or on the ground in some wild desert place; burning or setting adrift in canoes —these are the usual forms of disposal.

This brings us to perhaps the most important point, the two-fold contradictory tendency, on the one hand to preserve the body, to keep its form intact, or to retain parts of it; on the other hand the desire to be done with it, to put it out of the way, to annihilate it completely. Mummification and burning are the two extreme expressions of this two-fold tendency. It is impossible to regard mummification or burning or any intermediate form as determined by mere accident of belief, as a historical feature of some culture or other which has gained its universality by the mechanism of spread and contact only. For in these customs is clearly expressed the fundamental attitude of mind of the surviving relative, friend or lover, the longing for all that remains of the dead person and the disgust and fear of the dreadful transformation wrought by death.

One extreme and interesting variety in which this double-edged attitude is expressed in a gruesome manner is sarco-cannibalism, a custom of partaking in piety of the flesh of the dead person. It is done with extreme repugnance and dread and usually followed by a violent vomiting fit. At the same time it is felt to be a supreme act of reverence, love, and devotion. In fact it is considered such a sacred duty that among the Melanesians of New Guinea, where I have studied and witnessed it, it is still performed in secret, although severely penalized by the white Government. The smearing of the body with the fat of the dead, prevalent in Australia and Papuasia is, perhaps, but a variety of this custom.

In all such rites, there is a desire to maintain the tie and the parallel tendency to break the bond. Thus the funerary rites are considered as unclean and soiling, the contact with the corpse as defiling and dangerous, and the performers have to wash, cleanse their body, remove all traces of contact, and perform ritual lustrations. Yet the mortuary ritual compels man to overcome the repugnance, to conquer his fears, to make piety and attachment triumphant, and with it the belief in a future life, in the survival of the spirit.

And here we touch on one of the most important functions of religious cult. In the foregoing analysis I have laid stress on the direct emotional forces created by contact with death and with the corpse, for they primarily and most powerfully determine the behavior of the survivors. But connected with these emotions and born out of them, there is the idea of the spirit, the belief in the new life into which the departed has entered. And here we return to the problem of ani-

mism with which we began our survey of primitive religious facts. What is the substance of a spirit, and what is the psychological origin of this belief?

The savage is intensely afraid of death, probably as the result of some deep-seated instincts common to man and animals. He does not want to realize it as an end, he cannot face the idea of complete cessation, of annihilation. The idea of spirit and of spiritual existence is near at hand, furnished by such experiences as are discovered and described by Tylor. Grasping at it, man reaches the comforting belief in spiritual continuity and in the life after death. Yet this belief does not remain unchallenged in the complex, double-edged play of hope and fear which sets in always in the face of death. To the comforting voice of hope, to the intense desire of immortality, to the difficulty, in one's own case, almost the impossibility, of facing annihilation there are opposed powerful and terrible forebodings. The testimony of the senses, the gruesome decomposition of the corpse, the visible disappearance of the personality—certain apparently instinctive suggestions of fear and horror seem to threaten man at all stages of culture with some idea of annihilation, with some hidden fears and forebodings. And here into this play of emotional forces, into this supreme dilemma of life and final death, religion steps in, selecting the positive creed, the comforting view, the culturally valuable belief in immortality, in the spirit independent of the body, and in the continuance of life after death. In the various ceremonies at death, in commemoration and communion with the departed, and worship of ancestral ghosts, religion gives body and form to the saving beliefs.

Thus the belief in immortality is the result of a deep emotional revelation, standardized by religion, rather than a primitive philosophic doctrine. Man's conviction of continued life is one of the supreme gifts of religion, which judges and selects the better of the two alternatives suggested by self-preservation—the hope of continued life and the fear of annihilation. The belief in spirits is the result of the belief in immortality. The substance of which the spirits are made is the full-blooded passion and desire for life, rather than the shadowy stuff which haunts his dreams and illusions. Religion saves man from a surrender to death and destruction, and in doing this it merely makes use of the observations of dreams, shadows, and visions. The real nucleus of animism lies in the deepest emotional fact of human nature, the desire for life.

Thus the rites of mourning, the ritual behavior immediately after death, can be taken as pattern of the religious act, while the belief in immortality, in the continuity of life and in the nether world, can be taken as the prototype of an act of faith. Here, as in the religious ceremonies previously described, we find self-contained acts, the aim of which is achieved in their very performance. The ritual despair, the obsequies, the acts of mourning, express the emotion of the bereaved and the loss of the whole group. They endorse and they duplicate the natural feelings of the survivors, they create a social event out of a natural fact. Yet, though in the acts of mourning, in the mimic despair of wailing, in the treatment of the corpse and in its disposal, nothing ulterior is achieved, these acts fulfill an important function and possess a considerable value for primitive culture.

What is this function? The imitation ceremonies we have found fulfill theirs in sacralizing tradition; the food cults, sacrament and sacrifice bring man into communion with providence, with the beneficent forces of plenty; totemism standardizes man's practical, useful attitude of selective interest towards his surroundings. If the view here taken of the biological function of religion is true, some such similar role must also be played by the whole mortuary ritual.

The death of a man or woman in a primitive group, consisting of a limited number of individuals, is an event of no mean importance. The nearest relatives and friends are disturbed to the depth of their emotional life. A small community bereft of a member, especially if he be important, is severely mutilated. The whole event breaks the normal course of life and shakes the moral foundations of society. The strong tendency on which we have insisted in the above description: to give way to fear and horror, to abandon the corpse, to run away from the village, to destroy all the belongings of the dead one—all these impulses exist, and if given way to would be extremely dangerous, disintegrating the group, destroying the material foundations of primitive culture. Death in a primitive society is, therefore, much more than the removal of a member. By setting in motion one part of the deep forces of the instinct of self-preservation, it threatens the very cohesion and solidarity of the group, and upon this depends the organization of that society, its tradition, and finally the whole culture. For if primitive man yielded always to the disintegrating impulses of his reaction to death, the continuity of tradition and the existence of material civilization would be made impossible.

We have seen already how religion, by sacralizing and thus standardizing the other set of impulses, bestows on man the gift of mental integrity. Exactly the same function it fulfills also with regard to the whole group. The ceremonial of death which ties the survivors to the body and rivets them to the place of death, the beliefs in the existence of the spirit, in its beneficent influences or malevolent intentions, in the duties of a series of commemorative or sacrificial ceremonies—in all this religion counteracts the centrifugal forces of fear, dismay, demoralization, and provides the most powerful means of reintegration of the group's shaken solidarity and of the re-establishment of its morale.

In short, religion here assures the victory of tradition and culture over the mere negative response of thwarted instinct.

3 · A Functional View of Catholic Dogma

AUGUSTE COMTE

From the political estimate of Catholicism, we must next pass on to a brief review of its dogmatic conditions, in order to see how secondary theological doctrines, which appear to us socially indifferent, were yet necessary to the political efficacy of a system so complex and factitious that when its unity, laboriously maintained, was once infringed by the destruction of any one of its component influences, the disorganization of the whole was, however gradual, absolutely inevitable.

The amount of polytheism involved in Catholicism was as small as the needs of the theological spirit would at all admit. But there were accessory dogmas which, derived more or less spontaneously from the characteristic theological conception, have expanded into means more or less necessary to the fulfilment of its destination in regard to social progress. We must notice the most important of these.

The vague and variable tendency of theological conceptions impairs their social efficacy by exposing the precepts they supply to perpetual modification by human passions: and this difficulty can be met only by an incessant vigilance on the part of the corresponding spiritual authority. Catholicism had no choice, if the unity of its social function was to be preserved, but to repress the irreconcil-

SOURCE. *The Positive Philosophy of Auguste Comte,* translated by Harriet Martineau, New York: William Gowans, 1868, pp. 614–616.

able outbreaks of the religious spirit in individual minds by setting up absolute faith as the first duty of the Christian, because there was no other basis for moral obligation of other kinds. This was a real advance of the moral interests of society; for the great practical utility of religion in that age was that it permitted the provisional elevation of a noble speculative body, eminently adapted during its ascending period to direct the opinions and morals of mankind. It is from this point of view that the dogmatic, as well as the directly political character of Catholicism ought to be judged; for in no other way can we seize the true character of some doctrines, dangerous no doubt, but imposed by the nature or the needs of the system; and in no other way can we understand the importance formerly attributed by so many superior minds to special dogmas which might at first appear useless to the final destination, but which had a real bearing both upon the ecclesiastical unity and social efficacy of Catholicism. Some of these dogmas were the very means of the destruction of the system, by the mental and moral insurrection which they provoked. For instance, the dogma that the reception of the Catholic faith is the sole means of salvation was the only instrument for the control of theological divergence; but this fatal declaration, which involves the damnation of all heretics, involuntary as well as wilful, excited more deep and unanimous indignation than any other, when the day of emancipation arrived; for nothing is more confirmatory of the provisional destination of all religious doctrines than their gradually leading on to the conversion of an old principle of love into a final ground of insurmountable hatred; as we should see more and more henceforth amidst the dissolution of creeds, if their social action did not tend finally toward a total and common extinction. The dogma of the condemnation of mankind through Adam, which is, morally, more revolting than the other, was also a necessary element of the Catholic philosophy, not only for the theological explanation it supplied of human suffering, but, more specially, because it afforded ground for the scheme of redemption, on the necessity of which the whole economy of the Catholic faith is based. The institution of purgatory was happily introduced into the social practice of Catholicism, as a necessary corrective of the eternity of future punishment; for without it, there must have been either fatal relaxation or uncontrollable despair—both alike dangerous to the individual and society; whereas, by this intermediate issue both were avoided, and the religious procedure could be exactly adapted to each case. This was a case of political necessity; and another, yet more special, is that of the assignment of an absolutely divine character to the real or ideal founder of this great system, through the relation of such a conception to radical independence of the spiritual power, which is thus at once placed under an inviolable authority of its own, direct though invisible: whereas, under the Arian hypothesis, the temporal power, addressing itself immediately to a general Providence, must be less disposed to respect the intervention of the sacerdotal body, whose mystic head has been much lowered in rank. We cannot imagine, at this day, the immense difficulty of every kind that Catholicism had to encounter in organizing the separation of the two authorities; and therefore we can form no judgment of the various resources required by the struggle; among which resources this apotheosis is conspicuous, tending as it did to raise the Church in the eyes of monarchs; while, on the other hand, a rigorous divine unity would have favored, in an inverse way, too great a concentration of the social ascendancy. We accordingly find in history a varied and decisive manifestation of the obstinate predilection among the kings in general for the heresy of Arius, in which their class instinct confusedly discerned a way to humble the papal independence and to favor the social sway of temporal authority. The same political efficacy attached to the doctrine of the Real Presence, which, intellectually strange as it is, is merely a prolongation of the preceding dogma. By it, the humblest priest is invested with a perpetual power of miraculous consecration, which must give him dignity in the eyes of rulers who, whatever might be their material greatness, could never aspire to such sublime operations. Besides the perpetual stimulus thus administrated to faith, such a belief made the minister more absolutely indispensable: whereas, amidst simpler conceptions and a less special worship, temporal rulers might then, as since, have found means to dispense with sacerdotal intervention, on condition of an empty orthodoxy. If we proceeded from the dogma to consider the Catholic worship in the same way, we should find that (apart from the moral instrumentality in regard to individual and social action which it afforded) it had the same political bearing. The sacraments, in their graduated and well-combined succession, roused in each believer, at the most important periods of his life, and through its regular course, the spirit of the universal system, by signs specially adapted to the character of each position. In an intellectual view, the mass offers a most unsatisfactory spectacle, appearing to human reason to be merely a sort of magical operation, terminated by the fulfilment of a pure act of spirit-raising, real though mystical: but in a social view, we see in it a happy invention of the theological spirit, suppressing universally and irrevocably the bloody sacrifices of polytheism, by diverting the instinctive need of sacrifice which is inherent in every religious regime, and which was in this case daily gratified by the voluntary immolation of the most precious of imaginable victims.

D · DYSFUNCTION, VARIANT EVALUATION, AND CHANGE

1 · Dysfunctions and Variant Evaluations of Religion

ROBERT K. MERTON

One need not go far afield to show that the assumption of the complete functional unity of human society is repeatedly contrary to fact. Social usages or sentiments may be functional for some groups and dysfunctional for others in the same society. Anthropologists often cite "increased solidarity of the community" and "increased family pride" as instances of functionally adaptive sentiments. Yet, as Bateson[1] among others has indicated, an increase of pride among individual families may often serve to disrupt the solidarity of a small local community. Not only is the postulate of functional unity often contrary to fact, but it has little heuristic value, since it diverts the analyst's attention from possible disparate consequences of a given social or cultural item (usage, belief, behavior pattern, institution) for diverse

SOURCE. From Robert K. Merton, *Social Theory and Social Structure*, The Free Press: Glencoe, Illinois, 1957, pp. 27–30 and 42–46. Reprinted with permission of the publisher. Copyright 1957 by The Free Press, A Corporation. Copyright 1949 by The Free Press.

[1] Gregory Bateson, *Naven* (Cambridge [England] University Press, 1963), 31–32.

social groups and for the individual members of these groups.

If the body of observation and fact which negates the assumption of functional unity is as large and easily accessible as we have suggested, it is interesting to ask how it happens that Radcliffe-Brown and others who follow his lead have continued to abide by this assumption. A possible clue is provided by the fact that this conception, in its recent formulations, was developed by social *anthropologists*, that is, by men primarily concerned with the study of non-literate societies. In view of what Radin has described as "the highly integrated nature of the majority of aboriginal civilizations," this assumption may be tolerably suitable for some, if not all, non-literate societies. But one pays an excessive intellectual penalty for moving this possibly useful assumption from the realm of small non-literate societies to the realm of large, complex and highly differentiated literate societies. In no field, perhaps, do the dangers of such a transfer of assumption become more visible than in the functional analysis of religion. This deserves brief review, if only because it exhibits in bold relief the fallacies one falls heir to by sympathetically adopting this assumption without a thorough screening.

The Functional Interpretation of Religion. In examining the price paid for the transfer of this tacit assumption of functional unity from the field of relatively small and relatively tightknit nonliterate groups to the field of more highly differentiated and perhaps more loosely integrated societies, it is useful to consider the work of sociologists, particularly of sociologists who are ordinarily sensitized to the assumptions on which they work. This has passing interest for its bearing on the more general question of seeking, without appropriate modification, to apply to the study of literate societies conceptions developed and matured in the study of non-literate societies. (Much the same question holds for the transfer of research procedures and techniques, but this is not at issue here.)

The large, spaceless and timeless generalizations about "the integrative functions of religion" are largely, though not of course wholly, derived from observations in non-literate societies. Not infrequently, the social scientist implicitly adopts the findings regarding such societies and goes on to expatiate upon the integrative functions of religion *generally*. From this, it is a short step to statements such as the following:

> *The reason why religion is necessary* is apparently to be found in the fact that human society *achieves its unity* primarily through the possession by its members of certain ultimate values and ends in common. Although these values and ends are subjective, they influence behavior, and their integration enables this society to operate as a system.[2]

In an extremely advanced society

[2] Kingsley Davis and Wilbert E. Moore, "Some principles of stratification," *American Sociological Review*, April 1945, 10, 242–49, at 244 [italics supplied].

built on scientific technology, the priesthood tends to lose status, because sacred tradition and supernaturalism drop into the background . . . (but) No *society* has become so completely secularized as to liquidate *entirely* the belief in transcendental ends and supernatural entities. Even in a secularized society *some system* must exist for the integration of ultimate values, for their ritualistic expression, and for the emotional adjustments required by disappointment, death, and disaster.[3]

Deriving from the Durkheim orientation which was based largely upon the study of non-literate societies, these authors tend to single out *only* the apparently integrative consequences of religion and to neglect its possibly disintegrative consequences *in certain types of social structure.* Yet consider the following very well-known facts and queries. (1) When different religions co-exist in the same society, there often occurs deep conflict between the several religious groups (consider only the enormous literature on inter-religious conflict in European societies). In what sense, then, does religion make for integration of "the" society in the numerous multi-religion societies? (2) It is clearly the case that "human society achieves its unity [insofar as it exhibits such unity] primarily through the possession by its members of certain ultimate values and ends in common." But what is the evidence indicating that "non-religious" people, say, in our own society, less often subscribe to certain common "values and ends" than those devoted to religious doctrines? (3) In what sense does religion make for integration of the larger society, if the content of its doctrine and values is at odds with the content of other, non-religious values held by many people in the same society? Consider, for example, the conflict between the opposi-

[3] *Ibid.,* 246 [italics supplied].

tion of the Catholic Church to child-labor legislation and the secular values of preventing "exploitation of youthful dependents." Or the contrasting evaluations of birth control by diverse religious groups in our society.

This list of commonplace facts regarding the role of religion in contemporary literate societies could be greatly extended, and they are of course very well known to those functional anthropologists and sociologists who describe religion as integrative, without limiting the range of social structures in which this is indeed the case. It is at least conceivable that a theoretic orientation derived from research on non-literate societies has served to obscure otherwise conspicuous data on the functional role of religion in multi-religion societies. Perhaps it is the transfer of the assumption of functional unity which results in blotting out the entire history of religious wars, of the Inquisition (which drove a wedge into society after society), of internecine conflicts among religious groups. For the fact remains that all this abundantly known material is ignored in favor of illustrations drawn from the study of religion in non-literate society. And it is a further striking fact that the same paper, cited above, that goes on to speak of "religion, which provides integration in terms of sentiments, beliefs and rituals," does not make a single reference to the possibly divisive role of religion.

Such functional analyses may, of course, mean that religion provides integration of those who believe in the *same* religious values, but it is unlikely that this is meant, since it would merely assert that integration is provided by any consensus on any set of values.

Moreover, this again illustrates the danger of taking the assumption of functional unity, which *may* be a reasonable approximation for some non-literate societies, as part of an implicit model for *generalized* functional analysis. Typically,

in non-literate societies, there is but one prevailing religious system so that, apart from individual deviants, the membership of the total society and the membership of the religious community are virtually co-extensive. Obviously, in this type of social structure, a common set of religious values may have as *one* of its consequences the reinforcement of common sentiments and of social integration. But this does not easily lend itself to defensible generalization about other types of society.

We shall have occasion to return to other theoretic implications of current functional analyses of religion but, for the moment, this may illustrate the dangers which one inherits in adopting the unqualified postulate of functional unity. This unity of the total society cannot be usefully posited in advance of observation. It is a question of fact, and not a matter of opinion. The theoretic framework of functional analysis must expressly require that there be *specification* of the *units* for which a given social or cultural item is functional. It must expressly allow for a given item having diverse consequences, functional and dysfunctional, for individuals, for subgroups, and for the more inclusive social structure and culture. . . .

Ideology and the Functional Analysis of Religion

Again, it is instructive to turn, however briefly, to discussions of the functions of religion to show how the logic of functional analysis is adopted by people otherwise opposed in their ideological stance.

The social role of religion has of course been repeatedly observed and interpreted over the long span of many centuries. The hard core of continuity in these observations consists in an emphasis on religion as an institutional means of social control, whether this be in Plato's concept of "noble lies," or in Aristotle's opinion that religion operates "with a view to the persuasion of the multitude" or in the comparable judgment by Polybius that "the masses . . . can be controlled only by mysterious terrors and tragic fears." If Montesquieu remarks of the Roman lawmakers that they sought "to inspire a people that feared nothing with fear of the gods, and to use that fear to lead it withersoever they pleased," then Jawaharlal Nehru observes, on the basis of his own experience, that "the only books that British officials heartily recommended [to political prisoners in India] were religious books or novels. It is wonderful how dear to the heart of the British Government is the subject of religion and how impartially it encourages all brands of it." [4] It would appear that there is an ancient and abiding tradition holding, in one form or another, that religion has served to control the masses. It appears, also, that the language in which this proposition is couched usually gives a clue to the ideological commitment of the author.

How is it, then, with some of the current functional analyses of religion? In his critical consolidation of several major theories in the sociology of religion, Parsons summarizes some of the basic conclusions which have emerged regarding the "functional significance of religion":

> . . . if moral norms and the sentiments supporting them are of such primary importance, what are the mechanisms by which they are maintained *other than external processes of enforcement?* It was Durkheim's view that religious ritual was of primary significance as a mechanism for *expressing and reinforcing the sentiments* most essential to the *institutional integration* of the society. It can readily

be seen that this is clearly linked to Malinowski's views of the significance of funeral ceremonies as *a mechanism for reasserting the solidarity of the group* on the occasion of severe emotional strain. Thus Durkheim worked out certain aspects of the specific relations between *religion and social structure* more sharply than did Malinowski, and in addition put the problem in a different functional perspective in that he applied it to the society as a whole in abstraction from particular situations of tension and strain for the individual.[5]

And again, summarizing an essential finding of the major comparative study in the sociology of religion, Parsons observes that "perhaps the most striking feature of Weber's analysis is the demonstration of the extent to which precisely the variations in socially sanctioned values and goals in secular life correspond to the variations in the dominant religious philosophy of the great civilizations." [6]

Similarly, in exploring the role of religion among racial and ethnic subgroups in the United States, Donald Young in effect remarks the close correspondence between their "socially sanctioned values and goals in secular life" and their "dominant religious philosophy":

> One function which a minority religion may serve is that of *reconciliation with inferior status and its discriminatory consequences.* Evidence of religious service of this function may be found among all American minority peoples. On the other hand, religious institutions may also develop in such a way as to be *an incitement and support of revolt against inferior status.* Thus, the Christianized Indian, with due allowance for exceptions, has tended to be *more submissive* than the

[4] Jawaharlal Nehru, *Toward Freedom* (New York: John Day, 1941), 7.

[5] Talcott Parsons, *Essays in Sociological Theory,* 61 [italics supplied].

[6] *Ibid.,* 63.

pagan. Special cults such as those associated with the use of peyote, the Indian Shaker Church, and the Ghost Dance, all three containing both Christian and native elements, were foredoomed attempts to develop *modes of religious expression adapted to individual and group circumstances.* The latter, with its emphasis on an assured millennium of freedom from the white man, encouraged forceful revolt. The Christianity of the Negro, in spite of appreciable encouragement of verbal criticism of the existing order, *has emphasized acceptance of present troubles in the knowledge of better times to come in the life hereafter.* The numerous varieties of Christianity and the Judaism brought by immigrants from Europe and Mexico, in spite of common nationalistic elements, also *stressed later rewards rather than immediate direct action.*[7]

These diverse and scattered observations, with their notably varied ideological provenience, exhibit some basic similarities. First, they are all given over to the consequences of specific religious systems for prevailing sentiments, definitions of situations and action. These consequences are rather consistently observed to be those of reinforcement of prevailing moral norms, docile acceptance of these norms, postponement of ambitions and gratifications (if the religious doctrine so demands), and the like. However, as Young observes, religions have also served, under determinate conditions, to provoke rebellion, or as Weber has shown, religions have served to motivate or to canalize the behavior of great

[7] Donald Young, *American Minority Peoples* (New York: Harper, 1937), 204 [italics supplied]. For a functional analysis of the Negro church in the United States, see George Eaton Simpson and J. Milton Yinger, *Racial and Cultural Minorities* (New York: Harper & Brothers, 1953), 522–530.

numbers of men and women toward the modification of social structures. It would seem premature, therefore, to conclude that all religion everywhere has only the one consequence of making for mass apathy.

Second, the Marxist view implicitly and the functionalist view explicitly affirm the central point that systems of religion do *affect behavior,* that they are *not merely* epiphenomena but partially independent determinants of behavior. For presumably, it makes a difference if "the masses" do or do not accept a particular religion just as it makes a difference if an individual does or does not take opium.

Third, the more ancient as well as the Marxist theories deal with the *differential* consequences of religious beliefs and rituals for various subgroups and strata in the society—e.g., "the masses"—as, for that matter, does the non-Marxist Donald Young. The functionalist is not confined, as we have seen, to exploring the consequences of religion for "society as a whole."

Fourth, the suspicion begins to emerge that the functionalists, with their emphasis on religion as a *social mechanism* for "reinforcing the sentiments most essential to the institutional integration of the society," may not differ materially in their *analytical framework* from the Marxists who, if their metaphor of "opium of the masses" is converted into a neutral statement of social fact, also assert that religion operates as a social mechanism for reinforcing certain secular as well as sacred sentiments among its believers.

The point of difference appears only when *evaluations* of this commonly accepted fact come into question. Insofar as the functionalists refer to "institutional integration" without exploring the diverse consequences of integration about very different types of values and interests, they confine themselves to purely *formal* interpretation. For integration is a plainly formal concept. A society may be integrated around norms of strict caste, regimentation, and docility of subordinated social strata, just as it may be integrated around norms of open mobility, wide areas of self-expression and independence of judgment among temporarily lower strata. And insofar as the Marxists assert, without qualification, that all religion everywhere, whatever its doctrinal content and its organizational form, involves "an opiate" for the masses, they too shift to purely formal interpretations, without allowing, as the excerpt from Young shows to be the case, for particular religions in particular social structures serving to activate rather than to lethargize mass action. It is in the *evalua-*

tion of these functions of religion, rather than in the logic of analysis, then, that the functionalists and the Marxists part company. And it is the *evaluations* which permit the pouring of ideological content into the bottles of *functionalism.*[8] The bottles themselves are neutral to their contents, and may serve equally well as containers for ideological poison or for ideological nectar.

[8] This type of talking-past-each-other is perhaps more common than one is wont to suspect. Often, the basic agreement in the *analysis* of a situation is plentifully obscured by the basic disagreement in the *evaluation* of that situation. As a result, it is erroneously assumed that the opponents differ in their cognitive procedures and findings, whereas they differ only in their sets of values. . . .

2 · Ritual and Social Change: A Javanese Example

CLIFFORD GEERTZ

As in so many areas of anthropological concern, functionalism . . . has tended to dominate recent theoretical discussions of the role of religion in society.

Where the functional approach has been least impressive . . . is in dealing with social change. As has been noted by several writers (Leach 1954; Merton 1949), the emphasis on systems in balance, on social homeostasis, and on timeless structural pictures, leads to a bias in favor of "well-integrated" societies in a stable equilibrium and to a tendency to emphasize the functional aspects of a people's social usages and customs rather than their disfunctional implications. In analyses of religion this static, ahistorical approach has led to a somewhat overconservative view of the role of ritual and belief in social life. Despite caution-

SOURCE. *American Anthropologist,* Vol. 59, February, 1957, pp. 32–53.

ary comments by Kluckhohn (1944) and others on the "gain and cost" of various religious practices such as witchcraft, the tendency has been consistently to stress the harmonizing, integrating, and psychologically supportive aspects of religious patterns rather than the disruptive, disintegrative, and psychologically disturbing aspects; to demonstrate the manner in which religion preserves social and psychological structure rather than the manner in which it destroys or transforms it. Where change has been treated, as in Redfield's work on Yucatan (1941), it has largely been in terms of progressive disintegration: "The changes in culture that in Yucatan appear to 'go along with' lessening isolation and homogeneity are seen to be chiefly three: disorganization of the culture, secularization and individualization" (p. 339). Yet even a passing knowledge of our own religious history makes us hesitate to affirm such a simply "positive" role for religion generally.

It is the thesis of this paper that one of the major reasons for the inability of functional theory to cope with change lies in its failure to treat sociological and cultural processes on equal terms; almost inevitably one of the two is either ignored or is sacrificed to become but a simple reflex, a "mirror image," of the other. Either culture is regarded as wholly derivative from the forms of social organization—the approach characteristic of the British structuralists as well as many American sociologists; or the forms of social organization are regarded as behavioral embodiments of cultural patterns—the approach of Malinowski and many American anthropologists. In either case, the lesser term tends to drop out as a dynamic factor and we are left either with an omnibus concept of culture ("that complex whole . . .") or else with a completely comprehensive concept of social structure ("social structure is not an aspect of culture, but the entire culture of a given people handled in a special frame of theory" [Fortes 1953]). In such a situation, the dynamic elements in social change which arise from the failure of cultural patterns to be perfectly congruent with the forms of social organization are largely incapable of formulation. "We functionalists," E. R. Leach has recently remarked, "are not really 'anti-historical' by principle; it is simply that we do not know how to fit historical materials into our framework of concepts" (1954:282).

A revision of the concepts of functional theory so as to make them capable of dealing more effectively with "historical materials" might well begin with an attempt to distinguish analytically between the cultural and social aspects of human life, and to treat them as independently variable yet mutually interdependent factors. Though separable only conceptually, culture and social structure will then be seen to be capable of a wide range of modes of integration with one another, of which the simple isomorphic mode is but a limiting case—a case common only in societies which have been stable over such an extended time as to make possible a close adjustment between social and cultural aspects. In most societies, where change is a characteristic rather than an abnormal occurrence, we shall expect to find more or less radical discontinuities between the two. I would argue that it is in these very discontinuities that we shall find some of the primary driving forces in change.

One of the more useful ways—but far from the only one—of distinguishing between culture and social system is to see the former as an ordered system of meaning and of symbols, in terms of which social interaction takes place; and to see the latter as the pattern of social interaction itself (Parsons and Shils 1951). On the one level there is the framework of beliefs, expressive symbols, and values in terms of which individuals define their world, express their feelings, and make their judgments; on the other level there is the ongoing process of interactive behavior, whose persistent form we call social structure. Culture is the fabric of meaning in terms of which human beings interpret their experience and guide their action; social structure is the form that action takes, the actually existing network of social relations. Culture and social structure are then but different abstractions from the same phenomena. The one considers social action in respect to its meaning for those who carry it out, the other considers it in terms of its contribution to the functioning of some social system.

The nature of the distinction between culture and social system is brought out more clearly when one considers the contrasting sorts of integration characteristic of each of them. This contrast is between what Sorokin (1937) has called "logico-meaningful integration" and what he has called "causal-functional integration." By logico-meaningful integration, characteristic of culture, is meant the sort of integration one finds in a Bach fugue, in Catholic dogma, or in the general theory of relativity; it is a unity of style, of logical implication, of meaning and value. By causal-functional integration, characteristic of the social system, is meant the kind of integration one finds in an organism, where all the parts are united in a single causal web; each part is an element in a reverberating causal ring which "keeps the system going." And because these two types of integration are not identical, because the particular form one of them takes does not directly imply the form the other will take, there is an inherent incongruity and tension between the two and between both of them and a third element, the pattern of motivational integration within the individual which we usually call personality structure:

> Thus conceived, a social system is only one of three aspects of the structuring of a completely concrete system of social action. The other two are the personality systems of the individual actors and the cultural system which is built into their action. Each of the three must be considered to be an independent focus of the organization of the elements of the action system in the sense that no one of them is theoretically reducible to terms of one or a combination of the other two. Each is indispensable to the other two in the sense that without personalities and culture there would be no social system and so on around the roster of logical possibilities. But this interdependence and interpenetration is a very different matter from reducibility, which would mean that the important properties and processes of one class of system could be theoretically *de-*

rived from our theoretical knowledge of one or both of the other two. The action frame of reference is common to all three and this fact makes certain "transformations" between them possible. But on the level of theory here attempted they do not constitute a single system, however this might turn out to be on some other theoretical level (Parsons 1951:6).

I will attempt to demonstrate the utility of this more dynamic functionalist approach by applying it to a particular case of a ritual which failed to function properly. I shall try to show how an approach which does not distinguish the "logico-meaningful" cultural aspects of the ritual pattern from the "causal-functional" social structural aspects is unable to account adequately for this ritual failure, and how an approach which does so distinguish them is able to analyze more explicitly the cause of the trouble. It will further be argued that such an approach is able to avoid the simplistic view of the functional role of religion in society which sees that role merely as structure-conserving, and to substitute for it a more complex conception of the relations between religious belief and practice and secular social life. Historical materials can be fitted into such a conception, and the functional analysis of religion can therefore be widened to deal more adequately with processes of change.

The Setting

The case to be described is that of a funeral held in Modjokuto, a small town in eastern Central Java.[1] A young boy, about ten years of age, who was living with his uncle and aunt, died very suddenly but his death, instead of being followed by the usual hurried, subdued, yet methodically efficient Javanese funeral ceremony and burial routine, brought on an extended period of pronounced social strain and severe psychological tension. The complex of beliefs and rituals which had for generations brought countless Javanese safely through the difficult post-mortem period suddenly failed to work with its accustomed effectiveness. To understand why it failed demands knowledge and understanding of a whole range of social and cultural changes which have taken place in Java since the first decades of this century. This disrupted funeral was in fact but a microcosmic example of the broader conflicts, structural dissolutions, and attempted reintegrations which, in one form or another, are characteristic of contemporary Indonesian society.

The religious tradition of Java, particularly of the peasantry, is a composite of Indian, Islamic, and indigenous Southeast Asian elements (Landon 1949). The rise of large, militaristic kingdoms in the inland rice basins in the early centuries of the Christian era was associated with the diffusion of Hinduist and Buddhist culture patterns to the island; the expansion of international maritime trade in the port cities of the northern coast in the fifteenth and sixteenth centuries was associated with the diffusion of Islamic patterns. Working their way into the peasant mass, these two world religions became fused with the underlying animistic traditions characteristic of the whole Malaysian culture area. The result was a balanced syncretism of myth and ritual in which Hindu gods and goddesses, Moslem prophets and saints, and local place spirits and demons all found a proper place.

The central ritual form in this syncretism is a communal feast, called the *slametan*. Slametans, which are given with only slight variations in form and content on almost all occasions of religious significance—at passage points in the life cycle, on calendrical holidays, at certain stages of the crop cycle, on

changing one's residence, etc.—are intended to be both offerings to the spirits and commensal mechanisms of social integration for the living. The meal, which consists of specially prepared dishes, each symbolic of a particular religious concept, is cooked by the female members of one nuclear family household and set out on mats in the middle of the living-room. The male head of the household invites the male heads of the eight or ten contiguous households to attend; no close neighbor is ignored in favor of one further away. After a speech by the host explaining the spiritual purpose of the feast and a short Arabic chant, each man takes a few hurried, almost furtive, gulps of food, wraps the remainder of the meal in a banana-leaf basket, and returns home to share it with his family. It is said that the spirits draw their sustenance from the odor of the food, the incense which is burned, and the Moslem prayer; the human participants draw theirs from the material substance of the food and from their social interaction. The result of this quiet, undramatic little ritual is twofold: the spirits are appeased and neighborhood solidarity is strengthened.[2]

The ordinary canons of functional theory are quite adequate for the analysis of such a pattern. It can rather easily be shown that the slametan is well designed both to "tune up the ultimate value attitudes" necessary to the effective integration of a territorially-based social structure, and to fulfill the psychological needs for intellectual coherence and emotional stability characteristic of a peasant population. The Javanese village (once or twice a year, village-wide slametans are held) is essentially a set of geographically contiguous, but rather self-consciously autonomous, nuclear family households whose economic and political interdependence is of roughly the same circumscribed and explicitly defined sort as that demonstrated in the slametan. The demands of the labor-intensive rice and dry-crop agricultural process require the perpetuation of specific modes of technical co-operation and enforce a sense of community on the otherwise rather self-contained families—a sense of community which the slametan clearly reinforces. And when we consider the manner in which various conceptual and behavioral elements from Hindu-Buddhism, Islam, and "animism" are reinterpreted and balanced to form a distinctive and nearly homogeneous religious style, the close functional adjustment between the communal feast pattern and the conditions of Javanese rural life is even more readily apparent.

But the fact is that in all but the most isolated parts of Java, both the simple territorial basis of village social integration and the syncretic basis of its cultural homogeneity have been progressively undermined over the past fifty years. Population growth, urbanization, monetization, occupational differentiation, and the like, have combined to weaken the traditional ties of peasant social structure; and the winds of doctrine which have accompanied the appearance of these structural changes have disturbed the simple uniformity of religious belief and practice characteristic of an earlier period. The rise of nationalism, Marxism, and Islamic reform as ideologies, which resulted in part from the increasing complexity of Javanese society, has affected not only the large cities where these creeds first appeared and have always had their greatest strength, but has had a heavy impact on the smaller towns and villages as well. In fact, much of recent Javanese social change is perhaps most aptly characterized as a shift from a situation in which the primary integrative ties between individuals (or between families) are phrased in terms of geographical proximity to one in which they are phrased in terms of ideological like-mindedness.

In the villages and small towns these major ideological changes appeared largely in the guise of a widening split between those who emphasized the Islamic aspects of the indigenous religious syncretism and those who emphasized the Hinduist and animistic elements. It is true that some difference between these variant subtraditions has been present since the arrival of Islam; some individuals have always been particularly skilled in Arabic chanting or particularly learned in Moslem law, while others have been adept at more Hinduistic mystical practices or specialists in local curing techniques. But these contrasts were softened by the easy tolerance of the Javanese for a wide range of religious concepts, so long as basic ritual patterns— i.e., slametans—were faithfully supported; whatever social divisiveness they stimulated was largely obscured by the over-riding commonalities of rural and small-town life.

However, the appearance after 1910 of Islamic modernism (as well as vigorous conservative reactions against it) and religious nationalism among the economically and politically sophisticated trading classes of the larger cities strengthened the feeling for Islam as an exclusivist, antisyncretic creed among the more orthodox element of the mass of the population. Similarly, secular nationalism and Marxism, appearing among the civil servants and the expanding proletariat of these cities, strengthened the pre-Islamic (i.e., Hinduist-animist) elements of the syncretic pattern, which these groups tended to prize as a counterweight to puristic Islam and which some of them adopted as a general religious framework in which to set their more specifically political ideas. On the one hand, there arose a more self-conscious Moslem, basing his religious beliefs and practices more explicitly on the international and universalistic doctrines of Mohammed; on the other hand there arose a more self-conscious "nativist," attempting to evolve a generalized religious system out of the material—muting the more Islamic elements—of his inherited religious tradition. And the contrast between the first kind of man, called a *santri,* and the second, called an *abangan,* grew steadily more acute, until today it forms the major cultural distinction in the whole of the Modjokuto area.[3]

It is especially in the town that this contrast has come to play a crucial role. The absence of pressures toward interfamilial co-operation exerted by the technical requirements of wet-rice growing, as well as lessened effectiveness of the traditional forms of village government in the face of the complexities of urban living, severely weaken the social supports of the syncretic village pattern. When each man makes his living—as chauffeur, trader, clerk, or laborer—more or less independently of how his neighbors make theirs, his sense of the importance of the neighborhood community naturally diminishes. A more differentiated class system, more bureaucratic and impersonal forms of government, greater heterogeneity of social background, all tend to lead to the same result: the deemphasis of strictly geographical ties in favor of diffusely ideological ones. For the townsman, the distinction between santri and abangan becomes even sharper, for it emerges as his primary point of social reference; it becomes a symbol of his social identity, rather than a mere contrast in belief. The sort of friends he will have, the sort of organizations he will join, the sort of political leadership he will follow, the sort of person he or his son will marry, will all be strongly influenced by the side of this ideological bifurcation which he adopts as his own.

There is thus emerging in the town— though not only in the town—a new pattern of social living organized in terms of an altered framework of cultural classification. Among the elite this new pattern has already become rather highly developed, but among the mass of the townspeople it is still in the process of formation. Particularly in the *kampongs,* the off-the-street neighborhoods in which the common Javanese townsmen live crowded together in a helter-skelter profusion of little bamboo houses, one finds a transitional society in which the traditional forms of rural living are being steadily dissolved and new forms steadily reconstructed. In these enclaves of peasants-come-to-town (or of sons and grandsons of peasants-come-to-town), Redfield's folk culture is being constantly converted into his urban culture, though this latter is not accurately characterized by such negative and residual terms as "secular," "individualized," and "culturally disorganized." What is occurring in the kampongs is not so much a destruction of traditional ways of life, as a construction of a new one; the sharp social conflict characteristic of these lower-class neighborhoods is not simply indicative of a loss of cultural consensus, but rather indicative of a search, not yet entirely successful, for new, more generalized, and flexible patterns of belief and value.

In Modjokuto, as in most of Indonesia, this search is taking place largely within the social context of the mass political parties, as well as in the women's clubs, youth organizations, labor unions, and other sodalities formally or informally linked with them. There are several of these parties (though the recent general election severely reduced their number), each led by educated urban elites— civil servants, teachers, traders, students, and the like—and each competing with the others for the political allegiance of both the half rural, half urban kampong dwellers and of the mass of the peasantry. And almost without exception, they appeal to one or another side of the santri-abangan split. Of this complex of political parties and sodalities, only two are of immediate concern to us here: Masjumi, a huge, Islam-based political party; and Permai, a vigorously anti-Moslem politico-religious cult.

Masjumi is the more or less direct descendent of the pre-war Islamic reform movement. Led, at least in Modjokuto, by modernist santri intellectuals, it stands for a socially conscious, anti-scholastic, and somewhat puritanical version of back-to-the-Koran Islam. In company with the other Moslem parties, it also supports the institution of an "Islamic State" in Indonesia in place of the present secular republic. However, the meaning of this ideal is not entirely clear. Masjumi's enemies accuse it of pressing for an intolerant, medievalist theocracy in which abangans and non-Moslems will be persecuted and forced to follow exactly the prescripts of the Moslem law, while Masjumi's leaders claim that Islam is intrinsically tolerant and that they only desire a government explicitly based on the Moslem creed, one whose laws will be in consonance with the teachings of the Koran and Hadith. In any case, Masjumi, the country's largest Moslem party, is one of the major spokesmen on both the national and the local levels for the values and aspirations of the santri community.

Permai is not so impressive on a national scale. Though it is a nation-wide party, it is a fairly small one, having strength only in a few fairly circumscribed regions. In the Modjokuto area however, it happened to be of some importance, and what it lacked in national scope it made up in local intensity. Essentially, Permai is a fusion of Marxist politics with abangan religious patterns. It combines a fairly explicit anti-Westernism, anti-capitalism, and anti-imperialism with an attempt to formalize and generalize some of the more characteristic diffuse themes of the peasant religious syncretism. Permai meetings follow both the slametan pattern, complete with incense and symbolic food (but without Islamic chants), and modern parliamentary procedure; Permai pamphlets contain calendrical and numerological divinatory systems and mystical teachings as well as analyses of class conflict; and Permai speeches are concerned with elaborating both religious and political concepts. In Modjokuto, Permai is also a curing cult, with its own special medical practices and spells, a secret password, and cabalistic interpretations of passages in the leaders' social and political writings.

But Permai's most notable characteristic is its strong anti-Moslem stand. Charging that Islam is a foreign import, unsuited to the needs and values of the Javanese, the cult urges a return to "pure" and "original" Javanese beliefs, by which they seem to mean to the indigenous syncretism with the more Islamic elements removed. In line with this, the cult-party has initiated a drive, on both national and local levels, for secular (i.e., non-Islamic) marriage and funeral rites. As the situation stands now, all but Christians and Balinese Hindus must have their marriages legitimatized by means of the Moslem ritual.[4] Funeral rites are an individual concern but, because of the long history of syncretism, they are so deeply involved with Islamic customs that a genuinely non-Islamic funeral tends to be a practical impossibility.

Permai's action on the local level in pursuit of non-Islamic marriage and funeral ceremonies took two forms. One was heavy pressure on local government officials to permit such practices, and the other was heavy pressure on its own members to follow, voluntarily, rituals purified of Islamic elements. In the case of marriage, success was more or less precluded because the local official's hands were tied by Central Government ordinances, and even highly ideologized members of the cult would not dare an openly "illegitimate" marriage. Without a change in the law, Permai had little chance to alter marriage forms, though a few abortive attempts were made to conduct civil ceremonies under the aegis of abangan-minded village chiefs.

The case of funerals was somewhat different, for a matter of custom rather than law was involved. During the year I was in the field, the tension between Permai and Masjumi increased very sharply. This was due in part to the imminence of Indonesia's first general elections, and in part to the effects of the cold war. It was also influenced by various special occurrences—such as a report that the national head of Permai had publicly called Mohammed a false prophet; a speech in the nearby regional capital by a Masjumi leader in which he accused Permai of intending to raise a generation of bastards in Indonesia; and a bitter village-chief election largely fought out on santri vs. abangan grounds. As a result, the local subdistrict officer, a worried bureaucrat trapped in the middle, called a meeting of all the village religious officials, or Modins. Among many other duties, a Modin is traditionally responsible for conducting funerals. He directs the whole ritual, instructs the mourners in the technical details of burial, leads the Koran chanting, and reads a set speech to the deceased at the graveside. The subdistrict officer instructed the Modins—the majority of whom were village Masjumi leaders—that in the case of the death of a member of Permai, they were merely to note the name and age of the deceased and return home; they were not to participate in the ritual. He warned that if they did not do as he advised, they would be responsible if trouble started and he would not come to their support.

This was the situation on July 17, 1954, when Paidjan, nephew of Karman, an active and ardent member of Permai, died suddenly in the Modjokuto kampong in which I was living.

The Funeral

The mood of a Javanese funeral is not one of hysterical bereavement, unrestrained sobbing, or even of formalized cries of grief for the deceased's departure. Rather, it is a calm, undemonstrative, almost languid letting go, a brief ritualized relinquishment of a relationship no longer possible. Tears are not approved of and certainly not encouraged; the effort is to get the job done, not to linger over the pleasures of grief. The detailed busy-work of the funeral, the politely formal social intercourse with the neighbors pressing in from all sides, the series of commemorative slametans stretched out at intervals for almost three years—the whole momentum of the Javanese ritual system is supposed to carry one through grief without severe emotional disturbance. For the mourner, the funeral and postfuneral ritual is said to produce a feeling of *iklas*, a kind of willed affectlessness, a detached and static state of "not caring"; for the neighborhood group it is said to produce *rukun*, "communal harmony."

The actual service is in essence simply another version of the slametan, adapted to the special requirements of interment. When the news of a death is broadcast through the area, everyone in the neighborhood must drop what he is doing and go immediately to the home of the survivors. The women bring bowls of rice, which is cooked up into a slametan; the men begin to cut wooden grave markers and to dig a grave. Soon the Modin arrives and begins to direct activities. The corpse is washed in ceremonially prepared water by the relatives (who unflinchingly hold the body on their laps to demonstrate their affection for the deceased as well as their self-control); then it is wrapped in muslin. About a dozen santris, under the leadership of the Modin, chant Arabic prayers over the body for five or ten minutes; after this it is carried, amid various ritual acts, in a ceremonial procession to the graveyard, where it is interred in prescribed ways. The Modin reads a graveside speech to the deceased, reminding him of his duties as a believing Moslem; and the funeral is over, usually only two or three hours after death. The funeral proper is followed by commemorative slametans in the home of the survivors at three, seven, forty, and one hundred days after death; on the first and second anniversary of death; and, finally, on the thousandth day, when the corpse is considered to have turned to dust and the gap between the living and the dead to have become absolute.

This was the ritual pattern which was called into play when Paidjan died. As soon as dawn broke (death occurred in the early hours of the morning), Karman, the uncle, dispatched a telegram to the boy's parents in a nearby city, telling them in characteristic Javanese fashion that their son was ill. This evasion was intended to soften the impact of death by allowing them to become aware of it more gradually. Javanese feel that emotional damage results not from the severity of a frustration but from the suddenness with which it comes, the degree to which it "surprises" one unprepared for it. It is "shock," not suffering itself, which is feared. Next, in the expectation that the parents would arrive within a few hours, Karman sent for the Modin to begin the ceremony. This was done on the theory that by the time the parents had come little would be left to do but inter the body, and they would thus once more be spared unnecessary stress. By ten o'clock at the very

latest it should all be over; a saddening incident, but a ritually muted one.

But when the Modin, as he later told me, arrived at Karman's house and saw the poster displaying Permai's political symbol, he told Karman that he could not perform the ritual. After all, Karman belonged to "another religion" and he, the Modin, did not know the correct burial rituals for it; all he knew was Islam. "I don't want to insult your religion," he said piously, "on the contrary, I hold it in the utmost regard, for there is no intolerance in Islam. But I don't know your ritual. The Christians have their own ritual and their own specialist (the local preacher), but what does Permai do? Do they burn the corpse or what?" (This is a sly allusion to Hindu burial practices; evidently the Modin enjoyed himself hugely in this interchange.) Karman was, the Modin told me, rather upset at all this and evidently surprised, for although he was an active member of Permai, he was a fairly unsophisticated one. It had evidently never occurred to him that the anti-Moslem-funeral agitation of the party would ever appear as a concrete problem, or that the Modin would actually refuse to officiate. Karman was actually not a bad fellow, the Modin concluded; he was but a dupe of his leaders.

After leaving the now highly agitated Karman, the Modin went directly to the subdistrict officer to ask if he had acted properly. The officer was morally bound to say that he had, and thus fortified the Modin returned home to find Karman and the village policeman, to whom he had gone in desperation, waiting for him. The policeman, a personal friend of Karman's, told the Modin that according to time-honored custom he was supposed to bury everyone with impartiality, never mind whether he happened to agree with their politics. But the Modin, having now been personally supported by the subdistrict officer, insisted that it was no longer his responsibility. However, he suggested, if Karman wished, he could go to the village chief's office and sign a public statement, sealed with the Government stamp and countersigned by the village chief in the presence of two witnesses, declaring that he, Karman, was a true believing Moslem and that he wished the Modin to bury the boy according to Islamic custom. At this suggestion that he officially abandon his religious beliefs, Karman exploded into a rage and stormed from the house, rather uncharacteristic behavior for a Javanese. By the time he arrived home again, at his wit's end about what to do next, he found to his dismay that the news of the boy's death had been broadcast and the entire neighborhood was already gathering for the ceremony.

Like most of the kampongs in the town of Modjokuto, the one in which I lived consisted both of pious santris and ardent abangans (as well as a number of less intense adherents of either side), mixed together in a more or less random manner. In the town, people are forced to live where they can and take whomever they find for neighbors, in contrast to the rural areas where whole neighborhoods, even whole villages, still tend to be made up almost entirely of either abangans or santris. The majority of the santris in the kampong were members of Masjumi and most of the abangans were followers of Permai, and in daily life, social interaction between the two groups was minimal. The abangans, most of whom were either petty artisans or manual laborers, gathered each late afternoon at Karman's roadside coffee shop for the idle twilight conversations which are typical of small town and village life in Java; the santris—tailors, traders and store-keepers for the most part—usually gathered in one or another of the santri-run shops for the same purpose. But

despite this lack of close social ties, the demonstration of territorial unity at a funeral was still felt by both groups to be an unavoidable duty; of all the Javanese rituals, the funeral probably carries the greatest obligation on attendance. Everyone who lives within a certain roughly defined radius of the survivors' home is expected to come to the ceremony; and on this occasion everyone did.

With this as background, it is not surprising that when I arrived at Karman's house about eight o'clock, I found two separate clusters of sullen men squatting disconsolately on either side of the yard, a nervous group of whispering women sitting idly inside the house near the still clothed body, and a general air of doubt and uneasiness in place of the usual quiet busyness of slametan preparing, body washing and guest greeting. The abangans were grouped near the house where Karman was crouched, staring blankly off into space, and where Sudjoko and Sastro, the town Chairman and Secretary of Permai (the only non-residents of the kampong present) sat on chairs, looking vaguely out of place. The santris were crowded together under the narrow shadow of a coconut palm about thirty yards away, chatting quietly to one another about everything but the problem at hand. The almost motionless scene suggested an unlooked-for intermission in a familiar drama, as when a motion picture stops in the mid-action.

After a half hour or so, a few of the abangans began to chip half-heartedly away at pieces of wood to make markers and a few women began to construct small flower offerings for want of anything better to do; but it was clear that the ritual was arrested and that no one quite knew what to do next. Tension slowly rose. People nervously watched the sun rise higher and higher in the sky, or glanced at the impassive Karman. Mutterings about the sorry state of affairs began to appear ("everything these days is a political problem," an old, traditionalistic man of about eighty grumbled to me, "you can't even die any more but what it becomes a political problem"). Finally, about 9:30, a young santri tailor named Abu decided to try to do something about the situation before it deteriorated entirely: he stood up and gestured to Karman, the first serious instrumental act which had occured all morning. And Karman, roused from his meditation, crossed the no-man's-land to talk to him.

As a matter of fact, Abu occupied a rather special position in the kampong. Although he was a pious santri and a loyal Masjumi member, he had more contact with the Permai group because his tailor shop was located directly behind Karman's coffee shop. Though Abu, who stuck to his sewing machine night and day, was not properly a member of this group, he would often exchange comments with them from his work bench about twenty feet away. True, a certain amount of tension existed between him and the Permai people over religious issues. Once, when I was inquiring about their eschatological beliefs, they referred me sarcastically to Abu, saying he was an expert, and they teased him quite openly about what they considered the wholly ridiculous Islamic theories of the after life. Nevertheless, he had something of a social bond with them, and it was perhaps reasonable that he should be the one to try to break the deadlock.

"It is already nearly noon," Abu said, "things can't go straight on like this." He suggested that he send Umar, another of the santris, to see if the Modin could now be induced to come; perhaps things were cooler with him now. Meanwhile, he could get the washing and wrapping of the corpse started himself. Karman replied that he would think about it, and returned to the other side of the yard for a discussion with the two Permai leaders. After a few minutes of vigorous gesturing and nodding, Karman returned and said simply, "all right, that way." "I know how you feel," Abu said, "I'll just do what is absolutely necessary and keep the Islam out as much as possible." He gathered the santris together and they entered the house.

The first requisite was stripping the corpse (which was still lying on the floor, because no one could bring himself to move it). But by now the body was rigid, making it necessary to cut the clothes off with a knife, an unusual procedure which deeply disturbed everyone, especially the women clustered around. The santris finally managed to get the body outside and set up the bathing enclosure. Abu asked for volunteers for the washing; he reminded them that God would consider such an act a good work. But the relatives, who normally would be expected to undertake this task, were by now so deeply shaken and confused that they were unable to bring themselves to hold the boy on their laps in the customary fashion. There was another wait while people looked hopelessly at each other. Finally, Pak Sura, a member of Karman's group but no relative, took the boy on his lap, although he was clearly frightened and kept whispering a protective spell. One reason the Javanese give for their custom of rapid burial is that it is dangerous to have the spirit of the deceased hovering around the house.

Before the washing could begin, however, someone raised the question as to whether one person was enough—wasn't it usually three? No one was quite sure, including Abu; some thought that although it was customary to have three people it was not obligatory, and some thought three a necessary number. After about ten minutes of anxious discussion, a male cousin of the boy and a carpenter, unrelated to him, managed to work up the courage to join Pak Sura. Abu, attempting to act the Modin's role as best he could, sprinkled a few drops of water on the corpse and then it was washed, rather haphazardly and in unsacralized water. When this was finished, however, the procedure was again stalled, for no one knew exactly how to arrange the small cotton pads which, under Moslem law, should plug the body orifices. Karman's wife, sister of the deceased's mother, could evidently take no more, for she broke into a loud, unrestrained wailing, the only demonstration of this sort I witnessed among the dozen or so Javanese funerals I attended. Everyone was further upset by this development, and most of the kampong women made a frantic but unavailing effort to comfort her. Most of the men remained seated in the yard, outwardly calm and inexpressive, but the embarrassed uneasiness which had been present since the beginning seemed to be turning toward fearful desperation. "It is not nice for her to cry that way," several men said to me, "it isn't proper." At this point, the Modin arrived.

However, he was still adamant. Further, he warned Abu that he was courting eternal damnation by his actions. "You will have to answer to God on Judgment Day," he said, "if you make mistakes in the ritual. It will be your responsibility. For a Moslem, burial is a serious matter and must be carried out according to the Law by someone who knows what the Law is, not according to the will of the individual." He then suggested to Sudjoko and Sastro, the Permai leaders, that they take charge of the funeral, for as party "intellectuals" they must certainly know what kind of funeral customs Permai followed. The two leaders, who had not moved from their chairs, considered this as everyone watched expectantly, but they finally refused, with some chagrin, saying they really did not know how to go about it. The Modin shrugged and turned away.

One of the bystanders, a friend of Karman's, then suggested that they just take the body out and bury it and forget about the whole ritual; it was extremely dangerous to leave things as they were much longer. I don't know whether this remarkable suggestion would have been followed, for at this juncture the mother and father of the dead child entered the kampong.

They seemed quite composed. They were not unaware of the death, for the father later told me he had suspected as much when he got the telegram; he and his wife had prepared themselves for the worst and were more or less resigned by the time they arrived. When they approached the kampong and saw the whole neighborhood gathered, they knew that their fears were well founded. When Karman's wife, whose weeping had subsided slightly, saw the dead boy's mother come into the yard, she burst free of those who were comforting her and with a shriek rushed to embrace her sister. In what seemed a split second, both women had dissolved into wild hysterics and the crowd had rushed in and pulled them apart, dragging them to houses at opposite sides of the kampong. Their wailing continued in undiminished volume, and nervous comments arose to the effect that they ought to get on with the burial in one fashion or another, before the boy's spirit possessed someone.

But the mother now insisted on seeing the body of her child before it was wrapped. The father at first forbade it, angrily ordering her to stop crying—didn't she know that such behavior would darken the boy's pathway to the other world? But she persisted and so they brought her, stumbling, to where he lay in Karman's house. The women tried to keep her from drawing too close, but she broke loose and began to kiss the boy about the genitals. She was snatched away almost immediately by her husband and the women, though she screamed that she had not yet finished; and they pulled her into the back room where she subsided into a daze. After a while—the body was finally being wrapped, the Modin having unbent enough to point out where the cotton pads went—she seemed to lose her bearings entirely and began to move about the yard shaking hands with everyone, all strangers to her, and saying "forgive me my faults, forgive me my faults." Again she was forcibly restrained; people said, "calm yourself, think of your other children— do you want to follow your son to the grave?"

The corpse was now wrapped and new suggestions were made that it be taken off immediately to the graveyard. At this point, Abu approached the father, who, he evidently felt, had now displaced Karman as the man legally responsible for the proceedings. Abu explained that the Modin, being a Government official, did not feel free to approach the father himself, but he would like to know: how did he wish the boy to be buried—the Islamic way or what? The father, some-what bewildered, said, "Of course, the Islamic way. I don't have much of any religion, but I'm not a Christian, and when it comes to death the burial should be the Islamic way. Completely Islamic." Abu explained again that the Modin could not approach the father directly, but that he, being "free," could do as he pleased. He said that he had tried to help as best he could but that he had been careful to do nothing Islamic before the father came. It was too bad, he apologized, about all the tension that was in the air, that political differences had to make so much trouble. But after all, everything had to be "clear" and "legal" about the funeral. It was important for the boy's soul. The santris, somewhat gleefully, now chanted their prayers over the corpse, and it was carried to the grave and buried in the usual manner.

The Modin gave the usual graveyard speech, as amended for children, and the funeral was finally completed. None of the relatives or the women went to the graveyard; but when we returned to the house—it was now well after noon— the slametan was finally served, and Paidjan's spirit presumably left the kam-pong to begin its journey to the other world.

Three days later, in the evening, the first of the commemorative slametans was held, but it turned out that not only were no santris present but that it was as much a Permai political and religious cult meet-ing as a mourning ritual. Karman started off in the traditional fashion by announc-ing in high Javanese that this was a slametan in remembrance of the death of Paidjan. Sudjoko, the Permai leader, immediately burst in saying, "No, no, that is wrong. At a third day slametan you just eat and give a long Islamic chant for the dead, and we are certainly not going to do that." He then launched into a long, rambling speech. Everyone, he said, must know the philosophical-religious basis of the country. "Suppose this American (he pointed to me; he was not at all pleased by my presence) came up and asked you: what is the spiritual basis of the country? and you didn't know—wouldn't you be ashamed?"

He went on in this vein, building up a whole rationale for the present na-tional political structure on the basis of a mystical interpretation of President Sukarno's "Five Points" (Monotheism, Social Justice, Humanitarianism, Democ-racy, and Nationalism[5]) which are the official ideological foundation of the new republic. Aided by Karman and others, he worked out a micromacrocosm cor-respondence theory in which the indi-vidual is seen to be but a small replica of the state, and the state but an enlarged image of the individual. If the state is to be ordered, then the individual must also be ordered; each implies the other. As the President's Five Points are at the basis of the state, so the five senses are at the basis of an individual. The process of harmonizing both is the same, and it is this we must be sure we know. The discussion continued for nearly half an hour, ranging widely through religious, philosophical, and political issues (including, evidently for my benefit, a discussion of the Rosenbergs' execution).

We paused for coffee and as Sudjoko was about to begin again, Paidjan's father, who had been sitting quietly and expressionless, began suddenly to talk, softly and with a curiously mechanical tonelessness, almost as if he were reasoning with himself but without much hope of success. "I am sorry for my rough city accent," he said, "but I very much want to say something." He hoped they would forgive him; they could continue their discussion in a moment. "I have been trying to be iklas ("detached," "resigned") about Paidjan's death. I'm convinced that everything that could have been done for him was done and that his death was just an event which simply happened." He said he was still in Modjokuto because he could not yet face the people where he lived, couldn't face having to tell each one of them what had occurred. His wife, he said, was a little more iklas now too. It was hard, though. He kept telling himself it was just the will of God, but it was so hard, for nowadays people didn't agree on things any more; one person tells you one thing and others tell you another. It's hard to know which is right, to know what to believe. He said he appreciated all the Modjokuto people coming to the funeral, and he was sorry it had been all mixed up. "I'm not very religious myself. I'm not Masjumi and I'm not Permai. But I wanted the boy to be buried in the old way. I hope no one's feelings were hurt." He said again he was trying to be iklas, to tell

himself it was just the will of God, but it was hard, for things were so confused these days. It was hard to see why the boy should have died.

This sort of public expression of one's feelings is extremely unusual—in my experience unique—among Javanese, and in the formalized traditional slametan pattern there is simply no place for it (nor for philosophical or political discussion). Everyone present was rather shaken by the father's talk, and there was a painful silence. Sudjoko finally began to talk again, but this time he described in detail the boy's death. How Paidjan had first gotten a fever and Karman had called him, Sudjoko, to come and say a Permai spell. But the boy did not respond. They finally took him to a male nurse in the hospital, where he was given an injection. But still he worsened. He vomited blood and went into convulsions, which Sudjoko described rather graphically, and then he died. "I don't know why the Permai spell didn't work," he said, "it has worked before. This time it didn't. I don't know why; that sort of thing can't be explained no matter how much you think about it. Sometimes it just works and sometimes it just doesn't." There was another silence and then, after about ten minutes more of political discussion, we disbanded. The father returned the next day to his home and I was not invited to any of the later slametans. When I left the field about four months later, Karman's wife had still not entirely recovered from the experience, the tension between the santris and the abangans in the kampong had increased, and everyone wondered what would happen the next time a death occurred in a Permai family.

Analysis

"Of all the sources of religion," wrote Malinowski, "the supreme and final crisis of life—death—is of the greatest importance" (1948:29). Death, he argued, provokes in the survivors a dual response of love and loathing, a deep-going emotional ambivalence of fascination and fear which threatens both the psychological and social foundations of human existence. The survivors are drawn toward the deceased by their affection for him, repelled from him by the dreadful transformation wrought by death. Funeral rites, and the mourning practices which follow them, focus around this paradoxical desire both to maintain the tie in the face of death and to break the bond immediately and utterly, and they insure the domination of the will to live over the tendency to despair. Mortuary rituals maintain the continuity of human life by preventing the survivors from yielding either to the impulse to flee panic-stricken from the scene or to the contrary impulse to follow the deceased into the grave:

> And here into this play of emotional forces, into this supreme dilemma of life and final death, religion steps in, selecting the positive creed, the comforting view, the culturally valuable belief in immortality, in the spirit independent of the body, and in the continuance of life after death. In the various ceremonies at death, in commemoration and communion with the departed, and worship of ancestral ghosts, religion gives body and form to the saving beliefs . . . Exactly the same function it fulfills also with regard to the whole group. The ceremonial of death which ties the survivors to the body and rivets them to the place of death, the beliefs in the existence of the spirit, in its beneficent influences or malevolent intentions, in the duties of a series of commemorative or sacrificial ceremonies—in all this religion counteracts the centrifugal forces of fear, dismay, demoralization,

and provides the most powerful means of reintegration of the group's shaken solidarity and of the re-establishment of its morale. (In short, religion here assures the victory of tradition over the mere negative response of thwarted instinct) (ibid: 33–35).

To this sort of theory, a case such as that described above clearly poses some difficult problems. Not only was the victory of tradition and culture over "thwarted instinct" a narrow one at best, but it seemed as if the ritual were tearing the society apart rather than integrating it, were disorganizing personalities rather than healing them. To this the functionalist has a ready answer, which takes one of two forms depending upon whether he follows the Durkheim or the Malinowski tradition: social disintegration or cultural demoralization. Rapid social change has disrupted Javanese society and this is reflected in a disintegrated culture; as the unified state of traditional village society was mirrored in the unified slametan, so the broken society of the kampong is mirrored in the broken slametan of the funeral ritual we have just witnessed. Or, in the alternate phraseology, cultural decay has led to social fragmentation; loss of a vigorous folk tradition has weakened the moral ties between individuals.

It seems to me that there are two things wrong with this argument, no matter in which of the two vocabularies it is stated: it identifies social (or cultural) conflict with social (or cultural) disintegration; it denies independent roles to both culture and social structure, regarding one of the two as a mere epiphenomenon of the other.

In the first place, kampong life is not simply anomic. Though it is marked by vigorous social conflicts, as is our own saociety, it nevertheless proceeds fairly effectively in most areas. If governmental, economic, familial, stratificatory, and social control institutions functioned as poorly as did Paidjan's funeral, a kampong would indeed be an uncomfortable place in which to live. But though some of the typical symptoms of urban upheaval—such as increased gambling, petty thievery, and prostitution—are to some degree present, kampong social life is clearly not on the verge of collapse; everyday social interaction does not limp along with the suppressed bitterness and deep uncertainty we have seen focused around burial. For most of its members most of the time, a semi-urban neighborhood in Modjokuto offers a viable way of life, despite its material disadvantages and its transitional character; and for all the sentimentality which has been lavished on descriptions of rural life in Java, this is probably as much as one could say for the village. As a matter of fact, it is around religious beliefs and practices—slametans, holidays, curing, sorcery, cult groups, etc.—that the most seriously disruptive events seem to cluster. Religion here is somehow the center and source of stress, not merely the reflection of stress elsewhere in the society.[6]

Yet it is not a source of stress because commitment to the inherited patterns of belief and ritual has been weakened. The conflict around Paidjan's death took place simply because all the kampong residents did share a common, highly integrated, cultural tradition concerning funerals. There was no argument over whether the slametan pattern was the correct ritual, whether the neighbors were obligated to attend, or whether the supernatural concepts upon which the ritual is based were valid ones. For both santris and abangans in the kampongs, the slametan maintains its force as a genuine sacred symbol; it still provides a meaningful framework for facing death—for most people the only meaningful framework. We cannot attribute the failure of the ritual to secularization, to a growth in skepticism, or to a disinterest in the traditional "saving beliefs," any more than we can attribute it to anomie.

We must rather, I think, ascribe it to a discontinuity between the form of integration existing in the social structure ("causal-functional") dimension and the form of integration existing in the cultural ("logical-meaningful") dimension— a discontinuity which leads not to social and cultural disintegration, but to social and cultural conflict. In more concrete, if somewhat aphoristic terms, the difficulty lies in the fact that socially kampong people are urbanites, while culturally they are still folk.

I have already pointed out that the Javanese kampong represents a transitional sort of society, that its members stand "in between" the more or less fully urbanized elite and the more or less traditionally organized peasantry. The social structural forms in which they participate are for the most part urban ones. The emergence of a highly differentiated occupational structure in place of the almost entirely agricultural one of the countryside; the virtual disappearance of the semihereditary, traditional village government as a personalistic buffer between the individual and the rationalized central government bureaucracy, and its replacement by the more flexible forms of modern parliamentary democracy; the evolution of a multiclass society in which the kampong, unlike the village, is not even a potentially self-sufficient entity, but is only one dependent subpart—all this means that the kampong man lives in a very urban world. Socially, his is a *Gesellschaft* existence.

But on the cultural level—the level of meaning—there is much less of a contrast between the kampong dweller and the villager; much more between him and a member of the urban elite. The patterns of belief, expression, and value to which the kampong man is committed —his world-view, ethos, ethic, or whatever—differ only slightly from those followed by the villager. Amid a radically more complex social environment, he clings noticeably to the symbols which guided him or his parents through life in rural society. And it is this fact which gave rise to the psychological and social tension surrounding Paidjan's funeral.

The disorganization of the ritual resulted from a basic ambiguity in the meaning of the rite for those who participated in it. Most simply stated, this ambiguity lay in the fact that the symbols which compose the slametan had both religious and political significance, were charged with both sacred and profane import. The people who came into Karman's yard, including Karman himself, were not sure whether they were engaged in a sacralized consideration of first and last things or in a secular struggle for power. This is why the old man (he was a graveyard keeper, as a matter of fact) complained to me that dying was nowadays a political problem; why the village policeman accused the Modin not of religious but of political bias for refusing to bury Paidjan; why the unsophisticated Karman was astonished when his ideological commitments suddenly loomed as obstacles to his religious practices; why Abu was torn between his willingness to submerge political differences in the interest of a harmonious funeral and his unwillingness to trifle with his religious beliefs in the interest of his own salvation; why the commemorative rite oscillated between political diatribe and a poignant search for an adequate explanation of what had happened —why, in sum, the slametan religious pattern stumbled when it attempted to "step in" with the "positive creed" and "the culturally valuable belief."

As emphasized earlier, the present severity of the contrast between santri and abangan is in great part due to the rise of nationalist social movements in twentieth-century Indonesia. In the larger cities where these movements were born, they were originally of various sorts: tradesmen's societies to fight Chinese competition; unions of workers to resist plantation exploitation; religious groups trying to redefine ultimate concepts; philosophical discussion clubs attempting to clarify Indonesian metaphysical and moral notions; school associations striving to revivify Indonesian education; co-operative societies trying to work out new forms of economic organization; cultural groups moving toward a renaissance of Indonesian artistic life; and, of course, political parties working to build up effective opposition to Dutch rule. As time wore on, however, the struggle for independence absorbed more and more the energies of all these essentially elite groups. Whatever the distinctive aim of each of them—economic reconstruction, religious reform, artistic renaissance—it became submerged in a diffuse political ideology; all the groups were increasingly concerned with one end as the prerequisite of all further social and cultural progress— freedom. By the time the revolution began in 1945, reformulation of ideas outside the political sphere had noticeably slackened and most aspects of life had become intensely ideologized, a tendency which has continued into the postwar period.

In the villages and small town kampongs, the early, specific phase of nationalism had only a minor effect. But as the movement unified and moved toward eventual triumph, the masses too began to be affected and, as I have pointed out, mainly through the medium of religious symbols. The highly urbanized elite forged their bonds to the peasantry not in terms of complex political and economic theory, which would have had little meaning in a rural context, but in terms of concepts and values already present there. As the major line of demarcation among the elite was between those who took Islamic doctrine as the overall basis of their mass appeal and those who took a generalized philosophical refinement of the indigenous syncretic tradition as such a basis, so in the countryside santri and abangan soon became not simply religious but political categories, denoting the followers of these two diffuse approaches to the organization of the emerging independent society. When the achievement of political freedom strengthened the importance of factional politics in parliamentary government, the santri-abangan distinction became, on the local level at least, one of the primary ideological axes around which the process of party maneuvering took place.

The effect of this development has been to cause political debate and religious propitiation to be carried out in the same vocabulary. A koranic chant becomes an affirmation of political allegiance as well as a paean to God; a burning of incense expresses one's secular ideology as well as one's sacred beliefs. Slametans now tend to be marked by anxious discussions of the various elements in the ritual, of what their "real" significance is; by arguments as to whether a particular practice is essential or optional; by abangan uneasiness when santris lift their eyes to pray and santri uneasiness when abangans recite a protective spell. At death, as we have seen, the traditional symbols tend both to solidify individuals in the face of social loss and to remind them of their differences; to emphasize the broadly human themes of mortality and undeserved suffering and the narrowly social ones of factional opposition and party struggle; to strengthen the values the participants hold in common and to "tune up" their animosities and suspicions. The rituals themselves become matters of political conflict; forms for the sacralization of marriage and death are transformed into important party issues. In such an equiv-

ocal cultural setting, the average kampong Javanese finds it increasingly difficult to determine the proper attitude toward a particular event, to choose the meaning of a given symbol appropriate to a given social context.

The corollary of this interference of political meanings with religious meanings also occurs: the interference of religious meanings with political ones. Because the same symbols are used in both political and religious contexts, people often regard party struggle as involving not merely the usual ebb and flow of parliamentary maneuver, the necessary factional give-and-take of democratic government, but involving as well decisions on basic values and ultimates. Kampong people in particular tend to see the open struggle for power explicitly institutionalized in the new republican forms of government as a struggle for the right to establish different brands of essentially religious principles as official: "if the abangans get in, the koranic teachers will be forbidden to hold classes"; "if the santris get in, we shall all have to pray five times a day." The normal conflict involved in electoral striving for office is heightened by the idea that literally everything is at stake: the "if we win, it is our country" idea that the group which gains power has a right, as one man said, "to put his own foundation under the state." Politics thus takes on a kind of sacralized bitterness; and one village election in a suburban Modjokuto village actually had to be held twice because of the intense pressures generated in this way.

The kampong man is, so to speak, caught between his ultimate and his proximate concepts. Because he is forced to formulate his essentially metaphysical ideas, his response to such basic "problems" as fate, suffering, and evil, in the same terms as he states his claims to secular power, his political rights and aspirations, he experiences difficulty in enacting either a socially and psychologically efficient funeral or a smoothly running election.

But a ritual is not just a pattern of meaning; it is also a form of social interaction. Thus, in addition to creating cultural ambiguity, the attempt to bring a religious pattern from a relatively less differentiated rural background into an urban context also gives rise to social conflict, simply because the kind of social integration demonstrated by the pattern is not congruent with the major patterns of integration in the society generally. The way kampong people go about maintaining solidarity in everyday life is quite different from the way the slametan insists that they should go about maintaining it.

As emphasized earlier, the slametan is essentially a territorially based ritual; it assumes the primary tie between families to be that of residential propinquity. One set of neighbors is considered a significant social unit (politically, religiously, economically) as against another set of neighbors; one village as against another village; one village-cluster as against another village-cluster. In the town, this pattern has in large part changed. Significant social groups are defined by a plurality of factors—class, political commitment, occupation, ethnicity, regional origins, religious preference, age, and sex, as well as residence. The new urban form of organization consists of a careful balance of conflicting forces arising out of diverse contexts: class differences are softened by ideological similarities; ethic conflicts by common economic interests; political opposition, as we have seen, by residential intimacy. But in the midst of all this pluralistic checking and balancing, the slametan remains unchanged, blind to the major lines of social and cultural demarcation in urban life. For it, the primary classifying characteristic of an individual is where he lives.

Thus when an occasion arises demand-ing sacralization—a life-cycle transition, a holiday, a serious illness—the religious form which must be employed acts not with but against the grain of social equilibrium. The slametan ignores those recently devised mechanisms of social insulation which in daily life keep group conflict within fixed bounds, as it also ignores the newly evolved patterns of social integration among opposed groups which balance contradictory tensions in a reasonably effective fashion. People are pressed into an intimacy they would as soon avoid; where the incongruity between the social assumptions of the ritual ("we are all culturally homogeneous peasants together") and what is in fact the case ("we are several different kinds of people who must perforce live together despite our serious value disagreements") leads to a deep uneasiness of which Paidjan's funeral was but an extreme example. In the kampong, the holding of a slametan increasingly serves to remind people that the neighborhood bonds they are strengthening through a dramatic enactment are no longer the bonds which most emphatically hold them together. These latter are ideological, class, occupation, and political bonds, divergent ties which are no longer adequately summed up in territorial relationships.

In sum, the disruption of Paidjan's funeral may be traced to a single source: an incongruity between the cultural framework of meaning and the patterning of social interaction, an incongruity due to the persistence in an urban environment of a religious symbol system adjusted to peasant social structure. Static functionalism, of either the sociological or social psychological sort, is unable to isolate this kind of incongruity because it fails to discriminate between logico-meaningful integration and causal-functional integration; because it fails to realize that cultural structure and social structure are not mere reflexes of one another but independent, yet interdependent, variables. The driving forces in social change can be clearly formulated only by a more dynamic form of functionalist theory, one which takes into account the fact that man's need to live in a world to which he can attribute some significance, whose essential import he feels he can grasp, often diverges from his concurrent need to maintain a functioning social organism. A diffuse concept of culture as "learned behavior," a static view of social structure as an equilibrated pattern of interaction, and a stated or unstated assumption that the two must somehow (save in "disorganized" situations) be simple mirror images of one another, is rather too primitive a conceptual apparatus with which to attack such problems as those raised by Paidjan's unfortunate but instructive funeral.

servants, teachers, and clerks, and so will not be dealt with here.

[4] Actually, there are two parts to Javanese marriage rites. One, which is part of the general syncretism, is held at the bride's home and involves a slametan and an elaborate ceremonial "meeting" between bride and groom. The other, which is the official ceremony in the eyes of the Government, follows the Moslem law and takes place at the office of the subdistrict religious officer, or Naib. See Geertz, in press.

[5] For a fuller discussion of President Sukarno's *pantjasila* ideology and his attempt to root it in general Indonesian values, see Kahin 1952:122–127.

[6] For a description of a somewhat disrupted celebration of the end of the Fast holiday, Hari Raya (îd al-fitr) in Modjokuto, which shows many formal similarities to Paidjan's funeral, see Geertz, in press.

Notes

[1] The names of the town and of all individuals mentioned in this paper are pseudonyms. The field work extended from May 1953 until September 1954, with a two-month gap in July and August of 1953, and was undertaken as part of a co-operative project of six anthropologists and a sociologist under the sponsorship of the Center for International Studies of the Massachusetts Institute of Technology. A full description of the town and of the villages around it, prepared by the entire team, is in the process of publication. I wish to thank Victor Ayoub, Robert Bellah, Hildred Geertz, Arnold Green, Robert Jay, and Elizabeth Tooker for reading and criticizing various drafts of this paper.

[2] A fuller description of the slametan pattern, and of Javanese religion generally, will be found in my contribution to the forthcoming project report on the Modjokuto community study: Geertz, in press.

[3] For a description of the role of the santri-abangan distinction in the rural areas of Modjokuto, see Jay 1956. A third religious variant which I have discriminated elsewhere (Geertz 1956, and in press), the *prijaji,* is mainly confined to upper-class civil

REFERENCES CITED

DURKHEIM, ÉMILE
 1947   The elementary forms of the religious life. Glencoe, Illinois.
FORTES, MEYER
 1953   The structure of unilineal descent groups. American Anthropologist 55:17–41.
GEERTZ, CLIFFORD
 1956   Religious belief and economic behavior in a central Javanese town: some preliminary considerations. Economic Development and Cultural Change IV:134–158.
 N.D.   Religion in Modjokuto. (In press, Cambridge, Massachusetts.)
JAY, ROBERT
 1956   Local government in rural central Java. The Far Eastern Quarterly XV:215–227.
KAHIN, GEORGE MCTURNAN
 1952   Nationalism and revolution in Indonesia. Ithaca, New York.
KLUCKHOHN, CLYDE
 1944   Navaho witchcraft. Peabody Museum Papers, No. XXII. Cambridge, Massachusetts.

LANDON, K.
    1949   Southeast Asia, crossroad of re-
           ligions. Chicago.
LEACH, E. R.
    1954   Political systems of highland
           Burma. Cambridge, Massachu-
           setts.
MALINOWSKI, BRONISLAW
    1948   Magic, science and religion and
           other essays. Glencoe, Illinois,
           and Boston, Massachusetts.
MERTON, ROBERT
    1949   Social theory and social struc-
           ture. Glencoe, Illinois.

PARSONS, TALCOTT
    1951   The social system. Glencoe, Illi-
           nois.
PARSONS, TALCOTT and EDWARD A. SHILS
    1951   Toward a general theory of ac-
           tion. Cambridge, Massachusetts.
REDFIELD, ROBERT
    1941   The folk culture of Yucatan.
           Chicago, Illinois.
ROBERTSON-SMITH, W.
    1894   Lectures on the religion of the
           Semites. Edinburgh.
SOROKIN, P.
    1937   Social and cultural dynamics, 3
           vols. New York.

E · WORSHIP AND MANIFEST
AND LATENT FUNCTIONS

1 · *Objective and Subjective Worship*

JAMES BISSETT PRATT

In the two preceding chapters I have had occasion more than once to distinguish between two types of worship, one of which aims at making some kind of effect upon the Deity or in some way communicating with him, while the other seeks only to induce some desired mood or belief or attitude in the mind of the worshiper. The former of these types I shall refer to, for the sake of brevity, as *objective worship,* and the latter I shall call *subjective worship.* The distinction between the two seems to me so important that I doubt whether a thorough understanding of the various cults found in the different religions be possible unless this distinction be quite explicitly recognized. It is the key to many a ceremonial which without it must remain for most of us obscure, strange, and even ridiculous or shocking. This is true within the bounds of our own Christian religion. Consider,

SOURCE. James Bissett Pratt, *The Religious Consciousness,* New York: Macmillan, 1920, pp. 290–309 and 334–336. Reprinted with permission of the publisher. Copyright 1920 by The Macmillan Company. Renewed 1948 by Catherine M. Pratt.

for example, the impressions of the Protestant on first being present at a Catholic Mass, or the feelings of the Catholic on first attending a Protestant service. To the Protestant the mass seems fantastic; to the Catholic the evangelical worship appears godless. Each can understand the other only by appreciating the difference in aim: the leading purpose of the mass is the worship of God, that of the Protestant service is the subjective impression upon the minds and hearts of the worshipers.

Perhaps the most notable instance of objective worship is the Chinese official cult of Heaven, which can be performed *only* by the Emperor (or President), who does it on behalf of all the people. The same purely objective purpose stands out with equal directness in the Hindu temple ceremonials, especially in the regular daily *"puja"* of the officiating priest. Quite frequently there is no audience at this ceremony—no one is present but the priest who anoints the lingam, or strews flowers before the image, muttering certain sacred words of whose meaning he often has no notion and going through the ritual with the obvious single

143

purpose of *gratifying the god*.[1] Even when an audience is present the chief aim of the ceremony is plainly the adulation of the deity. The worshipers come because their god wishes their adoration and they can, perhaps, move him to grant their requests by prostrating themselves before the throne where, in his sacred image, he is seated. For the Hindu temple is in no sense a "meeting house." It is not built for the benefit of the human worshipers, but for the greater glory of God. The thought of going to the temple for the sake of the subjective effect which the *puja* might have upon one's own feelings is an idea that probably never enters into one Hindu head in a thousand. Occasionally, indeed, as I pointed out in the last chapter, there is a self-conscious attempt to gain this end, but it is relatively rare; and unquestionably the subjective effect is in innumerable cases attained even when the thought of it is quite absent from the mind. One need only watch the faces of the long line of heavy-laden humanity —especially of the widows—pouring quietly but steadily out of some temple of Shiva on the banks of the Ganges, to feel convinced that these dumb worshipers are taking home with them something of the same religious comfort and uplift which their sisters are finding in some little white meeting-house in far New England.

But the subjective benefits of cult and ritual which though often present in the less sophisticated forms of Hinduism remain almost unrecognized, come out quite explicitly in some of the very self-

conscious Hindu reform movements. An excellent example of this is to be found in the *Havan* ceremony of the Arya Samaj. The Aryas are an exceedingly rationalistic group of religious thinkers who are bent on the moral and intellectual reform of Hinduism, and who never lose an opportunity to attack and ridicule idolatry and the popular temple worship, as well as polytheism in all its forms. But from the very beginning of their reform movement they recognized so clearly the human need of a ritual, for the sake of its effects upon the worshipers, that the founder of the church, Swami Dayanand, in part invented, in part adopted from the Vedas, a ceremony remarkably well adapted in more ways than one to bring about the state of mind which the Samaj desires in its members. The audience gathers around a small pit, prepared for the occasion, and there the leaders make a sweet-smelling fire, pouring into it from time to time ladles of *ghi* or liquefied butter, to the accompaniment of a steady chanting of Sanskrit verses. This, Dayanand assured his followers, was an ancient Vedic rite, handed down for ages in the holy days when only the one God was worshiped, and practiced by the Rishis who wrote the Rig Veda. Here, then, we have visible and tangible elements brought into direct association with the religious belief; and a sacramental offering of them by the community and its representatives in such fashion as to symbolize the faith of all, and thus to bring social confirmation to the individual's religion, and to bind the whole of the group to the great and revered Past whose authority thus becomes a perennial spring of fervent religious sentiment. There is no thought whatever of the ceremony being a sacrifice to God or a way of pleasing Him. If you ask the Aryas why it is performed they will tell you it is for the sake of emphasizing their connection with Vedic times, and as a symbol of their devotion

[1] For the details of Hindu temple worship see Monier Williams, "Brahmanism and Hinduism" (4th Ed. New York, Macmillan: 1891), pp. 93–94, 144–45, 438–41; Farquhar's "Crown of Hinduism," pp. 313–14; Bhandarkar, "Vaishnavism, Saivism, and Minor Religious Systems" (Strassburg, Trübner: 1913), p. 81; and my "India and Its Faiths," Chap. II.

to all the world.[2] It forms the central part of their daily and weekly religious meetings, and the earnest religious feeling which it arouses among them is patent to every visitor.[3]

But the extreme examples of subjective worship are to be found in two other of the religions of India, namely Jainism and Buddhism. In their popular forms, both of these cults are fairly objective; but always in theory (at least in their original theories), and among their more intellectual followers in practice, they carry subjectivity to an extreme from which the professors of every other religion, eastern or western, would probably shrink. For the Jaina there is no God; instead, there is a mechanically moral but unconscious universe, and there are also twenty-four Tirthankaras or ideal beings who once lived and have long since passed into Moksha. These are conceived as still conscious, but they are quite unconscious of human affairs and can never be reached or in any way affected by human prayers or offerings. One might conclude from this that worship of them would be out of the question, at any rate for the more intelligent. This is by no means the case. At the ceremonies in Jaina temples you will find, at least occasionally, very intelligent and educated men, who are firmly convinced that nothing they do or say or think will reach the Tirthankaras, and yet who are as enthusiastic in making offerings and

intoning Sanskrit verses before a Tirthankara image as are any of their less enlightened brethren. I have talked with more than one of these men concerning their worship and they have insisted that they keep up the cult in this strict and scrupulous fashion because they find that its subjective effects upon them are decidedly beneficial—and this, in fact, is the orthodox Jaina theory upon the subject. Eight kinds of offerings are made to the images, and each of these has a symbolic meaning. Thus white rice represents knowledge, saffron rice beauty, etc.; and the presentation of these symbols, together with the Sanskrit verses chanted and the thought of the moral ideal for which the Tirthankara stands, all tend to bring new comfort and hope, new aspirations, and greater strength for the moral life.[4]

Buddhist theory, and to some extent Buddhist practice, carries this subjective worship if possible one step further. For in the religion as formulated by the Founder, and as still believed and practiced by a number of intelligent monks in Burma and Ceylon and also by some of the laity, there is not even so much to pray to as a conscious but unreachable Tirthankara. Buddhism, like Jainism, has two substitutes for God; one of them this miraculously moral but quite unconscious Cosmos with its inescapable Law of Karma; the other the ideal being, Gautama, the Buddha. But the Buddha has long since sunk into Nirvana, which in the opinion of the majority of the more learned and intelligent monks seems to be equivalent to nothingness. Not only is he beyond all our prayers and offer-

---

[2] I should add that the chief function performed by this ceremony in the opinion of the Arya Samajists is the *purification of the air*. This notion originated with Swami Dayanand, who expounds it at length in the passage of his authoritative book, the "Satyarth Prakash," in which he lays down the rules for the Havan ceremony. See Durga Prasad's translation of the "Satyarth Prakash" (Lahore, Virjanand Press: 1908), pp. 101–103.

[3] For further description see my "India and Its Faiths," pp. 208–210.

[4] See the chapter on the Jainas in my "India and Its Faiths," in which I have dealt in greater detail with this subject. For further descriptions of Jaina worship see Mrs. Sinclair Stevenson's "Notes on Modern Jainism" (Oxford, Blackwell: 1910), pp. 85–105, and her larger work, "The Heart of Jainism" (Oxford U. Press, 1915) Chap. XIII.

ings; he is not even conscious. In the words of many of the monks with whom I talked in Burma and Ceylon, "Buddha finish!" Yet these good atheists have by no means given up the cult. Morning and night, if they be monks, do they assemble in the hall of their monastery around the image of the Founder of their Faith, and offer fresh flowers and ancient praises in his honor. And most of them sometime during the day will go, together with little groups of faithful lay brothers, to some near-by pagoda, and there place a candle within the great shrine, and recite more verses and more praises. "Thus reflecting," says the Dina Chari-yawa, in recital of the duties of the novice, "he shall approach the dagoba, or the bo-tree, and perform that which is appointed: he shall offer flowers, just as if the Buddha were present in person, if flowers can be procured; meditate on the nine virtues of the Buddha with fixed and determined mind; and having worshiped seek absolution for his negligences and faults just as if the sacred things [before which he worships] had life." [5] In short the enlightened Buddhist is to act *"just as if"* he believed various things which he does not believe, because the performance of these acts has been found to be helpful in the production of a desirable inner state of mind. A Burmese Buddhist book says plainly, "It is bootless to worship the Buddha; nothing is necessary but to revere him and the memory of him. Statues are useful only in so far as they refresh the memory; for as the farmer sows the seed and gathers in the grain in due season, so will the man who trusts in the Buddha and holds fast by his sacred Law, obtain deliverance and pass into Nehban. The earth and the Buddha are alike in themselves inert." [6]

[5] Quoted in Hardy's "Eastern Monachism" (London, Partridge and Oxford: 1860), p. 25.
[6] Quoted by Shway Yoe (J. G. Scott) in "The Burman" (London, Macmillan: 1882), Vol. I, p. 221.

When we turn from India to Christendom we find again both objective and subjective worship—sometimes standing out from each other quite obviously, sometimes inextricably intermingled. Although both forms have been found many times over in both the great western branches of the Christian Church, objective worship comes out the more distinctly in Roman Catholicism, and subjective worship in Protestantism. The Catholic Church seems to consider the direct worship of God as much a part of its duty as the salvation of souls. In certain orders of nuns systematic efforts are directed toward making sure that the Blessed Sacrament is being constantly adored by pious sisters,[7] prostrate before it at every moment of the day and night. By a widespread custom in various parts of the Catholic world, laymen join with the "religious" once a year in consecrating "Forty Hours" to the adoration of the Sacrament.[8] A very considerable part of the day of every priest is occupied in saying the "Office." [9] This rather heavy requirement is but distantly if at all connected with the purpose of saving souls or of producing a subjective effect upon

[7] Four Orders have been founded and continued for this special purpose:—the "Religious of Perpetual Adoration" of Belgium, an order of the same name in Einsiedeln (Switzerland), the "Sisters of the Perpetual Adoration" (of Quimper, France), and the "Perpetual Adorers of the Blessed Sacrament,"—see Catholic Encyclopedia.
[8] "Questa divozione consiste nell'esporre il Santissimo Sacramento alla dorazione dei fedeli per tre giorni di seguito e per tredici o quattordici ore del giorno" ("Tutto con Me,"—Milano, Tipografia Santa Lega Eucaristica: 1908—p. 847).
[9] The Office varies on different days, but in general it may be said to consist of about one-seventh of the Psalter—the entire Psalter being thus recited once each week—plus certain liturgical formulas and responses, with special additional material for saints' days.

anyone. It aims primarily and chiefly *ad majoram Dei gloriam*. The conception is that God is pleased with this chorus of prayers and praises rising to Him in unison from all quarters of the globe. The same objective character of much of Catholic worship is to be seen in the very buildings themselves which we know as Catholic churches. As Henry Adams puts it, the nave was made for the people but the choir for God.[10] Especially noticeable is the arrangement for objective worship in the cathedrals of Spain, where the central portion of the nave is blocked up with the *coro* or choir, whose walls, rising on three sides, make it almost a separate building in the midst of the cathedral. Thus the view of the high altar is quite cut off from all parts of the church except the *coro,* the small space between it and the altar, and a minute section of each transept. The result is that only a few worshipers in the whole cathedral can see the altar,— a commentary in stone upon the purpose of the cathedral and of the services performed within it. The important thing is not that the worshipers should be able to behold and follow the service or be impressed by it, but *that God should be properly and gloriously worshiped.*

But it is not only in great cathedrals that the objective nature of Catholic worship is felt. The Catholic church in every part of the world, and no matter how humble in architectural design, means to be (as the Hindu temple means to be) not a meeting house for worshipers but a place where in a peculiar sense God dwells. The heart of Catholicism for its most spiritual children is its belief in the peculiar presence of God within the Sacrament; and it is this that makes the Catholic church mean so much more to the good Catholic than the Protestant meeting house can ever mean to anyone. To some minds the contrast is enormous. George Tyrrell tells us that at an early age he felt that "the difference between an altar and a communion table is infinite."[11] When a Catholic goes into a Protestant church he has an immediate sense that something is lacking. Involuntarily he looks for the altar with its hidden but ever present Host, and, not finding it, he realizes that the building is merely a place for people to meet together and think about God—not a temple in which one meets with God Himself in a peculiarly close and objective way. To be sure God is believed to be present in the Protestant church, but nowhere in particular and no more in the church than elsewhere. God is present everywhere in general, and nowhere in particular. In the Catholic belief, too, He is present everywhere in general, but He is also present in one place in particular. He is there in the wafer, mysteriously transformed in "substance" into His very body, upon the altar. Hence the glorious robes of the priest to do honor to the heavenly guest; hence the acolytes, the incense, the music, the candles. The objective nature of Catholic worship is plain in all these things; and especially when contrasted with the corresponding adornments of the Protestant service, notably its flowers. The Protestant church decks its buildings with flowers solely and admittedly for the congregation to see. They make the church pleasanter, possibly attract a few more people by their touch of color and beauty, and perhaps help to put some in a more spiritual

---

[10] "The choir was made not for the pilgrim but for the deity, and is as old as Adam or perhaps older. . . . The Christian church not only took the sanctuary in hand and gave it a new form, but it also added the idea of the nave and transepts, and developed it into imperial splendor. The pilgrim-tourist feels at home in the nave because it was built for him; the artist loves the sanctuary because he built it for God" ("Mont St. Michel and Chartres," Washington: 1912, p. 161).

[11] "Autobiography," Vol. I, p. 98.

frame of mind. The candles of the Catholic church are placed there not for man but for God. This is true of them whether publicly and officially or privately contributed. The woman who places her candle before the shrine of the Madonna has no thought in her mind of the effect it may have on other worshipers. The Madonna will see it and that is enough. It would be placed there just the same were no one expected to enter the church.

The same contrast between the objective and the subjective is seen again if we compare the acts and bearing of the minister with those of the priest in conducting the service. The minister as well as the priest may mean that God shall hear the words of the service, but he certainly also means that the congregation shall hear—both in order that they may pray with him and also in order to produce upon them, by his prayers and their prayers, the desired psychological effect. He not only prays; he "leads in prayer." His prayer he utters in a loud voice, that all may hear, as he stands facing the audience. And too often his prayer is of the sort intended in the oft-quoted description: "the most eloquent prayer ever addressed to a Boston audience."

Instead of this, the priest turns his back on the congregation, faces the altar where God is, and whispers his prayer in a voice too low to be heard by anyone and in a tongue unknown to all but his fellow priests. During most of the service he seems utterly oblivious to the presence of other worshipers. The Protestant clergyman on a rainy Sunday, when the church is cold and only twenty or thirty are present, may dismiss his hearers and give up the service. To the Catholic priest, the size of the congregation and the temperature of the building make no apparent difference. He comes into the church from the sacristy carrying the chalice and followed by his attendant, looking neither to the right hand nor to the left for his audience, with his eyes fixed only upon the altar where the body and blood of Christ are shortly to be seen; and he says his mass in exactly the same way whether the Church be thronged or he and the boy be the only human beings in the building.

For the mass is viewed by the Church not as a means for producing an effect but as something objectively worth while in itself—the mysterious sacrifice on the cross of God to God, miraculously repeated upon the altar. In the words of Frederic Harrison, "the Mass is a reality —if one admit its scientific extravagance —and for religious and moral efficacy the most potent institution that any religion in man's history can boast—'the most admirable of the Catholic institutions'—at once a tremendous drama, a searching discipline, an entire creed transfigured in a visible presentment of a spiritual doctrine." [12] The mass is the very center of Catholic worship and the heart of Catholic belief; and leading up as it does to the miracle upon the altar and the tremendously dramatic climax of the elevation of the Host, it has no rival in the whole round of religious ceremonial for impressiveness and for the production of deep but controlled religious emotion. To the unsympathetic and ignorant beholder it seems bizarre, but whoever enters sympathetically, intelligently, and imaginatively into the feelings of the worshipers kneeling around him, and for the moment takes their "objective" point of view of the peculiar and miraculous presence of the Divine, can hardly fail to find in it a new and unique and deeply religious experience. It was this almost unreplaceable stimulus to the religious sentiment that was left behind when our Protestant fathers went out from the old historic Church. And when this is understood one

[12] "The Positive Evolution of Religion" (New York, Putnams: 1913), p. 129.

sees how hopeless it must ever be to fill the place of this lost sense of the peculiar immediacy of the Supernatural and Divine by any use of candles or incense, intoned service and ringing of bells, or the voices of violins, cellos, and opera singers.

In other words, the subjective effect of the objective methods used by the Catholic Church is very considerable, even though aimed at only indirectly—in fact largely because it is aimed at only indirectly. To the reverent Catholic it makes little or no difference that he cannot hear the priest's words, and that if he could hear them they might be to him unintelligible. He may if he likes follow the service by means of the translation in his prayer book; but this he does not need and seldom tries to do. It is of no importance that he should. For he finds —and this sums up the subjective value of the mass—that a church in which mass is being said is an *excellent place to pray*, that the service gives him an intense realization of the closeness of God to human life, and that he goes away from it with a sense of spiritual refreshment.

So excellent in producing subjective effects are the objective methods of the Catholic Church that a benevolent atheist might conceivably do his best to forward the interests of Catholicism. If he were a wise as well as a benevolent atheist, however, he would probably keep his views of the truly subjective nature of worship entirely to himself. For once let the cat out of the bag, the desired result might become almost unattainable. And here we find both the strength and the weakness of purely objective methods. Given a body of worshipers who accept implicitly the belief back of the cult, and the effect of it upon their religious sentiments will be stronger than that which any direct attempt at influencing them could ever bring about. But the number of those for whom this is possible is likely to diminish steadily with the loss

of respect for authority and the spread of modern education, free thought, and rationalism. The Catholic Church has always shown remarkable insight into the psychology of the mystic and of the uneducated. Its whole history shows also an almost equally remarkable failure to understand the minds of the rationalistic and the lovers of free thought. For Protestants the mass fails of its subjective religious effect because they cannot share the Catholic belief in transubstantiation, and hence the direct Catholic kind of objective worship is for them impossible. And something like this loss of subjective impressiveness in the mass holds true for an increasing number of the more intelligent Catholics themselves. In Italy and France, for example, there are a great many good men—nominally Catholics—to whom the mass is simply foolishness. To them, the Latin mumbling of the priest is a useless repetition, and the incense and candles are a kind of earnest nonsense. Not believing strongly or at all in the real presence, and not being of the emotional or mystical type, they fail to get anything out of the service—and hence stay away. For men of this sort, the reading of fairly long and consecutive and well-chosen passages of Scripture, followed by an intelligent sermon on some moral problem, with the singing of a few good hymns, might be the ideal form of public worship. But this is, of course, very nearly the Protestant and "evangelical" form.

While, therefore, the Protestant worship can probably never minister to the religious feelings of people of the mystical and traditional type as can the more objective worship of the Catholic Church, to persons of the intellectual and moral type it probably furnishes the best solution. I speak of it as a solution, for the worship which is to appeal to these two types of mind is indeed a problem. On the one hand it must not demand of them a faith which is for them no longer possible, hence must include much frank and self-conscious effort to influence their faith and feeling directly; and on the other hand it cannot afford to leave out entirely the objective aspect of worship, for to do so would be implicitly to surrender certain essential parts of the faith upon which much of the subjective effect of worship is ultimately based. The problem of the Protestant Church has therefore been to find a combination of objective and subjective worship that will plant and nourish the religious sentiments, enliven the moral emotions, and at the same time will not antagonize the reason of its members. It will be noticed that I have mentioned here one aim very prominent in Protestant worship which receives but little stress in the public worship of the Catholic Church—namely the enlivening of the moral emotions. The Protestant Church seeks, quite self-consciously, so to construct its services as to reinforce the moral tendencies of its members with the strength which comes from deep religious sentiment.

The methods by which the Protestant Churches seek to solve their problem and to make their worship best fulfill its religious functions, are too well known to need description. Objective methods have by no means been completely discarded. There are presumably many congregations and individuals who still intend the hymns of praise which they sing—notably the Doxology—to be heard by the Deity. "The office of song in the sanctuary," writes Dr. Snowden in a recent book, "is to praise God. Worship seeks the highest form of expression which is poetry wedded to music, the rhythm of speech and song. Music is one of the art-paths to God." [13] An examination of our modern hymn-books, however, will show that the proportion of what we might call *objective* hymns is not large, and a

study of older hymnals in comparison makes it plain that the percentage is decreasing.[14] The chief function of the hymn is decidedly subjective. The leading form, and for many people the only form of objective worship left in the Protestant service is prayer. By nearly every religious Protestant this is regarded as truly objective in its nature—a direct address of the soul to the Deity; and it seems most unlikely that more than a very few have any thought when they pray of the subjective effects prayer may have upon them. Here, then, we find worship in the simple, direct, ancient sense. We find it, that is, wherever people actually do pray. How many of the congregation are praying in any real sense of the word during the "long prayer" is a question which only He who hears prayers could answer. If I may trust my own observation, and the expressions of those whom I have questioned upon the subject, no very large portion of the congregation "follow" the long prayer, and fewer still find it really helpful in producing even the prayerful attitude of mind.

Nearly all the details of the Protestant service, then, and also the service as a whole, are planned out with the deliberate purpose of producing certain psychological effects upon the congregation.

[13] "The Psychology of Religion," p. 245.

[14] Cf. super, "The Psychology of Christian Hymns," *Am. Jour. of Relig. Psy.*, III, 1–15. The history of the use of hymns in the Christian service gives an interesting example of the change from purely objective to largely subjective worship. In the mediæval church the hymns were all in Latin and were sung not by the congregation but by the choir alone—the obvious purpose being to praise God. The practice of writing hymns in the vernacular and having them sung by the congregation began with the Reformation—especially through the influence of Luther, Gerhardt, the Moravians, and the Methodists.—See Hewitt, "Paul Gerhardt as a Hymn Writer and His Influence on English Hymnody" (Yale University Press: 1918).

"The minister," writes Dr. Hartshorne, "has a definite purpose and a definite plan. He wishes to bring the congregation to a new point of view or to a new resolve. To this end he selects music, hymns, prayers, Scripture, and address, and weaves all into a harmonious whole which shall, in its total effect, induce the desired change in the minds of the audience. And consciously or unconsciously he makes use of the psychology of feeling and emotion." [15] How successful the average minister is in this aim, the reader will probably decide for himself. Dr. John P. Hylan issued a questionnaire on this subject, a few years ago, and the responses showed that the service, the church building, and even the day itself —the Sabbath—shed upon most of the respondents a certain subjective influence of a rather mild sort.[16] The success of different ministers and different churches in this effort of course varies enormously.

The tools, so to speak, by which this subjective effect is brought about are well known to us all. The architecture and its decorations help, and so does (to those who attend the same church all their lives) the close association between the familiar church interior and the religious impressions and aspirations of childhood. The creed, recited by the congregation in unison, has the effect already pointed out of reinforcing individual faith by social confirmation. Especially is the congregational singing of hymns productive of considerable religious feeling;[17] while the rendering of selections by the choir at times aids in producing the desired religious atmosphere—provided the selections be really religious and the rendering of them be sincere.[18] The "Scripture lesson" is usually too short to be of much influence. The aim of the sermon, the central part of most Protestant worship, seems to be threefold: to increase or correct the faith of the hearers, to nourish their religious sentiments, and to arouse, fortify, and redirect their moral convictions and emotions. It is here that the Protestant Church finds its great weapon in liberalizing and deepening religious thought and in directing the forces of the Christian community toward purity of private life and toward aggressive actions in the great struggle for social righteousness. The responses collected by Mr. L. W. Kline from various types of church-goers to the question, "Please state in what way sermons affect and benefit you," indicate plainly (so far, at any rate, as his respondents were typical) that it is the moral appeal of the sermon, especially when delivered with unmistakable earnestness and sincerity, that produces by far the greatest effect the preacher can hope for.[19]

[15] "Worship in the Sunday School" (New York, Columbia University: 1913) pp. 115–16.

[16] "Public Worship" (Chicago, Open Court: 1901). Chap. III.

[17] Dr. Müller-Freienfels reports the result of a statistical investigation of his own to the effect that hymn singing in which the worshiper himself takes part has a much greater emotional effect upon him than music to which he merely listens. This is, of course, what we should naturally expect. *Ztsft. f. Relspsy.*, IV, p. 371.

[18] All music tends to rouse some kind of emotion, but the state of mind incited by certain kinds of emotion may be almost inhibitory to the religious sentiment. Indeed according to President Faunce, "in most churches the task of the preacher is rendered vastly more difficult by the intrusion of incongruous or impertinent music. After the choir by elaborate performance has brought the congregation into the concert-mood, the preacher is expected to remove that mood and replace it by the temper of devotion." ("The Religious Function of Public Worship," *Am. Jour. of Theol.* XIV 5.—Jan., 1910).

[19] "The Sermon: A Study in Social Psychology"—*Am. Jour. of Relig. Psy. and Ed.* I, 288–300.

But while the Protestant Church has done well in laying great emphasis upon the sermon, it is a question whether it has not laid too little emphasis upon the rest of the service. A recent contributor to the *Atlantic* asserts, in half-earnest, that "nothing would be so beneficial as to have our pulpits silenced for a year. . . . The other phases of worship would be restored—the worship of prayer, confession, praise, and enlightened faith. Some of them are entirely gone from the churches. The people no longer pray but listen to the minister as he prays.[20] Worship has become a passive matter. The congregation has become an audience—a body of listeners."[21] In short, the Sunday morning church service, while often appealing quite admirably to the moral emotions and convictions of the worshipers, seems to many of its best disposed critics and lovers to be lacking exactly on the religious side. The reality of the more-than-human, the relation of the individual to the Determiner of Destiny, the intense emotional realization of the Cosmic—these things are no longer suggested to us in Church as they used to be to our fathers. Somehow in our smug security we seem armed against them, even when the preacher tries to bring them home to us. And the enormous throngs who never enter a church door are seldom reminded of them.

There is one kind of religious service which almost every one attends occasionally, no matter how skeptical he be, and one which seldom fails of producing upon all present a very deep effect. Strangely enough, moreover, it is seldom enumerated among the religious methods of the church. For an increasingly large number of people in our days the only form of religious service left is an occasional funeral. With the rarest of exceptions, the funeral is always a religious ceremony. Other former functions of the church, such as marriage, education, the care of the poor, etc., are being taken over by the civil authorities; but the disposal of the dead almost everywhere still remains in the hands of religion. And though the religious value of the funeral is seldom recognized, or at least seldom mentioned, it is very considerable. For in the presence of Death we find ourselves face to face with the dreadful and silent forces which lie beyond our control—the Cosmic Reality, our conscious relation to which *is* religion. Here we stand on the very edge of the mystery. The curtain for a moment is partly drawn and we get a glimpse of the cosmic process. We return to our little tasks, to be sure, all the more mystified, but with at least a renewed sense of the reality of the mystery. Compared with the savage or with the mediæval Christian, we moderns spend our lives almost entirely in the light of common day, in a world which science has made safe and commonplace. It takes something like Death to startle us out of our complacent scientific and practical attitude, and to reveal to us the vista of cosmic mystery which (in cruder forms) was ever present to our less scientific forbears. It is this sense of the Unknown, this realization of our own dependence, this intimation of a Power not to be exhausted by the study of science, this questioning of the Why, the Whence, and the Whither, this placing of ourselves for once in a cosmic setting—it is this that the funeral brings, and to this that it owes its uniquely religious value. It seems, indeed, almost an irrational celebration of our own defeat, yet so commanding is its position in the spiritual economy of our lives that we may feel fairly sure of its

[20] Query: Do they?
[21] G. P. Atwater, "The Ministry: An Overcrowded Profession." *Atlantic Monthly* for Oct., 1911, pp. 483–84.

retention as a religious ceremony to the end of human time.

But whether our Protestant Sunday service needs more of the solemnity and of the cosmic quality which the funeral possesses, or whether its chief need be more moral earnestness, more ritual, more preaching or no preaching at all, there seems at any rate to be a pretty general feeling that it needs something. Our various denominations are showing a very commendable dissatisfaction with their present methods and a willingness to experiment on new lines in the hope of finding some type of worship more generally satisfactory. We see them fumbling about, groping for light, trying new plans of popular appeal which range all the way from vested choirs to moving pictures. A fairly large body in many of the denominations feels the need of more ritual—a need which, as we have seen, is deeply founded in human psychology. New rituals are therefore being rapidly produced, but none of them seem quite to fill the need—a fact which might indeed have been anticipated considering the importance of a traditional sanction if the ritual is to be felt as appropriate and fitting. The problem of reshaping the Protestant worship is in fact peculiarly difficult. For it means discovering a method of nourishing the religious sentiments of people most of whom are of the intellectual and active types. And it must do this without the aid of the two most powerful means which other churches and religions make use of for the purpose—namely the kind of belief which makes elaborate objective worship easy and natural for large groups, and a ritual which has the authority and sanctity of generations behind it.[22]

[22] The Protestant Episcopal Church has a much less difficult problem; for it has inherited a ritual which not only is beautiful in itself, but is rich in the sanctity and authority of an age-long tradition. Such a ritual

Fortunately it is not the task of a writer on the psychology of religion to devise a solution for this problem. I shall therefore content myself here by pointing out one or two things. In the first place we must remember that no one solution is possible. The variations in human temperament and taste are so great that a very considerable diversity in ritual among Christian churches—even among those who *believe* exactly the same things —will always be not only desirable but necessary if the Church is to feed the needs of all. The union of Christian churches in their various philanthropic and missionary undertakings is doubtless very desirable; but a union of the

is peculiarly adapted to the production of the religious atmosphere; and the individual brought up within the Episcopal fold almost invariably finds his church an excellent place in which to pray. The problem for the Episcopalian is simply to make his ritual elastic and adapted to the growing and ever new needs of the times, while keeping it also conservative and ancient. He must, if he can, strike the golden mean between the old and the new, he must retain enough of the traditional to appeal to the religious sentiment and yet surrender enough and add enough to conform to the demands of modern thought and modern needs. Changes, therefore, should be made from time to time in the ritual, but such changes should be gradual and for the moment always slight. If an outsider might make one further suggestion, I would add that the Episcopal Church would at any rate make a much greater appeal to stray visitors from other folds if her clergymen would pay more attention to the intellectual content of their sermons and the moral significance of their themes. There are many excellent preachers within the Episcopal Church, but the clergyman too often appears to be satisfied with a deadly conventional treatment of an insignificant or antiquated subject, seeming to be under the impression that the banality of his remarks may be hidden under a large use of the "chancel voice."

Churches which should banish or even decrease the present diversity in ritual would be a real misfortune.[23]

No solution, moreover, seems to be possible which relies wholly on what I have called subjective methods. The attempt to produce merely subjective religious effects is always in danger of defeating itself. For religion, as we have seen, involves a belief which means to have objective validity; and if worship neglects this and directs all its efforts openly to the production of changes in social and psychical conditions, it may indeed remain a moral force, but it ceases to be religious and it loses all the emotional reinforcement that comes from the religious sentiment. I cannot, therefore, think that anything of much importance will be brought about by the adoption of prayer books or the processionals of vested choirs or anything else of a merely superficial sort. The difficulty with Protestant worship goes deeper than the surface, and until some more fundamental change is wrought, its mode of worship will remain always unsatisfactory. The worshiper in the Protestant Church must be made to feel, as the Catholic feels at the mass, that *something is really being done*—something in addition to the subjective change in his own consciousness. Let him understand that you wish him to come to church in order that you may make a psychological impression on him, and he will be in-

[23] The diverse ritualistic needs of men sharing practically the same beliefs is well illustrated by the case of those two good friends and excellent Christians, John Bright and William E. Gladstone. In his journal under date of September, 1873, while on a visit to Gladstone, Bright comments: "To Church. Service *high*. Three parsons. Mr. Gladstone most earnest in the singing, etc. To me much of the service seemed only fitted for very ignorant people." (Quoted in Trevelyan's "Life of John Bright," London, Constable: 1913, p. 415.)

creasingly likely to stay away. Or he may come to hear your opera singer, but his religious sentiment will remain untouched. If public worship is to be profitable to him he must find in it something more than that. In other words, what the Protestant service needs more than anything else is the development of the objective side of its worship. As we have seen, the principal objective element left in the Protestant service is prayer. Here, then, a beginning of the solution of the Protestant problem may be sought. The worshiper may be made to feel as he does not to-day that *in prayer something really happens*. This need not and should not mean that answer to special prayers and the influence of prayer upon war and weather is to be inculcated from the pulpit. It does mean that if the Protestant Church desires to make its worship more vital it should take great new pains to train its members, and especially its children, in the habit of prayer, and in the belief that somehow in prayer one puts oneself in touch with a supersensible world. The church should see to it that whatever else its Sunday service may neglect to do, it should bring to its worshipers an atmosphere of prayer, and a sense of the real presence of the Divine. Of course Protestantism has always made some effort in this direction, but when one compares the training in prayer and meditation which most of its young people receive with the best of the religious training given by the Catholic Church, one understands that there is a kind of *inwardness*, a sense of the vital reality of spiritual things, a feeling of need for spiritual reinforcement, which Protestantism has failed to foster.

But we must go deeper than this and ask ourselves the question whether we really believe that worship is any longer possible in the modern world at all. Plainly if objective worship be impossible for the intelligent, and if subjective without objective worship is self-delusion, there is an end of all worship for the modern man. Plainly also the second of the above hypothetical propositions is true—subjective worship without some objective worship cannot stand. The question, therefore, narrows down to this: Is any kind of objective worship possible for the man of our age? In answer to this it must be said plainly and first of all, that objective worship of the sort that aims to please the Deity is a thing of the past. The modern man cannot even attempt to participate in it without conscious hypocrisy. That is not the end of the matter, however. There is a kind of worship that is perfectly objective and sincere and that is quite as possible for the intelligent man of to-day as it was for the ancient:—namely that union of awe and gratitude which is reverence, combined perhaps with consecration and a suggestion of communion, which most thoughtful men must feel in the presence of the Cosmic forces and in reflecting upon them. Such was the attitude of Spinoza and Herbert Spencer. Such was the genuinely objective worship of the ancient philosophers of Greece and India, and of many of the Hebrew Psalmists and Prophets. In this act of instinctive self-abasement there is no aim of producing an effect upon oneself; the attitude is as objective as it is natural. Worship is therefore not something to be outgrown. Its forms change with the changing symbols, the changing robes with which men seek to deck out the Determiner of Destiny. The thing itself is as eternal as is man's finitude. The task of the church is to stimulate and direct this fundamental human impulse, with what wisdom it can supply.

The subjective benefits of prayer are so unmistakable that one who had lost all belief in any objective relation between the praying individual and a higher power, might very wisely continue to pray (if he could) purely for the sake of the reflex effects of prayer upon his own mind and character. The case cited a few pages back of a former student of mine who continues the use of petitional prayer merely for its subjective influence shows that this deliberate use of prayer as self-culture with no reference to any Being who shall hear and answer, is not only possible but (at least in rare cases) actual. The classical example of this sort of thing is, of course, to be found in Jainism and Buddhism. Though the more "advanced" Jaina monks have given up prayer altogether for meditation, very many of them, as well as many of the intelligent laymen, continue to pray, because experience has shown them that prayer, though inconsistent with their theory, is helpful in practice. Similarly the Buddhist monk in Mandalay quoted a few pages back, said to me: "The intelligent Buddhist does not pray for wealth nor health nor anything. He repeats certain phrases to the Buddha because of their good influence upon him. The whole thing is subjective and the effects to be expected are spiritual only. Of course the value of prayer in this sense is dependent on the state of mind of the man who prays."

The question whether prayer is nothing more than a mind state having a certain subjective value, such as auto-suggestion or the enjoyment of music, or whether it is also an objective relation between the prayerful soul and some sort of "Higher Power" above or "Spiritual World" round about, from Whom or from which new influxes of spiritual life may actually come—this is for metaphysics rather than for psychology. Psychology may and should point out, however, that the subjective effects of prayer are almost invariably due, directly or indirectly, to some real faith in the objective relation. A few Jaina and Buddhist monks, and a few earnest "emancipated" minds the world over, may succeed in reaping some subjective benefits from prayer after they have given up the belief in any external influence; but a large part of this effect they can reap only because of an early faith in some external influence, and also (probably) because at the moment of prayer they put themselves back temporarily into something like the believing state of mind. Except in so far as this is true, their "prayer" is merely meditation. That meditation may have excellent subjective effects is not to be denied, but no one with any knowledge of the psychology of religion will claim for it an influence equal to that which results from the earnest prayer of the man of faith. The subjective effects of prayer, in fact, seem to be roughly proportional to the strength of the faith of him who prays. The benefits which the Jaina and Buddhist monks reap from prayer are probably insignificant compared with those which come to the earnest believer in prayer as an objective means of communicating with the Divine. The number of persons, moreover, who would be able to get any beneficent results from prayer once they had lost their faith in its objective nature, is exceedingly limited. Few people possess the histrionic ability and the volitional control over the imagination requisite for any notable effects from prayer without faith, and few even of those who possess these abilities would think it worth while to make use of them in such prayer for the sake of possible subjective benefits. For every case like that of the unbelieving student quoted above who still continued to pray, probably fifty cases could be cited of those who had completely given up prayer because of loss of faith in it as an actual relation between man and God.

This being the case it is interesting to note the fervor with which certain psychological writers extol the value of prayer and in the same breath either state or imply that its value is due entirely to subjective conditions. These writers seem to have forgotten what Dr. L. P. Jacks has well called the "alchemy of thought," "to interpret experience is to change it." [24] For since the subjective value of prayer is chiefly due to the belief that prayer has values which are *not* subjective, it will with most persons evaporate altogether once they learn that it is *all* subjective. Hence if it be true both that the subjective value of prayer is very great and also that it is the only value which prayer possesses, this latter fact should be assiduously kept secret. The psychologist who knows it and publishes it broadcast is like the physician who should disclose to his patient the great value and the true nature of bread pills. "Take these," the doctor may be conceived as saying; "take three of these after each meal and seven after Sunday dinner, and they will completely cure you. They contain nothing but bread and have no value in themselves, absolutely none; but since you don't know this fact and are unaware that you are being fooled, their subjective effect upon you will be invaluable."

No, if the subjective value of prayer be all the value it has, we wise psychologists of religion had best keep the fact to ourselves; otherwise the game will soon be up and we shall have no religion left to psychologize about. We shall have killed the goose that laid our golden egg.

[24] "The Alchemy of Thought" (London, Williams and Norgate: 1911); p. 108.

2 · Inspirational Religious Literature: From Latent to Manifest Functions of Religion[1]

LOUIS SCHNEIDER AND SANFORD M. DORNBUSCH

ABSTRACT. *The very popular inspirational religious literature, sampled for the last seventy-five years, shows pronounced tendencies toward emphasis on salvation in this world, toward general decline of eschatological interest, and toward further secularization in the form of devaluation of suffering and instrumentalization of the deity. This last feature of instrumentalization, in combination with others, serves both to mark the emergence of a distinctive "spiritual technology" in the literature and to stress that its writers incline more or less deliberately to make what have been certain "by-products" of religious activity into "goals." The drive to make religion useful is possibly self-defeating.*

Inspirational religious literature is known to be enormously popular. The books of Norman Vincent Peale today, of Bruce Barton a generation ago, and of numerous of their close intellectual relatives and imitators have achieved

staggering sales.[2] Sociologists have left comment on the literature to journalists or theologians or gifted outsiders.[3] But it is of significance for the analysis of "cultural drift," with broad general implications. In this article, a brief survey of the literature and a summary of its dominant trends and themes, attention is

SOURCE. Reprinted from *The American Journal of Sociology*, Vol. LXII, No. 5, March 1957, pp. 476–481, by permission of the University of Chicago Press. Copyright 1957 by the University of Chicago.

[1] Grateful acknowledgment is made to the Center for Advanced Study in the Behavioral Sciences, Inc., and to the Laboratory of Social Relations of Harvard University for their support of the project which this paper reports in part. We are also grateful to Miriam Gallaher, Margaret Swenson, David Feldman, and Bruce Finney.

[2] A two-page advertisement in the *New York Times Book Review* (April 8, 1956) announces that Peale's *The Power of Positive Thinking*, "the best-loved inspirational book of our times, reaches its 2,000,000 copy anniversary." A generation ago it could be remarked that "few realize that the field of religious books often furnishes the most spectacular and continuing records in book sales. While novelists may vie with each other for records of a hundred thousand, there are continually springing up in the field of religious books titles that go far beyond that, and even into the million" (*Publisher's Weekly*, February 19, 1921, p. 513).

[3] See, however, Everett C. Parker, David W. Barry, and Dallas W. Smythe, *The Television-Radio Audience and Religion* (New York: Harper & Bros., 1955), for a sociological analysis of the output of inspirational religion on television and radio in New Haven. Other discussions are: William Lee Miller, "A Passionate Faith in the Great Whatever" (review of Edward R. Murrow's *This I Believe*), *The Reporter*, X (April, 1954), 46–48, and "Some Negative Thinking about Norman Vincent Peale," *ibid.*, XII (January, 1955), 19–24; and Gustave Weigel, "Protestantism as a Catholic Concern," *Theological Studies*, XVI (June, 1955), 214–32.

Detailed statistical verification of some points made here will be provided in a forthcoming paper, "American Inspirational Religious Literature, 1880–1955."

given to a special phase which is of considerable sociological import.[4]

The literature is by no means entirely unitary, but strains or trends in it exhibit prominent elements of unity.[5] Ralph Waldo Trine's *In Tune with the Infinite*, Bruce Barton's *The Man Nobody Knows*, Henry C. Link's *The Return to Religion*, and Peale's *A Guide to Confident Living* and *The Power of Positive Thinking* suggest for purposes of definition four criteria to which the items of literature should conform: (*a*) they assume the general validity of the Judeo-Christian religious tradition; (*b*) they aim to inspire with the hope of salvation here or in an afterlife; (*c*) they

recommend use of techniques to achieve salvation, in whatever sense salvation might be understood; and (*d*) they address themselves to the "everyday problems" or "everyday people." The books vary in the balance among the four points.

The general validity of the Judeo-Christian tradition is assumed in these works with significant vagueness. Specific theological doctrines, such as of Christ's soteriological mission, or specific theological discussions, as of Christ's status as a member of the Trinity, are hard to find. More likely, there will be found discussion of a transcendent "something" about which a professed theologian could say practically nothing. Daniel Poling confesses, "I began saying in the morning two words, 'I believe'—those two words with nothing added." [6]

The literature also holds forth the hope of some kind of salvation. In the seventy-five years covered in the survey eschatological interest has declined. But, while concern with the next world fades increasingly, salvation comes quite conclusively to mean salvation in this world: release from poverty or handicapping inhibition in personal relations or from ill health or emotional disequilibrium. But salvation in this secular sense is held forth as a definite hope and even a promise.[7]

---

[4] The article reports part of a study of a sample of over thirty best-sellers published since about 1880.

[5] Individual writers differ; e.g., there are marked differences between Peale and Harry Emerson Fosdick and between them and Bruce Barton or between all three and British writers who have found a sizable American public, like Harold Begbie, who in *Twice-born Men* (Boston: F. H. Revell, 1909) praised the "inspiration" afforded the poor of the London slums by the Salvation Army more than a generation ago, or like Daphne du Maurier, who ranges herself, in *Come Wind, Come Weather* (New York: Doubleday, Doran, 1940), with the followers of Frank Buchman. Catholic writers, like Bishop Sheen, are in quite a different universe, to which the characterization below will not apply well. This should not, however, suggest that there are no important resemblances between Catholic and other writers; many, for example, share the view that "social salvation" or social reform is to be achieved more or less exclusively through the reform of the individual and increased numbers of reformed individuals. Thus, Bishop Sheen, who avers that "world wars are *nothing but* macrocosmic signs of the psychic wars waging inside microcosmic muddled souls" (*Peace of Soul* [New York: Permabooks, 1954], p. 8) (italics ours), allies himself on this point with Daphne du Maurier and Henry C. Link.

[6] Quoted from *Parade: The Sunday Picture Magazine*, September 19, 1954, by Will Herberg, *Protestant—Catholic—Jew* (New York: Doubleday & Co., 1956), p. 282.

[7] So Emmet Fox: "If only you will find out the thing God intends you to do, and will do it, you will find that all doors will open to you; all obstacles in your path will melt away; you will be acclaimed a brilliant success; you will be most liberally rewarded from the monetary point of view; and you will be gloriously happy" (*Power through Constructive Thinking* [New York: Harper & Bros., 1932]), p. 23.

The inspirational literature bristles with techniques to attain peace and power which range from putting one's self "in tune with the infinite" by some intuitive twist of the psyche to sensing a deity in the chair by one's bed at night; from reconstructing failures as trifles or even as successes to whispering to one's self a promise of good things to come. These practices, finally, are represented as helpful to ordinary men and women in solving their everyday problems, but this point needs no elaboration here.

Elements of this kind may be found in a variety of other places, for example, in Augustine's *Confessions* or Thomas à Kempis' *Imitation of Christ*. But these documents differ in affirming faith unequivocally. Moreover, the salvation they envisage is not of this world. The ends they set out lack the concrete, tangible quality of such goals as business success or emotional "adjustment," and, consequently, they hardly bristle with the techniques with which the modern literature is filled. True, in a certain sense there is some overlap, as, for instance, in the case of prayer, which is often recommended; but there are obvious differences between devotional prayer and prayer that, not very subtly, is instrumental.[8] On the other hand, the literature, not only on its own recognizances, is in some sense "religious." Advertisements that promise to add six inches to the chests of scrawny men are "inspirational" in tone, but they make no pretensions to being religious and cannot qualify as inspirational religious literature.

A dominant trend in the literature through the decades is secularization; for instance, suffering has lost its "meaningfulness" and more and more is described as senseless misery, best gotten rid of. No longer divinely or transcendentally significant, suffering figures as a pathological experience calling for a psychiatrist or a minister trained in counseling. Again, the deity as represented in the literature is in process of transformation: his existence in some objective sense is no longer insisted upon, and he often approximates a consciously useful fiction. The "hero" appears more and more as the "well-adjusted" man, who does not question existing social institutions and who, ideally successful both in a business or in a professional sense,[9] feels no emotional pain. Finally, there is a strong bias

[8] A qualification rather unusual in the literature is: "Too often the whole value of a prayer is judged by emotional awareness of change in one's inner states, and if one does not feel differently after having prayed, he begins to wonder if there is anything to it." The writer adds, in even more unusual vein, that "to make such a test is to forget that prayer is directed toward God, not toward ourselves" (Georgia Harkness, *Prayer and the Common Life* [Nashville: Abingdon-Cokesbury Press, 1948], p. 66).

[9] Bruce Barton in one strategic sentence sets off two dominant strains in the literature in speaking of the life of Christ: "Stripped of all dogma, this is the grandest achievement story of all" (*The Man Nobody Knows* [Indianapolis: Bobbs-Merrill Co., 1925], p. 9). Surprisingly little attention has been given by sociologists to the success theme and the support for it in American religion, especially in view of the leads given by Weber and Tawney. The Reverend Russell H. Conwell's "Acres of Diamonds" speech, with its forthright assertion that "the foundation principles of business success and the foundation principles of Christianity, itself, are both the same" (*Acres of Diamonds* [New York: Modern Eloquence Corp., 1901], pp. 138–68 at p. 148) is a pertinent and well-known item, but Weber would also have been interested in numerous cognate items, such as the contention of Mrs. Stetson, the Christian Scientist, that poverty is a form of evil and error, while prosperity is both symbol and consequence of spirituality (see E. S. Bates and J. V. Dittemore, *Mary Baker Eddy: The Truth and the Tradition* [New York: A. A. Knopf, 1932], p. 381).

against the "unscientific" and for equating religion and "science." [10]

In American thought William James,[11] in effect, substituted, "I believe because it is useful" for "I believe because it is so"—or even, with Tertullian, "because it is impossible"—an idea which abounds in the inspirational religious literature. Or the best is made of both worlds in a combination such as, "I feel it is absurd; but, since it is useful, I shall insist that it is true." Thus, Henry Link avers, "I believe in God because I have found that without the belief in someone more important than themselves, people fail to achieve their own potential importance." And he adds later: "Agnosticism is an intellectual disease, and faith in fallacies is better than no faith at all." [12] Writers like Harry Emerson Fosdick will go only a certain distance in this direction. Fosdick asserts:

The explanation of the rise of cults like Christian Science and New Thought is obvious. While the old-line churches were largely concerning themselves with dogma, ritual, and organization, multitudes of folk were starving for available spiritual power with which to live. These cults arose to meet this need, and with all their mistaken attitudes . . . they have genuinely served millions of people by *translating religion into terms of power available for daily use.*[13]

But if Fosdick is willing to go only thus far, others are willing to go beyond him. The literature consistently emphasizes "God-power" as divine flow into men, sustaining and aiding them in some materially useful sense to the point where the deity often becomes simply a psychological device. The strain toward instrumentalization is so strong in Peale, for example, that one must by inference from his work assign to God as a primary function the dispensing of divine vitamins to men eager for health and wealth.

A kind of spiritual technology has also been developed, inseparable, of course, from the instrumental element. Standard religious procedures like prayer are constantly recommended, although often with a characteristic twist, as in Peale when he urges: "Learn to pray correctly, scientifically. Employ tested and proven methods. Avoid slipshod praying." [14] Self-exhortation, another frequently suggested procedure, undoubtedly has affinities with more "classical" religious procedures, as in: "I do believe," "Christ is with me," "In everything I do God helps," "I cannot lose." Again, stress is placed on special psychic states, perhaps with physical props simultaneously sug-

[10] Perhaps simply an exaggeration of an already fundamental strain in Protestant philosophy of religion and theology (cf. George F. Thomas, *Protestant Thought in the Twentieth Century,* ed. Arnold S. Nash [New York: Macmillan Co., 1951], pp. 99–100).

[11] Cf. his *Varieties of Religious Experience* (New York: Longmans, Green & Co., 1902) and *Essays on Faith and Morals* (New York: Longmans, Green & Co., 1949). From James comes, apparently, much of whatever intellectual stock in trade the inspirational literature manifests. "Believe," he says, at one point, "that life *is* worth living, and your belief will help create the fact" (*Essays on Faith and Morals,* p. 31). However, the literature, taking the stance that "faith is the answer," hardly bothers with instances in which the most devoted faith has not brought emotional calm or brought it only after long struggle, such as are often found in James.

[12] *The Return to Religion* (New York: Macmillan Co., 1936), pp. 34, 63. This may also be simply an exaggeration of trends found throughout American Protesantism (cf. Willard L. Sperry, *Religion in America* [New York: Macmillan Co., 1947], pp. 153–54).

[13] *As I See Religion* (New York: Harper & Bros., 1932), pp. 17–18 (italics ours).

[14] *A Guide to Confident Living* (New York: Prentice-Hall, Inc., 1948), p. 114.

gested—for example, a state of receptivity to "God-power." A notable set of recommendations depends upon converting spiritual principles into magic. Thus, as in some of the work of Lloyd Douglas, which is frequently only a fictional transcript of inspirational religious literature, he who gives without letting anyone know it is repaid a thousand fold, both magically and materially; he becomes a great success. An outcome not only of impossible physics but—in the light of the principle, "cast your bread upon the waters" and cognate exhortations—of a dubious spirituality, this can be described as spiritual technology.

Other trends include, as the quotation above from Fosdick illustrates, a definitely antiritualistic,[15] antidogmatic, antiinstitutional (antiorganizational) strain. The stress is most emphatically on religious "experience," as might be expected.

In marking the transition from latent to manifest functions of religion, one must distinguish between a *primary* and a *secondary* religious sequence. A good enough text for the primary sequence is afforded by the biblical prescription and promise, "Seek ye first the Kingdom of God, and all these things shall be added unto you." "Faith" is thus urged, but it is urged as primary; its possible "fruits" are only hinted at. The notion that Job might have been seeking to be "well adjusted" simply on the basis of the Book of Job is incongruous. The primary religious sequence may be roughly rendered, then, as follows: Faith → Action → "Results" (for example, emotional equanimity).[16]

---

[15] Cf., e.g., E. Stanley Jones: "Nothing is essential but God, and no rite or ceremony is essential in finding him" (*The Christ of Every Road* [Nashville: Abingdon Press, 1930], p. 150).
[16] An anthropologically or psychologically simplistic view is not being suggested. If "faith" can lead to "action," under "action" including ritual or ceremonial behavior, there

But the modern inspirational literature more or less deliberately reverses this sequence. It starts from the observation (here assumed to be correct) that what is loosely called "faith" *can* bring about "peace of mind" and cognate desired ends. It does not, so to say, start with "the Kingdom of God," that is, with what may be called "classical" religious belief, because the belief is thought to be *true*. (Of course, it may incidentally hold out for the truth of such doctrine as it happens to retain.) It relies on a secondary sequence that begins with a projection or presentation of the desirability of all manner of "good things," mainly wealth and emotional or physical health. This secondary sequence becomes, then, "Results" (in prospect) → Action → Faith (or, possibly, also "Results" → Faith → Action), "action" being largely on the lines of spiritual technology. The modern spiritual technology may in a number of ways be a substitute for older religious ritual. If it is acknowledged that at times, when men have believed sincerely and devotedly, serenity or calm has come to them, it has clearly often come as a *by-product*. Serenity, calm, and the like have been latent functions of religious faith and devotion. It is not necessary to claim that they have been *unqualifiedly* latent; differences of degree may well be crucial. But the inspirational religious literature makes these latent functions of religion manifest and pursues them as aims.

The shift from latent to manifest raises the question: Can the same "results" be obtained? A task facing sociological theory is the classification and explanation of cases in which the transition has

---

is no implication that this is a *necessary* sequence. It is quite possible for "action" to reinforce "faith" or for each to reinforce the other. Moreover, it is not suggested that a *necessary* outcome of "faith" is "peace of mind"; merely that this is *sometimes* the outcome.

different kinds of results. If, say, factory workers can be inspired by a demonstration of the full nature and final uses of the product to which their seemingly disjointed individual efforts have led, it does not follow that an analogous service will always be performed by a demonstration to the religious that their efforts to "find God" afford them "peace of mind." Nor is there any reason to think that faith will be enhanced if it is also shown, directly or by implication, that gaining peace of mind is the point of religious practice in the first place. Here, too, differences of degree are important. That the inspirational religious literature does not always make an outright and unqualified shift from latent to manifest but often stops short of an uninhibited assertion that the *object* of faith is to attain power or peace of mind is of sociological interest.

But the sheer fact that there has been a shift on the lines indicated is easily documented and, for that matter, not only in the inspirational religious literature. Thus, Marshall Sklare notes a similar development in Conservative Judaism:

> According to tradition, the Jew should observe the Sabbath because it is God's will that he do so. In appealing for a reinvigoration of the holiday, Conservatism, however, speaks in terms of *social utility*—in this case the potential contribution of observance to better mental health. Only secondarily is it suggested that the Sabbath may have something more than therapeutic significance, and, furthermore, no Divine sanctions are inferred. The performance of a religious obligation becomes a technique for achieving personality adjustment.[17]

[17] *Conservative Judaism* (Glencoe, Ill.: Free Press, 1955), pp. 121–122. Sklare also quotes from a wall poster that avers the Sabbath has afforded the Jew "a blessed opportunity for

Thus, curiously, the religious begin to look on their own activity in the manner of functionally oriented sociologists and psychologists. The question is whether, in doing so, they do not endanger the religious function; or perhaps these are all signs that faith has already lapsed, the efforts to exhibit its virtues being proof. In this connection it is pertinent to look back to a recent paper by William Kolb, who poses a "moral dilemma" for sociologists of religion who affirm the "integrating" function and necessity of belief in ultimates while themselves holding that belief to be illusory:

> To spread the idea that a belief in ultimate validity of values is necessary but illusory would be to destroy society through destroying or confusing this belief. Yet to urge people to accept the idea that there is an ontic realm of values while believing oneself that such an idea is false is deliberately to deprive people of the knowledge necessary for their freedom and dignity.[18]

Many of the purveyors of inspirational religion may represent a kind of halfway house. At one extreme we would find followers of the "old-time religion," unreserved believers that their creed has objective validity, who, at times, incidentally reap material benefits from it. At another extreme, are "positivistic" functional sociologists, quite prepared to find religion increasing the solidarity of the group, drawing the deviant individual back to it, and so on, while unconvinced themselves. Inspirational religion is somewhere between these extremes,

personality adjustment" and the opportunity, furthermore, "to preserve our psychological, physical, and spiritual equilibrium" amid the tensions of daily stress (*ibid.*, p. 122).
[18] W. L. Kolb, "Values, Positivism, and the Functional Theory of Religion: The Growth of a Moral Dilemma," *Social Forces*, XXXI (May, 1953), 309.

somewhat fluctuating and unsure, yet with a powerful instrumental bent. Faith, again, is "the answer"—enjoined in the first instance not because the religious content that it affirms is above all "true," but just because it is "the answer." The concentration on "the answer," the results, already half-suggests an "illusion." The presumed primary "truth," put into the background from the very absence of attention to it, becomes the more dubious the less stress it receives and the vaguer it gets. The impulse to make religion "useful" is understandable, but the deliberate effort to do so may be self-defeating.

F · OTHER STRESSES AND PERSPECTIVES: MEANING, NONCONSERVATIVE FUNCTIONS, AND FUNCTIONAL ALTERNATIVES

1 · Motivation of Religious Belief and Behavior

TALCOTT PARSONS

In whatever kind of society *some* human expectations, in the fulfillment of which people have acquired a deep emotional investment, are doomed to frustration. These frustrations are of two main types. One of them consists in the fact that men are "hit" by events which they either cannot foresee and prepare for, or control, or both; to which, however, they must make major adjustments, sometimes practical but always emotional. The type case of this kind of frustration is the occurrence of premature death. Certainly the fact that though we all know we have to die almost no man knows when he will die is one of the cardinal facts of the human situation. But not only for the person facing death himself, if he has time to think about it, but quite clearly for the survivors, there is a major problem of adjustment, for the simple reason that the human

SOURCE. Talcott Parsons, "Sociology and Social Psychology," in *Religious Perspectives in College Teaching*, pp. 293–299, edited by Hoxie N. Fairchild. Copyright 1952, The Ronald Press Company.

individual as an object of emotional attachment is of such fundamental importance. Even the loss of a "beloved enemy" can, we know, be very upsetting. Though religious orientations to death, which are universal and fundamental to religion, contain many shadings of belief about the "life after death," the fundamental feature of this orientation is not "wishful thinking." As one historian of religion has put it, "No major religion has ever claimed to be able to 'beat death.' " [1] The dead are dead, and cannot be brought back to life; but the living must still adjust themselves to that fact. From the point of view of the social scientist, what they believe and do in this situation has significance as a set of "mechanisms" which in some ways facilitate this adjustment. From the secular social point of view to hold funeral ceremonies does not "accomplish anything," the functions of such ceremonies are "latent," but they may none the less be highly important.

[1] A. D. Nock, in unpublished lectures.

In general it is extremely conspicuous that ceremonialism not only concerns the directly bereaved, but directly symbolizes the belongingness of the deceased and of the bereaved in larger social groupings. On the one hand these larger groups which are not so directly affected give their "support" to the bereaved, but on the other they set a "tone" for the occasion which in general says, "the traditional values of the society must be upheld." Death must be only a temporary interruption, the important thing on one level is to "get over it" and to go on living. Though it is by no means obvious, there are many features of funeral ceremonies which are closely similar to those of psychotherapy.

There are other types of uncontrollable events besides death which have what in certain respects is a similar bearing on human interests, natural catastrophes being one of them. Furthermore it should be noted that not only frustration in the usual sense, but unexpected and therefore "unearned" good fortune may also have an upsetting effect and require processes of adjustment. Perhaps our own Thanksgiving fits in that category. The Pilgrim Fathers may well have felt that they were extremely "lucky," or as they said, favored by God, to have survived their first terrible year in the wilderness at all.

A second type of frustrating experience is connected with what has come to be called in a special sense "uncertainty." By this is meant the very common type of situation where there is a strong emotional investment in the success of certain human endeavors, where energy and skill undoubtedly count for much, but where unknown and/or uncontrollable factors may and often do intervene to upset any "reasonable" balance between action and success. The exposure of agriculture the world over, with few exceptions, to the vagaries of uncontrollable and unpredictable weather, is one of the

most important examples. No matter how industrious and capable a farmer may be, his crops may be ruined by drought or flood. The field of health is another classical example, and there are a variety of others. The unpredictable character of human conduct in many fields, from love to war, is also prominent.

In all these situations rational techniques must of course loom large; no farmer ever grew good crops by magic alone. But these are the classical situations in which what anthropologists call magic flourishes. Whatever the distinction made, magic is always continuous with religion; it always involves some relation to the strains occasioned by uncertainty, and to human emotional adjustment to such situations. Magical beliefs and practices constitute, from the point of view of social psychology, mechanisms of adjustment to these situations of strain. They give an opportunity to "act out" some of the psychological products of that strain, thus to "place the blame" for the frustration—most conspicuous in the cases of belief in witchcraft. They give people the sense of "doing something about it" in areas where their rational techniques are powerless or untrustworthy. Above all they act as a tonic to self-confidence; they are a protection against allowing the risk of failure to lead to a fatalistic discouragement, the attitude that since success cannot be assured, it is no use trying at all. At the same time, magic may act as a stereotyping agency in situations where empirical knowledge and technique are applicable, and thus block technological advance—this in spite of the fact which Malinowski makes so clear, that magic cannot take the place of rational technique. The Trobriand Islander does not believe that he can make up for failing to cultivate his garden properly by more and better magic; it is a supplement, not a substitute.

The frustrations of established expectations of which we have been speaking pose "problems of meaning" in a double sense. On the one hand, man, being a culture-bearing animal, does not merely "take it" when things go as he does not expect. He has to give these things a meaning, in the first instance emotionally, so that his adjustments to such experiences can become integrated in the *system* of experience, which means among other things that his reactions are coordinated and organized with those of his fellows; he can communicate his feelings and receive adequate responses to his expressions of them.

But beyond this, as we have noted at the beginning of this section, the culture in which a social group lives constitutes a more or less integrated system. As such it must have a certain level of consistency; it must "cover" the principal ranges of men's experience in such a way that all of them to some degree "make sense," together as a whole.

Besides the direct problem of emotional adjustment to the frustration of particular experiences, the "generalization" which is involved in the integration of a cultural system brings up two further particularly crucial "problem" areas. The culture links the experience and expectations of any particular individual or sub group with those of others in a society. There is not only the question of why must this happen *to me*, or to those close to me, but why must it happen at all to anyone? Above all, since men universally seek gratification of their wishes and needs there is the generalized problem of suffering, of why men must endure deprivation and pain and so unequally and haphazardly, or, indeed, at all, and, since all societies must live by moral standards, there is equally the problem of "evil," of why men violate the moral standards of their society and why the "economy" of rewards and punishments fails, as it *always* does to some extent, to balance out. Good fortune and

suffering must always, to cultural man, be endowed with meaning. They cannot, except in limiting cases, be accepted as something that "just happens." Similarly it is impossible to live by moral standards and yet be wholly indifferent either to the extent of conformity with them or to the fate of conformists and violators respectively. It is necessarily disconcerting that to some degree "the good die young while the wicked flourish as the green bay tree."

The sociologist is in a position to state that some significant degree of discrepancy between expectations in both these respects and the actual state of affairs in a society is inevitable, though it varies greatly in degree and in incidence. Both expectations of gratification and moral standards vary from society to society, but this fundamental fact of discrepancy seems to be a constant, grounded in the nature of human personality, society and culture and their relations to each other.

This complex of circumstances constitutes from a certain sociological point of view[2] the primary focus of the differential significance of religion in human life. It is made up of aspects of the life situation to which, men being what they are, they cannot remain emotionally indifferent, and which at the same time in the long run they cannot evade. But adequate adjustment on either the emotional or the cognitive level to these situations cannot be worked out through the "ordinary" techniques and attitudes of practical utilitarian life. The content and incidence of the problems vary, but their presence is a constant. Almost another way of putting the essential point is to say that tragedy is of the essence of the human situation.

[2] More positive aspects of religion, independent of the strains inherent in the human situation, may be equally important, but are more difficult to get at in the context of the intellectual traditions of modern social science.

In one sense all religious ideas involve what may be called "transcendental reference"; this indeed is what has been meant here by saying that they concern the "supernatural." But this need not imply that the "locus of values" is put primarily in the "other" world. Indeed "naturalism" in the sense of sanctioning the interests of this life in health, wealth, happiness, long life, is more common than not in religious traditions. But the existence of the transcendental reference plus the tension which necessarily to some degree obtains between "ordinary" expectations and the discrepancies of experience with reference to them, may be related to a development by which the primary locus of value is placed in the transcendental sphere itself, in a life after death, or in some other form of "salvation" from the involvements of ordinary human social life. Indeed the problem of balancing the books of the human economy makes this very likely, though the "displacement" may not be into a transcendental world, but may emphasize a future state of human society, as in Western "progressivism" or "revolutionary" utopianism. Furthermore, the degree of radicality of repudiation of the things of "this world" may vary greatly, from a desire to "reform" some secondary unsatisfactory features of it, to the view that ordinary secular human life is intrinsically evil, that man is sunk in utterly hopeless degradation and sin, and that *only* in transcendental terms is any positive value whatever to be found.

Whatever the situation in these respects, the religious problem par excellence in the more generalized sense is the "justification of the ways of God to man," is "making sense" out of the totality of the human situation, both in the cognitive sense of a "theory" in which the discrepancies and the established order can be brought within a single view, and in emotional adequacy so that man can adjust to his own fate and that of the societies with which he is identified. Thus though religious ideas on the sophisticated levels are "philosophical" in content, we will not speak of them being religious so long as the basis of interest is merely intellectual, the solution of baffling cognitive problems. They become religious only so far as a commitment in emotion and action to their implications becomes involved, as, in that sense, to quote Durkheim, they are "taken seriously."

From the psychological point of view, then, religion has its greatest relevance to the points of maximum strain and tension in human life as well as to positive affirmations of faith in life, often in the face of these strains. It is most deeply and intimately involved with the "emotional" problems of men, precisely as these are related to the higher levels of culture, to the problems to which in the widest sense man finds it most difficult to adjust.

2 · *Medieval Millenarism: Its Bearing on the Comparative Study of Millenarian Movements*

NORMAN COHN

Preliminary Definitions

A necessary preliminary is to determine what meaning is to be given to the word "millenarian."

Its original meaning was narrow and precise. It referred to the belief held by some Christians on the authority of Revelation XX 4–6 that after His Second Coming Christ would establish a messianic kingdom on earth and would reign over it for 1000 years before the Last Judgment. According to the Book of Revelation the citizens of that kingdom will be the Christian martyrs, who are to be resurrected for the purpose 1000 years in advance of the general resurrection of the dead. In general Christian millenarians have interpreted that part of the prophecy in a liberal rather than a literal sense: they have equated the martyrs with the suffering faithful—themselves—and have expected the Second Coming in their lifetime.

It is natural that Christian theologians should in general insist upon this traditional sense of the term "millenarian." But we are concerned not with classifying beliefs from the standpoint of any Christian orthodoxy but with analysing certain types of behaviour in a variety of societies, not all of them even nominally Christian. The term "millenarism" is clearly intended to be understood here in that wider sense which in recent years

SOURCE. Norman Cohn, "Medieval Millenarism: Its Bearing on the Comparative Study of Millenarian Movements," from *Comparative Studies in Society and History*, Supplement II, 1962, pp. 31–43.

has become customary amongst anthropologists and sociologists and to some extent among historians too. Understood in this sense, "millenarism" becomes simply a convenient label for a particular type of salvationism.

It remains to define that type. At least for the purpose of this introductory paper I propose to regard as "millenarian" any religious movement inspired by the fantasy of a salvation which is to be

(a) collective, in the sense that it is to be enjoyed by the faithful as a group;

(b) terrestrial, in the sense that it is to be realised on this earth and not in some otherworldly heaven;

(c) imminent, in the sense that it is to come both soon and suddenly;

(d) total, in the sense that it is utterly to transform life on earth, so that the new dispensation will be no mere improvement on the present but perfection itself.'

(e) accomplished by agencies which are consciously regarded as supernatural.

Historical Perspectives

It is to be expected that a conference which is concerned to further the sociological interpretation of millenarian movements will give particular attention to comparatively recent movements, for only these have been studied, in detail and at first hand, by social scientists. It is nevertheless important to bear in mind that movements such as the Ghost Dance among the Indians of the American Northwest, the Cargo Cults in Melanesia, Sematism in Java, Jehovah's Witnesses in the United States and Europe and Africa, are but new installments of a story which began more than 2000 years ago.

The oldest form of millenarism of which much is known is the messianic hope of the Jews. Chapter VII of the Book of Daniel, which was composed about 165 B.C. at the height of the Maccabean revolt, is a millenarian manifesto which foretells how Israel will overthrow the Greek empire and thereafter dominate the whole world for all eternity. Similar fantasies abound in the militant apocalypses composed during the struggles which the Jews waged against the Romans from 63 B.C. to 72 A.D. Thus the Apocalypse of Baruch tells how the messiah will shortly break the power of Rome, exterminate all nations which have ever ruled over Israel and establish a kingdom which will last to the end of the world. Then pain, disease, untimely death, violence and strife, want and hunger will be unknown and the earth will yield its fruits ten-thousandfold. There is evidence that the party of the "zealots" who precipitated and led the war of 66–72 A.D., and of 131 A.D. was a truly millenarian movement, obsessed by such fantasies as these and convinced of the imminent coming of a supernatural messiah.

Those wars resulted in the destruction of the Temple, the annihilation of political nationality and the final dispersion of the Jews; and the messianic hope changed its form accordingly. The messiah was no longer expected to lead Israel to military victory or to establish a world-empire under Jewish domination but only to reassemble the scattered communities and reconstitute the national home. Nevertheless this was still a millenarian belief, for the messianic reign was still thought of as a new Golden Age in which God's plan for the world was to find its consummation. That Jewry has been able to endure an unparalleled series of catastrophes and still

survive has undoubtedly been due in part to the hold exercised by this collective fantasy. And it is most significant that whereas usually the coming of the messiah was relegated to some vague and distant future, it became a matter of tense, urgent expectancy whenever some major disaster occurred. It was during the massacres which ran from the eleventh to the fourteenth centuries that European Jewry first produced pretenders to the role of messiah; and each time the result was a wave of millenarian enthusiasm which often expressed itself in a sudden mass migration towards Palestine. The great expulsion from Spain and Portugal at the close of the fifteenth century was followed by the appearance of several messiahs who attracted large followings. Up to the seventeenth century Polish Jewry, which enjoyed a uniquely favourable position, was immune to messianic excitement; but during that century it was subjected to persecutions which culminated in the massacre of some 300,000 and resulted in permanent ruin—and at once we find Polish Jewry supplying the most enthusiastic followers of the most celebrated of Jewish messiahs, Shabbetai Zvi.

More than any other religion, Jewish religion centers on the expectation of a future Golden Age; and Christianity, developing out of Judaism, inherited that expectation. Moreover in the time of Jesus the Jews were much given to millenarian movements; and for many of its early adherents Christianity was just such a movement. Whatever Jesus himself may have meant when he talked of the imminence of the kingdom of God, it is certain that many Christians from the first to the fourth centuries, including such eminent Fathers of the Church as Papias, Irenaeus and Lactantius, expected a dispensation in which the earth would without cultivation produce unheard-of abundance of wine and corn and milk and in which the heathen would be handed over to servitude under the faithful. Such fantasies are indistinguishable from those in the Jewish apocalypses; even the very notion that the age of bliss will occupy the last thousand years before the End is of Jewish origin. And for Christians as for Jews the messiah was to be an avenger, annihilating the wicked, casting down the mighty, exalting the faithful. The one point of difference was that while the Jews were awaiting the coming of such a deliverer the Christians were awaiting his return.

Millenarism remained powerful in the Christian Church so long as Christians were an unpopular minority threatened with persecution. When in the fourth century Christianity attained a position of supremacy in the Mediterranean world and became the official religion of the Roman empire, the Church set out to eradicate millenarian beliefs. Little is heard of them for many centuries. Then suddenly they reappear, held now in more or less explicit opposition to the teaching of the Church. This new millenarism was far more complex than the old, drawing on a variety of ideological traditions and inspiring a variety of movements. Out of the proliferation of such movements in western Europe during the later middle ages and the Reformation period it is possible to identify a few principal types.

The earliest movements form as it were a Christian counterpart to the mass migrations of Jews towards Jerusalem. To medieval Christians Jerusalem was not only the scene of the passion and resurrection of Christ—it was also a symbol of that heavenly Jerusalem "like unto a stone most precious" which according to the Book of Revelation was to replace it at the end of time. Even the learned referred to it as "the navel of the world, the land fruitful above all others, like another paradise of delight"; and simple folk did not easily distinguish between the celestial and the terrestrial city. This fantasy of a miraculous realm, abounding both in spiritual and in material blessings, played a large part in many of the crusades which were launched between the end of the eleventh and the beginning of the fourteenth centuries—not however so much in the official crusades of professional warriors under the auspices of the pope as in the unofficial crusades of the poor. These movements arose from recurrent waves of popular excitement in which masses of men and women and young folk would follow some ascetic, miracle-working preacher on a wild, desperate expedition across unknown lands and seas until they perished. Ideologically these movements owed much to the works known as the medieval Sibylline Oracles, with their prophecy of a great emperor who is to arise before the Second Coming, massacre all Moslems, establish a Golden Age of plenty and make his way to Jerusalem. At least some of the leaders of the crusades assumed this role; while their hordes, seldom able to reach the Moslems, massacred Jews instead, and by the thousand.

These crusades of the common people constituted an enterprise which was carried on for generations in conscious rivalry with the official crusades. The poor claimed that their very poverty made them God's elect and ensured them the success which was denied to the knights; and they were apt to be set in motion by the news either that an official crusade was preparing or else that it had failed. What is most striking however is the part played in these movements by mass insecurity. The areas which saw the rise of popular crusades were always those areas north of the Alps that had a relatively dense population including landless peasants; Flanders, northern France, and the Rhine valley. In these areas many people, because they found themselves in such an insecure position reacted all the more sharply to any sudden, overwhelming threat. It is significant that at the time of the First Crusade of 1095 the areas which were swept by mass enthusiasm had for ten years been afflicted by famine and drought and for five years by plague; while the crusades of 1146, 1309 and 1320 were all preluded by famines. Nor must it be assumed that famine was a normal condition. In the long period 1225–1309, for instance, there were only three major famines in the Low Countries and along the lower Rhine; and each of these was accompanied either by a people's crusade or by some mass movement of a similar kind.

Flourishing at first in the shadowy margins of orthodox Catholicism, in the thirteenth century the popular crusades turned against the Church, which they condemned for its wealth and worldliness. In this they pointed forward to the next wave of millenarism, the movement known as Joachimism. The twelfth century had seen a rapid increase in the economic prosperity of western Europe; and this affected the way of life of the higher clergy. Abbots turned their monasteries into luxurious establishments, while bishops built palaces in which they could live in the same magnificent style as other great feudal lords. The greater circulation of money and the revival of trade enabled the papacy to develop a vast fiscal system, which in turn enabled it to fight political battles, to hire armies and to maintain a court of the utmost splendour—in fact, to behave just like a particularly powerful secular monarchy. Joachimism developed as a protest against this state of affairs.

Aroung the middle of the thirteenth century certain of the so-called "Franciscan Spirituals"—rigorous ascetics who had broken away from the main body of the Franciscan order over the issue of absolute poverty—began to produce their commentaries on the prophetic writings of the Calabrian abbot Joachim of Fiore, who had died half a century earlier. In these works Joachim was made to tell how in 1260 the Spirituals would inaugurate the Third and last Age, the age of the Holy Spirit, which would abrogate the Christian dispensation in the same way as that had abrogated the dispensation of the Old Testament and the Law. This would mark the beginning of the Millennium in which all men—including Jews, Moslems and other heathen, now converted—would be united in prayer, mystical contemplation and voluntary poverty. Other forged prophecies attributed to Joachim foretell how, as preparation for the millennial Church, the existing Church is to be chastised and the clergy massacred by the German emperor. When the year 1260 passed without bringing the awaited transformation the date was postponed again and again. In one form or another the Joachimite faith persisted down to the Reformation and even beyond, and it provided the ideology for various millenarian movements.

Inevitably the Joachimite Spirituals were condemned as heretics and persecuted accordingly; and this in turn increased their fury against the Church. They came to see it as the Whore of Babylon and the Pope as Antichrist and the Beast of the Apocalypse; and at the same time they came to expect a saviour from their own ranks to mount the papal throne as the "Angelic Pope" chosen by God to convert the whole world to a life of voluntary poverty. In the conviction that this was on the point of happening a certain Fra Dolcino collected, about the year 1300, a following of over a thousand armed men. Entrenched in the mountains of Piedmont the band waged ruthless war against the papal armies until, as was bound to happen, it was defeated and massacred. Dolcino was burnt as a heretic, but so great was his prestige that years later followers of his still chose to perish at the stake rather than deny their master.

Marxists have sometimes tried to interpret the millenarism of the Spirituals, and particularly the militant movement around Dolcino, as a protest by poor peasants against a church which was exploiting and oppressing them. This interpretation is certainly mistaken. Research shows that the Spirituals were drawn mainly from the more privileged strata of society, notably from the mixture of noble and merchant families which formed the dominant class in the Italian towns. Far from belonging to the poor peasantry, many of them had renounced great wealth in order to become poorer than any beggar. And when they condemned the wealth and worldliness of papacy and church they were protesting not against economic exploitation but against a defection of spiritual authority —indeed of the one divinely ordained authority which with its prescriptions and demands embraced the life of every Christian and which alone, through its sacraments, could offer him hope of salvation after death. Medieval men, accustomed to see in asceticism the surest sign of grace, naturally questioned the validity of a church which was manifestly unascetic. But uncertainty on so vital a matter was bound to engender intolerable anxieties. It was in response to these anxieties that the Spirituals elaborated their fantasy of the Millennium as one vast, all-embracing, poverty-loving church. And as in all millenarian fantasies, the imperfect existing order was to be replaced not by one less imperfect but by perfection itself. The age of the Holy Spirit was to be an age of supernatural bliss and harmony and its denizens were to enjoy a knowledge of God superior to that of Christ himself.

The Church was the chief agency traditionally charged with the task of regulating relations between men and the powers ruling the cosmos—but it was not the only one, for supernatural authority pertained also to the national monarchy. Medieval kingship was still to a large extent a sacred kingship; however restricted in his political powers, the monarch was a representative of divinity, an incarnation of the moral law and the divine intention, a guarantor of the order and rightness of the world. Joachimism was an international movement, but on the interpretation advanced above its appeal in a given country might reasonably be expected to be in inverse ratio to the prestige of the monarchy. And it would seem that this was indeed the case. Joachimism flourished most vigorously in Italy, where there was no national monarchy and where the Pope was himself a great territorial potentate. In France and England, where the prestige of the monarchy stood high, Joachimism had relatively little influence. In Germany, on the other hand, where there was a monarchy but one which was falling into ever greater impotence and discredit, Joachimism took a peculiar form. There the fantasy of the coming Angelic Pope was sometimes accompanied, sometimes even replaced, by that of the coming supernatural German emperor, a poverty-loving monarch sent by God to institute a world-wide messianic empire.

The Joachimites held that in the Third Age mankind would become a community of perfected beings, rejoicing in divine insight and needing guidance from neither church nor state; and they believed themselves to be inaugurating that dispensation. A very similar fantasy underlay the heterodox mysticism known as the Free Spirit, which flourished from the thirteenth century onwards and inspired a number of millenarian sects. But whereas for the Joachimites perfected beings were *ipso facto* ascetics, for the adepts of the Free Spirit they were *ipso facto* moral anarchists—total amoralists who could do whatever they chose without disquiet of conscience. Typically, a sect of the Free Spirit would be headed by a man claiming to be the Second Adam, engaged in establishing on earth a Third Age which would be at the same time a recreation of Paradise as it existed before the Fall. In theory the members of such a sect were free to commit murder or robbery and indeed every conceivable crime. In practice they seem merely to have practised free love among themselves and occasionally, by way of dramatizing the restoration of primal innocence, performed communal ceremonies in a state of ritual nakedness.

Although the individual sects were small, collectively they formed an underground movement which ramified across vast areas of Europe and preserved a certain ideological continuity over some five centuries. Like other heretical and millenarian doctrines, the Free Spirit was disseminated by wandering prophets who included many former monks and priests—but with this peculiarity, that they disseminated it chiefly amongst unmarried women and widows in the upper strata of urban society. In medieval Europe, with its constant wars and its celibate clergy, the number of women always far exceeded the number of possible husbands; and while spinsters and widows in the lower strata could always work and those in the aristocracy could always become nuns, in the prosperous merchant class they often found themselves both idle and despised. It was common for such women to become experimenters in religious experience, practising extreme mortifications and developing mystical ecstasies; and unlike nuns, they were little supervised by the clergy. It was amongst such women that adepts of the Free Spirit would make their way, in the guise of miracle-working holy men, inspired confessors and preachers. In

this manner the adepts built up, in conspiratorial secrecy, their millenarian groups dedicated to the reconquest of total innocence. The Millennium of the Free Spirit was an invisible empire, held together by the emotional bonds—which of course were often erotic bonds—between men and women.

The adepts of the Free Spirit were not social revolutionaries and did not normally seek followers amongst the poor—but as part of their creed of total emancipation they did conserve the one thoroughly revolutionary social doctrine known to the middle ages. That human beings had at first lived as a community of equals holding all things in common and knowing nothing of "Mine" or 'Thine" was a commonplace in the ancient world. The Fathers too held that such was the original intention of God, and from them the notion was taken over by the medieval scholastics and canonists. But it was certain adepts of the Free Spirit who, towards the end of the fourteenth century, first tried to call the egalitarian State of Nature out of the depths of the past and to present it as an attainable ideal. In doing so they provided the basis for a new form of millenarism. The Milennium could now be imagined as a recreation of that lost Golden Age which had known nothing of social classes or of private property. During the great social upheavals which accompanied the close of the middle ages various extremist groups were inspired by the conviction that at any moment the egalitarian, communistic Millennium would be established by the direct intervention of God.

It was always in the midst of some great revolt or revolution that the revolutionary millenarian group first emerged into daylight. This is equally the case with John Ball and his followers in the English peasants' revolt of 1381; the extreme Taborites during the early stages of the Hussite revolution in Bohemia,

1419–1421; Thomas Müntzer and his "League of the Elect" in the German peasants' revolt of 1525; and the Radical Anabaptists who, in the midst of a wave of revolts in the capitals of the ecclesiastical states in northwest Germany, established the "New Jerusalem" at Münster in 1534–1535. What is seldom realised—and what Marxist and right-wing historians have united in concealing —is how little these groups had in common with the mass uprisings which they tried to exploit. Yet to appreciate the contrast one has only to consider what kind of objectives the mass movements set themselves. Thus the English peasants, seeing new possibilities opened up by the labour shortage after the Black Death, were concerned to have manorial dues commuted for cash rents and villeinage replaced by wage labour. The Hussites were concerned to expropriate the church in Bohemia (and incidentally the German aliens who governed it) and, in varying degrees, to increase the status and independence of the laity as against the clergy. The German peasants, a prosperous and rising class, were concerned to increase the autonomy of their communities and to defend their traditional rights against encroachments by the new territorial states. In the ecclesiastical states of north-west Germany the powerful and wealthy guilds in the capital cities were concerned to restrict the economic privileges and immunities of the local clergy. These were all limited and realistic aims. On the other hand the aims of the millenarian group in each case corresponded not to the objective social situation and the possibilities it offered but to the salvationist fantasies of a handful of free-lance preachers; and they were accordingly boundless.

A millenarian revolt never formed except round a prophet—John Ball in England, Martinek Hauska in Bohemia, Thomas Müntzer in Thuringia, first Jan Matthys and then Jan Bockelson at Münster. Wherever the career of such a prophet can be traced, it turns out that he had been obsessed by apocalyptic fantasies for years before it occurred to him, in the midst of some social upheaval, to address himself to the poor as possible followers. And what he then offered them was not simply a chance to improve their material lot—it was also, and above all, the prospect of carrying out a divinely ordained mission of stupendous, unique importance. On the strength of supernatural revelations, the social conflict of the moment was presented as essentially different from other struggles known to history, a cataclysm from which the world was to emerge totally transformed and redeemed. A movement fighting such a battle under a divinely inspired leader inevitably regarded itself as an elite set infinitely above the rest of mankind, infallible and incapable of sin. Avowedly concerned to purify the world of sin in preparation for the coming of the Millennium, these movements commonly showed themselves very bloodthirsty indeed.

It has sometimes been argued that a revolutionary millenarian group fulfils the function of preparing the way for more realistic social movements. This was not the case with the movements which have just been described, for each of these appeared only when an organised insurrection of a decidedly realistic kind was already under way. The spectacle which presents itself is, rather, of a band of a few hundred dedicated enthusiasts struggling to master, in the interests of its own apocalyptic fantasy, a vast popular movement numbering tens or hundreds of thousands. And if the millenarian group differed vastly from the mass movement around it in aim and outlook and strategy, it differed just as much in social composition. The prophet himself was not normally, any more than in other millenarian movements, a manual worker or even a former manual worker, but an intellectual or half-intellectual. Ball, Hauska and Müntzer were all former priests turned free-lance preachers; while of Müntzer it is known that he was born to modest comfort and became a graduate with a voracious appetite for reading. Of the prophets at Münster Matthys was indeed a master-baker, but Bockelson was the bastard son of a village mayor, literate, and a failed cloth-merchant, while their manifestos were composed for them by Rothmann, another former priest. As for their following—it is significant that all these movements flourished in areas where there existed a population which had no institutionalised means of defending or furthering its interests.

The life of a settled peasant or a skilled artisan in medieval Europe was often a hard one but it did not normally lack a certain basic security. On the land the manorial regime was by no means a system of uncontrolled exploitation. The custom of the manor which bound the peasants also bound their lord; and in the village group peasants possessed an organisation which was highly efficient in defending traditional rights and even on occasion in extending them. The guilds in which the skilled artisans in the towns were organised were formidable bodies, perfectly capable of planning and leading a successful revolt against an obstinate overlord or an extortionate patriciate. But in the most populous and economically advanced areas of Europe there existed numbers of poor folk who had no such organisations behind them: in the countryside landless peasants and farm-hands, in the towns journeymen (who were forbidden to organise), unskilled workers (who had no guilds) and a floating population of beggars and unemployed. It was such people as these that provided the revolutionary prophets with their following.

In social composition not so very different from the popular crusades of earlier centuries, these last millenarian movements of the middle ages took place in a very different context. The society which bred them was a society profoundly disoriented by the defection of the traditional relationships crumbling under the pressure of the new capitalist economy. In more than a purely chronological sense these movements stand at the threshold of the modern world.

Sociological Comments and Queries

The future miraculous age of bliss can be imagined in many very different ways And being themselves so various, millenarian fantasies can appeal to people of the most varied kinds and in the most varied situations. The present survey of medieval millenarism deals with only a few of the immense number of variations revealed by historical, anthropological and sociological research. Even so, it may still prompt some general reflections which are relevant to the comparative study of millenarian movements.

It seems certain, then, that the rise of millenarian movements is favoured by certain specific circumstances—and all the more strongly when two or more of those circumstances are present together. It is possible to identify some of the circumstances which so operated in medieval Europe, and legitimate to enquire whether they have operated elsewhere too.

1. Catastrophe or the fear of catastrophe; e.g. the famines and plagues which preceded several popular crusades and similar movements; the massacres which preceded the mass movements of dispersed Jews towards Jerusalem. Are catastrophe or the fear of catastrophe particularly favourable to millenarian movements of a migratory kind?

Have we a related phenomenon in the recurrent migrations of the Apapokuva-Guarani of Brazil in search of the Land without Evil? It appears that such migrations were occurring already before the arrival of the Portuguese and are dictated by sudden panic fears, based on Guarani mythology, of the impending destruction of the whole world save only the Land without Evil. It is significant that by medieval Christians catastrophes were accepted as "signals" for the Second Coming and the Last Judgment; while for the Jews intensified persecution was traditionally expected to herald the coming of the messiah.

2. Supposed defection of the authority traditionally responsible for regulating relations between society and the powers governing the cosmos. Italian Joachimite movements around or in expectation of the last, "Angelic" Pope; German Joachimite movements around or in expectation of the final world-emperor—these have their counterparts in various Russian sects which from the time of the Raskol (1666) regarded the Czar as the Antichrist who had ruined the church as an agency of salvation. Some of these sects were millenarian, e.g. the Skoptsi, who in the nineteenth century numbered tens of thousands scattered all over Russia and including nobles, officials, army officers and rich merchants as well as peasants. The basic rule of the Skoptsi was that within their organisation (a clandestine but highly efficient one) all men must be castrated and all women must lose their breasts. The leader of the Skoptsi, Selivanov, was regarded as a reincarnation of Christ—but also as Czar Peter III, saved from his murderers and now biding his time to mount the imperial throne, hold the Last Judgment and establish a world-wide millennial kingdom of sexless beings. The case has its importance, for here is a millenarian movement which quite clearly cannot be interpreted in terms of class conflict or indeed of anything except religiously motivated anxiety.

It would be worth while to examine what part the defection of a ruler as cosmocrator may have played in non-Christian millenarian movements, e.g. after the collapse of the Burmese monarchy and the desecration of the Golden Palace at Mandalay. This could perhaps be treated as part of a more general question: Can one not detect in the genesis of a great number of millenarian movements, from medieval Europe to Java and from the Guarani of Brazil to the Taiping rebels in China, the working of mass anxiety concerning the stability and orderly functioning of the cosmos?

3. Emotional frustration in women of means and leisure but without social function or prestige. Throughout the history of Christianity this circumstance has contributed to the rise of revivalist movements and it still does so today. What ideal such a movement sets itself seems to depend chiefly on personal factors—in the first place on the particular personality of the prophet, which will appeal only to certain types of women. The antinomian and erotic millenarism of the Brethren of the Free Spirit does however indicate one recurrent possibility. Nineteenth-century France, for instance, saw similar sects spring up—e.g. the transformation of the Saint-Simonian movement under Barthélemy-Prosper Enfantin, in 1831–1833, and the clandestine sect around Jean-Antoine Boullan in the 1880's.

Do comparable movements occur in societies where the sexual life is less guilt-ridden than it has usually been in Christendom?

4. The existence, in a society which recognises that the relative power and prosperity of different sections (classes, ethnic groups, etc.) can change, of elements which canont organise for the purpose of defending and furthering their interests by secular means. This circumstance, which in Europe so greatly assisted revolutionary prophets from Ball to Bockelson, seems also to have provided the stimulus for many of the anti-

European millenarian movements which have flourished in Africa and Asia and the Americas during the past century. Central to this form of millenarism is the belief that the oppressors are about to be cast down, even annihilated, with the help of supernatural beings. Where medieval sectarians expected the return of Christ as judge and avenger, many of the "primitive" peoples of today and yesterday have awaited the return of their long-dead ancestors.

It is not, incidentally, only "nativistic" movements which imagine the Millennium as the restoration of a lost Golden Age—medieval millenarians did so too.

Has there ever been a millenarian movement which can confidently be attributed to this circumstance alone, or is this always reinforced by circumstances making for cosmic anxiety, as described above?

It remains to ask whether the above observations help towards a general sociological interpretation of millenarian movements.

They would seem at any rate to invalidate, as inadequate to the complexity of the matter, those current quasi-teleological interpretations (not all of them Marxist) which see millenarian movements as necessarily contributing to cultural evolution. As one's mind ranges from the Skoptsi to the Apapokuva-Guarani one is impelled, rather, to consider the psychic prerequisites for these movements, i.e. the common emotional needs of those who participate in them.

With all due tentativeness I shall now advance, as a possible topic for discussion, a general socio-psychological hypothesis concerning the causation of millenarian movements. Of course, to suggest that all millenarian movements arise in situations which have certain identifiable features in common is not to suggest that wherever such situations exist millenarian movements must in-

fallibly arise. Whatever other value it may or may not have, the following hypothesis has certainly no predictive value at all.

It is suggested, then, that the decisive causative factors are these:

1. Many traditional religious worldviews include a promise of a future age of bliss to be enjoyed by the faithful. This traditional promise provides the indispensable basis for a millenarian faith. It seems that in societies—such as that of ancient Greece—where the religious world-view has no place for such a fantasy, millenarism cannot develop. Where on the other hand such a fantasy is familiar it can sometimes be given the immediacy and particularity necessary to convert it into an effective millenarian ideology.

2. It is the prophet who carries out this adaptation of traditional lore and who becomes the bearer of the resulting ideology. If in addition the prophet possesses a suitable personality and is able to convey an impression of absolute conviction, he is likely in certain situations of emotional tension to become the nucleus of a millenarian movement.

3. It is perhaps possible to indicate how such situations of emotional tension arise. It seems that there is in many, perhaps in all, human psyches a latent yearning for total salvation from suffering; and that that yearning is greatly intensified by any frustration or anxiety or humiliation which is unaccustomed and which cannot be tackled either by taking thought or by any institutionalised routine. Where a particular frustration or anxiety or humiliation of this nature is experienced at the same time and in the same area by a number of individuals, the result is a collective emotional agitation which is peculiar not only in its intensity but also in the boundlessness of its aims.

4. Such a situation provides the perfect opportunity for a prophet promising a

collective salvation which is to be both immediate and total. It is the discharge of accumulated emotional tension that gives such energy to the resulting millenarian movement.

There remain many problems which the above hypothesis, even if it proved correct, would do nothing to clarify. Why, for instance, has Indian society been almost free from millenarian movements—even though in the prophecy of Vishnu's avatar as Kalki Hinduism has its own millenarian myth? Is it perhaps because a series of reincarnations ending infallibly in Nirvana offers the individual a more convincing prospect of total salvation than does the Christian hope (which must remain most uncertain) of heaven? And in general what are the factors, historical or immediate, which militate against the growth of millenarian movements? Is one such factor, operating in the West today, that strengthening of the ego which is said to be a characteristic modern trend?

Again: What relationship can be established between a given millenarian ideology and the religious world-view which underlies it? Is it true, for instance, that world-views (such as the Christian, the Jewish and the Moslem) which include the notion of a divine will working through history towards a preordained end provide a better climate for millenar-ism than world-views which know nothing of a divine purpose and see history as an unending series of cycles? Or is such a climate better only for some kinds of millenarism? In particular, is the fantasy of a "chosen people," divinely appointed to inaugurate and enjoy the Millennium, confined to those movements which are of Christian, Judaic or Moslem origin? Such movements often show signs of collective megalomania; would the same be true of millenarian movements which spring from other types of world-view?

And finally: To what extent can millenarism be self-generating? The Greek and Roman empires, normally so tolerant in matters of religion, persecuted Jews and Christians. Have we here examples of religious communities which, precisely because they regard themselves as agents of the divine will and predestined heirs to the millennial kingdom, call down persecution—and then, in response, develop still more strongly the millenarian aspects of their religions?

These are difficult problems indeed—and if we could solve them all we should no doubt find others as difficult confronting us. But then the aim of this conference is not, presumably, to produce a comprehensive sociology of millenarism but rather, by comparing the various groups of data available to it, to advance a little in that direction.

3 · Religion and Socialism

H. RICHARD NIEBUHR

The Methodist revival was the last great religious revolution of the disinherited in

SOURCE. H. Richard Niebuhr, *The Social Sources of Denominationalism*, pp. 72–76. Copyright 1929 by Henry Holt and Company. Reprinted by permission of Meridian Books, The World Publishing Company.

Christendom. And it was not wholly a popular movement. Perhaps that is one reason why it was the last. It is a striking fact that the revolutionary tendencies of the poor in the nineteenth century were almost completely secular in character, while in preceding eras they were always largely religious in nature. The socialism of 1848 and later years was closely akin in many ways to Anabaptism and Quakerism as well as to Lollardy and the Waldensian revolt. It cherished as these did the hope of an inevitable social renewal which would cast down the mighty from their seats and exalt them of low degree. Like these it provided the oppressed with an emotional escape from the weariness and grime of uneventful and profitless labor. Like these it brought to consciousness the latent sense of social solidarity and endowed the impoverished individual life with the significance of participation in a cosmic event. But for the angels who fought on the side of Baptists and Quakers it substituted economic laws, and in place of the early coming of the Son of Man it anticipated the class struggle and the dictatorship of the proletariat. What were the reasons for this change?

The conditions which preceded the rise of socialism were not dissimilar to those which formed the background of the religious revolutions of previous centuries. There was present the actual exclusion of the poor from churches grown emotionally too cold, ethically too neutral, intellectually too sober, socially too aristocratic to attract the men who suffered under the oppression of monotonous toil, of insufficient livelihood and the sense of social inferiority. There was present also the awakening of the disinherited to the consciousness of their human dignity and worth. But the result was not a religious revolt. On the contrary socialism often assumed the character of an anti-religious movement. Its secularism was doubtless due to many causes—to the growth of the scientific temper and of nineteenth-century materialism, to the prevalence of the mechanistic conception of life which industrialism fosters, to the determinism of the

Hegelian philosophy in which Marx had been trained, to the bare fact that the leaders of the movement were not religious men. But among the causes of this secularism the absence of an effective social idealism within any of the Christian churches was of especial importance. The last previous religious movements among the disinherited, Methodism and Pietism, had failed to follow in the steps of the Baptists and Quakers. They had allowed the millenarian hopes to lapse; they had substituted for the concept of the kingdom the symbol of heaven; they had been concerned with the redemption of men from the hell beyond the grave alone and had held out little promise of salvation from the various mundane hells in which the poor suffer for other sins besides their own. So they had failed to keep alive within the church those realistic hopes which had always been the source of new religious uprisings in the centuries before; and they had joined with the older churches in proclaiming a purely other-worldly hope. In any other century of Christian history this failure to keep alive the promise of social amelioration through Christian ethics and by divine miracle might have had less far-reaching results. In the century of inventions and of industrial production, in a time so largely occupied with the present world and its values, the absence of this social element from the preaching of the gospel was fatal to the religion of the disinherited. It is significant that much of the leadership of the social movement now came from a group which had been nurtured in the ideals of Old Testament prophecy, and which even when it lost its religious faith did not fail to give expression to ideals which had been derived from that religion. The leadership of the Jews in the social revolutions of the nineteenth and twentieth centuries had these religious sources; it was the only effective substitute for the Christian leadership which had once been unfailingly available in every crusade for justice but which had died out, perhaps as a result of attrition in a theological and other-worldly church.

The nineteenth century, it is true, did not entirely lack representatives of the naïve religious movements. The Salvation Army is an outstanding example of the manner in which a separate conventicle must be formed by the religious poor, who have been excluded from the denominations of their newly enriched brothers. But Booth was neither a Francis nor a Wesley. The movement he inaugurated was not a popular movement of spontaneous character; the very organization of the Army implied a home-mission enterprise rather than a religious and social awakening. Moreover the under-privileged of the modern era have been too greatly alienated from the gospel as well as from Christianity, whether by the silent forces of the industrial environment, or by the strident voices of Marxian apostles, or by the indifferent attitude of churchmen, for the Army to be able to repeat the successes of its victorious predecessors. Other contemporary movements of the religious poor toward the attainment of adequate religious experience and expression come to light in many a gospel tabernacle and evangelistic society and millenarian association. But the mass of the workers remains untouched; there is no effective religious movement among the disinherited today; as a result they are simply outside the pale of organized Christianity. Yet without the spontaneous movement from below, all efforts to repristinate the ethical enthusiasm of the early church and to reawaken the Messianic hope are unavailing. The churches which again and again have been recalled to consider a neglected message by the religious revolutions of the unfortunate are so much the poorer because there is no sect of the disinherited today. Even sectarianism is preferable to the absence of vital Christian conviction and expression among those whose hunger and thirst after righteousness is not any the less necessary to the world because it has natural roots.

4 · Extremism, Political and Religious

SEYMOUR M. LIPSET

Direct connections between the social roots of political and of religious extremism have been observed in a number of countries. In Czarist Russia, the young Trotsky recognized the relationship and successfully recruited the first working-class members of the South Russian Workers' Union (a revolutionary Marxist organization of the late 1890s) from adherents to religious sects.[1] In Holland and Sweden, recent studies show that the Communists are strongest in regions which were once centers of fundamentalist religious revivalism. In Finland, Communism and revivalist Christianity often are strong in the same areas. In the poor eastern parts of Finland, the Communists

SOURCE. Seymour M. Lipset, "Extremism, Political and Religious," from Seymour M. Lipset, *Political Man*, Garden City, New York: Doubleday, 1960, pp. 107–108. Copyright 1959, 1960 by Seymour M. Lipset. Reprinted by permission of Doubleday & Company.

[1] See Isaac Deutscher, *The Prophet Armed, Trotsky, 1879–1921* (London: Oxford University Press, 1954), pp. 30–31.

have been very careful not to offend people's religious feelings. It is reported that
many Communist meetings actually begin with religious hymns.[2]

This is not to imply that religious sects
supported by lower-class elements necessarily or usually become centers of political protest. In fact, such sects often
drain off the discontent and frustration
which would otherwise flow into channels of political extremism. The point
here is that rigid fundamentalism and
dogmatism are linked to the same underlying characteristics, attitudes, and predispositions which find another outlet
in allegiance to extremist political movements.

In his excellent study of the sources of
Swedish Communism, Sven Rydenfelt
analyzed the differences between two

socially and economically comparable
northern counties of Sweden—Vasterbotten and Norrbotten—in an attempt
to explain the relatively low Communist
vote in the former (2 per cent) and the
much larger one in the latter (21 per
cent). The Liberal party, which in
Sweden gives much more support than
any other party to religious extremism,
was strong in Vasterbotten (30 per cent)
and weak in Norrbotten (9 per cent).
Since the total extremist vote in both was
almost identical—30 and 32 per cent—
he concluded that a general predisposition toward radicalism existed in both
counties, containing some of the poorest,
most socially isolated, and rootless groups
in Sweden, but that its expression differed, taking a religious form in one
county, and a Communist in the other:
"The Communists and the religious radicals, as for instance, the Pentecostal sects,
seem to be competing for the allegiance
of the same groups." [3]

[2] See Sven Rydenfelt, *Kommunismen i Sve-
rige. En Samhallsvetenskaplig Studie.* (Kund:
Gleerupska Universitetsbokhandeln, 1954),
pp. 296, 336–37; Wiardi Beckman Institute,
Verkiezingen in Nederland (Amsterdam,
1951, mimeographed), pp. 15, 93–94; Jaako
Novsiainen, *Kommunism Kuopion lää nisssä*
(Helsinki: Joensuu, 1956).

[3] See W. Phillips Davison's extensive review
of Sven Rydenfelt, *op. cit.,* which appeared
in the *Public Opinion Quarterly,* 18 (1954–
55), pp. 375–88. Quote is on p. 382.

RELIGION AS CULTURE,

STRUCTURAL DIFFERENTIATION,

AND NONRELIGIOUS ACTIVITIES

THE subjects treated in Part Four constitute a very considerable portion of what may reasonably be subsumed under the general heading of sociology of religion. Four subjects are set out in sequence, two of these (namely, structural differentiation and culture and differentiation) being particularly closely related. Here, as elsewhere, an element of the arbitrary must be admitted, and the subjects might have been differently allocated. But there are good enough reasons, as will be evident, for putting together the several elements of concern in the sociology of religion suggested by the rubrics of religion as culture, structural differentiation, culture and differentiation, and religion and nonreligious activities.

Section A, on religion as culture, is intended to give stress to the view that religion as a cultural phenomenon, as a realm of meanings, values, and symbols, has not been well explored by sociologists. There has been some tendency

182

in the sociology of religion—happily, a tendency not unchallenged by others—to take for granted certain religio-cultural backgrounds, in particular, of course, the cultural background of Christianity, and even to concentrate on social processes in religion that are rather empty of cultural content (in so far as this is possible). It is in a sense true that culture as such does not greatly interest the sociologist, or at least that it does not interest the sociologist to the degree that culture as plainly and demonstrably influencing social interaction does. But there are dangers in hasty consignment of religion as culture to anthropologists or philosophers or historians or theologians, on the assumption that these specialists will "take care" of the matter. Religion as culture does heavily obtrude into human interaction; and even as meaning-value-symbol content, apart from any special influence on interaction, it should not be neglected if only because of the sheer potential of influence on interaction that it may have. Issues are involved in all this about which it is not needful to say much here. Religion as culture may be abstracted from the context of social interaction and treated analytically as a separate realm. This is a kind of methodological maneuver. And when this maneuver is effected, religion as culture can still in fact be extremely important in its influence on interaction. On the other hand, it is at least conceivable that a certain varying "quantum" of religion as culture may not be particularly effective or operative in relation to interaction at particular times. This is an empirical matter entirely. But however such ideas as these may be elaborated, it is still true that the over-all influence of religion as culture on social interaction is considerable.

In the first selection in Section A, Weber's item on asceticism, mysticism, and salvation, it is clear that the author has very much in view the effects on behavior of the religiocultural systems he seeks to analyze. He writes forth-rightly of "contrasts in effects upon behavior." Weber's item has intrinsic interest as a vital part of his thought in the sociology of religion. It may also serve to illustrate the very meaning of culture within the religious sphere. It may be remarked, incidentally, that of the outstanding sociologists of religion Weber perhaps particularly brings out the possibility that religious "ideas" can have a profound influence on practice. Yet Weber could and did realize (very much like Pratt) that, as he puts the matter in *The Religion of India*,[1] "*dharma*, that is, ritualistic duty, is the central criterion of Hinduism . . . Hinduism is primarily ritualism . . . The first question a Hindu asks of a strange religion is not what is its teaching (*mata*) but its *dharma*." Thus, Weber too was

[1] Max Weber, *The Religion of India*, Glencoe: The Free Press, 1958, p. 24.

aware of how important practice could be, at the least in the eyes of practitioners of certain religions. But the various issues this suggests can only be thus glancingly noted now, and cannot be carried closer to satisfactory statement or resolution than they were in the introduction to Part Three.

Ideally, after Weber's introductory item, additional selections should afford a thorough and systematic analysis of religion as culture. This is not possible. The necessary materials are simply not available. But an effort has been made to present items that, taken together, constitute a listing and exemplification of a few significant religiocultural processes (or conditions). The first of these, H. R. Niebuhr's study of "Christ Against Culture," illuminates a well-known type of religion that is opposed to "the world" —that is, to the world of culture and society. The conflict Niebuhr describes in elaborating this type is a common one and threatens constantly to break out even in religious orientations that are in principle quite different from the Christ-against-culture outlook. Christianity may generally be said to have a strong tradition of "tension" with the so-called world. Niebuhr's item may certainly be read as one that sets out a process (or condition) of conflict of religion with culture (although it is of course the case that in a thoroughly legitimate sense the Christ-against-culture orientation is itself a cultural phenomenon). Conflict or tension may also lapse, as indeed Niebuhr was well aware. (Portions of his book on *Christ and Culture*, from which the selection here is taken, are most relevant also to the phenomenon of lapse or absence of conflict between religion and the world). Religion can be absorbed by, or accommodated to, the world of culture and society. Elements of accommodation in this sense are rather strikingly suggested in Strizower's description of the case of the Jews of India, although it is quite clear that accommodation or absorption does not have its own way entirely in this case. Thus in these two readings by Niebuhr and Strizower religious conflict with and accommodation to the world of culture and society may be said to be set out as two of the simpler processes of the working of religion as culture—"simpler," or "simple," in broad outline, at any rate. (It is clear that religious conflict with and accommodation to the world may be taken as "conditions" and that their "processual" aspect, just as a matter of definition, comes to the fore when they are "dynamically" conceived.)

Religions move from one cultural and social context to another and religion accordingly exhibits a process that may be given the conventional anthropological label of cultural diffusion. The literature dealing with such diffusion is enormous. In a broad way, and to say no more, the entirety of the history of missionizing is relevant here. Diffusion might have been variously exemplified. Thus, the coming of Christianity to Japan is one among numerous other interesting cases on which there is a significant literature, and this is also one of a number of cases that might reasonably be argued to be more important in a "world historical" sense than the case which has here been chosen to exemplify diffusion of religion. But the case selected, treating Christianity and Islam among the African Mossi, has a contemporary relevance that is not without its own point, is conveniently self-contained, and assumes no special historical background as it is presented by Skinner; and it has the additional desirable feature of making some comparison between two of the so-called world religions—Christianity and Islam —as they attempt to make an impact among the Mossi. Religion of course appears here again as a cultural reality. As the cultural reality of Christianity or Islam, as one or another distinctive complex of meanings and values and symbols, Christian or Moslem, it comes to a portion of Africa where it encounters still another complex, and Skinner's item is an effort to clarify some aspects of the encounters involved.

Further, in connection with religion as culture, there is a highly significant outlook according to which religion as culture is subject to a process of what may be called inner or self-induced cultural "degeneration." This outlook is presented in the two very brief selections from Pitirim A. Sorokin's *Social and Cultural Dynamics* that conclude Section A of Part Four. In the first of these selections, Sorokin is concerned with the change from what he calls Ascetic Ideationalism to Active Ideationalism. Ascetic Ideationalism seeks to enhance "spiritual" ends, as it seeks to diminish nonspiritual ones; and it is detached from the world. Active Ideationalism, since it is still Ideationalism (and thereby, in Sorokin's terms, must still feature an important spiritual bias) is sympathetic to ascetic trends but, as its name suggests, it is oriented to the shaping of the life of others as well as of the self; and, very much to the point for present purposes, it has to operate in the "world"—again the world of culture and society. Operating in the world, it must be touched and transformed, one might even say contaminated, by the world. Sorokin writes, in the first passage from his work ("The Active Ideational Culture Mentality"): "In a way it is the tragic and immanent destiny of the Ascetic Ideational culture system to turn into the Active Ideational." He affords some analysis of how this comes about, and his main stress is on the circumstance that the world of actuality imposes certain necessities and constrains to certain compromises with pristine ideals. Thus Saint Paul, "the great organizer of Christianity," is caught more and more in the "web" of the "empirical world"; and primitive ascetic Christianity becomes tainted, as it were, with components of a world from which it cannot possibly hold itself entirely aloof once it seeks to mold it. The stress in the second passage from Sorokin here presented ("The Degradation of Culture by Masses") is obviously on something rather different, namely, degeneration of cultural content (whether specifically religious or not) through the "vulgarization" wrought by masses who do not attain certain levels of intelligence or cannot reach certain levels of spirituality. The material presented does not exhaust Sorokin's views on these matters. Thus, to note no more, elsewhere in his *Dynamics* (Volume 3, pp. 223–224) he observes that "Ideational culture . . . generates forces that work against its negativistic attitude toward the accumulation of wealth and the establishment of economic well-being" and emphasizes that the coming of masses of people, in veneration, to the abodes of such men as saints and hermits has often brought about a prosperity that has endangered or eliminated the asceticism sustained by the saints and hermits and their congeners. But the brief passages here made available are sufficiently suggestive of the general character of Sorokin's views on the process of inner "degeneration" of religion as culture. (Those unfamiliar with Sorokin's general cultural types—sensate, ideational, and idealistic—will find a brief presentation of them in the paper by Parsons reprinted in Section C of Part Four.)

A view remarkably similar to that held by Sorokin about the degeneration of religious culture through degradation or vulgarization by masses is entertained by Gustav Mensching and will be found set out in Section C on Culture and Differentiation. Indeed, Sorokin's material is not only related to that of Mensching in Section C but also to that of Parsons in Section C. The interplay among the component selections in Part Four will be further noted. At this point, it should be said once more that the religiocultural processes of conflict, accommodation, diffusion, and internal "degeneration" are designed to afford *instances* of religiocultural process. No pretense is made that a systematic listing or collation of such processes has been effected. It is my bias, if that is not already plain enough, that the entire field of religion as culture needs very careful cultivation by sociologists. What is here presented is barely suggestive of tasks that need to be undertaken.

Section B of the present Part deals with structural differentiation in religion. As the selection from Mensching on folk and universal religion indicates, there is an unevolved folk religion which ties together religious adherence and group or tribal adherence. Religious adherence and group affiliation are then simply inseparable, and this is the mark of folk religion. But in universal religion, as Mensching puts the matter, it is the individual who is "the subject of religion." The individual may then adhere to or believe in a universal religion (which in principle addresses itself to all individuals) while his tribal or national or other group affiliation becomes irrelevant. He may be a Christian though a Japanese, a Moslem though an Englishman, a Buddhist though a Frenchman. The distinction of folk and universal religion is important and it is clearly set out by Mensching. Indeed, it is even very useful to make a somewhat parallel distinction today, for certain purposes, as the item from Lenski's work in Section B shows. Lenski does not employ Mensching's terminology, but the distinction he makes between religion as *communal* and as *associational* has evident points of resemblance to Mensching's. There is a "people" or community of Jews and of Catholics and of Protestants (white and Negro); and for these there are communal bonds. There is a religious association of Jews and of others; and here the bonds are those that tie together persons who belong to the same specifically religious organization and make the same religious profession. Lenski bases some interesting and cogent analysis on this distinction. It is a distinction that will come to the fore again in this volume, in Section F of Part Five devoted to religion and problems in coexistence.

The material on the structural differentiation of religion is presented as Section B of Part Four for a number of reasons, although no very detailed justification for its inclusion at this particular point need be given. In refined analysis of religion as culture, the notion of structural differentiation is likely to be most useful. Thus, the stance that Niebuhr has described as Christ-against-culture is hardly conceivable, or flatly impossible, in a situation where an authentic folk religion in Mensching's sense flourishes. (And to say this is to state more than a mere tautology.) Folk religion definitely does not constitute a meaning-value-symbol complex that can stand over against and "criticize" the world of culture and society. The Christ-against-culture stance, on the other hand, quite clearly requires or demands and calls for a religious criticism of the world. A Christ-against-culture religious orientation is flatly incompatible with an undifferentiated folk-religious condition. That it is the case, once the notion of structural differentiation is to the fore, that distinctive cultural phenomena treated in the present readings can be better understood, will be further seen in the second selection (in Section C) in this Part from Mensching's work, on the masses, folk belief, and universal religion. Much of such incisiveness as Mensching's view of the "magical-primitive" character of folk belief has arises from

the circumstance that he can oppose that folk belief, derived from a folk-religious base, to the "high" or "elevated" religious conceptions that are associated with a universal religion. (Although the material on the masses, folk belief, and universal religion comes from an earlier work by Mensching than that from which the first selection in the present Part is drawn, it fits most conveniently at the later point at which it has been placed.) As an additional reason for including the topic of structural differentiation in its present place, doing so allows a certain convenience of transition to that final portion of Part Four that deals with religion and nonreligious activities. As Parsons notes in the paper "Christianity and Modern Industrial Society," religion "undergoes processes of differentiation in a double sense. The first of these concerns differentiation within religious systems themselves, the second the differentiation of the religious element from nonreligious elements in the more general system of action." In "folk" or "primitive" societies, generally and perhaps even definitionally speaking, there is considerable entanglement of religion and broadly nonreligious spheres of action, such as what we now think of as distinct spheres of economy or science. This plainly relates to differentiation in the second sense that Parsons refers to. And the "story" of differentiation is accordingly carried on in Section D of Part Four, with concentration, to be sure, on the relation of religion to some nonreligious spheres. (It is assumed that the latter are by common-sense criteria, in any case, sufficiently "nonreligious" on the face of them to require no special comment reinforcing their nonreligious character.)

This must suffice for suggesting the general "logic" of the structure of Part Four. After Sections A and B, Section C presents two pieces, one by Mensching and one by Parsons that have already been referred to. And the reason for inclusion of Mensching's piece under the Section on Culture and Differentiation has been indicated above. Parsons' many-faceted essay is included here for a number of reasons. Concern for differentiation is very evident in the essay. The challenge to some of Sorokin's relevant views of cultural development is also quite plain. Very significant, also, is the closely related challenge to some of the usual views of the "secularization" of the Western world, especially as that is expressed in Parsons' statement that, even though it is to risk "accusation of a Pharisaic complacency" to say so, nevertheless "in a whole variety of respects modern society is more in accord with Christian values than its forebears have been." Some interesting implications, too, might be drawn from the argument about denominational pluralism and political democracy that Parsons presents. Parsons claims that "careful study of voting behavior has shown that voting preferences are deeply anchored in the established involvement of the individual in the social structure." Voting preferences, then, the contention is, are not expressed by socially isolated sets or numbers of individuals or by individuals whose social contexts are irrelevant to their voting behavior. This raises questions about the very significant thesis of the inner degenerative tendency of "high" religion that has been set out in somewhat different ways by Sorokin and by Mensching. Thus we may ask whether the latter two do not rest their vulgarization or degeneration themes too much on the presumption of a constantly identical mass, whose constituent human units are for all relevant purposes just the same today, let us say, as they were in the time of the Buddha or of the Christ—with the same intellectual limitations and the same unconquerable promptings to accentuate the magical at

the cost of the spiritual, and the like, while social contexts for this persistent mass (as in the form of associations with "higher" groups) are either effectively nonexistent or actually ineffective. Perhaps, after all, some qualifications of the themes of Sorokin and Mensching may have to be made, even if it may initially seem that those themes are in all respects "obviously" right. It is so often necessary to say that matters need further investigation. The necessity is as plain in the matters here suggested as it is in a variety of others. Parsons' paper affords valuable pointers to the need for more evidence on a large number of questions vital for a genuinely and appropriately ambitious sociology of religion.

In Section D, a few selected aspects of relations of religious to nonreligious activities are stressed. Specifically, readings are presented that examine some relations of religion to economic activity, to science, and to politics. Section D may be said to be concerned with religion-as-culture on the one hand and with cultural although "nonreligious" phenomena on the other. But this is true in a broad and somewhat loose sense, and there are matters that come up in the readings chosen that may seem to take us some distance from strictly cultural phenomena. It would not be worthwhile, however, to analyze the readings in Section D in detail with a view to a meticulous discrimination of preoccupation with cultural matters from preoccupation with matters that might be said to be less strictly cultural. The several "fields" of economy, science and politics that Section D touches upon are conveniently presented under the heading of religion and nonreligious activities, and it is evident enough that some discussions are more nearly "cultural" than others. Thus, a portion of Needham's discussion of Buddhism and Chinese science is so set out (essentially in terms of value compatibilities and incompatibilities) that there need be no hesitation at all about labelling it "cultural." In other discussions, cultural reality is less directly to the fore.

In some of the matters touched upon in Section D, the literature on which one may draw is considerable, and much of that literature sets out controversies that cannot even be hinted at here. Stringent selection has once more been unavoidable. Max Weber's chapter on "Asceticism and the Spirit of Capitalism," from his famous *Protestant Ethic,* presents some of his essential views of the relations of Protestantism and capitalism. These views have been strongly defended and passionately criticized. Historians have understandably been much interested in them. The pertinent historical literature alone is sizable, and it must be given at least some attention by sociologists concerned with Weber's views. An historical selection has accordingly been included, namely a chapter by Scoville on the economic status of the Huguenots, drawn from his able recent monograph on the persecution of the Huguenots and the development of the French economy. Scoville has his own more or less distinctive and informative approach to some of the problems proposed by Weber's work, and he is eminently capable of speaking for himself. His essay may stand simply as one instance of an historian's response to the great stimulation that Weber's work has brought. It is worth remembering that Weber's own interest in the *Protestant Ethic* and capitalism was a very wide one, that he was concerned with the possible economic effects of other religions, and that he cast his concern in the form of comparisons, as in the case, for example, of Confucianism and Puritanism.[2] It is regrettable that compara-

tive material bearing on Weber's themes in this entire connection could not be included.[3]

To revert for the moment to history, one of the points in dispute about Weber's work relates to the question of what periods of time his views of the Protestantism-capitalism connection may be valid for, in so far as they are indeed valid. Thus, McNeill, a leading historian of Calvinism, who has a number of reservations about the connecting of Calvinism in particular with capitalism, nevertheless clearly seems to temper some of his reservations with the movement of time away from the figure of Calvin. Thus, he remarks that "by the early eighteenth century . . . the divine sanction of the acquisition as well as the charitable use of wealth had become a commonplace in most Christian minds, Calvinists included." McNeill even reminds us usefully, with respect to one pertinent point, that Weber himself had noted that for Calvin "the elect differ externally in no way from the damned."[4] Another well known historian has said that Calvin let loose a revolution which *he* neither wanted nor foresaw, although it is a revolution which "emerges from his dialectic."[5] It is important, then, to note the time references in the case study by Scoville. The latter's book, roughly, covers the years 1680–1720, and his central concern is with events and developments dating from about the time of Louis XIV's revocation of the Edict of Nantes in 1685. Scoville's is a case study in a series that appears to have

---

[2] See *The Religion of China,* Glencoe: The Free Press, 1951, Ch. 8.

[3] A well known pertinent recent work is Robert N. Bellah's *Tokugawa Religion,* Glencoe: The Free Press, 1957.

[4] See John T. McNeill, *The History and Character of Calvinism,* New York: Oxford University Press, 1954, pp. 421 and 222; Max Weber, *The Protestant Ethic,* New York: Scribner's, 1958, p. 110.

[5] Henri Hauser, *Les Débuts du Capitalisme,* Paris: Alcan, 1931, Ch. 2.

very little likelihood of ending soon. Students will probably never be fully satisfied with the evidence for and against Weber's views and may never even be fully agreed as to precisely what those views mean, but again it is eminently safe to suggest that the views have afforded and will continue to afford "great stimulation."

The readings from Weber and Scoville feature themes that are taken up in a framework of investigation of contemporary realities in the items by Greeley and by Bressler and Westoff. These items also reflect interest in the connections of Protestantism and science, a topic of both sociological and historical interest on which additional readings would have been most desirable. In the absence of such additional readings, it may at least be noted that Robert K. Merton has supplied one of the most distinguished and influential statements of the thesis that Protestant asceticism gave significant stimulation to the rise of modern science.[6] Here, too, as in the case of Protestantism and economy, time factors are of some importance. Thus, Merton has noted the possibility that a latter-day, more secularized religious orientation may give less support to value outlooks encouraging scientific endeavor than an earlier one. It should also be remarked that Merton's thesis about the influence of religion on science contains the view that it was *unintended* consequences of cer-

tain religious orientations that stimulated science, much as it has been contended that Calvin neither wanted nor foresaw the revolution that many believe Calvinism wrought in economic life.

Merton remarks that "the association between ascetic Protestantism and science has persisted to the present day," although it may not have the force it once had. But he adds, with regard to his whole notion of the association of Protestantism and science, that "as with any hypothesis, particularly in historical sociology, this one must be regarded as provisional, subject to review as more of the evidence comes in." [7] Both germane historical evidence and evidence pertaining to contemporary fact, indeed, go on accumulating. It has seemed appropriate, then, to allow room to two very recent studies bearing on Protestantism and Catholicism in relation to science (or scientific interests) and economic values—the studies by Greeley and by Bressler and Westoff. The studies do not, of course, raise all the questions we might like to ask, even about relevant contemporary circumstances, and they should also be taken with a certain tentativeness. Greeley wisely comments toward the end of his paper: "One survey does not a revolution make." [8] The so

---

[6] Robert K. Merton, "Puritanism, Pietism and Science," Ch. 18 in *Social Theory and Social Structure*, Glencoe: The Free Press, 1957. (See also the same author's *Science, Technology and Society in Seventeenth Century England*, Osiris 4, Bruges: Saint Catherine Press, Ltd., 1938, pp. 360–632.) Merton's views in this matter have been criticized. A very recent critic who directly disputes the reading of pertinent seventeenth-century evidence is Lewis S. Feuer, in *The Scientific Intellectual*, New York: Basic Books, 1963, Ch. 2.

[7] "Puritanism, Pietism and Science," op. cit., p. 605.

[8] Of course, this does not obviate the challenge to views of special affinities between Protestantism and science, or between Protestantism and high secular intellectual endeavor generally, that research of the type that Greeley has undertaken represents. It is of some interest that Greeley found, after the article here reprinted had been completed, that Jews are more likely to be in the "top twelve" graduate schools than are Protestants or Catholics, but that Protestants are no more likely than Catholics to attend such schools. (Personal communication to me from Greeley.) The absence of Protestant-Catholic differentiation in this sphere is again a pro-

common assertion, "more research is needed," is not only a piece of intellectual ritual; it also says concisely something that does have to be said time and again. As the kind of work presented by Greeley and by Bressler and Westoff goes on, it may well change the character of questions students ask about the relations of religion to economy and science (or other institutions). Given the nature of the research instruments that sociologists have been developing, the asking of questions gets shaped in distinctive ways. This involves the possibility that some questions historically and "classically" posed may not be answerable in their original form by modern techniques. (It may be remarked, incidentally, that this does not at all justify an immediate conclusion that the older questions are therefore "meaningless.") But it also presents the possibility that old questions may flower out and gain in penetration and subtlety.

Recent historical and sociological writing has given some stress to the view that there are elements in religion giving support to science. Whitehead thought that faith in the possibility of science as we know it was even a derivative of medieval theology. Such a view is obviously different from some older outlooks that religion (or at least "theology") stands in conflict with science. These outlooks were unquestionably often too simple and too arbitrarily selective. Yet there is perhaps a danger now of quite overlooking the measure of validity they have. We most certainly need not hold to the view that religion is everywhere and in every respect supportive, whether by intention or otherwise, of scientific endeavor—or of "modern" economic endeavor. There is another danger worth mentioning at this point. This is that with emphasis on religion as affecting science or economy (or other institutions), granting that influences in this line occur, it may be presumed that there is no reverse influence. But there can be no doubt that reverse influences do occur. Indeed, Merton, for one, noted that a science religiously nourished or stimulated could, once developed, react on the religious fostering agency—and even to the detriment of some of the intellectual bases of the latter. (The phenomenon of "feedback" is an eminently important one in social affairs.) Thus we return here, evidently, to the point that there *can* be conflict between religion and science, and the point even emerges from work initially designed to stress the positive effect of at least one important religious movement—ascetic Protestantism—on science.

It is at least very safe to say that the problems of the relations of religion and science are numerous and tangled, even within the confines of the relatively small questions about those relations that are suggested by the selections given. To give some additional sense of the complexities that can arise, a final selection on religion and science is taken from Joseph Needham's ambitious work on *Science and Civilization in China*—a selection on Buddhism and Chinese Science. Needham is clearly persuaded that "other-worldly rejection of this world seems to be formally and psychologically incompatible with science," and, equally clearly, he sees Buddhism as a world-rejecting religion. Yet Needham also says that there are ideas associated with Buddhism which might perhaps have given Chinese thinkers a disposition toward modern scientific notions. If problems of the kind thus suggested are far from "settled" for Western circumstances, they are undoubtedly more difficult still for Oriental circumstances. But Needham's

---

vocative finding. Yet it is perhaps still best to regard the studies by Greeley and by Bressler and Westoff as giving something of the "flavor" of one side of a significant controversy.

wrestling with the complexity of Buddhist influence on Chinese science may serve as an interesting example of an effort to disentangle elements in religious idea-systems that work in different directions as regards their effects on science.

The last two readings in Part Four can only provide some light on a severely limited number of problems of religion and politics. The essay by Max Weber is characteristically wide-ranging and affords useful historical and comparative perspectives. The short selection from Alford's *Party and Society* may serve as a brief statement of contemporary research interest in the connection between religious affiliation and political tendency. It may in a sense be said to pose a *problem* of differentiation, for it inevitably highlights the point that in various modern nations a peculiarly intimate connection between religious affiliation and political behavior exists, although this phenomenon appears within the framework of situations in which the sheer general differentiation of religion and politics is presumably widely understood.

A · ASPECTS OF RELIGION AS CULTURE

1 · *Asceticism, Mysticism, and Salvation Religion*

MAX WEBER

Concentration upon the actual pursuit of salvation may entail a formal withdrawal from the "world": from social and psychological ties with the family, from the possession of worldly goods, and from political, economic, artistic, and erotic activities—in short, from all creaturely interests. One with such an attitude may regard any participation in these affairs as an acceptance of the world, leading to alienation from god. This is "world-rejecting asceticism" (*weltablehnende Askese*).

On the other hand, the unique concentration of human behavior on activities leading to salvation may require the participation within the world (or more precisely: within the institutions of the world but in opposition to them) of the religious individual's idiosyncratically sacred religious mood and his qualifications as the elect instrument of god. This is "inner-worldly asceticism" (*innerweltliche Askese*). In this case the world is presented to the religious virtuoso as

SOURCE. Max Weber, "Asceticism, Mysticism, and Salvation Religion," from Max Weber, *The Sociology of Religion,* Boston: Beacon Press, 1963, pp. 166–183. Reprinted by permission of the Beacon Press, copyright 1963 by Beacon Press (English translation from the fourth edition of J. C. B. Mohr [Paul Siebeck] original edition in German).

his responsibility. He may have the obligation to transform the world in accordance with his ascetic ideals, in which case the ascetic will become a rational reformer or revolutionary on the basis of a theory of natural rights. Examples of this were seen in the "Parliament of the Saints" under Cromwell, in the Quaker State of Pennsylvania, and in other types of radically pietistic conventicle communism.

As a result of the different levels of religious qualification, such a congery of ascetics always tends to become an aristocratic, exclusive organization within or definitely outside the world of the average people who surround these ascetics. They operate on the principle of the social class system, in this regard. Such a religiously specialized group might be able to master the world, but it still could not raise the religious endowment of the average person to its own level of virtuosity. Any rational religious associations that ignored this obvious fact were bound sooner or later to experience in their own everyday existence the consequences of differences in religious endowment.

From the point of view of the basic values of asceticism, the world as a whole continues to constitute a *massa perditionis*. The only remaining alternative is a renunciation of the demand that the world conform to religious claims. Consequently, if a demonstration of religious fidelity is still to be made within the institutional structure of the world, then the world, for the very reason that it inevitably remains a natural vessel of sin, becomes a challenge for the demonstration of the ascetic temper and for the strongest possible attacks against the world's sins. The world abides in the lowly state appropriate to its status as a created thing. Therefore, any sensuous surrender to the world's goods may imperil concentration upon and possession of the ultimate good of salvation, and may be a symptom of unholiness of spirit and impossibility of rebirth. Nevertheless, the world as a creation of god, whose power comes to expression in it despite its creatureliness, provides the only medium through which one's unique religious charisma may prove itself by means of rational ethical conduct, so that one may become and remain certain of one's own state of grace.

Hence, as the field provided for this active certification, the order of the world in which the ascetic is situated becomes for him a vocation which he must fulfill rationally. As a consequence, and although the enjoyment of wealth is forbidden to the ascetic, it becomes his vocation to engage in economic activity which is faithful to rationalized ethical requirements and which conforms to strict legality. If success supervenes upon such acquisitive activity, it is regarded as the manifestation of god's blessing upon the labor of the pious man and of god's pleasure with his economic pattern of life.

Certain other manifestations of inner-worldly asceticism must be noted. Any excess of emotional feeling for one's fellow man is prohibited as being a deification of the creaturely, which denies the unique value of the divine gift of grace. Yet it is man's vocation to participate

rationally and soberly in the various rational, purposive institutions of the world and in their objective goals as set by god's creation. Similarly, any eroticism that tends to deify the human creature is proscribed. On the other hand, it is a divinely imposed vocation of man "to soberly produce children" (as the Puritans expressed it) within marriage. Then, too, there is a prohibition against the exercise of force by an individual against other human beings for reasons of passion or revenge, and above all for purely personal motives. However, it is divinely enjoined that the rationally ordered state shall suppress and punish sins and rebelliousness. Finally, all personal secular enjoyment of power is forbidden as a deification of the creaturely, though it is held that a rational legal order within society is pleasing to god.

The person who lives as a worldly ascetic is a rationalist, not only in the sense that he rationally systematizes his own personal patterning of life, but also in his rejection of everything that is ethically irrational, esthetic, or dependent upon his own emotional reactions to the world and its institutions. The distinctive goal always remains the alert, methodical control of one's own pattern of life and behavior. This type of inner-worldly asceticism included, above all, ascetic Protestantism, which taught the principle of loyal fulfillment of obligations within the framework of the world as the sole method of proving religious merit, though its several branches demonstrated this tenet with varying degrees of consistency.

But the distinctive content of salvation may not be an active quality of conduct, that is, an awareness of having executed the divine will; it may instead be a subjective condition of a distinctive kind, the most notable form of which is mystic illumination. This too is confined to a minority who have particular religious qualifications, and among them only as the end product of the systematic execution of a distinctive type of activity, namely contemplation. For the activity of contemplation to succeed in achieving its goal of mystic illumination, the extrusion of all everyday mundane interests is always required. According to the experience of the Quakers, God can speak within one's soul only when the creaturely element in man is altogether silent. In agreement with this notion, if not with these very words, is all contemplative mysticism from Lao Tzu and the Buddha up to Tauler.

These subjective and mystical beliefs may result in absolute flight from the world. Such a contemplative flight from the world, characteristic of ancient Buddhism and to some degree characteristic of all Asiatic and Near Eastern forms of salvation, seems to resemble the ascetic world view—but it is necessary to make a very clear distinction between the two. In the sense employed here, "world-rejecting asceticism" is primarily oriented to activity within the world. Only activity within the world helps the ascetic to attain that for which he strives, a capacity for action by god's grace. The ascetic derives renewed assurances of his state of grace from his awareness that his possession of the central religious salvation gives him the power to act and his awareness that through his actions he serves god. He feels himself to be a warrior in behalf of god, regardless of who the enemy is and what the means of doing battle are. Furthermore, his opposition to the world is psychologically felt, not as a flight, but as a repeated victory over ever new temptations which he is bound to combat actively, time and again. The ascetic who rejects the world sustains at least the negative inner psychological relationship with it which is presupposed in the struggle against it. It is therefore more appropriate in his case to speak of a "rejection of the world" than of a "flight from the world." Flight

is much more characteristic of the contemplative mystic.

In contrast to asceticism, contemplation is primarily the quest to achieve rest in god and in him alone. It entails inactivity, and in its most consistent form it entails the cessation of thought, the nemesis of everything that in any way reminds one of the world, and of course the absolute minimization of all outer and inner activity. By these paths the mystic achieves that subjective condition which may be enjoyed as the possession of, or mystical union with, the divine. This is a distinctive organization of the emotions which seems to promise a certain type of knowledge. To be sure, the subjective emphasis may be more upon the distinctive and extraordinary content of this knowledge or more upon the emotional coloration of the possession of this knowledge; objectively, the latter is decisive.

The unique character of mystical knowledge consists in the fact that, although it becomes more incommunicable the more strongly it is characterized by idiosyncratic content, it is nevertheless recognized as knowledge. For mystical knowledge is not new knowledge of any facts or doctrines, but rather the perception of an overall meaning in the world. This usage of "knowledge" is intended wherever the term occurs in the numerous formulations of mystics; it denotes a practical form of knowledge. Such *gnosis* is basically a "possession" of something from which there may be derived a new practical orientation to the world, and under certain circumstances even new and communicable items of knowledge. But even these items will constitute knowledge of values and non-values within the world. We are not interested here in the details of this general problem, but only in the negative effect upon behavior which is distinctive of all contemplation, an effect so opposed to the effect upon behavior of asceticism, in our sense of the latter term.

The contrast in effects upon behavior is self-explanatory, and pending a more thorough exposition, we may strongly emphasize here that the distinction between world-rejecting asceticism and world-fleeing contemplation is fluid. For world-fleeing contemplation must originally be associated with a considerable degree of systematically rationalized patterning of life. Only this, indeed, leads to concentration upon the boon of salvation. Yet, rationalization is only an instrument for attaining the goal of contemplation and is of an essentially negative type, consisting in the avoidance of interruptions caused by nature and the social milieu. Contemplation does not necessarily become a passive abandonment to dreams or a simple self-hypnosis, though it may approach these states in practice. On the contrary, the distinctive road to contemplation is a very energetic concentration upon certain truths. The decisive aspect of this process is not the content of these truths, which frequently seems very simple to non-mystics, but rather the type of emphasis placed upon the truths. The mystical truths come to assume a central position within, and to exert an integrating influence upon, the total view of the world. In Buddhism, no one becomes one of the illuminated by explicitly affirming the obviously highly trivial formulations of the central Buddhist dogma, or even by achieving a penetrating understanding of the central dogma. The only way to become illuminated is the aforementioned concentration of thought, together with the various other procedures for winning salvation. The illumination consists essentially in a unique quality of feeling or, more concretely, in the felt emotional unity of knowledge and volitional mood which provides the mystic with decisive assurance of his religious state of grace.

For the ascetic too, the perception of the divine through emotion and intellect is of central importance, only in his case it is of a "motor" type, so to speak. The ascetic's assurance of grace is achieved when he is conscious that he has succeeded in becoming a tool of his god, through rationalized ethical action completely oriented to god. But for the contemplative mystic, who neither desires to be nor can be the god's "instrument," but desires only to become the god's "vessel," the ascetic's ethical struggle, whether of a positive or a negative type, appears to be a perpetual externalization of the divine in the direction of some peripheral function. For this reason, ancient Buddhism recommended inaction as the precondition for the maintenance of the state of grace, and in any case Buddhism enjoined the avoidance of every type of rational, purposive activity, which it regarded as the most dangerous form of secularization. On the other hand, the contemplation of the mystic appears to the ascetic as indolent, religiously sterile, and ascetically reprehensible self-indulgence—a wallowing in self-created emotions prompted by the deification of the creaturely.

From the standpoint of a contemplative mystic, the ascetic appears, by virtue of his transcendental self-maceration and struggles, and especially by virtue of his ascetically rationalized conduct within the world, to be forever involved in all the burdens of created things, confronting insoluble tensions between violence and generosity, between empirical reality and love. The ascetic is therefore regarded as permanently alienated from unity with god, and as forced into contradictions and compromises that are alien to salvation. But from the converse standpoint of the ascetic, the contemplative mystic appears not to be thinking of god, the enhancement of his kingdom and glory, or the fulfillment of his will, but rather to be thinking exclusively about himself. Therefore the mystic lives in everlasting inconsistency, since by reason of the very fact that he is alive he must inevitably provide for the maintenance of his own life. This is particularly true when the contemplative mystic lives within the world and its institutions. There is a sense in which the mystic who flees the world is more dependent upon the world than is the ascetic. The ascetic can maintain himself as an anchorite, winning the certainty of his state of grace through the labors he expends in the effort to maintain himself as an anchorite. Not so the contemplative mystic. If he is to live consistently according to his theory, he must maintain his life only by means of what nature or men voluntarily donate to him. This requires that he live on berries in the woods, which are not always available, or on alms. This was actually the case among the most consistent Hindu *shramanas*, and it accounts for the very strict prohibition in all Hindu *bhikshu* regulations (and found also among the Buddhists) against receiving anything that has not been given freely.

In any case, the contemplative mystic lives on whatever gifts the world may present to him, and he would be unable to stay alive if the world were not constantly engaged in that very labor which the mystic brands as sinful and leading to alienation from god. For the Buddhist monk, agriculture is the most reprehensible of all occupations, because it causes violent injury to various forms of life in the soil. Yet the alms he collects consist principally of agricultural products. In circumstances like these, the mystic's inevitable feeling that he is an aristocrat with respect to salvation reaches striking expression, culminating in the mystic's abandonment of the world, the unilluminated, and those incapable of complete illumination, to their inevitable and ineluctable fate. It will be re-

called that the central and almost sole lay virtue among the Buddhists was originally the veneration of the monks, who alone belonged to the religious community, and whom it was incumbent upon the laity to support with alms. However, it is a general rule that every human being acts in some fashion, and even the mystic perforce acts. Yet he minimizes activity just because it can never give him certainty of his state of grace, and what is more, because it may divert him from union with the divine. The ascetic, on the other hand, finds the certification of his state of grace precisely in his behavior in the world.

The contrast between the ascetic and mystical modes of behavior is clearest when the full implications of world-rejection and world-flight are not drawn. The ascetic, when he wishes to act within the world, that is, to practice inner-worldly asceticism, must become afflicted with a sort of happy stupidity regarding any question about the meaning of the world, for he must not worry about such questions. Hence, it is no accident that inner-worldly asceticism reached its most consistent development on the foundation of the Calvinist god's absolute inexplicability, utter remoteness from every human criterion, and unsearchableness as to his motives. Thus, the inner-worldly ascetic is the recognized "man of a vocation," who neither inquires about nor finds it necessary to inquire about the meaning of his actual practice of a vocation within the world, the total framework of which is not his responsibility but his god's. For him it suffices that through his rational actions in this world he is personally executing the will of god, which is unsearchable in its ultimate significance.

On the other hand, the contemplative mystic is not in a position to realize his primary aim of perceiving the essential meaning of the world and then comprehending it in a rational form, for the very reason that he has already conceived of the essential meaning of the world as a unity beyond all empirical reality. Mystical contemplation has not always resulted in a flight from the world in the sense of an avoidance of every contact with the social milieu. On the contrary, the mystic may also require of himself the maintenance of his state of grace against every pressure of the mundane order, as an index of the enduring character of that very state of grace. In that case, even the mystic's position within the institutional framework of the world becomes a vocation, but one leading in an altogether different direction from any vocation produced by inner-worldly asceticism.

Neither asceticism nor contemplation affirms the world as such. The ascetic rejects the world's empirical character of creatureliness and ethical irrationality, and rejects its ethical temptations to sensual indulgence, to epicurean satisfaction, and to reliance upon natural joys and gifts. But at the same time he affirms individual rational activity within the institutional framework of the world, affirming it to be his responsibility as well as his means for securing certification of his state of grace. On the other hand, the contemplative mystic living within the world regards action, particularly action performed within the world's institutional framework, as in its very nature a temptation against which he must maintain his state of grace.

The contemplative mystic minimizes his activity by resigning himself to the order of the world as it is, and lives incognito, so to speak, as humble people have always done, since god has ordained once and for all that man must live in the world. The activity of the contemplative mystic within the world is characterized by a distinctive brokenness, colored by humility. He is constantly striving to escape from activity in the world back to the quietness and inwardness of his god.

Conversely, the ascetic, whenever he acts in conformity with his type, is certain to become god's instrument. For this reason the ascetic's humility, which he considers a necessary obligation incumbent upon a creature of god, is always of dubious genuineness. Therefore the success of the ascetic's action is a success of the god himself, who has contributed to the action's success, or at the very least the success is a special sign of divine blessing upon the ascetic and his activity. But for the genuine mystic, no success which may crown his activity within the world can have any significance with respect to salvation. For him, his maintenance of true humility within the world is his sole warranty for the conclusion that his soul has not fallen prey to the snares of the world. As a rule, the more the genuine mystic remains within the world, the more broken his attitude toward it becomes, in contrast to the proud aristocratic feeling with respect to salvation entertained by the contemplative mystic who lives apart from the world.

For the ascetic, the certainty of salvation always demonstrates itself in rational action, integrated as to meaning, end, and means, and governed by principles and rules. Conversely, for the mystic who actually possesses a subjectively appropriated state of salvation the result of this subjective condition may be antinomianism. His salvation manifests itself not in any sort of activity but in a subjective condition and its idiosyncratic quality. He feels himself no longer bound by any rule of conduct; regardless of his behavior, he is certain of salvation. Paul had to struggle with this consequence, among others, of mystical contemplation (*panta moi eksestin*); and in numerous other contexts the abandonment of rules for conduct has been an occasional result of the mystical quest for salvation.

For the ascetic, moreover, the divine imperative may require of human creatures an unconditional subjection of the world to the norms of religious virtue, and indeed a revolutionary transformation of the world for this purpose. In that event, the ascetic will emerge from his remote and cloistered cell to take his place in the world as a prophet in opposition to the world. But he will always demand of the world an ethically rational order and discipline, corresponding to his own methodical self-discipline. Now a mystic may arrive at a similar position in relation to the world. His sense of divine inwardness, the chronic and quiet euphoria of his solitary contemplative possession of substantively divine salvation, may become transformed into an acute feeling of sacred possession by or possession of the god who is speaking in and through him. He will then wish to bring eternal salvation to men as soon as they have prepared, as the mystic himself has done, a place for god upon earth, i.e., in their souls. But in this case the result will be the emergence of the mystic as a magician who causes his power to be felt among gods and demons; and this may have the practical consequence of the mystic's becoming a mystagogue, something which has actually happened very often.

If the mystic does not follow this path towards becoming a mystagogue, for a variety of reasons which we hope to discuss later, he may bear witness to his god by doctrine alone. In that case his revolutionary preaching to the world will be chiliastically irrational, scorning every thought of a rational order in the world. He will regard the absoluteness of his own universal acosmistic feeling of love as completely adequate for himself, and indeed regard this feeling as the only one acceptable to his god as the foundation for a mystically renewed community among men, because this feeling alone derives from a divine source. The transformation of a mysticism remote from the world into one characterized by

chiliastic and revolutionary tendencies took place frequently, most impressively in the revolutionary mysticism of the sixteenth-century Baptists. The contrary transformation has also occurred, as in the conversion of John Lilburne to Quakerism.

To the extent that an inner-worldly religion of salvation is determined by contemplative features, the usual result is the acceptance of the secular social structure which happens to be at hand, an acceptance that is relatively indifferent to the world but at least humble before it. A mystic of the type of Tauler completes his day's work and then seeks contemplative union with his god in the evening, going forth to his usual work the next morning, as Tauler movingly suggests, in the correct inner state. Similarly, Lao Tzu taught that one recognizes the man who has achieved union with the Tao by his humility and by his self-depreciation before other men. The mystic component in Lutheranism, for which the highest bliss available in this world is the ultimate *unio mystica,* was responsible along with other factors for the indifference of the Lutheran church toward the external organization of the preaching of the gospel, and also for that church's anti-ascetic and traditionalistic character.

In any case, the typical mystic is never a man of conspicuous social activity, nor is he at all prone to accomplish any rational transformation of the mundane order on the basis of a methodical pattern of life directed toward external success. Wherever genuine mysticism did give rise to communal action, such action was characterized by the acosmism of the mystical feeling of love. Mysticism may exert this kind of psychological effect, thus tending—despite the apparent demands of logic—to favor the creation of communities (*gemeinschaftsbildend*).

The core of the mystical concept of the oriental Christian church was a firm conviction that Christian brotherly love, when sufficiently strong and pure, must necessarily lead to unity in all things, even in dogmatic beliefs. In other words, men who sufficiently love one another, in the Johannine sense of love, will also think alike and, because of the very irrationality of their common feeling, act in a solidary fashion which is pleasing to God. Because of this concept, the Eastern church could dispense with an infallibly rational authority in matters of doctrine. The same view is basic to the Slavophile conception of the community, both within and beyond the church. Some forms of this notion were also common in ancient Christianity. The same conception is at the basis of Muhammad's belief that formal doctrinal authorities can be dispensed with. Finally, this conception along with other factors accounts for the minimization of organization in the monastic communities of early Buddhism.

Conversely, to the extent that an innerworldly religion of salvation is determined by distinctively ascetical tendencies, the usual result is practical rationalism, in the sense of the maximization of rational action as such, the maximization of a methodical systematization of the external conduct of life, and the maximization of the rational organization and institutionalization of mundane social systems, whether monastic communities or theocracies.

The decisive historical difference between the predominantly oriental and Asiatic types of salvation religion and those found primarily in the Occident is that the former usually culminate in contemplation and the latter in asceticism. The great importance of this distinction, even for our purely empirical consideration of religions, is in no way diminished by the fact that the distinction is a fluid one, recurrent combinations of mystical and ascetic characteristics demonstrating that these heterogeneous elements may combine, as in the monastic religiosity of the Occident.

In India, even so ascetical a planned procedure for achieving salvation as that of the Jain monks culminated in a purely contemplative and mystical ultimate goal; and in Eastern Asia, Buddhism became the characteristic religion of salvation. In the Occident, on the other hand, apart from a few representatives of a distinctive quietism found only in modern times, even religions of an explicitly mystical type regularly became transformed into an active pursuit of virtue, which was naturally ascetical in the main. Stated more precisely, there occurred along the way an inner selection of motivations which placed the primary preference upon some type of active conduct, generally a type pointing toward asceticism, and which implemented this motivational preference. Neither the mystical contemplativeness of St. Bernard and his followers, nor Franciscan spirituality, nor the contemplative trends among the Baptists and the Jesuits, nor even the emotional suffusions of Zinzendorf were able to prevent either the community or the individual mystic from attributing superior importance to conduct and to the demonstration of grace through conduct, though this was conceptualized very differently in each case. The stress upon conduct might be purely ascetic or it might be intersected by certain contemplative emphases. It will be recalled that Meister Eckhart finally placed Martha above Mary, notwithstanding the pronouncements of Jesus.

But to some extent this emphasis upon conduct was characteristic of Christianity from the very outset. Even in the earliest period, when all sorts of irrational charismatic gifts of the spirit were regarded as the decisive hallmark of sanctity, Christian apologetics had already given a distinctive answer to the question of how one might distinguish the divine origin of the pneumatic achievements of Christ and the Christians from comparable phenomena that were of Satanic or demonic origin: this answer was that the manifest effect of Christianity upon the morality of its adherents certified its divine origin. No Hindu could make this kind of statement.

There are a number of reasons for this basic distinction between mysticism and asceticism, but at this point it is only necessary to stress the following aspects of the distinction.

First to be considered is the fact that the concept of a transcendental, absolutely omnipotent god, implying the utterly subordinate and creaturely character of the world created by him out of nothing, arose in Asia Minor and was imposed upon the Occident. One result of this for the Occident was that any planned procedure for achieving salvation faced a road that was permanently closed to any self-deification and to any genuinely mystical subjective possession of god, at least in the unique mystical sense of "possession of god," because this appeared to be a blasphemous deification of a mere created thing. The path to the ultimate pantheistic consequences of the mystical position was blocked, this path being always regarded as having the character of an ethical justification before god, which ultimately could be accomplished and maintained only by some sort of active conduct within the world. This certification of the really divine quality of the mystical possession of salvation (certification before the ultimate judgment of the mystic himself) could be arrived at through the path of activity alone. Activity in turn introduced into mysticism paradoxes, tensions, and the loss of the mystic's ultimate distance from god. All this was spared to Hindu mysticism. For the Asiatic the world is something simply presented to man, something which has been in the nature of things from all eternity; while for the occidental, even for the occidental mystic, the world is a work which has been created or performed, and not even the ordinances of the world are eternal. Consequently, in the Occident mystical salvation could not be found simply in the consciousness of an absolute union with a supreme and wise order of things as the only true being. Nor, on the other hand, could a work of divine origin even be regarded in the Occident as a possible object of absolute rejection, as it was in the flight from the world characteristic of the Orient.

However, this decisive contrast between oriental and occidental religions is closely related to the character of Asiatic salvation religions as pure religions of intellectuals who never abandoned the concept of the empirical world. For the Hindu, there was actually a way leading directly from insight into the ultimate consequences of the *karma* chain of causality, to illumination, and thence to a unity of knowledge and action. This way remained forever closed to every religion that faced the absolute paradox of a perfect god's creation of a permanently imperfect world. Indeed, in this latter type of religion, the intellectual mastery of the world leads away from god, not toward him. From the practical point of view, those instances of occidental mysticism which have a purely philosophical foundation stand closest to the Asiatic type.

Further to be considered in accounting for the basic distinction between occidental and oriental religion are various practical factors. Particular emphasis must be placed on the fact that occidental Rome alone developed and maintained a rational law, for various reasons yet to be explained. In the Occident the relationship of man to god became, in a distinctive fashion, a sort of legally definable relationship of subjection. Indeed, the question of salvation can be settled by a sort of legal process, a method which was later distinctively developed by Anselm of Canterbury. Such a legalistic planned procedure of achieving salvation could never be adopted by the oriental religions which posited an impersonal divine power or which posited, instead of a god standing above the world, a god standing within a world which is self-regulated by the causal chains of *Karma*. Nor could the legalistic direction be taken by religions teaching concepts of Tao, belief in the celestial ancestor gods of the Chinese emperor, or, above all, belief in the Asiatic popular gods. In all these cases the highest form of piety took a pantheistic form, and one which turned practical motivations toward contemplation.

Another aspect of the rational character of a methodical procedure for achieving salvation was in origin partly Roman, partly Jewish. The Greeks, despite all the misgivings of the urban patriciate in regard to the Dionysiac cult of intoxication, set a positive value upon ecstasy, both the acute orgiastic type of divine intoxication and the milder form of euphoria induced primarily by rhythm and music, as engendering an awareness of the uniquely divine. Indeed, among the Greeks the ruling classes especially lived with this mild form of ecstasy from their very childhood. Since the time when the discipline of the hoplites had become dominant, Greece had lacked a social class possessing the prestige of the official nobility in Rome. Social relationships in Greece were in all respects simpler and less feudal. In Rome the nobles, who constituted a rational nobility of office of increasing range, and who possessed whole cities and provinces as client holdings of single families, completely rejected ecstasy, like the dance, as utterly unseemly and unworthy of a nobleman's sense of honor. This is obvious even in the terminology employed by the Romans to render the Greek word for ecstasy (*ekstasis*) into Latin: *superstitio*. Cultic dances were performed only among the most ancient colleges of priests, and in

the specific sense of a round of dances, only among the *fratres arvales*, and then only behind closed doors, after the departure of the congregation. Most Romans regarded dancing and music as unseemly, and so Rome remained absolutely uncreative in these arts. The Romans experienced the same distaste towards exercises in the *gymnasium*, which the Spartans had created as an arena for planned exercise. The Senate proscribed the Dionysiac cult of intoxication. The rejection by Rome's world-conquering military-official nobility of every type of ecstasy and of all preoccupation with individually planned procedures for attaining salvation (which corresponds closely to the equally strong antipathy of the Confucian bureaucracy towards all methodologies of salvation) was therefore one of the sources of a strictly empirical rationalism with a thoroughly practical political orientation.

As Christian communities developed in the Occident, they found this contempt for ecstatic procedures to be characteristic of all the various religions that flourished on essentially Roman territory. The Christian community of Rome in particular adopted this attitude against ecstasy quite consciously and consistently. In no instance did this community accept on its own initiative any irrational element, from charismatic prophecy to the greatest innovations in church music, into the religion or the culture. Early Christianity was infinitely poorer than the Hellenistic Orient and the community of Corinth, not only in theological thinkers but also, as the sources seem to suggest, in every sort of manifestation of the spirit (*pneuma*). Whether despite this lack of theology and *pneuma* or because of it, the soberly practical rationalism of Christianity, the most important legacy of Rome to the Christian church, almost everywhere set the tone of a dogmatic and ethical systematization of the faith, as is well known. The subsequent development of the planned procedures of salvation in the Occident continued along similar lines. The ascetic requirements of the old Benedictine regulations and the reforms at Cluny are, when measured by Hindu or oriental standards, extremely modest and obviously adapted to novices recruited from the higher social classes. Yet, it is precisely in the Occident that *labor* emerges as the distinctive mark of Christian monasticism, and as an instrument of both hygiene and asceticism. This emphasis came to the strongest expression in the starkly simple, methodical regulations of the Cistercians. Even the mendicant monks, in contrast to their monastic counterparts in India, were forced into the service of the hierarchy and compelled to serve rational purposes, shortly after their appearance in the Occident. These rational purposes included preaching, the supervision of heretics, and systematic charity, which in the Occident was developed into an actual enterprise (*Betrieb*). Finally, the Jesuit order expelled all the unhygienic elements of the older asceticism, becoming the most completely rational discipline for the purposes of the church. This development is obviously connected with the next point we are to consider.

The occidental church is a uniformly rational organization with a monarchical head and a centralized control of piety. That is, it is headed not only by a personal transcendental god, but also by a terrestrial ruler of enormous power, who actively controls the lives of his subjects. Such a figure is lacking in the religions of Eastern Asia, partly for historical reasons, partly because of the nature of the religions in question. Even Lamaism, which has a strong organization, does not have the rigidity of a bureaucracy. The Asiatic hierarchs in Taoism and the other hereditary patriarchs of Chinese and Hindu sects were always partly mystagogues, partly the objects of anthropolatric veneration, and partly—as in the cases of the Dalai Lama and Taschi Lama—the chiefs of a completely monastic religion of magical character. Only in the Occident, where the monks became the disciplined army of a rational bureaucracy of office, did asceticism directed toward the outer world become increasingly systematized into a methodology of active, rational conduct of life.

Moreover, only in the Occident was the additional step taken—by ascetic Protestantism—of translating rational asceticism into the life of the world. The inner-worldly order of dervishes in Islam cultivated a planned procedure for achieving salvation, but this procedure, for all its variations, was oriented ultimately to the mystical quest for salvation of the Sufis. This search of the dervishes for salvation, deriving from Hindu and Persian sources, might have orgiastic, spiritualistic, or contemplative characteristics in different instances, but in no case did it constitute "asceticism" in the special sense of that term which we have employed. Hindus have played a leading role in dervish orgies as far afield as Bosnia. The asceticism of the dervishes is not, like that of ascetic Protestants, a religious ethic of vocation, for the religious actions of the dervishes have very little relationship to their secular occupations, and in their scheme secular vocations have at best a purely external relationship to the planned procedure of salvation. Even so, the procedure of salvation might exert direct effects on one's occupational behavior. The simple, pious dervish is, other things being equal, more reliable than a non-religious man, in the same way that the pious Parsee is prosperous as a businessman because of his strict adherence to the rigid injunction to be honest.

But an unbroken unity integrating in systematic fashion an ethic of vocation in the world with assurance of religious salvation was the unique creation of ascetic Protestantism alone. Furthermore, only in the Protestant ethic of vocation does the world, despite all its creaturely imperfections, possess unique and religious significance as the object through which one fulfills his duties by rational behavior according to the will of an absolutely transcendental god. When success crowns rational, sober, purposive behavior of the sort not oriented exclusively to worldly acquisition, such success is construed as a sign that god's blessing rests upon such behavior. This inner-worldly asceticism had a number of distinctive consequences not found in any other religion. This religion demanded of the believer, not celibacy, as in the case of the monk, but the avoidance of all erotic pleasure; not poverty, but the elimination of all idle and exploitative enjoyment of unearned wealth and income, and the avoidance of all feudalistic, sensuous ostentation of wealth; not the ascetic death-in-life of the cloister, but an alert, rationally controlled patterning of life, and the avoidance of all surrender to the beauty of the world, to art, or to one's own moods and emotions. The clear and uniform goal of this asceticism was the disciplining and methodical organization of the whole pattern of life. Its typical representative was the "man of a vocation," and its unique result was the rational organization and institutionalization of social relationships.

Another major theory regarding the attainment of salvation rejects the individual's own labors as completely inadequate for the purpose of salvation. From this point of view, salvation is accessible only as a consequence of the achievement of some greatly endowed hero, or even the achievement of a god who has become incarnate for this very purpose and whose grace will redound to the credit of his devotees, *ex opere operato*. Grace might also become available as a direct effect of magical activities, or it might be distributed to men out of the excess of grace which had accumulated as a result of the human or divine savior's achievements.

·

2 · *Christ Against Culture*

H. RICHARD NIEBUHR

The first answer to the question of Christ and culture we shall consider is the one that uncompromisingly affirms the sole authority of Christ over the Christian and resolutely rejects culture's claims to loyalty. It seems to be both logically and chronologically entitled to the first position: logically, because it appears to follow directly from the common Christian principle of the Lordship of Jesus Christ;

SOURCE. H. Richard Niebuhr, "Christ Against Culture," from H. Richard Niebuhr, *Christ and Culture*, New York: Harper and Brothers, 1951, pp. 45–76. Used with permission of Harper and Row, Publishers, Incorporated. From cloth bound editions.

chronologically, because it is widely held to be the typical attitude of the first Christians. Both claims are subject to question, yet it must be conceded that the answer was given at a very early time in the history of the church, and that on the surface it seems to be logically more consistent than the other positions.

While various New Testament writings evince something of this attitude, none presents it without qualification. The first gospel contrasts the new law with the old, yet contains very explicit statements about the Christians' obligations to be obedient not only to the code of Moses but also to the requirements of the leaders of Jewish society.[1] The book of Revelation is radical in its rejection of "the world," but here the problem is complicated by the persecution situation in which Christians find themselves. Among the other writings, the First Letter of John contains the least ambiguous presentation of this point of view.

This little classic of devotion and theology has been treasured by Christians for its profound understanding and beautiful statement of the doctrine of love. It achieves the simple summary of Christian theology: "God is love," and the equally concise formulation of Christian ethics: "Love one another." It presents in their inseparable relation and in fugue-like manner the three themes of love: God's love for man, and man's for God, and brother's for brother. "In this is love, not that we loved God but that he loved us. . . . We love because he first loved us. . . . Beloved, if God so loved us, we ought also to love one another. . . . If any one says, 'I love God,' and hates his brother, he is a liar. . . . No man has ever seen God; if we love one another God abides in us and his love is perfected in us. . . . He who does not love his brother whom he has seen, cannot love God, whom he has not seen." [2] The central interest of the writer, however, is quite as much the Lordship of Christ as the idea of love. Indeed, Christ is the key to the whole kingdom of love, for "in this the love of God was made manifest among us, that God sent his only Son into the world, so that we might live through him"; and "by this we know love, that he laid down his life for us; and we ought to lay down our lives for the brethren." [3] The Christ who makes human love for God and neighbor possible by his demonstration of the greatness of God's love for man, the Christ who loves men to the point of laying down his life for them and who is their advocate in heaven, is also the one who requires what he has made possible. The writer of I John insists on obedience to the commandment of Jesus Christ no less than on confidence in the love of God.[4] The gospel and the new law are here thoroughly united.[5] Hence God requires two things: "This is his commandment, that we should believe in the name of his Son Jesus Christ and love one another, just as he has commanded us." [6] The dual commandment of love of God and neighbor, which the writer well knows,[7] has here undergone a certain transformation as a result of the recognition that the first movement of love is not from man to God but from God to man, and that the first requirement of the Christian life is therefore a faith in God that is inseparable from the believing acceptance of Jesus Christ as his Son. It is exceedingly important for the First Letter of John that Christians be loyal to no merely spiritual Christ but to a visible and tangible Jesus Christ of history, who is, however, not only the Jesus of history but the Son of God, inseparably united with the unseen Father in love and righteousness, in the power to achieve and the authority to command.[8] With these two themes of love and faith in Jesus Christ, other ideas, such as those of the forgiveness of sin, the gift of the Spirit and of eternal life, are closely connected; nevertheless these two define the Christian life; no one can be a member of the Christian fellowship who does not acknowledge Jesus as the Christ and the

[1] Mt. 5:21–48, 5:17–20; 23:1–3.
[2] I John 4, vv. 10–12 combined with vv. 19–20.
[3] Ibid., 4:9; 3:16.
[4] Ibid., 2:3–11; 3:4–10, 21–24; 4:21; 5:2–3.
[5] Dodd, C. H., The Johannine Epistles, 1946, p. xxxi.
[6] I John, 3:23.
[7] Ibid., 4:21.
[8] Cf. ibid., 1:1–3; 2:1–2; 2:22–24; 3:8b; 4:2–3, 9–10, 14–15; 5:1–5; cf. also Dodd, op. cit., pp. xxx–xxxvi; 1–6; 55–58.

Son of God and who does not love the brothers in obedience to the Lord.

This succinct statement of the positive meaning of Christianity is, however, accompanied by an equally emphatic negation. The counterpart of loyalty to Christ and the brothers is the rejection of cultural society; a clear line of separation is drawn between the brotherhood of the children of God and the world. Save in two instances[9] the word "world" evidently means for the writer of this letter the whole society outside the church, in which, however, the believers live.[10] The injunction to Christians is, "Do not love the world or the things in the world. If any one loves the world, love for the Father is not in him."[11] That world appears as a realm under the power of evil; it is the region of darkness, into which the citizens of the kingdom of light must not enter; it is characterized by the prevalence in it of lies, hatred, and murder; it is the heir of Cain.[12] It is a secular society, dominated by the "lust of the flesh, the lust of the eyes and the pride of life," or, in Prof. Dodd's translation of these phrases, it is "pagan society, with its sensuality, superficiality and pretentiousness, its materialism and its egoism."[13] It is a culture that is concerned with temporal and passing values, whereas Christ has words of eternal life; it is a dying as well as a murderous order, for "the world passes away and the lust of it."[14] It is dying, however, not only because it is concerned with temporal goods and contains the inner contradictions of hatred and lie, but also because Christ has come to destroy the works of the devil and because faith in him is the victory which overcomes the world.[15]

Hence the loyalty of the believer is directed entirely toward the new order, the new society and its Lord.

The "Christ-against-culture" position is not set forth here in its most radical form. Though love of neighbor has been interpreted to mean love of the brother— that is, the fellow believer—it is also taken for granted that Jesus Christ has come to expiate the sins of the world, which probably means in I John the expiation of the sins of all men, regarded more or less individually. Though there is no statement here that the Christian is obliged to participate in the work of the social institutions, to maintain or convert them, neither is there any express rejection of the state or of property as such. Doubtless the end of "the world" seemed so near to the writer that he found no occasion for counsel on these points; all that was required under the circumstances was loyalty to Jesus Christ and to the brotherhood, without concern for the transitory culture.

Similar, though less profound, expressions of the same attitude are to be found in other Christian writings of the second century, while Tertullian stated it in radical fashion. The best-loved books of the time, such as *The Teaching of the Twelve, The Shepherd of Hermas, The Epistle of Barnabas,* and the *First Epistle of Clement,* present Christianity as a way of life quite separate from culture. Some of them are more legalistic than I John, setting forth the meaning of Christ's Lordship almost solely in terms of the laws given by him or in Scriptures, and regarding the new life under divine mercy more as a reward to be earned by obedience than as free gift and present reality.[16] But whether grace or law is emphasized as the essence of the Christian life, in any case it is life in a new

[9] I John 2:2; 4:14.
[10] Cf. Dodd. *op. cit.,* pp. 27, 39–45.
[11] I John 2:15.
[12] *Ibid.,* 5:19; 1:6; 2:8–9, 11; 3:11–15.
[13] *Op. cit.,* p. 42.
[14] I John 2:17; cf. 2:8.
[15] *Ibid.,* 3:8; 5:4–5.

[16] Cf. Lietzmann, H., *The Beginnings of the Christian Church,* 1937, pp. 261–273.

and separated community. The idea which is common to second-century statements of this type is the conviction that Christians constitute a new people, a third "race" besides Jews and Gentiles. So Clement writes, "God, who seeth all things and who is the ruler of all spirits and the Lord of all flesh . . . chose our Lord Jesus Christ and us through him to be a peculiar people." [17] As Harnack has summarized the beliefs of these early Christians, they were persuaded that "(1) our people is older than the world; (2) the world was created for our sakes; (3) the world is carried on for our sakes; we retard the judgment of the world; (4) everything in the world is subject to us and must serve us; (5) everything in the world, the beginning and course and end of all history, is revealed to us and lies transparent to our eyes; (6) we shall take part in the judgment of the world and ourselves enjoy eternal bliss." [18] The fundamental conviction, however, was the idea that this new society, race, or people, had been established by Jesus Christ, who was its lawgiver and King. The corollary of the whole conception was the thought that whatever does not belong to the commonwealth of Christ is under the rule of evil. This came to expression in the doctrine of the two ways: "two ways there are, one of life and one of death, but there is a great difference between

the two ways." [19] The way of life was the Christian way. It was expounded by the rehearsing of the commandments of the new law, such as the commandments to love God and neighbor, the Golden Rule, the counsels to love the enemy and not to resist evil; certain injunctions drawn from the Old Testament were, however, also included. The way of death was described simply as the vicious course of life, so that the plain alternative was to be either a Christian or a wicked man. There seems to be in this Christian ethic no recognition of the fact that in a society where gospel rules are not acknowledged some rules are nevertheless in force; and that as there are virtues and vices in the domain of Christ so there are also virtues and vices relative to the standards of non-Christian culture. The line was sharply drawn between the new people and the old society, between obedience to the law of Christ and simple lawlessness; though some concession to the presence of divine government in and over cultural institutions is to be found in Clement's prayer "that we may be obedient to thy almighty and glorious name, and to our rulers and governors upon the earth." He recognized, as he goes on to say, that "Thou, Master, hast given the power of sovereignty to them through thy excellent and inexpressible might, that we may know the glory and honor given to them by thee, and be subject to them, in nothing resisting thy will." [20]

The most explicit and, apart from New Testament writers, doubtless the greatest representative in early Christianity of the "Christ-against-culture" type was Tertullian. One must hasten to add that he does not wholly conform to our hypothetical

[17] I Clement lxiv, 1; cf. Epistle of Barnabas, xiii–xiv.
[18] Harnack, A., Mission and Expansion of Christianity in the First Three Centuries, 1904, Vol. I, p. 302; cf. Gavin, Frank, Church and Society in the Second Century, 1934, which draws a picture of primitive Christian life—chiefly on the basis of Hippolytus' Apostolic Tradition—as dominated by the sense of its "corporate and social quality." "It was as if to say that the proudest boast of the believer was that he was a 'member.' His most essential quality was that he 'belonged.' " P. 3; cf. pp. 5, 8.

[19] The Teaching of the Twelve Apostles, i, 1; cf Barnabas, xix–xx; Shepherd of Hermas, Mand, 6, i.
[20] I Clement lx, 4–lxi, 1.

pattern, but demonstrates traits that relate him to other families and types. He is a Trinitarian who understands that the God Who reveals Himself in Jesus Christ is the Creator and the Spirit also; but within that context he maintains the absolute authority of Jesus Christ, "the supreme Head and Master of [God's promised] grace and discipline, the Enlightener and Trainer of the human race, God's own Son." [21] Tertullian's loyalty to Christ can express itself in such radical terms as the following: "Christ Jesus our Lord (may he bear with me a moment in thus expressing myself!), whosoever he is, of what God soever he is the Son, of what substance soever he is man and God, of what faith soever he is the teacher, of what reward soever he is the promiser, did, whilst he lived on earth himself declare what he was, what he had been, what the Father's will was which he was administering, what the duty of man was which he was prescribing." [22] In every case the primary Christian reference is to Christ "as the Power of God and the Spirit of God, as the Word, the Reason, the Wisdom and the Son of God," and the Christian confession is, "We say, and before all men we say, and torn and bleeding under . . . tortures we cry out, 'We worship God through Christ.' " [23] With this concentration on the Lordship of Jesus Christ Tertullian combines a rigorous morality of obedience to his commandments, including not only love of the brothers but of enemies, nonresistance to evil, prohibitions of anger and the lustful look. He is as strict a Puritan in his interpretation of what Christian faith

demands in conduct as one can find.[24] He replaces the positive and warm ethics of love which characterizes the First Letter of John with a largely negative morality; avoidance of sin and fearsome preparation for the coming day of judgment seem more important than thankful acceptance of God's grace in the gift of his Son.

Tertullian's rejection of the claims of culture is correspondingly sharp. The conflict of the believer is not with nature but with culture, for it is in culture that sin chiefly resides. Tertullian comes very close to the thought that original sin is transmitted through society, and that if it were not for the vicious customs that surround a child from its birth and for its artificial training its soul would remain good. The universe and the soul are naturally good, for God is their maker, yet "we must not consider merely by whom all things were made, but by whom they have been perverted," and that "there is a vast difference between the corrupted state and that of primal purity." [25] How much corruption and civilization coincide in Tertullian's thought is partly indicated in the reflection that Christ came not to bring "boors and savages . . . into some civilization . . . ; but as one who aimed to enlighten men already civilized, and under illusions from their very culture, that they might come to the knowledge of the truth." [26]

It becomes more evident when one notes what the vices are that he condemns and what the worldliness is that

[21] *Apology*, chap. xxi. This and the following quotations are taken from the translation of Tertullian's works in *Ante-Nicene Fathers*, Vols. III and IV.
[22] *The Prescription Against Heretics*, chap. xx.
[23] *Apology*, xxiii, xx.
[24] Cf. *Apology*, xxxix, xlv; *De Spectaculis; De Corona; On Repentance.*
[25] The quotation is from *De Spectaculis*, ii. For the doctrine of the natural goodness of the soul see *Apology*, xvii, *The Soul's Testimony*, and *A Treatise on the Soul*, chapter xxxix of which speaks of the corruption of the soul through customs; but cf. chap. xli.
[26] *Apology*, xxi.

the Christian is required to shun. The most vicious thing, of course, is social, pagan religion, with its polytheism and idolatry, its beliefs and rites, its sensuality and its commercialization.[27] Such religion, however, is interfused with all the other activities and institutions of society, so that the Christian is in constant danger of compromising his loyalty to the Lord. Tertullian, to be sure, rejects the charge that believers are "useless in the affairs of life," for, he says, "we sojourn with you in the world, abjuring neither forum, nor shambles, nor bath, nor booth, nor inn, nor weekly market, nor any other places of commerce." He even adds, "We sail with you, and fight with you, and till the ground with you; and in like manner we unite with you in your traffickings— even in the various arts we make public property of our works for your benefit." [28] This, however, is said in defense. When he admonishes believers his counsel is to withdraw from many meetings and many occupations, not only because they are corrupted by their relation to pagan faith but because they require a mode of life contrary to the spirit and the law of Christ.

So political life is to be shunned. "As those in whom all ardor in the pursuit of honor and glory is dead," writes Tertullian even in defense, "we have no pressing inducement to take part in your public meetings; nor is there aught more entirely foreign to us than affairs of state." [29] There is an inner contradiction between the exercise of political power and Christian faith. Military service is to be avoided because it involves participation in pagan religious rites and the swearing of an oath to Caesar, but chiefly

because it violates the law of Christ, who, "in disarming Peter, unbelted every soldier." How "shall the son of peace take part in battle when it does not become him even to sue at law?" [30] Trade cannot be prohibited with equal rigor, and there may even be some righteousness in business, yet it is scarcely "adapted for a servant of God," for apart from covetousness, which is a species of idolatry, there is no real motive for acquiring.[31]

When Tertullian turns to philosophy and the arts he is, if anything, more drastic in pronouncing prohibitions than he is in the case of the soldier's occupation. He has no sympathy with the efforts of some Christians of his time to point out positive connections between their faith and the ideas of the Greek philosophers. "Away," he exclaims, "with all attempts to produce a mottled Christianity of Stoic, Platonic and dialectic composition. We want no curious disputation after possessing Jesus Christ. . . . With our faith we desire no further belief." [32] In Socrates' daimon he discovers an evil demon; the disciples of Greece have for him nothing in common with "the disciples of heaven"; they corrupt the truth, they seek their own fame, they are mere talkers rather than doers. In so far as he must concede the presence of some truth in these non-Christian thinkers, he believes that they derived their insights from the Scriptures. The stain of corruption pervades the arts also. Literary erudition, to be sure, cannot be wholly avoided, therefore "learning literature is allowable for believers"; but teaching it must be discountenanced, for it is impossible to be a professor of literature without commending and affirming "the praises of idols interspersed therein." [33] As for the theater, not only the games with their

[27] *On Idolatry; Apology*, x–xv.
[28] *Apology*, xlii.
[29] *Ibid.*, xxxviii. Elsewhere, in chap. xxi, Tertullian remarks that "Caesars too would have believed in Christ, if either the Caesars had not been necessary for the world, or if Christians could have been Caesars."

[30] *On Idolatry*, xix; *De Corona*, xi.
[31] *On Idolatry*, xi.
[32] *Prescription Against Heretics*, vii; *Apology*, xlvi.
[33] *On Idolatry*, x.

levity and brutality, but tragedy and even music are ministers of sin. Tertullian seems to delight in his vision of the last judgment, when the illustrious monarchs who had been deified by men, the wise men of the world, the philosophers, poets, and tragedians, along with play-actors and wrestlers, will groan in the lowest darkness or be tossed in the fiery billows, while the carpenter's son they despised is exalted in glory.[34]

The great North African theologian seems, then, to present the epitome of the "Christ-against-culture" position. Yet he sounds both more radical and more consistent than he really was.[35] As we shall have occasion to note, he could not in fact emancipate himself and the church from reliance on and participation in culture, pagan though it was. Nevertheless he remains one of the foremost illustrations of the anticultural movement to be found in the history of the church.

II. Tolstoy's Rejection of Culture

We shall not undertake to describe how this *motif* in early Christianity was developed in the monastic movement, with its withdrawal from the institutions and societies of civilization, from family and state, from school and socially established church, from trade and industry. Eventually, of course, many sorts of monasticism arose and some of the varieties occupied positions quite distinct from those of Tertullian and the First Letter of John. Yet the main stream of the movement, as represented for instance by the *Rule of St. Benedict*, remained in the tradition of exclusive Christianity. Whatever contri-

butions it eventually made to culture, including the recognized social religion, were incidental byproducts which it did not intend. Its intention was directed to the achievement of a Christian life, apart from civilization, in obedience to the laws of Christ, and in pursuit of a perfection wholly distinct from the aims that men seek in politics and economics, in sciences and arts. Protestant sectarianism—to use that term in its narrow, sociological meaning—has given the same sort of answer to the question of Christ and culture. Out of the many sects that arose in the sixteenth and seventeenth centuries, protesting against the worldly church, both Catholic and Protestant, and seeking to live under the Lordship of Christ alone, only a few survive. The Mennonites have come to represent the attitude most purely, since they not only renounce all participation in politics and refuse to be drawn into military service, but follow their own distinctive customs and regulations in economics and education. The Society of Friends, never as radical, represents the type less adequately; though the family resemblance can be noted, especially in connection with the practice of brotherly love and the abstention from military service. By and large, however, the modern Quaker shows greater affinity to the opposite attitude in Christianity, the one which regards Christ as the representative of culture.[36] Hundreds of other groups, many of them evanescent, and thousands of individuals, have felt themselves compelled by loyalty to Christ to withdraw from culture and to give up all responsibility for the world. We meet them in all times and in many lands. In the nineteenth and early twentieth centuries they did not attract much attention, for most Christians seemed to be-

---

[34] *De Spectaculis,* xxx.

[35] Cf. Cochrane, C. N., *Christianity and Classical Culture,* 1940, pp. 222 ff., 227 ff., 245 f. For further discussions of Tertullian's ethics see Guignebert, Charles, *Tertullien, Étude sur ses Sentiments à l'Égard de l'Empire et de la Société Civile,* 1901, and Brandt, Theodor, *Tertullians Ethik,* 1929.

[36] The best discussion, within the compass of one work, of the ethics of medieval and modern sectarianism is to be found in Troeltsch, E., *The Social Teachings of the Christian Churches,* 1931, pp. 328 ff., 691 ff.

lieve that another answer to their problem had been finally established. But there was one man who in his own way and under the circumstances of his own time and place stated the radical position as vehemently and consistently as Tertullian. That man was Leo Tolstoy. He is worth our special attention, because of the great and dramatic manner in which he presented his convictions in life and art, and because of the pervasiveness of his influence in West and East, in Christianity and beyond it.

The great crisis Tolstoy met in his middle years was resolved, after many painful struggles, when he accepted the Jesus Christ of the Gospels as his sole and explicit authority. Noble by birth, wealthy by inheritance, famous by his own achievements as the author of *War and Peace* and *Anna Karenina,* he yet found himself threatened in his own life by the meaninglessness of existence and the tawdriness of all the values that his society esteemed. He could not rise from this despair into tranquility, and from the full stoppage of life into new activity, until he recognized the fallibility of all other authorities and acknowledged the teaching of Jesus as inescapable truth, founded on reality.[37] Jesus Christ was for Tolstoy always the great lawgiver, whose commandments were in accordance with man's true nature and with the demands of uncorrupted reason. His conversion centered in the realization that what Jesus had really done was to give men a new law, and that this law was based on the nature of things. "I have understood," he writes in describing the great change in his life, "Christ's teaching in his commandments and I see that their fulfill-

ment offers blessedness to me and to all men. I have understood that the execution of these commandments is the will of that Source of all from which my life also has come. . . . In its fulfillment lies the only possibility of salvation. . . . And having understood this, I understood and believed that Jesus is not only the Messiah, the Christ, but that he is really the Saviour of the world. I know that there is no other exit either for me or for all those who together with me are tormented in this life. I know that for all, and for me together with them, there is no way of escape except by fulfilling those commands of Christ which offer to all humanity the highest welfare of which I can conceive." [38] The literalness with which Tolstoy interpreted the new law, as found particularly in the fifth chapter of the Gospel according to St. Matthew, and the rigorousness of his obedience to it, made his conversion a very radical event. In the little book entitled *What I Believe* or *My Religion* he relates the the story of his effort to understand the New Testament, and of his release from struggle when he at last discovered that Jesus' words were to be literally interpreted, with all ecclesiastical glosses on the text eliminated. Then it became clear that Christ's commandments were a statement of God's eternal law, that he had abolished the law of Moses, and had not come, as the church inclined to say, to reinforce the old law or to teach that he was the second person of the Trinity.[39] Tolstoy believed that he was interpreting the gospel faithfully when he undertook to summarize this new law in five definite injunctions. The first commandment was: "Live at peace with all men and never consider your anger against any man justified. . . . Try in advance to destroy any enmity between yourself and others

---

[37] Cf. Preface to "The Christian Teaching," Vol. XII, pp. 209 ff. of *The Tolstoy Centenary Edition,* London, 1928–37. (This edition will hereafter be cited as *Works.*) Cf. also "A Confession," *Works,* Vol. XI, pp. 3 ff.; "What I Believe," Vol. XI, pp. 307 ff.

[38] "What I Believe," *Works,* Vol. XI, pp. 447, 448.
[39] *Ibid.,* pp. 353 ff., 370 ff.

that it may not flame up and destroy you." The second: "Do not make the desire for sexual relations an amusement. Let every man have a wife and each wife a husband and let the husband have only *one* wife and the wife only *one* husband, and under no pretext infringe the sexual union of one with the other." The "definite and practicable third commandment is clearly expressed: Never take an oath to anyone, anywhere, about anything. Every oath is extorted for evil ends." The fourth commandment destroys "the stupid and bad" social order in which men live, for simply, clearly, and practically it says: "Never resist the evildoer by force, do not meet violence with violence. If they beat you, endure it; if they take your possessions, yield them up; if they compel you to work, work; and if they wish to take from you what you consider to be yours, give it up." The final commandment, enjoining love of the enemy, Tolstoy understood as the "definite, important, and practicable rule . . . : not to make distinctions between one's own and other nations and not to do all the things that flow from making such distinctions; not to bear enmity to foreign nations; not to make war or to take part in warfare; not to arm oneself for war, but to behave to all men, of whatever race they may be, as we behave to our own people." [40] Through the promulgation of these five laws, Tolstoy believed, Christ had established the kingdom of God; though it is clear that the law of nonresistance was for him the key to the whole.

As in the case of other examples of this type which we have considered, the counterpart of such devotion to the commandments of Jesus Christ is a thoroughgoing opposition to the institutions of culture. To Tolstoy these seem to be

founded on a complex foundation of errors, including the acceptance of the inevitability of evil in man's present life, the belief that life is governed by external laws so that men cannot attain blessedness by their own efforts, the fear of death, the identification of true life with personal existence, and, above all, the practice of and belief in violence. Even less than Tertullian does he think that human corruption is resident in human nature; the evil with which men contend is in their culture only. Moreover, Tolstoy seems to have little understanding of the extent and depth to which culture enters into human nature. Hence he can center his attack on the conscious beliefs, the tangible institutions, and the specious customs of society. He is not content simply to withdraw from these himself and to live a semimonastic life; he becomes a crusader against culture under the banner of the law of Christ.

Every phase of culture falls under indictment. Though state, church, and property system are the citadels of evil, philosophy and sciences and arts also come under condemnation. There is no such thing as good government for Tolstoy. "The revolutionaries say: 'The government organization is bad in this and that respect; it must be destroyed and replaced by this and that.' But a Christian says: 'I know nothing about the governmental organization, or in how far it is good or bad, and for the same reason I do not want to support it.' . . . All the state obligations are against the conscience of a Christian: the oath of allegiance, taxes, law proceedings and military service." [41] The state and Christian faith are simply incompatible; for the state is based on love of power and the exercise of violence, whereas the love, humility, forgiveness, and nonresistance of Christian life draw it completely away

---

[40] *Ibid.*, pp. 376 f., 386, 390, 392 f., 398, 404. Cf. "The Gospel in Brief," *Works,* Vol. XI, pp. 163–167.

[41] "The Kingdom of God Is Within You," *Works,* Vol. XX, pp. 275 f.

from political measures and institutions. Christianity does not so much make the state unnecessary as sap its foundations and destroy it from within. The argument of such Christians as Paul who contend that the state performs an interim function in restraining evil does not appeal to Tolstoy, for he sees the state as the chief offender against life.[42] Against its evil there is no defense except complete nonparticipation, and nonviolent striving for the conversion of all men to peaceful, anarchic Christianity.

Though the churches call themselves Christian, they are equally far removed from the Christianity of Jesus. Tolstoy regards them as self-centered organizations that assert their own infallibility; servants of the state, defenders of the reign of violence and privilege, of inequality and property; obscurers and falsifiers of the gospel. "The Churches as Churches . . . are anti-Christian institutions," utterly hostile in their "pride, violence, and self-assertion, immobility and death" to the "humility, penitence, meekness, progress and life" of Christianity.[43] As in the case of states, reformation of such institutions is wholly inadequate. Christ did not found them, and comprehension of his doctrine will not reform but will "destroy the churches and their significance." [44] To this theme, as to the criticism of the state, Tolstoy returns again and again. The church is an invention of the devil; no honest man believing the gospel can remain priest or preacher; all the churches are alike in their betrayal of Christ's law; churches and states together represent the institutionalization of violence and fraud.[45]

Tolstoy's attack on economic institutions is equally intransigent. His own effort to renounce property while yet retaining some responsibility for its administration constitutes part of his personal tragedy. He believed that property claims were based on robbery and maintained by violence. More radical than second-century radical Christians and than most monks, he turned even against the subdivision of labor in economic society. It seemed to him to be the means by which privileged persons, such as artists, intellectuals, and their kind, absorbed the labor of others, justifying themselves by the belief that they were beings of a higher order than workingmen, or that their contribution to society was so great that it compensated for the harm they did by overburdening manual workers with their claims. The first supposition has been exploded by Christian teaching about human equality; the contribution made to society by the privileged is dubious when it is not patently mischievous. Hence Tolstoy urges the intellectuals, as well as landlords and military men in society, to stop deceiving themselves, to renounce their own righteousness, advantages, and distinctions, to labor with all their power to sustain their own lives and those of others by manual labor. Following his own principles, he attempted to be his own tailor and cobbler, and would have liked to be his own gardener and cook.[46]

Like Tertullian, Tolstoy also turned against philosophy and the sciences and arts in which he had been nurtured. The

---

[42] *Ibid.*, pp. 281 ff.

[43] *Ibid.*, p. 82.

[44] *Ibid.*, pp. 69, 101.

[45] Cf. "The Restoration of Hell," a remarkable little fable in which the re-establishment of the reign of evil on earth after Christ's victory is explained particularly by the invention of the church. The devil who invented it explains to Beelzebub, "I have arranged it so that men do not believe in Christ's teaching but in mine, which they call by his name." *Works*, Vol. XII, pp. 309 ff. Cf. also "Religion and Morality," "What is Religion?" "Church and State," "An Appeal to the Clergy," in the same volume.

[46] "What Then Must We Do?" *Works*, Vol. XIV, pp. 209 ff., 269 ff., 311 ff.

first two are not only useless, because they fail to answer the fundamental questions of man about the meaning and conduct of life, but are bad because they rest on falsehood. The experimental sciences devote great energies to confirm a dogma that makes the whole enterprise false, namely the dogma that "matter and energy exist," while they do nothing to ameliorate man's actual life. "I am convinced," writes Tolstoy, "that a few centuries hence the so-called 'scientific' activity of our belauded recent centuries of European humanity will furnish an inextinguishable fund of mirth and pity to future generations." [47] Philosophy leads us no further than to the knowledge that all is vanity; but "what is hidden to the wise and prudent is revealed to babes." The common peasant who follows the Sermon on the Mount knows what the great and wise cannot understand. "Special talents and intellectual gifts are needed, not for the knowledge and statement of truth but for the invention and statement of falsehood." [48] The artist Tolstoy could not make quite as complete a break with the arts. He at least made a distinction between good art and bad. To the latter category he consigned all his own former work, save for two small stories, all "genteel" art designed for the privileged classes, and even *Hamlet* and the *Ninth Symphony*. But he allowed a place for an art that was a sincere expression and communication of feeling, that had universal appeal, was comprehensible by the masses of men, and was in accord with Christian moral consciousness.[49] Hence in so far as he did not devote his

great literary talents to the writing of homilies and tracts on non-resistance and true religion, he produced parables and stories such as "Where Love Is There God Is" and "Master and Man."

Tolstoy of course no more conforms completely to our type than any other great individual conforms to a pattern. He is like the author of I John in his praise of love and his rejection of the "lust of the flesh, the lust of the eyes, and the pride of life." He is like Tertullian in the vehemence of his attack on social institutions. He is like the monks in his personal withdrawal into a life of poverty. But he differs from all these in his relation to Jesus Christ, for one finds in them a personal devotion to a personal Lord which is strangely lacking in Tolstoy. For him the law of Christ is much more significant than the person of the lawgiver. Maxim Gorky has remarked that when Tolstoy spoke of Christ there was "no enthusiasm, no feeling in his words, and no spark of real fire." [50] The writings in general bear out that judgment. Moreover, Tolstoy shows little understanding for the meaning of the grace of God manifested in Jesus Christ, for the historical nature of Christian revelation, for the psychological, moral, and spiritual depths of both corruption and salvation. Hence he was more of a legalist than even the legal Tertullian. Yet in modern history and under the conditions of the modern culture of which he was in part a product, Tolstoy remains a clear-cut example of anticultural Christianity.[51]

It would be easy to multiply illustrations of the type. Described one after the other they would constitute a very diverse group, including Eastern and Western Catholics, orthodox and sectarian Protestants, millenarians and mystics, ancient

---

[47] "What I Believe," *Works,* Vol. XI, p. 420; cf. "A Confession," Vol. XI, pp. 23 ff.; "On Life," Vol. XII, pp. 12 f.

[48] "Reason and Religion," *Works,* Vol. XII, p. 202; cf. "A Confession," Vol. XI, pp. 56 ff., 73 f.

[49] "What Is Art?" *Works,* Vol. XVIII, pp. 231 ff.

[50] Gorky, Maxim, *Reminiscences of Leo Nikolaevich Tolstoy,* 1920, p. 5.

[51] For full descriptions of Tolstoy's life and works see Aylmer Maude's *Life of Tolstoy* and Ernest J. Simmon's *Leo Tolstoy.*

and medieval and modern Christians. Yet their unity of spirit would also be apparent in their common acknowledgment of the sole authority of Jesus Christ and the common rejection of the prevailing culture. Whether that culture calls itself Christian or not is of no importance, for to these men it is always pagan and corrupt. Neither is it of first-rate significance whether such Christians think in apocalyptic or in mystical terms. As apocalyptics they will prophesy the early passing of the old society and the coming into history of a new divine order. As mystics they will experience and announce the reality of an eternal order hidden by the specious temporal and cultural scene. The significant question to be asked about Christians in this respect is not whether they think historically or mystically about the kingdom of God; but rather whether they are convinced of its nearness and are governed by this conviction, or whether they think of it as relatively remote in time or space and relatively ineffective in power. Neither are the differences between Protestants and Catholics decisive. Monastic characteristics reappear in Protestant sectarians; and a Lutheran Kierkegaard attacks the Christendom of post-Reformation culture with the same intransigence that marks a Wiclif's thrust against medieval social faith. Various and diverse though these men and movements are, they give a recognizably common answer to the problem of Christ and culture.

III. A Necessary and Inadequate Position

It is easy to raise objections to this solution of the Christian dilemma. Yet intelligent Christians who cannot conscientiously take this position themselves will recognize the sincerity of most of its exponents, and its importance in history and the need for it in the total encounter of church and world.

Half-baked and muddle-headed men abound in the anticultural movement as well as elsewhere; doubtless hypocrisy flourishes here too. Yet the single-heartedness and sincerity of the great representatives of this type are among their most attractive qualities. There has been a kind of Kierkegaardian "reduplication" in their lives, for they have expressed in their actions what they said in words. They have not taken easy ways in professing their allegiance to Christ. They have endured physical and mental sufferings in their willingness to abandon homes, property, and the protection of government for the sake of his cause. They have accepted the derision and animosity which societies inflict on nonconformists. From the persecutions of Christians under Domitian to the imprisonment of Jehovah's Witnesses in national-socialist Germany and democratic America, such people have been subject to martyrdom. In so far as Christian pacifists in our time belong to this group—not all of them do—their sufferings will seem to themselves and others to be more evidently due to obedience to Jesus Christ than is the case when a Christian soldier suffers and dies. Part of the appeal of the "Christ-against-culture" answer lies in this evident reduplication of profession in conduct. When we make it we seem to be proving to ourselves and others that we mean what we say when we say that Jesus Christ is our Lord.

In history these Christian withdrawals from and rejections of the institutions of society have been of very great importance to both church and culture. They have maintained the distinction between Christ and Caesar, between revelation and reason, between God's will and man's. They have led to reformations in both church and world, though this was never their intention. Hence men and movements of this sort are often celebrated for their heroic roles in the history of a culture which they rejected. What

Montalembert said of Benedict of Nursia applies in one way or another to almost all the great representatives of exclusive Christianity: "Historians have vied in praising his genius and clear-sightedness; they have supposed that he intended to regenerate Europe, to stop the dissolution of society, to prepare the reconstitution of political order, to re-establish public education, and to preserve literature and the arts. . . . I firmly believe that he never dreamt of regenerating anything but his own soul and those of his brethren, the monks." [52] Doubtless the individualistic ideal of soul-regeneration is not an adequate key to the attitude of radical Christians; but neither is the hope of social reform. In social reform they accomplish what they did not intend. Second-century believers who had no interest in the rule of Caesar prepared the way for the social triumph of the church and the conversion of the pagan world into a Christian civilization. Monasticism eventually became one of the great conservers and transmitters of cultural tradition; it trained many great ecclesiastical and political leaders of society; it strengthened the institutions from which its founders had withdrawn. Protestant sectarians made important contributions to political customs and traditions, such as those which guarantee religious liberty to all members of a society. Quakers and Tolstoyans, intending only to abolish all methods of coercion, have helped to reform prisons, to limit armaments, and to establish international organizations for the maintenance of peace through coercion.

Now that we have recognized the importance of the role played by anticultural Christians in the reform of culture, we must immediately point out that they never achieved these results alone or directly but only through the mediation of

[52] De Montalembert, *The Monks of the West,* 1896, Vol. I, p. 436.

believers who gave a different answer to the fundamental question. Not Tertullian, but Origen, Clement of Alexandria, Ambrose, and Augustine initiated the reformation of Roman culture. Not Benedict, but Francis, Dominic, and Bernard of Clairvaux accomplished the reform of medieval society often credited to Benedict. Not George Fox, but William Penn and John Woolman, changed social institutions in England and America. And in every case the followers did not so much compromise the teachings of the radicals as follow another inspiration than the one deriving from an exclusive loyalty to an exclusive Christ.

Yet the radically Christian answer to the problem of culture needed to be given in the past, and doubtless needs to be given now. It must be given for its own sake, and because without it other Christian groups lose their balance. The relation of the authority of Jesus Christ to the authority of culture is such that every Christian must often feel himself claimed by the Lord to reject the world and its kingdoms with their pluralism and temporalism, their makeshift compromises of many interests, their hypnotic obsession by the love of life and the fear of death. The movement of withdrawal and renunciation is a necessary element in every Christian life, even though it be followed by an equally necessary movement of responsible engagement in cultural tasks. Where this is lacking, Christian faith quickly degenerates into a utilitarian device for the attainment of personal prosperity or public peace; and some imagined idol called by his name takes the place of Jesus Christ the Lord. What is necessary in the individual life is required also in the existence of the church. If Romans 13 is not balanced by I John, the church becomes an instrument of state, unable to point men to their transpolitical destiny and their suprapolitical loyalty; unable also to engage in political tasks, save as one more group of power-hungry or security-seeking men. Given Jesus Christ with his authority, the radical answer is inevitable; not only when men are in despair about their civilization, but also when they are complacent, not only as they hope for a kingdom of God, but also as they shore up the crumbling walls of temporal societies for the sake of the men who might be buried under their ruins. So long as eternity cannot be translated into temporal terms nor time into eternity, so long as Christ and culture cannot be amalgamated, so long is the radical answer inevitable in the church.

It is an inevitable answer; but it is also inadequate, as members of other groups in the church can easily point out. It is inadequate, for one thing, because it affirms in words what it denies in action; namely, the possibility of sole dependence on Jesus Christ to the exclusion of culture. Christ claims no man purely as a natural being, but always as one who has become human in a culture; who is not only in culture, but into whom culture has penetrated. Man not only speaks but thinks with the aid of the language of culture. Not only has the objective world about him been modified by human achievement; but the forms and attitudes of his mind which allow him to make sense out of the objective world have been given him by culture. He cannot dismiss the philosophy and science of his society as though they were external to him; they are in him—though in different forms from those in which they appear in the leaders of culture. He cannot rid himself of political beliefs and economic customs by rejecting the more or less external institutions; these customs and beliefs have taken up residence in his mind. If Christians do not come to Christ with the language, the thought patterns, the moral disciplines of Judaism, they come with those of Rome; if not with those of Rome, then with those of Germany, England, Russia, America,

India, or China. Hence the radical Christians are always making use of the culture, or parts of the culture, which ostensibly they reject. The writer of I John employs the terms of the Gnostic philosophy to whose pagan use he objects.[53] Clement of Rome uses semi-Stoic ideas. In almost every utterance Tertullian makes evident that he is a Roman, so nurtured in the legal tradition and so dependent on philosophy that he cannot state the Christian case without their aid.[54] Tolstoy becomes intelligible when he is interpreted as a nineteenth century Russian who participates, in the depths of his unconscious soul as well as consciously, in the cultural movements of his time, and in the Russian mystic sense of community with men and nature. It is so with all the members of the radical Christian group. When they meet Christ they do so as heirs of a culture which they cannot reject because it is a part of them. They can withdraw from its more obvious institutions and expressions; but for the most part they can only select—and modify under Christ's authority—something they have received through the mediation of society.

The conservation, selection, and conversion of cultural achievements is not only a fact; it is also a morally inescapable requirement, which the exclusive Christian must meet because he is a Christian and a man. If he is to confess Jesus before men, he must do so by means of words and ideas derived from culture, though a change of meaning is also necessary. He must use such words as "Christ" or "Messiah" or "Kyrios" or "Son of God" or "Logos." If he is to say what "love" means he must choose among such words as *"eros," "philanthropia"*

[53] Cf. Dodd, C. H., *op cit.*, xx, xxix, xlii, *et passim.*
[54] Cf. Shortt, C. De Lisle, *The Influence of Philosophy on the Mind of Tertullian,* and Beck, Alexander, *Roemisches Recht bei Tertullian und Cyprian.*

and "*agape*," or "charity," "loyalty," and "love"—seeking one that comes close to the meaning of Jesus Christ, and modifying it by use in context. These things he must do, not only that he may communicate, but also that he may himself know whom and what he believes. When he undertakes to fulfill the demands of Jesus Christ, he finds himself partly under the necessity of translating into the terms of his own culture what was commanded in the terms of another, partly under the requirement of giving precision and meaning to general principles by adopting specific rules relevant to his social life. What is the meaning of Jesus' statements about the Sabbath in a society which does not celebrate such a day? Is it to be introduced and modified, or left aside as a part of an alien, non-Christian culture? What is the meaning of praying to a Father in heaven, in a culture with a cosmology differing radically from that of Palestine in the first century? How shall demons be cast out where they are not believed to exist? There is no escape from culture here; the alternative seems to be between the effort to reproduce the culture in which Jesus lived, or to translate his words into those of another social order. Furthermore, the command to love the neighbor cannot be obeyed except in specific terms that involve cultural understanding of the neighbor's nature, and except in specific acts directed toward him as a being who has a place in culture, as member of family or religious community, as national friend or enemy, as rich or poor. In his effort to be obedient to Christ, the radical Christian therefore reintroduces ideas and rules from non-Christian culture in two areas: in the government of the withdrawn Christian community, and in the regulation of Christian conduct toward the world outside.

The tendency in exclusive Christianity is to confine the commandments of loyalty to Christ, of love of God and neigh-bor, to the fellowship of Christians. Here also the other gospel requirements are to be enforced. But, as Martin Dibelius among many others has pointed out, "the words of Jesus were not intended as ethical rules for a Christian culture, and even if they were applied as such they were not sufficient to supply an answer to all the questions of daily life." [55] Other helps were needed; and they were found by early Christians in Jewish and Hellenistic-Jewish popular ethics. It is remarkable to what extent the ethics of second-century Christianity—as summarized for instance in *The Teaching of the Twelve* and the *Epistle of Barnabas*—contains material extraneous to the New Testament. These Christians, who thought of themselves as a new "race" distinct from Jews and Gentiles, borrowed from the laws and customs of those from whom they had separated what they needed for the common life but had not received from their own authority. The situation is similar in the case of the monastic rules. Benedict of Nursia seeks Scriptural foundation for all his regulations and counsels; but the New Testament does not suffice him, nor does the Bible as a whole; and he must find, in old reflections on human experience in social life, rules by means of which to govern the new community. The spirit in which both Scriptural and non-Scriptural regulations are presented also shows how impossible it is to be only a Christian without reference to culture. When Tertullian recommends modesty and patience, Stoic overtones are always present; and when Tolstoy speaks of nonresistance, Rousseauistic ideas are in the context. Even if no use were made of another inheritance besides that derived from Jesus Christ, the needs of the withdrawn community would lead to the development of a new culture. Invention, human achievement, temporal realization of

[55] Dibelius, Martin, *A Fresh Approach to the New Testament*, p. 219.

value, organization of the common life —all must go on in it. When the dogmas and rites of social religion have been abandoned, a new dogma and a new ritual must be developed, if religious practice is to go on at all. Therefore monks work out their own rituals in their monasteries, and Quaker silences become as formalized as masses; Tolstoy's dogmas are as confidently uttered as are those of the Russian church. When the state has been rejected, the exclusively Christian community has necessarily developed some political organization of its own; and has done so with the aid of other ideas than those derived from the injunction that the first shall be the servant of all. It has called its leaders prophets or abbots, its governing assemblies quarterly meetings or congregations; it has enforced uniformity by means of popular opinion and banishment from the society; but in any case it has sought to maintain internal order, not only generally but in a specific way of life. Prevailing property institutions have been set aside; but something more than the counsel to sell all and give to the poor has been necessary, since men had to eat and be clothed and sheltered even in poverty. Hence ways and means of acquiring and distributing goods were devised, and a new economic culture was established.

In dealing with the society which he regards as pagan, but from which he never succeeds in separating himself completely, the radical Christian has also always been required to take recourse to principles he could not derive directly from his conviction of Christ's Lordship. His problem here has been that of living in an interim. Whether exclusive Christians are eschatologists or spiritualists, in either case they must take account of the "meanwhile," the interval between the dawning of the new order of life and its victory, the period in which the temporal and material has not yet been transformed into the spiritual. They cannot separate themselves completely, therefore, from the world of culture around them, nor from those needs in themselves which make this culture necessary. Though the whole world lies in darkness, yet distinctions must be made between relative rights and wrongs in that world, and in Christian relations to it. So, Tertullian writing to his wife advises her to remain a widow if he should die first. He disclaims any motive of jealousy or possessiveness, for such carnal motives will be eliminated in the resurrection, and "there will at that day be no resumption of voluptuous disgrace between us." She is to remain a widow because Christian law permits only one marriage and because virginity is better than marriage. Marriage is not really good but only not evil; indeed, when Jesus says " 'They were marrying and buying' He sets a brand on the very leading vices of the flesh and the world, which call men off the most from divine disciplines." Hence Tertullian counsels his wife to accept his death as God's call to the great good of a life of continence. But thereafter he wrote a second letter in which he gave the "next best advice," to the effect that if she needed to remarry she should at least "marry in the Lord," that is, marry a Christian and not an unbeliever.[56] In the end one can find in Tertullian a whole scale of relative goods and evils in his estimation of orders in man's sex-life in the interval before the resurrection. Compared with virginity, marriage is relatively evil; a single marriage in a lifetime, however, is relatively good as compared with second marriage; yet if the evil of second marriage does take place, marriage with a believer is relatively good. If Tertullian were pressed

[56] "To His Wife," (Ante-Nicene Fathers, Vol. IV); cf. also "On Monogamy"; "On Exhortation to Chastity."

he might concede that if there were to be marriage with an unbeliever, a monogamous marriage would still be a better wickedness than polygamy; and even that in a disordered world polygamy might be relatively good compared to wholly irresponsible sex relations.

Other illustrations of the necessity for recognizing laws relative to the time of the interim and to the existence of a pagan society can be found in the history of Friends who are concerned that since there is a vicious institution of slavery slaves should be treated "justly"; and since there is buying and selling a fixed-price policy should prevail. One thinks, too, of Christian pacifists, who, having rejected the institutions and practices of warfare as wholly evil, yet seek to have armaments limited and certain weapons banned. Count Tolstoy's daughter has told the story of her father's tragedy, which was at least in part the tragedy of an exclusive Christian whose responsibilities did not allow him to escape the problems of the "meanwhile." For himself he could choose the life of poverty, but not for wife and children, who did not share his convictions; he did not want the protection of police, and did not need it; but he was a member of a family that required the guardianship of force. So the poor man lived on his own rich estate, unwillingly and with ambiguous responsibility; the non-resister was protected against mobs even at his death. Countess Alexandra relates a story that presents the problem dramatically, and indicates how even Tolstoy needed to recognize that conscience and the rule of right lay their claims on man in the midst of bad institutions. Since he had renounced property but remained bound to his family, responsibility for the management of the estate fell on his wife, who was poorly equipped for the task. Under her inadequate supervision, incompetent or dishonest stewards allowed the property to fall into general disorder. A horrible accident occurred as a result of maladministration—a peasant was buried alive in a neglected sandpit. "I seldom saw father so upset," writes his daughter. "'Such things can't happen, they can't happen,' he was telling mother. 'If you want an estate you must manage it well, or else give it up altogether.'"[57]

Stories of this sort, which illustrate the adjustments of radical Christians to a rejected and evil but inescapable culture, can be multiplied; and they delight their critics. But surely the delight is premature and unfounded, for such stories only underscore the common Christian dilemma. The difference between the radicals and the other groups is often only this: that the radicals fail to recognize what they are doing, and continue to speak as though they were separated from the world. Sometimes the contradictions are quite explicit in their writings; as in the case of Tertullian, who seems to argue against himself on such subjects as the value of philosophy and government. Often they are implicit, and come to expression only in contradictory conduct. In either case the radical Christian confesses that he has not solved the problem of Christ and culture, but is only seeking a solution along a certain line.

[57] Tolstoy, Countess Alexandra, *The Tragedy of Count Tolstoy*, 1933, p. 65; cf. pp. 161–165, and Simmons, *op. cit.*, 631 ff., 682 f. *et passim.*

3 · Jews as an Indian Caste[1]

SCHIFRA STRIZOWER

According to the 1951 census there are some 26,000 Jews in India. However, owing to emigration—chiefly to Israel—an estimate of 20,000 is much nearer the mark for today.

Indian Jewry is divided into three main groups. Some 14,000 Jews are known as Bene Israel—Children of Israel. Bene Israel maintain that their name suggests their origin, namely that they are descendants of members of the Ten Tribes of Israel who found their way into India in the second century B.C.E. Nowadays over two-thirds of the Bene Israel live in Bombay. Until very recently Bene Israel were divided into two endogamous units. To a large extent, Bene Israel resemble in physical features the people among whom they live, varying in skin colour from very light to dark brown. Their mother tongue is Marathi, one of the local languages; very many of them also speak English. The Jewish group on the south-west coast of India —reduced in numbers from 2,500 to 1,500 by emigration to Israel—is known as Cochin Jewry, although by no means all members of this group live in the town of Cochin. Cochin Jewry is divided into endogamous sub-groups: the White Jews, the Black Jews, and the Meshuararim. The latter are the underprivileged descendants of the manumitted offspring of unions between Cochin Jews and their slave concubines; they are also divided into two groups, one of which is attached to the White Jews and the other to the

Black Jews, according to descent. In comparison with the Black Jews, who resemble in physical features the people among whom they have been living for over a millennium, the White Jews, who are for the most part fair-complexioned, are newcomers who migrated to India but a few centuries ago. Nevertheless, both White and Black Jews claim domicile in India for some two thousand years. Malayalam, the local language, is their mother tongue; but virtually all the White Jews and some of the Black Jews also speak English. Some 4,000 Jews from Baghdad, with small additions from Aden, Afghanistan, and Iran, are known as Baghdadi. The first of the Baghdadi arrived in India in the late eighteenth century. There are Baghdadi communities of some 2,000 each in Bombay and Calcutta; there is also a small group of Baghdadi in Poona. Baghdadi are on the whole fair-complexioned. They consistently use English.

A few hundred European Jews, mainly from Germany and Austria, came to India in the nineteen-thirties. They live in Delhi, Calcutta, Madras, and especially in Bombay. Though the European Jews in Bombay often stress their differences from the Baghdadi, they join in Baghdadi social and religious activities.

While the Baghdadi tend to imitate the Europeans, the social systems of the Bene Israel and Cochin Jewry show great resemblances to that of the Hindus. In this paper I propose to furnish evidence bearing on the assimilation of one Jewish group, the Bene Israel, to the Hindu caste system.

Caste membership is acquired at birth,

SOURCE. Schifra Strizower, "Jews as an Indian Caste," from *The Jewish Journal of Sociology*, Vol. 1, April, 1959, pp. 43–57.

determines marriage, prescribes ritual, and is associated with a traditional occupation. The castes are conceived of as existing in different degrees of spiritual dignity; those of high degree, barred from hundreds of lowly tasks which are yet necessary for their existence, need the services of those of low degree, while those of low degree need the ministrations of those of high degree for their spiritual salvation. Contact between those of different degrees of spiritual dignity produces pollution in those of high degree; hence the castes must be kept apart. Above all, castes are kept apart by the ban on intermarriage and the restriction on commensality. The Hindu system, then, implies a mystically sanctioned, pre-ordained inter-dependence and at the same time it stresses the social separation of caste from caste.

But the caste system, Srinivas says, "is far from a rigid system in which the position of each component caste is fixed for all time. Movement has always been possible. . . . A low caste was able, in a generation or two, to rise to a higher position in the hierarchy by imitating the practices of the higher castes." [2]

Though the position of the Bene Israel within Indian society is not of the mystic and pre-ordained kind bound up with the religious conceptions of Hinduism, Bene Israel refer to themselves, and are referred to by their Indian neighbours, as a caste. Nor is this unusual. For caste, Srinivas writes,[3]

also provided the pattern for relations with non-Hindu groups. Christians and Muslims were regarded as castes, too, and they accepted such a status. Even revolutionary movements which had aimed at the overthrow of the caste system ended by either becoming castes themselves or reproduced the caste system within themselves. The main body of Hindus regarded these sects as castes and not as sects.

Again,

Even a change of religion [Hutton says][4] does not destroy the caste system, for Muslims, who do not recognize it as valid, are often found to observe it in practice, and there are many Muslim castes as well as Hindu; and when some reforming body breaks away from Hinduism and repudiates caste, it becomes something very like a new caste of its own. Jews and Christians also in India often form castes or bodies analogous to castes . . . the caste system has afforded a place in society into which any community, be it racial, social, occupational or religious, can be fitted as a co-operating part of the social whole, while retaining its own distinctive character and its separate individual life.

Bene Israel told me that their ancestors "belonged to those of the Ten Tribes which had escaped deportation after the fall of the Kingdom of Israel in the eighth century B.C.E. However, in order to avoid the persecutions which followed in the train of constant invasions by a host of conquerors," the ancestors of the Bene Israel left their home in 175 B.C.E. "and proceeded by a route not unknown in those times to India. But although they went to a new country, they brought with them their old misfortunes." For the ship in which the group travelled was wrecked off the Konkan on the west coast of India not far from Bombay. "Almost all the people were lost with all their belongings, and only seven couples were saved. The bodies of the drowned were washed ashore in the very village where the survivors had taken refuge and buried there. . . . The survivors had lost everything they had brought with them from their homes in the shipwreck and were in consequence reduced to a miserable plight, more easy to be imagined than described. . . . The descendants of the seven couples were cut off from their co-religionists until recent times. As their numbers increased, they spread over the Konkan." [5]

During their long isolation from their co-religionists, Bene Israel relate, they forgot Hebrew and a great part of Jewish ritual. However, they observed the Sabbath, some of the Holy-days, the dietary regulations and circumcision; they remembered the *Shema,* the confession of the Jewish faith, and repeated it on every occasion, such as that of circumcision, marriage, and death. Moreover, Bene Israel relate that "unions with alien women were frowned at because the group wished to adhere to Jewish religious principles, and also because the Hindus, on account of their laws, were against marriage between Bene Israel and non-Bene Israel." But Bene Israel acknowledge that "while in ignorance of much of Jewish religion, the community adopted some of the local customs—foreign, it is true, to Judaism, but harmless and innocent, and not savouring in the smallest degree of an idolatrous tendency."

Bene Israel maintain that some of the ritual which they observed during their long isolation from their co-religionists was very similar to that practised in Israel in 175 B.C.E.—internal evidence for their migration from Israel at that time. Moreover, Bene Israel point out that the festival of Hanukkah and the four fasts of national mourning, which were not observed by them during their long isolation, had not been introduced in 175 B.C.E. [6]

Obviously, it is not intended here to argue for or against the accuracy of Bene Israel historical memories. Nevertheless, it must be stated that those who have interested themselves in the Bene Israel hold that this group came to India from an Arabian country in the middle of the first millennium C.E. [7] Moreover, the internal evidence adduced by the

Bene Israel does not stand up to closer investigation. It may, of course, be possible to trace some similarity between the ritual observed by the Bene Israel during their long isolation from the main stream of Jewish life and that practised in Israel in 175 B.C.E. However, the question arises whether there is not a much greater similarity between the ritual observed by the Bene Israel and that practised in India. In other words, one wonders whether the ritual observed by the Bene Israel was not copied from Hindu example rather than adapted from the ritual of Israel in 175 B.C.E. Moreover, non-observance of the festival of Hanukkah and the four fasts of national mourning introduced after 175 B.C.E. cannot be accepted as evidence for the group's migration and isolation before their introduction, since Bene Israel did not observe some of the ritual which was certainly in use in Israel in 175 B.C.E.

Again, Godbey says: [8] "It is certain that any tradition of descent from ancient Israel . . . may have originated in some historic fact. This urges inquiry for the origin or meaning of . . . such tradition. . . . It should be recognized that all such peoples are the best judges" of whether they are descendants of the Ten Tribes of Israel or not. Nevertheless, it is possible that the Bene Israel tradition of descent from the Ten Tribes originated with travellers who encountered them and from whom the group adopted it. But whether or not the tradition of descent from the Ten Tribes is based on "some historic fact," it is of functional significance. For the claim to such descent, often put forward by Jewish communities which have been isolated for centuries from their co-religionists and assimilated by social systems not usually associated with Judaism, correlates with the strong Jewish belief in the survival of the Ten Tribes and their eventual reintegration into the main stream of Jewish life, and hence provides a basis for renewal of relations between these "peripheral" Jewish communities and the general body of their co-religionists.

Bene Israel tradition has it that their ancestors took to oil pressing soon after their arrival in India. Because they rested on the seventh day, Bene Israel were called "Shanwar Teli"—Saturday oil-presser caste. Even today a few of the 460 Bene Israel who have remained in the Konkan follow this occupation.

One wonders whether Bene Israel were the oil-pressers *par excellence* in this area. For Mr. S. V. Avalaskar, the Konkan historian, in a personal communication, writes:

Practically every village (especially the bigger ones) had one or two families of the Bene Israel. The Bene Israel abstained from the work of oil pressing on Saturdays, and the Konkan village community did not buy oil on Saturdays. This custom is being observed even today. The social restriction not to buy oil on the day when the Bene Israel oil-pressers did not press oil, appears to me very significant. . . .[9]

It seems that Bene Israel stood low in the hierarchy of Konkan society. Indeed, a member of the Bene Israel who had spent his youth in a Konkan village told me: "We Bene Israel get on well with the Hindus. Hindus are gentle people and kind, and they do not like strife. Yet twenty years ago the Hindus in the Konkan still thought that if Bene Israel touched the utensils which Hindus used for food the utensils became polluted. The Hindus thought of us as Teli caste, and oil pressing is humble, unclean work. But this has changed now."[10]

Another member of the Bene Israel community, Professor M. Ezekiel, writes of the humiliation and irritation he felt at being called "Teli":

. . . when we first arrived in Alibag, after the retirement of my father in 1905, we were shocked to be described

as Teli, and my mother as Telin, the feminine of Teli. I knew for certain that not for three generations had we known anyone in our family who had done the Oil-man's trade. Even in the John Elphinstone High School, most boys took delight in calling us by that very irritating name 'Teli'. I found to my surprise that some boys in the School had Ghanis or Oil-presses in their houses and their main source of income was the Oil-press. They were real Teli, but we always protested that we were not, not for some generations back. It may be there were some very far behind, we did not know . . . We felt it very humiliating to be designated Teli . . . We have risen far above that level and are now Doctors, Professors and even Principals of University Institutions.[11]

Like Hindu groups wishing to rise in public esteem, Bene Israel adopted some of the canons of behaviour of the higher castes.[12] For example, they refrained from eating beef and frowned at the re-marriage of all but the poorest of widows. Again, they were quick to point out that their dependence upon oil pressing was purely fortuitous, the result of their destitute position after the shipwreck, and not of a pre-ordained order of the universe which delegates this calling to those of spiritually low qualities.[13] Moreover, a number of Bene Israel succeeded in giving up oil pressing for agriculture; a few Bene Israel rose to high positions in the army and fleet of the local rulers.[14]

Assimilation to their Hindu neighbours is also reflected in Bene Israel thinking: ". . . the Hindu culture had sunk so deep into their bones," Ezekiel writes, "that in fact until very recently they believed that beef was prohibited to them in the Old Testament."[15] A member of the Bene Israel community told me: "I am an orthodox man, though I must admit that I have eaten beef once or twice."

A few Bene Israel asked me: "Do the orthodox Jews in England eat beef?" Again, Bene Israel said: "Is it necessary for a widow to re-marry? Of course, if she has not been provided for financially she may not be able to avoid it—but even then it is not nice for a widow to re-marry." A young woman of the Bene Israel community told me that her mother had been widowed very soon after marriage. Nevertheless, her mother's father would not consent to his widowed daughter's re-marriage: "Nowadays there are some people in the community who do not worry about widow re-marriage. But we are one of the best families in our community, so my grandfather could not allow his daughter to re-marry." The grandfather of this informant confirmed that he had persuaded his widowed daughter not to re-marry: "You may think of our practice as assimilation to the Hindu system. But we know that widow re-marriage is not prohibited in the Bible! And we Bene Israel do not prohibit widow re-marriage; we merely frown at it. But don't you think that the Hindu attitude to widow re-marriage goes one better than the Bible? So Bene Israel attitude to widow re-marriage goes one better than the Bible! Is not this a good thing?" [16]

It is not suggested here that Bene Israel, whose position in Konkan society was not of the mystic and pre-ordained kind, formed a caste proper. Nevertheless, it has been shown that features belonging to a true caste structure entered into the relations between Bene Israel and Hindus: like other groups, Bene Israel were associated with a traditional occupation; relations between Bene Israel and Hindus were governed by the concept of pollution; oriented in terms of the caste system, Bene Israel adopted some of the practices and values of those privileged and endowed with a higher dignity and, like other lowly placed groups, thereby attempted to raise their position

in Konkan society. Indeed, even Kehimkar, who maintains that Bene Israel "kept themselves aloof" and did not adopt Hindu values, on occasion reveals an orientation to the caste system: members of the Bene Israel family of Ashtamkar "resemble very much the Konkanasth Brahmins . . . ," he notes with great approval, and are "well known for speaking pure Marathi . . . equally good as [sic] that used by Brahmins . . ." [17]

Moreover, features belonging to a true caste structure also entered into the relations of Bene Israel with each other. Bene Israel were divided into two units, the Gora or White Bene Israel and the Kala or Black Bene Israel. The former are believed to be the pure descendants of the seven couples who landed in the Konkan, the latter are known to be the offspring of unions between Bene Israel men and non-Bene Israel women—though it is obvious from the skin colour of the Gora that some unions between their ancestors and non-Bene Israel must have taken place. [18] Indeed, there are Gora, White Bene Israel, who are darker than Kala, Black Bene Israel. It would seem therefore that Kala are the offspring of mixed unions which for some reason or other have been remembered, while unions between the ancestors of the Gora and non-Bene Israel have been forgotten—perhaps the ancestors of the Kala contracted unions with non-Bene Israel later than did those of the Gora.

Kehimkar maintains that Kala are the offspring of "illicit unions, either temporary or permanent," and not of inter-marriages proper. He suggests, moreover, that although the very existence of Kala "shows that the state of morality was one lower than it is now," illicit unions are less of an "abomination" than inter-marriages proper. [19] Similarly, Hutton relates: "It is not uncommon in some parts of India for a man of one caste to keep a concubine of a lower caste, or even a non-Hindu, and he is not outcasted by his caste fellows on that ground. . . ." But ". . . a person marrying outside the caste is ex-communicated." [20]

Until some years ago, Gora and Kala neither intermarried nor interdined. A woman of the Bene Israel community told me: "My mother used to get furious when Kala came near her cooking utensils, and would push them away. She would not allow Kala to touch any utensils which she used for food." Gora and Kala worshipped in the same synagogue. But Kala were given the sanctified wine, distributed in the synagogue after the service on Sabbaths and Holy-days, only after Gora had been served.

It appears that Kala rank could not be mitigated. Kehimkar relates that in 1846 a wealthy man who exercised great influence over the community

> attempted to introduce his own child born from an alien woman as a real Bene Israel by taking that child to a public feast to dine from the same dish with him and others; the Bene Israel strongly objected to it. As soon as the child sat at the table, the whole party present on the occasion dispersed, being greatly indignant at this attempt to remove the anciently recognized distinction between the real Israel and Black or Kala Israel. [21]

It is difficult to ascertain the correct number of Kala. Obviously, no one will admit to being Kala; and as a result of the diminishing discrimination against Kala in matters social and ritual it is difficult for the non-Bene Israel to identify them. [22] But while Gora no longer discuss the subject openly a Gora may point out a Kala behind his back, especially if he is on bad terms with him. In this manner I came across some fourteen Kala elementary families. Gora are not certain about the number of Kala, though they hold that there are more than fourteen Kala elementary families. A Gora told me: "Most people don't worry about Gora and Kala these days. After all, Gora and Kala observe the same religious practices. We are all equal! But when it comes to marriage, most Gora don't like their children to marry Kala. Yet there have been some marriages between Gora and Kala in recent years. [23] What to do?—But don't mention that I discussed the subject with you! Perhaps I should not have talked about it. Kala will be hurt. After all, now all are equal. I told you because you are interested in it from a sociological point of view. So it wasn't gossip!"

Gora and Kala were clearly not fully castes in the Hindu sense. There was but a one-sided dependence: Kala worshipped in the synagogue of the Gora, but Gora did not need the services of Kala. There was no differentiation in religious observances. There was no differentiation in occupation. But like Hindu castes, Gora and Kala were conceived of as existing in different degrees of spiritual dignity. Gora, believed to be of pure blood, were exalted, while Kala bore the stigma of their descent. [24] Moreover, the restrictions on social relations between Gora and Kala resembled the restrictions on social relations between Hindu castes.

Like the Hindus, Bene Israel lived in joint families. Sons brought their wives to their father's home, and daughters left after marriage. Informants told me that at least one of a man's sons was expected to marry his father's sister's daughter. Descent was reckoned in the male line.

Three *Kajis* [25] acted as priests and judges of the Bene Israel. The *Kaji* office was hereditary; moreover, *Kaji* hereditary privileges were confirmed by the local rulers.

According to Bene Israel tradition, the *Kaji* office was introduced by David Rahabi, a co-religionist. He is supposed to have stumbled upon the Bene Israel by accident.

Bene Israel are uncertain about the date of Rahabi's coming. Some hold that he came about a thousand years ago, others say that he came some five hundred years ago, etc. Because the word "Rahab" is occasionally used in the Bible to designate Egypt,[26] Bene Israel infer that Rahabi came from that country.

Although David Rahabi was convinced that the Bene Israel were the real descendants of the Hebrews [Kehimkar relates][27] he still wanted to test them further. He therefore, it is said, gave their women clean and unclean fish to be cooked together; but they promptly singled out the clean fish from the unclean ones, saying that they never used fish that had neither fins nor scales.

Being thus satisfied that the Bene Israel were indeed Jews, Rahabi initiated their first religious revival. He is supposed to have instructed three young men—Jhiratkar, Shapurkar and Rajpurkar—and these, thus trained, assumed the *Kaji* office.

Olsvanger, who published Kehimkar's book in 1937, comments: "What documents or references are there to prove the historicity of this David Rahabi?" [28] However, there is a document to prove the real existence of this man. For there is a Rahabi family in Cochin in whose unpublished family history, a manuscript written in Hebrew, I have read that a member of the family, David Ezekiel Rahabi, went to western India in the middle of the eighteenth century, in the course of his work for the Dutch East India Company, there encountered the Bene Israel, and reformed the Judaism that he found existent among them.[29] Kehimkar relates that a family with the surname Rahabi is found in Cochin;[30] nevertheless he maintains that David Rahabi did not come from Cochin. For such an admission would lead one to ask whether Rahabi was really the first

Cochin Jew to come across Bene Israel and would thus undermine the Bene Israel tradition that their isolation from their co-religionists until recent times—an isolation which, Bene Israel assert, accounts for their past orientation to the Hindu social system—was interrupted but once.[31]

Some time during the eighteenth century Bene Israel began to settle in Bombay. Informants said: "Employment and education could be found in Bombay, offering our people greater respectability and social advancement." Nowadays some 12,000 Bene Israel live in Bombay.[32]

The move to Bombay led to more than mere change of habitat and occupation. In the Konkan Bene Israel had been dispersed over many villages, forming part and parcel of the life in the village in which they found themselves. Spatial proximity and many common cultural forms made the Bene Israel as much members of their village community as of their caste group—perhaps more so, because their caste group happened to be a particularly dispersed one.[33] But the great possibilities of employment in the fast developing city encouraged the formation of a sizeable group, leading to more complex relations between co-members. Furthermore, the presence within the same locality of different groups, speaking different languages and having different cultural forms, encouraged intra-group cohesion. In Bombay Bene Israel emerged as a community, a strongly knit kind of group bound together by their common life.

Moreover, Bene Israel religious life flourished in Bombay: synagogues were built; periodicals devoted to instruction in the principles and practices of Judaism came into being; books of Jewish interest were translated into Marathi, the mother tongue of the Bene Israel; and so on. Furthermore, Bene Israel began to refer to themselves as "Jew caste." [34]

The second religious revival of the Bene Israel was assisted by the arrival of a small group of Cochin Jews in the early nineteenth century who, like David Rahabi, devoted themselves to the teaching of Judaism, but this time in a professional capacity. Paradoxically, the religious revival was helped forward by the activities of the missionaries. Bene Israel told me: "The translation of the Bible into Marathi by the missionaries was a great boon. For the first time the Bible reached the community in a language with which all were familiar, giving all an idea of Judaism, and greatly indebting them to the translators. Christian missions with their schools and classes have been an important means of speeding the community on the way to religious reform."

But the Baghdadi who came to Bombay in the late eighteenth century, Kehimkar relates, "have never as a community done any thing for the religious and educational welfare of the Bene Israel." [35] Nevertheless, it is suggested here that the Baghdadi played an important part in the nineteenth-century religious revival of the Bene Israel—and not only because the former, familiar with Hebrew and the minutiae of Jewish religious practices, provided the Bene Israel with an example of Jewish orthodoxy. For the Baghdadi had outstripped the Bene Israel in a number of ways. The leaders of the Baghdadi community pioneered in industry, providing employment for many thousands of people. They built museums and public libraries. They subsidized the entire religious, educational and charitable services of their community. Moreover, Bene Israel relate, "Baghdadi shared the privileges of the Europeans in India." At that time, then, Baghdadi not only enjoyed religious superiority, but also wealth and prestige. Concerned to raise their status in the Bombay hierarchy Bene Israel claimed alignment with their highly placed co-

religionists. No wonder then that Bene Israel religious life flourished in Bombay, emphasizing their oneness with the Baghdadi.

A closer examination of the veracity of some of the Bene Israel historical memories indicates that this is not an unfair interpretation of the group's orientation to Judaism and Jewry in the nineteenth century.

Bene Israel assert that they were completely isolated from their co-religionists for some two thousand years—an isolation which, Bene Israel assert, accounts for their past orientation to the Hindu social system. Nevertheless, there is evidence for the view that Bene Israel isolation from their co-religionists was much less complete than their historical memories suggest.

For example, Maimonides speaks of the Jews of India, and it is generally assumed that he is referring to the Bene Israel. Thus at least in the twelfth century the existence of the Bene Israel was not unknown to their co-religionists. [36]

Again, it seems certain that Rahabi was not the only Cochin Jew to visit the Bene Israel before the nineteenth century. For Buchanan writes about his visit to Cochin: [37]

The Black Jews communicated to me much interesting intelligence concerning their brethren the ancient Israelites in the East. . . . They recounted the names of many other small colonies resident in northern India, Tartary and China, and gave me a written list of SIXTY-FIVE places. I conversed with those who had lately visited many of these stations, and were about to return again. The Jews have a never-ceasing communication with each other in the East. Their families indeed are generally stationary, being subject to despotic princes; but the men move much about in a commercial capacity and the same individual will pass through many extensive countries. So that when any thing interesting to the nation of the Jews takes place, the rumour will pass rapidly throughout Asia.

As soon as Buchanan came to Bombay he was approached by the Bene Israel who had heard of his talks with the Cochin Jews and wanted to discuss the prophecies of Isaiah with him.[38] It is true that Buchanan met both these Jewish communities in the early nineteenth century, at a time when contact with their Cochin co-religionists is admitted by the Bene Israel; however, Buchanan implies that contact between the Jewish groups in the East was of long standing, and moreover not infrequent. It would be difficult to believe that the Cochin Jews had much contact with many small, obscure Jewish communities in far-away places, but were not in contact with the Bene Israel who lived on the same coast line as themselves.

Again, there is evidence that the Bene Israel were not as ignorant of Hebrew as is generally assumed. For in an old Bene Israel cemetery in the Konkan I noticed a gravestone with a Hebrew inscription dated 1715—proof that Bene Israel were then not unfamiliar with at least the rudiments of that language. But if, as seems certain, Rahabi met and taught the Bene Israel in the middle of the eighteenth century, it seems difficult to account for the existence of a Hebrew inscription some decades before his arrival, except on the assumption that Bene Israel never entirely forgot Hebrew or that Rahabi was not the first didactically inclined Jew to visit them.[39]

Closer examination of even the few data cited here thus strongly suggests that the Bene Israel were not as isolated from Jewry or as ignorant of Judaism as their historical memories imply. But before the move to Bombay the group's habitual relations had been with the Hin-dus. Bene Israel orientation to Judaism and their co-religionists took place at a time when the latter entered the social environment of the former as a highly placed group, an orientation which Bene Israel, not unnaturally, represent as a re-discovery.

It might be argued that all the data imply is that the Bene Israel change in orientation was facilitated by the entry of their co-religionists into the social environment; but that the data do not imply that the change in orientation was connected with the position of their co-religionists in the social environment. However, there was more to their co-religionists' entry into the social environment of the Bene Israel than mere orientation of the latter to the former. For Baghdadi argued that Bene Israel were more Indian than Jewish and refused to accord them "pure" Jewish status. The attitude of the Baghdadi led to much strife between the two Jewish communities of Bombay.

The Bene Israel concern over the Baghdadi attitude justifies the interpretation put forward here of the Bene Israel nineteenth-century religious revival. For Jewish communities can exist side-by-side, in a repetitive fashion, and in any number. Moreover, from the point of view of Judaism differences between Jewish communities, as long as they are compatible with its Code, merely denote the different sections, of equal status, in the extensive religious group. Hence from the point of view of Judaism Bene Israel had but little need to concern themselves with the Baghdadi who, as Dr. E. Moses, a leading member of the Bene Israel community, complained in a letter to the *Jewish Advocate*, an Indian-Jewish paper, in February 1945, "are foremost in running down the Bene Israel," denying them "pure" Jewish status. Bene Israel formed a viable Jewish community of their own. Why then the concern over the Baghdadi attitude?

It is suggested here that the Bene Israel concern over the Baghdadi attitude makes sense only when considered in relation to the damage in status within the local hierarchy which the former ascribed to the attitude of the latter. Such an interpretation is corroborated by the change which the relations between the two Jewish communities have undergone in recent years. Though virtually all Bene Israel informants in Bombay frequently complained about the Baghdadi attitude, many of them indicated that they could now afford to be less sensitive to Baghdadi criticism than before: "In the new India all are equal. Now Baghdadi are no better than Bene Israel. Now all are equal. Now what does it matter?" Other informants referred to changes in the economic position of the Baghdadi community: "Baghdadi could always get work in the Sassoon mills. But now the mills have been sold. Now all are equal." Some informants stressed the rights and obligations which were now blurring the boundary between Bene Israel and Baghdadi. For example, some Bene Israel children are now being admitted to the Baghdadi communal school; some Bene Israel teachers are now being employed in the Baghdadi communal school; during the last war Baghdadi invited Bene Israel to co-operate in defence activities rendered necessary by German anti-Jewish propaganda in India. "Baghdadi don't seem to claim an exclusive title to the true creed these days," an informant told me. "But this is not because Bene Israel are now more orthodox. It is because it doesn't matter so much these days. It is because Baghdadi can no longer play the part of the higher Jew caste." As elsewhere in India, where religious prestige is tied to secular power, loss of the latter tends to diminish the former.

The Bene Israel situation is, however, not unique within Jewry. For the world beyond the Jewish horizon—by no means as irrelevant as Judaism would make it appear to be—everywhere counteracts the circumscribing intentions of the Jewish Code and significantly affects the relations within Jewish communities and between them and their respective environments. Moreover, the world beyond the Jewish horizon interferes with the effectiveness of common religion as a principle of unity. The relations of Jewish communities with each other and between them and their respective societies thus provide material for the study of the basis and efficacy of various principles of social alignment.

Notes

[1] This paper is based on a field study carried out in Bombay. The study was financed by the Department of Educational and Cultural Reconstruction of the Conference on Jewish Material Claims Against Germany.

[2] M. N. Srinivas, *Religion and Society among the Coorgs of South India*, Oxford, 1952, p. 30. But mere imitation, L. Dumont and D. Pocock write in "Village Studies", *Contributions to Indian Sociology*, No. 1, The Hague, 1957, p. 35, "without some other economic or political factor brings about no change in the relative position of castes."

[3] Srinivas, ibid., p. 31.

[4] J. H. Hutton, *Caste in India*, 2nd ed., London, 1951, pp. 2, 115.

[5] Whenever I asked my informants for the source of their historical memories, they replied: "It's in Kehimkar's book." H. S. Kehimkar, a member of the Bene Israel community, wrote *The History of the Bene Israel of India* in 1897. The book was published in Tel-Aviv in 1937 (some decades after the author's death) by the good offices of Dr. Immanuel Olsvanger. A copy of Kehimkar's book is found in most Bene Israel homes.

[6] Allen H. Godbey, too, in his *The Lost Tribes: A Myth*, Duke University Press, 1930, p. 339, says that lack of knowledge of the festival of Hanukkah and the destruction of the temple by the Romans which led to the re-introduction of the four

fasts of national mourning) "seems decisive evidence of settlement in India long ere the Christian era . . ." (I shall refer to this point again.)

[7] For example, the *Gazetteer of the Bombay Presidency*, Bombay, 1885, vol. xviii, Part 1, p. 506, suggests that the Bene Israel came to India from the Persian Gulf or Aden in the sixth century C.E. J. Wilson, in his *Appeal for the Christian Education of the Bene Israel*, Bombay, 1866, relinquishes his previous opinion (put forward in his *Lands of the Bible*, Bombay, 1847, Vol. 2, pp. 667–79) that the Bene Israel are the descendants of the Ten Tribes, and suggests instead that they are Jews, descendants of the Kingdom of Judah, who came to India from the Yemen in the sixth century C.E.

[8] Godbey, ibid., p. 33.

[9] However, Professor G. S. Ghurye, who was good enough to discuss this point with me, suggested that if the Konkan village community abstained from oil buying on Saturdays, the abstention must be explained in terms of Konkan Hindu ritual and not in connexion with the Bene Israel oil-pressers. (But is it not possible that in course of time Konkan Hindus also came to connect abstention from oil buying on Saturdays with the Bene Israel oil-pressers who rested on that day? At any rate, Mr. Avalaskar seems to have done so.)

[10] This informant said too: "Perhaps I should not have told you this. Bombay Bene Israel would not have told you this. They don't want to remember about their status in the Konkan. But perhaps they don't remember. Bombay Bene Israel have been away from the Konkan for some generations. And they have risen. They are clerk caste in Bombay." (Bene Israel first came to Bombay in the middle of the eighteenth century.) I asked this informant how he accounted for the change in the relations between Bene Israel and Hindus in the Konkan in the last twenty years. He replied: "There has been much educational and also some economic improvement among Konkan Bene Israel. Besides Hindus are less orthodox now." H. S. Kehimkar in *The History of the Bene Israel of India*, pp. 51, 56, too, speaks of the low status of the Bene Israel in Konkan society. Kehimkar, however, attrib-

utes this to their membership of a non-Hindu religious group. But then Kehimkar aimed at establishing that Bene Israel always regarded themselves and were regarded by their Indian neighbours as members of the Jewish religious group, and that Jewry must therefore accord the Bene Israel 'pure' Jewish status. (The significance which attached to the Bene Israel demand to be accorded "pure" Jewish status will be discussed presently.) Though there are of course regional variations, it is worth while pointing out that M. N. Srinivas in "The Social System of a Mysore Village," in *Village India, Studies in the Little Community*, American Anthropological Association, Memoir No. 83, 1955, pp. 2, 22, while including the Muslims in his list of the castes of the village, does not suggest that their membership of a non-Hindu religious group automatically makes them as polluting as the lower castes. Srinivas acknowledges, however, that there are "excessive uncertainties as to their hierarchical position." Hutton, ibid., p. 82, writes: "Generally speaking, Muslims and Christians are regarded as inferior to Brahmans and Nayars in Malabar, but as less polluting than the lower castes . . ."

[11] M. Ezekiel, *The History and Culture of the Bene Israel in India* (a booklet), Bombay, 1948, pp. 26–7. Alibag is a Konkan township.

[12] It seems, however, that the attempts of the Bene Israel to raise their status in Konkan society by adopting canons of behaviour of the higher castes met with but limited success.

[13] Ezekiel, ibid., p. 8, writes: ". . . there was a rich oil merchant. . . . It was he who took pity on these destitute people and gave them work. . . . It is thus that they learnt the oil pressing business. . . ." I am told, however, that it is not unusual for Hindu castes of low status to claim similarly that their position is purely empirical and fortuitous, the result of bad luck—in spite of the Hindu teaching that condition in this life is the result of conduct in the last incarnation.

[14] In any case, occupational specialization "has it limits," M. N. Srinivas writes in "The Social System of a Mysore Village," *Village India, Studies in the Little Community*, p.

16, since no single village or group of a few neighbouring villages can support an indefinite number of non-agriculturists.

[15] Ezekiel, ibid., p. 64. It is by no means uncommon for Jewish groups to hold that practices and values adopted from the wider society are in line with practices and values enjoined by the Jewish Code. It must be admitted, however, that though a number of Bene Israel asked me whether orthodox Jews in England ate beef, virtually all Bene Israel now know that beef eating is not prohibited in the Old Testament. (Kehimkar, ibid., p. 24, implies that prudence rather than past ignorance of Jewish dietary regulations encouraged the Bene Israel to abstain from eating beef.)

[16] The ban on polygamy among Western Jews represents an example of assimilation on lines similar to the dislike for widow remarriage among the Bene Israel. (Western Jewry, however, only holds that the ban on polygamy is in line with the values of Judaism, and not that it "goes one better than the Bible.")

[17] Kehimkar, ibid., pp. 56, 61, 90.

[18] Gora Bene Israel told me: "It is not skin colour which tells us who is Kala. It is known in the community who is Kala. There are some Gora who are a little dark, but not because of mixed unions. Poverty and the excessive heat of India greatly affected the fair complexion of our ancestors."

[19] Kehimkar, ibid., p. 51. Recently, however, some marriages proper between Bene Israel men and non-Bene Israel women have taken place. Bene Israel told me: "Nowadays such a mixed union is preceded by the woman's conversion to Judaism." They were uncertain as to whether the offspring of this type of union are Kala.

[20] Hutton, ibid., pp. 71, 63–4.

[21] Kehimkar, ibid., p. 32. (Kehimkar was born in 1830, and it is possible that he witnessed this incident.)

[22] Among Bene Israel as well as among other Bombay groups, the immense elaboration of economic, educational, and general social activities is in modern times creating class divisions between caste fellows. Caste and class, though theoretically antithetical, are accommodating themselves to each other. Among the Bene Israel, class divisions tend

to replace the Gora and Kala groupings—hence the diminishing discrimination against Kala.

[23] During my stay in Bombay a marriage between Gora and Kala took place. An informant remarked: "The girl's father was terribly upsét. He tried to stop it. After all, in our community marriage is arranged by the parents. The girl's father is against love-marriage—especially against love-marriage between Gora and Kola. But the couple insisted. Nowadays some people do insist on love-marriage. So the father gave in. He did not like it! But what to do?"

[24] A similar mode of grouping exists among Cochin Jewry. Neither the White Jews nor the Black Jews need the services of their Meshuararim. But the latter worship in the synagogues of their respective communities, and, moreover, bear the stigma of their descent.

[25] *Kaji* is an Arabic term. It has been suggested that the Arabic terms in use among the Bene Israel support the view (referred to above) that this group came to India from an Arabian country. However, the Muslims in India, too, use the term *Kaji* for their priest and judge. Bene Israel insist that they learnt the Arabic terms in use among them from their Muslim neighbours in the Konkan.

[26] For example in Psalms lxxxvii. 4; lxxxix. 11.

[27] Kehimkar, ibid., p. 41.

[28] Kehimkar, ibid., p. 40, footnote by Dr. L. Olsvanger.

[29] The Rahabi family came to Cochin from Aleppo in the middle of the seventeenth century. The family soon played an important part in Cochin Jewry. (Pereyra de Paiva mentions the family in his *Noticias dos Judeos de Cochim*, 1686.) For many years the Rahabi acted as agents of the Dutch East India Company.

[30] Kehimkar, ibid., p. 41.

[31] Even the few Bene Israel who told me that they were inclined to doubt the accuracy of the group's historical memories and who, moreover, hold that Rahabi came from Cochin in the middle of the eighteenth century, nevertheless maintain that the group's isolation from Jewry until recent times was interrupted but once by the arrival of Rahabi.

[32] The remainder of the 14,000 Bene Israel in India form small groups in various parts of the country. For example, there are some 400 Bene Israel in Poona; 460 Bene Israel are dispersed over 17 villages in the Konkan; about 40 live in Delhi. About 2,000 Bene Israel live outside India. For example, 900 Bene Israel have emigrated to Israel; a few live in England; there is a community of 400 in the capital of Pakistan.

[33] M. N. Srinivas, *Religion and Society among the Coorgs of South India*, pp. 31–2 describes the structural situation in India as subject to opposed types of solidarity. On the one hand, ". . . members of the same caste living in different villages have a great deal in common." On the other hand, ". . . members of a village community, whatever their caste, have certain interests in common." Srinivas terms the solidarity common to the caste group "horizontal solidarity," the solidarity common to sections of different castes occupying different positions in the hierarchy and living in one locality "vertical solidarity."

[34] Kehimkar, ibid., pp. 256, 257, 261, etc., cites letters written by the Bombay Bene Israel in the nineteenth century to government officials in which the group refers to itself as "Jew caste" or "Jew caste or Israel caste." In the census reports, too, Bene Israel referred to themselves as "Jews." It is not suggested here that the community dropped the name "Ben Israel" entirely. But it is suggested that the term "Jew caste" occurs often enough to be significant.

[35] Kehimkar, ibid., p. 56. Kehimkar admits, however, that Solomon David Sassoon and his nephew Jacob E. D. Sassoon "have of late years shown the nobleness of their family and the magnanimity of their mind in studying the welfare of the Bene Israel, and have thereby set an excellent example to their countrymen, who, we trust, will now take it to heart, and follow in their footsteps."

[36] 'But the Jews of India', Maimonides wrote to the Jews of Lunel at the end of the twelfth century, "do not know the Written Law. They have nothing of religion except that they rest on Saturday and perform circumcision on the eighth day." As the Jews of Cochin are known to have been familiar with the Written Law (The Law of Moses), the prophets, and parts of the Talmud, it is assumed that Maimonides was referring to the Bene Israel.

[37] C. Buchanan, *Christian Researches in Asia*, 4th ed., London, 1811, p. 225.

[38] Buchanan, ibid., p. 233.

[39] Rahabi was born in 1720. In any case, Bene Israel maintain that Rahabi did not teach them the meaning of Hebrew. Yet the composition of a Hebrew inscription obviously requires some knowledge of the meaning of Hebrew.

4 · Christianity and Islam among the Mossi[1]

ELLIOTT P. SKINNER

The twin forces of Christianity and Islam are both seriously contending for the conversion of the pagan masses of the Western Sudan. Islam first penetrated this region during the 11th century and succeeded in converting many people to its faith. Christianity arrived on the

SOURCE. Elliott P. Skinner, "Christianity and Islam among the Mossi," from *American Anthropologist*, Vol. 60, June, 1958, pp. 1102–1119.

scene only 60 years ago, and has not had the time to win many converts. However, there remained many societies in this area which were largely pagan until European conquests exposed them almost simultaneously to the influences of both Christianity and Islam. One such society, the Mossi, has been described as the principal island of resistance to Islam in the Sudan (Gouilly 1952:52). André (1924:31) states that the Mossi "offered to the Animists an irreducible rampart against the invasion of Islam." And Delafosse concurs that the Mossi "seem to have been particularly hostile to Islam which has made no progress among them since the Hegira. And although an appreciable number of Moslem strangers (Yarsé) lived among them, they have almost all remained pagans" (1912, vol. 3:187).

The first Christian Catholic missionaries arrived in Mossi territory in 1900, just four years after French conquest. These missionaries were kindly if fearfully received by the people, who gave them land for building a mission and for cultivating crops. The Mossi helped the Christians cultivate these crops and willingly allowed the children to attend the mission school. Nevertheless, when the missionaries tried to convert the children to Catholicism, the parents objected and withdrew the children from school (Socquet 1956:62). The Protestant American "Assemblies of God" mission first worked among the Mossi in 1926, and in 1931 they reported that the outlook for conversions was "hopeful" (Cooksey and McLeish 1931:215). But from 1926 to date, the Protestants have made negligible progress in their conversions. There are today about 155,000 Moslems, 26,000 Catholics, and 1,760 Protestants in a Mossi population of over 1,500,000. These figures attest to the fact that despite a long history of resistance to foreign religious systems, many Mossi are now abandoning their traditional religion. But the figures also show that while Islam is gaining many converts, the Catholics are making only slight progress, and the American Protestants hardly any at all. There are obviously many reasons for the differential advance of these three religious systems. In this paper I will examine and analyze the processes by which these religious systems attempt to gain converts, and delineate the reasons for their differential success.

The Mossi who are now feeling the impact of external religious influences represent the unique example of a Sudanese group which has preserved its ethnic identity and political autonomy through all the vicissitudes of Sudanic history until French conquest in 1896. Tradition records that the first Mossi rulers left the Dagomba region in the Gold Coast (present-day Ghana) during the 11th century and moved into the bend of the Niger River, carving out three large kingdoms and smaller principalities in the process. At the head of these still extant kingdoms are rulers (*Moro Nabas*) who hold feudal-like control of the provinces, districts, and villages which comprise their domains. A complex hierarchical administrative apparatus extends the power of the rulers into the smallest village, and funnels taxes and tribute back to them. French conquest modified this highly efficient system but did not greatly change it. The Mossi state apparatus rests on an economy which produces cotton cloth, horses, sheep, cattle, and goats, but the main support of this large population—one of the densest in the Sudan—is grain agriculture. Today, some Mossi districts still have as many as 70 persons per square mile.

The Mossi are divided into stratified royal, noble, and commoner patrilineages. Characteristic of this lineage system is a process by which royal sublineages descend serially until they merge with the mass of commoner lineages. Below the lineages there were once large non-Mossi groups of serfs and slaves, but these people have now been grouped into lineages and have become Mossi. Patrilocal polygynous extended family households, grouped into villages, form the basic Mossi settlement pattern. Marriages are arranged between unrelated persons through the agency of lineage members who establish "friendly" relationships. The two friends might ask their lineage heads for women to exchange as wives, or the "friend" who has received more gifts from his opposite number will give over a wife. Because only the older men have women and goods at their disposal, they are usually the ones who receive wives. The result is that most young men have no wives and must content themselves with occasional lovers until they inherit wives from lineage members. The Mossi have a great fear of incestuous relations which bring down the wrath of the ancestors (the Keemsé).

Ancestor veneration is at the core of Mossi religious behavior. The recent ancestors are notified, through sacrifices, of the important events in the lives of their descendants, and they are expected to aid in solving everyday problems. The ancestors also invoke their sanctions against antisocial behavior among their descendants. Once a year the Mossi people, in concert with the Moro Nabas, appeal to their individual and collective ancestors for good crops, large families, and for the preservation of the dynasty. Often associated with the ancestors as propitiatory agents are local deities called Tengkougas (sing. Tenkougre) or earth shrines, visibly manifested by clumps of trees, mountains, rocks, or rivers. Tengsobas or earth priests appeal to the Tengkougas on behalf of the local populations for help in sickness, for rain and good crops, and for children. When proper sacrifices are offered to the Tengkougas, their spiritual agents, called kinkirsé, enter the wombs of women and are born as children. Twins and children who die young are regarded as "evil" kinkirsé who entered a woman without being invited. Nevertheless, many persons consider twins as special gifts to parents in favor of the earth deities.

The earth itself, Tenga, is one of the principal deities of the Mossi. Tenga is considered the wife of a male deity called Winnam, Windé, or Naba Zidiwindé. The true nature of Winnam is not clear. The Mossi say: "Winnam is the sun, and Winnam is God"; he is considered a sun god as well as a supreme deity. Winnam is venerated but he is not feared, because it is the dead ancestors who chastise evil-doers by affliction or death. When wicked people die they face the wrath of the ancestors in Keemsétenga, or land of the ancestors.

The Mossi have several concepts of the spiritual essence or animating principle of man. First there is the seega (pl. seesé), an entity found in all living beings; it leaves the body during sleep, and its adventures provide the dreams of men. The seega can be captured during its nocturnal wanderings or in places where large crowds congregate. If the seega is captured and eaten by a sorcerer, its owner will die. A man's shadow is also called his seega; persons about to die have no shadows, since their seesé have either been stolen or have left on their own account.

Another principle called the keema (pl. keemsé) is associated with the dead or with persons about to die. The keema of a dying man wanders around and often frightens people; as soon as he is dead, he is no longer referred to by name but is called the "keema." Keemsé is also the word used for the generalized ancestors who sanction the behavior of the living and who must be placated if people wish to have enough food, wives, children, and good health. A man's own keemsé take a vital interest in his affairs, in return for which they receive nourishment in the form of the seesé (animals do not have keemsé) of sacrificed animals.

The breath, called vousem, is also considered an animating principle by the Mossi and, since it leaves the body through the nose at death, they believe that a man's nose is the first thing to die. It is not clear how the seega is disposed of when the body dies. Some people say it remains forever about the haunts of man; others believe that it goes to a mountain called Plimpikou and disappears into a cavern. Still others believe that the seega becomes the keema and goes to Plimpikou, from whence the keemsé come to visit their descendants. It is difficult to determine whether the Mossi have always been vague about their traditional religious concepts or whether this uncertainty is the result of the influx of such foreign creeds as Islam and Christianity.

The first recorded contact between the Mossi and Moslems took place around 1328 when the Yatenga Mossi attacked, burned, and sacked Timbuktu, then held by the Dia dynasty of the Songhoi (Dubois 1896:251). For more than a century afterward, the Mossi pursued a turbulent and aggressive policy in the region of the Niger bend, pushing as far as Gourma, Walata, and Banku (ibid.: 127). They were finally defeated and routed by Sonni Ali in 1477. In 1499, when Askia the Great (El Hadj Mohammed ben Abou Bekr, usurper of the Songhoi throne from the Sonni dynasty in 1494) returned from his pilgrimage to Mecca, he launched a *jihad* or holy war on the Mossi who had rejected his ultimatum to adopt Islam. Askia defeated the Mossi, "devastated the towns and countryside, took men, women, and children as prisoners, and forcibly converted these captives to Islam" (Dubois 1896:127–128). The pagan Mossi and the Moslem Songhoi fought several other battles until Songhoi power was broken by the Moroccans, who conquered Timbuktu in 1590.

The Moslems made no further attempt to convert the Mossi by force, but Moslem pressure did not stop; it now came in the peaceful guise of Moslem merchants and Yarsé Moslem refugees from the Mandingo cities such as Timbuktu and Djenne, who received permission from the Mossi rulers to settle in the country. However, judging from the reports of the first Europeans to reach the Mossi, the Moslems lived under many restrictions and were forbidden by the Moro Nabas to recite their prayers in public places (Tauxier 1912:585–586). Despite these restrictions, the Moslems were able to extend their influence through conversion of the cadet sons of the rulers and conversion of at least one ruler of the Ouagadougou Mossi dynasty.

About 1780 Naba Kom, the son of Zombré and a Yarsé Moslem woman, permitted the Yarsé to live in the villages and sent one of them to the Gold Coast for religious instruction. His son, Naba Sagha, was involved in a civil war and replaced some dissident pagan district chiefs with his Moslem sons. The present ruling lineage of Nobéré (where I worked) is descended from Ngado, one of these sons.[2] But although the rulers permitted their younger sons to adopt Islam, they themselves and the heirs to the thrones remained pagan in order to maintain the bonds with the ancestors. The exception to this rule was Doulougou, the grandson of Sagha, who was elected Moro Naba despite being a Moslem. Now the spread of Islam was given new impetus: Yarsé proselyting increased, mosques were built in Ouagadougou and in the villages, and many Koranic schools were founded. But with Doulougou's death the rulers reverted to paganism and Moslem influence declined. Nevertheless, the learned Moslem Imams continued to serve at court and used their knowledge of the outside world for the benefit of the rulers.

The Moslem Mossi showed the greatest hostility to the first Europeans who arrived in the country. The Imam of Yako, under the influence of his Tidjani son (who had made the pilgrimage to Mecca), refused to have any dealings with Europeans. Furthermore, he convinced the Moro Naba that death awaited any ruler who granted an audience to a European. When the French attacked the Mossi in 1896, an Imam from Béré, a former pilgrim, told the ruler to flee and not depend on his ill-equipped soldiers to defeat the gun-bearing invaders. Lamberth reported that the Moslems told the defeated and demoralized Mossi that "as soon as all the blacks become Moslems, the whites will leave" (Tauxier 1912: 792).

No one knows how many Moslems were in Ouagadougou when the French arrived. Delafosse (1912, vol. 3:193) records that around the turn of the century there were about 42 Koranic schools with 230 students scattered around the country. Tauxier (1912:793), writing about the same period, states that there were 33 Koranic schools with about 358 students. No Koranic schools were reported for the Nobéré and Manga districts, but I know that there were several in the neighboring district of Béré. In 1926 there were 70 Koranic schools and 4,000 Moslems in Ouagadougou (seven percent of whom were non-Mossi). By 1944 there were about 240 schools and approximately 25,000 Moslems. The last census, 1954, did not record the number of Koranic schools but gave the figure of 60,000 Moslems in the Ouagadougou region.[3] The 4,000 Moslems of Nobéré comprise 42 percent of that district's population. With the exception of one Catholic school master and the Catholic catechist who came to the district during 1956, the population is pagan. It might be relevant to point out that Nobéré has the highest percentage of Moslems in Kombissiri, an administrative unit (a subdivision) which has 152,000 pagans, 23,000 Moslems, 3,000 Catholics, and about 100 Protestants.

As noted above, Islam first came into the Nobéré district with Ngado, who replaced a dissident pagan chief, but Ngado's lineal descendants reverted to paganism until a few years ago when the present district chief became a nominal Moslem. The cadet sons of Ngado did not revert to paganism, and today all the noble sublineages of the district are Moslem. We may note here that one of the main aspects of Islamic proselytization in this district, as elsewhere among the Mossi, has been the conversion of persons who do not hold strategic positions vis-à-vis the ancestors. The present chief is no exception to this rule, because he is only a nominal Moslem. His eldest son is the only one in the family who is not a Moslem—a status which is becoming increasingly difficult to maintain in a growing Moslem population. The chief himself became partially converted to Islam in gratitude to a Moslem Hausa trader who cured his illness. He recites the five daily prayers and observes most of the prescriptions of Islam, but he still drinks European beer, subscribes to many pagan rites and beliefs, and supervises the annual Péléga or sacrifice to the ancestors. This dual allegiance is politically expedient because the chief can function as the head of the Moslem community as well as the traditional head of all the people. He does have occasional difficulty with intolerant Moslems who wish him to become a devout Moslem, and with the traditionalists who claim that today the crops are smaller, the people sicker, and the women barren because of the neglect of the ancestors. However, with the approach of holy days, these differences are resolved in the interest of community harmony.

The chiefs of the villages under the overall command of the district chief are mainly pagan, since they are descended from the district chief replaced by Ngado. Yet they command villages inhabited by the noble Moslem sublineages of the ruling house as well as by commoner lineages. The village chief cannot become a Moslem because he too is responsible for sacrifices to the ancestors, without whose help his people would suffer. He does not take an active part in Moslem festivities, but receives the homage due a chief from the Moslems on these and other occasions. However, most village chiefs show an interest in Moslem affairs, and one of them, the chief of Vooko, built a prayer-circle (*misseri*) for Moslems who came to pay homage.

The pivotal role which the village chief plays in the exchange of wives between Moslems and pagans has led indirectly to the increase of the Moslem population. Before the French conquest he gave the Moslems more wives than he received from them. This unequal exchange, plus the nobles' prerogative of seizing the wives of pagans, contributed to the increase of the Moslems.

The conversion of Mossi to Islam is sometimes accompanied by a rupture in the relationships between persons involved in "friendships" with a view of obtaining wives. A great quarrel developed in the district between a pagan chief and a recent convert who refused to give the chief a daughter promised as a wife. The chief became furious and claimed that the Moslem had broken a promise made years ago, but the Moslem claimed that it was against his new religion to give his daughter to a pagan. It is not true that Moslems in the village do not exchange wives with pagans, but the Moslems often try to convert their pagan friends so that the brides will not have to revert to paganism. The chief's difficulty was that he could not become a Moslem because of his ritual and ceremonial relationship with the ancestors. The Moslem men do not have such difficulties with their pagan wives because most women follow their husband's dictates in religious and other matters. Many Moslem men attempt to prevent their wives from having sacrifices made to the ancestors, but if a woman really wishes such a sacrifice she can easily have it arranged through her pagan relatives. If a woman married to a Moslem refuses to observe Islamic practices, she is liable to divorce and runs the risk of having her children taken away.

Mossi anxiety over children is often instrumental in converting them to Islam. When a woman is barren or her young children die, she consults a soothsayer (*barga*). She is either told that her Tengkougre benefactor was not amply rewarded and recalled the children, or that her "Moslem" children (children who wished to be Moslems) were angry because they were given pagan names. In the latter case she is advised to make a gift to a Moslem and to ask her husband to build a Moslem prayer-circle outside his hut so that when her children "return" (are born again) they will see it. Finally, she is advised to give all her children Moslem names. I could discover no reason why the pagan soothsayers advise these anxious parents to adopt Islam, except that they hope that complicated prescriptions will be more efficacious. Nevertheless, so effective is this technique for gaining converts to Islam that even members of the family of the chief pagan priest are not immune to it. Furthermore, once a woman has a Moslem child, all her other children must be Moslems or they will die. A man whose children are all Moslem has no recourse except to adopt Islam if he wants a funeral, because his Moslem sons may not give him a pagan funeral.

Every Mossi, whether Moslem or non-Moslem, wishes a proper funeral, and now that travel has increased the fact of being Moslem or pagan is of great importance. Many young migrants to Ashanti have reported that their dead pagan comrades were unceremoniously disposed of, while the local Christians and Moslems took care of their dead coreligionists. But despite this fact, and the belief of administrators and missionaries, I found no evidence that the seasonal and other migration of Mossi youth to Ghana and the Ivory Coast have contributed very much to the spread of Islam. It is true that some of the thousands of Mossi who fled their homeland to escape forced labor or military service ultimately returned as Moslems, but the majority of seasonal migrants do not have enough contact with foreign populations for them to become Moslems. Most of the Mossi who migrate to Ghana work on cocoa farms far removed from large centers of population. It is also true that even those Mossi who worked for Moslems on the farms and found it expedient to "pray" (as the Mossi refer to conversion to Islam) soon reverted to paganism on their return in order to escape the displeasure of their lineage members. I have recorded several cases of pagans who became Moslems only when they returned from abroad to find their relatives all converted to Islam.

Today there are obvious rewards for those Mossi who embrace Islam; besides such tangible rewards as getting wives and children, there are the intangible ones of upward social mobility and greater prestige. It is important to note that most liberated slaves and serfs are now Moslems. Formerly these non-Mossi had low status, but today those who have been to Mecca bear such proud titles as *Hadji*. On the night before Ramadan, one of these men gave a talk before the Nobéré chief during which he chided the chief for his impiety and voiced the hope that the next chief would be a true Moslem. He admitted that the chief might interpret such a speech from a former serf as impertinence, but he begged him to accept the censure as coming from the servant of *Nabiyama* (the prophet). This same man had refused to pay homage to the chief at the annual sacrifice to the ancestors, and when admonished returned the daughter which the chief had given him as a wife. In earlier days a chief would not have given a daughter to a serf, and moreover, a disrespectful serf could be killed instantly.

Many French administrators and Christian missionaries allege that Mossi youth embrace Islam because they like the beautiful robes and red fezzes of the Moslems, but this is a naive explanation for the conduct of a highly sophisticated people. Most young men in Nobéré wear Moslem-type clothes because such clothes are the mode. Now that sun helmets, dark glasses, and women's raincoats with hoods are in vogue, pagans as well as Moslems wear them. What is of interest, however, is that when pagans become Moslems they wear cleaner clothes and affect a different style of life.

The local consensus is that Moslems are much better behaved than pagans because they do not swear, fight, or get drunk in public. The man chosen as Imam is required to have such characteristics as mercy toward evil-doers, benevolence, magnanimity, physical beauty, and virility. Yet many Mossi say that the Moslems can be worse than any other people. They accuse them of being charlatans, of selling Koranic verses as charms, and of committing murder by the use of magical formulae. Neither pagans nor Moslems believe that a man is necessarily good because he recites his daily prayers or goes to Mecca.

Moslems in the district follow most precepts of their religion: they recite the five daily prayers according to the rites of Tidjani (there are only two Moslems of the Hamada sect in the district and no members of the Hamallist sect), give alms to the poor, observe the month-long fast (called by the Mossi the *Karême*), celebrate the great festival of Ramadan and the lesser festivals, and aspire to make the pilgrimage to Mecca. Most of the Moslems can lead prayers, but only about one-tenth of their number can read and recite the Koran. However, today the masters (*karasambas*) of the 32 Koranic schools in the district are endeavoring to instruct the many boys and few girls in reading the Koran and understanding Moslem theology.

The Karême is observed by most adult Moslems in the community with the exception of invalids and working men.

Moslems say that the fast is intended to turn the minds of the people to God, and they distinguish between the Moslems "of the mouth" who break the fast and those "of the heart" who fast until Ramadan. The crescent moon of Ramadan is greeted with guns and general rejoicing and the following morning the Moslems gather at the tomb of Ngado to give praises to God; during the rest of the day they pay homage to the chief and visit their friends. However, a change in the traditional observance of Ramadan is expected, because one of the Moslem leaders objects to the ceremony at the tomb of Ngado. He feels that some Moslems are beginning to regard the tomb of the first Moslem as an earth shrine or Teng-kougre.

So far, only five of the more prominent Moslems in the district have made or are making the pilgrimage to Mecca. The first man made the voyage about seven years ago, and is now conducting a Koranic school in a neighboring district. His brother went to Mecca about two years ago and is now the senior *El Hadj* in the district. Of the two men who were on the pilgrimage when I arrived in the district, one has since died near the Red Sea and the other is still away. One other man left for Mecca and returned to the district during my stay. Most of the pilgrims now fly to Mecca; only two men followed the traditional route through Ghana, Kano, Lake Chad, the Anglo-Egyptian Sudan (now Sudan), and on to Mecca. In general, all pilgrims have used their own resources for the trip, but they receive some help from their lineage brothers and from the other Moslems in the district and in Ouagadougou.

The pilgrimage to Mecca represents the greatest event in the lives of the district Moslems. When the last pilgrim left, a great crowd gathered at his house and prayed for his safe journey, and some even accompanied him to Ouagadougou and remained there until he left. The Moslems and many pagans of the district, under the command of the district chief, cultivated his fields during his absence. And when the new El Hadj returned, a large crowd accompanied him to his house with shouts of joy. There he killed a sheep in thanksgiving, sprinkled the crowd with holy water from Mecca, and recounted his experiences. His listeners were impressed by his airplane flight and the description of Mecca, but they showed the greatest interest when he said that Meccan women covered their faces and that most Meccan men were monogamous. The local Moslems smiled when they heard this bit of news from one of their members, but I have seen them scowl when discussing the monogamous practice desired by the Christians.

The attitudes of Moslems differ very little from those of the other Mossi as regards children and polygyny. They say that they do not believe in the efficacy of ancestor veneration and do not "kill chickens" to the ancestors, but they maintain that it is a man's duty to have many wives so that he may have children to succeed him. Furthermore, since Mohammed himself decreed that his followers may keep four wives, provided they treat each with the same degree of kindness, there is no conflict between Islamic tenets and Mossi practice of polygny. The average Moslem has two wives, but even the few men in the district who have more than four wives do not appear overly concerned about transgressing the tenets of their faith. Mossi Moslems have not adopted the paternal parallel cousin marriage so common among other Moslems, and show surprise when told that Islam permits such marriages. However, they have modified their marriage behavior to harmonize with what they consider an Islamic tenet that "a man should not marry the widow of his father." The Moslem Mossi profess to look with horror on these marriages among their pagan brothers, preferring the levirate instead.

The Moslems' attitude toward the low status of women in Mossi society has not changed, and in one respect it can even be said that this attitude has been strengthened. Many Moslem wives now cover their faces, and many El Hadjis have attempted to place their wives in purdah by preventing them from going to the market for fear they would come in contact with pagan men. The development of this practice is running counter to the growing emancipation of Mossi women, who have just begun to leave their villages for periodic visits to the larger towns. Nevertheless, the important fact is that the Mecca pilgrims have the opportunity to see Moslem women playing roles which are forbidden or unknown to Mossi women. And while it is true that the Mossi pilgrims would not easily adopt and foster monogamy, their receptivity to new Islamic beliefs and customs might have a liberating effect on their treatment of women. Once institutional and cultural changes have been accepted by the El Hadjis, they are likely to spread quite rapidly throughout the society because men who have visited Mecca are believed to have returned filled with wisdom and understanding.

Christianity came to the Mossi on January 24, 1900, shortly after French conquest. As noted above, the first missionaries were well treated, but the Mossi balked at the attempts at conversion. Nevertheless, by 1919 the White Fathers of the Catholic missions had established several centers, among which was the district of Manga where this study was conducted. Manga is considered a Catholic district, but there are only 3,000 Catholics out of a population of 124,000— which also includes 9,200 Moslems and five Protestants. Thus, in contrast to Moslem Nobéré, which has no Catholics or Protestants, Manga, like most districts in Mossi territory, has a Moslem community.

The conversion of the Mossi in Manga to Catholicism follows the classical pattern of missionary proselytization in the country. Monsignor Socquet (1956:62) states that the Mossi always react to attempts at conversion with the statement: " 'We are looking at our chief,' that is to say, 'We will follow our chief in conversion as in all other matters. If he is favorable to it, then we will not go against his will.' " Socquet concludes: "It is thus understandable how important is the conversion of the chiefs, or, at least, their sympathy for our religion, in the spread of Catholicism." The missionaries may have been successful in the village of the Manga district chief because he was sympathetic to them, but they made few converts in the villages far from the district center or in the neighboring districts. In the Béré district, a few miles from Manga, the Catholics have made only 22 converts despite more than 15 years' work. In Manga, however, they were able to "recruit" most of the young children for their church and school. When an old man was asked why his children became Catholic, he tried to evade the question but finally replied that he did not control the minds of his children. Knowing the nature of administrative practice in the upper Volta before 1946, and the nature of Mossi family structure, we looked further for the answer.

Paradoxically, it comes from a Catholic missionary, André Dupont, who, seeking to discover the reason for the decrease of patients in the Catholic-controlled maternity clinics, asked:

Why have the maternity clinics which in 1942 served more than seventy mothers a month now serve only two or three? "We are no longer forced to go," reply the villagers. Was it the fear of sanction which accounted for the unanimous use of the clinics? Alas! It would seem to be so. The use of force and sanction have rendered odious an institution of charity. It would have been better if the mothers were only encouraged to use the clinics. "These natives do not understand," I am told sometimes. But how does one expect them to understand? (Dupont 1949:4)

Fear was certainly one of the reasons why the people in Manga embraced Catholicism. Before 1946 (the Brazzaville conference in 1944 abolished forced labor), men and women were recruited for work on the roads and on Ivory Coast plantations, and children were recruited for the schools. The district chiefs often gathered orphans and the children of their former serfs and sent them to the mission to fill the quotas, but many children and whole families voluntarily attached themselves to the missions. The reasons for so doing are legion, but in some cases it was simply the desire to accept the new religious faith.

Once at the mission the children were taught French and the tenets of Catholicism. Many of the boys later became catechists or priests and several girls went into the nunnery. However, the largest group of educated youths became the clerical personnel of the administration and were lost to missionary activity. Because the administration lacked French-speaking Mossi, the young people received good jobs. This desertion to the administration has become so serious that the missionaries at Manga have ceased to teach French to their catechists and now use the vernacular.

Conversion to Catholicism, bringing with it the knowledge of French, was formerly one of the sure roads to upward social mobility. Most Catholic teachers at Manga (and at Nobéré) are individuals who were recruited as unwilling schoolboys but today are the highest paid members of their lineages. Other gains have accrued to persons who become Catholics. For example, the people at Manga believe that the missionaries used their influence with the administration to have one of their converts, a younger son of the late chief, elected to the district chieftainship over his elder brother. This belief is probably unfounded, since the Moro Naba seems to be electing the literate sons of chiefs to their fathers' positions so that educated chiefs, and not educated commoners, can serve as members of French parliamentary bodies. Unfortunately, the people of Manga do not understand modern political problems, and have accepted the new chief only because of their traditional respect for the chieftainship.

The conversion of the Manga chief to Catholicism has not engendered many problems for his pagan subjects. The chief's primary duty—to begin the yearly ceremonial cycle of sacrifices to the ancestors—has been taken over by his father's brother, who is now considered the ritual head of the chiefly lineage. Nevertheless, to the chief still accrue the gains of this ceremony because his followers pay him homage and bring him gifts on his birthday, which comes at this period. Moslems in the community also pay their respects at this time, and they prefer his Catholic birthday celebration to the bloody sacrifices of chickens to the ancestors. On the other hand, the chief shows little of the common Catholic disapproval of Moslems and sends gifts to their leaders on the Moslem feast days. He also entertains the district Moslems when they come to pay him homage.

The Catholic chief does not act as a pivot in the exchange of wives between pagans of his lineage and the other lineages. This task now falls to his father's brothers. Nevertheless, as district chief he is constantly involved with the marital problems involving pagan parents and their Catholic children. The main source of the difficulty is that Catholic girls are encouraged to refuse to join their pagan husbands when so ordered by their parents. The mission not only insists that the girl freely choose her own husband, but encourages her to reject a polygynous union. Catholicism thereby interposes itself between the girls and their society, not only impairing the prestige of their fathers and lineages but also giving the girls more freedom than they would ordinarily possess.

The pagans claim that by encouraging girls to choose mates without parental consent, the Catholics are really taking the opportunity to obtain wives for young Catholic men. Paradoxically, there seems to be some truth in this, since Bouniol, a White Father, states:

A Mossi who is unable to acquire a wife by [traditional] means must either remain unmarried or seduce another man's wife . . . they must choose between celibacy and immorality.

Such a state of affairs creates many problems for the missions, especially as the system is recognized and sanctioned by the colonial authorities. . . . Young native Christians are obviously placed in a very awkward position. Their conversion angers their parents, who refuse to give them a wife; neither will their friends bestow a daughter upon them, because they know that they will not receive one in return, since a Christian may not give a daughter in marriage to a pagan. . . . *Consequently, unless the missionaries help them to find a wife, they must remain unmarried—a very discouraging prospect!* (1920:160 italics mine)

When a young Catholic receives a wife through the mission, he may visit her father and pay the customary respect by giving him kola nuts and brass coins. The father of a mission girl may accept or reject his son-in-law as he sees fit, but formerly he could not defy the power of the missions.

A pagan youth who wishes to marry one of the mission girls has to discuss the

matter with the priests and swear publicly that he will become a Christian. Before 1946 the young man had to fulfill his promise or be intimidated by the chief and the missionaries until he relented or fled the district. Today, however, the priests usually abandon their efforts to obtain the conversion of the young men after three months have passed. In some cases the young men take their wives and move to other districts, and return only after the girls have given up Catholicism. Despite the lure of wives from the mission, not many young men become Christians on this account because the Mossi are still concerned primarily with family relationships and the effect that conversion would have on these relationships.

The church's prohibition of polygyny is by far the most serious bar to the spread of Catholicism. Many men do not adopt Catholicism simply because they fear that monogamous marriages would not produce children. Father Paternot (Considine 1954:103) has cited a study purporting to show that Christian Mossi have more children than the pagans, but the ordinary people of the district would not accept the facts he presented. They cite their personal experience to the contrary. Dim Delobson (1934:136), a Mossi converted to Catholicism, states:

A certain number of Christians of my acquaintance whose wives did not have children during the first five years of marriage had recourse to magical practices in order to get children. These simple people thought that although they had an omnipotent God beside them, they could impudently— after all the good priests will not know about it—ask the little, but also powerful gods to grant them some material favors here on earth. When the gods' given children were taken for Holy Baptism, they were given Christian names instead of the names of the earth shrines, and they did not wear magical charms which would have indicated to the priest the real state of affairs. Nevertheless, the children were bathed in water to which magical potions were added, and when the mothers went to visit their parents, sacrifices of chickens were given to the benevolent Tengkougas.

The Mossi's strong desire for children is admittedly one of the main reasons for leaving the Catholic Church so that they can take other spouses in addition to barren ones. The church has now belatedly recognized this problem and, knowing that it cannot prevent men from taking plural wives, allows them to come to church but prohibits them from taking the Mass.

Many cultural factors besides the desire for children make polygyny important for the Mossi, and make conversion detrimental to the functioning of their family system. Because of lineage opposition to their conversions, some converts are forced to establish nuclear households —a practice out of harmony with the normal rhythm of Mossi life. The reason for this disharmony is that Mossi women married to Catholics must work alone instead of with co-wives and other women of the extended families. Even the Catholic husbands would not help their wives with household tasks requiring more than one person, nor would they violate tradition by chatting with their wives except at night in their huts. Another factor is that after the Mossi Christian woman has given birth to a child, she follows the traditional custom and goes back to her parents' home to remain there during the two or three years' lactation period. This imposes a great hardship on a Catholic husband because during this time he is left without wife or helpmate. In the extended family household there would have been women to take care of a man's material needs, and his mistresses would

have taken care of his sexual needs. The Catholic can and does ask the mission for a young girl to take care of his material needs, but of course she is not expected to satisfy his sexual desires. Obviously this arrangement is not satisfactory, and many Catholic men, with the acquiescence of their wives, keep mistresses. Dim Delobson comments:

> Ouagadougou has a large number of Christians, but does this mean that these people in their love for the church respect all her rules? Alas! there are a large number of Christians who oblige their lawful wives to leave the conjugal couch and make way for the accommodation of mistresses . . . in conformity with the old custom. But this is a subject which is too delicate to discuss further. I only note it in passing: *Noli me tangere* (1934:169).

Despite the influence of tradition on Mossi Catholics, I feel it would be a mistake to say that the complexity of Catholic dogma is one of the drawbacks to missionary success in this country. One Mossi has already been made a bishop of the Catholic Church, and most of the proselytizing in Manga falls on the two Mossi priests and the five Mossi nuns. Under the supervision of two White Fathers, the Catholic children and adults are acquainted with the dogma and rituals of the church. The festivals are well attended and celebrated with as much pomp as possible. Although the Mass is sung in Latin, the Mossi have adapted some of their traditional tunes to the Mass, and use their own language for prayers and hymns. Catholics observe all the sacraments including Confession—a sacrament which is hazardous from the Mossi point of view, because man must lay bare his innermost thoughts to the priests, who, in the final analysis, are Europeans and thus administrators.

It is true that even the staunchest Catholics in Manga have not abandoned all belief in traditional rituals and religious credos. For example, many Mossi Catholics believe in the existence of sorcerers, but the Catholic Church does not recognize the existence of sorcerers or such evil forces (I have met White Fathers who believe that there are unexplainable psychic and physical phenomena in Africa), and moreover has no way of dealing with them. "But," says Dim Delobson (1934:136), "the Mossi believes so strongly in the power of such entities, that even those converted to Christianity cannot always escape the action of malevolent practitioners." The result is that many Catholics desert the church when they believe that only traditional specialists can help them with personal problems. Catholic families easily abandon Christianity when told by shamans that to do so is necessary in order to have children. Unfortunately, the panoply of saints in modern French Catholicism does not seem to be able to syncretize with or displace the local deities, and thus come to the aid of the Mossi. This weakness of modern Catholicism in West Africa appears to make it unable to deal with many of the insecurities which arise in the daily lives of its adherents.

The American Protestant missionaries were never able to establish stations in either Manga or Nobéré because of the relative strengths of Catholicism and Islam in these two districts. However, they do have stations in Po and Koubri, 30 and 50 miles away. The 1954 census lists five Protestants in Manga, but I could find only one family head who had been a Protestant and that during the period when he worked for missionaries. It is interesting to note that when he returned to his native Manga he did not become a Catholic but embraced Islam instead. Although Protestants among the Mossi are trying very hard, they are working under three handicaps: (1) the opposition of the local administration, (2) their

own explicit cultural bias, and (3) the puritanical nature of their brand of American Midwestern Protestantism.

The first Protestant missionaries to arrive in 1926 reported: "There has often been opposition to the preaching of the Gospel in the district, and there is a continual under-current which has hindered many from accepting Christ" (Assemblies of God Mission 1934:14). Americans who wished to train the young Mossi to read and write found official opposition to the use of the vernacular for such purposes, and were obliged to receive French teaching certificates. When one recognizes that in those days less than one-tenth of one percent of the Mossi children were in schools (today the number is just over three percent) one cannot help feeling that any kind of education would have been useful to the Mossi. During the war the Pétain-oriented administration restricted the movements of the Americans and frightened off their converts. And finally, the Americans come under the general disapprobation with which the Mossi view most Europeans.

American Protestants are fairly well insulated from the Mossi population, and have only now begun to show any interest in Mossi culture and problems. Geoffrey Gorer, who visited the Mossi in 1935, wrote:

> There were some American missionaries in this village, a whole family living in a house filled with texts; I do not know what creed they preached, or with what success; they looked more like American missionaries than I had thought anyone could have done off the films . . . they spoke with a dispassionate "none of our business" disapproval of the ill treatment of the negroes, who they said were ruled entirely by fear (1935:149).

Many of the Protestant missionaries who are now working with the Mossi are still inclined to agree with the first missionaries' ethnocentric judgement of their customs:

> Moral standards are very low. Nothing is wrong until it is found out. Chastity is unknown . . . we questioned in vain many natives in search of a suitable Mossi word for "virgin." They all declared there was no such word in their language. . . . Many horrifying and degrading customs of theirs, we would not dare to put in print (Assemblies of God Mission 1934:12).

Given such reactions, it is not surprising that the Protestants take no opportunity to use "heathen" beliefs and practices to further their own work. When they do take an interest in village affairs, it is usually to aid some young woman having marital difficulties with her lineage members (Sanders 1953:43). Since most Mossi problems are ultimately concerned with women, one can take it as a general rule that they are not in sympathy with any religious system which aggravates this problem.

The American Protestants have the most puritanical religious regime of all the proselyting religions in this country. The Catholics forbid polygyny, and the Moslems prohibit the use of alcohol, but the American Protestants forbid polygyny, drinking native beer, smoking cigarettes, and chewing kola nuts. The result is that the Protestants find it difficult to gain converts, and are constantly weeding out "rice Christians" from their mission stations. One young Catholic informant said that he was very impressed with the Americans who drove up in their big cars and straightaway "cried out the Evangelists." Asked why the missionaries did not get converts, he said that the Mossi were afraid of whites. This response, while true, is inadequate, but as one former Protestant said to me, "With the Americans one can do nothing." So far the American Protestants have made little progress and it is safe to predict that the puritan brand of American Protestantism is not going to make much headway among the Mossi.

The old pagan priest, seeing the steady advance of the new religious systems, tells the visitor that the traditional ways of the ancestors are disappearing and that now the Mossi must follow one of three ways: Allah (Islam), Péredamba soré (Catholicism), or Americadamba soré (Protestantism). He is sad to see this happen, but even his grandchildren are now Moslems. In the struggle between Catholicism and Islam for adherents it is the general consensus that Islamic conversions are on the increase. Islam is gaining, not only because of the reasons already cited but also because the political situation, which has greatly changed since the Brazzaville conference in 1944, is still rapidly changing. Today the Moslems are gaining twenty converts to every Catholic convert, largely because the Mossi do not now fear official sanctions. For example, the Manga mission installed a Mossi catechist in Nobéré with the avowed purpose of gaining converts among Moslem and pagan children enrolled at the new state-run school. The people of the district initially refused to give their land for such a station, but were overruled by the administration through the chief. Although the teacher is a Catholic, he has not dared to encourage any of his students to join the church. The one pagan child who showed an interest in Catholicism was immediately ostracized and beaten by the other students. Shortly afterward, many Moslem parents attempted to withdraw their children from the school, claiming that the children could not attend Koranic classes and the public schools at the same time. But the teacher, realizing the source of their fear, told them that the school would remain entirely secular in nature.

The Imam at Nobéré is positive that now the White Fathers do not have "force" behind them, no conversions will be made in the district. He said that the Moslems here do not rely on force to convert the pagans, and leave them alone if they resist persuasion to embrace Islam.

Mossi politicians who, for the most part, were trained by the Catholics and are still supported by the church, are careful not to offend their pagan and Moslem constituents. One internationally-known Mossi politician told a Nobéré audience that he had a Moslem name in addition to his Catholic name, and that he even attended a Koranic school. Although this admission did not help him gain the votes of the Moslems, he carried the district because he was supported by the chief and received the votes of the pagans. The politicians are now under pressure from the people to expand the system of public schools so that the road to social mobility, through education, would be open to pagans and Moslems as well as Catholics. Even in Manga, where the government-supported parochial school is adequate for the school population, there are plans to build a public school. The special prerogative of the mission schools to use noncertificated personnel on their teaching staffs is now being attacked by teachers who themselves were trained in these schools. These teachers are demanding that the government either cease paying salaries to the unqualified teachers in the mission schools or else employ similar persons in the public schools. Thus one of the most important channels through which the Catholics obtained converts is being consciously narrowed.

Conclusion

The spread of Islam in Africa south of the Sahara is one of the significant cultural events in this area. Islam is not only spreading at the expense of the indigenous religious systems, but is taking precedence over Christianity brought to Africa by the conquering Europeans. The reasons cited for the success of Islam over Christianity are legion. They include: the adaptability of Islam in contrast to the rigidity of Christianity (Greenberg 1946:70; Goilly 1952:173; Marty 1917:283); the simplicity of Islamic doctrines, as opposed to the complexity of Christianity (Delafosse 1931: 236; Quellien 1910:38–39); and the "imponderable factors" brought about by European conquest (Goilly 1952:261–266).

In this paper I have shown that Islam has made greater progress than has Christianity among the Mossi because:

(1) Christianity has a negative appeal to the Mossi because it was brought by their conquerors. For the proud Mossi, Christianity is intimately linked with their first real invasion, defeat, and occupation by aliens in their long history. In contrast, Islam has penetrated the country by peaceful means after its initial failure at proselytization by means of the jihad.

(2) In the early period of this century, the European administration recruited Mossi men and women for forced labor at home and in the Ivory Coast, and recruited children for the mission schools. But as soon as forced labor was abolished and the Mossi could do as they wished, mission school and church attendance declined, and the Mossi mothers even refused to attend the Catholic maternity clinics. During this entire period, the Moslems were propagating the ideas that recruitment for forced labor and other injustices would cease only when all the Mossi embraced Islam.

(3) Catholicism attempted to break down the Mossi social system during the period when their political system was rendered practically impotent. But while the Mossi could not forcibly oppose the effects of French policy on their political system, they effectively neutralized the

church's attempts to disrupt their social system. In contrast to Catholicism, Islamic practices and tenets harmonized with many aspects of the Mossi social system, especially with regard to polygyny and the status of women. Many Mossi converted to Islam in order to fulfill the prescriptions of pagan shamans, who linked conversion with the acquisition of children to continue the lineage. Christianity did not admit the existence of the traditional supernatural forces, and evolved no techniques for dealing with the Mossi's belief in the efficacy of such forces. In the sphere of social mobility, Islam permitted the most illiterate emancipated serf to make a pilgrimage and return an honored El Hadj, while only the most brilliant scholar is able to become an official in the Catholic community.

(4) More of the young men who leave their homes to serve in the armed forces or spend long periods away as laborers return as Moslems than as Christians. There is, however, no evidence that the increased Islamization of the Mossi is due to the heavy seasonal migration of young men to Ghana and Ivory Coast.

(5) American Protestantism, although not associated with French administrative policy, was negatively received because its missionaries were Europeans (whites). Furthermore, the extremely intolerant Protestant attitude toward the traditional Mossi religion and the puritanical nature of their religion made their efforts at conversion highly unsuccessful.

(6) The increase of public schools is lessening the importance of Catholicism and the Catholic school as the only means of social mobility through education. The newly emancipated pagan and Moslem masses are forcing the Catholic-trained Mossi politicians to act in the interest of their constituents, even if at the expense of the missions and Catholicism. The Catholics have consecrated the first Mossi bishop and have installed him in his see, but the return of each plane-load of Mossi Hadjis from Mecca spreads Islam into the remotest villages.

Notes

[1] This article is an expanded version of a paper read at a meeting of the American Anthropological Association in Chicago, 1957. The field work on which this analysis is based was conducted among the Mossi of Ouagadougou from November 1955 to January 1957, and was made possible by a Fellowship from The Ford Foundation African Studies Program. Needless to say, all ideas contained herein are my own. During these months among the Mossi I lived both in the predominantly Moslem district of Nobéré, and in the district of Manga, which has a fairly large Catholic population. I am indebted to Conrad Arensberg, Joseph Greenberg, Marvin Harris, and Ben Zimmermann for many helpful suggestions.

[2] Tauxier (1912:792) reports that when he visited Pirigui village, situated to the north of Ouagadougou, he was surprised to discover that almost half of the nobles were Moslems. It is highly probably that here, also, were the descendants of a son of Sagha who replaced a dissident chief.

[3] These figures are only approximate since many thousands of persons are unreported. Again, many persons listed as Moslems are pagans who have taken Moslem names for ritual purposes.

References Cited

ANDERSON, JOHN NORMN DARYMPLE
1954   Islamic law in Africa. London, Her Majesty's Stationery Office.
ANDRÉ, P. J.
1924   L'Islam Noir: Contribution à l'étude des confréries religieuses islamiques en Afrique Occidentale, suivie d'une étude sur l'Islam au Dahomey. Paris, Geuther.
ASSEMBLIES OF GOD MISSION
1934   Report of the Assemblies of God Mission to the Mossi, Upper Volta. Springfield, Missouri, Gospel Publishing House.

BOUNIOL, JOSEPH
   1929 The White Fathers and their missions. London, Sands and Company.
CONSIDINE, JOHN JOSEPH
   1954 Africa, world of new men. New York, Dodd, Mead.
COOKSEY, JOSEPH J., and ALEXANDER MC-LEISH
   1931 Religion and civilization in West Africa. London, World Dominion Press.
DELAFOSSE, MAURICE
   1912 Haut-Sénégal-Niger. 3 vols. Paris, Emile Larose.
DELOBSON, DIM
   1934 Les Secrets des Sorciers Noirs. Paris, Librairie Émile Nourry.
DUBOIS, FELIX
   1896 Tombouctou la mysterieuse. Paris, Ernest Flammarion.
DUPONT, ANDRÉ
   1949 La Rapide évolution des Africains dans la Haute Volta. Paris, Marche Coloniaux, Année, no. 163. (Janvier 1.)
GORER, GEOFFREY
   1935 Africa dances. New York, A. A. Knopf.

GOUILLY, ALPHONSE
   1952 L'Islam dans l'Afrique Occidentale Française. Paris, Larose.
GREENBERG, JOSEPH
   1946 The influence of Islam on a Sudanese religion. New York, Monographs of the American Ethnological Society No. 10.
LE CHATELIER, A.
   1899 L'Islam dans l'Afrique Occidentale. Paris, G. Steinheil.
MARTY, PAUL
   1917 Études sur l'Islam au Sénégal. 2 vols. Paris, Leroux.
QUELLIEN, ALAIN
   1910 La politique musulmane dans l'Afrique Occidentale Française. Paris, Larose.
SANDERS, RAYMOND
   1953 Meet the Mossi. Springfield, Missouri, Gospel Publishing House.
SOCQUET, MSGR.
   1956 L'Église Catholic en Afrique Noire. Paris, Magazine de l'A.O.F. no. 15 (Aout).
TAUXIER, LOUIS
   1912 Le Noir du Soudan. Paris, Émile Larose.

5 · The Active Ideational Culture Mentality

PITIRIM A. SOROKIN

This as well as the other remaining forms of mentality are generally better known than the Ascetic Ideational; therefore, I shall be briefer in giving concrete illustrations of each of them and in indicating the great organizations, systems, and agencies which incorporate, endorse, and practice these forms.

Beyond the behavior of individuals and

SOURCE. Pitirim A. Sorokin, "The Active Ideational Culture Mentality," from Pitirim A. Sorokin, *Social and Cultural Dynamics*, vol. 1, New York: Bedminster Press, 1962, pp. 134–139. Copyright 1937, The Bedminster Press. Reprinted by permission.

small groups, the Active Ideational mentality is found in the great systems which spring to life from the Ascetic Ideational point of view. In a way it is the tragic and immanent destiny of the Ascetic Ideational culture system to turn into the Active Ideational. As soon as the Ascetic initiators attract the attention of other men, they begin to acquire followers. As the number of followers increases, an organization appears; and with it the pure Ascetic attitude—the attitude of complete indifference toward, and non-interference in, the affairs of the empirical world—becomes impossible. An "organization" or an "institution" is a phenomenon of this world. It requires management, direction, guidance, and the administration of many needs and relationships which are purely empirical. Thus, any Ascetic current, as soon as it grows in influence, becomes an organization; as soon as it becomes an organization, it necessarily becomes more and more Active Ideational; and the more Active, the more rapidly it grows. Such is the inevitable chain of transformation. Change comes also because it is impossible for large masses of the followers of an Ideational system to attain to, and remain upon, the high ground of Ascetic Ideationalism. Therefore, the transformation of the isolated Ascetic rivulets into a broad river is inevitably followed by the transformation of the Ascetic into the Active Ideational. But even at this stage there will remain within the organization a few who continue to follow the Ascetic point of view in contrast to the now Active Ideationalism of the majority. Such is the chain of destiny or "immanent causation."

One can see this in a great many cases. As soon as Brahmanism, or Buddhism, or Jainism, or Christianity, or Taoism, or, to take smaller groups, St. Francis of Assisi, or other hermits and ascetics, began to attract followers an organization appeared. Immediately the empirical world with its needs, affairs, relationships, pains and pleasures, sorrows and joys, poverty and property, sympathies and antipathies, became involved, and made pure Ascetic Ideationalism impossible for most members of the organization, and for the organization itself. The only form possible at this stage, when the moral powers of the current are still very strong and the demoralization of the stage of decay is as yet absent, is the Active Ideational. It stands for constitutions, rules, laws, and by-laws; often for empirical punishments and rewards, promotions and demotions, praise and blame; for the appearance of rulers and the

ruled; in brief, for an organized network designed to enforce empirically the moral standard of life among the members of the organization as well as among outsiders. "The salvation of one's own soul turns into the salvation of the souls of others." The transcendental and the other worldly phenomena return to the empirical world and are more and more entangled by it.

Read from this standpoint the history of the growth of Brahmanism, Buddhism, Christianity, or Taoism, or of a religious order or center, or of a settlement which grew about some hermit or ascetic, or of many a minor current of mysticism. Everywhere you will find this transformation from Ascetic to Active Ideationalism. When we read about the activities of St. Paul, the great organizer of Christianity, we notice at once (from his Epistles) how he had to busy himself with worldly matters, and how the empirical world caught him more and more in its web. He had to give instructions to the brethren about this and that, censure them for some things, warn them of others, prohibit some activities, encourage others; and most of the matters in which his flock involved him, from riots and politics to property and wealth, were of this world. In the Acts of the Apostles we read that even in the earliest Christian community in Jerusalem its members were required to "pool" all their property, and when Ananias or other members did not do this, punishment, even capital punishment, at once made its entry into this supposedly Ascetic Ideational group. And the more Christianity grew, the more this transformation progressed. It is true that the Ascetic aspect remained very strong during the earliest centuries of its history; but its Active aspect grew rapidly, especially from the time of its legalization (after A.D. 313 and 321). More and more Christianity had to enter into world affairs, and into affairs for the salvation of mankind as a whole. Up to the time of its demoralization, when it temporarily weakened and its Active Ideational form began to be contaminated with various Sensate forms, the Christian organization remained (until the fourteenth century approximately) predominantly Active Ideational, the Sensate, Idealistic mentalities being minor currents.[1]

The following quotations from the letters of Pope Gregory VII show concretely the nature, and the inevitability, of this Active Ideational mentality into which the Church was driven from Ascetic Ideationalism. Like all the great administrators of the Christian Church, and regardless of whether he wanted it or not, Gregory had to spend most of his energy in settling affairs of a worldly nature, trying to bring them nearer to the pure ideal of Christianity. "We urgently beg your Fraternity to crush out absolutely this absurd claim [upon a piece of property by one of the parties]," he commands in one of his letters of November 30, 1073. Similarly he had to fight adultery, the irregular sex life of the clergy, unlawful marriages of the low and the high, simony, avarice, bad political government, and so on. In order to enforce his Ideational commands he had to invoke, side by side with spiritual means, a full set of empirical rewards and punishments. The ideal remained purely Ideational; but reality made necessary the use of the empirical world in its most intensive and extensive forms. Thus, in a series of letters and commands to many

kings and princes urging them to join the Crusades, the objective is spiritual; but the motives given as inducements are of a different nature. "And be assured," he writes to Count William of Burgundy, "that you, and all who join you in this undertaking, will receive a *double*, nay, as we believe, a *manifold*, reward from Peter and Paul, chiefs of the Apostles." This sounds quite commercial, like a good profit on an investment.

However, he rarely forgets to stress, and to strive for, the purely spiritual values for which the Church stands. In this sense his position remains purely Ideational. "We exhort . . . to love God and your neighbor as yourself; to keep peace among you; to live in chastity . . . to devote yourselves to charity and hospitality," he writes to the people of Bohemia. Or writing to Beatrice of Tuscany (June 24, 1073), he says:

> It is fixed by the divine judge how much everyone is to suffer by adversity and how far he is to enjoy prosperity. Whoever, therefore, in times of temptation is led by fear of the one or hope of the other to stray from the right path shows that he neither hopes in God, nor respects the appeal of Holy Writ.

Or

> If, then, they [the spiritual as well as the secular rulers] seek only their own glory and the lusts of this world, they cannot live without confusion to themselves and to their people.

In most of his letters written to kings, princes, and rulers he concludes with the wish, "May Almighty God enlighten your minds and lead you into eternal glory," or "that you may through his [St. Peter's] merit be delivered from your sins," and so on—wishes which from the Sensate standard of our age would sound like an insult. In a letter against Philip I of France he writes:

---

[1] On a smaller scale the same is shown by history of many monasteries and orders. Most of them, in Egypt, Syria, or Europe, were "founded" by hermits and ascetics who did not want to found any organization. The Mount Athos monastic community may serve as an illustration. It grew around hermits and ascetics. The eremitical type of mentality conduct was there first, the organized "cenobitic" and "idiorhythmic" subsequently. See the cited works of Lake and Choukas.

Now everyone is committing every kind of abominable crimes. They regard neither divine nor human law. They make nothing of perjury, sacrilege, incest or mutual betrayal. Of all these things your king—who is to be called a tyrant rather than a king—is the cause and fountainhead under the inspiration of the Devil. Every stage of his life is stained with vice and crime. And since he began his wretched and unhappy reign . . .

All this sounds spiritual and Ideational, though not as pure and unearthly as "My kingdom is not of this world," and other mottoes of the Ascetic Ideational sort.

But when we read of the measures taken to enforce these pieces of advice, exhortations, or "commands," we discover that the empirical world is very much present. "By our apostolic authority we command you"—this often repeated phrase has the very sound of worldliness. And in giving warning, in applying anathema, in ejecting the disobedient from the Church, and in using other purely physical pressure (punishment, confiscation of property, and so on), Gregory VII almost invariably quotes his favorite passages in the Bible as his divine authority, in justification of his interference in all these world affairs: "If thou dost not speak to warn the wicked from his way, that wicked man shall die in his iniquity, but his blood will I require at thine hands," he often quotes from Ezekiel. "Cursed be the man who holds back his sword from blood." "Woe to him who keepeth back his sword from the incorrigible sinner." [2]

This shows that as soon as the Ascetic adaptation takes the form of an organiza-

[2] All these quotations are from *The Correspondence of Pope Gregory VII*, trans. by E. Emerton (New York, 1932), pp. 8, 15, 20, 23, 39–40, 62, 65, 76, *et passim*. Another conspicuous incarnation of this mentality is found in the Buddhist Emperor Açoka.

tion, the main duty and the main function of the organization becomes to "warn the wicked," because their sins would otherwise be the responsibility of the organization. It is driven to a policy of compulsory saving of the wicked; and this policy forces it not to "hold back its sword from the incorrigible sinner," and thus hopelessly involves it in the affairs of the empirical world.

Thus, as soon as the Ascetic Ideational form becomes, however unwillingly, the center of an organization, it is doomed to be transformed into an efficient Active Ideational system (unless it degenerates to the Sensate stage), and, for the masses striving to follow the Ascetic ideal, the level of Active Ideationalism is the highest attainable.

What has been said of Christianity may be said of any other system which was Ascetic at its beginning. I have already pointed to a similar phenomenon with respect to Taoism. The history of Buddhism and Sufism offers further examples. This means that the Active Ideational type of mentality has always been widely spread in such systems when they entered the stage of attracting a large following and assumed an organized or institutionalized form. It is their destiny (until they become demoralized and lose their vigor and spirituality, and fall into the snares of the Sensate mentality).

The Active Ideational culture mentality can come to existence also directly, without passing through the Ascetic stage. Many groups have always been emerging in that direct way. As an example we may take the system of mentality of Mih-Teich in China—the system that was perhaps the most powerful in the fourth and third centuries B.C. It was rigidly organized as a sect. It attempted actively to transform the empirical world; it fought luxury, degeneration, egotism, anger, greed, by all means, including especially the compulsion, and autocratic enforcement, of its prescriptions. Logically moving along this line, the doctrine came to its culmination: to the *compulsory* introduction and maintenance of universal solidarity and love.[3] Here, then, we meet the same warning of the wicked, the same use of the sword for his salvation, that we found in the formulas of Gregory VII. Whether we take Calvinism or the Inquisition or any other movement or machinery of compulsion aimed to

[3] For Mih-Teich and his system see J. Legge, *The Life and Works of Mencius* (Philadelphia, 1875), pp. 99–121; H. A. Giles, *Religion of Ancient China* (London, 1905), Vol. II; M. Granet, *op. cit.*, pp. 490 ff.; A. Forke, "Mo Ti," *Mitteilungen des Seminars für orientalische Sprachen* (1923).

save the sinners from perdition and to bring this empirical world nearer to the "Kingdom of God," they are all the incarnations of this type of culture mentality.[4]

[4] Akin to it are all such movements of compulsion as Robespierre's terroristic salvation of the Republic, Lenin's and Stalin's Proletarian Dictatorship, and even the overenthusiasm of advocates of Prohibition who propose a pitiless punishment of all who partake of alcoholic beverages. However, the aims in such movements are of this world—utilitarian, hedonistic, eudaemonistic. Therefore they belong to a special brand of Active "Epicureanism" and not to Active Ideationalism.

6 · The Degradation of Culture by Masses

PITIRIM A. SOROKIN

Taoism, Hinduism, Christianity, Confucianism of the intellectual stratum of either the Chinese, Hindu, or European society is one thing; in the mentality and culture of the respective lower classes it is another thing. Each of these religiophilosophical-ethical systems in its pure form is one of the sublimest and greatest systems ever created. In the mentality and culture of the lower classes of the respective societies, each of them is vulgarized to an enormous degree. What is Taoism or Hinduism of the masses of the lower classes but a collection of so-called "superstitious" rituals, magic beliefs, primitive ideas about God, soul, trans-

SOURCE. Pitirim A. Sorokin, "The Degradation of Culture by Masses," from Pitirim A. Sorokin, *Social and Cultural Dynamics,* Vol. 4, New York: Bedminster Press, 1962, pp. 259–260. Copyright 1937, The Bedminster Press. Reprinted by permission.

migration, and so on, which have little of the depth and sublimity of the system of Lao-Tse or Qwang-tsu, or of the Vedas, Upanishads and Brahmanas. The same is true of Christianity or Confucianism or any other religious and moral system. There is little in common between the Epicureanism of Epicurus and that of the mass of his followers, during his lifetime as well as after his death. The first was practically "Stoic" and a noble form of ethical eudemonism; the second assumes the most vulgar form of the flat hedonism of "wine, women and song," and *"Carpe diem."* The Darwinian theory of evolution in the mentality of the "enlightened" masses is but an atrocious idea that "man came from a monkey." The ideology of Marxian socialism in the mentality of the proletarian masses is but a call to "steal what has been stolen" and kill and eliminate the exploiters. "Positivism" (of A. Comte or others) means,[1] for the radical high-school or college student, a primitive mixture of atheism and progressivism. Even such ideas as the concept of a gentleman mean one thing in the culture of England of the eighteenth century; another for a *nouveau riche*, who by hook or crook has made money on the stock market and considers himself a gentleman; and still another for a "proletarian" who is raised by revolution to a position of prominence. The Gothic style, Bach's music, or Dürer's painting mean, for the culture of the lower classes, if by chance these values enter it, something very different from what they represent to the mentality of the connoisseurs and properly trained and qualified persons and groups. Dante's *Divine Comedy* or Shakespeare's *Macbeth* are, again, something quite different in the mentality and culture of the

lower and the upper classes. And so with almost any complex system or value.[2]

[1] This objective fact is the root of the tragedy of vulgarization and decisive disfiguring of any complex and great and sublime system of cultural values when it infiltrates and roots itself among the large masses. Such a success is invariably bought at the cost of its simplification and distortion. Often, after such a success, there remains little of the system as it was created by the author and a selected group of his disciples.

[2] The inevitable vulgarization of education itself, when it becomes universally diffused in all classes, is a further corroboration of the uniformity discussed. In ancient Hellenic society it became most widely diffused in the third century A.D. See M. I. Rostovtzeff, *The Social and Economic History of the Roman Empire* (Oxford, 1926), p. 375. It was so simplified and vulgarized that, among its other effects, we find a complete lack of either great writers, thinkers, or artists in that and subsequent centuries, instead of a great increase of these and a blossoming of culture, as many think. Similarly, the universal diffusion of education in our society has led, among other results, to the emergence of the "yellow press," "yellow movies," "educated ignorance," or, in the totalitarian states, to the diffusion of the governmental "intellectual chewing gum" with all the tabloid pseudo culture and flat mentality of both. And the more "universal" our colleges and universities, our B.A.'s and Ph.D.'s become, the lower becomes the standard of the universities and Ph.D.'s, the greater the superficiality and "trained incapacity" of the majority of the graduates. This is the reason, perhaps, why the crop of real creativeness of cultural values, among all those millions who have successfully passed the present curriculum of schools and universities, has been so disproportionately small.

B · STRUCTURAL DIFFERENTIATION

1 · Folk and Universal Religion

GUSTAV MENSCHING

1. Folk Religion*

We distinguish basic structures of religion and religious types within them. We come upon the phenomenon of basic structures when we investigate the historical circumstance that there are some religions which are confined to a single folk and others which have spread among many peoples. There are *folk religions* and *world religions*. The difference thus suggested among historical religions by no means has to do with territorial diffusion alone. Rather it rests upon a deeper structural differentiation of religion itself.

First it must be noted that, in folk religion of every kind, the *folk,* or in nature-religion the tribe, but in any case a vital community, is the carrier of the religion. The individual has not yet discovered himself but has a life quite bound up with that of the collectivity. On this foundation the historically earliest religious communities are of the vital type: family—and house—community, sib and tribe, folk and state. In early religion there are no specific religious communities aside from the vital, given communities of

SOURCE. Gustav Mensching, "Folk and Universal Religion" (from *Die Religion,* Curt E. Schwab, Stuttgart, 1959, pp. 65–77, translated by the editor).
* In translating, I have omitted a few references to religious documents. L.S.

birth. But these vital communities for their part have a sacred stamp and are at the same time religious communities.

The second structural factor in folk religion is that in that religion the "salvation" afforded consists in the condition of positive relationships of the folk community to the divinities that appertain to it. This condition of salvation of the folk community, into which the individual is born, and whose maintenance is the duty of the members of the folk society, is a mystic "life" which binds all together and to separate one's self from which means actual death. "The human being who precedes history or exists outside it leads . . . a double life. One is the unheeded life whose beginning is actual birth . . . the other is the true life, which begins with a rite . . . These two lives are not separate." (C. H. Ratschow, *Magie und Religion,* 1946, p. 43.)

The gods of folk religion are exclusively related to a particular folk and limited to that folk as their province of domination, so to put it. This holds not only for the folk as a whole but also for the vital communities that constitute it: family and sib, tribe and clan also have their proper gods. These gods accordingly lack universality. The idea of one's own gods is thus wholly reconcilable with the view that other peoples have gods proper to them. In the Israelite religion, for example, the claim of the Moabites against that of the Israelite God Jahweh is delimited and recognized. But there prevails between the folk and its divinities a strictly and exclusively binding relationship. Defection to foreign divinities is, thus, repeatedly designated in Israel as seriously sinful. Folk religion is in consequence of this by no means tolerant. But we are confronted by a typically folk-religious intolerance which I designate as inner-religious intolerance; for toward the outside one is tolerant insofar as one does not dispute the existence or right to existence of foreign gods.

The peculiarity of the particular folk involved and the relationship to the folk is substantially more clearly marked out in folk religion than in the universal religions. While the universal religions are in principle supra-national and owe their diffusion and ability to diffuse to this supra-national character, there is naturally and quite directly reflected in the folk religions the special spirit of the folk. This is especially clear (other factors, such as peculiarity of cultus, outlook on the gods, and the like, aside) in what is considered good and bad, in a word in *folk-religious* ethics. In the Teutonic religion, for example, ethical values are related to the weal and woe of the sib, so that the sib is the value standard of good and bad. The same relationship is present in the pre-Mohammedan folk religion of the Arabic tribes. And in Japanese Shinto serious "celestial sins" consist in offense against the interests of the folk community. The "ten commandments" of the Old Testament, also, are explicit folk-law, in which in the fourth commandment the continued existence of the folk is made contingent upon proper conduct toward father and mother and thus upon maintenance of the family. But aside from this relationship of ethic to folk, it may be shown in detail through comparison of the value-tables of different folk religions that,

through "preference" of one value over other recognized ethical values, the special spirit of the individual folk religion is determined. As another characteristic of the folk-religious ethic and thereby of the structure of the folk religion itself may be added the circumstance that the recognized ethical values (like the idea of God itself) still neither have nor claim universal validity. The above stressed folk connection of ethics thus means not only that values are related to the welfare and security of the folk but also that they have validity only within the domain of the particular folk. The stranger to folk and sib has no claim to friendly conduct: he is "hostis" (stranger and enemy), and the laws of behavior valid within the folk context are of no effect in relation to him. There is also lacking within the folk religious context the perception of the universality of ethical values and of their *unconditioned* validity—a validity unrestricted by the object of the ethical act or disposition. Good and evil are not yet absolute good and evil, but still the relatively good and evil, that which is valuable or harmful for the welfare and survival of the folk.

As the external circumstance of restriction to a folk points to fundamental structures which determine the character and limits of folk religion, so on the other hand the observation of the external *fate* of the folk religion within the folk world leads to a far more important recognition of essential changes in human existence itself. A glance at the history of religion shows that nearly all the folk religions experienced the fate of being replaced by universal religions. In detail, this happened in different ways. We can distinguish three different ways of replacement of aboriginal folk religion through a universal religion.

One set of folk religions evolved in the course of their history, in their later period, universal tendencies that came out of themselves, although with a maintenance of their folk-determined limited form and their own folk-religious tradition. This is the case, for example, in India. Universal tendencies indeed emerge early in the Vedas. We already encounter the intuition of the One in the earlier Rigveda. The many folk gods disappear behind the One (whether personally or neutrally conceived) and become simply names for the One. "The singers designate what is merely one by many names—Agni, Mitra, Matarishvan." In the Upanishads the basic structure is already that of universal religion, but the folk-religious *form* has remained. And also in Hinduism, which essentially builds on the Vedic tradition, we deal with pure universal religion (aside from the primitive folk religion of the broad masses, which is also maintained in every universal religion as "folk belief"), but again in the form of folk religion. The folk-religious tradition is not overcome; but it no longer determines essence, although it continues to determine external form. Similarly the *Israelite* religion offers in its evolution the picture of a self-universalizing religion. The real folk religion was founded through Moses on the demonistic foundation that remains clearly visible in the Old Testament in the worship of animals, the dead, ancestors, trees, springs, and stars. Through Moses the individual tribes became a single folk with a conscious and religiously experienced fate under a common God, Jahweh. Jahweh is unequivocally the folk god of Israel.

Through the agency of the great prophets of the eighth century before Christ there begins the universalization of the Israelite religion. But this religion preserves its folk-religious form into the present. The folk religion of *Iran* also won through the prophet Zarathustra a universal character but kept its folk-religious form. In Greece, where every polis had its gods, it was the great tra-

gedians who proclaimed a universal idea of God. Here indeed we have an example of the second form of universalization.

In a second set of folk religions universalization occurs as the folk religion is replaced or complemented by a foreign universal religion. This occurred, for example, in Greece by the agency of the mystery religions coming from abroad, which also came to Rome and appeared beside the Roman folk religion (the latter, for its part, never developed its own universal tendencies). The same process also occurred in Japan: the folk religion of Shintoism was complemented, from 552 A.D. on, by the foreign universal religion of Buddhism.

In a third set of folk religions, there occurred the establishment of a supranational *world religion*. On the ground of Indian folk religion Buddha founded Buddhism. On the ground of the Israelite folk religion and on that of the Arabic folk religion, Christianity and Islam were founded by Jesus and Mohammed respectively. Each of these three world religions came into a peculiar relationship to the field of its own folk-religious origin. The tension between Indian folk-religion and Buddhism led to the overcoming of Buddhism in the Indian field of origin. In the Israelite religious world also the tension, already present in the lifetime of Christianity's founder, between Israelite folk religion and Christianity, was preserved. In contrast to Buddhism in India, Christianity in Palestine never won a victory but remained a foreign religion which neither displaced nor complemented the original religion. But Buddhism, too, was influential in India only perhaps for a millennium. Then it wandered as a foreign religion into the Far East. Only on the ground of the Arabic folk religion did Islam come to replace the aboriginal religion.

In all cases, then, actual folk religion in religious history was replaced by universal religion. That occurred in a later time. The folk religions are early religions. But it is not enough simply to record this historical circumstance. It rests upon a structural change in the mode of existence of men themselves and thus upon *anthropological* presuppositions. There are precise correspondences between the mode of existence of early men and religious structure. Early man, as we may say briefly in connection with important work by G. van der Leeuw (*Der Primitive Mensch und die Religion*, 1937), lives in the unity of an undivided and unexamined life. He does not stand over against the world, but lives in it, and the fullness of powers that animate the world fills him also. In this stage, there is little that separates subject and object, or indeed object and object. Man is essentially participant in everything. The contours of things in the external world are fluid. In the depths of all phenomena and of man himself there is an ultimate essential identity. In brief, early man is not yet isolated from the elementary unity of life, has not yet fathomed himself as an ego and a self released from community and life-unity. Folk religion corresponds to this stage of human existence, for it is the religion of *unexamined elementary unity*. The various interpretations of the folk-religious stage of belief may be corrected from this perspective. One may characterize the stage of folk religion, with Paul, as a "time of ignorance," which was then overcome through the universal-religious knowledge of one's own religion. In terms of the science of religion it must be said that this theological interpretation does not do justice to historical circumstance. Anthropologically speaking, a universal religion would not have been possible in early times. We shall analyze the structure of universal religion in the next section. It will then be plain that as folk religion corresponded precisely to early human exist-

ence, so universal religion, which is a religion of later time, again corresponds to the *transformed* existence of recent man. The emergence of universal religion thus occurred in an historical moment in which it was a human necessity, since, to be sure, folk religion no longer answered man's condition.

But it is not only the flat theological interpretation of folk religion which now becomes corrected. The rationalistic interpretation of the course of religious history is corrected by the above perspective. Historical religions cannot be looked upon as variations, of essentially the same order, of a "natural religion," for there are profound structural differences among religions—differences that are left out of account in the abstraction of a meager "natural religion" as the common religion of man. The historical necessity of the transition from folk to universal religion may be perceived directly from the cognition of anthropological presuppositions.

2. Universal Religion

In the analysis of universal religion, we may also begin with external phenomena which point to profound inner laws and factors. The universality of the religions of which we affirm that they also have an inner structural community is in the first place external: these religions go beyond the boundaries of their religio-historical field of origin or their folk or country and diffuse among many different peoples without regard to race, culture, speech, or other distinctiveness. There is still another observation that points from the external to concealed laws. It is not only in regard to space (diffusion to many lands and peoples) but also in regard to time that the phenomenon of universal religion presents itself to us as a problem. The universal religions emerge in the history of religion at nearly the same time. Rudolf

Otto, in another connection and from different viewpoints, first referred to "the law of parallels in the history of religion." Otto speaks of the transition from myth to logos, from mythology to theology, and thinks that this significant step occurred nearly everywhere at the same time among civilized men—between 800 and 500 B.C. In my judgment, the phenomenon Otto had in view can be better described as a transition from the structure of folk religion to that of universal religion. In Greece, this transition took place in the period between Hesiod and Plato. Pythagoras founded his order in 530 B.C. Confucius died in China about 470 B.C. Lao-tse lived some centuries later, according to recent opinion. This development begins in India in the era of the Upanishads, about 800 B.C., and Buddha was alive in 500 B.C. In Israel also the same period is involved, for the prophets paved the way for the universalization of folk religion in the eighth century B.C. Even in Persia the reform of folk religion by Zarathustra probably falls in these same centuries. These parallels in time are strange. In the same centuries there stirs everywhere among men the longing for a new form of religion. What happened? Clearly, a *fundamental change in human existence* itself set in. But let us first be clear on what the structure of universal religion, which takes account of this altered situation in the human mode of existence, consists of.

The decisively new feature in the structure of universal religion is that in this religion it is no longer the collectivity, as in folk religion, but the *individual* who is the subject of religion. Whereas the individual in folk religion was a member of the over-arching community, through which he lived and in whose "sanctity" he participated, in all universal religion we encounter the individual who has become conscious of himself and presents distinctive religious problems.

For this is now the second fundamental factor: no longer is sanctity a given thing, sanctity that one could lose in folk religion in exceptional cases if one got detached from the salvation-community of folk and sib, but *the condition of non-salvation* is the given thing, and indeed a *personal* condition of non-salvation in which the individual finds himself. Salvation is desired, as is contact with divinity or the unity that is no longer given with membership in the great vital communities of sib and folk into which everyone is born. The vital community, indeed, lost its sacred character in later time and became profane. The individual himself perceives himself as detached from the numinous primitive ground of existence. Man did indeed become in growing measure master of the world and its powers as he became subject and the external world increasingly became object. But in his surrender to the world and its goods he lost elemental contact with the numinous world above. Therefore the individual must win anew a soteriological contact which had only to be cultivated and maintained in folk religion. Also on the ground of the individualized universal religion, in a later stage of organization, the effort is made to produce a situation analogous to that of folk religion, insofar as man wins salvation through membership in an objective soteriological organization (the church).

In universal religion *man* is the object of the message of salvation. Thereby a de-nationalization of religious concern takes place. We deal with the need for depth in human existence, flatly, and thus with every man's need. Universal religion is therefore not only externally universal, but has primarily an inner universality, in that it concerns everyone. And therefore in universal religion everywhere a universal offer of salvation is proclaimed over against the existing state of non-salvation. Salvation and man's existence depend on the taking up of this offer.

The universal message encounters a folk-differentiated humanity. The supranational proclamation of universal religion therefore had everywhere to be melted down. Re-minting and minting anew were necessary for all universal religions and were carried out everywhere in East and West. The universal message of salvation is consequently international in content, but in its form it appears in the history of religion in a variety of stampings, according to the spirit of the peoples it conquered. The folk-differentiation of mankind is thus no boundary for the diffusion of a universal religion; for, as the history of religion shows, it is certainly possible for other peoples to appropriate a universal religion which is foreign to them as regards its field of origin. Two thirds of mankind profess a foreign religion. The absolute limit of appropriation lies rather in men themselves, in their religious capacity for understanding or the lack thereof. The great founders of religions have meditated on the fact of their wide-reaching failure or of the downright unbelief which they encountered among men, and adduced an explanation correspondent with the basic character of their message. Buddha construed unbelief in such fashion as to understand it as a sign of immaturity in man's long journey of rebirth. Even the unbeliever will in time attain knowledge when he has attained the necessary stage of maturity. Jesus spoke of the calling to belief by the Father in Heaven, and similarly Mohammed conceived unbelief as the effect of a quite incalculable act of will on the part of the arbitrary Allah. But in any case there are assumed here firm barriers, immovable by men.

A further characteristic of universal religion lies in *the totality of its claim.* The religion of salvation claims the entire personality and existence of man. It is not a matter of modification on the periphery of human life, but of a profound level of existence, from out of which all sectors of human existence receive their new influence.

Folk religion also bound its members totally, for the existence of the secondary individual depended on the community of the folk, whose life was his life. In early religion also, man lives a full and redeemed life only when he lives a "united existence." This redemptive union, however, is given in antecedent folk-solidarity.

In the universal religion of later times there goes forth to the given isolation of the individual the message of salvation. This also aspires to achieve a "united existence," on a new basis, to be sure. But it can do so only if it penetrates to the depth where the disturbance of unity has taken place. Mysticism and prophecy, the two fundamental forms of universal religions, both claim, each in characteristic fashion, the whole man to the very roots of his existence: mysticism as it strives for the elimination of individual being, the merging of the individual in the One; prophecy as it seeks to re-establish the unity-in-belief (of the individual isolated and living remote from God) with the personally conceived savior-deity.

Universal religion, which has in actuality spread among numerous peoples, carries within itself the *tendency to diffusion.* In the pure folk religion, whose divinities are nationally and territorially delimited, there naturally does not exist the object of converting other peoples to one's own religion. On the contrary, the knowledge of one's own gods appears here as a value that puts one at an advantage over other people and that one would therefore rather keep secret than impart. Thus the Romans, for example, called out unknown gods from a besieged city in an act of "evocation" in order to take away divine aid from the besieged. In the folk religion with a universal content the tendency to diffusion is already manifest, as in Judaism, which in the time of Christ had conquered seven per cent of the inhabitants of the Roman Empire. This mission of Judaism broke down in view of the pure religious universalism of Christianity, since the Jewish religion held firm to the specifically folk-religious demand of entrance into the national community of the Jews. On these grounds the substantially universal religion of the Jews could not become a world religion. The same is true of Confucianism, for this too represented specifically Chinese outlooks and claims, side by side with a substantial universality (especially in the realm of ethics). It is thus evident that everywhere that universal contents emerge in a folk religion a tendency to diffusion becomes apparent. But this tendency nevertheless fails: not by reason of historical accident but out of innermost necessity, for on the one hand the universal content has not yet attained the depth in which the universally unredeemed condition of the existential isolation of latter-day man is shown, and on the other this same content, insofar as it is already universal, has not yet transcended its national boundaries and so failed to find understanding among alien peoples.

In the case of genuine world religions, on the other hand, these conditions are fulfilled. They touch upon the unredeemed condition of *man* and transcend the nation. The tendency to diffusion is omnipresent in them and has been everywhere successfully realized, to be sure in differing degrees. The difference in intensity of the desire to missionize is contingent on the essential structure of the universal religion. Mystic religions, which rather incline toward concealment (compare the arcana-discipline in the mystery religions), are less disposed to mission than the prophetic religions. Buddhism as a mystic world religion has nowhere represented a hard Either-Or, as have Islam and Christianity, the prophetic world religions. Buddhism, rather, has considered foreign notions of deity as pre-stages of the Buddhist knowledge of salvation and built them into its own system. But the prophetic religions are strictly exclusive and therefore sought the radical destruction of all alien religions in order to make the prophetic ones all-dominant. Hence Buddhism appears everywhere *beside* other religions. In Japan it came as a universal religion beside genuine Shintoism; in China beside Confucianism and Taoism; and in India, its land of origin, it remained existent, to be sure as a dwindling minority religion, beside Hinduism and Islam.

We return once more to the initially discussed question of *anthropological presuppositions*. It is evident that folk religion corresponded to the mode of existence of early times. This mode of existence was briefly described as that of unexamined unity. After the structure of universal religion (in connection with which it was plain above all that the religious focus is on the isolated individual) was explained, it was easily shown that universal religion corresponds precisely to the change in the mode of human existence that had supervened in the meantime. G. van der Leeuw has shown that in the evolution of mankind there may be clearly recognized the emergence of individual self-consciousness and, at the same time therewith, growing self-differentiation from a world increasingly becoming "object." The general development, the process of "becoming man" (van der Leeuw), amounts to a liberation and an achievement of independence on the part of the individual. But, negatively, this process at the same time involves a threat to man in the depths of his existence through isolation from the metaphysical primitive powers which, without residue, sustained and fulfilled the undiscovered individual within the primitive vital collectivity. The newly discovered ego strives for independence with all its newly awakened powers. All universal religions make answer to this human situation with unmistakable structural unanimity, for, as was shown, they all start from a fundamental break in the depths of human existence and seek in one fashion or another to establish a re-union with the holy. Accordingly, world religion is responsive not, one may say, to a newly recognized need (as an orthodox view of religion would have it) but to a newly arisen need of man awakened to self-consciousness in more recent time. It is from this standpoint that the inner meaning of the circumstance previously mentioned, that folk religions were everywhere replaced by universal religions, is to be understood. Folk religions were not forcibly constrained to their decline. Nor did they disappear

before the better or profounder truth of universal religions. They perished because they no longer answered to the newly developed condition of mankind. Of course, universal religion is to this extent the profounder and truer perception as over against folk-religious truth, but its truth would have been valueless in early history insofar as no question had arisen on the part of men to correspond to the answer given by universal religion. This interpretation of the phenomenon of late universal religion also dispenses us from the assumption demanded of us by the orthodox view of religion: that mankind remained in utter darkness and in unqualified, unredeemed error, for millennia, until at last the light of universal truth broke forth. There are no human errors of so fundamental a type. However primitive were the theoretical notions that men had of their gods, in religious substance they were surely oriented in the right direction in the given total situation. It was the gradual change of the total situation which first allowed the ripening of the aspiration toward new truth and deeper knowledge of God which was brought to mankind in the universal message of the world religions.

2 · Religion: Communal and Associational

GERHARD LENSKI

Socio-Religious Group Membership

In religion, as in all other phases of human activity, men are social beings. That

SOURCE. Gerhard Lenski, "Religion: Communal and Associational," from Gerhard Lenski, *The Religious Factor*, New York: Doubleday, 1961, pp. 17–21, 32–39. Copyright 1961 by Gerhard Lenski. Reprinted by permission of Doubleday & Company, Inc.

is to say, in their religious activities men constantly relate themselves to others. Religious activity stimulates social interaction and group organization, with the result that the religious life and activity of individuals comes to be organized in terms of a variety of religious groups.

Religious groups in the modern metropolis are a much more complex form of social organization than has generally been recognized. Far too often American sociologists have regarded them as merely one more type of specialized, formal association[1]—the counterpart of the corporation, the labor union, the Kiwanis club, or the PTA—except, of course, that the religious group is viewed as far less influential than most since it brings its members together for only an hour a week, and even then attracts but a minority of the population.

This view corresponds with certain obvious facts, but ignores others. It is the truth, but not the whole truth. The crucial fact which it ignores is that religious groups are basically *endogamous* (that is, group members normally marry others within their group),[2] with the result that interaction among members of a family normally involves interaction among members of the same religious group. The more deeply people have internalized the norms, or standards, of their group, the more their actions reinforce similar tendencies in other members of their family. In short, family groups (when religiously homogeneous) tend to function as subunits of the larger and more inclusive religious group.

This is not to say that Catholic families, for example, are *merely* subunits

of the Catholic church, any more than we would say that American families are merely subunits of American society. However, just as American families are subunits of our society, reinforcing by rewards and punishments those societal standards which they adopt for their own, so, too, religiously homogeneous families serve as subunits of the religious group, reinforcing its norms.

A second fact of major importance is that one's earliest years, so crucial in the development of personality and in the establishment of behavior patterns, are normally spent in the family group. Furthermore, during this period the child's chief relations are with his mother, whose contacts outside the socio-religious group are normally far more limited than those of the father.

A third fact of some importance is that friendly cliques (the other major type of primary group in our society) also tend to be religiously homogeneous. When this is true, these groups likewise tend to function as subunits of religious groups.

Collectively these facts are of great importance. They show that religious groups cannot be thought of merely as formal associations even in the modern metropolis. The system of social relationships which constitute each of the major religious groups in our society involves much more than the limited number of highly specialized and relatively impersonal relationships to which the associations give rise (e.g., relationships between priest and parishioner, Sunday school teacher and pupil, etc.). In addition to these there are a vast number of very generalized, highly personal, and very basic social relationships (such as those between friends or between the members of a family) which constitute an integral part of every religious group. *In short, religious groups are communal as well as associational type groups.*

---

[1] See, for example, Leonard Broom and Philip Selznick, *Sociology* (Evanston: Row, Peterson, 1955), pp. 440–41. See also, Harry M. Johnson, *Sociology: A Systematic Introduction* (New York: Harcourt, Brace, 1960), Chapter 16, where the discussion of religious groups is in terms of an associational-type group. Most other basic texts also seem explicitly or implicitly to equate the church with the religious group, at least in the modern metropolis. This same pattern may be found in Thomas F. Hoult's recent volume, *The Sociology of Religion* (New York: Dryden, 1958), pp. 152–68.

[2] Evidence is presented below to show that both families and friendly cliques tend to be religiously homogeneous.

Hence our analysis must take account of religious communities, or subcommunities, as well as religious associations.[3]

[3] This distinction between communities and associations has long been a major concern in sociological theory, but its relevance for systematic research has hardly begun to be exploited. Ferdinand Tönnies' volume, *Gemeinschaft und Gesellschaft,* has been the most important single work clarifying the distinction. According to Tönnies, associations (*Gesellschaften*) arise out of the desire of men to attain specific, but limited, ends without regard for the affective character of the social relationships required by their collective effort. Ties of cordiality and friendship are unnecessary in an association. In fact, those participating may even be personally hostile toward one another. By contrast, communities (*Gemeinschaften*) arise out of the natural attraction of like-minded persons for whom the social relationships established are an end in themselves, and not merely the means to some other end. Tönnies believed that there are no pure communities or associations in the real world, since all human groups contain elements of both. However, the relative proportions of communal and associational traits vary greatly from group to group, with important consequences for the life of men.

Other early sociologists were also aware of this important distinction. Max Weber made frequent use of it in his writings, borrowing directly from Tönnies. Durkheim's distinction between mechanical and organic solidarity was clearly a comparable distinction.

In most of the early literature on this subject, the major emphasis was on the decline of communal type social relationships and the growth of associational type relationships in modern society. The latter were typically seen as subversive of the former and hence there was a tendency for this important theoretical distinction to be taken over by the "professional viewers with alarm"—much to the detriment of modern sociological theory and research. It was not until Roethlisberger and Dickson's important study, *Management and the Worker* (Cambridge, Mass.: Harvard University Press, 1939), that it was discovered that formal associations not only do

To include both the communal and associational aspects of religious groups, I shall refer to them in the future as socio-religious groups. By using this somewhat cumbersome and less familiar term I hope to direct attention to three things. First, the groups to be examined are more than associations. Second, their subcultures reflect the experience and influence of the subcommunity *as well as* of the association, which means that these subcultures ought never be interpreted as merely by-products of, or derivations from, theology. Third, in Detroit race as well as religion defines the boundaries of group membership, a fact of crucial importance in the case of Protestantism.

In the metropolitan community of Detroit there are at present four major socio-religious groups, plus several minor ones. The major ones are, in order of size:

1. White Protestants   41 per cent
2. White Catholics   35 per cent
3. Negro Protestants   15 per cent
4. Jews   4 per cent

The remaining 5 per cent of the population is made up of persons with no religious preference, and of Eastern Orthodox, Negro Catholics, and a very small number of Moslems and Buddhists. The membership of individuals in these groups was determined simply on the basis of their response to a question asking for their religious preference and on the basis of their race.

---

not necessarily destroy communal type relationships, but may even give rise to them. Slowly, as the implications of this important study have come to be recognized, the full potentials of Tönnies' concepts have begun to be apparent. One of the major aims of this study is to demonstrate the value of these concepts as tools for enhancing our understanding of the nature of religious groups, the role they play in human societies, and the means by which they are able to play this role.

It may seem surprising that the Protestant population has been divided by race rather than denomination. This was done for the simple reason that the denominational groups within Detroit Protestantism no longer constitute self-contained socio-religious groups to any great degree, while the racial groups do. Both the religious and secular activities of Protestants in Detroit are highly segregated along racial lines. The two populations usually worship separately, and marriage and other primary-type relations seldom cut across the racial line. By contrast, there is a great amount of intermarriage among Protestants of different denominations, and with even greater frequency ties of friendship cut across denominational lines. Furthermore, there is a considerable movement back and forth across denominational lines within each racial group. The 1958 survey revealed that in only about one third of the Protestant families were both husband and wife lifelong members of the same denomination. . . . In all the other cases either the husband or wife, or both, had previously belonged to a different denomination. The limited importance attached to denominational loyalties is also emphasized by the fact that roughly half the Protestants in our sample said they would like to see their denomination merge with one or more other Protestant groups. . . . Finally, our data revealed very few significant differences among Protestant denominations which did not reflect differences in the class position or regional background of individual members . . . For all these reasons we have treated Protestantism as a unit, except as it is divided along racial lines. . . .

The Four Socio-Religious Groups: Strength of Group Ties

Let us now turn to our *dramatis personae*, the four major socio-religious

groups. There are a number of questions which should be answered before we examine the secular institutions of the community. To begin with, how do the groups compare with one another in terms of vitality?

When one examines the four major socio-religious groups in Detroit in the light of our distinction between the association and the subcommunity, it quickly becomes evident that each is a distinctive type of social organization. The Jewish and Catholic groups present the sharpest contrasts, so let us examine them first.

The Jewish Group

In the case of Judaism we are confronted with a group in which the religious associations have been seriously weakened. In Orbach's recent analysis of church attendance in the Detroit area (based on six of the first seven sample surveys of the Detroit Area Study), it was found that only 12 per cent of the Jews $(N = 192)$[4] reported regular weekly attendance at synagogue or temple.[5] Another 20 per cent reported attending at least once a month, and 56 per cent only on High Holy Days, or a few times a year. Twelve per cent did not attend at all.[6]

---

[4] This symbol $(N = 192)$ means that the percentage cited in the same sentence is based on 192 cases. . . .

[5] These data were assembled by H. L. Orbach and presented at a meeting of the Gerontological Society in a paper entitled, "Age and Religious Participation in a Large Metropolitan Area." A revised version of this paper is to be published in an issue of *Geriatrics* in 1960. The findings are based on the reported church attendance of nearly 7000 Detroiters.

[6] In a study of the Jewish group in an eastern seaboard city of 130,000, only 22 per cent reported attending synagogue at times other than High Holy Days. See Marshall Sklare and Marc Vosk, *The Riverton Study:*

On the basis of such evidence one might conclude that the ties binding the individual to the group are very weak. However, the 1958 survey indicates that while the *associational* bond is weak in the Jewish group, the *communal* bond is extremely strong. In fact, available evidence indicates that the communal bond in the Jewish group is as strong, or stronger than in any other group. For example, it was found that *all* of the Jewish respondents in our sample who were married (N = 24) were lifelong Jews married to a lifelong Jewish spouse.[7] When asked what proportion of their close relatives were Jewish, 96 per cent said that all or nearly all were Jewish. When asked the same question about their close friends, 77 per cent reported

that all or nearly all were Jewish. Such evidence makes it clear that while the ties binding individual Jews to their religious associations have been seriously weakened in modern times, the ties of communalism remain strong. If our sample is at all reliable, the great majority of Detroit Jews find most of their primary-type relationships within the Jewish subcommunity.

The Catholic Group

The white Catholic group presents a very different picture in every respect. On the basis of Orbach's six-year survey, it appears that more than 70 per cent of Detroit Catholics (N = 2374) attend Mass at least once a week and only about 5 per cent fail to attend at all. While there may be some measure of exaggeration in these figures,[8] it is certain that the ties binding the individual to the nuclear association are far stronger in Catholicism than in Judaism.

In the case of communal ties, the situation is exactly reversed. Catholics are far more inclined than Jews to marry and establish other intimate personal relationships outside their group. Sixteen per cent of the Catholic respondents in the 1958 survey reported that they were currently married to a non-Catholic. In addition still others had contracted marriages with non-Catholics who ultimately became Catholics, or themselves left the Catholic church as a consequence of

How Jews Look at Themselves and Their Neighbors (New York: The American Jewish Committee, 1957), p. 11. In Washington, D.C., 25 per cent reported attendance at least once a month. See Stanley Bigman, *The Jewish Population of Greater Washington in 1956* (Washington: The Jewish Community Council of Greater Washington, 1956), p. 100. These figures suggest that Detroit Jews are more active in synagogue than Jews on the East Coast.

[7] In the special interdecennial sample survey of 1957 the Bureau of the Census included a question on religious preference. One of the findings of this census was that over 96 per cent of all American Jews are married to persons currently professing to be Jews. For Catholics the comparable figure was 89 per cent. For all Protestants, both Negro and white, the figure was nearly 96 per cent. U.S. Bureau of the Census, *Current Population Reports: Population Characteristics*, Series P–20, No. 79 (February 2, 1958): see especially Tables 6 and 7. In interpreting these figures it must be kept in mind that Protestants are much more likely to marry Protestants merely because of chance, since 66 per cent of all Americans aged 14 and over are Protestants, while this is much less likely for Catholics and Jews, who constitute only 26 and 3 per cent of the population respectively.

[8] Those conducting sample surveys found long ago that there is some tendency for respondents to exaggerate their good qualities and minimize their poor qualities when being interviewed. Such exaggerations usually tend to be minor in character rather than blatant misrepresentations or falsification. In studies of behavior, such misrepresentations do not present a serious problem since there is reason for believing that exaggerations occur in roughly the same *proportions* throughout the population.

marrying a non-Catholic, so that 30 per cent of all those who were raised as Catholics married someone who was raised a non-Catholic.

In view of the high rate of inter-marriage between Catholics and non-Catholics, it is hardly surprising that a substantial minority of Catholics have a significant number of close relatives who are non-Catholics. Whereas 96 per cent of the Jews reported that all or nearly all of their close relatives were Jewish, only 79 per cent of the Catholics reported that all or nearly all of their close relatives were Catholics. There is an even more pronounced discrepancy with respect to ties of friendship. Whereas 77 per cent of the Jewish respondents reported that all or nearly all of their close friends were Jewish, the comparable figure for Catholics was only 44 per cent.

On the basis of such data we can see that Judaism and Catholicism represent two distinct types of socio-religious groups in the modern metropolis. In the Jewish group communal ties predominate, and ties with religious associations are extremely weak. In the Catholic group the relationship is reversed, though it would be an exaggeration to say that Catholic communal ties are weak.

The White Protestant Group

In the white Protestant group still another pattern emerges. The proportion of white Protestants who attend worship services regularly falls far below the Catholic figure, though not nearly so low as in the Jewish group. In Orbach's six-year survey it was found that roughly one third of the white Protestants in Detroit (N = 2887) attend worship services every Sunday. Slightly more than 20 per cent attend from one to three times a month, and 14 per cent never attend. The remaining third attend occasionally.

In communal solidarity and strength, however, white Protestants closely match white Catholics. Whereas 84 per cent of the white Catholics who were married reported that their spouse was of the same faith, 86 per cent of the white Protestants made the same statements. Whereas 70 per cent of those who were raised Catholics married someone raised a Catholic, 73 per cent of the white Protestants married someone raised a Protestant. Seventy-nine per cent of the white Catholics and 76 per cent of the white Protestants reported that all or nearly all of their close relatives were of the same faith. Finally, 44 per cent of the white Catholics reported that all or nearly all of their close friends were of the same faith; the corresponding figure for white Protestants was 38 per cent.

Judging from such evidence, it appears that the white Protestant group is the least cohesive of the three white socio-religious groups. It lacks the very strong communal bond of the Jewish group, and it lacks the very strong associational bond of the Catholic group. In terms of the *relative* strength of these two bonds, however, the white Protestant group resembles the Jewish group a bit more than the Catholic group since the communal bond seems to be somewhat stronger than the associational bond. However, this resemblance should not be exaggerated; the differences are still very real.

The Negro Protestant Group

In the Negro Protestant group the communal bond is extremely strong, owing to the discriminatory practices of whites. As Drake and Cayton noted in their book on Chicago Negroes, race relations in the North and South differ chiefly in the area of secondary-type relationships, or the more impersonal, contractual-type relationships.[9] In the

[9] St. Clair Drake and Horace R. Cayton, *Black Metropolis* (New York: Harcourt, Brace and Co., 1945), Chapter 6.

South these are segregated, in the North they are integrated. In the realm of primary-type relationships—intimate relations of kinship and friendship—segregation tends to be the rule in the urban North almost as much as in the rural South. Of necessity, therefore, the overwhelming majority of Negroes in Detroit marry other Negroes, and find their intimate personal relationships with others of their own race. Counterdiscrimination by Negroes themselves is also a factor.

While data were not obtained on these matters in the 1958 survey, it seems safe to estimate that not less than 98 per cent of Detroit Negroes are married to others of their race and also find their *close relatives* limited to their own race. With respect to *close friends,* it seems that an estimate of 90 to 95 per cent being limited to others of the Negro race would not be far wide of the mark.[10]

To some extent the estimates above exaggerate the degree to which Negro Protestants associate with other Negro Protestants, since a small minority of the Negro population consists of Catholics, non-believers, and adherents to non-Christian cults. However, since these groups constitute no more than about 10–12 per cent of the Negro population, their influence is not great. Furthermore, these Negro minorities seem to be partially assimilated to the subculture of the dominant Negro Protestant majority.[11]

[10] These estimates are based primarily on conclusions derived from the author's personal contacts with Negro students from the Detroit area attending the University of Michigan. Also it may be noted that in the 1958 Detroit Area Study, only 1 interracial marriage was discovered out of nearly 550 marriages.

[11] For example, Orbach's study of church attendance, op. cit., shows that the church-attendance patterns of Negro Catholics are virtually identical with those of Negro Protestants, and stand in sharp contrast to the much more regular attendance of white Catholics.

While the associational bond in the Negro Protestant group is not nearly so strong as the communal bond, it is nevertheless stronger than in any of the other socio-religious groups except the white Catholic. Nearly 40 per cent of Negro Protestants (N = 1030) attend worship services every Sunday, and more than three quarters attend at least once a month. Negro Protestants were tied with white Catholics in having the smallest percentage of persons who have completely divorced themselves from the nuclear religious associations. Only 5 per cent never go to church.[12]

Summary

For a summary of the evidence so far we may turn to Table 1, which shows

TABLE 1. *Relative Strength of Associational and Communal Bonds in the Four Major Socio-Religious Groups*

	STRENGTH OF BONDS:	
SOCIO-RELIGIOUS GROUP	ASSOCIATIONAL	COMMUNAL
Jews	Weak	Strong
White Catholics	Strong	Medium
White Protestants	Medium	Medium
Negro Protestants	Medium	Strong

that each of our four groups posseses a distinct combination of communal and associational attributes. Of the four, the white Protestant group seems to be the least cohesive, but is obviously in no danger of dissolution.

One final bit of evidence concerning group cohesion and solidarity was ob-

[12] The smallness of this figure for all four groups seems to indicate that for the overwhelming majority of persons who identify with one or another of the groups, the nuclear religious associations are of some importance, no matter how slight.

tained when we asked Detroiters whether they thought any of their friends or relatives would try to discourage them, or would be at all disturbed or unhappy, if they attempted to join another faith. . . . Judging from the vigor of the responses, it is clear that desertion of one's native group is regarded as closely akin to treason in many circles. For example, when a young Jewish housewife was asked whether her friends and relatives would try to discourage her from changing her faith she replied: "Yes—they'd kill me. My mother is very religious." In answer to the same question a young Catholic man said succinctly: "I'd get hung." A Lutheran housewife, a convert from Catholicism, described in some detail the vigorous efforts her friends and relatives made to dissuade her.

Nearly two thirds of all Detroiters stated that they thought their friends and relatives would try to discourage them if they attempted to join another group. The percentages in each group expecting this were as follows:

White Catholic	81 per cent
Jews	72 per cent
White Protestants	60 per cent
Negro Protestants	24 per cent

Those who said that no one would attempt to discourage them were then asked whether they thought any of their friends or relatives would be at all unhappy or disturbed if they made such a change, since even this kind of mild response would be something of a restraining influence. In the four major groups, an additional 10 per cent indicated that such a reaction was likely. In other words, fully 72 per cent of the total membership of these groups expected some objection if they sought to shift their allegiance. Omitting the Negro Protestants and taking the three white groups together, 82 per cent, or more than four fifths, expected *some* type of sanction. Broken down by groups, the figures were as follows:

Jews	96 per cent
White Catholics	87 per cent
White Protestants	75 per cent
Negro Protestants	28 per cent

These figures suggest that whatever the Jewish group lacks in associational vitality is more than compensated for by the strength of the communal bond.[13]

[13] In a study of an unnamed eastern seaboard community of 130,000 it was found that only 2 per cent of the Jewish parents interviewed had no objection to their children marrying a Gentile. Sklare and Vosk, op. cit., p. 33.

C · CULTURE AND DIFFERENTIATION

1 · *The Masses, Folk Belief and Universal Religion*

GUSTAV MENSCHING

The masses have a peculiar connection with universal religion, for on the one hand, to be sure, they do not understand the ideas of high religion, and on the other hand (partly out of their distortion of ideas, partly out of a primeval folk-religious heritage), they create a religion of their own which we call folk belief. We understand the term "masses" here in the sense of Gustave LeBon. The basic tendencies of the masses adduced by LeBon are indeed to the point, but they do not exhaust the character of the masses in general, and the purely religious primitive tendencies of the masses are not discussed by LeBon. Nevertheless, we may, in broad connection with LeBon's analysis, cite a number of general mass tendencies which, religiously speaking, work out in such fashion that they lead directly to folk belief and make the latter comprehensible.

1. Our problem is the comportment of the masses within a high religion. It must be added at once that this must be *organized* high religion, in order for the

SOURCE. A translation in abridged form by the editor from Gustav Mensching, *Soziologie der Religion*, Bonn: Ludwig Röhrscheid, 1947, pp. 137–148. [An occasional paraphrase, rather than translation, could not be avoided. L.S.]

problem to arise, for as long as high religion is and remains a matter of individuals who are deeply moved personally, masses in our sense have nothing to do with it. In that case, high religion is what it is supposed to be in its purity, a matter of conscious personal decision. And the communal religious structures of pure high religion are communities of committed individuals, but certainly not mass structures. This, LeBon has quite left out of consideration. For him, every union of divers persons is a mass, which without further specification is subject to the laws of the mass spirit. The view which we here defend is that the high-religious communal structures *may* become "massified." But they need not necessarily do so. *Organized* high religion, for example in the form of a church, on the other hand, has to do with masses, since it stands unqualifiedly open to all and actually has the tendency to take up within itself as many people as possible—and therefore the masses. But what are the tendencies of the masses which operate religiously?

(a) The masses are not moved by rational considerations but by dim, subconscious motives and feelings. The consequence is that the individual in the mass largely loses his individuality and independence. Thus the level of the masses is lowered to a primitive stage and becomes disposed toward the taking on of primitive forms of belief.

(b) The masses are credulous. The unusual and fantastic arouse their imaginative propensity and find credence with them. Hence the masses very easily construct legends and demand miracles of all sorts. They are most readily influenced by concrete representations and graphic events or reports of events. They ask for large guarantees, for the certainty of the visible and the empirically experienceable. Here there emerges incapacity for symbolic thought.

(c) The masses are one-sided. They cannot, in independent judgment, form a differentiated opinion, but can only accept or reject wholesale what they find in various doctrines. Only *unqualified* truths are accepted by them. Doubt and probing effort to attain truth and certainty are alien to them.

(d) The masses may be ethically good or bad. They show no necessary tendency to the ethically good. They are only externally subject to influence in either direction. They need external moral leadership. And they allow themselves to be guided by what "people" do, again with abandonment of one's own judgment and of rational and moral testing of convention. The moral level of the masses is actually very low. Organized high religion is wont to aim for a lowered ethics of the masses, for a lesser perfection beside the greater perfection of the virtuosos of piety.

(e) Tradition has great power over the masses. They abide by the usual and the accustomed with great tenacity. They guard against change and innovation and connect these with the sentiment of sacrilege. They clothe customary forms in a sacred invulnerability, on which the practical effect of transactions in the holy is made to depend. And here we already have the basic tendency of the masses which is decisive for folk belief: the primitive magical attitude.

(f) The masses are a sociological residue from the stage of the sacred folk community. The magical world-view corresponds to the latter; and in early time this world-view is mixed with religion, just as it is found in the masses in high religion. Primitive magical religion, again, is the most important factor in folk belief.

(g) Finally, the desire to be led and for leaders characterizes the masses, religious as well as other masses. The religious masses demand authoritative leadership by the representatives of a religious organization to whom nearly divine power and virtue are imputed. Priests are the leaders of the religious. They and the organizations they serve are expert in the handling of the masses.

2. The belief of the masses, "folk belief" in its most general and basic features, can be derived and understood from these most general tendencies.

(a) First we may note the amazing *sameness* of folk belief. In terms of content, folk beliefs everywhere in the world of religion resemble one another most astonishingly. As examples, Chinese and Indian folk belief are very similar. Frazer has referred to the universal sameness of folk belief and noted that in India the religion of the common people was really a belief in an immense number of spirits, many, if not most of them, malicious and harmful. He has remarked that as in Europe (under a veneer of Christianity) so in the Orient, belief in magic and witchcraft, in spirits and kobolds has constantly maintained itself popularly.

(b) The foundation of folk belief is magic. The masses believe in powers and forces that can be influenced by magical practice. The idea of mana is alive everywhere in the folk belief of religions. With the dynamic conception of mana there is often bound up a personalistic notion. "Power" appears in personal form, in large numbers of spirits, toward whom the appropriate behavior is on the lines of magical conjuring. It is obvious that many elements within the masses are especially disposed toward this elementary magic: women, standing closer to the primitive forces of life and more influenced by feeling than men; among occupational classes, peasants, whose life work brings them more closely into contact with and arouses presentiments about the dark and mysterious powers of the earth; hunters and sailors, whose occupations make them feel their dependence upon powers they cannot control by reason and vocational skills; soldiers, men hourly threatened by death who have always been ready to ensure themselves against the deadly shot by means of magical folk belief.

(c) All folk belief has a pronouncedly eudemonistic character. Happiness and prosperity, personal success of every kind —these are the aims served by the folk belief of all times and peoples. (Thus it comes about that folk belief degrades religious credo and cultus to the status of instrumentalities of earthly welfare, within high religion oriented to quite different things such as the salvation of the soul. The primitive reward—and—punishment theme, reckoning with the compensation of earthly merits, plays an important role in all folk belief.) The kind of installation a Japanese may have in the way of a Buddha-altar in a wall niche is designed for the happiness and prosperity of his family. A niche for a deity reminds us of the corner for God in Catholic and especially in Bavarian houses. But in both East and West this sort of installation arises from the primitive need for the proximity and solid presence of the holy.

(d) Here we come upon a further essential element of all folk belief: the nearness and differentiation and vividness of the divine reflect a primitive religious tendency of all masses. The inaccessible remoteness of the high-religious *single* divinity everywhere arouses in the masses the same feeling of aloneness and evokes the desire for mediation, for differentiation, for specialization of the divinely all-powerful in the form of an abundance of celestial beings which shall be close to man. This tendency of the masses is shown in Islam. As against the remote God in all his majesty and arbitrariness, the simple man of the masses feels the need for nearness through mediating powers. High Islamic religion does not satisfy the need of the masses. From the same tendency arises the cult of saints of the Catholic Church. The saints are near and trustworthy helpers in distress in life's daily concerns, who have their precisely delimited functional spheres.

(e) The desire for leadership noted above as a general tendency of the masses meets, in organized high religion, with the propensity to leadership and rule everywhere peculiar to the clergy. The organized priesthood therefore takes over, in all places, the handling of the masses as it demands and achieves their full subordination—for the demand corresponds to the masses' own disposition. But then the belief of these subordinated, subject masses—folk belief—becomes incorporated into the system of high religion.

In universal religion that has become firmly organized there necessarily arises a folk belief of the masses which maintains itself unchanged through the millennia since the masses also remain identical with themselves. If we look about us in the world of high religion we encounter everywhere the same mass belief that has been characterized in principle above.

1. Primitive folk belief again made its way into the old Mazdaism of Zoroaster. Mazdaism is indeed as much an example of the arousal of magic as it is of the reversion of the high-religious monotheism of Zoroaster to an outright polytheism.

2. Buddhism likewise everywhere shows the emergence of magical-primitive folk belief. Particularly within the church organization of Lamaism in Tibet, the entire world of folk religion is present in baffling profusion. Holy objects are built into or allowed entry into the figures of gods and saints in order to make them ritually effective. Thereby magical mana-power is conferred. All cult objects need this power and receive it by a consecration carried out according to set prescriptions. The characteristic instruments for typically folk-religious mechanization of piety are prayer-wheels, which, with the motion given by wind or water, effect increase of the virtues earned by their builders.

But folk belief again and again breaks through in other areas of Buddhism, for example in the Shingon and Tendai sects of Japan. (Tendai was founded by Dengyo Daishi, 767–822; Shingon by Kobo Daishi, 744–835.) Both built a tremendous system of ritual magic and prayer for all man's conceivable hurts and wishes: against illnesses, labor in birth, danger of fire, drought, robbery, apparitions, spirits of the forest, evil dreams, and so on. All sorts of apparatus are used to carry out the rituals involved.

Even the reform sect founded by Nichiren (born 1222 A.D.), which sought to keep itself free from magical folk belief, was not spared a re-awakening thereof. Amulets, all sorts of talismans, magical formulas, and magical transactions were widely diffused, and all this expression of folk belief was supported even by the priestly group which attended to mass dispositions.

The situation was similar in the Shin sect of Japanese Buddhism. Before the reformers, Honen Shonin (born 1133 A.D.) and Shinran Shonin (born 1173 A.D.) founded the Shin sect, religion was overgrown with all the forms of folk belief. Conjuring, recitation of sutras for the dead, oracles, interpretations of dreams, drawing of lots, magical choice of propitious days, astrology, divination, and so on, were widespread. The folk themselves were busy with calling upon the name of Buddha, with the reading and copying of holy texts, with pilgrimages, with offerings of flowers and incense, with the making of bells and temple paraphernalia and entire temples. They were preoccupied with vows and ascetic exercises. At the beginning of the twelfth century, the Tantric practices of the "left hand" spread for the first time in the above mentioned Shingon sect. This Tantrism regarded sexual union as means for the attainment of Buddhahood. Such was the orientation of the Tachikawa sect, which made rapid gains in those days. And in the recent past, also, shortly before 1868, the end of the Tokugawa period and the beginning of Japan's new political and religious order, there existed among the broad masses a folk belief ingeniously exploited by the Buddhist and Shintoist priesthood —although this belief has so little to do with higher religious ideas that it cannot in a strict sense be imputed to either Buddhism or Shintoism.

3. The same situation confronts us in Islam. Mohammed himself, believing in jinn and magical powers, made considerable concessions to folk belief, which accordingly developed the more profusely. Exorcism was a common substitute for medical science. Amulets with verses from the Koran or with symbolic, magically effective verses were worn. White magic is the special domain of dervishes. In the Islamic saint-cult, old cults repressed by Islam live on and fulfil the need of the masses to bridge over the distance to the one remote God through

mediating powers. Belonging to a religious order is valued by the masses as a potent means for the attainment of blessings in this world and the next. Members of the orders, in Islamic folk belief, dispose of a power of giving benediction, lending incomparable efficacy to amulets, pleas, and prescriptions. Some of the orders owe their particular success among the masses to the belief that their members eat snakes and scorpions without being harmed, can swallow fire and fragments of glass, and are invulnerable to weapons.

4. The Christian church organization, which actively opened itself to the masses, was of course also not spared folk belief. There are the holy objects employed by the folk for magical—eudemonistic uses, like holy water, willow catkin, amulets, rosaries, candles, bells, and so on. Primitive folk belief is evident in the multiplication of prayers recommended by the church; for here prayer itself becomes a meritorious sacrificial performance and can be employed for various purposes. But this signifies that the meaning of the Our Father, for example, which is expressed in supplications is no longer attended to and the

prayer is employed in its wholeness for concrete purposes, as becomes evident from the phrase "to say an Our Father for someone." Also in processions with the various ends that are to be gained by them, we confront ancient magical folk belief. As in Islam, so also in Catholicism the abstract monotheism of primitive Christianity is replaced by large numbers of holy powers and persons, by saints, angels, and archangels, and at the top of the celestial hosts there is the queen of heaven, Mary, the "Mother of God," to whom the most ardent forms of the Catholic cult are addressed.

The masses are a constant folk-religious residue. They remain the oppressive majority in universal religion also, and, on the basis of folk-religious primitive experience and driven by the primitive tendencies of religious masses, they believe in folk-religious manner and with folk-religious intention. However different religions are, folk-belief is similar in all the high religions. The primitive and ancient experiences of mankind are everywhere the same, and later men for the most part never transcend them. Differentiation first sets in over this elementary human stratum.

2 · Christianity and Modern Industrial Society

TALCOTT PARSONS

The present volume is conceived as a tribute to Professor Sorokin as a distinguished elder statesman of sociology, not only in the United States but also throughout the world. One of the highest achievements, particularly in a rapidly

SOURCE. Reprinted with permission of the publisher from *Sociological Theory, Values, and Sociocultural Change*, edited by Edward Tiryakian. Copyright 1963 by The Free Press of Glencoe, a division of the Macmillan Company.

developing discipline in its early phases of development, is to serve as a generator and focus of creatively important differences of opinion. Such differences pose problems which, though not solved or in any immediate sense soluble in the generation in question, still serve to orient the thinking of professional groups. For such differences to be fruitful there must be a delicate balance of commonly accepted premises, which make a fruitful meeting of minds possible, and difference of interpretation in more particularized questions which are open to some sort of empirical test.

In the sociological profession today Professor Sorokin and the present author are probably defined predominantly as antagonists who have taken widely different views on a variety of subjects.[1] The objective of this chapter is to take explicit cognizance of one, to me crucial, field of such difference of opinion, but to attempt to place it within a framework of common problems in the hope that consideration of the difference may help others toward a fruitful solution of these problems.

In the highly empirical atmosphere of American sociology in recent times there has been a tendency to neglect the importance of the great problems of the trends of development of Western society and culture in a large sense, of its place relative to the great civilizations of the Orient, and similar problems. Within this field the problem of the role of religion and its relation to social values stands in a particularly central position. In my opinion it is one of Sorokin's great services to have held these problems consistently in the forefront of concern, and to have refused to be satisfied with a sociology which did not have anything significant to say about them. In this fundamental respect Sorokin stands in the great tradition of Western sociological thought. This emphasis coincides with my own strong predilections, shaped as they were by European experience under the influences in particular of Max Weber and Durkheim.

It can, I think, safely be said that we share the convictions, first, of the enormous importance of the general evolutionary and comparative perspective in the interpretation of social phenomena and, second, of the crucial role of religion and its relation to values in this large perspective. When, however, we turn to more particular problems of spell-

ing out this context, differences of opinion emerge. A particularly important test case is that of the interpretation of the relations of religious orientation, values, and social structure in the course of that development in the modern Western world which has eventuated in modern industrialism. I propose to set over against a very schematic but I hope accurate outline of Sorokin's view, my own, which I think may be the kind of alternative which, though differing sharply from his view, may pose fruitful empirical questions on which future research may be expected to throw light. Only in this broadest contrast will I attempt to take account of the Sorokin position. My objective is not to present either a full statement or a critique of his conceptions as such, but to state my own as clearly as possible.

The heart of the Sorokin position which is relevant here I take to be his classification and use of three fundamental types of cultural orientation—the "ideational," "idealistic," and "sensate." [2] What may be called orientations in terms of the grounds of meaning on the one hand and values for social and personal conduct on the other, are treated as by and large varying together.

The ideational pattern is one which gives unquestionable primacy to transcendental and other-worldly interests in the religious sense. Reality itself is defined as ultimately beyond the reach of the senses, as transcendental. The goal of life must be to reach the closest possible accord with the nature of transcendent reality, and the path to this must involve renunciation of all worldly interests. Broadly speaking, other-worldly asceticism and mysticism are the paths to it. The ethical component which is so prominent in Christianity generally is not missing from Sorokin's conception. It takes, however, the form on which his later work has placed increasing stress: that of altruistic love, of pure **personal** selfless acts of love by individuals. In this discussion I would like to differentiate this form of altruism from the *institutionalization* of Christian ethics to become part of the structure of the society itself. It is the latter with which my analysis will be concerned.

The opposite extreme to the ideational pattern is the sensate. Here the empirical, in the last analysis the "material," aspect of reality is taken as ultimately real or predominant. In practical conduct the implication of a sensate view of the world is to make the most of the opportunities of the here and now, to be concerned with world success, power, and—in the last analysis—to put hedonistic gratifications first of all.

The idealistic pattern is conceived as intermediate between the two, not in the sense of a simple "compromise," but rather of a synthesis which can achieve a harmonious balance between the two principal components.

This basic classification is then used as the framework for outlining a developmental pattern leading, in the history of a civilization, from ideational to idealistic predominance and in turn from idealistic to sensate. Though very generally applied, the two most important cases dealt with in Sorokin's works are the civilization of classical antiquity and that of the Christian West. In both cases there was an early ideational phase which gradually gave way to an idealistic synthesis: in the classical that of fifth-century Greece, in the Western that of the high Middle Ages. The idealistic synthesis has then proceeded to break down into an increasingly sensate phase—in the classical case the late Hellenistic and Roman periods, in the Western the modern "capitalistic" or industrial period. Sorokin tends to regard the contemporary period, exemplified particularly in the United States, but also in the Soviet Union, as close to the peak of the sensate phase of development and destined for a general breakdown comparable to that of Greco-Roman civilization before a new ideational pattern can become established.

From one point of view the general developmental trend Sorokin outlines may be described as a progressive decline in the "religiousness" of the society and culture until a radical reversal is forced by a general societal breakdown. In the Western case the phase of early Christianity was the most religious, characterized by a primarily ascetic disregard for virtually all worldly interests, and the practice of brotherly love within the Christian community itself. Correspondingly, however, Christianity in this phase had little power to organize social relationships beyond the church. With the development of the idealistic phase, however, for a time it was possible to permeate secular life with at least an approximation of Christian ethics, but the balance was precarious and broke down relatively soon.

There may well be a considerable measure of agreement up to this point. Sorokin, however, clearly regards Protestantism, compared with medieval Catholicism, as primarily a step in the general decline of religiousness, and the secularism which has been prominent since the Age of the Enlightenment as the natural further step in the same direction. It is hence on the interpretation of Protestantism in the general process of Western social development and its sequel after the Reformation period that I would like to focus my own view. It will be necessary, however, to say a few things about more general theoretical orientation, and about the earlier historical phases as background for this analysis.

An Alternative Interpretation

There are two interrelated theoretical issues which need to be discussed briefly before entering into a historical analysis. These concern factors in the structure of a religious orientation itself on the one hand and the senses in which religious orientations and their institutionalization in the social system can undergo processes of structural differentiation on the other.

In the former respect Professor Sorokin seems to think primarily in terms of a single variable which might be called "degree of religiousness." This in turn tends to be identified with transcendental orientation in the sense of *other-worldliness* as defining the acceptable field of interest and activity. This is to say that, so far as religious interests are in any sense paramount in a motivational system, the religious person will tend to renounce the world and engage so far as possible in ascetic or devotional practices or mystical contemplation and purely spontaneous acts of love, reducing his involvement in "practical" affairs which involve institutionalized obligations to a minimum. He will therefore tend to be oriented to the reduction of all desires to participate positively and actively in worldly activities like political or economic functions. By the same token, positive commitment to such worldly interests and responsibilities is taken as an index of relative lack of religious interest.

Relative to the degree of religiousness we suggest the relevance of a second variable which we think is independent. This is the one which Max Weber formulated as the variation between other-worldly and inner-worldly orientation. Combined with a high degree of religiousness, the choice of one alternative leads to religious rejection of the world, the choice of the other to an orientation to mastery over the world in the name of religious values. There are further complications in the problem of a general typology of religious orientations, but suffice it to say for the present that I propose to explore the possibilities implicit in the hypothesis that Western Christianity belongs in the category of orientation which is high in degree of religiousness, with a predominantly inner-worldly orientation so far as the field of expected action of the individual is concerned. In ways I shall try to explain, this applies even to early and medieval Christianity, but becomes most clearly evident in "ascetic Protestantism." I feel that this hypothesis is excluded by Sorokin's assumption that religiousness *ipso facto* implies other-worldliness, supplemented only by spontaneous altruism.

The second main theoretical point concerns the question of differentiation. I think of religion as an aspect of human action. Like all other aspects, in the course of social, cultural, and personality development it undergoes processes of differentiation in a double sense. The first of these concerns differentiation within religious systems themselves, the second the differentiation of the religious element from nonreligious elements in the more general system of action. In the latter context the general developmental trend may be said to be from fusions of religious and nonreligious components in the same action structures, to increasingly clear differentiation between multiple spheres of action.

A special problem arises when we deal with a system over a sufficiently long period of time to include two or more stages in a process of differentiation. Structural parts of the system have to be named. It is in the nature of the process of differentiation that what was one part at an earlier stage becomes two or more distinct parts at a later. The simple logical question then is whether the name applied at the earlier stage is still used to designate any one of the parts surviving at the later. If the process is one of differentiation, clearly the surviving entity which carries the same name will be narrower in scope and more "specialized" in the later than it was in the earlier stage. It will then, by mere logic, have lost function and become less important than in the earlier phase. The problem then becomes one of analyzing the continuities, not only of the component called by the same name in the different stages, e.g., *religion,* but also of the senses in which the patterns of orientation given in the earlier stages have or have not been fundamentally altered in their significance for the system as a whole, considering the exigencies of the situations in which action takes place and the complex relations of this part to the other parts of the more differentiated system, e.g., the non-religious or secular.

It is my impression that Professor Sorokin has not given sufficient weight to these considerations and has tended to measure the influence of religion, from earlier to later stages, as if it were reasonable to expect maintenance of the same "degree of inclusiveness" in the direct "definition of the situation" for action which it enjoyed in the early stage of reference. Judged by this standard the degree of religiousness of Christian society has clearly suffered a progressive decline by the mere fact that the society has become functionally a more highly differentiated system of action than was the early "primitive" church.

The Setting of the Problem: Christianity—Society

As a first step it is necessary to outline a few essentials of the nature of the early Christian church and its relations to the secular society of the time. Its structure comprised, as is well known, a very distinctive synthesis of elements derived from Judaism, Greek philosophy, the Greek conception of social organization, and of course distinctive contributions of its own.

The Hebrew and the Greek patterns had in common the conception of a solidary, religiously sanctioned social unit, the organization of which was based on values fully transcending the loyalties of

kinship. In the Hebrew case it was the confederation of "tribes" bound to Jahweh and to each other by the Covenant. These units became fused into a "people" whose main orientation to life was defined in terms of the Law given to them by Jahweh, a firm collectivity structure defining its role as the fulfillment of God's commandments. In the historical course, by what precise stages need not concern us here, two crucial developments occurred. First Jahweh became a completely universal transcendental God who governed the activities not only of the people of Israel but of all mankind. Second, the people of Israel became, through the exile, depoliticized. Their religion was the essential bond of solidarity. Since this was no longer expressed in an independent political community, it was not exposed to the "secularizing" influences so importantly involved in political responsibility.

On the Greek side the *polis* was a comparable solidary confederation, in the first instance of kinship lineages. It was the "political" society almost par excellence, but one which eventually came to be based on the principle of the universalistic equality of citizens. Religiously it was oriented not to a transcendental God but to an immanent polytheism. The conception of the ultimate unity of divinity emerged in Greek civilization, but essentially as a philosophical principle the necessity of which was demonstrated by reason.

Seen against the background of Judaism and in certain respects also of the Greek component, the most important distinctive feature of Christianity of importance here was its religious individualism. In Judaism the primary religious concern was with the fate of the Jewish community as God's chosen people. In Christianity it became the fate of the individual soul; God was concerned with the salvation of individuals, not simply with the extent to which a social community as such adhered to His commandments.

This new conception of the relation of the individual soul to God might seem, given the fundamental transcendental character of the God of Judaism, to imply the virtual abandonment of concern with life in the world, to make the life of the Christian center primarily in devotional interests in preparing for the life to come. Indeed this strain in Christianity has always been a crucially important one and marks it off sharply from the main trend of Judaism. In this respect Christianity, however different its theological orientation, was closely analogous to Indian religion. But there was another aspect to Christian individualism: the fact that its adherents came to constitute a very special type of social collectivity on earth, the Christian church. The theological significance of the Christ figure as the mediator between God and man is central as defining the nature of man's relation to God, in and through the Church of Christ. It was the conception of the church which underlay the nature of the ethical conception of Christianity and was the basis from which the moral influence of Christianity could operate on secular society.

In theoretical terms this may be expressed by saying that the conception of the church, which implied the fundamental break with the Jewish law which Paul made final, constituted the *differentiation* of Christianity as a religious system (a cultural system) from the conception of a "people" as a social system. Given the Roman ascendancy in the secular society of the time, this differentiation was expressed in the famous formula "Render unto Caesar the things that are Caesar's" —i.e., the church did not claim jurisdiction over secular society as such.

At the same time this church was a solidary collectivity. The keynote here was the conception of "brothers in Christ." Its members were by no means

concerned only with their respective personal salvations, but with the mission of Christ on behalf of mankind. This had the dual meaning of an obligation to extend the Christian community by proselytizing and, within it, to organize its internal relations on the basis in the first instance of mutual brotherly love.

Though, religiously speaking, this was a radically individualistic doctrine, it was not an anarchistic, but what we have come to call an "institutionalized" individualism. The Christian doctrine of the Trinity, compared with Jewish unitarianism, is intimately connected with this development. Instead of a single "line" of relationship between an ultimately transcendental God and man, God became related to man *through* the Christ figure who was both God and Man, and Christ became the head of the Church, the "essence" of which was formulated as the third person of the Trinity, the Holy Spirit.

As I interpret it, this implied, correlative with the differentiation of the church from secular society, a differentiation *within* the religious system itself, in the broadest respect between the aspect of devotion and worship on the one hand, and the aspect of the Christian's relation to his fellow men on the other. The Christian community was constituted by the fact of common faith and common worship, but the contexts in which worship was paramount were differentiated from the context of love and charity which bound the community together in bonds of human mutuality.

From the present point of view this differentiation was just as important as the first, and intimately connected with it. The Jewish law had held the individual to highly detailed prescriptions of conduct which were "rationalized" for the most part only in the sense that they were declared to be Divine commandments. Now, as a member of the church he was held to a set of principles of conduct—the obligation to act in accord with the Holy Spirit. And though obviously directly connected with his commitment to God through faith, conduct in this world could be made to a degree independent of this, above all, in the sense that detailed prescriptions of behavior were not taken as religiously given but only the general principles of ethical action. Thus action decisions in particular cases had to be left to the conscience of believers and could not be prescribed by a comprehensive religious law. The context of worship was an independent context which generated motivation to act in accord with the spirit, but was not exactly the same thing as this action.

This differentiation occurred, however, within a genuine unity. The key theological problem here was the doctrine of the Creation and whether it implied an ontological dualism. In the great formative period this came to a head in the struggle with Manichaeism, and Augustine's fundamental decision against the latter broadly settled the issue. The sphere of the church as that part of man's life on earth directly dominated by the Holy Spirit was then a point of mediation between the direct expression of Divine will through Christ and the rest of the Creation. But the implication was that this remainder of the Creation could not be governed by an ontologically independent principle of evil and was hence inherently subject to Christianization.

Thus religious individualism, in the sense in which it became institutionalized in the Christian church, represented, relative to Judaism, a new autonomy of the individual on two fronts. In his own relation to God as an object of worship, the individual was released from his ascriptive embeddedness in the Jewish community. Whatever the relation of dependence on God implied in this, it was as an individual in the religious relation that he could be saved. There was also a new autonomy in his relation to the field of

human action, in the first instance as a member of the church and in his relations to his fellow members in brotherly love. The church was an association of believers, manifesting their attachment to God in their conduct in this world. The church was thus independent, not an ascribed aspect of a total society. There was hence, through these channels, a basic legitimation of the importance of life in this world, but in a situation where the church could reserve a basic independence from those aspects of secular society not felt to be permeated with the Holy Spirit.

Life in this world clearly includes human society. Indeed the church itself is clearly a social entity. But the early Christians judged the secular society of their time, that of the Roman Empire, to be ethically unacceptable, so the Christian life had to be led essentially within the church. This was connected with the Chiliastic expectation of an imminent Last Judgment. But gradually this expectation faded and the church faced the problem of continuing to live *in* the world and of attempting to come to some sort of long-run terms with the rest of the society outside itself.

I have stressed both the social character of the church and its radical break from the Jewish community because the pattern I have sketched formed a basic set of conditions under which Christian orientations could exert a kind of influence on secular society different from that which was possible to religion in the Jewish pattern. First, proselytizing on a grand scale was possible without carrying along the whole society immediately. While conversion to Judaism meant accepting full membership in the total Jewish community, a converted Christian could remain a Roman, a Corinthian, or whatever; his new social participation was confined to the church itself. There were important points at which the church potentially and actually conflicted with the societies of the time, but most of them could be solved by relative non-participation in "public affairs."

If in this respect the church limited its claims on its members, it also maintained a position of independence from which further influence could be exerted. It established a "place to stand" from which to exert leverage, and it developed a firm organization to safeguard that place. But the process was not to be one of absorption of the secular society into the religious community itself; it was rather one of acceptance of the fundamental *differentiation* between church and state, but the attempt to define the latter as subject to Christian principles.

There were certainly tendencies to a radical rejection of secular society in principle, but at least for the Western branch of Christianity by the time of St. Augustine the door was opened to the possibility that a Christian society as a whole could be attained. The most important vehicle for this trend was the building into Christian thought of the Greco-Roman conception of natural law. This implied a differentiation of life between spiritual and temporal spheres and a *relative* legitimation of the temporal, provided it was ordered in accordance with natural law. From this point of view, Roman society could be defined as evil, not because it was a secular society as such, but because as a society it failed to live up to norms present in its own culture.

The other principal focus of the process of Christianizing of society lay in the implications of the attempt to universalize Christian adherence within the society. Christianity was gradually transformed from a sect that remained aloof and in principle expected a Christian life only for the segregated special group of its own members into *the* church which was the trustee of the religious interests of the whole population. In proportion as this happened, persons in positions of responsibility in secular society automati-cally became Christians, and the question could not but arise of the relation between their church membership and their secular responsibilities. The focus of the emerging conception was that of the Christian monarch. The great symbolic event in this whole connection was the coronation of Charlemagne by the Pope. The symbolism of this event was dual. It was an act by the head of the church of legitimation of secular authority, which could be interpreted as the definitive ending of the conception of aloofness on the part of the church, of the position that it could take no moral responsibility in relation to the secular sphere. It also symbolized the acceptance by the monarch of the obligation to act, in his capacity as chief of government, as a Christian. Church and state then symbolically *shared* their commitment to Christian values.

It is not, in my opinion, correct to interpret this as the subordination of secular authority to the church. It was definitely a putting of the seal of religious legitimacy on the differentiation of the two spheres and their fundamental independence from each other as organized collectivities. But a true differentiation always involves at the same time an allegiance to common values and norms. In terms of the ultimate trusteeship of these values, the church is the higher authority. Perhaps a good analogy is the administration of the oath of office to an incoming American President by the Chief Justice of the Supreme Court. This clearly does not mean that the Chief Justice is the "real" chief of government and the President his organizational subordinate. What it means is rather that the Supreme Court is the ultimate interpreter of the Constitution, and the legitimation of presidential office by the Chief Justice is a symbolization of the subordination of the Presidency to constitutional law, which is equally binding on the Court.

In very broad outline this seems to be

the way the stage was set for the development of a process of the "Christianizing" of secular society, not, be it repeated, through absorption of secular spheres into the "religious life" in the sense of the life of the church or its religious orders, but by exerting influence on a life which remained by the church's own definition secular, hence, in the Catholic phase, religiously inferior to the highest, but still potentially at least quite definitely Christian.[3]

The first main phase was the medieval synthesis, which produced a great society and culture. But from the present point of view it must also be considered a stage in a process of development. The dynamic forces which led beyond the medieval pattern were in the present view inherent on both the religious and the secular sides. Brief consideration of some of the essential constituents which both went into the medieval synthesis and led beyond it will help to lay a foundation for understanding a little of the mechanisms by which a religious influence could be exerted on secular society.

First let us take the church itself. Differentiation of the church from secular society represented in one sense a renunciation of influence on secular life. There was no longer a detailed, divinely sanctioned law to prescribe all secular conduct. This may, however, be looked on as a kind of renunciation similar to that involved in a process of investment, a step toward a higher order of "productive" results in the future by a more roundabout process. Here resources are not simply mobilized to maximize short-run production. Some current resources are diverted into temporarily "unproductive" channels in uses which prepare a later production effort. To do this, however, this set of resources must be protected against pressures for their immediate consumption. In the religious case the church was such a base of operations which was kept secure from absorption

in the secular life of the time. Such pressures to absorption were indeed very prominent in the period after Constantine, in the West perhaps above all through the tendency of bishops to become heavily involved in secular political and economic interests.

The most important single fortress for the maintenance of the purity of religious orientation through this period was certainly the religious orders where segregated communities were devoted to a special religious life. Even this, however, had its this-worldly aspect, notably through the place taken by useful work in the Benedictine rule, which in many cases expanded into a generally high level of economic rationality. Furthermore the orders served as a highly important direct ground for the development of social organization itself; there were highly organized communities, administered in much more universalistic and less traditionalized ways than was most of the secular society of the time.

Secondly, however, that part of the church which served the laity through the secular clergy in the early medieval period underwent a major reform, significantly under monastic impetus. This of course is particularly associated with the Cluniac order and the name of Pope Gregory VII, himself a Cluniac monk. In one major aspect at least, it consisted of an extension of the monastic conception of purity of religious orientation to the roles of the secular clergy. There were two particularly important and closely related points here. One was the final defeat of the Donatist heresy and the firm establishment of the principle that priesthood was an office with powers and authority clearly separable from the person of the individual incumbent, or any particularistic network of relationships in which he might be involved. The second was the doctrine of clerical celibacy, which not only had not previously been enforced but also had not even been firmly established as a policy, and never was in the Eastern church.

These crucial reforms had two orders of significance. First, they served to consolidate and extend the independence of the church from secular influences. The particularly important extension was of course to the region of most direct and continuing contact with the laity through the secular clergy. Second, however, the structure of the medieval church came to serve, well beyond the Orders, as a model of social organization which could be extended into secular society. As Lea made so clear, in a society very largely dominated by the hereditary principle, clerical celibacy had a special significance.[4] Put in sociological terms, we may say that it made possible a social island which institutionalized a universalistic basis of role-allocation manifested in careers open to talent. The clergy was of course very far from being immune to class influence and at various times bishoprics and cardinalates were virtually monopolized by narrow circles of noble lineages. But this is not to say that the institution of celibacy and with it the barrier to inheritance of clerical office was unimportant.

There also was an intimate connection between the conception of clerical office which became crystallized in the Middle Ages and the building of much of Roman law into the structure of the church itself through canon law. In place of the relatively unrationalized and historically particularized Jewish law, the Christian church developed for its own internal use a highly rationalized and codified body of norms which underlay the legal structure of the whole subsequent development of Western society. Certainly the reception of secular Roman law in the late Middle Ages could not have happened without this.

Closely related to the church's use of Roman law was the place it made for the secular intellectual culture of antiquity. There is a sense in which this was already implicit in the place taken by Greek philosophy in theology itself. It was greatly reinforced by adoption of the conception of natural law as governing the secular sphere. Its medieval phase culminated in the very central place accorded to the work of Aristotle by Thomas Aquinas.

There was, however, also a structural aspect of the place of intellectual culture. Though in the earlier period it was only in the monasteries that the culture of antiquity was preserved and cultivated at all, as the medieval universities began to develop, the role of scholar and teacher assumed an important degree of independence both from the orders and from the hierarchy of the church. Though most of the schoolmen were monks, as scholars and teachers their activity was not directly controlled by their orders or chapters, nor by the bishops of the territories where they worked and taught. In terms of the crucial role of intellectual culture in later social development, notably through the rise of science, the structural basis of its independence is of an importance hardly to be exaggerated. This is perhaps the most critical single point of difference between the development of Western Christianity and of Islam, since in the latter case the influence of orthodoxy was able to suppress the independence of the scholarly class who had made such brilliant beginnings in the reception and extension of classical culture. The church's censure of Galileo should not be allowed to obscure the fact that, compared to other religious systems, Catholic Christianity made a place for an independent intellectual culture which is unique among all the great religions in their medieval phase.

There is one further important focus of the synthesis between medieval Christianity and the classical heritage. The universalism of Christianity held up a conception of a moral order for Christendom as a whole, with Christendom ideally expected eventually to comprise all mankind. This matched and was without doubt greatly influenced by the Roman conception of a universal sociopolitical order governed by a single universal system of law, a natural law coming to be institutionalized as the law of a politically organized society.

In basic Christian thinking, the Roman Empire as the secular order of the world had never ceased to exist. But since Charlemagne it could be defined as the *Holy* Roman Empire, as the normative framework of a universal Christian society. The empirical course of political development in Europe was to be such as to make this dream of unity under law in some respects progressively less realistic, at least for a very considerable period. Nevertheless the importance of the conception of a universal order should not be underestimated.

I have argued above that Christianity originally involved a cultural "marriage" between Judaic and Greco-Roman components. Though the early church repudiated the secular society of the contemporary Roman Empire, the above considerations make it quite clear that the normative aspect of classical culture was not repudiated; essentially a fundamental trusteeship of this heritage was built into the basic structure of the Christian church itself. It became the primary source from which this heritage was rediffused into the secular world and became the basis for further developments which somehow had failed to materialize in the ancient world. It is essential to my general argument here that this was a genuine integration.

Perhaps particularly from a Protestant point of view it is common to think of medieval Catholicism as mainly a pattern of compromise between a set of religious ideals and the exigencies of life in the world. It is quite true that, as Troeltsch so clearly brings out, the conception was that of a series of levels of closeness to

and distance from full contact with the Divine, with the monastic life at the top. But this is not to say that positive religious sanction was withheld from everything except devotional self-sacrifice, that for example natural law was thought of merely as a concession to human weakness. Very much on the contrary, a secular world governed by natural law was thought of as ordained by God, as the part of His Creation which was to serve as the field for man's activity. Secular society was, to be sure, a field of temptation, but also of opportunity to lead a Christian life. And an essential part of the Christian life came to be the control, if not the shaping, of secular society in the interest of Christian ideals.

Professor Sorokin is quite right, I feel, in regarding this as a synthesis rather than merely a compromise. But, as noted, it is my view that this was not the end of the road, the point from which the process of religious decline started, but rather an essential station on a road which has led much farther. A few more general things about the nature of the process need to be said. The point of view I am taking here is meant to be very far indeed from any idealistic "emanationist" conception of the process of social development.

A crucial initial point is the one stressed throughout, that the church was from the beginning *itself* a special type of social organization. We do not have to think of the cultural aspect of Christianity as socially "disembodied" and suddenly, by a kind of sociological miracle, taking over the control of a society. On the contrary, it developed, survived, and exerted its influence through the same kinds of processes of interaction between cultural and social systems which operate in other connections. First, we have noted, it maintained and consolidated its independence, and developed its own internal structure. Second, it became diffused so that, within the society in which it operated, it could assume that the whole population was, in the religious sphere, subject to its jurisdiction; it successfully eliminated all organized internal religious competition—by "propaganda" and various types of more or less political process.

It had in its own social structure institutionalized a set of values. Through the universality of membership in it, it had the opportunity to play a critical part in the socialization process for all members of the society. Though not directly controlling secular social organization, at certain levels of personality its "definition of the situation" and the importance of its special sanctions could, however imperfectly, be universalized. There was much revolt and much "backsliding," but relatively little indifference to the Christian point of view was possible. The long-run influence of such a set of forces should not be underestimated.

The church was not only an agency of reward for approved behavior and punishment of what it disapproved. It was a crucial focus of psychological support over a very wide range of human concerns—its role in administration of the *rites de passage* is a good index of this position. Finally it was a source of direct models, not only for values at the most general level, but for modes of organizing social relationship patterns at a relatively general normative level, in such fields as law, and careers open to talent.

This phase of the "Christianization" of secular society can, like others, be summed up in terms of a formula which has proved useful in other connections for the analysis of the progressive type of change in a social system.[5] Given a base in an institutionalized value system (in this case in the church) there have been three main aspects of the process. First there has been *extension* of the range of institutionalization of the values, above all through the influence on the laity

through the secular clergy. Secondly, there has been a process of further *differentiation*. The church itself has become further differentiated internally in that its sacramental system has been more clearly marked off from its administrative system, and its system of prescriptions for the ethical life of Christians through the canon law more clearly differentiated from both the others. At the same time the differentiation of the church *from* secular society has become more clearly marked. There has been a process of disengagement of the church from secular society through much more stringent control of the political and economic interests of bishops and clergy, and through sacerdotal celibacy. The beginnings of a revived Roman civil law have greatly aided in this process by more clearly defining the normative order of secular society.

Finally, third, there was a process of *upgrading* in terms of fulfillment of the requirements of the value system. Internally to the church itself this is the primary meaning of its internal reform, the strengthening of its administration, the elevation of standards in the orders and among the secular clergy. Externally, it was the gradual pressure toward a higher ethical standard among the lay population. The immense lay participation in enterprises like the building of the cathedrals is the most conspicuously manifest aspect of the general wave of "religious enthusiasm" in the Middle Ages.

The Reformation Phase

Perhaps the most important principle of the relation between religion and society which was institutionalized in the Middle Ages was that of the *autonomy* of secular society, of the "state" in the medieval sense, relative to the church, but within a Christian framework. The Christianity of secular society was guaranteed, not by the subjection of secular life to a religious law, but by the *common* commitment of ecclesiastical and temporal personnel to Christian faith. The Reformation may be seen, from one point of view, as a process of the extension of this principle of autonomy[6] to the internal structure of religious organization itself, with profound consequences both for the structure of the churches and for their relation to secular society. It may be regarded as a further major step in the same line as the original Christian break with Judaism.

The essential point may be stated as the religious "enfranchisement" of the individual, often put as his coming to stand in a direct relation to God. The Catholic Church had emancipated the individual, as part of its own corporate entity, from the Jewish law and its special social community, and had given him a notable autonomy within the secular sphere. But within its own definition of the religious sphere it had kept him under a strict tutelage by a set of mechanisms of which the sacraments were the core. By Catholic doctrine the only access to Divine grace was through the sacraments administered by a duly ordained priest. Luther broke through this tutelage to make the individual a *religiously* autonomous entity, responsible for his own religious concerns, not only in the sense of accepting the ministrations and discipline of the church but also through making his own fundamental religious commitments.

This brought faith into an even more central position than before. It was no longer the commitment to accept the particularized obligations and sacraments administered by the Church, but to act on the more general level in accordance with God's will. Like all reciprocal relationships, this one could be "tipped" one way or the other. In the Lutheran case it was tipped far in what in certain senses may be called the "authoritarian" direction; grace was interpreted to come

only from the completely "undetermined" Divine action and in no sense to be dependent on the performances of the faithful, but only on their "receptivity." In this sense Lutheranism might be felt to deprive the individual of autonomy rather than enhancing it. But this would be an incorrect interpretation. The essential point is that the individual's dependence on the *human* mediation of the church and its priesthood through the sacraments was eliminated and *as a human being* he had, under God, to rely on his own independent responsibility; he could not "buy" grace or absolution from a human agency empowered to dispense it. In this situation the very uncertainties of the individual's relation to God, an uncertainty driven to its extreme by the Calvinistic doctrine of predestination, could, through its definition of the situation for religious interests, produce a powerful impetus to the acceptance of individual responsibility. The more deeply felt his religious need, the sharper his sense of unworthiness, the more he had to realize that no human agency could relieve him of his responsibility; "mother" church was no longer available to protect and comfort him.

An immediate consequence was the elimination of the fundamental distinction in moral-religious quality between the religious life in the Catholic sense and life in secular "callings." It was the individual's direct relation to God which counted from the human side, his faith. This faith was not a function of any particular set of ritual or semi-magical practices, or indeed even of "discipline" except in the most general sense of living according to Christian principles. The core of the special meaning of the religious life had been the sacramental conception of the earning of "merit" and this was fundamentally dependent on the Catholic conception of the power of the sacraments.

From one point of view, that of the

special powers of the *church* as a social organization, this could be regarded as a crucial loss of function, and the Lutheran conception of the fundamental religious equivalence of all callings as secularization. My interpretation, however, is in accord with Max Weber's; the more important change was not the removal of religious legitimation from the special monastic life, but rather, the endowment of secular life with a new order of religious legitimation as a field of "Christian opportunity." If the ordinary man, assumed of course to be a church member, stood in direct relation to God, and could be justified by his faith, the *whole person* could be justified, including the life he led in everyday affairs. The counterpart of eliminating the sacramental mediation of the secular priesthood was eliminating also the special virtues of the religious. It was a case of further *differentiation* within the Christian framework.

Protestantism in its Lutheran phase underwent a process, analogous to that of the early church, of relative withdrawal from direct involvement in the affairs of secular society. With the overwhelming Lutheran emphasis on faith and the importance of the individual's *subjective* sense of justification, there was, as Weber pointed out, a strong tendency to interpret the concept of the calling in a passive, traditionalist, almost Pauline sense. It was the individual's relation to his God that mattered; only in a sense of nondiscrimination was his secular calling sanctified, in that it was just as good, religiously speaking, as that of the monk.

We have, however, maintained that the conception of the generalization of a Christian pattern of life was an inherent possibility in the Christian orientation from the beginning and it came early to the fore in the Reformation period in the Calvinistic, or more broadly the ascetic, branch of the movement. Here we may say that the religious status of secular

callings was extended from that of a principle of basic nondiscrimination to one of their endowment with positive instrumental significance. The key conception was that of the divine ordination of the establishment of the Kingdom of God on Earth. This went beyond the negative legitimation of secular callings to the assignment of a positive *function* to them in the divine plan.

In terms of its possibility of exerting leverage over secular society this was by far the most powerful version of the conception of the possibility of a "Christian society" which had yet appeared. First the stepwise hierarchy of levels of religious merit, so central to the Thomistic view, was eliminated by Luther. Then the individual became the focus not only of secular but also of religious responsibility emancipated from tutelary control by a sacramental church. Finally, precisely in his secular calling the individual was given a positive assignment to work in the building of the Kingdom.

The consequence of this combination was that, with one important exception, every major factor in the situation converged upon the dynamic exploitation of opportunity to change social life in the direction of conformity with religiously grounded ideals.

The basic assumption is that for Protestants the Christian commitment was no less rigorous than it had been for Catholics; if anything it was more so. In both Lutheran and Calvinistic versions the conception was one of the most rigorous submission of the individual's life to divine will. But in defining the situation for implementing this role of "creature," the Protestant position differed from the Catholic broadly as the definition of the preschool child's role relative to his parents differs from that of the school-age child's relation to his teacher. Within the family, important as the element of discipline and expectations of learning to perform are, the primary focus is on responsibility of the parents for the welfare and security of their children; the permeation of Catholic thought with familial symbolism along these lines is striking indeed.

In the school, on the other hand, the emphasis shifts. The teacher is primarily an agent of instruction, responsible for welfare, yes, but this is not the primary function; it is rather to help to equip the child for a responsible role in society when his education has been completed. To a much higher degree the question of how far he takes advantage of his opportunities becomes his own responsibility. Thus the function of the Protestant ministry became mainly a teaching function, continually holding up the Christian doctrine as a model of life to their congregations. But they no longer held a parental type of tutelary power to confer or deny the fundamentals of personal religious security.

If the analogy may be continued, the Lutheran position encouraged a more passive orientation in this situation, a leaving of the more ultimate responsibility to God, an attitude primarily of receptivity to Grace. (This is the exception referred to above—one of relatively short-run significance.) Such an attitude would tend to be generalized to worldly superiors and authorities, including both ministers and secular teachers. Ascetic Protestanism, on the other hand, though at least equally insistent on the divine origins of norms and values for life, tended to cut off this reliance on authority and place a sharper emphasis on the individual's responsibility for positive action, not just by his faith to be receptive to God's grace, but to get out and *work* in the building of the Kingdom. This precisely excluded any special valuation of devotional exercises and put the primary moral emphasis on secular activities.

Next, this constituted a liberation in one fundamental respect from the social conservatism of the Catholic position, in

that it was no longer necessary to attempt to maintain the superiority of the religious life over the secular. Hence one essential bulwark of a hierarchical ordering of society was removed. The Christian conscience rather than the doctrines and structural position of the visible Church became the focus for standards of social evaluation. This should not, however, be interpreted as the establishment of "democracy" by the Reformation. Perhaps the most important single root of modern democracy is Christian individualism. But the Reformation, in liberating the individual conscience from the tutelage of the church, took only one step toward political democracy. The Lutheran branch indeed was long particularly identified with "legitimism," and Calvinism was in its early days primarily a doctrine of a relatively rigid collective "dictatorship" of the elect in both church and state.

Third, far from weakening the elements in secular society which pointed in a direction of "modernism," the Reformation, especially in its ascetic branch, strengthened and extended them. A particularly important component was clearly law. We have emphasized the essential continuity in this respect between classical antiquity and modern Europe through the medieval church. Broadly, the revival of Roman secular law in Europe was shared between Catholic and Protestant jurisdictions; in no sense did the Reformation reverse the trend in Continental Europe to institutionalize a secular legal system. In England, however, as Pound has emphasized, Puritanism was one of the major influences on the crystallization of the common law in the most decisive period. This is very much in line with the general trends of Protestant orientation, the favoring of a system of order within which responsible individual action can function effectively. The protection of rights is only one aspect of this order; the sanctioning of responsibilities is just as important.

Perhaps most important of all is the fact that the change in the character of the church meant that, insofar as the patterns of social structure which had characterized it by contrast with the feudal elements in the medieval heritage were to be preserved, they had to become much more generalized in secular society. This is true, as noted, of a generalized and codified system of law. It is true of more bureaucratic types of organization, which developed first in the governmental field but later in economic enterprise. It is by no means least true in the field of intellectual culture. The Renaissance was initially an outgrowth of the predominantly Catholic culture of Italy, but the general revival and development of learning of the post-medieval period was certainly shared by Catholic and Protestant Europe. It is a significant fact that John Calvin was trained as a lawyer. And of course, particularly in science, ascetic Protestantism was a major force in cultural development.

It is particularly important to emphasize the breadth of the front over which the leverage of Protestantism extended because of the common misinterpretation of Max Weber's thesis on the special relation between ascetic Protestantism and capitalism. This has often been seen as though the point were that Protestantism provided a special moral justification of profit-making as such, and of that alone. In view of the deep Western ambivalence over the conception of profit, the role of ascetic Protestantism in this context could easily be interpreted as mainly a "rationalization" of the common human propensity to seek "self-interest," which is the very antithesis of religious motivation.

First, it will be recalled that Weber was quite explicit that he was not talking about profit-making in general, but only about its harnessing to systematic methodical work in worldly callings in the interest of economic production

through free enterprise. Weber was also well aware of a number of other facets of the same basic orientation to work in a calling, such as its basic hostility to various forms of traditionalism, including all traditional ascription of status independent of the individual, and its relation to science, a relation much further worked out by Merton.

Even Weber did not, however, in my opinion, fully appreciate the importance of the relation to the professions as a developing structural component of modern society, a component which in certain respects stands in sharp contrast to the classical orientation of economic self-interest.

The essential point is that private enterprise in business was one special case of secular callings within a much wider context. But it was a particularly strategic case in Western development, because of the very great difficulty of emancipating economic production over a truly broad front—on the one hand from the ascriptive ties which go with such institutions as peasant agriculture and guild-type handicraft, on the other hand from the irrationalities which, from an economic point of view, are inherent in political organization, because of its inherent connection with the short-run pressures of social urgency such as defense, and because of its integration with aristocratic elements in the system of stratification which were dominated by a very different type of orientation.

There is very good reason to believe that development of the industrial revolution *for the first time* could have come about only through the primary agency of free enterprise, however dependent this was in turn on prior conditions, among the most important of which were the availability of a legal framework within which a system of contractual relations could have an orderly development. Once there has been a major breakthrough on the economic front, however, the diffusion of the patterns of social organization involved need not continue to be dependent on the same conditions.[7]

Weber's main point about the Protestant ethic and capitalism was the importance of the subordination of self-interest in the usual ideological sense to the conception of a religiously meaningful calling; only with the establishment of this component was sufficient drive mobilized to break through the many barriers which were inherent not only in the European society of the time but more generally to a more differentiated development of economic production. Basically this involves the reversal of the commonsense point of view. The latter has contended, implicitly or explicitly, that the main source of impetus to capitalistic development was the *removal* of ethical restrictions such as, for instance, the prohibition of usury. This is true within certain limits, but by far the more important point is that what is needed is a powerful motivation to innovate, to break through the barriers of traditionalism and of vested interest. It is this impetus which is the center of Weber's concern, and it is his thesis that it cannot be accounted for by any simple removal of restrictions.

However deep the ambivalence about the morality of profit-making may go, there can be little doubt that the main outcome has been a shift in social conditions more in accord with the general pattern of Christian ethics than was medieval society, provided we grant that life in this world has a positive value in itself. Not least of these is the breaking through of the population circle of high death rates and high birth rates with the attendant lengthening of the average span of life. Another crucial point is the vast extension of the sphere of order in human relationships, the lessening of the exposure of the individual to violence, to fraud and to arbitrary pressures of authority.

So-called material well-being has certainly never been treated as an absolute value in the Christian or any other major religious tradition, but any acceptance of life in this world as of value entails acceptance of the value of the means necessary to do approved things effectively. Particularly at the lower end of the social scale, grinding poverty with its accompaniments of illness, premature death, and unnecessary suffering is certainly not to be taken as an inherently desirable state of affairs from a Christian point of view.

Another major theme of developments in this era which is in basic accord with Christian values is a certain strain to egalitarianism, associated with the conception of the dignity of the individual human being and the need to justify discriminations either for or against individuals and classes of them in terms of some general concept of merit or demerit. Certainly by contrast with the role of ascriptive discriminations in the medieval situation, modern society is not in this respect ethically inferior.

Also important has been the general field of learning and science. Perhaps the educational revolution of the nineteenth century was even more important in its long-run implications than was the industrial revolution of the late eighteenth century. It represents the first attempt in history to give large populations as a whole a substantial level of formal education, starting with literacy but going well beyond. Associated with this is the general cultivation of things intellectual and particularly the sciences through research. It is the marriage of the educational and industrial revolutions which provides the primary basis for the quite new level of mass well-being which is one major characteristic of the modern Western world. In both developments cultures with primarily Protestant orientations have acted as the spearheads.

The Reformation phase of Western development may be said to have culminated in the great seventeenth century, which saw the foundations of modern law and political organization so greatly advanced, the culmination of the first major phase of modern science, the main orientations of modern philosophy, and much development on the economic front. However important the Renaissance was, the great civilizational achievements of the seventeenth century as a whole are unthinkable without Protestantism. It coincided with a new level of leadership centering in predominantly Protestant northern Europe, notably England and Holland, and also with much ferment in Germany.

In spite of the very great structural differences, the essential principles governing the process by which society has become more Christianized than before were essentially the same in the Reformation period as in the earlier one. Let us recall that the Christian church from the beginning renounced the strategy of incorporation of secular society within itself, or the direct control of secular society through a religious law. It relied on the common values which bound church and secular society together, each in its own sphere, but making the Christian aspect of secular society an autonomous responsibility of Christians in their secular roles. My basic argument has been that the same fundamental principle was carried even farther in the Reformation phase. The sphere of autonomy was greatly enlarged through release of the Christian individual from the tutelage of the church. This was essentially a process of further differentiation both within the religious sphere and between it and the secular.

In all such cases there is increased objective opportunity for disregarding the values of the religious tradition and succumbing to worldly temptations. But the other side of the coin is the enhancement of motivation to religiously valued achievement by the very fact of being given more unequivocal responsibility. This process was not mainly one of secularization but one of the institutionalization of the religious responsibility of the individual through the relinquishment of tutelary authority by a "parental" church.

For purposes of this discussion the Reformation period is the most decisive one, for here it is most frequently argued, by Professor Sorokin among many others, that there was a decisive turn in the direction of secularization in the sense of abandonment of the values inherent in the Christian tradition in favor of concern with the "things of this world." As already noted, we feel that underlying this argument is a basic ambiguity about the relation of "the world" to religious orientations and that the Christian orientation is not, in the Oriental sense, an orientation of "rejection of the world" but rather in this respect mainly a source for the setting of ethical standards *for* life in this world. In line with this interpretation, the Reformation transition was not primarily one of "giving in" to the temptations of worldly interest, but rather one of extending the range of applicability and indeed in certain respects the rigor of the ethical standards applied to life in the world. It was expecting more rather than less of larger numbers of Christians in their worldly lives. It goes without saying that the content of the expectations also changed. But these changes indicated much more a change in the definition of the situation of life through changes in the structure of society than they did in the main underlying values.

Let us try to apply the same formula used in summing up the medieval phase to that of the Reformation. The most conspicuous aspect of extension was the diffusion of religious responsibility and participation in certain respects beyond the sacramentally organized church to the laity on their own responsibility. The central symbol of this was the translation of the Bible into the vernacular languages of Europe and the pressure on broad lay groups to familiarize themselves with it. The shift in the functions of the church from the sacramental emphasis to that of teaching is directly connected with this. This extension included both the elements of worship and that of responsibility for ethical conduct.

With respect to the church itself as a social system, the Reformation clearly did not involve further internal differentiation but the contrary. But it involved a major step in the differentiation of the religious organization *from* secular society. The Reformation churches, as distinguished from the sects, retained their symbiosis of interpenetration with secular political authority through the principle of Establishment. But the counterpart of what I have called the religious enfranchisement of the individual was his being freed from detailed moral tutelage by the clergy. The dropping of the sacrament of penance, the very core of Luther's revolt against the Catholic church, was central in this respect. Repentance became a matter of the individual's direct relation to God, specifically exempted from any sacramental mediation. This was essentially to say that the individual was, in matters of conscience, in principle accountable to no human agency, but only to God; in this sense he was *humanly* autonomous. This development tended to restrict the church to the functions of an agency for the generation of faith, through teaching and through providing a communal setting for the ritual expression of common anxiety and common faith.

There were two principal settings in which this differentiation of lay responsibility from ecclesiastical tutelage worked out. One was the direct relation to God in terms of repentance and faith. This was paramount in the Lutheran branch of the Reformation movement. The other was the primacy of moral action in the world as an instrument of the divine will, the pattern which was primary in ascetic Protestantism. In a sense in which this was impossible within the fold of Catholic unity on the level of church organization, both these movements become differentiated not only from the "parent" Catholic church but also from each other. Hence the ascetic Protestant branch, which institutionalized elements present from the beginning in Western Christian tradition, notably through Augustine, was freed from the kind of ties with other components which hindered its ascendancy as the major trend of one main branch of general Christian tradition. Clearly this is the branch which had the most direct positive influence on the complex of orientations of value which later proved to be of importance to modern industrialism.

The third point of upgrading is most conspicuous in the placing of secular callings on a plane of moral equality with the religious life itself. In crucial respects this shift increased the tension between Christian ideal and worldly reality. This increase of tension underlay much of the Lutheran trend to withdrawal from positive secular interests and the corresponding sectarian and mystical phenomena of the time. But once the new tension was turned into the channel of exerting leverage for the change of conduct in the secular world, above all through the imperative to work in the building of the Kingdom, it was a powerful force to moral upgrading precisely in the direction of changing social behavior in the direction of Christian ideals, not of adjustment to the given necessities of a non-Christian world.

The Denominational Phase

A common view would agree with the above argument that the Reformation itself was not basically a movement of secularization but that, in that it played a part in unleashing the forces of political nationalism and economic development—to say nothing of recent hedonism—it was the last genuinely Christian phase of Western development and that from the eighteenth century on in particular the trend had truly been one of religious decline in relation to the values of secular society. Certain trends in Weber's thinking with respect to the disenchantment of the world would seem to argue in this direction, as would Troeltsch's view that there have been only three authentic versions of the conception of a Christian society in Western history—the medieval Catholic, the Lutheran, and the Calvinistic.

Against this view I should like to present an argument for a basic continuity leading to a further phase which has come to maturity in the nineteenth and twentieth centuries, most conspicuously in the United States and coincident with the industrial and educational revolutions already referred to. From this point of view, the present system of "denominational pluralism" may be regarded as a further extension of the same basic line of institutionalization of Christian ethics which was produced both by the medieval synthesis and by the Reformation.

It is perhaps best to start with the conception of religious organization itself. Weber and Troeltsch organized their thinking on these matters within the Christian framework around the distinction between church and sect as organizational types. The church was the religious organization of the whole society which could claim and enforce the same order of jurisdiction over a total population as did the state in the secular sphere. The sect, on the other hand, was a voluntary religious association of those committed to a specifically religious life. The church type was inherently committed to the conception of an Establishment, since only through this type of integration with political authority could universal jurisdiction be upheld. The sect, on the other hand, could not establish any stable relation to secular society since its members were committed to give unequivocal primacy to their religious interests and could not admit the legitimacy of the claims of secular society, politically or otherwise, which a stable relation would entail.

This dichotomy fails to take account of an important third possibility, the denomination. As I conceive it, this shares with the church type the *differentiation* between religious and secular spheres of interest. In the same basic sense which we outlined for the medieval church, both may be conceived to be subject to Christian values, but to constitute independent foci of responsibility for their implementation. On the other hand, the denomination shares with the sect type its character as a voluntary association where the individual member is bound only by a responsible personal commitment, not by *any* factor of ascription. In the American case it is, logically I think, associated with the constitutional separation of church and state.

The denomination can thus accept secular society as a legitimate field of action for the Christian individual in which he acts on his own responsibility without organizational control by religious authority. But precisely because he is a Christian he will not simply accept everything he finds there; he will attempt to shape the situation in the direction of better conformity with Christian values. This general pattern it shares with all three of the church types, but not with the sect in Troeltsch's sense.

Two further factors are involved, however, which go beyond anything to be found in the church tradition. One of these is implicit in the voluntary principle—the acceptance of denominational pluralism—and, with it, toleration. However much there may historically have been, and still is, deep ambivalence about this problem, the genuine institutionalization of the constitutional protection of religious freedom cannot be confined to the secular side; it must be accepted as *religiously* legitimate as well. With certain qualifications this can be said to be the case in the United States today and, in somewhat more limited forms, in various other countries. From a religious point of view, this means the discrimination of two layers of religious commitment. One of these is the layer which defines the bases of denominational membership and which differentiates one denomination from another. The other is a common matrix of value-commitment which is broadly shared between denominations, and which forms the basis of the sense in which the society as a whole forms a religiously based moral community. This has, in the American case, been extended to cover a very wide range. Its core certainly lies in the institutionalized Protestant denominations, but with certain strains and only partial institutionalization, it extends to three other groups of the first importance; the Catholic church, the various branches of Judaism, and, not least important, those who prefer to remain aloof from *any* formal denominational affiliation. To deny that this underlying consensus exists would be to claim that American society stood in a state of latent religious war. Of the fact that there are considerable tensions every responsible

student of the situation is aware. Institutionalization is incomplete, but the consensus is very much of a reality.

The second difference from the church tradition is a major further step in the emancipation of the individual from tutelary control by *organized* religious collectivities beyond that reached by the Reformation churches. This is the other side of the coin of pluralism, and essentially says that the rite of baptism does not commit the individual to a particular set of dogmas or a particular religious collectivity. The individual is responsible not only for managing his own relation to God through faith *within* the ascribed framework of an established church, which is the Reformation position, but for choosing that framework itself, for deciding as a mature individual *what* to believe, and *with whom* to associate himself in the organizational expression and reinforcement of his commitments. This is essentially the removal of the last vestige of coercive control over the individual in the religious sphere; he is endowed with full responsible autonomy.

That there should be a development in this direction from the position of the Reformation church seems to me to have been inherent in the Protestant position in general, in very much the same sense in which a trend to Protestantism was inherent in the medieval Catholic situation. Just as Catholics tend to regard Protestantism in general as the abandonment of true religious commitment either because the extension of the voluntary principle to such lengths is held to be incompatible with a sufficiently serious commitment on the part of the church (if you are not willing to coerce people to your point of view are you yourself *really* committed to it?) or because of its legitimation of secular society so that church membership becomes only one role among many, not the primary axis of life as a whole. But against such views it is hard to see how the implicit individualism of all Christianity could be stopped, short of this doctrine of full responsible autonomy. The doctrine seems to me implicit in the very conception of faith. Asking the individual to have faith is essentially to ask him to *trust* in God. But, whatever the situation in the relation of the human to the divine, in *human* relations trust seems to have to rest on mutuality. Essentially the voluntary principle in denominationalism is extending mutuality of trust so that no *human* agency is permitted to take upon itself the authority to control the conditions under which faith is to be legitimately expected. Clearly this, like the Reformation step, involves a risk that the individual will succumb to worldly temptations. But the essential principle is not different from that involved in releasing him from sacramental control.

This is of course very far from contending that the system of denominational pluralism is equally congenial to all theological positions or that all religious groups within the tradition can fit equally well into it. There are important strains particularly in relation to the Catholic church, to Fundamentalist Protestant sects, to a lesser degree to very conservative Protestant church groups (especially Lutheran), and to the vestiges of really Orthodox Judaism. My essential contention is not that this pattern has been or can be fully universalized within Judaeo-Christianity, but that it is a genuinely Christian development, not by definition a falling away from religion. But it could not have developed without a very substantial modification of earlier positions within Protestantism. In particular it is incompatible with either strict traditional Lutheranism or strict Calvinism.

It was remarked above that the Reformation period did not usher in political democracy, but was in a sense a step toward it. There is a much closer affilia-

tion between denominational pluralism and political democracy. But before discussing that, a comparison between the two may help illuminate the nature of the problem of how such a system of religious organization works. Legitimists for a long period have viewed with alarm the dangers of democracy since, if public policy can be determined by the majority of the irresponsible and the uninformed, how can any stability of political organization be guaranteed? There is a sense in which the classical theory of political liberalism may be said to play into the hands of this legitimist argument, since it has tended to assume that under democracy each individual made up his mind totally independently without reference to the institutionalized wisdom of any tradition.

This is not realistically the case. Careful study of voting behavior has shown that voting preferences are deeply anchored in the established involvement of the individual in the social structure. Generally speaking, most voters follow the patterns of the groups with which they are most strongly affiliated. Only when there are structural changes in the society which alter its structure of solidary groupings and expose many people to cross-pressures are major shifts likely to take place. There are, furthermore, mechanisms by which these shifts tend, in a well-institutionalized democratic system, to be orderly.[8]

I would like to suggest that similar considerations apply to a system of denominational pluralism. The importance of the family is such that it is to be taken for granted that the overwhelming majority will accept the religious affiliations of their parents—of course with varying degrees of commitment. Unless the whole society is drastically disorganized there will not be notable instability in its religious organization. But there will be an important element of flexibility and opportunity for new adjustments within an orderly system which the older church organizations, like the older political legitimacy, did not allow for.

If it is once granted that this system of religious organization is not by definition a "falling away" from true religion, then its institutionalization of the elements of trust of the individual has, it seems to me, an important implication. On the religious side it is implicit in the pattern of toleration. Members of particular churches on the whole trust each other to be loyal to the particular collectivity. But if some should shift to another denomination it is not to be taken too tragically since the new affiliation will in most cases be included in the deeper moral community.

But such a situation could not prevail were the secular part of the system regarded as radically evil. The individual is not only trusted with reference to his religious participation, but also to lead a "decent" life in his secular concerns. Indeed I should argue, therefore, that for such a religious constitution to function, on the institutional level the society must present not a less but a more favorable field for the Christian life than did the society of earlier periods of Western history; its moral standards must in fact be higher.

There is a tendency in much religiously oriented discussion to assume that the test of the aliveness of Christian values is the extent to which "heroic" defiance of temptation or renunciation of worldly interests is empirically prevalent. This ignores one side of the equation of Christian conduct, the extent to which the "world" does or does not stand opposed to the values in question. If one argues that there has been a relative institutionalization of these values, and hence in certain respects a diminution of tension between religious ideal and actuality, he risks accusation of a Pharisaic complacency. In face of this risk, however, I

suggest that in a whole variety of respects modern society is more in accord with Christian values than its forebears have been—this is, let it be noted, a *relative* difference; the millennium definitely has not arrived.

I do not see how the extension of intra- and interdenominational trust into a somewhat greater trust in the moral quality of secular conduct would be possible were this not so. The internalization of religious values certainly strengthens character. But this is not to say that even the *average* early Christian was completely proof against worldly temptation, *independent of any support from the mutual commitments of many Christians in and through the church*. Without the assumption that this mutual support in a genuine social collectivity was of the first importance, I do not see how the general process of institutionalization of these values could have been possible at all except on the unacceptable assumption of a process of emanation of the spirit without involvement in the realistic religious interests of real persons.

However heroic a few individuals may be, no process of mass institutionalization occurs without the mediation of social solidarities and the mutual support of many individuals in commitment to a value system. The corollary of relinquishment of the organizational control of certain areas of behavior, leaving them to the responsibility of the autonomous individual, is the institutionalization of the basic conditions of carrying out this responsibility with not the elimination, but a relative minimization of, the hazard that this exposure will lead to total collapse of the relevant standards.

Let us try to sum up this fourth—denominational—phase of the line of development we have traced in terms of our threefold formula. First I would suggest that the principle of religious toleration, inherent in the system of denominational pluralism, implies a great further extension of the institutionalization of Christian values, both inside and outside the sphere of religious organization. At least it seems to me that this question poses a sharp alternative. Either there is a sharp falling away so that, in tolerating each other, the different denominations have become fellow condoners of an essentially evil situation or, as suggested above, they do in fact stand on a relatively high ethical plane so that whatever their dogmatic differences, there is no basis for drawing a drastic moral line of distinction which essentially says that the adherents of the other camp are in a moral sense not good people in a sense in which the members of our own camp are. Then the essential extension of the same principle of mutual trust into the realm of secular conduct is another part of the complex which I would like to treat as one of extension of the institutionalization of Christian values.

So far as differentiation is concerned, there are two conspicuous features of this recent situation. First, of course, the religious associations have become differentiated from each other so that, unlike in the Reformation phase (to say nothing of the Middle Ages), when there was for a politically organized society in principle only one acceptable church, adherence to which was the test of the moral quality treated as a minimum for good standing in the society, this is no longer true. The religious organization becomes a purely voluntary association, and there is an indefinite plurality of morally acceptable denominations.

This does not, however, mean that Christian ethics have become a matter of indifference in the society. It means rather that the differentiation between religious and secular spheres has gone farther than before and with it the extension of the individualistic principle inherent in Christianity to the point of the "privatizing" of formal, external religious commitment, as the Reformation made internal religious faith a matter for the individual alone. This general trend has of course coincided with an enormously proliferated process of differentiation in the structure of the society itself.

In this respect the religious group may be likened (up to a point) to the family. The family has lost many traditional functions and has become increasingly a sphere of private sentiments. There is, however, reason to believe that it is as important as ever to the maintenance of the main patterns of the society, though operating with a minimum of direct outside control. Similarly religion has become largely a private matter in which the individual associates with the group of his own choice, and in this respect has lost many functions of previous religious organizational types.

There seem to be two primary respects in which an upgrading process may be spoken of. Approaching the question from the sociological side, we may note that the development of the society has been such that it should not be operated without an upgrading of general levels of responsibility and competence, the acquisition and exercise of the latter of course implying a high sense of responsibility. This trend is a function of increase in the size of organization and the delicacy of relations of interdependence, of freedom from ascriptive bonds in many different ways, of the sheer power for destruction and evil of many of the instrumentalities of action.

Responsibility has a double aspect. The first is responsibility *of* the individual in that he cannot rely on a dependent relation to others, or to some authority, to absolve him of responsibility—this is the aspect we have been referring to as his *autonomy* in the specific sense in which the term has been used in this discussion. The other aspect is responsibility *for* and *to*, responsibility for results and to other persons and to collectivities.

Here the element of mutuality inherent in Christian ethics, subject to a commonly binding set of norms and values, is the central concern.

That the general trend has been to higher orders of autonomous responsibility is, in my opinion, sociologically demonstrable.[9] The central problem then becomes that of whether the kinds of responsibility involved do or do not accord with the prescriptions of Christian ethics. This is essentially the question of whether the general trend stemming from ascetic Protestantism is basically un-Christian or not. Granting that this trend is not un-Christian, the critical *moral* problems of our day derive mainly from the fact that, since we are living in a more complicated world than ever before, which is more complicated because human initiative has been more daring and has ventured into more new realms than ever before, greater demands are put on the human individual. He has more difficult problems, both technical and moral; he takes greater risks. Hence the possibility of failure and of the failure being his fault is at least as great as, if not greater than, it ever was.

There is a widespread view, particularly prevalent in religious circles, that our time, particularly some say in the United States, is one of unprecedented moral collapse. In these circles it is alleged that modern social development has entailed a progressive decline of moral standards which is general throughout the population. This view is clearly incompatible with the general trend of the analysis we have been making. Its most plausible grain of truth is the one just indicated, that as new and more difficult problems emerge, such as those involved in the possibility of far more destructive war than ever before, we do not feel morally adequate to the challenge. But to say that because we face graver problems than our forefathers faced we are doubtful of our capacity

to handle them responsibly is quite a different thing from saying that, on the same levels of responsibility as those of our forefathers, we are in fact handling our problems on a much lower moral level.

Our time by and large, however, is not one of religious complacency but, particularly in the most sensitive groups in these matters, one of substantial anxiety and concern. Does not the existence of this concern stand in direct contradiction to the general line of argument I have put forward?

I think not. One element in its explanation is probably that new moral problems of great gravity have emerged in our time and that we are, for very realistic reasons, deeply concerned about them. My inclination, however, is to think that this is not the principal basis of the widespread concern.

The present discussion has, by virtue of its chosen subject, been primarily interested in the problems of the institutionalization of the values originating in Christianity as a religious movement, which have been carried forward at various stages of its development. But values —i.e., moral orientations toward the problems of life in this world—are never the whole of religion, if indeed its most central aspect. My suggestion is that the principal roots of the present religious concern do not lie in *relative* moral decline or inadequacy (relative, that is, to other periods in our society's history) but rather in problems in the other areas of religion, problems of the bases of faith and the definitions of the ultimate problems of meaning.

The very fact that the process of the integration of earlier religious values with the structure of society has gone so far as it has gone raises such problems. The element of universalism in Christian ethics inherently favors the development of a society where the different branches of Christianity cannot maintain their earlier insulation from each other. The problem of the status of Judaism has had to be raised on a new level within the structure of Western society, one which came to a very critical stage in the case of German Nazism. It is a society in which all the parochialisms of earlier religious commitments are necessarily brought into flux.

But beyond this, for the first time in history something approaching a world society is in process of emerging. For the first time in its history Christianity is now involved in a deep confrontation with the major religious traditions of the Orient, as well as with the modern political religion of Communism.

It seems probable that a certain basic tension in relation to the "things of this world" is inherent in Christianity generally. Hence any relative success in the institutionalization of Christian values cannot be taken as final, but rather as a point of departure for new religious stock-taking. But in addition to this broad internal consideration, the confrontation on such a new basis with the non-Christian world presents a new and special situation. We are deeply committed to our own great traditions. These have tended to emphasize the exclusive possession of the truth. Yet we have also institutionalized the values of tolerance and equality of rights for all. How can we define a meaningful orientation in such a world when, in addition, the more familiar and conventional problems of suffering and evil are, if not more prevalent than ever before, at least as brought to attention through mass communications, inescapable as facts of our world?

It is the inherent tension and dynamism of Christianity and the unprecedented character of the situation we face which, to my mind, account for the intensive searching and questioning, and indeed much of the spiritual negativism, of our time. The explanation in terms of an alleged moral collapse would be far too simple, even if there were more truth in it than the evidence seems to indicate. For this would imply that we did not need new conceptions of meaning; all we would need would be to live up more fully to the standards familiar to us all. In no period of major ferment in cultural history has such a solution been adequate.

Notes

[1] Cf. Sorokin, *Fads and Foibles in Modern Sociology and Related Sciences* (Chicago: Henry Regnery, 1956).

[2] The most important general statements of his position are in *Social and Cultural Dynamics* (New York: American Book Company, 1937), Vol. I, Part 1, and *Society, Culture, and Personality* (New York: Harper, 1947), Part 7.

[3] In this general interpretation I follow in particular Troeltsch, *Social Teachings of the Christian Churches.*

[4] H. C. Lea, *The History of Sacerdotal Celibacy* (New York: Russell and Russell, 1957).

[5] Perhaps the fullest statement of this scheme is contained in T. Parsons and W. White, "The Link between Character and Society," in S. M. Lipset and L. Loewenthal (eds.), *Culture and Social Character* (New York: The Free Press of Glencoe, 1961).

[6] By autonomy I mean here *independence* of direct authoritarian control combined with *responsibility* defined in moral-religious terms. It is close to "theonomy" as that concept is used by Tillich.

[7] This thesis is further developed in my two essays published as Chapters III and IV of *Structure and Process in Modern Societies* (New York: The Free Press of Glencoe, 1959).

[8] Basing myself on the studies of voting behavior by Berelson, Lazarsfeld, *et al.,* I have analyzed this situation in " 'Voting' and the Equilibrium of the American Political System," in Eugene Burdick and Arthur J. Brodbeck (eds.), *American Voting Behavior* (New York: The Free Press of Glencoe, 1959).

[9] *Cf.* Parsons and White, *op. cit.,* for a brief statement of the case for this view.

D · RELIGION AND NONRELIGIOUS ACTIVITIES: ECONOMY, SCIENCE, POLITICS

1 · Asceticism and the Spirit of Capitalism

MAX WEBER

In order to understand the connection between the fundamental religious ideas of ascetic Protestantism and its maxims for everyday economic conduct, it is necessary to examine with especial care such writings as have evidently been derived from ministerial practice. For in a time in which the beyond meant everything, when the social position of the Christian depended upon his admission to the communion, the clergyman, through his ministry, Church discipline, and preaching, exercised an influence (as a glance at collections of *consilia, casus conscientiæ*, etc., shows) which we modern men are entirely unable to picture. In such a time the religious forces which express themselves through such channels are the decisive influences in the formation of national character.

SOURCE. Max Weber, "Asceticism and the Spirit of Capitalism," from Max Weber, *The Protestant Ethic and the Spirit of Capitalism*, New York: Scribner's, 1958, pp. 155–183. Reprinted with the permission of Charles Scribner's Sons. Translated by Talcott Parsons. Permission also granted from Allen and Unwin, the British publishers.

For the purposes of this chapter, though by no means for all purposes, we can treat ascetic Protestantism as a single whole. But since that side of English Puritanism which was derived from Calvinism gives the most consistent religious basis for the idea of the calling, we shall, following our previous method, place one of its representatives at the centre of the discussion. Richard Baxter stands out above many other writers on Puritan ethics, both because of his eminently practical and realistic attitude, and, at the same time, because of the universal recognition accorded to his works, which have gone through many new editions and translations. He was a Presbyterian and an apologist of the Westminster Synod, but at the same time, like so many of the best spirits of his time, gradually grew away from the dogmas of pure Calvinism. At heart he opposed Cromwell's usurpation as he would any revolution. He was unfavourable to the sects and the fanatical enthusiasm of the saints, but was very broad-minded about external peculiarities and objective towards his opponents. He sought his field of labour most especially in the practical promotion of the moral life through the Church. In the pursuit of this end, as one of the most successful ministers known to history, he placed his services at the disposal of the Parliamentary Government, of Cromwell, and of the Restoration, until he retired from office under the last, before St. Bartholomew's day. His *Christian Directory* is the most complete compendium of Puritan ethics, and is continually adjusted to the practical experiences of his own ministerial activity. In comparison we shall make use of Spener's *Theologische Bedenken*, as representative of German Pietism, Barclay's *Apology* for the Quakers, and some other representatives of ascetic ethics, which, however, in the interest of space, will be limited as far as possible.

Now, in glancing at Baxter's *Saints' Everlasting Rest*, or his *Christian Directory*, or similar works of others, one is struck at first glance by the emphasis placed, in the discussion of wealth and its acquisition, on the ebionitic elements of the New Testament. Wealth as such is a great danger; its temptations never end, and its pursuit is not only senseless as compared with the dominating importance of the Kingdom of God, but it is morally suspect. Here asceticism seems to have turned much more sharply against the acquisition of earthly goods than it did in Calvin, who saw no hindrance to the effectiveness of the clergy in their wealth, but rather a thoroughly desirable enhancement of their prestige. Hence he permitted them to employ their means profitably. Examples of the condemnation of the pursuit of money and goods may be gathered without end from Puritan writings, and may be contrasted with the late mediæval ethical literature, which was much more open-minded on this point.

Moreover, these doubts were meant with perfect seriousness; only it is necessary to examine them somewhat more closely in order to understand their true ethical significance and implications. The real moral objection is to relaxation in the security of possession, the enjoyment of wealth with the consequence of idleness and the temptations of the flesh, above all of distraction from the pursuit of a righteous life. In fact, it is only because possession involves this danger of relaxation that it is objectionable at all. For the saints' everlasting rest is in the next world; on earth man must, to be certain of his state of grace, "do the works of him who sent him, as long as it is yet day". Not leisure and enjoyment, but only activity serves to increase the glory of God, according to the definite manifestations of His will.

Waste of time is thus the first and in principle the deadliest of sins. The span of human life is infinitely short and precious to make sure of one's own election. Loss of time through sociability, idle talk, luxury, even more sleep than is necessary for health, six to at most eight hours, is worthy of absolute moral condemnation. It does not yet hold, with Franklin, that time is money, but the proposition is true in a certain spiritual sense. It is infinitely valuable because every hour lost is lost to labour for the glory of God. Thus inactive contemplation is also valueless, or even directly reprehensible if it is at the expense of one's daily work. For it is less pleasing to God than the active performance of His will in a calling. Besides, Sunday is provided for that, and, according to Baxter, it is always those who are not diligent in their callings who have no time for God when the occasion demands it.

Accordingly, Baxter's principal work is dominated by the continually repeated, often almost passionate preaching of hard, continuous bodily or mental labour. It is due to a combination of two different motives. Labour is, on the one hand, an approved ascetic technique, as it always has been in the Western Church, in sharp contrast not only to the Orient but to almost all monastic rules the world over. It is in particular the specific defence against all those temptations which Puritanism united under the name of the unclean life, whose rôle for it was by no means small. The sexual asceticism of Puritanism differs only in degree, not in fundamental principle, from that of monasticism; and on account of the Puritan conception of marriage, its practical influence is more far-reaching than that of the latter. For sexual intercourse is permitted, even within marriage, only as the means willed by God for the increase of His glory according to the commandment, "Be fruitful and multiply." Along with a moderate vegetable diet and cold baths, the same prescription is given for all sexual temptations as is used against religious doubts and a sense of moral unworthiness: "Work hard in your calling." But the most important thing was that even beyond that labour came to be considered in itself the end of life, ordained as such by God. St. Paul's "He who will not work shall not eat" holds unconditionally for everyone. Unwillingness to work is symptomatic of the lack of grace.

Here the difference from the mediæval view-point becomes quite evident. Thomas Aquinas also gave an interpretation of that statement of St. Paul. But for him labour is only necessary *naturali ratione* for the maintenance of individual and community. Where this end is achieved, the precept ceases to have any meaning. Moreover, it holds only for the race, not for every individual. It does not apply to anyone who can live without labour on his possessions, and of course contemplation, as a spiritual form of action in the Kingdom of God, takes precedence over the commandment in its literal sense. Moreover, for the popular theology of the time, the highest

form of monastic productivity lay in the increase of the *Thesaurus ecclesiæ* through prayer and chant.

Now only do these exceptions to the duty to labour naturally no longer hold for Baxter, but he holds most emphatically that wealth does not exempt anyone from the unconditional command. Even the wealthy shall not eat without working, for even though they do not need to labour to support their own needs, there is God's commandment which they, like the poor, must obey. For everyone without exception God's Providence has prepared a calling, which he should profess and in which he should labour. And this calling is not, as it was for the Lutheran, a fate to which he must submit and which he must make the best of, but God's commandment to the individual to work for the divine glory. This seemingly subtle difference had far-reaching psychological consequences, and became connected with a further development of the providential interpretation of the economic order which had begun in scholasticism.

The phenomenon of the division of labour and occupations in society had, among others, been interpreted by Thomas Aquinas, to whom we may most conveniently refer, as a direct consequence of the divine scheme of things. But the places assigned to each man in this cosmos follow *ex causis naturalibus* and are fortuitous (contingent in the Scholastic terminology). The differentiation of men into the classes and occupations established through historical development became for Luther, as we have seen, a direct result of the divine will. The perseverance of the individual in the place and within the limits which God had assigned to him was a religious duty. This was the more certainly the consequence since the relations of Lutheranism to the world were in general uncertain from the beginning and remained so. Ethical principles for the reform of the world could not be found in Luther's realm of ideas; in fact it never quite freed itself from Pauline indifference. Hence the world had to be accepted as it was, and this alone could be made a religious duty.

But in the Puritan view, the providential character of the play of private economic interests takes on a somewhat different emphasis. True to the Puritan tendency to pragmatic interpretations, the providential purpose of the division of labour is to be known by its fruits. On this point Baxter expresses himself in terms which more than once directly recall Adam Smith's well-known apotheosis of the division of labour. The specialization of occupations leads, since it makes the development of skill possible, to a quantitative and qualitative improvement in production, and thus serves the common good, which is identical with the good of the greatest possible number. So far, the motivation is purely utilitarian, and is closely related to the customary view-point of much of the secular literature of the time.

But the characteristic Puritan element appears when Baxter sets at the head of his discussion the statement that "outside of a well-marked calling the accomplishments of a man are only casual and irregular, and he spends more time in idleness than at work", and when he concludes it as follows: "and he [the specialized worker] will carry out his work in order while another remains in constant confusion, and his business knows neither time nor place . . . therefore is a certain calling the best for everyone". Irregular work, which the ordinary labourer is often forced to accept, is often unavoidable, but always an unwelcome state of transition. A man without a calling thus lacks the systematic, methodical character which is, as we have seen, demanded by worldly asceticism.

The Quaker ethic also holds that a man's life in his calling is an exercise in ascetic virtue, a proof of his state of grace through his conscientiousness, which is expressed in the care and method with which he pursues his calling. What God demands is not labour in itself, but rational labour in a calling. In the Puritan concept of the calling the emphasis is always placed on this methodical character of worldly asceticism, not, as with Luther, on the acceptance of the lot which God has irretrievably assigned to man.

Hence the question whether anyone may combine several callings is answered in the affirmative, if it is useful for the common good or one's own, and not injurious to anyone, and if it does not lead to unfaithfulness in one of the callings. Even a change of calling is by no means regarded as objectionable, if it is not thoughtless and is made for the purpose of pursuing a calling more pleasing to God, which means, on general principles, one more useful.

It is true that the usefulness of a calling, and thus its favour in the sight of God, is measured primarily in moral terms, and thus in terms of the importance of the goods produced in it for the community. But a further, and, above all, in practice the most important, criterion is found in private profitableness. For if that God, whose hand the Puritan sees in all the occurrences of life, shows one of His elect a chance of profit, he must do it with a purpose. Hence the faithful Christian must follow the call by taking advantage of the opportunity. "If God show you a way in which you may lawfully get more than in another way (without wrong to your soul or to any other), if you refuse this, and choose the less gainful way, you cross one of the ends of your calling, and you refuse to be God's steward, and to accept His gifts and use them for Him when He requireth it: you may labour to be rich for God, though not for the flesh and sin."

Wealth is thus bad ethically only in so far as it is a temptation to idleness and sinful enjoyment of life, and its acquisition is bad only when it is with the purpose of later living merrily and without care. But as a performance of duty in a calling it is not only morally permissible, but actually enjoined. The parable of the servant who was rejected because he did not increase the talent which was entrusted to him seemed to say so directly. To wish to be poor was, it was often argued, the same as wishing to be unhealthy; it is objectionable as a glorification of works and derogatory to the glory of God. Especially begging, on the part of one able to work, is not only the sin of slothfulness, but a violation of the duty of brotherly love according to the Apostle's own word.

The emphasis on the ascetic importance of a fixed calling provided an ethical justification of the modern specialized division of labour. In a similar way the providential interpretation of profit-making justified the activities of the business man. The superior indulgence of the *seigneur* and the parvenu ostentation of the *nouveau riche* are equally detestable to asceticism. But, on the other hand, it has the highest ethical appreciation of the sober, middle-class, self-made man. "God blesseth His trade" is a stock remark about those good men who had successfully followed the divine hints. The whole power of the God of the Old Testament, who rewards His people for their obedience in this life, necessarily exercised a similar influence on the Puritan who, following Baxter's advice, compared his own state of grace with that of the heroes of the Bible, and in the process interpreted the statements of the Scriptures as the articles of a book of statutes.

Of course, the words of the Old Testament were not entirely without ambiguity. We have seen that Luther first used the concept of the calling in the secular sense in translating a passage from Jesus Sirach. But the book of Jesus Sirach belongs, with the whole atmosphere expressed in it, to those parts of the broadened Old Testament with a distinctly traditionalistic tendency, in spite of Hellenistic influences. It is characteristic that down to the present day this book seems to enjoy a special favour among Lutheran German peasants, just as the Lutheran influence in large sections of German Pietism has been expressed by a preference for Jesus Sirach.

The Puritans repudiated the Apocrypha as not inspired, consistently with their sharp distinction between things divine and things of the flesh. But among the canonical books that of Job had all the more influence. On the one hand it contained a grand conception of the absolute sovereign majesty of God, beyond all human comprehension, which was closely related to that of Calvinism. With that, on the other hand, it combined the certainty which, though incidental for Calvin, came to be of great importance for Puritanism, that God would bless His own in this life—in the book of Job only—and also in the material sense. The Oriental quietism, which appears in several of the finest verses of the Psalms and in the Proverbs, was interpreted away, just as Baxter did with the traditionalistic tinge of the passage in the 1st Epistle to the Corinthians, so important for the idea of the calling.

But all the more emphasis was placed on those parts of the Old Testament which praise formal legality as a sign of conduct pleasing to God. They held the theory that the Mosaic Law had only lost its validity through Christ in so far as it contained ceremonial or purely historical precepts applying only to the Jewish people, but that otherwise it had always been valid as an expression of the natural law, and must hence be retained. This made it possible, on the one hand, to eliminate elements which could not be reconciled with modern life. But still, through its numerous related features, Old Testament morality was able to give a powerful impetus to that spirit of self-righteous and sober legality which was so characteristic of the worldly asceticism of this form of Protestantism.

Thus when authors, as was the case with several contemporaries as well as later writers, characterize the basic ethical tendency of Puritanism, especially in England, as English Hebraism they are, correctly understood, not wrong. It is necessary, however, not to think of Palestinian Judaism at the time of the writing of the Scriptures, but of Judaism as it became under the influence of many centuries of formalistic, legalistic, and Talmudic education. Even then one must be very careful in drawing parallels. The general tendency of the older Judaism toward a naïve acceptance of life as such was far removed from the special characteristics of Puritanism. It was, however, just as far—and this ought not to be overlooked—from the economic ethics of mediæval and modern Judaism, in the traits which determined the positions of both in the development of the capitalistic ethos. The Jews stood on the side of the politically and speculatively oriented adventurous capitalism; their ethos was, in a word, that of pariah-capitalism. But Puritanism carried the ethos of the rational organization of capital and labour. It took over from the Jewish ethic only what was adapted to this purpose.

To analyse the effects on the character of peoples of the penetration of life with Old Testament norms—a tempting task which, however, has not yet satisfactorily been done even for Judaism—would be impossible within the limits of this sketch. In addition to the relationships already pointed out, it is important for the general inner attitude of the Puritans, above all, that the belief that they were God's chosen people saw in them a great renaissance. Even the kindly Baxter thanked God that he was born in England, and thus in the true Church, and nowhere else. This thankfulness for one's own perfection by the grace of God penetrated the attitude toward life of the Puritan middle class, and played its part in developing that formalistic, hard, correct character which was peculiar to the men of that heroic age of capitalism.

Let us now try to clarify the points in which the Puritan idea of the calling and the premium it placed upon ascetic conduct was bound directly to influence the development of a capitalistic way of life. As we have seen, this asceticism turned with all its force against one thing: the spontaneous enjoyment of life and all it had to offer. This is perhaps most characteristically brought out in the struggle over the *Books of Sports* which James I and Charles I made into law expressly as a means of counteracting Puritanism, and which the latter ordered to be read from all the pulpits. The fanatical opposition of the Puritans to the ordinances of the King, permitting certain popular amusements on Sunday outside of Church hours by law, was not only explained by the disturbance of the Sabbath rest, but also by resentment against the intentional diversion from the ordered life of the saint, which it caused. And, on his side, the King's threats of severe punishment for every attack on the legality of those sports were motivated by his purpose of breaking the anti-authoritarian ascetic tendency of Puritanism, which was so dangerous to the State. The feudal and monarchical forces protected the pleasure seekers against the rising middle-class morality and the anti-authoritarian ascetic conventicles, just as to-day capitalistic society tends to protect those willing to work against the class morality of the proletariat and the anti-authoritarian trade union.

As against this the Puritans upheld their decisive characteristic, the principle of ascetic conduct. For otherwise the Puritan aversion to sport, even for the Quakers, was by no means simply one of principle. Sport was accepted if it served a rational purpose, that of recreation necessary for physical efficiency. But as a means for the spontaneous expression of undisciplined impulses, it was under suspicion; and in so far as it became purely a means of enjoyment, or awakened pride, raw instincts or the irrational gambling instinct, it was of course strictly condemned. Impulsive enjoyment of life, which leads away both from work in a calling and from religion, was as such the enemy of rational asceticism, whether in the form of seigneurial sports, or the enjoyment of the dance-hall or the public-house of the common man.

Its attitude was thus suspicious and often hostile to the aspects of culture without any immediate religious value. It is not, however, true that the ideals of Puritanism implied a solemn, narrow-minded contempt of culture. Quite the contrary is the case at least for science, with the exception of the hatred of Scholasticism. Moreover, the great men of the Puritan movement were thoroughly steeped in the culture of the Renaissance. The sermons of the Presbyterian divines abound with classical allusions, and even the Radicals, although they objected to it, were not ashamed to display that kind of learning in theological polemics. Perhaps no country was ever so full of graduates as New England in the first generation of its existence. The satire of their opponents, such as, for instance, Butler's *Hudibras*, also attacks primarily the pedantry and highly trained dialectics of the Puritans. This is partially due to the religious valuation of knowledge which followed from their attitude to the Catholic *fides implicita*.

But the situation is quite different when one looks at non-scientific literature, and especially the fine arts. Here asceticism descended like a frost on the life of "Merrie old England." And not only worldly merriment felt its effect. The Puritan's ferocious hatred of everything which smacked of superstition, of all survivals of magical or sacramental salvation, applied to the Christmas festivities and the May Pole and all spontaneous religious art. That there was room in Holland for a great, often uncouthly realistic art proves only how far from completely the authoritarian moral discipline of that country was able to counteract the influence of the court and the regents (a class of *rentiers*), and also the joy in life of the parvenu bourgeoisie, after the short supremacy of the Calvinistic theocracy had been transformed into a moderate national Church, and with it Calvinism had perceptibly lost in its power of ascetic influence.

The theatre was obnoxious to the Puritans, and with the strict exclusion of the erotic and of nudity from the realm of toleration, a radical view of either literature or art could not exist. The conceptions of idle talk, of superfluities, and of vain ostentation, all designations of an irrational attitude without objective purpose, thus not ascetic, and especially not serving the glory of God, but of man, were always at hand to serve in deciding in favour of sober utility as against any artistic tendencies. This was especially true in the case of decoration of the person, for instance clothing. That powerful tendency toward uniformity of life, which to-day so immensely aids the capitalistic interest in the standardization of production, had its ideal foundations in the repudiation of all idolatry of the flesh.

Of course we must not forget that Puritanism included a world of contradictions, and that the instinctive sense of eternal greatness in art was certainly stronger among its leaders than in the atmosphere of the Cavaliers. Moreover, a unique genius like Rembrandt, however little his conduct may have been acceptable to God in the eyes of the Puritans, was very strongly influenced in the character of his work by his religious environment. But that does not alter the picture as a whole. In so far as the development of the Puritan tradition could, and in part did, lead to a powerful spiritualization of personality, it was a decided benefit to literature. But for the most part that benefit only accrued to later generations.

Although we cannot here enter upon a discussion of the influence of Puritanism in all these directions, we should call attention to the fact that the toleration of pleasure in cultural goods, which contributed to purely æsthetic or athletic enjoyment, certainly always ran up against one characteristic limitation: they must not cost anything. Man is only a trustee of the goods which have come to him through God's grace. He must, like the servant in the parable, give an account of every penny entrusted to him, and it is at least hazardous to spend any of it for a purpose which does not serve the glory of God but only one's own enjoyment. What person, who keeps his eyes open, has not met representatives of this view-point even in the present? The idea of a man's duty to his possessions, to which he subordinates himself as an obedient steward, or even as an acquisitive machine, bears with chilling weight on his life. The greater the possessions the heavier, if the ascetic attitude toward life stands the test, the feeling of responsibility for them, for holding them undiminished for the glory of God and increasing them by restless effort. The origin of this type of life also extends in certain roots, like so many aspects of the spirit of capitalism, back into the Middle Ages. But it was in the ethic of ascetic Protestantism that it first found a consistent ethical foundation. Its significance for the development of capitalism is obvious.

This worldly Protestant asceticism, as we may recapitulate up to this point, acted powerfully against the spontaneous enjoyment of possessions; it restricted consumption, especially of luxuries. On the other hand, it had the psychological effect of freeing the acquisition of goods from the inhibitions of traditionalistic ethics. It broke the bonds of the impulse of acquisition in that it not only legalized it, but (in the sense discussed) looked upon it as directly willed by God. The campaign against the temptations of the flesh, and the dependence on external things, was, as besides the Puritans the great Quaker apologist Barclay expressly says, not a struggle against the rational acquisition, but against the irrational use of wealth.

But this irrational use was exemplified in the outward forms of luxury which their code condemned as idolatry of the flesh, however natural they had appeared to the feudal mind. On the other hand, they approved the rational and utilitarian uses of wealth which were willed by God for the needs of the individual and the community. They did not wish to impose mortification on the man of wealth, but the use of his means for necessary and practical things. The idea of comfort characteristically limits the extent of ethically permissible expenditures. It is naturally no accident that the development of a manner of living consistent with that idea may be observed earliest and most clearly among the most consistent representatives of this whole attitude toward life. Over against the glitter and ostentation of feudal magnificence which, resting on an unsound economic basis, prefers a sordid elegance to a sober simplicity, they set the clean and solid comfort of the middle-class home as an ideal.

On the side of the production of private wealth, asceticism condemned both dishonesty and impulsive avarice. What was condemned as covetousness, Mammonism, etc., was the pursuit of riches for their own sake. For wealth in itself was a temptation. But here asceticism was the power "which ever seeks the good but ever creates evil"; what was evil in its sense was possession and its temptations. For, in conformity with the Old Testament and in analogy to the ethical valuation of good works, asceticism looked upon the pursuit of wealth as an end in itself as highly reprehensible; but the attainment of it as a fruit of labour in a calling was a sign of God's blessing. And even more important: the religious valuation of restless, continuous, systematic work in a worldly calling, as the highest means to asceticism, and at the same time the surest and most evident proof of rebirth and genuine faith, must have been the most powerful conceivable lever for the expansion of that attitude toward life which we have here called the spirit of capitalism.

When the limitation of consumption is combined with this release of acquisitive activity, the inevitable practical result is obvious: accumulation of capital through ascetic compulsion to save. The restraints which were imposed upon the consumption of wealth naturally served to increase it by making possible the productive investment of capital. How strong this influence was is not, unfortunately, susceptible of exact statistical demonstration. In New England the connection is so evident that it did not escape the eye of so discerning a historian as Doyle. But also in Holland, which was really only dominated by strict Calvinism for seven years, the greater simplicity of life in the more seriously religious circles, in combination with great wealth, led to an excessive propensity to accumulation.

That, furthermore, the tendency which has existed everywhere and at all times, being quite strong in Germany to-day, for middle-class fortunes to be absorbed into the nobility, was necessarily checked by the Puritan antipathy to the feudal way of life, is evident. English Mercantilist writers of the seventeenth century attributed the superiority of Dutch capital to English to the circumstance that newly acquired wealth there did not regularly seek investment in land. Also, since it is not simply a question of the purchase of land, it did not there seek to transfer itself to feudal habits of life, and thereby to remove itself from the possibility of capitalistic investment. The high esteem for agriculture as a peculiarly important branch of activity, also especially consistent with piety, which the Puritans shared, applied (for instance in Baxter) not to the landlord, but to the yeoman and farmer, in the eighteenth century not to the squire, but the rational cultivator. Through the whole of English society in the time since the seventeenth century goes the conflict between the squirearchy, the representatives of "merrie old England", and the Puritan circles of widely varying social influence. Both elements, that of an unspoiled naïve joy of life, and of a strictly regulated, reserved self-control, and conventional ethical conduct are even to-day combined to form the English national character. Similarly, the early history of the North American Colonies is dominated by the sharp contrast of the adventurers, who wanted to set up plantations with the labour of indentured servants, and live as feudal lords, and the specifically middle-class outlook of the Puritans.

As far as the influence of the Puritan outlook extended, under all circumstances —and this is, of course, much more important than the mere encouragement of capital accumulation—it favoured the development of a rational bourgeois economic life; it was the most important, and above all the only consistent influence in the development of that life. It stood at the cradle of the modern economic man.

To be sure, these Puritanical ideals tended to give way under excessive pressure from the temptations of wealth, as the Puritans themselves knew very well. With great regularity we find the most genuine adherents of Puritanism among the classes which were rising from a lowly status, the small bourgeois and farmers, while the *beati possidentes,* even among Quakers, are often found tending to repudiate the old ideals. It was the same fate which again and again befell the predecessor of this worldly asceticism, the monastic asceticism of the Middle Ages. In the latter case, when rational economic activity had worked out its full effects by strict regulation of conduct and limitation of consumption, the wealth accumulated either succumbed directly to the nobility, as in the time before the Reformation, or monastic discipline threatened to break down, and one of the numerous reformations became necessary.

In fact the whole history of monasticism is in a certain sense the history of a continual struggle with the problem of the secularizing influence of wealth. The same is true on a grand scale of the worldly asceticism of Puritanism. The great revival of Methodism, which preceded the expansion of English industry toward the end of the eighteenth century, may well be compared with such a monastic reform. We may hence quote here a passage from John Wesley himself which might well serve as a motto for everything which has been said above. For it shows that the leaders of these ascetic movements understood the seemingly paradoxical relationships which we have here analysed perfectly well, and in the same sense that we have given them. He wrote: "I fear, wherever riches have increased, the essence of religion has decreased in the same proportion. There-

fore I do not see how it is possible, in the nature of things, for any revival of true religion to continue long. For religion must necessarily produce both industry and frugality, and these cannot but produce riches. But as riches increase, so will pride, anger, and love of the world in all its branches. How then is it possible that Methodism, that is, a religion of the heart, though it flourishes now as a green bay tree, should continue in this state? For the Methodists in every place grow diligent and frugal; consequently they increase in goods. Hence they proportionately increase in pride, in anger, in the desire of the flesh, the desire of the eyes, and the pride of life. So, although the form of religion remains, the spirit is swiftly vanishing away. Is there no way to prevent this—this continual decay of pure religion? We ought not to prevent people from being diligent and frugal; *we must exhort all Christians to gain all they can, and to save all they can; that is, in effect, to grow rich.*"

There follows the advice that those who gain all they can and save all they can should also give all they can, so that they will grow in grace and lay up a treasure in heaven. It is clear that Wesley here expresses, even in detail, just what we have been trying to point out.

As Wesley here says, the full economic effect of those great religious movements, whose significance for economic development lay above all in their ascetic educative influence, generally came only after the peak of the purely religious enthusiasm was past. Then the intensity of the search for the Kingdom of God commenced gradually to pass over into sober economic virtue; the religious roots died out slowly, giving way to utilitarian worldliness. Then, as Dowden puts it, as in *Robinson Crusoe,* the isolated economic man who carries on missionary activities on the side takes the place of the lonely spiritual search for the Kingdom of Heaven of Bunyan's pilgrim, hurrying through the market-place of Vanity.

When later the principle "to make the most of both worlds" became dominant in the end, as Dowden has remarked, a good conscience simply became one of the means of enjoying a comfortable bourgeois life, as is well expressed in the German proverb about the soft pillow. What the great religious epoch of the seventeenth century bequeathed to its utilitarian successor was, however, above all an amazingly good, we may even say a pharisaically good, conscience in the acquisition of money, so long as it took place legally. Every trace of the *deplacere vix potest* has disappeared.

A specifically bourgeois economic ethic had grown up. With the consciousness of standing in the fullness of God's grace and being visibly blessed by Him, the bourgeois business man, as long as he remained within the bounds of formal correctness, as long as his moral conduct was spotless and the use to which he put his wealth was not objectionable, could follow his pecuniary interests as he would and feel that he was fulfilling a duty in doing so. The power of religious asceticism provided him in addition with sober, conscientious, and unusually industrious workmen, who clung to their work as to a life purpose willed by God.

Finally, it gave him the comforting assurance that the unequal distribution of the goods of this world was a special dispensation of Divine Providence, which in these differences, as in particular grace, pursued secret ends unknown to men. Calvin himself had made the much-quoted statement that only when the people, i.e. the mass of labourers and craftsmen, were poor did they remain obedient to God. In the Netherlands (Pieter de la Court and others), that had been secularized to the effect that the mass of men only labour when necessity forces them to do so. This formulation of a leading idea of capitalistic economy

later entered into the current theories of the productivity of low wages. Here also, with the dying out of the religious root, the utilitarian interpretation crept in unnoticed, in the line of development which we have again and again observed.

Mediæval ethics not only tolerated begging but actually glorified it in the mendicant orders. Even secular beggars, since they gave the person of means opportunity for good works through giving alms, were sometimes considered an estate and treated as such. Even the Anglican social ethic of the Stuarts was very close to this attitude. It remained for Puritan Asceticism to take part in the severe English Poor Relief Legislation which fundamentally changed the situation. And it could do that, because the Protestant sects and the strict Puritan communities actually did not know any begging in their own midst.

On the other hand, seen from the side of the workers, the Zinzendorf branch of Pietism, for instance, glorified the loyal worker who did not seek acquisition, but lived according to the apostolic model, and was thus endowed with the *charisma* of the disciples. Similar ideas had originally been prevalent among the Baptists in an even more radical form.

Now naturally the whole ascetic literature of almost all denominations is saturated with the idea that faithful labour, even at low wages, on the part of those whom life offers no other opportunities, is highly pleasing to God. In this respect Protestant Asceticism added in itself nothing new. But it not only deepened this idea most powerfully, it also created the force which was alone decisive for its effectiveness: the psychological sanction of it through the conception of this labour as a calling, as the best, often in the last analysis the only means of attaining certainty of grace. And on the other hand it legalized the exploitation of this specific willingness to work, in that it also interpreted the employer's business activity as a calling. It is obvious how powerfully the exclusive search for the Kingdom of God only through the fulfilment of duty in the calling, and the strict asceticism which Church discipline naturally imposed, especially on the propertyless classes, was bound to affect the productivity of labour in the capitalistic sense of the word. The treatment of labour as a calling became as characteristic of the modern worker as the corresponding attitude toward acquisition of the business man. It was a perception of this situation, new at his time, which caused so able an observer as Sir William Petty to attribute the economic power of Holland in the seventeenth century to the fact that the very numerous dissenters in that country (Calvinists and Baptists) "are for the most part thinking, sober men, and such as believe that Labour and Industry is their duty towards God".

Calvinism opposed organic social organization in the fiscal-monopolistic form which it assumed in Anglicanism under the Stuarts, especially in the conceptions of Laud, this alliance of Church and State with the monopolists on the basis of a Christian-social ethical foundation. Its leaders were universally among the most passionate opponents of this type of politically privileged commercial, putting-out, and colonial capitalism. Over against it they placed the individualistic motives of rational legal acquisition by virtue of one's own ability and initiative. And, while the politically privileged monopoly industries in England all disappeared in short order, this attitude played a large and decisive part in the development of the industries which grew up in spite of and against the authority of the State. The Puritans (Prynne, Parker) repudiated all connection with the large-scale capitalistic courtiers and projectors as an ethically suspicious class. On the other hand, they took pride in their own superior middle-class business morality, which formed the true reason for the

persecutions to which they were subjected on the part of those circles. Defoe proposed to win the battle against dissent by boycotting bank credit and withdrawing deposits. The difference of the two types of capitalistic attitude went to a very large extent hand in hand with religious differences. The opponents of the Nonconformists, even in the eighteenth century, again and again ridiculed them for personifying the spirit of shopkeepers, and for having ruined the ideals of old England. Here also lay the difference of the Puritan economic ethic from the Jewish; and contemporaries (Prynne) knew well that the former and not the latter was the bourgeois capitalistic ethic.

One of the fundamental elements of the spirit of modern capitalism, and not only of that but of all modern culture: rational conduct on the basis of the idea of the calling, was born—that is what this discussion has sought to demonstrate —from the spirit of Christian asceticism. One has only to re-read the passage from Franklin, quoted at the beginning of this essay, in order to see that the essential elements of the attitude which was there called the spirit of capitalism are the same as what we have just shown to be the content of the Puritan worldly asceticism, only without the religious basis, which by Franklin's time had died away. The idea that modern labour has an ascetic character is of course not new. Limitation to specialized work, with a renunciation of the Faustian universality of man which it involves, is a condition of any valuable work in the modern world; hence deeds and renunciation inevitably condition each other today. This fundamentally ascetic trait of middle-class life, if it attempts to be a way of life at all, and not simply the absence of any, was what Goethe wanted to teach, at the height of his wisdom, in the *Wanderjahren,* and in the end which he gave to the life of his *Faust.* For him the realization meant a renunciation, a departure from an age of full and beautiful humanity, which can no more be repeated in the course of our cultural development than can the flower of the Athenian culture of antiquity.

The Puritan wanted to work in a calling; we are forced to do so. For when asceticism was carried out of monastic cells into everyday life, and began to dominate worldly morality, it did its part in building the tremendous cosmos of the modern economic order. This order is now bound to the technical and economic conditions of machine production which to-day determine the lives of all the individuals who are born into this mechanism, not only those directly concerned with economic acquisition, with irresistible force. Perhaps it will so determine them until the last ton of fossilized coal is burnt. In Baxter's view the care for external goods should only lie on the shoulders of the "saint like a light cloak, which can be thrown aside at any moment". But fate decreed that the cloak should become an iron cage.

Since asceticism undertook to remodel the world and to work out its ideals in the world, material goods have gained an increasing and finally an inexorable power over the lives of men as at no previous period in history. To-day the spirit of religious asceticism—whether finally, who knows?—has escaped from the cage. But victorious capitalism, since it rests on mechanical foundations, needs its support no longer. The rosy blush of its laughing heir, the Enlightenment, seems also to be irretrievably fading, and the idea of duty in one's calling prowls about in our lives like the ghost of dead religious beliefs. Where the fulfilment of the calling cannot directly be related to the highest spiritual and cultural values, or when, on the other hand, it need not be felt simply as economic compulsion, the individual generally abandons the attempt to justify it at all. In the field of its highest development, in the United States, the pursuit

of wealth, stripped of its religious and ethical meaning, tends to become associated with purely mundane passions, which often actually give it the character of sport.

No one knows who will live in this cage in the future, or whether at the end of this tremendous development entirely new prophets will arise, or there will be a great rebirth of old ideas and ideals, or, if neither, mechanized petrification, embellished with a sort of convulsive self-importance. For of the last stage of this cultural development, it might well be truly said: "Specialists without spirit, sensualists without heart; this nullity imagines that it has attained a level of civilization never before achieved."

But this brings us to the world of judgments of value and of faith, with which this purely historical discussion need not be burdened. The next task would be rather to show the significance of ascetic rationalism, which has only been touched in the foregoing sketch, for the content of practical social ethics, thus for the types of organization and the functions of social groups from the conventicle to the State. Then its relations to humanistic rationalism, its ideals of life and cultural influence; further to the development of philosophical and scientific empiricism, to technical development and to spiritual ideals would have to be analysed. Then its historical development from the mediæval beginnings of worldly asceticism to its dissolution into pure utilitarianism would have to be traced out through all the areas of ascetic religion. Only then could the quantitative cultural significance of ascetic Protestantism in its relation to the other plastic elements of modern culture be estimated.

Here we have only attempted to trace the fact and the direction of its influence to their motives in one, though a very important point. But it would also further be necessary to investigate how Protestant Asceticism was in turn influenced in its development and its character by the totality of social conditions, especially economic. The modern man is in general, even with the best will, unable to give religious ideas a significance for culture and national character which they deserve. But it is, of course, not my aim to substitute for a one-sided materialistic an equally one-sided spiritualistic causal interpretation of culture and of history. Each is equally possible, but each, if it does not serve as the preparation, but as the conclusion of an investigation, accomplishes equally little in the interest of historical truth.

2 · The Economic Status of Huguenots

WARREN C. SCOVILLE

At the outset, Protestantism appealed to Frenchmen in all social and economic classes: the intelligentsia and professional circles, the peasantry, the artisan and commercial groups in cities, and the nobility.[1] There had been no indication that one group or another would eventually dominate the movement. In the latter half of the sixteenth century and until 1629 the nobility exerted a strong influence. From a third to a half of the nobles turned from Catholicism to Protestantism. They sought to align the new religion on their side in the fight against the centralization of governmental authority and the power of the Guises, or they hoped to use it to further their own private interests. With the end of the Religious Wars in 1598, and after the fall of La Rochelle and the promulgation of the Edict of Alais in 1629,[2] the most powerful nobles

abjured their new faith and reëntered the Catholic Church; the lesser nobility remained Protestant but sank into political oblivion. As a result of the persecution immediately preceding and following the revocation, most of the latter group also abjured. The more faithful participated in the underground resistance movement during the next hundred years, and only a few emigrated.[3] Several hundred gen-

SOURCE. Warren C. Scoville, "The Economic Status of Huguenots," from Warren C. Scoville, The Persecution of Huguenots and French Economic Development, Berkeley and Los Angeles: University of California Press, pp. 131–155.

[1] Émile-G. Léonard, Problèmes et expériences du protestantisme français (Paris, 1940), p. 27; Henri Hauser, La Réforme et les classes populaires en France au XVIe siècle (Paris, 1899), passim; Johann-Caspar Moerikofer, Histoire des Réfugiés de la Réforme en Suisse, trans. G. Roux (Paris, 1878), p. 11.

[2] After Louis XIII and Richelieu successfully besieged the Protestant stronghold of La Rochelle, Protestants lost their right to maintain fortified places and thus ended the so-called Protestant state-within-the-state.

[3] Charles Benoist, Condition juridique des protestants sous le régime de l'Édit de Nantes et après sa révocation (Paris, 1900), p. 74; J.-A. Galland, Essai sur l'histoire du Protestantisme à Caen et en Basse-Normandie de l'édit de Nantes à la Revolution (1598–1791) (Paris, 1898), pp. 92–93; J. Jailliot, "Le Protestantisme dans le Rethelois et dans l'Argonne jusqu'à la révocation de l'Édit de Nantes," Revue d'Ardenne et d'Argonne, XIII (1905–1906), 214–215; Jean de la Monneraye, "La Révocation de l'Édit de Nantes et le protestantisme en Bas-Poitou au dix-huitième siècle," Revue du Bas-Poitou, 36th year (1923), 12; L. Rossier, Histoire des protestants de Picardie, particulièrement de ceux du département de la Somme (Amiens, 1861), p. 247; C. Weiss, "De la Conversion de la noblesse protestante au XVIIe siècle," Bulletin de la société de l'histoire du protestantisme français (hereinafter cited as BSHPF), I (1853), 47–50.

tlemen glassmakers (*gentilshommes ver-riers*) in the south and southwest of France were predominantly Protestant, and they continued to engage in intrigue and to cause the authorities considerable concern.[4] Their social and economic status, however, set them apart from other nobles.[5] On the whole, the regular nobility ceased to dominate the Protestant movement after 1629 and had practically nothing to do with it after 1685.

As the nobles withdrew, Protestantism shed its political nature, and its followers became stanch supporters of royal absolutism. They refused, for example, to aid the Prince of Condé when he and other nobles opposed the throne in Louis XIV's minority,[6] and even in the darkest hours of persecution they remained royalist and were prone to blame ministers and government advisers rather than the king himself for their plight.[7] Those who went into exile experienced difficulty in adjusting to the constitutional monarchy of England or to the republican forms of government in Holland and Switzerland. They continued to hope that the revocation edict would be rescinded and that they could return to their homeland as loyal subjects of their king. They even tried to persuade France's enemies to insist upon the reëstablishment of the Edict of Nantes as one of the terms in the peace treaties of Ryswick (1697) and Utrecht (1713).[8]

Although, as Professor Hauser has suggested,[9] one reason that Protestantism never supplanted Catholicism as the dominant religion in France may have been its failure to sink its roots deep enough into the peasantry in the sixteenth century, its adherents in the southern provinces were more or less normally proportioned among all social classes.[10] The area was heavily agricultural, and there was a clear numerical preponderance of peasants. The same was true in Dauphiné and the little area of Gex. In addition, there were widely separated rural clusters of Protestants in Normandy and other northern and central provinces. A Catholic missionary, nevertheless, could write of Protestantism in about 1681 that "nearly all those of this sect are nobles, merchants, or workers; there are very few from the lowest classes among them." [11] It is noteworthy that Huguenot peasants, though constituting a small minority of all peasants, were considered to be among the best cultivators in France. It was said in 1759, for example, that the "cantons peopled by Religionists in Languedoc, Cévennes, and Vivarais

[4] The intendant in Languedoc, for example, wrote Louvois on January 4, 1689, that he feared Protestant glassmakers in his province and in Foix would lead a revolt if they were not disarmed (Archives Nationales, A^1 902, doc. 15).

[5] Warren C. Scoville, *Capitalism and French Glassmaking, 1640–1789* (Berkeley and Los Angeles, 1950), pp. 84–87.

[6] *Testament politique du Marquis de Louvois, premier ministre d'Etat sous le Règne de Louis XIV, Roy de France, où l'on voit ce qui s'est passé de plus remarquable en France jusqu'à sa mort* (Cologne, 1695), p. 374; A. Crottet, "Les Préludes de la révocation de l'édit de Nantes dans le pays de Gex," *BSHPF*, I, 293.

[7] Jacques de Missècle, *L'Édit de Nantes et sa révocation* (2d ed.; Colmar, 1931), pp. 14–15; Émile-G. Léonard, "Le Protestantisme français au XVIIe siècle," *Revue historique*, CC (1948), 159–161, 166 ff.

[8] Frank Puaux, "Essai sur les négociations des réfugiés pour obtenir le rétablissement de la Religion réformée au traité de Ryswick (octobre 1697)," *BSHPF*, XVI (1867), passim.

[9] *Op. cit.*, pp. 33, 37.

[10] Émile-G. Léonard, *Histoire ecclésiastique des réformés français au XVIIIe siècle* (Paris, 1940), p. xii.

[11] Bibliothèque Nationale, *Fonds français*, MS 21622, fol. 97. Professor Léonard made the same point in regard to Normandy in his lectures at the Sorbonne in 1949, which I was privileged to attend.

are the best cultivated and the most productive despite the difficult terrain." [12]
And the intendant at La Rochelle somewhat begrudgingly admitted in 1699 that
there was no place in all his province of
Saintonge where the soil was better tilled
than on the island of Oléron, with its
heavy Protestant population.[13]

The Protestant Bourgeoisie

Special interest centers on the Protestants who were members of the *bourgeoisie*. Most scholars have agreed that
they dominated and typified seventeenth-
century Protestanism. Girolano Venier,
the Venetian ambassador at Paris, stated
in his summary report in 1688 that "the
Protestants, having no hope of advancement at court or in the army, had chosen
to reside in the provinces best adapted
to trade and had added greatly to the
wealth of the kingdom by their industry,
their financial operations, and their ship-
ping. . . . It is believed that two-thirds
of the business of the country was in
their hands." [14] A Huguenot magistrate
at Toulouse in 1664 affirmed that "nearly
all trade of this country is in the hands
of those of the Reputedly Reformed Re-

ligion." [15] The statesman Daguesseau
likewise wrote that "by an unhappy fate
the Protestants were the most skillful
artisans and the richest merchants in
nearly all branches of the arts." [16] And
Seignelay, as minister of the marine, de-
plored the fact that the directors of the
great commercial companies were for
the most part Protestant and ordinarily
employed only members of their sect on
their ships.[17] If an astute observer had
visited the great ports and cities throughout France at the time of the revocation,
he probably would have arrived at a
similar conclusion.

The Protestant merchants at Bordeaux
and in some of the smaller communities
in Guyenne were very influential. Bezons,
as intendant in that area, reported on
December 12, 1688, that several of them
were apparently planning to flee:

It would be very unfortunate for trade,
considering its present state, if several
of these merchants were to leave because it is they who have the most
money and who are responsible for the
greatest part of Bordeaux's commerce.
I would have arrested one of them for
having sold his household possessions
had I not feared that such action
would have destroyed trade entirely.
Trade is very badly disrupted at present. New converts are practically the
only individuals who undertake it, and
their habits and background give them
an advantage in carrying it on over all
other merchants.[18]

[12] Bibliothèque Nationale, *Fonds français*,
MS 7047, fols. 440 ff. M. le Comte de Saxe,
Maréchal of France, attested the same fact
in 1746 (Bibliothèque de la Société Protes-
tante, MS 339, fol. 28). See also Roger
Lacoste, "Notes sur la bourgeoisie du Ber-
geracois à la veille de la Révolution,"
BSHPF, LXXXIII (1934), 447–483.
[13] Bibliothèque Nationale, *Fonds français*,
MS 4287, fol. 37.
[14] Barozzi and Berchet, *Le Relazioni degli
Stati Europei lette al Senato dagli Ambas-
ciatori Veneti nel secolo decimosettimo*,
Series II, "Francia," Vol. III (Venice, 1857–
1863), as quoted by Henry Austen Layard,
"The Revocation of the Edict of Nantes."
Illustrated from State Papers in the Archives
of Venice," *Proceedings of the Huguenot
Society of London* (hereinafter cited as
PHSL), II (1887–1888), 150.

[15] *BSHPF*, XXXIII (1884), 135.
[16] Camille Rabaud, *Histoire du protestantisme dans l'Albigeois et le Lauragais depuis
la révocation de l'édit de Nantes (1685)
jusqu'à nos jours* (Paris, 1898), p. 104.
[17] Eugène Guitard, *Colbert et Seignelay con-
tre la religion réformée* (2d ed.; Paris,
1912), p. 116. See also Charles W. Cole,
*Colbert and a Century of French Mercantil-
ism* (New York, 1939), II, 91, 101.
[18] Archives Nationales, G⁷ 134.

Bezons's predecessor had complained four years earlier that Protestant brokers who had been ousted by royal order after 1680 still managed to control foreign trade at Bordeaux by using subservient Catholic middlemen as dummies and by capitalizing on their religion to obtain commissions from foreign buyers who were also Protestant.[19] Seignelay was distressed to learn on September 18, 1685, that Huguenots owned and operated nearly all vessels plying between Bordeaux and the American isles.[20] The same religious group practically monopolized the wine trade; occupied important positions in the markets for tobacco, oils, cheese, white lead, starch, and salt fish; figured prominently in the legal and other professions; more than held its own in various craft gilds, although outnumbered; and punished Catholics and new converts by blacklisting and refusing to employ them.[21]

La Rochelle, another important commercial center, was one of the greatest Protestant strongholds. The Huguenots there owned and operated most of the boats engaged in coastwise trade, armed and supplied French warships based at neighboring Rochefort, and accounted for a third of all sailors and half of the 1,200 marine officers in the area.[22] Bonrepaus, while intendant-general at the Rochefort arsenal, further confirmed the hegemony of Protestants in a letter to Seignelay on May 19, 1685:

> You know, Monseigneur, better than I that the trade of this country is in the hands of Religionists, and that we cannot take it from them at the present without causing it great harm because Catholics are not enterprising enough to take it over. The same may be said of shipping. The chief shipmasters are members of the Reputedly Reformed Religion and own most of the merchant vessels. These men do all in their power to keep Catholics from earning a living. . . . I do not have to dissemble with you. These Religionists occupy the top rank in all places hereabout, and they view Catholics, and especially new converts, as miserable creatures whose standard of living makes them despicable.[23]

There were also frequent complaints that a dozen or more wealthy Huguenots monopolized the wine and salt trade around La Rochelle. According to contemporary documents, it was they to whom most foreign buyers addressed their orders; it was they who received, weighed, and handled all the salt pro-

---

[19] A. M. de Boislisle, *Correspondance des contrôleurs généraux des finances avec les intendants des provinces,* I (Paris, 1874), 34; see also p. 91.

[20] Archives Nationales, B³ *registre* 48, fol. 331. See also Frederic C. Lane, "Colbert et le commerce de Bordeaux," *Revue historique de Bordeaux et du département de la Gironde,* XVII (1924), 188–189.

[21] Archives Nationales, G⁷ 134; TT 431, doc. 155; Bibliothèque Nationale, *Fonds français,* MSS 4287, fols. 49, 50; 7047, fols. 440 ff.; Paul Bert, *Histoire de la revocation de l'édit de Nantes à Bordeaux et dans le Bordelais* (*1653–1715*) (Bordeaux, 1908), pp. 3, 4, 41, 50; C. Weiss, "Mémoire sur les protestants de France au XVIIᵉ siècle," *Séances et travaux de l'Académie des sciences morales et politiques,* XX (1851), 103–105.

[22] Archives Nationales, TT 232, *dossier* 19, doc. 9; 435, doc. 10; 448, doc. 295; B² *registre* 55, fol. 235; B³ *registre* 48, fol. 271; Bibliothèque Nationale, *Fonds français,* MSS 4287, fol. 34; 7044, fol. 28; Prosper Boissonnade, "La Marine marchande, le port et les armateurs de la Rochelle à l'époque de Colbert (1662–1682)," in *Bulletin de la section de géographie: Comité des travaux historiques et scientifiques* (Paris, 1922), pp. 21, 36; Guitard, *op. cit.,* p. 44; Henry Lehr, *Les Protestants d'autrefois. Vie et institutions militaires,* II (Paris, 1907), 38 ff.

[23] Archives Nationales, B³ *registre* 48, fols. 289 ff. See also *ibid.,* fols. 314–317; Boissonnade, *op. cit.,* pp. 21–22.

duced by peasants in the region; it was they who offered employment to vast numbers; and it was they who rigged the prices, bribed the judges, and changed their buying policies so as to punish Catholics and reward Protestants. Bonrepaus joyfully reported to Seignelay on September 14, 1685, that he had recently converted three Rochelais merchants who owned several sailing vessels as well as a sugar refinery, and who provided a livelihood for some 700 or 800 families in La Rochelle. The Abbé de Cordemoy at La Tremblade, a little community near Rochefort, admitted in a letter dated January 1, 1695, that Protestants in Saintonge and Aunis and on the islands off the coast were so affluent that they even controlled the Judiciary. Most of the local judges were poor Catholics, he said, who often had bought their seats on the bench with borrowed funds. They hence found themselves financially embarrassed and often sold justice to the highest bidder. Huguenot litigants, who were among the wealthier individuals in the region, showered the judges with costly gifts and thus nearly always obtained favorable decisions from the court at the expense of poorer Catholics.[24]

The majority of the hundred or more Protestants in the Breton port of Nantes served as agents for important commercial houses in England and Holland and were counted among the city's richest inhabitants.[25] Nicolas Dumoustier, lieutenant general at Caen, had represented to Colbert as early as February 27, 1665,

that "the larger portion of the merchants of this city profess the Reputedly Reformed Religion; and, since they have better access to English and Dutch markets and more experience in dealing with merchants from England and Holland because their religion is the same, they handle all the trade in cloth and other merchandise which originates in this region."[26] When Dumoustier proposed that certain Catholics establish a royal manufactory of fine woolens in the Dutch tradition, as the Huguenots Massieu and Jemblin had recently done, they were "very distant" to his suggestion and doubtful of their success, "not having the entrepreneurial spirit or the facilities of these two Protestants."

In the three chief ports in Upper Normandy—Rouen, Le Havre, and Dieppe—a good many Protestants were wealthy merchants. According to one zealous Catholic, Norman ports shortly before the revocation were "filled with Huguenots who, in sharp contrast with Catholic merchants, always receive the most valued and best commissions from businessmen in England, Holland, Germany, Denmark, and Sweden."[27] The intendant accused several Protestant merchants at Rouen and Caen on January 26, 1685, of being responsible for a shortage of money in the area. According to him, they had recently become incensed over legal sanctions directed against their religion and had tightly closed their purses. These were the same individuals who a short time earlier had imported supplies from neighboring regions when a local shortage of grain threatened famine. The intendant, however, reassured the controller general that

[24] Archives Nationales, G⁷ 338; TT 232 dossier 19, doc. 9; B³ registre 48, fol. 302; Bibliothèque Nationale, Fonds français, MS 7045, fols. 33, 38–39, 40–42.
[25] Archives Nationales, TT 258, dossier 1, doc. 3; Émile Gabory, "La Marine et le commerce de Nantes au XVIIᵉ siècle et au commencement du XVIIIᵉ (1661–1715)," Annales de Bretagne, XVII (1901–1902), 369, 371–372.

[26] Dumoustier's letter has been reproduced in Paul-M. Bondois, "Colbert et le développement économique de la Basse-Normandie," Bulletin de la société des antiquaires de Normandie, XLI (1934), 43–45.
[27] Archives Nationales, TT 260, dossier 13, doc. 169.

the money shortage would not endure very long because the men, after all, were "merchants by profession who could not abstain from trade for very long." [28]

So many wealthy employers in Rouen were Protestant that religious disputes there often resembled an economic class struggle between a Catholic proletariat and a Protestant *bourgeoisie*.[29] In a memorandum of February 15, 1683, an inhabitant of Rouen noted that only about a fifth of the population of Dieppe was Protestant. Yet this minority—"richer than the others and . . . [with] nearly all trade within their hands"—dominated civic affairs by faithfully attending all public meetings and by skillfully using their wealth and economic power.[30] New converts and regular Catholics sometimes had to sue Protestant employers in order to collect back wages.[31] And as late as 1742 a frustrated Catholic merchant who had recently purchased a captaincy in the Norman militia to gain social and economic distinction complained bitterly that he had been cheated. All the colonels and other officers in his unit, he said, were of Huguenot extraction and steadfastly refused to recognize his rank or to consort with him.[32]

Protestants and new converts consti-tuted the most influential group of citizens in Nîmes, an important center in silk and woolen manufacturing. The intendant Bâville, who ordinarily was more prone to belittle than to exaggerate the importance of Huguenots, reported in 1699 that they "have a higher standard of living and are more active and more industrious than regular Catholics," and that Huguenot merchants, "skillful in trade and daring in enterprise, apply themselves well to commerce and have all the genius that is needed to succeed in their profession. . . . Even if all of them are still not devout Catholics, at least they have not ceased to be very good businessmen." [33] Several years before 1685 a Catholic had protested that Protestants dominated the gilds and municipal posts in Nîmes so completely that Catholics could not find employment.[34] Apparently the revocation did not alter matters significantly, for the Abbé de Saint-Maximin, who could boast of a doctorate from the Sorbonne, voiced the same complaint in 1737. "Catholics," he said, "being in the small minority and very poor, are gradually being alienated from the Church by self-interest or complaisance. . . . Since trade and manufacturing are entirely in the hands of Religionists, workers and artisans have to conform to the standards set by those upon whom they depend for good standing, protection, and employment." [35]

Reports from other cities had a similar tone. Huguenot manufacturers at Sedan operated almost half of the looms in that city and offered employment to

---

[28] Boislisle, *op. cit.*, I, 42.

[29] Léonard, *Problèmes et expériences du protestantisme français*, pp. 27–28; Émile-G. Léonard, "Une Église protestante de notables (Caen) devant la persécution et la révolution" (unpublished manuscript, 1940); Hauser, *op. cit.*, passim; Jean Bianquis, *La Révocation de l'Édit de Nantes à Rouen, essai historique* (Rouen, 1885), p. vii; Philippe Le Gendre, *Histoire de la persécution faite à l'église de Rouen sur la fin du dernier siècle*, ed. Émile Lesens (Rouen, 1874), p. xxi.

[30] Archives Nationales, TT 264, *dossier* 19, doc. 83.

[31] Guitard, *op. cit.*, p. 44.

[32] Léonard, "Une Église protestante de notables"; Galland, *op. cit.*, pp. 372–373.

[33] Bibliothèque Nationale, *Fonds français*, MSS 1490, fol. 138; 4290, fol. 323.

[34] Archives Départementales de l'Hérault, C. 1656, as reproduced in Paul Gachon, *Quelques préliminaires de la Révocation de l'Édit de Nantes en Languedoc (1661–1685)* (Toulouse, 1899), Appendix, pp. vii–viii; see also pp. 146–147.

[35] Archives Nationales, TT 247, doc. 94.

hundreds of workers;[36] those who were fleeing Saint-Quentin in September, 1685, had carried on most of the trade of the city and had precipitated its economic ruin with their departure;[37] and the intendant at Alençon complained on January 27, 1687, that new converts, "the richest inhabitants of this city," were deserting and would greatly decrease tax revenues from his province.[38] Protestants in Metz were among the city's wealthiest merchants and most successful industrialists and, according to the intendant, monopolized wholesale trade.[39] In 1668, the Catholic half of Montauban's population had paid in the aggregate only one-sixth as much in property taxes as the other half.[40] The few hundred Calvinists in Lyon were either Swiss and other foreigners who engaged in trade as representatives of foreign firms or Frenchmen who had made a name for themselves in banking, commerce, and publishing.[41] The intendant at Lyon,

after asserting in 1699 that the revocation had not caused a very great exodus from that city, commented that those who had fled "were rich and cut a good figure in trade and carried away with them a considerable amount of wealth."[42] As to be expected of a city the size of Paris, its colony of some 10,000 Huguenots did not dominate its economic life. Significantly enough, however, when an acute shortage of bread and grain threatened Paris in November, 1698, the lieutenant general of police turned first to a Protestant merchant as the person most capable of providing relief.[43]

It is also important for our purposes to know whether Protestants occupied key positions in particular industries. Most of the reports and letters of intendants and other government officials indicate that the Huguenot *bourgeoisie* not only was wealthy and inclined to trade but also provided employment for large numbers of Frenchmen in manufacturing. One writer has claimed that Protestants lent more support than Catholics to Colbert's efforts to encourage large-scale capitalistic forms of production and also helped to diffuse foreign technology at home by copying English and Dutch industrial methods observed during their frequent travels abroad.[44] The Dutch family van Robais, which established in 1665 the famous fine woolen works at Abbeville and kept sixty-five or more looms constantly at work, was Calvinist;[45] so were Massieu, Jemblin, and their descendants, who acquired the Dutch secret of making fine cloth from Spanish wool and long operated a famous factory at Caen.[46] Two

[36] *Ibid.*, TT 435, *dossier* 5; Boislisle, *op. cit.*, II (1883), 37–38; Stephen Leroy, "Les Protestants de Sedan au XVIIIᵉ siècle," *BSHPF*, XLV (1896), 339–340.

[37] Archives Nationales, G⁷ 85. See also Boislisle, *op. cit.*, I, 56; Alfred Daullé, *La Réforme à Saint-Quentin et aux environs, du XVIᵉ siècle à la fin du XVIIIᵉ siècle* (Le Cateau, 1901), p. 183.

[38] Archives Nationales, G⁷ 71.

[39] Maurice Thirion, *Étude sur l'histoire du protestantisme à Metz et dans le pays messin* (Nancy, 1884), pp. 394–398; Orthon Cuvier, *Les Réformés de la Lorraine et du pays messin* (Nancy, 1884), pp. 26, 44–45; Reginald Lane Poole, *A History of the Huguenots of the Dispersion at the Recall of the Edict of Nantes* (London, 1880), pp. 170–171 n.

[40] Ch. Garrisson, "La Population protestante . . . de Montauban," *BSHPF*, XLVI (1897), 120–121.

[41] John Viénot, *Histoire de la Réforme française, de l'Édit de Nantes à sa révocation (1598–1685)* (Paris, 1934), pp. 414–415; Natalis Rondot, *Les Protestants à Lyon au dix-septième siècle* (Lyon, 1891), p. 52.

[42] Bibliothèque Nationale, *Fonds français*, MS 4288, fol. 66.

[43] Boislisle *op. cit.*, I, 502.

[44] Weiss, "Mémoire sur les protestants," *op. cit.*, XX, 106.

[45] Archives Nationales, F¹² 822A.

[46] Bondois, *op. cit.*, 43–46; Léonard, "Une Église protestante de notables."

Huguenot entrepreneurs founded a manufactory at Elbeuf which specialized in strong white cloth and found great favor in Colbert's eyes;[47] other Protestants did the same at Louviers;[48] and a large number of clothiers and woolen manufacturers at Sedan and in various cities in Languedoc were of the same religion.[49] In July, 1684, a little more than a year before he outlawed their religion, Louis granted four Protestants exclusive letters patent to make heavy crepe in the Zurich fashion throughout Champagne and Bire for twenty years. They succeeded in launching their enterprise and in establishing it on a firm footing before persecution forced them to flee. In Lower Poitou, a region not given to large-scale industry, Huguenots made up most of the population in centers where woolens were manufactured under the putting-out system rather than by gilds or in households.[50]

At Nîmes and to a lesser extent at Tours the silk industry was in the hands of Protestant throwsters, dyers, weavers, and entrepreneurs.[51] Some even found employment in the silk mills at Lyon, a predominantly Catholic city, and acquired the secrets of making the damasks, taffetas, and velvets for which that city was famous. In Picardy—and even in Brittany at Nantes, Rennes, and Vitré —Huguenots maintained important works which turned out fine linen fabrics or heavy sailcloth.[52] They operated several paper mills in Auvergne and Angoumois, a large number of tanyards in Touraine and other provinces, so many glass factories that some writers have erroneously concluded that they controlled the industry, several sugar refineries along the Atlantic coast, many forges and metallurgical works producing all kinds of articles ranging from kitchenware to armaments, hat manufactories in Normandy, clock and watch works, and several printing establishments in the largest cities.[53] In 1685 three very wealthy Protestant families at Villière-le-Bel near Versailles were said to employ all members of their sect who lived in the same community to produce lace and silverware under the putting-out system.[54]

The position occupied by Huguenots in the realm of finance has already been mentioned. At Lyon those of Swiss nationality vied with Italian bankers for top rank. Throughout the eighteenth century they enjoyed comparative peace

[47] Cole, op. cit., II, 150–151.
[48] Weiss, "Mémoire sur les protestants," op. cit., XX, 106–107.
[49] Leroy, op. cit., pp. 339–340; Émile-G. Léonard, "Économie et religion, les protestants français au XVIIIᵉ siècle," Annales d'histoire sociale, II (1940), 16–17; Boislisle, op. cit., II, 37–38.
[50] François Baudry, La Révocation de l'édit de Nantes et le protestantisme en Bas-Poitou au XVIIIᵉ siècle (Trévoux, 1922), pp. 305–307.
[51] Bibliothèque Nationale, Fonds français, MSS 7047, fols. 440 ff.; 17315, fol. 55; Weiss, "Mémoire sur les protestants," op. cit., XX, 111; Armand Dupin de Saint-André, Un Coup d'oeil sur l'histoire du protestantisme en Touraine (Paris, 1901), p. 66; Gachon, op. cit., pp. 146–147.

[52] Weiss, "Mémoire sur les protestants," op. cit., XX, 109–110. According to a manuscript dated 1759, Huguenots ran seventeen houses in Picardy which produced "a prodigious quantity of linens which experience has shown they alone can do with success" (Bibliothèque Nationale, Fonds français, MS 7047, fols. 440 ff.).
[53] Archives Nationales, A¹ 902, doc. 15; Bibliothèque Nationale, Fonds Français, MS 7047, fols. 440 ff.; David C. A. Agnew, Protestant Exiles from France in the Reign of Louis XIV (2d ed.; London, 1871–1874), II, 136; Bianquis, op. cit., p. xl; Galland, op. cit., p. 105; Poole, op. cit., 8–9; Weiss, "Mémoire sur les protestants," op. cit., XX, 107 ff.
[54] Bibliothèque Nationale, Fonds français, MS 7052, fols. 314–315.

and quiet there,[55] whereas native-born financiers of the Protestant faith in most cities other than Lyon, Rouen, and Paris suffered sporadic harassment. Many Huguenots throughout the realm engaged in banking and lending operations, either as their main interest or, more frequently, as a side line. Catholics were often their debtors, and as such loudly complained upon occasion that Protestant creditors wreaked revenge on them for acts of persecution directed against their religion.[56]

The participation of Protestants and new converts in government finance further reveals their political and social status. Douen, one of the most meticulous and cautious students of French Protestantism, has counted forty-eight Protestants who filled important government financial posts under Sully, Louis XIII, and Mazarin from 1596 to 1650, and thirty-one others who were employed under Herwarth and Colbert from 1650 to 1680.[57] Herwarth, intendant of finance and later controller general, was himself a Calvinist and introduced many of his coreligionists into public office;[58] Samuel Bernard, perhaps the most important banker in Paris and the one who saved the government from bankruptcy at a critical moment, was of the same faith before his conversion; and John Law, of course, was Protestant until near the end of 1719 when he abjured.[59]

The eighteenth-century scholar Claude-Carlomau de Rulhière noted that a list of some 100 Huguenots who lived in Paris in 1686 included "the names of the principal persons who today [i.e., about 1785] engage in banking at Paris and who are still known as Protestants." [60]

Many Huguenots, especially where they constituted a significant minority, had also worked their way into public office as tax farmers, measurers of salt, notaries, law clerks, members of provincial parliaments, mayors, city councilmen, and officers of local militia. The explanation frequently given was that in many districts they were the only ones financially able to buy the charges or to post adequate bonds.[61]

Protestantism, Capitalism, and Penalization

It is difficult to evaluate the economic position of Huguenots in French society. A few contemporaries and later writers have argued that Protestants were not wealthier, more industrious and enterprising, or more successful in agriculture, finance, trade, or industry than the average Frenchman. Most spokesmen, like the nineteenth-century economist Sismondi, have taken the opposite viewpoint. Sismondi wrote: "Since the best part of trade and industry of France was in the hands of Protestants, their houses in provincial cities were furnished with expensive items, and their stores were stocked with merchandise; all these riches, placed at the mercy of dragoons, were destroyed, and nothing contributed so much to the impoverishment of France." [62]

[55] Rondot, op. cit., pp. 32–33, 51–52.
[56] See, e.g., Archives Nationales, TT 431, doc. 157.
[57] La Révocation de l'Édit de Nantes à Paris d'après des documents inédits (Paris, 1894), III, 395–401.
[58] Guillaume-Adam de Félice, Histoire des protestants de France (8th ed.; Toulouse, 1895), pp. 385–386; Guillaume-B. Depping, "Un Banquier protestant en France au XVIIᵉ siècle: Barthélemy Herwarth, contrôleur général des finances (1607–1676)," Revue historique, X–XI (1879), 286–287.
[59] BSHPF, XII (1863), 456.
[60] Bibliothèque Nationale, Fonds français, MS 7044, fol. 257.
[61] Archives Nationales, G⁷ 239, 337, 390; TT 232, dossier 19, doc. 9.
[62] Histoire des français (Paris, 1821–1844), XXV, 510.

The impartial historian of the twentieth century must recognize that Protestants who were well off financially, even though they may have constituted only a small percentage of the total, probably attracted the most attention from contemporary observers and government officials; their names were most often mentioned, and their economic position was most often noted, in the documents that have come down to the present day. Since the historian's knowledge of Huguenots largely depends upon extant records, and since the selective process determining which records would be preserved was itself biased, the possibility remains that government documents do not represent a reliable sample of relevant data. I believe, nevertheless, that the evidence as a whole strongly supports the view that the Huguenots exercised a greater influence on the French economy than their numbers would suggest.[63]

A direct correlation, no matter how marked, does not in itself establish a causal connection between two phenomena. The mere fact that Huguenots made a favorable showing in economic activity does not prove that Protestant ideology reinforced their economic drives or that Protestantism as a way of life conflicted with such drives less than Catholicism; but the high correlation of Protestantism and economic success has been taken by some scholars as presumptive evidence that some such causal connection existed. Many philosophers, sociologists, economists, and historians in the past decades have developed hypotheses as to the relationship between Protestantism and capitalism. Some writers have stressed the impact of the doc-

trines of predestination and man's calling upon economic behavior; others have found it significant that both Protestantism and free-enterprise capitalism rest upon individualism; others have pointed out that Protestant teachings were compatible with the rationalization of economic life whereas Catholicism was not; and some have thought that the Reformation, by multiplying religious sects and evoking heated debates over church dogma, weakened the influence of organized Christian religion over the everyday activities of individuals. Still others, while contending that Protestant countries had a higher rate of saving and investment than predominantly Catholic areas, have sought an explanation for this in the attitudes of the two religions toward interest. Other writers have suggested that in some places—England, for example—the Reformation shifted the ownership of certain natural resources from ecclesiastical to lay hands and that the allocation of these resources among alternative uses thereafter conformed more closely to rational economic principles than formerly. And some have stressed the impact upon capitalism of religious wars which dislocated production, destroyed property and life, and diffused technology through the migration of religious minorities skilled in economic processes and techniques.

There is little reason here to attempt a detailed critical evaluation of these various hypotheses—especially of those that pertain to the generalized relationship of Protestantism to capitalism and rest upon philosophical, sociological, and psychological premises. It should be pointed out, however, that even if a philosopher found that nothing in Calvinist dogma provided a more rational basis for intense capitalistic activity than did contemporary Catholic dogma, it is still possible that interpreters and followers of Calvin may have construed his teachings as exhorting or condoning the

[63] The fragmentary data pertaining to the property confiscated from those who fled France and the size of the estates left by new converts upon their death confirm this belief.

rational pursuit of profits.[64] If evidence of this exists, the economic historian cannot afford to neglect it.

One of the chief problems for the present study is to explain why the Huguenots in France were so successful in economic matters, and whether the direct correlation between their religion and their success in business was mainly fortuitous or, instead, had a reasonable causal basis. The hypotheses mentioned above may provide some clues, although a case study of the Huguenots, based upon historical facts, can in itself neither refute nor substantiate such broad generalizations abstracted from the world of ideas. One cannot conclude, for example, that the impact of Protestantism upon capitalism in France was identical with or necessarily similar to the results observed elsewhere. If for no other reason, this would be true simply because the position of the Huguenots in the seventeenth and eighteenth centuries was nowhere exactly duplicated. It is significant that Huguenots remained a small and in many respects a "penalized" minority, and as such were forced into a role similar to that played by other penalized minorities, whether the basis for penalization was racial, social, religious, political, or economic. Unlike some other Protestant groups, the Huguenots were part of a society that was determined to keep Catholicism as its official religion, a society whose ruler strongly opposed

heresy for reasons that did not always stem from personal religious piety. The mere fact that Calvinism differed in many ideological and practical ways from Anglicanism and Lutheranism, for example, would preclude identifying its effects on group and individual behavior with the effects of Protestantism in the abstract.

Max Weber, in *The Protestant Ethic and the Spirit of Capitalism*,[65] seized upon the twin doctrines of predestination and of man's calling as the crucial and unique core of Calvin's teaching. According to the first of these doctrines, God bestowed his grace and eternal salvation upon some and denied them to others, and nothing that the saved or the condemned could do could possibly alter God's plan. Hence "the relation between earthly and eternal recompense" was denied.[66] How, then, could such a doctrine, instead of inculcating a fatalistic attitude, encourage its adherents to enter into all forms of economic activity with a zeal approaching religious fervor? Weber thought he had found the answer in Calvin's concept of man's calling. Calvin taught that the world existed solely to glorify God and that the Christian elected to eternal life by God's grace was in duty bound to contribute to this glory, among other ways, through social achievement. Thus all social and economic activity that served the life of the community became an obligation of the elect, although it never could be a means of gaining grace. No matter into what station in life a person was born, no matter with what skills and capabilities he was endowed, he was obligated —like the three servants in the parable of the talents[67]—to make the most of what his Master had given him. He could

[64] Amintore Fanfani, R. H. Tawney, and Max Weber have all agreed that the effects of Protestantism upon capitalism were really unintentional and unconscious. According to Weber, its consequences were in large measure those "that the Reformers did not foresee, and indeed definitely did not desire, and which often differed from or conflicted with all that they hoped to obtain by their ideals" (see Fanfani, *Catholicism, Protestantism, and Capitalism* [New York, 1935], pp. 190–191).

[65] Trans. Talcott Parsons (New York, 1930).
[66] Fanfani, *op. cit.*, p. 205.
[67] Matt. 25:14–30.

not fulfill this obligation by building up a store of good deeds sufficient, on net balance, to compensate for his sins and occasional backslidings. Rather, the elect had to face up to his obligation continually. Good works, furthermore, were "indispensable as a sign of election" to the rest of the community, and constituted one way "of getting rid of the fear of damnation." [68] Thus Calvinism, as interpreted by Weber, taught that the chosen, who would ultimately have citizenship in the City of God, could find fulfillment for their lives in the city of man and at the same time best glorify God by devoting themselves to those callings for which they had been specifically endowed by divine ordinance. A spiritual monastic life was inherently no better or more godly than one devoted largely to mundane trucking and bartering.[69] It was easy, therefore, for the rank and file to distort the Calvinist dogmas of predestination and man's calling into the belief that success in one's profession could reveal the action of grace.[70] Viewed in this light, these dogmas may have acted as a powerful stimulus to economic activity.

Although Calvin held that no man should seek his own gain at the expense of others and that each Christian was "his brother's keeper," Protestantism in France embraced certain practices that tended to support individualism. The relationship of man to God was an individual relationship which did not require the intercession of priest or saint. The good Huguenot read the Bible himself,[71] conducted individual and family prayers, and believed that God through his omnipotence and omniscience was continually aware of his actions in the market place as well as in the church.

As Fanfani has pointed out,[72] in some respects the doctrine of predestination had the effect of separating life on this earth and life in eternity into watertight compartments. Whereas Catholicism was concerned with the subsistence of the whole of society and considered all temporal means and goals as subservient to the ultimate attainment of immortality, Protestantism represented "the stage at which religion perceives that business morality has legitimate foundations in the earth. If an action is to have no reward but its results, the rationaliz-

---

[68] Weber, *op. cit.*, p. 115.

[69] Henri Hauser believed that the central idea of Protestant morality was the secularization of sainthood. "Men of all classes and of all trades are predestined to salvation or to damnation; the only means, then, of collaborating with the work of God is to do the best you can in the profession in which God has placed you." ("L'Économie calvinienne," a paper presented at the "Exposition Jean Calvin et la Réforme français" held in 1935 by the Société de l'Histoire du Protestantisme français, and published in *BSHPF*, LXXXIV [1935]).

[70] See the extract from a circular published by the Crédit industriel d'Alsace et de Lorraine in July, 1932, in *BSHPF*, LXXXI (1932), 325.

[71] The Calvinist was just as familiar with the Old Testament as with the New; the Catholic Church emphasized the New Testament almost (but not quite) to the exclusion of the Old. Since the New Testament is fundamentally spiritual and primarily concerned with immortality, and since the Old Testament mainly concerns temporal matters and life on this earth, it may well be that Huguenots were led through their reading of the Bible and their church attendance to accept a more balanced view of temporal and spiritual matters than Catholics. This suggestion, if it has any merit at all, relates to the effect that the Bible may have had upon the rank and file of members rather than upon an exceptional minority of either sect. The historian, however, simply cannot ignore the fact that capitalism made great strides in many Catholic areas, especially before the Reformation.

[72] *Op. cit.*, pp. 29, 120 ff.

ing principle of action will remain that of the maximum result." [73] The compartmentalization of eternal goals and temporal goals hence weakened both traditionalism[74] and the subordination of economic to moral problems. In sanctioning the maximization of output over input, it placed a premium on technical improvements, savings, and the satisfaction of material (as contrasted with spiritual) human wants with the least expenditure of time and effort.

Calvinism's attitude toward interest, like the support it gave individualism and the rationalization of economic activities, may have had causal influence on the economic success achieved by French Huguenots as a group. John Calvin, born into a bourgeois world, lived most of his life in such commercial centers as Strasbourg and Geneva, where lending money at interest was a daily practice. Unlike the monkish Luther, he was brought up in a rather rapidly changing economic order, and was aware that the economic environment of his time was quite different from that of the Greeks or Romans or from that which had existed in the earlier days of Western civilization.[75] He saw the necessity of buying and selling, of lending and borrowing, and of taking interest. He admitted he could find no prohibition

against interest in the Scriptures; he refuted Aquinas' contention that money was sterile by pointing out that money could buy things which in turn could yield a surplus; he even refused to forbid his pastors to lend at interest, but advised them not to do so lest their actions be misunderstood by their parishioners; and he explicitly justified interest on loans made to merchants for business purposes or to landlords for the acquisition of more property. On the other hand, there is ample evidence that Calvin's approval of interest-taking was qualified: "I would not wish at all, in justifying it, to favor usury [i.e., interest-taking], and I would like to see even the phrase disappear from the earth." [76] Calvin urged his followers to lend sums to necessitous consumers, from whom no interest should be exacted, and to small businessmen, who could pay no interest and even showed little prospect of repaying the principal, in preference to merchants and manufacturers who offered adequate guarantees for high rates of return. In other words, while recognizing the validity of lending and interest, Calvin urged his disciples to temper their capitalist spirit with the Christian principle of charity. According to Hauser's apt summary, "Calvin made use of interest as an apothecary mixes poisons—a necessary remedy, perhaps indispensable, but oh! so dangerous." [77]

Even though Catholicism had long recognized unusual circumstances under which the collection of interest was permissible, and even though numerous subterfuges had been devised for circumventing the Church's proscription under usual circumstances, Calvin's views to some extent liberalized the Christian's attitude toward lending. But to assess the effect of his views on Huguenot be-

[73] *Ibid.*, pp. 207–208. Fanfani elsewhere (p. 198) noted that "once the idea was admitted that salvation was independent of works, with the idea of free enquiry, a Protestant was only acting in a logical manner if he accepted the rational order of the world as it resulted from the free operation of man. While the Protestant who still envisaged a 'should be' state was illogical. The fundamental principles of Protestantism lead inevitably to the sanctification of the real; the obstinate attempt to prescribe other worldly limits to the world is a remnant of doctrines that Protestantism seeks to overthrow."

[74] See Weber, *op. cit.*, pp. 58 ff.

[75] See Hauser, "L'Économie calvinienne."

[76] Quoted in *ibid.*

[77] *Ibid.*

havior is an entirely different and far more difficult problem. Some writers have maintained that French Protestants showed less restraint than Catholics in lending at whatever rates of interest they could get,[78] and contemporary documents provide abundant evidence that in some areas of the country they were, on net balance, creditors of their Catholic brethren. Some may argue, of course, that the approval of interest-taking itself led to the rise of a *rentier* class which was reluctant to engage in risky ventures conducted for profit, and hence discouraged the development of the capitalist spirit. This does not seem to have been true. Calvinism, like Puritanism, became the gospel of hard work, thrift, and temperance. In 1723 an exiled pastor, after advising the Huguenots who had remained behind in Languedoc to learn to live "in temperance, justice, and piety," urged them to give attention

. . . to the bad effects of intemperance, which weakens one's discernment, destroys health, [and] ruins families. Idleness is its mother. Be industrious and you will have neither the time nor the fancy to flatter your discernment with superfluities. Remember that you live in the presence of God, that virtues are your true glory, and you will not at all give yourselves over to all these vanities of which men of the world make their merit consist by reason of not having anything better.[79]

Despite the plausibility of postulating a causal relationship, either direct or indirect, between Calvinist doctrine (as interpreted by Calvin's disciples) and the highly successful economic activities of his followers in France, the fact remains that French Protestants constituted a "penalized minority" throughout most of the seventeenth and eighteenth centuries

and were conscious of the social and legal discriminations directed against them. This was a significant factor in their behavior, perhaps more significant than the impact of Calvin's doctrines of predestination and man's calling, or than the support his teachings gave to individualism and the rationalization of economic activity, or even than his qualified approval of interest-taking. According to Arnold J. Toynbee, penalization may act as a very powerful stimulus to individual and group behavior:

The dominant race [or, here, the dominant majority] is apt to reserve certain avocations as its own exclusive preserves, and to impose upon the penalized race [here, the minority] the necessity of cultivating other fields of social activity if it is to find a living at all. The "reserved" occupations usually include all those which have high social prestige—the priesthood, the business of government, the ownership of land, the bearing of arms, and the civilian "liberal professions"—as well as the fundamental economic activity of Society, which has usually been agriculture in the social economies of societies in process of civilization down to recent times. By a process of exhaustion the penalized race [minority] is apt to find itself virtually confined to the field of trade and handicraft; and, just because the field is narrow, the penalized race [minority] is stimulated to make this field all its own and to conjure out of it, by a *tour de force* which fills the dominant race [majority] with astonishment and resentment, a harvest of wealth and power which this Naboth's vineyard would hardly have yielded to hands not debarred from other handiwork.[80]

This idea did not originate with Toyn-

[78] See, e.g., Benoist, *op. cit.*, p. 305.
[79] Archives Nationales, TT 247, doc. 54.
[80] *The Study of History* (London: Oxford University Press, 1934), II, 217.

bee. An old Spanish proverb declared that "heresy promotes business spirit";[81] and Sir William Petty, in his *Political Arithmetic* (London, 1691), claimed that "trade is more vigorously carried on, in every state and government, by the heterodox part of the same; and such as profess opinions different from what are publicly established . . . and even in France itself, the Huguenots are, proportionately, far the greatest traders." [82] More recently, Émile-G. Léonard has expressed a similar belief: "Each minority, each dissident group—because it tempers the character of its members, because it exalts their individual capacities, because it protects them from improvidence and expensive vices—in normal circumstances sets them on the road of economic and social achievement." [83]

If, as seems to be true, there is a general psychological and sociological principle that individuals or groups are led to tap little-used and unsuspected sources of power within themselves and to "respond" vigorously when confronted with challenges like penalization, then it appears likely that those with strong spiritual beliefs, like the Huguenots, will have a better-than-average chance of attaining great success. The Huguenots who responded to the challenge of penalization by fleeing France found another stimulus in the strangeness of a new environment; but their assimilation into the society of their adopted countries became more or less complete after several generations. By the nineteenth and twentieth centuries they no longer stood out from the rest of the population as cap-

tains of trade and industry. The Huguenots and their descendants who refused to flee continued to constitute an easily identifiable minority in France, and this helps to explain why French Protestants in the twentieth century still maintain an importance in the economy which is more than proportionate to their numbers. The degree of their "penalization," however, has been greatly reduced since the eighteenth century, and concomitantly their relative superiority in finance, trade, and industry has diminished.[84]

The forms this penalization assumed in the seventeenth century have already been described. The Edict of Nantes in 1598 had promised all Protestants equality of opportunity in the professions, in public office, and in economic jobs; yet entry into judicial, top military, and administrative positions became less and less accessible to them after 1661. In various ways Louis XIV also narrowed, particularly after 1679, the range of economic opportunities open to Huguenots. By 1685 they were eligible for very few positions outside private industry, trade, and finance; and even several gilds had shut them out. If penalization had consisted solely of such legal restrictions as these, it would be difficult indeed to argue that Huguenots gained conspicuous success in business before the revocation mainly because this field remained the only major area where they could freely deploy their energies. Several years of exclusion from other occupations appears too short a period to have exercised a pronounced effect on the

[81] Quoted by F. L. Nussbaum, *A History of the Economic Institutions of Modern Europe* (New York: Crofts, 1937), p. 138.
[82] Reprinted in Edward Arber, *An English Garner* (London, 1883), pp. 343–344.
[83] "Économie et religion, les protestants français au XVIIᵉ siècle," p. 7. See also his "Le Protestantisme français au XVIIᵉ siècle," pp. 161, 177–178.

[84] Cf. Toynbee, *op. cit.*, II, 250. As Professor Jacob Viner has pointed out to me in private correspondence, the test as to whether penalization effectively motivates people should not be absolute success in business but, rather, success relative to economic opportunities. Even if Huguenots had been poorer than their Catholic neighbors, this would not in itself have invalidated the penalization argument.

economic activities of an entire minority. Yet several contemporaries have explained the economic success of Huguenots in terms of such penalization.[85] Such views would have been more appropriate for the eighteenth century, when legal sanctions were a potent factor. The explanation for the seventeenth century must be sought rather in the fact that much of the penalization never crystallized into formal law and explicit government pronouncement, but was more in the nature of spontaneous, unorganized economic and social discrimination by the Catholic majority.

As often happens with penalized minorities, the Huguenots who gained a foothold in public office or achieved positions of favor and prominence used their influence, insofar as possible, to place their brethren in similar ranks. Sully and Herwarth as finance ministers, for example, appointed a large number of fellow Protestants to important financial posts in government;[86] and Mazarin, Fouquet, and Colbert readily employed Protestants in important positions because of their honesty and zeal, and these appointees in turn favored others of their religion whenever occasion permitted.[87]

Another factor in the success of Huguenots appears to have been their willingness to remain in trade and industry even after they had made their fortunes. An individual who has remained anonymous prepared a long memorandum in 1787 in which he wrote: "One has not been able to exclude them from trade which, according to natural law, is a free profession; and that has been a very good thing for commerce and manufactures, which since 1685 have flourished in several cities precisely because Protestant families, enriched by this means, have not been able to leave their vocations in order to pass into the order of the nobility as have Catholic families." [88] The intendant at La Rochelle had complained to Colbert as early as 1664 that Catholic merchants engaged in outfitting naval vessels ordinarily deserted their trade for public office as soon as they had amassed a fortune.[89] The deputy of trade at Bayonne in 1701 listed the revocation of the Edict of Nantes with its Huguenot dispersion as an important factor in the deterioration of economic conditions. He claimed that Protestants, excluded "from the dignities and employs of the robe and sword," had been uniquely occupied with trade:

In a manner of speaking, they made commerce the sole subject of their meditations. It was their custom to marry their daughters to other merchants, and in this way they did not dissipate their capital. In all justice

[85] For example, the deputy of trade at Bayonne (Bibliothèque Nationale, *Fonds français*, MS 8038, fol. 434); the author of the "Mémoire sur le commerce de France" (*ibid.*, fols. 14–15); Pierre Jurieu (*Réflexions sur la cruelle persécution que souffre l'église réformée de France* . . . [2d ed.; n.p., 1685], p. 44); the author of *Testament politique du Marquis de Louvois* . . . (pp. 369–370); and the Venetian ambassador at Paris at the time of the revocation.
[86] Léonard believes that this, more than Weber's thesis of man's calling, was largely responsible for the success of Huguenots in the financial world ("Le Protestantisme français au XVIIe siècle," p. 169).
[87] Archives Nationales, TT 287, *dossier* 6, doc. 32; Bibliothèque Nationale, *Fonds français*, MS 7047, fol. 727; Boissonnade, *op. cit.*,

p. 18; Erman and Reclam, *Mémoires pour servir à l'histoire de réfugiés françois dans les états du Roi* (Berlin, 1782–1799), I, 81; Depping, *op. cit.*, p. 286; Émile Lesens, *Le Protestantisme dans le pays de Caux* (*ancien colloque de Caux, Havre et Dieppe excepté*), ed. Victor Madelaine (Bolbec, [1906]), p. 144.
[88] Bibliothèque Nationale, *Fonds français*, MS 7047, fol. 727.
[89] Boissonnade, *op. cit.*, p. 18.

one has to admit that there were a large number of individuals among them who were powerful and very intelligent in business affairs.[90]

Huguenot merchants enjoyed a distinct advantage over Catholics in trade with such Protestant countries as England, Holland, Switzerland, and certain German states. Foreign Protestants preferred to transact their business with Protestant Frenchmen; and Catholics in Bordeaux, La Rochelle, Nantes, and Rouen often complained of being practically excluded from foreign trade. Huguenot merchants usually sent their sons to Geneva, England, or Holland at an early age to develop contacts, to observe the practices of foreign traders and manufacturers, and to attend school. In this way they became familiar with new technical processes and commercial procedures.[91] Members of Huguenot families who fled France in the sixteenth or seventeenth century remained in close commercial contact with relatives who elected to remain at home, and served as their foreign brokers. In the eighteenth century several Huguenots had family connections in the major commercial centers of Protestant Europe which allowed them to build up small empires in international trade.

Calvinism, by recognizing fewer religious holidays than Catholicism, lengthened the work year for its followers by about 15 or 20 per cent. Through its emphasis upon religious education and individual study of the Bible, its intensive training of pastors, and its organizational and administrative structure, it helped to make Huguenots, on the average, more enlightened than their neighbors.[92] In a memorandum of uncertain date entitled "Design for the Reunion of the Church in France by a Conference Which Has Been Proposed by Cardinal Richelieu," the author confessed that one reason that Huguenots remained in their heresy was because few priests were capable of instructing them and of refuting their erroneous beliefs. "There are only a few Catholic clerics," he wrote, "who know anything about these matters, whereas there is not a single [Protestant] minister who knows not something to sustain them in their error."[93] On October 20, 1699, another writer expressed the belief that Protestants in Cévennes had developed traits that made them "sober, industrious, and active in trade for which they have the real spirit," and that all were determined to acquire an education so they could read, write, and master arithmetic.[94]

One perspicacious Frenchman named Beaumelle, about the middle of the eighteenth century, summarized and explained the position occupied by Huguenots in his country:[95] "Although Protestants comprise only one-tenth of the nation by numerical count, it is nevertheless certain that, measured by their riches and industry, they constitute at least one-eighth of the whole; these two million

[90] Bibliothèque Nationale, Fonds français, MS 8038, fol. 434.
[91] C. Weiss, Histoire des réfugiés protestants de France depuis la révocation de l'Édit de Nantes jusqu'à nos jours (Paris, 1853), I, 31; Weiss, "Mémoire sur les protestants," op cit., XX, 104–105; BSHPF, XXIII, 135–136.
[92] Weiss, "Mémoire sur les protestants," op. cit., XX, 105, 106.
[93] Bibliothèque Nationale, Fonds français, MS 20967, fol. 40.
[94] Ibid., MS 20966, fols. 272–281.
[95] Beaumelle turned his memorandum over to Claude-Carlomau de Rulhière, who was busily engaged in writing his Eclaircissements historiques sur les causes de la révocation de l'Édit de Nantes, et sur l'état des protestants en France, depuis le commencement du Règne de Louis XIV, jusqu'à nos jours (new ed.; Geneva, 1788); and the memorandum in manuscript form may be found in the Bibliothèque Nationale, Fonds français, MS 7047, fols. 440 ff.

subjects are worth perhaps three million Catholics." They are "more active than Catholics because they can become their equals only through activity." "The severity of the laws directed against them leads to perpetual self-examination." They are "aided and abetted by the principles of their religion" which render them "more enlightened" and "capable of grasping all new ideas" and borrowing new technical processes from abroad which will help them gain success. "Their zeal for work," "their frugality" and "old-time thrift," their opposition to "luxury and idleness," and their "great fear of the judgment of God" lead them to focus their energies and to justify their faith and nonconformity by unusual achievements in the economic realm.

Although Beaumelle did not explicitly label Huguenots a "penalized minority," it is quite clear that his interpretation of their behavior is not at variance with the interpretation presented in this chapter. No matter on what level an easily identifiable minority is penalized, the penalization itself may provide a challenge of sufficient impact to call forth remarkable achievements by the minority in certain areas of human endeavor. This appears to have been true of the French Huguenots. Excluded from many public offices after 1661 and discriminated against in the professions, in military and political assignments, and even

in many arts and crafts, they focused their energies on commerce, industry, and finance. Like many other penalized minorities in history, they took refuge in the free-price market where automatic impersonal forces either bestow rewards upon the more efficient or weed out the inefficient irrespective of their religious or social status. Although this interpretation of why Huguenots turned to business stresses their reaction to various sanctions, it is quite clear that their religious beliefs and practices influenced the outcome in two ways: (1) it was their religion that made Huguenots a penalized minority, and (2) the theological doctrines of Calvinism predisposed their response and allowed them to seek "compensation" for their penalization in economic activity.

The expulsion of an appreciable portion of an economically active minority might very well have had a pronounced effect upon any economy. Whether the emigration of some 200,000 Huguenots seriously crippled economic life in France during the last three decades of Louis's reign is, in fact, the central problem of the present inquiry. Before examining the evidence on this score, it seems advisable first to survey economic conditions from 1683 to 1717 and to indicate where and when signs of economic stagnation and deterioration appeared.

3 · Influence of the "Religious Factor" on Career Plans and Occupational Values of College Graduates[1]

ANDREW M. GREELEY

ABSTRACT. Previous studies have indicated a strong tendency toward antiscientism among American Catholics; in particular, the recent work of Lenski has suggested that Catholics will score low on indicators of economic rationality (the "Protestant Ethic"). These hypotheses are not substantiated by data gathered in a survey of June, 1961, college graduates. Catholics were as likely to go to graduate school, to choose an academic career, to specialize in the physical sciences, and to plan a life of research as Protestants, even under a battery of socioeconomic and demographic controls. Nor was there any indication that Catholics were any less inclined to economic rationality than Protestants. It is suggested that the differences between these findings and those of Lenski might be connected with the different ethnic compositions of the two samples. A re-examination of an earlier study supports this suggestion.

Considerable interest has been expressed recently in the use of religion as a predictor variable.[2] Gerhard Lenski has maintained that, across a wide range of political, economic, intellectual, and family-value dependent variables, religion is at least as efficient a predictor as social class.[3] He also suggests that Catholics will score lower on items indicating economic rationality (the "Protestant Ethic") and higher on items indicating antiscientism. In attempting to find explanations for the latter phenomenon, he discovers both conscious and subconscious forces at work:

On the basis of the findings of this study it appears that overt conflict

SOURCE. Andrew M. Greeley, "Influence of the 'Religious Factor' on Career Plans and Occupational Values of College Graduates," reprinted from *American Journal of Sociology*, 68, May, 1963, pp. 658–671, by permission of the University of Chicago Press.
[1] The author is grateful for the help of Professors James A. Davis and Peter H. Rossi in the preparation of this paper.

[2] One thinks especially of the voting and fertility studies: on fertility cf. Ronald Freedman, Pascal K. Whelpton, and Arthur A. Campbell, *Family Planning, Sterility and Population Growth* (New York: McGraw-Hill Book Co., 1959) and Charles Westoff, Robert Potter, Philip Sagi, and Elliot Mishler, *Family Growth in Metropolitan America* (Princeton, N.J.: Princeton University Press, 1961). On voting cf. Paul Lazarsfeld, Bernard Berelson, and Hazel Gaudet, *The People's Choice* (New York: Duell, Sloan & Pearce, 1944); Bernard Berelson, Paul Lazarsfeld, and W. N. McPhee, *Voting* (Chicago: University of Chicago Press, 1954); and Philip E. Converse, Angus Campbell, Warren E. Miller, and Donald E. Stokes, "Stability and Change in 1960: A Reinstating Election," *American Political Science Review*, June, 1961.

[3] *The Religious Factor* (Garden City, N.Y.: Doubleday & Co., 1960).

between the churches and the modern scientific movement . . . is only one of the factors accounting for the disinclination of Catholics to enter scientific careers. In our opinion, other less visible factors are equally important—perhaps far more important—especially influential is the basic intellectual orientation which Catholicism develops: an orientation which values obedience above intellectual autonomy. Also influential is the Catholic tendency to value family and the kin group above other relationships. In brief, at both the conscious and subconscious levels of thought and action, membership in the Catholic group is more likely to inhibit the development of scientific careers than is membership in either Protestant or Jewish groups. The implications of this for the future of American society are not difficult to discover.[4]

Lenski would find substantial agreement for his analysis from the self-critics within American Catholicism. Writers like O'Dea,[5] Weigel,[6] Ellis,[7] and others[8] attribute the intellectual deficiencies of American Catholicism to the absence of a scholarly tradition, clerical domination, fear of modern science, lack of concern for temporal values, materialism among the Catholic laity, low valuation on curiosity and initiative in Catholic training, and the tendency to encourage talented youth to enter the religious life. The findings of Knapp and his associates on the poor productivity of scholars by Catholic schools apparently confirm these conclusions.[9]

However, the Knapp data refer to graduates in the years before 1950, and the self-critics have materials that are even older. Lenski's study, although recent, was limited to the Detroit metropolitan area. A recent survey by the National Opinion Research Center (NORC) permits us to test the Protestant Ethic and antiscientism hypotheses against contemporary data from a national sample.[10] Some 35,000 questionnaires were administered to June, 1961, graduates from 135 colleges and universities in a study of career plans, academic experiences, and occupational values.[11] Since ques-

[4] Ibid., p. 255.
[5] Thomas O'Dea, American Catholic Dilemma (New York: Sheed & Ward, 1958).
[6] Gustave Weigel, "American Catholic Intellectualism—a Theologian's Reflections," Review of Politics, XIX (1957), 275–307.
[7] John Tracey Ellis, "American Catholics and the Intellectual Life," Thought, Vol. XXX (Autumn, 1955).
[8] Summarized in Frank L. Christ and Gerard E. Sherry, American Catholicism and the Intellectual Ideal (New York: Appleton-Century-Crofts, Inc., 1961).
[9] Robert H. Knapp and H. B. Goodrich, Origins of American Scientists (Chicago: University of Chicago Press, 1952), and Robert H. Knapp and Joseph J. Greenbaum, The Young American Scholar: His Collegiate Origins (Chicago: University of Chicago Press, 1953).
[10] The survey was carried out under grants from the National Institutes of Health, the National Science Foundation, and the United States Office of Education. The careers of the respondents will be followed for several years to come by a continuing series of surveys.
[11] The sample was of stratified-cluster design. All American colleges and universities were grouped into four strata based on previous productivity of students going on to graduate degrees. Then schools were sampled randomly within each stratum. Twenty-page questionnaires (with sixty-two questions, principally about future career and educational plans) were administered to all graduating seniors within these schools; the response rate was well in excess of 90 per cent for most schools. Schools in the more productive strata were oversampled. In order to compensate for the unequal sampling rates, the observations were then weighted proportionately to the reciprocals of these rates, thus providing unbiased estimates. An

tions about original and current religion were included in the questionnaire, it is possible to analyze the influence of religion on these dependent variables.[12]

The following hypotheses were constructed from the conclusions of previous studies to be tested against the NORC materials:

1. Catholics will be less likely to go to college.
2. Catholic graduates will be less likely to go to graduate school.
3. Catholics who go to graduate school will be less likely to choose the arts and sciences, that is, the academic fields.
4. Catholics in the academic fields will be less likely to go into the most scientific of sciences, that is, the physical sciences.
5. Catholics who go into the academic fields will be less likely to plan a research career.
6. Catholics who go into the academic fields will be less likely to be religious and more likely to be apostates.
7. Catholics will tend to overchoose large corporations as employers, business as an occupation, and security and the avoidance of high pressure as occupational values.

Previous research findings would also lead us to suspect that, on both the "intellectualism" and economic rationality scales devised in the hypotheses, Protestants would be intermediate between Catholics and Jews.

_____

indication of the interest of the students in the survey is that the response rate to a second questionnaire sent to the same graduates in June of 1962 was over 85 per cent.
[12] The part of the analysis reported in this paper was done on a 10 per cent representative subsample. The preliminary report on the total project is contained in James A. Davis *et al.*, *Great Aspirations: The Career Plans of America's June 1961 Collegiate Graduates* (Chicago: National Opinion Research Center, 1962).

The use of the word "intellectualism" in this paper needs to be clarified. It is clear that going to graduate school in the physical sciences and planning a career of research in this area, for example, are not necessarily indicators of intellectuality, much less of potential scholarship. It is argued merely that the first six hypotheses proposed above would seem to follow logically from those writings that question the intellectuality or at least the orientation toward science of American Catholics. If the hypotheses are not supported by the data, previous researches are not necessarily disproved, but at least must be seriously re-examined. It might well be true that Catholics are entering "intellectual" careers for reasons different, and somehow less "intellectual," than Protestants and Jews, but surely this explanation cannot be presumed.[13]

Table 1 shows the distribution of the 10 per cent subsample by original religion.[14] It will be noted that about one-fourth of the graduates are Catholic,[15]

[13] It is embarrassing but probably necessary to enter a word about personal bias. At the present state of American culture it may not be true that, if a Catholic researcher discovers some indications that Catholics are not as antiscientific as previously thought, his findings are immediately subject to grave suspicion. Nevertheless, let it be recorded that the six "intellectualism" hypotheses in this paper were not straw men; the writer is close enough intellectually and personally to the self-critics to have thought "before the data" that this study would provide grist for the self-critics' mill. The findings of the NORC survey were therefore something of a rude surprise.
[14] It was felt that the religion in which one was reared was the most important in shaping one's values, if indeed they were shaped at all by religion.
[15] The vagaries of the sampling process selected sixteen Catholic schools; some 45 per cent of the graduates whose religion was Catholic came from these schools. However,

TABLE 1. *Religious Distribution of 1961 College Graduates*

	PER CENT
Protestant	61
Catholic	25
Jew	8
Other	3
None	3

* N = 3,330; no answer = 67; total 10 per cent sample = 3,397.

approximately the same proportion of Catholics in the population of the United States.[16] An immediate reaction would be to maintain that the first hypothesis (Catholics are disinclined to go to college) is not supported. The matter is not that simple, however, since there are more Protestants who are rural or Negro and these two latter groups are less likely to go to college. The kind of comparison that would be most satisfactory would be between urban white Catholics and Protestants at the specific ages of college graduation.

There are, however, no available national population figures that permit such a comparison to be made. However, if the racial factor is taken into account, it appears that Catholics are still slightly underrepresented in the college population, comprising 28 per cent of the

white population[17] of the nation and 26 per cent of the white population of the NORC sample. On the other hand, it seems quite certain that the educational gap between white Protestants and white Catholics is narrowing rapidly; Catholics make up 18 per cent of the total population with college education but 25 per cent of the June, 1961, graduates, despite the fact that the proportion of the Catholic population at college graduation age is about the same as the proportion of the national population at this age.[18] One can, therefore, say of the first hypothesis that there is no strong evidence supporting it, and that whatever differences exist between Catholics and non-Catholics in college education seem to be diminishing rather rapidly.[19]

---

[17] The percentages in this sentence are based on data reported by Bernard Lazerwitz in "A Comparison of Major United States Religious Groups," *Journal of the American Statistical Association,* LVI (September, 1961), 568–79.
[18] *Ibid.*
[19] Significant demographic differences among the three religious groups were computed from the Davies *Table of Significant Differences* with a correction factor added because of the fact that the sample was taken by a cluster technique. The independent assessment of the significance of Protestant-Catholic, Protestant-Jewish, and Catholic-Jewish differences is not completely legitimate, owing to the intercorrelation among them. However, the complicated nature of the sampling technique left little other choice. It was not feasible to modify the χ^2 test to take into account the cluster sample. The differences between Protestants and Catholics, however, are still relatively minor in almost all instances, and the differences between Jew and gentile are enough to be of importance, even if the tests are relatively crude. It might be noted that in an analysis of the total weighted sample of some 55,000, to be published shortly by J. A. Davis of the NORC staff, the same conclusions with regard to the religious factor have been reached as are reported in this article.

---

as we hope to point out in another paper, the differences between Catholic graduates of Catholic colleges and Catholic graduates of other colleges were minimal on virtually all items herein reported. The differences that do exist would have the graduates of Catholic colleges scoring *higher* on "intellectual" and "Protestant" items than Catholic graduates of other colleges.
[16] For a discussion of the Catholic population in the United States see my "Some Information on the Present Situation of the American Catholics," *Social Order,* April, 1963, pp. 9–24.

Educational Exerience

Table 2 summarizes the different educational experiences of the three religious groups. Jews are more likely to have attended "quality" colleges.[20] They are also more likely to score high (upper 20 per cent) on the Academic Performance Index. (The difference between Catholics and Protestants approaches sig-

to college, although Catholic graduates are more likely than Protestants and Protestants more likely than Jews to concede to their fellow students a "liberal" orientation. Protestants have a somewhat higher percentage who feel loyal to their schools than the other two groups. Protestants found the biological sciences more interesting than the other groups, and Catholics found English

TABLE 2. *Summary of Differences on Educational Experiences (Percentage Distribution)*

EDUCATIONAL EXPERIENCES	PROTESTANT (P)	CATHOLIC (C)	JEW (J)	STATISTICAL SIGNIFICANCE P-C	P-J	C-J
School quality A or B	12	12	26	N.S.	.01	.01
High academic performance	19	15	26	N.S.	.05	.01
Appreciation of ideas: Purpose of college:						
Subjective	65	65	65	N.S.	N.S.	N.S.
Projective	35	44	27	.01	.01	.01
Positive school loyalty	77	71	71	.01	N.S.	N.S.
Course reactions:						
Science interesting	34	33	37	N.S.	N.S.	N.S.
Mathematics interesting	32	34	37	N.S.	N.S.	N.S.
Biology interesting	44	37	37	.01	.05	N.S.
Social science interesting	63	65	65	N.S.	N.S.	N.S.
English interesting	49	54	37	.01	.01	.01
N	(2,007)	(833)	(272)			

nificance; however, there is no difference between the two groups when a comparison is made of the upper half academically.) All three groups contain about the same proportion of graduates who would attribute a "liberal" purpose

[20] The quality of the schools was based on an index prepared from the scores of students in the colleges on the National Merit Scholarship examinations. The Academic Performance Index mentioned in the next sentence was based on grade-point average weighted for school quality.

more interesting than the other groups. Each course was rated separately, so the respondents were not forced to choose one course as their favorite. The former finding might result from the more rural origins of American Protestants and the latter from the supposed tradition of humanistic studies in the Catholic colleges. The Catholic interest in science and mathematics is not what previous findings would lead us to expect. Generally speaking, there was little in the way of major differences in reactions to courses.

Future Plans

Table 3 summarizes information on future plans of the college graduates of the three religious groups. The Jews are most likely to plan to attend graduate school in the coming year and Protestants

(according to the prediction), Jews over-choose small companies and self-employment (no difference between Protestants and Catholics on this item), and Protestants overchoose elementary education for future career employment.[22] In the choice of future occupations, Jews are

TABLE 3. *Summary of Differences on Future Plans (Percentage Distribution)*

FUTURE PLANS	PROTESTANT	CATHOLIC	JEW	P-C	P-J	C-J
				STATISTICAL SIGNIFICANCE		
Graduate school next year	28	33	47	.05	.01	.01
Per cent of graduate students in arts and sciences	43	46	39	N.S.	N.S.	N.S.
Career employer:						
Large company	25	33	26	.01	N.S.	N.S.
Small company	7	11	21	N.S.	.01	.01
Self	7	8	14	N S.	.05	.05
Education	36	27	27	.01	.01	N.S.
Career occupation:						
Science	7	6	8	N.S.	N.S.	N.S.
Social science and humanities	10	10	10	N.S.	N.S.	N.S.
Medicine	2	3	6	N.S.	.05	.05
Law	2	3	10	N.S.	.01	.01
Engineering	7	8	8	N.S.	N.S.	N.S.
Education	34	26	27	.01	.01	N.S.
Business	15	23	17	.01	N.S.	.01
Other professions	16	12	6	.05	.01	.01
Other	7	9	8			
N	(2,007)	(833)	(272)			

least likely. There is no significant difference in the proportions of each group going into graduate study in the academic fields. These findings are in direct opposition to the hypotheses derived from previous research. No support is found for the notion of Catholic anti-intellectualism.

Catholics overchoose large companies[21]

[21] The percentages on career employer do not add to 100 because only those items that showed a difference are included in Table 3.

more inclined to law and medicine, Catholics more inclined to business, Protestants more inclined to education and "other professions." No other differences are significant.

[22] It has been suggested that the Protestant lead in education is the result of the fact that Negro Protestants overchoose this field; they do, indeed, but no more than other Protestants, according to the NORC data. It should be noted also that Negro Protestants who graduate from college are just as likely to go to graduate school as white Protestants.

Occupational Values

Table 4 gives the reaction of the graduates of the three religious groups to the question: "Which of these characteristics would be important in picking a career?" The "Protestant Ethic" hypothesis is not supported for Catholic-Protestant differences. Catholics are more interested in making money than Protestants, no different in avoiding high pressure, and no different in the quest for security through

The Effect of Controls

Only three control variables seem to produce much in the way of a change in the measures described in the preceding paragraphs, so these three were combined into a new index—the Index of Background Characteristics (IBC). Each religious group was subdivided into eight subgroups based on sex, home-town size (over 100,000 or under 100,000), and socioeconomic status (SES) (upper half

TABLE 4. *Occupational Values, by Religion (Percentage Distribution)*

				STATISTICAL SIGNIFICANCE		
OCCUPATIONAL VALUES	PROTESTANT	CATHOLIC	JEW	P-C	P-J	C-J
Making a lot of money	21	27	38	.01	.01	.01
Chance to be creative	50	50	64	N.S.	.01	.01
Helpful to others	68	61	60	.01	.01	N.S.
Avoid high pressure	15	17	15	N.S.	N.S.	N.S.
World of ideas	39	35	50	N.S.	.01	.01
Freedom from supervision	18	17	21	N.S.	N.S.	N.S.
Slow and sure progress	33	32	25	N.S.	.05	N.S.
Leadership	34	40	40	.01	N.S.	N.S.
Same area	4	8	9	.05	.05	N.S.
New area	10	10	11	N.S.	N.S.	N.S.
Work with people, not things	57	55	56	N.S.	N.S.	N.S.
N	(2,007)	(833)	(272)			

slow, sure progress. They are also more interested in "leadership," which may or may not be a "Protestant Ethic" type of item. Protestants are more interested in being helpful to others, which, however praiseworthy it might be, is hardly in keeping with the economic individualism of the "Protestant Ethic." Jews score higher on monetary ambition but also on the desire for creativity, and on a chance to work in a world of ideas. The basic cleavage on occupational values is between Jew and Gentile, not between Protestant and Catholic.

or lower half). Even though the numbers in some of these subgroups are rather small and comparisons must be made with some care, there are enough respondents in the important groups (e.g., big-city, high-SES males) for each of the three religions to enable us to judge to what extent background characteristics are responsible for the similarities and differences above.

Catholics were six percentage points ahead of Protestants in plans for graduate school the autumn after graduation. This lead continues (by four points) in the key group of high-SES, large-home-town males and is also unaffected in all female groups (Table 5). Only among small-

TABLE 5. *Per Cent Going to Graduate School in Fall, 1961, by Religion and Background Characteristics*

	PROTESTANT	CATHOLIC	JEWISH
	MALE		
Large home town:*			
High SES†	44 (248)	48 (159)	55 (103)
Low SES	39 (161)	39 (161)	55 (48)
Small home town:			
High SES	35 (304)	38 (94)	36 (14)
Low SES	26 (431)	21 (115)	50 (4)
	FEMALE		
Large home town:			
High SES	29 (260)	28 (96)	44 (60)
Low SES	24 (92)	28 (67)	35 (23)
Small home town:			
High SES	15 (248)	29 (74)	27 (18)
Low SES	16 (263)	22 (67)	

* Large home towns are those with a population over 100,000.

† High socioeconomic status (SES) indicates those whose parents had attended college and had a white-collar job (professional or manager) or who had a white-collar job and made more than $7,500 a year even if they had not attended college or who had a blue-collar job, but made more than $7,500 a year and had attended college.

city, low-SES males do Catholics fall behind Protestants (5 per cent) in graduate-school plans; among large-city, low-SES males there is exact parity. In general, we can say that the surprising showing of Catholics in the matter of graduate-school plans cannot be explained away by background characteristics. In all but one of the eight comparison groups, Catholics are either ahead of Protestants in graduate-school plans or even with them. In the four groups in which there are enough cases to make a comparison, the Jewish lead over the other two groups continues, although it seems that among high-SES males from large home towns, the Jewish lead is substantially reduced (from thirteen to seven points ahead of Catholics).

We saw previously that there was virtually no difference among the three religions in those planning arts and science careers, despite the prediction that Jews would be more likely than gentiles to plan such careers and Protestants more likely than Catholics. Table 6, part A, shows a very interesting phenomenon for Jews. More than twice as large a proportion of low-SES Jewish males choose the academic professions as do high-SES males (although the reverse is true for Jewish girls). Indeed, high-SES Jewish males are much less likely to choose the academic life than either Protestants or Catholics. There is little difference between Protestants and Catholics in the large home towns, whether they be male or female, in their plans for academic careers, though the small home-town Protestant males are ahead of the Catholics and the small home-town Catholic females are ahead of the Protestants. We note once again no evidence for a disinclination of Catholics to go into the academic life, and a somewhat surprising underchoice of academia by well-to-do Jewish sons.

The reason for the underchoice of academia by this group becomes clear in Table 6, part B; almost two-fifths of the high-SES Jewish males from big cities are choosing the traditional professions of law and medicine, while only one-tenth of the low-SES Jewish males are making the same choice. Thus well-to-do Jewish sons choose the traditional professions and "lower" class sons choose the academic professions. Even though the numbers on which this last statement is based are somewhat small, it should be noted that the differences are statistically significant. The Catholic overchoice of the professions in comparison with Protestants holds up in all male categories.

Table 6, part C, supports the finding that primary and secondary education is the Protestant field. The Protestant lead

TABLE 6. *Future Career Plans, by Religion and by Background Characteristics*

TABLE 6   *(continued)*

A. PER CENT CHOOSING ACADEMIC PROFESSION (PHYSICAL SCIENCES, BIOLOGICAL SCIENCES, SOCIAL SCIENCES, HUMANITIES)

	PROTESTANT	CATHOLIC	JEWISH
		MALE	
Large home town:			
High SES	22 (248)	18 (159)	12 (103)
Low SES	18 (161)	20 (161)	28 (47)
Small home town:			
High SES	19 (304)	12 (94)	7 (14)
Low SES	17 (431)	11 (115)	25 (4)
		FEMALE	
Large home town:			
High SES	25 (260)	28 (96)	29 (60)
Low SES	14 (92)	15 (67)	13 (23)
Small home town:			
High SES	16 (248)	23 (74)	23 (18)
Low SES	9 (263)	7 (67)	

B. PER CENT PLANNING CAREER IN PROFESSIONS (LAW AND MEDICINE)

	PROTESTANT	CATHOLIC	JEWISH
		MALE	
Large home town:			
High SES	12 (248)	18 (159)	38 (103)
Low SES	7 (161)	10 (161)	9 (47)
Small home town:			
High SES	13 (304)	16 (94)	28 (14)
Low SES	4 (431)	7 (115)	0 (4)
		FEMALE	
Large home town:			
High SES	0 (260)	1 (96)	0 (60)
Low SES	1 (92)	0 (67)	4 (23)
Small home town:			
High SES	0 (248)	1 (74)	0 (18)
Low SES	0 (265)	2 (67)	

C. PER CENT PLANNING CAREER IN PRIMARY OR SECONDARY EDCUATION

	PROTESTANT	CATHOLIC	JEWISH
		MALE	
Large home town:			
High SES	11 (248)	7 (159)	4 (103)
Low SES	25 (161)	15 (161)	13 (47)
Small home town:			
High SES	15 (304)	12 (94)	0 (14)
Low SES	27 (431)	22 (115)	0 (4)

c. *(Continued)*

	PROTESTANT	CATHOLIC	JEWISH
		FEMALE	
Large home town:			
High SES	48 (260)	41 (96)	64 (60)
Low SES	59 (92)	57 (67)	74 (23)
Small home town:			
High SES	58 (248)	53 (74)	56 (18)
Low SES	68 (263)	69 (67)	

D. PER CENT PLANNING CAREER IN BUSINESS

	PROTESTANT	CATHOLIC	JEWISH
		MALE	
Large home town:			
High SES	30 (248)	35 (159)	30 (103)
Low SES	19 (161)	28 (161)	9 (47)
Small home town:			
High SES	26 (304)	36 (94)	43 (14)
Low SES	19 (431)	34 (115)	50 (4)
		FEMALE	
Large home town:			
High SES	10 (260)	15 (96)	7 (60)
Low SES	5 (92)	10 (67)	4 (23)
Small home town:			
High SES	3 (248)	4 (74)	11 (18)
Low SES	6 (263)	3 (67)	

over Catholics in this career is to be found in all groups with the exception of the low-SES, small home-town females (where there are so few Catholics that the finding is dubious). It is worth noting that Jewish girls are the ones most likely to choose education, while Jewish males are the least likely. It is also worth noting that while Protestant males are ahead of Catholic males in all categories in the choice of education, the lead is especially pronounced among the low-SES groups. Apparently education is the popular means of upward mobility for "poor" Protestant males just as the academic life is for "poor" Jewish males.

Something of the same phenomenon is to be observed among Catholics in the choice of business careers (Table 6, part D). Catholics are ahead of Protestants in choosing business in all categories (except the troublesome low-SES, small home-town females), but the biggest overchoice is among low-SES males. Each religious group apparently has its own favorite path of upward mobility—the Protestants choosing education, the Catholics choosing business, and the Jews choosing academia. For the first two groups the choice is merely an exaggeration of what the upper-SES groups are choosing, but for the Jews the choice is totally different from the upper-SES choice of the traditional professions.

Background characteristics have no effect on the ordering of the three religions as to the importance of money as an occupational value (Table 7). It is more important to Jews than to Catholics in all categories and to Catholics than to Protestants. The slight Catholic deficiency in the desire to be "original and creative" seems to result primarily from the performance on this item of low-SES Catholics in large home towns, regardless of sex, and of Catholic girls from large home towns. The Jewish lead in "people, not things" on the other hand is a high-SES phenomenon, probably not unrelated to the interest of this group in the professions of law and medicine. We find no evidence in these values of any anti-intellectualism or anti-economic achievement in Catholics.

To sum up this section, we may say that Catholics are more likely to choose business, Jews more likely to choose law and medicine, and Protestants more likely to choose education. All three groups are about equally represented in the arts and sciences. There seem to be different paths of upward mobility for the lower-SES members of each religion. One need not look too far for a historical explanation of the differences we have reported: the American public school system, whatever its present orientations, was surely Protestant in its origins and early history; the Jews, traditionally victims of prejudice, would be inclined to look to the profes-

TABLE 7. *Selected Occupational Values, by Religion and by Background Characteristics*

A. "MAKING A LOT OF MONEY"

	PROTESTANT	CATHOLIC	JEWISH
	MALE		
Large home town:			
High SES	30 (248)	38 (159)	56 (103)
Low SES	25 (161)	28 (161)	46 (48)
Small home town:			
High SES	29 (304)	35 (94)	36 (14)
Low SES	26 (431)	30 (115)	0 (4)
	FEMALE		
Large home town:			
High SES	12 (260)	16 (96)	18 (60)
Low SES	7 (92)	12 (67)	8 (23)
Small home town:			
High SES	10 (248)	12 (74)	33 (18)
Low SES	13 (263)	24 (67)	

B. "OPPORTUNITIES TO BE ORIGINAL AND CREATIVE"

	PROTESTANT	CATHOLIC	JEWISH
	MALE		
Large home town:			
High SES	59 (248)	58 (159)	61 (103)
Low SES	55 (161)	49 (161)	62 (48)
Small home town:			
High SES	47 (304)	41 (94)	43 (14)
Low SES	42 (431)	43 (115)	50 (4)
	FEMALE		
Large home town:			
High SES	59 (260)	53 (96)	68 (60)
Low SES	52 (92)	46 (67)	76 (23)
Small home town:			
High SES	56 (248)	56 (74)	72 (18)
Low SES	42 (263)	51 (67)	

C. "OPPORTUNITY TO WORK WITH PEOPLE INSTEAD OF THINGS"

	PROTESTANT	CATHOLIC	JEWISH
	MALE		
Large home town:			
High SES	46 (248)	46 (159)	54 (103)
Low SES	45 (161)	50 (161)	35 (48)
Small home town:			
High SES	46 (304)	45 (94)	64 (14)
Low SES	46 (431)	46 (115)	74 (4)
	FEMALE		
Large home town:			
High SES	71 (260)	68 (96)	72 (60)
Low SES	68 (92)	64 (67)	64 (23)
Small home town:			
High SES	72 (248)	64 (74)	61 (18)
Low SES	72 (263)	82 (67)	

sions as the best way to get ahead despite prejudice; and the Catholics as latecomers to the economic battles, would find that the business corporation was best suited to their needs. Whether there is anything in each religion that would predispose its members in these directions remains to be seen. It could be argued that the practical bent of rabbinic scholarship would incline the Jews to the professions, and the large organizational

as someone who was planning to go to graduate school in the arts and sciences the coming fall.[23] We note that the only significant difference in field of choice is the Protestant lead over Jews in the biological sciences. We note further that, in the career activities favored by members of the three religious groups, the Jews lead both other groups significantly in choosing research. There is no support for the hypotheses that Catholics will un-

TABLE 8. *Plans of Potential Scholars, by Religion (Percentage Distribution)*

	PROTESTANT	CATHOLIC	JEWISH	SIGNIFICANCE		
				P-C	P-J	C-J
Field of study:						
Physical sciences	30	32	33	N.S.	N.S.	N.S.
Biological sciences	14	11	9	N.S.	.01	N.S.
Social sciences	20	18	25	N.S.	N.S.	N.S.
Humanities	36	39	32	N.S.	N.S.	N.S.
Total per cent	100	100	99			
Total *N*	2,159	970	489			
Career activities:						
Teaching	73	73	76	N.S.	N.S.	N.S.
Research	62	60	73	N.S.	.05	.01
Administration	17	17	16	N.S.	N.S.	N.S.
Service	8	9	15	N.S.	.05	N.S.
None of these	2	2	4			

apparatus of the Catholic church would orient its members toward the large corporation. Perhaps even the "service" tradition of much of American Protestantism could be linked with primary and secondary education. But such propositions require much more careful investigation.

Potential Scholars

Table 8 begins an investigation of the potential scholars from the three religious groups (those with no religion are added). A potential scholar was defined

derchoose physical sciences or research. Table 9 compares religiosity rates[24] and

[23] A different deck of cards was used for the analysis reported in this paragraph. It represented all respondents who planned fall graduate school in the arts and sciences: $N = 3,816$. It will be noted that in this deck the proportion for each religious group is different from that in the deck analyzed in previous paragraphs. The reason for this is that the three groups enter arts and sciences graduate school in different proportions than they exist in the total population.

[24] The "group mean" is the percentage re-

apostasy rates[25] for "scholars" and the group mean on these rates for each of the religious groups.

There is a slight increase in apostasy among Catholic "scholars" (about 2 per cent), and the amount of irregular church attendance increases moderately; however, in neither apostasy nor irregular church attendance is the increase among Catholic "scholars" comparable to the increase among the other religious groups. There is no evidence that the apparently

As a conclusion to this section, we might note that in a resurvey a year after graduation, 87 per cent of the Jews, 81 per cent of the Protestants, and 80 per cent of the Catholics who said that they were going to graduate school the autumn after their graduation were in fact taking graduate-school courses; 24 per cent of the Jewish graduates of June, 1961, 22 per cent of the Protestants, and 21 per cent of the Catholics affirmed their eventual intention of getting the Ph.D. (al-

TABLE 9.   *Religious Orientation of Arts and Sciences Graduate Students (Per Cent)*

	PROTESTANTS		CATHOLICS		JEWS	
	GRADUATE STUDENTS	ALL PROTESTANTS	GRADUATE STUDENTS	ALL CATHOLICS	GRADUATE STUDENTS	ALL JEWS
Regular church attendance*	36	65	73	85	36	68
Irregular church attendance	33	20	16	6	37	16
Apostate	31	15	11	9	27	16
N	(2,159)†	(2,007)‡	(970)†	(833)‡	(489)†	(272)‡

* For Catholics, weekly or several times a month; for Protestants, at least once a month; for Jews, at least two or three times a year.

† Total sample.

‡ Ten per cent sample.

heightened interest in the academic life among American Catholics has led to a large scale movement away from the Church.

ligious or apostasizing in the total college population as measured by the survey; the "scholar mean" is the percentage in the scholar deck.

[25] Two questions were used to measure apostasy: "In what religion were you raised?" and "What is your present religious preference?" An apostate was defined as one who had listed "religion in which he was raised" as Protestant, Catholic or Jew, and listed his present religion as "none." It is to be noted that only among Catholics is there no appre-

though an approximately equal proportion of each group had not yet begun their academic work for the degree).

The Ethnic Factor

Only two predictions of our initial hypotheses have been supported. Catholics overchoose large corporations and busi-

ciable increase of apostasy among "scholars." This could mean that Catholics perceive little conflict between orientation to the arts and sciences as a career and religious membership or that Catholics are better able to compartmentalize their lives than members of the other groups. A forthcoming paper will discuss the fact of apostasy and the variation in rates within the three major religious groups.

ness as a career (although the general Jew-gentile differences emerge pretty much as expected). Why our findings are so different from Lenski's needs to be-explored. A possible explanation (suggested by Bernard Rosen[26] and others) is that the ethnic composition of the two Catholic samples might be considerably different. Lenski gives no data on ethnic subdivisions within the Catholic sample and no ethnic question was asked in the NORC survey. However, it is generally assumed that the Catholic population of Detroit has a very large Polish element. An earlier study made of graduate students by NORC[27] did ask an ethnic question and enables us to see whether there are any differences between the various Catholic ethnic groups. It seemed possible that those ethnic groups who came in the later waves, largely southern and eastern European groups, might be experiencing a somewhat slower acculturation process than the earlier groups and, therefore, would be less likely to go to college, to plan academic careers, and to be strongly oriented toward economic or academic achievement. Two items in the graduate-student study enabled us to measure the college plans and the self-confidence of the various ethnic groups within American Catholicism: a question about whether college was taken for granted in high school and a question about evaluation of one's own abilities. In Table 10 we note that the Irish-German-British wave was more likely to have taken college for granted when in high school and to have a higher estimate

[26] In his review of Lenski's book in *American Sociological Review*, XXVII (February, 1962), 111.
[27] This survey was reported by James A. Davis in *Stipends and Spouses: The Consumer Finances of Graduate Stuly in America* (Chicago: Universtiy of Chicago Press, 1962).

TABLE 10. *Differences among Catholic Ethnic Groups (Percentage Distribution)*

	IRISH-GERMAN-BRITISH	ITALIAN-SLAVIC	SIGNIFICANCE
College taken for granted	43	30	.01
High estimate of abilities	33	23	.05
N	(556)	(147)	

of its own abilities than the Italian-Slavic group. There seems to be sound reason for suggesting that the differences between Lenski's findings and those reported here might be connected with ethnicity. It would appear that perhaps ethnicity has not ceased to be an important factor for sociological concern.

The question remains as to whether the influence of the ethnic factor that we described in the preceding paragraph is truly ethnic or is rather the result of the fact that members of one group have simply less in the way of an American background, since their families have been in America for a shorter period of time. Will the ethnic effect vanish under a control for generation or socioeconomic status? In Table 11 we note that a control for father's occupation does not eliminate the two differences that had correlated with ethnicity. First-wave ethnic groups are more likely to have a higher estimate of their native ability than second-wave ethnic groups regardless of father's occupation, even though both increase their estimate of native ability as status improves. Further, ethnic groups of the first wave with white-collar background are more likely to have come from families where college education was taken for granted than such groups of the second wave. The reverse seems to be true of the lower class of both waves, although the case base is very small.

Nor does a control for generation eliminate the differences between the two waves. It is true that the early (first to third) generations of both waves have about the same percentage ranking their native ability high. However, the later generations of the first wave have far more self-confidence than the later gener-

suggests that the pure ethnic factor deserves much further investigation.

Summary

It was the purpose of this essay to examine certain hypotheses about the influence of the Protestant Ethic and of Catholic anti-intellectualism in light of the data gathered by a national cluster sam-

TABLE 11.   *Ethnic Variables by Father's Occupational Status and by Generation (Percentage Distribution)*

	HIGH ESTIMATE OF NATIVE ABILITY		COLLEGE TAKEN FOR GRANTED WHEN IN HIGH SCHOOL	
	FIRST WAVE*	SECOND WAVE†	FIRST WAVE*	SECOND WAVE†
Father's occupational status:				
Upper class‡	35 (424)	27 (80)	52 (424)	45 (80)
Lower class	32 (132)	18 (67)	15 (132)	19 (67)
Generation:				
1st to 3d generation§	26 (140)	23 (107)	31 (140)	36 (107)
4th or after	38 (416)	25 (40)	47 (416)	33 (40)

* Irish, German, British.
† Italian, eastern European.
‡ Non-manual occupation.
§ At least one grandparent not born in America.

ations of the second wave. Finally, the later generations of the first wave are substantially more likely to have taken college for granted than the later generations of the second wave (although the reverse seems to be true for the earlier generations). Since the number of respondents involved is rather small and since the interactions under controls are often ambiguous, we can hardly regard this analysis as definitive. However, the finding that differences in self-confidence and the taking of college for granted do not disappear even in the fourth generation of the two ethnic categories strongly

ple of college graduates. Only one item in the Protestant Ethic complex (the overchoice by Catholics of large corporations) and one item in the anti-intellectualism syndrome of the self-critics within the American Catholic church (the overchoice of business as a career) were supported. There was no substantial evidence of anti-intellectualism among Catholic college graduates. (And as we will report elsewhere there were no significant differences between graduates of Catholic colleges and Catholic graduates of other colleges.) The main lines of division on the variables examined were on the Jew-gentile axis rather than on the Protestant-Catholic axis. It was further suggested after a brief examination of materials from another survey that the differences between our findings and those of other investigators might have to do with the different ethnic composition of the samples and that, therefore, the ethnic factor was still an important one in American society.

The abandonment of previously held concepts does not and must not proceed precipitously. Many of the survey findings reported in this paper are at variance with ideas that have been popular both within and outside of the American Cath-olic community. One survey does not a revolution make. The NORC* data provide little support for theories of anti-scientism among American Catholics. Considerably more research will be required, however, before one can in fact argue that the values of Catholics with regard to scholarship are not different from their non-Catholic fellow Americans. It will then be necessary to determine whether this similarity represents a major social change and, if it does, what the mechanisms of this change have been.

* National Opinion Research Center, University of Chicago.

4 · Catholic Education, Economic Values, and Achievement[1]

MARVIN BRESSLER AND CHARLES F. WESTOFF

ABSTRACT. This study tests the hypothesis that at each of three educational levels Catholic males who are educated solely in religious schools will exceed those whose formal education was exclusively secular in the proportion of those who fail to (1) internalize the values of worldly success and (2) actually achieve superior socioeconomic status. The sample comprising 265 to 309 men is part of a larger probability sample of young married couples residing in the nation's seven largest Standard Metropolitan Areas. The data derived from questionnaire and interview materials include thirty items measuring commitment to work and mobility values, and five measures of monetary achievement and occupational status and mobility. In the value sphere only six of the ninety comparisons were significant with a reasonable probability that even these reflect nothing more than sampling variability; there were no statistically significant differences between the two groups in economic behavior. Accordingly, the hypothesis that among Catholics a

SOURCE. Marvin Bressler and Charles F. Westoff, "Catholic Education, Economic Values, and Achievement," reprinted from American Journal of Sociology, 69, November, 1963, pp. 225–233, by permission of the University of Chicago Press.
[1] The data used in this study were collected as part of a study of fertility conducted by the Office of Population Research, Princeton University, under the administrative direction of the Milbank Memorial Fund. It was supported by grants from the Carnegie Corporation and the Population Council, Inc. We wish to acknowledge our appreciation to the School of Education of New York University for defraying the costs of additional data processing in connection with this analysis, and to the Social Science Research Council for its award of a grant-in-aid to Marvin Bressler.

Catholic education is negatively related to achievement values or to subsequent economic success is completely rejected.

The continuing debate on the eligibility of religious schools for tax-supported financial assistance has provoked considerable speculation on the social consequences of a Catholic education. The legal, philosophical, and even metaphorical dialectics guiding the discussion have by now assumed a certain ritualistic predictability. Justice Black's strict interpretation of the establishment clause[2] is confronted by Justice Douglas' declaration that "we are a religious people whose institutions presuppose a Supreme Being." [3] Social cohesion is invoked against cultural pluralism, and the melting pot is once again offered as a counterimage to the symphony orchestra. But whatever their differences, both partisans and opponents of religious schools share the common conviction that a Roman Catholic education serves as a mechanism of indoctrination that reinforces the influence of home and church. In experimental terms this assumption may be expressed as the expectation that Catholic products of Catholic schools will differ in important respects from their coreligionists who have been exposed to secular educational institutions. We shall bring evidence to bear on the validity of this assumption for one critical sector of American life by exploring the influence of type of education on the values and achievement of worldly success.

The two most prominent studies in the meager research literature devoted to this issue are not comparable in design, in use of research techniques, or in their samples, and perhaps for these reasons arrive at opposite conclusions. In his *The Religious Factor*, Gerhard Lenski writes: "Evidently Catholic schools do not generally develop in boys those attitudes, values, beliefs, and intellectual orientations which make it possible for a man to enjoy the more demanding jobs in the modern metropolis." [4] This observation was most pertinent for middle-class men. By contrast, on the basis of their analysis of Strodtbeck's unpublished New Haven data, Rossi and Rossi conclude: "Although the differences between parochial and public high school students are not very large they do tell a consistent story: the parochial student, whether from a 'white collar' or 'blue collar' background, is less attached to his family group and more oriented toward the prevalent middle-class norms of occupational success." [5] However, since small numbers prohibited Lenski from holding educational level constant and Strodtbeck's data refer only to high-school students, it is altogether possible that these apparently contradictory findings are an artifact of the research process rather than genuinely irreconcilable depictions of empirical reality.

In the absence of unambiguous directives from concrete research findings, hypothesis formation must necessarily rely on plausible inferences derived from the main stream of sociological scholarship. Orthodox theory supports the expectation that Catholic education should reinforce historical tradition that has been antagonistic to the full expression of the individualistic ethic and the impulse for material acquisition. Thomist ambivalence on the morality of private property, the principle of the "just price," medieval injunctions against usury, the emphasis

[2] See *Everson v. Board of Education of the Township of Ewing, et al.*, 330 U.S. 1, 67 Sup. Ct. 504 (1947).
[3] See *Zorach v. Clauson*, 343 U.S. 306, 72 Sup. Ct. 679 (1952).
[4] Garden City, N.Y.: Doubleday & Co., 1961, p. 248.
[5] Peter H. and Alice S. Rossi, "Some Effects of Parochial School Education in America," *Daedalus*, Spring, 1961, p. 313.

on social justice, and the ethical imperative to share surplus wealth are all still
a durable part of the mood and substance
of Catholic teaching.[6]

These specific doctrinal restrictions on
accomplishment in the economic sphere
are presumably augmented in the Catholic educational establishment by an "atmosphere in which the spiritual and the
supernatural hold the primacy in the
hierarchy of temporal and eternal values." [7] In the words of Fichter: "Religion
permeates the curriculum and the child
is deliberately given to understand that
his relationship with God is the most important single aspect of his life on
earth." [8] It would appear a priori that so
much preoccupation with other-worldly
matters would impose severe restraints on
an achievement ethos and prove dysfunctional for the realities of economic
struggle.

By contrast, instruction in secular
schools is reputed to be relatively free of

religious symbolism, theological elucida-
tion, spiritual exhortation, and other pervasive religious influences. According to
one critic: "Our public schools and colleges are rarely anti-religious. They simply ignore religion. Obviously, if a child
is taught in school about a vast number
of things . . . for 25 hours a week,
eight or nine months a year . . . and if
for all this time matters of religion are
never seriously treated, the child can only
come to view religion as, at best, an in-
nocuous pastime preferred by a few to
golf or canasta." [9] It seems plausible that
a philosophy of instruction that transmits
the ethical standards of the Judeo-Christian tradition without supernatural sanctions might considerably reduce inhibitions impeding the rational pursuit of
financial gain.

These considerations strongly suggest
the hypotheses that, at each educational
level, religiously educated Catholics
should exceed secular-educated Catholics
in the proportion who (1) fail to internalize values that are presumably conducive to worldly success, and (2) actually fail to achieve superior socioeconomic
status. Moreover, one might reasonably
expect such differences to increase in
magnitude as additional increments of
years of education multiply the opportunities for the inculcation of Catholic
doctrine.

Data and Procedures

The data used to test the hypotheses
that Catholic men[10] educated in Catholic
schools are less committed to an achievement ethos and subsequently achieve less
than those educated in non-sectarian

---

[6] See, e.g., Matthew F. Brady, "Why American Catholics Conduct Schools," *The Role
of the Independent School in American Democracy* (Papers Delivered at a Conference
on Education [Milwaukee, Wis.: Marquette
University Press, 1956]): "To educate solely
for 'success' in life when we mean by success, comfort, ease, luxury, esteem, power,
is laudable to a degree but only a partial
objective of complete education. Again material consideration alone cannot fulfill the
longings, the ideals of man's soul, for his
spiritual nature cries out for fulfillment in
a realm that is above and beyond the omnipresent and encroaching world about him."
[7] Neil G. McCluskey, S.J., "The Catholic
School in Theory and Practice," quoted in
Philip Jacobson, "A Jewish Viewpoint on
Church-State-School Relations," in William
Brickman and Stanley Lehrer (eds.), *Religion, Government, and Education* (New
York: Society for the Advancement of Education, 1961).
[8] Joseph S. Fichter, *Parochial School* (Notre
Dame, Ind.: University of Notre Dame
Press, 1958).

[9] Bernard Iddings Bell, "Our Schools—Their
Four Grievous Faults," in C. Winfield Scott
and Clyde M. Hill (eds.), *Public Education
under Criticism* (New York: Prentice-Hall,
Inc., 1954), p. 63.
[10] The religious preference of the man was
determined by a question asked of his wife.

schools and colleges come from a longitudinal study of factors affecting fertility in metropolitan areas of the United States.[11] The sample design has several distinct advantages for testing such an hypothesis. In 1957 a probability sample of 1,165 native-white, once-married couples, all of whom had had their second child born six months earlier, and who were residing in one of the seven largest Standard Metropolitan Areas of the country, was interviewed by teams of professional interviewers. The main feature of such a sample for the present analysis is that it permits comparisons of economic behavior at a roughly similar stage in the life-cycle while eliminating other sources of variation extraneous to our interest.[12]

The data utilized in the present analysis are drawn from two sources. The information on education, socioeconomic status and mobility of the husband come from interviews with the wife. The items measuring attitudes toward achievement derive from a self-administered questionnaire that the husband was requested by his wife to complete and return by mail.[13]

Since the sample was drawn from the largest metropolitan areas in the country, the proportion of Catholics (nearly half) was larger than would have been found in a sample of the national population as a whole. For purposes of our analysis, however, we have reduced the sample to a total ranging between 265 and 309 men.[14] The major loss of cases resulted from our desire to purify the comparisons by eliminating Catholics who were educated partly in Catholic and partly in public schools and colleges. Although this purification resulted in the loss of a quarter of the Catholic men (105), most of the combinations were insufficiently frequent to be usable.[15]

The Catholic sample, as a whole, at the time of the first interview (1957) exhibited the following characteristics. All had two children, with the youngest child six months old, and lived in one of the largest cities or its suburbs. The average Catholic couple had been married four to five years, the man was twenty-eight years old and his wife twenty-six. The average earnings of the men in 1956 was $4,400 and about 43 per cent had white-collar jobs. Some 26 per cent had attended college, while 65 per cent had not gone beyond high school. Only 9 per cent failed to receive education beyond the elementary-school level.

Analysis

The strategy of our approach is to compare economic achievement attitudes and behavior of Catholic men educated solely in Catholic schools with the attitudes and behavior of those whose formal education was exclusively secular. Quite clearly, a wide variety of circumstances that might have affected their attitudes as well as their fortunes could have and

[11] The report summarizing the first phase of the study is in Charles F. Westoff, Robert G. Potter, Jr., Philip C. Sagi, and Elliot G. Mishler, *Family Growth in Metropolitan America* (Princeton, N.J.: Princeton University Press, 1961). A second volume will appear in 1963 that summarizes the prediction of fertility over a three-year period.
[12] The details of the sampling plan are discussed in Westoff *et al., op. cit.*, pp. 16–28.
[13] A total of 941, or 81 per cent, of the husbands returned usable questionnaires. Although this response rate is unusually high for mail questionnaires, there is some bias in the typical direction of favoring respondents from slightly higher socioeconomic levels.

[14] The range arises because in the analysis of economic behavior we were able to use data collected from the wife, but the attitudinal material came from the husband's questionnaire with the lower response rate.
[15] The most common pattern (thirty-six cases) was attendance at a Catholic elementary school and graduation from a public high school.

probably did intervene in the five to ten years that these men have been out of school. But the fact remains that we are interested in ascertaining whether a Catholic education has any lasting effects in the economic sphere, in many respects a more important consideration than any immediate differences that might exist while the individual is in school.

The items selected to measure attitudes toward achievement are a series of thirty statements that the man was asked simply to indorse or reject. The statements fall roughly into two classes: those measuring a commitment to the work life and those reflecting a drive for success.[16] The respondent was asked to contrast the value of work with leisure-time activities and other aspects of home life. Attitudes toward success were measured by two groups of items, one of which probed the importance the individual attached to getting ahead in work and another set that attempted to assess the strength of his mobility drive by inquiring whether he would be willing to sacrifice a number of different values (such as friends, leisure time, family, security, political and religious views) in order to get ahead.

These items are not, of course, statistically independent. On the contrary, they were designed originally to form a number of different scales that were also utilized in the present analysis in order to capitalize on greater reliability;[17] the scales failed to disclose any patterns dif-

fering from the individual items. The items were analyzed individually for this study with full knowledge that, although many do correlate with each other, there is a considerable amount of independence; this led to the hope that variations in items with different contents might provide some insights into the nature of any association with Catholic education.

Five measures of economic achievement were employed: the respondent's earnings for the year prior to the interview, the change in his earnings since his marriage, the social prestige[18] of his current occupation, and two measures of occupational mobility,[19] one from his occupation at the time of his marriage and the other a comparison of his present with his father's main occupation.

Because of the limited number of cases involved we are only able to differentiate three levels of education: elementary only (up to eight years), attended high school, and attended college. The majority of men in the first two categories are graduates, but most of those classified at the highest educational level spent less than four years in college.

In Table 1 the responses to thirty statements reflecting the achievement attitudes of Catholic men whose education was exclusively secular or Catholic are compared at each of three educational levels, for a total of ninety comparisons. These data fail to confirm the expectation that a Catholic education is associated with the devaluation of an achievement ethic. Statistical tests reveal that only six

---

[16] For reasons of economy the detailed wording of the items is not reproduced here. The reader interested in any such detail is directed to Westoff *et al., op. cit.,* pp. 383–400, where the full wording, the distribution of responses of the total sample, and the intercorrelations of items are presented.

[17] The scales constructed were commitment to work values, importance attached to getting ahead, general drive to get ahead, willingness to sacrifice social interests to get ahead, and willingness to sacrifice ideological values to get ahead.

[18] Scored on the North-Hatt occupational prestige scale based on the 1947 National Opinion Research Center poll. For a recent appraisal and revision of this instrument see Albert J. Reiss, Jr., *Occupations and Social Status* (New York: Free Press of Glencoe, Inc., 1962).

[19] Intragenerational and intergenerational occupational mobility scores were calculated by differencing the social prestige ratings of the occupations involved.

TABLE 1. *Proportion of Achievement-Oriented Replies* to Thirty Questions on Attitudes Toward Work and Success of Catholic Men Educated in Secular Schools Compared with Those Educated in Catholic Schools, by Highest Level of Educational Attainment*

ATTITUDINAL ITEM	ELEMENTARY SCHOOL		HIGH SCHOOL		COLLEGE	
	SECULAR	CATHOLIC	SECULAR	CATHOLIC	SECULAR	CATHOLIC
Relax at home or work	81	92	91	89	84	85
Work more satisfying than time spent at home	31	33	28	27	30	35
Would work regardless of inheritance	37	75†	58	52	45	50
Work makes life worthwhile	50	50	33	32	18	25
Main interests in life connected with work	31	50	42	62†	70	70
Regret going in present line of work	63	50	52	53	48	50
Work most satisfying part of life	50	50	38	49	61	45
Enjoy spare time activities or work	13	50†	32	38	50	75
Work just a way of making money	31	33	52	47	77	80
Opportunity most important aspect of work	81	92	68	64	50	50
Spent time thinking about improving chances	75	92	74	87	61	35
Achieving money and possessions very important	37	75†	58	52	50	40
Satisfied with present opportunities	62	83	53	53	68	75
Important to own things as good as friends do	56	58	47	44	41	40
Anxious to get much further ahead	69	83	81	89	67	90
Getting ahead one of most important things in life	62	58	64	64	50	65
Determination and ambition important qualities	75	92	66	64	34	25
To get ahead, would:						
Give up vacations for several years	75	75	77	84	59	89†
Leave friends	75	75	71	71	68	84
Live in undesirable neighborhood temporarily	81	50	44	47	41	63
Give up leisure time	75	92	70	84	68	89
Postpone having another child	56	42	48	38	27	21
Move family to strange part of country	87	75	60	67	73	74
Do less interesting or less enjoyable work	37	50	48	44	41	53
Not see family as much as would like	37	33	18	35*	24	41
Risk health	12	17	11	18	18	37
Keep quiet about political views	50	75	40	37	37	53
Take a less secure job	53	42	46	56	48	68
Send children to poorer schools	44	25	17	24	18	21
Keep quiet about religious views	19	33	17	11	19	5

* In two or three instances it is not unambiguously clear whether a positive or negative response reflects an orientation toward achievement. These instances were decided in terms of the direction of their correlation with other items.

† Difference between the two proportions significant at the .05 level as determined by χ^2 with 1 degree of freedom. The number of men who attended secular or Catholic schools is 16 and 12 for elementary school, 128 and 45 who attended high school, and 44 and 20, who attended college.

of the ninety comparisons are significant, with the reasonable probability that even these reflect nothing more than sampling variability.[20] Moreover, a straightforward analysis of the items that elicited any sort of differential response between the two

[20] Depending on the severity of the test applied, a plausible argument can be advanced that these data (1) are, (2) are not, con-

sistent with the findings reported by the Rossis (Rossi and Rossi, *op. cit.*). They are supported by the over-all direction of the associations, but not by the criterion of statistical significance.

groups shows that the proportion of achievement-oriented replies was higher for the Catholic-educated in fifty-one of seventy-five instances. It would be overstating the case to argue the obverse of our original supposition; there is insufficient evidence to demonstrate that a Catholic education actually *encourages* an allegiance to work and mobility values. But we can quite clearly reject the hypothesis that, among Catholics, religious education is negatively related to these values of worldly success.

One might reasonably maintain that such value statements are of doubtful reliability and even assuming high reliability, there may be reason to question

it is for Catholics educated in nonsectarian schools. Thus our negative conclusion can be extended to important measures of economic behavior as well as economic values and attitudes.

Implications

The lack of association between a Catholic education and distinctive patterns of socioeconomic values and achievements invites speculation both as to causes and consequences. These results are especially striking since the initial selection into religiously affiliated schools and colleges is from the most religious homes. Thus both formal and informal educational

TABLE 2. *Proportion of Catholic Men above Average* on Selected Measures of Socioeconomic Status and Social Mobility, by Type and Level of Education*

	ELEMENTARY SCHOOL		HIGH SCHOOL		COLLEGE	
	SECULAR	CATHOLIC	SECULAR	CATHOLIC	SECULAR	CATHOLIC
Earnings in 1956	30	47	56	58	78	75
Changes in earnings since marriage	25	33	45	34	47	33
Social prestige of occupation	25	20	38	44	81	100
Intragenerational occupational mobility	30	33	28	32	29	25
Intergenerational occupational mobility	50	43	33	28	58	59

* Above the median of the distribution of all men on each scale. For sample sizes see n. †, Table 1.

the predictive validity of such values for economic behavior. Most social scientists would argue that actual economic achievement is of greater importance than attitudes toward achievement. With such considerations in mind we compared the socioeconomic accomplishments of Catholics educated in the two educational systems (Table 2). The five measures of status and mobility described above produce fifteen comparisons for the three educational levels. In none of these fifteen comparisons is there any statistically significant difference in the proportions. Whether the variable involved is income, occupational status, or mobility, the proportion of Catholic men scored as "high" on achievement is the same for those educated in Catholic schools and colleges as

processes within the school should be mutually reinforcing.[21] Assuming that our inquiry is free of serious flaws in design or measurement, the sources of this seem-

[21] The comparative effects of home and school training on religious knowledge and values are the subject of a projected study, the plans for which are described in Joseph G. Keegan, "A Study of the Relationship between Religious Atmosphere in the Home and Amount of Catholic Education, on the One Hand, and the Religious Knowledge and Religious Attitudes of Male Catholics Attending College, on the Other," in Stuart Cook (ed.), *Research Plans in the Fields of Religion, Values and Morality and Their Bearing on Religious and Character Formation* (New York: Religious Education Association, 1962), pp. 47–55.

ing anomaly may lie in a faulty set of implicit assumptions that frequently guide sociological expectations. These are (1) Catholic schools teach a distinctively Catholic or at least "religious" stance on economic matters, (2) schools are an effective vehicle for the transmission of values, and (3) religion markedly influences attitudes and achievement in the economic sphere. Each of these assertions is open to considerable question.

We suspect, for instance, that orientations to worldly success proffered by the two school systems are more congruent than is ordinarily supposed. Sociologists of religion, following Max Weber, probably have overemphasized the monolithic unity of Church teaching on economic matters and neglected opposing tendencies within the Catholic tradition. Economic historians such as Amintore Fanfani have demonstrated that the ideals of hard work and thrift, a well-developed rationale for private property, and an intellectual climate favoring the expansion of commerce and industry, existed in Catholic Italy during the fourteenth and fifteenth centuries in the period of the rise of modern capitalism.[22] Similarly, H. M. Robertson has assembled impressive evidence from a variety of sixteenth- and seventeenth-century sources that reveal favorable Catholic responses to the idea of work as calling, worldly asceticism, bourgeois virtues, economic rationality and the consecration of la-

bor.[23] Pending further investigation, it would be premature to dismiss the possibility that this other side of Church tradition has become a viable part of the economic message of the contemporary Catholic school.

Even assuming that Catholic instruction is free of doctrinal ambivalence, formal education may be an indifferent instrument for the transmission of a durable and coherent value system. The least generous estimate is that the absence of pronounced differentials in this study may simply reflect a crisis of competence that is endemic throughout the entire American educational structure. The inculcation of a self-conscious and articulate philosophy of worldly success to average students possessing ordinary perception, intelligence, and motivation may well confound the talents of the classroom teacher in either Catholic or secular schools. A more persuasive explanation is that as only one of many socializing agencies, the school's sovereignty in the domain of values may be highly circumscribed. For example, in summarizing the available evidence on collegiate influences on values Brim concludes that the college curriculum influences one's knowledge more than one's values.[24]

It is possible, of course, that significant differentials by type of education did exist but were nullified by the experiences of the respondents in the years subsequent to their departure from school. Catholic and secular educational institu-

[22] *Catholicism, Protestantism, and Capitalism* (New York: Sheed & Ward, 1955).

[23] For some representative quotations from Catholic spokesmen see Robertson, "A Criticism of Max Weber and His School," in Robert W. Green (ed.), *Protestantism and Capitalism* (Boston: D. C. Heath & Co., 1959), pp. 74–75: "One must rise to obey God, who only allows us sleep for the body's needs and commands us, when these needs are satisfied, to busy ourselves with the work which He prescribes for us according to our state." Or, "One serves God by faithfully

serving one's Prince; one serves God by employing one's capital . . . according to all the rules of probity and justice. There are duties to be performed in all conditions of life, and it is in acquitting oneself of these duties that one is sanctified." Or, "one can work fruitfully for God, for men and for oneself."

[24] Orville G. Brim, Jr., *Sociology and the Field of Education* (New York: Russell Sage Foundation, 1958), pp. 69–70.

tions differ markedly in their formal aims, curriculums, and pedagogical practices and possibly in their immediate impact on students. They are, however, both engaged in converting latent talent into salable professional, vocational, and personality skills. As Catholic males who are products of either system are exposed to given quantities of education, their real worth in the market place and prospects for success in the struggle for scarce economic rewards are correspondingly fixed. Thus confronted by the actualities of the real world, most men may respond by adopting realistic levels of aspiration and a set of values that prove to be functional for their particular potentiality for economic achievement. A rational man occupied in solving his most fundamental problems of economic and personality survival may, in the long run, be anesthetized to the philosophical niceties of Thomist, Calvinist, or Deweyan dogma to which he had been originally exposed.

These reflections purporting to explain why Catholic men appear to be immune to differential educational influences also imply that religion may have dubious utility as an independent variate capable of discriminating achievement orientation and economic success. This conjecture is partially supported by an analysis of Catholic-Protestant differences employing the same procedures that were applied to the intra-Catholic comparisons. Thus, for example, the fact that only fourteen of ninety value items and two of fifteen measures of achievement are significantly different statistically between Protestants and Catholics, and not all of these even in the same direction, strongly suggests a potentially profitable area of inquiry.[25]

[25] After surveying the relevant literature and the data in his own study, Lenski (*op. cit.*) concludes that "it is reasonably safe to say that in the modern American metropolis socially significant differences exist in the rates of mobility among the four major socioreligious groups. The Jewish group seems

Any final conclusions about the influence of religion in the economic sphere must be postponed until such time as we are able to augment education with the numerous additional controls that would be

clearly to be the most successful, with white Protestants second, Catholics third, and Negro Protestants fourth" (p. 80). He concludes also that "as a general rule, commitment to the *spirit of capitalism* is especially frequent among white Protestants and Jews; is much less frequent among Catholics and Negro Protestants even when position in the class system is held constant" (p. 115). Therefore he finds that "it seems safe to conclude that religion makes a difference in the behavior of men in the realm of economic activity. We should not exaggerate the magnitude of this influence, but neither should it be minimized" (p. 114). Donald J. Bogue on the other hand finds that "Roman Catholic household heads tend to have higher incomes, for a given amount of schooling completed" but cautions that "these differences may be due to differences in the age of head, number and type of secondary earners, family structure, and occupation—as well as to cultural factors associated with religious affiliation" (*The Population of the United States* [Glencoe, Ill.: Free Press, 1959], pp. 707–8). Bernard Lazerwitz' extensive data can be interpreted as demonstrating that Catholicism is no bar to economic achievement. His tables show that in the late 1950's identical proportions of Catholics and Protestants (18 per cent) had family incomes of $7,500 or above and also that the distribution of Protestant and Catholic heads of families in white-collar occupations was virtually identical—21 per cent and 19 per cent, respectively ("A comparison of Major United States Religious Groups," *Journal of the American Statistical Association*, LVI, No. 295, 574). David C. McClelland's review of social-psychological studies on the achievement motive leads him to conclude "that while the Protestant and Catholic religious labels may have been significantly associated with certain value attitudes, they are not associated in any overall way with *n* achievement. More careful discriminations must be made within each required to construct a satisfactory index of religiosity.

All the *post factum* speculations advanced thus far, taken separately or in combination, suggest that the Catholic breadwinner, like other Americans, derives his orientations to worldly success from the norms of his several subcultures and the broader society. Both our data and our interpretations are thus compatible with the conclusions reached by Rossi and Rossi in their survey article on the effects of a parochial school education. The authors note: "We have been unable to find strong evidence that parochial-school Catholics are very different from other Catholics. The influence of the school is shown most dramatically in areas where the Church has traditionally taken a strong stand, for example, on support of religious education, or on the performance of religious duties. In other areas of life the parochial-school Catholic is only marginally differentiated from

other Catholics." [26] Their findings should, of course, be interpreted with considerable caution. The generalizability of the few existing studies[27] in this area is seriously restricted by sampling limitations including geographic specificity, small numbers, and inadequate representation at all grade levels. The Rossis were obliged to rely mainly on four studies that seldom differentiate among various levels of educational attainment and whose data have primary reference to Florida and the New England area.

Obviously, research on the influences of Catholic education must be further refined and extended in range if it is to be genuinely useful in clarifying the alternatives of public policy. Meanwhile, the available evidence fails to sustain those who either hope or fear that a Catholic education magnifies religious differentials in the economic sector or in other secular areas in American life.

---

of the religious sub-groups before one can arrive at any consistent differences in *n* achievement scores" (*The Achieving Society* [Princeton, N.J.: D. Van Nostrand Co., 1961], p. 364). There is no consensus on the relationship between religion and the economic sphere, but all investigators agree that further refinements and controls are needed. There obviously remains much to be done.

[26] Rossi and Rossi, *op. cit.*, p. 311.
[27] Our general conclusions are quite consistent with the findings from comparisons of Protestants and Catholics reported by Greeley in an article that appeared too late to be integrated more fully in this paper. See Andrew M. Greeley, "Influence of the 'Religious Factor' on Career Plans and Occupational Values of College Graduates," *American Journal of Sociology*, LXVII (May, 1963) 658–71.

---

5 · *Buddhism and Chinese Science*

JOSEPH NEEDHAM

It is for us . . . to attempt some estimate of the influence which Buddhism

SOURCE. Joseph Needham, "Buddhism and Chinese Science," from Joseph Needham, *Science and Civilization in China*, Cambridge: The University Press, 1956, vol. 2, pp. 417–422, 430–431.

exerted on Chinese science and scientific thought. There can be little doubt that on the whole its action was powerfully inhibitory. While in propitious circumstances the doctrine of inevitable ethical causation might conceivably have been extended to cover the whole field of natural causation, this certainly never

took place. Perhaps any beneficial influence which it might have had was wholly
overshadowed by the doctrine of *māyā*,
for how could a mere phantasmagoria
invite serious scientific study? How could
the mentality which averted the eyes
from it, and which sought salvation in
eternal release from it, encourage the investigation of it? And the negative attitude of Buddhism was as marked in what
it refused to discuss, as in its positive
doctrines, for cosmogony was among the
problems regarded as unknowable and
impenetrable. Alas, the "World," for the
Buddhists, was not only "the world, flesh,
and the devil," but the world of Nature
itself. According to early Buddhist rules,
the monk should keep the doors of his
senses guarded, and if he should see anything, devote no attention to its characteristics and details. Buddhism was not
interested in co-ordinating and interpreting experience, or finding reality in the
fullest and most harmonious statement
of the facts of experience, but in seeking
some kind of "reality" behind the phenomenal world, and then brushing the
latter away as a useless curtain.

There must, of course, have been exceptions to this, particularly after *mahāyāna* doctrine had arisen and was concentrating attention on the relief of the
pain and suffering of all creatures. Undoubtedly it gave an impetus to the study
of the sciences allied to medicine. This
may be seen, for example, in the biogra-
phy of the Central Asian missionary monk
Fo-Thu-Têng (fl. + 310), translated and
commented by A. F. Wright. On an
earlier page, details were given of the
books of Indian learning in subjects such
as pharmaceutical botany which were
made available in Chinese before the
Thang. But all were lost during the medieval period, and since the elements in
developed Chinese science which can be
traced to Indian sources are surprisingly
few, it does not seem that Buddhism
played an important part in moulding it,

though assuredly some science was carried from India to China by the monks.
Perhaps this was because the Buddhist
communities of monks and their lay supporters in China tended generally to form
a rather closed system, by no means so
intermixed with the indigenous magma of
social and intellectual life as were Taoism
and Confucianism.

In his famous lecture on "Evolution
and Ethics" T. H. Huxley gave a not unsympathetic account of Buddhist thought,
equating the inherited character of individual men with the load of *karma*.
Although he made it clear that he considered Buddhism as a whole an indefensible escape from the world of reality,
his observations were later seized upon
by Lafcadio Hearn, who in a characteristically elegant but philosophically vague
essay, sought to show that Buddhist
thought had anticipated the recognition
of the "ethical significance of the inex-
plicable laws of heredity." Such an attempt to show that Buddhist thought is
similar to, or at least not incompatible
with, the world-outlook of modern science, was carried further a decade later
in a more elaborate work by Dahlke, and
is now renewed by my friend John Blo-
feld. I regret that I find myself unable to
regard these efforts as more than *tours-
de-force* of religious apologetic. The question of compatibility within an individual
personality is of course one thing (as we
know from the celebrated case of Fara-
day), and that of historical effects and
influences quite another. It was natural
that in modern times Buddhists should
seek to reconcile their faith with modern
science, just as in Europe floods of literature have been devoted to the same problem as it affected Christianity.

In this connection I should like to cite
the works of another friend, Wang Chi-
Thung, the venerable engineer, one of
the few men who mastered the old learning under the Chhing examination system, and also the natural sciences of the

new world. Himself a student of the famous Buddhist scholar Yang Wên-Hui, he has tried, in books such as *Yin Ming Fu Chêng Li Lun Mo Hsiang* (Elucidations of the Buddhist Classics), to reconcile science and Buddhism.

These apologetics take as their starting-point the given situation, and do not go into the matter historically. Yet it remains strange that the law of *karma* was never extended so as to give rise to the concept of scientific law. "The operation of *karma*," as Streeter said, "was conceived not juristically as the punishment of a continuing ego, but naturalistically in terms of a law of cause and effect, which was thought of almost as mechanistically as in the physical sciences." Without anticipating here what will be said at a later point about the differentiation of the concepts of juridical and scientific law in East Asia as contrasted with Europe, one cannot but call attention to the remarkable failure of Buddhist ideas of law to give rise to natural science. There were presumably two reasons for this. First there was no incentive to do any serious thinking about the non-human, non-moral universe, conceived as it was in terms of *māyā*, a kind of disagreeable cinema performance which one was compelled to watch, or going on in a hall from which one had the greatest difficulty in getting out. Secondly, though the operation of the "law" of cause and effect as such may seem to modern minds quite obviously neutral morally, the moral functions attributed to it were really the only part which interested the Buddhists at all. In a sense, impersonal cosmic inevitability was only a superficial dress with which they clothed their profound religious belief in divine justice. It was therefore useless as a catalyst of causal science.

There are certain specific theories associated with Buddhism, it must be admitted, which probably had a broadening effect upon Chinese minds, and might perhaps have predisposed them for modern science. One was the conviction of the infinity of space and time, of a plurality of worlds, and of almost endless lapses of time, reckoned in *kalpas* (*chieh*). Buddhist writings often speak of the enormous number of beings existing, for instance, in a single drop of water or a mote of dust. This may be illustrated by a passage from a work at least as early as the + 6th century, the *Lokasthiti Abhidharma Śāstra* (*Li Shih A-Pi-Than Lun*), which is mainly concerned with the motions of the sun and moon. It might almost be talking of the "light-years" of modern astronomy.

Monks enquired of Buddha the Illustrious how distant Jambūdvīpa was from the Brahma World. Buddha replied, "It is very far. If, for instance, on the fifteenth day of the ninth month at full moon a man in the Brahma World should throw down a square stone a thousand feet long and broad, it would do no harm for a long time, for only in the following year at the same date would the stone reach Jambūdvīpa."

Another notion allows us to go further, and to say that it was probably responsible for the recognition of the true nature of fossils in China long before they were understood in Europe; this was the theory of recurrent world-catastrophes or conflagrations, in which sea and land were turned upside down, and all things returned to a state of chaos before redifferentiating into a normal world again. Four phases of these cycles were recognised, differentiation (*chhêng*), stagnation (*chu*), destruction (*huai*) and chaos or emptiness (*khung*). Later we shall see how this theory was taken over by the Neo-Confucians. And its heuristic value for palaeontology will clearly appear. But it may well be held that both these theories were broadly Indian rather than specifically Buddhist, so that Buddhism conveyed them to China rather than itself inventing them. In any case we cannot afford to dismiss them with a superior smile, for in our own time some of the most eminent astronomers (such as de Sitter) have found reasons for thinking that our universe may have undergone successive cycles of expansion and contraction.

Another point at which Buddhism made contact with Chinese scientific thought—it would be going rather too far to say either that it stimulated it in this direction, or that it added much to it—was in all that concerned the processes of biological change. This naturally involved both phylogeny and ontogeny. The doctrine of reincarnation or metempsychosis naturally aroused interest once more in those remarkable transformations in which the Chinese had always believed, generalising their correct observations of metamorphosing insects to imaginary metamorphoses of frogs and birds. If birds could turn into mussels, it was less surprising that men might do so too (if their load of bad *karma* was sufficiently heavy) or into *pretas* (hungry ghosts) if it was worse. Such were the ends of life-cycles, but the beginnings of life-cycles were equally interesting, and a certain tendency therefore manifested itself for a re-examination of embryology. Although the inhibitory factors operating on Chinese science prevented much of importance being done, we may yet trace a distinct parallel between the influence of Buddhist ideas in this connection in China, and the strong influence exerted upon European 17th- and 18th-century embryology by Christian theological theories (entry of the soul into the embryo, transmission of original sin, etc.). Let us give an example.

In the *Mêng Chai Pi Than* (Essays from the Mêng Hall) of Chêng Ching-Wang, we have an early + 12th-century (Sung) elaboration of the famous passage of *Chuang Tzu* already quoted on biological transformations. The author follows Chuang Tzu's thought, tries to analyse the changes, links them with the conception of the "ladder of souls," arrives at the idea of innate tendencies, and ends by a distinctively Buddhist interpretation. Chêng Ching-Wang wrote:

Chuang Chou said, "All things arise from germs (*chi*) and go back to germs." This is also recorded in the *Lieh Tzu* book, which has a more complete statement. When I lived in the mountains and quietly observed the transformations of things, I saw many examples of it. The outstanding ones are that earthworms turn into lilies, and that wheat, when it has rotted, turns into moths. From the ordinary principles of things (*wu li*) we cannot analyse these phenomena. (One would suppose that) whenever such a transformation occurs, there must be some perception (*chih*) which beings about an inclination (*hsiang*) for it.

Now the change from the earthworm into the lily is a change from a thing which possesses perception (*chih*) into a thing which has none. But the change from wheat grains into moths is just the opposite. When the earthworm winds itself in the earth into a ball during the stage when it is intending to change, the shape of the lily (bulb) is already formed. Wheat (grains) are changed into moths in one night; they appear like flying dust.

According to the Buddhists, these changes are brought about by extremely real and pure intentions. From these general and specific causes (*yin yuan*) such phenomena arise. Take the everyday fact of the hen hatching the egg, for example; we know that the egg comes from the hen itself, but how can you explain the fact that a hen can hatch a duck's egg, and even, as Chuang Tzu records, that a hen can hatch a swan's egg?

As for the change from the wheat (grains) into the moths, they are actually produced from the "seeds" (*chung*) of the moths, and the wheat is first altered (*hua*); if not, it could not change itself into moths.

From the above argument, whenever intentions (*nien*) grow up, whether good or bad, there must be some result. Hou Chi was born from a footprint; Chhi from a stone; these things are undoubtedly true. The *Chin Kuang Ming Ching* records that with constant flowing, water is changed into fish, which all have life from Heaven; this is beyond doubt. Unfortunately, I fear that many people do not believe it.

Here, then, we have, in the early + 12th century, a real effort to observe, and to understand, the nature of biological transformations, and it is obviously connected with Buddhist ideas concerning metempsychosis.

The case is similar for embryology. Hübotter has translated and annotated a Buddhist sūtra on pregnancy and foetal development, which we shall later examine. Verging on the same subject is the *Yuan Jen Lun* (Discourse on the Origin of Man) by the monk Ho Tsung-Mi (+ 779 to + 841), which has been translated by Haas. More on the Taoist side, but doubtless influenced by the same current, are the discussions in the *Sêng Shen Ching* (Canon on the Generation of the Spirits in Man), which must be earlier than + 500, and on which we have a valuable paper by Gauchet. Similar material is contained in the + 11th-century *Lo Shan Lu* of Li Chang-Ling . . .

All in all, however, the problem of analysing fully the antagonistic effects of Buddhism on East Asian science remains.

Perhaps it sprang from deeper causes than any which have so far in this Section been put into words. In the last resort, Buddhism was a profound rejection of the world, a world which, each in their different ways, both Confucianism and Taoism accepted. The Buddhists had what was essentially a "sour-grapes" philosophy; from the transience of all earthly joys and pleasures they deduced their unreality and worthlessness, but it was a *non sequitur*. Inhabitants as we are of a world so much more liberated from pain and fear by true knowledge of Nature, and its application in machines, it is extremely difficult to place ourselves in the position of the ancient and medieval Buddhists. The insecurity of life was then so great, disease and death were everywhere, life was cheap; and the little nuclei of human happiness, the lovers or the young parents of children, could be exploded in a moment by drought, by flood, or by the activities of warring armies, without the hope of finding one another again except by merest chance. In such circumstances it was understandable that men and women should centre their hopes, if not on another world, at least on a creed and a way of life which did not depend upon the security of this; it was understandable that the *meditatio mortis* should flourish; and it was natural that they should unite in calling the visible world ugly because they could not make it happy. The only surprising thing is that throughout these centuries Buddhism did not meet with even greater success, and that so large a number of Confucians continued to make the fundamental and significant affirmation that life *was* worth living in the well-ordered society, and that however bleak the immediate prospect might be, men would always arise who would practice what Confucius had taught as to *how* society could be well ordered. Similarly, the Taoists, walking, as ever, outside society, refused to give up their naturalistic and realistic world-picture. The external world was, for them, real and no illusion; the sage, by following after its phenomena, would learn how to control them. A sexual element was at the heart of all things, and asceticism, in so far as it was valuable at all, was simply a means to an end, the attainment of material immortality, so that the enjoyment of Nature and her beauty might have no end.

Here is the keynote. One of the preconditions absolutely necessary for the development of science is an acceptance of Nature, not a turning away from her. If the scientist passes the beauty by, it is only because he is entranced by the mechanism. But other-worldly rejection of this world seems to be formally and psychologically incompatible with the development of science.

6 · The Relationship of Religion to Politics

MAX WEBER

Every religiously grounded unworldly love and indeed every ethical religion must, in similar measure and for similar reasons, experience tensions with the sphere of political behavior. This tension appears as soon as religion has progressed to anything like a status of equality with the sphere of political associations. To be sure, the ancient political god of the locality, even where he was an ethical and universally powerful god, existed merely for the protection of the political interests of his followers' associations.

Even the Christian God is still invoked as a god of war and as a god of our fathers, in much the same way that local gods were invoked in the ancient *polis*. One is reminded of the fact that for centuries Christian ministers have prayed along the beaches of the North Sea for a "blessing upon the strand," in reaction to the numerous shipwrecks there. On its part the priesthood generally depended

SOURCE. Max Weber, "The Relationship of Religion to Politics," from Max Weber, *The Sociology of Religion*, Boston: Beacon Press, 1963, pp. 223–236. Reprinted by permission of The Beacon Press, copyright by Beacon Press (English translation from the fourth edition of J. C. B. Mohr [Paul Siebeck] original edition in German).

upon the political association, either directly or indirectly. This dependence is especially strong in those contemporary churches which derive support from governmental subvention. It was particularly noteworthy where the priests were court or patrimonial officials of rulers or landed magnates, e.g., the *purohita* of India or the Byzantine court bishops of Constantine. The same dependence also arose wherever the priests themselves were either enfeoffed feudal lords exercising secular power, or scions of noble priestly families, e.g., as during the medieval period in the Occident. Among the Chinese and Hindus as well as the Jews, the sacred bards, whose compositions were practically everywhere incorporated into the scriptures, sang the praises of heroic death. According to the canonical books of the Brahmins, a heroic death was as much an ideal obligation of the Kshatriya caste member at the age when he had "seen the son of his son" as withdrawal from the world into the forests for meditation was an obligation of members of the Brahmin caste. Of course, magical religion had no conception of religious wars. But for magical religion, and even for the ancient religion of Yahweh, political victory and especially vengeance against the enemy constituted the real reward granted by god.

The more the priesthood attempted to organize itself as a power independent of the political authorities, and the more rationalized its ethic became, the more this position shifted. The contradiction within the priestly preaching, between brotherliness toward fellow religionists and the glorification of war against outsiders, did not as a general rule decisively stigmatize martial virtues and heroic qualities. This was so because a distinction could be drawn between just and unjust wars. However, this distinction was a product of pharisaical thought, which was unknown to the old and genuine warrior ethics.

Of far greater importance was the rise of congregational religions among politically demilitarized peoples under the control of priests, such as the Jews, and also the rise of large and increasingly important groups of people who, though comparatively unwarlike, became increasingly important for the priests' maintenance of their power position wherever they had developed into an independent organization. The priesthood unquestioningly welcomed the characteristic virtues of these classes, viz., simplicity, patient resignation to trouble, humble acceptance of existing authority, and friendly forgiveness and passivity in the face of injustice, especially since these virtues were useful in establishing the ascendancy of an ethical god and of the priests themselves. These virtues were also complementary to the special religious virtue of the powerful, namely magnanimous charity (caritas), since the patriarchal donors desired these virtues of resignation and humble acceptance in those who benefited from their assistance.

The more a religion acquired the aspects of a "communal religion" (Gemeinde-Religiosität), the more political circumstances co-operated to lend a religious transfiguration to the ethic of the

subjugated. Thus, Jewish prophecy, in a realistic recognition of the external political situation, preached resignation to the dominion of the great powers, as a fate apparently desired by God. As this type of religion spread, several factors continued to lend distinctive religious value to the aforementioned feminine virtues of the subjugated. One such social factor was the assignment to the priests of control over the masses, which was first practiced systematically by foreign rulers like the Persians and later by native Jewish rulers. Other social factors were the distinctively unwarlike activities of the priests themselves and their universal experience of the particularly intense effect of religious stimuli upon women. But there tended in this direction much more than the "slave revolt" in the realm of morality under the leadership of the priests. In addition, every ascetic, and especially mystical and personal quest for salvation which emerged among those individuals who had left tradition behind took this line. This occurred because of the very nature of the autonomous laws of religion, which we have examined. Certain typical external situations also contributed to this development, e.g., the apparently senseless changes of limited and ephemeral small political power structures in contrast to universalistic religions and relatively unitary social cultures such as that of India. Two other historical processes operating in the opposite direction also contributed to the same development: universal pacification and the elimination of all struggles for power in the great world empires, and particularly the bureaucratization of all political dominion, as in the Roman Empire.

All these factors removed the ground from under the political and social interests involved in a warlike struggle for power and involved in a social class conflict, thus tending to generate an antipolitical rejection of the world and to favor the development of a religious ethic of brotherly love that renounced all violence. The power of the apolitical Christian religion of love was not derived from interests in social reform, nor from any such thing as "proletarian instincts," but rather from the complete loss of such concerns. The same motivation accounts for the increasing importance of all salvation religions and congregational religions since the first and second centuries of the Roman period. This transformation was carried out, not only or even primarily by the subjugated classes who in their slave revolts had become the carriers of special anti-political religions, but principally by those who had lost interest in politics, who were without influence in politics, or who had become disgusted by politics.

The altogether universal experience that violence breeds violence, that social or economic power interests may combine with idealistic reforms and even with revolutionary movements, and that the employment of violence against some particular injustice produces as its ultimate result the victory, not of the greater justice, but of the greater power or cleverness, did not remain concealed, at least not from the intellectuals who lacked political interests. This recognition continued to evoke the most radical demands for the ethic of brotherly love, i.e., that evil should not be resisted by force, an injunction that is common to Buddhism and to the preaching of Jesus. But the ethic of brotherly love is also characteristic of mystical religions, because their peculiar quest for salvation fosters an attitude of humility and self-surrender as a result of its minimization of activity in the world and its affirmation of the necessity of passing through the world incognito, so to speak, as the only proven method for demonstrating salvation. Indeed, from the purely psychological point of view, mystical religion must necessarily

come to this conclusion by virtue of its characteristically acosmistic and non-specific experience of love. Yet every pure intellectualism bears within itself the possibility of such a mystical development.

On the other hand, inner-worldly asceticism can compromise with the facts of the political power structures by interpreting them as instruments for the rationalized ethical transformation of the world and for the control of sin. It must be noted, however, that the coexistence is by no means as easy in this case as in the case where economic acquisitive interests are concerned. For public political activity leads to a far greater surrender of rigorous ethical requirements than is produced by private economic acquisitiveness, since political activity is oriented to average human qualities, to compromises, to craft, and to the employment of other ethically suspect devices and people, and thereby oriented to the relativization of all goals. Thus, it is very striking that under the glorious regime of the Maccabees, after the first intoxication of the war of liberation had been dissipated, there arose among the most pious Jews a party which preferred alien hegemony to rule by the national kingdom. This may be compared to the preference found among many Puritan denominations for the subjection of the churches to the dominion of unbelievers, because genuineness of religion can be regarded as proven in such churches. In both these cases two distinct motives were operative. One was that a genuine commitment in religion could be truly demonstrated only in martyrdom; the other was the theoretical insight that the political apparatus of force could not possibly provide a place for purely religious virtues, whether uncompromising rational ethics or acosmistic fraternalism. This is one source of the affinity between inner-worldly asceticism and the advocacy of the minimization of state control such as was represented by the doctrine of the "Manchester school."

The conflict of ascetic ethics, as well as of the mystically oriented temper of brotherly love, with the apparatus of domination which is basic to all political institutions produced the most varied types of tension and compromise. Naturally, the polarity between religion and politics is least wherever, as in Confucianism, religion is equivalent to a belief in spirits or simply a belief in magic, and ethics is no more than a clever accommodation to the world on the part of the educated man. Nor does any conflict at all between religion and politics exist wherever, as in Islam, religion makes obligatory the violent propagandizing of a true prophecy which consciously eschews universal conversion and enjoins the subjugation of unbelievers under the dominion of a ruling class dedicated to the religious war as one of the basic postulates of its faith, without however recognizing the salvation of the subjugated. The practice of coercion poses no problem, since god is pleased by the forcible dominion of the faithful over the infidels, who are tolerated once they have been subjugated.

Inner-worldly asceticism reached a similar solution to the problem of the relation between religion and politics wherever, as in radical Calvinism, it represented as God's will the domination over the sinful world, for the purpose of controlling it, of religious virtuosi belonging to the "pure" church. This view was fundamental in the theocracy of New England, in practice if not explicitly, though naturally it became involved with compromises of various kinds. Another instance of the absence of any conflict between religion and politics is to be found in the intellectualistic salvation doctrines of India, such as Buddhism and Jainism, in which every relationship to

the world and to action within the world is broken off, and in which the personal exercise of violence as well as resistance to violence is absolutely prohibited and is indeed without any object. Actual conflicts between concrete demands of a state and concrete religious injunctions arise only when a religion is the pariah faith of a group that is excluded from political equality but still believes in the religious prophecies of a divinely appointed restoration of its social level. This was the case in Judaism, which never in theory rejected the state and its coercion but, on the contrary, expected in the Messiah their own masterful political ruler, an expectation that was sustained at least until the time of the destruction of the Temple by Hadrian.

Wherever communal religions have rejected all employment of force as an abomination to god and have sought to require their members' avoidance of all contact with violence, without however reaching the consistent conclusion of absolute flight from the world, the conflict between religion and politics has led either to martyrdom or to passive antipolitical sufferance of the coercive regime. History shows that religious anarchism has hitherto been only a short-lived phenomenon, because the intensity of faith which makes it possible is in only an ephemeral charisma. Yet there have been independent political organizations which were based, not on a purely anarchistic foundation, but on a foundation of consistent pacifism. The most important of these was the Quaker community in Pennsylvania, which for two generations actually succeeded, in contrast to all the neighboring colonies, in existing side by side with the Indians, and indeed prospering, without recourse to violence. Such situations continued until the conflicts of the great colonial powers made a fiction of pacifism. Finally, the American War of Independence, which was waged in the name of the basic principles of Quakerism though the orthodox Quakers did not participate because of their principle of non-resistance, led to the discrediting of this principle, even inwardly. Moreover, the corresponding policy of the tolerant admission of religious dissidents into Pennsylvania brought even the Quakers there to a policy of gerrymandering political wards, which caused them increasing uneasiness and ultimately led them to withdraw from political participation in and co-responsibility for the government.

Typical examples of completely passive indifference to the political dimension of society, from a variety of motives, are found in such groups as the genuine Mennonites, in most Baptist communities, and especially in the numerous Russian sects in various places. The absolute renunciation of the use of force by these groups led them into acute conflicts with the political authorities only where military service was demanded of the individuals concerned. Indeed, attitudes toward war, even of religious denominations that did not teach an absolutely anti-political attitude, have varied in particular cases, depending upon whether the wars in question were fought to protect the religion's freedom of worship from attack by political authority or fought for purely political purposes. For these two types of warlike employment of violence, two diametrically opposite slogans prevailed. On the one hand, there was the purely passive sufferance of alien power and the withdrawal from any personal participation in the exercise of violence, culminating ultimately in personal martyrdom. This was of course the position of mystical apoliticism, with its absolute indifference to the world, as well as the position of those types of inner-worldly asceticism which were pacifistic in principle. But even a purely personal religion

of faith frequently generated political indifference and religious martyrdom, inasmuch as it recognized neither a rational order of the outer world pleasing to God, nor a rational domination of the world desired by God. Thus, Luther completely rejected religious revolutions as well as religious wars.

The other possible standpoint was that of violent resistance to the employment of force against religion. The concept of a religious revolution was not consistent with a rationalism oriented to an ascetic mastery of mundane affairs, which taught that sacred institutions and institutions pleasing to God exist within this world. This was the case in Christianity, and particularly in Calvinism, which made it a religious obligation to defend the faith against tyranny by the use of force. It should be added, however, that Calvin taught that this defense might be undertaken only at the initiative of the proper authorities, in keeping with the character of an institutional church. The obligation to bring about a revolution in behalf of the faith was naturally taught by the religions that engaged in wars of missionary enterprise and by their derivative sects, like the Mahdists and other sects in Islam, including the Sikhs—a Hindu sect that was originally pacifist but passed under the influence of Islam and became eclectic.

The representatives of the two opposed viewpoints just described sometimes took virtually contradictory positions toward wars that had no religious motivation. Religions that applied ethically rationalized demands to the political realm had necessarily to take a more fundamentally negative attitude toward purely political wars than those religions that accepted the institutions of the world as "given" and relatively indifferent in value. The unconquered army of Cromwell petitioned Parliament for the abolition of forcible conscription, on the ground that a Christian should participate only in those wars the justice of which could be affirmed by his own conscience. From this standpoint, the mercenary army might be regarded as a relatively ethical institution, inasmuch as the mercenary would have to settle with God and his conscience as to whether he would take up this calling. The employment of force by the state can have moral sanction only when the force is used for the control of sins, for the glory of God, and for combating religious evils—in short, only for religious purposes. On the other hand, the view of Luther, who absolutely rejected religious wars and revolutions as well as any active resistance, was that only the secular authority, whose domain is untouched by the rational postulates of religion, has the responsibility of determining whether political wars are just or unjust. Hence, the individual subject has no reason to burden his own conscience with this matter if only he gives active obedience to the political authority in this and in all other matters which do not destroy his relationship to God.

The position of ancient and medieval Christianity in relation to the state as a whole oscillated or, more correctly, shifted its center of gravity from one to another of several distinct points of view. At first there was a complete abomination of the existing Roman empire, whose existence until the very end of time was taken for granted in antiquity by everyone, even Christians. The empire was regarded as the dominion of Anti-Christ. A second view was complete indifference to the state, and hence passive sufferance of the use of force, which was deemed to be unrighteous in every case. This entailed active compliance with all the coercive obligations imposed by the state, e.g., the payment of taxes which did not directly imperil religious salvation. For the true intent of the New Testament verse about "rendering unto Caesar the things which are Caesar's"

is not the meaning deduced by modern harmonizing interpretations, namely a positive recognition of the obligation to pay taxes, but rather the reverse: an absolute indifference to all the affairs of the mundane world.

Two other viewpoints were possible. One entailed withdrawal from concrete activities of the political community, such as the cult of the emperors, because and insofar as such participation necessarily led to sin. Nevertheless, the state's authority was accorded positive recognition as being somehow desired by God, even when exercised by unbelievers and even though inherently sinful. It was taught that the state's authority, like all the institutions of this world, is an ordained punishment for the sin brought upon man by Adam's fall, which the Christian must obediently take upon himself. Finally, the authority of the state, even when exercised by unbelievers, might be evaluated positively, due to our condition of sin, as an indispensable instrument, based upon the divinely implanted natural knowledge of religiously unilluminated heathen, for the social control of reprehensible sins and as a general condition for all mundane existence pleasing to God.

Of these four points of view, the first two mentioned belong primarily to the period of eschatological expectation, but occasionally they come to the fore even in a later period. As far as the last of the four is concerned, ancient Christianity did not really go beyond it in principle, even after it had been recognized as the state religion. Rather, the great change in the attitude of Christianity toward the state took place in the medieval church, as the investigations of Troeltsch have brilliantly demonstrated. But the problem in which Christianity found itself involved as a result, while not limited to this religion, nevertheless generated a whole complex of difficulties peculiar to Christianity alone, partly from internal religious causes and partly from the operation of non-religious factors. This critical complex of difficulties concerned the relationship of the so-called "law of nature" to religious revelation on the one hand, and to positive political institutions and their activities on the other.

We shall have to go into this matter at somewhat greater length, both in connection with our exposition of the forms of religious communities and in our analysis of the forms of domination. But the following point may be made here regarding the theoretical solution of these problems as it affects personal ethics: the general schema according to which religion customarily solves the problem of the tension between religious ethics and the non-ethical or unethical requirements of life in the political and economic structures of power within the world is to relativize and differentiate ethics into an organic ethic of vocation and a contrasting ascetic ethic. This holds true whenever a religion is dominant within a political organization or occupies a privileged status, and particularly when it is a religion of institutional grace.

Christian doctrine, as formulated by Aquinas for example, to some degree assumed the view, already common in animistic beliefs regarding souls and the world beyond, that there are purely natural differences among men, completely independent of any effects of sin, and that these natural differences determine the diversity of destinies in this world and beyond. Troeltsch has correctly stressed the point that this formulation of Christian doctrine differs from the view found in Stoicism and earliest Christianity of an original golden age and a blissful state of generalized anarchistic equality of all human beings.

At the same time, however, Christianity interpreted the power relationships of the mundane world in a metaphysical way. Human beings are condemned— whether as a result of original sin, of an individual causality of *karma*, or of the corruption of the world deriving from a basic dualism—to suffer violence, toil, pain, hate, and above all differences in class and caste position within the world. The various callings or castes have been providentially ordained, and each of them has been assigned some specific, indispensable function desired by god or determined by the impersonal world order, so that different ethical obligations devolve upon each status. The diverse occupations and castes are compared to the constituent portions of an organism, in this type of theory. The various relationships of power which emerge in such a social system must therefore be regarded as divinely ordained relationships of authority. Accordingly, any revolt or rebellion against them, or even the raising of vital claims other than those corresponding to one's status in society, is reprehensible to god because they are expressions of creaturely self-aggrandizement and pride, which are destructive of sacred tradition. The virtuosi of religion, be they of an ascetic or contemplative type, are also assigned their specific responsibility within such an organic order, just as specific functions have been allocated to princes, warriors, judges, artisans, and peasants. This allocation of responsibilities to religious virtuosi is intended to produce a treasure of supernumerary good works which the institution of grace may thereupon distribute. By subjecting himself to the revealed truth and to the correct sentiment of love, the individual will achieve, and that within the established institutions of the world, happiness in this world and reward in the life to come.

For Islam, this organic conception and its entire complex of related problems was much more remote, since Islam rejected universalism, regarding the ideal social stratification as consisting of believers and unbelievers or pariah peoples, with the former dominating the latter. Accordingly, Islam left the pariah peoples entirely to themselves in all matters which were of indifference to religion. It is true that the mystical quest for salvation and ascetic virtuoso religion did conflict with institutional orthodoxy in the Muslim religion. It is also true that Islam did experience conflicts between sacred and profane law, which always arise when positive sacred norms of the law have developed. Finally, Islam did have to face certain questions of orthodoxy in the theocratic constitution. But Islam did not confront the ultimate problem of the relationship between religious ethics and secular institutions, which is the fundamental problem of the relation between law and religion.

On the other hand, the Hindu books of law promulgated an organic, traditionalistic ethic of vocation, similar in structure to medieval Catholicism, only more consistent, and certainly more consistent than the rather thin Lutheran doctrine regarding the *status ecclesiasticus, politicus,* and *economicus.* As we have already seen, the status system in India actually combined a caste ethic with a distinctive doctrine of salvation. That is, it held that an individual's chances of an ever higher ascent in future incarnations upon earth depend on his having fulfilled the obligations of his own caste, be they ever so disesteemed socially. This belief had the effect of inducing a radical acceptance of the social order, especially among the very lowest classes, the classes which would have most to gain in any transmigration of souls.

On the other hand, the Hindu theodicy would have regarded as absurd the medieval Christian doctrine, as set forth for example by Beatrice in the *Paradiso* of Dante, that the class differences which obtain during one's brief span of life upon earth will be perpetuated into some permanent "existence" in the world beyond. Indeed, such a view would have deprived the strict traditionalism of the Hindu organic ethic of vocation of all the infinite hopes for the future entertained by the pious Hindu who believed in the transmigration of souls and the possibility of an ever more elevated form of life upon this earth. Hence, even from the purely religious point of view, the Christian doctrine of the perpetuation of class distinctions into the next world had the effect of providing a much less secure foundation for the traditional stratification of vocations than did the steel-like anchorage of caste to the altogether different religious promises contained in the doctrine of metempsychosis.

The medieval and the Lutheran traditionalistic ethics of vocation actually rested on a general presupposition, one that is increasingly rare, which both share with the Confucian ethic: that power relationships in both the economic and political spheres have a purely personal character. In these spheres of the execution of justice and particularly in political administration, a whole organized structure of personal relations of subordination exists which is dominated by caprice and grace, indignation and love, and most of all by the mutual piety and devotion of masters and subalterns, after the fashion of the family. Thus, these relationships of domination have a character to which one may apply ethical requirements in the same way that one applies them to every other purely personal relationship.

Yet as we shall see later, it is quite certain that the "masterless slavery" (Wagner) of the modern proletariat and above all the whole realm of the rationalized institution of the state—the so-called "rascally state" (*Rackers von Staat*) so abominated by romanticism— no longer possess this personalistic character. In a personalistic order of status it is quite clear that one must act differently toward persons of different statuses. The only problem that may arise on occasion, even for Thomas Aquinas, is how this is to be construed. Today, however, the *homo politicus,* as well as the *homo economicus,* performs his duty best when he acts without regard to the person in question, *sine ira et studio,* without hate and without love, without personal predilection and therefore without grace, but sheerly in accordance with the factual, material responsibility imposed by his calling, and not as a result of any concrete personal relationship. In short, modern man discharges his responsibility best when he acts as closely as possible in accordance with the rational regulations of the modern power system. Modern procedures of justice impose capital punishment upon the malefactor, not out of personal indignation or the need for vengeance, but with complete detachment and for the sake of objective norms and ends, simply for the working out of the rational autonomous lawfulness inherent in justice. This is comparable to the impersonal retribution of *karma,* in contrast to Yahweh's fervent quest for vengeance.

The use of force within the political community increasingly assumes the form of a material and social order founded on a lawful state. But from the point of view of religion, this is merely an effective mimicry of brutality. All politics is oriented to the material facts of the dominant interest of the state, to realism, and to the autonomous end of maintaining the external and internal distribution of power. These goals, again, must necessarily seem completely senseless from the religious point of view. Yet only in this way does the realm of politics acquire a uniquely rational dynamic of its own, once brilliantly formulated by Napoleon, which appears as thoroughly alien to every ethic of brotherliness as do the rationalized economic institutions. The accommodation that contemporary ecclesiastical ethics is making to this situation cannot be discussed in detail here. In general the compromise takes form through reaction to each concrete situation as it arises. Certainly, the goal of the Catholic church is to salvage its ecclesiastical power interests, which have increasingly become objectified into a doctrine of the fundamental interests of the church, by the employment of the same modern instruments of power employed by secular institutions.

7 · Religion and Politics

ROBERT R. ALFORD

The connection between religion and politics arises as a problem only in nations which are not religiously homogeneous. Classical political thinkers such as Aristotle took it for granted that re-

SOURCE. Robert R. Alford, "Religion and Politics," slightly adapted from Robert R. Alford, *Party and Society: The Anglo-American Democracies,* Chicago: Rand McNally and Co., 1963, pp. 49–58.

ligious homogeneity was a condition of political stability, and they were right. Where opposing beliefs about ultimate values enter the political arena, they exacerbate struggles by preventing compromise.[1] In modern non-homogeneous

[1] For a modern form of the argument that religious homogeneity is necessary for political stability, see Leicester Webb, "Churches and the Australian Community" in E. D.

societies, three changes (occurring in different degrees in different societies) may have moderated conflicts over ultimate values: secularization, the weakening of religious belief in general; compartmentalization, the separation of religion from other areas of life; and homogenization, the convergence of many religions upon a vaguely-defined consensus on teaching and practice.[2] Actually all of these processes, or contradictory forms of them, may be going on simultaneously.

The largely Protestant societies such as the Anglo-American countries have possibly moved farther along these three paths of change than other countries. Protestantism, with its emphasis upon the separation of Church and State, undoubtedly has encouraged a secular norm in the behavior of parties and voters. Even where religious issues and motives exist, they have had to remain covert, because they are illegitimate in the political realm.

In this respect, the Anglo-American countries differ greatly from the continental European countries. Religious parties do not exist in the Anglo-American countries, in sharp contrast to such continental nations as Italy, France, Belgium, Norway, and the Netherlands. No parties based almost exclusively upon an appeal to religious values and identifications have gained any appreciable strength in the Anglo-American countries. Although some parties have gained most of their support from particular religious groups (the nationalist parties *Bloc Populaire* and *Union Nationale* in Quebec, and the splinter Labor party in Australia gain the great bulk of their support from Catholics), the parties have never based their appeals or programs upon this characteristic of their supporters. This difference between the Anglo-American countries and some of the continental European ones is almost a defining characteristic of the former: they are "secular, homogeneous" political systems.[2a]

One reason for this difference may be suggested. In the continental countries where religious parties are strong, religious freedom was won at the same time and was linked with the achievement of political freedom. The consequence was that to this day, religion, class, and politics have been closely linked. In Britain, on the other hand, these issues emerged separately and were solved separately; as a result, not only were Church and State legally separated, but also the development of legitimate issues and parties connecting the two was prevented.

Certain features of the Reformation in England in the 1500's, unlike those of the Reformations on the continent, may have contributed to the relatively high degree of separation of church and state and the legitimacy of religious pluralism in British political culture. Since varying political stratagems rather than a constant religious ideal initiated the English Reformation, a number of

French, ed., *Melbourne Studies in Education, 1958–1959* (Melbourne: Melbourne University Press, 1960), pp. 89–131, and his lecture "Politics and Polity" (Canberra, Australian National University, 1960). Western societies, as he sees it, are unified by certain political values closely associated with Christianity: the idea of justice and the concept that the polity is something toward which men who are conscious of moral freedom and responsibility will naturally be drawn.

[2] See Gerhard Lenski, *The Religious Factor* (New York: Doubleday, 1960), p. 9, for this usage of the term "compartmentalization." However, Lenski later uses the word for the opposite phenomenon: the tendency for the whole of life to be organized around religious membership. He cites the Netherlands and Lebanon as the best examples of the latter (p. 326 ff.).

[2a] See Chapter 1 of *Party and Society, op. cit.,* for a discussion of the political culture of the Anglo-American countries.

religious options came to exist. The political authority in England undertook to break Catholic power without any single religious ethic or ideology guiding its efforts; it followed a continually oscillating course of strategy vis-à-vis the Church in the period 1530–1560. The crown of England itself passed through many hands during this period, and every change of government brought a sharp change of position regarding the Church. After three decades of policy fluctuation, the political authority could no longer re-establish a single dominant religion. A minority of the population remained firmly Roman Catholic, but other minorities just as firmly adhered to one or another of the many church reforms and systems of dogma which had been pressed upon the English people in the preceding decades. The English state had by the 1560's missed its historic opportunity, as no other European state had, to take religious decisions out of the hands of the people. Religious pluralism and the separation of the state from a single coercive church were thereby established in England—and subsequently in its colonies—as in no other country.[3]

Thus, a firmer historical basis for the secularization of politics has existed in the Anglo-American countries than in certain continental nations. In the colonies, the institutional domination of Protestantism was even less of an issue, and the Catholic church has never been more than a minority religion except in certain regions such as Quebec.[4] It must

be emphasized again, however, that political secularization need not imply the secularization of the whole society. These are two parallel processes which need not be associated.[5]

Another reason for the rise of religious parties in continental Europe and their lack, so far, in the English-speaking countries has been the simple fact that the latter are predominantly Protestant, the former, predominantly Catholic. Where Catholics have made up a majority of the population, and therefore have had an opportunity to carry out Catholic social policies by political means, Catholic parties have arisen and Protestant parties have formed in reaction.[6] In the Anglo-American countries, the autonomous authority of the Catholic church to educate its own members has not been seriously challenged, and that church, as a consequence, has not made militant attempts to influence political life. A modus vivendi has been worked out which has not only strengthened the legitimacy of the national political system, but has made it unnecessary for religious parties to emerge. No religious group of any size in these systems

---

[3] Taken from a summary of results in Herbert Schoeffler, *Wirkungen der Reformation.* [Effects of the Reformation] (Frankfort am Main: Vittorio Klostermann, 1960), pp. 322–24. I am indebted to Reinhard Bendix for this source.

[4] See Seymour M. Lipset, *Political Man* (New York: Doubleday, 1960), pp. 83–85, for a discussion of the ways in which historical resolution of issues colors subsequent political struggles.

[5] In the Netherlands, for example, the percentage describing themselves as "free thinkers," with "no fixed religion," or as "churchless" has increased steadily in each subsequent Census since 1879 to a high of 17 per cent in 1947. Although undoubtedly this figure does not indicate the "real" degree of secularization—since in a country where so few are areligious there must be some pressure to admit being religious—even this trend does not accord with the contrary trend toward religious parties. See M. Fogarty, *Christian Democracy in Western Europe, 1820–1953* (London: Routledge & Kegan Paul, 1957), p. 357.

[6] See Seymour M. Lipset and Juan Linz, "The Social Bases of Political Diversity in Western Democracies" (MSS, Center for Advanced Studies in the Behavioral Sciences, Stanford, Calif., 1956) for some of the general formulations of this section.

has challenged one fundamental premise of a legitimate democratic state: either a secular political culture must exist in a society with more than one important religious group, or homogeneity of religious composition must exist within a state with an explicitly religious basis. It is a measure of the viability of Protestantism, combined with British political institutions and traditions, that each of the Anglo-American countries has to a great degree been able to assimilate the Catholics into a secular political culture.

This achievement stands out even more when the particular situation of Quebec in Canada is considered. Here most of the conditions favoring the development of a religious party are present: a minority religious group is the majority within one of the two largest political units within a federal state; ethnic differences are present; a different language is spoken; and a sense of opposition is felt toward a political party with a historical association with another religion and ethnic group (the Conservatives, based upon English Protestants). Yet no religious party has developed; rather, nationalistic parties flourish. In Latin Europe, in contrast, the connection between a distinctive ethnic culture and Catholicism has produced strong Catholic parties.[7]

In Canada alone of the four Anglo-American countries might we expect such a consequence. Catholics in the United States and Australia are more diverse ethnically and geographically than in Canada, and in Britain the secession of Ireland deprived that issue of its saliency (although even the Irish issue had more of a nationalistic than a religious flavor). This example indicates again that something distinctive about the political culture of the Anglo-American

ican countries affects even the regions and religious groups presumably most isolated from its influence. Quebec has taken the path of an extreme emphasis upon "Canadianism," stressing cultural autonomy within the framework of the Canadian federal union rather than struggling for a separate religiously homogeneous state or forming a religious party.[8]

French-Canadian nationalist parties have not even stressed their religious differences with English-Canada, although they could have easily done so. This failure to emphasize a possible source of regional political solidarity is another mark of the difference between the political culture of the Anglo-American and continental systems. The 1942 nationalist party in Quebec—the *Bloc Populaire*—grew in spite of the refusal of Catholic Action and Cardinal Villeneuve in Quebec to support the party. It clearly had a possible religious appeal and base, however, for the lower clergy welcomed it, seeing the new party as a possible avenue for reversing the "effects of the wartime industrialization upon French-Canadian family life and morals."[9] A religious appeal could conceivably have offset the new party's internal divisions over economic policy. Some of the leaders were crusaders for nationalization of industry, some were big businessmen, and an overriding appeal for religious unity could have tempo-

[7] R. V. Burks, "Catholic Parties in Latin Europe," *Journal of Modern History*, XXIV (September, 1952), 269–86.

[8] Clearly Quebec's policies are determined by many factors, including the fear of joining the "melting pot" United States, but the point here is simply that its nationalistic tendencies have not been reinforced by a serious attempt to raise religious issues. Religion has been only one of the aspects of French-Catholic culture which have been seen by Quebec nationalists as necessary to maintain.

[9] Mason Wade, *The French-Canadians, 1760–1945* (London: Macmillan, 1955), p. 956.

rarily dissolved those differences; yet none was made.[10]

Thus, the primary fact about the political relevance of religion in the Anglo-American countries is that it is *not* the primary fact of political life. The problem then becomes the extent to which religious groups exhibit distinctive patterns of political behavior, and to link this to differences and similarities in social and political processes. While the designation "secular and homogeneous" applies when comparing these societies with others, religion is relevant to political behavior in these countries, although in varying degrees.

Catholics in each of these countries are more likely to vote for the major Left party than are Protestants. In the United States, they are disproportionately Democratic; in Great Britain and Australia, Labor; in Canada, Liberal.[11]

Possible causes of the distinctive political behavior of Catholics in these four countries lie partly in their special religious beliefs which find expression in political issues, but also partly in their position historically as an immigrant and low-status minority in each country. Even in Britain, the Catholics have largely been of Irish descent and have been treated and have regarded themselves as an ethnic minority. Catholics entered the other countries as immigrant minorities and went into low-status occupations. These several characteristics have combined to produce a tendency to vote for the Left party. The Right parties have tended to represent the upper classes, which have also been Protestant and from majority ethnic groups; the Left parties have tended to represent the lower classes, which have been more likely to be Catholic and have minority ethnic status.

Some of these reasons for political differentiation along religious lines are likely to disappear, but some are relatively permanent—again depending on general processes of secularization and homogenization in the society at large. Distinctive Catholic values and institutions are not likely to disappear: thus the issues of religious education and political representation are always present in these countries. These issues take different forms in each nation, and to the extent that they exacerbate Catholic consciousness of minority status, either culturally or

[10] The assimilation of Quebec to a secular political culture must not be overstressed. The Catholic Church in Quebec has a number of rights not possessed by other churches. In addition, there are Catholic trade unions and other religious penetrations into institutions normally secularized in the Anglo-American countries. This in itself makes the extent of political secularism more notable.
[11] Documentation is given in the appropriate chapters of *Party and Society, op. cit.*, but major sources may be mentioned here. For the United States, see Bernard Berelson *et al.*, *Voting* (Chicago: University of Chicago Press, 1954), pp. 71, 333; and Angus Campbell *et al.*, *The American Voter* (New York: Wiley, 1960), pp. 301–6. For Great Britain, see P. Campbell *et al.*, "Voting Behavior in Droylsden in October, 1951," *Journal of the Manchester School of Economic and Social Studies*, XX (1952), 63; and Hans J. Eysenck, *The Psychology of Politics* (London: Routledge & Kegan Paul, 1954), p. 21. For Australia, see Louise Overacker, *The Australian Party System* (New Haven: Yale University Press, 1952), pp. 305–6; and R. N. Spann, "The Catholic Vote in Australia" in Henry Mayer, ed., *Catholics and*

the Free Society: An Australian Symposium (Melbourne: F. W. Cheshire, 1961), pp. 115–41. For Canada, see Robert M. Dawson, *The Government of Canada* (Toronto: University of Toronto Press, 1954), p. 510; and W. Filley, "Social Structure and Canadian Political Parties: The Quebec Case," *Western Political Quarterly*, IX (December, 1958), 900–14. The main focus in *Party and Society, op. cit.*, is upon Protestant-Catholic political differences, for reasons discussed in Chapter 4.

religiously, their voting patterns may deviate from those of Protestants. The historical association of a party with a low-status immigrant group may disappear more readily as Catholics move up in social status and ethnic differences disappear. To put it another way, the purely religious dimension of distinctive political behavior may emerge more clearly after the class and ethnic associations disappear.[12]

The lack of legitimacy of either religious parties or explicitly religious political appeals or even explicitly religiously-motivated voting in the Anglo-American countries does not necessarily mean that distinctive patterns of religious voting are likely to disappear even if the Catholics become completely assimilated ethnically and socio-economically. A compelling argument for the continuation of a Catholic deviation is the continuing failure of the Anglo-American societies to live up to Catholic social policies. The very notion of the separation of Church and State is against traditional Catholic stands.[13] Until the State becomes Catholic or Catholics abandon certain fundamental tenets—such as religious education, opposition to birth control, and other positions—such issues will always be a potential source of religiously-based political cleavage. This distinctiveness does not necessarily have to be exhibited by loyalty to their traditional party, of course.

Catholic voting behavior in these countries is under a complex set of contradictory cross-pressures. Assuming that there is an association between class and party, and one between religion and party, almost every possible combination of class position and party identification involves cross-pressures for Catholics. The matter is further complicated by the contradictory tendencies within Catholicism itself, for it is at one and the same time profoundly conservative religiously and, sometimes, powerfully progressive socially. The very success of the Church in holding its members close may intensify these cross-pressures, since religion cannot as easily become compartmentalized for Catholics as for Protestants.

Middle-class Catholics are under cross-pressures because their class position and the conservative component of Catholicism predisposes them to vote Right. But the historical association of their minority status and ethnic position with the Left party leads them to vote Left.[14] Working-class Catholics are also under cross-pressures because the class and ethnic components of their status and the progressive component of Catholicism predispose them toward a Left vote, but the conservative element of Catholicism draws them toward a Right vote. The political consequences of these complex cross-pressures have not been satisfactorily analyzed comparatively. However, cross-pressures have been held to lead to withdrawal from political activities.[15]

---

[12] The problem of what happens when a minority religious group becomes socially mobile is discussed with special reference to Australia in Chapter 7 of *Party and Society, op. cit.*

[13] The attempts by American Catholic intellectuals such as John Courtney Murray to reconcile pluralism with Catholic social theology are testimony both to the secular norm of the Anglo-American societies and the necessity for Catholic theology to remain essentially unquestioned.

[14] Apparently, as shown in Chapter 8 of *Party and Society, op. cit.*, not only middle-class status but also subjective middle-class identifications are necessary to reduce Catholic distinctive political behavior, at least in the United States.

[15] The finding of the 1940 Erie County study in the United States was that persons in cross-pressured situations voted less often and delayed their voting decision more than persons not under cross-pressures. See Paul

Two recent studies have found, in contrast to the earlier one, that Catholics do not withdraw from voting in situations of predicted cross-pressures. A study of voting among Catholics in Kingston, Ontario, in 1953 and 1955 found that Catholics in a conservative political climate voted as heavily as anyone else. And a study of middle-class Catholics in Detroit in 1957 and 1958 found that they did not withdraw from political activity.[16]

The conclusions to be drawn from these specific findings may be: (1) that the cross-pressures upon Catholics have lost their importance; or (2) that Catholics are not under cross-pressures because one of the presumed bases of pressure is not one in reality or because through some other process the person or group is "shielded" from such pressures; or (3) that the cross-pressure theory is invalid—membership in groups with differing political predispositions does not tend to reduce the level of political activity or does so only under certain special circumstances.

The conservative influences of Catholic religious beliefs and values are shown by a number of studies. Contrary to what one might expect, Catholics (in the United States and Canada, at least) who usually attend services and are involved in church-related activities are *not* more likely to vote for the traditional Left party of their group; they are, indeed, less likely to do so than those more removed from their church. Conversely, Catholics more involved in the social and associational life of the Catholic community (apart from its religious dimension), as one might expect, are more likely to vote for the traditional party than those less involved in such community life.[17]

These studies indicate the dual and sometimes contradictory political effect of Catholicism as an aspect of an ethnic subculture and Catholicism as a distinctive set of values embodied in religious institutions.

It need not be assumed that distinctive voting patterns are the only expression of religious values in politics or that a religious party is incapable of adjusting to changing situations. In the Netherlands, although the support given to various parties has changed little in the last fifty years, governmental coalitions have changed in their composition, and varying social philosophies have been implemented. Although almost all Catholics vote for the Catholic party, for example, conflicts of interest between Catholic workers and Catholic employers take place *within* the Catholic party. Shifts of power and influence are reflected in changes of leadership and, thereby, shifts of the alliances within the parliamentary coalitions (from alliances with the Protestants to cooperation with the socialists, or vice versa). Such methods may allow political differences to be resolved as

---

F. Lazarsfeld, *et al., The People's Choice* (New York: Columbia University Press, 1948).

[16] John Meisel, "Religious Affiliation and Electoral Behavior: A Case Study," *Canadian Journal of Economics and Political Science*, XXII (November, 1956), 481–96. See also Lenski, *op. cit.*, p. 132.

[17] See Lenski, *op. cit.*, p. 165; and Meisel, *op. cit.*, pp. 492–94, for parallel findings for the United States and Canada on this point. Meisel found that sisters and lay nurses in Canada were more likely to be Conservative voters than were rank-and-file Catholics. Lenski found that Detroit Catholics who attended church frequently were more likely to be Republican than non-attending Catholics, but that Catholics who associated frequently with Catholics were more Democratic than Catholics who associated frequently with Protestants. See Chapter 6 of *Party and Society, op. cit.*, for a discussion of the "natural" conservatism of British Catholics, although the data do not permit a direct test of this point.

effectively as do the methods more common in the Anglo-American countries.[18]

It can be argued that major pressures against religious and regional politics have been created by social changes due to urbanization and industrialization in countries with secular and universalistic political cultures. If fundamental religious and regional differences decline, even if the symbols of identity remain, these social bases of political cleavage may become irrelevant. As the problems faced by government become more national in scope, politics may increasingly be based upon the competitions of large organizations with national social bases, competitions with an "interest" or "class" content.[19]

[18] I am indebted to Carlos Kruytbosch for pointing this out to me. See Fogarty, *op. cit.*, for a detailed analysis of the religious parties in continental Europe.

[19] The study reported in *Party and Society*, *op. cit.*, examined, insofar as the data from 53 public opinion surveys conducted from 1936 to 1962 would allow, the simultaneous effect of regional, religious, and class factors in voting behavior in order to discover the relative importance of these three major components of political cleavage in the Anglo-American countries. In addition, changes in the importance of these factors were analyzed.

RELIGION AND SOCIETY

FEW sociologists of religion would contend that the matters dealt with in Part Five are far from the center of the field. Some might even contend that, together with concern with the mutual influences of the "religious" and the "nonreligious," these matters would nearly exhaust the significant content of the field. They are in any case clearly of sociological importance.

The fact of variation in religious practice according to a number of socially significant criteria is a familiar phenomenon. Section A of Part Five sets out some elements or constituents of this fact of variation. Considerable interest in variation has been shown by French sociologists of religion, among others. Particularly in recent years, French sociologists have been much motivated by the concern of the Catholic Church with variation. Low levels of religious practice must evidently in some sense concern the church, and it is inevitably interested in variations in practice within and between regions and cities and social classes. The church is hardly unaware of its own existence in relation to a particular kind of civilization and society, and it seeks understanding of that civilization and society, very often, of course, with the object of attaining what it conceives to

be better realization of its goals. It can hardly be indifferent to a variation in, say, church attendance between classes that often suggests that it has only a precarious hold on certain segments of the population, such as European workers. Indeed, it is hardly surprising, in view of strongly "practical" interests on the part of the Catholic Church (and, for that matter, on the part of other churches) that much work on social aspects of religion has amounted to what has been called "kirchliche Sozialforschung"—ecclesiastical or churchly social research: a type of research that does have a highly "practical" orientation and is designed to solve or help solve immediate and pressing church problems, but that is not particularly characterized by sociological imagination or theoretical vigor. "Practical" and "theoretical" interests *can* be rather superficially opposed, however, and, in particular, some of the work of the French sociologists of religion has blossomed out beyond the confines of "practical" parish problems and verged on issues that virtually any sociologist would acknowledge to transcend narrow —let us say parochial—concerns.

The first selection presented in Part Five, constituting two chapters from Boulard's little volume, *An Introduction*

374

to *Religious Sociology*, reflects some of the "practical" motivations and sources of the contemporary French interest in the sociology of religion. The French, once more, have repeatedly shown concern, as is easily understandable from their Catholic background, precisely with variation in practice, with abstention from Catholic duties, with the impact of industrialism on practice. This kind of concern, again, *need* not necessarily be incompatible with theoretical concern. Presentation of facts of variation may be said to be continued in the selection following the material by Boulard, namely Fogarty's résumé of some significant European data on religious practice shown to be variant by particular kind of religion (Catholic or Protestant) and by other criteria, notably by national grouping, sex, age, and class or stratum. Fogarty presents significant material in a few pages. His data are valuable but, as he himself suggests at the very beginning of his statement, statistics of the kind he sets out are "extremely tricky." (Improvements in them are constantly being sought.) Moreover, new data bearing on the same matters Fogarty deals with are coming in rapidly. One has only to look, for example, at some issues of the journal entitled *Archives de Sociologie des Religions* to note that work in this general area of practice and its variations according to a number of criteria is being actively pursued. By the same token, however, perhaps anything that could be offered in this area would run the risk of being at least in some part very quickly dated. And Fogarty's pages do set out some currently broadly reliable variations in religious practice in Western Europe. It is also decidedly to the point that they afford a brief introduction to the entire area of religion and social stratification, which has been a most important one for the sociology of religion and which must receive a good share of stress in the present Part Five.

The general matter of religion and stratification is at least already hinted at, indeed, in Boulard's material, in his brief discussion of "a new civilization based on technical progress." (It may be noted, by the way, that a strong "liberal" current may be found in much contemporary French sociology of religion, a current that runs in favor of the French working class and that is plainly sustained by some elements in present-day French Catholicism.)

The fact of variation is both socially important and socially contingent. And one of the most important forms of variation (as in church attendance or participation in church affairs) is class or stratum variation. Section B addresses itself to this directly. The brief, condensed statement by Isambert (one of the prominent French contemporaries) which begins Section B sets out some circumstances of the phenomenon of working class alienation from the church in a number of countries. The phenomenon may, with qualifications such as Isambert appropriately makes, be said, as he notes, to be a kind of sociological "law." It is less striking in the United States than it is generally in Western Europe. (Lazerwitz's material in Section C is pertinent here.) But this should surely not be allowed to obscure its importance. The sociology of religion is an area of sociological concern that can afford provincialism even less than others. And the entire phenomenon of working class alienation from the church has a historical background that should not be neglected, for its neglect could only impoverish sociological wisdom on the whole subject. Again space limitations cramp us. Isambert presents much pertinent (and, incidentally, rather complex) historical material for France in the volume entitled *Christianisme et Classe Ouvrière* from which the condensed statement in Section B is taken. Aside, of course, from the condensed statement, this could not be drawn upon, nor could other useful historical material. But some sense of relevant historical dimensions may be conveyed by Wickham's first article in Section B.[1] The theme of working class alienation from the church could hardly be missed in Wickham's account. To realize the object, in Section B, of bringing out some aspects of the situation relating to religion and stratification in England and France in particular, two articles are provided in the section after the extract from Wickham's historical sociology of the city of Sheffield. It is desirable to have some analysis of the religious attitudes of various classes or strata in the present day and this is provided by Émile Pin, who made a notable study in the 1950's of the social circumstances and correlates of religion in a parish of the city of Lyons. The statement by Pin is derived from particular, limited materials, and there would certainly be an element of risk in generalizing or extending it to all of France (as Pin is well aware, himself), but it has seemed eminently worth while to allow him to set out here, in English dress, the work he has been courageous enough to present.

Pin's work again suggests the influence of "liberal" currents in French Catholic thought (although one must hasten to add that his study of a Lyons parish contains a solid core of material whose validity is independent of any ideological stance). A number of sociologists and a number of priests with a sociological orientation have felt much sympathy with the famous worker priests who cast their lot so unequivocally with the French working class. It has seemed

appropriate (in a section designed to feature a certain interplay between England and France) after Pin's statement (which may give some sense of the relatively strongly proletarianized character of the French working class even into the present day) to allow a contrast between France and England that is set out (again by Wickham) on the subject of worker priests for France and for its cross-channel neighbor.[2]

The theme of stratification in England and France, presented in Section B, is carried on for the United States in Section C. But here the materials broach not only similar but also, inevitably, different stratification problems. The first paper in Section C, by Bernard Lazerwitz, sets out a number of "variations," but the term now has to be understood more broadly: Lazerwitz's work involves interest in more than religious practice (as it points, for example, to such partly religiously influenced phenomena as differential birth rates) and it is very much and very directly concerned with variations between

[1] A valuable recent work on religion and stratification, with historical references most pertinent to the story all too briefly set out in Section B, is K. S. Inglis' Churches and the Working Classes in Victorian England, London: Routledge and Kegan Paul, 1963.

[2] Those unfamiliar with the worker-priest movement and controversy will find most useful the volume entitled The Worker-Priests: A Collective Documentation, translated by John Petrie and published by the Macmillan Company, New York, 1956. Interesting discussion of the worker-priests will be found in the various essays of the volume from which the short statement by Wickham closing Section B of Part Five is taken: Priests and Workers, edited by David L. Edwards and published by SCM Press, Ltd., London, 1961. Had the present volume been planned to be comprehensive enough to be a source book as well as a reader, it might well have made room for some of the content of at least one of the documents that exercised an important influence on the worker-priest movement, namely Godin and Daniel's France, Pays de Mission? This has been made available in an English adaptation by Maisie Ward, France Pagan? The Mission of the Abbé Godin, New York: Sheed and Ward, 1949

or among religious groups—something that is of course especially understandable in a country that has the religious diversity of the United States. The nuances of the term variation need not be further gone into. Most of the content of Section C is, in any case, designedly a content that bears on stratification. It was noted just above that the material on the United States broaches both similar and different problems when we have European circumstances in view. With regard to similarities, we may note that Lazerwitz is clearly interested in studying possible church alienation of the "lower" strata in the United States, in so far as this can be done by probing church attendance. But it appears that the American situation is different *in degree* from that in much of Europe. Lazerwitz's data show a significant direct relationship between social status and frequency of church attendance, but the relationship is a modest one, whereas in Europe, as in much of France, it is frequently a very marked one. (However, work on the United States that has to do with problems of religion and social stratification must also clearly give much attention to different matters, and it is scarcely surprising that Lazerwitz should be interested in the hierarchy of education, occupation, and income, wherein Episcopalians, Jews, and Presbyterians rank highest, white and Negro Baptists lowest, and Methodists, Lutherans, and Roman Catholics in between.) There is more matter of importance in Lazerwitz's paper, but it needs no further comment here.

Still, problems of stratification suggested by the data for the United States that show only a moderate direct association of church attendance with social status continue to afford occasion for probing more closely the entire area of religion and stratification in this country. It is possible that the apparently relatively slight degree of lower stratum alienation from the churches in the United States, by comparison with European countries, does not tell the entirety of a relevant story. It may be that more religious segregation of the social classes is taking place in the United States than seems initially to be the case and that it takes on special forms—not by the staying away from church on the part of lower strata but by their affiliation with distinctive and "separated" churches. (There is in any case, of course, no question that denomination and class are closely connected.) The whole matter undoubtedly presents complexities and needs more investigation, but a relevant statement is afforded us by Gibson Winter (in the selection that follows the item by Lazerwitz) from a work in which he has argued in detail that middle class and upper class churches are increasingly segregated from workers and Negroes in the central areas of our cities—and increasingly preoccupied with problems (those of the "organization church") that do not and cannot interest the lower strata.

Finally, it seems worth while to document some aspects of religion and stratification within a particular American community. A conveniently brief documentation is afforded by Donald Cowgill for the fairly sizable city of Wichita, Kansas, in his paper on the ecology of religious preference in that city.

Religious phenomena are clearly affected by social circumstances of various sorts. "Religion" itself achieves social organization, and the terms church, sect, and denomination point to modes of organization that have attracted considerable attention and been the object of considerable reflection and analysis. It is also true that study of church, sect, and denomination at many points leads to issues in social stratification, and it is accordingly the more appropriate to place the materials having to do with these structures in Section D.

The section is introduced by a virtually

inevitable choice from Ernst Troeltsch, whose discussion of sect and church types has been most influential. It is almost equally "inevitable," after Troeltsch, to present some of the work of H. Richard Niebuhr, whose *Social Sources of Denominationalism* remains a most provocative study and should, ideally, be more extensively presented here. Each of the two brief passages from Niebuhr's work presents themes that continue to nourish research interest. In "The Churches of the Disinherited: I," Niebuhr points out that religion *can* itself be in degree socially contingent. He suggests that if independent religious forces supply "the energy, the goal, and the motive of sectarian movements," nevertheless social and economic factors have their influence also; and he even asserts initially that "the divisions of the church have been occasioned more frequently by the direct and indirect operation of economic factors than by the influence of any other major interest of man." It is good to have this emphasis, for the simple reason that it gives occasion to note the sheer circumstance that religion can be a "dependent variable." This is worth stress in a mass of readings that do not strongly feature that circumstance. Whether Niebuhr's broad observations in this context can be refined raises other issues; it is still most useful to have the observations in this volume, if only for the reason indicated. The concise sketch of the tendencies of the religion of "the disinherited" that is also offered in the first selection from Niebuhr has been one of the influential characterizations of that religion.

The second reading from Niebuhr's work in Section D is mainly important here for its noting of the propensity to liquidation of sectarian groups. "Most important," says Niebuhr, "among the causes of decline of revolutionary churches into denominations is the influence of economic success." He undoubtedly has a point, but its importance here

may be said to consist in some of the things it easily implies or readily reminds us of—for example, that exercise of thrift and industry and absention from luxury, "humble" virtues that these are, paradoxically tend to create a wealth that, as Weber pointed out after John Wesley, may well eliminate the virtues that nourished it. Here, Niebuhr's work, in conjunction with that of Weber and others, may be taken to point to some very important mechanisms in the liquidation (indeed, in a sense the self-liquidation) of sectarian groups; and the relevance of this to problems in social stratification is evident. (None of this should be understood to mean that all sects liquidate themselves nor indeed even that all sects must change into "denominational" or "churchly" forms.) In the second passage from his work, Niebuhr does, then, touch upon these matters, if all too glancingly, and the concern with problems of stratification in the remainder of the passage presented is evident.

After the two brief selections from Niebuhr, we are brought back to some central descriptive problems about church and sect by Earl Brewer's essay on "Sect and Church in Methodism." Brewer's work consists in a certain enrichment of meanings and in an interesting application of relevant terms to Methodism. Other investigations have been directed to different objects, and it would have been useful to include several papers that give a strong sense of the variety of the usages of the central terms, such as the term sect, employed in the analyses in this section. But despite variety and discrepancy in usages of the term sect, in particular, there is an obvious disposition in the literature to continue to struggle with the term and to describe with some precision the components that go into the corresponding phenomenon. Thus, Bryan Wilson, whose paper follows Brewer's, clearly neither wants to eliminate the term nor, indeed, to give it some quite arbitrarily delimited meaning; and Wilson's paper justifies itself as a richly suggestive contribution to its subject. It is likely, nevertheless, that sociologists of religion will continue to be not quite satisfied with this central term and will continue to look for strategic features of so-called sects, features that will have a maximum power in the organization of relevant data and the explanation of relevant behavior—more of such power than current analyses afford.

In this connection, it should be observed that work on sects in particular still has not been made to feel anything like the full potential impact of comparative studies. Even very able articles often fail to range as widely as they might. There are certainly phenomena that appear to have strong affinities with sects in the Western world to be found within such religious spheres as that of Japanese Buddhism or that of Islam. A search for strategic features of sects in general can hardly afford to neglect these relevant phenomena outside the West.

One more broad matter that can only be mentioned by the way but that is suggested by the comments just made as well as by much literature within the range of Section D is the matter of how profitable it is to develop taxonomies of sect, church, and denominational forms. Appreciable effort has been expended on such taxonomies, and some of the outcomes have been ingenious. The main lines of distinction are undoubtedly useful. Until the phenomena of sect, church, and denomination are better known, however, and there is a better sense of what their strategic features for the purposes of explaining religious behavior are, there is some danger that classificatory schemes in this field may degenerate into taxonomic play. The content of Section D is hardly immoderate in this regard.

The items collated in Section D may suggest other problems that cannot be given consideration. But consideration must be given to certain aspects of the functions of sects. The section is concluded with an article by Benton Johnson on the Holiness sects. The problems posed in this article are most important. A certain opposition may be said to be sharpened by Johnson's work. That opposition is between two kinds of functions of sects. One set of functions has to do with satisfactions for sect members who have distinctive needs for social justice, for righteousness, and for a religion that has a strong emotional flavor. Clearly, Niebuhr had this kind of sect functioning very much in view. The sects of "the disinherited," he argues, will set forth a distinctive salvation—a salvation whose terms suggest aspirations toward social and economic levelling or the like; and those sects will show appreciation of solidarity, equality, mutual aid, honesty, simplicity, humility; and emotional fervor is one of their common marks. The functions performed by sects that may be characterized in this way can be called *compensatory* and *maintenance* functions. They compensate "the disinherited" for their disabilities (as through dreams of a great justice to come) and operate to maintain or preserve their distinctive traits of mind and character and modes of organization (as through stressing that when Christ needed help he did not turn to sophisticated men of high position but to simple and lowly ones). If sects change and cease to perform functions within this first set, then "the poor," as Niebuhr puts it, referring in particular context to the poor left over after the Quaker organization had definitely become a denomination of a "respectable" sort—"the poor were left without a gospel." And those "left without a gospel" would presumably at least try again to found or find a sect movement that should function to meet distinctive moral and psychological requirements.

But there is another set of functions performed by sects which may be called *escalator* functions. Johnson's article on the Holiness sects highlights Holiness emphasis on such things as "self-application, consistency, and achievement." It is at any rate plausible that this emphasis should serve to effect "socialization of the lower class in the dominant values of the American society," as the abstract of Johnson's article puts the matter. To the extent that this is actually so (and certainly the empirical points involved need more work) the Holiness sects function escalatorwise to translate their members into "higher" reaches of American society. And there is no necessity to think that it is only Holiness sects which may function in this way. Reading of English Methodist history (as in work by Robert Wearmouth) often creates the impression that Methodists worked hard to instill "middle class values" in their working class or lower class adherents. (One of the numerous interesting questions in the context of sect and stratification has to do with the differentiation of certain values and attitudes and stratification within the sect itself. Presumably some who are still Holiness adherents are appreciably closer to middle class American values than other Holiness adherents; and so, also, Methodism has been internally differentiated.)

The sect then may be looked upon as to some extent a self-transforming (or even self-liquidating) enterprise. (Alternatively, we may say that *some* sects may be regarded as self-transforming or self-liquidating enterprises: we would not expect the pattern of self-transformation here suggested to occur in, say, what Wilson calls gnostic sects.) But what, precisely, is it that transforms itself? Is it the particular sect form? Or is it a particular generation or particular generations of adherents to the sect? Or, in time, is it both? Moreover, are we or are we not again dealing here with the kind of situation Weber was so well aware of— the situation in which the pursuit of the

old "Protestant" virtues of industry, thrift, and frugality produces economic welfare (so that "godliness" once more proves "conducive to economic success," as Niebuhr phrases the matter) and in which the economic success corrupts or destroys the virtues out of which it arose? This could account for much sectarian self-transformation (and, indeed, self-liquidation.) In this context, simplicity, honesty, soberness, and the like may make a contribution much like that of the other virtues noted. Is it possible that somehow, in functioning in the compensatory and maintenance direction, a sect may already be laying the ground for its own further (quite unintended) performance of escalator functions? Or is there an appreciable diversity, so that some sects perform compensatory-maintenance functions more or less exclusively, others escalator functions, while others still adroitly mix the two kinds of functions? And what are the exact mechanisms by which the two kinds of functions are effected? Is there a difference between a more or less automatic self-transformation (via feedback from results of economic activity), which works as it does because wealth breaks down "simple" sectarian virtues, and a self-transformation that occurs because of explicit and distinctive exhortations to sect members by their leaders? When and why is it no longer legitimate to stress *self*-transformation? Why do some sects transform readily and others not? How do inner elements making for change within sects relate to external elements making for change?

Numerous other and more refined questions might evidently be asked in these premises. The reader will also note that the outlines of a problem-complex are here suggested which indicate the affinity that exists between sociological questions in the large and questions in the sociology of religion in particular. If, as some of the above suggests, sects can function as agencies of upward mobility, the sociologist is at once and legitimately inclined to assimilate them for purposes of certain kinds of analysis to quite different kinds of structures that have nothing directly to do with "religion" at all. This hint of affinities must suffice. The reader will most certainly have suspected them before and will suspect them again. A certain vitality in the sociology of religion could hardly be sustained without them. (Sect and church and denomination, specifically, lead us back to stratification, *inter alia,* and stratification is one of the numerous things that bind sociology of religion to sociology at large.)

Religious activity is constantly sustained by social structures and organizations. Sects, churches, and denominations are among the organizations that sustain it. There are others, however, and Section E of Part Five is designed to remind us of the existence of a large field of potential analysis by sociologists of religion—the field, precisely, of structures and organizations aside from sects, churches, and denominations. Fichter's article on conceptualizations of the urban parish brings together some elements of Catholic thought on the parish and reveals a strong sense of the parish as a social structure. The very interesting paper on religious orders by E. K. Francis treats matters too rarely treated sociologically. These two papers may perhaps suggest the richness of yield that might come from thorough analysis of structures. Oriental materials as well as materials from the West are plainly important for a careful overview of structures that we may hope will be forthcoming before long. The offering of but two papers in Section E should certainly not induce the notion that this field is unimportant. In view of a number of circumstances, including the circumstance that some of the most cogent things sociologists have to say relate to organizations, this field could indeed become one of the most important encompassed in the sociology of religion.

Some sects attempt a kind of extreme withdrawal from the "world" whose encroachment they abhor or fear, and adherents of different faiths may at different times seek to adopt devices of insulation so that their contacts are kept at a minimum. But in a world wherein the instrumentalities of communication and transportation are ever more highly developed, it is very difficult to avoid contact, and it has in any case long been impossible to avoid it in a variety of places. Often enough, also, contact is recommended by interested persons and agencies, in the hope of achievement of consensus of one kind or another, in the hope of a larger amity, or the like. A considerable set of problems of sociological interest arises in connection with contact. The three papers contained in Section F suggest something of their character. It is clear that there are places in the modern world where there has been very peculiar difficulty about making reconciliations of community affiliation and specifically religious adherence. It is pertinent to recall the discussion in Part Four by Mensching of folk and universal religion and the distinction made by Lenski between religion as communal and as associational. The universal religions, it will be remembered, are supposed to be marked by their release from tribal or national bonds, and the folk religions by their indissoluble connection with a folk and its welfare. In Lenski's perspective, the particular people called Protestants, Catholics, or Jews constitute communal groups and thereby show a kind of "folk" aspect. The same people specifically religiously organized make religious associations. In the light of these distinctions, the struggle of the Nazis to "define" Jewishness is of special interest.

The first reading in Section F, from Raul Hilberg's extensive monograph on the destruction of the European Jews, is not directly concerned with problems in the sociology of religion, but affords significant material for some of them. Hilberg notes shrewdly that "it is important to understand that the sole criterion for categorization into the 'Aryan' or 'non-Aryan' group was religion. . . . After all, the Nazis were not interested in the 'Jewish nose.' They were interested in the 'Jewish influence.' " Theoretically, religion is "one thing," while communal affiliation is another. As was noted in the introduction to Part Four, in connection with Mensching's distinction, one may be a Christian though a Japanese, a Moslem though an Englishman, a Buddhist though a Frenchman. Or in Lenski's sense of the matter, one may be a Catholic by formal religious profession and yet live a life in one's community that is richly interlaced with the lives of non-Catholics. This does no violence whatever to Lenski's view. But for the sake of further clarity, it may be said that there are indeed communal groups in Lenski's sense, such as Protestants, Catholics, and Jews form, but that these communal groups also live together in a still *larger* community, their members often going to school together, sometimes intermarrying, and so on. This sort of co-living in the larger community transcending particular communal groups was rejected by the Nazis, certainly for the Jews. The Nazis insisted on a "folkish" (or "racial") identification of the latter. Adherence to the Jewish religion was taken by them as spiritually incompatible with being authentically "German." (It will also be evident from Hilberg that having Jewish "affiliations" in a *broader* sense than that of formal profession of the Jewish religion was important for the Nazis in "defining" Jewishness.) One could not, then, clearly, be at once Jew and German, in this outlook. It will be seen that this represents a special kind of effort in the modern world again to identify, to make inseparable from one another, folk and religion, as far as the Jews are concerned.

The difficulties of definition that Hilberg describes were of course related to other difficulties that came from the realities of German society. Note that, as Hilberg reports Lösener's arguments, "half-Jews had performed meritorious service. . . . there were many marriages between Germans and half-Jews." The Jews had lived and continued to live in the German community. They had indeed intermarried in appreciable numbers. Many Germans with Jewish relatives did not want to see them exterminated or even seriously discommoded. The communal bonds of the Jews in the *larger* German community could not be wished away. Repeatedly, throughout Hilberg's book, the difficulty created by such bonds in Germany or by like bonds in other countries emerges. The Nazis had to give "much thought . . . to such problems as couples in mixed marriage, the disruption of German-Jewish business relationships, and so on." To take but a single instance of these difficulties outside Germany, Hilberg notes that in Croatia, in 1944, a police attaché named Hans Helm had to admit (along with one Siegfried Kasche) that in certain respects the Jewish "problem" had not been "solved." Thus: "With respect to the mixed marriages and *Mischlinge,* Helm remarked that quite a few Croat leaders had strong family ties with Jews (some Cabinet members had Jewish wives). Furthermore, Helm pointed out, that question had not been solved in the Reich either." [3] Even the Nazis had to make concessions to the *larger* communal bonds of the Jews in Germany and elsewhere, and the constraint, arising from the strength of such bonds, to ease their strictures on Jews is undoubtedly influential in their wrestling with "definitions" of what a Jew is. The

[3] See Raul Hilberg, *The Destruction of the European Jews,* Chicago: Quadrangle Books, 1961, pp. 125–126 and 457–458.

definitions clearly reflect the circumstance that the closer some set of "Jews" came to having only a certain *minimum* of *larger* communal bonds in the German community, the more feasible it became for the Nazis to move toward outright extermination of that set.

Another important situation that features problems in community and the co-existence of religious groups is presented in David Moberg's brief paper on vertical pluralism in the Netherlands. The situation that he analyzes has attracted much attention from sociologists of religion. Moberg calls his paper "Social Differentiation in the Netherlands," and the reasons for doing so are quite plain. The paper might also have been called "Failure of Differentiation" for equally evident reasons: religious affiliation is not, as it were, allowed to go "on its own," not allowed a status relatively independent of numerous other concerns of life. It would be of interest to compare the Dutch situation with others, such as that of India and Pakistan, for points of resemblance and difference between the Dutch experience on the one hand and the Hindu-Moslem experience in India (with its prominent feature of a drive toward separate "communal" existence for different religious groups), on the other, but the possibilities this may suggest are closed off in these readings in favor of a final item in Section F that addresses itself to some of the psychological correlates of religious coexistence. Rosenberg is appropriately cautious about his findings, and much more knowledge is needed in the premises he gets into, as in so many others, but the theoretical and "practical" importance of the matters he stresses would appear self-evident.

Section G of Part Five consists of two papers designed to stress role conflict and strain. It would have been desirable, once again, to present more material in this section, or even to have a supplementary section, that would give additional emphasis to such phenomena as contradiction (as in the form of "status contradiction," in which, for example, a minister who has a relatively elevated status precisely in virtue of being a minister yet at the same time has a relatively depressed status because he is minister to a low-ranking group). Contradiction and strain and dilemma are incessantly and vitally involved in social life generally, as they are in religiosocial life in particular. (This observation may already prepare us for the "dialectical" quality of the paper by O'Dea that constitutes the final selection in Part Five.)

The short study by Campbell and Pettigrew of the role of Little Rock ministers in that city's racial crisis has a number of very interesting features. (The reader should not miss in it the incidental but significant references to the Little Rock sects and sect leaders.) There are, again, "strains" that affect ministerial roles, and Campbell and Pettigrew set out some psychologically relevant considerations that make it understandable that some of those strains should be borne by occupants of ministerial roles without excessive personal disorganization or discomfort. From an ideal moral viewpoint, one might at times even wish to see their discomforts enhanced, but Campbell and Pettigrew are concerned to attend to the exhibition of strains (and of mechanisms for their mitigation) that appertain to particular kinds of positions which involve particular kinds of relations to a variety of significant others. The interrelations of roles are again clarified, as in the case of Wilson's paper.

The second and final paper in Section G, by Cumming and Harrington, considerably enriches "common sense" about the clergyman's role as counselor, presents much information about that role not available to common sense and affords a number of findings that are of evident sociological interest. Its bearing on analysis of role is too apparent to call for any special comment; and the inevitability of appeal to the notion of strain will once more be noted.

A short item by O'Dea comprises Section H of the present Part. The item may be regarded as a kind of introduction to "dialectical" analysis of religion. We may ultimately, in the sociology of religion (as in other branches of the discipline of sociology), have to rely very heavily on analysis guided by the notion previously suggested that social life is shot through with contradictions, strains, and dilemmas. The relevance of a number of the particular things that O'Dea stresses to matters previously taken up will be noted.

Thus, it is not difficult to see the pertinence of some of what he has to say to the first discussion by Sorokin presented above in Part Four. Nor is it difficult to see that his article has relevance to the general phenomenon of transition from sectarian to denominational or churchly forms. O'Dea's article could not conceivably "summarize" everything that has been presented in Part Five, but, if my bias, already twice suggested in these last few paragraphs—to the effect that contradiction, strain, dilemma, paradox are extremely significant in social life at large and in religiosocial life in particular—has any merit, then it is fitting enough that this article should bring Part Five to a close.

A · VARIATIONS IN PRACTICE
AND SOCIAL STRATIFICATION

1 · *The Map of Religious Practice in Rural France; The Present Position of Geographical Research*

F. BOULARD

I

We shall deal first with the religious map of rural France, which is to be found at the end of these two chapters. Some preliminary remarks are necessary to give the key to it and to explain its scope.

1. The Key to the Map

Notice first of all that it is a map of *religious practice.* Clearly religious practice is not the whole of religious vitality. Yet it is a sign the importance of which is not to be underestimated; the canons make attendance at Mass and performance of Easter duties obligatory, so that a man is not, in a strict sense, Christian, unless he practises his religion.[1] In addition, this sign has the great advantage of being objective. If an incumbent takes the trouble to count those who come to

SOURCE. F. Boulard, "The Map of Religious Practice in Rural France," "The Present Position of Geographical Research" (Chs. 1 and 2, pp. 3–18, of F. Boulard, *An Introduction to Religious Sociology,* London: Darton, Longman and Todd, 1960).

Mass or those who make their Easter communion he can have accurate figures; and two successive incumbents in the same parish, who make the same count, can arrive at comparable figures. Yet it is well known that by using any other criterion of Christian vitality two successive incumbents could form almost contradictory judgments about the same parish. It is a mistake to neglect the objective criterion provided by religious practice.

Secondly, this is a *rural* map. The towns, taken for our purpose as areas with over two hundred inhabitants to the square kilometre, have been eliminated. So towns and their suburbs, such as Paris, Lyons and Marseilles, as well as mining districts and other industrial areas, such as those of Béthune, Lille and Le Creusot, are marked as black patches. Smaller towns are marked in the same manner as the country around them.

Finally, it is a map made up of *cantons.*[2] Sociological observation brings out the interplay of wholes and therefore should be based upon fairly large units; the canton, or sometimes the deanery, has

385

been chosen. We shall from time to time attempt to illuminate the findings of this small-scale geography by particular examples.

Three shades appear on the map, corresponding to the three types of parish which I tried to distinguish in *Problèmes Missionnaires de la France Rurale*. These shades represent areas of majority practice (category A), areas of minority practice retaining Christian traditions (category B) and mission areas (category C).[3]

The geographical limits of these areas have had to be defined by exact mathematical criteria. After considerable experiment the following have been decided upon:

Category A, where the majority of the population practises: between 45 per cent and 100 per cent of adults, 21 and over, make their Easter communion and in principle attend Sunday Mass.[4] Why is the lower limit put at 45 per cent? Because, with rare exceptions, minors practice in much greater proportion to their strength than adults, and thus 45 per cent practice of adults corresponds to at least 50 per cent practice of all ages. We are interested in the proportion of adults, because it is they who create in any place a climate in favour of or indifferent to religious practice, which in the latter case may sometimes go as far as hostility. The proportion of adults alone gives a firm basis for sociological observation. The practice of young people generally falls off when they enter adult life, on return from military service and founding a home. Figures of religious practice which lump together adults, young people and children, do not provide a suitable basis for scientific observation. This primitive method of counting should be abandoned.

Category B, where a minority practises, but the population retains Catholic traditions: minority of practising adults (44 per cent to zero), but (in contrast to category C) the whole of the population participates in the great religious events of life. Professor Le Bras calls this 'seasonal conformity', when the population conforms to the Christian traditions of France at the different seasons of life—childhood, adolescence, marriage, burial. People maintain their attachment to the Church by observing those rites which carry social significance.[5]

Category C, mission areas, partially detached from the Church: minimum of 20 per cent of children not baptised or not attending catechism. These are mission areas in the sense that part of the population deliberately and consciously is not, or is no longer, in the Church. For these people the Church is 'outside'. In order to define these areas we have added the uncatechised to the unbaptised, because a child baptised in a maternity hospital, if he subsequently receives no religious instruction can, from a pastoral point of view, be considered a non-Christian. He still has everything to learn about Christ and the Church.

These criteria for establishing the three categories have stood the test of use. They have created well-marked regions on the map, which were just those that an informed man would clearly distinguish from their neighbours, such as the Christian region in the West, the indifferent valleys of the Garonne in the dioceses of Toulouse and Montauban, or of the Allier in the diocese of Clermont-Ferrand, the depopulated mission area of Limousin, and so on.

There are also some dotted areas on the map. They make up category P, consisting of rural Protestant groups; these dotted areas are imposed upon the shading of the three Catholic categories. The geographical extent of Protestantism has been defined for the purpose of this map without reference to religious vitality. The criterion used is that of five hundred Protestants to the canton. The geography of Protestantism in France is interesting. It is based upon history and is made up of scattered colonies, apart from two great regions, one in the Cévennes in the diocese of Mende and Nîmes and the other which begins at Le Puy and crosses the dioceses of Viviers and Valence to branch out into the dioceses of Grenoble and Gap. A third important region must be added, which is quite distinctive in its history and in its religious allegiance, and that is the Alsatian block and its extension towards Montbéliard. There the Protestants are Lutherans, whereas the rest of Protestant France is Calvinist. The two groups, Lutheran and Calvinist, are numerically equivalent. An estimate for each group of about 100,000–120,000 rural Protestants, including children, should not be far from the truth.[6]

The sources of our map of religious practice are figures produced by incumbents on the occasion of canonical visitations or of religious sociology surveys. How valid are these figures? In towns, before a good survey method had been worked out and used, they often reflected only too clearly the optimism or pessimism of the incumbent.[7] In the country the incumbent could be aware of the real situation and could easily count. If he gave his figures some slight boosting to flatter his superiors or his own illusions, the margin of error was slight. The religious map's own logic and the fidelity with which the demarcation line between areas A and B cuts across the boundaries of dioceses makes it evident that the scale is right and that the margin of error is less than 10 per cent. All this refers mainly to the past, for today accuracy of replies is more and more the rule.[8]

2. Some Statistics

There is no correlation between any of the three categories and the size of population, although the assumption has some-

times been made that the Church is strongest in depopulated regions. Practising regions are not infrequently those of high population density, and dechristianised regions, regions of depopulation. In *La Croix* of 4 January, 1953 and *Les Cahiers du Clergé rural* of January 1953 I gave estimates of figures for the whole of France, town and country. These were drawn from the unique documentation of M. Le Bras' files and from my own files. The main points of these estimates are:

1. Those not baptised into the Catholic religion number between 2,000,000 and 2,700,000 (this figure is certainly the maximum).[9] Among these we should count 800,000 Protestants, 300,000 Muslims, about 250,000 Jews, etc. The unbaptised among those of Catholic descent cannot exceed 1,250,000, say 3 per cent. A similar percentage would represent those belonging to other religions. 94 per cent of the people of France are then baptised Catholics.

2. Of the rural cantons 110 out of a total of more than 3,000 are in category C—'mission areas'. To this category, however, must be added almost all the large towns.

3. Average figures of practising Catholics for each diocese have little meaning. In the department of the Deux-Sèvres (diocese of Poitiers), for instance, there are cantons in the north-west, which show a practice of over 90 per cent and in the south, communes with up to 60 per cent unbaptised among those of Catholic descent. How can an average uniting such extremes have any significance? How, *a fortiori*, can an average be given for the whole of France? Since, however, figures based on pure guesswork are in circulation, and are quoted without question, an overall estimate must be attempted.

Now that I have at my disposal complete records for over fifty dioceses in all parts of France,[10] I have been able to divide the country into thirty-four homo-geneous areas, and to apply to each area a well-established co-efficient of Easter communicants. In cases of doubt I have always used a lower figure.

This calculation produces 10,500,000 Easter communicants over the age of 14 out of 31,700,000 French people of the same age (from which must be sub-tracted at least one million non-Catholics over the age of 14). This gives a co-efficient of 34.2 per cent Easter com-municants over the age of 14 (taking town and country together). Converting the percentage of those over 14 into the percentage of those over 21 gives a prob-able figure of 30 per cent Easter com-municants among adults.[11]

3. The Meaning of the Map

The meaning of this religious map is not always appreciated. Clearly it is not an honours list of the Christian Church. The quality of a region's Christian life is not to be deduced from its religious prac-tice alone, while the division of religious practice into three classes could seem an over-simplification. In fact we are shown three fundamental positions which a re-gion can adopt towards the mission of the Church and which are determined by the criterion of religious practice. In terms of the Gospel parable we have different types of soil for the divine seed.

In category A, the homes of the district are represented in church on Sundays (45 per cent of adults, which usually means at least 60 per cent of the women). The pastoral ministry of the Church from the pulpit and in the confessional is in direct touch with public opinion. The mission of the Church is in organic rela-tion with society, in an authentically reli-gious sense.

In category B, only a minority goes to church. The climate of opinion does not conduce to church-going, but in distinc-

tion from category C everyone, with rare exceptions, is linked with the Church by the occasional offices at the high points of life. The Church here also is an or-ganic feature of society, though in a more cultural sense. It has to make use of these occasional contacts. Since the age-range of most families is wide, and since parish visiting is an accepted thing, these contacts are considerable. Pastoral policy on this basis is now a well-tried method.

In category C, a significant proportion of families has deliberately broken with the Church. The Church is no longer in touch with them. Before the gospel of Christ can be brought to them, the agent of mission must first be accepted into the human community which they form.

We can say in conclusion, and this is not to deny the usefulness of maps which record finer shades of religious practice, that we now possess a strategic map. In category A, the Church is in *regular* con-tact with the whole of the population. In category B, it is in *occasional* contact with the population. In category C, there is a *breakdown* of contact with a signifi-cant proportion of the population. These deep strategic differences explain why priests from A regions are often lost when they take over parishes of category B. They are forced to reorientate themselves and to adopt a new pastoral policy. These differences make it necessary—and this is in accordance with the missionary tra-ditions of the Church—for those working in C regions to be allowed pastoral and missionary methods other than those in force, often for good reasons, in regions which have retained their Christianity.

It is to be hoped that pastoral policy, home missions and lay movements of the Church may find insights useful for their work in this threefold classification. If they do, it would show clearly how valu-able the simple criterion of religious prac-tice can be as an authentic sign of reli-gious vitality.

References

[1] All baptised Catholics attaining the age of reason are bound by Canon Law (Lateran Council, 1215) to make their Easter duties, which is to communicate at the time of Easter; to make their confession once a year and to attend Sunday Mass. The age of reason is normally taken to be 7, which is the age of First Communion. (In some regions First Communion may be at 8, 9 or 10.) There is the custom peculiar to France of Communion Solennelle at the end of catechism, formerly at the age of 12, but now later as the school-leaving age extends. The time of Easter is usually from two weeks before to two weeks after Easter. It is different in some dioceses: in Paris it is from three weeks before to three weeks after. Confession normally precedes Easter communion.

[2] The canton is the second smallest administrative subdivision in France. In 1936 there were 87 departments, 362 arrondissements, 3,028 cantons: each canton contained an average of 12 communes. The deanery usually coincides with the canton as a result of Napoleon's reorganisation of civil and ecclesiastical boundaries, as the diocese does with the department. This coincidence of civil and ecclesiastical boundaries is an advantage to French religious sociology. There would be between 25 and 45 deaneries in a diocese and between 15 and 30 parishes in a deanery with few exceptions.

[3] Vol. 1, p. 111 ff. The following terminology has also been suggested: Area of majority Catholic observance (A); Area of minority observance but retaining Catholic traditions (B); Partially detached area (C).

[4] For the reason why the map uses as basis of calculation Easter communion rather than attendance at Sunday Mass see Intro. to Rel. Sociology, p. 107.

[5] "The seasonal conformists, the passers-by, whose religion consists of three rites—baptism, marriage, burial, and, often, solemn first communion of the children. People who never enter a church except when the bell tolls for them to inform the parish that they are observing the rites of their ancestors." G. Le Bras, Etudes de Sociologie Religieuse, vol. 1, p. 5.

[6] M. Emile G. Léonard, Le Protestant Français, p. 82, estimates the total to be 800,000, including towns. His map on p. 96 differs from mine because he relies upon the numbers of local communities and not on the total of individuals which they contain, and especially because he includes towns where Protestantism flourishes far more than in the countryside.

[7] See Intro. to Rel. Sociology, p. 112.

[8] The Cahiers du Clergé Rural, June–July 1952, published the sources from which the map was compiled for each diocese; in addition to these, surveys have been completed of the dioceses of Bayonne, Carcassonne, Chartres, Lyons, Périgueux, Quimper, Le Puy, Marseilles, Vannes, Verdun and Soissons.

[9] 2,700,000 is a maximum, since this figure is obtained by applying to adults the percentage of non-baptised among children today. This percentage is distinctly higher today than those for previous generations.

[10] Today (1 July, 1957) we have full information about every parish in 63 out of 87 dioceses.

[11] These figures are for the whole of France, town and country. In 1944 in Problèmes Missionnaires de la France Rurale, vol. 1, p. 136, I estimated, as far as fragmentary knowledge then allowed, 38 per cent adult Easter communicants and 57 per cent "seasonal conformists" for rural France. Ten years later these first approximations have been only slightly modified by our subsequently more detailed knowledge. A calculation, based on the rural population, excluding only the largest towns, i.e. those of over 100,000 inhabitants, gives the following: adult Easter communicants 36 per cent; seasonal conformists 60 per cent. It is reasonable to infer from this that figures for the purely rural population would be very like, if not identical with, those of Problèmes Missionnaires.

II

The Present Position of Geographical Research

1. Religious Geography

Our next question is important: *How has the present situation arisen?* Obviously it is a question to puzzle Christians, and each will have some kind of an answer. Let us try to forget what we think we know, and look at the problem afresh.

The map of religious practice in France has many things to teach us. Before it was drawn up it would have been natural to suppose that the juxtaposition of the different shades, which we use to record the religious level of each canton, would produce a patchwork without any recognisable pattern: and yet there is a *physiognomy*, for which we must now try to account.[1]

First of all we can discern a vast zone of low level of practice, which covers all the Centre of France and part of the North with its clearly marked headquarters in Paris. There is a second zone of this sort, centred on Bordeaux; a third is centred on Marseilles with an extension in Languedoc and Roussillon (from the diocese of Nîmes to that of Perpignan), both of which belong to the Mediterranean type of civilisation.

By way of contrast let us take those regions which have remained practising. These are regions which for long were isolated, such as the West which was integrated comparatively late into the life of the nation, or mountain areas. There are exceptions to this and they are particularly important. We shall come back to them later.

A corridor of indifference cuts through the Christian region of the South in the dioceses of Toulouse and Montauban: the Garonne valley. The important facts are that the valley contains lines of communication by river, road and rail, and that it attracts industrial development. It is along such routes that civilisation advances. It is the function of the Garonne valley to be a high road for men and ideas. Remember that in the early centuries of the Church other such valleys were the first to become Christian, the valleys of the Rhine and the Rhône, but then of course the advancing civilisation was Christian. We should take note of the fact, which we discuss later on, that the Church as a rule advances not by miracles but predictably, by going where men go. Marseilles and Lyons were evangelised long before the centre of France.

We are now in possession of two facts, the influence of large towns and the influence of channels of communication. The position is that a new spirit has gone out from the towns, which are always the sources of new civilisations, since new ideas ferment where men come together. This spirit follows the natural ways of advance and therefore may be held up, if only temporarily, by natural barriers. I prefer to speak of a spirit originating in towns rather than of the influence of town on country, since, for example, the rural area around Paris is not the most dechristianised rural region. It is a case of the influence of towns through the civilisation which they create and send out and which takes shape in some regions rather than in others because of factors favouring it.

Let us consider in more detail this fact that there is a *geography of religion*. It is a disconcerting fact, because we are so used to looking upon religious practice exclusively as an individual responsibility. Yet here we find that it is not only individuals that we must classify as practising, indifferent or cut off from the Church, but whole regions as well. It is true that we had a rough idea that there were Christian and dechristianised regions in France. Now we have this scientifically established, which makes the psychological impact of it far more powerful.

Working it out is a fascinating operation. First you get the figures for a diocese. Then you calculate for each canton the percentage of men and of women who make their Easter communion; then you take the average and put this figure on the map, translating it into its appropriate shade. As a rule the figures are obtained from diocesan forms which set out the cantons in alphabetical order, and so you shade in the map according to the vagaries of alphabetical order. As you fill in the empty spaces on the map you see blocks forming. Sometimes these blocks are very considerable. A region strong in religious practice spans almost all of ten dioceses in the West of France and a region of indifference runs from Arras to Dax, crossing all France without a single canton in which there is a majority of practising adults.

All this is so disconcerting that people complain of determinism. Yet it is a challenge to us to study the position more closely. We must beware of the naiveté of holding a view of human liberty which takes no account of social pressures.

We are dealing with a truth about collective behaviour. If we cross France from Brest to Strasbourg we find that a countryman between Brest and Angers performs his Easter duties; between Angers and Nancy he does not; between Nancy and Strasbourg he does. If a man changes his region, he soon changes his religious behaviour. Twenty-five years ago in the region south of Paris I used to observe the annual influx into the beet fields of casual labour from Brittany. Where they came from, 60 per cent of

men in their sixties (those who were then aged 35 to 40) today still go to Mass at Easter; in the Beauce, they never set foot inside a church.

The Nazi propaganda experts claimed that 85 per cent of men could be manipulated by propaganda and that only 15 per cent were capable of acting according to their personal convictions. I cannot guarantee the proportion; but the powerful influence of environment, when we are dealing with men in the mass, is quite undeniable. If one Breton comes from Brittany into the Beauce, I do not know beforehand if he will stop practising or not; he could belong to the 15 per cent. But if 200 Bretons taken at random are scattered about the Beauce, I can tell in advance that between 150 and 160 will fairly quickly give up all practice of religion, unless spiritual care of a special kind is arranged for them.

At this point we begin to see the deep roots of the present situation. When we ask about the dechristianisation of a parish, it is usual and natural to produce local reasons. But we must now recognise that there are immense regions of minority practice, and it becomes clear that we cannot explain the falling off or the maintenance of practice in such vast areas simply by local causes. There are general causes. This must entail a broad missionary policy, because the efforts of individual parishes can never stop religious decline.

2. The Impact of Industrialism

Let us go on to ask how hostile influences first enter a Christian region.

Take the religious geography of La Vendée (diocese of Luçon). Seen as a whole the region shows a clear division. While the south is a white zone of religious indifference, the northern two-thirds form a zone of very strong religious practice. If we look in more detail and take parochial geography, we find notable differences between neighbouring parishes, but these differences are part of the same total picture or tonality of a region. Thus there is no parish of 10 per cent practice in the north of La Vendée, nor of 100 per cent in the south. There are variations, for which there are local causes, but *within the same regional tonality*.[2]

Yet even in a very religious area whitish patches of lower practice do appear. On enquiry it usually turns out that these parishes have become industrialised. When a factory is built in a region of strong religious practice it introduces a tendency to religious indifference. A chain of weak practice can be traced crossing Brittany and finishing in the Bocage of Normandy. It is formed of parishes where there are quarries. Granite quarries and dechristianisation go together.

This new spirit of which we have been speaking, which originates in the towns, arrives by the agency of factories and industrial work. It also arrives through tourism and through temporary migrations. There are people who leave the country for work in St. Denis near Paris and return home infected by new ideas.

We are now in a position to define the characteristics of this new spirit.

1. It is the spirit of a *new civilisation based on technical progress,* a materialist civilisation which has not been 'baptised'. It is a complex of technical progress, which is good in itself, and of materialism. The one goes with the other.

2. This civilisation is moreover accompanied by an *economic system,* liberal capitalism, which possesses the fundamental vice that the factory is not operated for the benefit of those who work there, but primarily for the benefit of capital. This is bound to create anti-spiritual pressures upon men. These do not come from industrial work itself but from the economic fact that money is placed above men.

3. This civilisation has a *new culture* based on the empirical sciences. It produces a new type of man possessing a technological humanism, which may not be particularly anti-clerical but which tends to be positivist.[3]

4. Finally, it is an *atomising civilisation*. This means, in the words of Jean Labbens, one of the foremost sociologists of the younger generation in France:

We live in a civilisation divided into many different groups. Modern man is rather like a small investor who has put his money into too many different concerns to have real links with any of them. Disaffection from religion seems to be largely due to the fact that he belongs to too many groups and to too varied cultures with the consequence that no value can be binding upon him.

Even if membership of several groups works in favour of freedom of religious practice, because a man may use one group as a shield against the pressures of other groups, it is nonetheless true that this lack of concentration must encourage spiritual dilettantism.

We are faced with *a conflict of civilisations*. This is why whole regions are affected and why whole regions put up resistance to the new civilisation. It explains the magnitude of the Church's task. It is not a matter of preventing the churches from emptying or of finding means of filling them, which would be only a small part of the work, but of making Christianity actively present in the whole of the advancing civilisation. In France this huge task falls mainly on the specialised branches of Catholic Action.

There is no way of stopping the arrival of the new civilisation. Only one solution is open to us, which is to penetrate it to the core with the spirit of Christ.

Notes

[1] "Great variety, but not chaos" was M. Le Bras' guess in 1931.

[2] The map of religious practice *by parishes* published for Belgium confirms this, as do the well-produced surveys of the diocese of Séez, *Pratique Religieuse et Orientations Pastorales,* and of the diocese of Coutances, *Sociologie et Pastorale.*

[3] For fuller discussion of this see *Essor ou Déclin du Clergé Français?* p. 389 ff.

2 · *Religious Statistics*

MICHAEL P. FOGARTY

Statistics on the number of practising believers in different countries are extremely tricky. In the case of the Protestant churches it is difficult to attach any absolute meaning even to such figures as exist, since these churches have no clear-cut standard of what constitutes a "practising" member. The Catholic Church does have an apparently clear-cut standard; a practising Catholic is one who, as a minimum, has been baptised, is married in church, goes to Mass on Sunday, and goes to confession and Communion at least once a year, about Easter. But even this test has more pitfalls than might be supposed. A literal reading, for instance, of the very precise statistics in the *Kirchliches Jahrbuch* for Germany, grossed up by the factor proposed in its text, would suggest that no less than 115% of the Catholics of the city of Passau fulfilled their Easter duties in 1948; an exemplary performance indeed. However, there is no need here to have figures reliable to the last place of decimals. It is important in discussing Christian Democ-

SOURCE. Michael P. Fogarty, "Religious Statistics," from Michael P. Fogarty, *Christian Democracy in Western Europe,* London: Routledge and Kegan Paul, 1957, pp. 345, 348–357. Reprinted with permission of Routledge and Kegan Paul, the British publisher, and The University of Notre Dame Press, the United States publisher.

racy in, say, France, to know whether the proportion of Christian believers is 10%, 50%, or 90%, and how they are distributed about the country. It is not important, in a study on as broad a scale as this, to know whether the proportion is, say, 42% or 43½%. And broadly accurate figures do in fact exist for the whole Catholic population of France, Belgium, Holland, Germany, and many parts of Italy. There is also a good deal of information about Protestant belief and practice in Germany and Holland.

Religious Practice among Catholics

The number of regular Sunday churchgoers is probably the best single index to use, as it permits comparison between churches whose views on the nature and significance of the communion service differ violently, but which agree on the duty to keep holy the Sabbath. Among Catholics in France and French-speaking Belgium something like 35% or 40%—Table 1—would seem to be regular churchgoers. These include more women than men—Table 2—and more than their share of older people, people from the smaller towns and countryside, and non-manual workers. But this must not be over-stressed; for the table also shows that regular church-goers include substantial numbers from all areas and classes. For Italy there are no complete

TABLE 1. *Proportion of Baptised Catholics Who Practise Their Religion.* (*All figures relate, unless otherwise stated, to those members of the Catholic population who are obliged by Church law to attend Mass on Sunday and confession and Communion at Easter.*)

COUNTRY	DATE	SOURCE AND NOTES	OCCASIONAL CONFORMISTS — GREAT OCCASIONS OF LIFE (MARRIAGE, BIRTH, DEATH) %	GREAT FEASTS	REGULAR SUNDAY MASS %	EASTER DUTIES %	NOTES
Germany	1949	*Kirchliches Jahrbuch.* The overall figures are dragged down by those for three dioceses (Berlin, Breslau [German section], and Meissen [Saxony]) in East Germany. The best and worst dioceses in West Germany are:			59	65	Sunday Mass attendances are *actual* attendances on two Sundays in each year, and thus probably over-estimate the number of *regular* attenders. All figures are grossed up by *national* factors which may not be fully applicable to *individual* dioceses.
		Trier (incl. Saar and Koblenz)			76	80	
		Passau (Bavaria)			69	95	
		Hildesheim (Brunswick Hanover)			45	52	
	1952	Poll by Institut für Demoskopie, Allensbach, March 1952. West Germany only. Adults (voting age) [Corresponding Protestant figures]	19 [38]	23 [27]	48 [14]		The Institute's categories are "Seldom," "Irregular or occasional," and "Regular" churchgoers. The poll was of adults of voting age.
Holland	1946	Katholiek Sociaal-Kerkelijk Instituut. Dioceses of:					
		S'Hertogenbosch (S.E.)			97		
		Breda (S.W.)			97		
		Utrecht (Centre & North)			92		
		Haarlem (West coast)			76		
		Towns of:					
		Amsterdam			62		
		Rotterdam			59		All in the diocese of Haarlem.
		Den Haag			72		
Belgium	1946–51	*Lumen Vitae,* Oct./Dec. 1952 Regions:					
		Flanders			50		
		Brussels			60		
		Wallonia			41		Figures of varying reliability, relating to Sunday attendance, not necessarily to regular attendance.
		of which:					
		Liége			45		
		Hainaut (Mons-Tournai-Charleroi)			26		
		Province of Namur			63		
		Province of Luxemburg			76		
France—rural	1939	Boulard, *Problèmes Missionaires de la France Rurale,* Vol. I, p. 136 (1946)	←—59—→		←—39—→		Categories are "practising" and "occasionally conforming."
all	1952	Poll by Institut Français de l'Opinion Publique Regions:	25	9	40	51	Those who attend regularly at Sunday Mass are also assumed to perform their Easter duties. So 51% who perform E. duties (including the 40% of Mass-goers) and 34% conformists plus 15% living outside religion = 100% of all baptised Catholics.
		Brittany, Vendée, parts of Normandy			60		
		East (Alsace, Lorraine, etc.) and North (Depts. of Nord and Pas-de-Calais)			c.50		
		Paris			25		
		Rest			c.35		
Italy—Mantua (diocese)	1948	Leoni, *Sociologia e Geografia Religiosa di una Diocesi,* 1952			37	60	
Rome	c.1950–1	Droulers and Rimoldi, *La Sociologia Religiosa in Italia,* in *La Scuola Cattolica,* 1952			25–30		
Milan	1949				20–30	35–40	Very rough figures.
Emilia, Tuscany	1941–7						
Liguria					10–30		
Veneto and adjacent districts	1941–7				80–100		

TABLE 2. *Characteristics of Regular Adult Mass Attenders, France, 1952*

PERCENTAGE OF:

	ALL REGULAR MASS ATTENDERS	WHOLE ADULT POPULATION
Men	34	48
Women	66	52
Aged:		
20–34	28	33
35–49	30	30
50+	42	37
Class:		
Workers	17	
Clerks, civil servants	16	
Independents (traders, etc.), professional, managerial	17	
Farmers	27	
Retired, not gainfully occupied	23	
From places with:		
under 5,000 inhabitants	60	53
5,000–100,000	26	31
over 100,000	14	16

Source as for Table 19

Of baptised adult Catholics, the poll showed the following proportions to regard themselves as "lukewarm" or "non-practising":

PERCENTAGES

	LUKEWARM	NON-PRACTISING
All	17	26
Workers	20	35
Clerks	18	31
Independents, professional, managerial, etc.	n.a.	24
Farmers	18	n.a.
No profession	n.a.	18

figures, and those that are available come largely from problem areas such as Rome or Milan. The most illuminating figures are those from Fr. Leoni's study of the diocese of Mantua, which lies sandwiched between areas of high observance to the North and others of notoriously low observance southwards towards Bologna. Fr. Leoni studied only the country districts; taking good and bad together, his figure for regular churchgoers comes out very close to that found by Canon Boulard in the French country districts. There was a particularly marked surplus of men over women in the parishes of lowest observance, and a general tendency for white-collar workers and proprietors to show higher percentages of attendance than manual workers (Table 3). It

TABLE 3. *Sunday Mass Attendance by Catholics in the Diocese of Mantua, 1948, Rural Districts Only*

PERCENTAGE OF EACH CATEGORY IN EACH PART OF THE DIOCESE WHO ATTEND SUNDAY MASS

	UPPER MANTUA	MIDDLE	LOWER MANTUA	WHOLE DIOCESE
Sex				
Men and boys	37	25	16	27
Women and girls	58	47	36	46
Total	47	36	26	37
Age				
7–14	57	50	38	49
15–21	50	45	31	42
22 and over	45	29	21	31
Occupation (adults over 21 only)				
Owner—farmers, landlords	57	63	54	57
Civil servants, clerical workers	69	52	48	56
Tenant farmers	63	57	43	54
Business owners and managers: traders: independent craftsmen	43	40	31	37
Skilled workers: shop assistants	41	32	24	34
Semi- and un-skilled workers	36	28	23	28

From Leoni, *Sociologia e Geografia Religiosa di una Diocesi*, 1952 (Rome, Gregorian University), pp. 58 ff.

would probably not be far wrong to assume that regular Mass attendance in
Italy is of the same order as in France.
In Germany, on the other hand, it is
markedly higher, quite possibly of the
order of 55–60%. There are no separate figures for church attendance by
Catholic and Protestant men and women
in Germany. But taking the two denominations together (Table 4) there are

not exempt by reason of age, health, or
work or domestic responsibilities. But it
should be stressed that all the figures
given are built up to some extent by
estimation and approximation. And these
broad, nation-wide averages, like the
three great international zones marked
out in Chapter I of *Christian Democracy
in Western Europe*—the central belt, the
northern Protestant and southern and

TABLE 4. *Proportion of Men and Women of High and Low Incomes in Western
Germany Who Are Churchgoers (Catholic and Protestant Together), September–
November 1952*

	NUMBER IN SAMPLE	CHURCHGOING (%):				
		REGULAR	IRREGULAR	SELDOM	NEVER	TOTAL
Higher incomes (at least 250 DM a month)						
Men	1,427	24	23	28	26	100
Women	1,455	34	25	29	12	100
Lower incomes (below 250 DM a month)						
Men	971	26	24	29	21	100
Women	1,339	38	25	27	10	100
Total	5,192	31	24	28	17	100

From polls by the Institut für Demoskopie, Allensbach. Figures refer to men and
women of voting age.

rather more women than men regularly
attending. The proportions from high and
low income groups are about equal. In
Flanders the proportion of regular attenders to the whole population under obligation rises to about 60%. Though there
are no complete Mass attendance figures
for Holland, the high proportion of
Catholics who complete their Easter duties suggests that—except in the coastal
belt which includes Amsterdam and Rot-
terdam—regular Mass attendance may be
a good deal higher there than even in
Flanders.

So far as possible these are percentages
of those who are actually obliged by
Church law to attend Mass—that is, are

western Catholic deserts—naturally conceal great local variations. A zone of relatively high practice stands out in the
north-west of France (Brittany, Vendée,
parts of Normandy), right outside the
central belt. Belgium, on the other hand,
is right in the belt, but Liége and much
of the mining area on both sides of the
frontier near Mons and Charleroi are in
matters of religion depressed areas. It is
possible to quote country districts, some
of them large—as in the centre of France
—which have in effect reverted to paganism, and also town working-class parishes
where practising Catholics can be counted
almost on one hand. In three Rouen parishes, with a total working-class popula-

tion aged 14 and over of around 9,500, Michael Quoist found 3% of the workers at Mass on Sunday, including one docker out of 661 in the district. 2½% of miners working underground at Lens practise their religion, and 2¼% also (1¼% of men alone) of workers in a working-class suburb at Puteaux, Paris. In general, observance is weak in the big residential and industrial towns which have grown up through the last century, and to whose conditions the Church has been slow to adapt itself. It tends to be weaker among manual than among white-collar workers, and among men than among women. "Weak" means here a comparison by the standards of the surrounding culture. Catholic observance in Amsterdam is very poor indeed by Dutch standards, but would stand out as a triumph of Christian evangelism in Paris.

Religious Practice among Protestants

The data for the Protestant churches are much less revealing, and it is important to remember the difference of church practice and discipline. For a Catholic, to fail to attend church on Sunday is a mortal sin. For a Protestant it is certainly an offence, but one more easily excused. When using church attendance data as an index of religious belief and practice, it is probably fair to equate regular attendance by Catholics with regular *or periodic* attendance by Protestants. The figures suggest (rather than prove) that the proportion of active members in this sense of the Protestant churches tends to equal or exceed that of the Catholic Church where Protestantism is a minority, but to fall short where it is dominant. There are probably not more than a million Frenchmen in any way attached to the Protestant churches, a very small minority. The French Protestant churches themselves claim only about 800,000 members. But of these as many as two-

thirds may be in some sense practising; as compared with the 40% or so of Catholics who are fully practising, and the 50% or 60% who attend at least an occasional—usually Christmas or Easter —Mass. In Holland the "Gereformeerd" churches, with 10% of the total population nominally attached to them, have a high standard of practice. On the other hand the Dutch national church, the Hervormde Kerk, has shown till recently a marked lack of solidity in its own ranks, and has been the main source (Table 5) of recruits for the growing army of the "churchless", that is of those who in filling in their Census forms no longer claim to belong to any church community. A study by Professor Kruyt

TABLE 5. *Source of Growth in the Number of "Churchless" Dutchmen, 1930–1947*

(a) *Increase in the number of "churchless"*		496,000
of whom:		
Natural growth of the "churchless" population (14.4% of the total population in 1930)	160,000	
Net transfer from Catholic Church (36.4% of the population in 1930)	80,000	
Net transfer from the Hervormde Kerk (34.5% of the population in 1930)	250,000	

(b) *Net gains and losses to the Hervormde Kerk, 1930–47*

Losses		*Gains*	
By transfer to other Reformed Churches	10,000	By natural increase	520,000
Transfer to Remonstrants	7,500	Reaffiliation of the "Hersteld Verband"	8,000
Transfer to other religious groups	2,500		
Loss to "churchless"	258,000		
Balance: net increase	250,000		
	528,000		528,000

Losses and gains are given *net*. E.g. loss to "churchless" = transfers to "churchless" minus transfers from them.

All figures are approximate estimates by J. P. Kruijt, in *Sociologisch Bulletin*, published by Kerk en Wereld, 1949, No. 3.

about 1930 showed church attendance among the Hervormde to be typically from 5% to 20% of church members in the mainly Protestant regions, dropping to as little as 4% in Amsterdam. It was much higher, up to 60% and more, in predominantly Catholic areas.

So also in Germany. The poll (Table 1) which showed in March 1952 that 48% of all Catholic voters claimed to be regular churchgoers put only 14% of Protestants in the same category. If "regular" and "occasional" are taken together the figure is still 71% for Catholics against 41% for Protestants. Data on the main acts of "occasional conformity" point the same way. It seems (Table 6) that

TABLE 6. *Proportion of Marriages Between Two Catholics or Two Evangelicals (i.e. Mixed Marriages Excluded) Not Celebrated in Church (Germany)*

		(%)
Catholic couples	1948	5–10
Evangelical couples	1930	18
	1934	7
	1937	15
	1939	32

From *Kirchliches Jahrbuch* (Evangelical), 1950, p. 466, and *Kirchliches Handbuch* (Catholic), 1944–51, p. 277.

The *Kirchliches Jahrbuch*, 1951, pp. 349 ff., shows that from 1940 onwards the proportion of Evangelical marriages celebrated in church rose again, and may by 1945 have been not far above the figure for 1930.

not more than 5–10% of Catholic couples fail to marry in church; this even after the events of the war and postwar years, which led among other things to a fair number of Catholics obtaining civil divorces and then "re-marrying" (being ineligible for a church marriage) before the civil authorities. In the Evangelical churches, on the other hand, 15–20% of

the couples in which both partners were Evangelical married outside the church in the early 'thirties. After recovering to 5–10% in 1933–6 this proportion shot up to 32% in 1939. Though it later recovered, it has never again equalled the Catholic figure. In addition to being generally lower, Protestant Church attendance seems to be very sharply biased towards the middle class.

Others: The Churchless

The total of Protestants and Catholics does not of course add up to the whole number of people in western Europe. But it does take in the great majority; for the number of Orthodox, Jews, and Moslems, is negligible, and only a small (though probably still a growing) minority denies a connection with any religious group at all (Table 7). In the

TABLE 7. *People with No Religious Affiliation (France, Holland, Germany)*

	NUMBER	% OF TOTAL OR LOCAL POPULATION
W. Germany, Census of 1950		
Total	1,525,200	3.2
Highest "Land" (Hamburg)		13.6
Lowest "Lands" (Bavaria and Württemberg)		1.1
West Berlin, Census of 1950	324,950	15.1
Holland, total, Census of 1879		0.3
1889		1.5
1899		2.3
1909		5.0
1920		7.8
1930	1,144,600	14.4
1947	1,641,300	17.0
Highest province, 1947 (North Holland)		34.1
Lowest province, 1947 (Limburg)		1.3
France, Institute of Public Opinion poll, 1952. Very approximate.		15–25

The German and Dutch figures refer to those who returned themselves as "free-thinkers," "no fixed religion," or "churchless" at the Census. The French figures are made up of two components, "instructed in no religion" and "baptised Catholics living outside any religion—atheists." Both components are estimated.

West German Census of 1950 certain places turned out to have a substantial proportion of "free religionists and free-thinkers." Hamburg, for instance, had 13½%. But the proportion for the Federal Republic as a whole was only 3.2%; though even this proportion added up to the substantial absolute total of 1,-525,000. Holland has some 17% (from the Census of 1947) of "churchless," mainly along the north and west coast. In France it seems that around 20%—very approximately—of the people are either instructed in no religion, or else baptised Christians who would now declare themselves frankly atheists. A further 5% or so, more or less, are baptised Christians who, without being declared atheists, might well come within the Dutch definition of "churchless."

Summary

It is clear from these various figures that though Christian Democracy's "natural constituency" is limited it is still substantial. Upwards of 40%—in many regions far more—of the adult baptised Catholics of the countries for which statistics exist, and a substantial number of Protestants, are actively enough in touch with the Churches to rank as regular churchgoers, and there is a further fringe of occasional conformists. And though churchgoing is more marked in some regions and classes than in others, and has died altogether in particular small districts and sections of the people, there is still a good deal of it to be found in every *large* region and social group. A churchgoer is not necessarily a democrat, or even in more than a formal sense a Christian. But there is at any rate a greater *prima facie* chance of his being open to the appeal of Christian Democratic principles—presented specifically as such—than there is in the case of those who refuse the name of Christian and the right and duty of participation in Christian worship.

B · FURTHER ASPECTS OF STRATIFICATION

1 · Is the Religious Abstention of the Working Classes a General Phenomenon?

FRANÇOIS-ANDRÉ ISAMBERT

Results obtained from a variety of studies in France rather uniformly show a particularly low rate of church attendance for workers of both sexes, even if occupational groupings often leave much to be desired from a scientific point of view.

Is this something peculiar to France? It is hardly surprising that we have similar results in other countries of Catholic tradition. In Belgium, where studies comparable to those for France have been made, figures for the whole population are higher, but the ratios within the whole are similar.[1] Italy (at least Central and Northern Italy),[2] Catholic Spain and even the Latin American countries seem to show analogous phenomena.[3]

What of countries of multiple faiths? For Germany and Austria we have little evidence. But the few studies in which social classes are differentiated with respect to religion give results like those above. Thus, a study of Viennese Catholic parish finds the lowest rate of church attendance among workers, particularly male workers.[4] A Protestant study of

SOURCE. A condensation and summary by the editor, of F.-A. Isambert, *Christianisme et Classe Ouvrière*, Casterman, 1961, pp. 43–53. The summary omits considerable bibliographical and other detail.

[1] E. Collard, *La Carte de la Pratique Dominicale*, Mons, Ed. du Dimanche, 1952 (commentary in *Lumen Vitae*, 1952, no. 4), J. Kerkhofs, *Godsdienstpractijk en Sociaal Milieu*, Brussels, Cahiers de Lumen Vitae, 1958, 378 pp., maps, summarized in French and English (concerning Limburg); and the series of studies of the Center for Religious Studies of Brussels.

[2] Bibliography in P. Droulers and A. Rimoldi, "La Sociologie Religieuse de l' Italie," *Lumen Vitae*, 1951, nos. 1–2, pp. 81–99 and A. Rimoldi, "Les Etudes de Sociologie Religieuse en Italie," in *Sociologie Religieuse, Sciences Sociales*, Paris, Ed. Ouvrieres, 1957.
[3] Bibliography on Spain in Del Valle, in *Sociologie Religieuse, Sciences Sociales, op. cit.*, pp. 97–104. G. Kibedi, "Une Enquête en *Amérique Latine*. Influence du Milieu sur la Vie Religieuse et Morale de la Vie Ouvrière de Bogota," *Lumen* Vitae, 1951, nos. 1–2, pp. 313–330. Other studies have been made in Brazil, Chile, etc.
[4] Walter Suk, "Das Bild eines Grosstadtpfarre," in D. Goldschmidt *et al., Soziologie der Kirchengemeinde*, Stuttgart: F. Enke, 1960, p. 119.

the city of Reutlingen (Württemberg) also finds among workers the strongest tendency to stand off from the church.[5] As regards the Netherlands, the sample furnished by a study of the commune of Tilburg gives ground for surprise because of the high percentage of religious observance (95% of the parishioners perform their Easter duties and 80% attend Sunday services). But even here the proportion of abstainers is higher among the workers.[6] Other studies mark the particularly high number of non-members of the church among the workers of certain regions.[7]

It is conventional to say that the Anglo-Saxon countries are not subject to this sociological "law." Relevant facts need closer examination, and we must separate the case of England, a country with a low rate of religious practice, from that of the United States, where the rate is high and apparently on the increase. As regards England, most pertinent for us is a study of four parishes of the Church of England. This did not compare the occupational statuses of the members of the "congregation" (those participating in parish activities) with those of the population as a whole. But it did allow comparison of the members' occupational statuses with those of certain categories of "seasonal" churchgoers, and the evidence again suggests lower worker participation in church ac-

tivity.[8] But this is insufficient to clarify the total religious situation in England, and here we must rely on estimates dating from the beginning of the century. If we are to believe certain disillusioned estimates,[9] the situation is not improving from a religious point of view. The inquiry of 1906,[10] without directly dealing with socio-occupational criteria, does, by way of differentiation of urban areas, allow us to infer large-scale abstention on the part of the masses.

The United States seems initially to present a different situation. However, data such as those of Cantril [11] on class level and educational level and confessional affiliation and non-affiliation allow us, together with what has been said above, to cast some suspicion on the notion that the Anglo-Saxon countries, and particularly the United States, constitute exceptions to what closely resembles a sociological law. Without doubt, more evidence is needed and it would be useful to have future inquiries concentrating on these matters.

The term sociological "law" must be used cautiously. For one thing, our documentation bears only on Western countries, and although we know from other sources that in the countries of Eastern Europe the transformation of peasants into workers has negative consequences for their religious practice, and although we have reports of difficulties in the maintenance of Buddhism or Islam in recently

---

[5] Friedrich H. Tenbruck, "Die Kirchengemeinde in der Entkirchlichten Gesellschaft," *ibid.*, pp. 127–128.

[6] A. Van de Weijer, *De Religieuse Practijk in en Brabantse Industriestad*, Assen, van Gorcum, 1955, 274 pp. Cf. pp. 5–8 and 87–90.

[7] Cf. J. P. Kruyt, *De Onkerkelijkheid in Nederlands*, 1933 and M. Staverman, *Buitenkerkelijkheid in Friesland*, Assen, van Gorcum, 1954, 268 pp. Cf. also R. Vekemans, "La Sociographie du Catholicisme aux Pays-Bas," *Archives de Sociologie des Religions*, no. 3, pp. 129–136.

[8] R. H. Thompson, *The Church's Understanding of Itself*, London, Som Press, 1957, 112 pp.

[9] Cf. H. H. Farmer, "Fundamental Causes of Failure," in J. Merchant (ed.), *Has the Church Failed?* London, 1947, pp. 46–48 and W. G. Pack, *An Outline of Christian Sociology*, London, 1948, p. 131.

[10] C. F. G. Masterman, *The Condition of England*, 1909, p. 69 and *passim*.

[11] Hadley Cantril, "Economic Composition of Religious Groups," *American Journal of Sociology*, March, 1943, pp. 574–579.

industrialized populations—nevertheless, no precise information in this sphere warrants a generalization extending to all political and religious areas. Moreover, in the sector to which we are limited, against the background of a general tendency to religious abstention in urban classes of lower economic levels, there are significant variations. The religious adherence of the workers of Tilburg is clearly higher than that of the bourgeois contingent or than that of the agriculturists in many regions of the Netherlands. In certain American towns, workers recruited from a minority group tightly clustered about its parishes or national churches show an especially strong religious integration. Finally, historical variations play a considerable role. Thus there developed in the United States, during the second half of the nineteenth century and at a time when Catholicism was still very much a minority religion, a wave of apostasy from the Protestant chuches on the part of the working classes. But this religious abstention of the workers in America seems clearly to be lapsing since the beginning of the twentieth century, under the influence of Protestant Social Christianity and of the development of Catholicism. Within France itself it is perhaps too much to speak of a large-scale exchange of religious attitudes between bourgeoisie and proletariat.[12] Yet it is true that at the beginning of the nineteenth century the workers of certain regions (especially in Mediterranean areas) seemed closer to the Church than did urban middle classes there and that in the course of the nineteenth century there occurred a revival of Catholicism among the bourgeoisie. . . .

[12] G. Le Bras, Études de Sociologie Religieuse, vol. 2, p. 406.

2 · Church and People in the Years of "Decline and Fall," 1900 to the Present

E. R. WICKHAM

There are those who delight in ecclesiastical hypochondria, but there are few themes so tiresome and profitless as bewailing the decline of the churches. Apart from its futility, it rarely lays bare the facts of the case or points intelligent lessons that might be learned. We are merely depressed. But sound and dispassionate analysis of the decline and fall is nonetheless important, if only to deliver us from nostalgia, from the dead

SOURCE. E. R. Wickham, "Church and People in the Years of 'Decline and Fall,' 1900 to the Present," from E. R. Wickham, Church and People in an Industrial City, London: Lutterworth Press, 1957, pp. 166–178.

hand of the past, and to set us free for positive mission into a new future.

There certainly has been a large-scale collapse of membership in the past two generations, both in absolute figures and relatively to the size of the population. From the 'eighties to the present time, in the industrial and urbanized areas of the country the sequence has been a slackening of what we have called the "boom" in church-going (that is to say, a failure of the churches to maintain their proportion of the ever-increasing population, as they had succeeded in doing in Sheffield in the preceding generation), a steady "deflation," and an eventual "recession." The pattern is not identical for all denominations, and only the Roman Catholic Church shows absolute increase. All the other churches show absolute losses over the period. From the end of the century the over-all curve of aggregate attendances would show a gradual fall to the inter-war years, when a steepening downward trend takes place. The relative curve, of course, in view of the population increases, would show a steeper fall.

National and Local Statistics of Recession

Unfortunately there are no later census figures for Sheffield comparable to those of 1851 and 1881, which would have permitted the charting of a graph, but though a census to-day would show the extent of the collapse it would not enable us to trace the pattern of decline. The best we can do is to assemble a variety of known facts from different parts of the country, piece them together and form a general view of what has happened. The only instance of measurement roughly falling within the period of decline is that provided by Seebohm Rowntree for the City of York, where the adult population had risen from 48,000 in 1901 to 78,500 in 1948, while the adult attendances at churches of all denominations on an average Sunday had fallen from 17,060 to 10,220, representing a fall in the proportion of the adult population from 35.5 per cent to 13 per cent.[1] We can assume that in the larger industrial cities, such as Sheffield, the fall has been greater and from a lower initial percentage.

The *British Weekly* in 1955 published articles on the Decline of Nonconformity,[2] and showed that though the membership of the major Free Churches of

[1] *English Life and Leisure*, B. Seebohm Rowntree and G. R. Lavers, 1951.
[2] *British Weekly*, Mar. 10, 17, 1955.

England and Wales had continued to increase from 1900 to 1910, from that time, before the commencement of the First World War, a gradual fall in total membership has taken place; in 1935 membership was almost equal to that of 1901. But the decline of the Free Churches is more serious than the loss of membership suggests. At the beginning of the century, says the *British Weekly*, the Free Churches had as many "adherents" as they had members, but "by 1935 the situation had become similar to that of the present, in which it is rare to find a Free Church congregation that is larger than the membership of the church." The loss of adherents therefore is much larger than that of members, and points to the weakened habit of worship on the part of those who may not have been fully committed, as it also points to the greatly diminished influence of Nonconformity on the public at large. Nor even is this the whole picture. From the 'thirties the decline has steepened sharply. Thus in the Methodist Church since 1932, the year of union, the membership in Great Britain has fallen from 838,019 to 740,872 in 1948, with losses in every single year, since when there have been some slight accessions that may show a staunching of the loss. Again, the membership of the Congregational Churches of England and Wales has fallen from 299,906 in 1935, to 221,370 in 1955, a loss of 26 per cent, though the losses in recent years have been fewer than in the earlier ones.

There are some figures for Sheffield that illustrate the decline, and all of them show a more serious recession than the national picture. Thus the Congregational Church shows a complete tailing-off of building extension after the first decade of the century in spite of the huge area expansion of the City after that date, a static membership of 3,643 in 1904 and 3,841 in 1930, and then a drop to 3,345 in 1938, and 2,037 in 1955. The Baptist membership of the City fell by much the same percentage, from 1,709 in 1931 to 1,070 in 1954. Again in the same period there are losses from the Methodist Church, but as the national figures would suggest, they are less heavy than the other Free Churches, Thus in the eight "districts" that fall in the City boundary (though they also include some areas outside the City), the membership in 1932 was 15,960, and had fallen to 12,528 in 1954. It is interesting to note however that the Methodist recession, as the other Free Churches, is considerably greater in Sheffield than the national fall, and suggests the greater losses in the industrial towns from the 'thirties.

One of the most striking ways of grasping the decline is to look at the building chart. Free Church denominations which were building at a feverish rate in the years of the "boom" quite suddenly terminate their expansion in the early years of the century, notwithstanding the continuing increase in the population, from 380,793 in 1901 to 512,834 in 1951, during which time the boundaries of the City were enlarged, and in which after the First World War vast new housing estates were erected on the perimeter. The Wesleyans alone of the Free Churches continued to plant new buildings in the extending areas, and the Methodist Church has continued to do so since 1932, the year of union between the Wesleyan, the Primitive Methodist and the United Methodist Churches. But the two latter Methodist denominations had virtually ceased to build twenty years before the union took place. It showed the greatest decline for the most liberal of the Nonconformist churches.

The decline in the strength of the Established Church is harder to measure since there are no "membership" figures. Technically its numbers are always increasing with the population advance, but clearly this gives no indication of real strength. But we have some comparative figures for Sheffield that demonstrate the losses since the 'eighties. Thus the 1881 census of worship gave total attendances at adult services of the Church of England on an average Sunday of 33,835, at a time when the population of the City was 284,410. In 1956, with the population slightly over half a million, the comparable figure of total attendances is between 12,000 and 13,000.[3] It should be noted that the 1881 figure does not represent the high-water mark, but a point of comparison. Again there are figures of Easter communicants, which were rising until after the First World War: 11,901 in 1910, and 13,456 in 1916. In 1950 the total of Easter communicants was about 11,000. This shows a degree of stability in communicant membership, but it should be borne in mind that the centrality of the Holy Communion has been greatly stressed in the present century, and in many churches is now the only Sunday morning service, while at the same time the age of admission to Communion has fallen. The near maintenance therefore of communicant figures, good though it is, should be set in the context of changed pattern in the worshipping habits of the Church.[4] There is however one other broad qualification to be remembered in making any statistical comparison between Victorian and modern habits. To-day great numbers of practising Christians attend church only once on a Sunday, and many of them not every Sunday—so changed has become our social pattern of life into which

[3] Based on Articles of Enquiry to the Churchwardens at the Archdeacon's Visitation.
[4] The number of Easter communicants in the Church of England as a whole was rising steadily from 1891 (the first year in which figures were collected), until the mid-twenties. But this does not refute the over-all loss of worshippers in the period.

worship is to find its place. Undoubtedly it means that the present number of worshipping Christians is higher than a count on any average Sunday would suggest.

Nonetheless, with all the favourable qualifications that could be adduced, the statistical evidence, not to mention the evidence of our eyes, is sufficient to prove the deflation of the religious habits of the people. A rough but graphic indication of the change is to mark how church extension in the twentieth century provides smaller buildings than earlier periods, housing congregations that would have been considered diminutive half a century ago, and yet set in the midst of larger parishes and districts. And some denominations have not even made this reduced provision to the expanded city. But there is more to be said on the pattern of decline throughout the nation during this modern period, and sociological aspects of it deserve examination.

The Recession Nation-Wide

When did the "boom" tail off, and deflation commence? And why did it happen? These are questions we seek to answer in this chapter. Neither of them can be answered simply, and the latter question is particularly complex, despite the facile and varied reasons that are customarily given. Both questions will take us from Sheffield, partly through the absence of local data, but it is also dictated by the nature of the problem. The origins and growth of churches in relation to social groups is better studied in a single area, as we have done—without this treatment, the necessary generalization would obscure all the finer points and issues and invalidate the local documentation. But in studying the decline of nineteenth-century religious institutions, the over-riding factors are to be found in the eroding acids and positive leavens at work in society as a whole. The causes are to be found in the impacts

of events, ideas, new moods and aspirations that are nation-wide, and indeed far wider than this, penetrating every part of the modern world. It is of course the outstanding characteristic of the modern era, though one that has been developing through the generations of industrialism, that the local community, be it village or town, no longer lives to itself. The local, at a certain stage, becomes integrally related to the nation and the world beyond, and subject consciously or otherwise to the impact of inventions, events, and ideas of that world beyond. Unless we are woefully parochial, or wilfully blind, we are forced to think in large-scale general terms, and to set the affairs of the parish pump in a broad context. For good or ill, extending horizons, with whatever appears upon them, are part of growing into the modern world. There is good reason then for setting the problem of man's fidelity and infidelity into the large context.

The date of deflation and the beginning of the recession of the churches cannot be given with exactness. And naturally enough. Social customs do not change overnight, nor do they change uniformly over a nation, city, class, or identically within the various denominations which we have already seen to be related to a class structure of the nation, which is itself in process of change. At the same period it may be possible to trace both advance and decline. In Sheffield we have already noted that the 1881 figure of church attendance does not necessarily represent the high-water line; it shows a point of high participation, and certainly the Wesleyans continued to advance well beyond this date, as their membership figures and extensive building programme testify. Nor is there any reason to believe that the Church of England did not continue far beyond this date to maintain her proportion of the population. Certainly it is a matter of legitimate argument when decline beings in any particular area, as also the pattern of decline. What is more certain is that between 1881 and 1900 the peak was reached, passed, and slow deflation had commenced. Speaking broadly, it is probably true to say that the general over-all decline of church-going in the nation begins in the late years of the nineteenth century.

Evidence of Recession in London

The clearest available evidence of changing social habit in the matter of worship during this period relates to London, though, let it hastily be said, London is not Sheffield! But nonetheless there is striking evidence from the Capital. A census of religious attendance was taken in 1886 by the *British Weekly* newspaper, by a count on one particular Sunday, and again by the *Daily News* in 1903 by a count spread over that year. The figures are subject to all the criticisms and qualifications that can be made of such compilations, but they provide means of comparison between the two dates. In 1886 the population of Smaller London was 3,816,483, and by 1900 it had risen to slightly more than 4,500,000. At the earlier date the total attendance at all the churches on a Sunday was calculated to be 1,167,312, of which 535,715 were for the Church of England, and 369,349 were Nonconformist (excluding the Salvation Army figures). In 1903 the *Daily News* computed the total attendances to be 1,003,361,[5] of which 429,822 were Church of England and 416,977 Nonconformist (including the Salvation Army figure of 22,402). The voluminous analyses of the figures for the latter census are published in Mudie-Smith's *Religious Life of London;* they enable the Londoner to know the exact number of people at his church or chapel at the beginning of the century.

[5] Including children at church services, but excluding Sunday school figures.

Mudie-Smith also provides a chapter on the comparison between the figures for 1886 and 1903. While the population had increased by over half a million, the total attendances had fallen by something like 150,000. The decrease in attendance was almost wholly confined to the Church of England "and fairly uniform all over London, affecting rich, middle class and poor districts," while the Free Churches as a body were holding their numbers, but not significantly expanding with the increased population.

The reasons for the erosion of the Established Church in comparison to the Free Churches are many, but most important would be the sustained and greater momentum of Nonconformity in the middle-class and lower middle-class groups, their greater affinity with the social and political aspirations of those sectors of society, the undoubted superiority of the immense social organization of the Nonconformist churches, and possibly the development of the "week-end habit" that would play greater havoc with churches not imbued with the Nonconformist conscience. All of which is to say that if there were forces at work weakening all churches, there were social and centripetal forces at work in Nonconformist congregations that were lacking or far less strong in the parish churches.

Would Sheffield and other large industrial areas have shown a similar trend in these years? It is a pretty question, and the probable answer is that the boom continued later in Sheffield, even if the pattern of deflation was the same. The greater social stability of the industrial North and the absence of anything comparable to the Greater London hinterland, into which Londoners were spreading, would give greater persistence to established social habits anyway. And if it was a general characteristic of urban areas that the Free Churches maintained their hold longer than the Church of England, this would have been an added reason for persistence, since Sheffield was more strongly Nonconformist than London, in 1881 with 46,441 attendances as against 33,835 of the Church of England. But on the *timing* of the deflation we are not on firm ground. Sheffield in due course has probably caught up with London, if it has not even surpassed it in this matter!

Before departing from the London scene we may profitably examine some of the comments made on the 1903 figures, analysing the causes of deflation. As with every census available from 1851, the point is made for every section of London that the poor and the working classes are substantially estranged from the churches, even though some denominations are more successful than others. It may be noted, too, that the commentators were shocked by the paucity of attendances, alleged to be, after deduction for "twicers", only one in five of the population, that "four persons out of every five in London and Greater London are either careless or hostile as regards public worship," though *we* may add, as with all the census figures examined, how large the attendances appear to the modern eye. This stands out even more in the figures for Greater London, where the borough with the highest attendance, High Barnet, registered attendances of one in 1.66 of the population, and the lowest borough, of Tottenham, showed one in 6.06. A few of the many comments throw light on the general picture. Thus Charles F. G. Masterman, Fellow of Christ's College, Cambridge, had the task of interpreting the figures of South London; he deserves to be quoted as one continuously preoccupied with the burden of this study:

. . . In South London one man out of every six, and one woman out of every five, attends some place of worship at least once every Sunday . . . the poor (except the Roman Catholic poor) do not attend service on Sunday, though there are a few churches and missions which gather some, and forlorn groups can be collected by a liberal granting of relief. . . . The working man does not come to church. A few communities of Primitive Methodists, Baptists and Salvationists, and similar bodies, as a general rule represent his contribution to the religious life of the nation. . . . The tradesmen and middle class of the poorer boroughs exhibit an active religious life, mainly gathered in the larger Nonconformist bodies, especially the Baptists. . . .

On the side of the working people this is a period of unusual difficulty. The uprooting from the country and the transference to the town had caused a general confusion and disorder . . . dumped down in some casual street, unknown to his neighbours, unconnected with a corporate body or fellowship, he goes through life in a kind of confused twilight, dimly wondering what it all means. Material comfort and security is inevitably under these conditions his main interest; the memories of a life which is independent of the hard, visible, tangible boundaries become daily dimmer, as he clangs the hammer, or heaves merchandise, or manipulates hard material things . . . the failure is considerable from the side of the churches. The Anglican Church represents the ideals of the upper classes, of the universities . . . the large Nonconformist bodies represent the ideals of the middle classes, the strenuous self-help and energy which have stamped their ideas upon the whole of Imperial Britain. Each lives in poor districts, in them, not of them; each totally fails to apprehend a vision of life as reared in a mean street, and now confronting existence on a hazardous weekly wage from a block-dwelling or the half of a two-storied cottage. . . . We are recognised as meaning well, but our aims and ideals never become clearly intelligible. "What is he after?" "What does he get?" "What is behind it all?" are questions I have frequently heard as some church has bourgeoned out into fresh and ingenious enterprise. . . . We appear and we vanish. After a few months of this perplexing enthusiasm the curate or minister is called to another sphere of work, and disappears from the universe of those who had just, perhaps, commenced to realise that he possesses some traits of ordinary humanity. If we could only apprehend how entirely baffling and irrational all this must appear to those who are looking out of, instead of into, the abyss, our surprise would be less at the vastness of our failure than at the magnitude even of our poor success. Connected with this divergence we must recognise how scantily up to the present the Churches have identified themselves with those demands of Labour, which from the bottom of his heart the working man knows to be just. The battles of the past for social amelioration . . . have been fought apart from, and often with the open opposition of the larger religious organisations. . . .[6]

The passing of time has reinforced some of his caustic observations—that gigantic successful preaching centres merely draw from the local churches, and weaken them—"the water is not increased in quantity, but merely decanted from bottle to bottle . . . ," that "the morning and evening services of the Church of England, as normally performed, with their complicated and mysterious variations of canticles, prayers, and irrelevant readings of Scripture, are

[6] *The Religious Life of London*, ed. R. Mudie-Smith, 1904; ch. VII.

altogether bewildering to those not intimately familiar with the books from which they are compiled . . . ," and that "Sunday Schools conducted by mild-mannered and generous Buddhists would draw large and appreciative audiences." One further feature of London should be noted—the movement of population, first of the better-class people into the growing suburbs of Greater London, leaving solid masses of the poorer and less enterprising of the population, duly followed by the outward movement of the working classes into the suburbs, and the further emigration of the better classes. Nowhere did this happen on such a scale as in London of course, but London provides an acute illustration of what was happening in all the large towns of the country, and visibly in the city of Sheffield. Thus of London, George Haw, another man, almost obsessed it might be said with the problem of the working classes and their relationship to the churches, writes of the problem of Greater London:

. . . all the strong and prosperous people are running away from the inner belt of London as fast as they can; forgetting it, owning no responsibility for it, leaving it to the weaker, poorer, more weary ones. The manufacturers, their managers, and all the staff who take salaries as distinct from wages, come in the mornings, and go away in the evenings, and admit no responsibility, social or religious, for the crowded districts where their workplaces lie, and their workpeople live. The chronic poor and the small wage earners are left stranded, a class by themselves. It is a terrible thing the way London is separating itself into harsh divisions of class, into cities of the poor and cities of the rich. . . .

Of churchgoers in Greater London you might say they consist of two classes only—the upper middle class and the lower middle class. That is simply because suburban London in the main consists of these two classes. You get the same all the kingdom over. The residential suburbs of all cities fill the churches. It is in the nature of things therefore to find a higher proportion of churchgoers in Greater London than in London itself. The thing that calls for serious thought is that where the wage-earning class is pouring into Greater London, the church attendance declines. . . .

. . . Observe that where the working classes are crowding into Greater London, and the middle classes deserting them as they deserted them before, the church attendance is at the lowest. It stands at about the same proportion as in the working-class quarters of Inner London. If anything it shows a tendency to be lower. Willesden is now as poor in its church attendances as Stepney, Southwark or St. Pancras. . . . Willesden is becoming another St. Pancras; in its church life it has already become so.

. . . It may seem fairly satisfactory that in a big industrial borough like West Ham 1 in 4.80 of the inhabitants goes to a place of worship. But how many of the worshippers are working people? West Ham has still a large number of middle-class residents—that is, the class that makes up the majority of the churchgoers. . . . Take a church census of West Ham ten years hence, when the middle classes, who are now running away from it as fast as they can, will have almost entirely disappeared, and you will find the number of worshippers shrunken like a plant stricken with blight. Far quicker than in London itself, this decay of church life is spreading among the working-class districts of Greater London.[7]

[7] *ibid*, ch. XVII.

Mudie-Smith's composite volume is thus a treasury of information on the religious condition of London at the beginning of the century, and in the largest urbanized area of the country it enables us to date the slackening of the "boom" and the beginning of the "deflation," though for reasons we have considered it should be used with caution in judging the situation elsewhere. It also supplies impressive evidence of the estrangement of the working classes.

The statistical survey should be used as a companion volume to Charles Booth's monumental social survey of *Life and Labour of the People of London*, which was carried out between the years 1890 and 1900, of which seven volumes are devoted to a study of the religious life of the Capital. As so often with surveys uncongenial in their disclosures, it was not received with universal approbation, but beyond dispute he too showed the remarkable influence of class on religious observance, and that "wherever the regular working class is found, and in whatever proportion to the rest of the inhabitants, it seems equally impervious to the claims of religion . . . while those who do join any church become almost indistinguishable from the class with which they then mix, the change that has really come about is not so much *of as out of* the class to which they have belonged." With all the proper qualifications to be made for some denominations and within denominations, with due recognition of the widespread attendance at Sunday schools, and of the multifarious agencies of mission and charity whereby tracts of London, he averred, were "sodden with religion and unsaved," this estrangement of the adult working classes stands out from Booth's survey. And he puts his finger on the intractable sociological aspect of the mission problem. "Elaborate doctrinal teaching may be inculcated in childhood, but its influence is not likely to last unless maintained by the atmosphere of the home or unless supported by social usage. It is to social usage that the upper classes trust, and it is in the union of home and church that we find the strength of the Nonconformists. . . . Thus with regard to the working classes (and the poor) we seem to arrive at a deadlock. There is no hope of social usage, and to create religious homes a new generation of religious-minded parents must arise; while until we have the social usage or the religious homes all advance is stopped." The acute implications for the Church's mission posed by this sociological statement of the dilemma still await discovery.

Two Factors in the Nation "Unchurched"

We have strayed somewhat from the matter under particular consideration— the decline of the churches in the late nineteenth and early twentieth century. From this point two factors stand out, and both must be borne in mind. The one is the continued estrangement of the working classes, still enlarging, more and more colouring the urban and industrial areas, flooding into suburban areas. We have traced it at length, generation by generation, in the City of Sheffield. Their history, in this respect, is one of general continuity of habit, but with the decline of the denominations that had been more effective in reaching the working classes, with the political re-orientation of their leadership, and the solidification of their own pattern of life, and with the general weakening of religious faith in the whole nation, they were even more wholly outside the religious institutions as the twentieth century ad-

vanced. The other factor is the erosion within the churches themselves—a weakening adherence and progressive loss from the churches of their traditional supporters, whether upper, middle, or lower middle class, or even of the working classes where in small proportion to their numbers they were held.

These are the two factors that have found the churches so denuded in the course of the twentieth century; they are the two factors that in conjunction have left England so widely "unchurched." The two distinct histories coalesce in the twentieth century to form the mission problem of the nation; but, without an understanding that both have operated, we easily fall into a false analysis that ignores the persistent alienation of the urban industrial masses from the time of their very emergence in the new towns. That is to say, the losses in the twentieth century and the passing of time have obscured the more deepseated and historic problem of the alienation of the working classes. And the two factors still need not only separate analysis but separate treatment, since whatever changes may have taken place in standards of life and in the structure and outlook of the social classes—and great changes have taken place—the inherited attitudes and patterns of life of the working class, and those of the continuing very mixed middle classes, are very different. If Disraeli's "two nations" are now less sharply defined in economic terms, they are hardly less divided in cultural terms, with different attitudes towards religion and the churches even where non-membership is common to both. On this rock many well-intentioned evangelistic hopes have foundered.

3 · Social Classes and Their Religious Approaches

ÉMILE PIN

At the beginning of Chapter XI we formulated certain hypotheses concerning the respective religious approaches of the bourgeoisie and the working class, hypotheses whose value was to be tested by our questionnaire on religious practices. This matter was partially taken up in the last three chapters. We would like here, also using material from earlier chapters, notably that dealing with parochial works and religious movements, to assemble disparate elements and to reconstitute comprehensively each of the three approaches: the approach of the bourgeoisie, of the working class and of intermediate classes.

Obviously, our conclusions can be no more than provisional. It must be remembered that the scope of the documents used to formulate these conclusions is doubly limited: it is that of a single parish and, within this parish, that of a polling of opinion which cannot be attested as representative.

We shall also not hesitate in this last chapter to extend *the conclusions drawn from our statistics* by making use of the many conversations we have had over a four-year period with parishioners of every class. We are moreover certain that in doing this *we are not departing from the direction already taken: it is in an overall cultural adaptation or failure of adaptation that we must seek the origin of the links which we have discovered between religious practice and social class.* We have tried to remain

SOURCE. From Émile Pin, *Pratique Religieuse et Classes Sociales,* Paris: Éditions Spes, 1956, ch. XIV, pp. 395–408; translated by Stanley E. Gray.

within the area controlled by our statistical results, carrying our speculations beyond these only when this was useful in order to attain a comprehensive view.

I. The Religious Approach of the Bourgeoisie

Summary. Choosing from the many characteristics which can make up the religious behavior of a man, we had posited that the approach of the bourgeois was characterized by a certain individualism and by what we called "eschatologism."

Individualism leaves its mark on everything in the life of the bourgeois who has reached, through his own efforts, a worldly "salvation," does not depend on religion to regulate his existence, but rather appeals to it only to assure the continuation of this salvation in the other world.

What may we conclude from the study of our poll of opinions on religious practices?

Individualism and Communal Sense. The term "individualism" is pejorative. It indicates an explicit rejection of communal life. This rejection is unquestionably to be found in a certain number of those questioned, and the proportion is probably even greater in the parish at large. The practicing Catholics in question show distaste for communal forms of piety, especially for collective ritual gestures and hymns, a distaste which is an unmistakable indication of religious individualism. This individualism is far from typical of the majority of practicing bourgeois citizens. It may nevertheless be a sign of a particular tendency, a distortion of a value peculiar to the bourgeoisie, namely, an acute sense of the irreplaceable, unique character of every human person. And this value is undeniably a religious and a Christian value. It is to be found everywhere in the Gospel.

That a particular emphasis is placed on this value by the bourgeoisie is a fact revealed otherwise than in the distortions which the value engenders. The need for personal prayer, for meditation, has most often appeared in the bourgeoisie. It is particularly the bourgeois whose critical sense is disturbed by the naiveté of communal gestures. While remaining excellent Christians, and concerned with the Christian education of their children, there are mothers who insist that participation at mass should not be too passive, too much a matter of routine. What inspires this insistence?

Correction of the Hypothesis: The Demands of Urban Life. We have assumed that it came from a sort of fundamental disposition of the bourgeois. This is not false, but in order to be understood the disposition must be put back into the total context of bourgeois life. The disposition is an acquired one, for it is necessary for integration of the citizen into urban life. The complexity of urban civilization and the size of social units confront the urbanite with this alternative: he must either cultivate his personality, intelligence and character in order to resist anonymity and find a place in the social and cultural community, or he must disappear into this anonymity, refuse to comprehend his situation, and let his personality seep away into the many fissures which open up between the various aspects of his activity. Urban life, by its decomposition alone (the only link existing between the various theatres of urban activity is the anonymous one of public transportation) constrains the urbanite who wishes to pre-

serve the unity and stability of his personality to create or at least to increase a distance between his psychological life and his social life.[1] He can be himself only by separating himself, distinguishing himself from the "mass," by creating for himself a body of doctrine, of personal opinion.

Urban Christian life is molded on the same model as the rest of urban life. The Christian, or at least the Christian family, lives alone, without community of interests or support from without, left to itself, uncontrolled. The break is complete between the official organization of existence, the tolerant, liberal, even licentious environment of urban life on the one hand, and moral and religious norms on the other. It is up to each person, or at least to each family, to maintain, discover or invent its own mode of behaviour. Parishes function more as administrative centers than as effective groups, or at least so it seems on first sight. The Catholics who move into them or who leave them notify no one of their arrival or departure; no one pays attention to their presence or absence at church services. Only those persevere whose convictions are independent of the customs of their environment or who can manage to re-establish, through their culture and beyond these local customs, a community of mind and feeling within a universal Church, whose presence is scarcely visible in everyday life.[2]

[1] The distance between social life and psychological life is much less significant for the countryman (it may even disappear in so-called "primitive" societies). We do not think that the primary education received by children up to the age of fourteen or fifteen suffices for the formation of the personality of the future urbanite. For this, secondary studies seem necessary, with their disinterested approach and apparent lack of immediate utility.

[2] Is this not also the explanation for what we noted in Chapter X: that religious life is

Is it surprising that in such a situation the bourgeois Christian, who calculates the very conditions necessary for integration in the urban milieu (and also, we would say, for the integration of his own, private world) and who knows the importance of a well-structured personal life, should insist that these indispensable conditions be maintained for him? Must we label as an individualist the man who refuses to let his personal life be absorbed by a compelling, but also blinding and deadening collective spirit, when he has built up this life through hard effort and feels it threatened constantly by the laxity of his environment? [3]

Certainly, the Christian life is a life of charity, and the Christian bourgeois with his insistence on the formation of the individual may be tempted to forget it. He may be tempted to forget that it is through the Church, through the Christian community that he will be saved; but is he wrong, from a strictly religious point of view, to remember that the communal life will be authentic only if it is a grouping of adult and autonomous personalities?

It is not our intention here to approve or condemn anyone; we wish only to rid our hypothesis of whatever in it seemed too exclusive. It is not because the bourgeois has become accustomed to individualism in his secular life that he continues to be individualistic in his Christian life and in his assurance of salvation; it is rather, seen in a more comprehensive perspective, because urban existence itself and everything which is involved in it—including religious life—demands of him a resolutely personal attitude in his religious as well as in his secular life. This is at any rate the conclusion which we think may be drawn from the answers to the questionnaire on religious practices. It is evident, too, that the situation scarcely makes it easy for the bourgeois to understand the communal aspects of piety.

Religious Rites and the Transformation of Existence. If it has seemed necessary to revise the first part of our hypothesis, the second part on the other hand seems to need fewer modifications.

It is true that we have noted frequently mention of a change in mental attitude allegedly taking place in the parish.

But,

1. The very fact that there is question of a change would seem to prove that the former or spontaneous mental attitude needed or needs revision.

2. While the protests or at any rate the reticence concerning communal celebration of the mass appeared to stem from a justifiable religious need, the protests against sermons with a social message seem, excepting a few rare, carefully qualified criticisms, to come from a somewhat idealistic religious spirit.

3. The answers mentioned no visible amelioration in respect to professional life. This probably does not mean that such facts are non-existent, but it does seem that the daily preoccupations of the Christian bourgeois do not orient his attention in this direction.

4. It even seems that not all minds have as yet undergone the necessary mental readjustments, and that many of them are imbued with a class subjectivism which makes *social* inequality appear a necessary "evil," for which there is no remedy.

5. For many members of the bour-

___

thought of by the bourgeois as a private matter? It is not a matter for public discussion. Each person must decide his own convictions.

[3] "Prior to action, there is prayer; prior to prayer, faith, and faith is a gift. Too much action, as practised in the 'avant-garde' parishes, allures the young but does not arm them against themselves." (A family of the middle bourgeoisie.)

geoisie, perhaps still the majority, all of Christian life seems to consist in preparing oneself for a "correct" death, and not in making the significance of death a determining factor in the transformation of life.

6. It must be noted, however, that, partly as a result of a broad movement of thought and action, partly through the reaction of one generation against its predecessor[4] (in this case rather ambiguous), an important minority (certainly more than a hundred families) has undergone a profound change in mental attitude. Nevertheless, in a convention-ridden and cold world, this change in attitude lacks the means to express itself. It also lacks the means to transform existence. When expressed, it often appears more addicted to mere speech than productive of action, and we have put forward several hypotheses to explain this timidity.

7. Finally, is it necessary to add that this disembodied aspect of bourgeois religion cannot be separated from its other face, its "spiritual" character? French Catholicism is particularly sensitive to everything that could be considered a "temporal" or worldly compromise of religion, objecting even to whatever is efficacious in too practical a manner. The purity of the message is both claimed and proclaimed. This claim is undeniably a value, but it is not always easy to separate the wheat from the chaff. Every effective action assumes a choice among the various possibilities offered. Through idealism many Catholics in France refuse definite commitments which seem to them to express their ideal inadequately. France is the country of multiple political parties. The French bourgeoisie goes even further: it elects "independent" representatives. Among Catholic intellectuals, there are

those who are content to denounce, criticize, expose inconsistencies; but ultimately, what effective measures can emerge from an activity which deliberately remains negative? Evidently, between the more or less self-interested eschatologism of the bourgeois and the critical spirit of these intellectuals there is a continuity of a cultural type, although the *content* of their thought often appears diametrically opposed.

II. The Religious Approach of the Proletariat

Popular Culture. Popular culture is first of all definable in terms of what it lacks. Its members dispose of none of the means by which they might integrate themselves or find a recognized and stable place in urban society. They possess neither the financial reserves, nor the social connections, nor, most important, the cultural level and the personal education which would permit them to master complex situations and to separate the individual psychological life from the social life in which the individual is immersed. Suspicion, adolescent aggressiveness, uncooperativeness are normal in men who live in and must make their living from a world which does not possess by itself an immediate and visible coherence. Not only do they not understand this world, but further, they do not enjoy in it an equal share in the allotment of its most diverse advantages. The proletariat is in the first place proletarian because of its lack of intellectual and social education, then because of all the other deprivations suffered by its members, all of these deprivations being aggravated by the fundamental lack of adaptation. When rebuking the proletarian women for treating themselves to silk stockings and for buying up all the chickens at the market, the woman of the bourgeoisie was committing a double error: she was general-

[4] And also through a reaction on the part of newer elements of the bourgeoisie.

izing actions which, for lack of the means, could not have been repeated very often; but most important, she was judging, according to a bourgeois scale of values, attitudes which can only be understood when one has penetrated the chaotic and anarchic world of proletarian culture. In any event, the proletarian cannot *look ahead*, he can see no further than the immediacy of his job, the hovel and the neighborhood that he lives in. To see further, in space as in time, a different culture would be necessary. Does this mean that this incoherence is not compensated for by substitutes for culture? By no means. Every culture must, in the final analysis, form a coherent whole. The voids must be filled by explanatory "fragments." Two paths are open to the proletarian, the "horoscope" (and everything symbolized by the horoscope) and the simplistic explanations of the Party. Magic and Science. Magic for the women and science for the men. But we must not oversimplify. In this respect, there are men who are women and vice versa.

Superstitions. It is sometimes surprising to discover in the middle of the Twentieth Century, amidst the rationalism and the liberalism of our cities, a body of undying superstitions: What woman of a lower class neighborhood would walk under a ladder, would dare to light three cigarettes with the same match, offer a knife as a gift, step on a spider or see one in the morning without trembling, upset a salt shaker without the inevitable exorcising gesture, or be the thirteenth to sit down to the table? Others fear opening an umbrella indoors, marrying in May (this superstition is gaining prestige), dreaming of a baby, and there are those who rejoice at having encountered a hearse.[5] How many

women tremble upon consulting the weekly horoscope or pay visits to soothsayers, astrologers, fortune tellers and mediums? Others place confidence in childish devotions from which the religious meaning has entirely disappeared, as in those chain letters of prayers which circulate endlessly through the city. Several of our investigators receive these naïve formulations regularly in the mail.[6]

The bourgeois finds all of these superstitions amusing; he does not understand that they play an important role in popular culture, that of filling the empty spaces of a world which, without them, would be incoherent. The simplistic slogans of political parties play the same role.

Sects. Is it surprising that in this culture sects, in spite of the syncretism of their doctrine, their naïveté, their contradictions, attract a sympathetic audience? [7] Their success depends essentially on the restricted nature of the groups created.

---

[5] We have verified the existence of all these superstitions in the neighborhood studied.

[6] "Chain letter of Saint Anthony of Padua. I have confidence in you, do not break this chain because through it you will have a great surprise. Saint Anthony of Padua pray for us, for the things that concern us, for our house, give us happiness and health and grant our prayers. I have received this letter which brings good luck. It was begun in Auvergne and is to go around the world. Copy it 13 times, once each day to a person to whom you want to do good. On the 13th day you will have great joy. The priest who did this has earned 5 million. Miss Bertrand who broke the chain has been punished. Two soldiers who did it have earned a great fortune. Saint Anthony of Padua pray for us to the Lord our God. I have confidence in you. Do not break it."

[7] The Jehovah's Witnesses, and then the Christ's Witnesses have sought to proselytize in the neighborhood. The former have met with a certain amount of success. In one building, predominantly occupied by working class families, one of our investigators found three households converted to this sect.

By permitting each member to know the others and to be known by them, this restricted nature corresponds to a nonconceptual type of culture, in which immediate contact with persons and realities is the sole means of knowledge. Here we must make a slight correction in the hypothesis which we formulated at the beginning of Chapter XI. We had said that the proletarian could only adhere to a religion which reveals itself to be capable of creating a just world. We still think this. But the relative success of sects shows that the essential thing is not so much the result as it is the communion of action which aims at creating a just world. The militant members of the *Action Catholique Ouvrière* point out that the passive, timid and "socially uncommitted" attitude on the part of certain practicing Catholics from the lower class, or from the last ranks of the intermediate classes—that is to say on the part of those whom the proletarian may encounter in his daily life—is no less damaging to the image projected by religion than is the unconcern of the self-satisfied bourgeois. What the proletarian expects then of religion is neither the *immediate result* (or at least those who ask of religion no more than this show no religious sense), nor a simple, artificial communal life superimposed on a world of unjust inequality, but rather a *felt communion of action towards justice.* He will therefore be just as unfavorably impressed by purely verbal communal proclamations, by the passive and timid submission of his practicing Catholic co-workers, as by the injustice he endures at the hands of the Catholic of the upper bourgeoisie. The Communist Party is successful not so much in furnishing tangible results as in representing this communion. Furthermore, it has over the sects the advantage and the prestige of universality, a feature given by the amplitude of its struggle and its objectives. But it also knows how to take root locally, in restricted cells which inspire camaraderie. In its electoral campaign of December, 1955, the Party put great emphasis on door-to-door contacts. Its style and language appeal to immediate experience.

The Image of Urban Catholicism. Compared to this activity adapted to popular culture, urban Catholicism appears remote, theoretical, impersonal and ineffectual. We might say that it is involved in all those aspects of urban life which are beyond the intellectual and practical grasp of the proletarian. The proletarian may perhaps express his feeling by speaking of the association of religion and capitalism. But his vocabulary must be analyzed: capitalism is a vague term representing in his eyes the whole range of the unknown and complex conditions from which he suffers and which his *concrete and immediate mode of thinking* leads him to see as plotted by conscious, malevolent individuals: capitalists. The fact that it is precisely these capitalists who are assiduous at church, that it is their cars which crowd the streets around the churches on Sunday morning, that it is for them that the priests organize their finest ceremonies, and that it is with them that these priests most easily associate, furnishes the proletarian with the experiential content which will permit him to express himself, to explain his attitude subjectively. But that does not suffice, at least in our opinion, for an *objective* explanation. The primary factor is not the ineffectualness of religion in respect to the poverty of the proletarian, nor the association between religion and the wealthy. The primary factor is rather that, in everything which concerns the proletarian closely in his daily life, religion is absent and that, indeed, it operates in spheres and according to a *mode* which are inaccessible to him and without connection to daily life or the misery experienced daily. All this comes about for comprehensive cultural reasons. There are the "refinements" of ritual; the language of sermons; the Latin used in ceremonies; the restraint observed in conventions and conversation; the interposition of a system of concepts between those who converse; the presentation of religion to individuals to the accompaniment of an infinite respect for their personal liberty, which may give the impression of the wrong kind of "disinterestedness"; everything that "respectability" calls for; the keeping intact of private concerns—which, besides, is congruous with the size of the parishes. In our opinion, this is the obstacle between urban Catholicism and the proletariat, just as much as social injustice, even when this injustice is associated with the close, day-to-day experience of poverty.[8]

Has this not been proved inversely many times? Does not this same urban proletarian often return to the Church when he is even temporarily put again into the rural environment to which his mode of culture makes him adaptable? (Providing that the local clergy and religious institutions have remained adapted or have been able to adapt to the cultural type.) Should we accuse him of fickleness? No man is a pagan today who was a Christian yesterday and will chant the Credo again tomorrow. Should we not rather speak of cultural adaptation in one case and of an impassable gulf in the other?[9] It is not legitimate, then, to say

that the Breton loses his faith; we are not even authorized to say that he is forsaking religious observances in general, for the object of these observances is not the same in the one case as it is in the other.

Conclusion. In summarizing these reflections, we may conclude that a gulf is opened between the proletariat and urban Catholicism primarily through the agency of the *language* of words, of gestures and attitudes, and of cultural dimensions, customs and modes of feeling. We have on the one hand a world in which human relations are mediated by the concept, by critical reflection, by the knowledge born of education, by well defined social conventions; on the other, we have a world in which the only means of access to men and things is an immediate, felt contact.

On the one hand, we have a world in which inactivity and a somewhat ritualistic conception of religion are encouraged by the sense of death and of the vanity of earthly things (because the bourgeois has had the leisure to enjoy and to tire of them), by the desire to prolong eternally (and in a superior form) that worldly salvation which is at once so satisfying and so unsatisfying, as well as by an obscure desire to conserve acquired privileges.[10] On the other, we have a world in which the day-to-day experience of poverty inspires an urgent appeal to escape this poverty through some common, radical action.

On the one hand we find a world in which the cult of the unique person and the education of mind and character confer upon the individual a mental and social autonomy which may well express

---

[8] This having been stated, one may wonder whether this association is purely fortuitous and whether there is not a connection between the continuance of an unjustified social inequality and, if not religion, at least the whole range of those aspects of bourgeois culture which necessarily mark urban Catholicism in our country.

[9] Objections based on the example of dechristianized rural areas are not valid. To affirm that adaptation exists in certain rural areas is not the same as to affirm a universal adaptation of the Church to rural structures, and this for two reasons. First, because the

clergy is trained within the secondary urban culture; secondly, because cultures are in perpetual transformation; conserving a certain religious style does not assure its continuing adaptability.

[10] Even if there is an effort to alleviate the poverty which they engender.

itself as individualism or the rejection of what could be the sole means of reaching a practical goal: collective action. On the other, we have the conviction that only "man-to-man" cooperation and "unity" in action can achieve results.[11]

These are the principal aspects of the attitudes which seem to us to separate urban from proletarian culture, urban Catholicism from proletarian aspirations.

III. The Religious Approach of the Intermediate Classes

Intermediate Position. The intermediate classes are situated in a sort of purgatory where there is a possibility that virtue may be rewarded. They have escaped from the hell of the proletariat and are moving toward the "paradise" of the bourgeoisie, but have not yet reached it. The important characteristic here is hope, which provides the courage to face privations. The proletarian cannot look forward; he has neither the intellectual nor the material means. The intermediate classes are, on the other hand, blessed with foresight.

It is difficult to draw a line between the intermediate classes and the proletariat, at least if we rely upon easily discernible criteria. Income is on the average higher, as are standards of living and education, but the average includes extremes, and the lower extreme is hard to distinguish from levels attained by the working class. The demarcation exists, nevertheless, on a cultural plane. The point of departure for passage from lower to intermediate class seems to lie at the juncture of desire and possibility, of a desire for improvement often found in the young and the possibility of attaining this desire. This possibility is closely

related to housing conditions. The desire for improvement itself derives from a realization of this possibility, when a long enough time has elapsed since settlement in a neighborhood for a family to discover through experience a certain number of practical rules and means to get along in the urban labyrinth. It is not always for themselves that parents look for improvement, but often for their children—few in number—whom they urge forward.

This passage into the intermediate classes is marked by a break with the proletariat. For various reasons, particularly cultural ones, political opinions and ideologies may remain the same for some time, but not the mode of living, which changes.

Links with the neighborhood are cut, as with the working class. The family consolidates its efforts in order to realize through labor and thrift[12] a difficult and solitary breakthrough. The children, kept clean and properly dressed, must not play in the streets. They must be well behaved, thrifty and studious. Depending upon the level reached by their parents, the boys will endeavor to enter a professional school, a *lycée* if possible, or at the least a *cours complémentaire*.

The modest resources of the family afford no luxury, not even sufficiently comfortable circumstances to permit the enjoyment of social relations. The bourgeoisie feels nothing but indifference for these little people, who suffer from this indifference as their children do even more strongly. Reaching the age of fifteen to sixteen, these children want to emulate their friends of higher social strata, to imitate their parties, their sports, their hobbies. These attempts are merely a substitute, however, because their aspiration is not just to be able to do the same things, but to be effectively *admitted*.

[11] At the price of not being particular about the choice of collaborators. In any case, the cultural type itself does not favor subtle distinctions.

[12] Before the war of 1939–45 we would have used, still, the term "savings."

All those whose effort to advance has not been annihilated by the difficulties of life are particularly affected by the barriers which obstruct their access to the bourgeoisie, to its social intercourse, its *convivium* and its *connubium*. One might think that the families of the intermediate classes would try to create social links with each other, thereby establishing a sphere of social relations which would permit their integration. In reality, they do nothing of the kind. These families live in isolation, for no one of them enjoys the social prestige which would attract the others. It may be, too, that they do not possess the courage necessary to venture into the unknown, to break through barriers, to establish bridges. Theirs is a timidity imposed by a lack of culture, of social graces, of the assurance granted by positive knowledge. Not daring to intrude into an unfamiliar world, the families of the intermediate classes remain in a state of expectation, awaiting an invitation which would have to come from without, creating for them that which they themselves neither dare nor are able to achieve alone.

What They Demand of Religion. While the proletarian asks of the Church that it provide an active nucleus, a potential for vigorous action towards social justice, and while the bourgeois asks of it salvation in the other world, the intermediate classes wish the Church to afford a fraternal community. Something more than self-interest is to be seen in this demand. Such interest, while it cannot be identified with the religious demand, does predispose the little employee or modest shop foreman to attend to this aspect of religion, just as the proletarian and the bourgeois become sensitive to authentic religious values through their respective situations. Of course, if they were mutually exclusive, or affirmed unilaterally, these demands would cease to be religious.

The intermediate classes furnish the natural cement of parishes, provided that the parishes take the initiative to welcome them into the fold and to encourage their welcome by the other Christian members. As we have seen in Chapter IX, it is the intermediate classes who contribute almost the total participation in those parochial works which are intended to promote communal life and friendship. It is these classes which protest against the segregation of social milieux within the various sections of the *Action Catholique* movement, or against the bourgeois monopoly of positions of leadership. It is not that they fear the presence of the bourgeois; on the contrary, they judge this presence indispensable for the existence of a true community, but they would like the bourgeois to be able to participate through friendship and esteem for others, in a spirit of fraternal equality, and not, here again, in order to command or to make his superiority felt.

When cultures differ, so do the concrete manifestations of religious feeling. In other words, within this religious feeling the various component values, which are all rooted in the need for an absolute, take different hierarchical positions depending upon the culture. It would be false to claim that the whole of the religion of the proletarian, the bourgeois or the small employee can be reduced to each of the respective aspects which we have emphasized. But in each culture, there are several elements which are salient because of the particular conditions in which these cultures develop. These particular conditions in turn vary according to the culture. The elements which predominate in society as a whole play also their primordial role, and there is no doubt that in our industrial society, the role of technical and political elements is a leading one. These elements are not, however, the only ones. Furthermore, they do not act directly, but within those special inclusive social phenomena constituted by the various social classes. Again, within each of these classes, hierarchies are perceptible; we have pointed out the primary importance for religious adherence of *modes of knowledge*, an importance which has been insufficiently recognized, in our opinion.

In relation to these "cultures" and the basic personalities which develop within them, religions stand as structured, or better, as organized wholes in which the imprint of the past is deeply marked. It is a past influenced by the cultures which the religion has already assimilated, a past marked by former adaptations. Is there any reason to be surprised that when confronted with social classes not only different from one another but profundly opposed (not only in objectives but in mode of thought and way of life), religion's prior eagerness to adapt to a single class—a class which was perhaps a little too quickly identified with society as a whole—has created for the other contending social classes special difficulties in the matter of religious adherence? On the contrary, what would be surprising would be a different state of affairs.[13]

[13] As we have previously noted, spontaneous values proper to each culture are ambiguous and may engender atheistic outlook as well as religious adherence. A spontaneous atheism of both bourgeois and proletarian exists.

4 · Worker-Priests in Britain?

E. R. WICKHAM

What shall we say to the advocates of a worker-priest movement in Britain? It is interesting to note that the idea of a ministry engaged in secular professions was proposed as early as 1833 by Thomas Arnold in his *Principles of Church Reform*. One of his many proposals was for a revival of the order of deacons who would follow a secular calling to make a bridge between the secular and the sacred, the clergy and the laity, though with Arnold's strong emphasis on the minister as a scholar and a gentleman, we may doubt whether he had in mind the ordination of the early nineteenth century artisan!

The idea has been considered again, a number of times since the war. In the report to the Church Assembly, "Towards

SOURCE. E. R. Wickham, "Worker-Priests in Britain?" from David L. Edwards, ed., *Priests and Workers,* London: SCM Press Ltd., 1961, pp. 131–140.

the Conversion of England," in 1945, there was an appended note in "priests in industry" prepared by a sub-committee that recommended that "in some circumstances, a parish priest should be allowed to take a job in industry for a shorter or longer period," and that "in exceptional circumstances, an industrial worker should be ordained as a deacon or a priest, to remain in industry and exercise his ministry as an industrial worker." It went on to say:

If any large scale attempt is to be made to Christianize industry, it would be necessary to develop a strategy, which will depend upon a network of well organized and carefully trained cells. These cells will normally be led by laymen; but in some instances a number of allied groups may wish to submit to the Bishop the name of one of their members for ordination. It would be the duty of such a priest in industry to act as the authoritative representative of the Church in factory life, and to determine and correlate strategy. He would use his lunch-hours for propaganda work and instruction, and he would visit his fellow workers after factory hours. He would take a prominent part in Trade Union and municipal affairs.

These proposals were not embodied in the formal recommendations of the Commission, and no action was taken. We should note moreover that the recommendations were made at a time before either the French movement or the Industrial Mission projects in England had attained significance. We may think, too, that some of the proposals, as is understandable at this early period, showed greater zeal for tackling a problem than sensitive understanding of shop-floor life in an English factory. In fact, however, the whole report was rapidly forgotten.

The matter came up again in the councils of the Church in 1955. In that year a joint committee report of the Convocation of Canterbury on canon revision faced the question of "what changes are desirable and practicable in the law relating to the pursuit by a clergyman of a gainful secular occupation." The question was raised not only in relation to the possibility of increasing the number of clergy by ordaining men in secular occupations to supplement a diminished parochial ministry, but also to the ordination of men "who already occupy positions of pastoral responsibility," to whom priesthood could be a valuable addition to their ministry. It was suggested that among doctors, club-leaders and welfare officers there would be eligible candidates. The report, however, also wished to include the case of "ordaining men in industrial occupations" (i.e. worker-priests) for specifically industrial ministry, though the recommendations are set out with a caution lacking in the earlier

report, with less confidence of how they would exercise their ministry, and with a plea that it should be further studied by representatives of industry and trade unions as well as by the Church. Explicitly in the report this caution is related to the history of the French movement. But again, no practical conclusions resulted.

Despite the widespread if somewhat shallow interest of the post-war Church in industry, and despite the deep concern and concentrated work in industry in some few areas of the country, we have in fact not witnessed a worker-priest movement in England. There have been a few ordained men who have taken industrial jobs, and at the present time there are some half-dozen young priests working on the shop-floor of industry with the permission of their bishops. They should be sharply distinguished from some others, never very many, fortunately, who have taken "welfare" jobs, or other white-collar jobs, perhaps to eke out a small stipend. There are more Free Church ministers who for simple economic motives have been compelled to do this. But the handful of genuine worker-priests do insist that there is a strong case for the development of such a ministry, and there are several bishops who would support some such development, but rather through the ordination of men already in secular callings than by encouraging the regular ministry to engage in secular work. In this volume, strong advocacy for the non-clerical priest, the "lay-priest," the man in the situation who is a priest, is made in the contribution of Patrick McLaughlin.

What should we say to these proposals? What objectives are sought through them? Are they of promise, of significance and wisdom? Or is this a blind alley without significance, even undesirable? There are many things to be said, and my own experience and knowledge of this field of mission have led me to some fairly determined views. Certainly we should be willing to allow some controlled experiments in new forms of ministry, including ministries of the worker-priest type. They need to be modest, eschewing grandiose claims and free of publicity. We should beware of grasping the idea as the panacea or "solution" to a massive and intractable problem with deep historical and cultural roots. And the men involved need to be selected with very great care, for not every instinct for the radical gesture is to be trusted, and not every man with an uncomfortable urge has the wisdom or tenacity to discover whether it is valid or not. But the question needs to be put into a larger context before a clear and reasoned answer might be forthcoming. It needs to be argued in some detail.

Undoubtedly we face an acute missionary situation in Britain, though the situation varies considerably from place to place. For example, the Church in the urban, industrialized parts of South Yorkshire, East or South London, is reduced to a smaller, more imprisoned fraction of the community than, say, in the industrial connurbation of S.E. Lancashire. In the latter the Church has been more indigenous to the working-class culture and the "fringe" therefore is longer, for historical and sociological causes. But the variations notwithstanding, and not withstanding the recent increase in church attendance in better-class suburban and ex-urbanite areas, the acuteness of the mission problem in the urban industrial areas is undeniable. The case for a missionary Church devised for engagement as distinct from a Church solely pastorally-minded and organized, however expectantly, for maintenance, is as strong in Britain—certainly in England—as anywhere in Europe. Nor is this only an argument for a re-orientation of mind and emphasis in the parochial life and structure of the Church. With the best

will in the world the purely parochial expression of the Church (in fact almost its sole expression) cannot exert significant and planned influence on the fluid forces of modern industrial society or on its varied institutions, social, industrial and political projections, which cannot be tied down into those small geographical areas we call parishes. I have argued this point in particular relation to the industrial institutions of society in *Church and People in an Industrial City,* and it has never been contested by any informed social observer. Of course this in no way disparages the concept of the parish or the parish ministry which must remain the major expression of the Church's life, whatever new emphases or strategies may be required in our modern complex society. But it is to admit that there is a crying need for strategy and policy in the industrial city, in the urban conglomerate, the industrial diocese, to *influence* the *influences* of society, if one may put it that way, and that in any such strategy some new deployment of man power, some new expressions of ministry, will be required. This is sensed by those who advocate a worker-priest movement or the ordination of men remaining in their secular callings, though one suspects such advocacy is not always supported by a close knowledge of the industrial scene or by a theology of mission informed by a "feel" for Church-community relations appropriate to the British scene. Certainly neither zeal nor theory alone are sound guides in this field. The case then for the missionary strategy, for the redeployment of some selected and specially trained clergy to new tasks is overwhelming, but this is not necessarily to justify either a movement along the French lines, or a strategy based upon McLaughlin's particular theology of the Church and ministry. We must look at the French scene and compare it with our own.

The French and British Situations

At once we are bound to notice the very dissimilar contexts of the missionary problem in our two countries, separated though they are by such a narrow strip of water. A basic difference is to be seen in the class relationships, for our British society, class-ridden though it may be, has not seen the deep social fracture of the French scene. The French working class, if not Marxist *au coeur*, has been dominated by Communist organizations and leadership—a fact to note, notwithstanding the disarray of the Party since "Hungary," and its weakening electoral power since General de Gaulle's return to power in 1958. Lacking a large, politically significant, democratic-Socialist workers' party, the worker has long voted Communist and certainly the literature of the worker-priest movement shows the French working class as a clearly demarcated strongly self-conscious group, "proletarian," and often described in its own self-analysis as oppressed and degraded. Its slogans if not its tactics, are recognizably revolutionary and politically-messianic. The foreign observer may wonder how this should be with the steady economic growth of France since the war; he may be tempted to wonder if it may not be an increasingly anachronistic attitude, bound to weaken with the progressive prosperity of Western Europe. But be that as it may, evidence for the attitude is real enough, and France does not, seemingly, have the political instruments that might encourage the corporate embodiment of more democratic and confident instincts even if their existence is justified. All of this is historically explicable.

Historically understandable, too, is the deep rift between the Catholic Church in France and this working-class culture, a rift that is not due simply to factors in

this problem common to our two countries—such as the inadequacy of pastoral care in the vast amorphous urban parishes, or the sociological imprisonment of the Church within more privileged groups (in fact the nineteenth century bourgeois class in France was notoriously anti-clerical)—but to ideological causes themselves explicable in theological terms on the side of the Church, and to political and ideological ones on the side of the proletarian class. If we look only at the *extent* of the missionary problem in the two countries we are struck by the similarity. But how unlike if we probe deeper! There is nothing in France comparable to the British Labour Party, non-Marxist, woven of many strands, but deeply marked by ethical and Christian idealism, the consequence of its British soil and more concretely in many parts of the country of radical Nonconformity. Whatever criticisms can be levelled at the British Churches in their relationships with the working classes (and they are many indeed), it can be asserted that their Protestantism, their liberalism, and indeed their very divisions have saved them from that "heteronomy" (to use Tillich's term) that has its counterpart in the worst expressions of anti-clericalism and secular autonomy. The British Churches did little to avert it, but at least we can say of Britain that the "autonomy" of society is largely the product of secular forces and not in any major sense the consequence of the Church's "heteronomy." The result is that both political and religious institutions in Britain, unconsciously in inter-play, have led to quite different attitudes to Churches here than in France. This is not to minimize the gravity of the missionary problem in Britain, but it is to assert a difference of "feel" in that problem. The French worker tends to be anti-clerical in an ideological sense; the English industrial workers on a massive scale are estranged from the Church, indifferent to her and critical for reasons and rationalizations both erratic and shrewd. But, significantly, the British workman wants to justify and excuse himself for his separation from the Church. He wants to explain that "you can be a Christian without going to church," that the Churches are out of touch with real life, that she has failed in this situation and that . . . he will produce a hundred reasons for not "going to church," he wants to put himself in the right over against the Church—he often protests too vigorously. And if a minister of the Church, as a minister and a man, penetrates into his setting, at ease, on his level, without patronage, forthright in his words, he is accepted and welcomed, and after the initial torrent of attack on the Churches he can count upon the assertion that at last the Church is doing her proper job "in coming to the people." There is no evidence at all in the worker-priest literature from France that such an attitude obtains there. This distinction should not be painted in terms too black and white—as Godin has written: "if you have had dealings with the real pagans, you appreciate how much of Christ's teaching is still left in France," and in the English scene, on the other hand, there is a deeper secularism than is often apparent in a nation that has always shrunk from the apellation "atheist" and has no knowledge of a philosophic agnosticism. But the stain of the Churches runs widely over British society if thinly, even into groups that have been historically estranged from them. The cultural cleavage is less pronounced here without doubt. It can make the missionary task the more baffling; the problem is less clear-cut here, more subtle. But one can understand why the French priest, seeking acceptance in a cultural group so radically dissociated from the Church and the Church's culture, has himself felt impelled to make a radical disassociation from the conventional Church and ministry, from its cultural imprisonment and its political assumptions.

We should notice too the different mood of the two working classes. Whatever disabilities the British "working class" (not a phrase that social group is solidly attached to) suffers in the middle of the twentieth century, whatever promise and hopes of the immediate post-war years have not materialized, few would deny that social changes since the war have transformed its general condition. There has been a general rising standard of living, if all too slow and intermittent, and not withstanding the poor economic conditions of particular groups, such as unskilled men in certain industries, on datal rates, with little overtime and so on. Increased educational opportunity, the demand for more highly trained workers, day release to technical colleges —notwithstanding the deeper entrenchment of the middle-classes in their own educational advantages—are real enough on a wide scale, and can be expected to expand. The trades unions are accepted as an essential part of the industrial structure of the country and the periodic exceptions prove this general rule. Whatever disputes, tensions or disturbances occur, the mood of the unions is one of confidence and of considerable power. And from a material point of view, the cultural advance of the working class is evident, again notwithstanding many pockets of exception, many areas of cultural and material slum and the many seductions of "ad-mass."

The consequence of these social changes in British society since the war is that the "working class" is far from being an isolated, closed group. One must not generalize too much from the example, but in many a family where the father works in the factory as a labourer, the sons are growing up to be skilled workers, technicians, white-collar workers and managers. Again, despite the survival of pockets of severe under-privilege, the English worker is not to be regarded as degraded. He grumbles of course. He may be "alienated" on a large scale, but less in the Marxist sense than in a more imponderable sense, in that all modern men in our urban industrialized society are estranged from their true being, in our undirected and unmastered industrial society. Again, one does not want to paint this picture in too radical a contrast. It is a massive task to lift a nation with so vulnerable an economy as Britain. The so-called "equal educational opportunity" creates its own problems. The "affluent society" has a way of producing new cultural divisions and new social problems. And on the other hand, the French economy, we are told, has its own inner strength and carries the possible promise of a gradual dilution of the sense of class war.

There is of course a danger in such broad general comparisons. The working community in each nation, within different industries and areas of each nation, will have its own wide range of social attitudes, its areas of acute isolation and of open social advance, its areas of self-confidence and its areas of depression, its industrial groups that are forward-looking and those that are smouldering, aggressive and "bloody-minded," or even simply regressive and apathetic. This will be true of both countries. And this is to say that there can be cultural groups so broken from the rest of society, so estranged from a Church living in more privileged social groups even if as mutations within them, that the case for radical identification by something like a worker-priest movement can be argued. But we must look at the overall situation, the cultural trends and the prospects of the future, in devising a strategy of mis-sion, and this compels us to question whether it is a relevant strategy of mission in the contemporary British scene, in a society with a considerable degree of social mobility, a steady diminution of the "proletarian" group, and where a strong ideological sense of the working class is lacking. Baffling as the missionary task of the Church is here, the dramatic context of the French scene, as the French writers depict it, is simply lacking here. The situation here quite simply makes different demands on the Church and her ministry. In France, says Collonge, the worker-priests felt obliged to work for the "ruin of the social and political balance that we have at present" . . . "they did not try to dilute the class war—but on the contrary accepted the class war as a fact, like gravity, which must therefore be taken into account." The gulf between the Church and the working-class there was not simply wide —it would appear to be absolute. As Poulat says, "quite simply, the gulf between the social structures of the Church and those of the working class was too great, and was demonstrated to be much greater than we had thought at the outset . . . The industrial work of the priest was seen primarily as a means of contact with the workers which it was impossible to have otherwise. It did not arise out of theory; it was imposed by a situation. If other forms of contact should be found, this work would lose, if not its usefulness, at least its necessity." And so on. Clearly, the worker-priest movement derived its justification and importance from a complex of factors, some of which emerged only in the process—but they are not the factors that can be shown to be decisive in the British situation. Both the industrial-social scenes and the religious scenes are unlike.

C · AMERICAN PHENOMENA: VARIATION AND STRATIFICATION

1 · Religion and Social Structure in the United States

BERNARD LAZERWITZ[*]

The development of the sociology of religion for the United States has been seriously handicapped by a lack of data on large and varied populations. While many investigations have been made of the religious behavior of restricted groups and, recently, an excellent study has been done upon religion in Detroit,[1] reliable data for the entire nation have just become available. One sample survey conducted by the United States Census Bureau and several sample surveys conducted by the Survey Research Center of the University of Michigan and the National Opinion Research Center of the University of Chicago have furnished information which permits a detailed description and some analysis of religious behavior in the United States.[2] The Survey Research Center studies reported

upon here have stimulated detailed research on the social status of our major religious groups and upon the factors associated with attendance at religious services.

The religious composition of the adult population of the United States can be seen in Table 1. Protestants constitute 72 per cent of the adult population,[3] Roman Catholics 22 per cent, and Jews 3 per cent. By far the two largest Protestant denominational groups are the Baptists and Methodists who together total 38 per cent of the adult population.[4]

What about the future religious composition of the United States? Demographic research has documented a consistently higher birthrate for Roman Catholics. Hence, would it not be reasonable to expect future generations to show gradually increasing percentages of Roman Catholics?[5]

Such an expectation really represents a highly oversimplified view of population dynamics. First of all, a sizable percentage of Protestants have families as large as or larger than those of Roman Catholics. Data presented by Petersen in his book, *Population*, show substantial

[*]The author is indebted to the Survey Research Center of the University of Michigan for the generous permission to use and publish its religious survey data. Financial support for the analysis of the survey data was provided by the University of Illinois Research Board. The present paper, based on previous research by the author, was written expressly for this volume.

TABLE 1. *Religious Composition of the Adult Population of the United States*

RELIGIOUS GROUPS	PER CENT OF U. S. POPULATION 21 YEARS OLD OR OLDER[a]
Protestants	72%
Baptists	21
Methodists	17
Lutherans	7
Presbyterians	6
Episcopalians	3
Other Protestants	18
Roman Catholics	22
Jews	3
Other Religions	1
No Religion or Religion not reported	2
Nation	100%
Sample Size	5827
U. S. Adult Population[b]	108,051,172

[a] Based upon Survey Research Center data obtained in 1957 and 1958. The percentages pertain to the civilian population 21 years old or older.

[b] United States population 21 years old or older as reported by the 1960 Census of Population.

birthrates for Baptists.[6] Negroes, who are overwhelmingly Protestants, have high birthrates; Southern whites, also heavily Protestant, have high birthrates. Hence, the Protestant group, possessing over a three-to-one edge on Roman Catholics, contains more than enough high birth-rate adherants substantially to counteract (though not fully overcome) Catholic fertility.

Of even more interest are the fertility differences among the low birthrate, numerically smaller, higher status Protestant denominations, such as Presbyterians, United Church of Christ, and Episcopalians, and the high birthrate, numerically large, lower status Protestant groups such as the Baptists or more fundamen-

talist denominations. Demographically, one would be safe in predicting a significant shift in numbers in favor of the latter more traditionalistic Protestant denominations. But of great importance among Protestants is movement among denominations since large percentages of Protestants change to denominations other than the ones into which they are born. Information on the magnitudes of these dynamic intra-Protestants shifts is meager.[7] Nevertheless, it appears highly likely that birth differences among Protestant denominations are significantly reduced (perhaps eliminated) by the dynamics of adult denominational changes.

To complicate matters further, there is the question of conversion streams between the Protestant and Catholic communities. The future proportions of the population preferring the various Protestant faiths or the Roman Catholic faith cannot be considered without reliable data on conversions and the religious choices of children of mixed marriages. Such data are not available.

All this adds up to the futility of trying to predict the future religious composition of the United States without knowledge about the following.

(a) Future changes in Protestant and Catholic birthrates.

(b) Intra-Protestant movements away from denomination of birth to other denominations.

(c) Religious conversions between Protestantism and Catholicism.

(d) Membership results of mixed marriages.

(e) Size and religious composition of immigration to the United States.

The Social Status of Our Major Religious Groups

Comparisons among our major religious groups on the basis of education,

TABLE 2. *Amount of Education for Adults of Major United States Religious Groups, December, 1957*

RELIGIOUS GROUPS	SAMPLE SIZE	0–8 GRADES	SOME HIGH SCHOOL	4 YEARS HIGH SCHOOL	1–3 YEARS COLLEGE	4 YEARS OR MORE OF COLLEGE	TOTAL (%)
Nation	5827	33	20	28	10	9	100
Protestants	4185	33	21	27	10	9	100
Baptists	939	44	24	21	7	4	100
Whites	713	39	26	24	7	4	100
Negroes	226	63	20	11	3	3	100
Methodists	730	31	20	28	10	11	100
Lutherans	328	35	22	29	9	5	
Presbyterians	272	18	17	29	20	16	100
Episcopalians	119	8	14	25	25	28	100
Roman Catholics	1270	34	20	32	9	5	100
Jews	188	21	13	33	17	16	100

occupation, and income reveal substantial differences.[8] For example, Table 2 indicates that a status array can be formed with Episcopalians on top having 53 per cent with one or more years of college, followed by Presbyterians with 36 per cent and Jews with 33 per cent. In the middle are Methodists, Lutherans, and Roman Catholics. On the bottom are the Baptists, both whites and Negroes.

This interesting ranking of the religious groups recurs on occupation of family head as shown by Table 3. The Episco-palians have the largest professional percentage, followed by the Jews, and then the Presbyterians. The Jews have the largest percentage of owners, managers, and officials, followed by Episcopalians and Presbyterians. These three religious groups have very few farmers.

In the middle of the occupational pile are found the Catholic, Methodist, and Lutheran groups. On the bottom come the white and Negro Baptists.

Forty-two per cent of the Catholics are found in the skilled and semiskilled cate-

TABLE 3. *Occupation of Family Heads for Major United States Religious Groups, December, 1957*

RELIGIOUS GROUPS	SAMPLE SIZE	WITHOUT AN OCCUPATION	FARMERS	UNSKILLED	SEMISKILLED	SKILLED	CLERICAL AND SALES	OWNERS, MANAGERS, AND OFFICIALS	PROFESSIONS	TOTAL (%)
Nation	5827	18	9	9	15	18	10	12	9	100
Protestants	4185	17	10	10	15	17	10	12	9	100
Baptists	939	18	11	15	20	16	7	8	5	100
Whites	713	16	12	8	19	19	9	11	6	100
Negroes	226	18	8	34	21	10	4	1	4	100
Methodists	730	21	9	8	14	16	11	11	10	100
Lutherans	328	14	15	8	14	18	13	11	7	100
Presbyterians	272	17	4	8	7	17	14	20	13	100
Episcopalians	119	13	2	4	6	12	17	23	23	100
Roman Catholics	1270	15	4	10	20	22	10	11	8	100
Jews	188	14	0	1	9	9	16	32	19	100

gories. Except for the small number of Catholic farmers, the Catholic occupational distribution resembles that of the white Baptists.

This hierarchical pattern is further borne out by Table 4 on total family

a heavily southern group, and the South is still our underprivileged region.[9] The very high position of United States Jewry may come as a surprise to some.[10] When one remembers that heavy Catholic and Jewish immigration began about the same

TABLE 4.   *Total Family Income in 1956 for Major United States Religious Groups*

RELIGIOUS GROUPS	SAMPLE SIZE	UNDER $1000	$1000– $1999	$2000– $2999	$3000– $3999	$4000– $4999	$5000– $5999	$6000– $7499	$7500– $14,999	$15,000 OR MORE	TOTAL (%)
Nation	5827	7	8	10	13	15	15	13	16	3	100
Protestants	4185	8	9	11	13	14	15	12	15	3	100
Baptists	939	17	13	14	15	14	11	9	6	1	100
Whites	713	10	9	13	15	16	14	12	9	2	100
Negroes	226	27	20	17	15	9	5	5	1	1	100
Methodists	730	7	10	14	10	15	17	12	13	2	100
Lutherans	328	6	9	11	10	18	16	14	14	2	100
Presbyterians	272	5	6	9	12	14	14	14	20	6	100
Episcopalians	119	1	1	4	7	12	13	16	35	11	100
Roman Catholics	1270	4	7	8	12	17	17	17	16	2	100
Jews	188	1	2	5	9	10	15	16	31	11	100

income. On top, once more, are the Episcopalians with 46 per cent of their families earning $7500 or more, followed by the Jews with 42 per cent, and the Presbyterians with 26 per cent of their families earning $7500 or more.

In the middle one finds Catholics, Lutherans, and Methodists. On the bottom, once again, are white and Negro Baptists.

These education, occupation, and income data sort the religious groups into a social hierarchy of the following ranks:

Top: Episcopalians
     Jews
     Presbyterians
Middle: Methodists
     Lutherans
     Roman Catholics
Bottom: White Baptists
     Negro Baptists

While the differences among the Methodists, Lutherans, and Catholics are small, the bottom position of Negro and white Baptists comes as no surprise. The unfortunate position of the Negro in our society is well known. White Baptists are

time (the 1840's for Irish Catholics and German Jews; the 1880's for Eastern European Jews and other Catholic groups), the rapid rise of the Jewish group becomes extraordinary.[11]

In concluding this section, it should be mentioned that unpublished data from these surveys reveal that northern born white Baptists are quite urbanized and are heavily concentrated in blue collar occupational categories. In fact, northern born white Baptists exhibit an occupational distribution much like that of Roman Catholics. Southern born white Baptists, as expected, remain the lowest status white group and have a significant rural southern segment.[12]

Church Attendance and Social Status

After this examination of the rankings of our major religious groups on a number of social indices, let us turn to an exploration of church attendance.[13] Table 5 introduces data on frequency of church attendance. The national pattern of 45 per cent attending church regularly

TABLE 5. *Church Attendance During 1957 for Adults of Major United States Religious Groups*

RELIGIOUS GROUPS	SAMPLE SIZE	ATTENDS CHURCH				TOTAL (%)
		REGULARLY	OFTEN	SELDOM	NEVER	
Nation	5827	45	21	26	8	100
Protestants	4185	39	23	30	8	100
Baptists	939	41	31	22	6	100
Methodists	730	36	27	28	9	100
Lutherans	328	39	29	27	5	100
Presbyterians	272	41	20	29	10	100
Episcopalians	119	33	23	33	11	100
Roman Catholics	1270	72	13	11	4	100
Jews	188	13	21	51	15	100

(once a week or more); 21 per cent attending often (once, twice, or three times a month); 26 per cent attending seldom (a few times a year or less); and 8 per cent never attending is a Protestant pattern. Roman Catholics are frequent church attenders and Jews seldom attend. In short, the following three basic patterns of church attendance are found in the United States.

(1) A Catholic pattern typified by about 72 per cent attending church weekly.

(2) A Protestant pattern which has one-third to 40 per cent attending weekly, 20 to 30 per cent attending often and seldom, and 5 to 10 per cent reporting no attendance.

(3) A Jewish pattern which is predominately one of annual "High Holidays" attendance.

Tables 6 and 7 relate variations in attendance at religious services to education and occupation.[14] In Table 6 one can observe that church attendance increases with increasing number of years of schooling for Protestants and Catholics.[15] The percentage increases are fairly sizable as one moves up the educational scale with a nice breaking point occurring at the four years of high school level. Adults with less than a high school education clearly attend church considerably less than those adults who do have a high school education or better.

As Table 7 indicates, adults whose family heads have white collar occupations show more regularity of church attendance than adults whose family heads have nonfarm, blue-collar positions. Protestant adults whose family heads are farmers attend church as frequently as the white collar categories. This does not hold for the small group of Catholic farmers.

Apart from a slight reduction in church regularity for the lowest income categories, no pattern of association exists between income and church attendance within either the Protestant or Catholic groups. The classification of respondents by income results in enough low and middle income respondents who are frequent church attenders to eliminate any tangible association between income level and church-going.

Before pursuing further the degree of association between social status and church attendance, it might be interesting to report briefly the associations with church attendance of sex, age, and family

TABLE 6. *Frequency of Church Attendance by Years of School Completed*

FREQUENCY OF CHURCH ATTENDANCE

RELIGIOUS GROUPS	SAMPLE SIZE	REGULARLY	OFTEN	SELDOM	NEVER	TOTAL (%)
Protestants						
0–8 Grades	1381	33	26	31	10	100
Some high school	880	35	23	34	8	100
4 Yrs. high school	1128	42	21	31	6	100
1–3 Yrs. college	422	47	23	24	6	100
4 Yrs. or more of college	374	52	20	24	4	100
Roman Catholics						
0–8 Grades	436	63	17	13	7	100
Some high school	256	67	14	15	4	100
4 Yrs. high school	397	80	10	8	2	100
1–3 Yrs. college	117	79	10	9	2	100
4 Yrs. or more of college	64	89	9	1	1	100

TABLE 7. *Frequency of Church Attendance by Occupation of Family Head*

FREQUENCY OF CHURCH ATTENDANCE

RELIGIOUS GROUPS	SAMPLE SIZE	REGULARLY	OFTEN	SELDOM	NEVER	TOTAL (%)
Protestants						
Professions	372	47	23	23	7	100
Owners, managers, and officials	502	41	22	30	7	100
Clerical and sales	419	43	23	29	5	100
Skilled	711	35	21	36	7	100
Semiskilled	628	34	23	36	7	100
Unskilled	411	35	27	31	7	100
Farmers	410	44	30	20	6	100
Roman Catholics						
Professions	106	81	11	7	1	100
Owners, managers, and officials	139	83	8	5	4	100
Clerical and sales	132	81	11	5	3	100
Skilled	279	68	15	13	4	100
Semiskilled	254	66	16	13	5	100
Unskilled	131	62	21	11	6	100
Farmers	51	67	9	20	4	100

life cycle. The well known greater frequency of female church attendance appears in these data. What is of interest is that Protestant women report that they attend church 1½ times as much as Protestant men (46 per cent of the women report attending regularly while only 30 per cent of the men report regular attendance). Among Roman Catholics the sex difference is slight, with 75 per cent of Catholic women and 67 per cent of Catholic men reporting regular attendance.[16]

It has long been thought that adults become more religious as they age. When these survey data were analyzed for an association between age and church attendance, none appeared. There is no meaningful change in church attendance with age for either Protestants or Catholics apart from a lower rate of attendance among Protestants 21 to 24 years old. Perhaps church attendance is based upon patterns established fairly early in life and subject to little (if any) change with aging.[17]

Finally, relating family life cycle to church attendance reveals that young, single Protestants attend church the least. After marriage, regularity of church attendance rises, and it peaks for those

Protestants having children five years old or over. Apparently, when children are old enough to be sent to Sunday School, their parents tend to stay for religious services. With children no longer in the home, regularity of attendance drops. Roman Catholics do not show similar changes in church attendance with family life cycle.[18]

Alienation from Religion

A great deal of research has shown that the number of voluntary associations a person joins is sharply related to his social status.[19] Therefore, the variations in number of organization memberships with the various indices of social status employed in this chapter (education, occupation, and income) can be contrasted with similar variations between church attendance and these same indices. This will furnish a good indication of just how strongly responsive frequency of church attendance is to social status variations. Hence, the question being examined becomes: How strong are the variations in degree of attachment to religion that appear at various social levels?[20]

TABLE 8.   *Percentage Distribution of Memberships for Adults of Major United States Religious Groups*

RELIGIOUS GROUPS	SAMPLE SIZE	NUMBER OF MEMBERSHIPS				TOTAL (%)
		0	1	2	3 OR MORE	
Nation	2469	49	26	13	12	100
Protestants	1743	50	25	13	12	100
Baptists	525	58	25	10	7	100
Methodists	398	45	28	16	11	100
Lutherans	201	44	23	18	15	100
Presbyterians	172	45	18	18	19	100
Episcopalians	70	33	20	13	34	100
Roman Catholics	558	50	28	13	9	100
Jews	91	42	22	20	16	100

It would be best to start the investigation with Table 8 which gives the number of voluntary association memberships held by adults of various United States religious groups.[21] There is a marked degree of variation among the religious groups in their memberships. Indeed, they can be ranked as follows.

GROUP	RANK
Episcopalians	1
Jews, Presbyterians, Lutherans	2
Methodists	3
Catholics	4
Baptists	5

Episcopalians rank first on number of memberships in three or more organizations and Jews rank first on memberships in two organizations. The percentage distributions of Protestants, as a whole, and Roman Catholics are very much alike.[22]

As would be expected, there is strong agreement between the above rank order of religious groups on organization memberships and their previous rank order on social status. But, there is a negative association between group ranking on memberships and ranking on church attendance.[23] A religious group's social and economic status undoubtedly produces its degree of organizational activity while each group's history results in distinctive patterns of church attendance.

Checking memberships against various demographic variables reveals the following.[24]

(a) *Sex.* Protestant men are slightly more likely to be members of voluntary associations than are Protestant women. Catholic men are clearly more active in voluntary associations than are Catholic women.

(b) *Age.* Among Protestants and Catholics there is a slightly "U" shaped curve for the association between age and memberships. Starting from a point of low activity in the 21–24 years old group, organization memberships increase through the twenties and reach a fairly constant level from 30 to 44 years. Then there is a consistent reduction in activity until the 65 years of age or older category which sees a renewed low in number of memberships.

(c) *Family life cycle.* Protestant and Catholic young single people are fairly active in organizations, but amount of participation decreases after marriage. With the coming of children, the rate of participation rises and reaches its maximum for families with their youngest child 5 years old or older. When the children leave home, the now older parents reduce their rate of participation but remain considerably more active than are young married couples with no children.

This summary of data on organization memberships by religious grouping indicates strong associations between memberships and social variables. These associations are pronounced for both age and life cycle which, in turn, show little or no association with church attendance.

This sensitivity of membership to social position is clearly brought out by education, occupation, and income. Table 9 shows that within both the Catholic and Protestant groups there are direct and substantial associations between amount of education and number of organization memberships. The changes in zero membership and multimemberships are considerable as level of education increases.

Table 10 illustrates that within both religious groups there are direct associations between occupational status of family head and number of organization memberships. Protestant skilled and semi-skilled workers have identical patterns; Protestant farmers are more active organizationally than Protestant blue collar workers. In addition, within both the

TABLE 9.   *Percentage Distribution of Memberships by Years of School Completed*

		NUMBER OF MEMBERSHIPS				
RELIGIOUS GROUPS	SAMPLE SIZE	0	1	2	3 OR MORE	TOTAL (%)
Protestants						
0–8 Grades	584	63	26	7	4	100
Some high school	382	56	25	11	8	100
4 Yrs. high school	451	41	29	17	13	100
1–3 Yrs. college	166	32	25	18	25	100
4 Yrs. or more of college	160	25	17	22	36	100
Roman Catholics						
0–8 Grades	179	63	29	6	2	100
Some high school	110	52	31	11	6	100
4 Yrs. high school	176	46	26	16	12	100
1–3 Yrs. college	57	32	28	20	20	100
4 Yrs. or more of college	36	19	27	27	27	100

Protestant and Catholic faiths, there exist direct and substantial associations between memberships in any organization or membership in two or more organizations and total family income.[25]

Now, direct comparisons can be made between church attendance and number of organization memberships by contrasting Tables 6 and 7 with Tables 9 and 10. There are consistently sharper associa-

TABLE 10.   *Percentage Distribution of Memberships by Occupation of Family Head*

		NUMBER OF MEMBERSHIPS				
RELIGIOUS GROUPS	SAMPLE SIZE	0	1	2	3 OR MORE	TOTAL (%)
Protestants						
Professions	154	26	31	18	25	100
Owners, managers, and officials	194	34	24	16	26	100
Clerical and sales	165	37	27	18	18	100
Skilled	300	57	26	11	6	100
Semiskilled	238	56	26	13	5	100
Unskilled	156	68	18	6	8	100
Farmers	171	44	29	15	12	100
Roman Catholics						
Professions	52	37	25	17	21	100
Owners, managers, and officials	46	30	30	13	27	100
Clerical and sales	66	53	26	12	9	100
Skilled	107	45	30	19	6	100
Semiskilled	90	52	28	14	6	100
Unskilled	52	67	27	4	2	100
Farmers	17	65	23	6	6	100

tions between number of memberships and education and occupation than between these status indices and frequency of church attendance. On top of this, number of memberships varies with income while church attendance does not. Clearly, frequency of church attendance is sluggishly associated with social status when contrasted with number of memberships in voluntary associations.

These findings emphasize that there is relatively little alienation from religious institutions (as measured by church attendance) induced in people as a result of the factors determining their social status. In the United States attendance at religious services is considerably less socially restrictive and, indeed, is far more encouraged and practiced at all levels of our social structure than in Europe.

This body of findings for the United States is in sharp contrast with findings for much of Europe, where there exist wide divergences in church attendance throughout the social structure and the degree of alienation from religious institutions for people in lower social status positions is considerable.[26]

The relative success of United States religious institutions in maintaining strong ties with all segments of our society is a product of many factors, among the most important of which are the following ones.

(1) The circumstance that numerous United States religious groups, such as the Methodists or Baptists, have had marked historical associations with the lower classes.

(2) The lack of any official state church and the disestablishment of the official colonial churches starting with the American Revolution.

(3) The need for every United States religious institution to obtain adequate support in both financial and membership spheres on a completely voluntary basis.

(4) The ability of any dissatisfied segment of society to establish its own denomination in order to satisfy its specific spiritual needs.

In a recent statement, Lipset summarized this "success" of religion in the United States by pointing out that "a strong societal emphasis on achievement and equalitarianism (which in part may be perceived as a secular transvaluation ideology) combined with strong religious belief, particularly among the lower strata, should maximize the legitimacy of the existing distribution of privilege and thus minimize the conditions for left-wing extremist protest." [27]

Summary

The information presented in this chapter can be briefly summarized in the following points.

(a) The United States is religiously heterogeneous, but has very few adults without a religious preference.

(b) Major United States religious groups can be arrayed into a social status hierarchy with Episcopalians, Jews, and Presbyterians on top; Methodists, Lutherans, Roman Catholics, and Northern born white Baptists in the middle; and Negro and Southern born white Baptists on the bottom.[28]

(c) Catholics are frequent church attenders; about one-third to 40 per cent of Protestants attend church regularly; and Jews are predominantly annual "High Holidays" attenders.

(d) There is a moderate but significant direct relationship between increasing frequency of church attendance and increasing social status as measured by education and occupation.

(e) Jewish men attend synagogue 2½ times as often as Jewish women; Protestant women attend church 1½ times as often as Protestant men. Catholic women attend church slightly more often than Catholic men.

(f) These data fail to exhibit any association between increasing age and increasing church attendance. As to life cycle, Protestants with children five years old or older show a small rise in church attendance.

(g) Regularity of church attendance cannot be conceived of as merely another manifestation of over-all activity in voluntary associations. While some relationship does exist between these two factors, it seems that both are results of a complicated interplay of social status, demographic, and historical factors.

(h) Number of organizational affiliations responds strongly to social structural and life cycle variations and is probably a less complicated variable than church attendance. People with more education, larger incomes, more responsible occupations, and in the child-rearing stage of life, are coerced and persuaded into organization memberships and activities much more than people at lesser levels of education, income, and occupational status or who are not involved in child-rearing.

(i) Regularity of church attendance strongly reflects the religious emphases of specific religious groups and, somewhat sluggishly, social structure. Not surprisingly, church attendance, a fairly complex variable, depends, in addition, upon a whole range of religious feelings and attitudes. Finally, attendance at church in the United States is considerably less socially restrictive and, indeed, is far more encouraged and practiced at all levels of our society. This situation is in contrast to Protestant and Catholic Europe where the lower classes are often strongly alienated from their churches.

Technical Appendix

The information introduced here was gathered on three national probability sample surveys conducted by the Survey Research Center of the University of Michigan. Of these three surveys, two were conducted in the Spring of 1957, and the third survey was conducted in November, 1958.[29]

One national sample was selected for both 1957 surveys; it was then randomly divided at the final sampling stage for the two surveys. The third survey used the same primary and secondary sampling units employed for the first two surveys, but, of course, had different final stage sampling elements. The two sample designs used the 66 primary sampling units then employed on standard Survey Research Center studies; the selection procedures made use of the city directory and segmentation techniques developed by the Sampling Section of the Survey Research Center.

All interviewing was done by the regular field staff of the Survey Research Center. The religious question asked on the two 1957 surveys was: "What is your religious preference?" On the 1958 survey the question was: "Is your church preference Protestant, Catholic, or Jewish?" In addition, interviewers for the two 1957 surveys were instructed to ask this question if a respondent stated he (or she) was a Protestant: "What religious denomination is that?" The larger[30] of the two 1957 surveys obtained information on memberships in voluntary associations.

Since the samples analyzed are multistage, clustered ones, it is necessary to estimate statistical significance by use of the formula for the variance of the difference between two ratio estimators.[31] Low and high level estimates of significance have been obtained. The low level estimate is based upon the simple random sample formula for the standard error of the difference between two percentages; the high level estimate includes a generalized clustering factor derived from the variances of ninety-six specific ratio estimators. This high level is 1.4 times the low level.

When the difference between two percentages is less than twice the low level estimate, the two percentages are not considered significantly different. When the difference between two percentages is greater than twice the high level estimate, the two percentages are considered significantly different at the 95 per cent confidence level. When the difference between two percentages falls between twice the low and high level estimates, the question of significance is considered unresolved.

Occasionally, insufficient sample sizes block statistical significance. In such cases, the data have been inspected for consistent patterning. Hence, all conclusions stressed in the present article are based upon the presence of either statistical significance or consistent patternings and often upon both.[32]

Notes

[1] See Gerhard Lenski, The Religious Factor, Garden City, New York: Doubleday, 1961; Joseph H. Fichter, Social Relations in the Urban Parish, Chicago: University of Chicago Press, 1954; Michael Argyle, Religious Behavior, London: Routledge and Kegan Paul, 1958; Benson Y. Landis, "A Guide to the Literature on Statistics of Religious Affiliation with References to Related Social Studies," Journal of the American Statistical Association, 54 (June, 1954), pp. 335–357.

[2] The findings from the Census Bureau survey are reported in: United States Bureau of the Census. "Religion Reported by the Civilian Population of the United States: March, 1957," Current Population Reports, Series P-20, No. 79. The National Opinion Research Center material can be found in: Donald Bogue, "Religious Affiliation," The Population of the United States, Glencoe, Illinois; The Free Press, 1959, pp. 688–709.

[3] Of this 72 per cent, 9 per cent are Negro Protestants and 63 per cent are white Protestants. In addition, 93 per cent of adult Negroes prefer some Protestant denomination.

[4] The data did not permit the subdivision of any of the Protestant denominations into specific denominational organizations such as Northern or Southern Baptists.

For the nation as a whole, 16 per cent of adults 21 years old or over are white Baptists, 5 per cent are Negro Baptists; 15 per cent are white Methodists and 2 per cent are Negro Methodists. The Baptists and Methodists are the only major Protestant denominational groupings with large proportions of Negroes.

[5] For a major study which treats religious fertility differences, see Ronald Freedman, Pascal Whelpton, and Arthur Campbell, Family Planning, Sterility, and Population Growth, New York: McGraw-Hill, 1959, Chapters 4, 5, 9.

[6] William Petersen, Population, New York: The Macmillan Company, 1961, pp. 222–226.

[7] For a recent book that gives some data on interdenominational movement, see James Morgan, Martin David, Wilbur Cohen, and Harvey Brazer, Income and Welfare in the United States, New York, McGraw-Hill; 1962, pp. 339–341.

[8] Three surveys have been analyzed for Protestants, Roman Catholics, and Jews. Only two out of the three surveys obtained Protestant denominational preferences. The reader should bear this in mind when contrasting the number of interviews reported for all Protestants with that reported for Protestant denominations. Furthermore, only the Protestant denominations included in the various tables of this chapter were I.B.M. coded for the two surveys.

[9] These rank positions together with the data recorded in Tables 2 to 4, apart from sampling variations and some coding differences, are in substantial agreement with the data reported by Bogue, op. cit. He also reports 69 per cent of the white Baptists as living in the South in 1957.

[10] Numerical size can serve as a limiting factor on a group's social position. Relatively large religious groups, such as the Roman Catholics or Methodists, should have a more difficult time finding enough "better-off" social "slots" to enable as great a percentage of their groups to rank as high on education,

occupation, and income as the smaller Episcopalian and Jewish groups. On the other hand, such numerically smaller groups can find a comparatively larger number of high status social "slots" relative to their numbers. Considering chance alone, one would expect each religious group to form as great a percentage of the various social status levels as it does of the nation's population. Clearly, this is not the case.

[11] Additional data on these religious groups can be found in Bernard Lazerwitz, "A Comparison of Major United States Religious Groups," *Journal of the American Statistical Association,* 56 (September, 1961), pp. 568–579.

[12] Bernard Lazerwitz, *Residential Belt Locations and Some Regional Characteristics of Major United States Religious Groups.* University of Illinois, (dittoed paper).

[13] Church attendance is the one religious behavior factor which has been fairly well investigated and correlated with other social variables. Undoubtedly, a thorough investigation of the factors associated with variations in praying, bible reading, or attitudes toward traditional religious beliefs, such as life after death, would reveal far more complex and interesting patterns of religious living among our various religious bodies.

[14] The probability that the amount of church attendance reported by respondents is subject to upward bias has been pointed out by various researchers. Whatever bias exists in the church attendance data presented here will appear equally in relationships of the church attendance variable with other survey variables. Consequently, the various differences in associations between church attendance and such other survey variables should not be appreciably distorted by possible overestimations of church attendance.

[15] The small number of interviews with Jews precluded detailed analysis of the relation between synagogue attendance and education or occupation. The degree of investigation permitted by the data indicates a negative relationship between increasing education and frequency of synagogue attendance and none between occupational status and attendance at religious services. Lack of survey information prevents control for Jewish denominational preferences. Hence, it is

quite likely that these educational and occupational relationships with synagogue attendance reflect the differences between older, foreign born, more Orthodox Jews with lower educational and occupational status and their children and grandchildren who have achieved considerably more education and better occupations.

[16] Among Jews, men attend regularly 2½ times more frequently than women. This is a result of the Orthodox Jewish norm strongly emphasizing male attendance at services. While many Jews are no longer Orthodox, it is probable that the norm urging greater male attendance still operates among non-Orthodox Jews most of whom are the children or grandchildren of Orthodox forebears.

[17] Orbach has also found no association between age and church attendance in Detroit. See Harold Orbach, "Aging and Religion: Church Attendance in the Detroit Metropolitan Area," *Geriatrics,* 16 (October, 1961), pp. 530–540. A more thorough investigation by age cohorts of church attendance and other forms of religious activity would go a long way toward resolving the question of the effect of aging upon religious behavior and beliefs.

[18] The results of the investigation into the association between church attendance and the other study variables for the major Protestant denominations follow the trends reported for the entire Protestant group. For data on Baptists and Methodists and for a more detailed discussion of the factors associated with church attendance, see Bernard Lazerwitz, "Some Factors Associated With Variations in Church Attendance," *Social Forces,* 39 (may, 1961), pp. 301–309.

[19] An excellent bibliography of empirical work in the area of voluntary association memberships can be found in John C. Scott, Jr., "Membership and Participation in Voluntary Associations," *American Sociological Review,* 22 (June, 1957), pp. 315–326. See also Leonard Reissman, "Class, Leisure, and Social Participation," *American Sociological Review,* 19 (February, 1954), pp. 76–84, and Charles R. Wright and Herbert H. Hyman, "Voluntary Association Memberships," *American Sociological Review,* 23 (June, 1958), pp. 284–294.

[20] Admittedly, strength of attachment to

religion is imperfectly measured by frequency of church attendance. Equivalently, not all features of social position are indicated by education, occupation, and income. Nevertheless, good enough measures of religious attachment and social position are furnished by these factors. It would be most desirable to have ample national data, obtained by proper sampling and survey procedures, on many facets of religious behavior and beliefs for Protestants, Catholics, and Jews. Unfortunately, such information does not exist.

[21] The organization membership data could be derived from only one national survey instead of the three used for major religious groups and the two surveys used for Protestant denominations. Hence, sample sizes in this Table and in Tables 9 and 10 are smaller than those previously reported.

[22] Since the differences between white and Negro Baptists are small, the Baptist distribution accurately represents both racial groups.

[23] There is a negative Kendall's tau of − 0.2 between group rankings on organization membership and rankings on church attendance.

[24] Again, the available number of interviews permits these cross-classifications to be done only for Protestants and Catholics.

[25] For additional data on the relationship between membership in voluntary associations and frequency of church attendance, see Bernard Lazerwitz, "Membership in Voluntary Associations and Frequency of Church Attendance," Journal for the Scientific Study of Religion, 2 (Fall, 1962), pp. 74–84.

[26] To probe further these interrelations among church attendance, number of memberships, and social status, the data were subdivided by sex and religious preference and upper, middle, and lower status groups were then formed by jointly controlling for levels of education, occupation, and income. Then, for each group of upper, middle, and lower status Protestant and Catholic men and women, percentage distributions were computed on church attendance and number of voluntary association memberships. Among all these groups, there is a direct relationship between higher status ranking and increasing frequency of church attendance and

greater number of voluntary association memberships. But the status group percentage ranges are much larger for organization memberships than for church attendance.

[27] Seymour M. Lipset, "The Value Patterns of Democracy: A Case Study in Comparative Analysis," American Sociological Review, 28 (August, 1963), p. 530.

[28] Undoubtedly, denominations such as the United Church of Christ and Unitarians would fall into the top rank.

[29] The three surveys are described in Gerald Gurin, Joseph Veroff, and Sheila Feld, Americans View Their Mental Health, New York: Basic Books, 1960; Robert Davis, The Public Impact of Science in the Mass Media, Ann Arbor, Michigan: Institute for Social Research, 1958, mimeographed; Warren Miller, The Party and the Representative Process: A Progress Report on Research, Ann Arbor, Michigan: Institute for Social Research, 1959, mimeographed.

Comparisons of the sets of percentages obtained on the three surveys indicate the passage of 18 months produced only random changes. With these surveys combined into one, the data may be thought of as referring to a point in time midway between the Spring of 1957, and November, 1958, namely December, 1957.

[30] This survey was the one by Gurin, op. cit. It was decided to measure totality of organizational memberships held by individuals. Any added refinement on such an operational measure would have involved recoding of the interviews or required information not obtained on the survey. Furthermore, a numerical approach to voluntary association activity has been successfully employed in almost all previous research in this area.

[31] For a presentation of such a procedure see Leslie Kish and Irene Hess, "On the Variances of Ratios and of Their Differences in Multi-Stage Samples," Journal of the American Statistical Association, 54 (June, 1959), pp. 416–446.

[32] For a discussion of various means of handling the problem of evidence in secondary analysis of survey data see Richard Curtis and Elton Jackson, "Multiple Indicators in Survey Research," The American Journal of Sociology, 68 (September, 1962), pp. 195–204.

2 · The Exodus

GIBSON WINTER

Protestantism was on the move from 1870 to 1950; the major denominations of White Protestantism were moving outward from central city areas to the suburbs during most of this period. This decentralization of Protestantism was a reaction to changes in metropolitan population; it was also evidence of the uprooting of the congregations from their neighborhoods; in fact, neighborhoods became places of residence instead of communities. The net effect of this outward movement has been a growing insulation of the major denominations from the people of the central cities.

The Protestant exodus from the central city was partly a consequence of the upgrading of native-born White Protestants. Upgrading here means movement upward in social rank from manual to nonmanual work.[1] Whatever one's ideas about the equality of all kinds of work, Americans accord higher prestige to nonmanual work. Although many skilled workers receive higher incomes than the lowest ranks of nonmanual workers, the white collar is invariably a sign of higher social rank.[2] Native-born urban Whites had many opportunities to move from manual to nonmanual work between 1870 and 1950; in fact, this upgrading had been going on since the great immigrations of the mid-nineteenth century.

Upgrading in a metropolitan area usu-

SOURCE. Gibson Winter, "The Exodus," from Gibson Winter. *The Suburban Captivity of the Churches*, Garden City, New York: Doubleday, 1961, pp. 39–51 and 185–189 (notes). Copyright 1961 by Gibson Winter. Reprinted by permission of Doubleday and Company, Inc.

ally leads to residential movement away from the inner city. The growth of business and industrial establishments expands the area of the inner city; poorer populations are pushed toward the perimeter of this expanding center; working-class residential areas are invaded by the lowest ranks in the labor force; better residential areas feel the outward movement of the skilled ranks of the labor force; thus, outward movement and upgrading go hand in hand with urban expansion.[3] By 1920, population outside the central cities had begun to increase disproportionately; the suburban trickle had become a flood; movement from "dirty" work to "clean" work accelerated residential movement from the central city to the suburban fringe.[4]

White Protestants were in the vanguard of the suburban movement, being advantageously placed to benefit by the expansion in numbers of clean jobs. The outward tide of middle-class movement became simultaneously an exodus of White Protestantism.[5] Urban Protestantism became suburban Protestantism in less than a century. White Protestant outposts in central areas of the metropolis are today either heavily subsidized by nonresident congregations or struggling for survival against heavy odds. In the continuing metropolitan sprawl, Protestant churches are being established throughout the lower middle- and upper middle-class areas surrounding the central cities. Unless this tide is reversed, White Protestantism will have few remaining churches within the perimeter of the central cities by 1975; moreover, these remaining churches will be supported by upper-class groups in high-rent apartments or by clusters of middle-class people in selected areas of the city.[6] In the light of the broad population trend of recent decades, the suburbanization of Protestantism seems to be an inevitable consequence of the upgrading of native-born urban Whites.

The meaning of the upgrading of major denominations of White Protestantism is not very clear, since the old-line denominations were already identified with the middle classes in the latter part of the nineteenth century. Although no accurate studies of the social-class composition of these denominations are available, religious leaders often protested the alienation of Protestantism from the working classes at this time.[7] Many poorer areas of the major cities were stripped of churches in the latter part of the nineteenth century; in fact, Protestant congregations at this time were closely identified with the petty bourgeoisie and the upper classes; consequently, the notion of upgrading must be used with considerable caution.

The major denominations were upgraded in the course of the exodus from the central city by drawing their memberships more and more exclusively from people in nonmanual occupations; these denominations became increasingly identified with the middle class. The reduced proportion of manual workers in the churches came about in several ways: native-born White urbanites were being upgraded during this period, so that a "natural" upward mobility occurred;[8] moreover, the removal of church sites to better residential locations meant the abandonment of many members who could not move from the former location; churches of major denominations were thus sloughing off their lower-class members and adding new members in districts of higher prestige.[9] Major denominations were upgraded, therefore, as they identified themselves more closely with the middle class. These denominations have always had manual workers in their membership, but from 1870 to 1950 the percentage of manual workers in major denominations was sharply reduced.

Another kind of upgrading also occurred among major denominations. Although denominational congregations were primarily middle class in the latter part of the nineteenth century, their buildings were located in the central city areas. The cleavage between old-line Protestantism and the working class was created by social rather than physical distance. The size and nature of cities at this time made this development inevitable. Furthermore, shorter physical distances created real physical barriers in a time when rapid transportation was only beginning to alter the pattern of metropolitan life. The suburbanization of the major White denominations has enormously increased the physical distance between the Protestant churches and working-class people. If and when working-class people begin to move to the suburbs, as they now do in central sections of satellite areas, some of these physical barriers may be overcome. However, it has become less and less meaningful to charge denominational congregations with their responsibilities to the working classes and the Negro population, since an increasing proportion of denominational congregations are insulated from these segments of the population by the line which separates suburbia from the central city. In this sense, the upgrading of the major White denominations also means physical insulation from manual workers; most Protestant congregations are now thoroughly divorced from the residential locales of working people.

The upgrading of White Protestant congregations has both internal and external aspects. Internal upgrading came about by sloughing off lower-class members who were not in a position to move toward the suburbs; external upgrading resulted from increasing the physical distance between denominational churches and working-class people. Upgrading continues today, since central city churches are rapidly losing ground while suburban churches are increasing their memberships.[10] Collapse of central city churches means abandoning large numbers of the congregation to an inadequate ministry, while suburban gains mean increased recruitment from the upper social ranks. The Protestant exodus is an index of selective Protestant growth among the upper social ranks; it is also an index of the disengagement of major denominations from the people and problems of the central city areas. Whatever the constituency of Protestantism may have been in the nineteenth century, it became increasingly middle class and physically more insulated from the working classes during the Protestant exodus.

Population changes were the precipitating factor in the Protestant exodus; many congregations changed the location of their churches every decade or two after 1850.[11] Industrial expansion brought waves of immigration; the more prosperous church members moved outward with each new wave; in many cases, the congregations sold their buildings and built new churches in the better residential areas; in fact, the expansion of major cities can be traced by mapping the location and relocation of Protestant congregations.[12] Particular immigrations and in-migrations had distinctive effects on the major denominations: they led uniformly to Protestant movement, but the implications for Protestantism were not always the same. The specific character of these effects can be seen by considering the actual population movements.

Protestantism reacted against several types of population movement between 1870 and 1950. The *Roman Catholic* immigrations were obviously a serious

problem to the major denominations; concentrations of Roman Catholic immigrants made some residential areas untenable for Protestant congregations. When Roman Catholic concentration is combined with an expansion of commercial districts, a certain amount of Protestant movement is inevitable. Many church buildings were vacated during these great immigrations; more seriously, however, the Protestant retreat from largely Roman Catholic areas often meant the abandonment of minority groups of Protestants. In the early period of urban growth, the Protestant exodus meant stripping inner city areas of religious institutions, since Roman Catholic churches could not be established in sufficient numbers to meet the waves of immigration.[13]

Immigrations of *foreign-born Protestants* likewise confronted native-born Protestantism with serious problems; ethnic communities developed their own religious institutions, and foreign-born Protestants affiliated with them.[14] How much this tendency was aggravated by attitudes of native-born Whites would be hard to assess. It is clear, however, that local Protestants found foreign-born people strange and viewed them as aliens.[15] Some Protestant denominations developed foreign-language churches and missions for Protestant immigrants, but such congregations rarely mixed immigrants with the native-born.

St. Louis is an example of heavy Protestant immigration subsequently developing into separate streams of Protestantism. German-speaking Protestants developed their own institutions and followed a separate path of outward movement in the second generation.[16] Native-born Protestantism beat a retreat from the immigrant settlements, moving toward the residential areas of highest prestige. These movements meant a failure to solidify Protestant forces and a consequent abandonment of less mobile members of the native-born congregations.

In-migrations of *rural White Protestants* also confronted the major denominations with a problem; rural newcomers brought a different style of life, were confined largely to the lower rungs of the economic ladder, and were treated as aliens. Naturally, they gravitated to religious sects which fitted their own needs, as ethnics had attached themselves to ethnic communities. The Protestant retreat and the search by newcomers for a familiar style of religious observance contributed also to the alienation of rural Protestants from the major denominations. Since the sects were small groups and ministered to a fragment of the rural in-migration, the net effect of the exodus was to increase the unchurched populations of the central cities.[17] This problem continues to face the major denominations, since rural Whites are still pouring into the central cities. The significant fact about the retreat from rural newcomers is that these folk were traditionally Protestant.[18] The Protestant retreat, in this instance, meant a radical impoverishment of the ministry to these areas and unchurched large numbers of rural in-migrants. The derelict churches which remained could not provide adequate ministries for their own constituencies and lacked the vitality and interest to recruit substantially from the newcomer groups. These weakened churches provided vulnerable points for invasion by left-wing, fundamentalist groups.[19] Protestant gains in membership through movement to the best residential areas were counterbalanced by heavy losses in churches and memberships in the central areas of the city.

The pattern of *Negro in-migration* to metropolitan areas had somewhat different effects on the major denominations. Negroes entered urban areas with a Protestant tradition; nevertheless, they represented the most serious threat to White Protestantism of all the new population groups. Negroes had trickled into urban areas during the nineteenth century; there were small colonies of Negroes in the larger cities by the turn of the century; however, Negro in-migration increased rapidly during World War I, and after 1920 became a major source of metropolitan growth. In-migration of Negroes uniformly accelerated the withdrawal of White Protestantism; in fact, the two cultures were totally estranged.[20] Since World War II denominational leadership has taken a new tack and urged integration of Negroes into local White congregations, but this counsel requires a different kind of congregation to become more than a gesture.[21]

The retreat from the Negro occurred in a two-phase movement: higher-status congregations withdrew with the first threat of Negro invasion; middle- and lower middle-class congregations moved more slowly; consequently, the secondary withdrawal of Protestantism came about through attrition.[22] The lower-status congregations, in other words, suffered losses of membership for years before finally collapsing, holding consistently to the pattern of an all-White constituency.[23]

This two-phase retreat from the Protestant Negro indicates the special character of the Negro problem in the metropolitan area. Higher-status congregations moved every decade or so; the rumor of Negro movement was sufficient to prompt their exodus. The "tip-point" for higher-status congregations (meaning the point at which they perceive the area as Negro) occurred with the mere threat of Negro movement, rather than at the point of heavy Negro concentration. (Tip-point usually refers to that proportion of Negroes in a residential area which will cause most, if not all, Whites to leave—in other words, that point where an area swings to almost total Negro occupancy.) The tip-point for higher-status congregations corresponded roughly to the residential movement of their own constituencies prior to Negro movement, and was often preceded by movements of the Jewish community. Negroes did not occupy an entire neighborhood on first invading an area; consequently, many lower-status Whites continued to live there. Lower middle-class White congregations dwindled slowly as Negroes continued to increase in numbers in these areas; increases in the Negro population in Chicago from 1920 to 1940, for example, were not accompanied by significant increases in the residential space available to Negroes; the Negro population was simply crowded more densely into the available buildings within the Negro ghetto. The increase of Negro population meant a corresponding decrease in the number of Whites remaining in the area; the secondary tip-point for White Protestant churches seems to have been at roughly 40 per cent. When Negroes represented about two fifths of the residents of an area, all Protestant churches had moved or disbanded.[24] The retreat of higher-status Protestant churches at the first tip-point impoverished the Protestant ministry to the area; the secondary withdrawal at the 40 per cent tip-point caused the abandonment of the remaining White Protestant population.

The Supreme Court decision against restrictive covenants in 1948 accelerated residential movements of Negroes and closed the interval between the two tip-points. Today White Protestantism may disappear from a residential area in a matter of months. Very few higher-status congregations serve both Negroes and Whites; it is the middle-status congregations of the central city that bear the brunt of conflict at these points of racial intersection. Some of them have attempted to desegregate; few have been successful, however, since residential areas are almost totally Negro before

such an integrated pattern can offset the withdrawal of Whites. The Negro movement and White retreat have led to the withdrawal of major denominations of White Protestantism from many areas of the central city.

To the extent that Negroes gravitated to their own churches in the course of urbanization, they followed the pattern of the foreign-born and the rural Whites. Negro churches have varied considerably in quality: some Negro churches have had ministries of the highest quality and have shown concern for their membership; in general, however, the Negro community has been overchurched with struggling congregations and inadequately trained ministries. In retrospect, it is easy to say that the major denominations of White Protestantism might have corrected this situation through a more positive attitude toward the Negro newcomer; actually, it is too late to alter the situation.[25] Negro Protestantism will have to build an adequate ministry and religious life under the most difficult circumstances, for the overcrowding of Negro residential areas has caused the spread of urban blight with each new movement of the Negro population.[26] Inner city blight is rapidly consuming the total area of the central city, and, although the strongesr forces in Negro Protestantism have fought this blight and worked for better housing, the Negro churches are no more able to cope with this situation than the major denominations.[27] Every step toward an integrated church threatens the status of the Negro ministry; every attempt to build a strong congregation is undermined by the rapidly spreading blight. Encounters between White and Negro Protestantism still occur principally at the highest denominational levels, and most of these interchanges are superficial. The long tradition of social apartheid has eventuated in a schism of the first magnitude in metropolitan Protestantism.[28] The Protestant exodus brought in its wake an even deeper alienation of the major White denominations from Negro Protestantism.

The double tip-point in White Protestant withdrawal further accentuated the problem of desegregating local congregations. The initial retreat of high-status congregations left lower middle-class churches at the points of racial intersection. It is generally acknowledged that lower middle-class Whites have shown excessive prejudice against Negroes.[29] This is usually interpreted in terms of their marginal position; actually lower middle-class Whites pay disproportionately high rents in order to live in white-collar areas,[30] are extremely vulnerable to inflation, and fear anything which jeopardizes property values.[31] This vulnerable flank of Protestantism has repeatedly faced the Negro question. Higher-status congregations have shown no better acceptance of Negroes than lower middle-class Whites, and all hope for reconciliation dissolved with the retreat of stronger congregations from the central city. Lower middle-class Whites, left with dwindling congregations and shrinking church finances, formed the rearguard of the Protestant retreat from the central city; in fact, many middle-class Whites have kept a sense of social class identification with their more mobile compeers by resisting any attempts to desegregate the churches. Since many former residents continued for a time as members of the old church after moving away from the neighborhood, their less mobile associates maintained the life of the congregation unchanged out of loyalty to the church's former splendor.

The Protestant exodus can now be summarized: (1) *Roman Catholic immigrations* pushed Protestant congregations out of many areas of the central cities; to some extent, this was also true of Jewish immigrations at the turn of the century; these Protestant movements can be attributed to changes in the religious complexion of inner city areas, although the evidence suggests that many moves were premature and based on social class differences. These were almost inevitable movements for religious institutions whose principle of organization is the voluntary congregation; such churches move when the important members leave the area. (2) *Foreign-born Protestants* presented a different problem, since retreat in this instance caused a further fragmenting of Protestantism. (3) *The in-migration of White and Negro newcomers* also had a special effect; the Protestant retreat from these newcomers has created a schism in metropolitan religious life; the major White denominations are retreating to the suburban and satellite areas, while Negro and sectarian Protestantism are beginning to dominate central city areas. The major White denominations have moved toward exclusive identification with the White middle classes; in fact, they are insulating themselves geographically from the working-class people of the metropolitan areas. The net effect of population change has been an upgrading of the major denominations through social and physical insulation from the working classes.

Certain effects of the exodus on central city areas have been noted; the most important effect is an impoverishment of the Protestant ministry to the central city, which the growth of sectarian and Negro churches has not been able to offset. Thus, the areas of greatest social and physical need have enjoyed the least adequate ministries. Except for the large, high-status churches, ministerial tenure has been shortest in the central city churches; buildings have been poorest; programs, the least adequate. In general, the major denominations of White Protestantism have demonstrated a lack of relationship to the human struggle in the metropolis, except for occasional instances of institutional ministries.[32]

The story of metropolitan churches

from 1870 to 1950 is the record of a desperate struggle for survival in the midst of rapid change. The average tenure of Protestant churches during this period was slightly over a score of years. It will probably be the same for the new and often elaborate buildings in suburbia unless the total organization of Protestantism changes. The metropolitan struggle for homogeneous neighborhoods infected the churches so that the intrusion of outsiders usually meant the collapse of both the neighborhood and the local religious groups. The pressures of rapid change turned congregations in upon themselves, so that they became more and more preoccupied with survival, less concerned with ministry to their communities. Neighborhoods became pools for recruiting members suitable to the social class level of the congregation; the metropolitan area became a field in which to choose prosperous sites for new church buildings.[33] Ministry assumed secondary importance, because population change made sheer survival as a parish or congregation highly problematic. Like men in a concentration camp who think only of food, these antique institutions lost touch with neighborhood and metropolis in their desperate struggle to survive. The parish and congregation were never designed for ministry in a rapidly changing metropolis; the attempt to maintain such institutions from 1870 to 1950 simply led to an exodus from the central city, and will lead in the next few decades to the collapse of the congregations which are being started each week.

We shall return to the problem of the congregation in the metropolis; it is essential in the present context, however, to recognize that the exodus was not a matter of bad faith or irresponsible leadership. It is naïve to think that men with better intentions can change the trend of events, when the best will in the world

cannot make a congregation an instrument of ministry in a metropolis. What happened at the turn of the century is being repeated now in every major denomination. The attempt to perpetuate the local parish or congregation as a basic unit of the Christian Church is doomed to failure, although such local units will have to be the building blocks of a new and more adequate form of the Church in the metropolis. Before considering these aspects of the mission to the metropolis, however, the transformation in Protestantism which came with the exodus will have to be considered.

Identification with the New Middle Class

The disengagement of Christianity from the working classes has occurred several times before in the history of the churches, although the North African case is probably the most striking example. Christianity reached one of the peaks of its development in North Africa during the third and fourth centuries. St. Augustine, Bishop of Hippo, is undoubtedly the outstanding leader who emerged from North African Christianity; his thought set the course for the development of medieval Christianity, and he continues to be a rich source of philosophical and theological inspiration; nevertheless, within a few centuries North African Christianity disappeared without a trace. This collapse can certainly be attributed in part to the expansion of Islam; however, the core of the problem was the identification of North African Christianity with the upper social classes. The churches became centers of upper-class culture; consequently they lacked widespread support among the people. When Islam swept across North Africa, it erased Christianity.[34] Where Christianity has become identified with upper-class élites, it has lacked a substantial base in the working population and has been unable to weather social change.

The Chinese case is somewhat similar. Christianity never became rooted among the agrarian population of China. Every development of Nestorian Christianity in China disappeared within a century. The attempt to re-establish Christianity in the nineteenth century now seems doomed to collapse under the pressures of agrarian communism. The cases of North Africa and China involved complex cultural changes and many special factors; nevertheless, the identification of Christianity with upper-class élites or special subcultures has occurred in history and has eventuated in the disappearance of Christianity within a matter of centuries.

The identification of Christianity with the middle and upper classes occurred in recent centuries in Western Europe. This seems to be the primary factor in the decline of Christian churches in Sweden, England, and France. Christianity has deep roots in these countries, but urbanization has undermined it for centuries.[35] Urban Christianity in Western Europe has been concentrated among the bourgeoisie and has been alienated from the working classes; it is not uncommon in these countries for participation in worship to include only 10 to 15 per cent of the total population.[36] The European situation is complicated by the existence of established churches, for nominal memberships conceal the paucity of participation; moreover, the situation has caused deep concern to Christian leadership in Europe. The disappearance of Christianity from these countries, as from North Africa, could easily occur under the impact of a radical social revolution; for the moment, Christianity is resting its case with the bourgeoisie.

American Christianity does not seem to be following the European pattern.

The major denominations in America give evidence of a growth which would seem to belie the foregoing analysis of the identification of Protestantism with the middle and upper social classes. One would expect an attenuation of membership in the major denominations, if the sloughing off of lower-class membership actually occurred between 1870 and 1950.[37] The seemingly contradictory picture—identification of the churches with middle and upper classes and increasing numerical strength—deserves special consideration, since it sets a pattern for the future of major denominations in their ministry to the metropolis. The American situation, in other words, presents certain unique characteristics which distinguish it from the North African and Western European developments.

The growth of the major denominations, despite losses in the central city areas, can be accounted for largely by the expansion of the middle classes since 1870. The mobility of Protestant churches made it possible for them to capitalize on this increase in the size of the middle class. For example, in St. Louis in 1923 four fifths of the population of the growing suburb of Webster Groves were members of Protestant churches as compared to the one-third Protestant membership in the city.[38] The losses incurred by major denominations in their movement away from the central city areas were more than offset by gains in the middle-class areas.

Central city losses and suburban gains of the major denominations conceal a fundamental change in the character of the Protestant constituency. A new middle class was emerging between 1870 and 1950, and it was this new middle-class population that was recruited during the Protestant exodus; consequently, the growth of the major denominations was a new phenomenon in Christianity . . .

Notes

[1] *Social Mobility in Industrial Society* by Seymour M. Lipset and Reinhard Bendix (Berkeley and Los Angeles: University of California Press, 1959), Chapters II and III.

[2] *The American Class Structure* by Joseph A. Kahl (New York: Rinehart, Sec. Ptg. 1959), pp. 72 ff.

[3] Simply stated, this is the zonal hypothesis set forth by E. W. Burgess in *The City* by R. E. Park, E. W. Burgess, and R. D. McKenzie (Chicago: University of Chicago Press, 1925), Chapter II; this hypothesis has been subject to much criticism but provides a useful descriptive statement.

[4] *The Changing Shape of Metropolitan America, Deconcentration since 1920* by Amos H. Hawley (Glencoe, Ill.: The Free Press, 1956), pp. 161 f.

[5] See *1924*, op. cit., Chart 19, p. 71, for the movement of White Protestantism in St. Louis; for Springfield, Mass., see *Spring 1926*, op. cit., pp. 72 f.; and for the situation in Chicago in 1945 see *Comparative Study of Congregational and Other Protestant Churches in Chicago, 1945–1946* by A. T. Rasmussen (Chicago Congregational Union; mimeographed copy in Hammond Library, Chicago Theological School), pp. 53 ff. and 71 ff.

[6] Redevelopment areas, for example, such as Hyde Park-Kenwood in Chicago, eliminate low-cost housing by demolition and rebuild with private capital to the top income level within the area. Such areas can continue to support churches of the major denominations, but this type of redevelopment is slow and costly.

[7] *The Rise of the City* by A. M. Schlesinger (New York: Macmillan, 1933), pp. 330 f. and esp. footnote 3 for references.

[8] Joseph Kahl, op. cit., p. 259; note the decreasing importance of foreign immigration after 1920 and the increasing significance of Negro in-migration from rural areas.

[9] H. Paul Douglass and Wilbur Hallenbeck documented this process in their studies; see references to the unchurching of lower-class Protestants in *1924*, op. cit., pp. 46–71; *Spring 1926*, op. cit., pp. 41–45, 274, 296, 298; *1927*, op. cit., p. 412; *1929*, op. cit., Charts XVI–XVIII, pp. 33 f.; *1932*, op. cit.; reference to Hallenbeck's findings that in a supposedly Negro area left by Protestant churches, one third to one half of the school pupils were native-born White; *1935*, op. cit., pp. 250–53; Walter Kloetzli has drawn attention to this problem among the Lutheran churches in a study on congregational structure, where he notes that a central area of Chicago with 800,000 population which once had dozens of National Lutheran Council churches now has three and these are new missions. The working-class areas of the metropolis were literally denuded of churches of the major denominations with the exception of a few high-prestige outposts.

[10] The most detailed and convincing evidence of this process of central city losses and suburban gains was presented in *1948*, op. cit., Table XLIX, p. 156.

[11] In a study of 1044 city churches, the median age was 42 years and the median afe of occupancy was 25 years, *1926*, op. cit., pp 232 f.

[12] *1924*, op. cit., p. 224.

[13] See A. M. Schlesinger, op. cit., pp. 330 f.; it would seem from W. Hallenbeck's study that Protestant churches left areas long before the balance of Roman Catholic population was such as to make the area untenable (see *1929*, op. cit., pp. 69–72 and *Spring 1926*, p. 299). Thus, the definition of a Roman Catholic area (and, as we shall see, a Negro area) is psychological and not statistical.

[14] *The Social Systems of American Ethnic Groups* by W. Lloyd Warner and Leo Srole (New Haven: Yale University Press, 1945), Chapter VII; *Protestant–Catholic–Jew* by Will Herberg (Garden City, N.Y.: Doubleday, 1955), Chapters II and III; *The Uprooted* by Oscar Handlin (New York: Grosset & Dunlap, 1951).

[15] *1924*, op. cit., pp. 68, 73, 217; *1926*, op. cit., pp. 251 f.; *Spring 1926*, op. cit., p. 281; *1948*, op. cit., pp. 156 f.

[16] *1924*, op. cit., p. 65.

[17] H. Paul Douglass notes this fact in many of his studies, but the appendices of *1948*, op. cit., detail the proliferation of small churches in the lower socio-economic areas of Pittsburgh. It is notable that seventeen denominations account for 96 per cent of the Protestant church membership in Pitts-

burgh (p. 63); yet those denominations have shown relatively little growth since 1930 while the sects increased their membership disproportionately with little effect on the total Protestant membership (pp. 11 f., 87, 89, 189).

[18] *Some Social and Economic Characteristics of the Detroit Area Populations, 1952* (Ann Arbor, Mich.: The Detroit Area Study, mimeographed, 1952). Table I, 5, p. 19, shows that migrants of less than 17 years residence are 73 per cent Protestant to 21 per cent Roman Catholic, and of those from the South, 93 per cent are Protestant (Table II, 5, p. 29).

[19] "The Role of Socio-Economic Factors in American Fundamentalism" by Everett L. Perry (unpublished Ph.D. dissertation, University of Chicago, 1959).

[20] "The Church and Segregation in Washington, D.C., and Chicago, Ill." by Frank David Dorey (unpublished Ph.D. dissertation, University of Chicago, 1950), pp. 62–115 and Chapter V.

[21] *The Protestant Church and the Negro* by Frank S. Loescher (New York: Association Press, 1948), p. 66; *The Kingdom Beyond Caste* by Liston Pope (New York: Friendship Press, 1957), pp. 108 f.

[22] "Community Turnover on the South Side of Chicago" by Frank David Dorey (unpublished B.D. thesis, Chicago Theological Seminary, 1942), pp. 65 f.

[23] This process is most clearly disclosed in the Pittsburgh situation, *1948*, op. cit., Table XLIV, p. 156 and Appendices, but the present construction is hypothetical and needs further testing.

[24] This is hypothetical in terms of other experiences, but it is supported by *1932*, op. cit., p. 165.

[25] *The Negro's Church* by B. E. Mays and J. W. Nicholson (New York: Institute of Social and Religious Research, 1933) points out the lack of contact between Negro and White churches and ministers in this period; the same situation is suggested in *1948*, op. cit., see *Recommendations*.

[26] *Where Shall We Live?* Report of the Commission on Race and Housing (Berkeley: University of California Press, 1958), Chapter III.

[27] *An American Dilemma* by Gunnar Myrdal (New York: Harper, 1944), Chapter 40; *The Negro in the United States,* by E. F. Frazier, Rev. Ed. (New York: Macmillan, 1957), Chapter XIV, pp. 354 ff.; *The Religion of Negro Protestants* by Ruby Funchess Johnston (New York: Philosophical Library, 1956), pp. 175 f.; and on ministerial training, *1935*, op. cit., Chart XII, p. 113.

[28] Morton Grodzins, op. cit., Chapter I.

[29] *The Strange Career of Jim Crow* by C. Vann Woodward (New York: Oxford University Press, 1955); "The Political Role of the Church as Defined by Its Parishioners," by B. R. Ringer and C. Y. Glock, mimeographed, confirms this trend to conservatism among the religiously committed, less educated (generally lower middle class), and poorly informed members of the Episcopal churches; this is precisely the group in denominational churches that flanked Negro movements.

[30] Otis D. Duncan and Beverly Duncan in *Cities and Society,* op. cit., p. 295, note this high rent-income ratio among lower white-collar households in Chicago.

[31] *Where Shall We Live?* op. cit., pp. 19 f.

[32] Tenure of city pastors has been relatively short, but the differences in length of stay fit the general financial level of the churches. See *1926,* op. cit., p. 218; *1935,* op. cit., p. 117.

[33] Research on the churches amply documents these generalizations; *Spring 1926,* op. cit., pp. 72 f., 299; *1932,* op. cit., p. 12; *1935,* op. cit., pp. 251 f.; *1948,* op. cit., pp. 156 f.

[34] *The Renewal of the Church* by Visser t'Hooft (London: SCM Press, 1956), pp. 69 ff.

[35] *Church and People in an Industrial City* by E. R. Wickham (London: Lutterworth Press, 1957), esp. Chapters II–V.

[36] *Religious Behavior* by Michael Argyle (Glencoe, Ill.: The Free Press, 1959) Table 9, p. 37; also E. R. Wickham, op. cit.

[37] It should be evident that the theory of turnover of membership in the major denominations is constructed on the basis of changes in church sites and concentrations of unchurched people in central areas of the city. This construction now leaves the unresolved problem of Protestant growth to be considered.

[38] *1924,* op. cit., pp. 176, 241; see also

1932, op. cit., pp. 85 f.; H. Paul Douglass noted several times that this new membership was more nominal than participant. We undoubtedly have a transformation in the nature and meaning of church membership from 1870 to 1950 which inflates membership figures and conceals the central city losses.

3 · The Ecology of Religious Preference in Wichita*

DONALD O. COWGILL

Religious preference of 65,000 households in Wichita, Kansas, was ascertained by survey. Data were analyzed by census tracts, which were then grouped according to income levels. Findings, in general, conform to those of earlier studies of relationship between social class and religious identification, but some exceptions are noted. Thus, Roman Catholics were found in both wealthy and poor areas, whereas Jews were markedly concentrated in high-income areas.— EDITOR.

There have been many studies of the ecology of membership or attendance in specific churches. Harlan Paul Douglass developed this approach to the analysis of specific churches thirty-five years ago.[1] Since then the mapping of residences of church members, of those attending Sunday School, and of those participating in various other activities and programs of the church has become standard procedure.[2] One study even treats of the ecology of the pastor's residence in relation to the church which he serves.[3] Douglass and others have used the ecological distribution of members as one of the variables in developing a typology of churches.[4] However, all such studies and typologies concentrate upon membership or participation in relation to the location of the individual church. They are more relevant to the study of institutions than to the study of people or of communities.

Perhaps the studies most relevant to this one are the many researches on community stratification which have noted the correlation between social class and church membership. Within individual cities, the most commonly found rela-

SOURCE. Donald O. Cowgill, "The Ecology of Religious Preference in Wichita," *The Sociological Quarterly*, 1, January, 1960, pp. 87–96.
* Paper read at the annual meeting of the Midwest Sociological Society in Lincoln, Neb., April 16–18, 1959.

[1] See H. Paul Douglass, *How to Study the City Church* (Garden City, N. Y.: Doubleday, Doran, 1928); also *The Springfield Church Survey* (New York: George H. Doran, 1926); *The St. Louis Church Survey* (New York: George H. Doran, 1924); *1000 City Churches* (New York: Harper, 1926).

[2] See, for example, *A Parish Workbook for City Churches* (New York: Congregational Christian Churches, 1956).

[3] Stanley H. Chapman, "The Contemporary Pastorate," *American Sociological Review*, 9:597–602 (Dec., 1944).

[4] See Stuart A. Queen and David B. Carpenter, *The American City* (New York: McGraw-Hill, 1953), pp. 291–92. The distinction between "metropolitan" churches and "neighborhood" churches rests largely upon the greater dispersion of membership for the metropolitan churches as contrasted with a compact ecological distribution of members of neighborhood churches.

tionships between religious affiliation and social class might be stated as follows:

(1) Upper class persons are preponderantly Protestant; Catholics comprise less than their share of the socially elite of most American cities.

(2) A high proportion of Catholics is found in the lower economic classes.

(3) Within the Protestant faiths, there is considerable variation in social status by denomination:

    (a) Episcopalians, Presbyterians, and Congregationalists tend to be heavily represented in the middle and upper classes.

    (b) Most typical of those in the middle classes are the Methodists and Lutherans.

    (c) The lower classes tend to be composed of Baptists and representatives of fundamentalist and evangelistic sects such as Pentecostal and Holiness.

(4) Jews show considerable variability in social status with some tendency toward concentration in upper-middle and upper-class status.[5]

To the extent that social status is reflected in the ecological pattern of residence, we might expect to find differentiated patterns of residence according to religious preference, but nowhere have such patterns been systematically studied for a representative sample or a complete population with the emphasis upon religious preference rather than upon membership or attendance at a particular church.

[5] See, for example, Liston Pope, "Religion and the Class Structure," *The Annals of the American Academy of Political and Social Science*, 256:84–91 (1948); Hadley Cantril, "Educational and Economic Composition of Religious Groups," *American Journal of Sociology*, 47: 574–79 (Mar., 1943); W. Lloyd Warner and Paul S. Lunt, *The Social Life of a Modern Community* (New Haven: Yale University Press, 1941), p. 359; August B. Hollingshead, *Elmstown's Youth* (New York: John Wiley, 1945), Ch. 5; Louis B. Bultena, "Church Membership and Church Attendance in Madison, Wisconsin," *American Sociological Review*, 14:384–89 (June, 1949).

Method of Wichita Study

During the last week of January and the first week of February of 1958, the Wichita Council of Churches sponsored a Teaching Mission in which many churches of the city engaged in intensive study and analysis of their programs. As one part of the Mission, these churches, assisted by still others who were not free at that time to participate in other phases of the Mission, conducted a city-wide census of religious preference and affiliation. Each of the participating churches furnished a core of volunteer census-takers who attended instruction sessions and on the appointed afternoon, February 2, called on householders in previously designated areas. Call-backs were made within the next several days on those who were not at home.

This was a massive operation in which 5,500 volunteers turned out on one afternoon to ring 80,000 doorbells. In spite of the ambitiousness of the project, most of the calls were completed on schedule, and within a few days returns were available on some 65,000 householders. These represented approximately 80 per cent of the households within the census area at the time.

These 65,000 have been painstakingly classified by hand according to the religious preference of the mother of the family, or in her absence, the head of the house. It was not feasible to obtain the preference of all of the individuals in Wichita, and for some individuals, particularly young children, such data are not very meaningful anyway. In spite of some mixed marriages and some difference of church membership and preference on the part of family members, religion is still very much a family affair in America, and it is not at all illogical that a census of religion should be carried out with families as the units rather than individuals. In any event, the family was treated as the unit in the Wichita census, and the entire family was classified, as stated above, according to the preference of the mother. This procedure was based upon two assumptions: first, experience has shown that when differences of religion do exist within a family, the children usually follow the preference of the mother; and second, misassignment of individuals on this basis will probably balance out in the total census, and therefore, it is probable that a census of families will show about the same distribution among the various denominations and faiths as would a complete census of individuals.

In the original census, we asked for general religious preference, for the name of the specific church of which one might be a member, and the name of the church usually attended. Usually these three items agreed, but sometimes they did not. The disagreements were of many kinds: some had preferences but did not belong and did not attend, some belonged and did not attend, some preferred one church but attended another, etc. Preference was ultimately used, rather than church membership or attendance, as the basis of classification because it appeared more generally valid and was available on a greater proportion of the sample. Furthermore, less is known about religious preference; after all, membership and attendance figures are always available as institutional statistics, but rarely in America have we a chance to see the religious orientation of the entire population, not just that of those who go to church.

The interpretations of the relationships between denominational preference and social and economic status in the city which are given in this report rest fundamentally upon the social and economic patterns brought out in an earlier study, A *Pictorial Analysis of Wichita*.[6]

Preferences of People of Wichita as a Whole

Wichita has been called a city of churches, and the number and variety of its religious institutions seems to give some warrant for such an appellation. There are 320 individual churches listed in the directory of churches published by the Wichita Council of Churches. These churches represent about sixty-six different denominations or faiths.

These appear to be sufficient in quantity and diversity to accommodate nearly all of the inhabitants. Only 4 per cent of the families of the city are classified as having no religious preference and only a few prefer religious institutions which are not included among the churches of the city. In fact, one follower of Father Divine, one Buddhist, and two Mohammedans appear to be the only ones in Wichita who would not be able to affiliate with a congregation of their faith if they so desired.

Whether Wichita has more diversity or leans more toward certain types of religion than other communities cannot be specifically established since we have no comparable census in other cities. It would be interesting to discover whether Mencken's reference to the "Bible Belt" is reflected in the religious make-up of Wichita, but there is little comparative information from other places.

The best evidence of this order, by coincidence, was published at the same time as the Wichita census. This is a sample of the population of the United States taken by the Bureau of Census in March, 1957.

[6] Donald O. Cowgill, A *Pictoral Analysis of Wichita* (Wichita: Community Planning Council and University of Wichita, 1954).

The question asked on this national survey was, "What is your religion?" This appears closely comparable with ours which was, "What is your religious preference?" In both cases the answer was usually given in terms of the names of organized religious institutions, whether or not the respondents were actually members of those institutions.

Table I shows the percentages for major denominations and faiths in Wichita

TABLE 1. *Religious Preferences of Families of Wichita Compared with the Population of the United States*

	PERCENTAGE U.S.A., 1957*	PERCENTAGE WICHITA, 1958
Protestant	66.2	81.5
Baptist	19.7	18.6
Lutheran	7.1	3.8
Methodist	14.0	21.0
Presbyterian	5.6	7.9
Other Protestant	19.8	31.2
Roman Catholic	25.7	11.8
Jewish	3.2	0.4
Other Religion	1.3	2.1
No Religion	1.3	2.1
Religion not reported	0.9	....†

* U.S. figures from Bureau of the Census, Current Population Reports: *Population Characteristics*, Series P-20, No. 79 (Feb. 2, 1958), p. 6.

† Those not reporting are not included in our tables.

and in the United States as a whole. It appears that Wichita has a far greater proportion of Protestants than the nation as a whole. In Wichita more than four out of five persons are Protestant, whereas, in the country as a whole, the ratio for adult individuals is two out of three. Of course, the obverse of this is that there are relatively fewer Catholics and Jews in Wichita than in the United States as a whole. Wichita is largely

native, and old American; it contains only a small proportion of recent immigrants or even second generation immigrant families, a large proportion of whom were Catholic and Jewish. The major centers of Catholic and Jewish populations are the port cities of the east. Wichita, an inland city, has not received as high a proportion of these migrants and consequently does not have as high proportions of Catholics and Jews.

Obscured within the ratios of other religions, showing Wichita with somewhat greater proportions, is the small but significant proportion of adherents of the Orthodox Greek Catholic faith stemming from an historical settlement of Syrians in Wichita.

Within the Protestant denominations, Wichita appears to have a high proportion of Methodists, Presbyterians, and "other Protestant" denominations. The national report does not give any breakdown of the "other Protestant" classification, hence we can only surmise the relative proportion of different faiths. We suspect that one reason for the high percentage of families in this category in Wichita is the high ratio of adherents of the Disciples of Christ (Christian) Church, 11 per cent of the total. The second reason for this excess in Wichita in the "other Protestant" category may be the occasion for Mencken's label "The Bible Belt." There are small but significant numbers of followers of many fundamentalist and evangelistic sects which when added together comprise a considerable proportion of the total.

Selected Ecological Patterns

In the larger study,[7] of which this is a summary, ecological maps of the residen-

[7] Donald O. Cowgill and La Verna F. Wadsworth, *Religious Preferences of the Families of Wichita* (Wichita: The Community Planning Council, 1958).

tial distribution of adherents of some forty denominations and faiths were prepared and analyzed. It is not possible to reproduce those maps here, nor can we discuss the patterns for all forty denominations. Instead, we shall attempt to describe typical patterns for different social classes, the patterns of distinctive faiths —Catholic and Jewish, patterns reflecting ethnic groups—Negro and Syrian, and the pattern for those who said they had no preference.

Income and status differentials are reflected strikingly in the distribution of adherents of many Protestant denominations. Those expressing a preference for the Episcopal church are found predominantly in the higher income sections of the city. This confirms the findings of the various stratification studies which have noted the concentration of Episcopalians in the upper classes.[8] The fact that the area in the vicinity of the University of Wichita also shows a high ratio of Episcopalians, probably indicates that there is an educational as well as an income component in the appeal of this denomination. In spite of the fact that there is an Episcopal church in the Negro district, the proportion of Episcopalians there is low, as it is in all sections with limited income and low occupational status.

Several other denominations, most particularly, Presbyterian and Congregational, have similar patterns. These, too, tend to conform to the expectations derived from the stratification studies, but the very definite correlation between Congregationalism and economic status in Wichita seems to refute Bergel's statement that "they are numerically not strong enough in the South and Middle West to play an important role in the class structure."[9] In Wichita, they made

up 2.3 per cent of the total, a slightly higher percentage than that of the Episcopalians.

The Methodist denomination appears typical of those whose greatest strength is in the middle classes. Methodists constitute a plurality in most of the census tracts with average incomes or above except for a few of the very highest income areas in which, as noted above, Episcopalians, Presbyterians, and Congregationalists are more numerous. And on the other hand, it should be noted that the poorest sections of the city had the fewest Methodists (when African Methodist Episcopal and Christian Methodist Episcopal are treated as separate denominations.) Thus, Methodism is below average in the wealthiest sections of the city and lowest in the poorest sections. This appears to warrant the judgment that it is strongest in the middle classes.

This may indicate that Methodists by and large have a somewhat higher status in Wichita than in some other communities since Warner found heavy representation in the lower classes in Yankee City,[10] and Liston Pope notes the same tendency in national polls.[11]

In the same general classification, appear the Unity Church, Lutheran, Disciples of Christ, Evangelical and Reformed, Friends, Latter Day Saints, and United Presbyterian. The Unitarian and Church of Christ Scientist tend to draw from the upper-middle-class range in Wichita.

The Pentecostal denomination gives a good representation of a church whose adherents are drawn chiefly from the lower income classes. This is shown in Wichita by a high frequency of followers in the multiple-housing areas adjacent to the central business district, in a mixed Mexican-Negro district opposite the stockyards, and in several other areas of

[8] See, for example, Warner and Lunt, op. cit., and Pope, op. cit., p. 86.
[9] Egon Ernest Bergel, Urban Sociology (New York: McGraw-Hill, 1955), pp. 315–16.

[10] Warner and Lunt, op. cit., p. 359.
[11] Pope, op. cit., p. 86.

low income status. Very few Pentecostals live in the upper income sections, or even in the areas of the middle income range. This conforms with the findings of Pope.

Other denominations with closely similar patterns include Jehovah's Witnesses, Salvation Army, and Four-Square Gospel. Also predominantly lower class, but drawing from a somewhat broader range than these are the Nazarene, Adventist, Baptist, Assembly of God, Church of Christ, Church of God, and United Brethren churches. Baptist churches generally draw a plurality of preferences in the low income sections of the city.

These data suggest that there are few Protestant denominations that do not reflect some specialization in relation to social classes and ecological area. However, this cannot be said of the Roman Catholic church in Wichita. There is a high proportion of Catholics in some upper income areas as well as in some very poor areas such as the central business district and the Mexican district. Likewise, the tracts with few Catholics range all the way from very poor in the stockyards area and the Negro district to an upper middle-class section.

This pattern appears to differ from the findings of many of the stratification studies in which Catholics are concentrated in the lower classes.[12] It is the author's judgment that this indicates a real difference. Wichita has relatively few Catholics (only 12 per cent) and, with the exception of a small Mexican settlement, few of these are recent immigrants. As an inland city whose industrialization dates from World War II, Wichita received little of the immigration which contributed so heavily to the Catholic population in Northeastern cities and which at least temporarily led to a loading of the lower classes in those cities with Cath-

olics. Recent migrants to Wichita have been more Baptist than Catholic.

Perhaps another way in which Wichita deviates from a national norm or pattern of Northeastern cities is in the stratification of its Jewish population. It is not unusual to have a fairly high proportion of Jews in the upper classes,[13] but the residential concentration of Jews in the upper income areas of Wichita is so great that a stranger looking at the map might conclude that there was a ghetto. However, close examination would reveal that in no tract do Jews constitute as much as 4 per cent of the total population, and it is also evident that the areas of maximum density of Jewish families in Wichita are the elite areas of the city.

Another aspect which may be of interest to sociologists is the extent to which the Jewish population has moved away from the location of their synagogues. One synagogue is about one and one half miles from the center of the city, the other is approximately two miles out, while nearly all of the Jewish population lives still farther out with the center of this population being about four miles to the east of the center of the city. Since the same phenomenon was reported by Chapman[14] fourteen years ago in New Haven, we may raise several interesting questions: Do Jews move toward the suburbs at a more rapid rate? Is there more reluctance (or difficulty) in moving a synagogue than in the removal of a church of another faith?

There are several denominations whose distribution can be explained only in terms of race and the ecology of race in Wichita. For example, the distribution of families giving African Methodist Episcopal as their religious preference quite clearly outlines the main Negro district. It underscores and confirms the highly

[12] *Ibid.;* Warner and Lunt, *op. cit.,* p. 359; Bultena, *op. cit.,* p. 386.

[13] Liston Pope shows 22 per cent.—*Op. cit.,* p. 86.
[14] Chapman, *op. cit.,* p. 86.

rigid residential segregation pattern in Wichita cited by this author previously.[15] The same pattern emerges for two other denominations whose membership is primarily Negro: Christian Methodist Episcopal and National Baptist.

Another finding of this study is that the proportion of those who gave "no church" as their preference is highest in the low income section of the city. This is in accord with Hollingshead, who notes the lack of church membership and attendance from the lower classes.[16] However, Bultena found little variation in church membership and attendance in Madison by social classes.[17]

In summary, the ecological study of religious preference in Wichita conforms in general with earlier studies of the correlation between social class and church membership, but at the same time reveals some variations and unique qualities. Episcopalians, Presbyterians, and Congregationalists show marked concentration in high income sections. Concentrations in areas characterized by medium incomes were for those giving preference to Unitarian, Christian Scientist, Unity and Lutheran, Methodist, Christian, Evangelical and Reformed, Friends, and Mormon churches. The poorer sections of the city tended to have more Nazarene, Adventist, Baptist, Assembly of God, Church of Christ, Church of God, United Brethren, Jehovah's Witnesses, Salvation Army, Four-Square Gospel, and Pentecostal followers. Roman Catholics were found in both wealthy and poor sections, but the Jews were markedly concentrated in high income areas. Followers of the African Methodist Episcopal, the Christian Methodist Episcopal, and the National Baptist denominations were found almost exclusively in the highly segregated Negro residential district, and those with no church preference were predominantly in the poor sections of the city.

[15] Donald O. Cowgill and Mary S., "An Index of Segregation Based on Block Statistics," *American Sociological Review*, 16:825–32; Donald O. Cowgill, "Trends in Residential Segregation of Non-Whites in American Cities, 1940–1950, *American Sociological Review*, 21:43–48 (Feb., 1956).

[16] Hollingshead, *op. cit.*, p. 117.

[17] Bultena, *op. cit.*, p. 386.

D · SECT, CHURCH, DENOMINATION, AND STRATIFICATION

1 · Sect-Type and Church-Type Contrasted

ERNEST TROELTSCH

The importance of this element is the fact that at this point, alongside of the Church-type produced by Christianity in its sociological process of self-development, there appears the new type of the sect.

At the outset the actual differences are quite clear. The Church is that type of organization which is overwhelmingly conservative, which to a certain extent accepts the secular order, and dominates the masses; in principle, therefore, it is universal, i.e. it desires to cover the whole life of humanity. The sects, on the other hand, are comparatively small groups; they aspire after personal inward perfection, and they aim at a direct personal fellowship between the members of each group. From the very beginning, therefore, they are forced to organize themselves in small groups, and to renounce the idea of dominating the world. Their attitude towards the world, the State, and Society may be indifferent, tolerant, or hostile, since they have no desire to control and incorporate these forms of social life; on the contrary, they tend to avoid them; their aim is usually either to tolerate their presence alongside

SOURCE. Ernst Troeltsch, "Sect-Type and Church-Type Contrasted," from Ernst Troeltsch, *The Social Teaching of the Christian Churches* (trans. Olive Wyon), London: Allen and Unwin, 1931, vol. 1, pp. 331–343.

of their own body, or even to replace these social institutions by their own society.

Further, both types are in close connection with the actual situation and with the development of Society. The fully developed Church, however, utilizes the State and the ruling classes, and weaves these elements into her own life; she then becomes an integral part of the existing social order; from this standpoint, then, the Church both stabilizes and determines the social order; in so doing, however, she becomes dependent upon the upper classes, and upon their development. The sects, on the other hand, are connected with the lower classes, or at least with those elements in Society which are opposed to the State and to Society; they work upwards from below, and not downwards from above.

Finally, too, both types vary a good deal in their attitude towards the supernatural and transcendent element in Christianity, and also in their view of its system of asceticism. The Church relates the whole of the secular order as a means and a preparation to the supernatural aim of life, and it incorporates genuine asceticism into its structure as one element in this preparation, all under the very definite direction of the Church. The sects refer their members directly to the supernatural aim of life, and in them

457

the individualistic, directly religious character of asceticism, as a means of union with God, is developed more strongly and fully; the attitude of opposition to the world and its powers, to which the secularized Church now also belongs, tends to develop a theoretical and general asceticism. It must, however, be admitted that asceticism in the Church, and in ecclesiastical monasticism, has a different meaning from that of the renunciation of or hostility to the world which characterizes the asceticism of the sects.

The asceticism of the Church is a method of acquiring virtue, and a special high watermark of religious achievement, connected chiefly with the repression of the senses, or expressing itself in special achievements of a peculiar character; otherwise, however, it presupposes the life of the world as the general background, and the contrast of an average morality which is on relatively good terms with the world. Along these lines, therefore, ecclesiastical asceticism is connected with the asceticism of the redemption cults of late antiquity, and with the detachment required for the contemplative life; in any case, it is connected with a moral dualism.

The asceticism of the sects, on the other hand, is merely the simple principle of detachment from the world, and is expressed in the refusal to use the law, to swear in a court of justice, to own property, to exercise dominion over others, or to take part in war. The sects take the Sermon on the Mount as their ideal; they lay stress on the simple but radical opposition of the Kingdom of God to all secular interests and institutions. They practise renunciation only as a means of charity, as the basis of a thorough-going communism of love, and, since their rules are equally binding upon all, they do not encourage extravagant and heroic deeds, nor the vicarious heroism of some to make up for the worldliness and average morality of others. The ascetic ideal of

the sects consists simply in opposition to the world and to its social institutions, but it is not opposition to the sense-life, nor to the average life of humanity. It is therefore only related with the asceticism of monasticism in so far as the latter also creates special conditions, within which it is possible to lead a life according to the Sermon on the Mount, and in harmony with the ideal of the communism of love. In the main, however, the ascetic ideal of the sects is fundamentally different from that of monasticism, in so far as the latter implies emphasis upon the mortification of the senses, and upon works of supererogation in poverty and obedience for their own sake. In all things the ideal of the sects is essentially not one which aims at the destruction of the sense life and of natural self-feeling, but a union in love which is not affected by the social inequalities and struggles of the world.

All these differences which actually existed between the late Mediaeval Church and the sects, must have had their foundation in some way or another within the interior structure of the twofold sociological edifice. If, then, in reality both types claim, and rightly claim, a relationship with the Primitive Church, it is clear that the final cause for this dualistic development must lie within primitive Christianity itself. Once this point becomes clear, therefore, it will also shed light upon the whole problem of the sociological understanding of Christianity in general. Since it is only at this point that the difference between the two elements emerges very clearly as a permanent difference, only now have we reached the stage at which it can be discussed. It is also very important to understand this question thoroughly at this stage, since it explains the later developments of Church History, in which the sect stands out ever more clearly alongside of the Church. In the whole previous development of the Church this question was less vital, for during the early centuries the Church itself fluctuated a great deal between the sect and the Church-type; indeed, it only achieved the development of the Church-type with the development of sacerdotal and sacramental doctrine; precisely for that reason, in its process of development up to this time, the Church had only witnessed a sect development alongside of itself to a small extent, and the differences between them and the Church were still not clear. The problem first appears clearly in the opposition between the sacramental-hierarchical Church conception of Augustine and the Donatists. But with the disappearance of African Christianity this opposition also disappeared, and it only reappeared in a decisive form after the completion of the idea of the Church in the Gregorian church reform.

The word "sect," however, gives an erroneous impression. Originally the word was used in a polemical and apologetic sense, and it was used to describe groups which separated themselves from the official Church, while they retained certain fundamental elements of Christian thought; by the very fact, however, that they were outside the corporate life of the ecclesiastical tradition—a position, moreover, which was usually forced upon them—they were regarded as inferior side-issues, one-sided phenomena, exaggerations or abbreviations of ecclesiastical Christianity. That is, naturally, solely the viewpoint of the dominant churches, based on the belief that the ecclesiastical type alone has any right to exist. Ecclesiastical law within the modern State definitely denotes as "sects" those religious groups which exist alongside of the official privileged State Churches, by law established, groups which the State either does not recognize at all, or, if it does recognize them, grants them fewer rights and privileges than the official State Churches. Such a conception, however, confuses the actual issue. Very often in

the so-called "sects" it is precisely the essential elements of the Gospel which are fully expressed; they themselves always appeal to the Gospel and to Primitive Christianity, and accuse the Church of having fallen away from its ideal; these impulses are always those which have been either suppressed or undeveloped in the official churches, of course for good and characteristic reasons, which again are not taken into account by the passionate party polemics of the sects. There can, however, be no doubt about the actual fact: the sects, with their greater independence of the world, and their continual emphasis upon the original ideals of Christianity, often represent in a very direct and characteristic way the essential fundamental ideas of Christianity; to a very great extent they are a most important factor in the study of the development of the sociological consequences of Christian thought. This statement is proved conclusively by all those who make a close study of the sect movements, which were especially numerous in the latter mediaeval period—movements which played their part in the general disintegration of the mediaeval social order. This comes out very clearly in the great works of Sebastian Franck, and especially of Gottfried Arnold, which were written later in defence of the sects.

The main stream of Christian development, however, flows along the channel prepared by the Church-type. The reason for this is clear: the Church-type represents the longing for a universal all-embracing ideal, the desire to control great masses of men, and therefore the urge to dominate the world and civilization in general. Paulinism, in spite of its strongly individualistic and "enthusiastic" features, had already led the way along this line: it desired to conquer the world for Christ; it came to terms with the order of the State by interpreting it as an institution ordained and permitted by

God; it accepted the existing order with its professions and its habits and customs. The only union it desired was that which arose out of a common share in the energy of grace which the Body of Christ contained; out of this union the new life ought to spring up naturally from within through the power of the Holy Spirit, thus preparing the way for the speedy coming of the Kingdom of God, as the real universal end of all things. The more that Christendom renounced the life of this supernatural and eschatological fulfilment of its universal ideal, and tried to achieve this end by missionary effort and organization, the more was it forced to make its Divine and Christian character independent of the subjective character and service of believers; henceforth it sought to concentrate all its emphasis upon the objective possession of religious truth and religious power, which were contained in the tradition of Christ, and in the Divine guidance of the Church which fills and penetrates the whole Body. From this objective basis subjective energies could ever flow forth afresh, exerting a renewing influence, but the objective basis did not coincide with these results. Only thus was it possible to have a popular Church at all, and it was only thus that the relative acceptance of the world, the State, of Society, and of the existing culture, which this required, did no harm to the objective foundation. The Divine nature of the Church was retained in its objective basis, and from this centre there welled up continually fresh streams of vital spiritual force. It was the aim of the leaders of the Church to render this basis as objective as possible, by means of tradition, priesthood, and sacrament; to secure in it, objectively, the sociological point of contact; if that were once firmly established the subjective influence of the Church was considered secure; it was only in detail that it could not be con-

trolled. In this way the fundamental religious sense of possessing something Divinely "given" and "redeeming" was ensured, while the universalizing tendency was also made effective, since it established the Church, the organ of Divine grace, in the supreme position of power. When to that was added the Sacrament of Penance, the power of spiritual direction, the law against heretics, and the general supervision of the faith, the Church was then able to gain an inward dominion over the hearts of men.

Under these circumstances, however, the Church found it impossible to avoid making a compromise with the State, with the social order, and with economic conditions, and the Thomist doctrine worked this out in a very able, comprehensive theory, which vigorously maintained the ultimate supernatural orientation of life. In all this it is claimed that the whole is derived, quite logically, from the Gospel; it is clear that this point of view became possible as soon as the Gospel was conceived as a universal way of life, offering redemption to all, whose influence radiates from the knowledge given by the Gospel, coupled with the assurance of salvation given by the Church. It was precisely the development of an objective sociological point of reference, its establishment on a stable basis, and its endeavour to go forward from that point to organize the conquest of the world, which led to this development. It is, however, equally obvious that in so doing the radical individualism of the Gospel, with its urge towards the utmost personal achievement, its radical fellowship of love, uniting all in the most personal centre of life, with its heroic indifference towards the world, the State and civilization, with its mistrust of the spiritual danger of distraction and error inherent in the possession of or the desire for great possessions, has been given a secondary place, or even given up altogether; these features now appear as mere factors within the system; they are no longer ruling principles.

It was precisely this aspect of the Gospel, however, which the sects developed still farther, or, rather, it was this aspect which they were continually re-emphasizing and bringing into fresh prominence. In general, the following are their characteristic features: lay Christianity, personal achievement in ethics and in religion, the radical fellowship of love, religious equality and brotherly love, indifference towards the authority of the State and the ruling classes, dislike of technical law and of the oath, the separation of the religious life from the economic struggle by means of the ideal of poverty and frugality, or occasionally in a charity which becomes communism, the directness of the personal religious relationship, criticism of official spiritual guides and theologians, the appeal to the New Testament and to the Primitive Church. The sociological point of contact, which here forms the starting-point for the growth of the religious community, differs clearly from that upon which the Church has been formed. Whereas the Church assumes the objective concrete holiness of the sacerdotal office, of Apostolic Succession, of the *Depositum fidei* and of the sacraments, and appeals to the extension of the Incarnation which takes place permanently through the priesthood, the sect, on the other hand, appeals to the ever new common performance of the moral demands, which, at bottom, are founded only upon the Law and the Example of Christ. In this, it must be admitted that they are in direct contact with the Teaching of Jesus. Consciously or unconsciously, therefore, this implies a different attitude to the early history of Christianity, and a different conception of Christian doctrine. Scripture history and the history of the Primitive Church are permanent ideals,

to be accepted in their literal sense, not the starting-point, historically limited and defined, for the development of the Church. Christ is not the God-Man, eternally at work within the Church, leading it into all Truth, but He is the direct Head of the Church, binding the Church to Himself through His Law in the Scriptures. On the one hand, there is development and compromise, on the other literal obedience and radicalism.

It is this point of view, however, which makes the sects incapable of forming large mass organizations, and limits their development to small groups, united on a basis of personal intimacy; it is also responsible for the necessity for a constant renewal of the ideal, their lack of continuity, their pronounced individualism, and their affinity with all the oppressed and idealistic groups within the lower classes. These also are the groups in which an ardent desire for the improvement of their lot goes hand in hand with a complete ignorance of the complicated conditions of life, in which therefore an idealistic orthodoxy finds no difficulty in expecting to see the world transformed by the purely moral principles of love. In this way the sects gained on the side of intensity in Christian life, but they lost in the spirit of universalism, since they felt obliged to consider the Church as degenerate, and they did not believe that the world could be conquered by human power and effort; that is why they were always forced to adopt eschatological views. On the side of personal Christian piety they score, and they are in closer touch with the radical individualism of the Gospel, but they lose spontaneity and the spirit of grateful surrender to the Divine revelation of grace; they look upon the New Testament as the Law of God, and, in their active realization of personal fellowship in love, they tend towards legalism and an emphasis upon "good works". They gain in specific

Christian piety, but they lose spiritual breadth and the power to be receptive, and they thus revise the whole vast process of assimilation which the Church had completed, and which she was able to complete because she had placed personal Christian piety upon an objective basis. The Church emphasizes the idea of Grace and makes it objective; the sect emphasizes and realizes the idea of subjective holiness. In the Scriptures the Church adheres to the source of redemption, whereas the sect adheres to the Law of God and of Christ.

Although this description of the sect-type represents in the main its prevailing sociological characteristics, the distinctive significance of the sect-type contrasted with the Church-type still has a good concrete basis. (There is no need to consider here the particular groups which were founded purely upon dogma; they were indeed rare, and the pantheistic philosophical sects of the Middle Ages merge almost imperceptibly into sects of the practical religious kind.) In reality, the sects are essentially different from the Church and the churches. The word "sect", however, does not mean that these movements are undeveloped expressions of the Church-type; it stands for an independent sociological type of Christian thought.

The essence of the Church is its objective institutional character. The individual is born into it, and through infant baptism he comes under its miraculous influence. The priesthood and the hierarchy, which hold the keys to the tradition of the Church, to sacramental grace and ecclesiastical jurisdiction, represent the objective treasury of grace, even when the individual priest may happen to be unworthy; this Divine treasure only needs to be set always upon the lampstand and made effective through the sacraments, and it will inevitably do its work by virtue of the miraculous power which the Church contains. The Church

means the eternal existence of the God-Man; it is the extension of the Incarnation, the objective organization of miraculous power, from which, by means of the Divine Providential government of the world, subjective results will appear quite naturally. From this point of view compromise with the world, and the connection with the preparatory stages and dispositions which it contained, was possible; for in spite of all individual inadequacy the institution remains holy and Divine, and it contains the promise of its capacity to overcome the world by means of the miraculous power which dwells within it. Universalism, however, also only becomes possible on the basis of this compromise; it means an actual domination of the institution as such, and a believing confidence in its invincible power of inward influence. Personal effort and service, however fully they may be emphasized, even when they go to the limits of extreme legalism, are still only secondary; the main thing is the objective possession of grace and its universally recognized dominion; to everything else these words apply: *et cetera adjicientur vobis*. The one vitally important thing is that every individual should come within the range of the influence of these saving energies of grace; hence the Church is forced to dominate Society, compelling all the members of Society to come under its sphere and influence; but, on the other hand, her stability is entirely unaffected by the fact of the extent to which her influence over all individuals is actually attained. The Church is the great educator of the nations, and like all educators she knows how to allow for various degrees of capacity and maturity, and how to attain her end only by a process of adaptation and compromise.

Compared with this institutional principle of an objective organism, however, the sect is a voluntary community whose members join it of their own free will.

The very life of the sect, therefore, depends on actual personal service and co-operation; as an independent member each individual has his part within the fellowship; the bond of union has not been indirectly imparted through the common possession of Divine grace, but it is directly realized in the personal relationships of life. An individual is not born into a sect; he enters it on the basis of conscious conversion; infant baptism, which, indeed, was only introduced at a later date, is almost always a stumbling-block. In the sect spiritual progress does not depend upon the objective impartation of Grace through the Sacrament, but upon individual personal effort; sooner or later, therefore, the sect always criticizes the sacramental idea. This does not mean that the spirit of fellowship is weakened by individualism; indeed, it is strengthened, since each individual proves that he is entitled to membership |by the very fact of his services to the fellowship. It is, however, naturally a somewhat limited form of fellowship, and the expenditure of so much effort in the maintenance and exercise of this particular kind of fellowship produces a certain indifference towards other forms of fellowship which are based upon secular interests; on the other hand, all secular interests are drawn into the narrow framework of the sect and tested by its standards, in so far as the sect is able to assimilate these interests at all. Whatever cannot be related to the group of interests controlled by the sect, and by the Scriptural ideal, is rejected and avoided. The sect, therefore, does not educate nations in the mass, but it gathers a select group of the elect, and places it in sharp opposition to the world. In so far as the sect-type maintains Christian universalism at all, like the Gospel, the only form it knows is that of eschatology; this is the reason why it always finally revives the eschatology of the Bible. That also naturally explains the

greater tendency of the sect towards "ascetic" life and thought, even though the original ideal of the New Testament had not pointed in that direction. The final activity of the group and of the individual consists precisely in the practical austerity of a purely religious attitude towards life which is not affected by cultural influences. That is, however, a different kind of asceticism, and this is the reason for that difference between it and the asceticism of the Church-type which has already been stated. It is not the heroic special achievement of a special class, restricted by its very nature to particular instances, nor the mortification of the senses in order to further the higher religious life; it is simply detachment from the world, the reduction of worldly pleasure to a minimum, and the highest possible development of fellowship in love; all this is interpreted in the old Scriptural sense. Since the sect-type is rooted in the teaching of Jesus, its asceticism also is that of primitive Christianity and of the Sermon on the Mount, not that of the Church and of the contemplative life; it is narrower and more scrupulous than that of Jesus, but, literally understood, it is still the continuation of the attitude of Jesus towards the world. The concentration on personal effort, and the sociological connection with a practical ideal, makes an extremely exacting claim on individual effort, and avoidance of all other forms of human association. The asceticism of the sect is not an attempt to popularize and universalize an ideal which the Church had prescribed only for special classes and in special circumstances. The Church ideal of asceticism can never be conceived as a universal ethic; it is essentially unique and heroic. The ascetic ideal of the sect, on the contrary, is, as a matter of course, an ideal which is possible to all, and appointed for all, which, according to its conception, united the fellowship instead of dividing it, and according

464   Religion and Society

to its content is also capable of a general realization in so far as the circle of the elect is concerned.

Thus, in reality we are faced with two different sociological types. This is true in spite of the fact (which is quite immaterial) that incidentally in actual practice they may often impinge upon one another. If objections are raised to the terms "Church" and "Sect", and if all sociological groups which are based on and inspired by monotheistic, universalized, religious motives are described (in a terminology which is in itself quite appropriate) as "Churches", we would then have to make the distinction between institutional churches and voluntary churches. It does not really matter which expression is used. The all-important point is this: that both types are a logical result of the Gospel, and only conjointly do they exhaust the whole range of its sociological influence, and thus also indirectly of its social results, which are always connected with the religious organization.

In reality, the Church does not represent a mere deterioration of the Gospel, however much that may appear to be the case when we contrast its hierarchical organization and its sacramental system with the teaching of Jesus. For wherever the Gospel is conceived as primarily a free gift, as pure grace, and wherever it is offered to us in the picture which faith creates of Christ as a Divine institution, wherever the inner freedom of the Spirit, contrasted with all human effort and organization, is felt to be the spirit of Jesus, and wherever His splendid indifference towards secular matters is felt, in the sense of a spiritual and inner independence, while these secular things are used outwardly, there the institution of the Church may be regarded as a natural continuation and transformation of the Gospel. At the same time, with its unlimited universalism, it still contains the fundamental impulse of the evangelic

message; the only difference is that whereas the Gospel had left all questions of possible realization to the miraculous coming of the Kingdom of God, a Church which had to work in a world which was not going to pass away had to organize and arrange matters for itself, and in so doing it was forced into a position of compromise.

On the other hand, the essence of the sect does not consist merely in a one-sided emphasis upon certain vital elements of the Church-type, but it is itself a direct continuation of the idea of the Gospel. Only within it is there a full recognition of the value of radical individualism and of the idea of love; it is the sect alone which instinctively builds up its ideal of fellowship from this point of view, and this is the very reason why it attains such a strong subjective and inward unity, instead of merely external membership in an institution. For the same reason the sect also maintains the original radicalism of the Christian ideal and its hostility towards the world, and it retains the fundamental demand for personal service, which indeed it is also able to regard as a work of grace: in the idea of grace, however, the sect emphasizes the subjective realization and the effects of grace, and not the objective assurance of its presence. The sect does not live on the miracles of the past, nor on the miraculous nature of the institution, but on the constantly renewed miracle of the Presence of Christ, and on the subjective reality of the individual mastery of life.

The starting-point of the Church is the Apostolic Message of the Exalted Christ, and faith in Christ the Redeemer, into which the Gospel has developed; this constitutes its objective treasure, which it makes still more objective in its sacramental-sacerdotal institution. To this extent the Church can trace its descent from Paulinism, which contained the germ of the sacramental idea, which, however, also contained some very un-ecclesiastical elements in its pneumatic enthusiasm, and in its urgent demand for the personal holiness of the "new creature."

The sect, on the contrary, starts from the teaching and the example of Jesus, from the subjective work of the apostles and the pattern of their life of poverty, and unites the religious individualism preached by the Gospel with the religious fellowship, in which the office of the ministry is not based upon ecclesiastical ordination and tradition, but upon religious service and power, and which therefore can also devolve entirely upon laymen.

The Church administers the sacraments without reference to the personal worthiness of the priests; the sect distrusts the ecclesiastical sacraments, and either permits them to be administered by laymen, or makes them dependent upon the personal character of the celebrant, or even discards them altogether. The individualism of the sect urges it towards the direct intercourse of the individual with God; frequently, therefore, it replaces the ecclesiastical doctrine of the sacraments by the Primitive Christian doctrine of the Spirit and by "enthusiasm". The Church has its priests and its sacraments; it dominates the world and is therefore also dominated by the world. The sect is lay Christianity, independent of the world, and is therefore inclined towards asceticism and mysticism. Both these tendencies are based upon fundamental impulses of the Gospel. The Gospel contains the idea of an objective possession of salvation in the knowledge and revelation of God, and in developing this idea it becomes the Church. It contains, however, also the idea of an absolute personal religion and of an absolute personal fellowship, and in following out this idea it becomes a sect. The teaching of Jesus, which cherishes the expectation of the End of the Age and the Coming of the Kingdom of God, which gathers into one body all who are resolute in their determination to confess Christ before men and to leave the world to its fate, tends to develop the sect-type. The apostolic faith which looks back to a miracle of redemption and to the Person of Jesus, and which lives in the powers of its heavenly Lord: this faith which leans upon something achieved and objective, in which it unites the faithful and allows them to rest, tends to develop the Church-type. Thus the New Testament helps to develop both the Church and the sect; it has done so from the beginning, but the Church had the start, and its great world mission. Only when the objectification of the Church had been developed to its fullest extent did the sectarian tendency assert itself and react against this excessive objectification. Further, just as the objectification of the Church was achieved in connection with the feudal society of the Early Middle Ages, the reappearance of the tendency to form sects was connected with the social transformation, and the new developments of city-civilization in the central period of the Middle Ages and in its period of decline—with the growth of individualism and the gathering of masses of people in the towns themselves—and with the reflex effect of this city formation upon the rural population and the aristocracy.

2 · The Churches of the Disinherited: I

H. RICHARD NIEBUHR

One phase of denominationalism is largely explicable by means of a modified economic interpretation of religious history; for the divisions of the church have been occasioned more frequently by the direct and indirect operation of economic factors than by the influence of any other major interest of man. Furthermore, it is evident that economic stratification is often responsible for maintaining divisions which were originally due to differences of another sort. Social history demonstrates how a racial class may retain its solidarity and distinction by becoming an economic class, and religious history offers examples of churches which were originally racial in character but maintained their separateness under new conditions because the racial group developed into an economic entity. It is true, of course, in this case as in that of others, that no one element, the religious or the economic or the racial, operates alone. Economic classes tend to take on a cultural character and economic differences between groups result in educational and psychological distinctions between them. The interaction of the various factors is well exemplified in the history of immigrant groups in the United States. These are distinguished at first by racial or national character, but they are usually also the lowest groups in the economic and cultural scale during the first genera-

SOURCE. H. Richard Niebuhr, "The Churches of the Disinherited: I," from H. Richard Niebuhr, *The Social Sources of Denominationalism*, Hamden, Conn.: The Shoe String Press, 1954, pp. 26–33. Copyright 1929 by Henry Holt and Company. Reprinted by permission of Meridian Books, The World Publishing Company.

tion and, therefore, their distinction from other groups is triply fortified. Their churches, as a result, are distinguished economically and culturally as well as racially from the denominations of previous immigrants who have risen in the economic scale while losing their specifically national or racial character.

An exclusively economic interpretation of denominationalism would, because of this interaction, be as erroneous as the exclusively economic interpretation of political history is bound to be. It is quite unjustifiable, above all, to leave the religious factor itself out of account in dealing with religious movements. Only because the inspiration of such movements is religious do they develop the tremendous energy they display in history. Yet an exclusively religious interpretation, especially a doctrinal one, is likely to miss the point of the whole development even more completely than does an exclusively economic explanation. For if religion supplies the energy, the goal, and the motive of sectarian movements, social factors no less decidedly supply the occasion, and determine the form the religious dynamic will take. Were spiritual energies to develop unchecked they would scarcely issue in the formation of such denominations as now compose Christianity. Religious energies are dammed up, confined to narrow channels, split into parallel streams, by the non-religious distinctions and classifications of Christians. The source of a religious movement, therefore, need not be economic for its results to take on a definitely economic character. On the other hand, economic conditions may supply the occasion for the rise of a new religious movement without determining its religious value. In any case, however, the character of the denomination issuing from the movement is explicable only if the influence of economic factors be taken into consideration.

So regarded, one phase of the history of denominationalism reveals itself as the story of the religiously neglected poor, who fashion a new type of Christianity which corresponds to their distinctive needs, who rise in the economic scale under the influence of religious discipline, and who, in the midst of a freshly acquired cultural respectability, neglect the new poor succeeding them on the lower plane. This pattern recurs with remarkable regularity in the history of Christianity. Anabaptists, Quakers, Methodists, Salvation Army, and more recent sects of like type illustrate this rise and progress of the churches of the disinherited.

Not only the religious revolutions of the poor, however, have left their impress on the denominational history of Christendom. One may also speak with G. K. Chesterton of the revolt of the rich against the poor. Some of the earlier churches of the Reformation received much of their specific character from their alliance with rising commercialism and set forth an interpretation of Christianity conformable with their major economic interests. To this group belong especially the Calvinistic churches, as has been shown by Weber, Cunningham, and Tawney. Other sects, whose origins are not so readily identifiable with economic movements, have preserved their separate character because of the economic status of their members and are distinguished from their sister denominations less by doctrine than by their wealth and the consequent conservatism of ethics and thought.

That astute historian of the social ethics of the churches, Ernst Troeltsch, once wrote: "The really creative, church-forming, religious movements are the work of the lower strata. Here only can one find that union of unimpaired imagination, simplicity in emotional life, unreflective character of thought, spontaneity of energy and vehement force of need, out of which an unconditioned faith in a divine revelation, the naïveté of complete surrender and the intransigence of certitude can rise. Need upon the one hand and the absence of an all-relativizing culture of reflection on the other hand are at home only in these strata. All great community-building revelations have come forth again and again out of such circles and the significance and power for further development in such religious movements have always been dependent upon the force of the original impetus given in such naïve revelations as well as on the energy of the conviction which made this impetus absolute and divine." This passage not only describes the character of the religious movements which originate in the culturally lower strata of society but also indicates wherein the religious expatriation of these classes consists and shows the dialectic of the process which gives rise to ever new movements.

The religion of the untutored and economically disfranchised classes has distinct ethical and psychological characteristics, corresponding to the needs of these groups. Emotional fervor is one common mark. Where the power of abstract thought has not been highly developed and where inhibitions on emotional expression have not been set up by a system of polite conventions, religion must and will express itself in emotional terms. Under these circumstances spontaneity and energy of religious feeling rather than conformity to an abstract creed are regarded as the tests of religious genuineness. Hence also the formality of ritual is displaced in such groups by an informality which gives opportunity for the expression of emotional faith and for a simple, often crude, symbolism. An intellectually trained and liturgically minded clergy is rejected in favor of lay leaders who serve the emotional needs of this religion more adequately and who, on the other hand, are not allied by culture and interest with those ruling classes whose superior manner of life is too obviously purchased at the expense of the poor.

Ethically, as well as psychologically, such religion bears a distinct character. The salvation which it seeks and sets forth is the salvation of the socially disinherited. Intellectual naïveté and practical need combine to create a marked propensity toward millenarianism, with its promise of tangible goods and of the reversal of all present social systems of rank. From the first century onward, apocalypticism has always been most at home among the disinherited. The same combination of need and social experience brings forth in these classes a deeper appreciation of the radical character of the ethics of the gospel and greater resistance to the tendency to compromise with the morality of power than is found among their more fortunate brethren. Again, the religion of the poor is characterized by the exaltation of the typical virtues of the class and by the apprehension under the influence of the gospel of the moral values resident in its necessities. Hence one finds here, more than elsewhere, appreciation of the religious worth of solidarity and equality, of sympathy and mutual aid, of rigorous honesty in matters of debt, and the religious evaluation of simplicity in dress and manner, of the wisdom hidden to the wise and prudent but revealed to babes, of poverty of spirit, of humility and meekness. Simple and direct in its apprehension of the faith, the religion of the poor shuns the relativizations of ethical and intellectual sophistication and by its fruits in conduct often demonstrates its moral and religious superiority.

Whenever Christianity has become the religion of the fortunate and cultured and has grown philosophical, abstract, formal, and ethically harmless in the process, the lower strata of society find themselves religiously expatriated by a faith which neither meets their psychological needs nor sets forth an appealing ethical ideal. In such a situation the right leader finds little difficulty in launching a new movement which will, as a rule, give rise to a new denomination. When, however, the religious leader does not appear and religion remains bound in the forms of middle-class culture, the secularization of the masses and the transfer of their religious fervor to secular movements, which hold some promise of salvation from the evils that afflict them, is the probable result.

The development of the religion of the disinherited is illustrated not only by the history of various sects in Christianity but by the rise of that faith itself. It began as a religion of the poor, of those who had been denied a stake in contemporary civilization. It was not a socialist movement, as some have sought to show, but a religious revolution, centering in no mundane Paradise but in the cult of Christ. Yet it was addressed to the poor in the land, to fishermen and peasants, to publicans and outcasts. In Corinth as in Galilee, in Rome as in Antioch, not many "wise after the flesh, not many mighty, not many noble were called"; and this condition continued far down into the third century. Origen and Tertullian as well as the opponents of Christianity, notably Celsus, bear ample testimony to the fact that "the uneducated are always in a majority with us." But the new faith became the religion of the cultured, of the rulers, of the sophisticated; it lost its spontaneous energy amid the quibblings of abstract theologies; it sacrificed its ethical rigorousness in compromise with the policies of governments and nobilities; it abandoned its apocalyptic hopes as irrelevant to the well-being of a successful church. Now began the successive waves of religious revolution, the constant recrudescences of religions of the poor who sought an emotionally and ethically more satisfying faith than was the metaphysical and formal cult Christianity had come to be. Montanism, the Franciscan movement, Lollardy, Waldensianism, and many similar tendencies are intelligible only as the efforts of the religiously disinherited to discover again the sources of effective faith. Yet on the whole it is true that the Roman Church, with its ritual, its pageantry, and its authoritative doctrine, supplied to the unsophisticated groups a type of religion which largely satisfied their longings; for under the necessity of adapting itself to the inundation of the northern tribes it

had evolved a system of leadership and worship congenial to the naïve mind and had learned to set forth salvation in terms not abstract but tangible and real though remote. The Roman Church, despite the evident failings of scholasticism and papal policy and sacerdotal luxury, was unable to maintain its integrity not so much because it did not meet the needs of the low strata as because it did not sufficiently accommodate itself to the new middle classes represented by humanism, the new capitalism and nationalism, as well as for reasons not primarily connected with the economic and cultural stratification of society.

3 · The Churches of the Disinherited: II

H. RICHARD NIEBUHR

The Quakers, no less than their predecessors among the churches of the poor, soon settled down to an "equable respectability." They accommodated themselves to the social situation and confined their efforts toward social reformation to the work of gaining converts to their faith, to the works of charity and to occasional efforts to influence public opinion on social questions. A number of factors were responsible for this decline in revolutionary fervor. The effect of persecution has been pointed out. Another important factor in the development of such denominations from revolutionary groups to settled social bodies, content with their place in the scheme of things, is the substitution of a second generation, which

SOURCE. H. Richard Niebuhr, "The Churches of the Disinherited: II," from H. Richard Niebuhr, *The Social Sources of Denominationalism*, Hamden, Conn.: The Shoe String Press, 1954, pp. 54–59. Copyright 1929 by Henry Holt and Company. Reprinted by permission of Meridian Books, The World Publishing Company.

holds its convictions as a heritage, for a first generation which had won these convictions painfully and held them at a bitter cost. But most important among the causes of the decline of revolutionary churches into denominations is the influence of economic success. The churches of the poor all become middle-class churches sooner or later and, with their need, lose much of the idealism which grew out of their necessities. There is no doubt of the truth of Max Weber's contention that godliness is conducive to economic success. From the days of Paul at Thessalonica onward, Christianity has not failed to exhort its adherents "that with quietness they work and eat their own bread," while at the same time it has commanded them to abstain from luxury, but, having "food and covering," "therewith to be content." Monastic asceticism, supported by a dualistic view of life, carried the second of these ideas to its extreme, and was rejected by Protestantism, but the Reformers introduced in place of the "extra-worldly" asceticism of the monks an "intra-worldly" asceticism, which regarded work in trade and vocation as the primary duty of life and a service to God; yet they continued to condemn any indulgence in the comforts and luxuries of life as sinful. Restrictions on consumption accompanied by emphasis upon production have their inevitable result in an economic salvation which is far removed from the eternal blessedness sought by the enthusiastic founders of the Protestant sects, but which is not less highly valued by the successful followers of later generations. This process, which is repeated again and again in the history of Christian sects, also took place in the case of the Quakers. In the second and third generations, with the aid of the prosperity prevailing in the days of good Queen Anne, this church of the disinherited became a more or less respectable middle-class church that left the popular movement from which it originated far behind. It continued to hold the tenets of its social program but now as the doctrines of a denomination rather than as the principles of inclusive social reconstruction. In America, especially, the economic rise of the Quakers was speedy and permanent.

Once more, therefore, the poor were without a gospel. The Millenarian hopes which had fired the popular movement of the seventeenth century with enthusiasm were definitely left behind. The ethics of Jesus was dissolved completely into a mild morality of respectability. Eighteenth-century England, ecclesiastical and academic as well as political, feared nothing so much as enthusiasm. Its reaction against the tense emotionalism of Civil War and Revolutionary days, its disillusionments, its lack of vital energies, exhausted as it was by the turbulent passions of religious and political revolt, left it sterile and cold in religion, enamored only with the bleak beauty of mathematically-minded philosophy or, more frequently, indifferent to the claims

of any ethical or religious idealism. Lecky, describing the religion of the period, writes, "The sermons of the time were almost always written, and the prevailing taste was cold, polished and fastidious." "As is always the case, the habits prevailing in other spheres at once acted on and were influenced by religion. The selfishness, the corruption, the worship of expediency, the scepticism as to all higher motives that characterized the politicians of the school of Walpole; the heartless cynicism reigning in fashionable life which is so clearly reflected in the letters of Horace Walpole and Chesterfield; the spirit of a brilliant and varied contemporary literature, eminently distinguished for its sobriety of judgment and for its fastidious purity and elegance of expression, but for the most part deficient in depth, in passion, and in imagination, may all be traced in the popular theology. Sobriety and good sense were the qualities most valued in the pulpit, and enthusiasm and extravagance were those which were most dreaded."

Whatever were the contributions which the Enlightenment made to the progress of religion—and that they were important none need doubt—it is evident that the period had nothing to offer the untutored and the poor by way of escape into emotional salvation nor by way of promise of social redemption. "The interval between the accession of Anne, in 1714, and the death of George II, in 1760, is a period in the religious history of England to which neither Churchmen nor Dissenters can look back without shame and regret," writes Fisher. "Puritanism had not only lost a great part of its influence, but also a great part of its vigor. A prevalent indifference and scepticism, the spread of vice, partly a heritage from the last Stuart kings, and the ignorance of the clergy, did not lessen a whit the acrimony of ecclesiastical disputes." Lecky has drawn a vivid picture of the low estate of the clergy. They were largely recruited from the lower economic classes, it is true, and so they might have been in a position to interpret Christianity to the people; but, on the one hand, they were too closely attached to the gentry, from whom they derived their livings, to feel any real concern for the needs of their fellows, while, on the other hand, too many were grossly ignorant of the content of Christianity and without appreciation of its meaning. Bishop Burnet wrote in 1713 of those who came to be ordained that "they can give no account, or at least a very imperfect one, of the contents even of the Gospels, or of the Catechism itself." The "moral and intellectual decrepitude" of the universities, which were "the seed-plots of English divinity," in part reflected, in part brought about the low estate of the clergy.

Such was the religious situation. Social and economic conditions presented a different aspect. England was more prosperous in the first half of the eighteenth century than it had been for many years. But that prosperity, as is usually the case, only tended to accentuate class differences by flaunting in the faces of the poor the luxury which they helped to create but could not share, and by calling forth in the fortunate that sense of superiority which flourishes where possession has no relation to merit. Class distinctions were apparently more real in the days preceding and during the Methodist revival than they had been at any time since the rise of Puritanism. This stratification of society played its part in excluding from the churches of the nobility and the middle class the unwanted and uninterested poor —uninterested in the comfortable, æsthetically pleasant, and morally soft religion of the well-to-do.

During the second half of the eighteenth century, moreover, this tendency toward stratification in English society was greatly accelerated by the industrial revolution. The old ties which had bound laborer and employer together in the feudal relationships of agriculture or in the patriarchal connection of master and apprentice were broken by the coming of the factory. The wage system and uncertainty of employment, rising capitalism and the competitive order, the growth of the cities and the increase of poverty widened the cleft between the classes. Lecky summarizes the situation by writing that "wealth was immensely increased, but the inequalities of its distribution were aggravated. The contrast between extravagant luxury and abject misery became much more frequent and much more glaring than before. The wealthy employer ceased to live among his people; the quarters of the rich and of the poor became more distant, and every great city soon presented those sharp divisions of classes and districts in which the political observer discovers one of the most dangerous symptoms of revolution."

4 · Sect and Church in Methodism

EARL D. C. BREWER

The sociology of religion may be defined as the scientific study of religion as a social institution, including its interrelationships with other social institutions and other aspects of society and culture.[1]

SOURCE. Earl D. C. Brewer, "Sect and Church in Methodism," *Social Forces*, 30, 1952, pp. 400–408.

[1] For other definitions and efforts to delimit the field see L. L. Bernard (ed.), *The Fields*

This definition not only differentiates it from other approaches to religious phenomena[2] but makes it cognate with other special sociologies dealing with major social institutions, e.g., family, state, economic organization, education, recreation. The sociology of religion would be dependent upon general sociology, then, for both its theory and methods. Special dependence would attach to that part of general sociology which centers upon social institutions which B. Malinowski regarded as "the legitimate isolate of cultural analysis,"[3] and which Talcott Parsons called "the logical focus of sociology."[4] Such theoretical dependence should be mutual since investigations in a given social institution might be expected to have implications for other social institutions if not, indeed, for modification and amplification of general theory. This affinity of the sociology of religion for other special sociologies dealing with social institutions does not, of course, mean that it is not intimately related to and dependent upon other fields of sociology, e.g., community, race, ecology, regionalism, social change, population, social stratification, as well as social psychology and sociology of knowledge.

Most definitions of the concept, "social institution," fall between the rather specific use of Znaniecki in limiting the term to "such official, impersonally patterned functions and statuses of members of any organized social group . . ."[5] and the more general view of Panunzio that social institutions may be regarded as "those systems of concepts, usages, associations, and instruments which, arising from the experiences of mankind, order and regulate the activities of human beings which are necessary to the satisfaction of basic needs. They are the basic systems of human activities, having considerable permanence, universality, and inter-penetrative independence."[6]

Regardless of the level of generality involved or the specific aspects emphasized, most sociologists and anthropologists who make extensive use of the concept "social institutions"[7] devise categories or type-parts as analytical tools.

These may be summarized and applied to a specific religious body or institution, to use the term in a restricted sense. Thus, a religious institution may be said to be composed of conceptual and ideological elements; usages, ritual and behavioral patterns; associational and organizational elements; and material and instrumental aspects which channelize the activities of human beings toward the satisfaction of basic needs, in this case, commonly recognized as religious. The conceptual and ideological elements

and Methods of Sociology (New York: Farrar and Rinehart, 1934), p. 165; Joachim Wach, Sociology of Religion (Chicago: University of Chicago Press, 1944), p. 374; Arthur L. Swift, Jr., New Frontiers of Religion (New York: The Macmillan Co., 1938), p. vii.

[2] Joachim Wach, op. cit., pp. 1–17.

[3] Bronislaw Malinowski, A Scientific Theory of Culture (Chapel Hill: University of North Carolina Press, 1944), p. 51.

[4] Talcott Parsons, "The Position of Sociological Theory," American Sociological Review, 13 (April 1948), p. 161.

[5] Florian Znaniecki, "Social Organization and Institutions," in Georges Gurvitch and W. E. Moore (eds.), Twentieth Century Sociology (New York: Philosophical Library, 1945), p. 211.

[6] Constantine Panunzio, Major Social Institutions (New York: Macmillan Co., 1939), p. 27.

[7] For examples, see William Graham Sumner, Folkways (Boston: Ginn and Co., 1906), p. 53; F. Stuart Chapin, Contemporary American Institutions (New York: Harpers, 1935), p. 412; J. O. Hertzler, Social Institutions (Lincoln, Nebraska: University of Nebraska Press, 1946, revised); B. Malinowski, op. cit., pp. 52–53; John Gillin, The Ways of Men (New York: D. Appleton-Century Co., 1948), p. 492; Constantine Panunzio, op. cit., p. 27.

would include the manner in which the particular institution conceptualizes the field of religion; works out its evaluational system; rationalizes its own origin, development, and mission; defines its attitude toward and relationships with other religious institutions, other social institutions, and other aspects of society. The usages, rituals, and behavioral patterns include all customs, ceremonials, rituals and other patterned ways of behavior expected of groups or of individuals in those aspects of their behavior related to the institution. The associational or organizational elements include the groups which compose the institutional structure, such as members and leaders occupying various statuses and playing numerous roles, perhaps in terms of institutional offices. The material or instrumental category includes such items as physical property, financial status, and such symbolic traits as language and the cross—in a word, all material and symbolic instruments used by the institution. This scheme deals with the internal structure of an institution. The character of many of these categories will naturally depend upon the functional relationships sustained by the particular structural units to the total institution. In addition, its position in the social structure, the geographic distribution, the relationships with other institutions of the same system, with all other social institutions as well as with other aspects of culture and society—all these factors are of importance in a structural-functional analysis of a given institution.

The use of this concept with its type-parts as a research tool for handling raw data descriptive of the institution-ways of one or more religious bodies would result in only a rough and static classification of the descriptive material. For a conceptual scheme to have dynamic elements and to be structured in a manner adequate to house correctly framed working hypotheses regarding sequential pat-

terns of change in religious bodies, including the interrelationships between such changes and social change in general, these categories from social institutional theory would need to be related to a typology of religious bodies drawn from studies in the sociology of religion and to constructed types of societies with which to treat societal change.

From Max Weber, especially his student, Ernst Troeltsch, to Howard Becker and his student, Milton Yinger, there has been repeated use of the terms "sect" and "church" to designate "distinct sociological types" of religious bodies.[8] The cumulative results of this theoretical endeavor may be related to the structural categories of social institutions to arrive at a preliminary statement of a constructed sect-type and church-type of religious institution.

A. THE EXTREME SECT-TYPE is, internally, polarized about a small, primary group with face-to-face relationships, with relatively undifferentiated leadership of a charismatic character which roots its authority in direct religious experiences and contact with Christ as Head of the Church; and, externally, withdraws into small groups, sets up conflict patterns with secular institutions, and attempts to substitute its own internal religious fellowship for wider socialization.

1. The sect-type, *in its conceptual and ideological type-part,* arises in revolt against, and commonly breaks away from, a church-type religious institution.

[8] See Earl D. C. Brewer, Methodism in Changing American Society (unpublished Ph.D. dissertation, University of North Carolina, 1950), for a brief review of this theoretic work which, in addition to these persons, deals with the contributions of John M. Mecklin, Liston Pope, F. H. Giddings, Richard Niebuhr, R. E. Park and E. W. Burgess, R. L. Sutherland and J. L. Woodward, Ellsworth Faris, J. Wach, Reinhold Niebuhr, H. W. Reed, Forest Weller, and A. W. Eister.

It appeals to the New Testament and the Primitive Church as ideals with emphasis on religious equality and brotherly love; poverty, and frugality; radical individualism in religious experience; redemption through subjective experience rather than through objective grace; and personal achievement in ethics and religion. There is general criticism of sacramentalism, official spiritual guides and theologians, and the various so-called excesses of the church-type institution. Christ is considered the head of the fellowship of believers. It renounces the idea of dominating the "world" and confines itself to domination of the selected few. There is general hostility or indifference toward the "world," toward ruling classes and state authority, and dislike of technical law and of the oath. There is concern with utopian patterns of thought and a resurgence of biblical eschatology as the only form of universalism.

2. *In its associational and organizational type-part,* the sect-type is a personal fellowship of small, voluntary, select, and exclusive groups. Adult baptism and conversion are the methods of gaining membership-character. Members are drawn largely from the lower classes of the society. Membership is maintained by the quality of religious life and may be discontinued by personal decision or by dismissal for failure to maintain the standards of the group. Typical characteristics of primary face-to-face groups are exhibited in the statuses and roles of members and leaders. These groups prefer isolation to compromise with larger aspects of society. They are dispersed and irregularly distributed as "culture pockets." The leaders are unprofessional, untrained, and arise largely from the group itself. They possess charisma of the person rather than of the office and are legitimatized by a sense of personal call. There is little or no overhead, hierarchical organization beyond the local group.

3. *In the category of usages, ritual, and behavioral patterns,* the sect-type is at war with many folkways and mores of the general culture and tends to replace these with strict norms and patterns of behavior for its membership. Membership is dependent upon observance of such patterns of behavior, many of which relate to areas not commonly regarded as religious. Patterns of worship and other ceremonials are simple, austere, and casual with large participation by the full membership of the group. Behavior patterns are characteristically those of small primary groups.

4. The sect-type, *in the material and instrumental aspects,* is characterized by poverty. Meetings of groups may be in homes or in simple, inexpensive meeting houses with meager equipment. There is little use of distinctive symbolic instruments. The leadership is either without pay or with very nominal income. Financial contributions are irregular, small in amount per capita, and on a free will basis. Few, if any, philanthropic, welfare, educational, and service agencies of a formal nature are supported. Mutual aid and other such communal sharing is done on a small primary group basis.

B. THE EXTREME CHURCH-TYPE is, internally, polarized about a large, widespread membership with emphasis upon objective institutionalization of the means of grace and salvation, ministered through a hierarchical priesthood, whose bureaucratically differentiated legal-traditionalistic leadership is validated by historical succession from the Founder of Christianity; and is, externally, ideally coterminous with society, accommodates itself to secular institutions, compromises and attempts to dominate and control them.

1. The church-type, *in the conceptual and ideological type-part,* arises out of an elaboration of an earlier sect-type religious institution in an effort to conserve gains and to adjust to a more complicated situation. It roots back in Jewish priestly

elements, the compromises of the early disciples, and the conservative elements in Paul. It appeals to Jesus as Man-God working in history, to the validity of the Christian tradition, and to apostolic authority expressed in the institutional church. Emphasis is upon the objective validity of the institution as a means of grace and salvation and the necessity to dominate the entire area of influence, to wipe out or absorb all opposing religious movements, and to accommodate to and control all secular institutions. Elaboration of conceptual or doctrinal structure, a deep sense of history, a tendency to rationalize and justify institutional existence, and primary concern with ideological, as opposed to utopian, modes of thought characterize the church-type. It is conservative and exhibits a success complex.

2. *In its associational and organizational category,* the church-type is made up of members from all classes and geographic areas of the society. It is thus widespread and inclusive, if not co-extensive with the given society. Persons are born into a relationship with the church-type organizations and infant baptism and confirmation are stages in passing into full membership. Membership-character is maintained by formal relationships to institutional procedures and may be discontinued at death or through excommunication for institutional reasons. The leadership is professional and specialized. It possesses charisma of the office and statuses and roles are organized into a bureaucratic hierarchy. It develops into the legal-rational and/or traditionalistic types of elaborate organizational structure.

3. The church-type, *in the area of usages, ritual and behavioral patterns,* generally accepts the folkways, mores and morals of prevailing groups of the general culture. It attempts to re-interpret alien patterns in keeping with its own interests and to adjust its own patterns to absorb them. Elaborate rituals and ceremonials are developed for all the major experiences of individual and group life. In specifically religious behavior, e.g., worship and sacramental rites, large responsibility is delegated to the priesthood. Performances become extremely elaborate, professional, colorful.

4. *In its material and instrumental elements,* the church-type institution is wealthy. Church buildings tend toward the cathedral type with ample, if not ornate, appointments and equipment. It is rich in symbolic instruments. Ownership of vast properties characterizes the church-type. The income is from property and taxes or tithes on a compulsory or semi-compulsory basis. The professional leadership is well paid. Widespread philanthropic, welfare, educational, and service agencies of a formal character are supported.

Assuming continua connecting these polar types, it would be possible to analyze data descriptive of a given religious body with respect to placement along such continua. The same procedure would hold for the comparative placements of several religious bodies at a given time or of a single body at different periods in its institutional life. Conceptually, the extent to which religious institution-ways of a given body approximated the constructed sect-type (or church-type) in their structural-functional manifestations they would be termed sect-ways (or church-ways) and the organization exhibiting them a sect-type (or a church-type) religious institution.

This typology has been useful as a conceptual scheme within which certain propositions regarding religious institutional change could be tested. For example, attention has been focused upon The Methodist Episcopal Church and the pattern of change occurring in it from the decade of organization, 1780–1790, to the decade of unification with other

Methodist bodies, 1930–1940. The general hypothesis was that it had moved from the sect-type toward the church-type of religious institution during this period. The conceptual scheme proved fruitful in furnishing the elements necessary for the deduction of working sub-hypotheses, the necessary guidance regarding the types of data needed to test the hypothesis, the categories for classifying such descriptive material, and, finally, the tools for a dynamic analysis of the data in terms of the major hypothesis itself. The study involved an examination of the major primary records deposited by The Methodist Episcopal Church with special attention to the reconstruction of the structural-functional characteristics of the body at four points in the one hundred fifty year period. In addition to "vertical probings" of the terminal decades, two intermediate decades at fifty year intervals (1830–1840 and 1880–1890) were used.

Limiting attention to the terminal periods only, a very brief summary of the data will indicate the extent to which Methodism approximated the sect-type in 1780–1790 and the church-type in 1930–1940. The first summarization of material is for Methodism during the decade of organization.

1. In the beginning, American Methodism was largely a transplantation of English Methodism. This was certainly true ideologically. The early Methodist movement in England had arisen in revolt against the church-type Church of England. There was an appeal to New Testament Christianity and the Primitive Church, yet early Methodism accepted many of the elements of Christian tradition as introduced by Wesley in modification of the patterns of the Church of England. The American Church conceived its mission in Wesleyan terms: "To reform the Continent and to spread scriptural holiness over these lands." The term "scriptural holiness" involved a highly personalized conception of salvation, rationalized the God-man relationship in Arminian terms, with the expectancy of a highly emotionalized process of repentance, salvation, sanctification and Christian perfection. Religious achievement was measured in terms of the "witness of the spirit" and of personal effort in morals and economics. At the same time, there was emphasis upon social reform in terms of bringing criticism to bear upon selected social problems, such as slavery. Social salvation involved essentially the salvation of persons from society. Early persecution of Methodism in America forced a measure of withdrawal from and conflict with society. However, there was general support of the Federal Government, endorsement of private property, and organization and support of schools and orphanages. Thus, there was limited accommodation to, and to some extent, criticism of prevailing political and economic institution-ways. Ideologically, then, Methodism was basically sect-type in the beginning although it never freed itself of some church-type traits inherited from the Church of England.

2. In the area of groups and organizations, Methodism was small in membership and scattered along the eastern seaboard. Its congregations were relatively isolated from the rest of society, with a sharp differentiation between members and non-members. Its membership was drawn predominantly from the lower classes of early American society. A religious experience of salvation was necessary for church membership, though the children of members might secure infant baptism. Membership character was continued by approximating through personal effort the moral standards demanded by the group. Discipline and expulsion of members for behavior deviations were frequent. Methodists were held together in primary groups with intimate sharing of experiences in class

meetings and bands. Mutual aid was practiced in religious, social and economic affairs. The local societies or congregations were generalized groups of the total membership with subdivisions into classes and bands for more intimate relationships. These local congregations or groups of laymen had a conference of preachers superimposed upon them. This clerical group possessed, in embryonic form, the basis of the professional ministry structured along specialized bureaucratic hierarchical lines. Thus, the organization of laymen was along sect-type lines, while the conference of preachers was a church-type inheritance from the Church of England.

The chief dividing line in the status-roles and institutional offices separated laymen and clergymen. A generalized role of class leader was differentiated among lay members. Ordained preachers gave full-time service to a circuit or a group of societies on an itinerating basis. Between the visits of these traveling preachers local activities were carried on largely by lay leadership. The preachers were not required to pass educational standards in the beginning but were constantly urged to read and sell books. There was great emphasis on "the call of the Holy Ghost to preach," but in addition, the candidate had to be voted into the conference of preachers before receiving permission to preach. Thus, the basic charisma of the person had to be supplemented by charisma of the office.

3. In the area of usages, ritual and behavior patterns, some of the strongest sect-type characteristics were exhibited. Personal behavior prescriptions were handed down by Wesley against excesses in food, clothing, and shelter. Prohibitions against all recreational activities, slave-holding, drinking, quarreling, taking advantage of a brother in economic affairs, and so on, were imposed. There were positive prescriptions for simple, honest, hard-working personal character

traits with emphasis upon mutual aid and support. There was recommended a formal liturgy for Sunday services and ritual forms for such ceremonies as marriage, burial, baptism, Lord's Supper, and ordination. These were modified from the Church of England. The formal liturgy was rejected and the ritual forms greatly simplified before acceptance in American Methodism. The emphasis was upon informal worship and preaching services, with simple revivalistic songs. Thus, in this area, too, there was the interplay of dominant sect-ways with the formal church-ways inherited from the Church of England.

4. In its material aspects, early American Methodism approximated the sect-type almost completely. The lower class people who gave allegiance to Methodism were poor and the societies were characterized by relative poverty, with dependence upon irregular "freewill" offerings for the support of full-time preachers and missionary and other connectional enterprises. Preachers received a common income, which was hardly sufficient to meet actual expenses. There were emotional appeals for collections. The Church was from the beginning involved in the printing business. The local societies met in homes, brush arbors, simple chapels, and in the open fields. The chapels had little equipment and few comforts. There was decided opposition to rented pews, cushions, crosses, stained-glass windows and other so-called excesses characteristic of the church-type religious institution. In this area, the young religious body approximated most closely the sect-type, yet it was through its involvement in the printing business and in other economic enterprises that rationalism entered earliest into the ordering of the bureaucratic structure of the religious institution.

One hundred and fifty years later both Methodism and American Society exhibited characteristics differing greatly from those of the early days of the Republic. To mention only the population changes, the United States had increased from nearly four millions to more than one hundred thirty-one millions of people, while Methodism had grown from fifty thousand to over seven million in membership. These changes in population and in church membership were associated with other structural-functional modifications in American Society and in Methodism. Confining attention to the Methodist Episcopal Church, a summary of its institutional characteristics points to a movement away from the sect-type and toward the church-type.

1. During the decade before Unification the ideology of the Methodist Episcopal Church involved a conception of its own mission in terms of maintaining itself as a dominant religious body and in reforming society in keeping with a liberal theological interpretation of religion, with special emphasis upon the social gospel. Salvation was rationalized as a progressive growth in grace, symbolized by membership in the Church. Religious achievement was measured in terms of church attendance and financial support of the work of the church. There was selective accommodation to the dominant folkways and mores of American society. There was acceptance of the basic societal values and participation in major social institutional activities. For example, in 1936 the Methodist Episcopal Church identified itself with democracy as completely as ever the Roman Catholic Church did with feudalism during the Medieval Period. It was in sect-type conflict with specific activities, such as legalized liquor, drinking, and gambling. Nevertheless, its social ethics dealt directly with social problems and institution-ways, as well as with personal behavior patterns. There was a growing appreciation of the traditions of Christianity, especially the Protestant branch of it, and an increasing appeal to and use

of the institution-ways of all Christian bodies, for example, the hymnody. There was new concern with its own history and traditions. Ideologically, then, Methodism had definitely moved toward the church-type, although there were remnants of the sect-type as seen in conflict patterns with certain folkways and mores.

2. In the area of groups and organizations, the membership of Methodism was spread geographically over the entire United States, although it made up less than five per cent of the total population. There was little differentiation between members and non-members. Methodist churches were not persecuted by or withdrawn from the rest of society. The total membership was drawn from all classes of society but given local congregations might be made up predominantly of members from one class. Church membership was based on a formal statement of faith, infant baptism, a training program in the meaning of church membership, and a decision to join the church. Active membership character was maintained by attendance upon services or financial contributions or both. Discipline and expulsion of members were rare, and then more often for failure to support the institution than for personal deviation and behavior. Personal relationships of members tended to become secondary and formal, especially in cities where members often were not personally acquainted. Specialized groups of members emphasized fellowship meetings to overcome this contractual type of interpersonal relationships. A variety of specialized boards, committees, and groups existed in the local church. These were related to an interlocking hierarchy of organizations above the local church level. A complex set of conferences and other administrative units formed a complex hierarchy in the church at large. Thus, in its groups and organizations, Methodism had moved from the relatively simple local societies and confer-

ence of preachers to a highly differentiated bureaucracy.

In keeping with the differentiation in types of groups, specialized lay leadership roles emerged, such as Sunday School teachers, stewards, trustees, chairmen of committees, and secretaries. Many activities of the church were carried on by this specialized lay leadership. Full-time ordained and professionally trained ministers had responsibility for the major functions of the church, although a local ministry was continued. The call to preach received less emphasis than educational standards in determining status in annual conferences. The charisma of the person was thus weakened at the expense of charisma of the office, with emphasis upon structuralization of clerical authority along traditional and legal-rational lines. These specialized lay and clerical status-roles were structured in a complex hierarchy of offices within the bureaucratic religious institution.

3. In the area of usages and behavior patterns, there was growing acceptance of prevailing folkways and mores of society with exceptions in such personal behavior as prohibitions against drinking alcoholic beverages for all Methodists and against the use of tobacco on the part of ministers. There was basic acceptance of and accommodation to various social institutional areas as organized in American Society, with criticisms in terms of particular deviations from Methodist ideology. An example is found in the accommodation to recreation-ways but with criticism of gambling. Also, there was accommodation to divorce but prohibition against remarriage of divorced persons by Methodist clergy, except under certain circumstances. Generally, there was more attention to institution-ways than to personal behavior patterns. There was increased formality in worship and preaching services with a hymnody representing all types of Christian music, including chants and anthems. There

were much more elaborate forms for various ritual performances, although in some cases the meaning of the ceremonies had been changed in keeping with liberal theology. There was a large increase in the number of life situations for which ceremonials were prescribed. This was seen in the development of a Methodist *Book of Worship* or "Prayer Book" and the increased emphasis in professional training on the correct performance of worship and ceremonials. It is obvious that in this area Methodism was becoming more increasingly church-type, although with a hold-over of certain sect-type tendencies.

4. Just as in the beginning the poverty of Methodism made it sect-type in its material aspects, so after one hundred and fifty years, it was in this area that it had achieved perhaps its most striking approximation of the church-type religious institution. Methodism had a larger stake in the economic life of America with income, buildings, and equipment in the billion dollar class. Its income was derived through fairly systematic contributions from members and from investments. There was support of orphanages, homes for the aged, settlement work, hospitals, educational institutions, and so on. Economic rationalism permeated this involvement in the economic order, including financial plans from the local church through all conferences and organizations. Ministers were better and more systematically paid than one hundred and fifty years earlier. Also, instead of mutual income arrangements, each individual congregation paid its own minister, an accommodation to individual enterprise economics. Church buildings were as elaborate as a local congregation could afford. In large cities, these attained cathedral proportions, with adequate space for fellowship and educational activities and with elaborate furnishing and equipment. Increasing use of the cross, vestments, and other symbols

of traditional Christianity moved Method-ism toward the church-type.

It is obvious from this brief summary of the data that Methodism was basically sect-type in 1780–1790 and that it had moved toward church-type characteristics by 1930–1940. Including the intermediate periods under analysis, a rough approximation of this total movement is shown in Figure 1. A warning should be

type elements in the structural-functional characteristics, as was true in 1780–1790, the position on the continuum would be near the sect-type end and would reflect the relative dominance of the sect-type over the church-type characteristics, in the judgment of the investigator. Other positions along the line would represent the same process.

A modification of this hypothesis is

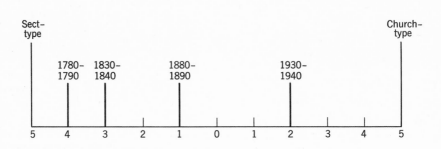

Figure 1. Approximation of the Position of the Methodist Episcopal Church Along the Sect-Church Continuum in Stated Decades at Fifty-Year Intervals, 1780–1790 to 1930–1940
Source: Based on Earl D. C. Brewer, Methodism in Changing American Society (unpublished Ph.D. dissertation, Chapel Hill: University of North Carolina, 1950), pp. 587–650.

made against interpreting this figure in terms of a calibrated scale measuring quantified data. The level of typological construction used in the conceptual scheme of this study would obviously support only an interpretive judgment as to the extent of movement along this continuum. That judgment is that such a movement has taken place at an accelerating rate, and the figure is simply a graphic way of summarizing that fact. This leads to a further point about a position on this continuum. What does it mean to say that Methodism was nearer one end of it than the other? The conclusion has already been reached that at any given period the religious body actually exhibited characteristics drawn from each end of the continuum. If the sect-type traits tend to dominate the church-

now possible. The Methodist Episcopal Church began with a heavy dominance of sect-type over church-type traits and has moved along the sect-church continuum to a point where there is a moderate dominance of church-type over sect-type characteristics. This movement has taken place at a slightly accelerated rate and may be expected to continue, following the unification of this religious body with two other branches of Methodism to form The Methodist Church. The extent of the movement is limited, however, by the dissenting tradition and the emergence of the denomination-type of religious body characteristic of this tradition in American society.

A second major problem of the sociology of religion has to do with the inter-relationships between the changing patterns within religious institutions and the changes in society as a whole. This requires a conceptual scheme adequate to deal with societal change. In this particular study a typology of social change as constructed by Howard W. Odum was employed. It is built around the ideal types of folk culture and state civilization, the assumption of a trend from the first toward the second, of the interaction between the two, and of the possibility of an equilibrium or balance between them.[9] Using this as an organizing framework the assumption was made that American society had started at the folk-cultural level and had moved toward the characteristics of a state civilization. Broad descriptive historical materials were collected, under this assumption, dealing with settlement and population characteristics, agriculture and industry, state and government, and, in briefer fashion, with other basic social institutions, such as the family, education, and recreation. Summarizing the conclusions of this work, it was found that the European settlement of America did not approximate the folk cultural level as closely as the earlier Mongolian settlement and that it had, with an accelerated tempo, moved toward the characteristics of the state civilizational type, though stabilizing at the present at a point short of the totalitarianism demanded by the extremes of the constructed type.[10]

Finally, it was possible to deal with the interrelationships between religion and society within the scheme of this study. Such questions as: To what extent are these constructed types culture bound, especially the sect-church typology, to

European societies with state churches? What is the interrelationship, if any, between these two typologies: the one dealing with social change in general and the other concerned with religious institutional change? Would it be possible to relate folk culture and the sect-type religious institution in such a manner as to say that the latter is a sub-unit of the former? Would it be possible to do the same for the state civilizational type of society and the church-type of religious body? What significance, if any, do these considerations have for understanding the relationships between religion and other aspects of changing American Society?

Without detailing the results of such theoretical considerations,[11] the summary conclusion may be reached that the sect-church typology with appropriate modifications is useful in a scientific analysis of religious institutional data in American Society. Furthermore, the limited level of state civilization reached in America and the movement of religious groups toward the denomination-type along the sect-church continuum reflect reciprocal interactive causal factors making of the civilization a multi-group society with a causally structured culture exhibiting a wide range of alternative patterns. It may be concluded, then, that there is a rough "correlation" between the denomination-type of religious institution and the level of state civilization reached in the United States. Secondary and segmental interaction patterns structured in a bureaucracy tend to develop within the religious institution as in other aspects of state civilization and accommodative relationships with other social institutions are characteristic of this level of the church-type. This stage of American Society in its movement toward the characteristics of the state civilization is oriented more toward the "secular" than the "sacred" constructed type in ideology and struc-

[9] For a statement of this typology of social change see Howard W. Odum, Notes on the Changing Structure of Contemporary Society (unpublished paper, Department of Sociology, University of North Carolina, 1948).
[10] For the details see Earl D. C. Brewer, *op. cit.*, pp. 66–208.

[11] For these details see *ibid.*, pp. 651–703.

ture.[12] These "secular" characteristics are naturally reflected in the religious institutions, especially those of the denomination-type. Liberalism in theology, economic rationalism, legalistic bureaucracy, and segmented and secondary relationships are examples of this tendency. These developments are subversive of the older and more "sacred" and sect-type institution-ways and have called up the "fundamentalistic" reaction to such "modernistic" secularism. It is likely, however, that the extreme church-type religious institution would dictate a prescribed faith in much the same way that an extreme state civilization would be totalitarian in its scope and demands. Thus, there appears to be mutual tolerance and support in the level of state civilization reached by the state and government and the level of church-type reached by Methodism and other dominantly denomination-type religious bodies in the United States.

Yet the sect-type religious organization can only partially be identified with folk culture. Religion in folk societies tends to conform to and sanction prevailing folkways and mores which is a church-type adaptative trait. If, however, the term "folk" is used in Odum's sense as representing a ". . . universal, societal constant in a world of variables . . . ,"[13]

[12] Howard Becker, "Sacred and Secular Societies," *Social Forces*, XXVIII (May 1950), 361–376.
[13] Howard W. Odum, *Understanding Society* (New York: The Macmillan Company, 1947), p. 13.

then the sect-type group possesses kinship with it when used to describe an ever-present and essential primary group aspect of every religious institution. This sect-element is present in the most elaborate and complex church-type institutions. In Medieval Catholicism, for example, this sectness was expressed in monastic orders and societies sanctioned by the Church and often representing the dynamic, growing edge of it. Too, there were groups during this period which had revolted from the Church and maintained themselves as persecuted sects fermenting the Protestant Reformation and the dissenting tradition. In a sense, then, sect-forces furnish the dynamic and sect-forms the structure for the "remnant" element in a decaying religion and the "revival" element in a growing religion. Although this statement should be considered in the nature of a conclusion in need of further study it would, if confirmed, tend to identify this aspect of the sect-type with the folk element in society. It is probable that these phenomena represent "folk forces" operating through religious institutions. If this be true it would help to explain the "cultural lag" between religious institutions and other social institutions. Indeed, it would make possible a tentative interpretation of the sect in terms of the folk and thus generalize the theoretical structure at this point. It would tend to confirm Odum's use of religious phenomena in his search for folk elements in society.

5 · An Analysis of Sect Development

BRYAN R. WILSON

The maintenance of original value orientations and of pristine charac-

SOURCE. Bryan R. Wilson, "An Analysis of Sect Development," *American Sociological Review*, 24, February, 1959, pp. 3–15.

ter is a crucial problem area encountered by institutions, particularly in the face of changing external or internal social circumstances. The tensions engendered in such conditions are clearly evident in sects, which provide a valuable institutional type for analysis, in that they have an explicit value commitment, are clearly circumscribed organizations, and are peculiarly self-conscious of their relations with the wider society. Some sects are markedly successful in the preservation of undiluted values of protest; others, notably those which gradually become denominationalized, are much less so. This paper seeks to distinguish and characterize distinctive types of sect, and to use such characterizations to determine the specific elements, and combinations of elements, which promote or retard such development.

The tendency for sects to become denominations has frequently been noted, and on the basis of this tendency the generalization has sometimes been made that a sect-type organization can exist for only one generation, that in the second generation the sect (and the cult in Becker's use of the term) becomes a church or a denomination.[1] Yet, if one survey existing religious organizations, it is evident that, in both the sociological and the everyday use of the term, some sects persist as such over several generations. In view of the fact that some sects have undeniably gravitated towards a denominational structure, however, we need to know just what factors in the organization and circumstances of sects promote or retard this development.[2]

Since sects are not all of a piece, we need to distinguish and delineate certain sub-types which should prove of greater predictive utility than does the grosser concept of the sect, and with which we may pass from crude hypothesis to more fully developed theory. Once these sub-types have been identified we may turn to the elements in sect organization which are focal points of tension. It is here hypothesized that sects experience different types of tension which vary according to their own constellation of values, as well as the circumstances of their origin. In response to such tensions, in the attempt at their management, we may expect to find the genesis of processes which cause some sects to develop into denominations, others to wither, some to be exterminated, some to fragment, and some to remain, over several generations, as sects.[3] This paper considers the following elements: the cir-

[1] H. Richard Niebuhr, *The Social Sources of Denominationalism,* New York: Holt, 1929, p. 19; Howard Becker, *Systematic Sociology on the Basis of the Beziehungslehre and Gebildelehre of Leopold von Wiese,* New York: Wiley, 1932; Liston Pope, *Millhands and Preachers,* New Haven: Yale University Press, 1942, pp. 118 ff.
[2] J. M. Yinger, *Religion in the Struggle for Power,* Durham: Duke University Press, 1946, suggested an alternative development for the sect, into an "established sect." More recently Yinger has suggested that established sects develop because they emphasize the evil nature of society, while denominationalizing sects are those which stress the reduction of individual anxiety and guilt— a conclusion generally consistent with the analysis proposed here; see Yinger's *Religion, Society and the Individual,* New York: Macmillan, 1957, pp. 151–152. Recognition of the limitations of the Niebuhr hypothesis is offered in the context of a discussion somewhat different from the above by Benton Johnson, "A Critical Appraisal of Church-Sect Typology," *American Sociological Review* 22 (February, 1957), pp. 88–92. For another approach to this process, see Harold W. Pfautz, "The Sociology of Secularization: Religious Groups," *American Journal of Sociology* 61 (September, 1955), pp. 121–128.
[3] The type of analysis to be followed owes much to the work and the suggestions of Philip Selznick; see especially his book, *The Organizational Weapon,* New York: McGraw-Hill, 1952.

cumstances of sect emergence, the internal structure of sect organization, the degree of separateness from the external world, the coherence of sect values, and group commitments and relationships.

Characterization of Sect and Denomination

Typically a *sect* may be identified by the following characteristics: it is a voluntary association; membership is by proof to sect authorities of some claim to personal merit—such as knowledge of doctrine, affirmation of a conversion experience, or recommendation of members in good standing; exclusiveness is emphasized, and expulsion exercised against those who contravene doctrinal, moral, or organizational precepts; its self-conception is of an elect, a gathered remnant, possessing special enlightenment; personal perfection is the expected standard of aspiration, in whatever terms this is judged; it accepts, at least as an ideal, the priesthood of all believers; there is a high level of lay participation; there is opportunity for the member spontaneously to express his commitment; the sect is hostile or indifferent to the secular society and to the state.[4]

In elaboration of this general identification of the sect, it might be added that although sects differ among themselves in their characteristic social relationships, the commitment of the sectarian is always more total and more defined than that of the member of other religious organizations. The ideology of the sect

[4] The characterization of the sect here proposed is in many respects more general than the "type-constructs" offered by Becker, Yinger, and Pope in the works cited above, and by E. D. C. Brewer, "Sect and Church in Methodism," *Social Forces* 30 (May, 1952), pp. 400–408. It omits such characteristics as subjectivism, informality, the expression of fervor, and poverty, since these characteristics appear to belong to certain subtypes only.

is much more clearly crystallized, and the member is much more distinctly characterized than is the adherent of the larger denomination or church. The behavioral correlates of his ideological commitment also serve to set him and keep him apart from "the world." Sects have a totalitarian rather than a segmental hold over their members: they dictate the member's ideological orientation to secular society; or they rigorously specify the necessary standards of moral rectitude; or they compel the member's involvement in group activity. Ideological conformity may be achieved by compulsory participation, but the system of control varies widely.[5] Not only does the sect discipline or expel the member who entertains heretical opinions, or commits a moral misdemeanor, but it regards such defection as betrayal of the cause, unless confession of fault and appeal for forgiveness is forthcoming.

The *denomination*, in contrast, shows the following features: it is formally a voluntary association; it accepts adherents without imposition of traditional prerequisites of entry, and employs purely formalized procedures of admission; breadth and tolerance are emphasized; since membership is laxly enrolled, expulsion is not a common device for dealing with the apathetic and the wayward; its self-conception is unclear and its doctrinal position unstressed; it is content to be one movement among others, all of which are thought to be acceptable in the sight of God; it accepts the standards and values of the prevailing culture and conventional morality; there is a trained professional ministry; lay participation occurs but is

[5] Thus in Christian Science, for example, doctrinal purity is maintained without members being compelled to participate in an intense round of group activity. Illustrative material is largely from the writer's own research into sects and sect literature in England; for these cases and for cases where the facts are widely known or well established, specific citations are omitted.

typically restricted to particular sections of the laity and to particular areas of activity; services are formalized and spontaneity is absent; education of the young is of greater concern than the evangelism of the outsider; additional activities are largely non-religious in character; individual commitment is not very intense; the denomination accepts the values of the secular society and the state; members are drawn from any section of the community, but within one church, or any one region, membership will tend to limit itself to those who are socially compatible.[6]

Characterization of Types of Sect

Given these general types of organization, we need to distinguish the sub-types of sects.[7] The basis of the present clas-

[6] This characterization of the denomination stresses many points similar to those suggested by Pope, op. cit., pp. 120 ff., but avoids making a direct comparison of sect traits and denominational traits, as well as the implication that sect characteristics automatically undergo mutation and become denominational traits.

[7] An earlier categorization of sects is offered by E. T. Clark in The Small Sects in America, Nashville: Abingdon Press, 1937, which uses rather diverse criteria, including attitudinal, doctrinal, and organizational elements. In the classification offered here the distinction advanced by Howard Becker, op. cit., between sects and cults, and more recently employed by W. E. Mann, Sect, Cult and Church in Alberta, Toronto: University of Toronto Press, 1955, is abandoned; movements styled as cults by Becker and Mann are here subsumed in a more generalized typification of the sect, and as a sub-type would figure principally among gnostic sects. For an extremely suggestive classification of sects, which has come to my notice since this paper was written, but which shares certain similarities with the categorization here proposed, see Peter L. Berger, "The Sociological Study of Sectarianism," Social Research 21 (Winter, 1954), pp. 467–485.

sification is the characterization of types of mission which might be discerned among sects. Generally these types of mission rest on the ideological and doctrinal character of sects, and serve as useful indicators of the clusters of other characteristics to be found in each type. For our purposes within the framework of Protestant Christianity, four broad types may be discerned. Such a classification is not necessarily exhaustive, nor necessarily exclusive of alternative types. It rests essentially on the response of the sect to the values and relationships prevailing in society. This response, in the nature of sectarianism as we have already described it, is necessarily one of greater or lesser rejection. The Conversionist sects seek to alter men, and thereby to alter the world; the response is free-will optimism. The Adventist sects predict drastic alteration of the world, and seek to prepare for the new dispensation—a pessimistic determinism. The Introversionists reject the world's values and replace them with higher inner values, for the realization of which inner resources are cultivated. The Gnostic sects accept in large measure the world's goals but seek a new and esoteric means to achieve these ends— a wishful mysticism. This classification is sociological rather than psychological; the responses are built into particular institutions. The implications of these four depictions are elaborated in the following characterizations, and although the empirical correlates of each type are not explored, the implications themselves are not simply logical extensions of the hypothesized types of response. What is here suggested is that, given particular responses within the context of Christianity, these further corollaries may be expected.[8]

[8] The basic types of response here proposed may be compared to the typology of modes of individual adaptation in Robert K. Mer-

1. The Conversionist sect is one whose teaching and activity centers on evangelism; in contemporary Christianity it is typically the orthodox fundamentalist or pentecostal sect. It is typified by extreme bibliolatry: the Bible is taken as the only guide to salvation, and is accepted as literally true. Conversion experience and the acceptance of Jesus as a personal saviour is the test of admission to the fellowship; extreme emphasis is given to individual guilt for sin and the need to obtain redemption through Christ. Despite the theoretical limit on the number who can gain salvation, the sect precludes no one and revivalist techniques are employed in evangelism. It is distrustful of, or indifferent towards, the denominations

_____

ton's "Social Structure and Anomie" (*Social Theory and Social Structure*, Glencoe, Ill.: Free Press, 1957, pp. 131 ff.). There is some correspondence between introversionist sects and the retreatist response, revolutionist sects and the rebellious response, and gnostic sects and the innovative type. Merton's conformist case is clearly not appropriate to sects, nor is the ritualist, unless one admits some schisms of the Catholic church and even then the case is doubtful. See also, Karen Horney, *The Neurotic Personality of Our Time*, New York: Norton, 1937.

It is clear that a given sect may well shift in its response to the external society, and whilst remaining a protest group, alter the terms of its protest. Our analysis here is primarily concerned with the process of accommodation—the conditions under which sects become denominations or fail to do so. A development unexplored here is the sect which, whilst remaining a sect, changes character by changing its response; frequently the shift will be of emphasis rather than of complete transformation. There is some evidence to show that revolutionist sects, under circumstances of external duress, have altered their response to one of introversion. The processes here involved would require further analysis in the light of the sociological variables underlying such changes, both as internal and external factors.

and churches which at best have diluted, and at worst betrayed, Christianity; it is hostile to clerical learning and especially to modernism; it is opposed to modern science, particularly to geology and to evolutionary theories; it disdains culture and the artistic values accepted in the wider society. Examples are to be found in the Salvation Army and the Pentecostal sects.

2. The Adventist—or revolutionist—sect focuses attention on the coming overturn of the present world order: in contemporary Christianity it is the adventist movement. It is typified by its emphasis on the Bible, and particularly of its exegesis of the allegorical and prophetic books from which the time and circumstances of the second advent of Christ is discerned. The conventional eschatological ideas of heaven and hell are regarded as false, and the resurrection of the dead for judgment is accepted as the principal eschatological event. Christ is regarded as a divine commander, not only as a saviour, and a high moral standard is based on the moral precepts of Jesus. Participation in the new kingdom will be limited and only those who have maintained doctrinal and moral rectitude will be eligible; admission to the fellowship is by thorough understanding of necessary doctrine, and not by affirmation of conversion. Evangelism is undertaken by way of preaching the word but quick conversions are not sought and revivalism is despised as emotional and misguided. The established church is regarded as fulfilling the role of the anti-Christ: clerical learning is despised (but science is depreciated only in so far as its doctrines conflict with adventist biblical exegesis) and the professional ministry is vigorously opposed. Separation from the world is a more crucial interdiction than are restrictions placed upon certain worldly activities. The sect is hostile towards the wider society and looks forward to its over-

throw.[9] Examples are Jehovah's Witnesses and the Christadelphians.

3. The Introversionist—or pietist—sect directs the attention of its followers away from the world and to the community and more particularly to the members' possession of the Spirit; in recent Christianity it is exemplified in the pietist sect. Such a sect is typified by reliance on inner illumination, whether this be regarded as the voice of conscience or the action of the Holy Ghost. The Bible is a source or stimulant of inner inspiration and ethical insight; doctrine is of lesser importance in that the letter has surrendered to the spirit, the deepening of which is a central preoccupation. The sect develops a particular *Weltanschauung* and considers itself an enlightened elect; inner values may be regarded as incommunicable and eschatological ideas are unarticulated or of little significance. No evangelism is undertaken and a strong ingroup morality is developed; the sect withdraws from the world, or allows its members to be active in the world only for human betterment at the behest of conscience and at the periphery of social concern. It is indifferent to other religious movements. It admits of no spiritual directors or ministers. Examples include some Holiness movements, Quakers, and the Society of the Truly Inspired (Amana Community).

4. The Gnostic sect emphasizes some special body of teaching of an esoteric kind. In contemporary Christianity it is a sect offering a new or revived interpretation of Christian teaching. It accepts the Bible as allegorical and complementary to its own gnosis; conventional Christian eschatology is replaced by a more optimistic and esoteric eschatology; Christ is a wayshower, an exemplar of truth, rather than a saviour. Christian mystical teachings, such as the Trinity, are replaced by other more exclusive mysticism, the significance of which the adherent can hope only gradually to penetrate; doctrine includes teachings which replace secular scientific explanations, and offer a cosmology, an anthropology, and a psychology of their own. The utility of the gnosis for everyday life is emphasized, particularly in the achievement of worldly success, self-realization, health, material well-being and happiness. Conversion is an alien concept to the Gnostic sect, but instruction and guidance is offered to the outsider or the neophyte; there are stages in understanding: enlightenment "unfolds." There is a charismatic leader (or a succession of such leaders) who pronounces wisdom; ministers are usually styled as teachers or guides, and ministerial functions are subdivided among laity with appropriate qualification. Other churches are regarded with indifference as ignorant or backward; secular knowledge is seen as valid and useful relatively, except where it contravenes sect teaching. The cultural standards of the society are accepted and even utilized: the Gnostic sectarian does not withdraw from the world but seeks to use his special knowledge for his own advancement, or that of the movement, in the world. These traits are found, for example, in Christian Science, New Thought sects, Koreshanity, and the Order of the Cross.[10]

[9] The similarities of the adventist type sect and the revolutionary political movement have been brought out by Donald G. MacRae in "The Bolshevik Ideology," *The Cambridge Journal*, 3 (December, 1954), pp. 164–177, and are also dealt with in Bryan R. Wilson, *Sects and Society*, London, Heinemann and Berkeley, University of California Press, 1961. See also Werner Cohn, "Jehovah's Witnesses as a Proletarian Movement," *The American Scholar*, 24 (Summer, 1955), pp. 281–298.

[10] The types here hypothesized are primarily Christian, and each type finds some support within Christian scriptures. Whether such a classification could be usefully employed for

Circumstances of Sect Emergence

The conditions under which sects emerge may, for analytical purposes, be divided into three elements: the method by which the sect comes into being, the specific factors of stimulus, and the external social conditions prevailing.

1. The principal methods of sect emergence are by spontaneous development around a local charismatic leader, by schism, and by organized revival. In the case of a sect emerging around a leader much will depend on his teaching and his organizational ability. Some such sects disappear when the leader dies or departs. Others, particularly those in which the leader offers a new gnosis which is consonant with the age, spread and retain their identity. The gnosis may be a new combination of ideas or the retailing of older ideas to a new audience.[11] Thus the optimism, feminism, and success-orientation of the New Thought sects and of Christian Science fitted well with American ideals at the end of the nineteenth century. If the leader offers a variant of traditional Christianity, however, then such a group is likely to remain local and, if persisting, eventually to make common cause with other fundamentalist movements or with the funda-

mentalist wing of one of the larger denominations, usually the Baptists. Many independent missions of this type joined with the pentecostal sects in England during the first three decades of this century. But if such sects spread they appear to be particularly likely to become denominationalized, as the distinctive needs of members change—assuming that there is no constant stream of new admissions to keep alive the pristine spirit of the movement.

The schismatic sect tends to be vigorous as long as its protest against the parent body remains significant, and as long as the rival group exists as a challenge; in this period it is likely to grow only by accretions from the parent body. Subsequently, as the issue of disagreement wanes in importance, such a schismatic group may adjust to continuance as a sect, may decay in the absence of opposition, or may partially and gradually rejoin the parent body. Illustrations of such processes are afforded in the history of the Plymouth Brethren in England, and of the Christadelphians in England, the United States, Canada, and Australia.

Organized revival is the method of development most usual to fundamentalist sects, and may well begin in a nondenominational spirit. Success, however, tends to impose organizational responsibilities and, if there are distinctive teachings, sects tend to emerge. The Full Gospel Testimony and the Elim Foursquare Gospel Church in England are examples of this development, the teachings being pentecostal. Such groups usually experience rapid growth and high turnover of personnel; since they rely on revivalists for stability and permanence there is, in the nature of the case, an acceptance of trained functionaries, and in this respect a tendency towards denominational development.

2. The specific factors of stimulus of sect emergence are usually found in the

---

other major religions is doubtful in that, although revolutionist and introversionist sects appear to be common to many religions, and the gnostic sects occur in some, conversionism is perhaps less widespread. The situation is sometimes confused with regard to the relative positions of orthodoxy and sectarianism, and by the difference between the relationship of religion and the state which prevails in many non-Christian countries and the pattern which has generally obtained in the West.

[11] This syncretistic approach is typical of gnostic sects: many such movements have drawn on diverse sources for their teachings. See, for example, Bryan R. Wilson, "The Origins of Christian Science," *The Hibbert Journal*, 225, Jan. 1959, pp. 161–170.

stresses and tensions differentially experienced within the total society. Change in the economic position of a particular group (which may be a change only in relative position); disturbance of normal social relations, for instance in the circumstances of industrialization and urbanization; the failure of the social system to accommodate particular age, sex, and status groups—all of these are possible stimuli in the emergence of sects. These are the needs to which sects, to some extent, respond. Particular groups are rendered marginal by some process of social change; there is a sudden need for a new interpretation of their social position or for a transvaluation of their experience. Insecurity, differential status anxiety, cultural neglect, prompt a need for readjustment which sects may, for some, provide. The maladjusted may be communities, or occupational groups, or dispersed individuals in similar marginal positions. The former cases are more typical for the emergence of Conversionist, Adventist, and Introversionist groups, the latter for the Gnostic sects. Sudden social dislocation, as experienced in urbanization and industrialization, appears to be a frequent circumstance in which Conversionist sects emerge, while Adventists and Introversionists have arisen in the midst of longer persisting deprivation.

3. The external social conditions are not easily distinguished from the stimulus factors considered above, but taken in their widest sense it is evident that there are different consequences for sects according to the political and moral character of the society in which they emerge. In feudal, authoritarian, or totalitarian societies, the sect is persecuted; if it persists it will do so only as a clandestine organization. It will tend to be hostile to the world (whether or not this was its original orientation) and may, in reality or in fantasy, project this hostility upon society. The very early Quakers, the Fifth Monarchy Men, and the numerous pietist and millennial movements in Europe from the thirteenth to the eighteenth centuries, illustrate this reaction.[12] An alternative development in the past has been for the sect to migrate and seek an environment where it could live according to its own standards. The achievement of such isolation has, in itself, consequences for sect organization and promotes communistic arrangements. Examples here are the Rappites, Amana Society, and other movements flourishing in eighteenth and nineteenth century America after migrating from Germany.[13] In such circumstances, to which more specific reference is made below, the sect is unlikely to show marked denominational tendencies.

In democratic or pluralist societies the sect is not pushed into the search for isolation, and although revolutionary type movements (Adventist) may emerge, they are likely to maintain their separation from the world by other methods. Clearly, during rapid social change the various stimulus factors discussed above are more likely to become operative, and it is empirically well established that sects proliferate in periods of social unrest. In this connection, some very general propositions have been offered on the basis of data drawn from the United States in the period from 1800 to the present time. This was a society undergoing almost uninterrupted expansion, rapid social change, high mobility, intense urbanization, and successive waves of immigration (from which its proletariat was continually re-recruited). In face of

[12] On European millennial movements see Norman Cohn, The Pursuit of the Millennium, London: Secker and Warburg, 1957.
[13] For a recent brief account of such movements, see Henri Desroche, "Micromillenarismes et Communautorismes Utopiques en Amérique du Nord du XVIIe au XIXe Siècle," Archives de Sociologie des Religions, 4 (Juillet-Décembre, 1957), pp. 57–92.

these developments the original social values were undergoing constant modification through differential acceptance by diverse ethnic and religious groups. In short, this was a highly atypical context from which to make generalizations concerning the development of sects. The absence of tradition and of stable class differences, the promotion of denominational competition, and the expectation of growth and development resulted in extreme accommodation which helped sects rapidly to evolve into denominations—almost as part of a "success-pattern." In this situation even the Quakers could develop a schism which accepted a ministry and became virtually a denomination. The external social circumstances, rather than the intrinsic nature of the sect as such, must here be invoked to explain why sects become denominations.[14]

The Internal Structure of Sect Organization

A feature of sects in contemporary society is that they tend to develop some sort of centralized organization, however minimal. This development has been prompted by the need for communication between dispersed communities, the increase in mobility, and the growing impact of legislation on sects, particularly in wartime. Central organization in itself, however, is not to be equated with a denominational tendency, since central control may be effectively employed to prevent such trends, as with Jehovah's Witnesses.[15] On the other hand, such

agencies may be a departure from the original sect ideal—their development may be a response to some external threat to the sect's values, but they also imply the surrender of other values. The most significant question about this development would seem to be whether or not those who acquire responsibilities in the central agencies of the sect become professional *public* functionaries—where functions become institutionally differentiated and specialization of roles occurs.

The initial position of the sect, where there is no local charismatic leader, is the occupation of offices by members in rotation, by lot, or by seniority, and subsequently to institute the lay leader, usually chosen by the group for his particular abilities. Once the concept of special training of such leaders is admitted, then a step to denominationalism has been taken. Training implies lack of parity between leaders and members, it compromises the radical democracy of the sect and the ideal of the priesthood of all believers. Spontaneity disappears, and leaders employ the status symbols of their profession, seeking equal esteem with the pastors of other movements.[16]

Such a radical departure from sect values does not normally occur abruptly, nor does denominational character rest on this one factor alone. Obviously, different types of sect show a different proclivity to this development. We can fully expect sects highly concerned with evangelism and revivalism to be most prone to evolve in this way. If missionaries and revivalists are being supported by the group, the value of special training is likely to be accepted and will

[14] For a discussion of internal and external factors in a clinical, as distinct from a typological, examination of sect development, see Bryan R. Wilson, "Apparition et Persistence des Sectes dans un Milieu Social en évolution," *Archives de Sociologie des Religions*, 5 (Janvier–Juin, 1958), pp. 140–150.

[15] See H. H. Stroup, *Jehovah's Witnesses*, New York: Columbia University Press, 1945; also E. Royston Pike, *Jehovah's Witnesses*, London: Watts, 1954; Werner Cohn, *op. cit.*

[16] The equivocal position of the ministry emerging within a sect which is undergoing transformation to a denomination, is discussed in Bryan R. Wilson, "Role Conflicts and Status Contradictions of the Pentecostal Minister," *American Journal of Sociology*, LXIV, 5, March, 1959, pp. 494–504.

probably be provided within and by the organization itself. The economies of scale may well induce the movement to train more people than can readily be absorbed in the mission field, or than can be supported there, whilst there is also a limit to the number of active revivalists who can operate on behalf of a particular movement. The replacement of local lay pastors by trained ministers is then a likely consequence. Something like this sequence can be seen in the development of pentecostal sects in Britain. Of other groups, the sect known as the Church of God in the British Isles and Overseas has full-time itinerant revivalists who preach in the meeting houses in place of local lay leaders. This development may be regarded as a stage in the same general process, retarded in this instance by the sect's strong anti-ministerial ideology.

This type of development is most probable in the Conversionist sects. The orthodox fundamentalist sect stands nearest to traditional Christianity and may have had its own origins in some larger movement with a ministry, whose organization might be accepted even if its teachings are rejected. The Adventist sect resists organizational change in its confident expectation of an early end to the present dispensation and is, in any case, hostile to any institution associated with the established order. Similarly, the pietist (Introversionist) sect is ideologically resistant to the development of a ministry and, moreover, is not concerned with evangelism. In that the adventists evangelize they do so without the use of revivalist techniques. The Gnostic sect, while usually instituting a system of special instruction, does so for the private and personal benefit of the member and not as a qualification for any particular office in the movement, even though in practice the more highly taught are likely to gain easier admission to leadership positions. Worship is not usually of major importance to the Gnostic sect and when professional functionaries do arise they are more likely to be private counsellors than public ministers.

Elites emerge in sects both at the local level and, once centralized agencies have arisen, also at the center. They may be elected by the generality, but they tend to become self-recruiting both locally and at the center. Central control of local leaders may also occur, and when it does the local elite will be the group which interprets, explains, and rationalizes the activity of the central group. In such movements there is a distinct centripetal tendency of responsibility: allegiance is to "headquarters," "the central board," "the executive." Christian Science and Jehovah's Witnesses both typify this organizational structure. The existence of such elites has no specific implication for the development of the sect into a denomination for the crucial matters are whether the elite is specially trained and whether its function becomes that of a professional ministry. What may be noted, however, is that centralized movements appear to be better able to prevent schism than movements in which the central agencies are less well articulated and in which centripetal responsibility has not developed.

Schism is a feature of sects and of churches more than of denominations (except in the early period of denominational development). (This is partly because sects and churches tend to possess a much more clearly articulated structure of doctrine and organization than do denominations.) Otherwise, schism usually centers on the question of purity of doctrine, and successful schism usually finds its leader in the very inner elite of the movement.[17] Schism of this kind

[17] For an excellent illustration of this point, see A. K. Swihart, *Since Mrs. Eddy*, New York: Holt, 1931; for further examples in Christian Science and other movements, see B. R. Wilson, *Sects and Society, op. cit.*

serves to preserve the distinctive sectarian character of the organization since the schismatic groups tend to become the keepers of each other's consciences in relation to the maintenance of traditional values. The two groups compete for the same public, and frequently appeal to the same sources and authorities in legitimation of their position, thus engendering a competitive struggle to prove the purity of their doctrine and social practice. The Plymouth Brethren, the Mennonites, and the Christadelphians provide illustrations of this development.

Degree of Separateness from the World

The relationship which a sect permits itself and its members to the external world is of vital importance to the nature of its continuance. In some measure, and by some methods, the sect is committed to keeping itself "unspotted from the world": its distinctness must be evident both to its own members and to others. To this end there are two principal types of mechanism, *isolation* and *insulation*. Isolation may be consciously designed, or unconsciously accepted. It may be vicinal isolation in which social isolation is necessarily implied, but this is readily achieved only by groups which accept a communistic type of organization; such organization, in turn, acts as a further isolating device. Sects which have aspired to be self-contained in this way, and have sought to avoid the "alien" even in those spheres where most sects are prepared to treat with him, have usually been of the Introversionist type. Clearly, such a radical mechanism for the achievement of self-maintenance would mean too profound a change in sect character for Conversionist sects, while the expectation of an early overturn of normal social relations makes such action premature for Adventists. Gnostic sects usually lack the community basis for such a venture and

seek their separateness from the world in different ways. Isolation may also be linguistic, a condition illustrated by the various bodies of Mennonites, Hutterites, and Doukhobors. Finally, isolation may be simply the injunction to maintain social separateness from the alien; this is urged by most sects, even the evangelical.

Insulation consists of behavioral rules calculated to protect sect values by reducing the influence of the external world when contact necessarily occurs. Of course, insulation may be a latent function of the moral demands of sect teaching, the justification for which is biblical or revealed prescription; the sect leaders and the members themselves, however, often become aware of the real value of such precepts. Distinctive dress is such an insulating device, characteristic of some Mennonites, early Quakers, and Hutterites. Group endogamy is a more widely used method of insulation and is the rule for most Adventist and Introversionist sects, the expectation in many Conversionist sects, and the preferred form, if marriage is approved at all, in Gnostic sects.

The Coherence of Sect Values

Separateness from the world is clearly a part of the general constellation of values embraced by sects. The coherence of such values and the tensions which their acceptance involves are discussed below. However, it is analytically possible to distinguish between tensions arising from the conflict of this particular value and others embraced by the sect and the tensions resulting from the conflict between sect ideals and the ideals of the wider society, and ultimately with those of the state.

The principal tension between the demand for separateness and other sect values arises in the injunction, accepted by many sects, to go out and preach the gospel. Evangelism means exposure to the world and the risk of alienation of the evangelizing agents. It means also the willingness to accept into the sect new members. This throws a particular weight on the standards of admission if, through the impact of recruitment, the sect itself is not to feel the effect of members who are incompletely socialized from the sect's point of view. The more distinctive are sect doctrines and the more emphatic the insistence on strict standards of doctrinal understanding, the less likely it is that the sect will suffer from its evangelism. The Introversionist and Gnostic sects do not experience this type of tension since they do not evangelize the alien, or seek to do so only by formalized procedures. The Adventist sect regards it as one of its responsibilities to preach the kingdom, to forewarn the world of events portending, and to gather a remnant, but it sends its evangelizing agents into the world only after their doctrinal understanding has been thoroughly tested and their allegiance well tried. Equally it does not expect rapid returns, but subjects those who wish to join the movement to examination of their doctrinal knowledge. The Conversionist sects, which are fundamentalists, experience this tension most fully and have evolved least protection for themselves on these vulnerable points. Their agents are young, their doctrine often less sharply distinguished from that of the denominations, and their tests of good faith inadequate, subordinate to conversionist enthusiasm, and easily, if unwittingly, counterfeited by the emotionally overwrought in the revivalist situation.

The recruitment of the second generation is also an aspect of evangelism. There are similar problems of the tests of admission and the process of socializing the in-comers. Niebuhr, and subsequently Pope, pin-pointed a key tension for sect organization in recognizing the significance of accepting the second genera-

tion.[18] It is an oversimplification to say, however, that the second generation makes the sect into a denomination. As indicated above, such development depends on the standards of admission imposed by the sect, the previous rigor with which children have been kept separate from the world, and on the point at which a balance is struck between the natural desire of parents to have their children included in salvation and their awareness of the community view that any sort of salvation depends on the maintenance of doctrinal and moral standards. Obviously, whether the sect tends to embrace whole families or simply individuals is a significant matter. In general, Gnostic sects, which tend to have an individualistic appeal and do not emphasize the normal type of separation from the world, have more difficulty in winning the allegiance of the second generation than have other sects. Pietistic and Adventist sects, enjoying both doctrinal distinctiveness and the allegiance of whole families (supported by endogamous injunctions) and also tending to have exacting standards for would-be joiners, are apt to hold their second generation without damage to sect identity. The fundamentalist Conversionist groups —who often appeal to individuals, have a less clearly articulated difference of doctrine from the denominations, and whose standards of admission are simple acceptance of a Saviour—are most likely to be affected by the degree of adherence of the second generation.[19]

The sect's desire to be separate from the world and its concerns—and the values which express that separateness—results in certain distinct tensions for the organization and for its members. For

[18] Niebuhr, op. cit.; Pope, op. cit.
[19] Both Niebuhr and Pope base their generalizations on the examination of what we have called Conversionist sects; if the classification presented above is valid, it should reduce errors in predicting the development of sects.

each sect there must be a position of optimal tension, where any greater degree of hostility against the world portends direct conflict, and any less suggests accommodation to worldly values. The typical issues of this conflict of values include: divergence of sect and external society on what constitutes true knowledge (which leads to conflict concerning education); the refusal of sects to recognize the legitimacy of society's legal arrangements and the refusal to accept conventionalized sacred practices such as oath-swearing; withdrawal of the sect from the political arrangements of society, refusal to vote, to salute national emblems, and the like; conscientious objection to participation in military activities of the state; the refusal to recognize the marital and familial regulations imposed by the state; objection to state medical regulations; disregard of economic institutions of society, as in the refusal to register land ownership or to join labor unions.

The means used by the sect to cope with these particular tensions is crucial for the persistence of sect organization. The sect may depart from the accepted moral rules of the wider society, but beyond a certain point the sect comes into conflict with even the democratic state in the pluralist society. The state does not always win in such conflicts, as the exemptions from oath-swearing, flag-saluting, military service, and medical regulation, all illustrate. But the sect itself, in pursuit of its values, in its search for exemption, may experience change of character. It must, for instance, develop agencies to treat with the state; to preserve its values it may be thrust into new types of social action, new contact with worldly organization—perhaps even fighting its case in the law courts of "the world," although this conflicts with the desire of most sects to be a law unto themselves. Action to reduce external tensions may in this way generate new

internal tensions as the sect departs from older practices and values.

Thus when Christian Scientists joined with other unconventional healing movements to resist state legislation concerning medical care, they appeared, to some members, to compromise their stand that Christian Science alone could really heal. When, in Britain in the first World War, Christadelphians developed an organization to seek exemptions from military service, they allowed the activities of the state to induce them to establish committees at a national level, which conflicted with their ideal of minimal organization and prompted dissension and schism. When the branch of the Doukhobors called the Sons of Freedom, facing the demand of the state that it regulate its marriages and accept secular schooling, resort to arson and violence, they trespass on their own pacifist ideals.[20] Clearly in such cases of challenge and response there may readily be the beginnings of sect change in that the sect develops agencies more like those of denominations, and admits, by the back door, the values prevalent in the wider society.

If the sect is to persist as an organization it must not only separate its members from the world, but must also maintain the dissimilarity of its own values from those of the secular society. Its members must not normally be allowed to accept the values of the status system of the external world. The sect must see itself as marginal to the wider society, and even when the marginality of extreme poverty, for example, has objectively disappeared, the consciousness of the inapplicability of the standards of the outside world must be retained. Whatever the changes in their material circumstances, the group must persist in

[20] On the Doukhobors, see H. B. Hawthorn (Ed.), *The Doukhobors of British Columbia*, University of British Columbia Press, 1955.

the feeling of being a people apart, if it is to persist. Status must be status within the sect, and this should be the only group to which the status-conscious individual makes reference. Yet for the proselytizing sect this is often accomplished only with difficulty since the social status of its members may radically affect its prospect of winning recruits. Even the sect of the very poor is usually pleased when a prominent personage is converted and often accords him a place of honor because of his status in the wider society. The classic cases of sects developing into denominations (usually accompanied by schism from the parent body on the part of those poorer members who resist the growth of formality and other denominational characteristics) illustrate just such a conflict of sect values: between genuine separateness from the world and the desire for social respectability.[21]

As we have seen, the Adventist and Introversionist sects are more fully insulated against this type of value conflict. Nor does this type of tension occur in the Gnostic sects which insulate the two areas ideologically by teaching, in many cases, that the material world is less real. Although the member might gain status in the group if improvement in his material circumstances can be attributed to his special sect-inculcated knowledge, still the two levels of experience are clearly distinguished.

Finally, we may note the significance

[21] The history of Methodism, the Church of the Nazarene, and some Pentecostal groups illustrate this process. See, for example, E. D. C. Brewer, op. cit.; W. R. Goldschmidt, "Class Denominationalism in Rural California Churches," American Journal of Sociology, 49 (January, 1944), pp. 348–355; Oliver R. Whitley, "The Sect to Denomination Process in an American Religious Movement: The Disciples of Christ," Southwestern Social Science Quarterly 36 (December, 1955), pp. 275–282.

of exclusiveness in the development of sects. The more fully the sect sees itself as a chosen remnant, the more fully will it offer resistance to the broadening process which is implied in becoming a denomination. Such resistance is more likely to be successful, however, if the sect has an aristocratic ethic concerning salvation—if it sees itself as a chosen elect, limited in size by divine command. Sects which emphasize free-will and the availability of Christ to all (even if they accompany such a teaching with an expectation that not many will in fact avail themselves of the opportunity), and which thus accept a general Arminian position theologically, are much more likely to practise evangelism and to seek rapid growth than are the others.[22] The Conversionist sects inherit this theological position and accept this mission, whereas the Adventist sects, who accept the command to preach the truth, nonetheless make truth difficult to obtain. Both Introversionist and Gnostic sects emphasize a gradual unfolding of grace or truth to the individual; although, par-

[22] Arminian type theology, as distinct from Calvinism, would appear to be a significant factor in promoting the growth of sect to denomination; Benton Johnson's statement (op. cit.), that this development is largely confined to voluntarist Calvinist sects, is in need of clarification. That some Calvinist groups could pass from sect to established church was made possible by the unusual circumstances of the settlement by sectarians of new territories. (It is doubtful whether the establishment of the Calvinist church at Geneva could be described as a sect-to-church process.) Elsewhere the Calvinist sects which developed into denominations did so only as their Calvinism gave way to a more Arminian and less exclusive teaching, as with the Baptists in England. Those groups which have retained Calvinistic teaching in anything like its pristine rigor have not fully experienced denominational development, e.g., the Strict and Particular Baptists whose organization remains essentially sectarian in character.

ticularly in the Gnostic groups, there is no sense of absolute exclusiveness, in both types there is an emphasis on an elect.

Group Commitments and Relationships

At some level the individual member's commitment to the sect must be total. This may mean the acceptance of a leader's commands, or a general ideological commitment, or a more specific doctrinal commitment, or a commitment to regulate all social and moral affairs entirely as the sect directs. In the Gnostic sect commitment tends to be simply to the leader or to the general ideological position of the movement; the member must acquire the *Weltanschauung* of the sect if benefit of its special gnosis is to be gained. There are few moral correlates of this ideological position, and those which do exist are typically personal aids to self-fulfilment, for example, abstinence in matters of diet and in use of drugs, tobacco, and alcohol. The Introversionist sects (which may or may not have recognized leaders, and whose leaders may or may not claim distinctive charisma) add to the commitment of the member a distinct moral commitment: certain types of behavior are expected, and there is a strong commitment to the fellowship itself. The Adventist group demands commitment to specific doctrine and specific morality, which further implies commitment to the brethren themselves. The Conversionist sects, while expecting doctrinal and moral rectitude, are less sharply exclusive in demands towards the fellowship as such and are even prepared to extend their general idea of community to embrace "all born-again believers."

Introversionist and Adventist sects are distinctly *Gemeinschaften*. Fellowship is an important value for all members: fellow-members are "brethren"; relation-

ships as far as possible are primary; the local meeting is a face-to-face group. The individual is a sect-member before he is anything else, he is expected to find his friends within the group, group endogamy is the rule, and there is expulsion of the wayward and lax. The membership is a membership of families rather than of individuals and sect values are mediated by the kin-group. The Introversionists are sharers of an inner and unseen truth; the Adventists are participants in revolutionary intrigue. The Conversionist sect shares these general characteristics only partially: its concept of brotherhood extends beyond sect boundaries and its standards are less rigorous. It accepts individuals more lightly, socializes them less intensely, and loses them more easily—all of which disturbs the strong sense of community. Its appeal is to the individual seeking salvation, and consequently it is less typically composed of families. The Gnostic sect is much more frankly a *Gesellschaft:* the individual's relationships to other devotees are secondary to his commitment to the ideology and the leadership. Brotherhood is an alien concept. Discipline is for disloyalty, not for specific moral misdemeanor. The impersonality of relationships may even be regarded as ideal, since the gnosis, "the principle," is what matters. Since there are fewer behavioral correlates of sect affiliation, the member, socially, may hide his membership and so avoid the disapproval of the outside world.

Conclusions

Our analysis has brought out a number of items which are subject to variation as between different types of sect and which help to determine the likely development of such movements. Thus it is clear that sects with a general democratic ethic, which stress simple affirmation of intense subjective experience as a criterion of admission, which stand in the orthodox fundamentalist tradition, which emphasize evangelism and use revivalist techniques, and which seek to accommodate groups dislocated by rapid social change are particularly subject to denominationalizing tendencies. These same tendencies are likely to be intensified if the sect is unclear concerning the boundaries of the saved community and extends its rules of endogamy to include any saved person as an eligible spouse; if its moral injunctions are unclearly distinguished from conventional or traditional morality; and if it accepts simple assertion of remorse for sin as sufficient to re-admit or to retain a backslidden member. Denominationalization is all the more likely when such a sect inherits, or evolves, any type of preaching order, lay pastors, or itinerant ministers; when revivalism leads to special training for the revivalists themselves (and so leads to a class of professionals who cease to rely on "love-offerings" but are granted a fixed stipend); and when the members are ineffectively separated from the world, a condition enhanced by proselytizing activities.

It is clear that the types of sect which we described as Conversionist are most likely to fulfil the conditions which transform sects into denominations and are least likely to enjoy the circumstances preventing this process. The Adventist and the Introversionist types appear to be best protected from this development, although by different mechanisms: they fulfil few of the conditions supporting this evolution and often enjoy or create the factors which retard it. The Gnostic sect is in some ways less clearly protected, but its distinctive ideology performs in some measure the functions which social insulating mechanisms perform for other types.

In a broad way, we can see why certain earlier studies of sects fell into errors of prediction, since the conclusions rested on the experience of certain types of sects, sects which existed in very particular social circumstances, and accommodated people whose social marginality and sense of anomie were often temporary and a consequence of inadequate readjustment to rapidly changing social conditions. Of course, to predict the development of any given sect requires examination in close detail of its circumstances. Once these are known, however, the foregoing analysis should provide a guide for the interpretation of these facts.

6   Do Holiness Sects Socialize in Dominant Values?

BENTON JOHNSON

ABSTRACT. *Exception is taken to the adequacy of the prevailing sociological view that the function of Holiness religion is to offer underprivileged groups an emotional and other-worldly escape from the realities that beset them. This article presents evidence for the view that Holiness religion may also function as an agency of the socialization of the lower class in the dominant values of American society.*

SOURCE. Benton Johnson, "Do Holiness Sects Socialize in Dominant Values?" *Social Forces*, 39, May, 1961, pp. 309–316.

Introduction

It is the thesis of this paper that one of the most important functions of the Holiness movement in American Protestanism is the socializing of marginal, lower class groups in the values commonly called middle class, or more broadly, in the dominant, institutionalized values of the larger society. This thesis cannot now be conclusively proved, but enough evidence exists to give it substantial credibility. Some of this evidence has been gathered by other investigators in the course of research on other problems involving Holiness groups. Much of the evidence was gathered by the author in his own research on Holiness sects.[1] For the most part the available material requires us to limit whatever generalizations are drawn to the group of white Holiness adherents in the South.

At first glance there seems to be much evidence to support a contrary view. Holiness church life is markedly different from upper and middle class Protestant church life. For example, Holiness groups encourage their members to display strong, uninhibited religious feelings at their public meetings. This striking emotionalism is not at all like the staid and dignified tone of worship at higher social levels. Holiness groups are fundamentalist in theology and other-worldly in outlook, and this too is counter to the less dogmatic, less other-worldly tone of

[1] G. Benton Johnson, Jr., A Framework for the Analysis of Religious Action with Special Reference to Holiness and Non-Holiness Groups (Unpublished doctoral dissertation, Harvard University, 1953). The purpose of this research was to compare the religious values of Holiness groups with those of non-Holiness evangelical groups on the same socio-economic level and in the same locality. A set of value conflict questions was asked verbally of 20 subjects with high religious commitment. Half of these were Holiness and half of them were non-Holiness in affiliation. The research sites, which were both rural and urban and included some mill villages, were in North Carolina. Evidence directly substantiating the present thesis was not deliberately gathered by this previous research, but much of what was gathered does uphold it.

belief in many Protestant churches. Finally, the legalistic approach to "morals" of the Holiness bodies contrasts with the increasingly permissive and tolerant attitude toward such matters that is characteristic of the middle and upper classes. It is our contention, however, that these differences should not be allowed to obscure the more fundamental fact of similarity of basic value orientation between Holiness groups and the more privileged classes. We will show that many of the strikingly different features of the Holiness groups probably function as mechanisms of socialization. And we will see that there is evidence that the values in which Holiness adherents are socialized are similar to the dominant, institutionalized values of the larger society.

Most previous research conducted on Holiness groups has not been concerned with the present problem. Broadly speaking, previous sociological invesigation has presented the following picture of the Holiness movement: (1) it offers an other-worldly, escapist, and emotional compensation for low socio-economic status; (2) the movement is not interested in attacking directly the institutional causes of this low status, and is hence indifferent to the major social and economic problems of the time. We have no quarrel with this exposition as far as it goes, but we do insist that it is only a partial sociological analysis. In a very few places in the present literature there are allusions to the phenomenon which we shall treat. Boisen states that Holiness sects give their members "hope and courage and strength to keep going in the face of difficulties," and adds that "Insofar as they succeed in doing this, their economic and social status is likely to be raised." [2] Holt remarks, after characterizing the social views of Holiness groups as "reactionary" rather than "rev-

[2] Anton T. Boisen, "Economic Distress and Religious Experience," Psychiatry, 2 (May 1939), p. 194.

olutionary or constructive," that nevertheless, these sects "are successful in inspiring hope and a type of behavior in individuals which may raise their individual or group status above that of their class." [3] Somewhat more to the present point, Yinger briefly states that "Many individual adherents are helped, by the self-discipline that the sect encourages, to improve their own status," but immediately adds that "the sect is irrelevant to the social and cultural causes that continue to create such disprivileged individuals." [4] The emphasis in all but one of these statements is on courage in the face of adversity, and the consequence, in all the statements, is considered to be upward social mobility.

In contrast, our emphasis will be on the fact that the Holiness groups encourage an orientation toward the world that constrains their members to adopt both motivationally and behaviorally an outlook similar in many respects to that of higher, more privileged social strata. Upward mobility may be an important long-term consequence of this orientation, but more fundamental is the possession of the orientation itself, which governs the believer's behavior toward the secular world. This orientation which the Holiness sects espouse is a variant of what Weber has called the ethic of innerworldly asceticism.[5] Most authorities concede that there is an important connection between this orientation toward the

world and the values and structure of industrial capitalism, specifically, and the dominant values of American society, more broadly. These values have been described frequently by sociologists.[6] Central to all descriptions is the emphasis on individual achievement of concrete goals by the consistent application of appropriate means. Closely related to the central achievement theme is the emphasis on democracy, individualism, mobility, and moral respectability. We will argue that the specifically religious values of Holiness groups converge with several features of the secular value system. If this is so, it will be plausible to suggest that a latent function of Holiness groups is the socialization of their adherents in the dominant societal values.

Theologically, the Holiness movement is a part of a larger movement within American Protestantism that has reacted against the austerities of Calvinism and has instead stressed the general availability of salvation and the possibility of the believer's achieving a kind of spiritual perfection. Of Arminian and Wesleyan parentage, Holiness theology has gone on to elaborate the stages by which the believer attains perfection. The so called Pentecostal branch of the Holiness movement, to which nowadays the term Holiness is popularly applied, conceives of three such stages. The mandatory "initial evidence" of arriving at the third and last stage is the believer's utterance of syllables of an unknown tongue. The Holiness movement is also heir to the tradition of revivalism. Many well-known

[3] John B. Holt, "Holiness Religion: Cultural Shock and Social Reorganization," *American Sociological Review*, 5 (October 1940), p. 741.
[4] J. Milton Yinger, *Religion, Society, and the Individual* (New York: The Macmillan Company, 1957), p. 173.
[5] Max Weber, *The Protestant Ethic and the Spirit of Capitalism*, Trans. by Talcott Parsons (New York: Charles Scribner's Sons, 1930). See especially chap. 4, "The Religious Foundations of Worldly Asceticism," pp. 95–154.

[6] See especially the following works: Robin M. Williams, Jr., *American Society* (New York: Alfred Knopf, 1951), pp. 388–442; Clyde Kluckhohn and Florence R. Kluckhohn, "American Culture: Generalized Orientations and Class Patterns," in Lyman Bryson, Louis Finkelstein, and R. M. McIver (eds.), *Conflicts of Power in Modern Culture* (New York: Harper & Bros. 1947), pp. 106–128.

orgiastic or emotional phenomena are common in Holiness meetings and some demonstration of strong feeling is considered an appropriate sign of attaining the various stages of perfection. The Holiness movement is fragmented into numerous sects. Some of these sects are congregational in polity but a number of them are episcopally organized.

Our concern will be with the Holiness groups of Pentecostal persuasion. We will also restrict ourselves to a consideration of the formally organized denominations in the Pentecostal tradition. There are many small groups, some confederated, some existing as individual "store front" congregations, that are in the Pentecostal movement. They seem especially prevalent among Negroes. We will not be concerned with these groups. It is freely admitted that the sociological generalizations which we hope to draw as to the effect of the Holiness movement on the value orientations of its adherents may not apply to the isolated "store front" variety of Pentecostal religion.

The Emphasis on Conversion

The great majority of the members of these newer Holiness sects of the Pentecostal persuasion are of low socioeconomic status.[7] But it has also been established that lower class persons tend to be less involved in religious activities than any other class of the population.[8]

[7] See Liston Pope, "Religion and the Class Structure," *Annals of the American Academy of Political and Social Science*, 56 (March 1948), pp. 84–91; also Walter Goldschmidt, "Class Denominationalism in Rural California Churches," *American Journal of Sociology*, 49 (January 1944), pp. 348–355.
[8] Hadley Cantril, "Educational and Economic Composition of Religious Groups: An Analysis of Poll Data," *American Journal of Sociology*, 48 (March 1943), p. 577; Frank D. Alexander, "Religion in a Rural Community of the South," *American Sociological Review*, 6 (April 1944), p. 245.

Holiness groups are especially strong in the southern states.[9] Now it is probably accurate to assume that the southern white lower class is less imbued with the dominant values of the society than any other large group of native non-Catholic whites in the country. Writing on this class in Old City, Davis and Gardner note:

By and large, lower-class behavior and ideology may be said to be characterized by a disdain for the government and laws which they see as creations of the upper class and middle class, a disdain for churches and associations and for the moral and religious values.[10]

The ordinary lower class person, and especially in the South, is not exposed to a constant set of socializing pressures emphasizing middle class work and achievement values, as is the person at higher social levels. In view of his initial commitment to values that are different from those of higher social classes, the lower class person if he is to adhere to these higher values, must make a "decision" or a reformulation of motivations, considerably more hard for him than for the middle class person who has really never had any serious choice to make. The borderline that he must cross is a sharp one. It is not chiefly an economic or occupational borderline but an evaluational and motivational borderline. And it is a

[9] Holt, *op. cit.*, p. 742.
[10] Allison Davis, Burleigh B. Gardner, and Mary R. Gardner, *Deep South* (Chicago: University of Chicago Press, 1941), p. 80. See also pp. 79–83 and 118–136 of this book. For other portrayals of the values of the southern white lower class, see W. J. Cash, *The Mind of the South* (New York: Alfred Knopf, 1941), pp. 42–44, 44–53, 308–309, etc.; also Leonard W. Doob, "Poor Whites: A Frustrated Class," in John Dollard, *Caste and Class in a Southern Town* (New York: Harper & Brothers, 1937), pp. 445–484.

borderline which, in view of his background and possible continued participation in lower class circles, the individual is in danger of crossing again in the opposite direction.

The great attention that Holiness and other sects pay to the phenomenon of conversion is highly suggestive of the fact that these groups endeavor to reorient the individual's motivations and values in fundamental ways. Holiness believers usually insist that they and their colleagues are "changed" at the time of conversion. Most of these groups draw a sharp and rigid line between the converted and the unconverted. Like the emphasis on conversion, the drawing of this line again suggests that a value conflict of some importance is involved.

What impels individuals to become members of Holiness sects and, we assume, to cross a value orientational borderline? Prior to any important reformulation of motives there is likely to be an experience of heightened frustration or deprivation. A number of observers of the Holiness groups suggest that many join in order to compensate for the frustration occasioned by their low socioeconomic position. As Holt points out, the areas within the South that have experienced the greatest growth of Holiness groups have been those characterized by an expanding economy, chiefly of an industrial nature, but also of an agricultural and recreational character.[11] It is very likely, as some have suggested,[12] that in these areas the awareness among lower class persons that they are underprivileged has been sharpened as they have increasingly been obliged to earn a livelihood in fairly regimented organizations under the supervision of persons of higher status than themselves. In view of this heightened sense of being on the bottom of society, Holiness reli-

gion enables the lower class individual to deny that he is really on the bottom in any meaningful sense. As Liston Pope has put it, Holiness religion allows the individual to "substitute religious status for social status."[13] Or, as Goldschmidt has written, Holiness relation "denies the existence of this world and its woes; it denies the values in terms of which they [the adherents] are the underprivileged and sets up in their stead a putative society in the Kingdom of God, where, because of their special endowments . . . they are the elite."[14]

The Acceptance of Secular Society

That important reformulations of values or motives take place when a person joins a Holiness sect seems pretty well agreed on. But we have not yet established the direction which this reformulation takes other than to note that most observers emphasize that the otherworldliness of Holiness belief inclines the individual to make a kind of fantasy-like retreat from what many would call social reality.

Let us grant that Holiness sects place great emphasis on getting to heaven and correspondingly devalue the pursuit of empirical, social ends as ultimate goals in themselves. Still, we assume that these sects are obliged to adopt some orientation toward secular activities. Basically, such an orientation must reject or accept the values and institutions of society.

Yinger, Pope, and others have rightly pointed out that although Holiness groups preach against "worldliness" they do not attempt an organized protest against any important features of the social system.[15] Now if a group espouses

[11] Holt, op. cit., pp. 742–743.
[12] Ibid., p. 745; also Yinger, op. cit., p. 167.
[13] Liston Pope, Millhands and Preachers (New Haven; Yale University Press, 1942), p. 137.
[14] Goldschmidt, op. cit., p. 354.
[15] Pope, Millhands and Preachers, pp. 164–166; Holt, op. cit., p. 741; Yinger, op. cit., pp. 170–173.

values in considerable opposition to those of the larger society, that group *must* face the problem of its relation to that society and the problem of how, specifically, to institutionalize its own values. This leads it to formulate a social policy aimed at securing these values in the face of opposition. The two possible polar types of such a social policy are outright attack on the larger social structure and a relatively total withdrawal from that society into exclusive religious communities. Holiness groups are not interested in "social action" or in attempts to reform society broadly so as to make it more "Christian" in any structural sense. Neither are they interested in forming themselves into segregated, tightly knit, self-sufficient communities.

Either the social action orientation or the withdrawal orientation would seem to be necessary adaptations if Holiness groups were seriously at odds with secular society. This leaves the alternative that Holiness groups basically accept society as constituted. There is evidence which can be immediately noted in support of the view that some kind of acceptance pattern characterizes the adaptation of these sects to the larger society. Even when we consider the many rules to which Holiness sects hold their members, these members are still for the most part left entirely free to participate in ordinary secular life. The church does not in any significant way attempt to be a regulator or coordinator of all its members' activities. Although the Holiness believer is held to certain distinct standards, he is able to pursue any legitimate private interest without being answerable to the congregation.

Although Holiness adherents are inclined to emphasize their distinctiveness and particularly their separation from "the things of this world," an examination of what they usually mean by this sentiment fails to reveal a sweeping rejection of secular norms. What Holiness people usually mean when they speak of their anti-worldliness is that they are opposed to religious disbelief and to a violation of their own normative standards. One Holiness pastor, when asked by the author to describe the chief evils of modern times, complained that "women will go downtown nude—I mean not wearing anything you'd call decent dress." Another pastor was concerned with "the material outlook on life . . . , playing it high, wide and handsome." As we shall see, however, his objection is not to involvement in money-making activities per se, but to involvement without proper motivation and discipline.

Further evidence of the very restricted nature of the Holiness opposition to the ways of contemporary society is seen in the interest which some of our respondents showed in being respected in their own communities. An eagerness to be acknowledged as a legitimate movement by outsiders may be taken as a sign that the movement is not really so "different" and that it embodies beliefs and norms that outsiders might admire. A minister of the Pentecostal Holiness Church expressed great pride that he had been invited to sit on the platform at the public high school commencement exercises along with the usual group of Baptist, Methodist, and Presbyterian ministers. He acknowledged that when a Holiness church is founded in a community, ill will and opposition often arise. "They'll point us out and not want to have anything to do with us. . . . Call us liars and funny people," he said. This attitude is based on ignorance, according to the pastor, for "after they see what we really are they usually quiet down." Holiness people are simply "clean and decent folks" in his opinion. The emphasis on winning respect and acceptance of the non-Holiness community by showing them "what we really are," namely "clean and decent folks," seems to imply that there are important normative similarities between Holiness people and non-Holiness people.

The Primary of Ascetic Norms

Still, acceptance of secular values can be a passive matter or it can be positive. There is evidence for the view that the Holiness acceptance of much of society and its values is of a positive and not of a passive nature. We make this statement because of the predominating influence of a form of Calvinist inner-worldly asceticism in determining the Holiness orientation toward the world. This asceticism underlies the specific norms to which Holiness adherents are held. These norms closely correspond, both in general orientation and in particulars, to the rules commonly incumbent on members of the older revivalistic denominations at an earlier stage of their development. Members of Holiness sects are forbidden to consume alcoholic beverages, to dance, to gamble or to play cards, to "smoke, dip or chew" tobacco. They may not attend places of "worldly amusement" such as plays, movies, fairs, ball games, or poolrooms. They may not engage in mixed bathing; women may not use makeup or wear short skirts, short sleeves, short hair or ornamental jewelry. Profanity is forbidden, and strict Sabbath observance is enjoined. Obligations, including debts, must be faithfully discharged. There are a few other specific commandments varying from denomination to denomination and from congregation to congregation, but the above list is the hard core of those categorical behavioral injunctions, chiefly of a prohibitive nature, to which most Holiness sects subscribe.

Almost all these rules are directed toward the suppression of the esthetic, the erotic, the irrational chance-taking or immediately pleasurable aspects of life. As Weber has argued, the "destruction of spontaneous, impulsive enjoy-ment"[16] implied in such ascetic rules is related to the attempt which certain religious systems make to induce their adherents to devote their lives to the systematic pursuit of overriding ends.[17] We assume that in general asceticism is a mechanism of the regulation of the gratification needs of individuals. It is especially important in a situation where behavior patterns stressing rational, purposeful activity are being inculcated. By cultivating the attitude of affective neutrality which is appropriate to any goal attainment process asceticism keeps the actor's gratification needs focused on the *ultimate* goal of action (salvation) by avoiding distracting or tempting gratifications that might enhance regressive tendencies or reinforce alienative motivations.

What is the relationship of these ascetic norms to the general observation that Holiness adherents are emotionally uninhibited? Much has been written about the fact that the emotionalism of Holiness meetings is erotically charged, that it appeals to persons who are emotionally "starved," and that it serves for lower class persons what more sublimated pursuits of immediate gratification serve for middle and upper class persons. No doubt all this is true, but from our standpoint the principal consequence of Holiness emotionalism is to secure and maintain the motivational commitment of individuals to the kind of life implied by the ascetic rules.

This commitment to asceticism is secured by playing on the individual's desire to escape punishment and find reward. The punishment is Hell. The reward is Heaven. The traditional Christian conception of man, destined without grace to go to Hell to suffer eternal torment, is usually presented at Holiness meetings. At the same time a "way out"

[16] Weber, *The Protestant Ethic*, p. 119.
[17] *Ibid.*, pp. 105, 166–169.

is offered that promises eternal joy instead. These alternatives are portrayed in the most vivid manner so as to induce the hearers actually to experience the extremes involved. Very likely the promise of immediate relief from a sense of general deprivation and meaninglessness is especially attractive to members of socially depressed strata. The "blessed assurance" of salvation is held to be attainable forthwith, as a kind of "foretaste of glory divine." Although Holiness religion does encourage a person to become satiated with the joy that he is saved, if he is to enter into full membership in the sect he must pay a price for this joy. The price is that he must frame his life according to the ascetic norms of the congregation. Hence for the full sect member the emotional permissiveness of Holiness meetings is likely to be seen as an opportunity to strengthen commitment to the obligatory norms of the group.

It is the ascetic norms and not the experiencing of a state of spiritual exaltation that are the substance of the day-to-day religious role of the Holiness believer. There are a number of common features of Holiness sects which attest to this fact. First, whereas an individual believer is only required to experience the initial stage of grace, that is of conversion itself, *all* members are required to abide by the set of ascetic rules which is typically referred to as the "discipline." Secondly, it is largely infraction of these rules that calls forth strong negative sanctions on the part of the congregation. Holiness sects are not typically lenient where infraction is concerned. They often practice a form of excommunication known as "disfellowshipping" or reading the offender out of the congregation. Finally, it is not possible among Holiness sects for an individual to claim a kind of spiritual exemption from these rules owing to his having received higher spiritual or emotional blessings. Quite the contrary: de-

spite the fact that he may have received such a blessing, he is subject to negative sanctions if he fails to abide by the "discipline" of the sect. This policy is not the subject of controversy in Holiness circles and it is theologically supported by the Wesleyan doctrine of the possibility of a fall from grace.[18]

The Effects of Holiness Commitment

So far we have argued that far from being diffusely alienated from secular society, Holiness sectarians are positively oriented to it in terms of an ethic of inner-worldly asceticism. This ethic is regarded as having made its most significant secular impact on the economy. Therefore, it is important to investigate whether Holiness adherents tend to possess traits or attitudes which make for their successful integration into productive enterprises. Liston Pope has pointed to the fact that many mills in the South encourage the establishment of churches among their workers by giving land, buildings, and financial support. From the mills' standpoint this encouragement has been more than a pious gesture. It has been given with the expectation that the churches will produce a more dependable kind of worker, in short, that they will inculcate traits in laborers that

[18] These and other considerations have led the author to the conclusion that most Holiness sects are *ethical* in the sense in which this term has been defined by Weber. According to Weber, an ethical religion is one that stresses the ordering of everyday life according to a set of supernaturally legitimated norms. Such a religion stands in contrast to one that stresses contemplative or orgiastic union with the supernatural. See Max Weber, "The Social Psychology of the World Religions," in *From Max Weber: Essays in Sociology* (Trans. and ed. by Hans H. Gerth and C. Wright Mills; New York: Oxford University Press, 1946), pp. 287–291.

are desirable from a managerial or production point of view. Almost without exception the churches so subsidized are Protestant and in the tradition of inner-worldly asceticism. Pope states:

> There is no doubt in the minds of employers that churches have succeeded, and still succeed, in providing better workers for the mills. Statements by employers in Gaston County may be taken as representative of employers throughout the brief history of the Southern textile industry.[19]

Although at the time of Pope's research in 1939 the mills tended predominantly to support non-Holiness evangelical denominations such as the Baptists, he did note an increasing tendency for them also to support Holiness sects, apparently as the employers came to recognize that these sects did not "upset the routine of the life of workers." [20]

Pope's interest in the mills' encouragement of churches was centered about the opportunities for control of the workers by the mill management that this situation affords and in the generally conservative social doctrine espoused by most churches whether subsidized or not.[21] This is a legitimate, and we think, valid analysis. But our interest here is in the simple fact that Protestant churches are directly encouraged by industrial concerns which feel it to be "good business" in the sense of enhancing the profit opportunities of the firm by providing a disciplined labor supply. A mill pastor very frankly spoke of this to the author in the following manner:

> Take these mills around here. They figure that church people make a bet-

ter type than other people and they know what they're saying. X Mills, for instance, they invest from 80 to 100 thousand dollars a year in churches. . . . They say it's a good investment because the fellow who goes to church regularly is a more efficient worker in the long run. Maybe here is a better workman, but he gets drunk. Well, he spends his weekend drinking and he's no good on Monday. A company can't have half of its force staying out on Monday. . . . Some people don't wait for the weekends either, they go out on a spree every night. In other words, the Christian man in the long run would prove the more efficient workman because he can be dependend on.

The emphasis is on efficiency and steadiness, and a direct connection between these virtues and the ascetic norm of abstention from alcohol is noted. Pope notes that southern mill officials lay particularly strong emphasis on the fact that the church going employee is thought to be a steady and reliable worker. Nonchurch going employees may be as efficient, but they are more prone to absenteeism and to quitting the job, both of which have been serious problems to the southern textile industry.[22] We have argued before that asceticism is associated with a generally methodical long-term devotion to concrete tasks. The evidence presented by Pope establishes the plausibility of the proposition that the Holiness and other inner-worldly ascetic sects in the South actually do produce workers who consistently apply themselves to the tasks set for them in the industrial work situation.

Consistent self-application to one's work is not only a vital condition for building and maintaining a highly productive economy, it is one of the oft-mentioned characteristics of the dominant American value system. Self-application

---

[19] Pope, *Millhands and Preachers,* p. 29.
[20] *Ibid.,* p. 140.
[21] See especially Pope's chapter on "Churches and Sects," pp. 117–140, and his chapter on "The Control of Churches by Mills," pp. 143–161, both in *Millhands and Preachers.*
[22] Pope, *Millhands and Preachers,* pp. 29–30.

can be, and in many unskilled work roles possibly must be, essentially a routine matter requiring little initiative or independent decision-making. According to Weber, however, a further distinguishing characteristic of the ethic of inner-worldly asceticism is the concept of the *calling*. Self-direction, mastery, and positive achievement in occupational tasks are its central themes. Such an orientation is more appropriate to managerial and entrepreneurial roles than to lower level occupational positions. If, as we argue, the Holiness sects socialize in dominant values through the medium of an emphasis on the ethic of inner-worldly asceticism, they should produce values which stress mastery and self-direction.

What evidence is there that this is so? The author asked ten Holiness ministers in intensive interviews a question in which they were required to choose between two conflicting, generalized orientations toward life. One of these orientations was a statement of the self-direction and mastery theme of the ethic of the calling. The other orientation was stated so as to imply a less achievement-minded, more cautious outlook on life, and possibly to imply (if the respondent so chose) a rejection of the goal attainment process altogether. The question is reproduced below as it was read to the respondents:

> Two young Christian men are talking about what they are going to do with their lives. One of them says that in his life he is going to aim high. He is going to use his opportunities as they come to him day by day, he is going to develop his talents to the utmost; he is even going to risk failure by setting his own aims so far beyond that he may only partly attain them. The other man says, no, that in his life he isn't going to bite off more than he can chew, that he would rather do a little bit all right than make a big mess out

of something that he can't handle. Now if you had to give aid and encouragement to one of these two young men, which one would you agree with?

Only one respondent to this question tended in any manner to deny the desirability of positive goal attainment in the occupational area. All the rest of the informants, regardless of whether they chose the first or second orientational alternative, demonstrated a positive approval of the goal attainment process. Almost all of those who chose the second orientational alternative called attention to the importance of ascetic or traditional moral norms. They did so, however, in order to set guides and limits to the achievement process and not in order to pose asceticism as a complete way of life. One minister of the Assemblies of God was disturbed at the prospect of "going after success for its own sake." A minister of the Pentecostal Holiness Church did not want a man's overriding ambition to cause him to "*push* himself anywhere that he wasn't prepared for." Still, this same minister held that "the higher positions will come if we've been consistent with our self-improvement."

Half the respondents voiced the kind of enthusiastic endorsement of the occupational goal attainment process that would have gratified an investigator such as Max Weber. All of them showed a clear comprehension and acceptance of the ethic of the calling. The following response was given by a Church of God pastor:

> I think it pays to have a vision. That's a wonderful thing to have. If you have God in your life then I think you'll always go forward and never backward. You have to stress your goal and what you're aiming for and go forth to get it. . . . If you ain't got no vision then you're going to say, "No I can't do it." You're going to say

good enough is good enough. Determine what you want to do, then press on, don't be defeated.

A minister of the same denomination echoed similar sentiments when he stated, "Where there's no aspiration, there's nothing done, there's no heights taken." Still another minister of the Church of God said that he had advised his son in school not to be "content with being in the middle of that class or at the tail end of it—be at the very top of it." He went on to remark that people "ought to desire to excel in their work," and "make up their minds to do well."

In many ways the most striking response was made by the minister of the Assemblies of God whose stricture against "material things" was noted above. In the present context he said:

> Well, I believe God has a plan for every one of us. If we accept Him then we're obligated to follow that plan for the glory of God. . . . When we're doing what God has planned for us we ought to give God our very best. We ought to aim high, like the man said. If you had a call to the grocery business, then you ought to be ambitious for the glory of God, to be successful for Christ's sake. That other man is a drifter. He's not interested in the glory of God. He's not industrious, just doesn't care. I'm trying to think of some Scripture. One that comes to mind is, "Be not slothful in business." . . . When I went into the painting business I said I was going to be the best in the business. And I was.

If we add this pastor's views on greed and worldly pleasures as well as his joy over his salvation and spiritual perfection, we can round out our presentation of the Holiness orientation toward life: It is other-worldly in the sense of expecting the greatest personal joy in the hereafter, but it involves as a condition of this the devotion to doing the will of God in this world. This will can be realized in almost any kind of activity, but it demands consistent output of effort, a denial of distracting pleasures, and a focus on achievement. The positive emphasis on self-application, consistency, and achievement, are the principal Holiness themes that directly converge with dominant American values.

E · OTHER RELIGIOUS STRUCTURES

1 · *Conceptualizations of the Urban Parish*[1]

JOSEPH H. FICHTER

The social structure of an urban Catholic parish is highly complex. At first glance this would not seem to be true, because the casual observer probably sees nothing but a large number of people who satisfy their religious needs at a particular parish church. On closer analysis, however, it will be noted that any social unit of a few thousand persons logically structures its social relations according to multiple patterns. It seems true also that the social scientist not only can but must conceptualize the parish in multiple ways in order to achieve meaningful analysis.

The analytical tool of multiple conceptualizations of the parish is obviously not an invention of the social scientists. Besides other approaches, a person could study the parish historically, theologically, canonically, and sociologically, and the sociological approach itself allows for numerous conceptual frameworks. The editors of a recent study of the

Catholic parish in America remark that "there are, of course, several possible approaches to the living reality which is the parish," and they exemplify this patent observation by saying that the parish can be an institutionalized administrative unit, a social group in its own right, or a component of the larger ecclesiastical unit.[2] A quarter of a century ago Harbrecht spoke about the three-fold aspect of the parish and discussed briefly the *legal* aspect from canon law, the *religious* aspect from pastoral theology, and the *socioethical* aspect from moral philosophy.[3]

This varied conceptualization of the urban American parish is not the same as the detailed subdivisions under which the parish is studied in the numerous textbooks and commentaries on the Code of Canon Law. These writings have in the past referred to different kinds of parishes in the Church, but they have now settled upon the three major types

SOURCE. Reprinted from Joseph H. Fichter, *Social Relations in the Urban Parish,* Chicago: University of Chicago Press, 1954, pp. 181–194 (ch. 14) by permission of the University of Chicago Press.
[1] An expansion of a paper read at the fifteenth annual meeting of the Southern Sociological Society, Atlanta, Georgia, March 28, 1952 (see *Social Forces,* XXXI, No. 1 [October, 1952], 43–46).

[2] C. J. Nuesse and Thomas J. Harte (eds.), *The Sociology of the Parish* (Milwaukee: Bruce Publishing Co., 1951), p. 3.
[3] John Harbrecht, *The Lay Apostolate* (St. Louis: B. Herder Book Co., 1929), p. 21. This book was designed to analyze only the last-named aspect and was subtitled, "A Social Ethical Study of Parish Charity Organizations for Large City Parishes."

as territorial, personal, and mixed.[4] One of the first books written on the subject of pastors and parishes after the promulgation of the canon law of 1918 presented the following detailed subdivisions of the Catholic parish: (a) parishes and quasi-parishes; (b) territorial and personal; (c) secular and religious; (d) incorporated and independent; (e) removable and irremovable; and (f) exempt and nonexempt.[5] These various aspects of the parish, some of which are overlapping, must be known by the student of canon law, but they are not important to our present purpose.

The student of society may find it fruitful to analyze the normal large urban Catholic parish under any of the following aspects. Each varies in importance as a conceptual frame of reference for the research scientist. The parish may be considered (a) a legal corporation; (b) a superimposed association; (c) an institutionalized association; (d) a communal group; or (e) a cluster of subgroupings. It is also helpful for some purposes to conceive the parish as (f) a network of family relations and (g) a series of statistical categories. Even this list is not, of course, exhaustive or all-embracing.

(a) The parish is a *legal corporation* according to two systems of law, the canonical code of the Church and the civil code of the state. Having its own canon law, the Catholic Church does not recognize or admit the right of the state to make laws governing the existence and operation of the parish, but in the *de facto* situation there are numerous in-

stances in which the Catholic parish takes cognizance of the civil law.[6] This is not merely a reference to the acceptance of, and compliance with, codes which prescribe regulations concerning building, sanitation, fire prevention, etc. Incorporating as a legal entity under the laws of the state has been considered a helpful convenience by American parishes and dioceses.

The juridic notion of a pastor in Canon 451 implies that the parish is a moral person, a legal entity, a canonical corporation. A whole section of the Code (Canons 451–86) deals with the rights and obligations of pastors and necessarily discusses the parishioners.[7] The pastor is a priest or a moral person to whom a parish is intrusted with the care of souls to be exercised under the authority of the local ordinary. Scores of commentaries have been written concerning the canonical relationship between pastor and parishioners, and a further discussion of this aspect would be superfluous here.

The status of the parishioners in this canonical corporation, however, seems worthy of note, especially as it relates to the Catholic lay people in American cities. Abbo and Hannan remark that "the body of the faithful certainly constitutes a collectivity of which the law takes definite notice, since it is they for whom the pastor is appointed. In American civil law, this collectivity, if legally incorporated, is the repository of the

---

[4] See T. Lincoln Bouscaren and Adam C. Ellis, *Canon Law: A Text and Commentary* (2d rev. ed.; Milwaukee: Bruce Publishing Co., 1951).

[5] Ludovicus Fanfani, *De iure parochorum* (Rome: Marietti, 1924), pp. 3–7. For a more recent work on this subject see Laurentius Agius, *Summarium iurium et officiorum parochorum* (Naples: D'Auria, 1953).

[6] See Charles Augustine, *The Canonical and Civil Status of Catholic Parishes in the United States* (St. Louis: B. Herder Book Co., 1926), and for several interesting cases of pastors and parishioners before the civil courts see *ibid.*, pp. 305–25.

[7] See Bouscaren and Ellis, *op. cit.*, chap. v, pp. 188–227, and their definition from the point of view of the people, "a community of the faithful to which has been assigned its own rector with ordinary power in the internal forum for the care of souls."

rights and duties of the parish. It is not so under the law of the Church. If, then, it is said that the law of the Code does not deny juridic recognition to the body of the faithful as a collectivity, it is meant that it accords them this recognition in a very limited sphere, i.e., that of having all the resources of the parish, spiritual and temporal, administered in their behalf." [8]

As a legal corporation formed under the civil law of most states,[9] the urban Catholic parish has as its purposes and objectives "the holding and administering of property, real, personal and mixed, so that the same may be devoted to religious purposes, for the benefit of those who attend the Roman Catholic Church belonging to this corporation."

The members of this legal corporation under civil law also constitute the board of five directors who manage, administer, and control it. These are the "civilly" legal officers of the parish. The bishop is *ex officio* president; the vicar-general of the diocese is the vice-president; and the pastor holds the combined offices of secretary and treasurer. The two remaining members of the board are lay parishioners, formerly called "trustees," who are appointed by the bishop, usually for a term of two years. They are almost always successful professional and businessmen.

In practice, all legal and fiscal business of the parish is conducted by the secretary-treasurer, the pastor. The corporation charter forbids him to contract any debt over two hundred dollars and stipulates that "no real estate belonging to the corporation shall be sold, mortgaged or disposed of in any way without the vote and consent of all the five Directors."

The obvious intent of the parochial charter is that the effective legal control of the parish be in the hands of the clergy. The history of lay trusteeship in the parishes of the United States has demonstrated the wisdom and practicality of this arrangement.[10] The pastor, who is himself subject to higher authority in the administration of the parish, usually recognizes that the practical advice of the lay trustees can be very valuable. At the same time the laymen usually understand that their function is consultative rather than directive. The pastor is obliged to meet with them only on important financial decisions.

It is clear that the parishioners are not stockholders in this legal corporation, but they contribute the money and properties which the corporation administers. They are the "repository of the rights and duties" and the beneficiaries of the religious services and of the charitable, educational, and literary purposes for which the corporation was legally constituted. The two lay members of the board are not their elected representatives. Viewed in this light of civil law, the urban American parish is neither a spontaneously organized structure nor a mass-controlled organization. The lay people have no formal authority, direct or indirect, over the parochial corporation, but the corporation is an instrument of service to them.[11]

---

[8] John Abbo and Jerome Hannan, *The Sacred Canons* (St. Louis: B. Herder Book Co., 1952), I, 445–46. For a further contrast between the canonical and the civil legal corporation see Augustine, *op. cit.*, pp. 110–27.

[9] The description of the parochial legal corporation given here is found in the official synodal publication of various American dioceses.

[10] For a brief and reliable discussion of trusteeism see Theodore Maynard, *The Story of American Catholicism* (New York: Macmillan Co., 1941), pp. 187–96, 235–37.

[11] This arrangement differs sharply from that of contemporary French-Canadian parishes. There the *fabrique*, or corporation, owns the real estate given by the parishioners for public worship; "it is the proprietor of the parish church, the rectory, and the sums of money assigned for the upkeep of those buildings

(b) The urban Catholic parish may be called a *superimposed association* in the sense that the conditions for its existence are fixed by Rome through the local bishop. Canon 216 of the Code points out that every diocese must be divided into definite territorial areas, each with its own permanent pastor, people, and church.[12] Thus, the religious association of lay Catholics in any given parish is not a matter of choice by the people themselves as long as they reside within the designated boundaries. In practice, of course, some of the lay persons in any parish attend neighboring Catholic churches for religious services, and some participate in other parochial activities there, but a formally imposed and morally obligatory relationship still remains between them and the pastor of their own parish.

Of more importance than the territorial assignment of people to a definite parish is the fact that the general framework of their religious functions and objectives is also prescribed by church authorities outside the parish.[13] This means

that, whenever the parishioners assemble for religious activities, they follow a pattern of worship and devotion which is *essentially* the same throughout the whole Catholic Church. The liturgical rituals of the Church, in so far as they are designed for public and corporate worship, can be termed ideal patterns of social relations. The moral and social behavior of parishioners, normatively posited in commandments, precepts, and rules of the Church, is also superimposed.

This accounts for the basic cultural universality of all Catholic parishes. At a certain minimum level there is permitted no variation, and this minimum is always centered around the essential values of the Roman rite. The regulatory patterns governing auricular confession, the form of Eucharistic consecration, and the administration of the other sacraments are rigidly fixed by the canon law of the Church. At another level there are regulatory patterns fixed in each diocese by the bishop. For example, a bishop may dispense his diocese from abstinence on those Fridays which concur with national holidays or patronal feasts, while another bishop may refuse to do so. Each diocese has its own synodal decrees which are obligatory only on the parishes of that diocese.

From a sociological point of view this superimposition of basic cultural patterns from outside the parish is probably the greatest difference between the Catholic parish and the Protestant congregation. The latter has a wide range of selection which may be developed by its minister and participants. This is evidenced not only in the creedal divergences but also in the variety of worship services among the various denominations, as well as among the various con-

---

and the celebration of the liturgical ceremonies." A lay warden is elected by the parishioners every year, and the three most recently elected wardens form the board of administrators. They "set limits to the authority of the parish priest; they also set limits to the authority of the bishop." This is written by the Most Reverend Maurice Roy, archbishop of Quebec, in *The Parish and Democracy in French Canada* (Toronto: University of Toronto Press, 1950), pp. 17 ff. Some American dioceses are "corporation soles," so that the parishes are merely part of the single local corporation, the diocese.

[12] See also the discussion in *Dynamics of a City Church*, Vol. I of *Southern Parish* (Chicago: University of Chicago Press, 1951), chap. 2, "What Is the Parish?"

[13] Hiller's concept of the "institutional group" is partly similar to our concept of the parish as a "superimposed association" in that the cultural system of the Church provides a

common value-orientation for the members of the parish (Ernest T. Hiller, "Institutions and Institutional Groups," *Social Forces*, XX, No. 3 [March, 1942], 297–306).

gregations within the same denomination. These groupings tend much more to be institutionalized associations, in the sense discussed below, than superimposed associations.

(c) The Catholic parish may also be conceptualized as an *institutionalized association*.[14] This is the fact which makes each parish a unique social phenomenon, different from every other parish. In other words, the patterned relationships in each urban parish have become institutionalized *locally*, by and for these particular people over a period of several generations in this designated territory of so many city blocks. In this sense, the parochial social system may be said to be a product of its own members.

As Wach remarks, "the sociologist of religion, interested in the study of the cultic group, cannot be satisfied with reviewing its theology as the foundation of the theory and practice of fellowship among its members."[15] Even the most sympathetic observer will note that the facts of social life in the urban parish frequently fail to conform to the expectations of social thought and behavior implied in the moral and dogmatic teachings of the Catholic Church.

This is simply another way of saying that, while there are many similarities among Catholic parishes all over the world, there are also distinctive features in each. The associative processes and patterns are formed, maintained, and transmitted by these particular parishioners. They are affected by the age and sex composition, the occupational, marital, economic, and class status of the parishioners, as well as by the manner in which the parishioners perform the roles consonant with these statuses. They are affected by the various personalities which individuate each human interaction, by the goals toward which the roles actually function, and by the strong secular values of the American urban and industrial milieu.

(d) The fourth way in which the Catholic parish may be conceptualized is that of a *communal group*[16] that is, of a number of people who are held together primarily by their high religious values. Clinchy, who is a close observer of religious behavior, says that "the central element in the structure of a group's existence is religion. . . . The heart and will of every culture lie in the beliefs of the group: that is, its religion. Without convictions about what is good, and without specific beliefs about its goals and the means to attain them, the group's *esprit* will decline, and the group will perish."[17]

This concept of the parish as a communal group rests upon the negative notion that the group will perish unless it holds values of a high order. This is one of Sorokin's most emphasized sociological principles: that people are truly integrated by their "systems of meanings

[14] The term "institutionalized group" used by Znaniecki seems to combine both concepts used above, "superimposed association" and "institutionalized association." His definition denotes "groups which are essentially cooperative products of their own members, but whose collective functions and statuses are partly institutionalized by other social groups" (Florian Znaniecki, "Social Organizations and Institutions," in *Twentieth Century Sociology*, eds. Georges Gurvitch and Wilbert E. Moore [New York: Philosophical Library, 1945], p. 212).

[15] Joachim Wach, "Sociology of Religion," in *Twentieth Century Sociology*, p. 428.

[16] MacIver's "communal type" of society, as distinguished from the "associational type," includes a number of factors other than high values (see R. M. MacIver and Charles H. Page, *Society: An Introductory Analysis* [New York: Rinehart & Co., 1937], pp. 8–12, 218–29).

[17] Everett Clinchy, "The Efforts of Organized Religion," *Annals of the American Academy of Political and Social Sciences*, CCXLIV (March, 1946), 128.

and values." [18] Thomas and Znaniecki also use this principle when they call a parish "a kind of great family whose members are united by a community of moral interests." [19] Finally, Donovan remarks that "the members of the parish, both clerical and lay, share in a unity which stems from their common religious beliefs and which finds expression in their joint participation in group functions." [20]

These observations constitute the hypothesis that the *sharing of common values* is the essential sociological and psychological factor of the Catholic parish as a group. Empirical research indicates that the *sharing of functions* is a much more practical factor of unity. In simple terms this means that, when people do things together which they think are worth doing, they tend to be drawn together. The interacting influence of co-operative functions seems to increase the group appreciation of values, which in turn leads to progressive interaction.

It is quite possible that smaller village parishes tend toward the ideal of the communal group. In the large urban parish, however, the great majority of lay persons seem to use the local church as a kind of "service station" for their religious needs: a place to go to Mass and confession, get married, and have their children baptized and their old folks buried. Their communal "social" bond

with the priests and other parishioners is analogous to that which an automobile owner has with the gas-station manager and with the latter's other customers. It is somewhat like the professional relationship between dentist and patients.[21]

While the concept of a genuinely integrated communal group does not apply to the whole urban parish as a social aggregate, this does not mean that primary, communal relationships are completely absent from the parish. As a matter of fact, there is at the heart of every urban parish a group of parishioners who are united primarily through their high religious values. It appearrs that only these can fulfil Thomas and Znaniecki's definition of the parish as a "great family."

(*e*) The fact that various functions are performed and various objectives attained in an organized way leads to the fifth concept of the urban parish as a cluster of *subgroupings*. Each of these has it own objectives, activities, and membership. The pastor is theoretically and ex officio the highest authority in all of them. Their ultimate objective must in some way conform to that of the parish as a whole: the sanctification and salvation of souls. But their immediate objectives help to specify the various groups.

It has been noted that the total parochial association is superimposed and maintained according to universal standards of the Catholic Church. Much more latitude is allowed in the origin and maintenance of the parochial subgroupings. The original impetus for the formation of a group comes sometimes from the people and sometimes from the pastor. Occasionally its formation may be requested by the bishop.

---

[18] Pitirim Sorokin, *Society, Culture and Personality* (New York: Harper & Bros., 1947), p. 127.

[19] William I. Thomas and Florian Znaniecki, *The Polish Peasant in Europe and America* (New York: A. A. Knopf, 1927), I, 275.

[20] John D. Donovan, "The Sociologist Looks at the Parish," *American Catholic Sociological Review*, XI, No. 2 (June, 1950), 68. Wach (*op. cit.*, p. 428) similarly says that "religious communities are constituted by loyalty to an ideal or set of values which is the basis of their communion."

[21] Brogan developed a similar analogy (D. W. Brogan, "The Catholic Church in America," *Harper's*, CC, No. 1200 [May, 1950], 40–50).

These "parish societies" may be classified in many ways, according to age and sex composition, marital status, and religious conditions of membership, although these norms are not in every instance defined. They may be placed on a continuum indicating the degree of success or failure they have experienced in striving for their objectives. They may be divided as formally imposed or locally initiated, who originated them and where.

Probably the most useful sociological approach is that which considers the main functions and goals of the parish subgroupings or "societies." (1) The *liturgical* groups are those which assist at the religious services performed in the church itself. The Acolyte Society, the choir, and the ushers take a more or less direct part in the services; the Ladies' Altar Society provides the appurtenances of the sanctuary. (2) The *sociospiritual* groups are sufficiently distinctive in their functions and objectives to be considered separately from those in the above category. They are organized into social groups for the primary objective of sanctification. They include, for example, the Children of Mary, the sodalities, the junior and senior Holy Name societies, and the Nocturnal Adoration societies. (3) In the category of *educational* groupings are included the parents' clubs, the Confraternity of Christian Doctrine, and study clubs of various kinds. (4) The *ameliorative* groups do the corporal works of mercy, St. Vincent de Paul conferences for men and the Daughters of Mercy for women. In a sense they act as the parochial "relief agencies" for the needy families and individuals of the parish. (5) Finally, the primarily *recreational* objectives are pursued in the Boy and Girl Scouts, Brownies and Cubs, boys' and girls' sport teams, and in the adult committees which promote these groupings.

It must be pointed out, however, that these formally organized subgroupings do not embrace all the parishioners in any parish. Although membership in these voluntary groupings is open to all (except the very youngest children), it is probably true to say that no American urban parish can claim that more than a third of its members are participants in the parochial organizations. Numerically therefore this concept suffers the same limitations as does the parish when considered as a communal group. It cannot be accorded a total application to the parish.

(*f*) The concept of the urban American parish as a *network of family relations* is more subtle and more difficult to analyze. While it is probably false to assert that "religion runs in families," we have found that participation in parochial programs is frequently a "family affair." We noted this particularly in parish organizations: sons and daughters tend to be active in the youth groups when their parents are active in the adult societies of the parish.

In the actual functioning of the urban parish, however, there tends to be a discrete relationship of the individual qua individual to the parish center rather than a "group" relationship as a member of a family. In this the Catholic parish differs most markedly from the Jewish congregation, wherein a man is a member of the congregation as head of the family and others become members through him. In most urban parishes it is a notable fact that the members of a family do not usually attend Mass and other services together. If there are small children in the family, the parents attend Mass separately; the children of school age have their own Mass, at which attendance is obligatory; and the adolescents may go to still another Mass with their friends rather than with the members of their family. The majority of parishioners, however, come to the church without a partner or companion.[22]

It is interesting to note that pastors frequently estimate the size of the parish by the number of families rather than by the number of individuals who live in the parochial territory. Even in one of the largest downtown churches where over six thousand persons attend Mass every Sunday, most of them from hotels and rooming-houses, the pastor still says, "Our parish is made up of only about one hundred and fifty families."[23] This is probably a residual pattern of thinking derived from the era when community, family, and parish tended to be identified. It is also probably the result of the continued system of keeping the census files by families, according to which the data on all members of the family are kept on the same card.

From the point of view of the parishioners themselves, a consciousness of "family membership" in the parish appears to be present only in the nuclear parishioners and those of long residence. This occurs not only because these people are closer to the parish center but also because they are closer to one another. Continuous day-by-day association of the

[22] This is probably not true in suburban parishes or in places where most parishioners go to church in automobiles. Our statistical checks were made in city parishes where the church is within walking distance of most residences.

[23] He refers, of course, to those who have a domicile, or quasi-domicile, in the parish. The transients, called *peregrini,* are not in a strictly canonical sense termed "parishioners" (see Canon 94, nn. 2, 3). Harbrecht (*op. cit.,* pp. 23–24) holds that the canonical axiom, "Quisquis est in paroecia, est de paroecia," applies even in this case. This fluid group constitutes a *de facto* category in the downtown parish, and the pastor quoted in the text remarked that "it would be impossible and illogical to leave them out of consideration in the actual operation of the parish."

social researcher with these families brings out this fact more clearly than any over-all statistical analysis could achieve. These families know the main "Catholic families" of the parochial area; they identify themselves with them and are able to give a quite reliable account of their religious status.

The concept of the parish as a network of family relations is scientifically meaningful as a criterion of the transition from the relatively communal to the relatively associational structure of the urban parish. As an analytical tool for the understanding of the parish, this concept has greater scientific significance in the former type than in the latter. This is precisely because the importance of family membership in the parish tends to fade during a period of several decades, particularly in the urban parish of multiple dwellings. It would be fruitful to contrast this urban situation with the fast-growing suburban parishes, where the majority of families are relatively young and where there is frequently a deliberate attempt to foster community spirit and parish loyalty.

(g) Besides the six general conceptualizations so far described, it seems useful also to think of the urban parish as a series of *statistical categories* into which the membership falls. The significance of a classification of parishioners lies in the comparison of one category with another and of each with the religious ideals and practices which the parish is promoting. In the first volume of *Southern Parish* these categories were employed in many ways according to age, sex, marital status, socioeconomic status, length of residence, amount of schooling, nationality background, etc.

One of the most frequently employed devices in this regard among American sociologists is the attempt to correlate denominational membership with social status. The influence of the Warner

516   Religion and Society

school and the preoccupation of some American sociologists with social stratification have resulted in a number of studies indicating the status of denominations.[24] This has not been pursued to its congregational or parochial refinement, even though it is obvious to any observer that some parishes have "higher status" because they are in better neighborhoods. Internally, however, most urban Catholic parishes include a fairly broad stratification. The correlation of religious fidelity with socioeconomic status is one of the most obvious applications of this concept in the sociology of the parish.

The use of these categories is a practical device for answering many questions concerning the religious observances of the large city parishes. Using age and sex categories, we have been able to show that parishioners of both sexes reach a religious ebb in their thirties and that at all ages females show better religious performance than males.[25] By rearranging the categories in various ways, we have found that single persons are more faithful to religious duties than married persons, those in Catholic marriages better than those in mixed marriages, certain ethnic groups better than others, etc. The value of this approach seems greatest to the parish priest who wishes to probe the weaknesses and recognize the strengths of his parish population in their formal religious observances.

Statistical categories based on religious practices have led to a convenient stratification of the urban parish. For example,

[24] W. R. Goldschmidt, "Class Denominationalism in Rural California Churches," American Journal of Sociology, XLIX, No. 4 (January, 1944), 348–55; Liston Pope, Millhands and Preachers (New Haven: Yale University Press, 1942).

[25] See "The Profile of Catholic Religious Life," American Journal of Sociology, LVIII, No. 2 (September, 1952), 145–49.

the functional deficiencies of the parish may be measured by the size and composition of the "dormant" category, made up of those who are in the parish but not of it. The "marginal" parishioners constitute a number of people who are on the fringe of the parochial aggregate. "Modal" parishioners are the largest number of the ordinary "practicing" Catholics in the area. The relatively small class of "nuclear" parishioners is at the center of parish life, while an even smaller number may be called the "leadership group." Foregoing chapters of this book analyzed these major categories in some detail.

This brief account of seven ways in which the complex social structure of an urban Catholic parish can be abstractly analyzed is not meant to be exhaustive. A conceptual framework is valuable, after all, only in so far as it serves the specific purpose of the social scientist. There is probably no "best way" in which to conceptualize a social unit except the way which best helps the scientist to give meaning to his data. It is possible, therefore, that numerous other approaches may be devised and employed for fruitful empirical research.

We have found, for example, that the study of small informal cliques and of the various subneighborhoods of the parish provide a fascinating insight into the social relations of parishioners. The friendship cliques are not strictly parochial, like the organized subgroupings discussed above, but they tend to show the degree to which primary relationships are carried on with both Catholics and non-Catholics. The subneighborhoods are roughly defined areas surrounding a corner drugstore, grocery store, and/or bar. There are from thirty to forty such areas in the normal residential urban parish. They are valuable sources of knowledge concerning the type of both casual and frequent contacts which parishioners have with their immediate neighbors.

Running through almost all these approaches, however, are two concepts which are basic to the understanding of the urban parish; the first may be termed *functional,* and the other *structural.* The functional approach analyzes the social roles of the persons-in-action within the parochial system. For example, there can be no question but that the key persons in the operation of any Catholic parish are the priests. This is true not only of the direct "care of souls" but also of the whole problem of maintaining the social structure as a going concern. Thus the pastoral roles may be separately analyzed.[26]

Other full-time functionaries in the parish (schoolteachers, secretaries, janitors, etc.) play social roles which cannot be neglected, the study of which tends to give insight into the operation of the total parochial system. They are subsidiary roles which have been institutionalized over a period of time, and they are collectively important in achieving the general objectives of the parish. Also open to analysis are the roles of the lay persons who are acting either as individuals or as group members in the various voluntary activities which occur in every urban parish.

[26] See *Social Relations in the Urban Parish,* chap. 10, discussion of the priest's roles.

The structural approach ties together all these roles in the rank ordering and communicational system of the parish. The so-called "chain of command" or bureaucracy of any social unit is frequently unobtrusive and informal. This is an important factor, and sometimes a crucial one, in the urban culture where parishioners, like other Americans, have become imbued with the democratic ideology. Crisis situations bring to the fore the fact that in the ultimate analysis the parish is administered by the priests and not by the laity.

The evolving urban parish in America, where culturally attuned priests are the administrators, seems to be steering a psychologically difficult course between two extremes. The ecclesiastical constitution cannot allow the "congregational system" wherein the lay people run the church, while the active vocation of the parishioner would wither under an "authoritarian system" wherein the lay people are mere passive subjects of church administration. The priest-parishioner relationship is, of course, reciprocal. The laity cannot do without the clergy; the clergy cannot do without the laity. The relationship of these statuses has become structured in the parish and must be assumed to exist in all the various conceptualizations which have been suggested in this chapter.

2 · *Toward a Typology of Religious Orders*

E. K. FRANCIS

ABSTRACT. *From a sociological viewpoint two phenomena have to* *be distinguished: the community of religiosi and the religious order properly speaking. The former corresponds to the psychological group and the familistic or Gemeinschaft type, while the latter represents an organized group of the Gesellschaft*

SOURCE. E. K. Francis, "Toward a Typology of Religious Orders," reprinted from *American Journal of Sociology,* 55, March, 1950, pp. 437–449 by permission of The University of Chicago Press.

type. The principal historical types are analyzed to show the stages from the pure community of religiosi to the fully developed order: monasticism, as a total way of life; the canons regular and military orders combining life "in religion" with the status of priests or knights "in the world"; the friars, who tend toward a purposive organization in the service of the church; and, finally, the Jesuit order, the mature product of a long evolution, with its professional devotion to the objective institute, rationality, individualization, and depersonalization of intragroup relations.

The present article is an attempt to apply a specifically sociological frame of reference to the analysis of a class of religious phenomena commonly referred to as "religious orders." [1] As we shall see, how-

[1] This paper is the result of studies made in a manner frequently unsystematic during more than ten years and involving largely direct observation of life in the different orders and interviews with many of their members. Thus it is impossible to make always exact reference to sources of information. I am indebted to the Reverend Philip L. Hanley, O.P., and Dr. Gerhart B. Ladner, both of the Notre Dame faculty, for their valuable suggestions as to the wording of certain passages, and to the Reverend Josef A. Jungmann, S.J., of the University of Innsbruck, for checking the parts on the Jesuit order. The printed source material, though extensive, includes publications which, as a rule, treat the subject from an historical or theological rather than from a sociological viewpoint. The only major sociological monograph is Gustav Gundlach's essay on the Jesuit order, *Zur Soziologie der katholischen Ideenwelt und des Jesuitenordens* (Freiburg: Herder, 1927). The same author has also contributed a more general article on the subject to the *Handwörterbuch der Soziologie*. Much information on the subject in

ever, this classification which is suggested not only by common-sense notions but also by the terminology adopted by other disciplines, particularly history, is inadequate from the viewpoint of the sociologist.

The subject of our discussion is the different forms under which life "in religion" has been organized in the Roman Catholic church. A person who leads a life "in religion," as distinguished from life "in the world," will be called a religiosus (plural: religiosi) to avoid the ambiguity of the English equivalent "religious." Life in religion implies a manner of conduct which by the church is recognized as being different from that expected of any ordinary religious person, and which is based on some promise to accept certain obligations considered as being morally superior and conducive to a state of greater spiritual perfection, in addition to the duties shared by all members of the church.[2]

I

Life in religion need not imply membership in any religious order properly

general and on the different orders is contained in all the larger encyclopedias, particularly the *Enciclopedia universal ilustrada europeo-americana.* The most complete survey of the field will be found in Max Heimbucher, *Die Orden und Congregationen der katholischen Kirche* (2 vols.; Paderborn: Schöningh, 1933).

[2] In modern canon law the term "religiosus" is used with a more limited meaning referring specifically to some form of common life and the vows of obedience, chastity, and poverty: "Status religiosus seu stabilis in communi vivendi modus, quo fideles, praeter communia praecepta, evangelica quoque consilia servanda per vota obedientiae, castitatis et paupertatis suscipiunt, ab omnibus in honore habendus est" (*Codex juris canonici,* canon 487).

speaking, for religiosi may also belong to communities which are not organized as orders. This distinction between the community of religiosi and the religious order is sociologically significant. The ideal type of the monastic community conforms to the type of a relatively small personalized group and coincides with what has been termed a psychological group, all of whose members exist as a group in the psychological field of each individual.[3] The religious order, on the other hand, is a far more abstract and complex form of social organization, referred to in sociological literature variously as institutional group or association (E. T. Hiller), social organization (F. Znaniecki, Krech and Crutchfield), abstract collectivity (L. v. Wiese and H. Becker), or organized group (P. A. Sorokin). Here the definition of the group in the minds of its members as well as of the out-group is based on abstract notions as to who belongs to the group, as to the (total or segmental) roles of the individual members within the group, and as to the value system common to the group, that is, primarily as to what Sorokin has termed the "law-norms" of a group;[4] this definition is, furthermore, based on symbols, cultural products, enforcing agents and techniques, rather than on the direct experience of every

member as a concrete person and of the group as composed of these concrete persons.[5]

The community of religiosi represents an intimate face-to-face group which, in the extreme case, performs practically all the functions of the natural family short of biological procreation. Though the pure type will be found but rarely under modern conditions, early monastic communities indeed represented highly personalized and localized groups all of whose members existed explicitly as a group in the psychological field of each individual. Moreover, its candidates for membership were frequently adopted at a tender age and underwent at least later childhood training within the community to the exclusion of practically all out-group contracts.

By contrast, the religious order tends to substitute more impersonal, segmental, and abstract relationships among the members of its local establishments, more properly called "convents," [6] that is, gathering places rather than communities. Its members are no more bound by the typically monastic *stabilitas loci* (permanence of residence in one place) to the community by which they have been received into religion but can be moved and do move in the course of their lives from one convent to another, or even may take up residence in other places if the purpose or interests of the order should require it.

The sociological implications of this distinction are obvious. The monastic novice enters a specific monastery. During his training period he is systematically being reeducated and remodeled, above all by participation in the intimate

---

[3] Cf. David Krech and Richard S. Crutchfield, *Theory and Problems of Social Psychology* (New York: McGraw-Hill Book Co., 1948), p. 368.

[4] Cf. his *Society, Culture and Personality: Their Structure and Dynamics* (New York: Harper & Bros., 1947), pp. 71–85. Although in general agreement with Sorokin's description of the law-norms as the essence of any organized group (*ibid.*, p. 77), we would prefer to substitute the more neutral term C-norms (or the constituent normative system underying every kind of organized groups or O-groups), for reasons to be discussed in some other context.

[5] Cf. Krech and Crutchfield, *op. cit.*, p. 369.

[6] Although in the English language the word "convent" now denotes nunneries, it can be quite properly applied to the local establishments of any order.

life of the concrete, rather small, face-to-face group, by exclusive interaction with all its members, and by indoctrination with its group ways (or observances). Only after his *conversio morum*,[7] that is, his complete conversion to the mores of this particular group, has been assured, is he received into it as a full member, a professed monk, and by his vows becomes an integrated part of the group, severing for his lifetime all ties with the outside world. Even today most of the members of the stricter orders (Trappists, cloistered nuns) after joining the organization are on principle not allowed to have any social contacts except with the members of their own community, and even these are rigorously restricted by such provisions as the rule of perpetual silence.

In the Jesuit order, on the other hand, which is the most developed form of a typical order, the unit is not the local community but the order as such which for administrative purposes is subdivided into provinces or territorial units. These include several local establishments some of which are set aside for the specific purpose of training future members. These training centers, however, are not

meant to become the permanent residence of the candidates; on the contrary, Jesuits may expect to be moved on short notice not only within their own country but literally to any spot on the earth where the order needs them. Any permanent attachment either to persons or places is definitely discouraged, while mingling with the "world" is implied in the Jesuit's life-goal of active apostolate. Complete segregation from outside contacts is maintained only during training and the periodical retreats which may last for as long as a month. Beyond this, withdrawal from the world is observed not by well-defined and integrated groups but individually, and this largely on a purely psychological level in the form of that inner "detachment" so greatly emphasized by St. Ignatius of Loyola.[8] Membership in the Jesuit order and other organizations of the same type has thus an entirely different meaning from that in a Benedictine abbey. While monastic life is essentially a collective undertaking, the Jesuit type of order aims at the efficient organization of specially trained individuals as determined by utility and purpose. The former is of the *Gemeinschaft* (Tönnies), familistic (Sorokin), and essentially primary (Cooley) group type, while the latter is of the *Gesellschaft* or contractual type of social groups. As we will see further below, the other types of religious orders represent intermediary stages between these extremes.

In view of these basic differences between the various types of religious

---

[7] This phrase is actually included in the formula of the vow required from the monk according to the Rule of St. Benedict. A different reading is *conversatio morum*, which is at present used, but its interpretation has caused considerable controversy. However, in the formula of profession included in the Rule of the Order of Templars, which is based on that by St. Benedict, we find the following revealing passage: "Vis assumere tibi conversationem fratrum nostrorum?" Cf. Henri de Curzon, *La Règle du Temple* (Paris: Renouard, 1886), p. 167. Although another manuscript has the traditional *conversatio morum*, the incident proves nevertheless that the meaning given to the phrase conforms with our interpretation: What is expected of the new member is a promise to accept the ways and mores of this particular community as his own.

[8] Cf. *Spiritual Exercises*, "Foundation." Gundlach, *op. cit.*, p. 59, describes this detachment or indifference as "die Fähigkeit, sich ungehindert von persönlicher Voreingenommenheit im alleinigen Hinblick auf das transzendentale Endziel zu entscheiden" (the faculty of making one's decisions exclusively in view of the transcendental final goal and without being impeded by any personal bias).

orders, the question arises as to their common sociological denominator, disregarding theological implications for the present purpose. One of the generic factors of all phenomena of this kind seems to be isolation. Everywhere, though in different degrees, we find the idea of a withdrawal from the "world" in order to be able to devote one's self to a set of higher, spiritual, values. Thus asceticism, that is, self-denial of good commonly enjoyed or pursued by the society from which one withdraws, wholly or partially, appears as an essential characteristic of life in religion. The specific end which is supposedly facilitated by this withdrawal is the attainment of certain religious ideals which the person feels cannot be achieved to the same degree or with the same assurance of success in his "normal" social setting. Life in religion always implies the minimization or rejection of some, and the maximization of other, values included in the culture within which the religiosus is living physically. However, this renunciation of the "world" is never complete but always a highly selective modification of given sociocultural patterns. For in many respects the religiosus remains imbedded in his original society; he emphasizes one of its central value complexes while considering others as an obstacle to its full realization. Moreover, he reorganizes his own way of life accordingly by assuming a new social role which is eventually accepted and even institutionalized by the larger society.

II

Our preceding discussion suggests that religious orders, though based on the relative segregation of their members from the ordinary run of life, are always functionally interrelated with a given sociocultural system. However, once they have become institutionalized, they show the same tendency as all institutions, namely, to perpetuate themselves as historical types of organized groups independent of the major cultural changes which affect society at large. Of course, a religious order may also establish houses outside its original environment (foreign missions) and thereby transplant its typical pattern into an alien society. All the major types of religious orders which have come into existence in the Western world in the course of the last fifteen centuries can still be found in many parts of the world, with the sole exception of the military orders, at least in their original meaning. They must be understood on the basis of the historical culture in which they have originated.

We have seen that the common ground where all orders meet is a religious ideal characterized by a selective emphasis given to certain portions of biblical precepts of conduct which the church as such has not made absolutely binding upon all its members but whose practice has been left to the free choice of individuals or groups of individuals aspiring at a greater religious perfection. As long as the church itself consisted of small and segregated groups of fervent believers, and as long as it had preserved all the vigor of a social movement, little distinction was made between life in the world and life in religion. This distinction was eventually suggested mainly by three events in the later stages of church history.

1. The religious persecutions of the third century found individual believers reacting in three typical ways: by martyrdom, apostasy, or flight to places remote enough to allow their escape from the secular arm. The latter course is directly responsible for the organization of the first monastic communities in the deserts of the Near East, but the idea persisted and actually spread after the original reason had disappeared.

2. The church, in its gradual adapta-

tion to the requirements of life in the world, was ever harassed by zealots and heretical sects who accused it of disloyalty to the various ascetical precepts which can be found in the Bible or can be read into it. While the church consistently rejected moral extremism as expressed by various sects, it also considered the formation of celibatarian groups under its own supervision as a safety valve counteracting both sectarianism and license.

3. Finally, in the course of the fourth century, when the church became an accepted institution, ecclesiastical life at large lost much of its original exclusiveness and grew "worldly." Thus people endowed with a more than average religious zeal and mystical urge tended to withdraw from this new public activity of the church and to retire as hermits into the wilderness. From hermitism there is only a small step to coenobitical life which was brought about by the union of several anchorites into monastic communities. Both St. Anthony, who is often acclaimed as the father of hermits, and St. Pachomius, the author of one of the first monastic rules, are typical of this period of transition from the church as a religious movement to the legally instituted state church.

Monasticism[9] was introduced to the West under the direct influence of these oriental models and was fostered in the fourth and fifth centuries by the progressive disintegration of the social order in the Latin Empire. Here St. Augustine, who had been inclined to consider the

[9] Cf. Dom Cuthbert Butler, *Benedictine Monachism: Studies in Benedictine Life and Rule* (2d ed.; New York: Longmans, Green & Co., 1924); Dom John Chapman, *Saint Benedict and the Sixth Century* (New York: Longmans, Green & Co., 1929); also the article "Monastic and Family Life" by E. K. Francis, which was published anonymously in the Benedictine periodical *Pax* (Gloucester: Prinknash Abbey, 1940).

sack of Rome in 410 as a symbol of the impending collapse of ancient civilization, organized his parochial and diocesan clergy into a community along monastic lines. It was his example and certain of his writings, some of them spurious, particularly the so-called "Rule of St. Augustine," which were largely responsible for the emergence of one of the two original types of religious orders in the West, the canons regular. Toward the end of the same century, another famous lawgiver for religious communities, St. Benedict of Nursia, fled from law school into the wilderness, despairing of the traditional mission in public service which was to be his lot as the scion of a distinguished family. In 528 he laid the foundations of the first Benedictine monastery at Monte Cassino.

Now it should be clear that Western monasticism did not originate with St. Benedict. In his time the movement had already spread throughout Italy, Gaul, and particularly Ireland, whence it was brought to northern and Central Europe. It seems, however, that the successful abbot was commissioned by the civil authorities to compile a legal code, along the lines of codifications initiated under Diocletian, which would regulate the life of all those who put themselves outside the ordinary parochial and diocesan organization of the church by choosing a life in religion.

Thus Western monasticism, which became identical with Benedictinism, is clearly based on the culture of Christian antiquity. It was in no way a purposive organization but rather a style of life which gradually found a common form of expression and eventually was institutionalized by both church and state. The unit is not the "order" but the local community of religiosi patterned after the model of the patriarchical patrician family and the Roman villa or estate. Its economy and daily routine follow closely the traditional pattern. The *pater familias* now becomes the abbot, although his dominant position is given a new meaning by making complete renunciation of one's own will to the will of God as represented in his person, the one pillar of Benedictine spiritualism. Only in the designation of a successor to a deceased abbot does the Rule necessarily deviate from the model of the natural family and adopt electoral procedures copied from contemporary political institutions.

With the sole exception of the abbot, the monks are conceived as minors without any personal status or property apart from that held by the community as such under his trusteeship. Nevertheless, Christian concepts did introduce an element of individualism by recognizing personal moral responsibility and the ideal of personal perfection. The Benedictine idea of personality, however, comes closest to the Hellenic model of the *anthropos kalos k' agathos* (ἄνθρωπος καλὸς κἀγαθός), the harmoniously developed natural and spiritual man who avoids all extremes, even those of religious zeal. Thus Benedictine frugality is not conceived as a life-goal in itself as with the Franciscans but rather as one ascetical means among others to achieve a type of life conducive to union with God. It could probably be said that the monastic style of life is characterized by its regular rhythm of daily routine and by the harmony between work and worship; between physical, intellectual, and spiritual activities; between a charitable understanding for human needs and rigorous discipline.

Although the monastic community is primarily a way of life for its members, the *opus Dei,* that is, the common performance of the daily liturgy as an incessant act of worship of God's majesty, could be called its main objective. This is also the point where monasticism becomes integrated into the life of the church and obtains its specific function as an organ of liturgical worship. Thus, in

their relations to the hierarchical organization of the church, the Benedictines have met probably with fewer difficulties than any other religious order; until recent times, they have never shown any ambition to make themselves the champions of any particular doctrine, religious practice, or movement within the church.

While the original spiritual basis of monasticism has barely changed throughout its long history, it did undergo several modifications. These were usually a result of the need for periodic revivals of the ancient observances and for the inner reform of communities which had lost their initial fervor. The first of these reform movements was initiated by the Abbey of Cluny. By 1109 there were about two thousand dependent monasteries forming an association which looked to Cluny as their head and regularly held general chapters attended by all the local superiors under the chairmanship of the abbot of the motherhouse. A century after Cluny the organization of Citeaux was founded, which went a step further beyond this and similar "congregations" of Benedictine abbeys and priories, by imposing hierarchical controls and a common set of norms and observances upon all its affiliated communities. The Cistercian order may thus be compared with a constitutional monarchy under the abbot-general as the sovereign head and with the general chapter as its supreme agency or parliament.

The communities of hermits (and, since the eleventh century, orders of hermits such as the Carthusians) appear as a variety of the basic monastic pattern. Originally there were three types of hermits: (1) those who, like St. Jerome or St. Nicholas of Flüe, lived in almost complete isolation, at least for part of their lives, as individuals and without any kind of organization; (2) those who gathered together in the same neighborhood and maintained a loose organization for mutual protection and edification such as certain anchorites in the Egyptian desert; (3) and those who built their cells near some community of monks. The Rule of St. Benedict actually makes provisions for hermits who would attach themselves in a very loose way to a monastery. Present-day orders of hermits follow the second type, but their organization is much more definite and formal. Although each hermit inhabits his separate cell or little building which he leaves only on rare occasions, the members of a local establishment are united under a common government, have common economic institutions, and even meet periodically. Thus they may be said to form a stable community of religiosi with a rigorously limited pattern of social interaction.

Although attempts have been made to trace the tradition back to St. Augustine, the various communities of canons founded during the earlier Middle Ages in accordance with the Augustinian model and Rule were doubtlessly influenced by the high prestige which monastic life in its Benedictine form of expression was then enjoying, it being considered as a more perfect state even than priesthood itself.[10] The gradual en-

[10] Thomas Aquinas, e.g., teaches that among the priestly hierarchy only the episcopal status but not that of the other clergy is to be considered as one of perfection. See *Summa theologiae*, II-II, Q. 184, particularly Art. 6: "Unde manifestum est quod non omnes praelati sunt in statu perfectionis sed soli episcopi"; and Art. 8: "Ergo videtur quod religiosi sint perfectiores quam archidiaconi vel presbyteri curati," to which Thomas seems to agree when he answers: "Et ideo comparatio status religionis ad eorum [i.e., presbyterum] est sicut universalis ad particulare et sicut holocausti ad sacrificium." The best treatment of the canons regular is to be found in François Petit, *La Spiritualité des Prémontrés aux XIIe et XIIIe siècles* (Paris: Vrin, 1947).

forcement of celibacy upon the secular clergy also suggested that the latter should imitate the common life of monastic communities, and the Fourth Lateran Council of 1059 exhorted the clergy to live wherever possible in religious communities while pursuing their pastoral duties. Thus particularly the clergy attached to cathedral and other large churches were organized into canonical chapters which were essentially modeled after monastic principles and forms of life. However, the enforcement of one of the monastic ideals, namely, the renunciation of one's personal property, caused great difficulties, since canons were usually chosen from noble and wealthy families. The problem was eventually solved by making a distinction between communities of secular canons, that is, priests who retained their family property, and canons regular who accepted all the monastic principles and ideals; like the monks, they were exempt from episcopal jurisdiction and formed independent communities of religiosi under their own abbots without however giving up their sacerdotal and pastoral functions.

The most important of the many organizations of canons regular which sprang up during the eleventh and twelfth centuries was the order of Prémontré, founded by St. Norbert in 1121–26. It not only was contemporary with that of Citeaux but followed the Cistercian pattern also in its structure. Although the local community is still the basic unit and the canon is primarily a lifelong member of the abbey in which he has been professed, all the local superiors are required to attend the annual general chapter, while regular visitations of all dependent monasteries are carried out by the motherhouse. Moreover, a member had the right to appeal from the decision of a local superior to the abbot of Prémontré and finally to the visitor, who would refer the matter to the general chapter in the last instance. This was an important step beyond the unrestricted personal rule of the abbot as visualized by St. Benedict, but it parallels certain aspects of the Cistercian form of centralized organization.

The Premonstratensians, like other canons regular, could be considered as an attempt to adapt the basic pattern of monasticism to the needs and responsibilities of a particular status group within secular society, namely, priests. Monasticism had fully developed the guiding principles and forms of organization for life in religion and had become the accepted institution for all those seeking greater religious perfection. Priests, on the other hand, were bound to the "world" by their apostolic mission. The combination of the way of life in religion with the duties of priests in the "world" resulted in an interesting modification of the basic monastic pattern. As we know, the monks whom St. Benedict had in mind were as a rule not ordained priests and were to live completely segregated from the outside world devoted only to work, contemplation, worship, and their own perfection. Even the few ordained monks within a community would serve merely its own spiritual needs. Thus the recitation of the psalms (the Divine Office, later incorporated in the so-called breviary the recitation of which has been made compulsory for all priests as well as monks) and not the Mass stood in the center of Benedictine liturgy. This is radically changed with the idea that the canons, though following the monastic way of life for most of the time, should nevertheless continue to perform their ministerial functions, particularly preach and offer Holy Mass. Thereby the original complete segregation from the world has to be given up, and adjustments have to be made with regard not only to liturgical spirituality but also to the greater emphasis given to studies as compared with manual labor and to the greater facility in leaving the monastic inclosure at least temporarily. Finally, we find for the first time the notion that life in religion is not simply a way of life as against life in the world but serves a definite purpose in aiding the church's apostolic mission in the world.

The situation is somewhat similar with regard to the military orders.[11] Despite a vast literature on their political and cultural achievements (and shortcomings), actually too little is known of their social organization and inner day-by-day life to permit a conclusive sociological analysis. The few remnants of military orders still in existence have undergone profound changes, usually by becoming orders of priests of the conventional type, or mere confraternities of noblemen, so that their original pattern cannot be reconstructed from observation. Moreover, it seems that their organization was often vague and subject to frequent changes under the impact of local conditions or historical events. As far as we can see, the idea of the military order had apparently its origin mainly in the fraternities of laymen, so numerous during the Middle Ages, who attached themselves to some existing organization of religiosi and in part imitated their way of life so as to gain the spiritual benefits but also certain advantages of a more legal and secular nature which they were enjoying. Among the latter, incidentally, was the exemption from episcopal jurisdiction, both ecclesiastical and secular, which carried, for instance, the right of receiving the sacraments and a Christian

[11] Cf. J. Prutz, *Die geistlichen Ritterorden* (Berlin, 1908); J. Delaville le Roulx, *Les Hospitalliers en Terre Sainte et à Chypre* (Paris, 1904); E. J. King, *The Rule, Statutes and Customs of the Hospitallers, 1099–1310* (London: Methuen, 1934); Curzon, *op. cit.*; and for the Spanish military orders the respective articles in the *Enciclopedia universal ilustrada europeo-americana.*

burial even in localities which were under the ecclesiastical interdict.

In approaching the present subject, we must above all realize the enormous value attached to membership in an institution of religious perfection in an age when the salvation of one's own soul was everybody's foremost concern. Again we find an attempt to combine life in religion with life in the world and a blending of a secular status group with that of religiosi. The ideal of Christian knighthood in itself had already a religious connotation, which is so clearly expressed in the French version of the Rule of the Temple with the following words: "En cele religion est florie et ressuscitée orde de chevalerie. Laquele orde desprisoit amor de justise, ce que apartenoit a son office, et non faisoit pas ce que devoit: ce est defendre povres, veves, orfelines et yglises." [12] That these together with the defense of Christianity against the infidels and the conquest of the Holy Land were essentially functions in the service of the church, similar though on a different level from those performed by canons regular, was eventually recognized by granting several organizations of knights the canonical status of true orders of religiosi with all the privileges, exemptions, and benefits due to them. But even with regard to the traditional obligations of religiosi the elaborate penal code as well as the section on conventual life included in the Rule of the Temple give sufficient proof of the fact that the professed knights, sergeants-at-arms, and chaplains were subject to the same severe regimen as the most rigorous orders of monks.[13] Considerable adjustments had to be made in view of their participation in military campaigns and the position and duties of the many dignitaries and officers, but sometimes also with reference to individual property and even matrimony.

The military order had usually a complex economic organization, an elaborate administrative mechanism, and a hierarchical government with a complicated system of elections and delegated powers. Nevertheless, the rule of the high master seems to have been strictly centralistic and rather autocratic. The whole structure appears guided much more by the secular concepts of medieval feudalism than by the classical notions of monasticism. It thus had difficulties in maintaining the basic elements of life in religion against the many secular ambitions and responsibilities of its members, much more so than the canons regular, whose clerical status made the combination with monastic ideals more congruent and workable.

III

The friars or mendicants indicate the next stage in the development of religious orders. Their principal representatives, the Dominicans and Franciscans,[14] started out as it were at opposite poles, only to blend with each other eventually to such an extent that most observers find it rather difficult to distinguish them in

[12] "In this religious order, the order of knighthood flourishes and has been revived. Which [latter] order despises the love of justice, which belongs to its office, and is not doing what it ought to do: namely, defend the poor, widows, orphans and churches" (Curzon, op. cit., pp. 12-13).

[13] Ibid., pp. 153-64, 285-336, and 170-215. The status of sergeants was offered to those brethren who were not of noble birth.
[14] See G. R. Galbraith, The Constitution of the Dominican Order (Manchester: University Press, 1925); Raphael M. Huber, A Documented History of the Franciscan Order . . . , 1182-1517 (Milwaukee: Nowiny Publishing Apostolate, 1944); and Edward Hutton, The Franciscans in England, 1224-1538 (Boston, 1928).

their modern forms as different types. Both are a product of the revolutionary social changes which characterize the later Middle Ages. We must think above all of the breakdown of feudal agrarianism and the rise of urban society, the restlessness and relative mobility of the masses, the problems of the new proletariat, and the spread of learning and rational thought among ever wider social strata. All this found bishops, secular clergy, and the older orders largely unable to cope with the spiritual needs of their flock, who were in a state of general ferment. Significantly enough, the Franciscans built their little churches mainly in the suburbs outside the city walls, while the convents of the Dominicans are to be found near the quarters of the burghers and the seats of learning in the centers of old cities.

Even before the friars had made their appearance, we saw that life in religion had gradually acquired definite purposive aspects as against the original concept of a total way of life in segregation from the world. The orders came more and more to be considered as specialized armies in the service of the church. It had become customary to exempt all religious orders from episcopal jurisdiction and to put them directly under the authority of the Holy See. But the relationship between the Roman Curia and the military orders had been especially emphasized in the fight against the infidels, which was a matter of the whole church rather than of its basic territorial units, the individual bishoprics. This idea is taken up by the friars who put themselves explicitly as *milites Christi* at the disposal of his vicar on earth, the pope. But the fight shifted from the enemy without to new enemies within, the various heresies and the general social disorder engendered by the upheaval.

What St. Francis (1182–1226) ap-

parently set out to create was not so much a religious order as a religious movement, a loose confraternity of inspired disciples with nothing more to keep them together than a brief program of exalted ideals taken from the New Testament, and an urge to bring about the inner reform of Christianity, and even mankind, by propagating the imitation of Christ, thus understood, through personal example and exhortation. In its beginning, at least, the Franciscan movement was essentially based on personal devotion to the founder and his charismatic leadership. It swept aside all the barriers of segregated life and denounced the traditional means of economic support which had lent to the older orders their solid foundation. Although the Poverello of Assisi lived to see his movement gradually converted into a more objectivized, stable, and thus also more permanent institution for religiosi, up to this day his order, now split into three separate organizations (including the Capuchins), seems to have preserved some of the charismatic aspects of the original movement. Perhaps this is also responsible for the fact that the Franciscans, more than most other orders, have found themselves so frequently in conflict with the hierarchical organization of the church; but at the same time also for the great attraction they ever have had for the many followers of the "Poverello" of Nazareth, which at present makes them the largest religious family in the Catholic church.

St. Dominic (1170–1221), on the other hand, himself a canon regular and a contemporary of St. Francis, deliberately built up an elaborate centralized organization of religiosi as an efficient instrument for a definite purpose, namely, the conversion of heretics by means of the spoken word. In this way, the Order of Preachers became the first real order in the full meaning of the word as used

in this context. Nevertheless, much of
the original pattern of life in religion is
still retained. Outwardly, a Dominican
convent resembles a monastic community
in its routine, government, and discipline.
According to Galbraith, it would seem
that in the beginning the friar was, theoretically at least, still a member of the
house in which he had been professed.
In practice, however, this relation was
often limited to the obligation of praying
for the members of the original community, while in every other respect he
was linked to the place where he happened to work at any given time. Today,
Dominicans are primarily members of a
given province. Moreover, the vow of
obedience is not made to the local or
provincial prior but to the master-general
of the whole order.

The concept of authority too has undergone radical changes. The Benedictine abbot was the absolute paternal
master of a given family of religiosi and
their "living rule" in all temporal as well
as spiritual matters. The Dominican
prior, on the other hand, is rather a minister of the community with strictly
limited rights and functions. All major
decisions as to economic affairs or the
reception of novices have to be made
in conjunction with the local chapter. A
republican form of government pervades
the whole organization. The representatives of the local houses in the provincial
chapters and of the provinces in the
general chapter are no more the respective local or provincial superiors alone,
as was the case in the Cistercian organization, but besides the official functionaries there are delegates elected for the
specific purpose of representing the membership of the subordinate units. The
final authority of the order is vested in
the general chapter, the legislative assembly of the representatives of the
provincial chapters, which delegates
powers to the master-general, the provincial and conventual chapters and their

officers. While there is no need to go
into the details of the Dominican constitutions, it is important to realize that
St. Dominic and his successors were
bent on creating the most efficient organization which would allow the training of
an army of specialists and their use to the
best advantage of the church for the
salvation of souls.[15]

Accordingly the observances which
had been so characteristic of life in religion were either reduced to rather
perfunctory performance such as the
common office, or eliminated as waste of
time and effort like manual labor. The
specialist who was to be made free to
devote all his effort to the accomplishment of the order's objective was the
eloquent and cool-headed preacher well
equipped to disprove heresies, to argue
the Catholic faith as a self-consistent,
reasonable doctrine, and to attract sympathy for the cause by the austerity and
simplicity of his personal demeanor. The
ideal of communal poverty, which the
Dominicians adopted similar to the Franciscans, now appears in its proper light.
As Galbraith remarks in a somewhat
pointed manner: "With St. Francis the
wedding of the Lady Poverty was an
object in itself. St. Dominic consented to
the surrender of temporal goods only
because he thought it would make his
followers more free to study and to
preach."[16] While the renunciation not
only of personal but also of communal
property (somewhat mitigated in the
course of time) was to Dominic a means
for eminently practical and rational ends,
it was to the Franciscans a primary

[15] This idea is clearly stated in the constitutions of the Order of Preachers: ". . . et
studium nostrum ad hoc principaliter arden-
terque summo opere debeat intendere ut
proximorum animabus possimus *utilis* esse";
and again: ". . . cum ordo noster *specialiter*
ob predicationem et animarum salutem ab
initio noscatur institutus fuisse. . . ."
[16] *Op cit.*, p. 179.

ascetical ideal congruent with their specific image of Christ, which concentrates upon his poor life on earth, particularly its beginning and end.

The Society of Jesus, the last of the typical forms to be studied under which life in religion has been organized, appears as the mature product of a long evolution. All the principles in which its structure is anchored had been known and practiced long before St. Ignatius of Loyola. The trend toward centralization and constitutionalism has its source as far back as in Citeaux, perhaps even Cluny; pastoral care was emphasized by the canons regular; the military orders had already put themselves at the direct disposal of the pope; specialization, efficiency, and mobility were typical ideas of St. Dominic; and the tendency toward individualism has its parallel in the Franciscan movement. Yet, all this was brought to a climax in the Jesuit order where it overshadows the original, monastic model of life in religion to such an extent that the latter is almost lost to sight.

Life in religion, as understood by the Jesuit type of religious order, is no more a total way of life, not even essentially in contrast to life in the world. It is rather a specialized occupation aimed at influencing the world by mingling with it. The constitutions of the Society of Jesus state as its objective the care for the salvation and perfection of the souls, not only of its own members but with equal emphasis on their fellow-men.[17]

Gustav Gundlach, himself a Jesuit scholar, offers an interesting analysis and interpretation of the constituent norms underlying this type of organized group. According to him, an order is a permanent community of life (*Lebensgemeinschaft*) which is based on a typical image of the living Christ common to all its members.[18] The image of Christ characteristic of the Jesuit order is "der Sohn, der . . . für die religiöse Zentrierung jeder Zeit und jedes Lebens kämpft und dafür um Mitarbeiter wirbt. . . . Christus als hilfesuchender Kämpfer gegen die Entgottung der Welt."[19] From this follows the dynamic ideal of work which probably is the most pronounced trait of the Society of Jesus. For by his knowledge of co-operating with the Divine Grace in guiding the world to God, the Jesuit is spurred to utmost activity toward success. "Bei aller Betonung der . . . 'guten Meinung,'" writes Gundlach, quoting the *Summarium constitutionum*, 1, "erhofft man im Orden von der Tätigkeit 'Frucht.'"[20] To achieve the greatest possible success, a purposive rational method is adopted which is ever ready to re-examine traditional standards. Thus the original liturgical functions of the community of religiosi are now completely abolished as a hindrance to ef-

---

[17] "Finis huius societatis est non solum saluti et perfectioni propriarum animarum cum divina gratia vacare, sed cum eadem impense in salutem et perfectionem proximorum incumbere" (*Examen generale*, cap. 1, par. 2). We are quoting from one of the earlier editions: *Constitutiones Societatis Jesu; cum earum declarationibus* (Rome: Collegium Romanum, 1640). The literature on the Jesuits including the publications of original documents is very extensive. Besides the con-

stitutions, see particularly the *Spiritual Exercises* by St. Ignatius of Loyola and the *Ratio studiorum* of 1599, both available in many editions. Cf. also Gundlach, *op. cit.*, and Ludwig Koch, S.J., *Jesuiten-Lexikon: Die Gesellschaft Jesu einst und jetzt* (Paderborn: Bonifacius-Drukerei, 1934).

[18] *Op. cit.*, p. 50.

[19] ". . . the son [of God] who is fighting for the religious orientation of every age and every life, and who is recruiting collaborators for it. . . . Christ, as the warrior against the secularization of the world, asking for help" (*ibid.*, p. 94).

[20] "Despite all the emphasis put on the good intention, the order is expecting that this activity will bear fruit" (*ibid.*, p. 98).

fective work. This rationality is also shown in the realistic consideration given to concrete conditions and to the prospects of any given procedure. While Gundlach stresses the specific religious motivation of the Jesuit order, he admits that "its idea of work comes close to that of Capitalism" as understood and analyzed by Max Weber and his school.[21]

As every other type of order, the Society of Jesus is strongly influenced by the spirit of the time in which it originated. This is also revealed in its positive evaluation of the world. According to Gundlach, it tries to distinguish clearly between the divine and the human factor in social life and history and is ever ready "to adopt whatever appears valuable in the development of the human factor" regardless of any traditions to the contrary.[22] Indeed, the Jesuits have time and again acted as an *avant-garde*, able to assimilate new ideas and trends, without prejudice against innovation and cultural change affecting the world within which they are operating.

Modern also is the whole structure of the order with its decided emphasis put on rational organization in view of a purpose which, as Gundlach indicates with reference to W. Eliasberg, would be impossible to achieve "without the rational, that is technically correct, use of means." [23] It requires from its members complete professional devotion to the common enterprise and unconditional discipline. On the other hand, it is based on a detailed code of work and administration and on a most rigorous centralization. When viewing the Jesuit constitutions, we should avoid drawing comparisons with modern systems of civil government, for the Jesuit order is conceived much less as a self-governing society than as an agency in the service of

the church, more like a modern army or corporation. Its supreme head is the pope, as the vicar of Christ, to whom the highest rank of Jesuits, the *professi*, are personally bound by a fourth vow declaring their readiness to carry out, unconditionally and without questioning, whatever command or mission he would give them within the scope of the Society.[24] From him the general of the order receives his directives as to the work to be done and as to general policies. Within the order itself, however, the general has total spiritual jurisdiction and wields extraordinary authority as its chief executive intrusted with complete responsibility for the whole institute. Either directly or by delegation through subalterns, it is the general who admits and dismisses members, determines their rank, promotion, and work, and who exercises the closest supervision over all and sundry through a clever system of written communications and reports. On the other hand, he himself is bound by the constitutions and is elected for life by the general congregation. However, neither the general nor the provincial assemblies have the same governmental functions as the chapters of many of the older orders. Their composition is in part determined by office, rank, and seniority. Although endowed with legislative powers, they seem to serve above all as mechanisms for the election of the general and of his assistants, a sort of cabinet with consultative functions. However, the *procuratores*, who are elected by the provincial congregations and are much like their ambassadors, do have, theoretically at least, the right to demand the convocation of a general congregation to censure and even depose an unworthy general.[25]

[21] *Ibid.*, p. 100.
[22] *Ibid.*, pp. 104–5.
[23] *Ibid.*, pp. 80–81.
[24] Cf. Koch. *op. cit.*, p. 986.
[25] Cf. Parts VIII and IX of the *Constitutiones*, and Koch, *op. cit.*, articles "General," "Generalversammlung," and "Verfassung."

Although the members of the order, particularly those below the rank of *professi*, are required to reside in one of its local establishments, the notion of a local house forming a permanent or even temporary community is gone; it appears more as a residence and workshop for its casual inmates: as army barracks under a commanding officer who receives his instructions from the provincial chief of staff and ultimately from the high command at the Roman Curia. Originally the exercise of authority did follow patriarchical patterns, and as late as 1923 a general congregation decreed that relations between subordinates and superiors should be guided, in a paternal manner, by clemency, kindness, and charity.[26] Yet, as Koch reminds us, since Claudius Aquaviva, general of the Society from 1581 to 1615, bureaucratic procedures have become prevalent.[27] In the last analysis, each professed member of the order appears as an interchangeable and self-sufficient part, fully trained and equipped to fill his post if need be single-handed. The Jesuits are not so much brethren as comrades-at-arms, sometimes described as a corps of officers destined to lead the people's army of the militant church.

It is this organizational aspect of the system which also seems to explain the great stress laid upon obedience and authority, for, as the Weber school has pointed out, emphasis on organization as against personal relations together with strictest discipline and subordination under a centralized management are necessary correlatives to individualization and a prerequisite for keeping a perfectly functioning machine, consisting of living, rational matériel, co-ordinated and in working condition. Thus simply viewed as a type of social organization, the Jesuit order does reveal many of the characteristics commonly associated with modern complex society and organized groups of the *Gesellschaft* type which, like an army, industrial plant, or business corporation, require rigorous conformity with rational norms of administration yet at the same time lay claim to the personalities of individual members only in so far as they serve the purpose of the institution.

The Jesuit type of order is the mature product of a long evolution. It is also its final expression, for no new type of life in religion has appeared since, though some see in Don Bosco's Oratory, others in the Visitation Nuns of St. Francis of Sales, the same creative genius which was at work in similar foundations of the past. The numerous other organizations which have come into existence in modern times are usually patterned after the Jesuits. They seem to emphasize one aspect of the Jesuit system here, while suppressing some other details there in ever new variations, but none seems to have added anything fundamentally novel to the basic pattern.

[26] Cf. *Epitome* 22, pars. 3 and 7, as quoted by Koch, *op. cit.*, article "Verfassung."
[27] Koch speaks of "einem sachlich bis ins kleinste vorgesehenen Geschäftsgang" (*ibid*).

F · PROBLEMS IN COEXISTENCE: COMMUNITY AND CONFLICT

1 · Definition

RAUL HILBERG

A destruction process is a series of administrative measures which must be aimed at a definite group. The German bureaucracy knew with whom it had to deal: the target of its measures was Jewry. But what, precisely, was Jewry? Who was a member of that group? The answer to this question had to be worked out by an agency which dealt with general problems of administration—the Interior Ministry. In the course of the definition-making, several other offices from the civil service and the party became interested in the problem. . . .

The problem of defining the Jews was by no means simple; in fact, it was a stumbling block for an earlier generation of anti-Semites. Hellmut von Gerlach, one of the anti-Semitic deputies in the Reichstag during the 1890's, explained in his memoirs why the sixteen anti-Semitic members of the legislature had never proposed an anti-Jewish law; they could not find a workable definition of the concept of Jew. All had agreed upon the jingle:

SOURCE. Raul Hilberg, "Definition," from Raul Hilberg, *The Destruction of the European Jews,* Chicago: Quadrangle Books, 1961, pp. 43–53.

Never mind to whom he prays,
The rotten mess is in the race.
[*Was er glaubt ist einerlei
In der Rasse liegt die Schweinerei.*]

But how to define race in a law? The anti-Semites had never been able to come to an agreement about that question. That is why "everybody continued to curse the Jews, but nobody introduced a law against them." [1] The "simple" people who wrote the Nazi Party program in 1920 did not supply a definition either; they simply pointed out that a member of the community could only be a person of "German blood, without regard to confession."

When the Interior Ministry drafted its first anti-Jewish decree for the dismissal of Jewish civil servants, it was confronted by the same problem which had troubled the anti-Semites and the early Nazis. But the bureaucrats of the Interior Ministry attacked the problem systematically, and soon they found the answer.

[1] Hellmut von Gerlach, *Von Rechts nach Links* (Zurich, 1937), pp. 111–13. The author, an anti-Semitic deputy, quit the faction in disgust.

The decree of April 7, 1933,[2] provided that officials of "non-Aryan descent" were to be retired. The term "non-Aryan descent" was defined in the regulation of April 11, 1933,[3] as a designation for any person who had a Jewish parent or a Jewish grandparent; the parent or grandparent was presumed to be Jewish if he (or she) belonged to the Jewish religion.

The phraseology of this definition is such that it could not be said to have run counter to the stipulations of the party program. The ministry had divided the population into two categories: "Aryans," who were people with no Jewish ancestors (i.e., pure "German blood"), and "non-Aryans," who were all persons, Jewish or Christian, who had at least one Jewish parent or grandparent. It should be noted that the definition is in no sense based on racial criteria, such as blood type, curvature of the nose, or other physical characteristics. Nazi commentators, for propagandistic reasons, called the decrees "racial laws" (Rassengesetze),[4] and non-German writers, adopting this language, have also referred to these definitions as "racial." [5] But it is important to understand that the sole criterion for categorization into the "Aryan" or "non-Aryan" group was religion—to be sure, not the religion of the person involved but, in any case, the religion of his ancestors. After all, the Nazis were not interested in the "Jewish

nose." They were interested in the "Jewish influence."

The 1933 definition (known as the *Arierparagraph*) did give rise to difficulties. One problem arose from the use of the terms "Aryan" and "non-Aryan," which had been chosen in order to lend to the decrees a racial flavor.[6] Foreign nations, notably Japan, were offended by the general implication that non-Aryans were inferior to Aryans. On November 15, 1934, representatives of the Interior Ministry and the Foreign Office, together with the chief of the party's Race-Political Office, Dr. Gross, discussed the adverse effect of the *Arierparagraph* upon Far Eastern policy. The conferees had no solution.

The Foreign Office reported that its missions abroad had explained the German policy of distinguishing between the *types* of races, rather than the *qualities* of the races (*Verschiedenartigkeit der Rassen,* rather than *Verschiedenwertigkeit der Rassen*). According to this view, each race produced its own social characteristics, but the characteristics of one race were not necessarily inferior to those of other races. In short, racial "type" comprised physical and spiritual qualities, and German policy attempted no more than the promotion of conditions which would permit each race to develop in its own way. However, this explanation did not quite satisfy the Far East states, who still felt that the catch-all term "non-Aryan" placed them into the same category with Jews.[7]

There was another difficulty which

---

[2] Reichsgesetzblatt (RGBl) I, 175.
[3] RGBl I, 195.
[4] For example, the commentary by Wilhelm Stuckart and Rolf Schiedmair, *Rassen- und Erbpflege in der Gesetzgebung des Reiches* (5th ed.; Leipzig, 1944).
[5] One Jewish historian went so far as to call the medieval practice of identifying new Christians as former Jews "racial." See Cecil Roth, "Marranos and Racial Antisemitism— A Study in Parallels," *Jewish Social Studies,* 1940, pp. 239–48.

[6] Actually, the term "Aryan," like "Semitic," is not even a race designation. At best, it is a term for a linguistic-ethnic group.
[7] Circular letter by Pfundtner, February 9, 1935, NG-2292 (Nuremberg Documents). Bülow-Schwante (Foreign Office) to missions and consulates abroad, May 17, 1935, enclosing circular letter by the Ministry of Interior, April 18, 1935, NG-3942.

reached into the substance of the measure. The term "non-Aryan" had been defined in such a way as to include not only full Jews—that is to say, persons with four Jewish grandparents—but also three-quarter Jews, half-Jews, and one-quarter Jews. Such a definition was considered necessary in order to eliminate from official positions all persons who, even in the slightest degree, might have been carriers of the "Jewish influence." Nevertheless, it was recognized that the term "non-Aryan," aside from embracing the full Jews, included also a number of persons whose inclusion in subsequent, more drastic measures would result in difficulties. In order to narrow the application of subsequent decrees to exclude such persons, a definition of what was actually meant by "Jew" became necessary.

At the beginning of 1935 the problem received some attention in party circles. One of the meetings was attended by Dr. Wagner, then *Reichsärzteführer* (chief medical officer of the party), Dr. Gross (Race-Political Office), and Dr. Blome, at that time secretary of the medical association, later Deputy *Reichsärzteführer*. Dr. Blome spoke out against a special status for part-Jews. He did not want a "third race." Consequently, he proposed that all quarter-Jews be considered Germans and that all half-Jews be considered Jews. Reason: "Among half-Jews, the Jewish genes are notoriously dominant." [8] This view later became party policy, but the party never succeeded in imposing that policy on the Interior Ministry, where the decisive decrees were written.

On the occasion of the Nuremberg party rally, Hitler ordered, on September 13, 1935, that a decree be written—in two days—under the title "Law for the Protection of German Blood and

Honor." Two experts of the Interior Ministry, Ministerialrat Medicus and Ministerialrat Lösener, were thereupon summoned to Nuremberg by plane. When they arrived, they found Staatssekretäre Pfundtner and Stuckart, Ministerialrat Seel (civil service expert of the Interior Ministry), Ministerialrat Sommer (a representative of the Führer's Deputy Hess), and several other gentlemen in the police headquarters, drafting a law. Interior Minister Frick and Reichsärzteführer Wagner shuttled between Hitler's quarters and the police station with drafts. In the midst of the commotion, to the accompaniment of music and marching feet, and in a setting of flags, the new decree was hammered out. The law no longer dealt with "non-Aryans" but with "Jews." It prohibited marriages and extramarital intercourse between Jews and citizens of "German or related blood," the employment in Jewish households of female citizens of "German or related blood" under the age of 45, and the raising by Jews of the Reich flag.[9] None of the terms used were defined in the decree.

On the evening of September 14, Frick returned to his villa from a visit to Hitler and told the exhausted experts to get busy with a draft of a Reich Citizenship Law. The *Staatssekretäre* and *Ministerialräte* now went to work in the music room of Frick's villa, to write a citizenship law. Soon they ran out of paper and requisitioned old menu cards. By 2:30 A.M. the citizenship law was finished. It provided that only persons of "German or related blood" could be citizens. Since "citizenship" in Nazi Germany implied nothing, no interest attaches to the drafting of this decree, except insofar as the civil servants stuck in a provision to the effect that "full Jews"

---

[8] Affidavit by Dr. Kurt Blome, January 17, 1946. NO-1710 (Nuremberg Documents).

[9] Law for the Protection of German Blood and Honor, September 15, 1935, RGB1 I, 1146.

could not be citizens. This implied a new categorization, differentiating between Germans and part-Jews, on the one hand, and such persons, regardless of religion, who had four Jewish grandparents, on the other hand. Hitler saw this implication immediately and crossed out the provision.[10]

The attitudes of the party and of the civil service toward part-Jews had now emerged quite clearly. The party "combatted" the part-Jew as a carrier of the "Jewish influence"; the civil service wanted to protect in the part-Jew "that part which is German." [11] The final definition was written in the Interior Ministry, and so it is not surprising that the party view did not prevail.

The authors of the definition were Staatssekretär Dr. Stuckart and his expert in Jewish affairs, Dr. Lösener. Stuckart was then a young man of 33. He was a Nazi, a believer in Hitler and Germany's destiny. He was also regarded as a party man. There is a difference between these two concepts. Everyone was presumed to be, and was accepted as, a Nazi unless by his own conduct he insisted otherwise. But not everyone was regarded as a party man. Only those people were party men who held positions in the party, who owed their positions to the party, or who represented the party's interests in disagreements between the party and other hierarchies. Stuckart was in the party (he had even joined the SS in an honorary capacity); he had risen to power more quickly than other people; and he knew what the party wanted. But in this last respect Stuckart was not an all-out party man;

he refused to go along with the party in the definition business.

Stuckart's expert on Jewish affairs, Dr. Bernhard Lösener, had been transferred to the Interior Ministry after long service in the customs administration. Definitions and Jewish affairs were an entirely new experience to him; yet he became an efficient "expert" in his new assignment. Ultimately he drafted, or helped draft, 27 anti-Jewish decrees.[12] He is the prototype of other "experts" in Jewish matters, whom we shall meet in the Finance Ministry, in the Labor Ministry, in the Foreign Office, and in many other agencies.

The two men had an urgent task to perform. The terms "Jew" and "German" had already been used in a decree which contained criminal sanctions. There was no time to be lost. The final text of the definition corresponds in substance to a memorandum written by Lösener and dated November 1, 1935.[13] Lösener dealt in his memorandum with the critical problem of the half-Jews. He rejected the party's proposal to equate half-Jews with full-Jews. In the first place, Lösener argued, such a categorization would strengthen the Jewish side. "In principle, the half-Jew should be regarded as a more serious enemy than the full Jew because, in addition to Jewish characteristics, he possesses so many Germanic ones which the full Jew lacks." Second, the equation would result in an injustice. Half-Jews could not emigrate and could not compete with full Jews for jobs with Jewish employers. Third, there was the need of the armed forces, which would be deprived of a potential 45,000 men. Fourth, a boycott against half-Jews was impractical (the German people would

---

[10] The history of the two laws is taken from the affidavit by Dr. Bernard Lösener, February 24, 1948, NG-1944-A. Final version of the Reich Citizenship Law, dated September 15, 1935, in RGBl I, 1146.

[11] See letter by Stuckart, March 16, 1942, NG-2586-I.

[12] See list compiled by Lösener in his affidavit of February 28, 1948, NG-1944-A.

[13] Stuckart to Foreign Minister von Neurath, November 1, 1935, enclosing Lösener memorandum, NG-3941.

not go along). Fifth, half-Jews had performed meritorious services (recital of names). Sixth, there were many marriages between Germans and half-Jews. Suppose, for example, that Mr. Schmidt finds out, after ten years of marriage, that his wife is half-Jewish—a fact which, presumably, all half-Jewish wives keep secret?

In view of all these difficulties, Lösener proposed that the half-Jews be sorted into two groups.[14] There was no practical way of sorting half-Jews individually, according to their political convictions. But there was an automatic way of dealing with that problem; Lösener proposed that only those half-Jews be counted as Jews who belonged to the Jewish religion or who were married to a Jewish person.

The Lösener proposal was incorporated into the First Regulation to the Reich Citizenship Law, dated November 14, 1935.[15] In its final form, the automatic sorting method separated the "non-Aryans" into the following categories: Everyone was defined as a Jew who (1) descended from at least three Jewish grandparents (full Jews and three-quarter Jews), or (2) descended from two Jewish grandparents (half-Jews) and (a) belonged to the Jewish religious community on September 15, 1935, or joined the community on a subsequent date, or (b) was married to a Jewish person on September 15, 1935, or married one on a subsequent date, or (c) was the offspring of a marriage contracted with a three-quarter or a full Jew after the Law for the Protection of German Blood and Honor had come into force (September 15, 1935, or (d) was the offspring of an extramarital relationship with a

three-quarter or a full Jew, and was born out of wedlock after July 31, 1936. For the determination of the status of the grandparents, the presumption remained that the grandparent was Jewish if he or she belonged to the Jewish religious community.

Defined not as a Jew but as an individual of "mixed Jewish blood" was (1) any person who descended from two Jewish grandparents (half-Jewish), but who (a) did not adhere (or adhered no longer) to the Jewish religion on September 15, 1935, and who did not join it at any subsequent time, and (b) was not married (or was married no longer) to a Jewish person on September 15, 1935, and who did not marry such a person at any subsequent time (such half-Jews were called Mischlinge of the first degree), and (2) any person descended from one Jewish grandparent (Mischling of the second degree). The designations "Mischling of the first degree" and "Mischling of the second degree" were not contained in the decree of November 14, 1935, but were added in a later ruling by the Ministry of Interior.[16]

In practice, therefore, Lösener had split the non-Aryans into two groups, Mischlinge and Jews. The Mischlinge were no longer subjected to the destruction process. They remained non-Aryans under the earlier decrees and continued to be affected by them, but subsequent measures were, on the whole, taken only against "Jews." Henceforth, the Mischlinge were left out.[17]

The administration of the Lösener decree, and of the Arierparagraph which preceded it, was a complicated procedure which is interesting because it affords a

[14] The nature of these arguments is quite interesting, since they could have been used equally well to argue against all anti-Jewish measures.
[15] RGB1 I, 1333.

[16] Stuckart, Rassenpflege, p. 17.
[17] For summary of anti-Mischling measures from 1933 to 1944, see Hilberg, The Destruction of the European Jews, pp. 268, 273n, 274.

great deal of insight into the Nazi mentality. In the first place, both decrees were based on descent: the religious status of the grandparents. For that reason, it was necessary to *prove* descent. In this respect, the decrees affected not only "non-Aryans;" *everybody* who wanted to be employed by the Reich, or in the party, had to search for the records of his ancestors. An applicant for a position (and, in many cases, an office holder) required seven documents: his own birth or baptismal certificate, the certificates of his two parents, and the certificates of all four grandparents.[18]

Prior to 1875–76, births were registered only by churches.[19] Thus the churches were drawn into the administration of the very first measure of the destruction process. They did their part of the job as a matter of course. Oddly enough, however, the office holders themselves were not prepared to offer their full co-operation. As late as 1940, the chief of the party's foreign organization had to remind his personnel to submit the documents. Most employees in the office had simply ignored an earlier directive for submission of records, without even giving an excuse or explanation for failure to comply.[20] Of course, in part at least, the lack of prompt compliance was simply due to the difficulty of procuring the necessary papers.

Even in the early thirties, a whole new profession of licensed "family researchers" (*Sippenforscher* or *Familien-*

forscher) had appeared on the scene, to assist applicants and office holders in finding documents. The Sippenforscher compiled *Ahnentafeln* ("ancestor charts"), which listed parents and grandparents. Sometimes it was necessary to do research on great-grandparents also. Such procedures, however, were limited to two types of cases: (1) applications for service in such party formations as the SS, which, in the case of officers, required proof of non-Jewish descent from 1750, and (2) attempts to show that a Jewish grandparent was actually the offspring of Christian parents. This latter procedure was possible, because a grandparent was only *presumed* to be Jewish if he (or she) belonged to the Jewish religion. In the same way, inquiry into the status of the great-grandparents could be used to the detriment of an applicant. For if it were shown that a Christian grandparent had actually been the child of Jews, the grandparent would be considered a Jew, and a "downward" classification would result.[21]

The final decision about the correctness of the facts was made by the agency which had to pass on the applicant, but in doubtful cases a party office on family research (the *Sippenamt*) rendered expert opinions for the guidance of agency heads. There was, in that connection, a very interesting category of doubtful cases: the offspring of extramarital relationships. The status of these individuals raised a peculiar problem. How was one to classify someone whose descent could not be determined? This problem was divided into two parts: individuals with Jewish mothers and individuals with German mothers.

In cases of offspring of unmarried Jewish mothers, the *Reichssippenamt* ("Family Research Office") presumed that any child born *before* 1918 had a

---

[18] For detailed specifications, see, for example, the Merkblatt für den Abstammungsnachweis of the Reichsfilmkammer, October, 1936, G-55.

[19] *Pfarrämter.* After 1875–76, registrations were performed by the state's *Standesämter. Reichsfilmkammer Merkblatt*, October, 1936. G-55.

[20] Order by Gauleiter Bohle, May 31, 1940, NG-1672.

[21] Stuckart, *Rassenpflege*, p. 16.

Jewish father and that any child born *after* 1918 had a Christian father. The reason for this presumption was a Nazi hypothesis known as the "emancipation theory," according to which Jews did not mix with Germans before 1918. However, after 1918 the Jews had the opportunity to pursue the systematic disintegration (*Zersetzung*) of the German people (*Volkskörper*). This activity included the fostering of extramarital relationships. In commenting upon this theory, Amtsgerichtsrat ("Judge") Klemm of the party's Legal Office pointed out that it was quite true that Jews were guilty of this practice but that, after all, the practice was intended only to violate German *women*. It could hardly be assumed that a Jewish woman undertook pregnancy in order to harm the German *man*. According to the criteria used by the *Reichssippenamt*, complained Klemm, a Jewish mother could simply refuse to tell the office who the father was, and her child would automatically become a *Mischling* of the first degree.[22] Klemm's comments were probably quite correct. This was perhaps the only Nazi theory which worked to the complete advantage of a number of full Jews.

The "emancipation theory" does not seem to have been applied to the offspring of unwed German mothers. The reason was simple: the Party's *Reichssippenamt* rarely, if ever, got such cases. If it had gotten them, just about all of Germany's illegitimate children born after 1918 would have been classified as *Mischlinge* of the first degree. But since

[22] Amtgerichtsrat Klemm, "Spricht eine Vermutung für die Deutschblütigkeit des nicht feststellbaren Erzeugers eines von einer Jüdin ausserehelich geborenen Kindes?" *Deutsches Recht*, 1942, p. 850, and *Die Judenfrage* (*Vertrauliche Beilage*), July 1, 1942, pp 50–51.

the Party did not get the cases, the illegitimate offspring of a German mother remained a German, with all the rights and obligations of a German in Nazi Germany. However, there were a few instances when a Jew or *Mischling* had acknowledged paternity of a German mother's child. In some of these cases, persons who had been classified as *Mischlinge* went to court, pointing out that the legal father was not the actual father and that, therefore, there was ground for reclassification. For such cases, the Justice Ministry laid down the rule that the courts were not to inquire into the motives of the person who had acknowledged fatherhood and that they were to reject any testimony by the mother, "who is only interested in protecting her child from the disadvantages of Jewish descent."[23]

The cumbersome task of proving descent was not the only problem which complicated the administration of the decrees. Although the definition appeared to be airtight, in the sense that —given the facts—it should have been possible at once to determine whether an individual was a German, a *Mischling*, or a Jew, there were in fact several problems of interpretation. Consequently, we find a whole number of administrative and judicial decisions which were designed to make the definition more precise.

The principal problem of interpretation hinged on the provision in the Lösener decree according to which half-Jews were classified as *Mischlinge* of the first degree if they did not belong to the Jewish religion and were not married to a Jewish person on or after September 15, 1935. There was no legal difficulty in determining whether a person was married; marriage is a clearly defined legal

[23] Directive by Ministry of Justice, May 24, 1941. *Deutsche Justiz*, 1941, p. 629.

concept. But the determination of criteria for adherence to the Jewish religion was not so simple. Whether a half-Jew was to be classified as a Jew or a *Mischling* of the first degree ultimately depended on the answer to the question: Did the man regard himself as a Jew?

In 1941 the Reichsverwaltungsgericht (Reich Administrative Court) received a petition from a half-Jew who had not been raised as a Jew and who had never been affiliated with any synagogue. Nevertheless, the court classified the petitioner as a Jew because there was evidence that, on various occasions since 1914, he had designated *himself* as a Jew in filling out forms and official documents, and he had failed to correct the impression of the authorities that he was a Jew. Toleration of a presumption was sufficient conduct for the purpose of classification as a Jewish person.[24]

In a later decision the Reichsgericht (highest court in Germany) ruled that conduct was not enough; the attitude disclosed by the conduct was decisive. The particular case concerned a young woman, half-Jewish, who had married a half-Jew (*Mischling* of the first degree). The marriage consequently did not place her into the Jewish category. Now, however, there was the matter of her religion.[25] The evidence showed that in 1923 and 1924 she had had Jewish religious instruction upon the insistence of her Jewish father. In subsequent years she accompanied her father to the synagogue, once a year, on Jewish high holy days. After her father died in 1934, she discontinued visits to the synagogue, but,

in asking for a job in the Jewish community organization, she listed her religion as Jewish. Until 1938, moreover, she was entered as a member of a synagogue. The court decided that she was *not* Jewish. The evidence showed that she had resisted her father's attempt to have her formally accepted with prayer and blessing into the Jewish religion. She had visited the synagogue not for religious reasons but only in order to please her father. In asking for a position with the Jewish community organization, she was motivated not by a feeling of Jewishness but solely by economic considerations. As soon as she discovered her entry in the Jewish community list, she requested that her name be struck out.[26]

The attitude and intention of the individual was decisive in another case, which is very interesting from a psychological point of view. A half-Jew who had married a German woman in 1928 had thereupon ceased to be a member of his synagogue. In 1941 the Jewish community organization in Berlin, which was then performing important functions in the destruction process, suddenly demanded information about the man's personal finances, and when this information was refused, the Jewish community went to court, claiming that the defendant had quit his synagogue but not his religion. The court rejected the Jewish organization's argument, pointing out that the Jewish religious community had no legal personality and no public law status. Consequently, any man who had quit his synagogue had quit his religion at the same time, unless there was evidence that he still regarded himself as a Jew. There was no such evidence in this case. To the contrary, the defendant

[24] Decision of the Reichsverwaltungsgericht, June 5, 1941. *Deutsches Recht*, p. 2413; also in *Die Judenfrage* (*Vertrauliche Beilage*), February 1, 1942, pp. 11–12.

[25] In the Jewish practice, the *mother's* religion is decisive in determining the religion of the half-Jewish child.

[26] Decision of the Reichsgericht/3. Strafsenat, August 13, 1942. *Deutsches Recht*, 1943, p. 80, and *Die Judenfrage* (*Vertrauliche Beilage*), February 1, 1943, pp. 11–12.

had provided proof of his membership in party organizations, and in every other respect the court was satisfied that this man had intended to sever his connections with Jewry when he stepped out of the synagogue.

This decision was one of the few which was assailed by the party's Race-Political Office. A lawyer of that office, Dr. Schmidt-Klevenow, referring to the fact that the Jewish community itself had claimed the defendant to be a member, asked whether the court had to be "more pontifical than the pontiff (*papstlicher als der Papst*)." [27]

From all these decisions, the judiciary's concern with half-Jews is quite evident. This concern was the product of a desire to balance the protection of the German community against the destruction of the Jews. When a person was both German and Jewish by parental descent, the judges had to determine which element was dominant in the man. To do this, they only had to be a little more precise than Lösener had been in asking the question of how the individual had classified himself.

The court interpretations of the Lösener decree illustrate once more that there is nothing "racial" in the basic design of the definition. In fact, there are a few very curious cases in which a person with *four* German grandparents was classified as a Jew because he belonged to the Jewish religion. In its decision one court pointed out that Aryan treatment was to be accorded to persons who had the "racial" requisites "but that in cases when the individual involved feels bound to Jewry in spite of his

Aryan blood, and shows this fact externally, his attitude is decisive." [28] In another decision, by the Reich Finance Court, it was held that an Aryan who adhered to the Jewish religion was to be treated as a Jew for the duration of his adherence to the Jewish faith. According to the court, an individual "who is racially a non-Jew, but who openly claims membership in the Jewish community, belongs to the community and therefore has placed himself in the ranks of the Jews." [29]

Even while the judiciary closed the loopholes of the Lösener definition by making it more precise, it became necessary, in an increasing number of cases, to make exceptions on behalf of individuals whose categorization into a particular group was considered unjust. In creating the *Mischlinge*, Lösener had constructed a so-called third race, that is, a group of people who for administrative purposes were neither Jews nor Germans. The *Mischlinge* suffered from three discriminations: (1) they were excluded from the civil service and the party; (2) they were restricted in the army to service as common soldiers; and (3) they could not marry Germans without official consent.[30]

Because of these discriminations, pressure for exceptional treatment was applied by colleagues, superiors, friends,

[27] Decision of an Amtsgericht, affirmed on appeal, reported in *Deutsches Recht*, 1941, pp. 1552–53. Summary of case with comment by Schmidt-Klevenow in *Die Judenfrage* (*Vertrauliche Beilage*), September 1, 1941, pp. 61–63.

[28] Decision by Oberlandesgericht Königsberg, 4. Zivilsenat, June 26, 1942, in *Die Judenfrage* (*Vertrauliche Beilage*), November 1, 1942, pp. 82–83.

[29] Decision by the Reichsfinanzhof, February 11, 1943. *Reichssteuerblatt*, 1943, p. 251, and *Die Judenfrage* (*Vertrauliche Beilage*), April 15, 1943, pp. 30–31. This case, as well as the case cited above, concerned individuals who had accepted the Jewish religion upon marriage to a Jewish woman.

[30] Later, *Mischlinge* were denied admission to the bar and suffered from discriminations in the schools.

and relatives. Consequently, in 1935 a procedure was instituted for the reclassification of a *Mischling* into a higher category, i.e., *Mischling* of the first degree to *Mischling* of the second degree, or *Mischling* of the second degree to German, or *Mischling* of the first degree to German. This procedure was known as *Befreiung* ("liberation"). There were two kinds, "pseudo-liberations" and "genuine liberations" (*unechte Befreiungen* and *echte Befreiungen*). The pseudo-liberation was a reclassification based upon a clarification of the facts or of the law. It was achieved by showing, for example, that an allegedly Jewish grandfather was not really Jewish, or that a presumed adherence to the Jewish religion had not existed. The "real liberation," however, was granted upon showing the applicant's "merit." [31] Applications for real liberations were routed through the Interior Ministry and the Reich Chancellery to Hitler if the petitioner was a civilian, and through the Army High Command and the Führer Chancellery if the petitioner was a soldier.[32]

The recipients of this favor were sometimes high officials. Ministerialrat Killy of the Reich Chancellery, a man who performed significant functions in the destruction of the Jews, was a *Mischling* of the second degree. His wife was a *Mischling* of the first degree. He had joined the party and had entered the Reich Chancellery without telling anyone about his origin. When the decree of April 7, 1933 (*Arierparagraph*), was issued, Killy informed Lammers about the state of affairs and offered to resign. Lammers thought the situation quite grave because of Killy's wife but advised Killy not to resign. Thereupon, Lammers spoke to Hitler, who agreed to Killy's continuing service. Then on Christmas Eve in 1936, while the Killy family was sitting around the tree and opening gifts, a courier brought a special present: a *Befreiung* for Killy and his children.[33]

The "liberations" increased in volume to such an extent that on July 20, 1942, Lammers informed the Highest Reich Authorities of Hitler's desire to cut down on their number. The applications had been handled too "softly" (*weichherzig*). Hitler did not think that the blameless conduct of a *Mischling* was sufficient ground for his "liberation"; the *Mischling* had to show "positive merit," which might be proved if, for example, without awareness of his ancestry he had fought for the party uninterruptedly and for many years, prior to 1933.[34]

Lest we leave the impression that the tendency to equate *Mischlinge* with Germans was unopposed, we should point out that there was another tendency to eliminate the "third race" by reclassifying *Mischlinge* of the second degree as Germans and transforming all *Mischlinge* of the first degree into Jews. This pressure, which came from party circles and the police, reached its zenith in 1942; however, it never succeeded.

Thus we find that the Lösener definition remained the basis of categorization throughout the destruction process. Even though some different definitions were later adopted in some occupied countries and Axis states, the basic concept of these early decrees remained unchanged.

In summary, here is a recapitulation of the terms and their meanings:

[31] Stuckart, *Rassenpflege*, pp. 18–19.
[32] Affidavit by Blome, January 17, 1946, NO-1719.
[33] For Killy's adventures, see his testimony in Case No. 11, transcript pp. 23, 235–23, 267.
[34] Lammers to Highest Reich Authorities, July 20, 1942, NG-4819. The Lammers letter was based on remarks by Hitler at the dinner table. See Henry Parker (ed.), *Hitler's Tischgespräche im Führerhauptquartier 1940–1942* (Berlin, 1951), entries for May 10, 1942, and July 1, 1942, pp. 303, 313.

$$\text{Non-Aryans} \begin{cases} \end{cases}$$

Mischlinge of the second degree:
  Persons with one Jewish grandparent
Mischlinge of the first degree:
  Persons with two Jewish grandparents who did not
belong to the Jewish religion and were not married to a
Jewish person on September 15, 1935
Jews:
  Persons with two Jewish grandparents, if they belonged
to the Jewish religion or were married to a Jewish person
on September 15, 1935, and persons with three or four
Jewish grandparents

2 · Social Differentiation in the Netherlands*

DAVID O. MOBERG

ABSTRACT. *Dutch social differentiation is based upon religious in addition to socio-economic considerations. Religious distinctions cause division of institutions and activities into Catholic, Protestant, humanistic, and neutral "columns." Tentative consequences of this system of vertical pluralism are summarized. Reasons for its persistence in spite of efforts to break it down are suggested.*

In the Netherlands differentiation along socioeconomic lines is quickly apparent to the observer who seeks evidences of it. Social status or, as the Dutch say, "rank" colors all social relationships. Social differentiation is also apparent along

SOURCE. David Moberg, "Social Differentiation in the Netherlands," *Social Forces*, 39, 1961, pp. 333–337.
* The author is grateful to Professors J. P. Kruijt of the University of Utrecht and William Petersen of the University of California at Berkeley for constructive criticism of earlier versions of this paper. The participant observation upon which it is partly based occurred in 1957–58 while the author was a Fulbright lecturer in sociology at the University of Groningen, the Netherlands.

religious lines, and it is with these that this paper is concerned. Cutting vertically across the class structure are several *zuilen* (columns or pillars) which are related to the religious faith of their members, each of which is an almost self-sustaining unit.

A person may spend his entire life with very few contacts with persons and influences outside of his own "column." He may be born in a confessional hospital and educated through the trade school or university level in confessional schools. His employment will be found with someone of his own religious affiliation, for there is evidence that hiring of personnel is sometimes on a discriminatory basis by religion. He will join a trade union, professional society, or occupational association for persons of his religion. His civic and social organizations and activities are likely to be organized along denominational lines, even if they center primarily around gymnastics, bird-watching, music bands, or teetotalism. He will marry someone from his own religious denomination, read its daily newspaper and weekly or monthly magazine, listen to its radio broadcasts, vote for its political candidates, rear his children in its schools, go on vacation trips sponsored by a confessional travel club for persons of his religious faith, attend only churches of his denomination, symbolically wear his wedding ring on the right ring finger if he is a Protestant and on his left if he is Catholic, and finally be buried in the churchyard. His isolation from persons of other religious faiths is likely to be broken only in certain community celebrations, business contacts, and other occasional life experiences unless he deviates from the position of faithfulness decreed by his church. Only the upper economic and professional classes and persons who have no close church ties find it easy to cross the barriers erected between the various religious groups, and the unchurched seldom are welcome beyond their own "secular" circles.

The process by which the ideologically oriented groups which are present in society are increasingly gathered up into an organizational social control system consisting of distinct "columns" is called the *verzuiling*. The resulting system tends to overgrow the ideal values through its stress upon formal organization and to provide ideological justification or rationalization for the organizational pattern.[1]

No other language has a direct equivalent for the word *verzuiling*.[2] The nearest English cognates are the concepts of sub-cultures, pluralism, "unity in diversity," special interest groups, and pressure groups. If somehow all of these were woven together and given in addition an ideological and religious twist, we might come near an understanding of the term.

Following Fogarty's precedent, I shall refer to it as "vertical pluralism."[3]

The three basic "columns," Catholic, Protestant, and humanistic, are sometimes subdivided into several additional ones, and besides them are neutral groups attempting to be general organizations for all people. Only the Catholic column is clearly monolithic. As a Dutch sociologist has said,

All other columns are built up of small pieces and fragments, stand crisscrossed and higgledy-piggledy, and (what is still more strange for pillars) more or less cross over each other. One can perhaps speak much better than pillars of an entire brushwood of ramificating branches and tangled trees.[4]

An over-all estimate of the relative strength of the three main "pillars" is based upon parents of primary school children: 34 percent are Roman Catholic, 28 percent Protestant, and 38 percent neutral.[5] However, only 51 percent of the votes cast in the 1959 elections were for the confessional political parties.[6]

Manifest and Latent Consequences of Dutch Vertical Pluralism

In summarizing some results of the *verzuiling*, the difficulties of separating causes from effects and of discerning the manifest and especially the latent consequences of any characteristic or part of society must be kept in mind. The following are presented as tentative and subject to modification with increased

[1] J. A. A. Van Doorn, "Verzuiling: Een Eigentijds Systeem van Sociale Controle," *Sociologische Gids,* III (March–April 1956), pp. 41–49.
[2] S. E. Steigenga-Kouwe, "Verzuiling en Bevolkingsgroei," *Socialisme en Democratie,* Verzuilingsnummer (January 1957), pp. 40–46.
[3] Michael P. Fogarty, *Christian Democracy in Western Europe, 1820–1953* (London: Routledge & Kegan Paul, 1957), pp. 41–47.
[4] Hilda Verwey-Jonker, "De Psychologie van de Verzuiling," *Socialisme en Democratie, Verzuilingsnummer* (January 1957), pp. 30–39.
[5] *Ibid.*
[6] J. P. Kruijt, personal correspondence.

knowledge. They are based upon a combination of personal participant observation and reports by Dutch and American scholars. The more manifest among them are presented first, and all of them obviously overlap with each other.

1. Vertical pluralism increases spatial and ideological isolation of the members of the major religious groups. Isolation is apparent in a number of areas, all of which form an interesting network and reinforce each other.[7] These include mass communications, social welfare, education, adult education, libraries, recreational and leisure-time activities, cultural associations, politics, occupations, economic affairs, and even sociological research.

2. The solidarity of religious groups is increased. The constraint of the group over the individual is made to operate in ways that would be impossible without it in modern society.[8] The religious bodies are strengthened by their competition with one another. They are continually on the alert to protect their distinctive positions. Conflict with external foes contributes to increased internal strength.

3. The unique values of the religious groups are protected. Indoctrination is invariably more effective when accompanied by a high degree of censorship to prevent the spreading of "false ideas." The *verzuiling* helps prevent out-marriage of youth in the churches to a degree that would be impossible without it.[9] Alien ideas not in keeping with the

teachings of a religious institution are not as quickly disseminated to the faithful as they would be if there were no religious segregation.

4. Individuals are given identity by the ideological positions to which they adhere. Social pressures compel individuals to identify themselves as belonging to one of the major columns. This undoubtedly squelches a certain amount of nonconformity, but it also leaves few persons in the position of being mere faces in the lonely crowd. Persons who wish to remain "neutral," however, are automatically identified as being secularists or humanists with the implication that they are anti-religious, unless they are part of religiously oriented subgroups similar to the major columns within the Labor Party.

5. Vertical pluralism in theory makes explicit the practical implications of religious doctrine. Nevertheless, there are serious questions as to whether specific translations of doctrine into practice or policy are the *only* applications possible on the basis of the doctrines held by the confessional parties. Conflicts between mutually desirable but incompatible policies arise because the application of differently accepted principles results in the contradictions which inevitably emerge when one value is advanced at the expense of another. In the realities of political struggles it is rarely possible to discern clearly and in detail the practical policies dictated by religious principles. Principles stand against other principles to confuse the religiously oriented political leader. A "casuistry of practical expedience" almost inevitably results from the blending of religious and political dogmatism.[10]

[7] For a brief description by an American observer see John W. Dykstra, "Holland's Religious Segmentation," *Christian Century*, LXXII (October 19, 1955), 1207–1208.
[8] J. P. Kruijt, "Sociologische Beschouwingen over Zuilen en Verbuiling," *Socialisme en Democratie*, Verzuilingsnummer (January 1957), pp. 11–29.
[9] See A. Pomman, *Geografische en Confessionele Invloeden Bij de Huwelijkskeuze in Nederland* (Leiden: H. E. Stenfert Kroese, 1951).
[10] H. Stuart Hughes, "How Democratic Is Christian Democracy?" *Commentary*, XXV (May 1958), 379–384.

6. Scholarly work is labeled by vertical pluralism. Persons reared in Dutch society cannot avoid involvement in the values associated with the *verzuiling* and are compelled to take sides. Knowing their ideological position is essential to understand and evaluate properly their contributions.[11] (Perhaps it would be an advantage for Americans to have their scholarly biases so easily identifiable!)

7. Vertical pluralism contributes to personnel shortages. One result of the spreading of urbanization and the accompanying specialized division of labor is a scarcity of trained personnel in many specialized positions of social work, education, medical care, and other vocational fields. Vertical pluralism often requires a duplication of personnel in the corresponding institutions supported by the confessional groups within a community which would be unnecessary if there were cooperation enough to support a single larger public institution. In addition, vertical pluralism often leads to the requirement of special religious qualifications not directly relevant to the performance of a task. This prevents otherwise qualified persons from filling certain positions. Shortages of personnel and problems of recruiting specialized workers are thus multiplied.

8. The economic costs of vertical pluralism are great. The necessity to provide for a separate school system for each major religious group in a community and additional duplication in social work, radio, television, health funds, and related areas undoubtedly increase the total costs of these services. These increased costs are distributed to all taxpayers

through government support of such activities. They are not maintained only by those who believe they reap a special benefit through their independent institutions.[12]

9. School attendance problems are multiplied. Attendance cannot be regulated on the basis of attendance districts alone, for a child may find it necessary to cross an entire city to attend a school of his own religion. In rural areas the problems of transportation also impose a heavier burden on parents than would prevail with a single school system. The problems are similar to those faced by minority group members in American communities which have a dual school system, but the Dutch system is a triple or quadruple one.

10. Educational efficiency may be reduced. Duplication of basic facilities to maintain separate school systems increases the expenditures and tends to decrease the services provided per unit of expenditure per pupil. To whatever degree education is more efficient in large institutions because of increased specialization of teachers, greater attention to individual variations of abilities and interests, heterogeneity of student bodies, and more efficient grouping of students in ideal-sized classes, the Dutch educational system suffers. Homogeneity along ideological lines helps preserve the purity of the ideological groups, but it also impoverishes the minds of students who are not encouraged to recognize that interpretations and contributions of groups other than their own can increase understanding of problems and point toward their solutions.

11. Vertical pluralism contributes to increased population pressure. The growth of population is encouraged by

[11] For an example see William Petersen, *Planned Migration: The Social Determinants of the Dutch-Canadian Movement* (Berkeley: University of California Press, 1955, p. 19, note 6.

[12] S. Miedema, "De Kosten van de Verzuiling," *Socialisme en Democratie*, Verzuilingsnummer (January 1957), pp. 47–58.

the values of neo-Calvinists and Roman Catholics because increased numbers contribute to increased political influence and power. Both groups, to be sure, have logical philosophical-theological values which encourage population growth, but their practical interpretations appear to be based partly upon the struggle for power. Traditional values stimulating population growth are encouraged and institutionalized by competition of religious bodies to the detriment of economic and social well-being at the same time as the nation actively sponsors emigration to help alleviate population pressures.[13]

12. Vertical pluralism contributes to misunderstanding and tensions between the religious groups and thus diminishes national solidarity. Separation promotes ignorance of other groups; ignorance promotes misunderstanding, failure to recognize the needs of others, and rigid ethnocentrism.[14] Children are taught their history lessons from different ideological viewpoints. Hostility toward outgroups is increased by political propaganda. In "throw-away" leaflets distributed to our door during the 1958 elections were statements indicating that each confessional political party claims to be God's own party, with the implication that equivalent counterclaims of the others are fraudulent. Religious teachings stress the dangers of contact with persons from other religious denominational families. Personal impressions from association with Catholics, Protestants, and secularists indicate to the writer that there are deep latent tensions between the Dutch religious groups. This personal observation is verified by the opinions of other Americans who have been in the Netherlands.[15]

13. Vertical pluralism carries ecclesiastical dogmatism into political life. When religious leaders in an authoritarian church take sides on political issues, laymen dare not challenge or contradict their clergy on secular topics for fear of being condemned as "modernists" or heretics under other labels.[16] In 1954 a strongly worded pastoral letter by the Dutch Catholic Bishops severely and formally censured Catholics who had joined the Labor Party.[17] While not absolutely forbidding Catholics from being members of the Labor Party, the Church strongly advises them against it. Thus political affairs often become questions of faith and morals in a nation of vertical pluralism.

14. The ultimate goals of Dutch politico-religious leaders are not democracy and freedom but the promulgation of doctrines and practices related to their religious ideologies. Whenever democratic and religious values compete and appear to be incompatible, democratic values are subordinated to religious considerations. "When religion itself appears threatened, the Christian Democrat is obliged to make a painful choice. To save his religious faith, he may be obliged to sacrifice his political principles . . ."[18] Authoritarianism based upon dogma or, in the case of Protestants, upon belief in the supreme authority of the World of God is elevated above the principles of individual liberty and democracy.[19]

15. Community solidarity and efficiency are diminished. Not only is group set against group in political affairs, but even when there are community-wide activities with cooperative planning there must nearly aways be representation from all major confessional groupings of

[13] Petersen, op cit., esp. pp. 15–41.
[14] Kruijt, "Sociologische Beschouwingen . . . ," op. cit.
[15] For example, see Dykstra, op. cit.
[16] Hughes, op. cit.
[17] Fogarty, op. cit., p. 390.
[18] Hughes, op cit., p. 384.
[19] See Fogarty, op. cit., pp. 159–160.

the community. As a result, incompetence is often evident; considerations of religious politics are placed above competence in the appointment or selection of personnel for community organizations and committees. Even when federated activity cuts across the religious columns, actual association of persons with different religious views takes place only among the small proportion of the population which holds positions of leadership. "Water-tight" partitions separate the rank-and-file members.[20]

16. Personal initiative is reduced by vertical pluralism. While the Dutch often criticize Americans as being "mass men," it is probable that they are actually much more so themselves. Organizations dominate nearly every area of life. To quote a Dutch-American scholar who worked on a research project in Amsterdam,

The indigenous tri-partitism adds to the complexity . . . with this welter of organizations there is little left for the individual to do. He is likely to become dependent upon and lost in the organization. The rank-and-file member has little or no opportunity to exercise his own personal responsibility. Outside of his organization he is likely to feel lost.[21]

Segments of the population that have no special organization to represent them are forgotten.

17. Personal liberty is diminished in a system which discourages or forthrightly condemns the ideas of groups other than one's own. The person who lives in a closed system which exposes him to only one world view, one religious system, and one interpretation of God's working in the universe undoubtedly has much less personal freedom than the one who is given the opportunity of examining numerous of these viewpoints and evaluating them against each other to make his own choice of his philosophy of life. To be sure, the Dutch groups are not completely insulated from each other, but the lower the socio-economic position of their members, the more sound-proof this insulation becomes. A Dutch scholar opposed to the *verzuiling* has said that modern totalitarianism differs little ideologically from the confessional state. The rights and freedom of individual persons are infringed upon by extreme vertical pluralism.[22]

18. Vertical pluralism may contribute to personality problems. It is conceivable that social demands to separate from those who are considered "worldly" or impure may contribute to mental illnesses and personality deviations in the modern urban world in which complete separation is impossible. Personal hypocrisy in which the claims of religious organizations are accepted and adhered to in theory but are denied in the facts of everyday living may also be encouraged by this system.

Conclusion

It would be an error to imply that the Dutch people generally do not want vertical pluralism to continue. If a majority wished to stop its directly political aspects, such as tax-fund support to confessional schools, hospitals, welfare agencies, radio studios, and other partially or wholly tax-supported church-related activities and organizations, they could easily do so through their democratic political institutions. A survey of church-member families in a working-class area

[20] J. P. Kruijt, "Sociologische Beschouwingen . . . ," *op. cit.*

[21] John T. Daling, "A Look at the Dutch (I)," *The Reformed Journal,* VII (May 1957, 26.

[22] G. Ruygers, "Politieke Doorbraak en Verzuiling," *Socialisme en Democratie,* Verzuilingsnummer (January 1957), pp. 59–64.

of Utrecht discovered that 92.5 percent of the Catholics, 98 percent of the neo-Calvinists, and 59 percent of the Netherlands Reformed parents wanted their children to attend confessional elementary schools, and substantial proportions also wished to maintain other aspects of vertical pluralism.[23]

Many intellectuals are convinced that the benefits of the system are outweighed by its costs and therefore actively engage in political and educational activities designed to effect a "breakthrough" (*doorbraak*) in the walls of separation that isolate the confessional groups from one another. Yet a small but gradually diminishing majority of the people desire the continuance of the *verzuiling* and believe that it is wholesome for the nation as well as for the churches.

Social control is a major element in the retention and extension of the system. Consciousness of kind is also involved, and the separate organizations serve an educational function in helping persons adjust to social demands and fit into social roles. Vertical pluralism is like a sieve or strainer in the hands of religious leaders by which they test new elements proposed as additions to the culture and keep away from the faithful those which they deem undesirable. It is a source of propaganda, for each religious group with its own subculture and its own system of values hopes victoriously to

make the entire nation take the course of action which it believes to be the most desirable. The strong desire of the Dutch for consistency between their faith and their relationships to the world thus plays a significant part in the maintenance of the system of vertical pluralism.[24]

The natural resistance of social institutions to change, the vested interests of political and administrative leadership in political parties, schools, social welfare agencies, and other institutions and associations, and above all the value systems of the Dutch people and their religious bodies make it unlikely that the "breakthrough" will be successful soon.

> The strong inclination of our [Dutch] people to ideologize leads to solidarity and in the societal area to *verzuiling*. . . . The [*verzuiling*] tendency itself lies in the final analysis in the nature of religion itself as the highest and central value of human life; it holds no less for the laicized forms of religion, the so-called world-outlook.[25]

With its source in religious faith, Dutch vertical pluralism can be expected to remain, especially in the school system, as long as a majority of the population retain the basic tenets and current interpretations of their Catholic and Calvinistic faith.[26]

[23] J. P. Kruijt, "Levensbeschouwing in Groepssolidariteit in Nederland," in Nederlands Sociologische Vereniging, *Sociologisch Jaarboek XI* (Leiden: E. J. Brill, 1957), 34–41.

[24] Verwey Jonker, *op. cit.*
[25] J. A. Ponsioen, "Notities Voor de Sociologische Bestudering van de Verzuiling," *Sociologische Gids, III* (March–April 1956), 20, 22.
[26] See Fogarty, *op. cit.*, pp. 379–384, 387–390.

3 · The Dissonant Religious Context and Emotional Disturbance

MORRIS ROSENBERG

ABSTRACT. *Contextual dissonance refers to a situation in which the individual's social characteristics differ from those of the population by which he is surrounded. Data from a sample of high-school students suggest that children reared in a dissonant religious context are somewhat more likely to have low self-esteem, to manifest psychosomatic symptoms of anxiety, and to experience depressive affect. Experiences of prejudice appear to contribute to these results. Among those in dissonant contexts, children reared in "culturally dissimilar" neighborhoods appear more likely than others to manifest symptoms of emotional disturbance.*

I. Introduction

The influence of the individual's social context upon his attitudes and behavior has been pointed up in a number of recent sociological studies.[1] Several of these studies have highlighted the importance of the discrepancy between, or concordance of, the individual's social characteristics and those of the population by which he is surrounded. For example, it may be a very different experience for a white child to be raised in a Negro neighborhood than for a Negro child to be raised in the same neighborhood; for a Catholic child to be raised in a Protestant neighborhood than for a Protestant child to be raised in the same neighborhood; for a middle-class child to be raised in a working-class neighborhood than for a working-class child to be reared in this social context. In other words, it is not simply the individual's social characteristics nor the social characteristics of those in the neighborhood in which he lives which are crucial, but the *relationship* between the two—their concordance or discordance—which is of central significance.

In this paper, we wish to examine the relationship between one such dissonant context—the religious context—and certain signs of psychic or emotional disturb-

SOURCE. Morris Rosenberg, "The Dissonant Religious Context and Emotional Disturbance," reprinted from *American Journal of Sociology*, 68, July, 1962, pp. 1–10 by permission of The University of Chicago Press.
[1] Alan B. Wilson, "Residential Segregation of Social Classes and Aspirations of High School Boys," *American Sociological Review*, XXIV (1959), 836–45; Robert K. Merton and Alice S. Kitt, "Reference Group Behavior," in R. K. Merton and P. F. Lazarsfeld (eds.), *Continuities in Social Research: Studies in the Scope and Method of "The American Soldier"* (Glencoe, Ill.: Free Press, 1950), pp. 71 ff.; Paul F. Lazarsfeld and Wagner Thielens, *The Academic Mind* (Glencoe, Ill.: Free Press, 1958), *passim;* Leonard Pearlin and Morris Rosenberg, "Nurse-Patient Social Distance and the Structural Context of a Mental Hospital," *American Sociological Review*, XXVII, No. 1 (1962), 56–65. A methodological discussion of contextual analysis appears in Paul F. Lazarsfeld, "Problems in Methodology," in R. K. Merton, L. Broom, and L. S. Cottrell, Jr. (eds.), *Sociology Today* (New York: Basic Books, 1959), pp. 69–73.

ance. Does a Catholic child raised in a Protestant neighborhood, for example, show more symptoms of anxiety and depression than one reared in an environment inhabited mostly by his coreligionists? Does such an experience affect his self-esteem? Does a dissonant context have the same effect upon the other religious groups? Does it make a difference *what* the nature of the dissonant context is, for example, is it a different experience for a Catholic child to be raised in a Protestant neighborhood than it is for him to be raised in a Jewish neighborhood? These are some of the questions to which the present research is addressed.

Our data are drawn from questionnaires administered to high-school juniors and seniors in ten high schools in New York State. The population of New York State public high schools was stratified by size of community, and the sample of schools was selected from this population through use of a table of random numbers. Three separate but overlapping questionnaires were administered alternately to the respondents; each student completed one questionnaire. Some of the data to be presented, then, come from different questionnaire forms.

II. Religious Dissonance and Emotional Disturbance

In the course of completing questionnaires dealing with the values, goals, and self-conceptions of youth, these high-school upperclassmen were told:

This section deals with the neighborhood in which you grew up. If you lived in more than one neighborhood, think of the neighborhood in which you lived *longest*.

Think back to the time when you were in grammar school. Generally speaking, what was the religious affilia-

tion of most of the people in the neighborhood in which you lived?

Respondents were then asked to fill in the approximate proportions of each religious group in these neighborhoods. It was thus possible to compare those who were predominantly surrounded by coreligionists in childhood, those whose neighborhoods were about evenly divided between members of their own and another religion, and those who were in a distinct religious minority.

Table 1 suggests that the experience of living in a dissonant religious context has certain psychic consequences for the individual exposed to it. In every case, we see, students who have been raised in a dissonant social context are more likely than those who have been reared in a consonant or mixed [2] religious environment to manifest symptoms of psychic or emotional disturbance. For example, Catholics raised in non-Catholic neighborhoods are more likely than Catholics raised in predominantly Catholic or half-Catholic neighborhoods to have low self-esteem, to feel depressed, and to report many psychosomatic symptoms.[3]

[2] "Consonant" means that almost all or about three-quarters of the people in the neighborhood were of the same religion as the respondent; "mixed" means that about one-half were of the same religion; and "dissonant" means that one-quarter or almost none were of the same religion.

[3] The measure of self-esteem is a ten-item Guttman scale which, through the use of "contrived" items (see S. A. Stouffer *et al.* "A Technique for Improving Cumulative Scales," *Public Opinion Quarterly*, XVI [1953], 273–91) yields a seven-point scale. The reproducibility is 93 per cent and the scalability is 72 per cent. The items in this scale, with which respondents were asked to strongly agree, agree, disagree, or strongly disagree, are the following: (1) On the whole, I am satisfied with myself. (2) At times I think I am no good at all. (3) I feel that I have a number of good qualities. (4) I am able to do things as well as most other

TABLE 1. *Contextual Dissonance and Self-Esteem, Psychosomatic Symptoms, and Depression, by Religious Affiliation*

| | CATHOLICS | | PROTESTANTS | | JEWS | |
| | IN NON-CATHOLIC NEIGHBOR-HOODS (PER CENT) | IN CATHOLIC OR MIXED NEIGHBOR-HOODS (PER CENT) | IN NON-PROTESTANT NEIGHBOR-HOODS (PER CENT) | IN PROTESTANT OR MIXED NEIGHBOR-HOODS (PER CENT) | IN NON-JEWISH NEIGHBOR-HOODS (PER CENT) | IN JEWISH OR MIXED NEIGHBOR-HOODS (PER CENT) |
MEASURE						
Self-esteem:						
Low	41	29	31	25	29	18
Medium	30	25	27	30	10	23
High	30	46	42	45	61	60
No. of respondents*	(37)	(458)	(164)	(241)	(41)	(80)
Psychosomatic symptoms:						
Many	65	55	54	48	55	51
Few	35	45	46	52	45	49
No. of respondents	(37)	(467)	(164)	(245)	(42)	(77)
Depressive affect:						
Depressed	20	18	22	11	28	16
Not depressed	80	82	78	89	72	84
No. of respondents	(35)	(429)	(148)	(221)	(39)	(70)

* The difference in number of cases in the tables is due to the fact that "no answers" have been omitted from the calculations. Most of the "no answers" have been so classified because they did not complete all the items in each scale or score because of lack of time. Since several of the "depression" items appeared near the end of the questionnaire, the largest proportion of "no answers" appears on this scale.

Similarly, Protestants or Jews raised in dissonant social contexts are more likely than those reared in neighborhoods inhabited chiefly or equally by their co-

people. (5) I feel I do not have much to be proud of. (6) I certainly feel useless at times. (7) I feel that I'm a person of worth, at least on an equal plane with others. (8) I wish I could have more respect for myself. (9) All in all, I am inclined to feel that I am a failure. (10) I take a positive attitude toward myself.

Depressive affect is measured by a six-item Guttman scale with a reproducibility of 95 per cent and a scalability of 75 per cent. The items in this scale, which were randomly distributed throughout the questionnaire, are the following: (1) On the whole, how happy would you say you are? (2) On the whole, I think I am quite a happy person. (3) In general, how would you say you feel most of the time—in good spirits or in low spirits? (4) I get a lot of fun out of life. (5) I wish I could be as happy as others seem to be. (6) How often do you feel downcast and dejected?

The psychosomatic symptoms score is based upon ten of the fifteen symptoms which appeared in the Neuropsychiatric Screening Adjunct used by the Research Branch of the United States Army in World War II. The development and validation of these psychosomatic items are presented in Shirley A. Star, "The Screening of Psychoneurotics in the Army: Technical Development of Tests," in S. A. Stouffer et al. *Measurement and Prediction* (Princeton, N.J.: Princeton University Press, 1950). The items utilized were: (1) Do you ever have trouble getting to sleep or staying asleep? (2) Do your hands ever tremble enough to bother you? (3) Are you bothered by nervousness? (4) Have you ever been bothered by your heart beating hard? (5) Have you ever been bothered by pressures or pains in the head? (6) Do you ever bite your fingernails now? (7) Have you ever been bothered by shortness of breath when you were not exercising or working hard? (8) Are you ever troubled by your hands sweating so that they feel damp and clammy? (9) Are you ever troubled with sick headaches? (10) Are you ever bothered by having nightmares (dreams that frighten or upset you very much)?

religionists to manifest these signs of emotional disturbance. These three measures are, of course, highly related to one another, but they are neither conceptually nor empirically identical. Whatever measure is used, the results are essentially similar.

The effect of the dissonant context does not appear to be a large and powerful one; many of the differences are quite small. While some of these differences are not statistically significant and some others are barely so, note that the results are all perfectly consistent. For all nine comparisons made, those in the dissonant context are without exception more likely than others to manifest these symptoms of psychological disturbance. For this reason, these results may merit attention.

It is important to note that there is no clear difference in emotional distress between those raised in neighborhoods inhabited *almost exclusively* by coreligionists and those reared in areas in which only *about half* the members are coreligionists. This result would suggest that whether everyone in the neighborhood is of one's group is less important than whether there are *enough* of them to give one social support, a feeling of belongingness, a sense of acceptance. Thus, two groups may well look down upon one another, but each group may take pride in itself. Even though members of each group may challenge and attack the other, every individual still has a group with which he can identify. It is only when the individual is in the distinct minority, when it is impossible for him to restrict his associations to members of his own group, that the deleterious psychological consequences of the dissonant religious context become evident.

III. The Effect of Discrimination

The child who is isolated from his religious group thus tends to face his immediate environment without the sustenance of group support. It is not difficult to envision the experiences he might undergo. The nature of ethnocentrism is such that the majority group tends to define the minority out-group member as different and inferior. Specifically, this may take the form of excluding the minority-group member from participation in activities, taunting him, hurling derogatory epithets at him, or using the abundant variety of instruments of cruelty of which children are capable.

To examine this question we asked our respondents: "When you were a child, were you ever teased, left out of things, or called names by other children because of . . . your religion?" Table 2 shows that within every religious group students reared in the dissonant context are much more likely than those raised in a consonant or mixed context to have experienced such taunting or exclusion on the basis of religious affiliation.

Such discrimination, we would expect, can hardly fail to have some effect upon the psychic state of the individual. And Table 3 shows that this is so. Within each religious group, those who have experienced discrimination are more likely to have low self-esteem, more likely to have many psychosomatic symptoms, and more likely to be depressed. This is true for all nine comparisons made. The most conspicuous relationship is found between the experience of prejudice and the report of psychosomatic symptoms. Such psychosomatic symptoms represent physiological indicators of anxiety, and there is reason to believe that they are closely associated with neuroticism.[4] This would suggest that the child who experiences prejudice is more likely to develop feelings of fear, anxiety, insecurity, and tension—a striking testimony to the penalty in human happiness and

---

[4] See Star, *op. cit.*, chaps. xiii–xiv.

TABLE 2. *Dissonant Context and Subjection to Religious Discrimination by Religious Affiliation*

	CATHOLICS		PROTESTANTS		JEWS	
QUESTION	IN NON-CATHOLIC NEIGHBOR-HOODS (PER CENT)	IN CATHOLIC OR MIXED NEIGHBOR-HOODS (PER CENT)	IN NON-PROTESTANT NEIGHBOR-HOODS (PER CENT)	IN PROTESTANT OR MIXED NEIGHBOR-HOODS (PER CENT)	IN NON-JEWISH NEIGHBOR-HOODS (PER CENT)	IN JEWISH OR MIXED NEIGHBOR-HOODS (PER CENT)
"When you were a child, were you ever teased, left out of things, or called names by other children because of your . . . religion?"						
Ever*	22	5	22	6	48	26
Never	78	95	78	94	52	74
No. of respondents	(37)	(454)	(162)	(238)	(42)	(78)

* "Ever" refers to those who answered "often," "sometimes," or "rarely."

psychic well-being paid by the innocent and unwitting victims of prejudice.

We have seen that students raised in dissonant social contexts experience greater psychic disturbance than others, that such students are more likely to have experienced prejudice, and that those who have experienced prejudice are more likely to manifest such disturbance. This would suggest that one reason students in the dissonant context are more disturbed is that they have experienced such prejudice. In order to see whether this is so, we have examined the relationship

TABLE 3. *Experience of Prejudice and Self-Esteem, Depression, and Psychosomatic Symptoms, by Religious Affiliation*

	PER CENT EXPERIENCED PREJUDICE IN CHILDHOOD					
	CATHOLICS		PROTESTANTS		JEWS	
MEASURE	EVER	NEVER	EVER	NEVER	EVER	NEVER
Self-esteem:						
Low	36	30	37	29	24	23
Medium	40	26	26	27	20	18
High	25	44	37	45	55	59
No. of respondents	(40)	(601)	(62)	(494)	(61)	(112)
Psychosomatic symptoms:						
Many	74	54	64	48	55	44
Few	26	46	36	52	45	56
No. of respondents	(40)	(613)	(61)	(496)	(59)	(112)
Depressive effect:						
Depressed	56	40	53	34	39	36
Not depressed	44	60	47	66	61	64
No. of respondents	(36)	(561)	(51)	(452)	(51)	(102)

of contextual dissonance to psychic disturbance, controlling experiences of prejudice; the method of control employed is "test factor standardization." [5] The results show that in eight out of nine cases the relationship between contextual dissonance and emotional disturbance is reduced when prejudice experiences are controlled. The relationships do not, however, completely disappear.

These data would suggest, then, that the experience of discrimination does contribute to the psychological consequences of contextual dissonance but that it does not account for them completely. To be reared in a dissonant context thus reflects more than the experience of being taunted, ridiculed, attacked, or excluded on the basis of one's group affiliation. What is also probably involved is the insecurity which stems from lack of integration in a group, issuing from a feeling of social isolation, a sense of being "different," an absence of "belongingness." It is apparent why such experiences may be associated with an individual's level of self-acceptance as well as his feelings of anxiety and depression.

Differential Responsiveness to Discrimination. While the data in Table 3 suggest that all the religious groups are emotionally responsive to the effects of prejudice, attention is drawn to the fact that they are not *equally* responsive to it. Specifically, it appears that Catholics and Protestants are more affected by the experience than Jews. Why the Jewish children, who have experienced by far the most prejudice, should be least affected by it is not certain. Perhaps the prejudice against Jews in the society is so pervasive that its expression is taken for granted; perhaps Jewish children are

[5] This procedure is described in Morris Rosenberg, "Test Factor Standardization as a Method of Interpretation," *Social Forces* (forthcoming).

taught early to expect such slights and to harden themselves against them; perhaps, since discrimination plays such a relatively large role in the lives of Jewish children, they may tend to react to it by attributing the fault to the discriminator rather than to themselves. Whatever the reason, our results suggest that the group which experiences the most prejudice is, in terms of our indicators of emotional disturbance, least affected by it, whereas the group which, in our sample, experiences the least prejudice is most affected by it. Many of the most serious victims of prejudice, then, are those in the majority group.

IV. Contextual Specification

Given the fact that children reared in a dissonant religious context are more likely to suffer the pangs of self-contempt, to feel depressed, and to experience various psychosomatic manifestations of anxiety, the question arises: are certain dissonant contexts more prejudicial to the individual's psychic well-being than others? Perhaps Catholics living in Protestant neighborhoods are less affected by their minority group position than Catholics in Jewish neighborhoods. Perhaps Jews in Protestant neighborhoods are less affected than Jews in Catholic neighborhoods. In other words, while we have seen that the dissonant religious context appears to have a bearing upon one's psychic and emotional state, it may be that certain contexts are "more dissonant" than others.

Considering only those students who have been reared in a dissonant religious context, we have compared the levels of self-esteem, depression, and anxiety of members of each religious group reared in neighborhoods occupied chiefly by members of the other two religious groups. Table 4 suggests the following: (1) that Catholics in Protestant areas experiences less emotional disturbance

TABLE 4. *Psychic States of Students in Different Religious Contexts*

	CATHOLICS IN PREDOMINANTLY		PROTESTANTS IN PREDOMINANTLY		JEWS IN PREDOMINANTLY	
MEASURE	PROTESTANT AREAS (PER CENT)	JEWISH AREAS (PER CENT)	CATHOLIC AREAS (PER CENT)	JEWISH AREAS (PER CENT)	PROTESTANT AREAS (PER CENT)	CATHOLIC AREAS (PER CENT)
Self-esteem:						
Low or medium	68	75	58	78	20	45
High	32	25	42	22	80	55
No. of respondents	(28)	(8)	(149)	(9)	(10)	(20)
Psychosomatic symptoms:						
Many	68	62	56	62	55	60
Few	32	38	44	38	45	40
No. of respondents	(28)	(8)	(150)	(8)	(11)	(20)
Depressive affect:						
Depressed	19	25	23	25	11	29
Not depressed	81	75	77	75	89	71
No. of respondents	(26)	(8)	(138)	(4)	(9)	(21)

than Catholics in Jewish areas; (2) that Protestants in Catholic areas experience less disturbance than Protestants in Jewish areas; and (3) that Jews in Protestant areas experience less disturbance than Jews in Catholic areas. Since we are dealing only with those in dissonant contexts, the number of cases is small and the results therefore cannot be considered reliable.[6] Further studies utiliz-

[6] It may be noted that there are discrepancies in the total number of cases classified as "dissonant" in Tables 1 and 4, particularly among Jewish respondents. One reason is that a number of respondents reported that they grew up in "Christian" neighborhoods. Jewish students who gave this reply were classified in Table 1 as growing up in non-Jewish neighborhoods, but it was not possible to determine whether these neighborhoods were Catholic or Protestant. Hence, these cases have been omitted from Table 4. Another reason is that in Table 4 we are dealing with those who grew up in *predominantly* (all or three-quarters) Catholic, Protestant, or Jewish neighborhoods. We have thus omitted, for example, Catholics reared in approximately half-Protestant-half-Jewish neighborhoods; Protestants reared in half-Catholic-half-Jewish neighborhoods; and Jews reared in half-Catholic-half-Protestant neighborhoods.

ing a larger number of cases would be required to strengthen these conclusions. Nevertheless, it is relevant to note that in eight out of nine comparisons made, the results are in agreement with the conclusions cited above. Since such a high level of consistency obtains, these results appear to warrant further analysis.

Though we lack a sufficient number of cases for statistical adequacy, there is another way of approaching the problem. If some principle can be enunciated which is consistent with these findings, it would increase our confidence that the observed differences are real and meaningful. The principle we propose to account for these findings is the concept of *cultural similarity or dissimilarity*. We will suggest that, if an individual lives in a culturally dissimilar neighborhood, then this context is "more dissonant" than if he lives in a culturally similar neighborhood.

To recapitulate, our data suggest that Catholics in Protestant neighborhoods are less disturbed than Catholics in Jewish neighborhoods; that Protestants in Catholic neighborhoods are less disturbed than Protestants in Jewish neighborhoods; and that Jews in Protestant neighborhoods are less disturbed than Jews in Catholic neighborhoods. If these results are due to the fact that more dissonant contexts are associated with more emotional disturbance, then it would have to be shown (1) that Catholics are culturally more similar to Protestants than they are to Jews; (2) that Protestants are culturally more similar to Catholics than they are to Jews; and (3) that Jews are culturally more similar to Protestants than they are to Catholics. Before we can determine whether this is so, it is first necessary to discuss the nature of "cultural similarity."

Cultural Similarity. The question of cultural similarity is a complex one. In gross terms, of course, it is obvious that American and British societies have more cultural elements in common than, say, American and Chinese societies. If one were to make a more detailed comparison of two cultures, however, one would have to compare their traditions, customs, mores, values, perspectives, philosophies, art, technology, goals, ideals, etc. Given our limited data, such comparisons are manifestly impossible. We have, however, selected one area which would generally be considered culturally relevant—the area of values.

If we consider a value to be "a conception of the desirable which influences the selection from available modes, means, and ends of action," [7] then there are four areas in our study which appear to fit this description: (1) self-values— which traits, qualities, or characteristics does the individual consider important in judging himself? (2) maternal values —for what types of behavior was the individual most likely to gain the approval of his mother? (3) paternal values—for

what types of behavior was the individual most likely to gain the approval of his father? and (4) occupational values—what satisfactions, gratifications, or rewards is the individual most concerned with obtaining from his life's work? [8]

A simple procedure for comparing the similarity of religious groups was employed. With regard to each item, we asked whether the proportion of Catholics choosing the item was closer to the proportion of Protestants choosing it or to the proportion of Jews; whether the proportion of Protestants choosing it was more similar to the proportion of Catholics or of Jews; and whether the proportion of Jews choosing it was more similar to the proportion of Protestants or of Catholics. This involved forty-four comparisons of self-values, five comparisons of maternal values, six comparisons of paternal values, and six comparisons of occupational values.

Table 5 indicates that, in each of the four value areas under consideration, Catholics were more often similar to Protestants than they were to Jews; Protestants were more often similar to Catholics than they were to Jews; and Jews were more often similar to Protestants than they were to Catholics.

Of course, we cannot be certain that

---

[7] Clyde Kluckhohn *et al.* "Values and Value-Orientations in the Theory of Action," in T. Parsons and E. A. Shills (eds.), *Toward a General Theory of Action* (Cambridge, Mass.: Harvard University Press, 1954), p. 395.

[8] Self-values included such items as: ambitious; clear-thinking or clever; hard-working or conscientious; dependable and reliable; etc. Parental values were measured by asking whether mothers and fathers were most likely to approve of the child for being strong and aggressive; for doing well in school; for getting along with other children; etc. Occupational values dealt with whether the individual was most concerned with using his abilities at his work, gaining status and prestige, having the opportunity to be creative and original, etc. The list of occupational values is drawn from Morris Rosenberg, *Occupations and Values* (Glencoe, Ill.: Free Press, 1957), pp. 141–42.

TABLE 5. *Comparisons of Cultural Similarity or Dissimilarity*

NO. OF COMPARISONS

GROUP COMPARED	SELF-VALUES	MATERNAL VALUES	PATERNAL VALUES	OCCUPATIONAL VALUES
Catholics more similar to Protestants	27	5	6	4
Catholics more similar to Jews	11	..	..	2
Equal	6	..	..	..
No. of comparisons	44	5	6	6
Protestants more similar to Catholics	29	3	4	4
Protestants more similar to Jews	12	1	1	2
Equal	3	1	1	..
No. of comparisons	44	5	6	6
Jews more similar to Protestants	22	4	2	4
Jews more similar to Catholics	15	1	1	2
Equal	7	..	3	..
No. of comparisons	44	5	6	6

similar results would appear if other areas of culture were considered. Assuming, however, that these are reasonable indicators of cultural similarity, this would mean that some contexts are "more dissonant" than others in the manner specified.

With these results, we can now return to our earlier discussion of varying dissonant contexts. As we noted in Table 4, Catholics in Protestant areas generally showed less disturbance than Catholics in Jewish areas; Protestants in Catholic areas showed less disturbance than Protestants in Jewish areas; and Jews in Protestant areas showed less disturbance than Jews in Catholic areas. In each of these three comparisons, those who were reared in a "more dissonant" religious context appeared to experience greater disturbance than those reared in a "less dissonant" context. These results would suggest that it may not only be a question of *whether* the context is dissonant,

but *how* dissonant it is, which has implications for mental health.

It is obvious, of course, that given the small number of cases in this section of the report and the breadth of the concepts involved, one can only advance such a generalization with the utmost tentativeness. It can only be stated that the results are consistent with such a conclusion. Further studies utilizing more adequate samples and broader indicators of cultural similarity would be required to support or falsify this conclusion.

V. Discussion

We have seen that children raised in dissonant religious contexts are in subsequent years more likely to manifest disturbances in self-esteem, depressive affect, and psychosomatic symptoms. Our data do not suggest that the dissonant social context is a powerful factor in producing these signs of emotional disturbance, but the consistency of the results suggests that it may be a real factor. We doubt whether the dissonant context often produces these psychological consequences independently of other factors. Rather, we would be inclined to assume that its main influence is exercised upon those already predisposed to psychological disturbance; those standing near the cliff are pushed ever closer to it or actually over it. The child who is uncertain about his worth becomes all the more doubtful when others define him as different and inferior; the child who is tense becomes all the more tense when threatened by others; the child who is moderately depressed becomes more so when he is rejected by his age mates. But if these predispositions did not exist, it is doubtful whether the dissonant religious context per se would be powerful enough to generate such consequences.

Let us, however, attempt to spell out in greater detail how the dissonant social context might exercise its influence on one of the psychological consequences discussed, namely, self-esteem. Our data have suggested that children raised in a dissonant religious context have lower self-esteem than those raised in a consonant context, and that the more dissonant the context, the smaller the proportion who accept themselves. One factor which undoubtedly plays a role is prejudice in its direct and unabashed form. Thus, children who have been raised in a dissonant context are far more likely than others to report that they have been teased, called names, or left out of things because of their religion, and those who have had such experiences are less likely to accept themselves. It may be that this effect is intensified the more dissimilar the individual's group affiliation and that of his neighborhood. To be taunted, jeered at, or rejected by one's peers might well be expected to leave its imprint upon the individual's picture of himself.

But it is probably more than simple prejudice, narrowly conceived as hostility to members of a group, which is responsible for these results. Beyond this, actual cultural dissimilarity may produce rejection. It is characteristic of cultural groups that they tend to feel united on the basis of shared norms, values, interests, attitudes, perspectives, goals, etc. Ease of communication and a sense of solidarity spring directly from such similarity of thought and feelings. The likelihood that an individual will be accepted into the group is thus not only a question of whether he is socially defined as different by virtue of his group membership, but also by whether he *actually is* different—in interests, values, "personality" traits—by virtue of the fact that he has, perhaps through his parents and relatives, absorbed the values of his own membership group. For example, a Jewish child may learn from his parents, relatives, etc., that it is extremely im-

portant to be a good student in school. If he is raised in a Catholic neighborhood, where, according to our data, less stress is placed upon this quality, then he may be scorned by his peers as a "grind," an "eager beaver," an "apple polisher," etc. At the same time he may place little value on being "tough," a "good fighter," etc.; these qualities, more highly valued in the group by which he is surrounded, may give him the reputation of being a "sissy." If cultural dissimilarity does have such an effect, then it is likely that the greater the cultural dissimilarity, the greater the effect.

The point, then, is that qualities which may be accepted or admired in one's own group may be rejected by members of another group. Hence, there is a real likelihood that one will feel different when in a dissonant social context, and this sense of difference may lead the individual to question himself, doubt himself, wonder whether he is unworthy.

The same factors may operate to generate depression and anxiety. While it is not possible to enter into detail at this point, there is theoretical and empirical reason for expecting disturbances in self-esteem to be associated with depression and anxiety. It is thus possible that the relationship between the dissonant context and depression and anxiety may in part be mediated through its influence on the self-picture. In addition, the tension generated by prejudice, the threat of attack, the lack of social support, the feeling of isolation, the possible feeling of helplessness, could all be expected to contribute to depression and anxiety among those predisposed in that direction.

It is also possible that the effect of contextual dissonance may be heightened by living in a neighborhood chiefly inhabited by people who are, in the broader society, defined as a minority group. To be an "outsider" in a predominantly Catholic or Jewish neighborhood appears to be associated with greater emotional disturbance than to be an "outsider" in a Protestant neighborhood. It is thus possible that Catholics and Jews, defined as "minority groups" in the broader society, develop stronger religious group solidarity within their own neighborhoods. Hence, the youngster who lives in a neighborhood chiefly inhabited by members of such solidary religious groups, but who is himself not a member of the group, may experience particularly strong feelings of isolation.

We noted earlier that contextual consonance or dissonance can only be defined by the *relationship* between the individual's social characteristics and the social characteristics of those by whom he is surrounded. Thus, we have spoken of a context as dissonant if the individual is immersed in an environment whose predominant social characteristics are different from his own. In principle, the social characteristic under consideration might be race, religion, social class, nationality, etc., or it might be a social quality defined by a narrower environment. In this sense, then, a white child in a Negro neighborhood, a Negro child in a white neighborhood, a working-class child in a middle-class neighborhood, a Catholic child in a Protestant neighborhood, an Irish child in a Polish neighborhood would all be imbedded in dissonant social contexts. But this does not mean that

all dissonant contexts would be expected to have the same effect. First, to be a middle-class child in a working-class neighborhood may be quite different from being a working-class child in a middle-class neighborhood. In other words, *relative status* ranks may have an influence, even though both contexts are equally dissonant. Second, to be of Spanish origin in an Italian neighborhood may have little effect if nationality is not a highly *salient* group characteristic. Third, the effect of contextual dissonance might vary with the *clarity of social definition*. Thus, social classes are not sharply and unequivocally defined, and the awareness of class difference may be vague if contiguous classes are involved. For these reasons, conclusions concerning the effect of religious dissonance cannot simply and readily be transferred to other kinds of dissonant contexts.

The quality of religious affiliation thus has certain properties which are not necessarily characteristic of other social qualities. Membership in the group is quite clear and unequivocal; it is a socially salient characteristic; and it tends to be subject to differential social evaluation in the broader society. Whether other group characteristics lacking certain of these qualities, or possessing others, would produce similar results under conditions of contextual dissonance can only be determined by further research.

G · ROLE CONFLICTS AND STRAIN

1 · Racial and Moral Crisis:
The Role of Little Rock Ministers[1]

ERNEST Q. CAMPBELL AND THOMAS F. PETTIGREW

ABSTRACT. *Three reference systems
—the self, the professional, and the
membership—are variables bearing
on behavior in moral dilemmas.
These are used to explain the apparent inconsistency between attitude and behavior of ministers in
the racial crisis current in Little
Rock, Arkansas. Certain institutional characteristics compelled the
minister to give a peaceable atmosphere in his congregation precedence over social reform. Certain
institutional arrangements, working
propositions, techniques of com-
munication, and the reactions of ex-* *tremists helped the minister to control the development of guilt while
remaining inactive during his city's
racial crisis.*

This paper analyzes the conduct of the
ministers in established denominations
in Little Rock, Arkansas, during the crisis
over the admission of Negro students to
the Central High School in the fall of
1957. How do ministers behave in racial
crisis, caught between integrationist and
segregationist forces?

One might expect that Little Rock's
clergymen would favor school integration. All the major national Protestant
bodies have adopted forceful declarations
commending the Supreme Court's desegregation decision of 1954 and urging
their members to comply with it. And
southern pastors have voted in favor of
these statements at their church conferences—and sometimes have even issued similar pronouncements to their
own congregations.[2] But the southern

SOURCE. Ernest Q. Campbell and Thomas F.
Pettigrew, "Racial and Moral Crisis: The
Role of Little Rock Ministers," reprinted
from *American Journal of Sociology*, 64,
March, 1959, 509–516 by permission of The
University of Chicago Press.
[1] This study was supported by a grant from
the Laboratory of Social Relations, Harvard
University. The authors wish to express their
gratitude to Professor Samuel A. Stouffer for
his suggestions. Two brief popular accounts
of aspects of this study have appeared previously: "Men of God in Racial Crisis,"
Christian Century, LXXV (June 4, 1958),
663–65, and "Vignettes from Little Rock,"
Christianity and Crisis, XVIII (September
29, 1958), 128–36.

[2] For example, local ministerial groups issued
such statements in New Orleans, Louisiana;
Richmond, Virginia; Dallas and Houston,
Texas; and Atlanta, Macon, and Columbus,
Georgia. For a review of national church
statements see "Protestantism Speaks on Jus-
tice and Integration," *Christian Century*,
LXXV (February 5, 1958), 164–66.

man of God faces serious congregational opposition if he attempts to express his integrationist beliefs publicly in the local community. The vast majority of southern whites—even those living in the Middle South—are definitely against racial desegregation.[3]

The purpose of this study is to determine how the ministers of established denominations in Little Rock behaved in the conflict. In analyzing their behavior, we treat self-expectations as an independent variable. This is contrary to the usual course, in which the actor is important analytically only because he is caught between contradictory *external* expectations. The standard model of role conflict treats ego as forced to decide between the incompatible norms of groups that can impose sanctions for nonconformity. This model—which is essentially what Lazarsfeld means by cross-pressures—skirts the issue of whether ego imposes expectations on itself and punishes deviations. Pressure and sanction are external to the actor. Hence the typical model tends to be ahistorical in the sense that a finite number of cross-pressuring groups are used to predict the actor's behavior. It is assumed that the actor cannot have developed from periods of prior socialization any normative expectations for his behavior which would have an independent existence.[4]

This additional variable—the actor's expectations of himself—is especially meaningful in the analysis.

Though it is a city of approximately 125,000, Little Rock has much of the atmosphere and easy communication of a small town. It is located in almost the geometric center of the state, and physically and culturally it borders on both the Deep South-like delta country to the east and south and the Mountain South-like hill country to the west and north. Thus Little Rock is not a city of the Deep South. Its public transportation had been successfully integrated in 1956, and its voters, as late as March, 1957, had elected two men to the school board who supported the board's plan for token integration of Central High School. And yet Little Rock is a southern city, with southern traditions of race relations. These patterns became of worldwide interest after Governor Faubus called out the National Guard to prevent desegregation and thereby set off the most publicized and the most critical chain of events in the integration process to date.

Only two ministers devoted their sermons to the impending change on the Sunday before the fateful opening of school in September, 1957. Both warmly

---

[3] A 1956 National Opinion Research Center poll indicated that only one in every seven white southerners approves school integration (H. H. Hyman and P. B. Sheatsley, "Attitudes toward Desegregation," *Scientific American*, CXCV [December, 1956], 35–39). A 1956 survey by the American Institute of Public Opinion showed that in the Middle South—including Arkansas—only one in five whites approved of school integration (M. M. Tumin, *Segregation and Desegregation* [New York: Anti-Defamation League of B'nai B'rith, 1957], p. 109).

[4] By showing that the actor may have a predisposition toward either a particularistic or

a universalistic "solution" to role conflicts in instances where the particularistic-universalistic dimension is relevant, Stouffer and Toby link the study of personality to that of role obligations in a way rarely done (Samuel A. Stouffer and Jackson Toby, "Role Conflict and Personality," *American Journal of Sociology*, LVI [March, 1951], 395–406). This study, however, treats the personal predisposition as a determinant of conflict resolution rather than a factor in conflict development. Much the same is true of Gross's analysis (Neal Gross, Ward S. Mason, and Alexander McEachern, *Explorations in Role Analysis: Studies of the School Superintendency Role* [New York: John Wiley & Sons, 1958], esp. chaps. xv, xvi, and xvii).

approved of the step and hoped for its success. Other ministers alluded to it in prayer or comment. It was commonly believed that a majority of the leading denominations' clergy favored the school board's "gradual" plan. This impression seemed confirmed when immediately after Governor Faubus had surrounded Central High with troops fifteen of the city's most prominent ministers issued a protest in, according to the local *Arkansas Gazette*, "the strongest language permissible to men of God."

When Negro students appeared at the high school for the first time, they were escorted by four white Protestant ministers and a number of prominent Negro leaders. Two of the four whites are local clergymen, one being the president of the biracial ministerial association, the other, president of the local Human Relations Council. Many of the more influential ministers of the city had been asked the night before to join this escort. Some demurred; others said they would try to come. Only two appeared.

On September 23, the day of the rioting near Central High School, several leaders of the ministerial association personally urged immediate counteraction on the mayor and the chief of police. Later, support was solicited from selected ministers in the state to issue a declaration of Christian principle, but dissension over the statement prevented its publication. Indeed, *no* systematic attempts were made by the clergy to appeal to the conscience of the community. Such statements as individual ministers did express were usually—though not always—appeals for "law and order" rather than a Christian defense of the principle of desegregation.

Several weeks after the rioting, plans for a community-wide prayer service began to develop. Care was taken to present this service in as neutral terms as possible. Compromise and reconciliation were stressed: never was it described as organized prayers for integration. And indorsements came from both sides of the controversy—from President Eisenhower and from Governor Faubus. As one of the sponsors put it: "Good Christians can honestly disagree on the question of segregation or integration. But we can all join together in prayers for guidance, that peace may return to our city." The services in the co-operating churches were held on Columbus Day, October 12. All the leading churches participated, with only the working-class sects conspicuously missing. The services varied widely from informal prayers to elaborate programs, and attendances varied widely, too, and totaled perhaps six thousand.

These "prayers for peace" may best be viewed as a ritualistic termination of any attempts by the clergy to direct the course of events in the racial crisis. The prayers had met the national demand for ministerial action and the ministers' own need to act; and they had completed the whole unpleasant business. Despite sporadic efforts by a small number to undertake more effective steps, the ministers lapsed into a general silence that continued throughout the school year.

We began our work in Little Rock in the week after the peace prayers. Following a series of background interviews and a careful analysis of ministerial action as recorded in the press, twenty-nine detailed interviews with ministers were held.[5] Twenty-seven of them are Protestants and two are Jewish; the Roman Catholics did not co-operate.

This sample was not selected randomly; the so-called "snowball technique" was used in order to include the most influential church leaders. This in-

[5] Thirteen additional interviews were held with the sect leaders of an openly pro-segregation prayer service. None of these were members of the ministerial association or were in personal contact with any ministers of the established denominations. A detailed report on them will be published.

volves asking each interviewee to name the members of the Little Rock clergy that he considers to be "the most influential." The first interview was made with an announced leader of the peace prayers, and interviewing was continued with all the men mentioned as influential until no new names were suggested. We added a number of ministers who were not named but who had taken strongly liberal positions during the crisis. Thus our sample is most heavily weighted with the pastors of the larger churches with the greatest prestige and the pastors of smaller churches who had assumed active roles in the conflict. These two groups, we anticipated, would have to contend with the greatest amount of incompatibility in role.

Most of the interviews were held in the church offices. Rapport, which was generally excellent, was partly secured by the authors' identification with southern educational institutions. A detailed summary, as nearly as possible a verbatim account, was placed on Audograph recording equipment shortly after the completion of each interview. Information in three broad areas was sought, and to this end a series of open-ended questions was developed. A series of questions was aimed at determining whether the respondent was a segregationist or an integrationist. A segregationist here is defined as one who prefers racial barriers as presently constituted; an integrationist is one to whom the removal of legal and artificial barriers to racial contact is morally preferable to the present system.[6]

Each interviewee was asked to give a complete account of what he had done

and said in both his parish and in the community at large regarding the racial crisis. If he had not been active or vocal, we probed him for the reason and to learn if he had felt guilty over his failure to state the moral imperatives.

A final set of questions dealt with the pastor's perception of his congregation's reaction to whatever stand he had taken. If pressure had been applied on him by his parishioners, we probed him to learn exactly what pressure had been used and how.

The segregationist. Only five of the twenty-nine clergymen we interviewed were segregationists by our definition. None was avidly so, and, unlike segregationist ministers of the sects, none depended on "chapter-and-verse Scripture" to defend his stand. All men in their late fifties or sixties, they did not think that the crisis was a religious matter. One of them was a supervising administrator in a denominational hierarchy. Although all five were affiliated with prominent denominations, they were not among the leaders of the local ministerial body.

These five men have not been publicly active in defending segregation.[7] Each was opposed to violence, and none showed evidence of internal discomfort or conflict. All five co-operated with the neutrally toned prayers for peace. As one of them commented, "You certainly can't go wrong by praying. Praying can't hurt you on anything."

The inactive integrationist. Inactive integrationists had done enough—or believed they had done enough—to acquaint their congregations with their sympathy with racial tolerance and integration, but during the crucial weeks of the crisis they were generally silent. These, representing as they do all major

---

[6] Using the interview, three judges, the two authors and a graduate assistant, independently rated each respondent as either a segregationist or an integrationist. Agreement between the three raters was complete for twenty-seven of the twenty-nine cases.

[7] Again, this is in contrast to the sect segregationists. One sect minister is president and another is the chaplain of the local Citizens' Council.

denominations, varied considerably as to age and size of church served. Included among them were virtually all the ministers of high prestige, many of whom had signed the protest against Governor Faubus at the start of the crisis and later were advocates of the peace prayer services. Some had spoken out in favor of "law and order" and in criticism of violence. They had not, however, defended the continued attendance of the Negro students in the high school, and they had not challenged their members to defend educational desegregation as a Christian obligation. They were publicly viewed as integrationists only because they had supported "law and order" and had not defended segregation.

Altogether, the inactive integrationists comprise sixteen out of the twenty-nine of our sample. Because it was not a random sample, we cannot draw inferences regarding the division of the total ministerial community or of ministers of established denominations into integrationist and segregationist camps. However, since the sample underrepresents the uninfluential ministers who had not been in the public eye, during the crisis, we may conclude that a large majority of Little Rock's men of God did not encourage their members to define the issue as religious, nor did they initiate actions or participate in programs aimed at integration.

The active integrationist. Eight of our respondents can be designated as active integrationists because they continued to defend integration in principle and to insist that support of racial integration is nothing less than a Christian imperative. They were, on the whole, young men who have headed their small churches for only a few years. Most were disturbed that the churches of the city were segregated; some have urged their churches to admit Negroes. Most of the active integrationists had

serious difficulty with their members because of their activities, evidence of which was lowered Sunday-morning attendance, requests for transfer, diminished giving, personal snubs and insults, and rumors of sentiment for their dismissal. One had concluded that his usefulness to his congregation had ended and accordingly had requested to be transferred. By the end of 1958, several others had been removed from their pulpits.

One thing all twenty-nine of the sample had in common was a segregationist congregation.[8] Without exception, they believed that the majority of their members were strong opponents of racial integration. The highest estimate given by any integrationist of the proportion of his congregation which supported his views was 40 per cent; the median estimate for segregation was 75 per cent. Only three interviewees thought that a majority of their members would "accept" a strong public defense of integration by their minister.

Personal integrity, alone, would lead the liberal Little Rock minister to defend integration and condemn those who support segregation. However, the minister is obligated to consider the expectations of his church membership, especially inasmuch as the members' reactions bear upon his own effectiveness.

When an individual is responsible to a public, we distinguish three systems as relevant to his behavior: the self-reference system (SRS), the professional reference system (PRS), and the membership reference system (MRS). The SRS consists of the actor's demands, expectations, and images regarding himself. It may be thought of as what the actor

[8] Our study of a modest sample of church members bore out the ministers' estimates of predominantly pro-segregation sentiment in their congregations.

would do in the absence of sanctions from external sources. We have already seen that typically the SRS would support racial integration.[9] The PRS consists of several sources mutually related to his occupational role yet independent of his congregation: national and regional church bodies, the local ecclesiastical hierarchy, if any, the local ministerial association, personal contacts and friendships with fellow ministers, and, probably, an image of "my church." Finally, the MRS consists simply of the minister's congregation. We have already seen that it favored segregation or at least ministerial neutrality.

The net effect of three reference systems seems to favor the cause of integration. Were they equal in strength, and were there no contrary forces internal to any of them, this conclusion is obvious. The minister would then feel committed to support the official national policy of his denomination; his knowledge that fellow ministers were similarly committed would support him, and the local hierarchy would encourage him to make this decision and reassure him should his congregation threaten disaffection. These external influences would reinforce his own values, resulting in forthright action in stating and urging the Christian imperatives. However, internal inconsistencies in the PRS and the SRS restrain what on first examination appears to be an influence toward the defense of integration.

The professional reference system. Two overriding characteristics of the PRS minimize its liberalizing influence. First,

[9] Although groups make demands, impose sanctions, and significantly affect the actors' self-expectations and self-sanctions, nevertheless, we treat the self-reference system as an independent variable in role conflict. This system seems especially significant where personal action is contrary to the pressure of known and significant groups.

most of its components cannot or do not impose sanctions for non-conformity to their expectations. Second, these parts of the PRS that can impose sanctions also impose other demands on the minister, inconsistent with the defense of racial integration before members who, in large part, believe in racial separation and whose beliefs are profoundly emotional.

The inability to impose sanctions. The national and regional associations that serve as the official "voice of the church" are not organized to confer effective rewards or punishments on individual ministers. Especially is this true in the case of failure to espouse national racial policy or to act decisively in the presence of racial tension. This is even more true of the local ministerial association; it does not presume to censure or praise its members. Conversely, the local church hierarchy is an immediate source of sanctions. It has the responsibility of recommending or assigning parishes, and of assisting the pastor in expanding the program of his church.

The probability and the nature of sanctions from fellow ministers among whom one has personal contacts and friends are somewhat more difficult to specify. However, it does not appear likely that he is subject to sanctions if he does not conform to their expectations by liberal behavior on racial matters. Should he indorse and actively support segregationist and violent elements, this would be another matter. If he is silent or guarded, however, it is not likely to subject him to sanction. The active integrationists in Little Rock expressed disappointment at the inaction of their associates while at the same time suggesting possible mitigating circumstances. There is no evidence that personal or professional ties had been damaged.

Among the various components of the PRS, then, only the local ecclesiastica, which does not exist for some, and, to a considerably lesser extent, fellow ministers, are conceivable sources influencing the minister's decision to be silent, restrained, or forthright.

Conflicting expections and mitigated pressures. The role of the minister as community reformer is not as institutionalized (i.e., it does not have as significant a built-in system of rewards and punishments) as are certain other roles associated with the ministry. The minister is responsible for the over-all conduct of the affairs of the church and is judged successful or unsuccessful according to how they prosper. He must encourage co-operative endeavor, reconciling differences, and bring people together. Vigor and high morale of the membership are reflected in increased financial support and a growing membership, and his fellow ministers and his church superiors are keenly sensitive to these evidences of his effectiveness. His goal, elusive though it may be, is maximum support from all members of an ever growing congregation.

The church hierarchy keeps records. It hears reports and rumors. It does not like to see divided congregations, alienated ministers, reduced membership, or decreased contributions. Responsible as it is for the destiny of the denomination in a given territory, it compares its changing fortunes with those of rival churches. In assigning ministers to parishes, it rewards some with prominent pulpits and punishes others with posts of low prestige or little promise. However exalted the moral virtue the minister expounds, the hierarchy does not wish him to damn his listeners to hell—unless somehow he gets them back in time to attend service next Sunday. Promotions for him are determined far less by the number of times he defends unpopular causes, however, virtuous their merit, than by the state of the physical plant and the state of the coffer.

Now it is especially commendable if the minister can defend the cause and state the imperative with such tact or imprint that cleavages are not opened or loyalties alienated. If, however, the moral imperative and church cohesion are mutually incompatible, there is little doubt that the church superiors favor the latter. One administrator told two of his ministers, "It's o.k. to be liberal, boys; just don't stick your neck out." Indeed, ecclesiastical officials advised younger ministers, systematically, to "go slow," reminding them of the possibility of permanent damage to the church through rash action.

Under these circumstances pressure from the national church to take an advanced position on racial matters loses much of its force. The minister is rewarded *only* if his efforts do not endanger the membership of the church: "Don't lose your congregation." Similarly, the prospect of an unfavorable response from his congregation protects him from the (possibly liberal) church hierarchy; he need only point to what happened to Pastor X, who did not heed the rumblings in his congregation. The higher officials, themselves keenly aware of local values and customs, will understand. And his fellow ministers, too, are, after all, in the same boat. They give him sympathy, not censure, if he says, "My hands are tied." An informal rationale develops that reassures the pastor: "These things take time," "You can't change people overnight," "You can't talk to people when they won't listen." There is strong sympathy for the forthright pastor who is in real trouble, but he is looked on as an object lesson. Thus the ministers reinforce each other in inaction, despite their common antipathy to segregation.

The self-reference system. We still must reckon with the demands the minister imposes upon himself. It is obvious that the actor has the power of self-sanction, through guilt. A threatening sense of unworthiness, of inadequacy in God's sight, cannot be taken lightly. Similarly, to grant one's self the biblical commendation "Well done" is a significant reward. We have said that the self is an influence favoring action in support of desegregation. Can the inactive integrationist, then, either avoid or control the sense of guilt?

Our data are not entirely appropriate to the question. Nevertheless, four circumstances—all of which permit of generalization to other cases—appear at least partially to prevent the sense of guilt. These include major characteristics of the ministerial role, several ministerial values and "working propositions," certain techniques for communicating without explicit commitment, and the gratifying reactions of extreme opposition forces.

The role structure. The church, as an institutional structure, sets criteria by which the minister may assess his management of the religious enterprise; it does *not* offer criteria by which to evaluate his stand on controversial issues.[10] This encourages, even compels, the minister to base his self-image, hence his sense of worth or unworth, on his success in managing his church. Thus, if church members do not share his goals, three types of institutionalized responsibilities restrain him in reform.

In the first place, the minister is required to be a cohesive force, to "maintain a fellowship in peace, harmony, and Christian love," rather than to promote dissension. Thus some ministers prayed during the Columbus Day services that members "carry no opinion to the point of disrupting the Christian fellowship."

Second, he is expected to show a progressive increase in the membership of his church. Pro-integration activity, lacking mass support, is likely to drive members to other churches.

Finally, his task is to encourage maximum annual giving and to plan for the improvement and expansion of the plant. It is hardly surprising that several inactive integrationists who were engaged in vital fund-raising campaigns shrank from action that might endanger their success.

Working propositions. The minister makes certain assumptions about his work that reduce the likelihood of guilt when he does not defend moral convictions that his members reject. He is, first, a devotee of education, by which he means the gradual growth and development of spiritual assets—in contrast to his counterpart of an earlier period, who was more likely to believe in sudden change through conversion. He also believes that communication with the sinner must be preserved at all costs ("You can't teach those you can't reach") and for long enough to effect gradual change in attitude and behavior. A crisis, when feelings run high, is not the time to risk alienating those one wishes to change. For example, Pastor X acted decisively but, in so doing, damaged or lost his pastorate: "Look at him; he can't do any good now."

Communication techniques. The minister may avoid committing himself unequivocally.[11] Some use the "every man a priest" technique, for example, the stating of his own opinion while expressing tolerance for contradictory ones and reminding his listeners that their access to God's truth is equal with his. Others use the "deeper issues" approach; generalities such as the brotherhood of man,

[10] Blizzard does not find a "community reformer" or "social critic" role in the ministry (see Samuel W. Blizzard, "The Minister's Dilemma," *Christian Century*, LXXIII [April 25, 1956], 508–10).

[11] For a full description and illustration of such techniques as used in Little Rock see our *Christians in Racial Crisis: A Study of Little Rock's Ministers* (Washington, D.C.: Public Affairs Press, 1959).

brotherly love, humility, and universal justice are discussed without specific reference to the race issue, in the hope that the listener may make the association himself. Still another course is to remind listeners that "God is watching," that the question of race has religious significance and therefore they should "act like Christians." There is also the method of deriding the avowed segregationists without supporting their opposites. The "exaggerated southerner" technique, which may be supplementary to any of the others, involves a heavy southern drawl and, where possible, reference to an aristocratic line of planter descent.

These techniques do not demand belief in integration as a Christian imperative. Further, except for the "every man a priest" technique, they do not commit the speaker to integrationist goals as religious values; the listener may make applications as he chooses. The speaker, on the other hand, can assure himself that the connections are there to be made; he supplies, as it were, a do-it-yourself moral kit.

Reaction of the opposition. The ministerial body in Little Rock, except for pastors to dissident fundamentalist sects, is defined by agitated segregationists as a bunch of "race-mixers" and "nigger-lovers." For example, the charge was made that the peace prayers were intended to "further integration under a hypocritical veneer of prayer" and that the sect pastors sponsored prayers for segregation "to show that not all of the city's ministers believe in mixing the races." Indeed, ministers of major denominations were charged with having "race

on the mind" so that they were straying from, even rejecting, the biblical standard to further their un-Christian goals.

The effect of opposition by segregation extremists was to convince certain inactive integrationists that indeed they *had* been courageous and forthright. The minister, having actually appropriated the opposition's evaluation of his behavior, reversing its affective tone found the reassurance he needed that his personal convictions had been adequately and forcefully expressed.

Were the force of the membership reference system not what it is, the professional reference system and the self-reference system would supply support to integration that was not limited to "law and order" appeals and the denunciation of violence. However, since "Don't lose your congregation" is itself a strong professional and personal demand, the force of the PRS is neutralized, and the pressure from the SRS becomes confused and conflicting. Inaction is a typical response to conflicting pressures within both the internal and the external system.

It is not surprising, then, that most Little Rock ministers have been far less active and vocal in the racial crisis than the policies of their national church bodies and their sense of identification with them, as well as their own value systems, would lead one to expect. Rather, what is surprising is that a small number continued to express vigorously the moral imperative as they saw it, in the face of congregational disaffection, threatened reprisal, and the lukewarm support or quiet discouragement of their superiors and peers.

2 · Clergyman as Counselor

ELAINE CUMMING AND CHARLES HARRINGTON

ABSTRACT. *The clergyman's role as counselor is examined with reference to its articulation with the whole deviance-controlling system. His activities appear to vary with the characteristics of his congregation and his own educational level. It is proposed that the effect is produced by certain strains, some of which inhibit the development of a system of divided labor between clergymen and other deviance-controlling agents, particularly social workers.*

This is the second report from a group of studies designed to discover how the task of controlling deviance in society is divided among the various integrative agents and agencies.[1] In this paper we report a study of the clergyman's description of his counseling role and an analysis of this role with emphasis upon its articulation with the rest of the controlling system.

Helping is a traditional activity of the clergy[2] and, as such, has received con-

siderable attention from social scientists. Recent studies have shown that a large number of people turn to clergymen when they are in trouble.[3] Studies of our own have shown that the clergyman ranks with the doctor as the first contact made outside the kinship and friendship circle during the onset of mental illness.[4] Most people appear to be satisfied with the help that they get from the clergyman.[5] As Eaton and his co-workers point out, "Clergy are close to many people during crucial periods of the life cycle. . . . For those who know they need help the clergy is accessible without a waiting list or an intake worker to screen applicants. And going to a clergyman does not require a self-admission of help-

SOURCE. Elaine Cumming and Charles Harrington, "Clergyman as Counselor," reprinted from *American Journal of Sociology*, 69, November, 1963, pp. 234–243 by permission of The University of Chicago Press.

[1] A revision of a paper read to the annual meetings of the American Sociological Association, Washington, D.C., 1962. The research reported was supported in part by NIMH Grant 4735, principal investigator, Elaine Cumming. Acknowledgment is made of the assistance of the staff of the Mental Health Research Unit, Syracuse, N.Y., and its director, John Cumming, under whose auspices the studies are taking place.
[2] See Benton Johnson, "The Development of

Pastoral Counseling Programs in Protestantism: A Sociological Perspective," *Pacific Sociological Review*, I (Fall, 1958), 59–63, and Robert S. Michaelsen, "The Protestant Ministry in America: 1850 to the Present," in H. Richard Niebuhr and Daniel D. Williams (eds.), *The Ministry in Historical Perspective* (New York, 1956).
[3] *Action for Mental Health: The Final Report of the Joint Commission on Mental Illness and Health* (New York, 1961).
[4] See Elaine Cumming, "Phase Movement in the Support and Control of the Psychiatric Patient," *Journal of Health and Human Behavior*, III (Winter, 1962), 235–41 (also see Bruce D. Dohrenwend, "Some Aspects of the Appraisal of Abnormal Behavior by Leaders in an Urban Area," *American Psychologist*, XVII, No. 4 [1962], 190–98).
[5] Gerald Gurin, Joseph Veroff, and Shiela Feld, *Americans View Their Mental Health*, Vol. IV of a series of monographs published by the Joint Commission on Mental Illness and Health (New York, 1960).

lessness on the part of the client."[6] In spite of his popularity, the clergyman's counseling role appears to some who have studied it to be "poorly defined,' "diffuse," and "conflicted." [7] Other observers have suggested that the clergyman has a peculiarly difficult role because of his sensitivity to the values and norms of his congregation.[8] Indeed, the clergyman is probably alone among integrative agents in being a member of the group he controls.[9]

In some respects the clergyman resembles the other helping and controlling agents in the community. All have poli-

cies and norms governing who may call upon them for what kinds of help and who should be referred for more specialized attention. These policies and norms set the agent apart as a recognizable system of action and define the "boundary conditions" that both separate him from, and relate him to, other systems. Concretely, an agent's boundary conditions determine the accessibility of his services to clients and other agencies, and help to regulate the patterns of mutual dependency—that is, the division of labor—among agents.

The clergyman's relationships with the remainder of the controlling system, the permeability of the boundary around his role as counselor, and his own helping practices can all be expected to resemble those of other agencies in some ways, but the major hypothesis tested in this study is that, *because the clergyman differs from other agents of social control in being normatively involved with his congregation, his behavior, including his articulation with these other agents, should be influenced by the characteristics of that congregation.*

I. The Study

In Syracuse, New York, a sample of sixty-one churches was selected. They included ten Roman Catholic, six Episcopal, three Lutheran, three Eastern Orthodox, eight Methodist, seven Presbyterian, five Baptist, ten fundamentalist, three Jewish, and six churches of other Protestant denominations. The sample was selected from the total universe of churches in Syracuse after they had been stratified by size, neighborhood status, and denomination, the latter grouped into five categories—Roman Catholic, liturgical Protestant, other Protestant, fundamentalist Protestant, and Jewish. The stratification yielded eighty cells; the sixty-one that contained churches were randomly

[6] Joseph W. Eaton *et al.*, *Pastoral Counseling in a Metropolitan Suburb* (Pittsburgh: Southeastern Community Guidance Association [4232 Brownsville Rd.], 1961).
[7] See Samuel Blizzard, "Role Conflicts of the Urban Parish Minister," *City Church*, VII (September, 1956), 13–15, and Allan W. Eister, "Religious Institutions in Complex Societies: Difficulties in the Theoretic Specifications of Functions," *American Sociological Review*, XXII (August, 1957), 387–91; see also Warren O. Hagstrom, "The Protestant Clergy as a Profession: Status and Prospects," *Berkeley Pub. Soc. Instit.*, III, No. 1 (Spring, 1957), 1–12; Waldo Burchard, "Role Conflicts of Military Chaplains," *American Sociological Review*, XIX, No. 5 (1954), 528–35; and Blizzard, *op. cit.*
[8] See Joseph H. Fichter, S.J., *Social Relations in the Urban Parish* (Chicago: University of Chicago Press, 1954), chap. x; Burchard, *op. cit.*; Ernest Campbell and Thomas F. Pettigrew, "Racial and Moral Crisis: The Role of Little Rock Ministers," *American Journal of Sociology*, LXIV (March, 1959), 509–16; Michaelsen, *op. cit.*, Lee Braude, "Professional Autonomy and the Role of the Layman," *Social Forces*, May, 1961.
[9] For a general discussion of this point see Talcott Parsons, *The Social System* (Glencoe, Ill.: Free Press, 1950), chap. x; Charles Kadushin, "Social Distance between Client and Professional," *American Journal of Sociology*, LXVII (March, 1962), 517; and Campbell and Pettigrew, *op. cit.*

sampled.[10] One clergyman from each of fifty-nine churches was interviewed as a representative of that church.[11] In churches with more than one clergyman, a pastor was allocated for interview by the clergyman in authority, usually on the basis of his interest in counseling. The results, therefore, should be generalized to the counseling activities of churches in Syracuse, not to the city's clergymen.

Three types of variables were examined: the characteristics of the clergyman and his congregation, the nature of the problems counseled, and the articulation of the clergyman's counseling role

with the remainder of the system. Each clergyman was asked to describe his congregation in terms of his age, income, residence, and occupation. With this information, the socioeconomic statuses that had been assigned to the churches on the basis of neighborhood reputation alone were modified. Finally, thirty-one of the fifty-nine churches were classified as upper or middle class and twenty-eight as working class.[12] The size of the congregation and the age and education of the clergyman himself were noted.

Each clergyman was asked to describe the problems brought to him for counseling and the extent of his counseling activities. Forty-one different types were distinguished from these descriptions. In Table 1 they have been divided into problems that more than half of the reporting clergymen counsel, and those that more than half of those reporting refer for service elsewhere. The problems are also grouped, in terms of their social characteristics, into three categories: (1) transition states, (2) deviant behavior, and (3) exigencies. The categories are rough, and decisions to include types in one category rather than another are sometimes based on the interviewer's interpretations, but they are an attempt to develop theoretical classifications of problems that can be expected to be differently handled by the clergy.

Transition states are the adjustment problems inherent in the life-cycle that everyone can expect to encounter. They include adolescent sex problems, need for vocational guidance, loneliness in old age or widowhood, bereavement, and

[10] Church names and addresses were taken from the City Directory; local church officials contributed further details. Size was classified as follows: small, up to 150 total members; medium, 150–500; large, 500–1,000; and very large, over 1,000. Neighborhood status was taken from Charles V. Willie, "Socioeconomic and Ethnic Areas" (unpublished Ph.D. dissertation, Syracuse University, 1957). The neighborhoods were classified as upper, middle, lower, and mixed metropolitan. The empty cells in the stratification plan are accounted for chiefly by the absence of small Roman Catholic churches and large fundamentalist churches. The latter group included the so-called store-front churches, seven of which no longer existed at the time of the research. These were replaced by further random choices from the cells. The sample included 10 of the 22 Roman Catholic churches, 6 of the 12 Episcopal, 3 of the 7 Lutheran, 3 of the 11 Eastern, 8 of the 17 Methodist, 7 of the 8 Presbyterian, 5 of the 15 Baptist, 10 of the 21 fundamentalist, 3 of the 8 Jewish, and 6 of the remaining 15 churches of other Protestant denominations. This represents, in terms of the grouping used, 45 per cent of the Roman Catholic, 40 per cent of the liturgical, 47 per cent of the other Protestant, 48 per cent of the fundamentalist, and 37 per cent of the Jewish churches.

[11] Two fundamentalist clergymen refused to be interviewed, although eight attempts were made in each case.

[12] Downtown churches with congregations of mixed economic status were classed as middle class, while those with only a few elderly wealthy people and a majority of very poor parishioners were classed as working class. The latter churches were once fashionable, but have been left in areas of transition and decay.

TABLE 1. *Incidence and Disposition of Problem Types*

	CLERGY REPORTING		PER CENT REFERRING (OF THOSE REPORTING)
	NO.	PER CENT ($N = 59$)	
Problems less than half reporting clergy refer:			
Transition states:			
Premarital counseling	49	83.1	42.9
Marriage and parent-child counseling	38	64.4	18.4
Counseling adolescents	29	49.1	17.2
Loneliness in old age or widowhood	29	49.1	13.8
Bereavement	14	23.7	00.0
Adjustment to puberty	14	23.7	00.0
Problems associated with the menopause	6	10.2	16.7
Adjustment to retirement	4	6.8	00.0
Deviant behavior:			
Marital conflict	37	62.7	48.6
Parent-child conflict	32	54.2	18.8
Criminal and quasi-criminal behavior	28	47.5	28.6
Infidelity	25	42.5	20.0
Depression and pathological guilt	21	35.6	47.6
Hostility, aggression, acting out	11	18.6	45.4
Sexual deviations	9	15.3	44.4
In-law and intergenerational disputes	9	15.3	11.1
General interpersonal conflict	9	15.3	33.3
"Neuroses" and "phobias"	7	11.9	42.8
Irresponsibility and immaturity	7	11.9	14.3
Neglect of children	6	10.2	33.3
Exigencies:			
Adjustment to interfaith marriages	16	27.1	6.3
Adjustment to physical illness	14	23.7	14.3
Adjustment to interethnic marriages	9	15.3	00.0
Unemployment (temporary financial aid)	7	11.9	28.5
Counseling kin of ill clients	6	10.2	16.7
Adjustment to economic dependency	3	5.1	00.0
Problems more than half reporting clergy refer:			
Transition states:			
Problems of child-bearing and adoptions	7	11.9	85.7
Deviant behavior:			
Vague mental disorders	45	76.3	71.1
Unwed mothers	42	71.2	78.6
Alcoholism	36	61.0	69.4
Sexual problems in marriage	22	37.3	63.6
"Psychoses," "paranoia," "schizophrenia"	15	25.4	73.3
Divorce and separation	15	25.4	66.7
"Psychopaths" and "mental defectives"	4	6.8	100.0
Exigencies:			
Insufficient income	42	71.2	57.1
Physical illness	18	30.5	88.9
Child care and support	18	30.5	55.6
Legal problems (non-criminal)	11	18.6	63.6
Housing problems	9	15.3	77.7
Senility	8	13.6	62.5
Transients	6	10.2	83.3

transient maladjustments. Clergymen would be expected to deal with these problems frequently.

Deviant behavior includes infidelity, criminal or quasi-criminal behavior, unwed motherhood, severe marital conflict, mental, emotional, and sexual disturbances, psychoses and neuroses, and chronic inability to get along with others. It would be reasonable to expect clergymen to refer many of these "pathological" problems.

Exigencies are essentially environmental; they include lack of money, unemployment, cultural conflicts and discontinuities, and adjustments to physical illness. The clergyman would be expected to refer those problems that he lacks concrete resources for solving and to counsel those not needing concrete help.

Each clergyman in the sample reported collaborating with others in the deviance-controlling system. These collaborations include contacts with nonprofessionals acting as informal sources of social control as well as with those professionally concerned with the control of deviance. A clergyman who participates in a system of divided labor with others can be thought of as having a high level of activity across the boundary of his counseling role.

A boundary activity score was computed from the clergyman's responses. Each clergyman was given one point for each of three signs of articulation with the larger controlling system. Thus, a score of two or three reflects relatively high boundary activity, while a score of zero or one, low activity and a relatively impermeable role boundary. The three indexes themselves form a Guttman-type scale. The items are:

1. *Receipt of referrals or information about clients from sources outside the congregation.* This characteristic was considered to reflect the accessibility of the clergyman as a helper, and also

others' recognition of this role in the helping system. Forty-two clergymen reported this item.

2. *At least one referral by the clergyman to an outside agency in the month prior to the interview.* This activity was taken to indicate that the clergyman perceives certain problems as outside his competence. Referrals indicate that he allows people to leave his sphere of influence and also that he perceives himself as acting with others in a system of divided labor. Twenty-eight clergymen reported this item.

3. *An active rather than a passive form of referral.* Some clergymen participate more actively in the referral process than others; these report that they telephone agencies to inquire if a service is available, make appointments for parishioners, or even accompany them to the agency. Other clergymen suggest to a client or parishioner where he may go for help but make no actual contact with the agency. These we call passive referrals. A passive style of referral suggests that the clergyman is less accessible for co-operative solutions of problems and is less influenced by the norms of the agency world. Twenty-six clergymen reported active participation in referrals.

The counseling of non-parishioners is another indication of the clergyman's accessibility, and forty-nine of the fifty-nine clergymen report this activity. While it does not discriminate well among them, and is therefore not included in the boundary score, this accessibility of the clergyman distinguishes him, together with some church-sponsored charitable agencies, from secular helping agencies, all of which have formal criteria of admission.

II. Findings

As the articulation of the clergyman's counseling role was the focus of this study, the boundary activity score was examined for its relationship with the other variables. It is not, however, considered to be an independent variable. All the relationships reported appear to be causally reversible.

As Table 2 shows, boundary-activity

TABLE 2. *Number of Clergymen by Boundary-Activity Score and Denomination*

		BOUNDARY SCORE*	
DENOMINATION	TOTAL NO.	0–1	2–3
All clergymen	59	25	34
Roman Catholic	10	2	8
Liturgical Protestant	12	5	7
Other Protestant	26	10	16
Fundamentalist	8	8	0
Jewish	3	0	3

* Fundamentalists have a significantly higher proportion of 0 and 1 scores than all other clergymen. $P = .0005$ by Fisher's exact test.

score is independent of denomination, except for the eight fundamentalists, all of whom have scores of 0 or 1. It seems reasonable to attribute the low scores of these pastors to the fact that they are leaders of small exclusive sects, but we will return to this point later. For the remainder of the clergymen in our sample, the boundary characteristics of the counseling role must be dependent on factors other than denomination and its associated theological differences.

Among the social-structural variables that have been linked to the clergyman's practices and attitudes are congregation size and socioeconomic class.[13] In Table

3 we see that boundary score is directly associated with the socioeconomic level of the congregation, and that within the working-class churches size is also associated. It may be, however, that size is itself related to status; the larger working-class churches tend to have stable congregations while the smaller ones are more likely to be "store-front" churches with impoverished or transient congregations.

Bearing in mind that clergymen of the largest middle-class churches have the most permeable role boundaries and those of the smallest working-class churches the least, we note that the twenty small working-class churches include seven of the eight fundamentalists, the remaining thirteen being distributed among all the remaining denominations except Roman Catholic. Controlling for church size and socioeconomic level, we find that although six of these seven fundamentalists have scores of zero, compared with six of the thirteen other remaining clergymen, this difference is not significant.[14] In short, for all churches, differences in the boundary activity appear to be associated with differences in characteristics of congregations other than denomination.

When the characteristics of the clergymen are examined, differences in bound-

[13] See Fichter, *op. cit.*, and Russell R. Dynes, "Church-Sect Typology and Socio-economic Status," *American Sociological Review*, Vol. XX (October, 1955); Thomas F. Hoult, *The Sociology of Religion* (New York, 1958); Max Weber, *Essays in Sociology* (New York, 1946); Louis Bultena, "Church Membership and Church Attendance in Madison, Wisconsin," *American Sociological Review*, XIV (1950), 364–388; and Walter Goldschmidt, "Clan Denominationalism in Rural California Churches," *American Journal of Sociology*, LXI (1944), 348–55.

[14] We have suggested above that the fundamentalists are qualitatively different from other denominations, but it is possible that, as they are the smallest and poorest churches, they represent only the final type in a series with graded boundary permeability. The numbers are so small, however, that the issue remains open.

ary score are not found to be significantly associated with age. The proportion of young clergymen, 23-34 years of age, having high boundary scores is 60 per cent, which is approximately the same as the comparable proportion of 67 per cent of the clergy who are 60 years of age and older. The proportion having high boundary scores of those who are 35-44 is 52 per cent, and of those who are 45-59, 62 per cent. This is surprising because younger clergymen might be expected to have received training for their counseling roles that would bring them into contact with social workers, physicians, psychologists, and so on, and, because of this, might possibly have become integrated into the deviance-controlling system. Details of each clergyman's training as a counselor were not available, however, so a direct test of this hypothesis is not possible.

The clergymen were divided into two groups according to whether or not they had received higher education at other than a theological or Bible school. While their level of education was found to be associated with boundary score, a much closer association was found between boundary score and the *concordance* between the clergyman's education and the socioeconomic status of his congregation.[15] Educated clergymen in middle-class churches and less-well-educated clergymen in working-class churches are considered concordant with their congregations. Educated clergymen in working-class congregations were considered discordant. There were no less-well-edu-

cated clergymen in middle-class congregations. An examination of the boundary scores of the clergymen classified according to their concordance with their congregation reveals that twenty-eight of the thirty-one clergy concordant with their middle-class congregations have high boundary scores, as compared with six of the fifteen clergy discordant with their working-class congregations and none of the thirteen clergy concordant with their working-class congregations. Comparing just the two working-class groups, the boundary score is significantly higher ($P = 0.018$, Fisher's exact test) among the discordant group than among the concordant group. The clergymen of middle-class congregations have been shown in Table 3 to have

TABLE 3. *Number of Clergymen by Boundary-Activity Score and Congregation Size and Class*

CONGREGATION TYPE	NO.	BOUNDARY SCORE 0-1	BOUNDARY SCORE 2-3
All congregations	59	25	34
Middle-class congregations	31	3	28*
More than 1000 members	16	1	15
Less than 1000 members	15	2	13
Working-class congregations	28	22	6*
More than 1000 members	8	3	5†
Less than 1000 members	20	19	1†

* Middle-class clergy have more high scores than working-class. $\chi^2 = 25.8$, degrees of freedom = 1, $P < 0.0001$.

† Clergymen of large working-class congregations have more high scores than those of small congregations. $P = 0.003$, Fisher's exact test.

[15] The middle-class concordant clergy includes: four Roman Catholic, five Episcopal, three other liturgical, sixteen Protestant, and three Jewish. The working-class discordant group includes: six Roman Catholic, one Episcopal, two other liturgical, five Protestant, one fundamentalist. The clergy concordant with working-class congregations includes: five Protestant, seven fundamentalist, and one liturgical.

higher boundary scores than those of working-class congregations. We see, then, that boundary score is strongly associated with concordance between the clergyman and his congregation, even when class is held constant.

Clergymen with high boundary scores report a higher rate of counseling activity[16] than those with low scores. Of the seventeen with a large case load, fifteen have high boundary scores. At the other extreme, only three of the fifteen with small case loads have high boundary scores. The group with medium case loads occupies an intermediate place with sixteen of the twenty-seven having high boundary scores. These differences are statistically significant ($z = 3.91$; $P < .00005$, Wilcoxon signed ranks). In addition, the clergy with high boundary scores also report more types of problems in all three categories. This may mean that the impermeable boundary reduces the numbers of applicants, or it may mean that there are few applicants and thus the clergyman is not called upon to make the kind of contact that would give him a high boundary-activity score. Furthermore, those clergymen who have more contacts with the rest of the deviance-controlling system and who also see a larger number of clients may discriminate more finely between similar problems and thus tend to report a larger number of types. For example, a clergyman who counsels one marital problem a year calls it just that; a clergyman counseling fifty marital problems and referring ten of them to other agencies may differentiate those associated with cultural conflict from those arising from sexual maladjustment, and so on.

The clergymen from this sample of churches, regardless of their boundary conditions, report that they refer many more clients to other agents than are referred to them and they refer to many agencies that never reciprocate with referrals to them. In all, they report refer-

ring to more than 50 agencies—and the average clergyman refers to 5.4. The most popular referral targets are Planned Parenthood Association, County Welfare Department, Alcoholics Anonymous, and physicians—all agencies specializing in a specific concrete service. The clergy themselves receive referrals from an average of only 0.63 agencies, most commonly from physicians. Many Protestant clergymen expressed discontent with this asymmetry of referrals.[17]

In other studies in this series, it has been noted that social workers appear to consider clergymen "too judgmental" and have complained of their inability to "give up" the client. Clergymen, on the other hand, appear to suspect social workers of an "amorality" that will undermine their parishioners' spiritual values. Some clergymen say that social workers "hold onto" clients longer than is necessary; they complain that social agencies will not give them information that they need in order to help the parishioner.

In summary, we have found the following:

1. The hypothesis that the articulation of the clergyman's counseling role to the remaining deviance-controlling system is related to the characteristics of the congregation is lost regarding denomination, but upheld regarding size and socioeconomic status. This relationship is not, however, a simple one—concordance between education and socioeconomic status predicts boundary activity quite accurately, but discordance does not predict at all.

2. Clergymen with low boundary scores report less counseling and describe fewer types of problems brought for

---

[16] The size of the clergyman's case load was ranked by two coders independently, using answers to all relevant interview questions. All differences were then resolved between the coders.

[17] For a discussion of this strain see George Todd Kalif, "Pastoral Use of Community Resources," *Pastoral Psychology*, November, 1950.

counseling. Nevertheless, clergymen from all types of congregations report counseling all of the three major types of problems. Deviant behavior is referred frequently; transitional problems and exigencies, less frequently.

3. The clergyman refers more clients than he receives and he uses more agents than use him. This asymmetry is related to both the readiness of the average person to approach a clergyman for help and the tensions between clergymen and some other supporting and controlling groups.

We can now discuss some possible interpretations of these findings and in particular suggest new variables that might throw more light on the clergyman's counseling role. Before doing so, however, it should be repeated that the analysis rests upon the clergyman's image of his counseling role, and although for some purposes this does not matter, systematic distortions might lead to an erroneous picture of the clergyman's position in the total integrative system.

III. Discussion

The findings of this study might be interpreted in a number of ways. It might be proposed that different norms develop in congregations of different social-structural types and that these norms might differ in regard to the amount of time properly spent by the clergyman on nonspiritual matters. Perhaps the most parsimonious interpretation, however, can be developed by considering the clergymen's role in the greater system and particularly the strain to which it is subject. These strains are of two kinds—those concerned with disparities between the clergyman's reference groups and his membership groups and those concerned with the position of the clergyman as counselor in the larger deviance-controlling system.

Strains between reference groups and membership groups. The clergyman's membership in his congregation can be expected to have three important outcomes. First, he will develop, in interaction, some sentiments that he shares with them. Second, he will develop, again through interaction, diffuse, solidary bonds with some members, and third, he will be identified with his congregation by those outside it.

If the clergyman has a college education he will be likely to share some attitudes with other college-trained professionals including social workers, psychologists, and physicians; such a clergyman might be expected to appear on committees with other professionals and also to know them socially.[18] Referrals from clergymen of middle-class churches should be facilitated by shared values and personal friendships, and the larger the church, the more such bridges it is likely to have. Finally, social workers and psychiatrists who know a clergyman personally are more likely to exempt him from the stigma of "judgmental clergyman," and to consider him "professionalized" or "sophisticated," and thus to co-operate with him in the management of some clients. Such a relatively conflict-free situation may well lie behind the high boundary scores of the educated clergymen of middle-class congregations.

[18] Seven clergymen within our sample are board members of agencies affiliated with the Community Chest. Of these, six are from middle-class congregations, as we would expect. The lone clergyman from a working-class congregation seems a special case. He has retired from administrative positions in denominational agencies and has recently agreed to come out of retirement to minister to a small congregation that cannot afford to hire a full-time clergyman because it is in a depressed transitional area of town. His position in an agency board—a church affiliated one—seems to be a function of his past activity in agencies rather than his present ministry.

In contrast to these educated clergymen, those in working-class congregations cannot expect so high a level of compatibility among their own attitudes, those of their congregations, and those of the agency system. Such clergymen will not have access to outside resources through overlapping memberships, although they may have personal friendships among other professionals, share many viewpoints with them, and use them as reference groups. Many studies have shown, however, that these same professionals prefer middle-class clients,[19] and the clergyman, if he has personal contacts among agency professionals, will know this and perhaps be reluctant to risk a rebuff by interceding for his parishioners. Such a situation has the conditions necessary for a classical role conflict and may be the reason for the lesser use of the agency system reported by this group of clergymen. If, on the other hand, the clergyman does not have personal contacts among professionals, he will not be subject to the same conflict, but the professionals will tend to identify him with this congregation and be doubly reluctant to accept referrals of working-class clients from an unknown, working-class, and "judgmental" clergyman. If this is so, these latter clergymen should resemble the final group, the less-well-educated clergymen in the working-class churches, and a critical test of the formulation would lie in seeing whether the discordant clergymen who referred clients had personal contacts in the target agencies while those who did not refer had none.

In working-class churches where the clergyman's lack of higher education renders him concordant with his congregation, we would expect the clergyman to have a solidary relationship with his congregation but little access to the agency system. This, together with the agencies' own preference for middle-class clients, may explain the scant use made of outside resources by these clergymen.

It is interesting that less-well-educated clergymen do not appear in our sample in middle-class churches, although it is a theoretical possibility for some Protestant denominations. Such a situation may be inherently unstable because the clergyman would be expected to have difficulty establishing bonds with either the congregation or the agency system while at the same time bonds that existed between the latter groups might be expected to exclude him.

Strains between the clergyman and the rest of the controlling system. We have hypothesized that role conflicts arise when certain kinds of clergymen minister to certain kinds of congregations. Some other types of strains can be thought of as affecting all clergymen because of the relationship of their role to the rest of the system.

The first type of strain seems to arise just because the clergyman is a familiar and accessible figure whom people feel they can approach. His accessibility forces him into a referral role. He sorts and sifts those who come to him, and allocates those that he cannot help to other services—often after a period of trial-and-error counseling. This allocation process involves defining the parishioner as sick or deviant, and he is almost always reluctant to do this when the problems are transitional or arise in exigencies. For example, clergymen often give financial help during temporary unemployment so that parishioners will be spared the humiliation of applying for public assistance. In other words, unless the clergyman is totally isolated from the control system, his position in it imposes on him the obligation of allocating clients

[19] See Jerome K. Myers and Leslie Schaffer, "Social Stratification and Psychiatric Practice: A Study of an Out-Patient Clinic," *American Sociological Review,* XIX (June, 1954), 307–10.

to services, and this involves him in decisions that are difficult to make. It also involves him in an automatic asymmetry with respect to the rest of the agency system. He cannot at once be the allocator and the target agent,[20] and so he perceives himself as giving more than he gets.

Besides the strain arising from the clergyman's position, strains inhere in the counseling function. Although there is an increasing specialization among agencies offering the so-called face-to-face services, it is questionable that counseling can be distinguished clearly from intensive casework. Because of haziness about where one leaves off and the other begins, considerable attention is paid to the training required for each. Pastoral counseling is perceived as requiring less training than casework, and so the social worker tends to regard the clergyman as an amateur. His feeling of responsibility for the total client is interpreted as "incomplete professionalization" and his willingness to deal with the respondent's moral well-being is seen as judgmental— a term of anathema. All of this need not lead to conflict if the clients qualifying for casework services were clearly different from those qualifying for counseling. Our studies suggest, however, that the clergyman and the social agency compete for what is often called the "motivated

[20] In this he differs from the physician. In our own studies we have found (see, e.g., n. 4) that the general practitioner is also a gatekeeper in the sense that people turn to him when informal resources fail, but he receives as many patients by referral as he sends to other agencies, and thus does not perceive himself as supplying other people with patients and receiving none in return.

client," and this competition exacerbates the tension between the two groups. The helping task might be divided between clergymen and social workers either on the basis of function or on the basis of the target population, but as neither is done, each tends to regard the other redundant. Such solidarity as exists between clergyman and social worker is based on a commonality of interest, as we have argued above, and not on interdependence. The clergymen of this study appear to have much less strain in their dealings with physicians, lawyers, housing authorities, and other agents whose specific functions do not overlap with their own.

Finally, the membership of the clergyman in the group he counsels puts him in a position similar to that of the physician who will not treat his family and dislikes treating his friends. For all clergymen, this strain may act as an encouragement to refer. Those whose structural situation cuts them off entirely from the world of social agencies may be reducing the strain by circumscribing their counseling activities.

Returning to our point of departure— the division of labor among the integrative agents—we can see that the clergyman's position in the system involves him in a dual role. He is a counselor, but because he is approached so early in the search for help, he is called upon to allocate many clients to other agencies. The frustration that the clergyman experiences because of the asymmetry of his relationship with other agents appears to be offset by the rewards attendant upon his historic role as counselor— a role that he views as an intrinsic part of his ministry.

H · DILEMMAS IN INSTITUTIONALIZATION

1 · Five Dilemmas in the Institutionalization of Religion

THOMAS F. O'DEA

An institutional complex may be viewed as the concrete embodiment of a cultural theme in the on-going life of a society, as the "reduction" of a set of attitudes and orientations to the expected and regularized behavior of men. These institutionalized expectations include definitions of statuses and roles, goals, and prescribed and permitted means, and they articulate with the culture of the society and with the personality structures that the socialization processes have produced in a given society.[1]

It is the great virtue of social institutions from the point of view of the functioning of social systems that they provide stability in a world of inconstancy. The unusual and creative performance of the hero, sage or saint, though of great exemplary and genetic importance, is too unpredictable to become the basis of everyday life. The human world would be an unsteady and incalculable affair indeed were it chiefly dependent upon

such phenomena. Yet the achievement of the necessary stability involves a price. It involves a certain loss of spontaneity and creativity, although these are often found operating in some measure within the expectations of institutional patterns.

The founded religions display this fundamental antinomy in their histories. They begin in "charismatic moments" and proceed in a direction of relative "routinization." This development necessary to give objective form to the religious movement and insure its continuity may in Weber's terms proceed either in a traditional or a rational-legal direction.[2] Such routinization is an unavoidable social process, and as such represents for religious institutions a many-sided and complex paradox.

The charismatic moment is the period of the original religious experience and its corresponding vitality and enthusiasm.

SOURCE. Thomas F. O'Dea, "Five Dilemmas in the Institutionalization of Religion," *Journal for the Scientific Study of Religion*, 1, October, 1961, pp. 32–39.
[1] See Talcott Parsons, *The Social System*, The Free Press, Glencoe, Illinois, 1951.

[2] Max Weber, *The Theory of Social and Economic Organization*, Talcott Parsons, and A. M. Henderson, tr., Oxford University Press, New York, 1947, pp. 363ff. Also From Max Weber; *Essays in Sociology*, Hans Gerth and C. Wright Mills, tr. Oxford University Press. New York, 1946, pp. 53, 54, 262ff, 297, 420.

Since . . . this experience involves the deep engagement of the person involved with a "beyond" which is sacred, it is unusual in a special sense. It would remain a fleeting and impermanent element in human life without its embodiment in institutional structures to render it continuously present and available. Yet in bringing together two radically heterogeneous elements, ultimacy and concrete social institutions, the sacred and the profane, this necessary institutionalization involves a fundamental tension in which five functional dilemmas take their origin.

In other words, religion both needs most and suffers most from institutionalization. The subtle, the unusual, the charismatic, the supra-empirical must be given expression in tangible, ordinary, and empirical social forms. Let us now examine the five dilemmas which express this fundamental antinomy inherent in the relation of religion to normal social processes.

1. The Dilemma of Mixed Motivation

In the pre-institutionalized stage of a religious movement, the classical type of which is the circle of disciples gathered about a charismatic leader, the motivation of the followers is characterized by single-mindedness. The religious movement does satisfy complex needs for its adherents, but it focuses their satisfaction upon its values and their embodiment in the charismatic leader. The charismatic call receives a wholehearted response. With the emergence of a stable institutional matrix, there arises a structure of offices—of statuses and roles—capable of eliciting another kind of motivation, involving needs for prestige, expression of teaching and leadership abilities, drives for power, aesthetic needs, and the quite prosaic wish for the

security of a respectable position in the professional structure of the society.

The contrast we have drawn between the earlier and later stages is not absolute as we can see in the Gospel where we read of the disciples of Jesus concerning themselves with who shall be highest in the kingdom. (Mt 18:1, Mk 10:37) Yet such self-interested motivation is in the charismatic period easily dominated by the disinterested motivation of the charismatic response.[3] Moreover, while the charismatic movement offers security to its adherents, it does so quite differently than do the statuses of well institutionalized organizations.

It is precisely because of its ability to mobilize self-interested as well as disinterested motivation behind institutionalized patterns that institutionalization contributes stability to human life. Yet if this mobilization of diverse motives is its great strength, it is paradoxically also its great weakness. It may in fact become the Achilles' heel of social institutions. The criteria of selection and promotion within the institutional structure must of necessity reflect the functional needs of the social organization and emphasize performance and therefore will not distinguish very finely between the two types of motivation involved. Thus it may develop that the self-interested motivation will come to prevail. There will then result a slow transformation of the original institutional aims, in many cases amounting to their corruption. When the institution so transformed is suddenly confronted by threat or crisis, the transformed motivation and outlook may reveal itself as impotence. Careerism that is only formally concerned with institutional goals, bureaucratic rigorism of a

[3] Talcott Parsons has most clearly shown how social structure is a balance of motivation. See his *The Social System* and *Essays in Sociological Theory,* The Free Press, Glencoe, Ill., 1959.

type that sacrifices institutional goals to the defense or pursuit of vested interests,[4] and official timidity and lethargy are some evidences of the transformation.

Such developments give rise to movements of protest and reform, ever recurring phenomena in the history of the founded religions. The Cluniac reform of the Middle Ages offers a striking example as does the Protestant Reformation of the 16th century.

This dilemma of mixed motivation is found not only among those who occupy important positions in the religious organization. It is also characteristic of changes in the composition of the membership with the passing of the charismatic movement and the founding generation. The passing of the founding generation means that the religious body now contains people who have not had the original conversion experience. Many are born members and their proportion increases with the years. The selection process which voluntary conversion represented often kept out of the organization precisely the kinds of persons who are now brought up within it. Already in the year 150 A.D., Hermas in THE SHEPHERD draws a most unflattering picture of some of the lukewarm "born Christians" in the Church.

2. The Symbolic Dilemma: Objectification versus Alienation

Man's response to the holy finds expression not only in community but also in acts of worship.[5] Worship is the fundamental religious response but in order to survive its charismatic moment worship must become stabilized in established forms and procedures.[6] Thus ritual develops, presenting to the participant an objectified symbolic order of attitude and response to which he is to conform his own interior disposition. Worship becomes something not immediately derivative of individual needs, but rather an objective reality imposing its own patterns upon the participants.

Such objectification is an obvious prerequisite for common and continuous worship, for without it prayer would be individual and ephemeral. The symbolic elements of worship are not simply expressions of individual response, but have an autonomy enabling them to pattern individual response. Yet here too the element of dilemma appears. The process of objectification, which makes it possible for cult to be a genuine social and communal activity, can proceed so far that symbolic and ritual elements become cut off from the subjective experience of the participants. A system of religious liturgy may come to lose its resonance with the interior dispositions of the members of the religious body. In such a case the forms of worship become alienated from personal religiosity, and whereas previously cult had evoked and patterned response and molded personal religiosity after its own image,[7] now such an over-extension of objectification leads to routinization. Liturgy then becomes a set of counters without symbolic impact upon the worshippers. It may of course

[4] Robert K. Merton, *Social Theory and Social Structure*, The Free Press, Glencoe, Illinois, 1957. See especially "Social Structure and Anomie," pp. 131–160.

[5] An important book, recently reissued, on this subject is *Worship*, Evelyn Underhill, Harper Torchbook, Harper & Brothers, New York, 1957. There is much modern liturgical research, for example see *Liturgical Piety*, Louis Gouyer, University of Notre Dame Press, Notre Dame, Indiana, 1955. See also *Early Christian Worship*, Oscar Cullman, A. Stewart Todd and James B. Torrence, tr. SCM Press, London, 1953.

[6] *Christian Worship: Its Origin and Evolution*, Louis Duchesne, M. L. McClure, tr. Gorham, New York, 1904.

[7] See *Liturgy and Personality*, Dietrich von Hildebrand, Longmans, Green and Co., New York, London, Toronto, 1943.

retain its element of sacredness through the very fact of its obscurity and mystery, a situation conducive to the development of a semi-magical or magical attitude.

This process may be seen in the Christian history of the Middle Ages when it became necessary for Churchmen to replace the lost correspondence between external act and gesture and interior psychological disposition in the Mass with an elaborate secondary allegorization such as that of Durandus which appears so ridiculous in the light of modern liturgical research. One result of such alienation of symbolic systems is to weaken the social character of worship with a consequent weakening of the solidarity of the religious community. Individual prayer as a concomitant of public rites replaces communal worship.

What we have indicated with respect to cult could also be traced out with respect to graphical and musical expression as well. Here too, overextension of the objectification of symbols can turn them into counters, themes can degenerate into clichés, and at times symbols may become simply objectively manipulatable "things" to be used for achieving ends. In the last case religion becomes semi-magic. Parallels can be made with verbal symbolism where the statement of important religious insights in words suffers routinization and a consequent alienation from interior religiosity and deep understanding occurs. Profound statements then become merely facile formulae.

The alienation of symbolism is one of the most important religious developments and its possibility and likelihood derives from the fact that the religious symbol is in itself an antinomy—an expression *par excellence* of the dilemma of institutionalizing religion.[8] To symbol-

[8] See Mircea Eliade, *Comparative Patterns of Religion,* Sheed and Ward, New York, 1958.

ize the transcendent is to take the inevitable risk of losing the contact with it. To embody the sacred in a vehicle is to run the risk of its secularization. Yet if religious life is to be shared and transmitted down the generations the attempt must be made.

Historians have too often failed to see the importance of this dilemma, although the history of religious protest movements is full of evidence of just how central it is. The symbol—word, gesture, act, or painting, music and sculpture—provides the medium of genuine communication and sharing and thereby the basis for socializing the religious response. When it is lost a central element in the religious life disappears. Moreover, when the resonance between the external and internal is lost, the symbol often becomes a barrier where previously it had been a structured pathway. It then becomes the object of aggression. Hence it is that the English Reformation concentrated so much of its fire upon the Mass, the priest as the celebrant of the Mass, the destruction of altars, stained glass, statues, etc. The radical anti-symbolism of the Puritans derives from the same experience of lost resonance with the established liturgy. This is one kind of protest that can arise as a response to this dilemma. In the Catholic and Protestant movements for liturgical renascence to be seen in our own day we see another kind of response to these developments.

3. The Dilemma of Administrative Order: Elaboration versus Effectiveness

Max Weber showed that charismatic leadership soon undergoes a process of routinization into a traditional or rational-legal structure made up of a chief and an administrative staff. There is an elaboration and standardization of procedures and the emergence of statuses and roles within a complex of offices. One important aspect is the development in many cases of a distinction between the office and its incumbent, which has become characteristic of the bureaucratic structures of the modern world. The Catholic Church has been the chief prototype in this evolution of the concept of office in European society.

It is characteristic of bureaucratic structure to elaborate new offices and new networks of communication and command in the face of new problems. Precedents are established which lead to the precipitation of new rules and procedures. One result may indeed be that the structure tends to complicate itself. This state of affairs evolves in order to cope with new situations and new problems effectively. Yet such self-complication can overextend itself and produce an unwieldly organization with blocks and breakdowns in communication, overlapping of spheres of competence, and ambiguous definitions of authority and related functions. In short, developments to meet functional needs can become dysfunctional in later situations. Weber noted that bureaucracy of the rational-legal type was the most effective means for rational purposeful management of affairs. Yet the word bureaucracy has not become a pejorative epithet in the folklore of modern Western societies for nothing. The tendency of organization to complicate itself to meet new situations often transforms it into an awkward and confusing mechanism within whose context it is difficult to accomplish anything.

This dilemma of the necessity of developing a system of administrative order versus the danger of its over-elaboration must be seen in relation to the first dilemma—that of mixed motivation. For the involvement of secondary motivation in bureaucratic vested interests complicates this third dilemma considerably. Genuine organizational reform becomes threatening to the status, security and self-validation of the encumbents of office. The failure of many attempts at religious and ecclesiastical reform in the 14th and 15th centuries is significantly related to this third dilemma and its combination with the first. The Tridentine insistence on organizational reform in the Catholic Counter Reformation as well as the great concern of the Protestant Reformation with the forms of ecclesiastical organization indicates that contemporaries were not unaware of this aspect of their problems.

Certainly such self-complication of procedures and offices is one of the elements involved in Arnold J. Toynbee's observation that an elite seldom solves two major problems challenging its leadership, for successful solution of the first transforms and incapacitates it for meeting the second.

4. The Dilemma of Delimitation: Concrete Definition versus Substitution of Letter for Spirit

In order to affect the lives of men, the import of a religious message must be translated into terms that have relevance with respect to the prosaic course of everyday life. This translation is first of all a process of concretization. It involves the application of the religious insight to the small and prosaic events of ordinary life as lived by quite ordinary people. In that process the religious ideas and ideals themselves may come to appear to be of limited prosaic significance. Concretization may result in finitizing the religious message itself. For example, ethical insights are translated into a set of rules. Since rules, however elaborate, cannot make explicit all that is implied in the original ethical epiphany, the process of evolving a set of rules becomes a process of delimiting the import of the original message. Translation becomes a betraying transformation. Moreover, the more elaborate the rules become in the attempt to meet real complexities and render a profound and many-sided ethic tangible and concrete, the greater the chance of transforming the original insight into a complicated set of legalistic formulae and the development of legalistic rigorism. Then, as St. Paul put it, the letter killeth but the spirit giveth life.

Yet the fact is that the ethical insight must be given some institutionalized concretization or it will remain forever beyond the grasp of the ordinary man. The high call of the ethical message may well, however, be reduced to petty conformity to rules in the process. Brahmanic developments of ritual piety, Pharisaic rituals in late classical Judaism and legalism in Catholicism offer three examples. This fourth dilemma may be compounded with the third and the over-elaboration of administrative machinery be accompanied by a deadening legalism. It may also become compounded with the second and the delimitation of the religious and ethical message may contribute to and be affected by the loss of interior resonance of the verbal and other symbols involved.

5. The Dilemma of Power: Conversion versus Coercion

The religious experience exercises a call. In Otto's words, its content "shows itself as something uniquely attractive and *fascinating*." [9] Moreover, the propagation of the religious message in Christianity has involved an invitation to interior change. This interior "turning" or "conversion" is the classical beginning of the religious life for the individual. With institutionalization of the religious movement, such a conversion may be replaced by the socialization of the young so that a slow process of education and training substitutes for the more dramatic conversion experience. Yet even in

[9] Rudolf Otto, *The Idea of the Holy*, J. W. Harvey tr., Oxford U. Press, London, 1923.

this case, the slower socialization in many instances serves as a propaedeutic for conversion. Christians, both Catholic and Protestant, agree that the act of acceptance must be voluntary, involving such interior turning.

However, as religion becomes institutionalized it becomes a repository of many of the values from which much of the life of the society derives its legitimation. Thus the preservance of religious beliefs and even the maintenance of the religious organization can come to be intertwined with societal problems of public order and political loyalty. This tends to become the case whether or not there is a legal separation of church and state.

In addition, since religion is dependent upon interior disposition and since that disposition is subject to numerous unexpected shocks and is always weak among those merely nominally religious, there is always the subtle temptation for religious leaders to avail themselves of the close relation between religion and cultural values in order to reinforce the position of religion itself. A society may find itself unable to tolerate religious dissent, since such dissent is seen as threatening the consensus upon which social solidarity rests. Religious leaders may be tempted to utilize the agencies of a society so disposed to reinforce the position of their own organization.

While such an interpenetration of religious adherence and political loyalty may strengthen the position of religion in the society, it may also weaken it in important respects. It may antagonize members of the religious body who are political oppositionists, and it may antagonize political oppositionists who otherwise might have remained religiously neutral. Second it may produce an apparent religiosity beneath which lurks a devastating cynicism. History offers many examples of such a coalescing of religious and political interests. Punitive use of the secular arm, the later confessional states in both Catholic and Protestant countries with their "union of throne and altar," and the real though unofficial identification of Protestantism with American nationalism and even nationality in the 19th century offer some cases.

A genuine dilemma is involved. Religion cannot but relate itself to the other institutions of society since religious values must be worked out to have some relation to the other values of a particular cultural complex. Since religion is concerned with ultimate values which legitimate other values and institutions, a relation with established authority and power structures is unavoidable. Such partial identification of basic values in religion and culture tends to strengthen both religious conformity and political loyalty. Yet with the progressive differentiation of society, the confusion of the two soon tends to be detrimental to both. It weakens the bonds of the religious community by weakening voluntary adherence and thereby diluting the religious ethos and substituting external pressures for interior conviction. It weakens the general society by narrowing the possibility of consensus among the population by insisting on a far greater area of value agreement than would in fact be necessary to the continued life of society. Yet some relation between the functionally necessary values in a society and the ultimate sanction of religion is necessary and it necessarily involves a relation between religious institutions and power and authority structures.

Anyone acquainted with the religious wars of the 16th century will readily recognize this dilemma as one important element involved. The long and painful travail of the development of religious freedom was made more difficult by such a confusion of religious and societal interests. Moreover, this confusion caused many men to welcome secularization

since it brought a measure of liberation from the fanatical conflicts of the preceeding period.

These five dilemmas represent five sides of the central dilemma involved in the institutionalization of religion, a dilemma which involves transforming the religious experience to render it continuously available to the mass of men and to provide for it a stable institutionalized context. The nature of the religious experience tends to be in conflict wth the requisites and characteristics of the institutionalization process and the resultant social institutions. From this incompatibility there derive the special problems of the functioning of religious institutions delineated in this paper. Some of these antinomies have their analogues in other social institutions. Yet there is reason to suspect that because of the unique character of the religious experience, its elements of incompatibility with institutionalization are more exaggerated than is the case with other areas of human activity. Yet *mutatis mutandis* these dilemmas are applicable to other institutions as well. Indeed the present theoretical formulation represents one way of apprehending general instabilities inherent in social processes or more precisely in the relation between institutionalization and spontaneous creativity.

Such instabilities have been studied— in some cases for a very long time—in terms of other categories of analysis. The first and fifth dilemmas are related to the problem of restraining force and fraud which besets all societies, and which has been a concern of European political philosophy since the Middle Ages. Yet our treatment reveals important new elements. It gets away from an ethical treatment to an analysis of inevitable tendencies in the development of social organizations and their changing relation to their participants. The second, third and fourth dilemmas are really special forms of that general social process that Weber called "the routinization of charisma." Our formulation has, however, indicated facets of the problem which Weber did not pursue. Actually the fifth dilemma is discussed, in substantially the form presented here, by Talcott Parsons in his book, *The Social System.* He was the first to use the term "dilemma of institutionalization" which he applied to this fifth dilemma.[10]

The present formulation obviously bears a close resemblance to Troeltsch's treatment of the perennial tension between the transcendent call of the New Testament and the world, giving rise to the ecclesiastical tendency to compromise and the sectarian rejection of compromise with the world. The present treatment, however, calls attention to other and more subtle aspects of the "world" which need considerable empirical investigation. For example nowhere is the social and psychological problem of the alienation and "wearing out" of symbolism given the kind of investigation it deserves. Nor are the functionally unavoidable elements involved in the dilemma of mixed motivation the object of the kind of research which is needed if we are to understand on both sociological and psychological levels what actually is involved in the day to day functional problems of religious institutions.

The present statement does attempt to indicate how we can go beyond all these previous formulations and tries to gather their insights into a consistent scheme dealing with one important dynamic set of factors internal to the functioning of religious movements and bodies. It is a conceptual scheme derived chiefly from the history of Christianity, and particularly of Catholicism. In no way does it pretend to be an overall framework for

[10] *The Social System,* Talcott Parsons, The Free Press, Glencoe, Illinois, 1951, pp. 165–166.

the sociology of religion, but rather to be what Merton called theory of the middle range dealing with one side or aspect of the complex phenomenon of institutionalized religion. A further examination of the meaning of ultimacy in the religious experience, for example, would throw meaningful light on the element of authoritarianism in much of the history of institutionalized religion in the West. For it is precisely this recognition of and response to the ultimate which, when objectified in institutionalized forms, has in the past led to ecclesiastical imperialism and authoritarian rigor.

In the present paper we have simply attempted to indicate the importance of an internal functional analysis of religious institutions based upon their own peculiar inner structure which derives from the particular religious experience upon which they happen to have arisen. Then we turned to follow out such an analysis with respect to one aspect of the founded religions, that derived from the basic antinomy involved in an institutionalization of religion. The present statement has the advantage of articulating with other theoretical developments in sociology today. It is consistent with theory in the field of the analysis of social systems, and with much theory and research upon bureaucratic structure. Its emphasis upon emergence relates it to work done by both sociologists and social psychologists on small groups. Moreover, it introduces the historical dimension into the heart of sociological analysis. The understanding of behavior in old established religious bodies requires some knowledge of the transformations which the group has undergone in its past history. Finally it indicates the relation of certain of these historical processes to human motivation and its transformation and expression in institutional forms.

While specific to the field of the study of religious institutions the present analytical scheme points to a fundamental dilemma involved in all institutionalization. It may be stated with stark economy as follows: what problems are involved for social systems in their attempt to evolve workable compromises between spontaneity and creativity on the one hand and a defined and stable institutionalized context for human activity on the other? Spontaneity and creativity are the very stuff of human vitality and the source of necessary innovation. Yet social institutions are necessary as the context for action for without them life would dissolve into chaos. Moreover, men inevitably evolve stable institutionalized forms. The present emphasis provides some element of corrective to the kind of "sociologism" which sees the ready-made, the emerged, the products of past interaction as so important that the importance of the new, the emergent, the coming to be, is missed.

Part Six

ON THE RELIGIOUS SCENE

IN THE UNITED STATES

ALTHOUGH some material on the religious scene in the United States has been included in this volume, it certainly has not been enough to render anything like a "comprehensive" view of that scene. Nor can it be claimed that the present terminal Part Six of the volume supplies materials necessary for a genuinely comprehensive view. The title of the present Part is indeed intended to give a suggestion of incompleteness. But the readings in the Part are nevertheless offered as items that set out with some skill matters that are important in connection with religion in the United States—and such matters must obviously have a rather special interest both for American sociologists concerned with religion and for American students of religion generally.

The first reading, Will Herberg's Harlan Paul Douglass Lecture on "America's Three-Religion Pluralism," presents a view of religion in the context of American culture and society and of the relations of the three main American faiths to one another that is most provocative and that has been highly influential in some intellectual circles. Herberg sup-

plies one of the more interesting modifications and elaborations of the original church-sect dichotomy. His work has other evident points of contact with matters previously encountered in this volume. The reader may wish to refer again to Parsons' article in Part Four, in the light of what Herberg has to say. He should note the particular way in which Herberg treats Wesley's argument about riches and religion.

Whether Herberg is right or not in his notion that current American religious developments will in the short run intensify, but in the long run alleviate, Protestant-Catholic tensions, the reality of tensions on the religious scene is plain and undeniable. In the second selection in Part Six, Pfeffer exhibits tensions in the broad arena of "religion and the state." [1] Perhaps nothing published between book covers could be

[1] Those interested in the detail of the history of relations of religion and state in the United States are referred to the often fascinating compilation by Anson Phelps Stokes, entitled *Church and State in the United States,* New York: Harper and Brothers, 1950, 3 vols.

quite "up to date" in the area of Pfeffer's concern, and events of importance have occurred even in the few years since he wrote the item presented, but Pfeffer deals with his topic in such fashion that his work dates rather less readily than that of a good many others.

Herberg's and Pfeffer's items are followed by a selection of a quite different order, namely, Glick's paper on "Intermarriage and Fertility Patterns among Persons in Major Religious Groups." This not only treats of matters obviously important to religious groups themselves but presents materials of a kind that should be closely scrutinized for clues to the problem of how much acceptance there is of a common "Americanism," whether this Americanism is taken as some "common denominator" of the several faiths or as something transcending or not especially relevant to religious variations. One may surely presume that the extent of intermarriage and its "preferred" lines should cast light upon such a problem. Again, Glick's paper reminds us usefully that there are aspects of activity either "religious" or closely associated with "religion" which can be "counted." The paper may be said to be one of an entire type, for other specimens of which, regrettably, space could not be found. Had the needed space been available, representatives of the type might have been grouped under some such title as "Religion and Enumerable or 'Indexable' Behaviors." And under such a title it would have been appropriate to include additional materials on religion and fertility, as well as on, say, religion and differential suicide rates and rates of mental illness and alcoholism. Glick's paper will have to stand for the entire type or sociological genre although it has its affinities with Lazerwitz's paper in Part Five.

If the paper by Glick represents a somewhat abrupt shift from the first two selections in Part Three, a considerable shift is again made in the following selections by Norval Glenn and Bernard Lazerwitz, which concentrate on highly significant minority groups. Glenn's item is of course concerned to afford a sociological analysis of what may reasonably be said to be the numerically (and in many other ways) most important minority in the United States, which happens also to be a racially more or less distinct element in the population at large. It will be seen that Glenn's paper covers a good deal of Negro religious activity. By contrast, the paper by Lazerwitz on Jews in and out of New York City may in a sense be said not to cover "religion" at all, but only some social correlates and attributes of being Jewish and non-Jewish within New York and outside it. Hence it is quite true that Lazerwitz's paper is by no means fully cognate with that of Glenn. Nevertheless, it does deal with matters of clear importance for a sociological analysis of Jewry in the United States (and presents a remarkable amount of useful information in brief compass). And certainly it deals with a second large American minority which, together with the Negro minority, is often taken as one of the two most important of such groups in the country.

Once again—for Part Six is designed to be varied although brief—the next two papers represent something of a shift. The items by England on Christian Science and by O'Dea on Mormonism, for their part, deal, not with what are frequently taken as America's two outstandingly important minorities but with what have often been regarded as its two distinctive and distinctively important minority religions. Neither paper deals with the religion involved in great detail, and for such detail the considerable literature on each of the religions should of course be consulted. Yet these papers also offer a good deal of material within the restricted space in which they set out their themes and careful reading of them will reveal at least mention of a number of matters that should not be overlooked merely because they are not elaborated or not made central. Thus, England refers to the "middle class" character of Christian Science, a feature of that religion (or of its adherents) that is important in its own right and *may* also be of some importance in relation to the considerable preoccupation with matters of health that England's work suggests. O'Dea's paper on the Mormons presents what must here serve as a last word on the themes of church and sect.

The last item in Part Six, De Tocqueville's very brief speculation about why some Americans manifest "a sort of fanatical supernaturalism," can hardly be represented as a "sociological analysis," but it has a certain interest, nevertheless, as coming from an able observer who had a number of cogent things to say about religion in the United States; and it may also serve neatly to point to one of the

inevitable gaps in Part Six: the gap left by omission of material on some of the "wilder," highly colorful American sects and cults. Not even a "portrait" of American religion with frankly descriptive aims could well afford to omit these colorful entities. And a reasonably comprehensive and imaginative sociological analysis of the American scene definitely could not omit them. The I Am Movement, various Spiritualist groups, Father Divine's Peace Mission, and a host of others[2] may not always lend themselves easily to the explanation that De Tocqueville proposes for "fanatical spiritualism" but, "modern" and unenvisaged by De Tocqueville as some of them are, they will certainly be suggested to the more informed by the language that the French commentator employed.

[2] See, for example, Charles S. Braden, *These Also Believe: A Study of Modern American Cults and Minority Religious Movements*, New York: Macmillan, 1950.

1 · Religion in a Secularized Society: Some Aspects of America's Three-Religion Pluralism

WILL HERBERG

The basic fact defining the contemporary religious situation in this country is the transformation of America, in the course of the past generation, from a Protestant nation into a three-religion country. It is necessary to examine somewhat more

SOURCE. Will Herberg, "Religion in a Secularized Society: Some Aspects of America's Three-Religion Pluralism" (Lecture II of the 1961 Harlan Paul Douglass Lectures), *Review of Religious Research*, 4, Fall, 1962, pp. 33–45.

closely the nature of this transformation, and its concomitant circumstances.

Writing just about thirty years ago, André Siegfried described Protestantism as America's "national religion," and he was largely right, despite the ban on religious establishment in the Constitution. Normally, to be born an American meant to be a Protestant; this was the religious identification that, in the American mind, quite naturally went along with being an American. Non-Protestants felt the force of this conviction almost as strongly as did the Protestants; the Catholic and the Jew experienced their non-Protestant religion as a problem, perhaps even as an obstacle, to their becoming full-fledged Americans; it was the mark of their foreignness. In a very real sense, Protestantism constituted America's "established church."

This is no longer the case. Today, to be born an American is no longer taken to mean that one is necessarily a Protestant; Protestantism is no longer the obvious and natural religious identification of the American. Today, the evidence seems to indicate, America has become a three-religion country: the normal religious implication of being an American today is that one is either a Protestant, a Catholic, or a Jew. As I have already suggested, these three are felt, by and large, to be three alternative forms of being religious in the American way; they are the three "religions of democracy," the "three great faiths" of America. Today, unlike fifty years ago, not only Protestants, but increasingly Catholics and Jews as well, feel themselves to be Americans not apart from, or in spite of, their religion, but in and through it, because of it. If America today possesses a "church" in the Troeltschean sense—that is, a form of religious belonging which is felt to be involved in one's belonging to the national community—it is the tripartite religious system of Protestant-Catholic-Jew.

This transformation of America from a Protestant into a three-religion country has come about not as the result of any marked increase in Catholics or Jews —the Protestant-Catholic ratio has not changed drastically in the past half century, and the proportion of Jews in the general population has probably been declining. It has come about as a consequence of the process discussed in the first lecture whereby the socioreligious group has emerged as a primary sub-

community in American society, replacing the older ethnic group in that capacity. I will say no more about the process itself, but I do want to explore certain aspects of the three-religion pluralism to which it has given rise.

Secularization and Religious Group Types

The sociology of secularization has been widely discussed, and many attempts made, since Troeltsch, to relate degree of secularization with organizational type. Professor Harold W. Pfautz has suggested a series of five organizational forms, in order of increasing secularization, as follows: the cult, the sect, the institutionalized sect, the church, and the denomination. Understanding by secularization the widening gap between conventional religion and operational religion, there is much to be said for this series of organizational types. I think, however, that the present-day American situation suggests certain qualifications and elaborations.

The cult, to begin with, seems to exhibit the lowest degree of secularization possible in modern society. For the member of the cult fellowship, there is a minimum distinction between conventional religion, operative religion, and existential religion, though it may be noted that in this country cult members are sometimes members of established denominations as well. The cult is not so much at war with the world and its ways as outside of them.

Cults suffer a high degree of mortality. If a cult survives, it becomes a sect, and undergoes the familiar sociological changes in size, leadership, associational structure, and the like. The sect follower has already advanced on the road to secularization, but it is hard to say how far since the sect too is not very stable. Sooner or later, it either disappears, or else develops into something quite different: in Europe, it generally became a church; in this country, however, the line of development has been toward the denomination, which in America, has come to mean something quite distinctive. A variant is the institutionalized, or "established," sect.

In the strict Troeltschean sense of the term, this country has not had a church since colonial times. The church, in this sense, is essentially the national community on its religious side, the national community religiously organized. Even where the transplanted religious bodies set up in the English colonies on the Atlantic Coast were churches to begin with, widespread religious dissidence, coupled with the diversity of population, soon broke the formal religious unity and induced an incipient denominationalism. Denominationalism became the established religious pattern in the wake of the great revival movements; and in denominationalism we have a further and very advanced stage of secularization. For denominationalism, in its very nature, requires a thoroughgoing separation between conventional religion and operative religion, and this is the mark of secularization.

The denomination, as we know it in this county, is a settled, stable religious body, very like a church in many ways, except that it sees itself as one of a large aggregate of similar bodies, each recognizing the proper status of the others in legitimate coexistence. The denomination in America is not at all the "nonconformist sect" that it is in Europe; or rather, it is the "nonconformist sect" become central and normative. It differs from the church in the European acceptation of the term in that it would never dream of claiming to be the national ecclesiastical institution; it differs from the sect in that it is socially established, thoroughly institutionalized, and nuclear to the society in which it is found. So firmly entrenched is the de-

nominational idea in the mind of the American that even American Catholics have come to think in such terms; theologically, the Catholic Church, of course, continues to regard itself as the one true church, but in their actual social attitudes American Catholics, hardly less than American Protestants or American Jews, tend to think of their church as a kind of denomination existing side by side with other denominations in a pluralistic harmony that is felt to be somehow of the texture of American life.

Obviously, the denominational system implies the emergence of a "common religion" distinct from the conventional religion of the denominations, for without such a "common religion" the society in which the denominations find their place in mutual legitimation would hardly be able to hold together. Denominational pluralism, on the American plan, means thoroughgoing secularization.

It is interesting to observe the process by which the successful sect becomes a denomination, and to follow the corresponding stages of secularization. Long ago, John Wesley, who was a keen observer of religion as he was a powerful evangelist, noted the forces that were at work undermining the religious revival he had launched.

Wherever riches have increased [Wesley pointed out], the essence of religion has decreased in the same proportion. Therefore, I do not see how it is possible in the nature of things for any revival of religion to continue long. For religion must necessarily produce both industry and frugality, and these cannot but produce riches. But, as riches increase, so will pride, anger, and love of the world in all its branches. How, then, is it possible that Methodism, that is a religion of the heart, though it flourishes now as the green bay trees, should continue in this state? For the Methodists in every place grow diligent and frugal; consequently, they increase in goods. Hence they proportionately increase in pride, in anger, in the desire of the flesh, the desire of the eyes, and the pride of life. Is there no way to prevent this—this continual decay of pure religion?[1]

What Wesley was here describing was not only the inner contradiction in every revival of religion; he was also describing the dynamics of the transformation of the sect into a denomination. For the sect is essentially an "outsider" group: it is largely composed of elements who see themselves "disinherited," outside the culture, with no stake in it, with no participation in its values. The sectarian ethos and the sectarian ideology reflect this "outsider" stance. This was substantially the position of the mass of the early Methodists, as it still is the condition of the "fringe" groups in this country today. But in a mobile society, "outsiders" do not long remain "outsiders." Within a generation or two, encouraged by the very virtues which religious sectarianism breeds, many of the sect following grow prosperous, gain economic substance, and thus improve their social status. Their hostility to the culture diminishes as they move closer to the center, and they begin to share many of its values: they send their children to college, their preachers to seminary; they build impressive churches, with a more or less elaborate institutional superstructure, including Boy Scouts and Sunday schools. Their sectarian ideology grows mellow, loses its rough edges, and becomes little more than a set of ritualistic formulas. Their ministers sometimes even join the local ministerial association. In short, the sect is well on the way toward becoming a denomination, a small denomination, usually, but a denomination nevertheless.

It should be noted that, despite Wesley's account, this process is not simply one in which "pure religion" is corrupted by economic prosperity, itself the consequence of the "industry and frugality" which, according to Wesley, "religion must necessarily produce." It is rather that economic prosperity, in modern Western society, brings its beneficiaries closer to the nuclear culture and its values, thus undermining their "outsider" stance and the extremism and hostility it breeds. Thus the movement from sect to denomination is a movement from the margin to the center of society, and therefore a movement from the sectarian ideology to the "common religion" of the society. The movement from sect to denomination is therefore a movement of rapid secularization.

Actually, what happens is much more complicated than this account would suggest. Economic prosperity and cultural advance appear to exert a double effect: on the one side, they impel better advantaged members of the sect to leave the sect and join a recognized denomination; on the other side, they tend to raise the entire sect in the sociocultural scale on the way to denominational status.

The first movement is difficult to document since it is composed of millions of unrecorded personal or family decisions; yet every observer is well aware that it is going on. As to the second movement —the elevation of the entire sect to denominational status—the evidence is easily at hand. Such great denominations as the Baptists and Methodists in this country came out of sects in precisely the way described; and somewhat later, the Campbellites, against their own intention, gave rise to the Disciples of Christ. Because it emerged so late, the Disciples became only a small denomination by American standards; the field had already been well charted out by the others.

Exactly the same process is taking place before our very eyes today. The Nazarenes, over a large part of the coun-

try, are indistinguishable from small Protestant denominational churches. The Assemblies of God have their liberal arts
colleges and graduate schools of religion;
their men's associations, their women's
councils, and their Sunday schools; their
publicity, promotion, and public relations agencies, including an international
radio program. But the most astonishing
illustration is provided by the Jehovah's
Witnesses. The Jehovah's Witnesses
would certainly seem to constitute the
model sect group: a "disinherited," "outsider" group, militant, growing, arrayed
against the culture and its values, promoting a typically sectarian ideology. Yet in
a recent issue of a Witnesses journal,
there appeared in article on "How to
Dress Well." In this article, the Witnesses
are told that neatness is the first requirement, that they should never wear a
patterned sports jacket with patterned
slacks, that shoes and socks should com-
plement, not clash with, clothes, and
other such bits of esoteric wisdom. This
article, I think, is of immense significance. It shows several things: it shows
that large numbers of Witnesses are now
able and eager to dress well, but simply
do not know how since they come from
a strata of society where such things are
not learned at the mother's knee; it shows
also that the Jehovah's Witnesses leadership is very much concerned that they
learn what they want to know, and in
general that Witnesses learn to fit into
lower-middle-class suburbia and be accepted by it. Obviously, the sectarian
"outsider" stance is beginning to give
way, some of the values of the culture
at least are being accepted, and others
will be at an accelerating rate. Jehovah's
Witnesses do not yet constitute a denomination, not even in the sense in
which the Nazarenes or the Assemblies
of God do; but the Witnesses are on their
way, and the way is the way of growing
secularization.

This way leads from the cult, to the

sect, to the denomination. With the denomination, secularization reaches its
most advanced stage. But, in the American system, denominations have their
groupings within a scheme of mutually
legitimated coexistence: specifically, they
group themselves into the three great
socioreligious subcommunities known as
the "three great faiths." We can thus
carry the series further: *cult-sect-
denomination-socioreligious community*.
Despite denominational rivalries at top
administrative levels, American Protestants and American Jews—Catholics
do not enter the picture here since their
"denominational" lines are within the one
church—American Protestants and American Jews, especially the younger people,
are becoming less denominational-
minded, tending to identify themselves
as Protestants or Jews rather than by denominational labels, choosing where they
can "united" or "community" churches,
or converting existing churches along
such "nondenominational," "ecumenical"
lines. This process—in which denominations are increasingly being articulated
within the religious community—seems
to be already well under way.

Now I want to get back to the trifaith
system. What I should like to suggest is
that, whereas America does not have a
church in the Troeltschean sense as an
organized institution, America does possess an overall religious entity that corresponds to the Troeltschean church,
and that is the trifaith system of Protestant-Catholic-Jew. This is the kind of
religious belonging that today, normally
and naturally, goes along with being an
American; it is, in a real sense, the nation
on its religious side.

If there is any truth to this view at all,
it would seem that there is still a further
stage of secularization beyond the religious community. The series can now
be completed: *cult-sect-denomination-
socioreligious community-trifaith system*.
Beyond, this, secularization cannot go. In

the trifaith system, conventional religion and operative religion have been almost completely separated and almost completely syncretized.

Three-Religion Pluralism and Religious Group Tensions

The transformation of America from a Protestant nation into a three-religion country has also exerted a far-reaching influence upon the patterns of religious group tension in this country. Let us examine some aspects of the situation, with an eye to the problem of secularization.

It is my contention that the transformation of America from a Protestant nation into a three-religion country, along with the concomitant upward movement of the Catholic population in the sociocultural scale in the course of the past generation, has had a double effect: in the short run, it has tended to exacerbate and sharpen Protestant-Catholic tensions; in the long run, however, I think, the very same process will tend to alleviate these tensions and mitigate their sharpness. And this duality of operation is closely connected with significant generational differences in outlook and attitude.

It is not difficult to see why the processes we are considering should make for a certain exacerbation of tensions. Protestants in this country are now faced with the prospect of the loss of accustomed status. The mass of the older Protestants have had their attitudes formed in an America that understood itself as a Protestant nation; the country, in a very real sense, was theirs, belonged to them, was their home. Now, within one generation, their own generation, the country has, almost literally, been taken away from them, to be parcelled out among the "three major faiths": what was once their own home they are now being compelled to share with two interloper groups. No wonder they feel dispos-

sessed; no wonder they feel threatened. There was a time, not so long ago, when the middle-class Protestant in this country hardly came across a Catholic in those community institutions and organizations that really counted. There were, of course, many Catholics around, but they were largely at the margin of society, laborers and servant girls, hewers of wood and drawers of water. But within the past generation American Catholics have advanced dramatically from a peripheral, foreign, lower-class group to a nuclear, middle-class American community. Today, the Protestant, wherever he turns in community life, confronts Catholics on every side; no wonder he is convinced that Catholics have multiplied enormously and are taking over the country, whatever the statistics may say. Once, too, the general American institutions were simply Protestant institutions. Protestants did not need any separate organizations of their own, because the general community organizations and institutions were Protestant and obviously theirs. Jews and Catholics, on the other hand, and incidentally Negroes too had begun their very existence in American life as minority groups, requiring special institutions, organizations, and agencies to represent and protect them, and these institutions, organizations, and agencies they rapidly built up. Today, Protestants, in most parts of the country, can no longer take the general community institutions for granted as theirs; but (aside from the Negro group) they have not managed to develop any significant institutions of their own, or at least did not get to developing these till very late. As a consequence, they frequently find themselves at a great disadvantage and are very resentful at the "separatism" of the Catholics and Jews, whose institutions they denounce as "divisive" and "un-American." All in all, the older Protestants in most parts of the country find themselves in a very frustrating position; it is no wonder that they have tended to develop an outlook that the editor of the *Christian Century* has very aptly, and with not too much exaggeration, described as "Protestant paranoia."

Where the older Protestants are faced with the grave threat of loss of accustomed status, American Catholics, on their side, are exceedingly anxious over their newly acquired status in American society; they are status-anxious. They feel that their recently achieved status as Americans, and as good middle-class Americans, is not being adequately acknowledged by the older masters of American society, the Protestants; and they therefore tend to be belligerent and resentful. They are suspicious and touchy, easily tempted to self-assertiveness and to gross overcompensation. But, above all, they feel hampered and closed in, denied their proper recognition; they see themselves ever anew threatened with exclusion and segregation. They therefore tend to develop what the editor of the *Christian Century*, to match the "Protestant paranoia," has called "Catholic claustrophobia."

Aside from these quasi-clinical designations, it is not difficult to see why, in this transition period from a Protestant to a three-religion country, there should be a certain exacerbation of Protestant-Catholic tensions, and of Protestant-Jewish tensions, too, in those places where Jews have made a sudden appearance in significant numbers in an older Protestant community. But, by the same token, there is every reason to expect an alleviation of tensions in the longer run.

We already have sufficient evidence to suggest that there are significant generational differences in attitudes that relate to religious group tensions. Younger Protestants tend to take a very different view, and to respond very differently, from the older members of their group;

and this is true, though not so markedly, for the younger Catholics as well. It is well known, for example, that on the so-called "Jack Kennedy" question, which the Gallup organization has been asking for the past twenty years—I mean the question: "If your party nominated a generally well-qualified man for the presidency this year, and he happened to be a Catholic, would you vote for him?"— the younger voters have uniformly taken a far less anti-Catholic attitude; and this attitude they have tended to retain as they have grown older, so that there is a marked long-range trend in the same direction. Whereas in 1940, 31 per cent of the respondents answered "no"—they would *not* vote for a Catholic, even though he was a well-qualified man and a member of their party—by 1956, the proportion had fallen to 22 per cent. In that year (1956), the "no" vote was 31 per cent for respondents 50 years of age and over, 17 per cent for those between 30 and 49, and only 14 per cent for those between 21 and 29. This pattern is borne out by every other available bit of information, including community studies.

Again, it is not difficult to see why this should be so. The younger Protestants have not had their attitudes formed in an America that was a Protestant nation, but rather in an America that was emerging as a three-religion country; consequently, they do not feel particularly dispossessed, threatened, or overwhelmed. On the contrary, to them Catholicism is a legitimate part of American religion, one of the "three great faiths," while Catholics are just good, middle-class Americans, an integral part of the American people. The response one gets from these younger Protestants—I am thinking of a community survey of a New England town not yet published, a town once entirely Protestant, now about half Catholic—the response one gets from these younger Protestants is something sociologists ought readily to understand. It runs something like this: "What's all the excitement about? So they *are* Catholics! But they're our kind of people, and after all, we're all Americans, aren't we?"

As Catholics become more obviously "our kind of people," and equally Americans with the rest of us, as American opinion becomes more and more defined by the generation that has grown up in a three-religion country, the group tensions that now disturb us will tend to allay. This would appear to be a safe prognostication.

It seems worth noting, I think, that this analysis of Protestant-Catholic tensions proceeds without any reference to the social and religious issues that are alleged to divide the two communities. This is not because I regard these issues to be of no importance; on the contrary, I think they are issues of great importance, which deserve careful consideration on their own account. But I do not believe that they are so much the source of the tension as the expression of it. They become issues precisely because they arise in an already established context of tension and become vehicles of this tension and antagonism. Moreover, even though they have become issues in Protestant-Catholic conflict, they are not usually questions on which Protestants are aligned all on one side, and Catholics all on the other; on the contrary, on every one of these questions there are differences and divisions within both communities, with sizable minorities in each group crossing the lines.

However that may be, it will be observed that the better relations emerging between Protestants and Catholics are grounded in the "common religion" of American belonging—"After all, we're all Americans!"—and its predominance over the conventional religions of the three groups, not in opposition but in comprehension. In other words, the promising alleviation of religious group tensions would appear to be due to the

advancing secularization of American life and religion. However we may feel about secularism, this should be noted and appreciated. It is the advanced state of secularization in the three-religion pluralism of contemporary America that is the decisive factor in the emergence of better religious group relations in this country.

Yet there is another side to the story, which may not be ignored. If, for the great mass of Americans, the new tolerance is a by-product of the emerging solidarity of the secularized "common religion," for a small group of theologically concerned people, something very like it comes from the opposite direction. Of recent years, we know, there has been a rapprochement, in America as in Europe, between theologically concerned Protestants and Catholics, even between theologically concerned Christians and Jews, precisely as a consequence of their theological concern. It is not the "common religion" of the American Way that binds them; it is rather their common Christian, their common Biblical, faith and understanding. Indeed, suspicion of the American Way as a substitute-religion serving Americans as their ultimate context of meaning and value is a common premise. Whereas, for the great mass of Americans, the operative formula is "After all, we're all Americans," for the theological elite, it would run something like, "After all, we're all Christians, standing on the same Bible," or, where Jews are included, "After all, we acknowledge the same God and recognize in Abraham our common father in the faith." The two attitudes are often confused under the vague rubrics of "tolerance," "unity," and "ecumenicity"; but they are very, very different and ought to be carefully distinguished.

The intergroup situation in this country at the present time is thus a very complicated one. There is a significant sweep toward better understanding as a result of extensive secularization at one end, and of a theologically oriented reaction against secularization at the other. .In between are masses of Americans 'caught in the grip of the transition from the old America to the new, from the Protestant nation to the three-religion country, and driven to fear, hostility, and a kind of defensive aggressiveness as a result. 'or completeness, we ought to mention small groups of anti-religious secularists and self-styled "liberals" who find in anti-Catholicism a more viable, and even more respectable, form of anti-religion. As Peter Viereck has well pointed out: "Catholic-baiting is often the anti-Semitism of the liberals." But these elements are dwindling, and the prospect is definitely for a steady improvement of intergroup relations among the religious communities. And largely this is the result of increasing secularization, either directly, or indirectly by way of reaction.

Three Emerging Generalizations

How shall we evaluate the sweeping secularization of American life and religion? No theological assessment will here be attempted. But there are certain things that will occur to every serious observer of American religion who has reflected on recent developments.

Secularization, which has been advancing at an increasing pace in Western society ever since the high Middle Ages, has taken a special and characteristic form in the United States, reflecting the special and characteristic pattern of acculturation of the many diverse groups of immigrants who have come to make up the American people. First, the emergence of the well-known system of multi-denominational pluralism; then, the recasting of American society in terms of the socioreligious community, in which the denominations are typically grouped: these are the two major phases of the

structural development of American religion since the early nineteenth century. Each of these phases marks a further stage of secularization.

The restructuring of American society along the line indicated has transformed America from the Protestant nation it has been since its beginning into a new kind of socioreligious entity—a three-religion country, in which social identification takes place by way of religious belonging. This transformation has obviously had far-reaching consequences, which are by no means all of one piece.

1. Religious belonging has become a mode of defining one's American identity. In this way, the two great non-Protestant religions—Catholicism and Judaism—have acquired American status and been granted a place in the three-religion system. Catholics, Jews, Lutherans, and others, who remember how formidable an obstacle to the preservation and communication of their faith the taint of foreignness once was, will not be altogether ungrateful for what has happened. And all Americans may be thankful for the new spirit of freedom and tolerance in religious life that the emergence of the tripartite system of the three great "religions of democracy" has engendered; it makes increasingly difficult the sinister fusion of religious prejudice with racist or nationalist chauvinism. But these gains have come out of a thoroughgoing secularization of religion, in which conventional religion—Protestant, Catholic, and Jewish—has been integrated into the "common religion" of the American Way and made to serve a nonreligious function. As a result, American religiousness has been growing increasingly vacuous—a religiousness of belonging, without religious commitment, religious concern, or religious passion. To many religiously concerned people, this seems a very high price to pay.

2. Religious belief today tends to be

assimilated to the ideas and values of the American Way. The conventional religions—Protestantism, Catholicism, and Judaism—are typically understood as variant expressions of the "common faith" which all Americans share by virtue of their participation in the American Way of Life. Consequently, religion enjoys a high place in the American scheme of things, higher today, perhaps, than at any time in the past century. But it is a religion thoroughly secularized and homogenized, a religion-in-general that is little more than a civic religion of democracy, the religionization of the American Way. Here, too, the price may be a very high one to pay.

3. Religious group relations in this country, despite a certain exacerbation for the moment, seem headed for a very considerable improvement in the foreseeable future. Every American will welcome this prospect, and will welcome it without qualification. But again, it is coming largely, though not entirely, as the consequence of a secularizing evacuation of conventional religion. The price here, too, is a heavy one.

It is not my purpose to draw any balance sheet. All I have attempted to do is to call attention to certain aspects of the secularization of religion in contemporary America that may help illumine the paradox with which we began our discussion, the paradox that America is at once the most religious and the most secularistic of nations. I hope it is now possible for us to see in what way this paradox is true, and what this paradox has come to mean for the social and religious life of America.

Explanatory Note

1. Quoted in Robert Southey, *Life of Wesley and the Rise and Progress of Methodism* (2nd Amer. Edition; Harper, 1847), Vol. II, p. 308.

2 · Religion and the State

LEO PFEFFER

Religious Liberty in Catholic Dogma, History, and Practice

Perhaps nowhere else is the clash between Catholic dogma and libertarianism more dramatically manifested than in the relation of religion to the state, and more specifically in the matter of religious liberty. The dogma of Catholicism is not hospitable to concepts of freedom in matters of faith. A religion that considers itself the only true faith and its rites the only way to salvation is

SOURCE. From Leo Pfeffer, *Creeds in Competition.* Copyright by Leo Pfeffer, 1958. Used by permission of Harper and Row, Publishers.

not likely to be sympathetic to the claims of what it deems erroneous and heretical beliefs, nor of the demands of weak if not inherently evil men to espouse those beliefs.

Let it be said at the outset that the creed of Calvinism, of established Anglicanism or, for that matter, of biblical or Talmudic Judaism is hardly more liberal in matters of faith. None of these religions, however, permanently influenced the evolution of American principles of church-state relations, and all of them have long adjusted themselves to those principles. The adjustment of Catholicism is more recent and still not entirely completed. Moreover, as we shall shortly see, Protestantism and Judaism are, perhaps unfairly, suspicious and somewhat skeptical about the wholeheartedness and permanence of that adjustment—considerably more so than they are about the adjustments made by Calvinism, Anglicanism, and Judaism.

In any events, it is Catholic antipathy to religious liberty that constitutes the most frequent ground of attack upon it by non-Catholics. They find much in Catholic dogmatic literature that expresses this hostility. Frequently cited by non-Catholic critics is the editorial appearing in the April, 1945, issue of *Civilta Cattolica*, organ of the Jesuit order in Rome:

The Roman Catholic Church, convinced through its divine prerogatives of being the only true Church, must demand the right of freedom for herself alone, because such a right can only be possessed by truth, never by error. As to other religions, the Church will certainly never draw the sword, but she will require that by legitimate means they shall not be allowed to propagate false doctrine. Consequently, in a state where the majority of people are Catholic, the Church will require that legal existence be denied to error, and that if religious minorities actually exist, they shall have only a *de facto* existence, without opportunity to spread their beliefs. . . . In some countries, Catholics will be obliged to ask full religious freedom for all, resigned at being forced to cohabit where they alone should rightfully be allowed to live. But in doing this the Church does not renounce her thesis, which remains the most imperative of her laws, but merely adapts herself to *de facto* conditions, which must be taken into account in practical affairs. . . . The Church cannot blush for her own want of tolerance, as she asserts it in principle and applies it in practice.

Catholic dogmatic commitment to the exclusiveness of its own truth and to the falsity of other claims to truth would appear logically not only to justify this position but to require it. Thus, say Ryan and Bloand in their authoritative *Catholic Principles of Politics*, "the fact that the individual may in good faith think that his false religion is true gives him no more right to propagate it than the sincerity of the alien anarchist entitles him to advocate his abominable political theories in the United States, or than the perverted ethical notions of the dealer in obscene literature confer upon him a right to corrupt the morals of the community." Catholic dogma does not recognize any difference between the falsity and evil of anarchism or obscenity and the falsity and evil of non-Catholic religions. Nor does it acknowledge the moral right of a political state to recognize a difference between them or to treat them differently. It is, said Leo XIII, no more lawful for the state than for the individual to disregard differences in religions and hold them all to be equal.[1]

It can hardly be denied that the history of Christianity reveals many instances in which the Roman Catholic Church called upon the coercive arm of the state to enforce its claim to exclusive possession of religious truth and to suppress other beliefs as error and evil. It was St. Augustine who justified the persecution of heretics on the ground that it was more benevolent that heretics should be purged of their sin than that they should die unsaved, "for what is a worse killer of the soul than freedom to err?" The long and bloody history of the Holy Inquisition remains the most tragic manifestation of Roman Catholic dogma that error has no right to exist.

Fortunately these pages of history have long been turned and are not likely to

[1] See below, p. 610, for the statement by Leo XIII.

602   On the Religious Scene in the United States

be reopened. But, critics of Catholicism charge, even today the practical consequences of Catholic aversion to freedom in matters of conscience can be observed. Spain is invariably pointed to as a case history of the treatment of non-Catholic religions in a nation in the Catholic tradition. While Spanish law states that "none shall be molested for their religious beliefs or the private practices of their worship," it also states that "no other ceremonies or external demonstrations than those of the Catholic religion shall be permitted." Protestants, it is true, are not persecuted by the government; their ministers enjoy freedom of the pulpit, and their children receive religious education in their Sunday schools, using in their classrooms Protestant religious books that their parents may freely print for their own use. In short, Protestants have full freedom of *private* religious practice.

But Protestants do not have full freedom to practice their religion publicly. Their chapels may not display exterior evidence of the nature of the service conducted within the walls. Protestants may not publish or import Bibles for general circulation; they may not open new churches or reopen closed ones without a special permit, which may be arbitrarily refused. Protestant proselytizing, propagandizing, and even public demonstrations are forbidden. Other than Sunday schools, Protestants may not conduct religious schools but must send their children either to Catholic schools or to the public schools, and even in the latter their children must participate in Catholic instruction.

The Catholic Reply

This, then, is the charge leveled against Catholicism and the Catholic Church. What is the Catholic reply? In substance, the reply of American Catholics is that while every individual state-ment made in the indictment is true, the whole is false. It is false because it is not the whole truth. The picture revealed by the whole truth is radically different from that presented by a deliberate selection of some truths.

Consider, for example, the Inquisition and other instances of medieval Catholic persecution of heretics. These are neither denied nor defended by American Catholics. What they object to is the presentation of these instances as an aspect of the history of Catholicism rather than an aspect of the history of civilization. In the Middle Ages, Catholics in power engaged in persecution and oppression not because they were Catholics but because they were persons in power during an era when persons in power normally engaged in persecution and oppression. The proof lies in the conduct of non-Catholics in power. If Catholics persecuted non-Catholics, so did non-Catholics persecute Catholics and different non-Catholics. It was not a Catholic, but Luther, the father of Protestantism, who said that "heretics are not to be disputed with, but to be condemned unheard, and whilst they perish by fire, the faithful ought to pursue the evil to its source and bathe their hands in the blood of the Catholic bishops." Again, it was the Protestant Calvin who said that "whoever shall now contend that it is unjust to put heretics and blasphemers to death, will, knowingly and willingly, incur their very guilt."

In this country, Catholics point out, the persecutors and oppressors have been exclusively Protestant. The Quakers who were put to death in New England were the victims of Protestantism, not Catholicism. The heretics who filled the jails of Virginia in Madison's day were put there by Protestants, not Catholics. In United States history, Catholics point out, Protestants have never been persecuted by Catholics, even in Maryland when it was a Catholic-controlled colony, whereas

Catholics have been persecuted by Protestants. The full and true picture does not consist merely of a tale of Catholic persecution but is delineated in the words of the United States Supreme Court in a 1947 decision:

> With the power of government supporting them, at various times and places, Catholics had persecuted Protestants, Protestants had persecuted Catholics, Protestant sects had persecuted other Protestant sects, Catholics of one shade of belief had persecuted Catholics of another shade of belief, and all of these had from time to time persecuted Jews.

What is true of earlier persecutions is true of the contemporary scene. Protestants are oppressed and discriminated against in Spain, not because Spain is a Catholic state but because it is a totalitarian state, and it is in the nature of a totalitarian state to oppress and discriminate against minorities. Non-Catholic totalitarian states oppress and discriminate against religious and ethnic minorities no less than do Catholic totalitarian states: witness atheistic Soviet Russia on the one hand or Moslem Saudi Arabia on the other. Conversely, democratic countries in the Catholic tradition grant liberty to religious minorities no less than do non-Catholic states: witness Ireland, for example, whose constitution acknowledges the special position of the Catholic Church and of the Catholic religion, professed by the great majority of the citizens, and yet accords full religious freedom to Protestants, Jews, and other non-Catholics.

The statements on religious error and religious freedom found in Catholic dogma present a different and more difficult problem for Catholic spokesmen. The difficulty lies in their reluctance to give what is probably the most effective answer. These statements are based upon papal pronouncements made during the centuries, and the high estate held by respect for authority in the Catholic scheme of things makes it difficult and embarrassing for Catholics to say what they otherwise would say—that these pronouncements are not to be taken too seriously.

Actually, that is what in effect is said by such leading Catholic thinkers as John Courtney Murray and Heinrich Rommen. And they are not merely saying it to the non-Catholic world, but are arguing it eloquently within Catholicism. The papal pronouncements, they say, must be understood in the context of the time, place, and situation in which they were uttered. They are not to be understood nor were they intended to be understood as absolutes, true for all times and in all circumstances. They were promulgated as defensive measures to protect the Church and Catholicism when they were in danger and under attack. They are not to be taken as either required or desirable even in countries which are overwhelmingly Catholic in their population. As Rommen has said, "the modern Bill of Rights and the inviolability of the sincere conscience must be jealously respected by a Catholic civilization, if ever the dream of a wholly Catholic world is to be realized."

It remains true, however, that what is generally considered as authoritative Catholic thought does not go this far. The papal pronouncements are accepted as correct in principle. The authoritative organs of the Catholic Church in America, such as the *American Ecclesiastical Review,* contest the validity of Father Murray's contention that even in a Catholic state freedom to err must be respected. To them, in principle, freedom of worship remains, in the words of the *Catholic Dictionary,* "the inalienable right of all men to worship God according to the teaching of the Catholic Church."

The Catholic position is that a sharp

distinction must be made between principle and practice. Ryan and Boland, *Civilta Cattolica*, the *Catholic Dictionary*, and the papal encyclicals on which these and similar pronouncements are based are all correct in principle, but they have no practical significance and no relevance to interreligious relations in the United States. These doctrines are applicable only to a Catholic state, that is, one in which all or almost all of the inhabitants are Catholics. Since there is not the slightest chance that this will happen in America in the foreseeable future, there is no reason for fear on the part of non-Catholics. Many Catholics believe that Protestants and Jews use the dogmatic statements on religious liberty in Catholic teachings as a stick to beat Catholics with, and not as an expression of real concern.

Nor do Catholics rest on the defensive. They express particular grievance at Protestant and Jewish concern about restrictions on religious liberty in Catholic countries. They contrast this with Protestant and Jewish silence with respect to restrictions on Catholics in such Protestant countries as Sweden, or the exclusion of Jesuits from Switzerland, or the infringements on religious liberty in Israel, or, above all, the persecution of the Catholic Church and its clergymen in countries under Communist control. The comparative silence of Protestantism and Judaism when Catholic religious freedom is infringed, they suggest, casts doubt upon the sincerity of Protestant and Jewish protests against similar infringements in Catholic countries.

The Faiths and Freedom

The positions of the three faiths in respect to religious freedom can be summarized somewhat as follows. American Protestantism expresses unqualified commitment to full religious freedom. It has made a complete adjustment to the liber-

tarianism of the alliance of dissent and humanism. The Calvinist and the Episcopalian denominations (which have by now merged into Protestant dissent) no less than the Baptists and the Quakers assert the right, both in principle and in practice, to differ in matters of faith, to worship freely, and to propagate one's beliefs without hindrance. Whether with historical accuracy or not, American Protestantism proudly considers religious freedom the peculiar creation of Protestantism and cannot conceive of any society or any set of circumstances that would justify restrictions on freedom to worship and freedom to preach and teach in accordance with the dictates of conscience.

American Judaism is also fully committed to religious freedom. It, too, has completely and happily adjusted itself to the libertarianism of the alliance. With the exception of a small Orthodox fringe, it avows a commitment in principle as well as in practice, and does not approve such infringements on religious freedom as may be practiced in Israel. Judaism takes its own particular pride in religious freedom, asserting that the war of the Jews under the Maccabees against the Seleucids in the second century before Christ was the first recorded struggle for religious freedom.

In America only Catholicism is faced with the problem of reconciling with the libertarian ideal dogmatic pronouncements antipathetic to that ideal and to American concepts of religious freedom. This it seeks to do by drawing a distinction between a theoretical completely Catholic state and an actual pluralistic America. Many non-Catholics remain skeptical and consider Catholic avowals of acceptance of the American libertarian ideal as merely a compromise of expediency. Catholics recognize this skepticism, and realize the difficulty of their position. However, they see no alternative other than abandoning their belief that Catholicism is the one religion founded by Jesus Christ for all, and this they are not prepared to do.

Catholics urge that their differences with non-Catholics on the subject of religious freedom are purely differences of theory, having no practical relevance to the American scene. In one respect, however, the differences are not academic and have practical and tangible consequences. The statements of position of organized Protestantism and Judaism include within the mantle of protection of religious freedom the nonreligious, and even the anti-religious. Catholic churchmen show no sympathy to this view. Throughout their writings one discerns a complete absence of tolerance for those who are "against God." Religious freedom belongs to those who are religious. The First Amendment secures freedom "of religion," not freedom "from religion"; the purpose of the guaranty is to protect the citizens in the exercise of their religion, not in the exercise of irreligion. The basic difference between America and Soviet Russia lies in the acceptance or rejection of God, and any American who rejects God is potentially if not actually an enemy of the nation and as such certainly has no right to teach and propagate his evil doctrines. American Catholicism sees no material difference between atheism and communism, and deems it the obligation of the government and the people to defend themselves equally against both evils.

Separation of Church and State

The principle of religious freedom and the separation of church and state—the latter phrase was coined by Jefferson—is as uniquely American a concept and experiment as anything can be said to be. A system of society wherein the secular state lacked jurisdiction over the relationship of man to God or the gods was certainly without precedent in human history. It had never occurred to any but a few visionaries that it might be wrong for a secular ruler to dictate to his subjects how they should worship God or for priests to dictate to the state how it should conduct its secular affairs. It was the United States alone that conceived and proved the workability of the idea that, as Lord Bryce put it, religious organizations should be "unrecognized by law except as voluntary associations of private citizens."

The principle of freedom and separation was based upon the dual concept of voluntariness in matters of belief and government without inherent powers but limited to those specifically conferred upon it. It was given a constitutional protection in the opening words of the Bill of Rights: "Congress shall make no law respecting an establishment of religion, or prohibiting the free exercise thereof." This came about because in 1791, when the Bill of Rights (the first ten amendments to the Constitution) was adopted, the two most potent cultural forces in America were Protestant dissent and secular humanism; both were committed to it, and they combined to establish it as a fundamental principle of the American political system.

The concept of voluntariness in matters of belief has been called the great tradition of the American churches. More properly, it is the great tradition of the American dissenting churches. It is also the tradition of the secular-humanist political leaders who shared in the establishment of our democratic system. Their writings contain innumerable references to the evil, tyranny, and inefficacy of coercion in the realm of conscience. Both also agreed that political government has only such powers as are delegated to it and that the power to intervene in religious affairs was not granted to political government. Hence, the new government then being established should have no power to make any law respecting an establishment of religion or prohibiting its free exercise.

The two groups arrived at the common ideological meeting place from different directions. To the leaders of Protestant dissent the source of all temporal power was God, and He had not seen fit to delegate power over religion to temporal governments. The Baptist Roger Williams pointed out that the Ten Commandments were written by God on two tablets. On one side were the commandments which concern man's relation to God, e.g., "Thou shalt have no other gods before me," "Thou shalt not make unto thee any graven image," etc. On the other side were those concerning man's relationship to man, e.g., "Thou shalt not kill," etc. By placing a line of demarcation between the two tablets, God expressed His wish that transgressions of obligations between man and man shall be subject to the jurisdiction of man's tribunals, but the relationship of man to God shall be exclusively within God's jurisdiction.

A later Baptist leader, Samuel Stayman, preached that the "jurisdiction of the magistrate neither can nor ought to be extended to the salvation of souls." John Leland, Baptist leader in Virginia, wrote a tract in the same year that the First Amendment was adopted, entitled "Rights of Conscience and therefore Religious Opinions not recognizable by law." In this tract Leland said that "government has no more to do with religious opinions of man than with the principles of mathematics." Isaac Backus, spokesman for the Massachusetts Baptist Churches at the time of the Revolutionary War and the Constitution, in arguing against the use of tax-raised funds for religious purposes, said: "The free exercise of private judgment and the inalienable rights of consciences are too high a rank and dignity to be submitted to the decrees of councils or the imperfect laws

of fallible legislators. . . . Religion is a concern between God and the soul with which no human authority can intermeddle. . . ." And a few years before adoption of the First Amendment, another important segment of American Protestant dissent, the Presbyterian Church, argued against taxation for religious purposes on the ground that

The end of Civil government is security to the temporal liberty and property of Mankind; and to protect them in the free Exercise of Religion—Legislators are invested with powers from their constituents, for these purposes only; and their duty extends no further—Religion is altogether personal, and the right of exercising it unalienable; and it is not, cannot, and ought not to be, resigned to the will of society at large; and much less to the Legislature—which derives its authority wholly from the consent of the people; and is limited to the Original intention of Civil Associations.

The last quotation shows clearly the alliance between Protestant dissent and rationalist humanism, for it reflects the social contract theory of Locke and Rousseau. This theory was widely accepted in the latter half of the eighteenth century and upon it was based the Declaration of Independence and the American libertarian system of democratic government. According to the theory of the social contract, governments, in the words of the Declaration of Independence, "are instituted among men, deriving their just powers from the consent of the governed." A government, therefore, has only such powers as are granted to it by the governed, and if it seeks to exercise powers not granted to it, it is guilty of tyranny and usurpation.

The rationalists and deists who found their inspiration in the social contract believed that, as Madison put it, "in matters of religion no man's right is

abridged by the institution of civil society, and that religion is wholly exempt
from its cognizance." The reason for this,
they argued, is that matters of conscience are by their very nature inalienable, and therefore jurisdiction over them
was not and could not have been delegated to political government in the social contract. The views of this group
were epitomized in Paine's statement in
Common Sense: "As to religion, I hold it
to be the indispensable duty of government to protect all conscientious professors thereof; and I know of no other
business which government hath to do
therewith."

In 1786, but one short year before
the Federal Constitutional Convention
met in Philadelphia, Protestant dissent
and rationalist humanism joined forces
to defeat a bill introduced in Virginia
whose purpose was to provide tax funds
for the teaching of religion. The major
factor in the defeat of the bill was Madison's "Memorial and Remonstrance,"
which set forth fifteen arguments against
the measure. These arguments fell principally into two classes: those predicated
on the concept of voluntariness in matters of conscience, and those on the concept that religion is outside the jurisdiction of political government—the two
aspects of what five years later was to
become the religion clause of the First
Amendment. Immediately on defeat of
the bill, the alliance put through Jefferson's great Virginia Statute Establishing
Religious Freedom which also reflected
the dual concept of voluntariness and no-
jurisdiction.

Flushed with success, the alliance had
no real difficulty a year later in keeping
out of the proposed Federal Constitution
any invocation or even reference to God,
and in making that instrument a purely
secular document whose listed purposes
carefully excluded anything pertaining
to religion. In fact, the only reference
to religion in the entire document was
the negative one prohibiting religious
tests for Federal office, a provision that
the drafters fully realized could open
the door for "Jews, Turks and infidels"
to become President. Other than this no
provision guaranteeing religious liberty
was expressly stated, the reason being
that such a provision was believed unnecessary since the Federal government
would in any event have no jurisdiction
in religious affairs. This explanation, however, proved unsatisfactory, and four
years later the First Amendment was
added to the Constitution expressly bar-
ring laws respecting an establishment of
religion or prohibiting its free exercise,
i.e., no-jurisdiction and voluntariness.

The Meaning of the
No-Establishment Clause

For more than a century and a half the
United States Supreme Court had no
occasion to spell out definitively the
meaning of the no-establishment clause
—itself a silent yet significant witness to
the effectiveness of the Protestant dissent-secular humanist alliance in shaping
American politico-cultural patterns. It
was only when in the mid-twentieth
century the dominance of the alliance
was challenged by Roman Catholicism
that the Court was called upon to determine whether the no-establishment clause
had made the philosophy of the alliance
the supreme law of the land. It was no
coincidence that the issue should reach
the Supreme Court in a case involving
a Roman Catholic attack upon the principle established by the alliance that tax-
raised funds must not be used in support
of religion.

This occurred in 1947 in the famous
parochial school bus case, *Everson* v.
Board of Education. In that case, while
upholding by a vote of five to four the
validity of using tax-raised funds to trans-
port children to parochial schools, the
Court spelled out the meaning of the

First Amendment in the following definitive language:

> The "establishment of religion" clause of the First Amendment means at least this: Neither a state nor the Federal Government can set up a church. Neither can pass laws which aid one religion, aid all religions, or prefer one religion over another. Neither can force nor influence a person to go to or remain away from church against his will or force him to profess a belief or disbelief in any religion. No person can be punished for entertaining or professing religious beliefs or disbeliefs, for church attendance or non-attendance. No tax in any amount, large or small, can be levied to support any religious activities or institutions, whatever they may be called, or whatever form they may adopt to teach or practice religion. Neither a state nor the Federal Government can, openly or secretly, participate in the affairs of any religious organizations or groups and *vice versa*. In the words of Jefferson, the clause against establishment of religion by law was intended to erect "a wall of separation between Church and State."

The statement, which was reiterated by the Supreme Court the following year in the McCollum released-time case, shows clearly that the Court had interpreted the First Amendment as conferring the force of constitutional law on the principles of the Protestant dissent-secular humanist alliance. The statement imposes upon government an obligation to abstain from intervention in religious affairs and from granting governmental aid or support to religious institutions. As Lord Bryce had earlier noted, it expresses the view that in the United States religious associations are merely voluntary associations of private persons whose activities must be considered by the government as exclusively private and not subject to support out of tax-raised funds. It imposes an obligation of neutrality on government not merely as between different religions but also as between religion and non-religion, and indeed between religion and anti-religion.

That, said the Supreme Court, is what the fathers of the Constitution and of the First Amendment intended. And they intended it not because they were hostile to religion; the fact that the deeply pietistic dissenting sects strove for this is conclusive proof that its motivation was not unfriendliness to religion. The fathers of our republic, said the Court, were convinced that the cause of religion could best be served if the government maintained a strict hands-off policy and if it maintained a high and impregnable wall between church and state. They were convinced too that the best way to keep from these shores the religious bloodshed, persecution, and intolerance that had plagued the old world was to maintain such a wall between church and state in the new world.

This definitive interpretation of the no-establishment clause evoked considerable criticism from a number of sources. It was argued that the Supreme Court had misread the Constitution and had misinterpreted the intent of its framers. It was not the purpose of the First Amendment to divorce religion from government or to impose neutrality between believers and non-believers but only to meet in a practical manner the problems raised by a multiplicity of competing sects. This was done by requiring the government to be neutral as among these sects and forbidding it to favor one at the expense of the others. The amendment was not intended to bar the government from aiding and supporting religion and religious institutions so long as the aid and support is granted equally and without preference to some faiths and discrimination against others.

The proof of this, according to the critics of the Supreme Court's interpretation, is to be found in the history of our country and in the society about us. Throughout its history our governments, national and state, have co-operated with religion and shown friendliness to it. God is invoked in the Declaration of Independence and in practically every state constitution. Sunday, the Christian Sabbath, is universally observed as a day of rest. The sessions of Congress and of the state legislatures are invariably opened with prayer, in Congress by chaplains who are employed by the Federal government. We have chaplains in our armed forces and in our penal institutions. Oaths in courts of law are administered through use of the Bible. Public officials take an oath of office ending with "so help me God." Religious institutions are tax exempt throughout the nation. Our Pledge of Allegiance declares that we are a nation "under God." Our national motto is "In God We Trust" and is inscribed on our currency and our postage stamps.

These and many other similar illustrations of governmental co-operation with religion, say the critics of the Everson-McCollum principle, show conclusively that the purpose of the First Amendment was not to erect an absolute, unpenetrable wall between religion and government nor to make our nation Godless. The amendment, they say, prohibits preferential treatment and imposes an obligation of neutrality on the part of government as among the different religious groups, but not as between religion and non-religion, nor as between God-fearers and atheists.

The intensive criticism the Everson-McCollum principle received during the four years between the McCollum case and the New York City released-time case, *Zorach* v. *Clauson,* quite likely influenced the Supreme Court. For the decision in the Zorach case shows some retreat from the broad scope of the Everson-McCollum principle. "We are," said the Court, "a religious people whose institutions presuppose a Supreme Being." The First Amendment "does not say that in every and all respects there shall be a separation of Church and State." It requires only that "there shall be no concert or union or dependency one on the other."

Despite this language, it is doubtful that the Zorach decision is to be interpreted as a repudiation of the Everson-McCollum principle. The Court expressly stated that it adhered to the McCollum decision, a decision which . . . is consistent only with the broad interpretation of the First Amendment expressed in the Everson and McCollum cases. The Court in the Zorach case also went out of its way to say that under the First Amendment "Government may not finance religious groups nor undertake religious instruction"—a disability required only if the broad interpretation of the Everson and McCollum cases is accepted.

It is clear from this that the difference as to the intention of the fathers of the First Amendment and of the meaning of the amendment is not a mere academic exercise in American history. The difference in interpretation has practical consequences of tremendous importance. If the amendment is interpreted narrowly to prohibit only preferential aid, then it is permissible for Congress and the states to appropriate public funds for the support of religious education so long as all church schools are included in the program without favoritism or discrimination. Also it is permissible for the public schools to teach religion so long as each child is taught his own religion or the common elements of the major religions are taught to all children. If the broad Everson-McCollum interpretation is followed, neither government financing of religious education nor religious instruction in the public schools is permissible.

These practical consequences explain the differences among the religious faiths on the correctness or incorrectness of the Supreme Court's interpretation of the First Amendment. That religious groups should divide on this might seem strange at first sight. One would suppose that while historians could well differ as to a particular historical fact such as the intent of the fathers of our Constitution, the difference would not be reflected in, much less determined by, the difference in their religious affiliations. So too, while lawyers and law professors might differ as to the correct interpretation of a constitutional provision, that difference would seem to bear no logical relationship to whether they are Protestant, Catholic, or Jewish. Yet it is not as surprising as it would seem at first. It is human to read history and the Constitution as one would want history and the Constitution to be, and the deeper the want the more convinced one is that the interpretation is correct. In any event, the differences among (and, in the case of Protestantism, within) the religious groups as to the meaning of the First Amendment and separation of church and state reflect completely their diverse positions on specific practical issues of public importance, as well as their differences in accepting or challenging the political and cultural patterns shaped by the alliance of Protestant dissent and secular humanism.

Church and State in Catholicism

Even more than religious liberty, the notion that church and state should be separated and political government be secular is alien to Catholic dogma. For Catholicism a secular state is by its very nature a denial of God, since the supremacy of God requires that He be acknowledged and worshiped by all that He created, including the rulers of states. In speaking of the duty of government officials to profess and practice God's revealed religion, Pope Pius XI stated that there is no "difference in this matter between individuals and societies, both domestic and civil; for men joined in society are no less under the power of Christ than individuals." Catholic dogma on the relation of church and state was thus expressed by Leo XIII:

Justice therefore forbids, and reason itself forbids, the State to be godless; or to adopt a line of action which would end in godlessness—namely, to treat the various religions (as they call them) alike, and to bestow upon them promiscuously equal rights and privileges. Since, then, the profession of one religion is necessary in the State, that religion must be professed which alone is true, and which can be recognized without difficulty, especially in Catholic States, because the marks of truth are, as it were, engraven upon it. This religion, therefore, the rulers of the State must preserve and protect, if they would provide—as they should do—with prudence and usefulness for the good of the community.

As in the case of religious freedom, Catholic churchmen in the United States explain that these principles, though valid in theory, are inapplicable to a multi-religious society such as exists in America. Here the state cannot be expected, nor is it required, to acknowledge the exclusive truthfulness of the Catholic faith or to accord that faith sole or even preferential recognition. It is permissible for the state to conduct its affairs as if all religions were equally true, or, perhaps more accurately, it is permissible for the state not to pass judgment on which religion is the only true one. Hence, it is permissible for the state to bestow its favors and privileges equally upon all accepted religions.

This does not mean that the state even in America may be secular or Godless. On the contrary, American governments are as obligated to recognize the existence and supremacy of God through public and official acts of acknowledgment and worship as are governments in Catholic states. Catholicism holds that all governments, including those representative of populations of many sects, are morally obliged to engage in official acts of state worship and state acknowledgment of God. To this aspect of Catholic belief and to the growing influence of such belief on American culture can largely be attributed the recent manifestation of religion on the part of our government and our government officials, from the public religiosity of President Eisenhower and his aides to the inclusion of "under God" in the Pledge of Allegiance.

It is immediately obvious that the broad interpretation of the First Amendment expounded in the Everson and McCollum cases is completely incompatible with Catholic dogma, even as adjusted for application in non-Catholic states. It is also obvious that the narrow interpretation which would limit the meaning of the amendment to a ban on preferential treatment of any one faith is admirably in harmony with Catholic doctrine on the relationship of religion and government in non-Catholic states. It is therefore less than surprising that American Catholicism should vigorously oppose the Everson-McCollum principle and with equal vigor urge that the narrow interpretation of the First Amendment is the only valid one. Nor is it surprising that Catholic churchmen and spokesmen should indicate a strong dislike for the phrase "separation of church and state," calling it at various times a "shibboleth," "fraudulent," "un-American," etc., preferring to frame their arguments in terms of the no-establishment clause of the First Amendment.

The most authoritative expression of the Catholic position is to be found in a statement issued by the Catholic bishops through the National Catholic Welfare Conference several months after the McCollum decision was handed down in 1948. The statement, which is too long to be set forth here in full, declared:

To one who knows something of history and law, the meaning of the First Amendment is clear enough from its own words: "Congress shall make no laws (sic) respecting an establishment of religion or forbidding (sic) the free exercise thereof." The meaning is even clearer in the records of the Congress that enacted it. Then and throughout English and Colonial history "an establishment of religion" meant the setting up by law of an official Church which would receive from the government favors not equally accorded to others in the cooperation between government and religion—which was simply taken for granted in our country at that time and has, in many ways, continued to this day. Under the First Amendment, the Federal Government could not extend this type of preferential treatment to one religion as against another, nor could it compel or forbid any state to do so.

If this practical policy be described by the loose metaphor "a wall of separation between Church and State," that term must be understood in a definite and typically American sense. It would be an utter distortion of American history and law to make that practical policy involve the indifference to religion and the exclusion of cooperation between religion and government implied in the term "separation of Church and State" as it has become the shibboleth of doctrinaire secularism. . . .

We, therefore, hope and pray that the novel interpretation of the First

Amendment recently adopted by the Supreme Court will in due process be revised. To that end we shall peacefully, patiently and perseveringly work. . . .

We call upon all Catholic people to seek in their faith an inspiration and a guide in making an informed contribution to good citizenship. We urge members of the legal profession in particular to develop and apply their special competence in this field. We stand ready to cooperate in fairness and charity with all who believe in God and are devoted to freedom under God to avert the impending danger of a judicial "establishment of secularism" that would ban God from public life.

The substance of this statement of the Catholic position has been repeated countless times by Catholic churchmen and spokesmen. I have not found a single Catholic cleric or Catholic publication that dissents from it. The unanimity with which these views are held among American Catholics and the vigor with which they are defended make it fatuous to argue that there is no "Catholic" position on separation of church and state and the meaning of the First Amendment.

Separation and American Jewry

As it is not surprising that American Catholicism found the narrow interpretation of the First Amendment to be the only true and valid one, so it is no more astonishing that American Judaism found the broad interpretation expressed in the Everson and McCollum decisions to be the only true and valid one. For, as we have seen, Judaism happily adjusted itself to the American libertarianism which was articulated in the Everson-McCollum principle.

Because of the structural differences between Catholicism and Judaism, it is not to be expected that the same unanimity will be found in Judaism as in Catholicism. There are, undoubtedly, some rabbis who agree with Will Herberg, Jewish professor of theology at Drew University, and with the Catholic Church that the Everson-McCollum principles do not correctly reflect American traditions, nor the true American spirit, which is religious rather than secular. At least, one finds dissent among the rabbinate where no dissent is to be found among the Catholic priesthood.

It remains true, however, that there is substantial unanimity in American Judaism in support of the broad interpretation of the First Amendment announced by the Supreme Court in the Everson and McCollum cases. In 1955, a subcommittee of the United States Senate Committee on the Judiciary, under the chairmanship of Senator Thomas C. Hennings, Jr., of Missouri, instituted a study of the status of constitutional rights in the nation. Among the questions investigated was the extent of public agreement or disagreement with the Supreme Court's interpretation of the First Amendment in the Everson and McCollum cases. A statement of views was submitted to the committee by the Synagogue Council of America, consisting of and representing the six national organizations that comprise organized American Judaism—Reform, Conservative, and Orthodox, both at the rabbinic and congregational levels. In its statement, the Synagogue Council expressed its conviction "that the provision against establishment of religion in the First Amendment bars non-preferential as well as preferential aid to religion," and that "the First and Fourteenth Amendments impose upon government in American democracy an obligation of strict separation, an obligation that precludes all material aid to religion by Congress and the states whether accorded on a preferential or non-preferential basis."

The statement pointed out that when

the McCollum case was before the Supreme Court and the broad interpretation announced in the Everson case was under attack, the Synagogue Council, representing American Judaism, had submitted a brief as "friend of the court" urging the Supreme Court not to retreat from the broad interpretation. Since then, whenever the Synagogue Council expressed a statement of policy in areas where religion and government meet and interact, the Council has consistently reiterated its adherence to the Everson-McCollum principles and to the broad interpretation of the First Amendment.

Organized Jewry has not expressed itself publicly on the numerous governmental manifestations of religiosity such as including "under God" in the Pledge of Allegiance or putting "Pray for Peace" on postage stamp cancellations. That not a single member of either House of Congress voted against any of these measures is good evidence that it is not politic to be "against God," a reality which even the rationalist Jefferson recognized and took into account. The silence of American Jewry, a minority that is just beginning to enjoy equality of status, is therefore understandable. Yet it is safe to say that most Jewish organizations, religious as well as secular, are not happy about the increasing religious coloration of governmental action.

The Protestant Dilemma

The position of American Protestantism in respect to the meaning and scope of the First Amendment is neither as definite nor as uniform as that of Catholicism and Judaism. Protestantism is faced with a dilemma. On the one hand most Protestant groups, even such denominations as Congregationalism and Episcopalianism which vigorously but vainly fought disestablishment, today claim the principle of separation of church and state as a purely Protestant

creation. They deem it a great contribution to America and to Western civilization generally, and are extremely proud of it. Also they assert the principle as the basis for, and justification of, their almost unanimous opposition to such measures as the grant of tax-raised funds to parochial schools or to an exchange of ambassadors with the Vatican. At the same time most Protestant organizations are committed to compulsory Sunday observance laws, to certain aspects of religious education in connection with the public school system (such as released-time programs and Bible readings), and to other instances of governmental aid to religion which cannot easily be reconciled with the broad interpretation of the First Amendment announced in the Everson and McCollum decisions.

The offspring of the Protestant dilemma is ambivalence and the offspring of ambivalence are ambiguity and confusion and not a little self-deception. Compulsory Sunday observance laws are defended as health rather than religious measures, even though their chief defenders are such unsecular organizations as the Lord's Day Alliance and the Catholic Church. There is some flirting with the narrow interpretation of the amendment when Protestants argue that an exchange of ambassadors with the Vatican would be a preferential treatment of the Catholic Church, although, as they quickly point out, Protestant opposition would not be disposed of by adding an exchange of representatives with the World Council of Churches. The same sort of flirtation appears in the argument that public aid to parochial schools would constitute preferential treatment of the Catholic Church, although it is not explained why Protestants and Jews cannot establish their own parochial schools (as indeed they have to a small extent) and share equally in the state's favor.

Most Protestants recognize, even if

they do not admit, the unavoidable dilemma and the basic self-contradiction of their specific positions. A few on the left will express outright approval of the broad interpretation with full understanding and acceptance of its implications and consequences on such specifics as Sunday laws and religion in the public schools. A few on the right, on the other hand, will approve the narrow interpretation with full understanding and acceptance of its implications and consequences on such specifics as representation at the Vatican and grant of tax-raised funds to parochial schools.

The majority solve the dilemma by pretending it does not exist. They simply avoid expressing a definite position on the scope of the First Amendment and the meaning of separation of church and state. The Senate Judiciary subcommittee had no doubts about the Catholic position on the question, nor about the Jewish position. But it must have been quite perplexed as to what the Protestant position is. The National Council of Churches, in its statement submitted to the subcommittee, simply disregarded the pointedly worded question put by the subcommittee and stated its position in the following characteristically ambiguous language:

> The National Council of Churches holds the first clause of the First Amendment to the Constitution of the United States to mean that church and state shall be separate and independent as institutions, but to imply neither that the state is indifferent to religion nor that the church is indifferent to civil and political issues.

It is at least probable that most Protestant clergymen and organizations approve the recent overt manifestations of religiosity on the part of government in the United States. Moreover, even among the minority that disapproves, disapproval is predicated not so much on considerations of church-state relations as on the questionable value and sincerity of such superficial verbalizations. A few Protestant voices, however, have indicated uneasiness on constitutional grounds. The extent of Protestant disapproval cannot be gauged by the volume of articulated objection, for it is almost as difficult for Protestants to be publicly "against God" as it is for Jews.

3 · Intermarriage and Fertility Patterns among Persons in Major Religious Groups*

PAUL C. GLICK

Neither vital statistics nor decennial census figures have provided nationwide statistics on marriage and family patterns among the several religious groups, even though religion has been one of the central characteristics of

SOURCE. Paul C. Glick, "Intermarriage and Fertility Patterns among Persons in Major Religious Groups," *Eugenics Quarterly*, 7, March, 1960, pp. 31–38.

American culture. A part of the gap can now be filled by data collected by the

* Paper presented at the annual meeting of the American Sociological Society held in Seattle, Washington, August 27–29, 1958. The views expressed in this paper are those of the author and not necessarily those of the U. S. Bureau of the Census. The assistance of Wilson H. Grabill in the preparation and review of this paper is gratefully acknowledged.

U. S. Bureau of the Census in March 1957, in connection with the Current Population Survey. (1) This nationwide survey covered a sample of 35,000 households selected scientifically to represent all elements in the population of the nation. An analysis of some of the results of this survey is presented in this paper.

The question on religion was worded as follows: "What is your religion—Baptist, Lutheran, etc.?" The question was restricted to persons 14 years old and over, because some religious groups regard baptized infants as members and others count as members only persons who have "joined" at about 12 to 14 years of age or older. This difference in practice would undoubtedly affect the replies to such a question for persons under 14. In the 1957 survey, the answers to all questions were voluntary; only one per cent failed to give a reply to the question on religion.

The intent of the question was to elicit each person's religious preference, though the same reply would be expected from most of the people regardless of the phrasing of the questions. A preference question maximizes the proportion of the people who can be classified into the several religious groups and avoids the necessity of prescribing such a limiting criterion for inclusion as membership or attendance, both of which present some serious problems of definition. A preference question has the shortcoming, however, of drawing into the count for a given denomination some persons whose attachment to the group is nominal. It is possible that differences between the religious groups with respect to subjects discussed below would have been more distinct if the groups had been more narrowly defined.

Demographic Characteristics

Separate response categories were provided on the enumeration document for each of the six largest religious groups, as shown by official membership figures: Roman Catholic, Baptist, Methodist, Lutheran, Jewish, and Presbyterian. Other categories were also provided for "other Protestant," "other religion," and "no religion." For these groups, data were tabulated for persons 14 years old and over and, in addition, estimates of the number under 14 years old in each of the major groups were made by classifying family members under 14 according to the religion reported by the family head and his wife (if any). In families with mixed marriages, the author classified half of the children according to the religion reported by the head and half according to that of the wife. (See footnotes in Table 1.)

The findings in Tables 1 and 2 show that two out of every three persons in the United States in 1957 (66 per cent) were reported as (or estimated to be) Protestants, one out of every four (26 per cent) as Roman Catholics, three per cent as Jewish, one per cent as reporting some other religion, and three per cent as reporting no religion; one per cent made no report on religion.

Age. Figures on Protestants (by color), Roman Catholics, and Jews by key age brackets—young dependent ages, major productive ages, and old age—bring out the following points: At the extremes, nonwhite Protestants had a far larger proportion of young dependents than the Jews (42 per cent versus 28 per cent). White Protestants and Roman Catholics were intermediate and had about the same proportion of young dependents (34 and 36 per cent, respectively). At the same time, nonwhite Protestants had the smallest proportion in the productive ages and the Jewish population had one of the largest. In the old age bracket were smaller percentages of Protestant nonwhites and Roman Catholics than white Protestants and Jewish persons.

TABLE 1. *Civilian Population in the Major Religious Groups by Age, for the United States: March 1957*

RELIGION AND COLOR	TOTAL CIVILIAN POPULATION[1]		PER CENT BY AGE				MEDIAN AGE (YEARS)
	NUMBER	PER CENT	ALL AGES	UNDER 18 YEARS[1]	18 TO 64 YEARS	65 AND OVER	
Total	168,122,000	100.0	100.0	34.9	56.4	8.7	29.9
Protestant	111,533,000	66.3	100.0	35.1	55.7	9.2	29.9
White	95,330,000	56.7	100.0	34.0	56.2	9.8	30.9
Nonwhite	16,203,000	9.6	100.0	41.8	52.4	5.7	24.2
Roman Catholic	44,040,000	26.2	100.0	36.3	56.7	6.9	28.5
Jewish	5,013,000	3.0	100.0	27.8	62.2	10.0	36.6
Other religion and not reported	3,264,000	1.9	100.0	24.9	62.6	12.5	37.2
No religion	4,272,000	2.1	100.0	30.0	59.7	10.3	32.8

[1] Figures for children under 14 years old were estimated from religion reported by family head and wife. About 4 million of the 49 million children under 14 lived in families with head and wife reporting different religions; one-half of these children were assumed to have the religion of the head and one-half the religion of the wife. Ratio of persons 14 to 17 years old to persons 14 to 19 years old assumed to be the same for each religious group.

SOURCE: Derived from U.S. Bureau of the Census, "Religion Reported by the Civilian Population of the United States: March, 1957," *Current Population Reports*, Series P-20, No. 79.

The median ages provide a convenient means for summarizing the differences in age groupings. Thus, the median age for nonwhite Protestants was 24 years, that for Roman Catholics was 29 years, that for white Protestants, 31 years, and that for Jews, 37 years.

The age differences reflect such factors as differences among the religious groups with respect to major period of immigration of the persons (or of their ancestors) and with respect to their birth and death rates during past decades. Persons reporting "other religions" include mainly Eastern Orthodox Catholics and Orientals, many of whom migrated to the United States several decades ago and are now in old age. A relatively large proportion of those reporting no religion were in the adult age groups. It would be of interest to know how many of the middle-aged and older persons reporting no religion would have reported one in their earlier years, and to know how many of them would have reported each religion.

Sex. The percentage of *men* who were reported as Catholics was the same as the percentage of women who were reported as Catholics; likewise for Jewish men and women (Table 2). But three per cent more of the men than women reported no religion and three per cent more of the *women* than men reported themselves as Protestants. It would be

TABLE 2. *Religion Reported for the Civilian Population 14 Years Old and Older by Color and Sex, for the United States: March 1957*

RELIGION AND COLOR	BOTH SEXES		MALE, PER CENT	FEMALE, PER CENT
	NUMBER	PER CENT		
Total, 14 and over	119,333,000	100.0	100.0[1]	100.0[2]
White	107,361,000	90.0	90.1	89.8
Nonwhite	11,972,000	10.0	9.9	10.2
Protestant	78,952,000	66.2	64.7	67.5
Nonwhite	10,477,000	8.8	8.4	9.1
Baptist	23,525,000	19.7	19.4	20.0
Nonwhite	7,253,000	6.1	5.8	6.3
Lutheran	8,417,000	7.1	7.1	7.0
Methodist	16,676,000	14.0	13.5	14.4
Nonwhite	2,067,000	1.7	1.7	1.8
Presbyterian	6,656,000	5.6	5.3	5.8
Other Protestant	23,678,000	19.8	19.3	20.4
Roman Catholic	30,669,000	25.7	25.7	25.7
Nonwhite	774,000	0.6	0.6	0.7
Jewish	3,868,000	3.2	3.2	3.2
Other religion	1,545,000	1.3	1.4	1.2
No religion	3,195,000	2.7	4.1	1.4
Nonwhite	414,000	0.3	0.5	0.2
Religion not reported	1,104,000	0.9	1.0	0.9

[1] Based on 57,470,000 males 14 years old and over.

[2] Based on 61,863,000 females 14 years old and over.

SOURCE: Same as Table 1.

informative to know how many of the men reporting no religion worked in relatively isolated places where there were no religious organizations, and how many were merely indifferent toward religion.

Color. Seven-eighths of the nonwhites, as compared with five-eighths of the whites, were reported as Protestants. Six per cent of the nonwhites and 28 per cent of the whites were reported as Roman Catholics. So nearly are all nonwhites Protestants that almost any generalization which applies to nonwhite Protestants applies likewise to all nonwhite persons.

Region. In the South, 83 per cent of the persons of all races were reported as Protestants, as compared with 42 per cent in the Northeast and 69 per cent in the North Central region and the West. Approximately half of those reported as Roman Catholics and two-thirds of those reported as Jewish were living in the Northeast. The Northeast had the smallest proportion reporting no religion and the West had the largest (4 per cent).

Residence. Among persons reported as Jewish, 96 per cent lived in urban areas. The corresponding proportion was 79 per cent for those reported as Roman Catholics, 57 per cent for those reported as Protestants, and 54 per cent for those reporting no religion.

The unequal distribution of persons in the several religious groups according to the key demographic variables is relevant to the following discussion of family data on religion. (2)

Intermarriage

In view of the fact that about two-thirds of the adults in the United States are reported as Protestants, it would be theoretically possible for every Roman Catholic and every Jewish person to marry a Protestant. In such a hypothetical situation, rates of interfaith marriages for the Roman Catholics and Jews would be 100 per cent but that for Protestants would be less than 50 per cent.

Again, if religious ties were not strong and if other factors, such as race, social class, and geographic location were not to affect the selection of partners in marriage, persons in each religious group would tend to marry persons in any religious group on a random basis. In actual practice, of course, Protestants generally marry Protestants, Catholics generally marry Catholics, and Jews generally marry Jews. The question under discussion is the proportion of the couples who marry in or marry out of their religious group.

From the survey results on religion, it was possible to estimate the actual extent of intermarriage, for comparison with the amount which would have been "expected" on a random basis. Computations were made for married couples in which the husbands and wives were reported as Protestant, Roman Catholic, or Jewish. In this study, a Protestant husband with a Protestant wife was considered as a couple belonging to the same religious group, regardless of whether they were members of the same or different Protestant denominations.

The findings showed that 94 per cent of the married couples consisted of husbands and wives of the same major religious group. If the couples had been paired off without regard to the religion of their marriage partner, only 56 per cent of them would have had a spouse of the same religion; 44 per cent would have been married to a person in one of the other two major groups. In Table 3 corresponding figures are shown for each of the groups.

Among the couples with either a Protestant husband or a Protestant wife, both the husband and wife were Protestants in 91 per cent of the cases; in the remaining 9 per cent, one of the spouses was reported as a Roman Catholic or a Jew. For couples involving at least one Roman Catholic, 78 per cent were unmixed Roman Catholic couples and 22 per cent were mixed Catholic-Protestant or Catholic-Jewish couples. And for couples involving at least one Jewish partner, 93 per cent were unmixed Jewish couples and 7 per cent were mixed Jewish-Christian.

If all of these couples had consisted of persons of one of the religious groups or another at random, 47 per cent of the Protestants would have been in mixed marriages, instead of the actual 9 per cent. In other words, there were actually only about one-fifth (19 per cent) as many Protestant-Catholic or Protestant-Jewish couples as would have been expected on a random basis.

The rate of mixing was only slightly larger for couples with one or both Roman Catholic spouses. Thus, the actual mixture rate for Catholic spouses was 22 per cent and the expected rate was 84 per cent, making the actual rate only about one-fourth (26 per cent) as large as the expected rate. The minor differences which appear to exist between the mixture rates for Protestants and Catholics suggests that there is a higher rate

TABLE 3. *Actual Intermarriage Rates and Intermarriage Rates "Expected" if Husbands and Wives were Distributed at Random, for Married Couples in the United States with Husband and Wife Protestant, Roman Catholic or Jewish: March 1957*

RELIGION OF HUSBAND AND WIFE	MARRIED COUPLES		"EXPECTED" PER CENT IF RANDOM INTER- MARRIAGE	RATIO OF ACTUAL TO "EXPECTED" MIXED MARRIAGES
	ACTUAL NUMBER	ACTUAL PER CENT		
One or both Protestant	26,916,000	100	100	—
Protestant—				
Protestant	24,604,000	91	53	—
Roman Catholic or Jewish	2,312,000	9	47	.19
One or both Roman Cath.	10,657,000	100	100	—
Roman Catholic—				
Roman Catholic	8,361,000	78	16	—
Protestant or Jewish	2,296,000	22	84	.26
One or both Jewish	1,356,000	100	100	—
Jewish—				
Jewish	1,258,000	93	2	—
Protestant or Roman Cath.	98,000	7	98	.07

SOURCE: Same as Table 1.

of Catholic-Jewish than Protestant-Jewish intermarriage; the sample figures on such couples are quite small.

For couples with one or both Jewish partners, the ratio of the actual mixed marriage rate to the expected marriage rate was only about one-third that of Protestants or Catholics. Specifically, only 7 per cent of the couples with at least one Jewish partner had a Christian partner, whereas fully 98 per cent would have done so if they had married without regard to the religion of their partner in marriage. Hence, only 7 per cent as many Jewish persons outmarried as would have been expected by chance alone. The relatively low intermarriage rate for Jewish persons is no doubt a result in part of such factors as geographic concentration of Jewish population in urban neighborhoods.

In interpreting these "intermarriage" (or interfaith) mixtures, it should be recognized that some persons change their religion after marriage to conform to that of their spouse, that some enumerators may have failed to follow the instruction to ask for the religion of each person in the household rather than to assume that all had the same religion as the respondent, and that some respondents may have, for one reason or another, misreported the religion of one of the spouses. Probably most of these factors would tend to make the Census Bureau's household survey figures show less mixture among the three major religious groups than marriage records show. (3)

Moreover, intermarriage among denominations within the Protestant group is not reflected in the preceding discussion. There may well be more cultural resistance to intermarriage of persons in some of the widely different Protestant denominations than between Protestants and Catholics or Jews, but the available data did not throw light on this subject. Some persons reporting no religion may have ceased affiliating themselves with any religious group as a consequence of a conflict between their religion and that of their spouse. It is noteworthy, in this connection, that one million children under 14 years of age were living in families where the head reported no religion, whereas only about one hundred thousand children were in families where the wife reported no religion.

Finally, this study has not dealt with such related topics as differences in age at marriage and in the proportion who ever marry among the several religious groups. Thus, the findings may be affected by the extent to which Protestants tend to marry younger than Catholics and Jews and to which Catholics have a larger proportion in religious and educational work who never marry.

Fertility

Differences in the fertility rates for the several religious groups were measured in terms of the average number of children ever born per 1,000 women who had ever married (Table 4). Separate figures were compiled for women of childbearing age (15 to 44 years) and for women past the childbearing age (45 years and over). The rates for women of childbearing age are probably of more current interest than those for older women because they come closer to revealing eventual differences in reproductivity among women in the several religious groups who have been at the height of their childbearing during recent years; however, the rates for these women are affected somewhat by differences in age at marriage and in the timing of births after marriage.

For women of childbearing age, those reported as Baptists had the highest fer-

TABLE 4. *Cumulative Fertility Rate (Number of Children Ever Born per 1,000 Ever Married Women), by Religion Reported, for the United States: March 1957*

| | CUMULATIVE FERTILITY RATE | | |
| | WOMEN 15 TO 44 YEARS OLD | WOMEN 45 YEARS OLD AND OVER | DIFFER- |
RELIGION			ENCE
Total	2,218	2,798	580
Protestant	2,220	2,753	533
Baptist	2,359	3,275	916
Lutheran	2,013	2,382	369
Methodist	2,155	2,638	483
Presbyterian	2,001	2,188	187
Other Protestant	2,237	2,702	465
Roman Catholic	2,282	3,056	774
Jewish	1,749	2,218	469
Other, none, and not reported	2,069	2,674	605

SOURCE: U.S. Bureau of the Census, *Statistical Abstract of the United States, 1958*, Table 40. Based on data from Current Population Survey.

tility rate. To some extent this finding may be attributed to the fact that about one-third of the Baptists are Negroes, and the fertility rate for Negroes is about 20 per cent above that of whites. Moreover, a majority of the Baptists—whether currently in urban areas or rural—have probably grown up in the environment of the rural South, where the fertility rates are above those for the nation as a whole.

Despite the common belief—and evidence from other studies—that Catholics have larger families than other persons, (4) the Current Population Survey showed that the fertility rate for Roman Catholic married women of childbearing age in the country as a whole was not significantly higher than that for married Protestant women in the same age group. (The fertility rates standardized for age, not shown in Table 4, were virtually identical for the two groups, namely, 2,206 for Protestants and 2,210 for Roman Catholics.) The explanation lies, in part, in the fact that twice as large a proportion of Protestants as Catholics live in rural areas, and rural fertility rates are about one-fourth again as high as those in urban areas. Moreover, Protestants probably marry at a younger age than Catholics, on the average. Thus, although urban Catholic women may have higher fertility rates than other urban women, the survey figures indicate that Catholic women as a group in the entire nation do not have higher fertility rates than other women.

The fertility rate for Jewish women of childbearing age who had married was only about three-fourths as large as that for Protestant and Catholic women. As pointed out early in the paper, virtually all Jewish population in this country is found in urban areas, but the fertility rates for Jewish women was about 14 per cent below that for urban women of all religions combined. Also, according to independent studies, a relatively large proportion of Jewish workers is found in the professional and other white collar occupations, which require more than the average amount of education. (5) Women with husbands in such occupations tend to have 5 to 15 per cent fewer children than the national average. (The sample included only about 500 Jewish ever-married women 15 to 44 years old. This fact serves both as a caution in evaluating the results and as one of the reasons why the data are not shown in greater detail by related subjects.)

The (cumulative) fertility rates in Table 4 for women 45 years old and over reflect the fertility experience of earlier generations. Here, again, the Baptist women led all the rest, but the Roman Catholic women of this older age range had about ten per cent more children on the average than the entire group of Protestant women. The rate for the older Jewish women, as for the younger ones, was about three-fourths as high as the national average.

The fertility rate for women of childbearing age was about 600 points lower than that for women above childbearing age. This difference is not a mere reflection of the incomplete fertility of the younger women; it also arises, in part, from the fact that, despite the upturn in the birth rate during the 1940's, fertility rates today are still considerably lower than they were 40 or 50 years ago. The point to observe here, however, is that the difference between the fertility rates for women in the two broad age groups varied widely among the several religious groups. For example, the differences between the fertility rates of older and younger women among Baptists and Roman Catholics—clearly the most fertile of the older women—were the largest (about 800 to 900 points). At the other extreme, the Presbyterians had one of the lowest rates among both the younger and older women, and the difference for this denomination was the least (only about 200 points). These and other facts suggest a long-time trend toward the convergence of fertility rates among the religious groups.

Summary and Conclusions

The nationwide sample data collected by the Bureau of the Census in 1957 show that, among married couples with the husband and wife reported as Protestant, Roman Catholic, or Jewish, about one-fourth to one-fifth as many couples included only one Protestant partner or only one Catholic partner as would have been expected if the persons had married without regard to religion. By contrast, one-fourteenth as many couples included only one Jewish partner as would have been expected on a random basis. Thus, the findings provide statistical evidence that intermarriage occurs much more readily among Protestants and Catholics than between Jewish persons and Christians.

Moreover, Protestant and Roman Catholic married women of childbearing age had borne approximately equal numbers of children per woman, on the average, even though a much larger proportion of Protestants live in, or grew up in, rural areas where fertility rates are relatively high. Among Jewish women of childbearing age and of older ages, the fertility rates were about three-fourths as high as those for the country as a whole. Differences between rates for those of childbearing age and rates for older women suggest a trend toward convergence of the fertility levels among women in the major religious groups.

Undoubtedly, the differences between the major religious groups with respect to marriage and fertility patterns which have been shown by the survey data reflect differences in the age, color, geographic, and socioeconomic distributions of these groups as well as differences in religious doctrines with regard to family behavior.

References

[1] Two Census publications contain all of the statistics published from this study: U. S. Bureau of the Census, "Religion Reported by the Civilian Population of the United States: March 1957," Current Population Reports, Series P-20, No. 79; and Statistical Abstract of the United States, 1958, table 40.

[2] An extensive bibliography of statistical studies on religion is presented by Benson Y. Landis in "A Guide to the Literature on Statistics of Religious Affiliation with References to Related Social Studies," Journal of the American Statistical Association, Vol. 54, No. 286, June 1959, pp. 335-357.

[3] See Harvey J. Locke, Georges Sabagh, and Mary Margaret Thomes, "Interfaith Marriages," Social Problems, Vol. IV, No. 4, April 1957, pp. 329-333. On pages 332 and 333 the authors state: "In 1955, of all Catholic marriages 27 per cent were valid interfaith marriages. If those not sanctioned by the Church were added to these, there would be an even higher per cent of interfaith marriage." The rate is based on marriages reported in the Official Catholic Directory, rather than a cross-section of the population. The interfaith marriage rate is defined as "the per cent which interfaith marriages are of all marriages involving members of a given religious group" (p. 329). See also Loren E. Chancellor and Thomas P. Monahan, "Religious Preference and Inter-Religious Mixtures in Marriages and Divorces in Iowa," The American Journal of Sociology, Vol. LXI, No. 3, November 1955.

[4] A selected bibliography on studies of fertility differentials among religious groups is presented by Charles F. Westoff in "Religion and Fertility in Metropolitan America," Thirty Years of Research in Human Fertility: Retrospect and Prospect, Milbank Memorial Fund, New York, 1959, pp. 117-134. See especially Dudley Kirk, "Recent Trends of Catholic Fertility in the United States," Current Research in Human Fertility, Milbank Memorial Fund, New York, 1955, pp. 93-105. Kirk uses official Catholic statistics in examining the trends and current level of Catholic fertility in the United States.

[5] See Stanley K. Bigman, The Jewish Population of Greater Washington in 1956, The Jewish Community Council of Greater Washington, Washington, 1957, pp. viii-ix. In the Washington area, as in many other areas with relatively large Jewish populations, numerous professional and white collar jobs are available. See also Chapter 23, "Religious Affiliation," in Donald J. Bogue, The Population of the United States, The Free Press, New York, 1959.

4 · Negro Religion and Negro Status in the United States*

NORVAL GLENN

That religion can influence and be influenced by power relations and other aspects of social structure is exemplified by the religion of American Negroes. Many Negro religious beliefs and practices are, among other things, aids to adaptation to a subordinate status. Although Negro religion serves many of the same social and individual needs that are served by the religion of other people, it has in addition served a number of needs that grow out of discrimination, prejudice, and the initially inferior status of American Negroes. Religion has in some ways tended to retard the progress of Negroes in American society, and in other ways it has promoted Negro advancement.

That Negro religion and Negro status are and have been mutually influencing is certain, but the relationship is complex and there is considerable controversy among students of religion and of race relations as to its exact nature. The following questions have particularly been of concern: (1) In what respects is the religion of American Negroes unique? Are there many beliefs and practices peculiar to Negroes, or are most so-called Negro religious traits shared by past or present white religious groups? (2) To what extent are the dominant characteristics of Negro religion a reflection of the past and present status of Negroes in American society and to what extent do they grow out of an African cultural heritage and the uneven exposure of Negroes to different elements of white culture? (3) In what ways has

* Written for this volume.

Negro religion retarded the worldly advancement of Negroes and in what ways has it promoted advancement? Have the effects of Negro religion upon Negro economic and occupational status been in the balance positive or negative?

Some Broad Negro-White Religious Differences in the United States

This essay is addressed to each of these questions and to several more specific ones that grow out of them. The evidence is not such as to afford a definitive answer to each question, but an examination of available evidence relating to these issues can illuminate several aspects of the relationship between Negro religion and Negro status and can cast some light upon the more general relationship between religion and society.

Both Negroes and whites in the United States are predominantly Protestant, but a larger percentage of the Negroes are Protestant. Almost 90 per cent of the Negroes are Protestant compared with about two-thirds of the whites (see Table 1). Of all Negro-white religious differences, this one is most easily explained. The majority of American Negroes were converted to Christianity during the period of slavery and during the decades following the Civil War. At that time most Negroes lived in the South where, except for Louisiana and Maryland, few of the whites were Catholic. Therefore, Catholics were at a distinct disadvantage in their attempts to win Negro converts. Many of the hard-won Catholic gains among Negroes were lost after emancipation when many Negro Catholics, seeking more complete independence from whites, renounced Catholicism and joined all-Negro Protestant congregations.[1] The espousal of racial equality and integration by the Catholic church has recently aided the Catholic cause among Negroes,[2] but the number of Negro Catholics still is relatively small.

TABLE 1. *Religion Reported for Persons Fourteen Years Old and Over, by Color and Sex, United States, 1957*

PERCENTAGE DISTRIBUTION

RELIGION	WHITE		NONWHITE	
	MALE	FEMALE	MALE	FEMALE
Protestant	62.4	65.1	85.4	89.4
Baptist	15.1	15.2	59.1	62.0
Methodist	13.1	14.1	17.0	17.5
Other Protestant	34.2	35.8	9.3	9.9
Roman Catholic	27.8	27.9	6.4	6.6
Jewish	3.6	3.6	—	0.1
Other religion	1.3	1.2	1.5	1.5
No religion	4.0	1.3	5.4	1.7
Religion not reported	0.9	0.9	1.3	0.7

SOURCE: Bureau of the Census, *Current Population Reports,* Series P-20, No. 79, February, 1958.

The data in Table 1 show that nonwhite Protestants (most of whom are Negroes) are highly concentrated in the Baptist denominations whereas a majority of the white Protestants are in other denominations. The regional distribution of Negroes when most of them were converted to Christianity partially accounts for the difference, since white Baptists were more numerous in the South than elsewhere. Also, Baptist missionaries were

[1] Edwin Scott Gaustad, *Historical Atlas of Religion in America,* New York: Harper and Row, 1962, p. 149.
[2] E. Franklin Frazier, *Negroes in the United States,* rev. ed., New York: The Macmillan Co., 1957, p. 363.

more zealous than most others in their attempts to convert Negroes, and the emotional services and simple theology of the Baptists of that time had greater appeal among the uneducated Negroes than did most competing brands of Protestantism. Of the other denominations, only the Methodists, who also had emotional services, won a sizeable number of Negro converts.

The fact that most of the Negro converts joined Baptist and Methodist churches could in itself account for a great deal of the present difference between Negro and white religion. Yet much of the Negro-white difference cannot be accounted for in this way since it is within the broad categories of Baptists and Methodists. Negroes have their own Baptist and Methodist church bodies, which are in effect separate denominations and which bear only a tenuous relationship (in some cases only a historical relationship) to the white Baptist and Methodist church bodies. Negro and white Baptists still evince some broad doctrinal similarities, but there has been considerable divergence both in doctrine and in types of services since the separate Negro church bodies were formed before and immediately after the Civil War.[3]

[3] The earliest Negro converts to Christianity became members of mixed congregations, but they were usually segregated into a separate gallery or else were only allowed to watch and listen to the service from a side door. Many Negroes eventually became dissatisfied with their subordinate status in the predominantly white congregations and withdrew and formed their own congregations. In other instances, as the proportion of Negroes in a congregation grew, the remaining whites withdrew and left it all-Negro. By the Civil War few mixed congregations remained and some separate Negro church bodies had been formed. After emancipation the Negro congregations were expelled from the predominantly white church bodies in the South, and the religious separation of

There has been a similar divergence of Negro and white Methodist doctrine and services.

Recent public opinion polls indicate that the basic religious beliefs of Negro and white Protestants in the United States are very similar, but that on some issues Negro and white Protestants are not as closely in agreement as are white Protestants and white Catholics. The responses of white Catholics, white Protestants, and nonwhite Protestants to several religious questions asked in a 1957 Gallup Poll are shown in Table 2.[4] For several reasons, these data must be interpreted with caution. The "quota" sampling used for public opinion polling does not allow one to estimate accurately what the sampling error is likely to be, and, especially in the case of the rather small nonwhite sample, the error could be more than negligible. That is, all nonwhites might have responded somewhat differently to the questions than did the 152 nonwhites in the sample. In addition, the questions are of a very general nature, and probably evoked from many respondents conventional responses not based upon deep conviction and sincere belief. The tendency to give conventional instead of sincere responses may have been greater among nonwhites than among whites, since Negroes are likely to give more

conventional responses to white interviewers than to Negro interviewers,[5] and most if not all of the Gallup interviewers were white. Nevertheless, it is highly likely that the larger differences in responses to the questions in Table 2 reflect actual differences in practice and belief among the three categories of people compared.

Although these poll data indicate that church attendance is not greater among Negroes than among white Protestants and is not as great among Negroes as among white Catholics, there is some evidence that, in accordance with popular belief, Negroes on the average have stronger religious interests than whites. For instance, a much larger percentage of the nonwhites in the sample said that they regularly listened to or watched religious services on radio or television. On the other hand, a greater percentage of the nonwhites perceived a decrease in the influence of religion in American life, a difference that may reflect a decline in the importance of religion among Negroes relative to its importance among whites. Additional evidence for such a trend is discussed below.

The responses to questions on religious belief indicate a greater tendency for Negroes to be traditional, fundamentalist Christians. For instance, a larger percentage of the nonwhites said that they believed in the existence of a Devil, that one has to believe every word of the New Testament to be a Christian, and that one cannot be a Christian if he does not go to church. The differences are great enough that sampling error or a greater tendency for Negroes to give conventional responses to white interviewers is not likely to account for them. On the other

Negroes and whites became virtually complete.
[4] The author is indebted to the American Institute of Public Opinion and to the Roper Center for Public Opinion Research for permission to use these data here. These data were tabulated and analyzed in a project conducted by the author and Professor Leonard Broom and financed by the Hogg Foundation for Mental Health at the University of Texas.

In 1957 approximately 95 per cent of the nonwhites in the United States were Negroes; therefore, the nonwhite data are essentially for Negroes.

[5] Aaron M. Bindman, "Minority Collective Action against Local Discrimination: A Study of the Negro Community in Champaign-Urbana, Illinois," unpublished M.A. thesis, University of Illinois, 1961.

TABLE 2. *Responses of White Catholics, White Protestants, and Nonwhite
Protestants to Religious Questions, National Sample, 1957*

White Catholics:	$N =$	370
White Protestants:	$N =$	1024
Nonwhite Protestants:	$N =$	152

Did you yourself happen to attend church in the last seven days?

	WHITE CATHOLICS	WHITE PROTESTANTS	NONWHITE PROTESTANTS
Yes	77.0	43.7	43.4
No	23.0	56.2	55.3
No response	0	0.1	1.3
	100.0	100.0	100.0

At the present time, do you think religion as a whole is increasing its influence on American life or losing its influence?

	WHITE CATHOLICS	WHITE PROTESTANTS	NONWHITE PROTESTANTS
Increasing influence	79.7	68.2	50.7
Losing	6.5	13.7	35.5
Same	10.0	11.0	6.6
Don't know	3.5	6.8	5.9
No response	0.3	0.3	0.3
	100.0	100.0	100.0

Do you ever make a point of listening to or watching religious services on the radio or television?

	WHITE CATHOLICS	WHITE PROTESTANTS	NONWHITE PROTESTANTS
Yes, regularly	25.9	37.5	63.8
Yes, sometimes	50.3	44.6	27.6
No, never or prac- tically never	23.8	17.9	7.9
No response	0	0	0.7
	100.0	100.0	100.0

Do you believe that Jesus Christ was the son of God or just a man?

	WHITE CATHOLICS	WHITE PROTESTANTS	NONWHITE PROTESTANTS
Son of God	94.3	91.6	92.8
Just a man	1.6	3.5	2.6
Just a story	0.3	0.1	0.7
Uncertain	3.0	3.6	3.3
No response	0.8	0.2	0.6
	100.0	100.0	100.0

Do you believe that there is or is not a Devil?

	WHITE CATHOLICS	WHITE PROTESTANTS	NONWHITE PROTESTANTS
Is	64.6	61.3	73.0
Is not	20.3	26.4	14.5
Uncertain	14.6	11.4	10.5
No response	0.5	0.9	2.0
	100.0	100.0	100.0

Do you think that a person can be a Christian if he doesn't believe that every word of the New Testament is true?

	WHITE CATHOLICS	WHITE PROTESTANTS	NONWHITE PROTESTANTS
Yes	72.4	65.2	49.3
No	16.8	25.7	36.8
Uncertain	10.3	8 2	11.2
No response	0.5	0.9	2.7
	100.0	100.0	100.0

Do you believe there is or is not life after death?

	WHITE CATHOLICS	WHITE PROTESTANTS	NONWHITE PROTESTANTS
Is	71.4	78.4	76.3
Is not	16.2	9.1	11.2
Uncertain	12.4	12.1	9.2
No response	0	0.4	3.3
	100.0	100.0	100.0

Do you think a person can be a Christian if he doesn't go to church?

	WHITE CATHOLICS	WHITE PROTESTANTS	NONWHITE PROTESTANTS
Yes	72.4	81.9	66.4
No	21.6	14.1	27.0
Uncertain	5.4	3.3	3.3
No response	0.6	1.7	3.3
	100.0	100.0	100.0

Should the churches keep out of political matters or should they express their views on day-to-day social and political questions?

	WHITE CATHOLICS	WHITE PROTESTANTS	NONWHITE PROTESTANTS
Keep out	44.6	45.2	29.6
Express views	49.2	45.6	59.2
No opinion	6.2	7.5	7.9
No response	0	1.7	3.3
	100.0	100.0	100.0

hand, whites and nonwhites did not differ appreciably in stated belief in the divinity of Christ and in life after death.

A greater percentage of the nonwhite

respondents said that churches should express their views on day-to-day social and political questions, a difference that reflects the greater concern that Negro churches and Negro clergymen have actually had with at least some major political and social issues. Although some lower-class Negro preachers have eschewed concern with "affairs of the world," Negro preachers have generally played a leadership role that has entailed concern with a wide range of secular affairs. During slavery the plantation preachers emerged as Negro spokesmen who begged the masters for favors and in return encouraged docility among the slaves. After emancipation the preachers retained their mediative role as Negro spokesmen and representatives of the interests of whites. Since the church was the only Negro institution even nominally free from white control, it became the most important organization in the Negro community and took on numerous functions in addition to strictly religious ones. Where and when the stance of Negroes vis-à-vis whites became less compliant and acquiescent, the preachers, as the established Negro leaders, were expected to be "race leaders," to work for the improvement of Negro status. By contrast, in the white community there has been greater institutional specialization and a more differentiated leadership, and the functions of the church have been more strictly of a religious nature.

Some of the differences between the responses of whites and nonwhites to the poll questions can be accounted for by differences in average educational and economic status. For instance, poorly educated and poor people tend to be more traditional in their religious views. However, when the responses of white and non-white Protestants within broad educational levels were compared, much of the difference remained.[6] At each level, a

larger percentage of nonwhites said that they listened to or watched religious services on radio or television, that religion is losing influence in American life, that there is a Devil, that one cannot be a Christian if he does not attend church, and that churches should express views on day-to-day social and political questions.

These survey and poll data reveal only some very general differences between Negro and white religion. As the comparison is extended to more specific characteristics, it must necessarily become more impressionistic. Furthermore, the comparison becomes complicated by the fact that both Negro religion and white religion in the United States are now highly differentiated and no realistic comparison can be made of Negro religion as a whole and white religion as a whole. Therefore, each of the more common and characteristic forms of Negro religion must be dealt with separately and compared separately with the more common forms of white Protestantism.

The Religion of Rural Southern Negroes

The religious services of rural Southern Negroes differ from the usual white Protestant service mainly in that they are less formal and there is more participation by the congregation.[7] Many Negro

---

[6] The comparison was made within each of the following broad educational levels: (1) from zero to eight years of school completed, (2) from one to four years of high school completed, and (3) one or more years of college completed. On the average, whites within each level had slightly higher educational attainments than nonwhites, but these differences were hardly large enough to account for the differences between the white and nonwhite responses.

[7] This description of the religion of rural Southern Negroes is based upon several sources, but especially upon E. T. Krueger, "Negro Religious Expression," *American Journal of Sociology*, vol. 38 (1932–1933),

religious services are so informal and spontaneous that they appear to be without order or pattern. Any member of the congregation who feels inclined to express his feelings is likely to do so, usually in the form of singing, prayer, or shouting. Several persons may participate at one time, and the expression of ecstasy by one person is likely to precipitate similar expression by others. The service is divided into a long presermon stage, during which a state of rapport and mutual responsiveness is built up among the participants, and the sermon, during which the emotion, excitement, and responsiveness of the congregation reach a climax, if the preacher is successful, and the exultation of the participants leads to an orgiastic outpouring of shouting and singing, often accompanied by such physical manifestations as dancing, jerks, and seizures.

The sermon is likely to be relatively incoherent, consisting of soliloquies, character dialogues, Biblical tales, exhortations, and praises to the Lord, not held together by any unifying theme. Since the preacher is often illiterate or semiliterate, his knowledge of the Bible and of theology often is learned by word of mouth rather than from reading, and his accounts of Biblical events often are garbled. However, since the emphasis of the service is upon affect rather than cognition, the theological knowledge of the preacher bears no close relationship to his popularity. If he has good histrionic ability, if he can spin an exciting narrative in which God, the angels, and the Devil are realistic entities who play a direct role in human affairs, and if he can "shout" his congregation, he is considered a success.

pp. 22–31; and John Dollard, *Caste and Class in a Southern Town*, New Haven: Yale University Press, 1937, Chapter XI, "Caste Patterning of Religion."

The preacher denounces sin frequently, but he speaks even more often of a glorious afterlife. References to hell are rare relative to references to heaven. The emphasis is upon creating joy and mirth rather than upon instilling guilt and fear. Sorrows, poverty, drudgery, oppression, and troubles in general are momentarily forgotten in a vivid anticipation of a heaven in which there is no cotton to pick, no white mistresses' floors to scrub, no merchants to be indebted to, and no landlords to be dependent upon.

The origins of this religion are obscure and are the subject of considerable controversy. Some students of Negro religion profess to detect a similarity between some of the religious beliefs and practices of rural southern Negroes in the United States and of African Negroes. For instance, it is claimed that the swaying motions of the preacher and the rhythm that characterizes the singing, preaching, and audience response closely resemble the motions and rhythm in some African religious ceremonies.[8] Herskovits finds a common interest in water in the religious beliefs and ceremonies of American and African Negroes.[9] He attributes not only these similarities but also the strong religious interests of American Negroes to their African past. Although he agrees with most other scholars who have studied Negro religion that the religious beliefs and practices of Negroes in the United States provide compensation for their underprivileged status, he believes that their African cultural heritage causes them, "in contrast to other underprivileged groups elsewhere in the world, to turn to religion rather than to political action or other outlets for their frustration . . ."[10]

[8] M. J. Herskovits, *The Myth of the Negro Past*, New York: Harper and Brothers, chapter 7.
[9] *Ibid.*, chapter 7.
[10] *Ibid.*, p. 207.

Several other scholars—E. Franklin Frazier and Arthur H. Fauset among others—do not believe that there was any important carry-over of African religious beliefs or practices into the religion of Negroes in the United States.[11] African religion, according to this view, was dependent upon tribal organization, and, along with most other African culture, failed to survive the conditions of slavery in the British colonies in the New World. The characteristic forms of religious expression of Negroes in the United States, according to these scholars, grew out of the contact of Negroes with the religious revivals that swept the American frontier starting with the Great Awakening of 1734 and continuing until the last quarter of the 19th century. Therefore, the religion of rural southern Negroes is merely the evangelical religion that characterized the American frontier, modified to meet the unique needs of the slaves and freedmen. The frontier brand of evangelical Protestantism has generally disappeared among whites as they have become better educated, more sophisticated, and more prosperous, but it has survived in modified and elaborated form among southern rural Negroes, who have been isolated from the main stream of cultural change and economic advancement.

The latter view seems more nearly correct. Although there are similarities between the religious practices of African and American Negroes, the similarities between the religion of American Negroes and the religion of whites on the frontier are even greater.[12] The shouting, the

[11] For instance, see E. Franklin Frazier, op. cit. p. 334; and Arthur H. Fauset, Black Gods of the Metropolis, Philadelphia: University of Pennsylvania Press, pp. 101–104.
[12] Herskovits admits the similarity between rural southern Negro religion and white frontier religion, but he believes that the former influenced the latter (Op. cit., p. 225).

emotional seizures, the spontaneous outpouring of emotion, the rapport and mutual responsiveness among the congregation—all were prevalent in the white revival services, and, indeed, can still be found in several white lower-class sects. The Negro spirituals are uniquely Negro and whereas they may show some African influence, there is no doubt that many of the feelings, longings, and beliefs they express grew out of Negro experience on American soil. Some of the inflections of the voice and body movements of the Negro preacher and some of the responses of the audience are also uniquely Negro, and it is here that African influence is most likely. However, these characteristics of the Negro service could, like the spirituals, be largely American developments.

Although the sources of the dominant characteristics of the religion of rural southern Negroes are obscure and have been the subject of much debate, the functions of these characteristics are relatively clear. The emotionalism and the strong otherworldly orientation of this traditional religion of American Negroes have made the Negroes' subordinate status more bearable. The religious services have provided tension release, excitement, and escape in an existence characterized mainly by hardship, drudgery, and vicissitudes of various kinds. The focus upon the afterlife has promised the Negro "pie in the sky by and by when you die" and has had a soporific and diversionary influence. This type of Negro religion has not encouraged efforts for the improvement of the status of the Negro in the here and now and has tended to accommodate and reconcile him to an inferior status. From emancipation almost to the present, the Negro church was the main influence in orienting Negroes to the dominant white population, and there is almost unanimity among scholars of American race relations that the over-all

630   On the Religious Scene in the United States

influence of the church has been more toward acquiescence and docility than toward rebelliousness and protest.[13]

The accommodative influence of the Negro church has not resulted entirely from the emotionalism and otherworldliness of Negro religion. With the restoration of white supremacy in the South after Reconstruction, the Negro preachers came under the more or less direct control of whites. The preacher often was largely dependent upon whites for financial support or credit for his church, and often the very land on which the church stood was the property of whites. Indirect influence upon the preacher could be exercised through his congregation, who as individuals were usually in debt to whites and dependent upon them for jobs or tenure on the land. If all other means of control failed, the preacher was threatened with violence.[14] Therefore, when Negro preachers admonished their congregations to "turn the other cheek" and to love and be submissive to their white oppressors, they were influenced by more than Christian theology and morality.

Weber and others have pointed out that some forms of religion—especially some kinds of Protestantism—have promoted the economic advancement of their adherents by advocating a type of asceticism that is conducive to material success. These forms of religion have promoted the impulse renunciation and deferment of gratification that are essential to economic and other kinds of worldly advancement. However, there is little or no evidence that the Negro religion of

the rural South has had this effect. In spite of the frequent condemnation of sin by the preachers, the religion is not ascetic. Participation in the services more often brings a feeling of expiation of sin than a feeling of guilt. The emotional service provides an opportunity for impulse expression rather than being an influence for impulse renunciation. Dollard believes that the southern lower-class Negro religion plays exactly the opposite role from that usually ascribed to religion in a Puritanical society.[15] Instead of stressing self-control and denial of the appetites, this type of Negro religion gives the Negro, through ceremonials that relieve his guilt, poise and freedom as he enjoys the sensual pleasures of life.

Although Negro religion in the rural South has not generally been an important influence for Negro advancement, it has not been in all respects detrimental to Negro status and welfare. Since whites have looked upon the church with favor, influential preachers have been able at times to gain local concessions and individual favors for Negroes and to mitigate the harshness of white domination. Good relations between the church and high-status whites have strengthened the paternal benevolence toward Negroes that has characterized high-status whites in the South. Although in the long run this paternalism may have retarded Negro progress, in the short run it has been beneficial to Negro welfare. In addition, the church has helped to maintain solidarity in the Negro community and has thereby made possible cautious pressure for improvement in Negro status. The church is an organizational basis with great latent capacity, although this capacity has not yet been significantly realized, for racial advancement in the rural South. Also, some of the Negro church bodies have founded and partially

[13] For instance, see George Eaton Simpson and J. Milton Yinger, *Racial and Cultural Minorities*, rev. ed., New York: Harper and Brothers, 1958, pp. 582–586; E. Franklin Frazier, *op. cit.*, p. 336; John Dollard, *op. cit.*, p. 248; and Gunnar Myrdal, *An American Dilemma*, New York: Harper and Brothers, pp. 861–863.

[14] Myrdal, *op. cit.*, p. 861.

[15] *Op. cit.*, p. 249.

supported colleges for Negroes. These colleges generally are mediocre or poor in quality, but, in the absence of many better Negro colleges, they have played an important role in Negro education in the South.

Even when the influence of the church has been clearly not conductive to Negro progress, there are distinct limitations in the view that religion has been an independent causative agent that has kept Negroes down. Perhaps Negro religion in the South has been more a reflection of than an influence upon Negro-white relations. As white supremacy was restored and as Northern whites abandoned Southern Negroes during the latter decades of the 19th century, perhaps the only possible stance of Negroes vis-à-vis whites, short of suicidal rebellion, was an accommodative one. If this view is correct, then the emotionalism and otherworldliness of the Negro church were more means of accommodation than reasons for it. The relative lack of emphasis upon self-denial and impulse renunciation in Negro religion in the rural South may reflect the fact that the material rewards of such asceticism have been relatively meager for the southern Negro and that, given the relative lack of economic and educational opportunities, there has been little to be lost from a hedonistic, nonascetic orientation to life. This nonascetic orientation, which may grow largely out of lack of opportunities for Negro advancement, in turn is reflected in a nonascetic religion.

Yet, Negro religion is not a completely malleable and merely epiphenomenal factor in Negro-white relations. Although some of the dominant characteristics of Negro religion probably resulted in large measure from the subordinate status of Negroes and from their lack of opportunity to improve that status, these characteristics have in turn reinforced and helped to perpetuate Negro subordination. As opportunities for advancement have become greater, earlier adaptations of the Negro, including religious ones, have tended to inhibit action to take advantage of the new opportunities. When there has been pressure for change from other quarters, the southern Negro church has often been a conservative force.

The Religion of Urban Negroes

In recent years even Negro religion in some rural areas and small towns in the South has departed considerably from the traditional type of rural southern religion described above; Negro religion in the cities, both in the South and elsewhere, has departed much more.[16] The greatest change has been among the growing urban Negro middle class, whose religious services and beliefs do not differ in any important way from those of white Protestants of similar education and economic standing. The services are relatively formal and ritualized, the clergymen are well educated, the sermon is well organized and does not have a strong emotional appeal, and there is no strong otherworldly emphasis. However, there are few all-Negro congregations in which the services are as formal and the theology espoused by the minister is as modernistic as in the higher-status white congregations, such as the Episcopal, Presbyterian, and Congregationalist. Most Negro middle-class congregations are more nearly comparable to white Baptist and Methodist congregations that consist mainly of a mixture of people from the upper-manual and lower-white-collar occupations. The theology is essentially conservative. A literal interpretation is

[16] This description of urban Negro religion is based upon several sources, but especially upon E. Franklin Frazier, *op. cit.*; and St. Clair Drake and Horace R. Cayton, *Black Metropolis,* New York: Harcourt, Brace, and Co., 1945, chapters 15, 19, 20, 21, 22, and 23.

likely to be given of the scriptures, and such tenets of traditional Christianity as the virgin birth of Christ usually go unchallenged.

The major difference between the middle-class Negro congregations and their white counterparts is that the Negro minister is usually a more prominent community leader and is more concerned with secular affairs—especially race relations. The middle-class clergyman, in accordance with his general leadership role and the central importance of the church in the Negro community, has, since he first appeared, been expected to work for the advancement of the race. Since his congregation is prosperous enough to support him and his church, he is not dependent upon whites and has much greater freedom than the southern rural preacher to engage in race activities. However, the nature of the race activities that he has engaged in and advocated has varied with and reflected the general mood of the Negro middle class; he generally has not taken the initiative with new forms of protest and betterment activities. For instance, middle-class Negro clergymen in the cities of the South generally advocated cautious gradualism in race activities until the mid-1950's, when there was an upsurge of protest sentiment among urban Negroes in the South. Since then, middle-class Negro clergymen have come to the forefront in working for basic changes in the status of southern negroes, but most of them did not embrace the more vigorous techniques of protest until other leaders, including the professionals in the Negro protest and betterment organizations, took the initiative and gained widespread support.

Likewise, the race activities of middle-class Negro clergymen in the North have reflected the prevalent middle-class views of race relations. When the doctrine of the "double-duty dollar" was a popular proposed solution to Negro economic difficulties, it was often preached from the pulpits in middle-class and mixed-class churches.[17] As boycotts, picketing, demonstrations, and similar techniques became popular, the middle-class clergymen generally gave them support and in many cases provided leadership for the new types of activities. For instance, ministers have led the "selective patronage" movement in Philadelphia, which has placed economic pressure upon business firms to force the employment of Negroes. In the North, even more than in the South, middle-class ministers have had to take a more active and militant role on behalf of race causes or else abdicate their traditional leadership status in favor of leaders more attuned to the current Negro mood of protest.

However, urban middle-class Negro religion, like rural southern Negro religion, has not been a completely malleable and dependent factor in Negro-white relations. Although neither religious ideology nor religious leaders were in any important way responsible for the increased restiveness and mood of protest among Negroes during the mid-1950's, they have been influential in the selection of techniques of protest and in channeling expressions of discontent. Negro Christianity, with its doctrine that it is sinful to hate, is probably largely responsible for the emphasis upon nonviolent techniques of protest and for the repeated affirmations of love for the white man that characterize the southern civil rights movement.[18] Martin Luther King, Jr., a clergyman and the leading exponent of "passive resistance" and nonviolent tech-

[17] This doctrine is the belief that patronage of Negro-owned businesses will create more and better jobs for Negroes and will lead to a general improvement in Negro economic status.
[18] See James W. Vander Zanden, "The Non-Violent Resistance Movement against Segregation," American Journal of Sociology, vol. 68 (March, 1963), pp. 544–550.

niques of protest, has formulated an ideology that reconciles the mood of protest with such Christian values as passivity and love for enemies. By helping to remove the traditional religious restraints upon vigorous protest activity, King has given impetus as well as direction to the civil rights movement.[19]

The religion of urban lower-class Negroes is highly varied, but in general it is much more like the traditional rural

Negro religion than like urban middle-class religion. The services generally are again highly emotional, and there is often shouting and singing similar to that in the southern rural churches. With a few exceptions, the lower-class churches and sects are very otherworldly and less concerned with secular affairs than the middle-class churches. Their clergymen are less active in race activities, or not active at all. Their psychological functions to their adherents are similar to those of the rural churches, but, as is pointed out below, their effects upon the status of their members apparently are more often favorable.

A majority of the lower-class urban Negroes are Baptists, and the services and beliefs of lower-class Baptist congregations are most similar to those of the southern rural churches. The preachers are better educated and more sophisticated on the average than the rural preachers, but the difference is not great. The urban Baptist preachers are more concerned with sin and the Devil, perhaps because the influences that tend to draw people away from the church are greater in the city. Although the condemnation of sin from the Baptist pulpits is vehement, the church is not conspicuously successful in promoting the ascetic behavior it advocates or in preventing family instability. A larger number of women than of men are active in the church, and only in those families in which both husband and wife are "churched" does religion have much effect on family life. According to Drake and Cayton, the "influence of the church on lower-class sex and family life seems to be confined to moderating public brawling and to creating a group of women who try to make their children 'respectable' and encourage them to assume a middle-class family pattern even though they themselves, due to 'weakness of the flesh' or bitter experiences with men, do not maintain stable family rela-

[19] King assumed an active role in Negro protest activities earlier than did most Southern ministers. However, since he did not become active (nor did he enter the ministry) until a mood of protest was already prevalent among middle-class Negroes in the South, he does not constitute an exception to the generalization that the stance of middle-class clergymen in race relations has reflected rather than shaped to any appreciable extent the prevailing sentiments of the Negro middle class. King rose to national prominence and his career as a race leader was launched when he helped to organize the bus boycott in Montgomery, Alabama, in 1955. The boycott was precipitated by the arrest of a middle-class Negro woman who refused to give up her seat in a bus to a white person. The idea of boycotting the busses originated with a group of middle-class Negro women, and a large percentage of the more prominent Negroes in Montgomery concurred with it. The middle-class ministers of the city could hardly have avoided involvement in the boycott; King and several of the others organized and led it. Ministers of lower-class and mixed-class congregations were also drawn into the movement, largely through their association with the middle-class ministers in the ministerial alliance. These ministers were in large measure responsible for gaining the cooperation of lower-class Negroes that was essential to the success of the boycott. Without the leadership and diligent efforts of the ministers, the boycott probably would not have succeeded. However, they were not primarily responsible for it. (See Martin Luther King, Jr., *Stride Toward Freedom*, New York: Ballantine Books, 1958.)

tions . . ." [20] Perhaps the Baptist doctrine of "once saved, always saved" is conducive to periodic lapses into sin by believers, and tends to prevent the sustained self-denial and renunciation of pleasure needed for upward mobility.

Some of the other lower-class denomnations and sects apparently are more successful in their battle against sin. These include the Holiness sects, that rank second only to the Baptists in number of members in the urban Negro lower class. The Holiness sermons, even more than the Baptist ones, dwell upon the importance of living a "clean life," devoid of liquor, illicit sex, tobacco, fighting, and swearing. The "saints," as the Holiness members call themselves, believe that Christians must live free from all sin, and that they can do so if they are "sanctified" or "set apart from the world." Those who consider themselves sanctified make a strong effort to avoid behavior they consider to be sinful, and apparently many are successful. However, as with the Baptists, most of the believers are women, and this limits the effectiveness of the religion in promoting family stability and upward mobility.

The over-all effect of the Holiness religion on the status of its adherents is ambiguous. The Holiness sects are among the most otherworldly of the urban Negro religious organizations and perhaps have the most emotional services. Therefore, they tend to have the same escapist, diversionary functions as the rural churches. Since the "saints" believe that religion should not be mixed with "affairs of the world," the Holiness clergymen have been among the least active of Negro religious leaders in activities for racial advancement. The feeling that they are saints who live free from all sin gives the believers a compensatory feeling of superiority over all "unsanctified" persons, Negroes and whites alike, and this may lessen their desire to rise in worldly status. The Holiness preachers are often harsh in their criticism of "strainers and strivers," and few of the members of their congregations seem to have strong mobility aspirations. The "spiritual upward mobility" offered by the Holiness religion serves as a psychological substitute for upward occupational and economic mobility, and therefore the religion may inhibit efforts for worldly advancement. However, the effect of the Holiness religion upon the status of its adherents may not be adverse in the balance. Although the Holiness members may disclaim interest in "laying up treasures on earth," a latent function of their "sinless" existence is likely to be a greater accumulation of wealth and greater job stability than are typical of their lower-class "unsanctified" brothers. Furthermore, a complete substitution of spiritual advancement for worldly advancement is likely to be made only by persons for whom the latter seems unattainable and who would not have been upwardly mobile to any great extent anyway.[21]

[20] Drake and Cayton, *op. cit.*, p. 615.

[21] The view that the otherworldliness of the Holiness sects tends to lower the aspirations for worldly success of the Holiness believers is challenged by Benton Johnson ("Do Holiness Sects Socialize in Dominant Values?" *Social Forces*, vol. 39 (May, 1961), pp. 309–316). According to Johnson, the separation of the Holiness people from "the things of the world" does not entail a sweeping rejection of secular norms nor an abandonment of such "worldly" goals as economic, occupational, and academic success. Rather, the "worldliness" inveighed against by the Holiness preachers is the pursuit of immediate gratification in such ways as to jeopardize both the goal of salvation of the soul and long-range goals of worldly success. The values in which the sects socialize their members are broadly similar to the dominant middle-class values of American society, are in sharp contrast to the values of the unchurched lower class, and are conducive to material success. Johnson points

Some of the many small cults that have sprung up among lower-class urban Negroes apparently have been more conducive to the material advancement of their adherents than have the Holiness sects. The Father Divine Peace Mission Movement, the Moorish Science Temple, the United House of Prayer, the Nation of Islam (Black Muslims), and dozens of smaller cults founded by charismatic leaders have, like the Holiness sects, emphasized impulse renunciation, especially in regard to sex, and apparently have been more successful in bringing about sustained ascetic behavior among their believers.[22] Since these cults have generally been less otherworldly than other lower-class Negro religious organizations, they have been less likely to influence their members to abjure worldly success. For instance, the Black Muslims do not believe in an afterlife, and Father Divine offered his followers a Kingdom of

Heaven on earth rather than in a life to come. The leaders of some of these cults have explicitly encouraged their followers to accumulate wealth, and some of the cults have themselves engaged in business activities.

The Black Muslim movement apparently has been especially effective in producing a bourgeois way of life among its believers, even though like the other cults it has recruited its membership almost entirely from the most disadvantaged segments of Negro society.[23] Its members are forbidden to drink, smoke, engage in premarital or extramarital sex relations, or engage in many types of recreational activities that are common among lower-class urban Negroes. Women are treated with deference and respect, although they are relegated to an inferior status in the organization. Men are encouraged to support their families and to exercise strict control over their wives and children, not as in the maternal family that is typical of the Negro lower class. Unlike the Christian churches and sects, the Muslims have attracted more men than women, and therefore their effect upon family stability has presumably been greater. Installment buying is forbidden, conspicuous consumption is discouraged, and thrift and industry are encouraged. Many former criminals, prostitutes, and narcotic addicts have joined the movement, and they have reformed and remained reformed as long as they have remained in the movement. It is Lincoln's impression, at any rate, that few such persons have reverted to former types of behavior.[24]

The Baptist and Holiness organizations espouse similar standards of behavior, but an infraction of a rule within the

---

out that any appreciable upward mobility of the lower-class person must be preceded by reorientation from the prevailing lower-class values to middle-class values, and he believes that conversion to the Holiness religion often effects this change in value orientation. Return of the convert across the value orientation borderline tends to be deterred by the Holiness acceptance of the Wesleyan doctrine of the possibility of a fall from grace and by the threat to "disfellowship" or expel members who fail to abide by the ascetic rules of the Holiness religion.

If Johnson's view is correct, the effects of the Holiness religion upon economic status should be in the balance decidedly favorable. However, Johnson based his generalizations upon observation of *white* organized Holiness congregations in the South, and he points out that they may not apply to the "store-front" Holiness congregations that are especially prevalent among Negroes.

[22] For a good description of some of these cults and for an analysis of their functions and the bases of their appeal, see Arthur H. Fauset, *op. cit.*

[23] See C. Eric Lincoln, *The Black Muslims in America*, Boston: Beacon Press, 1961; and E. U. Essien-Udom, *Black Nationalism*, Chicago: University of Chicago Press, 1962.
[24] *Op. cit.*, pp. 82, 114–115.

Muslim organization is followed by sanctions that are certain (if officials know of the infraction) and relatively severe.[25] A semimilitary body within the movement, the Fruit of Islam, is charged with detecting offenses and deciding upon punishment for the offenders. A habitual offender is not likely to escape detection by this body for long. The most severe penalty is expulsion from the organization, and the satisfactions derived from participating in the movement apparently are great enough to most Muslims that threat of expulsion is a rather effective deterrent to prohibited behavior. However, internalized standards may well be more effective than the sanctions of the Fruit of Islam in controlling the behavior of Muslims.

The Muslim doctrine of black superiority is conceivably to a large extent responsible for the behavioral changes wrought in the Muslim converts. Lower-class Negroes are looked down upon both by whites and middle-class Negroes, and it is a fair presumption that these negative attitudes occasion some lack of self-respect and some feelings of self-hatred, unless there is extreme isolation from the attitudes and noncognition of them. American Negroes of all classes have tended to accept the prevailing white evaluation of Negroes and of Negroid physical features, and since the Negro's image of himself is partially a reflection of the attitudes of whites toward him, it tends to be a negative image.[26] Because

this negative evaluation of the Negro by whites and by himself is appreciably focussed upon his physical features, no attempts at achievement or self-improvement can completely relieve Negro feelings of inferiority. The Christian religion can help the Negro overcome his negative self-evaluation by substituting otherworldly for worldly standards of evaluation; for instance, the "sanctified" Negro Christian may feel superior in the eyes of God. But it is doubtful that this substitution of standards is often complete enough that the Negro Christian gains a fully satisfying self-image. He may respect his spiritual self while still hating his physical self—including his Negroid features—and such an ambivalent self-image is not conducive to maximum efforts at self-improvement.

The Muslim ideology, by contrast, substitutes one set of worldly standards for another. Through a myth of the origin of the races and through an elaborate and glorified history of the "so-called Negroes," [27] the blacks are made physically, mentally, and morally superior to whites. The Negro who accepts these standards can feel superior merely because he has dark skin and kinky hair. He has a firm basis for self-respect, and this self-respect can be made complete by the adoption of behavior deemed appropriate to a superior people. Therefore, his self-image may be less ambivalent than that of the "sanctified" Christian, and his attempts to maintain and enhance it may lead to more sustained and diligent efforts at self-improvement.

During the late 1950's, Muslim membership in Northern and Western cities

[25] Errant members are often expelled from the Holiness sects, but no systematic means of detecting offenders are employed, while such means are employed by the Muslims.
[26] See Kenneth B. Clark and Mamie P. Clark, "Racial Identification and Preference in Negro Children," in Theodore M. Newcomb and E. L. Hartley (eds.), Readings in Social Psychology, New York: Henry Holt and Co., 1947; Robert Johnson, "Negro Reactions to Minority Group Status," in Milton L. Barron (ed.), American Minorities, New York: Al-

fred A. Knopf, Inc., 1957; and Charles S. Johnson, Growing Up in the Black Belt, Washington, D. C.: American Council on Education, 1941, p. 259.
[27] The Muslims object to the word Negro and therefore refer to Negroes as blacks or so-called Negroes.

started to grow rapidly. Although a very small percentage of American Negroes have become Muslims,[28] many others have been influenced by the movement and have become Muslim sympathizers. The growth of the movement reflects widespread discontent among lower-class Negroes with their status and with the rate of improvement of their status. The goals of the movement, which are separatist rather than integrationist, reflect disillusionment with the prospects for Negroes to gain true equality in a society dominated by whites. The decade of the 1950's was a period of increased egalitarian rhetoric and of highly publicized court rulings favorable to Negroes, and these and other developments increased Negro aspirations for advancement and equal treatment and tended to dispel any remaining disposition to accommodation of Negroes to their inferior status. And yet many lower-class Negroes experienced no perceptible change in their lot in life. In fact, many experienced a deterioration in their economic condition as unemployment spread among unskilled and semiskilled workers. To many it seemed that the liberal whites and the Negro leaders, including the ministers, had promised much and delivered little in the way of tangible gains. The Muslim leaders offered alternative means to Negro advancement, and instead of promising equality with whites years and decades in the future, they offered an immediate feeling of superiority.

The Muslim movement might be looked upon as a widespread reaction against the accommodative influence of Negro Christianity, but such a view needs qualification. The Muslim leaders have e nced a keen awareness—in fact, an exaggerated awareness—of the fact that

historically neither the Christianity of Negroes nor the Christianity of whites has been greatly beneficial to Negro status. However, it seems unlikely that many of the Muslim converts arrived at an understanding of the traditional effects of Negro religion upon Negro status before they heard the Muslim teachings. Most of them seem to have been primarily attracted by the Muslim ideology and leadership rather than repelled by Christianity. Nevertheless, the Muslim teachings have made many Negroes aware of the traditional accommodative influence of Christianity, and this awareness has been one of the factors that recently have forced Christian ministers to play a more militant role in activities for recial advancement.

Trends in Negro Religion in the United States

Three major trends have been discernible in Negro religion during the past several decades—all closely related to changes in Negro status. First, as the Negro population has become more differentiated socially, culturally, and economically, Negro religion likewise has become more varied. Departures from the traditional southern rural Negro religion have become more numerous and more pronounced. Several of these departures are discussed above.

The second major trend is for religion to become less important among Negroes and for religious organizations and leaders to become less influential.[29] Whereas the importance of religion to whites may have increased during recent decades, the bases for the uniquely eminent role of Negro religion have been undermined.

[28] Lincoln estimated in 1961 that Muslim membership was about 100,000, or less than one-half of one per cent of the Negroes in the United States.

[29] Myrdal, op. cit., pp. 863, 875–878; Simpson and Yinger, op. cit., pp. 588–589; Drake and Cayton, op. cit., pp. 418–421, 653; and Maurice R. Davie, Negroes in American Society, New York: McGraw-Hill, 1949, p. 193.

The great interest of Negroes in religion has resulted partially from their lack of opportunity to participate in other institutional spheres, and as opportunities for other kinds of participation have become greater, the importance of religious activity has become less. As more Negroes have become well educated and gained entry into upper-level occupations, the prestige and influence of the Negro preacher have become relatively smaller. The Negro politician, the professional "race leader," and the Negro intellectual, among others, have challenged the traditional leadership of the minister. As other occupational opportunities have become greater, fewer Negroes have "felt the call" to preach. The data in Table 3 show

TABLE 3.   *Number of Employed Male Clergymen per 10,000 Population, by Race, 1940, 1950, and 1960*

	WHITE		NEGRO	
	NUMBER	NUMBER PER 10,000 POPULATION	NUMBER	NUMBER PER 10,000 POPULATION
1940	115,958	9.8	17,102	13.3
1950	142,110	10.5	18,150	12.1
1960	181,347	11.4	13,955	7.4

SOURCE: United States Census reports for 1940, 1950, and 1960.

the decline from 1940 to 1960 in the number of employed male Negro clergymen per 10,000 Negro population—a decline that was accompanied by an increase in white clergymen. This decline in part reflects a tendency for Negroes to demand educated clergymen in the place of untrained "jackleg" preachers and for the average size of congregations to increase, but it probably also reflects the declining relative attractiveness of the ministry to young Negro men. It may, but does not necessarily, reflect a decreasing demand for the services of religious functionaries.

Drake and Cayton report that during the depression of the 1930's there was a widespread feeling among lower-class Negroes in Chicago that the church was a "racket." [30] Financial difficulties faced by the churches led to intensified campaigns to raise money, which in turn contributed to this feeling. The disillusionment was not so much with religion as with preachers and the church. Many people correctly perceived that the motives of many Negro preachers were primarily mercenary, and there was a tendency to attribute mercenary motives to those preachers whose primary motives were in fact religious. During the prosperous era since the beginning of World War II, complaints that the churches are a "racket" seem to have declined and another kind of dissatisfaction has become more prominent. Negro economic and occupational gains during the labor shortage of World War II, favorable court rulings on civil rights, and several other developments have raised Negro aspirations and made Negroes more insistent in their demands for first-class citizenship. Many middle-class Negroes have come to look upon the otherworldly and emotional Negro religion as a hindrance to Negro advancement, as in fact it often has been, and have become critical of Negro preachers for the relatively inactive role that most of them have (until recently) played in working for basic changes in Negro status. Some of these Negroes have turned away from religion and others have placed pressure upon clergymen to play a more active role in the civil rights movement.

This pressure from members of congregations, competition from secular leaders, and, to a lesser extent, competition from the Black Muslims and the Catholics have forced Negro clergymen to take a more active and militant role in the drive for Negro equality—and this

[30] *Op. cit.,* pp. 419–421.

is the third major trend in Negro religion. The accommodative type of Negro religion is being replaced by a religion that is concerned at least as much with the worldly status and welfare of Negroes as with the salvation of their souls. This trend has been most pronounced with urban middle-class religion, but as a mood of protest spreads to all segments of the Negro population, the only kind of religion that can thrive among any class of Negroes will be a kind that is in harmony with that mood. It is to be expected that pressing Negro needs and growing aspirations for economic and social advancement will exercise a selective influence upon the elements of the traditional religion. The accommodative elements are likely to be deemphasized, and those portions of the Bible that appear to support demands for economic and social justice are likely to be given greater emphasis. At the same time, however, certain elements of the traditional religion will continue to condition, shape, and restrict the forms of Negro protest, although their influence may not be as great as it has been in the past.

5 · Jews In and Out of New York City[1]

BERNARD LAZERWITZ

Recent studies of United States religious groups have shown that Jewry has attained high levels of education and income and is very concentrated in white-collar occupations.[2] For a variety of reasons, these research endeavours have not touched upon internal differences within this major division of world Jewry. One of the most important of such differences arises out of the very heavy concentration of Jews in New York City. Indeed, data gathered for this article indicate that 44 per cent of the Jews of the United States live in New York City where they form 30 per cent of the population of this great city.[3]

Any contrast between New York City Jews and Jews residing in other United States communities involves three basic sociological factors: (1) numerical density, (2) selective out-migration from New York City, and (3) immigration into New York City of large numbers of Jewish refugees since the mid-thirties.

SOURCE. Bernard Lazerwitz, "Jews In and Out of New York City," The Jewish Journal of Sociology, 3, December, 1961, pp. 254–260.

What effect does their numerical density have upon the social structure of New York City Jews? Jewish publications frequently state that only in New York City does a Jewish "working class" still exist. Since Jews are such a large proportion of New York City, is it not reasonable to expect that they must work in fewer white-collar and more blue-collar occupations than do Jews in other American communities?[4] After all, even New York City can support only so many doctors, lawyers, and store-keepers.

On the other hand, where Jews are a small part of a community, economic limitations upon the available number of high status occupations would be less of a factor. Such Jews can have a very large proportion of their numbers in professional and other white-collar positions.

Selective out-migration from New York City calls attention to the fact that many economically successful Jews move out of New York City to the suburbs. Also, well educated Jews can, and do, move to any area of the country that offers economic and social attractions regardless of the (initially) small size of Jewish communities in such economically developing areas.[5] Hence, disproportionate numbers of Jews who are not as well prepared for occupational activity remain behind in New York City.

Thirdly, the immigration into New York City of many Jewish refugees has added an "under-privileged" sector to its Jewish population. Large numbers of these recent immigrants (as with the preceding waves of Jewish immigrants) are handicapped by language problems, interrupted or inadequate education, and lack of reserve savings.

Therefore, it is hypothesized that New York Jewry, as a whole, has less education, lower incomes, and more blue-collar workers than the rest of United States Jewry.

The Findings

The information presented here was gathered on three national surveys conducted by the Survey Research Centre of the University of Michigan. Two of these surveys were conducted in the spring of 1957, and the third was done during November 1958. A description of the nature of these three surveys together with tables of sampling errors can be found in a recent issue of the *Journal of the American Statistical Association*.[6]

Table 1 compares the religious com-

TABLE 1. *Religious Composition of the United States and New York City: December 1957*

RELIGIOUS GROUPS	UNITED STATES	NEW YORK CITY
Protestants	71.4	21.3
White	63.5	9.2
Negro	7.9	12.1
Roman Catholics	22.4	46.0
Jews	3.2	29.6
Other religions	0.9	1.3
No religion	2.0	1.7
Religion not reported	0.1	0.1
Total	100.0	100.0
Sample size	5827	283

position of New York City with that of the United States. It shows that New York City is indeed a place of residence for American minority groups. White Protestants just about disappear; Negroes show a 50 per cent increase over their national percentage;[7] Catholics are more than twice as numerous and Jews ten times as numerous as their national averages. Eighty-eight out of a hundred New Yorkers are Roman Catholics, Jews, or Negroes while 64 out of a hundred citizens of the United States are white Protestants.

TABLE 2. *New York City Catholic and Jewish Groups Contrasted with National Protestant and Catholic Groups and non-New York City Jewish Group by Education*

		AMOUNT OF EDUCATION				
RELIGIOUS GROUPS	N	0–8 GRADES	SOME HIGH SCHOOL	4 YEARS HIGH SCHOOL	1–3 YEARS COLLEGE	4 YEARS OR MORE OF COLLEGE	TOTAL (%)
U.S. Protestants	4,185	33	21	27	10	9	100
U.S. Catholics	1,270	34	20	32	9	5	100
N.Y.C. Catholics	132	54	21	18	5	2	100
N.Y.C. Jews	82	29	18	29	13	11	100
Non-N.Y.C. Jews	105	16	8	36	19	21	100

TABLE 3. *New York City Catholic and Jewish Groups Contrasted with National Protestant and Catholic Groups and non-New York City Jewish Group by Income*

TOTAL FAMILY YEARLY INCOME

RELIGIOUS GROUPS	N	UNDER $1000	$1000–$1999	$2000–$2999	$3000–$3999	$4000–$4999	$5000–$5999	$6000–$7499	$7500–$14,999	$15,000 OR MORE	TOTAL (%)
U.S. Protestants	4,185	8	9	11	13	14	15	12	15	3	100
U.S. Catholics	1,270	4	7	8	12	17	17	17	16	2	100
N.Y.C. Catholics	132	6	6	14	16	19	19	9	10	1	100
N.Y.C. Jews	82	4	2	7	13	17	15	15	25	2	100
Non-N.Y.C. Jews	105	1	2	4	5	4	15	15	37	17	100

Starting with high school graduates and continuing up the educational scale, non-New York City Jews outrank New York City Jews as shown by Table 2. Indeed, New York City Jews have just slightly more education than Protestants show nationally. Again, New York City Catholics rank below the national Catholic education percentages and are considerably below their fellow Jewish New Yorkers on education.

These patterns repeat themselves for the income data in Table 3. New York City Jews earn less than non-New York City Jews, and New York City Catholics earn less than their national grouping. New York City Jews are somewhat above national Protestant income percentages and earn more than their Catholic fellow townsmen.

Occupation percentages are shown in Table 4. Obviously, New York City Jews have a considerably higher percentage of skilled and semi-skilled workers than non-New York City Jews do. Once again, the previously mentioned patterns reappear with New York City Jews showing more white-collar workers than the national Catholic percentages which are higher, in turn, than the white-collar figures for New York City Catholics.

Table 5 gives synagogue attendance figures for the two Jewish groups. New York City Jews show slightly less regularity of synagogue attendance than do non-New York City Jews.[8] Finally, Table 6 indicates that both New York City Jews and Catholics have a larger foreign-born percentage than their two comparison groups.

The hypothesis that New York City Jews rank below non-New York City Jews on education, income, and occupation has been verified. In addition, the

TABLE 4. *New York City Catholic and Jewish Groups Contrasted with National Protestant and Catholic Groups and non-New York City Jewish Group by Occupation of Family Heads*

OCCUPATION OF FAMILY HEADS

RELIGIOUS GROUPS	N	PRO-FESSIONS	OWNERS, MANAGERS, OFFICIALS	CLERICAL AND SALES	SKILLED	SEMI-SKILLED	UNSKILLED	WITHOUT AN OCCU-PATION
U.S. Protestants*	4,185	9	12	10	17	15	10	17
U.S. Catholics*	1,270	8	11	10	22	20	10	15
N.Y.C. Catholics	132	3	6	10	21	19	23	18
N.Y.C. Jews	82	17	23	18	12	15	2	13
Non-N.Y.C. Jews	105	21	38	15	7	4	0	15

* Excludes 10% of U.S. Protestants and 4% of U.S. Catholics who are farmers.

TABLE 5. *New York City and non-New York City Jewish Groups Contrasted by Synagogue Attendance*

| | SYNAGOGUE ATTENDANCE | | | |
| | ONCE A MONTH OR MORE | A FEW TIMES A YEAR | NEVER | TOTAL (%) |
RELIGIOUS GROUPS				
N.Y.C. Jews	28	53	19	100
Non-N.Y.C. Jews	38	50	12	100

data indicate an equivalent relationship between New York City Catholics and the educational, income, and occupational achievements of Catholics throughout the United States. The problem, then, becomes one of trying to suggest the causal mechanisms behind these lower rankings of New York City dwellers.

The exact interrelationships among the three factors previously proposed to account for the New York City rankings cannot be obtained from available sources of information. However, some added clarification is possible.

First of all, New York City's Jewish and Catholic populations contain twice as many foreign born adults as do non-New York City Jews or Catholics throughout the United States. Unfortunately, the number of interviews with the foreign born is too small to permit adequate investigation of their age structure. Nevertheless, these foreign born contingents are not all derived from pre-

TABLE 6. *New York City Catholics and Jews Contrasted with the National Catholic and non-New York City Jewish Groups by Per Cent Foreign Born*

RELIGIOUS GROUPS	PER CENT FOREIGN BORN
U.S. Catholics	16
N.Y.C. Catholics	31
N.Y.C. Jews	44
Non-N.Y.C. Jews	21

quota immigration days and must include very sizable numbers of more recent immigrants.

Furthermore, it is well known that for at least a decade the economically "better-off" New York City Jews and Catholics have been moving out of the five boroughs into the surrounding suburbs. This leaves behind an increasing concentration of economically less successful Jews and Catholics.

Catholics are not more concentrated in New York City than they are in other large communities (such as Boston, Chicago, or Cleveland) that have sizable proportions of Catholics. Consequently, numerical concentration does not exert more pressure upon New York City's Catholic adults than on United States Catholics as a whole.

Jews are disproportionately concentrated in New York City.[9] But the differentials between Jews in and out of New York City are not unlike those between the two sets of Catholic percentages upon which no differentiating factor of concentration would be operating. Furthermore, Jews do not make up so large a percentage of New York that they would absolutely be forced into a variety of lower status occupations.[10] Apparently, then, the factor of Jewish numerical concentration is least important among the three factors proposed to explain the differentials in the Jewish data.

In short, it is likely that New York City's Jews and Catholics have their relatively less "desirable" education, income, and occupation distributions in large part because of in-migration of foreign born adults and out-migration of economically more successful adults who possess good education and are white-collar workers.

Note that New York City Jews outdistance New York City Catholics on all three social status variables. Within the social structure of their city, the New York Jewish group ranks at the top on income, education, and occupational status. Nationally, the Jewish group is outranked only by the Episcopalians on these three social status variables.[11] Hence, our two Jewish groups show equal ability to "get ahead" within their respective social environments.

The Jews of New York City do not appear to be more religiously active than are Jews in the rest of the country, if attendance at services is permitted to serve as the criterion. Even though there are Orthodox extremes in New York, there are enough Jews with lesser degrees of religious attachment to lower frequency of attendance at services.

A final item of interest can be obtained from the slight changes in "no religion" percentages of Table 1. One cannot claim that the percentage of adults who state they have no religion differs in New York City from the national percentage, despite the much higher percentage of Jews in New York City. United States Jews (both in and outside New York City) are known to be highly secularized and religiously indifferent, but not enough New York City Jews would declare themselves without a religion to raise that city's "no religion" percentage a noticeable amount. Nor is there any evidence that Jews, in any meaningful numbers, declared themselves Protestants or Catholics.

The willingness of New York City Jews to declare themselves Jews, of course, represents a religio-ethnic reaction to a question on religious preference. In addition, it seems to indicate that almost all Jews, among many ways of reacting to their Jewishness, prefer to choose Judaism to Christianity or complete secularism.

Perhaps the great size of the New York Jewish community promotes greater attachment to the Jewish group. Most non-New York City Jews live as parts of relatively large size Jewish communities so that the added group identification resulting from sheer numbers operates on them. If small-city or small-town Jews find the road to assimilation easier to travel, they represent a very small portion of the United States Jewish population.

It is easy to make too much out of the small New York City "no religion" percentage. But if this percentage were three or four times the national average, what interpretation would be given to the data? Clearly, it would be concluded that a sizeable group of New York Jews had declared themselves to be without a religion. Many Jews may not be happy with today's Judaism, but they prefer it to Christianity or nothing at all.

Notes

[1] The author wishes to thank the Survey Research Centre of the University of Michigan for permission to use its data. Financial support for this project was contributed by the University of Illinois Research Board. Mr. Louis Rowitz was the research assistant for this project.

[2] For a presentation of data on the social status and demographic characteristics of United States religious groups, together with a bibliography of similar studies, see: Bernard Lazerwitz, "A Comparison of Major United States Religious Groups", *Journal of the American Statistical Association*, September 1961.

[3] For a discussion of New York City Jews, see the chapter by Ben B. Seligman on "The Jewish Population of New York City: 1952" in Marshall Sklare (Editor), *The Jews*, Glencoe, Illinois. 1958.

[4] This assumes a legal structure and a degree of relations between Jews and non-Jews that would permit Jews relatively free access to the total range of community occupations.

[5] This is more of a hypothesis about the migration patterns of United States Jews than a statement of known facts.

[6] Lazerwitz, op. cit.

[7] To confirm the ability of a sample size as small as that employed here to give a reasonably accurate picture of New York City, it may be noted that the 1960 United States Census of Population reported that

Negroes compose 14 per cent of New York City's population.

[8] United States Jews are characterized by a low frequency of synagogue attendance. Roman Catholics and members of all major Protestant denominations attend religious services with greater regularity than do Jews.

[9] Of the Jews interviewed on these surveys, 76 per cent resided in large cities. Among the Jews residing in large cities, 57 per cent lived in New York City. Therefore, the con-

trasts between New York City Jews and non-New York City Jews is not primarily one between suburbanites and "inner city" residents.

[10] The best series of data would be one comparing Jews residing in cities having decreasing proportions of Jews. Unfortunately, such detailed information does not exist.

[11] Not enough interviews were obtained with New York City Episcopalians to do a separate analysis of the group.

6 · Some Aspects of Christian Science as Reflected in Letters of Testimony

R. W. ENGLAND

ABSTRACT. *An analysis of published Christian Science letters of testimony provides information concerning the membership, dynamics, and bases of appeal of this religion. Urban females of mature years who suffered from physical or mental ills constituted the largest category of communicants. Christian Science practice involves some quasi-psychiatric mechanisms, with the professional healer playing a role akin to that of the psychotherapist.*

Scholars have paid scant attention to the characteristics of members of specific minor religious sects and cults,[1] even

SOURCE. R. W. England, "Some Aspects of Christian Science as Reflected in Letters of Testimony," reprinted from *American Journal of Sociology*, 59, March, 1954, pp. 448–453 by permission of The University of Chicago Press.
[1] Hadley Cantril and Muzafer Sherif, "The Kingdom of Father Divine," *Journal of Abnormal and Social Psychology*, XXXIII (April, 1938), 147–67; Erdmann D. Beynon, "The Voodoo Cult among Negro Migrants in Detroit," *American Journal of Sociology*, XLIII (May, 1938), 894–907; E. K. Francis, "The Russian Mennonites: From Religion to

though a considerable body of general theory exists (usually oriented around concepts of personal and social disorganization), dealing with the factors presumably responsible for voluntary affiliation with social movements of all kinds.

To what sorts of people do "fringe" religious groups appeal? What factors stimulate and maintain adherents' interest, particularly in such movements as New Thought, Divine Science, Christian Science, Theosophy, Spiritualism, or Bahai—groups which Clark classifies as egocentric and esoteric sects[2] and which may be regarded as conspicuous departures from the three major religious systems of American culture? It may be perfectly true that the basic stimulus to such membership is some form of dis-

Ethnic Group," *American Journal of Sociology*, LIV (September, 1948), 101–7; John B. Holt, "Holiness Religion: Cultural Shock and Social Reorganization," *American Sociological Review*, V (October, 1940), 740–47; Allan W. Eister, *Drawing-room Conversion* (Durham: Duke University Press, 1950); Hadley Cantril, *The Psychology of Social Movements* (New York: Wiley, 1941).
[2] Elmer T. Clark, *The Small Sects in America* (New York: Abingdon-Cokesbury Press, 1949), p. 24.

organization and that most of the adherents will manifest lives disorganized in some degree, but knowing this throws little light upon the specific appeal factors of particular sects or on the characteristics of their members.

Aside from the participant-observer method, or a deductive approach based upon a study of a sect's history and "theology"—the latter often incomprehensible to the scientifically trained—the use of schedules, questionnaires, case histories, and personal documents is extremely difficult. Followers of these sects are apt to be hostilely sensitive to searching inquiries by outsiders: The "we-they" aspect of group relationships looms large in their behavior. However, in the case of one large sect—Christian Science—there exist in published form several thousand unsolicited documents (letters of testimony) written by its adherents. These letters have, for many years, been regular features of the *Christian Science Journal* and the *Christian Science Sentinel,* periodicals with a wide and respectful circulation among "Scientists."

This study, based on an analysis of a sample of five hundred letters, is an attempt to learn something of the characteristics of those to whom this religion appeals, the bases of the appeal, and the nature of the dynamics of Christian Science as far as its followers are concerned. The study is supplemented by the writer's knowledge of this religion resulting from his one-time participation in it.

The census bureau lists the United States membership of the Church of Christ, Scientist as 268,915, with an additional 139,758 Sunday School scholars between five and twenty years of age.[3] Christian Science is apparently an urban, middle-class religion. In 1936, 94.9 per cent of the formal membership was reported as living in urban areas.[4] The average value of the urban church edifices of this group was $48,818 compared with a national urban average of $44,583.[5] Women predominate among the congregations, for the sex ratio of the Church of Christ, Scientist is the lowest of any of the leading denominations in the United States: for each 100 female members there are but 31.3 males.[6]

An extended exposition of Christian Science doctrine is contained in Mary Baker Eddy's *Science and Health, with Key to the Scriptures* (Boston, 1906). Only enough essentials will be presented in this paper to permit clearer understanding of later sections of the article. Briefly, Christian Science teaches that the power of Divine Mind can manifest itself at the behest of believers by curing ills, harmonizing interpersonal relationships, providing material needs, and by otherwise ameliorating one's lot upon the mortal plane of existence. The only "reality" is the reality of God; all else is illusion. Traditional Christian virtues are identified with God. Inharmony, such as sickness, poverty, and war, is the illusory product of mortal mind and of error. When a Christian Scientist finds himself in a state of inharmony—ill, unemployed, discouraged—he repeats to himself certain formulas, reads *Science and Health* and the Bible, and may finally consult a practitioner if harmony is not restored. The practitioner, an authorized faith-healer, responds by either coming in person to "assert the Truth" or engages in absent treatment by asserting the Truth from his home or office. The recipient of such aid is then billed, much as one is billed by a physician or dentist,

---

[3] Bureau of the Census, *Religious Bodies: 1936,* Washington, D.C., 1941) II, Part, I, 390–91, 399. No later figures are available, since release of membership data is prohibited by the rules of this church.

[4] *Ibid.,* Part I, p. 390.
[5] *Ibid.,* I, 104–5.
[6] *Ibid.,* p. 23.

the amount of the fee depending upon the extent of treatment needed.[7]

Letters of Testimony

The publication of testimonies for Christian Science was first systematized in an early edition of Mrs. Eddy's textbook under the chapter title "Fruitage." Subsequent editions retained this section, although up through the final edition of 1906 the letters were usually identified only by the writers' initials and the names of their home communities. Shortly after the founding, in 1883, of the *Christian Science Journal*, a regular department within this organ was instituted which published testimonial letters. By 1906 the editors were including the full names and community addresses of most of the writers. The *Christian Science Sentinel*, created in 1898, carried then, and still carries, letters of testimony under a similar policy. These written statements (totaling to date about six thousand in the *Journal* alone) are a source of data to the student of religious behavior.

A sample of 500 letters was obtained from Volumes XLVII, LVII, LVIII, and LXIV of the *Journal* for the years 1929, 1939, 1940, and 1946. The letters were read serially within the four volumes. Of the 500, 406 (81 per cent) were from women; 94 (19 per cent) were from men—this is roughly comparable to the sex ratio within the formal membership, where males constituted (in 1936) about 24 per cent of the total.

[7] Present-day Christian Scientists are not forbidden all medical aid; in situations involving compound fractures, serious hemorrhages, certain dental troubles, and disabling pain, medical or dental care is permissible provided the patient resumes divine treatment as soon as his condition permits. Modifications of this kind have been partly responsible for the elevation of Christian Science to the ranks of the "respectable" sects.

Of the 406 females, 310 (76 per cent) were married—or had been married—and 96 were single. This was determined from the *Journal's* practice of including "Miss" or "Mrs." before the women's names. Thus, of all the letters, 62 per cent were from married (or widowed or divorced) females. Internal evidence indicates that the bulk of these married women were between thirty-five and sixty years of age. No estimates were possible in respect to ages of the male communicants or the unmarried women.

Factors Motivating and Sustaining Interest in Christian Science

An examination of the 500 letters indicated that two distinct classes of writers existed: (1) those who mentioned the prevalence in their lives of chronic adverse conditions *prior* to their becoming acquainted with Christian Science and

TABLE 1. *Reasons for Becoming Christian Scientists, by Sex and Type of Motive*

TYPE OF MOTIVE	MALES	FEMALES
To alleviate distressing conditions	38 (40.4%)	217 (53.4%)
Other	56 (59.6%)	189 (46.6%)
Total	94 (100.0%)	406 (100.0%)

$X^2 = 5.12; P < .05.$

(2) those who made no such mention. Since there exists a distinct tendency among Christian Scientists to attribute as many cures as possible to their religion, one might infer that the writers of class 2, since they made no such mention, had not been suffering prior to becoming Scientists. In other words, their reasons for following this faith were

originally other than for purposes of alleviating distressing conditions. Some 49 per cent of the writers were in this category, suggesting that approximately half the sample became interested in Christian Science because of specific troubles, while half were motivated by other factors.

A breakdown on the basis of sex in respect to these categories proved of interest (see Table 1). A significantly greater proportion of females than of males was apparently motivated to become Christian Scientists by reasons of prior distressing conditions.

It was clear that the writers' discussions of their symptoms and diseases were so fraught with confusion stemming from their ignorance of medicine and mental hygiene that classifications within this type of problem would be meaningless. However, a possible classification did appear feasible in terms of the principal troubles (four kinds) which were, in varying degree, instrumental in stimulating an interest in Christian Science:

(a) Those involving health: included here are functional and organic disorders and bodily injuries.

(b) Those concerned with financial difficulties: these include poverty, unemployment, business problems, etc.

(c) Those stemming from the use of tea, coffee, tobacco, and alcohol, roundly condemned by Mrs. Eddy, and the existence of presumably undesirable personality traits or attitudes likewise disapproved by her.

(d) Conditions of vaguely defined unhappiness: bereavement, depressed feelings, family discord, worries.

While these four categories are not mutually exclusive, particularly a and d, they arise empirically from the letters of persons in class 1, those whose problems predated their interest in Christian Science. In terms of individual cases, however only one of the four types of trouble mentioned above appeared to provide the principal motivation for each writer, even though she may have mentioned troubles in more than one category.

The distribution of males and females of class 1 among the four types of distressing conditions is small except for type a. However, none of the men complained of previous troubles of type d, while 6 per cent of the single and 8 per cent of the married women did.

A fundamental distinguishing feature of Christian Science theology is its explicit and emphatic denial of the reality of the physical world, the evidence of the senses being merely an illusion resulting from the activities of mortal mind. The principal characteristic of applied Christian Science is the denial of the necessity for medical aid except under the circumstances mentioned in footnote 7. The 500 letters indicate, however, that Christian Scientists take a lively interest in their adjustments to presumably non-existent persons and situations and exhibit considerable concern for the well-being of their bodies and minds. The most frequent topics discussed, and the primary subjects of 93 per cent of the 500 letters, were alleged cures of illnesses and the maintenance of health by applications of Christian Science. The curing of sickness and the maintenance of physical well-being appear to be the predominant factors sustaining interest in this religion.

Ninety-six per cent of the letters from women and 79 per cent of those from men concerned matters of health; the proportional difference is statistically significant, suggesting that the medical aspects of Christian Science are more important for females than for males (see Table 2).

Attitudes of Mind

Some significant attitudes and ways of thinking which may be characteristic of Christian Scientists generally are discernible from an examination of the 500 letters.

1. In *Science and Health*, Mary Baker Eddy warns her followers of the dangers attendant upon the possession of knowledge of physiology, anatomy, and medicine:

> The action of mortal mind on the body was not so injurious before inquisitive Eves took up the study of medical works. . . . You can educate a healthy horse so far in physiology that he will take cold without his blanket, whereas the wild animal, left to his instincts, sniffs the wind with delight. . . . Treatises on anatomy, physiology, and health, sustained by what is material law, are the prompters of sickness and disease. It should not be proverbial, that so long as you read medical works you will be sick [pp. 176, 179].

The grain of truth contained in Mrs. Eddy's argument cannot be gainsaid, but her fears that Christian Scientists might become prey to such dangerous knowledge were groundless. The medical, anatomical, and physiological knowledge held by the 500 writers was apparently very limited and, in some cases, totally absent.

Perhaps most conspicuous was an apparent ignorance of or indifference to the natural healing powers of the human body. Thus, a vast number of minor ailments, ranging from athlete's foot to the common cold, were treated and cured by the application of Divine Truth. Furthermore, there is, among the 500 communicants, considerable attention given to types of disorders so insignificant as to be of practically no consequence so far as one's daily life is concerned. Chapped hands, lone warts, a burned fingernail, hangnails, vague fleeting pains, and momentary dizziness were not infrequently the "healings" for which testimony was given. Man, like most or-

TABLE 2. *Factors Sustaining Interest in Christian Science, by Sex and Type of Problem*

TYPE OF PROBLEM	MALES		FEMALES	
Health	75	(79.8%)	392	(96.5%)
Other	19	(20.2%)	14	(3.5%)
Total	94	(100.0%)	406	(100.0%)

$X^2 = 33.85; P < .05.$

ganisms, is subject to myriad minor and temporary ills which are of little importance to general health. The doctrines of Mary Baker Eddy, however, endow even these pathological minutiae with special meaning, for they become evidence of the workings of mortal mind. When they vanish, as they almost inevitably must, Christian Scientists give credit not to their resilient organisms but to their religion. Thus, by virtue of the peculiar emphases of their faith and the peculiar functioning of the human body, Scientists have a constant and automatic source of evidence confirming their beliefs.

It is, however, the alleged healing of serious disorders with which Christian Science is associated in the popular mind and upon which are based its more dramatic aspects. The Christian Science textbook, as well as other writings of Mrs. Eddy, contains many descriptions of remarkable cures which have since become an important part of the lore of this religion. These writings constitute a core of illustrative proofs with which every Christian Scientist is familiar.

Humiston,[8] a physician, has analyzed 84 cases of cures reported in these early writings. His discussion makes it very

[8] Woodbridge Riley, Frederick W. Peabody, and Charles E. Humiston, *The Faith, the Falsity and the Failure of Christian Science* (New York: Fleming H. Revel Co., 1925), p. 322.

clear that laymen are not competent to diagnose themselves accurately, to distinguish symptom from disease, or to use medical terms correctly. The doubts cast by Humiston must necessarily reflect on the 500 letters used in the present study. This precludes analysis of them on the basis of types and seriousness of ills treated by Christian Science. Instead, the writer offers two observations based upon impressions rather than upon objective analysis:

(a) Married women complained of a greater variety of illnesses than did persons in the other two groups, and their complaints involved more serious disorders.

(b) The number of cancers, tumors, broken bones, and cases of pneumonia and acute appendicitis which were self-diagnosed by the writers seemed large. To a devout Scientist, calling in a physician is an admission of failure and of lack of faith, but since a physician's services are often necessary for correct diagnoses of serious maladies, it seems likely that most of the more dramatic cures are due simply to mistaken diagnosis. In scores of letters the writers describe how they broke their skulls, dislocated organs, awoke in the night with pneumonia, decided that mysterious lumps were cancers, or found themselves in other ways serious victims of mortal mind. Their next move was to begin divine treatment, either with or without a practitioner's aid. Elated and gratified when their skulls mended, their organs returned to place, their pneumonia and cancers vanished, they wrote letters of testimony to the *Journal*.

2. Unquestionably, an important aspect of Christian Science theory and practice is its relationship to disorders of psychogenic significance. However confused and contradictory Mrs. Eddy's thinking may have been, she was exploring an early bypath of what we know today as psychosomatic medicine. *Science*

and Health contains many references to the role of suggestion, belief, conviction, and emotions (hate, envy, vengefulness) in the genesis of bodily complaints, hopelessly entangled as they were with the author's theology.

There is much evidence, reflected in letters of testimony, suggesting that the curative powers of Christian Science practice involve certain elements of psychotherapy.

(a) The practitioner's role seems not unlike that of the psychiatrist or psychiatric social worker.[9] The following excerpts from two testimonies are typical of the attitudes of most of the 500 writers toward practitioners:

It took three years to complete the healing and I had the help of several practitioners at different times. I am grateful to them all for help and inspiration. It was a great joy and privilege to work with them.[10]

I can never express enough gratitude to the practitioner who helped me from the beginning, because during the first three months that I read *Science and Health* by Mrs. Eddy, I did not understand it. I would talk with the practitioner several times each day on the telephone, and I have always had a feeling that if it had not been for her untiring, unselfish, and loving encouragement, understanding and help during this most

[9] There were, as of 1951, approximately 8,500 practitioners in the United States, most of them women. These persons had received advanced training in Christian Science healing techniques ("Christian Science Practitioners and Teachers," *Christian Science Journal*, Vol. LXIX [1951], Appendix). Practitioners and their addresses are listed yearly in the *Journal*. The number 8,500 is an estimate made by the writer from a sample count of these names.

[10] *Ibid.*, LXIV (1946), 515–16.

trying time, I should have lost my way entirely.[11]

The practitioner becomes an object of affection, a rock of security, a confessor, and a source of hope, as well as a technical healer. Scores of letters contain effusive praise of practitioners whose care has been loving, kindly, thoughtful, and comforting. Such attitudes are akin to those of patients toward psychiatrists and other psychotherapists, although the phenomenon of transference is probably more clearly present in the latter cases than in the former, where formal psychotherapeutic techniques are absent.[12]

(b) One task of the bona fide psychotherapist is to help his patients to recognize the role played by emotional conflicts, to realize that many ills may be functional rather than organic in origin—in other words, to provide his patients with new concepts of the meaning of illness. Among the 500 letters is considerable evidence that Christian Scientists tend likewise to acquire new definitions of illness, which become emotionally as well as intellectually integrated parts of their behavior. Such reorientation is indicated in the following excerpts:

. . . I saw that Christian Science does not heal matter, but destroys all manner of disease (which is wrong thinking objectified on the body) through the realization of perfect man and perfect God. As I continued to affirm these truths I was healed.[13]

. . . In fact, it [Christian Science] has changed my whole thinking, and

has given me a sure foundation, something I can depend upon in times of trouble, whether it be sickness or lack of any sort.[14]

And from an especially perceptive believer:

I awakened on the morning of the recital with my throat so sore that I felt I should be unable to sing. . . . *I realized that fear was at the root of my difficulty,* and that I needed to keep my thoughts above matter. I read only *Science and Health,* and when I went to the recital that evening and sang . . . my teacher said I had never sung so well.[15]

Conclusions

The data used in this study were prepared from the edited documents of enthusiastic followers of Mary Baker Eddy. It is clear, therefore, that the conclusions must be regarded as highly tentative and are perhaps best presented in the form of hypotheses useful for further studies of this religion, as follows:

1. The largest single group from which the adherents of Christian Science are drawn are urban, middle-class, married females who are suffering from bodily disorders of physical or emotional origin.

2. Over half, but by no means all, of those becoming interested in Christian Science are motivated by specific troubles, with problems of health predominating.

3. The tendency to become associated with this religion because of specific troubles is more characteristic of women than of men.

4. The most tangible return gained from adherence to the faith, and the most significant influence for a sustained

[11] *Ibid.,* LVIII (1940), 346–47.
[12] Indeed, of the 500 letters, only one indicated a definite patient-psychiatrist relationship, although such experiences are probably not rare among Christian Scientists: "So little did I expect relief for my knee that I did not mention it at first *but for weeks poured out my financial and domestic troubles*" (*ibid.,* p. 576; italics mine).
[13] *Ibid.,* XLVII (1930), 469.
[14] *Ibid.,* p. 104.
[15] *Ibid.,* LVII (1939), 56. (Italics mine.)

interest, centers about the alleged power of the religion to cure bodily disorders.

5. Christian Science practice involves at least two aspects of professional psychotherapy: transference and a hazy perception that illnesses can be of emotional origin.

6. The role of the practitioner is akin to that of the psychotherapist, and much of the alleged effectiveness of this religion in relieving ills rests upon the establishment of a quasi patient-psychiatrist relationship between the sufferer and her practitioner.

7 · Mormonism and the Avoidance of Sectarian Stagnation: A Study of Church, Sect, and Incipient Nationality

THOMAS F. O'DEA

ABSTRACT. In the development of Mormonism ten factors combined to enable it to escape sectarian stagnation. Instead there emerged a large ecclesiastical organization which is the organized core of the Mormon people, who have evolved a subculture and homeland and for whom religious fellowship is impenetrated by the total bonds of community and family. The study illustrates both the relationship of religious fellowship to incipient nationality and the importance of a unique concatenation of events in social causation.

One of the many churches founded in the region south of the Great Lakes in the first half of the nineteenth century, the Church of Jesus Christ of Latter-Day Saints, or the Mormon church, alone avoided the stagnant backwaters of sectarianism. Founded in New York State in

SOURCE. Thomas F. O'Dea, "Mormonism and the Avoidance of Sectarian Stagnation: A Study of Church, Sect, and Incipient Nationality," reprinted from American Journal of Sociology, 60, November, 1954, pp. 285–293 by permission of The University of Chicago Press.

1830 by a small group of men, it has today more than a million members in the United States and in its mission countries of Europe and the South Seas. It is the only religious body to have a clear majority of the population in a single state (Utah), and it has been the central and strategic group in the settlement of the intermountain West. Of its numerous dissident bodies, five survive, the largest of which has 100,000 members; the smallest, 24. The former, the Reorganized Church of Jesus Christ of Latter-Day Saints, is an important denomination in parts of the Middle West.[1] From its founding the Mormon church has set out to establish the Kingdom of God on earth and had created—once in Ohio, twice in Missouri, and once in Illinois—settlements in which this ideal was to be realized, only to see them consumed by external conflict and internal dissent. Finally, in 1847, the Mormons, harassed

[1] Elmer T. Clark, The Small Sects in America (New York: Abingdon-Cokesbury Press, 1937). Clark gives the following dissidents besides the Reorganized Church: Bickertonites, Hedrickites, Strangites, and Cutlerites. None of these groups had over 1,500 members; the Cutlerites had about two dozen and practiced community of property.

and persecuted, dispossessed of all but faith, leadership, and superb organization, crossed the plains and settled in the Utah desert. There, relying on these spiritual and sociological assets, they established a regional culture area bearing the pronounced imprint of their peculiar values and outlook.

This article attempts to answer two questions: (1) What enabled the Mormon church to avoid sectarianism? (2) If the Mormon church did not become a sect, is it then an ecclesiastical body or "church" in the sense in which that term has been understood in the sociology of religion since Ernst Troeltsch? [2] In answering these two questions, two others —of more general interest—suggest themselves; the first of interest to sociological theory, the second to the growing concern with interdisciplinary research: (3) Is the accepted dichotomy, church or sect, conceptually adequate to handle the empirical data in the sociology of religion? (4) Can sociological analysis alone adequately explain the emergence of one type of social structure as against another?

Presented here are the findings of a larger study of Mormon values and Mormon social institutions,[3] a study which involved an analysis of Mormon theology and religious teaching, the development of Mormon social institutions—ecclesiastical, political, economic, and educational—and a community study based upon participant observation in a rural village, the characteristic product of

[2] See Joachim Wach, The Sociology of Religion (Chicago: University of Chicago Press, 1944), pp. 195 ff.
[3] This research was done as part of the Values Study Project of the Laboratory of Social Relations of Harvard University and was supported financially and otherwise by the project. It will be published in the forthcoming monograph by the writer entitled "Mormon Values: The Significance of a Religious Outlook for Social Action."

Mormon efforts at settlement in the West.[4]

Church and Sect

Ernst Troeltsch and Max Weber define a sect as a body of believers based upon contracted or freely elected membership in contrast to the institutional ecclesiastical body or church in which membership is ascribed. "Born into" and "freely chosen" signify the vital distinction. Park and Burgess, Simmel and von Wiese, and, following them, Becker elaborate this definition.[5] For them a church or ecclesia is characterized by the following: (1) membership on the basis of birth; (2) administration of the means of grace and its sociological and theological concomitants—hierarchy and dogma; (3) inclusiveness of social structure, often coinciding with ethnic or geographical boundaries; (4) orientation to the conversion of all; and (5) a tendency to compromise with and adjust to the world. The sect, on the contrary, is characterized by (1) separatism and defiance of or withdrawal from the demands of the secular sphere, prefering isolation to compromise; (2) exclusiveness, expressed in attitude and social structure; (3) emphasis upon conversion prior to

[4] See Evon Z. Vogt and Thomas F. O'Dea, "A Comparative Study of the Role of Values in Social Action in Two Southwestern Communities," American Sociological Review, XVIII, No. 6 (December, 1953), 645–54; and Lowry Nelson, The Mormon Village (Salt Lake City: University of Utah Press, 1953).
[5] Robert R. Park and Ernest W. Burgess, Introduction to the Science of Sociology (Chicago: University of Chicago Press, 1921), pp. 50, 202–3, 611–12, 657, 870–74; Howard Becker, Systematic Sociology: On the Basis of the "Beziehungslehre und Gebildelehr" of Leopold von Wiese: Adapted and Amplified (New York: John Wiley & Sons, 1932), pp. 624–28.

membership; and (4) voluntary election or joining.

The sect is often persecuted and is always ascetic. It usually rejects hierarchy and endeavors to implement the "priesthood of believers" in an egalitarian if narrow social organization. As H. Richard Niebuhr has observed, sectarianism, strictly defined, cannot outlast the founding generation[6] and, as Liston Pope has shown, often does not last it out.[7] The birth of children to the freely electing sectaries and the worldly success which so often crowns sectarian frugality and industry result in that adjustment to the world which Weber has called "the routinization of charisma." To cover this phenomenon, von Wiese and Becker introduce a third type, as does Niebuhr—the denomination. "Denominations are simply sects in an advanced stage of development and of adjustment to each other and the secular world." [8]

There have been attempts—often highly suggestive—to characterize the sectarian personality.[9] Von Wiese and Becker introduce a fourth type—the cult in which religion is private and personal; and Wach introduces another—the independent group. This latter is a semi-ecclesiastical body which starts out resembling a sect and through slow transformation and organizational differentiation becomes much more like a church.

Wach's chief example is the Mormon church. This classification is perceptive, but arguments will be given below to show that it is inadequate.

Wach also points out the impossibility of applying any of the above criteria with rigor. Accepting the importance of sociological criteria and of theological and philosophical doctrines in differentiating sects from other religious bodies, he concludes that the characteristic attitude is most pertinent—an attitude which claims to be "renewing the original spirit of the absolute or relative beginnings" of a religious movement.[10] In what follows the criteria of von Wiese and Becker and of Wach are applied to Mormonism.

The Avoidance of Sectarianism

The Mormon church claimed to be a divine restoration of the Apostolic Church after centuries of apostasy. The mark of the new dispensation was contemporary revelation. Through the prophet, Joseph Smith, the Lord was believed to have called the elect. The result was the church which was founded in western New York, at the time a near-frontier and the scene of a great religious enthusiasm.[11] To its converts it offered security—a resolution of the outer conflict and inner turmoil of denominational confusion and one which claimed the sanction of divine revelation. Convinced of a covenant to build the Kingdom of God on earth, the Latter-Day Saints attempted to establish their settlements on the basis

[6] H. Richard Niebuhr, The Social Sources of Denominationalism (New York: Henry Holt & Co., 1929), pp. 17 ff.
[7] Liston Pope, Millhands and Preachers: A Study of Gastonia (New Haven: Yale University Press, 1942).
[8] Becker, op. cit.
[9] See John L. Gillin, "A Contribution to the Sociology of Sects," American Journal of Sociology, XVI (1910), 236 ff.; Robert P. Casey, "Transient Cults," Psychiatry IV (1941), 525 ff.; and Ellsworth Faris, "The Sect," chap. v of The Nature of Human Nature (New York: McGraw-Hill Book Co., 1937).

[10] Wach, op. cit., pp. 194–96. For an excellent discussion of the church-sect problem see ibid., pp. 195–205, and especially his later "Church, Denomination, and Sect," chap. ix in Types of Religious Experience (Chicago: University of Chicago Press, 1951), pp. 187–208.
[11] Whitney B. Cross, The Burned-over District: The History of Enthusiastic Religion in Western New York, 1800-1850 (Ithaca: Cornell University Press, 1950).

of the Law of Consecration, or United Order of Enoch, a plan announced by the prophet-founder which reconciled Christian socialism with private initiative and management.[12] This law was withdrawn in 1838 after some seven years of experiment marked by contentions and jealousies, and tithing was substituted for it.

The Mormon church placed great emphasis upon the restoration of Hebrew ideals and upon the revival of Old Testament practices and institutions. The Saints were, they believed, a modern Israel: called by God, party to the covenant, and about to be gathered unto Zion. Polygamy was but one, although the most notorious, example of such revivals. In restoration and peculiarity, two important aspects of the Mormon Gospel, the attitudes of renewal and exclusiveness characteristic of sects were palpably present.

While commitment to building the Kingdom was sectarian in so far as it required withdrawal from the world and refusal to accommodate to the routine demands of secular life, it certainly had other possible implications. The idea of a Christian commonwealth was capable of quite nonsectarian interpretation. Moreover, the withdrawal from "Babylon" did not involve a repudiation of worldly pursuits, for in the City of God, the New Jerusalem, business, family life, government, and even armed defense would be acceptable and accepted. Na-

[12] See Doctrine and Covenants 42:30–36; also 51:1–16; 70:3, 9; 104; 82; and 92. This is a standard scriptural work of the Mormon church and contains the revelations of Joseph Smith. See also Leonard Arrington, "Early Mormon Communitarianism," *Western Humanities Review*, VII, No. 4 (autumn, 1953), 341–69; and also Arthur E. Bestor, Jr., *Backwoods Utopias: The Sectarian and Owenite Phases of Communitarian Socialism in America: 1663–1829* (Philadelphia: University of Pennsylvania Press, 1950).

ture was not seen as corrupted, and the vitiating effect of original sin upon preternatural virtue was denied—a most unsectarian doctrine. Work and recreation were both accepted and sanctified. Against the sectarian notions of renewal and exclusiveness must be placed the nonsectarian possibilities of building a Christian society and the doctrine of human goodness—of total "undepravity."

Yet other groups had set out to build the Kingdom, and whatever nonsectarian possibilities lie hidden in the idea of a Christian commonwealth were never made apparent. How many sects built isolated little communities where prosperity followed upon the sectarian ascetic of work and thrift? Such settlements often reached a membership of a thousand and then stopped growing. Others experienced "swarming," that is, excess numbers, usually in excess of a thousand, migrated and established a new settlement emulating the mother-community but independent of its authority. This was the common sectarian fate. How were the Mormons to avoid it and realize the nonsectarian possibilities of their vision?

The Kirtland attempt to build the Kingdom failed because of internal dissent, external opposition, and economic distress—the last the most important. The Saints then migrated to Missouri and there at two points—Jackson County and Far West—endeavored to construct the New Jerusalem. Their strange doctrines claiming contemporary converse with God, their frugality and industry and consequent prosperity, their talk of making the region a "promised land," and their northern manners accentuated by rumors of abolition sentiments aroused the animosity of their neighbors. Consequently, they were driven from the land, and, crossing the Mississippi, the only eastward move in their long wanderings, they entered Illinois, where they built another city. Nauvoo, on the east bank of the river, saw the arrival of converts in great numbers, the first fruits of the European harvest. But there, too, hostility followed the Saints, and rumors that the leaders were practicing polygamy—rumors that turned out to be true—and a more defiant attitude from the Mormon leadership increased gentile antagonism. In 1844 Joseph Smith was murdered at Carthage jail, and in the next three years the Saints were driven from Nauvoo. In 1847, after a period of disorganization and hardship, they migrated to Utah under the leadership of Brigham Young.

In the West the church gained the respite needed for its internal recovery and at the same time the relative isolation required for establishing a civilization whose institutions would be informed by Mormon conceptions and Mormon values. In the 1880's and 1890's, however, the Mormon-gentile conflict broke out anew with considerable acuteness, the issues now being polygamy and the admission of Utah to the Union. After harsh federal legislation and prosecution of Mormon leaders, the church abandoned polygamy and accommodated itself to the demands of the larger American community into which it was reintegrated. Yet relative isolation had done its work—Utah and the surrounding region remained a Mormon culture area, although the implicit claim to it as an exclusive homeland was given up. Moreover, Mormon peculiarity and self-consciousness remained.

In this early period of Mormon history many marks of sectarianism were present: not only the attitude of renewal and exclusiveness but voluntary election as the basis of membership, withdrawal from the secular community, asceticism which placed a high value on hard work, persecution which increased in-group cohesion, and the conception of the priesthiod of believers. The last doctrine, however, was not interpreted in terms of an egalitarian congregationalism.

Rather it found expression in an hierarchical priesthood organization, authoritarian in structure and function. As the church grew, as its early charismatic leadership became more institutionalized in the leading offices, and as it had to stand against external threats, the early congregationalism gave way more and more to authoritarian rule.

What factors militated against the development of a typical sect in this situation? Two were already mentioned: (1) *the nonsectarian possibilities of building the Kingdom which could require so much subtle accommodation* and (2) *the doctrine of natural goodness, by way of which nineteenth-century American optimism entered Mormon religious consciousness to blend there with the chiliastic expectations of a restorationist movement.* Yet the former alone could not effect the avoidance of sectarianism, as the record of so many other groups makes so clear; nor could the latter, although, when combined with other factors effective in the concrete situation, both could affect the issue in a powerful and pervasive manner. These two factors combined with the following eight to effect the issue:

3. *Universal missionary understanding of the notion of "gathering the elect."* The Mormon notion of peculiarity was exclusive, but it was not necessarily sectarian in the strictest sense. It was rather committed to missionary work—to calling the elect from the world. This was of great consequence when taken together with several other factors, despite its being a rather sectarian idea of missionary work.

4. *The temporal appropriateness of the doctrine in the late 1830's.* A generation before, the "gathering of the elect" might have been understood in terms of calling the elect from the neighboring counties. But in the second decade of the nineteenth century, American Protestantism had discovered a bigger world.

The Mormons came upon the scene in time to inherit the newer and broader definition. The universal understanding of calling the elect combined with the new world-wide definition of the mission field worked against a sectarian issue.

5. *The success of missionary work.* The ability of the Mormon Gospel to bring meaning and hope to many, in America and in Europe, especially England and Scandinavia, resulted in thousands of converts. With increased numbers, the notion of the holy city which the Saints were called to build now took on dimensions hardly compatible with sectarianism. Nauvoo had a population of 20,000 when Chicago had 5,000.

6. *The withdrawal of the Law of Consecration.* Had the Law of Consecration worked, the Mormons might have built another successful communitarian settlement of which our history has seen so many. The failure of the Law, on the other hand, deprived them of a blueprint, rigid conformity to which could have been interpreted as the only permissible economic ethic, thereby lending a sectarian narrowness to their activities and inhibiting growth. Moreover, the Law was withdrawn by Joseph Smith in a revelation which still held up its ideals as the will of God. As a result the flexibility of charismatic leadership was transmitted to the institutionalized church in economic matters, and its spirit vivified economic experiment for the next century, while a killing economic literalism was successfully eschewed. This is all the more striking, since in scriptural interpretation Mormons have generally been literalists.

7. *The failures and consequent necessity of starting again.* The need to start over again four times in sixteen years also contributed to flexibility preventing a set routine from developing which could then have been imposed on new problems, thereby limiting growth and contributing to a sectarian atmos-

phere and structure. Combined with the withdrawal of the Law of Consecration, this made a dogmatism of minutiae impossible.

8. *The expulsion from the Middle West.* The Middle West, the continent's most attractive ecological area, was destined to draw large numbers of non-Mormon settlers. In such a situation it would have been quite impossible for the Mormon church to have maintained any hegemony, spiritual, political, or economic. Instead it would in all likelihood have become one of a number of denominations accommodating to each other and to the secular world and thus would be reintegrated into the general American community with which it shared so many common roots as another small and unimportant Protestant group.

9. *The choice and the existence of a large, unattractive expanse of land in the West.* The Mormon leadership deliberately chose an unattractive region to gain the necessary respite that isolation would give and resisted the seductions of more pleasant prospects. The existence of this arid region was something over which they had no control. It was unquestionably a prerequisite for the future form of their community. The result was the opening-up of a huge area waiting to be converted from desert, supporting a scant nomadic population, to a Mormon culture area based upon irrigation farming. This also gave the necessary time in isolation for Mormon social institutions to emerge and to "set."

10. *The authoritarian structure of the church and the central government which it made possible.* The existence of a charismatic leader in the early stages of Mormon church history whose right to rule was believed to be based upon divine election and the consequent authoritarian and hierarchical structure of church government permitted scattered settlement in the West under central direction. Such authoritarian characteristics

were strengthened by the external conditions of conflict and hardship. Centrifugal tendencies in the West were restrained when not completely inhibited. The priesthood structure and the routinization of prophetic rule might in other circumstances have been completely compatible with sectarianism, yet in the western settlement they combined with open and relatively empty and isolated land, and missionary success and consequent emigration, to make large-scale settlement possible under central government. This combination ruled out the last chance of sectarianism.

These last eight factors, then, combined to militate against a sectarian issue to the Mormon experiment and to bring into existence the Mormon church of the present day. Instead of becoming a sect, the church became the core of a large culture area. In these eight factors and their combination we have the answer to our first question.

Neither Church nor Sect

The Mormon church is excluded by definition from the category of church or *ecclesia*, unless it has become one in the course of its development. Similarly with regard to the category of denomination: since we have defined denominations as "routinized sects," Mormonism, having avoided sectarianism, at the same time avoided denominationalism. However, to be of genuine interest, these two statements must be true in more than a formal sense—they must be more than mere analytical inferences from definitions. The question is then: Has the Mormon church become an ecclesiastical body in the course of its evolution?

Despite the avoidance of typical sectarian structure and isolation, the Mormon church has displayed and retained many sectarian characteristics. Most important are: (1) a sense of peculiarity, of election, and of covenant, which is reinforced by explicit theological doctrine; (2) a tendency to withdrawal from the gentile world (this is now most frequently expressed in admonition and symbolic practices, yet it found large-scale expression in the Church Welfare Plan with which the Mormon church sought to meet the great depression as a separate body capable of considerable autarchy); (3) a commitment to "warning the world" and "gathering the elect," the implications of which have been more routine and less dramatic since the accommodation which followed the defeat of the church on the polygamy issue; and (4) chiliastic expectations, still important not only among rural groups but in the writings of some leaders of the church.

While the Mormons have never identified group membership with peculiarity of dress as sectarists have frequently done, the strict interpretation of Joseph Smith's no-liquor, no-tobacco counsel at the present day serves an analagous function and has become the focus of the expression of exclusivist sentiments. Moreover, although persecution has stopped, the memory of it preserves ingroup solidarity and strengthens loyalty.

Yet despite the notae of the sect, the basic fact in Mormon history since 1890 has been the accommodation of the church to the demands of the larger gentile community. The abandonment of polygamy—that camel at which so many strained but which became so identified with loyalty that all were willing to suffer in its defense—was the surrender of what had become the typical Mormon institution. Economic experimentation—the communism of the United Order, for example—became less characteristic of Mormon activities, and, in general, the secular demands of Babylon displaced the earlier enthusiasm for the New Jerusalem. Even the successes of earlier fervor strengthened the trend to accommodation. Having become the dominant group over a large culture area, the Mormon church experienced the conservatism of the successful, which was not likely to upset a working equilibrium. The involvement of church leadership in established political, economic, and educational institutions, the education of children, the comparatively long-established hierarchy and dogma—all display ecclesiastical features of Mormon organization. The demand for conversion and the aversion to the ecclesiastical practice of infant baptism were soon institutionally compromised in the baptism of the eight-year-old children of Mormon families.

This combination of sectarian characteristics with structure, policy, and circumstances similar to many *ecclesiae* suggests that the Mormon church is a mixture of the pure categories outlined in our typology. Joachim Wach, recognizing this problem—specifically about the Mormons and generally in such typologies—has characterized the Mormon church as an independent group with semiecclesiastical organization.[13] It is, for Wach, neither church nor sect; it is an independent group through whose organization its members have access to the necessary means of salvation.

In terms of theology and group structure there is considerable justification for Wach's classification. Yet, in larger terms, there is more to be said. The Mormon restoration was not only a Christian renewal; it was a Hebrew revival. Mormondom conceived itself as a modern Israel. This alone is not uncommon in Christian experience, and we are likely to take it for granted. Yet in the Mormon case, contemporary conditions of life were to give the revival of Hebrew ideals a more genuine content than would have been possible in smaller groups in less demanding circumstances. The acceptance of a model is always important in the patterning of subsequent behavior,

[13] *The Sociology of Religion*, pp. 194–97.

and in the Mormon case the model of the chosen people could not but affect Mormon belief and behavior: polygamy is but the most notorious example.

Guided by this model, the Saints withdrew from the modern Babylon to build the modern Zion. Owing to circumstances over which they had little control, they found themselves wandering in the wilderness. They had sought but part of the Israelitish parallel; circumstances had provided the rest. For sixteen years they were driven about, attempting four times to build their city. Their size, the extent and duration of their suffering, and the way in which defeat several times crowned the most palpable successes combined to transform the bread and water of sectarian affliction into the real presence of national potentiality. Common effort in success and in failure, common suffering from elemental and human adversaries, even common struggle with arms against common enemies, all these lent to the symbolic emulation of ancient Israel an existential reality which devoted sectaries in more (or less) fortunate circumstances could hardly surmise. Mormonism lived its Exodus and Chronicles, not once but many times. It had its Moses and its Joshua. Circumstances had given it a stage upon which its re-enactment of biblical history was neither farce nor symbolic pageant.

Throughout this intense group experience—an experience which produced a genuine folk tradition in a decade and a half—Mormon family life and Mormon economic and political activity continued. During this time the Mormons courted and married, begat children and reared them, and established ties of consanguinity and affinity—made more numerous and complex by polygamy—which reinforced and impenetrated those of membership in the church. Economic activity, both co-operative and private, and political necessities, established further bonds. Moreover, in the years of wandering the Saints spent their lives in largely Mormon surroundings. This was even more true in the years that followed 1847, when geographical reinforced social isolation.

Fellowship in the Gospel became—and remains today—supported by and imbedded in a matrix of kinship. The circumstance of enforced nomadism and of successive resettlement, brought about by no design of the Saints and yet in close emulation of their Hebraic model, was experienced in a manner that would guarantee its transmission as informal family history as well as the more formally taught Church history. In each attempt at settlement a group increasingly conscious of itself as a chosen vessel established its holy city—its spiritual and temporal homeland—only to be driven out under circumstances that strengthened in-group loyalty and increased self-consciousness. In Utah a homeland was finally found where "the desert would blossom as the rose," and all previous Mormon history was reinterpreted as precursory of this final fruition in "the place which God for us prepared." The death of Joseph on the eastern side of the Mississippi was the final act of the first stage, as was that of Moses on the borders of the land of Canaan. It was the first stage in the development of incipient nationhood. The members of the Church of Jesus Christ of Latter-Day Saints had become—to use the significant term often used most casually by the Mormons themselves—the "Mormon people." Moreover, the Mormon people had found a homeland. The ties of religious faith were reinforced by those of blood and marriage, of common group memories often involving suffering and heroism, of common economic and cultural aspirations—and now by a region whose very physiognomy would become symbolic of another and perhaps greater group achievement, the successful settlement in the desert.

The Mormons were not completely unaware of what they had become. It is true that their American patriotism, which was an article of faith with them, inhibited any movement for national independence, and they tended to see their own religious homeland as part of a secular manifest destiny. Yet the latter was certainly subordinate to a religious conception of Zion in the mountaintops. In 1850 the Mormons established the state of Deseret—much larger than present-day Utah—and applied for admission to the Union. The covenant people would become an American state rather than an independent nation. In Nauvoo they had been virtually a state within a state through grant of a special charter from the Illinois legislature, and all previous attempts to build the city were characterized by considerable autonomy. The Civil War had not yet settled certain limitations of autonomy, nor had postwar developments in politics, economics, and technology made autonomy seem so far-fetched as one might imagine in today's conditions. Moreover, it must be recalled that, in moments of passion in the Mormon-gentile conflict, separatism and secession were openly considered and that armed, if inconclusive, conflict with federal forces did take place.

The Mormons had gone from near-sect to near-nation. The Zionism of the nineteenth-century Mormons stopped short of the national fulfilment of the Jewish Zionism of the twentieth century. Yet the Saints had in large part realized the implications of the model which had guided them in such auspicious circumstances. If their own patriotism combined with their defeat in the Mormon-gentile conflict to inhibit the full fruition of national sovereignty, Mormondom, nevertheless, became a subculture with its own peculiar conceptions and values, its own self-consciousness, and its own culture area. The Mormons, in a word, had become a people, with their own subculture within the larger American culture, and their own homeland as part of the American homeland.

Conclusion

We have now answered the first two questions. A peculiar concatenation of ten factors—ideal, matters of conceptions and values; historical, matters of unique concomitance or convergence in time; and structural, matters of social structure —combine to explain how the Mormon church escaped sectarianism. In escaping the fate of an isolated sect which had been the nemesis of so many other restorationist religious groupings, it did not become either a denomination or a church in the sense of the accepted definitions, although it displayed characteristics of both. Rather, the emulation of the Old Testament Hebrews in the unsettled conditions of the nineteenth-century Middle and Far West resulted in the emergence of a Mormon people—a phenomenon not unlike the emergence of nations and empires from religious groups in the past or in our own day. The development of nationhood, such as we have seen in contemporary Jewish Zionism, or in the fulfilment of the aspirations of Indian Islam, was inhibited by American patriotic convictions on the part of the Latter-Day Saints themselves and by the integrating power of the larger American community, yet the flare-up of separatist sentiment in the heat of conflict suggests the possibilities of development had circumstances been different.

What of the third and fourth questions asked above?

The dichotomy of church and sect and their derivatives—independent group and denomination—do not exhaust the possibilities which are offered by empirical research in the sociology of religion. The development of a people with a peculiar culture and with developed self-consciousness as well as a native region identified with themselves and their group "myth" is another possibility as was realized in the history of Mormonism.[14]

The final question is whether sociological analysis alone can adequately explain the emergence of one type of social structure as against another. Ten factors have been given as preventing the Mormon church from becoming a sect despite a theological and sociological tendency in the sectarian direction. Eight of these have been presented as particularly effective. It should be noted that, of these, all but the third and tenth factors are matters of historical contengency. That is, in the cases of factors 4 through 7 unique convergence of specific events must be considered in any adequate explanation. These matters could hardly have been predicted from, or be explained in terms of, a purely sociological frame of reference. It would seem that sociology in the uncontrolled field situation—and most significant problems are still in that category—must not attempt to solve its problems in terms of abstract schemata which do not take account of

[14] After I had worked through my data to the conclusion that Mormonism developed into something like an incipient nationality I found the following paragraph in Park and Burgess, *op. cit.*, pp. 872–73: "Once the sect has achieved territorial isolation and territorial solidarity, so that it is the dominant power within the region that it occupies, it is able to control the civil organization, establish schools and a press, and so put the impress of a peculiar culture upon all the civil and political institutions that it controls. In this case it tends to assume the form of a state, and become a nationality. Something approaching this was achieved by the Mormons in Utah." Although Park did nothing more with the idea, its statement here leaves little to be desired in clarity—a strong argument in favor of more familiarity with the masters of American sociology!

historical contingency and which abstract from time. From another point of view it may be said that intellectual analysis of the content of conceptions and values often gives a much richer understanding and a much safer lead concerning their implications for social action than do categorizations in terms of highly abstract schemata. Yet this difficulty seems less formidable than the historical. The inability of sociological analysis alone to predict or explain the emergence of one type of social structure as against another must be granted at least in the present example.

This concession has great significance for sociology whether in the planning of research or in the training of specialists. It proves again the importance of interdisciplinary co-operation. This may be either what Linton used to call several disciplines under one skull or collaboration between social scientists and scholars across departmental lines. In larger research it must certainly mean the latter.

8 · Why Some Americans Manifest a Sort of Fanatical Spiritualism

ALEXIS de TOCQUEVILLE

Although the desire of acquiring the good things of this world is the prevailing passion of the American people, certain momentary outbreaks occur when their souls seem suddenly to burst the bonds of matter by which they are restrained and to soar impetuously towards heaven. In all the states of the Union, but especially in the half-peopled country of the Far West, itinerant preachers may be met with who hawk about the word of God from place to place. Whole families, old men, women, and children, cross rough passes and untrodden wilds, coming from a great distance, to join a camp-meeting, where, in listening to these discourses, they totally forget for several days and nights the cares of business and and even the most urgent wants of the body.

Here and there in the midst of American society you meet with men full of

SOURCE. Alexis de Tocqueville, *Democracy in America* (ed. Phillips Bradley), New York: Alfred A. Knopf, 1946, vol. 2, pp. 134–135.

a fanatical and almost wild spiritualism, which hardly exists in Europe. From time to time strange sects arise which endeavor to strike out extraordinary paths to eternal happiness. Religious insanity is very common in the United States.

Nor ought these facts to surprise us. It was not man who implanted in himself the taste for what is infinite and the love of what is immortal; these lofty instincts are not the offspring of his capricious will; their steadfast foundation is fixed in human nature, and they exist in spite of his efforts. He may cross and distort them; destroy them he cannot.

The soul has wants which must be satisfied; and whatever pains are taken to divert it from itself, it soon grows weary, restless, and disquieted amid the enjoyments of sense. If ever the faculties of the great majority of mankind were exclusively bent upon the pursuit of material objects, it might be anticipated that an amazing reaction would take place in the souls of some men. They would drift at large in the world of spirits, for fear of remaining shackled by the close bondage of the body.

It is not, then, wonderful if in the midst of a community whose thoughts tend earthward a small number of individuals are to be found who turn their looks to heaven. I should be surprised if mysticism did not soon make some advance among a people solely engaged in promoting their own worldly welfare.

It is said that the deserts of the Thebaid were peopled by the persecutions of the emperors and the massacres of the Circus; I should rather say that it was by the luxuries of Rome and the Epicurean philosophy of Greece.

If their social condition, their present circumstances, and their laws did not confine the minds of the Americans so closely to the pursuit of worldly welfare, it is probable that they would display more reserve and more experience whenever their attention is turned to things immaterial, and that they would check themselves without difficulty. But they feel imprisoned within bounds, which they will apparently never be allowed to pass. As soon as they have passed these bounds, their minds do not know where to fix themselves and they often rush unrestrained beyond the range of common sense.

Index of Authors